HISTORIES

OF THE JEWISH PEOPLE

OF PINELLAS COUNTY, FLORIDA

1883-2005

Hebrew Dates 5643-5766

Dr. Herman Koren
Professor Emeritus
Indiana State University

 Published by Temple B'nai Israel, Clearwater, Florida-2007

DEDICATION

To the Jewish women and men of Pinellas County, Florida. The pioneers, those that came later, and those yet to come. Those who have and who will generously contribute to society. They will continue to enhance the beauty and sacred lives of all people, and make this part of the West Coast of Florida, a true example of goodness and continuity of Jewish life. This book, which honors all of these Jewish people and people everywhere, is full of heart and soul and joy and sorrow, and is not just a dry reference.

Some Special Thoughts

"You never get poor by giving to charity" Lena Hess, grandmother of Reva Kent

"...I also enjoy the feeling of responsibility to seek out the truth..." David Rothblatt, father of Bunnie Katz

"Our heritage is truth of our past. Thereby, we understand ourselves and our hope for generations yet to arrive." Sidney Colen

"History is not names, dates, and places, but the record of human beings responding to their environment." Rabbi Jacob Rader Marcus, Founder and Director of the American Jewish Archives

Symbolism of the Book Cover

The book cover must be read from right (front cover), across the spine, to left (back cover). At the upper right hand corner is a small old synagogue from which the joyful Jewish people are carrying Torahs under a wedding canopy to the new synagogue (on the back cover). The marchers are accompanied by men, women and children who are happily welcoming the Torah as if they were welcoming a new bride and groom at their wedding. Since the word "kiddushin" is used for the wedding vows, where the man and woman become consecrated to each other, it is appropriate that this word, which comes from the root word of "kodesh," "holy," be used for the interaction between the people and the Torah. At the upper left corner of the cover is an Ark, a holy cabinet for the Torahs.

On the spine of the book there is a woman. She symbolizes the binding force that keeps Jewish life together. The woman brings strength, dignity and love to the marriage. She creates a home out of a house and a house of God out of a beautiful structure dedicated to God. The little girl symbolizes the future.

As the people march and dance with the Torahs to their new spiritual home, they carry the word of God with them as they move into a new phase of their lives. They have now completed several mitzvahs. They have built a new home for God's word. They have transmitted God's word from generation to generation. They have chosen life and good for all of the people.

© 2007 by Temple B'nai Israel, St. Petersburg, FL

ISBN 978-1-4243-1541-3

Library of Congress Control Number: 2006908230
Printed in the United States of America

FINANCIAL CONTRIBUTIONS
FOR
PUBLICATION OF THIS BOOK

PLATINUM SPONSORS

Anonymous
Alan and Nancy Bomstein
Dr. Elinor Gordon
Reva Kent
Mr. and Mrs. Walter Loebenberg

GOLD SPONSORS

Jeffrey Grossman
Jewish Press

SILVER SPONSORS

Mrs. Marilyn Benjamin
Mr. and Mrs. Gerald Benstock
Sylvia Berg
Orin and Bertha Cohen
Leonard and Shirley Collman
David and Joan Fyvolent
Roland Fox
Lila Lawrence
Mr. and Mrs. Irvin Miller
Dr. and Mrs. Morris LeVine
Sylvan Orloff
Marc and Laurie Reiskind

A WORD FROM THE RABBIS

In place of a foreword, it seemed appropriate to ask each rabbi of Pinellas County to share a thought that he or she would find meaningful on the occasion of the publication of this unique document. This document represents the history and aspirations of the entire Jewish community. The rabbis are especially qualified to do this because of their significance in the Jewish community, as well as the general community, as spiritual leaders, educators and community leaders.

Dr. Bertram W. Korn, pulpit rabbi, scholar, historian, humanitarian, patriot (Navy chaplain-Admiral), dynamic and energetic community leader best describes what a rabbi is and what he or she does and the significance of the rabbi in the community. "...To be a Rabbi is to commit yourself to unceasing sacrifice. To be a Rabbi is to be aware always of the best in people and to help to overcome the worst. To be a Rabbi is to study without cessation the insights of our age-old heritage and the contemporary contours of the human situation. To be a Rabbi is always to try to comprehend the ways of God and explain them to humanity; and to try to comprehend the ways of humanity and explain them to yourself. To be a Rabbi is to pour out love to all you meet, even the unlovable and the unloving, especially those who mock and scorn the tradition which you love. To be a Rabbi is to strive endlessly for the unattainable, to reach for eternity, to struggle with God for God and godliness, never to be content with what you have wrought or taught or interpreted. To be a Rabbi is to know that the prophets and sages of old stand in judgment on everything that you say or do, and that your work in turn cannot be evaluated until many decades, even generations, have passed. To be a Rabbi is to be a goad to the indifferent and uncomprehending, and a patient servant of the humblest of the servants of God. To be a Rabbi is to stand firm for ideals which are enduring in strong truth, and to be prepared to surrender every thought and opinion which is your own. To be a Rabbi is to share the honor and dignity of leadership of this most ancient people, and to experience all the anguish of its sorrow and the pains of each of its individual members. To be a Rabbi is to know that there is so much more for you to do to help that many lifetimes will not suffice. To be a Rabbi is always to stand before the people not for yourself but for them, for the best that is in our history and for the best that is in them today. To be a Rabbi is to know the blessing of being called "My Teacher" by those who love you and will always remember you."

The Rabbis' Responses

Rabbi J. Leonard Azneer of St. Petersburg said, " The St. Petersburg Jewish community may rejoice in what it has created. It has built the religious, educational and social agencies necessary for Jews to live a secure and fulfilling Jewish life. This generation and those that preceded it are proud of its accomplishments. But what of the future, which will require that we maintain what we have built, and respond to new challenges?

In this connection, rabbinic wisdom reminds us that our destiny lies in the hearts and hands of our children. It cautions us, "Do not refer to them as your children, but as your builders." Our challenge is to inspire today's children to become the architects and builders of the Jewish community of tomorrow. I pray "So may it be."

Rabbi Arthur I. Baseman, Temple B'nai Israel, Clearwater said, " What is the task of the Rabbi, not as he faces his congregation or his community, but as he looks at himself. The Rabbi's task, as I have tried to live it, is first and foremost, to remain a human being. A rabbi is always a rabbi, whether in the pulpit in a robe, or on the beach in a bathing suit. The task then is not to be simply a human being without being a rabbi, but rather to make certain the rabbi remains a human being in all that he does. Secondly, the Rabbi's task is be certain that his family is given the love and care that he would hope every Jew would give to his or her own family. The Rabbi's family must never resent the shul or the fact that he is a Rabbi. A Rabbi must build a Jewish family and a Jewish home for his own loved ones. Thirdly, a Rabbi's task is to meet the challenge of strengthening Jewish religious commitment and it is to wrestle mightily against the religious apathy, ambivalence, and antipathy that often surround him. A Rabbi's task is to champion life-long Jewish learning and Jewish practice, and demonstrate the beauty and blessing that our Jewish tradition can bring to our lives and our Jewish identity. It is to be present with people at the heightened moments of their lives, whether happy or sad, to be welcoming and inclusive, and to create a sacred community. Finally, it is to model the three indispensable and fundamental acts of Jewish identity–an involvement with prayer and worship, a dedication to study and the pursuit of knowledge, and the performance of deeds of gracious, loving kindness and caring.I read that after a very intense military operation the Jewish military commander summed up his report with the inspiring and magical words "Beshelanu Amadnu"–"We stood up to what is ours." The expression meant, "We rose to the occasion," or "We have successfully carried out what was asked of us."At the conclusion of his career, a Rabbi hopes to be able to say to God, his congregation, and to himself "Beshali Amaditee"–"I stood up to what is mine".

Rabbi Kenneth Bromberg (deceased) Rabbi Emeritus of Congregation Beth Shalom of Clear**water** said, that the Rabbi/congregation is a human mix of strengths and weaknesses. As in a good marriage, the loving task is to ameliorate each other's weaknesses and develop each other's strengths. The focus of his professional life, as inscribed on his tombstone, was "to understand and ponder, study and teach, preserve and fulfill the teachings of the Torah." He said, "A rabbi is first and foremost an adult Jewish educator." "For a rabbi to fulfill his historic role as a teacher of Judaism to his community, it is clear that he must never stop being a student."Rabbi Bromberg achieved this effortlessly in his day-to-day contacts with congregants, colleagues, and members of the larger community. His teaching was two directional. He was an active listener who respected the wisdom of individuals and groups and a teacher who knew the appropriate time and place to make a presentation meaningful and useful. He said, quoting the Ethics of the Fathers, "Much have I learned from my teachers; more have I learned from my colleagues; most have I learned from my students."

Rabbi Bromberg made a plea for a healthy Jewish congregational and communal life through increased education of the Jewish people. He said, "Every year of my professional life, I become more and more convinced that the most enfeebling aspect of American Jewish life is the deep and widespread ignorance of the foundations of Judaism-its history, thought, beliefs and practices.... (This can be corrected by) a general increase in the level of substantive Jewish knowledge and therefore deeper, more credible discussion and decision-making."(This is the reason why there are so many educational programs in all the synagogues in Pinellas County, Florida and the U.S.)

Rabbi Gary Klein of Temple Ahavat Shalom of Palm Harbor said, "Judaism can be a very powerful force for good in our lives and in the world. Judaism can enhance our ethical sense and nurture our compassion. It can also help us become more appreciative of the important experiences and people in our lives. This appreciation increases the joy we experience during happy times and softens the pain that sadness brings.

Synagogues and other institutions should be second homes for members of the community and should enhance our pride in being Jews. I believe Pinellas County's synagogues fulfill these goals very effectively by enabling their members to join in worship, celebration, study and deeds of service to the Jewish and general communities. Synagogues are joined in this endeavor by other Jewish organizations. These include our local chapters of the American Israel Public Affairs Committee, Hadassah, Jewish Women International, Primer-Promoting Responsibility in Middle East Reporting, Jewish National Fund, our local Israel Bonds Organization, Gulf Coast Jewish Family Services, our local Federation, and Kent Jewish Community Center. Our Gulf Coast Jewish Family Services serves not only our own people, but also those in need who are part of the larger community. By doing this it enables our Jewish community to fulfill so many mandates of our tradition.

I am very pleased to be a rabbi in Pinellas County and to be the spiritual leader of Temple Ahavat Shalom. During the eighteen years that I have served here, I have seen a relatively small, but wonderfully powerful, Jewish community set an example of commitment to the most important teachings of Judaism."

Rabbi Jacob Luski of Congregation B'nai Israel of St. Petersburg said, " A correspondent from the New York Times came to interview Professor Saul Lieberman at the Jewish Theological Seminary on the occasion of the publication of his famous commentary on the Tosefta. The reporter found the distinguished professor poring over the pages of many books that were scattered on tables and desks, all around the room. As he watched Dr. Lieberman turn from one massive volume to another, he followed him from book to book and was puzzled. "What is this?" he asked. "This is the Bible." "And what is this?" And "This is the Mishna," the scholar replied. "What is the Mishna?" "It is an elaboration of the Bible; the rabbis who lived at that time interpreted the Bible in the light of their day." " I see, and what is this?" "This is the Gemara." "What is the Gemara?" "This was written even later. The sages who lived at that time elaborated upon the Mishna and reinterpreted it in the light of the times in which they lived." "And what is this?" "This is Rashi. He was a renowned commentator, who lived in France many years later and he interpreted Jewish law in the light of the times." And "And what is this?" "This is Maimonides, the great philosopher and teacher, who lived in Spain and rendered new interpretations in the light of his day." The reporter looked at Dr. Lieberman in amazement. "In other words," he said, "Judaism is a conversation between generations isn't it?" Professor Lieberman reacted immediately. "That is the best definition of Judaism I have ever heard, a conversation between generations."

We in Pinellas County continue the conversation between the generations. It is good to pause and reflect on the many successes and accomplishments of our community. In its ninth decade, Congregation B'nai Israel of St. Petersburg continues to expand and present the best of Conservative Judaism in our community. Our varied programs present Judaism as it challenges us today to live meaningful Jewish lives in the 21st-century. As we look to a bright future, we can be proud of our accomplishments as a Congregation in maintaining the conversation between the generations."

Rabbi Shimon Moch of Congregation B'nai Emmunah of Tarpon Springs said, "Rabbis have the difficult responsibility of working to strengthen the greater Jewish and general communities while they are trying to strengthen their particular congregations. The teachings of the sages repeat the refrain: Talmud Torah, without ma'aseh—learning without good works—means little. The sages also teach, "Talmud Torah keneged kulam—The study of Torah is equal in importance to all other mitzvot," principally because it leads us to the practice of all those other mitzvot. Rabbis must challenge their congregations to apply the teachings of Torah that they have together mastered, and transform them into ma'aseh, "deed." They must rouse their members to follow the prophetic call for social responsibility for the less fortunate among us and for furthering important issues involving social justice in our community. We rabbis have the challenge to help our congregations and the Jewish Community to change the way we think about our roles and our responsibility as Jews interacting with the world.

The dictum of Hillel, "If I am not for myself, who will be for me, and if I am for myself (alone), what am I, and if not now, when?" applies to synagogues and Jewish communities as much as it does to individuals A strong Jewish community stands up for its members and for Jews everywhere. It organizes and works to strengthen Jewish life here and throughout the world. The various institutions within the Jewish Community work together cooperating on programs and strategies for uniting and activating the Jewish Community. At the same time, a strong Jewish community will work for the betterment of the general community and will devote considerable energy to heal community wounds, and to uplift those within the community whom society has left behind. In a strong and worthy Jewish Community, general knowledge exists throughout the greater community, of the considerable, significant and critical roles that the Rabbis and many Jewish lay leaders play in building a stronger, more progressive and cohesive community, that includes all faiths, races, nationalities and groups.

How history judges the role of the Pinellas County Jewish Community in building a greater general community will largely testify to how effective our rabbis have been as teachers of Torah. This history of our Jewish Community will record much of the record of our past involvement. I pray that, beyond helping us to know our past, it helps us to better further our divine charge of being "a light for the nations."

Rabbi David J. Susskind, Rabbi Emeritus of Temple Beth-El said, " The majestic synagogues and temples, in north and south Pinellas county, had their antecedents in the second half of the 20th century, in the period when all of America was experiencing a revival of Jewish ethnicity. Temple Beth-El, the congregation that I was elected to serve in 1957, had been in service for a quarter of a century. During that time, seven rabbis had served in its pulpit. Mine was the opportunity to become acquainted with more than a few 'founders' of the congregation. The generation I came to serve became the 'builders' of the temple. Two hundred plus member families contributed to the building of a new structure with a uniquely designed sanctuary, social hall, chapel, library, administrative offices, and school wings. The temple was now equipped and I promptly instituted all the activities, programs, and services that comprise the function of a modern suburban synagogue in the 20th century.

I now enjoy the status of Rabbi Emeritus having served in the pulpit and community for thirty (30) plus years. My mantra for the temple was,"where faith and friendship meet"and so it did as we grew and prospered. It is now my abiding joy to witness many a former student at whose birth I celebrated or whose bar/bat mitzvah or confirmation I blessed or at whose wedding I officiated, assume positions of leadership in congregational life. Indeed it is a pleasure to behold Temple Beth-El as the spiritual and cultural center for a next and new generation of Jews in the 21st century."

Rabbi Michael Torop of Temple Beth-El of St. Petersburg said, "Rabbi Hanina said: I have learned much from my teachers, and from my colleagues more than from my teachers,but from my students more than from them all." (Babylonia Talmud, Tractate Ta'anit 7a)

Learning is a powerful experience. Teaching is a sacred responsibility. Each opportunity to explore Judaism with others brings a sense of renewal and enrichment. As a rabbi serving this wonderful community of St. Petersburg, I am truly both teacher and student, for there is rarely a moment when the process of teaching others does not challenge me to learn as well. When I see faces reflecting a deeper understanding and appreciation of the richness of our heritage, I feel fulfilled.

Education transforms lives. With Temple Beth-El, I have the opportunity to work in partnership with a congregation to create a true learning community. Our tradition values learning for its own sake, but there is a higher purpose as well. Learning leads to empowerment. Empowerment leads to action. The more we know about Judaism, the more effective we will be in applying Jewish values, ethics and teachings to the many different facets of our lives. We can become, as Abraham Joshua Heschel, z"l, suggests, "textpeople," Jews who bring the texts of Jewish tradition to life in the way that we think, feel and act. Both explicitly through what I teach, and implicitly through what I do, I hope to be a catalyst for others to develop their own expression of this ideal.

Judaism is filled with opportunities we call "teachable moments." These are unparalleled opportunities to infuse a given moment with the wisdom of the ages. There are times in each and every day, in all that we do as rabbis, that remind us that learning can be woven into many different experiences; it is through our shared commitment to integrate Judaism into our lives that we create a vibrant community.

When a community is inclusive and embraces the value of learning for all ages, from the youngest of our precious toddlers to the oldest of our esteemed elders, we discover anew the power of God in our lives. The sages believed that when we share words of Torah, the *Shekhinah*, the intimate presence of God is in our midst. Today, when the sacred seems to continually elude our grasp, a serious educational partnership between a rabbi and his or her congregation can help guide our spiritual quest.

Rabbi Danielle Upbin of Congregation Beth Shalom of Clearwater said, "L'dor Va'dor – from generation to generation it is incumbent upon the Jewish people to tell our stories. Our stories teach us about struggle and success, about overcoming being a minority, about strength of character and about belief and practice. We re-experience the stories of our people through constant study and through looking within the great books of our people. Through our lens on the past, a great voice calls out to us, commanding: "Zachor"

– Remember who you are. Remember your stories. Remember your heritage. Remember your peoplehood. Our children must not only study our ancient history, practices and laws, but also the names and deeds of our more recent ancestors. The stories of our founding fathers and mothers of the Jewish community in Pinellas County connects us back to the ancient Torah-values of kindness, generosity, strength, community, righteousness and iconoclasm.

The transmission of history from one generation to another is intricately bound up in our rituals, prayers and everyday experiences as Jews. We are commanded to know where we come from as a light to guide us on the path to where we are headed. This process of seeking understanding includes becoming familiar with many facets of our history. The children of our day will merit from this text as a resource of their own personal history. It will provide them with a profound sense of their roots in this county, as well as give them a taste of the struggles and emancipations that paved the way for them to thrive here as individuals with limitless opportunity and freedom to be Jewish."

Rabbi David Weizman of Congregation Beth Shalom of Clearwater said, "My teacher, Rabbi Morris Shapiro, tells this story about his grandson: When he was just old enough to speak, the child climbed up on the table, stood eye to eye with me and said, "Look Zeda, I am taller than you." Some time in 1942, Rabbi Shapiro, then only a boy himself, was singled out by the kappos of his shtettle in Poland to be, perhaps, the sole survivor of his village because of his extraordinary scholarship in Talmudic studies. They knew that the survival of the Jewish people depended on the preservation of Torah learning. So just as Rabbi Akiva taught one book of the Torah to each of five students during the time when the Romans were burning the Torah, young Morris Shapiro would one day teach his students. Many years later, Rabbi Shapiro's students were amused by the irony of his grandson's comment, for few stood taller than he did. The story is meant to teach us that each generation stands on the shoulders of the proceeding one. But the measurement of our spiritual life is much more ambiguous. How do we describe the development of our identity as individual human beings? When I have met with families before a funeral, I usually meet with as many family members as possible. They have the family photos out on the coffee table. One image leads to a story that jogs the memory of the next until people discover things that they never knew about the deceased or about their family history. In essence, each one is finding their own history as well. So much of our stories are lost because we never think they are important enough or interesting enough to record in any way, and then one day, after we are gone, a grandchild may ask, "who am I named after, and what were they like in life?" Let us take the time now to make a record, and may our stories serve as the shoulders for the generations to come."

ACKNOWLEDGMENTS

Of special significance is Sister Alma Mary Anderson, Professor of Graphic Design, Indiana State University, for taking on and carrying out the huge responsibility to make the manuscript camera ready. She and our colleague, Dr. Paul Hightower, Professor of Communications, Indiana State University, traveled to Pinellas County and spent an entire week taking photographs and scanning existing pictures in order to make them part of the story. Paul Hightower is well known for his excellent camera work and how he has made the taking of pictures a unique form of communications. Sister Alma Mary Anderson is world-renowned in her work on graphic design in the field of environmental health. She directs the graphic design graduate students at Indiana State University, two of whom, Sister Patricia Linehan and Sharon Cordray, were invaluable assistants. She has done all of the computer art work for the author's previous books in environmental and occupational health. Professor Anderson drew, by computer, the very unique cover, which represents the growth of Judaism and the movement forward of the wisdom of the Torah from generation to generation..

Thanks to Deborah Lynn Friedman for your beautiful and inspiring music and the use of Tifilat Haderech in the manuscript, Publisher, Sounds Write Productions.

My thanks to the many hundreds of individuals throughout Pinellas County, the State of Florida, and the United States who contributed material to this book. The names and organizations of the contributors may be found throughout the book as well as in the bibliography. My special thanks to Rabbi Arthur I. Baseman, who was there with me from the very beginning and convinced others of the essential nature and significance of this project. He also wrote the introduction to the chapter on Jewish Values. Bob Mintz, President, and the rest of the officers, Executive Committee and Board of Trustees of Temple B'nai Israel of Clearwater who supported the history project and agreed to publish this Pinellas County Jewish history. The Board of Rabbis and the rabbis individually gave enormous help in providing people and material to make the writing of this book possible. Thank you to Harriet Johnson, Reference Librarian of the St. Petersburg Public Library; the libraries of the cities of Largo, Clearwater, Tarpon Springs, Jacksonville, and Key West in Florida; St. Louis, Missouri; University of South Florida; Charleston, South Carolina; Savanna, Georgia; Philadelphia, Pennsylvania; Providence, Rhode Island; and all of the other libraries throught the country that helped verify the accuracy of information. Robin Yellin, family historian, was of great help in obtaining information about the early Jewish people of Pinellas County. Bunnie Katz provided much unique material about the St. Petersburg Jewish community and made many excellent suggestions. Elaine Wides was extremely helpful in providing information on Temple Beth-El and doing additional research on the early settlers of St. Petersburg. Shirley Collman provided a considerable amount of material about the Jewish people of Clearwater and North County. Reva Kent provided much material about the origins of several synagogues as well as community wide organizations. Ellie Gordon rescued the author when he was inundated with material. She organized all the paper into folders, which helped substantially with the research. All those who participated in the oral histories (names noted in the bibliography) provided many personal documents, as well as the names and phone numbers of other individuals who would be helpful in researching the Jewish history. My wife, Donna, worked hard on this project. She has always been my sounding board and has provided for me an extraordinary loving life which allows me to be continuously productive.

PROOFREADERS

A work of this nature takes the skills and knowledge of a variety of people to proofread the manuscript for accuracy and readability. Each of the chapters related to specific synagogues and organizations were submitted to them to determine if the work had been done accurately. Beyond that, a group of four people proofread the entire manuscript and made excellent contributions. They were: Sr. Alma Mary Anderson, Professor of Graphic Design, Indiana State University, Randi Cohen, Acquisitions Editor, CRC Press, Robert Green, writer, thirty years with Reuters News Agency. Donna Koren, Advisor and Consultant.

INTRODUCTION

The history of the Jewish Community of Pinellas County is part of a continuum of 4,000 years of Jewish life, love, respect, and an acknowledgment of the one God. A God who gave us the Torah, who nurtures us and who has provided for us the opportunity to create a more perfect world. Judaism teaches us that people are sacred and that we must treat other people with honesty, compassion, and kindness. We are taught that life is to be revered and that the world is to be cherished and protected. We have been offered good or evil, life or death. We have chosen of our own free will, good and life. This history is a retelling of this choice and the effect it has had on us, our children, as well as the total community of Pinellas County, Florida, the United States, and the world. This history is also part of a "conversation between generations" which was the best definition of Judaism that Professor Saul Lieberman had ever heard.

To properly understand Pinellas County Jewish history, it is necessary to better understand the lives of the Jewish people who arrived in America from colonial times on, how they arrived here, what they did, who they were, why they came, when they came, where they settled, and the results of their being here. Certain specific United States Jewish communities are briefly discussed because they relate to the Jewish story in Florida or more specifically Pinellas County. Also, it is necessary to understand some of the trends in society that affected Jewish life, including certain select world Jewish communities and events, particularly Jewish experiences in Europe. The Jewish people formed uniquely Jewish organizations. They contributed to, as well as led, many other community organizations in order to raise their families properly, enhance society, and ultimately leave the world a better place to live in. In the end, the names of these individuals, their good deeds, and the names of the collective Jewish people, should be like honey on the tongues of all of humanity. Above all else, the Jewish people are dedicated and committed to the care and improvement of human life. We believe in treating all people with compassion, kindness, and dignity.

This history will discuss the Jewish people of Pinellas County, its synagogues and its congregants, and its organizations, past and present, as a record of the lives and efforts of a unique group of people, who individually and collectively performed the work needed to raise families, contribute to society, and bring honor to the Jewish people and the community at large. This history is a beautiful chapter in an ongoing story of our Jewish way of life in Pinellas County, Florida, the United States, and the world from the first immigrants arrival in colonial times to present days in Pinellas County-2005. This story is about various aspects of Jewish life and contributions to our society. Finally, we are preparing this history to perform the mitzvah of teaching God's love, word, and goodness to our children, and those of generations to come.

The heart of Jewish life is the home. The soul of Jewish life is the Shabbat service. At our synagogues, Shabbat services are restful, beautiful, spiritual, full of music, loving and caring. The whole congregation becomes a mispucha, from the youngest to the oldest. The haunting sounds of the Mi Sheberach (the communal prayer to God to help heal our friends and relatives as well as ourselves), the gentleness of our rabbis and cantors, and the warmth of the congregational response, carry us forth in our quest for healing and helping others, and our oneness with our God. Our Judaism is reaffirmed in our desire to do good deeds. Ultimately, it is these good deeds, many of which are sponsored by the synagogues and Jewish organizations, which weave the lovely fabric, that is Judaism.

The manuscript is organized into 26 chapters, a table of contents, "A Word from the Rabbis", a "Family Album", an appendix, a bibliography and a comprehensive index. Chapter 1 is a discussion of the past history and trends in Jewish American life and selected world events which affected the American Jewish experience. It is a summary of the events, external and internal, that affected the Jewish people in the United States, Florida, and Pinellas County. It is also a recording of select Jewish people and their contributions, who helped create a uniquely Jewish American lifestyle, that we experience today. Chapter 2 is a brief history of Florida and the Tampa Bay area. Chapter 3 is a history of the Jewish people in Florida, excluding the Tampa Bay area. Chapter 4 is a brief description of the Tampa Bay area Jewish history. Chapter 5 is a condensed history of Pinellas County. Chapter 6 is an exploration of the roots of the Jewish community of Pinellas County, from 1883-1920. Chapter 7 explores the Jewish community of St. Petersburg and South County, from 1920-2005. Chapter 8 discusses the Jewish community of Clearwater and North County, from 1920-2005. Chapters 9-16 are histories of the various synagogues that are currently functioning in Pinellas County. The degree of detail in each of the histories is based strictly on the information that was available to the researcher at the time of the historical study. It has nothing to do with the significance of a given synagogue, its practices, or its congregants. There will be gaps chronologically in the years cited, because information was not available at the time of the study, for both these synagogues and Jewish organizations. Where the available information about the synagogue is very limited, the discussion will be either in Chapter 7 or Chapter 8 depending on its location rather than being in a separate chapter. Chapter 17-25 are histories of the other Jewish organizations in the community. The degree of detail of each of these organizations is also based strictly on the information that was available to the researcher at the time of the historical study. Obviously, all organizations are of great significance to overall Jewish life and community life. Chapter 26, Jewish Values, describes the value system that Jewish people use as a basis for their lives and the lives of their families. It incorporates the essence of Judaism which is positive community involvement in order to create a better world. The Jewish Family Album, provides a unique opportunity for all members of the Jewish community and their families, past and present, to be recognized and honored by family and/or friends, for their lives and good deeds, already completed or anticipated to be completed. It allows all people to see and celebrate the joy of being Jewish and the work they do to help make this world a better place. The appendix provides a list, in chronological order, of the Presidents of all of the synagogues, sisterhoods, brotherhoods, youth groups, organizations, etc. based on information available to the researcher. The bibliography provides a listing of major sources utilized in the book. However, because of space limitations hundreds of minor references had to be left out. The index is probably the most important part of the entire book because an individual can go to this source and find out where a given event or person can be located within the reference. This adds immeasurably to the value of the book.

The book, as a whole, creates a story of important events and the Jewish people, their contributions to their families, their Jewish community, and to the outer community in which they live and participate. In addition, it is a resource book for future researchers, who want to expand upon the information which has been documented and presented.

Purpose

The purpose of this project is to gather, store, and review documents and oral histories, in order to prepare a comprehensive, but concise, history of the Jewish pioneers and the many special people that followed them. Also there is information concerning the founding of Jewish organizations and synagogues in Pinellas County, how they came to be, and their positive effect on the surrounding communities. Throughout the text, there is listed the names of most of the Jewish people that came in the early years to Pinellas County. There is an attempt to provide dates of birth, dates of death, occupations, places of residence and business, marital partners, and any other related information, that is available, in order to provide for present and future researchers a source book of information concerning these people. All names are listed in the index for easy access. The completed document is factually accurate and serves as an example to large Jewish communities and all faith-based communities throughout the United States on how to conduct large community research about people and organizations, and how to preserve their own documents and present the information in a systematic, comprehensive, but concise manner. Ultimately the history is a tool for better understanding both by Jewish people and non-Jewish people alike, thereby acting as a positive force against the few who feel hatred is their way of life. Most importantly, this work is for our children and children's children to better recognize what has been given to them through their heritage and their Jewish community and family. It should become a major tool in helping the children develop a proper philosophy of Jewish life and life in general. It should help them understand that God is in their life, but they have the freedom of will to make good or bad choices, which ultimately affects others. Paraphrasing the Shema, you shall teach the love of God faithfully to your children, by setting an example by doing good deeds. What better way to accomplish this than by preparing a history of the lives and good deeds of our Jewish people, and what it means to help others to make this a happier, healthier, safer and more prosperous world, where all people are granted freedom from fear and want, and share a lovely fellowship in seeking God in their own way.

ABOUT THE AUTHOR

Dr. Herman Koren is the recipient of the Walter S. Mangold Award for 2005. This is the most distinguished award in the environmental health science field in the United States and possibly globally. Herman Koren, R.E.H.S.,M.P.H.,H.S.D., graduated from Temple University with a Bachelor of Arts degree in chemistry and biology in 1955. He graduated from the University of Michigan School of Public Health with a Master of Public Health degree in environmental health in 1959. He graduated from Indiana University with a Doctorate of Health and Safety degree with concentration in environmental health in 1972. He is Professor Emeritus, founder and former director of the Environmental Health Science Program and the Environmental Health Internship Program at Indiana State University at Terre Haute. He also founded and directed the Supervision and Management Program I and II. He has been an outstanding researcher, teacher, consultant, and practitioner in the environmental health field, and in the occupational health, hospital, medical care, and safety fields for the past fifty years. In addition to innumerable publications and presentations at national meetings, he is the author of seven books in many editions, which he has written over the last thirty years. His books include: Environmental Health and Safety, Pergamon Press; Handbook of Environmental Health, Vol I, Biological, Chemical and Physical Agents of Environmentally Related Disease ,CRC Press; Handbook of Environmental Health, Vol II, Pollutant Interactions in Air, Water, and Soil, CRC Press; Management and Supervision for Working Professionals, Vol I and Vol II, CRC Press; Illustrated Dictionary and Resource Directory of Environmental and Occupational Health, CRC Press; and Commemorative Book-150th Anniversary of the Jewish Community in Terre Haute, Indiana–1849-1999, United Hebrew Congregation.

Dr. Koren has served as a district environmental health practitioner and supervisor at the local and state level. He was an administrator at a 2,000 bed hospital. He was on the editorial board of the Journal of Environmental Health and the former Journal of Food Protection. He is Founder Diplomate of the Intersociety Academy for Certification of Sanitarians, Fellow of the American Public Health Association, a fifty year member of the National Environmental Health Association, founder of the Student National Environmental Health Association, and the founder and twenty-five year advisor of the Indiana State University Student National Environmental Health Association (Alpha Chapter). Dr. Koren developed the modern internship concept in environmental health science. He has been a consultant to the U.S. Environmental Protection Agency, the National Institute of Environmental Health Science, and numerous health departments and hospitals. He has served as the keynote speaker and major lecturer for the Canadian Institute of Public Health Inspectors. He was recipient of the Blue Key Honor Society Award for outstanding teaching and the Alumni and Student Plaque and citations for outstanding teaching, research, and service. The National Environmental Health Association has twice honored Dr. Koren with Presidential citations for "Distinguished Services, Leadership and Devotion to the Environmental Health Field" and "Excellent Research and Publications." In 1984, Dr. Koren, who had been active in the United Hebrew Congregation, a Reform temple, became the historian for the Jewish community of Terre Haute, Indiana. He volunteered to write "The 150-Year History of the Jewish Community of Terre Haute, Indiana, published in 1999. This helped fulfill a major interest that he had had since childhood in learning about the history of a people. He applied the knowledge and skills that he had learned through his scientific education and writings to the local Jewish history. He subsequently, while acting as historian, served in the various offices including President of the congregation. In 2001, he once again volunteered to write the "Histories of the Jewish People of Pinellas County, Florida." Temple B'nai Israel of Clearwater accepted this offer and agreed to publish the book.

TABLE OF CONTENTS

BACKGROUND

PINELLAS COUNTY

SYNAGOGUE HISTORIES

JEWISH ORGANIZATIONS

CHAPTER 1

AMERICAN JEWISH EXPERIENCE (INCLUDING SELECTED WORLD EXPERIENCES)

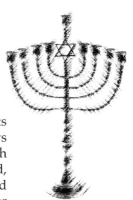

Biblical Times

The migration of the Jewish people to the United States over the last 350 years has its roots in the Bible and the various countries of the Diaspora. The Jewish people have always been on the move from the time of the famine of approximately 3,700-4,000 years ago which led them into Egypt from Canaan. The story continues, the Jewish people first prospered, were then repressed or conquered and finally moved on to a new country. This occurred again and again in the Babylonian exile of 586 BCE; the occupation of Palestine by Alexander the Great about 333 BCE; the rule of Palestine by the Ptolemaic Greeks based in Egypt about 300-200 BCE; the rule of Palestine by the Seleucid Greeks based in Syria from about 200-167 BCE; the rule of Palestine by Rome from 63 BCE to about the year 600. During all that time and to the present, the Jewish people continued to worship one God and sang or chanted their prayers to the one God of all people.

Jewish Liturgical Music

Jewish liturgical music is music used in the religious services of the Jewish people. It can be performed by anyone with appropriate training, but typically is led by a musical worship facilitator, Cantor, cantorial soloist, choir, or Rabbi. It was first performed as the chanting of the prose books of the Bible. Later, the prayers and biblical poetry were chanted. The Bible and the Talmud record that spontaneous music was common among the ancient Jewish people on all important occasions, both religious and secular. Jewish liturgical music is first described as an integral part of worship in II Samuel 6, and I Chronicles 6:16-17. The people Israel used string, wind, and percussion instruments along with singing and dancing. There are many examples of choral singing in the Bible. At the dedication of Solomon's Temple, 288 skillful Levite musicians performed. There were 24 groups of 12 each. The forms of singing were solo, choral, and responsorial. The levitical choir sometimes had a director who also led the singing. The first instruments mentioned in the Bible are the kinnor, a lyre, and the ugab, which may have been a vertical flute. Also ceremonial horns of little music value were the chatzotzra, which was a trumpet and the shofar, a ram's horn. After Solomon's Temple was built, music became an essential part of the Temple practice. The instruments used were: the nevel, a harp; the halil, a double flute that reportedly sounded like an oboe (It was one of the newer instruments, and was not allowed to be played on the Sabbath because of its unique and nontraditional sound.); the asor, a 10-stringed instrument probably like a psaltery; and the magrepha, an instrument with a powerful sound used to signal the beginning of the service. Cymbals which were originally used in the Temple were restricted, apparently for stylistic reasons, but remained part of the Temple service.

After the destruction of Jerusalem in 70 A D by the Romans and the Jewish people dispersed throughout the world, the chanting of prayers was preserved as the Jews traveled to all lands. The chanting formed the basis for modern traditional synagogue music. However, the music traditions of the early synagogues excluded the playing of musical instruments, because of rabbinic prohibition. This prohibition was based on the fact that the playing of instruments was considered to be work, which was not allowed on the Sabbath. Also, the use of instruments was discontinued as an act of mourning. The Bible inferred that instruments were associated with the Temple and with Jerusalem. Since the Temple and Jerusalem were both gone, instruments were no longer needed.

The early synagogues' liturgical music had a mourning quality because of the destruction of the Temple. There was a Rabbinic ban on secular and merry songs resulting in a service heavy in penitence. The fear of promiscuity led to the separation of men and women and ultimately to singing in the synagogue only by men.

Diaspora

Jewish people moved to Greece over 2,300 years ago and to Rome about 2,000 years ago. In the year 212, Jewish people became citizens of the Roman Empire in large communities in Spain, France, South Germany, Italy, Greece, and Asia Minor. From the year 300 to 600, there were many restrictions put on the Jewish people. They continued to migrate to many countries, seeking to create a better way of life for them and their families, and attempting to leave severe discrimination behind them. Around the year 800, Charlemagne and the Pope invited Jewish people to settle in the Holy Roman Empire. Jewish merchants were welcomed in a large number of countries. However, once again, the Jewish people were on the move. Jewish people were expelled from England in 1290 and from France for the second time in 1394.

Kabbalah

Kabbalah originated about 100 C. E. or earlier. It is an aspect of Jewish mysticism consisting of a large body of speculation on nature, divinity, the origin and fate of the soul, and the role of human beings. It consists of meditative, devotional, mystical and magical practices which were taught only to a select few people and therefore is regarded as an esoteric offshoot of Judaism. It was influenced by the biblical phenomenon of prophecy, where the prophet is chosen by God to announce his words to the multitude. Kabbalah as a movement can be traced to the 12th century. It later became a source for Hasidism.

Russian Jewish Community

It is believed, by tradition and legend, the Jewish people arrived in Armenia and Georgia either from the 10 lost Tribes around 721 B. C. E. or with the Babylonian exile in 586 B. C. E.. There are ruins, recordings and inscriptions on tombstones which talk about the existence of important Jewish communities in the Greek colonies on the shores of the Black Sea. Religious persecution in the Byzantine Empire caused many Jewish people to emigrate to these communities. During the seventh century Muslims and Persians fought constantly. This led to many Jewish people moving to the Caucasus Mountains and beyond. In subsequent generations these communities maintained relations with the centers of Jewish learning in Babylonian and Persia. Jewish people traveled regularly through Slavonic and Khazar lands on their way to India and China. They traded textiles, hides, spices and arms.

The kingdom of the Jewish Khazars is part of ancient Russian literature and referred to as the "Land of the Jews." During that time Jews were living in Kiev under the protection of Prince Vladimir. When the inhabitants of the town in 1117 rebelled against Prince Vladmir II, they also attacked the houses of the Jews. The invasion of the Mongols in 1237 brought much suffering to the Jewish people of Russia.

From the beginning of the 14th century the Lithuanians gained control over western Russia. The Lithuanians granted the first extensive privileges to the Jewish communities at the end of the 14th century. Under Poland-Lithuania there was extensive Jewish emigration and large-scale settlement from Poland to the Ukraine, Volhynia and Podolia from the middle of the 16th century to the end of the century. This was a time of significant Jewish growth and prosperity. In 1648-1649, the Chmielnicki massacres devastated the Jewish people of the Ukraine and several years later, the Muscovite armies did not allow Jews in the cities of Belorussia and Lithuania that they had captured. The principality of Moscow, which became the nucleus of the future Russian empire, had a terrible attitude toward the Jewish people and all foreigners in general. They were considered to be heretics and agents of the enemies of the state. Ivan IV, Ivan the Terrible (1530-1584), annexed the town of Pskov and ordered all Jewish people to convert to Christianity. Those who didn't were drowned in the river. Russian rulers in the following two centuries issued repeated decrees to keep Jewish people out of Russia.

At the beginning of the reign of Catherine

II, Jewish people were authorized to enter the country for trading purposes only. Because of hostile public opinion, she rescinded the order. During the ensuing wars that Russia conducted with its neighbors, Jewish people from territories that were conquered became part of the Russian empire. During the first phase of the Russian empire from 1772-1881, the Jewish people continued to carry out their economic functions with Poland-Lithuania. These Russian Jews where a distinct middle class. Many of them earned their livelihood from the leasing of villages, flour mills, forest, inns and taverns. Others were merchants, shopkeepers, or hawkers. The rest were craftsmen who worked for both landowners and peasants.

From 1772-1881, the Jewish people who lived in the regions annexed by Russia from the surrounding countries, were a distinct social class. Before they were middle-class individuals but now their economic position steadily deteriorated as they were confined to the Pale of Settlement and they grew rapidly in population. At first, Jewish children were admitted to all levels in the school system and the Jewish communities were also allowed to open their own schools. In 1817, Alexander I outlawed the blood libel which had caused terror and suffering to the Jewish communities of the 18th Century. By 1822, there was a systematic expulsion of the Jewish people from the villages, especially in the provinces of Belorussia.

Under Nicholas I (1825-1855), the Russian government sought to resolve the "Jewish Problem" through cruelty, suppression, and coercion. In 1827, he ordered the conscription of all boys from ages 12 to 25 years into military service. Those under age 18 were sent to special military schools. The Jewish people were expelled from Kiev and other areas. All individuals who were not considered to be useful to society, including small tradesmen and poorer classes, were to be conscripted into the army.

Alexander II (1855-1881) helped reform Russia. He emancipated the peasants in 1861 from their servitude to the landowners. He adopted a milder policy toward the Jewish people but still tried to assimilate them into Russian society. Jewish people became part of economic, political and cultural life which aroused a sharp reaction from Russian society. Many newspapers engaged in anti-Jewish agitation. There was a substantial population explosion among the Jewish people which increased the numbers from 2,350,000 in 1850 to over 5 million in 1900. This led to large numbers of shopkeepers, peddlers, brokers, and craftsmen.

In March 1881, revolutionaries assassinated Alexander II. There was much confusion throughout the country and the revolutionaries urged the people to rebel. The Russian government found a scapegoat. They said that the Jewish people were the cause of all of the hardship for the peasants and the misfortune of the country. Anti-Jewish riots or pogroms broke out in the towns and villages of southern Russia. These pogroms were repeated in 1882, 1883, and 1884. The new Czar, Alexander III, encouraged terrible discrimination against the Jewish people. He also enacted a series of laws which had a profound effect on their lives. Thus, the great wave of emigration received its final shove and the Jewish people of Russia and other Eastern European nations headed to the United States for freedom and security.

German Jewish Community

As Jewish people were present in France by the year 200 CE, they were also probably present in the German states somewhere in that time period. On July 1, 1244, C.E. Frederick, God Duke of Austria and other lands, wrote a charter for the Duchy of Austria granting the Jewish people special privileges as a distinctive racial and religious group. This charter was of great significance because it was soon adopted with some changes by most East European countries, including Hungary, Bohemia, Poland, Silesia and Lithuania. The charter was a very reasonable one which encouraged money lending among the Austrian Jews and probably was used to attract more Jewish people with money to the outlying German state. The Duke guaranteed Jewish people ample opportunity to sell their wares and lend money while being secure of life and limb. The German attitude was diametrically opposed to the French attitude toward the Jewish people. In 1194, Philip Augustus needed money. He confiscated Jewish wealth and he used the horrific blood libel that Jewish people committed ritual murders to have blood for their religious ceremonies.

Spanish Jewish Community

The golden age of the Spanish Jewish community occurred between 900-1480. The Moorish leaders of Spain typically were tolerant and multicultural. They respected and protected minorities. Jewish people, although only one half of a percent of the population, made up 10% of the urban population, and in the large cities of southern Spain, 15-20 percent. They were predominantly represented in crafts and commerce, but also in agriculture and medicine. In 929, Al Rahman III declared Al-Andulus an independent caliphate with its capital at Cordoba. It was during this time that there was a sudden development of a flourishing, creative and highly independent Jewish community in Spain. Hasdai ibn Shaprut (905-975), a remarkable person, diplomat and statesman encouraged Jewish scholarship, both secular and religious. Because of his high standing at the Cordoban court, he brought the Jewish community into a new era of scholarship. Under his patronage, Dunash ibn Labrat revolutionized Hebrew poetry by writing it in Arabic meter. Hasdai's personal secretary, Menahem ibn Saruq, pioneered the scientific study of the Hebrew language. Yeshivot were established, foreign scholars welcomed and Hebrew books imported. In 1009 the Cordoban caliphate collapsed and Islamic Spain divided into numerous small principalities with their capitals becoming cultural and commercial centers. The relatively tolerant rulers welcomed Jewish financiers, economic experts, writers, scholars and scientists.

The Moorish leaders were interested in science and the arts, and invited scholars from all over the world to come and serve the Calip and later other leaders. Jewish people, Moors, and Christians lived together and worked together in basically a tolerant atmosphere. Jewish people adopted Moorish customs and studied Arabic, the Koran, Hebrew and Jewish scriptures, especially the Talmud. The Jewish people and the Arab scholars read the original writings of the Greek philosophers. The Jewish philosophers studied Plato and Aristotle and developed new philosophies incorporating the theories of these two great men into Jewish theology and thinking. They wrote exquisite poetry, grammar and mathematical treatises. An interest in Arabic grammar led to the development of Hebrew grammar and revival of the Hebrew language.

Maimonides

The great rabbi, physician, statesman, and philosopher Moses Maimonides (Rambam), was born in Cordoba, Spain in 1135. He studied Torah under his father, Maimon, and Rabbi Joseph Ibn Migash. The family fled to Morocco after the fall of Cordoba to the Almohads. In Morocco, he gained most of his secular knowledge while studying at the University of Fes. During this time, he composed his commentary on the Mishneh. He briefly lived in Jerusalem and prayed in a synagogue on the Temple Mount and then finally settled in Fostat, Egypt, where he became the doctor for the Grand Vizier Alfadhil and/or the Sultan Saladin of Egypt. While in Egypt, he composed most of his life's work, including: "The Book of Commandments;" "The Mishneh Torah," a comprehensive code of Jewish law; "The Guide to the Perplexed," a philosophical work harmonizing and differentiating Aristotlian philosophy and Jewish theology; and many other works. Although much of his writing was done away from Spain, his grounding in scholarship came from the Spain of his youth. He was the ultimate example of the achievement of the Jewish people. His philosophy of life and interpretation of previous Jewish writings are as valid today as they were almost 900 years ago.

Polish Jewish Community

The history of Jewish people in Poland and in the cities of Przemysl and Lvov may be used as examples of the migration to Eastern Europe where large numbers of Jewish people helped build the countries in which they lived. They had successful

Moses Maimonides

societies and good lives. However, along with success came discrimination. The need to adapt to these acts meant creating their own religious and civil structure and culture, becoming martyrs to their religion, or once again migrating to another area. The first Jewish people who arrived in Poland as in other parts of the world, were merchants who were multilingual. In Poland in 965 or 966, Ibn Moses came from Muslim Spain to the Holy Roman Empire and Slavonic countries on a trade and diplomatic journey. He was the author of the first extensive account about Poland. As the feudal system started to disintegrate, towns were born and money was needed. This led to the settlement of Jews in Poland. Jews started arriving in 1097 or 1098 leading to the establishment of the Polish State. During the time of the Crusades, Jewish people were banned in Bohemia and Germany and therefore came to Poland. From 1132-1202, the ruler of Poland employed Jews as engravers, technicians, and supervisors of all workers. Many of the coins had Hebrew inscriptions on them. In 1264, the Jewish people were given special privileges and were exempted from local courts. The Jewish people were involved in long-distance trade, guilds, agriculture, and some even owned landed estates. By the 14th century, they had settled in some 35 towns, including Przemysl and Lvov.

Galicia was an independent principality during the Middle Ages. It became part of Poland during the 1300's. It flourished as a center of Polish culture and education as well as Jewish culture and education. It served as a source of the movement for Polish independence. In 1203, Jewish people were allowed to own land in Galicia. This area had rich deposits of petroleum, natural gas, coal, iron, lead, salt, sulfur, and zinc. It also had excellent farmland, where farmers raised livestock, barley, oats, potatoes, rye, sugar beets, and wheat. There were beautiful forests which supplied lumber. Lvov was founded in this beautiful area by Lev, founder of the independent principality of Galicia, in the 1200's. The whole area was ultimately claimed by Russia, the Ukraine, and Germany.

From 1333-1370, Casmir the Great issued a series of charters protecting Jews. In 1356, Jews were granted autonomy in their communal affairs. From 1388-1390, Grand Duke Vitovt granted privileges to Jewish people and protected them. In 1399, the first persecution of Jewish people occurred in Poland.

From 1501-1648, over 500,000 Jewish people lived in Poland, which was 5% of the population. They improved their economic status by engaging in the crafts as well as the various trades. They made food, leather, textile products, clothing, and were involved in the production of gold, pewter, and glass. They not only exported Polish products and cattle but became established merchants to many countries. They became financiers because they extended credit to many people. Clothing manufacturing and sales became principle occupations.

Later Spanish and Portuguese Jewish Community

By 1492, King Ferdinand and Queen Isabella expelled the Jews from the entire Spanish country. To escape persecution and intimidation, thousands of Jewish people were baptized, but still practiced their Jewish beliefs in secret. They were called marranos. The Spanish Inquisition burned these people at the stake. The Spanish King and Queen claimed that they were purifying the Spanish community, but in fact, this was an excuse to seize the tremendous wealth of the Jewish community and destroy their positive influence on society.

In 1492, ever moving on to seek new commercial ventures and because of discrimination, many Jewish people helped fund the Columbus expeditions. The first settlers in what became the United States, may have been Marranos (including Spanish and Portuguese). It is believed that Alphonso de la Calle, second mate, Maestro Bernal, physician, Rodrigo Sanchez, Comptroller, Luis de Torres, interpreter, all on Columbus's expedition, were marranos. Some historians believe that converted Jews were on Juan Ponce de Leon's voyages of 1513 and 1521 to the Florida Gulf Coast. In 1539, Hernando de Soto's large expedition, which landed at or near Tampa Bay, included people of Jewish descent, possibly merchants and traders. It is also believed that Marranos came along with the Spanish to St. Augustine in 1665.

Portugal became the initial home for some 150,000 Jewish people. Five years later, the Portuguese king ordered them out of the country, except for those who would convert. The Jewish people went to the Spanish colonies in the New World, such as Cuba, and the Portuguese colonies, such as Brazil. Brazil's first governor was a Jewish person who had converted. In fact, there were so many Jewish people in two of the provinces that Sephardim owned and operated the largest number of Brazil's sugar refineries by the 1650s. Many of the Jewish people who came to the New World had been in Europe, and were merchants, artisans, importers and exporters, physicians, engineers, and high-level government officials. Every year, 20 or 30 of these individuals were arrested as suspected marranos and shipped back to Portugal for trial by the Inquisition. Their children were sent to African islands to die.

Netherlands Jewish Community

The Netherlands won its independence from Spain in 1561. The Protestant Dutch accepted anyone, including Jewish people who were escaping from the oppression of the Inquisition in Spain and Portugal. In 1593, the first shipload of Jewish people arrived in the Netherlands. The Jewish people were allowed full physical security and were permitted to own synagogues and practice their own religion. Although they were now Dutch they still considered themselves to be Portuguese. The Protestant Dutch were merchants and recognized the potential usefulness of Jewish traders and financiers. By 1612, there were 10 Jewish brokers in the Amsterdam Stock Exchange. By 1621, a group of Jewish people became organizers and important shareholders in the Dutch West India Company.

Recife

In 1630, the Dutch laid siege to Recife, capital of the Brazilian province of Pernambuco. In order to weaken resistance, they pledged civil equality for all of the inhabitants, whether they were Roman Catholics or Jews. Many of the converted Jews accepted the terms of the Dutch

and went back to their original religion. Other Jewish people from Amsterdam, England, the Balkans and Central and Eastern Europe came to this wonderful place where Jewish people could live free. In 1642, they organized the first Jewish congregation in the New World, brought over the first Rabbi to the Americas, Isaac Aboab da Fonseca, from Amsterdam, built a synagogue, opened Hebrew schools, and built a kosher slaughterhouse. By 1650, there were approximately 1,500 Jewish people there. In 1645, Portugal started a 10-year effort to regain its colony. Many of the Jewish people, because of fear of the Inquisition, converted to Catholicism but continued to live secret Jewish lives.

In the 1640's, Jewish life was deteriorating in both the old and new worlds. The Cossacks attacked Poland killing more than 200,000 Jews and destroying 700 Jewish communities. At the same time, Jewish people were outlawed in England; forced to wear the yellow star in Rome; and subjected to the Inquisition in Mexico where 108 Jews were killed including 13 who were burned alive.

In January 1654, the colony at Recife surrendered to the Portuguese. The Portuguese commander was an enlightened person and therefore granted full pardon to all people involved in the insurrection, including the Jewish people. However, he was under orders to introduce the Inquisition. As a result of this conquest and because of fear of the Inquisition, within three months, the entire Jewish population left in 16 ships, 14 of them going to the Netherlands. One of the ships went to the Dutch West Indies, which had become a large naval base and commercial depot and soon a major place for the Jewish population of importers, and plantation owners. The other ship ended up in colonial America.

Shabbtai Zevi

Shabbtai Zevi, the son of a Dutch Jew, in the 1640's proclaimed himself to be the Messiah. The Jewish people were going through such terrible times that many of them accepted his proclamation as the truth. The Jewish people from Amsterdam to Constantinople were in a frenzy. They wanted to believe in him in order to correct the awful world in which they were living. When the Muslims threatened to kill him, he converted to Islam.

Hasidism

In Poland in the mid 1600s, there was a struggle between the traditional rabbinic Judaism and radical Kabbalah influenced mysticism, especially after the messianic movement of Shabbtai Zevi. Hasidism was a response to the needs of the common people in its simple, stimulating and comforting faith. Its aim was to create a new type of religious person, one who placed emotion above reason and rites, and religious exaltation above knowledge. True religion was not religious scholarship, but a sincere love of God combined with warm faith and belief in the importance of prayer. The ordinary person filled with a sincere belief in God, and whose prayers came from the heart, was more acceptable to God than the person who was very learned in Jewish law and obeyed it implicitly. Many of these prayers were offered to God in the form of music.

Hasidism was a message of joy amidst the somber life and hardship of the times. It became the most authentic product of the Jewish shtetl (small town). Hasidism was closely related to other Orthodox Jewish groups, however it de-emphasized Talmudic learning and was centered around the teaching of its founder, the Baal Shem Tov. Hasidism believed that God could be found not only in the spiritual world, but also in the material world. God could also be found in mundane work.

Baal Shem Tov

The "Baal" Shem Tov, Rabbi Israel ben Eliezer (1700-1760), founder of the Hasidic movement, became part of Eastern European Jewish life at a time when Jewish morale was extremely low. Shabbtai Zvi, who claimed he was the Messiah, was proven to be a fraud. This left the Jewish people despondent and disheartened. Their hope for a better life was gone. In addition, the Jewish community was divided between those who had power and wealth, typically the scholars and businesspeople, and those who were relatively uneducated

and in poverty. This made Judaism highly unattractive to the majority of the people in those areas. The "Baal " Shem Tov started a movement that appealed to the masses and made the individuals have a sense of worth and dignity. He returned the community to a meaningful and vibrant Judaism by using the major ingredient of Simcha or joy. What better way to show joy than to incorporate happy music into all aspects of life including religious services. He quoted the Psalmist, "Serve the Lord with joy-come before Him with singing." He said, "Only through simcha can we attain communion with God." The "Baal" Shem Tov lived what he taught. He spent much of his time in the fields among the shepherds absorbing their melodies and making song a natural part of his body and soul. The Hasidic people borrowed liberally the music of their host countries and made the melodies an outpouring of their souls. Each small community had its own distinct style and many of these styles and the music have become part of our worship services and our lives.

After the Baal Shem Tov died he was followed by a succession of rabbis known as Rebbes (leaders), who were descended from him. Rabbi Shneur Zalman(1745-1812) of Liada became the leader of Hasidism in Lithuania. He was the founder of Chabad, and chose its name. The Chabad originated in a small town in Russia called Lubavitch translated "town of love." Thus the movement is called the Chabad Lubavitch or just chabad. (The word Chabad is a Hebrew acronym for chochma (wisdom), bina (understanding), and da'as (knowledge). The name Chabad reflects the intellectual accessibility of the mystical teachings of the Kabbala).Rabbi Dovber (1773-1827), the second Rebbe of the Chabad, was the son of Shneur Zalman and the father of Rabbi Menachem Mendel (1789-1866). These rabbis were followed by Rabbi Shmuel(1834-1882), Rabbi Sholom Dovber (1860-1920), Rabbi Joseph Isaac Schneerson (1880-1950), and Rabbi Menachem Mendel Schneerson (1902-1994).

Russian Expansionism

From 1772-1815, more than 1,200,000

Polish and Lithuanian Jews came under Russian rule as a result of Russia's westward expansion. In 1795, laws were passed confining Jewish people to the Pale of Settlement in Russia. This brought further pressure on the Jewish people, including extreme poverty, serious financial crises and increasing discriminatory acts. A limited number of Jewish people escaped from these areas and came to America.

COLONIAL JEWISH COMMUNITY

In 1585, Joachim Gans was the first documented Jewish person to land on the shores of America. He was a metallurgist with considerable skill in the smelting of copper who accompanied an expedition of explorers to Roanoke, North Carolina. This expedition originated in Plymouth, England.

On February 24, 1654 , the Dutch schooner Valck left Recife (which is now northern Brazil). A Spanish privateer seized the ship and made it drop anchor in Jamaica, a Spanish colony. Everything was stolen except for the clothing and furniture. Several of the baptized Jewish people were arrested by the Inquisition. The twenty three professing Jewish people were rescued by a French vessel and were allowed to leave with the Gentile majority. The Jewish people included four men, six women, married and widowed, and thirteen children. They were Dutch, Italian, and some of Central European ancestry. They stopped first in Cuba and then sailed into the mouth of the Hudson River at New Amsterdam (New York). They arrived in America in early September 1654 and settled on the East Coast. Prior to that time Jacob Barsimson, a Jewish Hollander, had arrived in New Amsterdam on August 22, 1654. There were an estimated twenty five Jewish people in the colonies. In March 1655, five Jewish families and three unmarried males sailed directly from Holland to New Amsterdam. They were merchants and patriots.

Many of the Jewish people had learned at an early age what oppression was. They knew about restrictions, humiliation, and tyranny, and reacted in a very positive manner to the unrestricted commerce and opportunity for success, which did not exist in the lands of their birth. The initial restrictions imposed on the Jewish people by Governor Peter Stuyvesant had been reversed by the Dutch West India Company.

Asser Levy and the Jewish people fought for the right to be part of the militia and perform guard duty on the walls of the fort. The Jewish people knew from centuries of persecution, that to have democracy and all its rights, you must also assume responsibility for all people. This was the beginning of Jewish people serving with great distinction in the Armed Forces of the United States, in all wars and conflicts, and eventually led to the creation of the Jewish War Veterans.

New York Jewish Community

The British conquered New Amsterdam and changed the name to New York. The Treaty of Breda of 1667 guaranteed that Britain would give full rights of worship, trade, individual property, and inheritance to all inhabitants of the former New Netherlands, now New York. Although they were initially refused permission to build a synagogue and even had to pay taxes to the Anglican Church, in a few decades these restrictions lapsed and the Jewish people were able to possess property. In 1700, there were between two hundred and three hundred Jewish people in the country, with about 20 families in New York. The Jewish people in New York were allowed to worship openly in their own rented facilities. They were permitted to vote in elections, serve on juries and act as executors of estates. In 1718, Jewish people served as constables in three of New York's seven wards. In 1728, the first synagogue, Shearith Israel, was erected. Fifty seven men and four women contributed to the building of the synagogue. In addition, contributions came from the Spanish-Portuguese congregations in London, Amsterdam, Curacao and Suriname. The first synagogue was opened on Mill Street in an old grist mill.

Other Colonies

In the early years in New England Jewish people were not tolerated. However, after 1688, the colonial minister of New

England became British and the royal governors became more tolerant. In 1656, Jewish people were permitted resident rights in Quaker Pennsylvania and Anglican New Jersey. In Maryland, the Jewish legal status was in great peril because of the fear of Catholic people taking over the colony again. The laws of Maryland enjoined Jewish public worship and political rights of any sort. In Anglican Virginia during the colonial period, Catholics, dissenters, and Jews were granted no rights. In South Carolina, the philosopher John Locke wrote the constitution that excluded Catholics but included Jews, heathens and dissenters.

Gerschom Mendes Seixas

In 1768, Shearith Israel of New York appointed 23-year-old Gerschom Mendes Seixes as its hazzan or reader. As the only religious official in the congregation he functioned as spiritual leader, interpreter of religious law, supervisor of kashrut, performer of marriages and funerals and all the duties associated with ordained rabbis. He received his Jewish education primarily from his father. He was not a college graduate, but was self educated in Talmud and secular literature, including Christian texts. During the American Revolution, even though the congregation was split on the issue, he was a strong advocate for American independence. He convinced the majority of the congregants to close the synagogue rather than come under British occupation. In 1780, Seixas relocated to Philadelphia to become hazzan of Mickve Israel. Although he personally abhorred war he regularly called on God to bless the Revolution, the Congress and George Washington and the patriot armies. He said, "We consider the American cause to be just because of its emphasis on individual liberty and independence which is a blessing for America's Jewish people." In 1784, he was persuaded to return to New York and to Shearith Israel, where he served until his death in 1816.

Seixas was one of three clergymen who participated in the inauguration of George Washington in 1787. Seixas devoted much of his time and prestige to encouraging charity for the poor. He preached that being rich was not a sign of grace, nor poverty a sign of disgrace. He believed that the very purpose of a person's life was to help others, whether they were recognized or not recognized for their contribution. When he died, Seixas was mourned throughout the city of New York.

Philadelphia Jewish Community

The first known Jewish person to live in Philadelphia was Nathan Levy in 1735. He was a merchant and shipper and had acquired a small piece of land between 8th and 9th St. on the north side of Walnut Street. This later became the first Jewish cemetery in Pennsylvania. By 1750, the approximately 100 Jewish families living in Philadelphia earned their livelihood in relative security. During the American Revolution, many Jewish people moved to Philadelphia because they were not loyal to the British crown and most of the other cities were occupied by the British. The old house of worship was in a cramped building on tiny Elfreth's Alley in the center of Philadelphia. Rev. Seixas, along with other newcomers, and Mordechai Mordechai, a local congregant, received permission from the synagogues in London and Amsterdam to adapt the interior design of the new Portuguese-Spanish style structure of Philadelphia to match those existing in Europe. The Philadelphia congregation received financial help from Jewish communities in Newport, New York, Curacao, London and Amsterdam. Mikveh Israel, which became the first dedicated synagogue in Philadelphia in colonial times, was opened officially on September 13, 1783. Bernard and Michael Gratz, among others, were founders of the synagogue. The first Hebrew Sunday school started there.

Bernard and Michael Gratz

Bernard Gratz arrived in the colonies in 1754, and his brother, Michael, arrived in 1759. They both settled in Philadelphia, where they became promoters and merchants who opened up vast territories to trade and exploration. Their specialty was the fur trade. The brothers became revolutionaries and freely accepted their responsibility to help the emerging United States. The

Gratz Brothers helped to manufacture and to supply gunpowder and firearms to Washington's troops. They served on numerous boards and made many financial contributions to the Jewish and non-Jewish communities. Both of them contributed to the new public library in Philadelphia, which was started by Benjamin Franklin. In both their homes there were large libraries filled with many books.

Rebecca Gratz

Rebecca Gratz, the granddaughter of Simon, an eminent Jewish businessman, felt that the Jewish people would disappear through intermarriage if Jewish children were not given a proper education in Judaism. Rebecca was from the Michael Gratz part of the family. She was born in 1781 and became the foremost American Jewish woman of the 19th century. Rebecca was extremely well read and associated with many literary figures, including Washington Irving and Sir Walter Scott. She was a fervent patriot, profoundly religious woman, and a widely known activist for poor women. She was the founder and secretary of Philadelphia's earliest nonsectarian woman's philanthropic organizations, including the Female Association for the Relief of Women and Children in Reduced Circumstances, as well as the Philadelphia Orphan Society. Rebecca Gratz, despite being Jewish, was selected to sit on many boards of charitable organizations. Rebecca's brother, Simon, helped start the Gratz Liberal College for the Arts and Sciences in Philadelphia. She also served on the board of the Academy of Fine Arts. The author attended Simon Gratz High School in Philadelphia.

Charleston Jewish Community

It has been reported that in 1680, a handful of Jewish people sailed into Charles Towne Harbor. In 1695, the first official record of a Jewish person was recorded in the colony of Carolina. It indicated that he was an interpreter, possibly between the Spanish and Indians and the new English settlers. He must have arrived several years prior to that time in order to learn the Indian language. The records of the time were very sketchy. In 1697, sixty four men were made citizens of Carolina, including four Jews. There was no mention made of women. From 1697 on, the Sephardic Jews, who were very Orthodox, came from London and from the Caribbean islands. In the early 1700s, there was a record of a Jewish marriage. By 1723, there were enough Jewish people to form a congregation. They worshiped in each other's homes and in small halls. In 1740, all colonists, including Jews, were made citizens of the Province of Carolina and were permitted to own property and hold colonial governmental offices. Although the colony limited the franchise to Protestants, the Jewish people were able to continue to trade, to worship, to execute legal documents, and to sit on juries.

In 1749, Kahal Kadosh Unveh Sholom (Holy Congregation Mansion of Peace) was founded. Moses Cohen, who had come from London, was a prime supporter and was listed as the Chief Rabbi of the congregation. The first hazan was Isaac da Costa. Both of these men were influenced by the Bevis Marks Synagogue in London, England. In the beginning the congregation was strictly Orthodox in the Sephardic manner, with the services in Hebrew and Spanish. They were very repetitive and long, possibly lasting four hours or more. Fines were given for missing a Sabbath service, for arguing with a trustee, and for refusing a Torah honor.

In 1754, the first Jewish cemetery was dedicated.

The College of Charleston, founded in 1770 and chartered in 1785, is the oldest municipal College in America. In 1836 the city of Charleston assumed responsibility for the College. Included in their programs today is a Chair of Jewish Studies with a director and full-time staff.

In 1780, the Jewish congregation rented two upper rooms in a stone house and used them as the congregation's first sanctuary known as the "Old Synagogue.'

In 1784, the Hebrew Benevolent Society, the oldest one in America, was founded. Currently, there are over 300 male members. For whatever reason, women have never participated in this group.

In 1786, the Portuguese group purchased their own cemetery to be separate from the German congregation, although the original cemetery was large enough for both groups.

From 1790-1820, Charlestown had the largest Jewish population in the United States, more even than New York or Philadelphia.

In 1791, there were enough Jewish people in the community to build their first synagogue. They were chartered and changed the name to Kahal Kadosh Beth Elohim (Holy Congregation, House of God). At that time there were fifty three Jewish families in Charleston with about 220 people.

In 1794, the first Sephardic orthodox synagogue building was completed and dedicated. The Orthodox worship continued until 1838 when a serious fire destroyed that part of the city.

In 1801, the Hebrew Orphan Society, the oldest orphan society in America, was founded in Charleston. The membership was limited to thirty six people. The membership over these many years has been handed down from father to son, from family to family.

In December of 1824, forty seven Jewish people from Charleston, South Carolina, petitioned the leaders of Beth Elohim to make major changes in the Shabbat service. They asked that each Hebrew prayer in the service be followed immediately by an English translation. They also asked that new prayers be offered reflecting contemporary American life and that the rabbi offer a weekly sermon in English that would explain the Scriptures and apply them to everyday life. They also asked that the services be shortened. The leaders of the congregation refused to consider the petition. On November 21, 1825, Isaac Harby, the leader of the Reformed Society of Israelites, who led the breakaway from Congregation Beth Elohim of Charleston, South Carolina gave a speech to his new congregation about the rationale for being Reform rather than Orthodox. He did not seek the abandonment of the ancient language, Hebrew, from the religious service, but rather wanted to use the English language most of the time to be able to express prayers to God in the language of the nation to bring greater dignity to every prayer, every ceremony, and create a warmth of true devotion. He

wanted to discard rabbinical interpolations, avoid useless repetitions, to recite the Torah and the prophets in the original Hebrew followed by select translations into English, to make the service more meaningful. He also believed in giving a lecture about the law and explaining its meaning so that both young and old could learn about the essence of Judaism. He believed in order to live in America and to share the blessings of liberty, the Jewish people had to be looked upon by others as God fearing people whose language and customs could be understood by the general community. He felt that a religious law which was not rooted either in a spiritual or physical nature of people was only binding as long as it was useful. The Orthodox congregations felt that Reform Judaism was a sect because it was forming a new code for public worship, embracing instrumental and vocal music, using a chorus of male and female voices with Jewish and non-Jewish people, and changing the name of the house of worship from synagogue to temple. It also disturbed these individuals that the leaders were not rabbis but rather doctors. The Orthodox summed up their discussion by saying that the Reform move their lips in sanctity while they hold deception in their hearts. During the 19th century there were many sermons, lectures, articles, editorials and debates which were both highly ideological and recriminatory. Because of financial problems these individuals rejoined Beth Elohim.

In 1841, the German majority, together with the Reform Society of Israelites, took over the leadership and installed an organ. They became the first congregation in America to use instrumental music in the services. After several attempts at lawsuits, the Orthodox group resigned and formed Sherith Israel. In 1861, they rejoined and worked out a compromise. Both synagogues had a great number of members in the Confederate forces, which left both congregations lacking in funds. Once again the Reform and Orthodox groups could not get along and a suit ensued. The Orthodox group finally resigned and organized their own congregation, Brith Sholom Synagogue.

In 1859, the B'nai B'rith Lodge was

founded. It was then disbanded and finally reorganized in 1905.

Early Eastern European Migration

By 1700, Jewish people were coming from Poland and Russia to America because of a series of wars between Poland, Ukraine, Russia, Turkey and Tarters. The Army, especially from the Ukraine, used the war as an excuse to kill thousands of Jews, who were noncombatants.

Savannah Jewish Community

On July 11, 1733, forty two pioneering Jews from England came to Savannah, Georgia. Most of the Jewish people were from Portugal and, in addition, there were two German Jewish families. In 1732, the Jewish community of 6,000 living in London were faced with the poverty of their newly arrived coreligionists. They decided to help establish and generously supported the new colony of Georgia and also provided money for their fellow Jews to sail to the colony and to set up their homes. The Sephardic Synagogue also provided a Torah scroll written on deerskin and a circumcision box. The congregational archives of the first synagogue currently contain the original Torah, and letters from George Washington, Thomas Jefferson, James Madison, and several other Presidents. Governor Oglethorpe, when he learned that everyone was permitted to settle except Catholics, placed the new Jewish people on the fringes of his own tract of land, rented them a place to worship, and gave them a plot for their cemetery. Over a period of time, other Jewish people arrived. They were Sephardic and Ashkenazic, farmers and tradesmen. They got along very well with their neighbors. The Savannah Jewish community did not follow the usual sequence of obtaining a cemetery, building a mikvah, and establishing a congregation. Instead, they established the congregation first, then obtained the cemetery, and finally built the mikvah. In July, 1735, they agreed to open a synagogue. However, the construction of the building for the synagogue was delayed because of the arrival of new Jewish families who were Ashkenazic. The Sephardic Jews followed one set of rituals, whereas the Ashkenazic Jews followed another one. The Sephardic Jews left for a period of time around 1742 because Spanish soldiers had landed nearby and they were concerned that they might face the Inquisition. By 1774, enough Jewish people came back to Savannah to reform the congregation and celebrate the eve of Yom Kippur in a room furnished as a chapel by Mordecai Sheftal, in the home of his father Benjamin. During the Revolutionary War, Mordecai Sheftal became the highest ranking Jewish officer of the Revolutionary forces with the rank of deputy commissary general to the Continental troops in South Carolina and Georgia. He and his son were captured by the British and imprisoned in Antigua. Eventually they were traded for two captured British officers.

On July 7, 1786, the synagogue was reorganized and officers were elected. Services were held regularly, and at one time attendance numbered seventy three males and females. On November 20, 1790, Governor Edward Telfair granted the congregation a perpetual charter as a synagogue. By 1818, the growth of the Jewish population in Savannah had increased to numbers sufficient enough to build a synagogue. The small wooden structure was destroyed by fire on December 4, 1829, but the Torahs and Ark were saved. A new brick building was consecrated on the same site in 1841 by Reverend Isaac Leeser of Philadelphia. In 1853, the congregation finally could afford a permanent spiritual leader, who was Reverend Jacob Rosenfeld. He served until 1862. On February 11, 1868, the congregation took its first steps toward becoming Reform, by eliminating the second day of festivals. However, it was not until 1894, when members were permitted to go without hats during services.

Aaron Lopez

In 1737, in Lisbon, Antonio José da Silva, a distinguished Portuguese poet was thrown into prison because he has secretly remained faithful to his Jewish heritage. He was denounced as a heretic and was burned at the stake in a public ceremony before thousands of people. An eight-year-old boy, also a secret Jew, Aaron Lopez swore that he would leave this horrible intolerance as soon as he was able. When he became a man he arrived in Newport, Rhode Island and openly affirmed his Jewish faith. When the Revolutionary War started he was one of the great masters of New England commerce. He had thirty ships sailing worldwide. He jeopardized his fleet, his fortune and his life when he supported the American cause. He was like many Jewish people who came later. They were loyal Jews but more importantly loyal Americans.

French and Indian War

During the French and Indian War of 1754-63, Sampson Simpson and Jacob Franks were purchasing agents for the British Armed Forces. Simpson, Hyman Levy, Jacob Franks, and Judah Hays leased gun bearing privateers to the British Navy. Jewish people became importers, real estate investors, fur traders, and owned merchant vessels. They did an excellent trade with the Dutch West Indies, which also had a large Jewish population dating back to the 1500's. There were approximately 150 Jewish men and their families in Providence, Rhode Island. They built the local economy.

Touro Family

In 1758, the Touro family arrived in Newport, Rhode Island. Young Isaac became a cantor at the local synagogue. One of his sons, Abraham, went to New Orleans where he built a large shipping business. Abraham then moved to Boston, opened a shipyard in New Bedford, and achieved much financial success and recognition. When he died in 1825, he left many bequests to Jewish, local, and state charities. His younger brother, Judah, also made a fortune as an importer in New Orleans. Judah served as a civilian volunteer in the American army during the war of 1812. He was severely wounded and nearly lost his life. He contributed to a multitude of Jewish and non-Jewish charities and established New Orleans' first free public library and its first public infirmary. He left a fortune exceeding one million dollars which supported a variety of Jewish and many non-Jewish institutions, including hospitals, orphanages, and other nonsectarian programs.

In 1763, the Touro Synagogue of Congregation Jeshuat Israel of Newport, Rhode Island was dedicated. It is the oldest synagogue building in the United States. It was declared a national historic site in 1946 and a commemorative stamp was issued in its honor in 1982.

1776

By 1776, out of a total population of about three million people in the colonies, there were approximately 2,000 Jewish people, with roughly 300 to 350 of them in New York and additional large Jewish populations in Newport, Rhode Island, Philadelphia, Pennsylvania, Charleston, South Carolina, and Savannah, Georgia. Another source gave the following statistics: United States Jewish population, 2,500; Newport, Rhode Island, 76, New England, 150; New York, New York, 246, New York state, 350; Philadelphia, Pennsylvania, 122, Pennsylvania, 250; Charleston, South Carolina, 300; Richmond, Virginia, 28, Virginia, 200; Savanna, Georgia, 15, Georgia, 100. It is very difficult to determine the exact number of Jewish people in America during the early years since various historical sources often quote different numbers. Most of the Jewish people were traders, retailers, and artisans. Another source said that Charleston, South Carolina had a Jewish community of 600 families and was almost as prosperous as Newport, Rhode Island. These people were led by a few merchants with trade connections, especially in the West Indies. They were very important to the frontier communities. Among this group of Jewish men were David and Moses Franks, Bernard and Michael Gratz, Joseph Simon, Andrew Levy, Samuel Judah, and Haym Salomon.

Haym Salomon

Haym Salomon became a member of the Liberty Boys, an organization that fought the British during the Revolutionary War. One day he read a letter printed in the newspaper stating that, "Our poor soldiers are reduced to the very edge of famine, their patience is exhausted by sufferings, and their spirit is almost broken." Salomon sent a letter to

General George Washington expressing his eagerness to serve the army by financing some of its deserving officers. He gave General Von Steuben 1,000 pounds and then financed the Pulaski Legion of light infantry and foot soldiers. By the fall of 1780, the Continental Army had not received pay for five months. George Washington wrote to Robert Morris, the Minister of Finance, that food was extremely scarce, the situation was desperate, and the Army was threatening mutiny. He asked Robert Morris to please contact Haym Salomon for help. Robert Morris sent a messenger to deliver a letter to Mr. Salomon on Yom Kippur at Mikvah Israel Synagogue. The letter stated, "The terrible emergency of the moment necessitates my turning to you at this hour. The office of finance has been unable to procure sufficient funds to cover the enclosed notes, which must be discounted immediately. I have exhausted even my personal sources of aid. Since all else has failed, I must beg of you to act immediately with whatever resources you have to satisfy our distress." When the messenger was asked how much money was needed, he replied $20,000. Haym walked to the Bema and told the rabbi that he had to address the congregation. The rabbi said that a financial communication on Yom Kippur is forbidden. The congregation was in an uproar. Hyam explained that more soldiers were dying from starvation and cold than from British bayonets and that $20,000 was needed immediately. In fifteen minutes pledges for the $20,000 had been raised and after sundown the money would be delivered to Mr. Morris. This unselfish devotion to America has been consistent with the 4,000 year tradition of Jewish people contributing their money and their lives to help other people live a better life. It is also part of the 4,000 year unbroken belief of Jewish people in one living God and their need to be God's helper here on earth.

United States Constitution and Bill of Rights

In 1787, the United States Constitution, and in 1791, the Bill of Rights, outlawed religious tests as qualifications to hold any office or public trust and forbade Congress from making any law respecting the establishment of a religion in the country. Jewish people had gained by law their religious rights in the United States.

Jewish Soldiers and Sailors in the Colonies

Jewish people also made many contributions to the armed forces of the United States as well as in politics. They served with great distinction as officers, as well as enlisted men.

Lieutenant Colonel Solomon Bush, a high ranking Jewish officer in the Continental Army, was decorated for his bravery in action. He was the first Jewish person considered for cabinet rank, when he applied for Postmaster General of the United States. He did not receive the position, although he was highly honored by his fellow Americans. He was a devoted Mason and became a grandmaster for the State of Pennsylvania. Solomon's father was Matthias who came to New York City in the 1740s and later moved to Philadelphia or Germantown. He became a naturalized citizen in 1749. He married into the prominent Simon Gratz family and became a leader in the synagogue established in Philadelphia in the 1760s. He was a merchant and shipowner, and during the French and Indian War, an Army purveyor.

On August 1, 1776, following the signing of the Declaration of Independence by the colonies Francis Salvador was killed leading a little army of 330 men who were defending the frontier settlers against the Cherokee Indians who had been incited by the British. He was the first Jewish person to die in the American Revolution. He had previously distinguished himself as the financial adviser to the South Carolina Assembly. He was the first of many Jews who would die in defense of the United States of America over the next 229 years.

Mordecai Sheftal was a leader in the Revolutionary movement against the British in Georgia. He was named by the Revolutionary Government, Commissioner General of Purchases and Issues to the Militia of Georgia.

The Cardoza family were war heroes and jurists. David settled in Charleston

South Carolina, in 1775, enlisted in the South Carolina Army, and fought many times against the British. His brother, Isaac, was among many Jewish men who fought to defend Charleston Harbor against the British. His brothers, Moses and Abraham, were also involved in the American Revolution. David's son, Jacob Newton, was an outstanding economist.

Albert Jacob Cardozo, born in 1825, was elected to the New York Supreme Court. His son, Benjamin Nathan, born in 1870, became a member of the United States Supreme Court.

Naval captain Levi Myers Harby was involved in the Seminole Indian War in Florida in 1828. He previously had been involved in many naval battles including the crushing of the Barbary Pirates. When he was sixty eight years old, the Civil War started. He was given command of the fighting ship Neptune by the Confederacy.

Captain Mordecai Myers was both a military hero and a politician. He joined a military company under the command of Colonel John Marshall, who later became the Chief Justice of the United States Supreme Court. In the war of 1812, he became a hero when he saved more than 200 men and their military supplies by using great energy, skill, and risking his own life. He later became the first Jewish mayor of Schenectady, New York.

Commodore John Ordroneaux fought the British in the War of 1812. Commodore Uriah P. Levy, a naval hero, served the United States from the War of 1812 until 1862. He ended the practice of flogging sailors as inhumane and senseless.

Dr. David Camden De Leon, the fighting doctor, although he had no military experience, took command of American troops whose officers had all been killed. This occurred during the Mexican War of 1845. He turned defeat into victory by rallying the soldiers and counter attacking. He was twice cited for his gallantry, including a Congressional citation. He previously had been involved in the Seminole War in Florida.

Jewish people have always been patriots and have performed at the highest level of their capabilities to help defend this country, which had given them a chance to develop to their ultimate capabilities, to have freedom of speech and religion, and to provide a better way of life for their families and for society at large. In keeping with this distinguished and honorable pattern, the author's father, Charles Koren, who was an immigrant from Russia in 1908, served twice in World War I. Because he was dying of influenza, he was given a medical discharge. When he recovered, he enlisted a second time to help defend his country and this time received an honorable discharge.

1790-1800

In 1790, there were approximately 3,000 Jewish people in the country. They had originally come from a variety of countries including Brazil, the Netherlands, Germany, Poland, Russia, etc.. George Washington wrote a letter to the Hebrew Congregation of Newport, Rhode Island. He restated the Constitution and Bill of Rights when he proclaimed that liberty is an inherent natural right and assured the Jewish community that the United States government, "Gives to bigotry no sanction, to persecution no assistance." George Washington's letter affirmed that the United States would be a place where Jews were welcomed as equals.

In 1798, Emma Lazarus' great-grandfather, Samuel, and Gerschom Mendes Seixas founded the Kalfe Sedakah, a society for those stricken by yellow fever in the epidemic that occurred that year. Relief was given to all people regardless of religion or national origin. Gerschom was the first native born rabbi in the United States. He was the rabbi of Congregation Shearith Israel, a Spanish and Portuguese Synagogue in New York City, in 1768. He fathered 26 children. He and most of his congregation left New York City in 1776 when the British were approaching during the American Revolutionary War. Most of his congregation went to Philadelphia while he went to Stamford, Connecticut. In 1780, he went to Philadelphia and helped found the new synagogue, Mikveh Israel, where he served as rabbi for two years. In 1784, he returned to New York. He was the first rabbi in America to give his sermons in English. He gave sermons dealing with Jewish participation in the life of the state and made appeals for the support of the American Revolution. His son David established the Deaf and Dumb Institute of Philadelphia.

By the late 1700s, the pioneering Jewish people in Philadelphia established the routes for merchandise to flow from the Jewish companies into the territories in exchange for the furs coming out of those lands. The Jewish companies helped outfit the George Rogers Clark Expedition to Vincennes Indiana in 1799, and were part of the opening of the Northwest territory. Jewish peddlers proceeded through the Cumberland Gap into Indiana, Illinois, Kentucky and westward.

Jewish Religious Movements

There were formal differences of opinion about all things religious among Jewish people going clear back to the Maccabean revolt which is the basis for the story of Chanukkah. The Jewish people fought for twenty five years to get out from under their oppressors. Afterwards they split into three groups: the Essenes, Sadducees, and the Pharisees. The Essenes were an aesthetic and mystical group devoted to strict discipline living in isolation from the world and probably wrote the Dead Sea Scrolls. They may have influenced early Christianity through their mystical teachings. The Sadducees evolved out of the Hellenistic elements of Judaism. The movement was made up of the priests and aristocrats of Jewish society. They were conservative religiously but liberal socially. They believed in a narrow and unchanging interpretation of the written Torah and did not believe in the oral Torah. The Temple and sacrificial services were at the center of worship. They adopted the Greek culture which was predominant in the outer community. The Pharisees believed that God gave the Jewish people both a written and oral Torah and that both were equally binding, but opened to reinterpretation by the rabbis. They were devoted to the study of the Torah and education for all people.

After being conquered by Rome, a fourth group, the Zealots, appeared. This group was nationalistic in character. They favored war with Rome and believed death was preferable to Roman control.

They were the defenders of Masada. The Pharisees were the only ones that survived the destruction of the Temple. Afterwards, for many centuries, there were no organized differences of opinion within Judaism. There were some differences in practices and customs depending on where you lived.

In the ninth century, a sect known as the Karaites arose. They denied the existence of the oral Torah and did not believe in rabbinical interpretation. Everything was inspired by God and therefore anything done by people would have flaws in it. The opposing group was known as the Rabbanites. They relied upon rabbinical interpretation to determine what was appropriate in enforcing religious law.

The concepts of Orthodox, Conservative, and Reform Judaism, as we know them today, have only been developed during the last 200 years. (Hasidism, a form of orthodoxy, has been previously discussed). Basically Orthodox groups differ from Conservative and Reform by their definition of Judaism and their beliefs about Torah and Halakhah (The legal path that should be followed.), which in the case of Orthodox is inviolate. Reform believe in the right of the individual to decide what is proper faith or practice. Reform is an evolving religion based on sacred principles. Conservative is a coalition of many diverse elements ranging from almost Orthodox to almost Reform. The conservative movement can preserve tradition but at the same time believe that Judaism is a living organism and constantly evolving.

Orthodox Judaism

Orthodox Jewish people vary from ultra to modern, however this group is the most traditional of the Jewish people and follow all of the dietary laws, observe all of the holidays and enforce segregation of the sexes in prayer. The term Orthodox denotes a conservative and ritualistic outlook as viewed from the perspective of liberalism. Orthodox Jews believe that God gave Moses the whole Torah on Mount Sinai, including the Written Torah and the Oral Torah, which is an oral tradition explaining and interpreting the Written Torah. Among the Orthodox Congregations, there is a diverse range of issues which have not been resolved. They include: the importance or legitimacy of mysticism; policies toward Zionism and Jewish nationalism; the religious status of the State of Israel; educational philosophies; leadership philosophies; cooperation with non–Orthodox Jewish people; etc.. Modern Orthodox Judaism attempts to adapt Orthodox Judaism in interaction with the surrounding non-Jewish modern world. It emphasizes that if this interaction is guided by Jewish values, it will be desirable and intellectually and physically good. They believe that Jewish people should live by Jewish principles of faith, but have a relaxed standard for traditional laws and customs. Rabbi Israel Azriel Hildesheimer, the rabbi of Eisenstadt, Hungary in 1851, and Rabbi Samson Raphael Hirsch of the principality of Oldenberg in 1830, and chief rabbi of Moravia in 1847, were the most influential religious leaders in the Modern Orthodox Movement at its inception. They established schools and wrote numerous documents concerning the introduction of German methods of instruction and secular branches of learning into the Jewish schools. This was a time when there was great dissension between Reform and Orthodox Judaism.

Reform Judaism

Reform Judaism began in Germany in the late 1700s and early 1800s. Some sources choose the beginning of the Reform movement between 1810 and 1820 with the congregations in Seesen, Hamburg and Berlin, Germany, where fundamental changes occurred in traditional Jewish practices and beliefs, such as mixed seating, the use of German in the services, single day observance of festivals, and the use of a cantor/ choir. Reform Judaism was influenced and inspired by scholars who were analyzing a new openness to what was going on in the world around them. A number of these Jewish scholars sought to abandon traditional beliefs and practices that did not seem to apply to that time period, while asserting their Jewishness in new ways. They argued that Halakhah or Jewish law was a process and not fixed forever in ancient times. They therefore did not have to practice the dietary laws or separate men from women in public worship. Only the moral laws were binding and those teachings which asserted the divine nature of the human spirit and sought to promote a just society. Reform Jewish people believe that the Torah was written by people inspired by God rather than given directly by God to the Jewish people. The Torah is sacred, but its laws are not strictly observed if they are outdated. Jewish men and women not only sit together in the Temple but also participate in all aspects of Jewish rites and rituals and may serve as rabbis or cantors. Between 1790 and 1830, there were many aesthetic changes in Jewish worship among Reform Congregations. They included: decorum in synagogue; instrumental and choral music; sermons in English or German on theological themes; confirmation ceremonies; removal of prayers considered to be obsolete; removal of material on the sacrificial cult; removal of theologically problematic passages; and redefinition of the rabbi's role as a theologian and pastor. Between 1840 and 1880, Reform Judaism grew rapidly because of the involvement of highly skilled scholars and rabbis. Reform teaching today is far less radical than in the 19th Century. Reform is committed to supporting the State of Israel as well as the major goals of achieving justice and peace for all people. Preservation of some traditional Jewish practices is important, including the use of Hebrew in worship.

Conservative Judaism

The Conservative Movement originated in Germany in the 1850s. It centered around the Jewish Theological Seminary of Breslau, founded in 1854. It was led for the first 20 years by Zecharias Frankel. It was created by Jewish people who thought that the Reform Movement of that day was excessive in its changes in prayer and rituals. They were not interested in necessarily preserving Orthodox Judaism as it was received from their fathers, but rather developing Jewish life in a way that would allow for necessary changes without destroying or impairing its essential tradition. Conservative Judaism emerged in the United States in the late 19th Century. It falls somewhere in between the Orthodox and Reform Movements.

The conservatives believe that the Torah is sacred but assert that certain laws and customs should be adapted to the modern world. Men and women may sit together. Conservative Judaism maintains that the truths found in Jewish scriptures and other Jewish writings came from God, but were transmitted by humans and contain a human component. They generally accept the binding nature of Jewish law, but believe that the law should change and adapt, absorbing parts of the predominant culture which relate to Jewish values.

1800-1820

By 1800, there were about 3000 Jewish people in the country, mostly along the eastern seaboard of the United States. Synagogues had been established in New York, Newport, Rhode Island, Richmond, Virginia, Philadelphia, Savannah and Charleston, South Carolina. There were three rabbis in the West Indies but none in the United States. Many of them did not become part of the Jewish story later because it was almost impossible to maintain their Judaism. It was a lot easier to intermarry and have their descendents have another religion. A group of them from Poland and Russia emigrated because they had lost all their municipal rights and were being taxed more than anyone else for the debts incurred by the countries. These Jewish people, those that preceded them, and those that came in later generations, changed America and America helped shape the Jewish-American identity. In Europe, Jewish people did not think of themselves as one people. They were either Sephardic Jews whose ancestors came from Spain and Portugal or Ashkenazic Jews, who came from Central and Eastern Europe. The Sephardic Jews spoke Ladino as their Jewish language and the Ashkenazic Jews spoke Yiddish. These Sephardic Jews were usually better educated and wealthier. The two groups did not socialize or even intermarry. They had their own synagogues. Within the Ashkenazic Jewish population there were further subdivisions based on their countries of origin. Basically, because of the non-Jewish population, Jewish people began to think of

themselves as a group of equal citizens in the United States and together stood up for their civil rights. However, they stood apart when it came to the establishment of synagogues and development of means of worship. For purposes of worship and socializing these Jewish people were divided into different sects or denominations known as movements.

In the 1800s, the first golden age of Southern Jewish life occurred. Thousands of immigrant Jews, drawn by family and the Mississippi River trade, after arriving in New York, New Orleans and Galveston, Texas, continued their journey into the South. Cotton was king and merchandise was needed by people everywhere. Jewish peddlers and merchants responded to this need and became part of the story of America. After the boll weevil infestations destroyed much of the cotton crop and the large discount and retail chains arrived, the young Jewish people left the small towns for college and for more promising careers in the large metropolitan areas.

In 1815, after Napoleon's defeat, Jewish people lost the rights of citizenship in several countries. Many Jewish people converted to Christianity to maintain these rights. Some Jewish people, who did not want to convert, decided to leave for the new world.

Between 1815 and the Civil War, two million German speaking Europeans migrated to the United States. This was due to the ruination left by the Napoleonic wars. Many of the Jewish people had no future and the young Jewish men were not even permitted to marry.

Jewish Sunday Schools and Sisterhoods

In 1818, Rebecca Gratz established a small religious school for her siblings and their children. She felt it was essential for Jewish people, living as minorities in a Christian world, to understand their Jewish heritage. She established the first Hebrew Sunday School and Jewish Orphanage. A Jewish orphanage was necessary because at a nonsectarian one, converting the Jewish children would be part of the process of helping them. In 1819, she helped establish the Female Hebrew Benevolent Society to create a Jewish presence in the charitable community. She believed that charitable work done quietly was an appropriate extension of a woman's role. She also believed that women were uniquely responsible for preserving Jewish life in America and there was a special opportunity in which women could be fully Jewish and fully American. In 2002, Evelyn Fyvolent Samuels of St. Petersburg Florida, age 102 years old, was proud of having lived this way her entire life.

In 1835, Rebecca urged the Female Hebrew Benevolent Society to develop a Jewish educational program modeled on the Christian Sunday schools. In 1838, this was accomplished, the school was opened, and sixty students enrolled. Rebecca became the school superintendent and served for more than twenty five years. The school was coeducational and met once a week. The lessons were taught in English instead of Hebrew. The school was run entirely by women. Rebecca Gratz died on August 27, 1869, a woman of valour.

The first Jewish Sunday school in the South and the second in the United States was founded in Charleston, South Carolina in 1838 by Sally Lopez (1806-1902). It was called"The School of Israel" and was administered by "The Society for the Religious Instruction of Jewish Youth." It was modeled after the Sabbath school begun by Rebecca Gratz in Philadelphia. Rebecca would write out lessons in a copybook and forward them to Charleston every week. Sally would make copies and distribute them to the teachers.

In 1842, Penina Moise became the superintendent of the school. She had fifty students in four classes. Five boys and one girl were confirmed in a ceremony in 1855 at Beth Elohim. Penina (1797-1880) was one of the first female poets published in America. She wrote most of the hymns for Beth Elohim's first hymnal which was published in 1842.

1820-1840

Until 1820 there were about one hundred Jewish people entering the United States each year. This hardly made up for those intermarrying. It was an immigration largely of small-town Jews, who were mostly single men. They were young middle-class Jews who were ambitious and enterprising. Many of them were artisans. Only about one third of them were recorded as peddlers. They sold mainly clothing and groceries. In the 1820's, in southern Germany, the Matrikel laws forbade young Jewish people from marrying and forming a family in the community where they lived. This, with other social and economic factors, created a desire for political emancipation. The young Jewish men also wanted to avoid conscription into the Army. They came to the United States, started earning money, and then sent for their brothers and sisters, mothers and fathers and girlfriends. By 1825, the Jewish population had increased to approximately 4,000- 6,000 people.

Between 1820-1880, the Jewish population of the United States rose from 4,000-6,000 to 250,000 people, Some were born here but many were immigrants, who once again escaped from discrimination in Europe. Most imigraants were German Jews. After Napoleon was defeated in Europe, Jewish people lost their citizenship, and life became very difficult. They had to fight to survive economically and politically. They came to America in large numbers for religious, economic and political freedom. The German immigrants were very industrious and eager to become part of American life. Many of them started out as small peddlers, saved some money, and opened small stores in towns located at the borders of civilization. Stores in such cities as Cincinnati, Pittsburgh, and Philadelphia became large department stores. Along with them came the concept of the Reform Movement. Even though Reform did not succeed in Germany where it started, it took root in the United States.

Chicago Jewish Community

In 1832, Jewish people came to Chicago from Prussia, Austria, Bohemia, and sections of modern-day Poland. Chicago's first Jewish congregation, Kehilat Anshe Mayriv, was formed in 1847, and the congregation built the first synagogue in 1851. B'nai Sholom was founded in 1852. Chicago's Sinai, the city's first Reform congregation, was founded in 1861. Jewish people continued to come into the city in the ensuing years. Between 1880 and 1900, fifty five thousand Russian and Polish Jews crowded into the Maxwell Street market neighborhood. Yiddish became the language of choice. Dozens of Hebrew schools, Yiddish theaters, and forty Orthodox synagogues were built within walking distance of Halstead and Maxwell Streets. The Jewish community continued to expand. Some members of this community, including the Jacobs family, settled in St. Petersburg in the 1920s. The Rutenberg family, who came from Chicago, settled in Clearwater in the early 1950s. These families and others provided a much-needed boost to the growth of Pinellas County and Pinellas County Jewish life.

Reverend Isaac Leeser

In the 1830s, Reverend Isaac Leeser developed the Bible-centered approach to American Judaism. Leeser, being a traditionalist, apparently taught that everything stated within the Bible was to be strictly followed. Leeser emphasized the use of sermons, the translation of the Hebrew Bible into English, and the translation of Sephardic and Ashkenazic prayer books into English. He promoted the study of Hebrew. In 1834, he published "The Jews and Mosaic Law," a defense of the revelation of the Bible and the Jewish people's adherence to this principle. In 1837, he published a 590 page book of his sermons and assorted essays on such themes as God, the Holidays, the Messiah, and women's participation in Jewish communal enterprises. His work was entitled, *Argumentative and Devotional on the Subject of the Jewish Religion*, and delivered at the Synagogue Mikveh Israel in Philadelphia, in the years 5590-5597 (1830-37). In 1838, he issued *The Hebrew Reader*. A year later he issued the "*Catechism for Younger Children*, which was prepared for a newly established Sunday School in Philadelphia. The Catechism was dedicated to Miss Rebecca Gratz, Superintendent of the Sunday School for Religious Instruction of Israelites in Philadelphia.

In April, 1843, he published the first edition of *The Occident and American Jewish Advocate*, the first Jewish periodical in the United States. In 1848, he edited and translated *The Book of Daily Prayers for Every Day in the Year According to the Custom of the German and Polish Jews*. In 1853, he published a translation of the entire Bible, which was the first by a Jewish person, into the English language. In 1862, he wrote to President Lincoln asking that a Jewish chaplain be appointed to the Army. This was accomplished on September 12, 1862, when the Reverend Jacob Frankel of Congregation Rodeph Sholom became the first rabbi to serve as a military chaplain in the United States. In 1867, he was instrumental in establishing the first rabbinical seminary in America, Maimonides College, which lasted until 1873. His most urgent message was to promote Jewish education. Jewish children were not learning about the Jewish people and their traditions. Reverend Leeser, the leader of the Orthodox Jewish Community and Rabbi Isaac Mayer Wise, the leader of the Reform Jewish Community, had a dream to create Jewish organizational unity. They wanted to start a Union of American Jewish congregations. At that time it did not work. By 1850, there were 160 congregations in the United States, but their spiritual leadership and educational programs were very poor.

Reverend Leeser was born December 12, 1806, in Prussia, and was an orphan at an early age. He received his secular education at a gymnasium and his religious education from two prominent rabbis. When he was eighteen, he traveled to the United States to join his uncle in Richmond, Virginia to begin a business career. He also assisted the local religious functionary, the Reverend Isaac B. Seixas. In 1829, an article that Leeser published in defense of Judaism brought him to the attention of the public and he was invited to be the religious leader of the Philadelphia Congregation Mikveh Israel. For the next forty years, he was the most prolific American Jewish writer and the most creative Jewish person seeking to turn the Jewish people into a single community. He died in 1869.

1840-1860

By 1840, there were only about 200 Jewish families left from the first settlers who belonged to congregations. The rest of the Jewish people who came between 1620 and 1839 had disappeared into hundreds of Christian families. However, there was now a total of about 15,000 Jewish people, many of them new German immigrants. There were twenty one large congregations in the United States, with fifteen of them being German speaking. Already schisms had appeared in various synagogues because the Jewish people were separating along ethnic lines in their prayer services but not in their duty to help each other. In 1795, a group of German Jewish immigrants broke away from Philadelphia's Mikveh Israel to form the German Hebrew Society which became Rodeph Sholem. In 1825, the German congregants of New York's Shearith Israel formed their own synagogue, B'nai Jeshurun. German Jews were forming German speaking congregations in Cincinnati and other midwestern communities. Many German Jewish immigrants easily adopted Reform Judaism which opened most of Jewish ritual to women with the exception of ordination.

Atlanta Jewish Community

The first Jewish settlers arrived in Atlanta in the 1840s. The Jewish people were a significant part of the economy and contributed substantially to the cultural, educational, and political life of the society. Most of Atlanta's Jews came to the city from other parts of the country. They started as peddlers and then developed partnerships with relatives and friends. They obtained dry goods on credit from Baltimore and New York wholesalers to sell cheaply and on credit to establish their stores.

In 1850, twenty six Jews lived in Atlanta, most of whom came from Germany. By the time of the Civil War, their numbers had doubled. They still had insufficient people to start a synagogue, but they were able to form the Hebrew Benevolent Society in 1860 (a different source said 1865) to provide insurance, and burial benefits. It served as the first formal Jewish religious organization. By 1865, Atlanta had 600 Jewish people.

On January 1, 1867, the Rev. Isaac Leeser of Philadelphia presided over the first Jewish wedding. He encouraged the people to form a new congregation to replace the one started in 1862 that had folded. The Hebrew Benevolent Congregation received its charter four months later and began building a synagogue in 1875. The congregation swung back and forth between Orthodox and Reform and finally became a Reform synagogue when it hired a Rabbi from Hebrew Union College. In 1881, Jewish immigrants started coming from Eastern Europe. They made their livelihoods through small businesses. They obtained goods on credit and became peddlers and then moved on to open stores. A B'nai B'rith Chapter was started in 1870 followed by men's and women's benevolent associations.

Damascus Blood Libel

Despite the rancor exhibited by the Orthodox and Reform Jews toward each other, when it came to defending Jewish people abroad, all American Jewish people spoke as one. The earliest collective action by American Jews was their response to the Damascus blood libel of 1840. In the spring, in the ancient capital of Syria, an Italian friar and his Muslim servant mysteriously disappeared. His daughter and monks charged Jews had kidnaped and murdered the two men to use their blood for Passover matzo. This is an ancient, extremely false accusation against the Jewish people, used by individuals to provide justification for rape, murder and pillage. Under torture, two witnesses named several prominent Damascus Jews as the killers. The accused Jewish people were arrested, tortured and sentenced to death. Local officials seized sixty three Jewish children to compel others to reveal where the blood was hidden. In the summer of 1840, when word of these outrages reached America, the organized English Jewish community had already sent the respected Sir Moses Montefiore to the Sultan of the Ottoman Empire to protest what was happening in Damascus. Although, there was no national organization or recognized leader of the

15,000 person American Jewish community, there were many public rallies and meetings held at the synagogues. The congregants sent considerable correspondence to President Martin Van Buren asking him to intervene in Damascus. President Van Buren ordered American diplomats in Constantinople and Alexandria to tell the Ottoman rulers of Syria of the horror felt by all Americans over what was being done to the Jewish people. Because of the pressure from America, Britain and France, the Overlord of Syria ended the torture of Jewish prisoners and ordered their release. He also ordered that the Jewish community be protected. The Ottoman Sultan issued a decree that the blood libel had no reasonable foundation in truth and Jews must possess the same advantages and enjoy the same privileges as other subjects, especially the free exercise of their religion.

B'nai B'rith

On October 13, 1843, twelve young German Jews who were New York retailers met at the Sinsheimer Café and formed B'nai B'rith, "Children of the Covenant." Henry Jones was the leader. Their mission was to unite the Israelites in the work of promoting their highest interests and those of humanity; develop and elevate the mental and moral character of the Jewish people; develop the principles of philanthropy, honor, and patriotism; help the widows and orphans, as well as others in dire need. They collected five dollars from each member to establish a widow and orphans fund, sick fund, and a burial fund. From 1843-1868, B'nai B'rith grew from a dozen men in one lodge to many thousands of men in more than 100 lodges.

In 1851, B'nai B'rith joined the founders of the secular Jewish learning movement in promoting Jewish education. Local members built New York's and the nation's first Jewish Community Center, which included a Jewish public library. During the Civil War, B'nai B'rith members assumed leadership roles in opposing General Ulysses Grant's attempt to expel Jews from several states until President Abraham Lincoln revoked the order. This was the beginning of efforts to protect Jewish people and later to bring to justice people that massacred innocent civilians of all races and religions. As time went on, considerable effort was used to help educate the immigrants and to integrate them into society.

B'nai B'rith has served local communities since 1868, when it launched its first disaster relief campaign during a time of serious flooding. After the Civil War, it opened the Cleveland Orphans Home. In 1899, in Denver, it opened the National Jewish Medical and Research Center to study lung and immune diseases. All these local and national charitable projects have continued to the present day.

The first B'nai B'rith lodge abroad was founded in Berlin in 1882. One organized in Vienna was the place where Sigmund Freud presented his theories and remedies, because he was shunned by his professional peers. Dr. Chaim Weizman, Israel's first President, helped establish B'nai B'rith in Manchester, England.

In 1900, B'nai B'rith sent $25,000 to the poverty stricken victims of pogroms in Galicia, Russia. In 1901, B'nai B'rith helped several thousand immigrants throughout the United States, thereby removing them from the ghettos of New York.

In October,1913, B'nai B'rith and Sigmund Livingston founded the Anti-Defamation League (ADL) to fight anti-semitism around the world. The Charter reads "The immediate object of the League is to stop, by appeals to reason and conscience and, by appeals to law, the defamation of the Jewish people. Its ultimate purpose is to secure justice and fair treatment to all citizens alike and to put an end forever to unjust and unfair discrimination against and ridicule of any sector or body of citizens."

Livingston established the ADL because of past discrimination against Jewish people and in direct response to the case of Leo Frank, a Jewish factory manager from Georgia who had been arrested on murder charges and lynched by a mob while awaiting trial. Further investigations proved that he was innocent of the crime. The only thing he was guilty of in the eyes of the lynchers was being Jewish.

As the charter indicated, the ADL fights against all forms of discrimination, bigotry and racism. They have opposed the Nazis, Ku Klux Klan, Henry Ford, Father Charles Coughlin and the German-American Bund. In 2004 it had a budget of over $40 million with twenty nine offices in the United States and three offices abroad.

In the early 1920s, B'nai B'rith saved the lives of thousands of Jewish people. They spent $250,000 adopting 600 European war orphans and established a Mexican bureau when Ellis Island's was closing to new immigrants. Approximately 10,000 Jewish people were able to enter Mexico and then come on to the United States.

In 1923, at the University of Illinois, B'nai B'rith started the first Hillel Foundation chapter. In 1924, it founded Aleph Zedek Aleph (AZA) an organization for teenage boys. In 1927, it founded B'nai B'rith Girls (BBG).

In 1934, it drew up a mass petition against the brutality of the Nazi government and cosponsored mass protest meetings in all major cities of the United States.

Isaac Mayer Wise

There was a tremendous need for organized religion to develop and maintain a Jewish presence in the United States. Rabbi Isaac Mayer Wise, well educated and articulate tried to accomplish this, in later years, by founding the formal organizations of the Reform Jewish Movement in the United States through the establishment of the Union of American Hebrew Congregations in 1873, Hebrew Union College in 1875, and the Central Conference of American Rabbis in 1889. Rabbi Wise was born on March 29, 1819, in Steingrub, Bohemia. He was a brilliant student, who at age nine, had learned all he could about the Bible and the Talmud from his father, who was a teacher. He then went on to study with his grandfather, who was a physician, for a period of three years, until his grandfather died. He continued his studies in a variety of schools and then completed his formal education by attending the University of Prague and the University of Vienna for three years. In 1842, at age twenty three, he appeared before a rabbinical court of three well-known rabbis, was given many oral and written examinations, and was ordained as a rabbi. In 1844, he married Theresa Bloch

and had ten children. Since he was unable to practice with freedom in Bohemia, he left for New York, arriving on July 23, 1846. He changed his spelling of his name from Weiss to Wise. He served as rabbi of Congregation Beth El in Albany, New York, for four years, where he initiated reforms in the religious services, including choral singing, confirmation to replace bar mitzvah, and allowing women to sit with men at services. His actions resulted in dismissal by the board of directors. A group of congregants formed a new Reform congregation, Anshe Emet, and established him as their rabbi. In 1854, Rabbi Wise went to Cincinnati, Ohio to become the rabbi of Beth Eichim, a Reform congregation. He remained there for the rest of his life. He died March 26, 1900. He like, Reverend Isaac Leeser, tried to organize all Jewish congregations into one large Jewish federation of congregations. Whereas Leeser failed totally, Rabbi Wise was successful in bringing all of the Reform congregations together in a national organization.

Rabbi Isaac Mayer Wise

German Jewish Immigration

Cincinnati, because of its location on a curve in the Ohio River, became a natural gateway to the markets of Ohio, Indiana, and Kentucky. By 1840, there were approximately 115,000 people living there, with about 1,500 Jewish people.

The German Revolution of 1848 created the need for the Jewish people to seek emancipation from the problems of the old world and a need to live in a new society where they could be free, independent, and prosperous. Intellectual Jews decided to leave Germany and add to the growing strength of the United States. By late 1848, there were 50,000 Jewish people, with most of them living in the big cities. By 1850, there were seventy seven Jewish congregations in twenty one states.

The new wave of German immigrants came to the United States, including many Jewish people who were older than the original German Jewish immigrants. Many of them were part of the Reform Movement, because they could achieve civic equality and social acceptance in their surrounding community. They went into peddling and small trade which later developed into substantial businesses. They were in search of democracy in America and as part of this developed religious, philanthropic, and fraternal organizations. The German immigrants, including the German Jews, augmented the older German communities of Cincinnati and St. Louis. German Jews worked very hard and founded many German societies, organizations, and institutions. They also worked very hard to help each other and to develop new Jewish communities. An example of this was Terre Haute, Indiana, where land was purchased for a burial ground in 1845. In 1849, eight to ten families formed the Terre Haute Israelite Burial Society, a verein. This was a Jewish mutual benefit society and also functioned as a burial society, a credit union, and a means of help for its members or the poor, in times of sickness or difficulty. This was the beginning of the Jewish community of Terre Haute, Indiana. On March 28, 1858, thirty three members of the burial society, an informal Jewish community, formed a formal burial society and formal Jewish community by becoming the Terre Haute Zions Gemeinde, a Jewish congregation, burial society, and fraternal order to help Jews in time of need. Shortly thereafter they rented a facility for a Synagogue. In 1894, the Jewish people of Tampa, Florida would follow the same pattern in founding Schaarai Zedek.

By 1850, there were between 50,000 and 100,000 Jewish people in the country. Earnestine Rose helped to organize the first National Woman's Rights Convention, which met in Massachusetts. For thirty years, she was active in the National Woman's Suffrage Association. Jewish people became active and were founders of music societies, theater societies, book publishers, and a large variety of charities.

St. Louis Jewish Community

In 1852, The Occident, which was published in Philadelphia, included an article about Jewish life in St. Louis. Isaac Leeser, the editor, who toured the country to find all of the Jewish communities existing and to meet as many Jewish people as possible, arrived in St. Louis on December 12, 1851. He was a guest of the Bondi (originally Bondy) family. Isaac Leeser discovered a large body of Israelites living in St. Louis. They were divided into three congregations. The original one was Polish and there was also a German Congregation as well as a Bohemian Congregation. Before his arrival and during his time in St. Louis, there was an attempt to unify the three congregations into a United Hebrew Congregation and to construct a suitable place of worship, a place of education and edification, and a place for all Jewish people to socialize. This did not occur, despite the eloquent appeals and presentations by Isaac Leeser over a period of several months. Although the differences between the three congregations' customs varied little, there were problems because of the amount of poetical prayers to be recited on certain days and the prayers to be included or omitted in the services. The three congregations disagreed intensely about these matters.

Mr. Leeser was detained in St. Louis for many months because of the harsh winter. While there, he met many of the approximate 1000 Jewish people who were residents. He said that the Jewish people started coming about 1840 and developed into a vibrant and successful part of St. Louis society. They chiefly engaged in commerce, dry goods, clothing, millinery, cap-making, jewelry, and grocery businesses. A few were mechanics. Some were professional men such as lawyers and doctors. August Bondi was initially a clerk in a retail clothing store. Later, he studied law.

It was to this established Jewish community in St. Louis that Edward A. Blum, his father, his mother, his brother and his sister arrived around 1860. Like August Bondi, he went in search of success on another frontier, Tarpon Springs, Florida. He and his family became the first Jewish people to settle in Pinellas County. In 1883, like August Bondi, he became an honest and efficient postmaster and later became a charter member of the Council of Tarpon Springs.

August Bondi

August Bondi, great grandfather of Jane Bondi Rutenberg, became the great American-Jewish freedom fighter who rode with John Brown in Kansas. He became a

Probate Judge and occasionally acted as Superintendent of Public Instruction. He fought dishonesty among administrators and guardians and forced them into honest settlements. His honesty caused his loss for reelection by nine votes. In 1878, he became a Royal Arch Mason. In 1879, he was elected Police Judge and reelected in 1881 and in 1883. In 1883, August Bondi was appointed to the State Board of Trustees for Charitable Institutions. Because he went after those who were accepting graft, he was removed by the governor. He later became a postmaster who was efficient and honest. He was a person of conscience who fought for the rights of people of all races and religions who were oppressed. He and his family always practiced their Judaism despite the frontier conditions they encountered in Missouri and Kansas.

Jewish Community Centers

In 1854, in Baltimore Maryland, the first Young Mens Hebrew Association opened to provide support for Jewish immigrants, help ensure that there would be a Jewish community, provide Jewish continuity, and provide a place for recreation as well as learning. This was the beginning of the Jewish Community Center Movement. Along with increasing immigration in the late 19th century, similar associations opened up as libraries, cultural centers, and settlement houses to help the immigrants and the Jewish people already in United States learn English, new customs, civic responsibilities, and how to become part of their new democratic home. The Council of Young Mens Hebrew and Kindred Associations was founded in 1913 to coordinate and promote the efforts of the independent centers. During World War I, the organization secured funds to enlist rabbis for service in the military and called a conference of several different Jewish organizations which became the forerunner of the Jewish Welfare Board in 1917. This group developed a comprehensive infrastructure for taking care of the welfare of Jewish military personnel. The Jewish Welfare Board became the National Association of Jewish Community Centers and YM-YWHAs. In the 1950s and 1960s, the Jewish Community Centers built large modern facilities to serve the suburban Jewish populations. Their ultimate goal was to: create a community of learning Jews who were respectful of Jewish differences; create knowledgeable Jews who were committed to Jewish values and practices; create knowledgeable and committed participants in synagogue life, Jewish communal and cultural life; and promote the nation of Israel as a central part of Jewish identity. The Jewish Community Center Association now serves over one million people through 275 centers and camps.

1860s and the Civil War

By 1860, there were 10,000 Jewish people in Cincinnati, and the St. Louis Jewish community had also grown in size. Jewish people also sought their fortunes along the lower Mississippi Valley settling in Memphis, Natchez, Vicksburg, Shreveport, Baton Rouge, and New Orleans. Jewish people worked extensively in the clothing trades, which led to many small stores and later department stores owned by Jewish families throughout the country. Jewish people pioneered the technique of installment payments to make the purchase of goods reasonable for the average person. Jewish manufacturers in the Eastern United States supplied Jewish wholesalers who in turn supplied Jewish retail merchants and peddlers. Eventually the peddlers went from carrying packs on their backs to horse and wagons to permanent stores. Many of the first stores owned in small and large communities were owned by Jewish people. These Jewish people were coming to the United States because their attempt to achieve equality in Europe had been destroyed and they were being severely persecuted.

By 1861, there were 200,000 Jewish people in the United States with approximately 150,000 of them being German Jews. They were divided by their loyalty to the north and south, since they were affected by their regional influences rather than their religious teaching. There were about 6,000 Jews serving in the Union forces and about 3,000 Jews serving in the Confederate forces. Many of them had previous experience fighting in the armies of their countries of birth, such as Poland.

Colonel Edward S. Salomon was the commander of the 82nd Illinois Volunteer Infantry, which included more than one hundred Jewish men, at the battle of Gettysburg on July 1-3, 1863. Despite the highly intense charge of 15,000 Confederate troops under General George E. Pickett, he and his men repulsed them. For his bravery and leadership, he was honorably promoted to brigadier general. There were eight Jewish generals in the Union forces and six Jewish Medal of Honor winners among the enlisted men: Sergeant Leopold Karpeles, Benjamin B. Levy, Henry Heller, Abraham Cohn, David Orbanski and Isaac Gause. The Medal of Honor winners were ordinary citizens, but brought great honor to the United States and to the Jewish people because of their extreme bravery.

The most important of the Southern Jewish men was Judah P. Benjamin, Confederate Secretary of State. He was born to a Sephardic family in the West Indies. He spent his adolescence in Charleston, briefly attended a university, then studied law privately. He was admitted to the bar in New Orleans. Judah attained wide recognition because of his legal writings. He was a political conservative. In 1842, he was elected to the Louisiana Legislature and ten years later became the first Jewish person to serve in the United States Senate. In 1856, he was offered an appointment by President Franklin Pierce to become the first Jewish justice of the United States Supreme Court. But he turned down the appointment. He was a leader of the Southern view and advocated that the South secede from the Union when Lincoln was elected. Being a prominent Jewish leader for the South contributed to discrimination against Jewish people after the Civil War.

Despite the important contributions to both causes in the Civil War, there was considerable official discrimination and popular xenophobia in the North. Jewish troops were denied their own chaplains, since the Volunteer Bill made provisions only for Christian clergymen. A special appeal had to be made to President Lincoln to remedy this. No comparable problem was found in the Confederacy. There was considerable prejudice, however, toward immigrant Jews in the armed services. When things went wrong, the Jewish businessmen in the South were blamed. As the prices of scarce items went up, again it had to be the fault of the small Jewish businessman, since he was the most visible person there. Judah P. Benjamin became a scapegoat for everything that was wrong in the South.

In the North, Jewish soldiers suffered intolerable harassment and abuse. Jewish people were blamed for anything that went wrong. Anyone that had a foreign accent was a traitor or a spy. General Ulysses S. Grant, angry at the Northern traders who came to the South as cotton speculators, issued an order keeping out all cotton speculators, Jews, and other vagrants. On December 17, 1862, General Grant issued Order #11, stating that the Jews violated every regulation of trade and were therefore expelled from the Military Department of Tennessee, which also included most of Mississippi and much of Kentucky, within twenty four hours. This applied to men, women, and children no matter what they did. This was the worst displacement of people without cause, until the internment of Japanese-Americans in 1942. Twenty four hours was an incredibly short time to try to accomplish this unbelievable task. The Jewish men alerted the newspapers by using telegrams and letters and the Jewish communal leaders reacted throughout the North and the South. Typically Union Army Jewish soldiers were welcome in Southern Jewish congregations. Northern Jewish communities raised funds for Southern Jewish synagogues. It did not matter if the people were from the North or South, the Jewish people would stick together and not allow such acts to occur. A meeting was held with President Lincoln who was shocked and embarrassed by the Jewish ordeal in the South. He issued an order to cancel the infamous Order number 11. Many newspapers criticized Grant for a lack of judgment and even for bigotry. Others refused to criticize him because he had become such an important person in the Union Army. At that time, General Grant refused to express regrets for his actions. In the election of 1868, the Jewish people were blasted again for not wanting to vote for the hero. As President, General Grant worked for the rights of Jewish people living both in the United States and abroad. However, the damage had been done. A new upsurge of anti-Jewish sentiment was now the way of life in the United States. Many of the stereotypes of the Jewish people, which had originated in Europe, were now in vogue in the United States, and many of the discriminatory acts would follow.

1870s

By 1870, there were 200,000 Jewish people in the United States. In the 1870s and 1880s, there was an explosive growth of urban poor. The immigration of several million people from Eastern Europe would only add to this growing problem. There was official police anti-Semitism in New York followed by outbreaks of police anti-Semitism in Chicago, Philadelphia, and Boston. The Jewish people were disliked by other immigrant groups because they dressed differently, spoke a different language, Yiddish, and they looked different. Many Jewish people, who had already been helping to relieve the suffering of others, sharply increased their efforts in improving the lives of, especially, women and children. The Hebrew Technical School for Girls was established in 1880 to provide an industrial education for young Jewish women. It taught them cutting and fitting of dresses, sewing, millinery, bookkeeping, typewriting, business penmanship, and housework.

Hebrew Orphan's Asylum

The Hebrew Orphan's Asylum of Atlanta was established in 1876 to serve the B'nai B'rith 5th District. This facility became the home for hundreds of Jewish children from the Southeast from 1876 to 1930. The Jewish children were not only raised in the Atlanta Hebrew Orphan's Home, name changed in 1899 after the B'nai B'rith gave up its control over the facility, but also were educated here. Loans were provided to them for college tuition. When the need for the orphanage diminished, the agency sold the home and began to support foster parents. In order to upgrade its mission, the organization became the Jewish Children's Service.

They began to help the Jewish children through grants to various communities to help them start local programs to help the youth of that community. The name was officially changed in 1948. In 1988, the name was once against changed to the Jewish Educational Loan Fund. Interest-free loans were now being provided to Jewish students who lived in the affiliated communities throughout the Southeast.

Joseph Seligman and Discrimination

In 1877, the beginning of Jewish social rejection by the outer community started. The banker, Joseph Seligman, a personal friend of former President Grant, a respected and powerful government adviser, leader of many charities, and the most prominent Jewish person in the United States, went to Saratoga, New York with his family to stay at the Grand Union Hotel. He expected his usual suite to be waiting for him. Instead, the desk clerk read him a prepared statement: "Mr. Seligman , I am required to inform you that Judge Hilton, the administrator of the Grand Union Luxury Hotel, had given instructions that no Israelite shall be permitted in the future to stop at this hotel." The reason for this rejection was both personal and vindictive, but it had a far-reaching effect on Jewish people in various parts of the United States. Now it was in vogue to reject Jewish people at hotels because it had been done at the Grand Union Hotel. This action became known as the Grand Union Affair. The owner of the hotel was A. T. Stewart Company, a mercantile conglomerate. Mr. Stewart, who had gotten along well with Mr. Seligman in the past, was incensed because Seligman could have been Secretary of the Treasury, but did not want the position. Stewart, who afterwards was named Secretary of the Treasury, was rejected by the Senate. Also, Seligman was elected to the Committee of 70, a group of prominent New Yorkers whose specific purpose was to eradicate the Tweed political machine, and Stewart was not elected to this group. Judge Henry Hilton was a political crony of Stewart and member of the Tweed political machine. Judge Hilton blamed a decline in business at the hotel on the Jewish people. He said that Christians were uncomfortable being around Jewish people. This was a hateful statement and a hateful action based on his own prejudice and not fact.

A new Jewish image of excess wealth and ostentatiousness was promoted in a variety of books and magazines. This was part of the culture of increasing hostility to the Jewish people by a small but vocal group of non-Jewish people that did not represent the larger community. However, the more frequently something is presented, even though it is not right, the more apt people become to expect this to be the truth. Restrictions spread everywhere including many of the social clubs that the Jewish people had originally founded and could no longer participate in. This discrimination was not only in the Eastern United States but also in the South. Jesse Seligman was Vice President of the Union League Club of New York, but resigned in 1893 when his son was blackballed because of his religion. Jesse Seligman was a confidant of President Grant and some of his successors. For over twenty years he was the President of the Hebrew Benevolent and Orphan Asylum of New York and was an original member of the Board of Trustees of the Baron de Hirsch Fund.

Jewish people had served as mayors of cities including Tampa, Presidents of the chamber of commerce, Presidents of banks, and Presidents and directors of many other organizations. Social prejudice had become the norm now. Jewish people responded by forming their own social clubs and other Jewish organizations. Soon there was a network of excellent Jewish resorts along the Atlantic Seaboard. The less affluent middle class Jewish people joined fraternal societies and clubs, which flourished for many generations. Jewish businesses continued to grow and expand in the largely non-Jewish outer world, since they were so extremely important to the economy and communities that they served.

It is of great significance and interest to understand the contributions of the Seligman family to the welfare of the United States of America. There were numerous Jewish financial contributions to the Union forces in the Civil War. When the Civil War began, the North could not sell Union bonds abroad, although the South had no such problem. This created tremendous financial difficulties. The Seligman Brothers, by means of their international banking firm, J. and W. Seligman & Company, broke the no credit wall when they sold over $200 million worth of bonds from their Frankfurt, Germany office. At that time, the North owed the Seligman family over one million dollars for clothing purchased from their dry goods store.

1880-1900

From the 1880s on, Jewish people experienced the initial impact of exclusion from the better hotels, resorts, and clubs. The social rejection presented no serious obstacle to legal or political security. However, there was always an implicit threat that this would follow. A surge of religious and other novels, including hundreds of books, reflected a common stereotype of zealous, even fanatical Jewish people, who wanted to impose their will on the overall society. They enforced the erroneous and blasphemous idea that the Jewish people committed deicide.

By 1880, the Jewish population of the United States had grown to between 230,000 and 280,000 with a new post Civil War immigration of about 60,000 people. Of 200 American congregations, only twelve were not Reform and most of the Reform were radical.

The Great Migration

In 1881, after the assassination of Alexander II, the pogroms started and the great migration from Eastern Europe began. Although some Jewish people went from Russia, Romania and Poland to live in agricultural communities in Palestine, the largest group of Jewish immigrants came to the United States to escape severe discrimination, poverty, high taxation, and the physical fear of pogroms. From the smallest children to the oldest members of the family, the Jewish people lived in fear of severe beatings, rape, destruction of their home, and death. The major Russian pogroms occurred between 1881-1884 and 1903-1906. Many of the Jewish people came from the Pale of Settlement, which was an area restricted to Jewish people stretching from the Baltic Sea to the Black Sea. These Jewish people had typically lived in small towns and were largely urbanites. They brought with them a rich Yiddish culture, which was expressed through newspapers, the arts, and especially the theater. Yiddish was more than merely a language of utility used in everyday speech and writing.

This creative energy of the Jewish people, who had no other outlet in their surrounding society expressed themselves through literature, poetry, drama, music, and religious and cultural scholarship. Yiddish described a vibrant internal life that had developed in the ghettos and shtetles of Eastern Europe. Yiddish literature had existed for hundreds of years as folk tales, legends, and religious homilies. The Yiddish language dated back about 1,000 years. It was derived from High Germanic dialects to a complete language that incorporated parts of Hebrew, Aramaic, Slavic, and Romance languages. It was written in Hebrew characters and spoken chiefly in Eastern European Jewish communities and by immigrants of these communities throughout the world.

The Eastern European Jewish people had a strong sense of religiosity, which identified itself with life in the shtetls and small cities from which they had come. They were orthodox from the point of view of religious services and religious rituals, including keeping a kosher home and using only Hebrew in services. They were at odds with their coreligionists, who were typically reform and more assimilated into society. The German Jews typically used the language of the country they were living in. They therefore used either German or English and did not bother to learn Yiddish. These Western European Jewish people wanted to desperately become part of their surrounding society and not be identified with something which they considered to be old-fashioned and of little or no value. This massive migration would last until 1920. During this forty year period, more than two million Eastern European Jews emigrated to the United States.

Emma Lazarus

In 1881, Emma Lazarus, angry at the Russian pogroms which followed the assassination of Czar Alexander II, went to Wards Island to help the terror stricken survivors, men, women and children, who crowded its facilities. She responded to an article in the Century Magazine which justified the pogroms, blaming the victims, and defending the Czarist government, by writing a defense of Judaism and the Russian Jew, entitled "Russian Christianity versus Modern Judaism," in May, 1882. In 1883, she wrote the sonnet inscribed on the pedestal of the Statue of Liberty in New York Harbor.

"Give me your tired, your poor,
Your huddled masses
yearning to breathe free,
The wretched refuse
of your teeming shore.
Send these the homeless,
tempest-tossed to me,
I lift my lamp beside the golden door!"

Emma Lazarus was born in 1849 and died in 1887. In her short time on earth she made numerous and lasting contributions with her poetry and by using her life as an example of the goodness that can be brought forth by an American Jewish woman. Although in her early years, she wrote little about the Jewish people, in her latter years she worked assiduously to build the spirit of Jewish enthusiasm. She promoted the broad system of physical and intellectual education adopted by the ancestors of the Jewish people, worked for the alleviating of the suffering of oppressed Jews and all other people, and promoted the larger principles of religion, liberty, and laws upon which Judaism is founded and upon which all Jewish people of all types and opinions could come together in harmonious unity.

Adolphus Simeon Solomons

In 1882, Adolphus Simeon Solomons helped establish the American Red Cross. Many of the meetings, to plan and prepare to join the International Red Cross, were held in the District of Columbia, in his home. The proposal to form the Association of the American Red Cross and incorporate it was held there. He was a publisher who was held in great esteem by the Jewish and general communities. He was a soldier patriot who in 1840 at age fourteen, enlisted in the New

York state Militia and served for seven years. He organized the first training school for nurses in Washington and the Washington House Association which provided shelter for homeless men. He was also an officer of the Provident Aid Society, the Emergency Hospital of the Society for the Prevention of Cruelty to Animals and many other charities. In New York, he helped organize Mount Sinai Hospital and the Montefiore Home for Chronic Invalids. When he died in 1910, he left a legacy of charity, helping the sick and poor, and working with ,as well as organizing, Jewish organizations that helped all people.

Pittsburgh Platform

In 1885, Reform rabbis from around the United States met from November 16 to November 19, in Pittsburgh, with Rabbi Isaac Mayer Wise presiding, to issue a series of Reform principles. This meeting was a continuation of the Philadelphia Conference of 1869, which was the continuation of the German Conference of 1841 to 1846. The major principles as reworked by the author follows:

1. We recognize that every religion attempts to grasp the concept of God in every mode, source or book of revelation held sacred to that group;
2. We recognize that Judaism presents the highest conception of the God-idea in our Holy Scriptures and as developed and spiritualized by Jewish teachers in accordance with the moral and philosophical progress of their respective ages;
3. We maintain that Judaism preserved and defended, despite continuous struggles and trials under enforced isolation, the God-idea as the central religious truth for the human race;
4. We recognize the Bible as a record of the consecration of the Jewish people to its mission as the priest of the one God, and value it as the most potent instrument of religious and moral instruction;
5. We believe that the modern discoveries of scientific researchers related to nature and history are not antagonistic to the doctrines of Judaism and that the Bible reflects the primitive ideas of its own age in explaining divine providence and justice;
6. We recognize in Mosaic law a system of training the Jewish people for its mission during its national life in Palestine, and today except as binding only its moral laws and utilize only such ceremonies as elevate and sanctify our lives, and reject those that are not adapted to modern civilization;
7. We believe that such Mosaic rabbinical laws as related to diet, priestly purity, and dress are not in keeping with modern spiritual elevation;
8. We recognize that in this modern era of enlightenment, the approaching of the realization of Israel's greatest hope for the establishment of the kingdom of truth, justice, and peace among all people, the Messianic era;
9. We consider ourselves no longer to be a nation, but a religious community and therefore do not expect to return to Palestine, sacrificial worship, where the restoration of any of the laws concerning the Jewish state (obviously this stand on what was to become Zionism changed dramatically and the Reform Jewish Movement supported the Jews of Palestine and the State of Israel);
10. We recognize in Judaism a progressive religion ever striving to be in accord with reason and preserving our historical identity;
11. We recognize Christianity and Islam as being daughter religions of Judaism and appreciate their mission to aid in the spreading of monotheistic and moral truth;
12. We acknowledge that the spirit of broad humanity helps fulfill our mission and therefore extend the hand of fellowship to all who cooperate with us in the establishment of the reign of truth and righteousness among men;
13. We assert the doctrine of Judaism that the soul is immortal which is grounded in the belief of the divine

as nature and the human spirit finding bliss in righteousness and misery in wickedness;

14. We reject as ideas not rooted in Judaism, the belief in bodily resurrection and in Hell and Paradise as places for everlasting punishment and reward;

15. We believe in the spirit of the Mosaic legislation, which strives to regulate the relations between rich and poor, that it is our duty to solve, on the basis of justice and righteousness, the problems presented by the contrasts and evils of the present organization of society.

Samuel Gompers

In 1886, Samuel Gompers, a former cigar maker, was elected to be the President of the American Federation of Labor, which had been recently organized. With the exception of one year, he held that position until he died on December 13, 1924. He was born in London on January 27, 1850 to Dutch Jewish parents. He had four years of schooling and at age ten became an apprentice shoemaker. His father taught him how to become a cigarmaker and at age seventeen, he started to make cigars on his own. He joined the Cigar-makers' Union. In 1877, after striking for better conditions, the Union collapsed because of a lack of money and member discipline. He reorganized the cigar-makers, provided international officers for all unions, developed a strike fund, and established benefits for sickness, accidents, and unemployment. Other labor unions followed the example of the Cigar-makers' Union. In 1881, a new federation of unions was formed called the Federation of Organized Trades and Labor Unions of the United States and Canada. This became the American Federation of Labor. He felt that both labor and capitalists were essential in the management of business. He was Vice President of the National Civic Federation, an organization which sought to promote stable labor relations through collective bargaining and personal contact between labor leaders, industrialists, and bankers. In World War I, he supported President Woodrow Wilson's policies and organized the War Committee on Labor. For forty years he was the dominant figure in the labor movement and encouraged and was the leader of the working person and the trade union. He created a free and strong American labor movement.

Jewish Theological Seminary

On January 2, 1887, the Jewish Theological Seminary opened its doors to its first students. From this one-room school, the seminary has grown over the years to three impressive campuses in New York, Jerusalem and Los Angeles. The faculty of the four schools–Rabbinical School, Cantors Institute, Graduate School and Seminary College of Jewish Studies, has trained leaders for both the Conservative movement and the Jewish community throughout the world. The Ramah camps, Jewish Museum and Eternal Light, which came much later contributed to the Jewish community and community at large for the last 117 years.

Nathan Straus

In 1888, Nathan Straus became one of the owners of R. H. Macy & Company. He provided restrooms, a depositor's account system, medical care, and an inexpensive lunch room for the Macy employees. He became park commissioner in New York City from 1889 to 1893 and President of the New York City Board of Health in 1898. He turned down the nomination for mayor of the city. He always helped people. During the horrible winter of 1892-93, he distributed food to the poor and sold a million and a half buckets of coal for five cents each. The following winter he gave away more than 200,000, five cent tickets good for coal, food or lodging. He also established lodging houses that provided bed and breakfast for five cents. He supported the pasteurization of milk and started a campaign to educate the public. In 1911, he was appointed by the President of the United States to be the only delegate to the Third International Congress for the Protection of Infants, held in Germany. In 1931, when he died, President Taft called him the greatest Jewish person of the last twenty five years. In reality, he had been great his entire life, because he cared more for others than for accumulating personal wealth.

Census Study

In 1889, the Bureau of the Census studied 18,000 Jewish families, who were first or second generation Central Europeans. Of this group, fifty percent were wholesale or retail merchants; twenty percent were accountants, bookkeepers, or clerks; two percent were bankers, brokers or company officials; five percent were professionals; less than one percent were peddlers. In the South, where Jews made up less than one percent of population, they had a profound influence on merchandising.

By 1890, there were between 400,000 and 475,000 Jewish people in the country. Pogroms in Europe, along with every form of persecution and extreme poverty, forced the Jewish people to migrate from Poland, Russia, Ukraine etc..

Emile Berliner

In 1890, Emile Berliner became involved in the fields of hygiene and health. He organized and founded the Society for the Prevention of Sickness. In 1907, he organized the first milk conference in Washington, DC for the pasteurization of milk and the improvement of its quality. He was very active in trying to stop the spread of tuberculosis and wrote many articles on hygiene and preventive medicine. In 1887, he invented the flat disk to replace the cylinder on Thomas Edison's phonograph. He experimented on various forms of electricity and telephones.

Maud Nathan

Maud Nathan was a social worker and suffragist. She helped found the Consumers League of New York, an organization dedicated to bettering the working conditions of female retail clerks. She found that the stores were filthy, there was sexual harassment on the job, and women worked sixty hours a week for two or three dollars. She not only fought this but, also realizing that because women did not vote they did not have the ability to change the minds of the legislators, devoted a lifetime to helping women get the right to vote.

Lillian D. Wald

In 1891, Lillian D. Wald graduated as a nurse from the New York City Hospital. At age 22, she entered Woman's Medical College to study to become a doctor. As part of her postgraduate training, her assignment was to organize a plan for home nursing to meet the needs of the poor immigrant families on the Lower East Side of New York. When she saw how miserably these poor people lived, she dropped out of medical school and decided to move to the neighborhood and to open an office there. She soon had four nurses and then moved to 265 Henry Street, which was her base for forty years. She was the founder of the Visiting Nurse Society. She and her staff gave help to everyone regardless of race or religion. By 1913, her staff not only provided health care in homes but also in public schools, which led to the New York Board of Health's organizing and staffing the first public nursing system in the world. From the Henry Street Settlement, she educated mothers and their daughters in home nursing, cooking and sewing. This helped provide self-help organizations for the working girl and led to the realization that women could provide an avenue for self-expression and break away from traditional role expectations. Advice manuals and journals were written or translated into Yiddish to help Americanized immigrant Jews with instructions in manners, hygiene, parenting, sexuality, and birth control. The staff also provided education, recreation, and special activities for families and children.

Hannah Greenbaum Solomon

In 1893, Hannah Greenbaum Solomon founded the National Council of Jewish Women, the oldest active Jewish woman's volunteer organization in America. The goals of the Council were to teach all Jewish women their obligation to their religion and community. Hannah was elected as the first President and served until 1905. She was then chosen to be Honorary President for Life. She was active in all aspects of philanthropy and civic life in Chicago. In 1884, she and her sister Henrietta Frank, who was the President of the Chicago Woman's Club, caused the club to become much more involved in the problems of children and women. She helped found the Chicago Juvenile Court and was on the board of the Chicago Civic Federation.

Jewish Chautauqua Society

In 1893, the Jewish Chautauqua Society was founded in Philadelphia by Reform Rabbi Henry Berkowitz to help teach all people, no matter what background, tolerance and understanding of Judaism. In 1909, Dr. Philander P. Claxton, later U.S. Commissioner of Education, suggested to Rabbi Berkowitz that the society assign rabbis to lecture at universities to help Christians develop a better understanding of Jews and Judaism. In 1911, Rabbi Julian Morganstern gave the first JCS college lecture at the University of Tennessee. In 1922, sixty four lectures were given by rabbinic scholars at twenty three universities in nineteen different states. In 1939, the National Federation of Temple Brotherhoods assumed the sponsorship of the JCS as its educational project. In 1940, lectures were given at 134 colleges. In 1943, the society enrolled 3,085 individual annual members. In 1944, three new phases of JCS activity were introduced: donating Jewish reference books to college libraries; assigning rabbis on invitation of church denominational groups to serve as teachers or counselors at Christian Church Youth Camps; sponsoring the first JCS resident lectureship on Judaism at Howard University, Washington D.C. From that point on, the Jewish Chautauqua Society has been deeply involved in providing speakers, educational materials, books, and other assistance to large numbers of people in a variety of settings, including hundreds of colleges and universities. For over 120 years, the Jewish Chautauqua Society has progressively provided more and more knowledge and education about Jews and Judaism, has brought about an appreciation in the Jewish people of their history, religion and culture, and has built bridges of understanding between peoples of all faiths and cultures.

Panic of 1893

After the Panic of 1893, when agricultural overproduction and falling prices caused serious financial problems, the Jewish people were blamed for what had occurred.

In addition, southerners who had gone to Atlanta and other cities to find jobs and couldn't were encouraged by bigots to blame the Jewish people. The reality was that the Jewish financiers were trying to create a better world in the United States and were helping not only Jewish people, but more frequently, the general community. It should also be noted that many more non-Jewish financiers than Jewish financiers existed at the time, and the Jewish people by and large were not as involved in high finance as they were in other aspects of society.

1896

An article in *Harpers Weekly* and *North American Review*, as well as material written by Mark Twain, appeared stating that American Jews did not serve and fight in the Civil War. It is obvious that the information was totally wrong. On March 15, 1896, 78 Jewish veterans met in New York City to refute this statement and thereby organized the Hebrew Union of Veterans, the precursor group to the Jewish War Veterans of the USA. The veterans had a right to be angry, since many of the 6,000 Jewish men who served in the Grand Army of the Republic had been killed or wounded and many of the men received various decorations and medals, including six Congressional Medal of Honor. The Civil War veterans and many Jewish veterans that followed from all of the wars of the 20th and 21st century, including World War I and World War II, pledged to maintain a true allegiance to the United States; to combat anti-Semitism and to combat bigotry; to assist other comrades and their families in times of need; to gather and preserve the records of patriotic service performed by Jewish people; and to honor the memories and protect the graves of Jewish veterans. In 1897, Twain apologized to the veterans for his anti-Semitic remarks.

Meanwhile, T. Herzl wrote a book called *The Jewish State*. He said that we had to do more than pray for the Messiah to come to reestablish the State of Israel. We had to work actively toward this end. He established a new movement known as Political Zionism (the love of Zion or

Israel). The small number of Jews who began to settle in Israel in 1882 now started to increase.

1898

On February 15, fifteen Jewish sailors died out of a total of 266 American crew men dead, when the battleship Maine was sunk. This was a precursor of the Spanish-American War, which lasted for three months. Adolph Marix, Executive Officer of the ship, and later a Vice Admiral in the United States Navy was Chairman of the Board of Inquiry that investigated the mysterious sinking. Adolph, a Jewish young man, was appointed by Abraham Lincoln to the United States Naval Academy. When the United States declared war on Spain on April 21, 1898, the first volunteer was a Jewish doctor, Colonel Joseph M. Heller. About 5,000 Jewish men served in this war. 104 Jewish men died. The first Rough Rider commanded by Colonel Teddy Roosevelt, who died was a sixteen year-old Jewish boy. Jewish men served in greater proportion than did the remainder of the United States citizens.

Back in the United States, the conservative Jewish movement broke with the conservative orthodoxy of Eastern Europe. This was essentially the opportunity for the conservative movement to try innovative changes while still maintaining considerable ritual.

Sisterhoods

The individual sisterhoods of the reform, conservative and orthodox congregations followed a common pattern of activities. They started as religious housekeepers of these synagogues, provided for various events, raised funds for many needed projects, helped support religious education, provided assistance to the needy and elderly, and made these synagogues into warm and significant places of worship. National Sisterhood organizations followed at a later time

1900–1920

By 1900, there were between 938,000 and a little over one million Jewish people in the country and more than 600 congregations had been established. Jewish people were more frequently involved in the practice of their religion in a formal manner. Further, Jewish intellectuals were among the people challenging the foundations of the social order. The leader of this movement was Theodore Roosevelt. There was an outcry for democratic government, better cities, and the curbing of corporate power. Lincoln Steffens, a great American reformer and journalist wrote "The Shame of the Cities." He documented corruption in American cities asserting that in some of the cities there was a little corruption aided by powerful businessmen. As an example, he wrote that Philadelphia was, "... corrupt and contented." Such incidents as the Triangle Shirtwaist Company fire, the terrible conditions in which the garment workers had to live and work, and the contamination of food, as shown in Upton Sinclair's book, *The Jungle*, moved the reformers to push for dramatic changes in society.

In the early 1900s, Jewish women helped organize the International Ladies Garment Workers Union. This was formed in reaction to the horrible working conditions that new immigrants, especially women, were exposed to in New York City. The author's mother, Gussie Wax Koren, who was employed by her great-uncle in a doll factory at age sixteen led the entire group of mainly women and some men out on strike because of the working conditions. She won concessions and the workplace was a safer place.

Union of Orthodox Jewish Congregations of America

About 1904, the Union of Orthodox Jewish Congregations of America was founded. It became the primary coordinating agency for Orthodox Jewish Congregations in North America. It provides programs in education, outreach, social services, Kosher supervision, youth work through the National Conference of Synagogue Youth, advocacy for the developmentally disabled, political action, ethical and moral education, synagogue support services, Torah, Jewish holidays, and an extensive web site for all people. Similar to all movements, orthodoxy has its right, center, and left wings and there are new Yeshivot for training rabbis in each of these areas. Associated programs of the Union are: Aish HaTorah, an organization which concentrates on adult learning; Edah, an organization which is fully committed to Torah, halakah (Jewish law) and the quest for kedushah (holiness) through open intellectual inquiry in secular and religious areas, and involvement in the social, political, and technological realities of the modern world; Joseph Soloveitchik Institute, an organization which trains young men and young women who have made a commitment to day school education; National Council of Young Israel, an organization of nearly 150 Orthodox congregations which works mostly with rabbis and does some congregational consulting; National Jewish Outreach Program, an organization which attempts to bring back Jewish adults to their religion; Rabbinic Council of America, an organization which serves over 1,100 Orthodox rabbis internationally and also offers a full range of services to chaplains, administrators, and educators; and Yeshiva University, an organization which is internationally famous for its Albert Einstein College of Medicine and Benjamin N. Cardozo School of Law. Yeshiva University, founded in 1886, is the premier training ground for mainstream Orthodox rabbis in North America. Its graduate programs also include social and community service and cantorial studies.

The Protocols of the Elders of Zion

In 1905, the Tsarist secret police tried to hold back the coming revolution by calling it a Jewish plot and used as their evidence falsified documents entitled, " The Protocols of the Elders of Zion". The original concept for these accusations go back to 1864, when a French journalist wrote a political satire about Emperor Napoleon III. Four years later, a German novelist plagiarized the original work and changed the conspiracy for world domination from Napoleon III to a secret meeting of Jewish Elders in Prague. According to the falsified documents, during the Zionist Congress of 1897, a group of Jewish wise men outlined 24 protocols to enslave the Christian world,

by first taking control of the International banking system. The American Jewish Committee commissioned an experienced and respected journalist, Herman Bernstein to produce a rebuttal of the Protocols. In his book, *The History of a Lie*, Bernstein proved the origins of the Protocols, how they were altered from the original text, and the subsequent lies developed by the Russian police. However, Henry Ford, an extremely anti-Semitic person, who transferred his hatred of financiers into an anti-Jewish crusade, supported the *Dearborn Independent*, which prepared a series of articles entitled "The International Jew." This was a highly derogatory and inflammatory set of materials based on the Protocols, that was published weekly from 1920 to 1922, and then periodically for another five years. Ford ordered his chain of automobile dealers to function as subscription agents, even assigning quotas to them. By 1927, Ford was involved in several suits brought by Jewish people. His business was suffering and he finally ended his anti-Jewish campaign. In 1938, Henry Ford accepted the Grand Cross of the German Eagle at the personal request of Adolph Hitler. In 1940, he stated to the British newspapers that international Jewish bankers had caused the outbreak of World War II. Henry Ford did so much for the economic growth of the United States when he first introduced the mass-produced automobile and paid his workers a living wage. Unfortunately he let his own personal and narrow views of financiers become a hatred of Jewish financiers. He had a lifelong hatred of the Jewish people which led him to be instrumental in influencing millions of people to become bigots and blame the problems of society on the Jewish people, a very small but highly motivated and dedicated group of patriots and outstanding citizens in their communities.

In 1905-1907, a wave of pogroms in Russia caused by the Black Hundreds resulted in severe living conditions and even death for large numbers of Jewish people. This led to the peak years of Jewish immigration to the United States in 1906–1907.

In 1906, the Jewish Encyclopedia was completed in New York City. It was considered to be the most important accomplishment in the science of Judaism.

By 1910, there were between 1.5 million and 2.3 million Jewish people in the United States. Of this group, there were many people of distinction several of whom will be discussed because of their unique contributions to the growth and development of the United States.

Jacob Henry Schiff

Jacob Henry Schiff bridged the late 19th and early 20th century. He was born on January 10, 1847 in Germany, a descendent of a distinguished rabbinical family that could trace its lineage to 1370. In 1865, he emigrated to the United States and became a citizen. He married Theresa Loeb on May 6, 1875, and then joined her father's firm. In ten years he was named Chief Executive Officer because of his financial abilities. He died on September 25, 1920.

Schiff was a great financier, philanthropist, and dedicated patriot of this country. Through his corporation, Kuhn, Loeb & Company, he helped finance the development and growth of Westinghouse Electric, U.S. Rubber, Armour, American Telephone and Telegraph and many other major corporations. He served as a director and adviser to numerous insurance companies, banks, and other corporations. He was a prime mover in helping to consolidate and expand the American railroad system. He was prominent in floating loans for the United States government and for foreign nations who worked with the United States government. He funded innumerable Jewish and non-Jewish philanthropies, and established and developed many of them. He was very concerned about humanity and sickness and therefore contributed heavily to Montefiore Hospital in New York. He served as its President for thirty five years and visited the hospital weekly to make sure that the care that was given was exemplary

Rabbi Stephen Samuel Wise

Rabbi Stephen Samuel Wise was a social reformer who helped bridge the gap between the old established American Jewish community and the eastern European immigrants who came at the beginning of the 20th century. He was a co-founder of the National Association for the Advancement of Colored People in 1909 and he helped mediate and arbitrate labor disputes. In 1911, the Triangle Shirtwaist Company fire, in which 146 women lost their lives, had a tremendous effect on him. Thereafter, he fought relentlessly against sweatshops in unsafe factories. When Hitler came to power in 1933, Rabbi Wise organized Jews and non-Jews against Nazi Germany and helped form a boycott of German goods.

Julius Rosenwald

Julius Rosenwald was a prominent philanthropist. In 1910, he joined Sears Roebuck & Company and served as its President until 1925 and then as its chairman until he died in 1932. President Woodrow Wilson appointed him as a member of the Advisory Commission of the Council of National Defense in 1916. He was sent on many missions at home and abroad by the Secretary of War. He was very active in charities for Jewish causes, as well as non-Jewish causes. Rosenwald equated Judaism to service to humanity and he believed Jews were a people, not a nation. He helped feed the hungry children in Germany after World War I and helped establish colleges in Syria and Constantinople. He contributed almost $4 million to help build black YMCA-YWCA buildings throughout the United States. He, like Booker T. Washington, believed that the salvation of the black people lay in education and, therefore, he contributed very heavily to this effort. He established the Julius Rosenwald Fund in 1917 and by 1919, it had grown to $30 million. From 1900 to 1950, the Rosenwald foundation gave away over $700 million in today's dollars. Among many projects, Mr. Rosenwald contributed to the construction of nearly 5,400 schools for black children in the South. After World War I, an estimated 60% of American blacks who completed primary school had been educated in a school built by Rosenwald. He was involved with the Chicago Planning Commission, was President of the Federation of Jewish Charities, and built and gave to the city of Chicago the Museum of Science and Industry.

Hadassah and Henrietta Szold

Henrietta Szold was born in Baltimore in 1860. She was the daughter of the eminent Baltimore Rabbi, Benjamin Szold, who was one of the founders of the original Federation of American Zionists. Her father's interests in Palestine Jewish life helped nurture her own interests in helping the Jewish people there. Henrietta received a typical women's secondary education and then taught for a decade and a half at a girl's finishing school. Because of her concern about immigrants, on her own time she joined a group of dedicated volunteers in organizing the country's first night school devoted entirely to immigrants. From 1889 to 1893, she would get up at 4:30 a.m. to prepare assignments for her night-school teachers, conduct her own daytime classes, and then teach her night-school classes until 11:30 p.m. She was the Secretary of the Jewish Publication Society from 1893 to 1916 and created the yearly edition of the *American Jewish Yearbook*.

Henrietta Szold, on the holiday of Purim, February 24, 1912, at Temple Emanu-El, founded Hadassah. She brought together thirty eight Jewish women from the New York's Zionists studies groups and urged them to form the new organization dedicated to the health care of the Jewish people in Palestine. She was elected President. In 1909, with her mother, she had gone to Palestine, where she was shocked by the poverty and disease of the Jewish people. When she came home, she was eager to help her fellow Jewish people. She persuaded the philanthropist Nathan Straus to help underwrite the cost of the nurses for a five-year period. They sent two nurses, Rose Kaplan and Rachel Landy, to Jerusalem to set up health care stations. The two nurses sailed with the Strausses on January 1, 1913 and opened an office in Jerusalem in March of that year. The sign identifying the clinic read, "American Daughters of Zion, Nurses Settlement, Hadassah." They treated 5,000 patients in their first year.

The second convention of the Daughters of Zion meeting in 1914, formally adopted the name of Hadassah for the organization because of the group's medical efforts in Palestine. Henrietta was then elected the first President of the national group. By 1916, Hadassah had 4,000 members and Henrietta Szold was given the responsibility for organizing the American Zionist Medical Unit in Palestine. In 1918, Hadassah sent forty four doctors and nurses to Palestine with $50,000 in equipment and medicines. In 1920, when Henrietta was sixty years old, she went to Palestine to direct the operations of the medical clinics. When Hebrew University was founded in 1925, Henrietta Szold quickly encouraged the medical unit to join with the educational unit to create a modern medical institution. In 1936, it became the Hadassah Hospital, one of the most respected, modern medical centers in the world. Henrietta remained in Palestine until her death in 1945.

Today, Hadassah is the largest Zionist organization in the world and one of the largest women's organizations in the United States. It supports the Hadassah Medical Center as well as providing funds for a variety of other programs such as: religion in the public schools; image of Jewish women in the media; Jewish education events; Jewish education study guides and publications; Jewish family education; Hadassah Foundation; Hadassah Leadership Academy; Hadassah Missions; Hadassah mitzvah day; Hadassah tutoring programs; healthy women's programs; Hebrew studies; Legislative Action Center; violence against women; children at risk; and young women/young leaders. Hadassah sponsors cutting age research in numerous health related specialties and sends emergency teams worldwide. Hadassah now has 300,000 members in chapters throughout the United States and Hadassah International has units in thirty four countries on four continents. Hadassah is the largest volunteer organization in the United States committed to healing, teaching, and research on the physical, spiritual and cultural levels.

Dr. Solomon Schechter

On February 23, 1913, Dr. Solomon Schechter, President of the Jewish Theological Seminary brought together a group of twenty two synagogues with a common mission, the development and perpetuation of Conservative Judaism, and formed the United Synagogues of Conservative Judaism. In 1992, it was renamed the United Synagogue of America. The first act of the organization was to form the Department of Education in order to provide program supervision, standards, textbooks, and curricula. In 1952, eight synagogues issued the " Guide to Standards for Congregational Life." In 1959, it issued a "Statement of Standards for Synagogue Practice," which became binding upon all affiliated congregations. These standards are modified periodically.

Solomon Schechter was born in 1847 (1850?) to a Lubavitch Hasidic family, in Romania, and was educated at the University of Berlin. He went to England in 1882 and in 1890 was made lecturer in Talmud at Cambridge. In 1902, he became the second President of the Jewish Theological Seminary in New York City, which he developed into a center of learning and the beginnings of the Conservative Movement. His greatest academic fame came from his discovery of the Cairo Geniza, an extraordinary collection of more than 100,000 pages of medieval Jewish texts that were preserved in an Egyptian synagogue. The find revolutionized the study of Medieval Judaism.

Schechter always emphasized the centrality of Jewish law in Jewish life. He said, "...Judaism is absolutely incompatible with the abandonment of the Torah." He believed in strict Jewish traditionalism, but was dissatisfied with his Hasidic upbringing, since it did not allow for any kind of change to become a modern religion. He died in 1915.

Sigmund Livingston

Sigmund Livingston, an attorney born in Bloomington, Illinois, persuaded the B'nai B'rith to sponsor the Anti-Defamation League. The immediate objective was to stop the defamation of the Jewish people and to secure justice and fair treatment for all citizens. During the period of mass immigration many of the individuals coming from Europe brought with them the anti-Jewish prejudices that they had in their former countries. In addition, the Jewish people, besides being isolated in Eastern Europe were different in education, manner of dress, culture, and occupation. Even their virtues antagonized people because Jewish people frequently had a powerful family feeling, a strain of intellectualism, and a need and willingness to work long hours to survive. Jewish people were nonconformists and nonconformists attracted bullies and bigots. In the early years, the Anti-Defamation League's primary concern was the protection of American Jews from all forms of discrimination. During World War I, discrimination increased sharply because of wartime tensions, because of the Ku Klux Klan, and a select group of individuals who hated Jewish people. Sigmund Livingston died in 1945 after thirty two years of dedicated service as a national chairman.

Louis D. Brandeis

Louis D. Brandeis was born on November 13, 1856 and died on October 5, 1941. He served as an Associate Justice of the United States Supreme Court for 22 years, eight months, and eight days. He was a son of Jewish immigrants and was raised in Louisville, Kentucky, where his father was a successful grain merchant. He entered Harvard Law School at age eighteen and earned the highest average in the school's history, graduating in 1877. He was an extraordinary lawyer, public figure and Zionist. For Brandeis, the law was a means of shaping social, economic, and political affairs. He believed that the law had to operate on the basis of two assumptions: that the individual was the basic force in society and that the individual had limited capabilities. His intent was to stretch the individual's potential to its limit. He had a huge role in securing the "Right to Privacy." He wrote about this extensively in the *Harvard Law Review* of December 15, 1890.

Russian Revolution

In March 1917 (February, according to the old Russian calendar which was changed in 1918), the Russian people rebelled against Czar Nicholas II. The October Revolution took place in November 1917, when V. I. Lenin and the Bolsheviks, later called Communists, seized power. Communist Russia gradually became the Soviet Union by conquering Georgia, Ukraine, and eastern Armenia. This had a profound effect on the Jewish people of the Ukraine and later Poland. Over 140,000 Polish Jews went to Palestine. Between 1927 and 1938, nearly 200,000 Polish Jews left the country with 74,000 going to Palestine, 34,000 to Argentina, and 28,000 to the United States. The rest went to other countries.

World War I

On April 2nd, 1917, United States declared war against Germany. This war, which began in Europe in August of 1914, initially emphasized American neutrality. By 1917, President Wilson, fearing a world dominated by imperial Germany, and angry over the violation of neutral rights on the oceans, declared war. Volunteer enlistments were asked of all United States citizens. Although Jewish people represented only 3.2 percent of the total population, 5.73 percent joined the country's Armed Forces. Congressman Julius Kahn of California, Chairman of the House Military Affairs Committee said, "... Jews at all periods in the world's history have been ready to make the supreme sacrifice whenever the land that gives them shelter demands it. I know, that I voice the sentiment of the overwhelming majority of the Jews in the United States when I say that we will do our share toward keeping old Glory floating proudly in the skies so that it may continue to shelter under its folds the downtrodden and the oppressed of every land." More than 250,000 Jewish people served in the Armed Forces in World War I. Approximately 3,500 died and more than 12,000 were wounded. They won innumerable commendations for bravery.

The war affected the lives of millions of industrial workers including women, blacks, farmers, and other minorities. Despite the horrors that occurred, prosperity had now been brought to the American economy. There was a burst of moral-reform movements, but the wartime spirit brought forth new racial violence and fresh anti-radical hysteria. During the war years, about 500,000 blacks migrated North from their traditional homes in the South looking for job opportunities in the war industries. After the Russian Revolution there were red scares everywhere. In 1919, there was a string of bombings and among the victims was Attorney General Mitchell Palmer. He led raids and arrested around 700 suspected communists and anarchists.

Balfour Declaration

On November 2, 1917, the British government declared the establishment of a Jewish home in Palestine when it issued the Balfour Declaration. This was, in fact, a decision of the British Cabinet, in consultation with Jewish leaders, and was issued as a letter from Arthur James Balfour to Lord Rothschild. It stated, "His Majesty's Government views with favor the establishment in Palestine of the National Home for the Jewish people, and will use their best endeavors to facilitate the achievement of this object, it being clearly understood that nothing shall be done which may prejudice the civil and religious rights of existing non-Jewish communities in Palestine by the rights and political status enjoyed by Jews in any other country."

Bernard Mannes Baruch

Bernard Mannes Baruch served through three wars as an adviser to the Presidents who called upon him for his expertise and excellent judgment. President Wilson appointed him to the Advisory Commission of the Council of National Defense, and the War Industries. When he accepted these appointments he resigned his position with industry, liquidated his holdings, sold his seat on the New York Stock Exchange and purchased millions of dollars of liberty bonds. He played active roles in the administrations of Presidents Wilson, Harding, Hoover, Roosevelt, and Truman. During World War II, he was deeply involved in working on many committees that helped the war effort.

Irving Berlin

Irving Berlin epitomized the Jewish relationship to the United States of America. He wrote patriotic songs in World War I and World War II, and a total of over 900 songs, nineteen musicals, and the scores of eighteen movies which gave pleasure, meaning and happiness to the land that he adopted and adopted him in turn. He wrote "Easter Parade," "White Christmas," and other songs which made the total community happy. When he wrote in 1939, "God Bless America," sung by Kate Smith, he introduced to the people of the United States a second national anthem, because of its patriotism and popularity. He donated a large sum of money to a variety of charities. He was born on May 11, 1888 in Russia and died on September 22, 1989 at the age of 101 years, in the United States. He left a wonderful legacy of music, and once again reinforced the Jewish need to provide charity for all those who cannot help themselves.

1920-1940

The early to mid-1920s was a time of prosperity in the United States, as well as industrial and technological growth created by a new and booming electrical industry and the invention of the affordable automobile. This was followed by the worst depression in the history of the United States. In 1925-1926, the great housing boom and speculation, especially in Florida, went bust.

In 1920, there were between 3,300,000 and 3,600,000 Jewish people in the United States. The people of the country wanted calm after the uproar of World War I, which caused higher taxes and involvement in the foreign affairs of the world. The United States became a nation of isolationists. They wanted to retreat from the world and only participate in American events. American culture and society changed dramatically as a wave of new lifestyles and ideas in music and literature erupted. While some people thought this was wonderful, others felt that no good could come from this new way of life. The Volstead Act of 1919, which tried to control the mores of people helped foster gangsterism and a sense of wildness among the upperclass community. Boom times had arrived. Anything was possible and everyone could make money quickly. The 19th Amendment to the Constitution of the United States was passed in 1920, granting women the right to vote, and therefore increasing their power in the political world. This was a natural outgrowth of all their hard work in passing the 18th Amendment, in 1919, which prohibited the

sale of non–medical use of alcohol. Prenatal and baby care centers were also created in rural areas.

The Ku Klux Klan, revived in 1915 after being disbanded in 1869, was now operating at maximum strength. Fundamentalists, such as Billy Sunday, insisted on the divinity of the Bible and were angered by the theory of evolution. The Immigration Acts of 1921 and 1924 established a quota system, which resulted in a sharp reduction of Jewish people as well as others, who wanted to come to the United States. There were also quotas in law schools, medical schools, other professional schools, and colleges. Despite this, the Jewish children of the immigrants went to college in far higher numbers then the total community. The Jewish need for education drove families to make enormous sacrifices to send their children to college. In 1927, there were approximately 4,200,000 Jewish people in the United States. The stock market crashed on October 29, 1929 and the panic led to bank foreclosures all over the United States. An international Depression resulted. During the 1930s, there were many virulent anti-Jewish groups including the Ku Klux Klan. Charles E. Coughlin, a Canadian born priest, who had a newspaper called " Social Justice," and a radio program, which reached twenty six states from Maine to Colorado, was another anti-Jewish voice. He had invested very heavily in silver and owned nearly 500,000 ounces. Outraged by this exposure, he blamed his problem on the Jewish conspiracy. By 1937, his radio broadcasts were taking on a more fascist cast, as he praised Mussolini, and supported Hitler.

In 1931, The Jewish Braille Institute of America was organized by the National Federation of Temple Sisterhoods and the United Synagogue Council of America. These two organizations, representing the Jewish Women of the Reform and Conservative Movements in the United States, have been deeply involved, for many years, in working with blind people.

Franklin D. Roosevelt was elected President in 1932. He established extensive programs to restore the economy, reform financial systems and institutions, and tried to recover prosperity. Millions of people listened to the radio news, musical programs, and comedy shows. By 1937, there were between 4,600,000 and 4,800,000 Jewish people in the United States.

Albert Einstein

Albert Einstein also epitomized the Jewish relationship to the United States of America. His scientific work was outstanding and unmeasurable. As a person, he constantly opposed oppression and hatred. Although he felt that the development of an atomic bomb was horrific, he urged President Roosevelt to develop one before the Germans could. This famous letter that he wrote helped change the course of history. His legacy is his enormous scientific contributions, his fight against bigotry, his fight against the use of nuclear weapons, and his enormous love for humanity.

Rabbi Mordechai Kaplan

In 1934, Rabbi Mordechai Kaplan founded Reconstructionism. His aim was to remake Jewish life. He defined Judaism as a religious civilization which includes prayer, Hebrew as a language, Israel, literature, art, drama, etc.. His aim was to make Judaism as meaningful as possible to American Jews. He established Jewish centers as places where Jews could experience all aspects of Jewish life, from Jewish culture to prayer. He combined the Jewish Community Center with the synagogue and had a significant impact upon modern Jewish life and Jewish thought.

Kaplan was born in Lithuania in 1881. He received a traditional Jewish education in Vilna and immigrated along with his family to the United States in 1889. Becoming disenchanted with the orthodox theology he increasingly sought non-orthodox approaches to Judaism. He graduated from City College of New York and was ordained a rabbi at the Jewish Theological Seminary of the conservative movement. In 1909, at age 28, Kaplan began to teach at the Jewish Theological Seminary, first as chair of the Teachers Institute and then as a professor of the philosophy of religion. He helped create the Young Israel Modern Orthodox movement with Rabbi Israel Friedlander.

Because his theology continued to evolve he was considered to be a heretic by the Orthodox movement.

Kaplan was profoundly influenced by the new social science of sociology and progress in the physical sciences. The Jewish Virtual Library says of Rabbi Kaplan, "... He came to see Judaism not as a religion, but as a civilization, characterized not only by beliefs and practices, but by language, culture, literature, ethics, art, history, social organization, symbols and customs. He promoted the notion of a synagogue-center which offered not only religious prayer services, but study programs, drama, dance, song, sports and exercise."

In 1935, Kaplan wrote, *Judaism as a Civilization*, a book which became the foundation of the new Reconstructionist Movement. Kaplan taught that we need a reconstruction of the religious foundations of Judaism in light of our understanding that Judaism is a religious civilization. He promoted democracy in the synagogue and advocated monetary membership, elected leadership, and a respect for the religious opinions of all individuals. He instituted the bat mitzvah in the conservative movement when he brought his daughter at age 12 to read the Haftarah on the Sabbath. He continued to study and teach until his death at age 102 in 1983.

The four key aspects of Kaplan's thought included:

1. Judaism is an evolving religious civilization. Despite our dispersion throughout the world our common history is the source of our covenant.
2. God is the power which makes possible personal salvation rather than a supernatural force in the universe. God can not abridge the laws of nature for God is synonymous with natural law.
3. Prayer is necessary because it helps us become conscious of our conscience, the force within which we are able to construct our relationships and realize salvation. Community prayer focuses attention on the needs of everyone. Worship releases emotion and helps orient us in a positive psychological direction.

4. Chosenness is an expression of Jewish obligation to God and humanity. A personal messiah in the form of a human being is not part of Judaism.

These two decades were a period of increasing political and social unrest in many parts the world. The Nazis came to power in Germany as a result of the Germans' sense of injustice, and nationalistic frustration from World War I and its aftermath. The Jewish people's right to live a normal life, and in fact even to live, was now endangered.

This was a time of insecurity and uncertainty among the European Jewish people. There were over six million Jewish people, with over three million in Poland. In Lvov, in 1921, there were 76,800 Jewish people making up 35% of the total population. By 1931, there were 99,600 Jewish people making up 31.9% of the total population. In Przemysl, in 1921, there were 18,360 Jewish people making up 38.3% of the population. By 1931, there were 17,300 Jewish people making up 34% of the population. These two towns serve as examples of the Jewish communities in Poland. 52.2% of Jews were involved in Trades, 10.8% were involved in crafts, 6.5% were involved in industry, 14.1% were involved in clerical positions, 6.2% were in a professional field or were teachers, 2.5% were involved in agriculture, 4.0% were unemployed, and 3.7% were part of the miscellaneous categories.

There was a significant portion of people who had academic education and therefore these areas had excellent social and cultural programs. In Przemysl there were about 100 Jewish lawyers, about 100 Jewish physicians, pharmacists, artists, writers, musicians, actors, and government officials. The town had a library that contained 40,000 volumes in Polish and other languages. Once a week there were lectures on literary and scientific topics in the library. The last chairman of the library was a Jewish teacher. They also had merchants' organizations and credit unions. A prominent person in the merchants' organizations was Yosef Rinde, grandfather of John and Toni Rinde, who owned a large retail/wholesale store specializing in toys and religious icons.

In 1933, with Hitler in power, the official program of extreme discrimination against the Jewish people started throughout Europe. The Jews were ruined economically, persecuted, removed from all positions of power and prestige, and finally eliminated. Riots, street fighting, and all forms of violence were used to achieve this goal.

On November 9 and November 10, 1938, Kristallnacht, the night of broken glass, occurred. It was a highly organized series of anti-Jewish riots, carried out by the Nazis in Germany and Austria. 7,000 Jewish shops, businesses and homes were vandalized and ransacked, 267 synagogues were burned, and 30,000 Jewish men were deported to concentration camps (Dachau, Buchenwald, Sachsenhausen). The Nazis levied a fine of one billion marks against the Jewish community to restore the damage that had been inflicted upon them. On November 12, 1938, Nazi leaders decided to overtly destroy Jewish life in the Third Reich. This was the beginning of the "Final Solution."

Worldwide Nazi Influence

In 1938, hatred toward the Jewish people by the Nazis was not confined to Europe. It was found in every part of the world where there was Nazi influence. The following is a first-person account by eighteen year old Shirley Collman of Tampa. It is a story that was repeated, with certain variations, numerous times in various parts of the world. It also is a story that talks about the haves and have nots of society.

"I graduated from Plant High School in Tampa in January of 1938. In those days they had midterm graduations. I planned to attend the University of Tampa in September. My aunt and uncle in South America gave me a graduation present to visit them until college started. I was there for seven months. My uncle worked for Standard Oil of New Jersey.

I traveled by bus to New York City. It was safe to do this at this time. I was met by friends of the family, Sam and Helen Rothstein. They took me to Bayonne, New Jersey where I boarded a German oil tanker. The other passengers looked after me.

The first thing I saw when I boarded the tanker was a large picture of Adolph Hitler. There were more of them in the dining room and in every area that the crew had to pass. Each time they (the crew) came into the room they would stop, salute the picture and say "Heil Hitler."

One of the company couples from the ship insisted that I stay with them. They took me to shop in Aruba, an area of rough wooden stalls. They had perfumes, Japanese embroidered items, and other imports. The area was filthy dirty at that time. All the roads were dirt roads.

I took another overnight smaller boat for a couple of days and then a primitive rail car. Once I was in Maracaibo, my aunt met me. We took another boat to La Salina where the oil camp was on Lake Maracaibo. My uncle had been assigned a nice house with nice furniture. My aunt had to buy the meat in the open market in the little town of La Salina. The meat was fly infested. The company had a nice clubhouse and a well populated bar. New movies were shown in the open air twice a week.

We went into Maracaibo by boat once a month to go to a grocery store to get our staples and sundries, etc.. After the first time, my aunt sent me by myself to do the shopping. The store sent the groceries right to the boat. My treat was to have a lunch wherever I wanted to. Unfortunately, I saw some terrible things in the city. I saw anti-Jewish rallies and parades and more pictures of Hitler. There was a large German population even before the war. The poverty was horrendous. There were only two classes of people, the haves and the have nots. There was much, much syphilis and other sicknesses. Men with open sores begged to get food. Pitiful!"

Occupied Countries

Worldwide, Germany was on the march, and the Nazis were spreading hate and intolerance. Austria was annexed in 1938. The Nazi-Soviet Non-Aggression Pact (Molotov-Ribbentrop Pact) was signed on August 23, 1939. In a secret protocol, Article II, the two countries agreed that the spheres of influence would be bounded approximately by the line of the rivers Narev, Vistula, and San. They also agreed that they would decide later if an independent Poland was warranted. Poland was invaded by Germany on September 1, 1939. The Holocaust had begun and 6 million Jewish people and several million others were eventually eliminated in the death camps.

Przemysl, Lwow, and Lublin, Poland

Przemysl residents were treated like all Jewish communities in European cities. The Germans operated according to a predetermined plan with precision and cruelty. They carried out expulsions and murders. From a population of about 20,000 Jewish people there were only about 300 alive after the war.

Stella and Maurice Rinde

Excerpts of the memoirs of Maurice Rinde (John's father) also known as, Wiktor Kroczykowski, an identity he assumed sometime in early 1942 with forged papers, helps paint a picture of the times in Poland. His story is an example of the terror Jewish people had to live through in Nazi occupied countries. Maurice had been living with his wife, Stella, and two children, John and Irene, in Przemysl, which had 60,000 inhabitants, one third of them Jews.

The late 1920s in Europe were a bad time for Jewish people because of the after effects of World War I, but this was nothing compared to the 1930s. On Thursday, September 7, 1939, the city was bombed and a great number of casualties occurred. Since the people underestimated what the Germans would do, only male Jews aged eighteen to sixty were considered in danger. The male Jews fled the city leaving their wives, children and elderly people behind. By September 15, they reached the border of Poland, Russia and Rumania, and crossed the river into Rumania. However, they were denied admission to Rumania and turned back to return home. Since they were traveling mainly on foot, this process took several weeks. In the meantime Przemysl was briefly occupied by the Nazis. The Germans rounded up prominent Jews from lists previously prepared in order to deport them. They came looking for Maurice, who luckily was on his way to Rumania to escape deportation.

According to the provisions of the previously mentioned Nazi-Soviet Nonaggression Pact, Poland was partitioned shortly after the country surrendered and

Przemysl came under Russian control. There followed a short period of time while the Germans withdrew and the Russians walked in, that the Ukrainians caused havoc. With the men gone, masses of Ukrainian farmers equipped with clubs and other concealed weapons started a pogrom in the city. Jewish men in the Russian army that were in the city had machine guns and orders to shoot anyone that attacked the Jewish people. This put a stop to the pogrom. It took the Jewish men of Przemysl several weeks to return home.

Life under the Russian occupation was harsh. Now a person was not persecuted for being Jewish, but rather for being rich. Being a capitalist in Russia was a serious crime. Capitalists were denied a work permit which was tantamount to deportation to Siberia, not to mention expropriation of all possessions. The Russian occupation led to the nationalization of the Rinde's factory and confiscation of their apartment, cash, jewelry, silver place settings, crystals, furniture, and personal belongings. During the severe winter of 1939/40, the Rinde family left for Lwow, a bigger city, sixty five miles away. There Maurice, posing as a "proletarian worker," took a Soviet bookkeeping course so that he could get a job. The salary only covered about 40 to 50% of his and his family's living expenses, food, but not clothing. He was fired repeatedly because he had a " criminal past," which meant that he had owned a factory, or was a capitalist.

Meanwhile the Germans, in their occupied territories, issued several special orders. One, issued October 26, 1939, stated that Jews in the ages of fourteen to sixty must perform forced labor and the first forced labor camps were organized at the end of 1939.

1940-1946–World War II

Germany's Blitzkrieg, or lightning, war led to the occupation of many Western European nations. The Jewish people of Europe were in extreme danger. A German order dated January 24, 1940, stated that the right to hold property by Jewish people was abolished. A German order dated

January 26, 1940, deprived Jewish people of the right to travel or to change their place of residence anywhere in Poland. Further, the Jewish communities had to make contributions of gold, silver, furs and other precious objects. The ration of food allowed to the Jewish population was to be much smaller and far worse than that of the other inhabitants of the country. A German order dated November 23, 1940 compelled Jewish people to wear special marks.

On June 21, 1941, the war between Germany and Russia broke out and German occupation occurred. Germans issued orders affecting every aspect of daily life and the penalty for failure to obey was an automatic death sentence. Everybody was required, under penalty of death, to report to his work, but the Jewish people were rounded up, beaten, mistreated, and killed at the whim of the soldiers. Sometimes they were brought to work to perform the dirtiest tasks, which had to be done by hand only. No tools were allowed. Everybody that was not Jewish had the right to stop someone who was suspected of being Jewish and take him or her to the Germans. This happened when a young Ukrainian boy stopped Maurice and sent him to a German soldier. Since other people were gathered around the soldier, Maurice just walked on as if he were not Jewish. Jewish people hid out in homes, offices, factories and warehouses. Roundups were going on continuously and a group of Ukrainians seized a large number of Jewish people and turned them over to the Germans. One day, an employee who had a grievance (dating back to the Russian occupation) against the company he worked for under Maurice's supervision, had him arrested. The man arrived with two Ukrainian militiamen and took him to German police headquarters. Maurice spoke fluent German and was able to talk himself out of the situation. He was constantly in fear that he would be exposed and executed.

German officers constantly stole the possessions of the Jewish people. They went into the apartments of the Jewish people, made selections of whatever they wanted and took them. If they were nice they paid 1% to 10% of the value of the things they were taking. If they weren't nice they didn't pay anything. The German officers would then stop Jewish people in the street, who were easily identified because they had to wear armbands, and make them carry the stolen goods to the German's quarters.

Along with the other Jewish people, the Rinde family suffered from severe hunger. They were allowed four ounces of bread a day. When Maurice would be able to buy a black bread on the Black Market, the children, ages four and six, would consume it in minutes. When a German general was killed, an order was issued to kill a group of prominent Jews including Maurice Rinde, but luckily they couldn't find him. About seventy Jewish men were executed.

Soon Maurice and his family were expelled from their apartment and forced to move to the ghetto where they had to share an apartment, consisting of two bedrooms and an eat-in kitchen, with another family. John had been kept out of the first grade but was taught by a tutor. In three months, he had completed all of the material for first grade and then started to learn Hebrew. John read fluently, like a third-grader. Upon subsequent escape from the ghetto, he had to be told to forget the Hebrew, which he promptly did.

Jewish people were not allowed to go out into the street after 8 p.m.. Without pay, they worked from 5 a.m. to 8 p.m. shoveling snow, cleaning streets and unloading cargo, and felt lucky when they weren't beaten, imprisoned, deported, or murdered. One day Maurice's sister, Tuna, was caught without her armband and was murdered.

By early 1942, the Hitler gangsters started their "final solution of the Jewish question," which was the institution of the gas extermination chambers. The first step was taken in Lwow, where the population of Jewish people was 93,000 and 33,000 were sent off, supposedly, to work camps. Instead they were sent to die in the first gas chamber in Belzec.

On July 26, 1942, the SS attempted to carry out their first large-scale resettlement action against the Jews of Przemysl. This meant their liquidation. A fifty one year old reserve German officer and lawyer from Breslau, Dr. Albert Battel, an Oberleutenant,

who was the adjutant to the local military commander, Major Max Liedtke, along with the major, ordered the bridge over the river San, the only access into the Jewish ghetto, to be blocked. When the SS attempted to cross to the other side, the Sergeant-major in charge of the bridge threatened to open fire unless they withdrew. Previously, Dr. Battel had demanded that the Jews who worked in the Wehrmacht not be deported, even though they did not have Gestapo stamps. The Gestapo had refused to comply with this demand. Later that afternoon, an army detachment under the command of Oberleutenant Battel broke through the SS cordoned-off area of the ghetto and used army trucks to remove up to 100 Jewish people and their families to the barracks of the local military command. These Jewish people were placed under the protection of the Wehrmacht and therefore did not die in the Belzec extermination camp. This action saved the lives of Stanley and Lusia Igel, and their child Toni Igel Rinde. Dr. Battel's conduct was so embarrassing that the entire affair was investigated and the results sent to Heinrich Himmler and Martin Borman, second in command to Hitler. Himmler swore that after the war Dr. Battel would be arrested. Dr. Battel, who had arrived in January 1942, was transferred elsewhere in September 1942. In 1944, Dr. Battel was discharged from the army because of heart disease. He went home to Breslau, but was drafted into the Volkssturm. He was captured by the Russians and then was released. He was unable to regain his law practice because of the de-Nazification program. He died in Hattersheim near Frankfurt, Germany. On January 22, 1981, Yad Vashem recognized Dr. Albert Battel (posthumously) for his heroic stand against the SS and his saving of a large number of Jewish lives.

Luisa and Stanley Igel

On July 27, people were ordered to assemble in the ghettos and were either murdered or taken away to concentration camps. A special guard accompanied the roentgenologist, Dr. Rinde (John's uncle), with his wife and daughter, because a complaint had been filed against him by a German that he had treated Arian patients. They were sent to Belzec concentration camp and were later executed. On August 8, 1942, John Rinde's grandparents, rather than face deportation by the Gestapo, committed suicide by swallowing a cyanide pill.

The Jewish people who lived in Europe and survived the Holocaust had either escaped to the woods, fought the Germans as partisans, passed as Gentiles, were given away as children to be raised as Gentiles until the parents could recover them, or lived through the concentration camps. For the purposes of this book, it would be impossible to tell all of the individual stories of these Holocaust survivors. (Maurice Rinde's memoirs were made available to the author by his son, John.)

Gradually the ghetto was shrinking, as more and more people were forcibly deported, ostensibly to work camps. However, it became clear to those who were willing to face the facts that the deportation was to death camps rather than work camps. People with vision and means started to make plans to escape from the ghetto. To that end, the Rinde family obtained forged ID papers, under the name Kroczykowski, identifying them as Catholics. They then awaited an appropriate moment to escape. The moment came at the start of the next round up, in the summer of 1942. The process began by placing the children with Christian families to avoid having them murdered. John, who was seven years old, lived in a Christian woman's apartment, where he was alone during the daytime and was not allowed near any windows to avoid being seen. Irene, who was only five years old, was placed with a teacher who had her play with her own child. A Ukrainian boy recognized the little girl and threatened to report her. She was taken back to the old apartment where a doctor and his wife said that the child belonged to them. The doctor, his wife and the child were rounded up by the Germans, but then released when he said he had an important task to perform at the hospital. A janitor from the local school went to fetch the child and brought her to her parents. With the roundup continuing and the fear that the children would be found out, Maurice took John, and his wife took the little girl, and went off separately to seek shelter in the same building. Maurice

and John hid in a four story building which was used for the manufacture of honey. Maurice's cousin, who spoke perfect German, was the manager of the company. Maurice gave bribes to everyone and his wife posed as an employee with her daughter. They hid in a small side room and stayed in one place all day long. They spend over two weeks in this hiding place until the deportation drive was over.

Maurice decided that he and the family had to move on to a new location, Lublin, where they could establish their new identity. They went by train late at night. When they passed Belzec on the train, the experienced Polish travelers closed the windows to avoid the smell of the burning bodies from the death camps.

Maurice had to obtain a job permit and permission to settle in the city, in order to have an apartment assigned to him. This was no small feat. Maurice enrolled in a bookkeeping course and earned a certificate which allowed him to work.

The first apartment assigned to the Rindes was in the old Jewish ghetto, all the Jews having recently been deported. This was a dirty place close to the railway station where the landlady had two rooms with six beds in each room. Maurice and John shared one bed while Stella and Irene shared a second one. Although they all presented documents to the landlady, she knew that they were Jewish, but did not reveal this information to anyone. One of the landlady's daughters worked for the Department of Labor. Maurice was able to utilize this information later to help not only himself, but other people. He obtained a second legal document and was able to eventually obtain an apartment. The apartment consisted of one room which was approximately thirty six square meters in size and had to serve as sleeping quarters as well as a kitchen for four people. Broken pieces of glass were used to cover the windows. They found old secondhand furniture. Maurice was also able to get back from a Ukrainian, who had hidden their belongings, a fur coat, two down comforters , some pillows, and a pair of shoes, which had gold and jewelry hidden in the heels. They obtained further forged documents. During this period of time they met other Jewish people who had forged documents and who were living as Christians. There was constant harassment by the police who were always demanding to see everyone's papers in order to trap any hidden Jews. The children were constantly warned not to reveal that they were Jewish. They were told to play quietly and avoid saying anything.

Maurice told the Germans that he was a certified bookkeeper and that because there was a shortage of bookkeepers, he could help run a company. He needed a job urgently, because those who were unemployed would be shipped off to labor camps. He was able to secure one because he not only had bookkeeping skills, but also spoke German fluently. Polish people, who were not essential to the running of the city, were evicted from Lublin because it was going to become once again a German city. Maurice was able to help people within the factory as well as the owners, because of his knowledge of German and his contacts in the labor office.

Maurice's brother, Henry, and his wife, Leonora, and Stella's brother-in-law, Joseph Bigelizen, were living in a desperate situation in hiding. Henry placed his two daughters, Roma, age nine, and Fila, age twelve, in a convent, and with his wife came to live with Maurice and the family. Henry always carried a cyanide pill with him in case he would be deported. Maurice found an empty house where the widow of a railway employee had been evicted to make room for the Germans. Since the Germans didn't want the house, Maurice was able to take possession of it and now had a place to hide his relatives. The house had one big room, one big kitchen, a foyer, an attic, an outhouse, a well and a big garden, where potatoes and vegetables were cultivated. Maurice took his relatives at night, by a horse driven car, and hid them in the house. Henry received word that his two daughters could no longer stay in the convent, because other children were calling them Jews. The Polish lady who placed them there removed them and brought them to Maurice's house where the children were hidden. The children arrived in a terrible condition. They were severely malnourished

and had frost bitten fingers. Maurice bought a metal oven and installed it in the cellar, where the family spent the days in the winter. In the summer they sat in the attic with light coming in only through a small window which was 12 inches by 24 inches. They had to stay away from the window so they would not be seen from the outside. To provide adequate food for everyone, they had two milk deliveries, one at 8 a.m. and one at 9 a.m.. Other food had to be bought on the black market. The nine of them lived together until the war was over. Maurice's story was repeated over and over again during this time as some people were able to escape the extermination of the Jewish people by living as Christian Polish people.

The Rindes managed to survive in this fashion, with many close calls and incidents until Lublin was liberated by the Soviets in the summer of 1944. Although the Jewish people were no longer being murdered, conditions were still very harsh.

United States Jewish People

In the United States, it was necessary to combat the foreign policy of isolation as fostered by Charles Lindberg and the American First Committee. Meanwhile, by 1940, between 4,700,000 and 5,000,000 Jewish people lived in the United States.

From 1940 to 1960, there were years of turmoil and then finally progress toward a better society. On the home front, all Americans, including Jewish Americans, made extraordinary efforts to protect the country and help win the war. Evelyn Fyvolent Samuels and her work for the American Red Cross was a fine example of this kind of effort. Charles Koren, who had already served twice in World War I now became an auxiliary policemen in World War II and served in this post for five years as a volunteer. After the war, the fight against communism became the major concern of the country. The Marshall Plan of 1947, and the Truman Doctrine of 1947, were directed at the rebuilding of Europe and fighting a Communist takeover.

Jewish men and women willingly joined the United States Armed Forces because their values were the same as those expressed by President Franklin

Roosevelt in his message to Congress in January, 1941 when he proposed lend-lease legislation to support Great Britain, who was already involved in World War II. President Roosevelt stated that Four Freedoms should prevail everywhere in the world. "In the future days which we seek to make secure, we look forward to a world founded on four essential human freedoms: freedom of speech and expression–everywhere in the world; freedom of every person to worship God in his own way–everywhere in the world; freedom from want which will secure to every nation a healthy peacetime life for its inhabitants –everywhere in the world; freedom from fear, which means a world-wide reduction of armaments to such a point and in such a thorough fashion that no nation will be in a position to commit an act of physical aggression against any neighbor–anywhere in the world."

In World War II, over 550,000 Jewish men and women served in the armed forces of the United States. Jewish women were active in a variety of capacities, including the military, as assembly-line workers, and in a variety of defense industries. About 11,000 Jewish service people were killed and over 40,000 were wounded. Over 52,000 decorations, citations and awards were given to the Jewish heroes. Whereas the Jewish people represented 3.3 percent of the total American population, 4.23 percent served in the Armed Forces. About 60 percent of all the Jewish physicians in the United States under 45 years of age were in the service. President Franklin D. Roosevelt praised the fighting abilities and service of Jewish men and women. General Douglas MacArthur said, "I am proud to join in saluting the memory of fallen American heroes of the Jewish faith."

In January, 1943, a temporary organization, the interim committee of the American Jewish Assembly, began laying plans to provide aid to the post-war European Jewish community. The American Jewish Conference grew out of this effort. Jewish leaders provided enormous assistance to the survivors of the Holocaust. The American Jewish Assembly helped advise the United States on Jewish affairs at the inception of the United Nations.

In June, 1944, Congress passed the G.I. Bill of Rights. This provided living allowances, tuition fees, supplies, medical treatment, and loans for homes and businesses. Its purpose was to help stimulate economic growth and provision for new factories and equipment. It provided a vast opportunity for young people to go to college and buy new homes. Many Jewish service people took advantage of this wonderful opportunity to improve themselves and help build a substantial career for the future.

In 1945, the radio program, "Eternal Light," was founded and sponsored by the Jewish Theological Seminary. Religion became interesting and entertaining as well as inspirational. People of all faiths listened each Sunday to this program. These individuals voiced their enthusiasm and approval by sending letters to the radio studio. In 1950, the radio series was honored nationally during Brotherhood Week for making the most outstanding contributions to mutual understanding of religion. It had been previously honored the same way. The program was primarily written for and about ordinary people and their problems. Ancient stories, as well as recent stories, were presented by current individuals. Each story was told simply, directly and dramatically in language that everyone knew and could understand. Spiritual uplift and moral integrity were properly incorporated in every story, which was meant to impress and inspire the listener.

In 1946, the Employment Act was passed by Congress. President Truman promised economic growth and established the Council of Economic Advisers to assist the President in maximizing employment, production, and purchasing power.

The Emma Lazarus Federation in the 1940s fought racial injustice, anti-semitism, promoted women's rights, promoted the State of Israel, world peace, and promoted consumer issues. Once again the Jewish women had come to the forefront, not only as the mainstay of the family and repository of tradition, but also as intellectual human beings who worked very hard to resolve the problems of society.

At the end of World War II, there was a sharp increase in population due to the baby boom resulting from the return of the armed forces from abroad. The economy flourished and the Jewish community flourished with it. As the Jewish people moved to suburban communities, new reform and conservative synagogues were formed. The Havurah Movement in large synagogues provided an opportunity for members to join small and more intimate prayer and socialization groups. This was a time when there was a sharp increase of Jewish people coming to Florida.

The United States Army became desegregated in 1948, thereby allowing African-Americans to become part of the integrated forces. This led to examination and widespread recognition that society at large was not integrated and that changes had to be made.

State of Israel

On November 29, 1947, the United Nations partitioned Palestine into two states. On May 14, 1948, Israel proclaimed independence and the United States recognized the State of Israel. The Arabs immediately rejected the proclamation and declared war against Israel. Israel was admitted to the United Nations in 1949.

Brandeis University

Brandeis University, named after the first Jewish justice of the United States Supreme Court, Lewis D. Brandeis, was founded in 1948. It was the gift of the American Jewish community to higher education to provide a high level nonsectarian university with a commitment of total excellence in education. The university, founded by eight Boston businessman and nurtured by thousands of supporters, was the former home of Middlesex College in Waltham, Massachusetts.

Eight Boston women conceived the idea of forming an organization whose main purpose was to support the libraries of the fledgling university, which did not have an endowment or alumni. They named their tiny group "The Brandeis University National Women's Committee." From the beginning, when they contributed $2000 to the library, they have built this organization into four outstanding libraries and have

contributed over $30 million. They have grown from eight people to over 65,000 women, in 127 chapters throughout the United States. The women had their first library in a stable with a total of 1000 books chosen by the librarian. Thanks to the efforts of the women this small, vigorous research university has developed the resources necessary to become outstanding in many areas of education and research.

The Fair Deal

In President Truman's State of the Union message in 1949, he proposed the Fair Deal. It enlarged the New Deal of President Roosevelt by adding housing, conservation, economic security, health insurance, federal aid to education, agricultural subsidies, an increase in the minimum wage, expanded Social Security, flood control, slum clearance, expanded public power, soil conservation, and the building of low income housing units. This, plus the need for housing generated by returning veterans, led to a sharp expansion in the economy of the entire country and a new era in the expansion of various parts of Florida including the Central West Coast. Business opportunities increased proportionately.

1950s

On June 24, 1950, North Korean troops attacked the Republic of Korea thereby starting the Korean War. Once again, Jewish men and women were part of the armed forces and helped protect Korea and prevent the spread of communism.

In 1950, there were between 4.5 million and 5 million Jewish people in the United States. The Conservative Movement permitted their congregants to drive to the synagogue on the Sabbath and congregants were allowed to use electricity on the Sabbath.

The Supreme Court's decision of Brown versus Board of Education of Topeka, in 1954, held that "separate but equal" violated the equal protection clause of the 14th Amendment of the Constitution of the United States and was thereby unconstitutional. This was followed by the Montgomery bus boycott in December 1955, where Rosa Parks, a black woman, refused to give up her seat to a white man and was therefore arrested. This led to a massive bus boycott in Montgomery, Alabama. In 1956, the United States Supreme Court ruled that the segregation of public transportation was unconstitutional. The Civil Rights Act of 1957, established a permanent commission on Civil Rights with investigative powers but did not guarantee the right to vote for black people.

From 1952 to 1960, President Eisenhower started the process of developing the most extensive public-works program in United States history, the Interstate Highway Act. This created for the country a tremendous expansion into the suburbs and into many rural areas. For Florida, this program created financial incentives which had only been surpassed by the coming of the railroads. Eisenhower also extended Social Security benefits and raised the minimum wage. This contributed to more older people coming to Florida. In 1960 there were between 5,300,000 and 5,500,000 Jewish people in United States. The number of Jewish people coming to Florida increased sharply.

1960-1970

In the early 1960s, the Civil Rights Movement exploded. There was tremendous frustration because of blatant racism epitomized by segregated schools, segregated housing, lack of voting rights in various areas, and a poor standard of living. Black leaders such as Martin Luther King Jr. rose to positions of power. The National Association for the Advancement of Colored People, co-founded by Jewish people became a powerful legal force in arguing cases in front of the United States Supreme Court leading to the Civil Rights Act of 1957 and Voting Rights Act of 1965. A lot of the funding of this organization came from the Jewish community. Jewish people marched with the blacks to attempt to gain civil rights that all Americans were entitled to, and enjoyed. Rabbi David Susskind of Temple Beth El in St. Petersburg, Florida was one of these marchers. Jewish people even gave their lives for this effort. In 1963, Rev. King gave his famous "I Have a Dream" speech at the historic

Civil Rights March on Washington D.C. on August 28, 1963. The Civil Rights Act of 1964, public accommodations section, outlawed segregation in public areas. The Voting Rights Act of 1965 prohibited the use of literacy tests as part of voter registration. The Civil Rights Act of 1968, barred discrimination in housing sales or rentals. The Civil Rights Acts not only helped the black population, but also helped other minorities, including Jewish people purchase or rent housing in areas that were limited by deed restrictions.

In 1965, President Lyndon Johnson proposed new social legislation which led to the liberalization of immigration laws. It abolished the restrictions and quota system previously used by the United States to determine where immigrants could come from. In later years, it allowed Russian Jewish immigrants to come to the United States in substantial numbers.

In 1967, Israel fought the Six Day War against the Arab states. It succeeded because of a massive shipment of highly sophisticated weaponry from the United States. In 1973, during Yom Kippur, once again Syria and Egypt, supported by Russia, led an all-out war against Israel. The Jewish people of the United States, along with many other people in the world, came to the assistance of Israel, the only true democracy in the Middle East. All the support and the greed of the oil producing countries led to the oil crisis of the late seventies and of the early eighties.

In 1969, the Environmental Protection Agency was created by President Nixon to enforce standards of Water and Air Quality. The protection of the environment plays an important role in Jewish life.

The Conservative Movement made many changes in the late sixties and early seventies. Family seating was allowed in synagogue. Women were allowed to be part of the minyan and permitted to read the Torah. Women were ordained as rabbis between 1977 and 1979.

Jacob Birnbaum
The Struggle for Soviet Jewry

In1964, Jacob Birnbaum, who had come from England the previous year, started a movement to convince the American Jewish community to rise up against the spiritual genocide of Soviet Jewry. He said that only American Jews had the resources and connections to make a difference and to get Soviet Jewish people a better life and even the ability to emigrate to Israel or the United States.

The Stalin era had ended and the Soviet Union, desperate for technology and trade, and fearful of China, increasingly turned to the United States for help making the Soviets more susceptible to economic pressure.

In the Soviet Union, there were three million Jewish people, a quarter of the world's Jewish population. Jewish people were now denied permission to train their clergy in their own seminaries, to have national theaters in their own language, and to express their Jewish identity in any other form. Although 450 synagogues had survived the Stalin era, by 1963, only 96 synagogues were now open. Jewish people were accused of undermining the Soviet economy and some of them after public trials were executed. Further the Russians had changed their decades-old policy of forcing Jews out of the country and now would not even let them go.

Unfortunately, the major Jewish organizations warned that protests against Soviet Jewish problems would backfire. In the spring of 1964, Birnbaum fought against these two forces–the Soviet determination and American Jewish paralysis. Within a decade, American Jews, the State of Israel and a Soviet-Zionist dissident movement brought the struggle of the Jewish people to the entire international community. By the 1980s, the movement was so successful that President Ronald Reagan made Jewish emigration a centerpiece of his campaign of pressure against the Soviets. This campaign led to the freedom of over one million Soviet Jews.

Jacob Birnbaum was born in Hamburg, Germany in 1926. His grandfather, Nathan Birnbaum, invented the term Zionism and served as secretary general of the first Zionist Congress in Basel in 1897. Jacob's father Asher was a leading Yiddish scholar who moved from Germany to London in 1933. He worked for the British government and thereby read the desperate letters from Europe about what was happening to the Jewish people there. He told his son Jacob about the misery that Jewish people faced in countries that hated and distrusted them.

Jacob developed a passion for helping the Soviet Jewish population because of his grandfather's passion for the Eastern European Jewish community and his father's frustration at being unable to help prevent the destruction of the Jewish community. Jacob had previously worked with Holocaust teenagers in the 1950s, Algerian Jewish immigrants in 1962 and other Jewish groups. In the United States Jacob took his clue for how to stimulate action to save the Jewish Russian community from the Holocaust as a warning of what might happen, and the civil rights movement as an example of the good that could happen.

1970-1975

In 1970, there were between 5,400,00 and 6,000,000 Jewish people in United States. In the 1970s and 1980s there had been a redefinition of the role of the female in Orthodox Judaism. Female activism resulted in women's prayer groups, birth ceremonies for girls, Talmud study for girls and women, women in leadership positions within Orthodox congregations, and in some cases, women reciting the kiddush, the kaddash, and the blessings over bread.

On October 13, 1970, Golda Meir, Prime Minister of the State of Israel received an Honorary Degree of Doctor of Humane Letters. When she thanked Dr. Nelson Glueck she said, "... We are an ancient people and we speak of thousands of years as if they were but days or weeks. Just a few weeks ago we celebrated the 19th hundredth anniversary of the destruction of the Second Temple. 1,900 years, and still Jewery survives, scattered in all corners of the earth!...I refer to Jews whose heroism enabled them to remain Jewish in a spiritual national sense. Often we lament the divisiveness which exists within the Jewish people and we speak (too often, in my opinion) in an exaggerated way about our failings and shortcomings. Yet we possess this remarkable capacity of remaining a united people despite the many differences and varieties which persist among us. We are indeed, if I may be permitted to say so, the most non-conformist of peoples – at least we are non-conformist in our relationship to each other. Each of us is impelled to express himself or herself with great individual emphasis and firmness, yet despite it all, our unity as a people remains strong after the lapse of so many centuries and in the face of almost impossible circumstances...." Golda Meir succinctly expressed who the Jewish people are, why there are a variety of expressions of the Jewish religion, and why Jewish people typically work together to help each other and to help others who are in need.

Dr. Nelson Gluek

In 1971, the world communities, Jewish and non-Jewish alike, lost an internationally renowned rabbi, educator, scholar, archaeologist, builder, visionary, interfaith champion, a zealous fighter for religious freedom, and humble man of God, Dr. Nelson Gluek. He made numerous archaeological discoveries in the Middle East on the basis of readings in the Bible. During the 1930s, he verified the boundaries and dates of the ancient kingdoms of Edom, Moab and Ammon, as well as discovered King Solomon's copper mines and identified King Solomon's seaport and fortress. During and after World War II, he provided strategic contributions to Allied military intelligence based on his intimate knowledge of Palestinian topography. He was known affectionately by all as "The Professor." Under his guidance, Hebrew Union College grew to a complex of four schools in Cincinnati, Los Angeles, New York City, and Jerusalem. He opened for his dearest friend, Professor Jacob Rader Marcus, the American Jewish Archives and Periodical Center. He sponsored numerous other projects including: the Interfaith Program, the Graduate School in Jerusalem and the mandatory year of study in Israel. He merged the Jewish Institute of Religion with Hebrew Union College. His own scholarship was prodigious. He wrote hundreds of articles and several books and he made the Scriptures come alive through his discoveries in the holy land. Dr. Alfred

Gottschalk wrote about Nelson Glueck, "We have lost much. This profoundly mystical and often brooding man brought together in his being the faith of our fathers of which he spoke so much and the free reign of the intellect through which he chartered our people's history and joined the past with full force with the burning present." Nelson was a shy man who hated crowds and bigness. He had a good heart and he practiced loyalty to his friends, his family, his country, the State of Israel, and to God. He and his wife Helen, whom he loved with a gentle, yet remarkable passion, looked forward to their remaining years of fruitful work in Jerusalem. Unfortunately, he died all too soon. Helen, a Research Professor of Hematology, would now have to do it alone.

1975-1980

In 1975, the Helsinki Accord stated that Jewish people in the Soviet Union had the right to rejoin their families elsewhere. Many organizations, including the American Bar Association and the Florida Bar Board of Governors, supported resolutions on the Deprivation of Human and Legal Rights for Soviet Jews.

In 1977, ARZA, Association of Reform Zionists of America, was formed. It is committed to religious pluralism and social justice in the State of Israel.

On September 17, 1978, the Camp David Accords brought a peace treaty between Egypt and Israel with President Carter as the matchmaker. Although this treaty helped, subsequent attempts at bringing peace to the Arab-Israeli conflict have not been successful.

In 1979, Ethiopian Jews started to be airlifted to Israel. This humane rescue mission, called "Operation Moses," was due to the general state and desperation of the Ethiopian Jewish community. Because the cost of transporting the people, educating them, and absorbing them into Israeli society was so high, the American Jewish community was asked to help with the funding. The Pinellas County Jewish community was asked to fund 20 individuals at $6,000 each.

1980-1990

In 1980, there were between 5,500,000 and 5,900,000 Jewish people in the United States.

In the 1980s, the Aaron Diamond Foundation decided to distribute $150 million in a 10-year period. George Soros, one of many Jewish people who contribute millions of dollars yearly to help others, continued to contribute huge sums of money to help people of all races, religions and nationalities.

In 1985, a system was developed to mark and identify Torah scrolls. After more than two years of intensive research, a process involving the use of micro perforations gained approval of leading religious authorities, security experts and congregant officials. Each Torah in the United States, Canada, Israel, and around the world will have a unique code and a corresponding certificate of registry. The Universal Torah Registry was created in consultation with a synagogue, rabbinic, communal and law enforcement groups because of a series of Torah thefts in the United States and around the world. This process is essential because, throughout the history of the Jewish people, individuals have risked their lives to protect the Torah, the scroll that links our past to our present and makes manifest our covenant with God. It is the fabric of our Jewish life and its threads are tied to our hearts and our minds.

On December 9, 1986, there were community wide rallies for Soviet Jewry in Pinellas County, entitled "Our Message to Moscow: Free the Jews of Silence." The plight of the Soviet Jews was dismal and though organizers hoped that by having rallies all over the country would cause something to happen which would help these people.

Statement on Jewish Unity

In 1987, the Presidents of the Rabbinical Assembly (Conservative), the Central Conference of American Rabbis (Reform), and the Rabbinical Council of America (Orthodox) decided that despite the range of differences between Reform, Conservative and Orthodox Judaism, as Jewish people, everyone had to work together in order for all to be beneficiaries of the Jewish religion.

Kassel Ableson, President, Rabbinical Assembly, Milton H. Polin, President, Rabbinical Council of America, and Jack Stern, President, Central Conference of American Rabbis issued the following brief:

"STATEMENT on JEWISH UNITY"

"You are One and Your name is One; and who is like Your people Israel one nation on earth". Thus do Jews affirm their commitment to the One God and to the unity of the People of Israel.

But are the words of this prayer true today, at least with regard to the People of Israel? Are we Jews-Orthodox, Conservative and Reform-still one people or have the bonds of unity been torn asunder?

Recent events and strident statements reported in the media appear to highlight the differences in religious belief and practice that divide us rather than unite us. How do we express our distress over the polarization of the "people Israel, one nation on earth?"

We are Jews by virtue of the Covenant, or Covenants, that God made with our ancestors and with us. There are, in fact, two Covenants; one a Covenant of Fate, the other a Covenant of Faith.

The Covenant of Fate is our history and destiny. We have a common past, shared experiences. We have suffered together at the hands of tyrants from Pharaoh to Hitler, who made no distinction between Jews whether they were Orthodox, Conservative or Reform, whether religious or secular, whether Zionist, non-Zionist or anti-Zionist, whether committed or assimilated. The tragedies in our history have been inflicted upon us by others; whether our destiny will also be imposed upon us by others or will result from our loving concern for each other, we shall always be united in a Covenant of Fate.

The Covenant of Faith involves our understanding of and commitment to God and Torah. Our understanding of this Covenant tends at time to produce differences of opinion even deep divisions within the People of Israel. Notwithstanding these real differences, there's nothing that prevents us from dialogue and cooperation on matters of mutual concern.

Together we pray that our joint endeavors in these areas of Jewish life will develop friendship and trust and hasten the day when "God will be One and His name One" and His people Israel will truly be "one nation on earth."

Chabad Lubavitch

In 1988, Chabad Lubavitch went into cyberspace. The father of this program was Rabbi Yosef Yitzchak Kazen (1954–1998), considered by many as a pioneer of Jewish education on the Internet. He spent thousands of hours digitizing documents that could be downloaded by other people especially Jewish people. Chabad.org's mission is to, "Utilize internet technology to unite Jews worldwide, and power them with knowledge of their 3,300-year-old tradition, and foster within them a deeper connection to Judaism's rituals and faith." Their philosophy is as follows: "Everything in this world was created for a divine purpose. All forms of modern technology can and should be harnessed to make the world a better place and, in the case of Jews, to spread Judaism in the widest possible manner."

Religious Action Center for Reform Judaism

In 1989, the Religious Action Center for Reform Judaism suggested a fine addition to the Passover observance. The center asked that Jewish people embrace the traditional custom of ridding their homes of chamets (leaven) prior to Passover, by providing this food for the hungry. The number of homeless people in America was estimated at two to three million. Over thirty two million Americans lived below the poverty line. This was but one of many programs sponsored by all of the Jewish communities to provide food for the hungry. Jewish people feel pain when less fortunate individuals are without food.

1990-2000

The Civil Rights Act of 1991 allowed women, people with handicaps, and religious minorities to collect punitive damages for intentional on-the-job discrimination. It widened the definition of discrimination and forced businesses to respect citizen's rights of equality. In 1992, there were 5,828,000

Jewish people in the United States.

In 1993, the PLO-Israel Peace Treaty was signed by Arafat and Rabin. This historic Treaty allowed Palestinian self-rule in parts of Israel, protected Israelis in Palestinian areas, recognized the existence of Israel and the PLO as legitimate entities, who would live in peace side-by-side. Unfortunately, this dream has never been realized and the slaughter of innocent people continues to go on, day after day, even in the year 2005.

Rabbi Jacob Rader Marcus

On November 18, 1995, Dr. Jacob Rader Marcus died. Although he was a reform rabbi, he was truly a rabbi for all of the Jewish people of the United States and the world. He was the preeminent historian of American Jewish History, and the Founder / Director of the American Jewish Archives. At age ninety three, he addressed the Central Conference of American Rabbis. At age ninety nine, he was still teaching a course at Hebrew Union College. He was a trail-blazer for American Jewish historiography. His credo was, "History is not names, dates, and places, but the record of human beings responding to their environment." It is this credo that has influenced the author to spend probably an inordinate amount of time discussing the lives and contributions of a vast number of people to the Jewish and general communities.

2000-2005

Rabbi Alexander Schindler

On November 15, 2000, Rabbi Alexander Schindler, one of the greatest leaders of the Jewish people, died. He had served as President of the Union of American Hebrew Congregations and, in that capacity, transformed the movement into a vigorous force in American religious life. He had an unrelenting commitment to issues of peace, social justice, equality, and compassion. Rabbi Schindler saw Judaism as a dynamic religion that evolved through its dialogue with tradition. He insisted on the full equality of women in Jewish religious life. His life was a journey which constantly reflected his great concern for all disadvantaged people. Rabbi Schindler created the Reform movements "Outreach" programs which enabled Reform congregations to welcome all Jewish people as well as non-Jewish spouses into the congregation. He was a motivating person behind the Reform movements' adoption of patrilineal descent. That is, the child of either a Jewish mother or a Jewish father is Jewish. From 1976 through 1978, he served as the Chair of the Conference of Presidents of Major American Jewish Organizations. Rabbi Eric Yoffie, in a tribute to his mentor said, "His (Rabbi Schindler's) was a voice of optimism and hope and his leadership was characterized by charisma, intense personal warmth, and extraordinary poetic oratory...being in his presence was a joy; hearing him speak was a delight. His soaring vision brought us to new heights and he will be sorely missed."

National Jewish Population Survey

In October 2002, the United Jewish Communities released some of the findings of its National Jewish Population Survey of 2000-2001. They are as follows: there are approximately 5.2 million Jewish people in the United States compared to 5.5 million in 1990; the Jewish population is aging; adults aged 18 and older make up 81 percent of the Jewish population, while children make up only 19 percent; Jewish adults 65 and older are 19 percent of the total population; nine percent of the Jewish population is 75 or over; the Jewish population is 49 percent male and 51 percent female; the marital status of Jewish people is similar to non-Jewish people; Jewish people are having fewer children with 52 percent of Jewish women ages 30 to 34 having not had any children compared to 27 percent of all American women; 85 percent of adult Jews were born in the United States, with a good many of the foreign-born coming from Russia; 43 percent of the Jewish population lives in the northeast portion of the United States, whereas only 22 percent live in the South compared to 35 percent for non-Jewish people; the Jewish population is very well educated with 24 percent holding graduate degrees and 55 percent having earned at least a bachelor's degree, compared to non-Jewish people with five percent holding graduate degrees and 28 percent holding at least a bachelor's degree; the majority of Jewish people, 62 percent, are employed either full or part time; the majority of employed Jewish people work in management, business and professional/technical positions, 59 percent compared to 40 percent of the non-Jewish population; although the median household income of the Jewish population is about $50,000, 19 percent of all Jewish households are low income. The approximate Jewish population of Florida is 628,000, of the total population of over 16 million people or 3.9 percent.

In order to conduct this survey more than 5 million phone calls were made to 1.3 million telephone numbers in all 50 states and the District of Columbia. The survey was rigorous and scientifically exacting. It represents all segments of the American Jewish population. The United Jewish Communities Research Department directed the research project in collaboration with its National Technical Advisory Committee, a distinguished group of academics and federation professionals. The United Jewish Communities represents 156 Jewish Federations and 400 independent communities across the country. Note that the American Jewish Yearbook 2000 from the American Jewish Committee reported 6,136,000 Jewish people in the United States in the year 2000. The American Jewish Year Book 2002 from the American Jewish Committee 2002, reported 6,155,000 Jewish people in United States in the year 2002. The difference in the numbers between the two reports might be due to the way in which the data was gathered. Today, there are over 5,000 congregations throughout the United States.

Jewish Charity

In 2002, Jewish people throughout the United States continued to give large sums of money to a variety of causes to make our lives better and to take care of the poor and needy. The Goldman Fund, which focuses on environment, population, social services, and Jewish affairs proposed a change in distribution of monies, which would increase the flow of cash to the various charities while rapidly distributing its resources to take care of current needs. In 2002, the trustees made grants of about $50 million from the $430 million Richard and Rhoda Goldman fund in San Francisco.

Pope John Paul II

On April 2, 2005, the Jewish community, as well as the world, lost a great religious leader. Pope John Paul II made the concept and reality of better Jewish-Catholic relations a centerpiece of his religious policy. He condemned anti-semitism, commemorated the Holocaust and established diplomatic relations with Israel. Pope John Paul II was a man of peace and a friend of the Jewish people. In his twenty seven years in the papacy, he created more goodwill and love for the Jewish people than the previous 2000 years of world history. His own personal experience with the Holocaust, when many of his own friends, neighbors and classmates died simply because they were Jewish, had a profound effect upon his thinking. In April, 1986, Pope John Paul II was the first pope to visit a Jewish house of worship, the Great Synagogue in Rome, since the visit of the first Pope, Peter. He warmly embraced Rome's chief rabbi and prayed with the congregation. In March 2000, he made a historic visit to Israel. He went to Jerusalem's Western Wall, bowed his head in prayer and slipped a note into the cracks between the stones. He said, "we are deeply saddened by the behavior of those who in the course of history have caused these children of yours to suffer, and asking your forgiveness, we wish to commit ourselves to genuine brotherhood with the People of the Covenant."

On April 9, 2005, Rabbi Mitchell Wohlberg's Shabbat sermon was dedicated to Pope John Paul II. Rabbi Wohlberg said in part, "The passing of Pope John Paul II was a loss not just for Christians but for all humanity. He was not only a church leader but a world leader–not only a prince of the Church but a prince of a man. He was a remarkable human being. John Paul, the actor, the playwright, the athlete, the skier, the philosopher, the politician, the moralist, the ethicist, the poet, the ecumenist...But he was more than that. When I saw the pictures of his body first lying in state I realized that was the same room where I had an audience with him. And I remembered how, when I came face-to-face with him and looked in his eyes, I knew that I was the presence of a man of God...

Pope John Paul II accomplished much during the course of his lifetime. He spread the message of peace and concern for the poor and the sanctity of life to the four corners of the globe...

We the Jewish people, have lost a good friend in the passing of John Paul...From our perspective, he was what the Bible describes as the "Kohen hagadol m'echav– the priest who was greatest from amongst all his brothers." ...We can only pray to God that we will have one like him again. T'hi nishmoso tsrurah b'tsror hachayim– May his soul be bound up in the bond of eternal life. Amen."

CHAPTER 2

BRIEF HISTORY OF FLORIDA AND TAMPA BAY AREA

The Spanish explorer and treasure hunter, Don Juan Ponce de Leon, first saw Florida on Easter, March 27, 1513. He claimed the land for Spain and named it La Florida, Land of Flowers. In 1519, he came to the peninsula and landed men from three small ships. He visited Tampa Bay in 1521. Between 1513 and 1563, the government of Spain had six expeditions to settle Florida, but all failed. One of them was led by the Spanish explorer, Panifilo de Narvaez, who landed at Tampa Bay in 1528 with 300 men. He was not interested in the beauty of the area, but rather where he could find the gold, that the Indians had told him about. Most of his men died as well as Panifilo. Hernando de Soto landed in the Bay Area in 1539. He also sought gold and went as far as the Mississippi River to find it, even though half of his men had died.

The French established a fort and colony on the St. John's River in 1564. They threatened the Spanish treasure fleets which sailed along the Florida shoreline. Don Pedro Menendez de Aviles, Spain's most experienced admiral, was sent by King Philip II to explore and colonize. On August 28, 1565, the Feast Day of St. Augustine, he arrived off the coast of Florida. Eleven days later, he and his 600 soldiers and settlers came ashore and named the Indian village of Seloy, St. Augustine. He destroyed the French garrison on the St. John's River and then defeated the French fleet. St. Augustine was founded forty two years before the English colony at Jamestown, Virginia and fifty five years before the Pilgrims landed on Plymouth rock in Massachusetts. In 1668, the pirate Captain John Davis plundered the town. A fort was built and it was able to repulse attacks in 1702 and in 1740 by the governors of South Carolina and Georgia. In 1763, England acquired Florida from Spain in exchange for Cuba. This allowed Jewish people to settle legally in Florida.

In1765, an English chartmaker mapped the Pinellas coast. In 1783, the English lost the colonies and the Bahamas and ransomed them by trading Florida back to Spain, in the Treaty of Paris, which was signed September 3. In 1790, the King of Spain offered land grants to foreigners, who agreed to settle in East Florida for at least ten years. Many new residents came into Florida, including escaped slaves. In 1818, Andrew Jackson made several military forays into Florida and fought the Indian people. This was later called the First Seminole War.

On July 10, 1821, U.S. troops took possession of the territory of Florida and Spain left forever. Andrew Jackson established a new territorial government on behalf of the United States. Florida was a wilderness with tiny settlements of native Indian people, African-Americans, and Spaniards. People from older Southern plantation areas of Virginia, the Carolinas, and Georgia, arrived in considerable numbers. In 1821, a yellow fever epidemic killed many newcomers. In 1824, Tallahassee was chosen as the new capital city because it was halfway between the existing governmental centers of St. Augustine and Pensacola.

As Florida's population continued to grow, so did the pressure on the federal government to remove the Indians from their lands. The white people wanted the land and also wanted to remove the sanctuaries the Indians provided for runaway slaves. The Seminole Indians were constantly fighting the settlers and this resulted in the Seminole War of 1836. As President, Andrew Jackson, spent $20 million and the lives of many U.S. soldiers, Indians, and U.S. citizens to force the removal of the Seminole Indians.

The first known white settlers arrived in the Bay Area around 1823, when a New York City pioneer named Robert J. Hackley moved in and built a plantation. In 1824, the federal government put the Seminole Indians on a reservation near the Hackley plantation. The government built Fort Brooke to oversee the reservation. The fort later changed its name back to the original Indian name of Tampa.

Key West was discovered by Ponce de

Leon in 1513. The island was originally known as the Isle of Bones, because it was littered with the remains of an Indian battlefield or burial ground. The city was first permanently occupied in 1822, when it became a small naval depot, whose purpose was to rid the area of pirates. The settlement was incorporated in 1828 and, four years later, became the county seat of Monroe County. The city grew and prospered on fishing and the salvaging of shipwrecks on the nearby reefs. Later, the city became famous for cigar manufacturing with imported Cuban tobacco made by Cuban refugees. Sponging became part of the commercial function of the city. By 1890, Key West was the richest and largest city in Florida. However, after 1900, the major industries declined, and there was a steady decline in population between 1919 and 1935. World War II brought prosperity back to Key West with the population more than doubling between 1940 and 1960.

In 1834, Hillsborough County was created by an Act of Congress out of Alachua County and the area grew in population and importance. The future Pinellas County was part of this area.

In 1836, the first railroads began to operate in Florida. This was the beginning of the great expansion of the territory. Now there was adequate transportation for the first time.

By 1840, white Floridians were trying to develop the territory and gain statehood. The population had reached 54,477 people with African-American slaves making up almost half of the population. Steamboat navigation was well established on the Apalachicola and St. John's Rivers and railroads were being planned. The territory's economy was based on agriculture with plantations concentrated in middle Florida between the Suwanee and Apalachicola rivers. The owners of the plantations established the political tone for all of Florida until after the Civil War.

On March 3, 1845, Florida became the 27th state admitted to the Union. Officially, the capital of Florida was now moved from St. Augustine to the new town of Tallahassee. William D. Moseley was elected as the first governor, and David Levy Yulee, one of Florida's leading proponents for statehood, became a United States senator.

On September 25, 1848, a powerful hurricane hit the Tampa Bay area. Despite this natural disaster, there was further growth in the area.

By 1850, the population of the State of Florida had grown to 87,445 including about 39,000 African-American slaves and 1,000 free blacks. Slavery became the dominant issue of this new state. Most of the Florida voters, who were white males, ages 21 years or older, did not oppose slavery. At the same time, the Indian problem was resolved during the Third Seminole War from 1855-1858. Only a few hundred Seminoles survived by hiding in the Everglades. Black people, who were escaped slaves, were denied sanctuary from the Indians.

In the 1860 Presidential election, no Floridians voted for Abraham Lincoln. Shortly thereafter, on January 10, 1861, Florida seceded from the Union. A few weeks later, Florida joined the Confederate States of America.

During the Civil War, the coastal towns and forts of Florida were occupied by the Union forces while the interior of the state remained in the Confederate hands. Florida provided about 15,000 troops and significant amounts of supplies to the Confederacy. Tampa became an important port for the Confederacy. Salt, citrus, and other supplies were sent out on blockade runners, until the Union Navy captured the town. About 2000 Floridians, black and white, joined the Union Army.

After the Civil War, the ports of Jacksonville and Pensacola once again flourished because of the demand for lumber and forest products to rebuild the nation's cities. Freed slaves provided a much-needed source for this labor-intensive work. The plantations' production of cotton started to diminish and the land came under cultivation by tenant farmers and sharecroppers, both African-American and white.

The Civil War did not have a great affect on the economy of Florida. The expansion of the railroads throughout the United States, and especially in Florida contributed to an economic boom. Florida, produced a wealth of agricultural products, including cotton, tung oil, livestock, fruits and vegetables, that served the nation through its network of railroads and ports. It produced virtually every agricultural product imaginable year-round, including citrus fruit, which was highly sought after.

By 1880, Florida's population reached an estimated 270,000 people. Large-scale commercial agricultural, cattle raising and industries such as cigar manufacturing caused a dramatic expansion in the economy. Large-scale building of railroads occurred and the tourist industry started to become an essential part of the economy of the state. The same ships and railroads that took the agricultural goods out of Florida brought the tourists to enjoy the beautiful weather, especially during the winter.

In 1884, Henry B. Plant built the railroad which connected Tampa to Jacksonville and North Florida. During the 1880s and 1890s, Mr. Plant spend millions of dollars developing the tourist industry inTampa, while building the 3.5 million-dollar Tampa Bay Hotel, which now houses the University of Tampa.

In 1885, Henry Flagler arrived in St. Augustine. He developed the old Spanish town into a major resort for leisure travelers. He built fine hotels and other facilities. His Florida East Coast Railroad provided a transportation link between New York and St. Augustine.

Vicente Martinez Ybor

In 1886, Vicente Martinez Ybor established the cigar industry, which became world renowned. He was born in Valencia, Spain in 1818, and at the age of fourteen went to Havana, Cuba. He founded his own cigar factory in 1853. In 1869, he moved his cigar factory to Key West because of labor unrest in Cuba. In Key West he found a very serious drawback, the lack of a transportation system. In 1885, Ybor negotiated with the Tampa Board of Trade to set up a cigar factory. Tampa provided favorable financial terms and Ybor, as well as several of his fellow factory owners built cigar factories there. Ybor City became the crown jewel of the cigar industry, producing over 400 million cigars a year and it helped promote unprecedented growth

within the area. At the height of tobacco production, there were about seventy cigar factories employing 30,000 people. Ybor was responsible for developing Ybor City when he constructed a large number of workers' cottages. He was different from other manufacturers in that he allowed the workers to purchase their homes rather than rent them. These people became a stable workforce because it allowed them a special sense of independence and self-respect. Ybor died in 1896 and was buried in Oaklawn Cemetery. In 1886, Ybor City became a large Jewish business center along with creation of the cigar industry.

Spanish-American War

In 1898, during the Spanish American War, Tampa became the primary port for American troops to go to fight the Spanish in Cuba. The soldiers and other people associated with the war found the climate in the Tampa Bay area to be wonderful and this stimulated a new boom for the area. By the turn-of-the-century, Florida's population and per capita wealth was increasing rapidly. The potential for the "The Sunshine State" appeared endless.

1900-1920

Although the first gas powered automobile was produced in quantity by Oldsmobile in 1901, it was not until Ford began producing his Model T in 1908, that modern automobile mass production occurred. The coming of the automobile for the ordinary person led to the further expansion of Florida. It became commonplace to vacation in Florida and many visitors decided to make this beautiful part of America their permanent home. This led to a continuing economic boom for the state.

World War I served to further stimulate Florida's economic growth. Not only did Florida continue to produce all types of agricultural goods and provide forest products, but its climate offered excellent year-round training for all branches of the armed forces. Florida's ports became the hosts for naval bases. Army, Air Force and other marine facilities added substantially to the presence of service people here.

Networks of cities and roads continued to grow to support the war effort and contributed to the economic expansion and the following land boom.

By the 1920s, real estate speculation brought a sizable population boom. The large number of real estate developments quickly attracted buyers, and land in Florida was sold and resold. Profits and prices for many developments reached highly inflated levels. In 1926, Florida's economic bubble burst when money and credit ran out. The banks and investors abruptly stopped trusting the paper millionaires. Severe hurricanes in 1926 in 1928 further damaged the economy.

In 1929, the Great Depression began. At the same time, the Mediterranean fruit fly invaded the state, and the citrus industry was devastated. Florida citrus production was cut by about 60%, which led to further economic problems.

During the 1930s, those who had money still came to Florida as tourists. The New Deal, under President Roosevelt, provided jobs and money through a variety of agricultural programs, the National Recovery Administration, the Civilian Conservation Corps, the Works Progress Administration, the Social Security Act, etc.. Also aiding the economy of the state was Florida becoming the largest citrus producer.

In World War II, 1941-1945, the economy of Florida improved dramatically. Once again because of its mild climate throughout the year, the state became a major training center for soldiers, sailors, and airmen of the United States and its allies. Highway and airport construction accelerated, and by the end of the war Florida had an up-to-date transportation network ready for use by residents and visitors. By 1945, an endless stream of people began to come to Florida. Many of the service people who trained in Florida came back as permanent residents or at least as tourists.

After the war a significant increase in population occurred in Florida and the Tampa Bay area. Florida's economy became more diverse. Tourism, cattle, citrus and phosphate industries were joined by a large number of new industries, which expanded the number of jobs available to residents and brought even more people to the state. Housing construction, mall and business construction, and infrastructure such as roads, hospitals, strip malls, schools, police and fire facilities, synagogues and churches have provided countless jobs and large sums of money for the Florida economy. Retirees, as usual, brought money, which was used for necessities as well as luxuries.

In 1951, on December 24, Harry T. Moore, Florida NAACP leader, and his wife were murdered in Orange County because of Moore's efforts to register Florida African Americans to vote. Unfortunately, unreasoning people still tried to promote racism within the state.

Currently, new industries including electronics, plastics, construction, real estate, aeronautics, international airports, port facilities, international banking, etc. continue to contribute to the growth of Florida. Attractions, such as a large theme parks in the Orlando area, beaches and plenty of sunshine bring over forty million visitors to the state from across the United States and around the world. The U.S. space program has provided considerable media attention.

CHAPTER 3

HISTORY OF JEWISH PEOPLE IN FLORIDA EXCLUDING TAMPA BAY AREA

In 1763, after the British took over Florida, Jewish people were able to acquire land and property in Pensacola. Joseph de Palacios, Samuel Israel, and Alexander Solomons migrated to Pensacola, bought property, opened stores, and developed business ties with the Caribbean and England's North American colonies. Isaac Monsanto arrived in 1769. Isaac Mendes came in 1776 from Jamaica to Pensacola. These men and other Jewish men who came later had close ties to fellow Jews in Savannah, Georgia, and Charleston, South Carolina. In 1783, David Moses, a Polish Jew was operating a hide store in St. Augustine. By 1820, there were an estimated thirty to forty Jewish people in Florida.

"Florida Jewish Heritage Trail"

Thanks to Rachel B. Heimovics, freelance writer, and, Marcia Zerivitz for writing, and the Samuel L. Ziff Jewish Museum of Florida for publishing " Florida Jewish Heritage Trail," in the year 2000. As a result, there is significant factual information about some of the Jewish pioneers of the 1800s and early 1900s. Some of these individuals will now be discussed, while others will be merely listed. To gain further information about the Jewish experience in Florida, it is wise to obtain and read a copy of this publication, which can be obtained from the Jewish Museum of Florida, 301 Washington Ave., Miami Beach, FL 33139-6965.

Moses Elias Levy

In 1819, Moses Elias Levy had already made a fortune in shipping when he came to north central Florida. He purchased 92,000 acres of land, where he started a Jewish colony, Pilgrimage Plantation, in Micanopy. Jewish people, fleeing persecution in Europe, came here. Moses bought sugar cane and fruit trees for the plantation. Moses Levy was among the earliest and largest developers of land in Florida. The plantation was burned down at the beginning of the Second Seminole War in 1835.

Moses Levy, an Orthodox Jew, was also one of the founders of Micanopy. Moses, the father of David Levy Yulee, was born in 1781 in Morocco, went to St. Thomas, West Indies, moved to Havanna and then to Florida. He became a naturalized citizen in 1822. He wanted to rescue Jewish people who were being persecuted as well as abolish slavery. He stood for free education in Florida and was a charter officer of the Florida Education Society. By the 1840s, he owned 100,000 acres throughout the state. He died in 1854.

Samuel and Louisa Myers

In 1821, Samuel and Louisa Myers came to Pensacola where he practiced law, helped organize the local militia, and served on the city council. The following year, they had a daughter, Louisa, the first documented Jewish birth in the state of Florida.

David Levy Yulee

In 1836, David Levy Yulee was admitted to the Florida Bar. He was born in St. Thomas, West Indies on June 12, 1810, and at age nine, was sent to Norfolk, Virginia to attend a private school. He studied law in St. Augustine, Florida and then later practiced there. He was a delegate to the Florida Constitutional Convention in 1838, served in several other offices, was elected to the United States Senate, and served from July 1, 1845 to March 3, 1851. He was again elected to the United States Senate in January 1855 and served until he resigned on January 21, 1861. Because he supported the Confederacy, he was a prisoner at Fort Pulaski in 1865. He built the first railroad across the state, was President of several railroad companies, and was known as the father of Florida's railroads. His greatest impact on the Bay Area came through his gyrations with his Florida railroad. He would release information incorrectly, stating that his railroad would move to Tampa, which caused development euphoria followed by bitter letdowns. He was hung in effigy at the Hillsborough County Court House after one of these intense disappointments. He was really trying to keep others from competing with his railroad. He died in New York City on October 10, 1886.

1836-1845

In 1836, Col. Abraham C. Myers, a West Point graduate, was Chief Quartermaster in the Seminole war. Fort Myers is named after him. In 1838, Raphael Jacob Moses, a fifth-generation American Jew came to St. Joseph from Charleston, South Carolina. He practiced law and participated in politics until he moved to Georgia in 1849. In 1840, a Jewish peddler, Gerschom ben Yosef, was killed by Indians near St. Augustine. He was one of many peddlers who traveled throughout the state. On March 3, 1845, when Florida achieved statehood, there were less than 100 Jewish people out of a population of 66,500.

Philip Dzialynski

In 1853, Philip Dzialynski brought a Torah to Jacksonville. He was born in 1833, in Posen, Prussian Poland. After his first wife, Ida, died during the Civil War, he moved his growing family to Savannah and started to build contacts in north Florida and south Georgia. He was a Hebrew scholar, led the city's B'nai B'rith Jacob Congregation and helped found the Savannah Hebrew Collegiate Institute. He later moved to Tampa to start a business and finally came back to Jacksonville.

Robert Williams

In the early 1850s, Robert Williams and his bride, Helena Dzialynski, moved to Florida. Robert settled in Jasper in 1854 and Helena moved with her family to Jacksonville around 1850. In 1865, the Williams family moved to Tallahassee. Robert opened a store, became a cotton planter, and also became active in civic affairs. He installed the first streetlights in Tallahassee. He often lead the prayers on Jewish holidays in Tallahassee and donated a Torah for worship services. The Torah is still in use at Temple Israel of Tallahassee. The Williams family flourished and the five daughters married Jewish men from

the Cohen, Apte, Hirschberg and Diamond families, who became civic, business, and religious leaders of the Tallahassee community. By 1860, there were 15 Jewish people in Tallahassee.

Jacksonville Hebrew Cemetery

In 1857, when six Jewish people died of yellow fever in Jacksonville, the first Jewish cemetery and first Jewish institution, Jacksonville Hebrew Cemetery, was formed. As was true in Terre Haute, Indiana in 1849, a Jewish cemetery was essential because of Jewish law, which requires that a Jewish person be buried in a Jewish cemetery and not a cemetery of another religion. In a nonsectarian cemetery, Jewish graves must be in a separate section. In Terre Haute, Indiana, eight to ten Jewish families formed the Terre Haute Israelite Burial Society, a verein (a Jewish mutual benefit society that also functions as a burial society containing a chevra kadisha, a credit union and help for its members or the poor in times of sickness or difficulty). This was the first Jewish institution in the city. A cherva kadisha is literally a holy society, whose function is to prepare bodies for Jewish burial. Jewish prayer books, which are disintegrating, and other ritual items are also buried in a Jewish cemetery.

Early Jewish Businessmen

Jewish people were involved in growing tobacco and manufacturing cigars during the 19th and 20th centuries. Charles and Hannah Peyser marketed cigars from 1860-1920 in Ocala. In 1861, when David Levy Yulee extended the railroad to Cedar Key, he opened up the entire area to commerce. It provided a way for transporting the lumber and manufactured byproducts of turpentine, brooms, and pencils across Florida.

Other Jewish people who have made outstanding contributions to the Jewish and general communities of Florida include: the Benjamin family of Alachua County and Ocala, 1867 to 1937; Jacob Raphael Cohen of Orlando and Tallahassee, 1860s to 1890; B.H Lilienthal, Palatka, 1874 to 1895; Marcus Loeb, Palatka, early 1880s to 1896; Lewis Baer, Pensacola, 1876 to late 1800s; Samuel, Morris, Julius and Jacob Cohen (Cohen's

Department Store), Jacksonville, 1870 to the 1980s; Morris and Sarah Wolfson and family, Jacksonville, early 1900s to 1980s; Moses Endel, who carried a Torah to Gainesville in 1865, Endel Brothers Department Store; Marcus Frank, Ocala, 1899 to 1950; Charles Rheinauer, Ocala, fashionable clothing stores, 1882 through the 1900s; Isaac Maas clerked for the Rheinauers in the early 1880s, before he joined his brother Abraham in Tampa to found the Maas Brothers Department Store; and many others.

In the 1870s and early 1880s, Phillip Dzialynski helped to spark civic and business life in Polk County and vicinity. He was involved in real estate, citrus groves, and exported local products to Europe. He died in Jacksonville on January 16, 1896. His wife, Mary, died in Jacksonville on November 5, 1935. His brother, Morris, served as mayor and municipal judge in Jacksonville.

In 1879, Henry Brash was elected mayor of Marianna. He was the first of about eighty Jewish men and women who have served as mayors in Florida.

Early Jewish Synagogues and Organizations

In 1869, in Pensacola, land was given to Temple Beth El for a Jewish cemetery. In 1871, a Jewish cemetery was opened in Gainesville, Florida. It was dedicated in 1872.

In 1874, the first B'nai B'rith Chapter in the state of Florida was founded in Pensacola. In 1876, the Progress Club, a Jewish social organization, opened in Pensacola. The same year, the first Jewish congregation in Florida, Temple Beth El, of Pensacola was chartered.

In the 1880s, many Jewish congregations were chartered. They included: Ahavath Chesed Congregation, Jacksonville, 1882; Rodeph Sholom, Key West, 1887; and United Hebrews of Ocala, 1887.

Key West

In the late 1800s, many Jewish people entered the United States through Key West. Such men as Joseph Wolfson, Abraham Wolkowsky and David L. Rippa made many contributions to Key West. In 1884, Joseph Wolfson , a Romanian, migrated to Florida. He was on his way to Tampa when the ship encountered bad weather and he was forced to land off the coast of Key West. He found a small community of Jews already living there and mistakenly thought he had landed in Tampa. He sent for his family to join him there. In1885, Abraham Wolkowsky arrived in Key West from Romania. In 1887, Jewish peddlers were going from house to house with packs of dry goods, laces, etc. The City Council imposed a license of $1000 each on peddlers causing the Jewish business people to stop peddling and open stores. This led to a further influx of more Jewish families because of potential business opportunities. They sold clothing, groceries, cigars, dry goods, and furniture. Other Jewish merchants were Appel, Aronwitz, Einhorn, Holtzberg, Lewinsky, Markowitz, and others. Abraham started out as a peddler and soon opened a clothing store. He married Rebecca Lewinsky, the daughter of another early Key West Jewish family. The Rippa family had early contact with the Jewish people of Tampa. A member of the family was buried in the Jewish cemetery in Tampa in the late 1890s. The family is related to the Bobos and the Habers of Tampa and Terre Haute, Indiana. In 1912, Henry Flagler completed the Overseas Railway, an extension of the Florida East Coast Railway to Key West.

1890s

In the 1890s, Jewish people continued to come into Florida enhancing existing Jewish communities and expanding into other areas. In 1890, the LaVilla Neighborhood of Jacksonville became a Jewish enclave of Eastern European Jewish immigrants. It contained its own businesses, the YMHA, and the Orthodox synagogue, B'nai Israel, founded in 1901. The estimated Jewish population of Florida was 2,500. By 1893, Jewish people started to settle southeast Florida, following Henry Flagler's new railroad.

1900s

The history of the Jewish people in Florida from 1900 to the present is extensive and beyond the scope of this book. Therefore, the following history of the Jewish people of the Tampa Bay area and especially Pinellas County will be the focus of the ongoing history of Jewish people in Florida. However, a few observations and facts concerning the total Florida Jewish community are needed. Jewish businesses, agriculture, homebuilding, professions, and all other phases of commercial activity increased sharply when nationwide economic conditions improved substantially, and with the increased migration of Jewish people to this part of the United States. Jewish retirees came from the north to live out the remainder of their lives in sunny and airy climates. The retirees along with the young people founded new synagogues, Jewish organizations, and participated actively in the affairs of the general community. The Jewish people contributed huge sums of money and time to many nonprofit organizations in order to improve and enhance the lives of all people. They involved themselves in public service and projects. On pages 41 and 42 of the "Florida Jewish Heritage Trail," is a list of Jewish men and women who have served in the executive branch of government, the legislative branch of government, and the judiciary at the state and federal level.

South Florida

In 1928, some Jewish people moved to south Florida, but most remained in north Florida, with about 40 percent of the total in Jacksonville. The estimated Jewish population in Florida was 10,000. In 1933, David Sholtz, the governor of Florida was Jewish. In 1940, the estimated Jewish population of Florida was 25,000. In the 1940's, Miami had the largest Jewish population of approximately 5,000 people. In the 1950s, the general use of air-conditioning and jet planes brought a massive amount of Jewish people to settle in south Florida. In 1959, about 10,000 Cuban Jews came to Florida to be free. In 1960, the estimated Jewish population of Florida was 175,000. In 1984, the MOSAIC project was created and an intensive study was made of the Jewish people of the State of Florida. MOSAIC: "Jewish Life in Florida," depicting the

Jewish experience from 1763 to the present, became an exhibit which traveled to thirteen cities from 1990-1994. In 1995, the MOSAIC became the Jewish Museum of Florida which was housed in a former synagogue that was Miami Beach's first congregation, built in 1936. Jewish people have come to Florida from many places but especially from the northeastern United States, Caribbean, and South America. In the year 2000, the estimated Jewish population of Florida was 800,000.

CHAPTER 4

TAMPA BAY AREA JEWISH HISTORY

Before 1842, there were few residents other than Indians in the Tampa Bay area. Substantial numbers of settlers did not arrive in the Tampa Bay Region until after the conclusion of the Second Seminole War in 1842. This was the beginning of permanent Jewish residents in this area. Emmaline Ouentz Miley and her husband William were probably the first permanent Jewish settlers in the Tampa Bay area. Emmaline was born August 16, 1814 and came from Europe to Charleston, South Carolina. When she was eighteen, William Goodman Miley proposed marriage. She refused the proposal until William had agreed to sell his slaves and buy no more. They were married Dec. 25, 1833 and settled in the vicinity of Montgomery, Alabama. William and Emmaline and their five children, William Goodman, Emily, Samuel Augustine, David Montgomery, and Loven made the overland journey to Hillsborough County's Lake Thonotosassa region. Eventually there were thirteen children. The family cleared land and built a log cabin. Because of the presence of Seminole Indians, they had to make several hurried trips to Fort Brooke at Tampa for protection. During the Civil War she continued to cultivate a citrus grove despite the loss of several children and her husband. She lived in Hillsborough County until her death on Dec. 11, 1907.

Early Merchants

In 1844, George Giddens, Tom Pollack, and Jesse Pollack came from Alabama to join the Mileys. In 1857, Samuel Cline & Max White moved a clothing store to Tampa. They moved their store from St. Augustine after the 1857 panic.

In 1869, Phillip Dzialynski came back to Florida and became a wholesale grocer and commissioned merchant in Tampa. This was considered to be wonderful for the Tampa business community because he was a man of stature. In August, George Blum, a native of Bavaria, announced that he and his New Orleans partner, David Kloppenburg, would buy farm produce at the highest market price in cash. This was very important for the cash starved community in Tampa Bay. Mr. Gustave Lewinson, a merchant from New York, leased the steam operated Saw Mill. He and Edward Bettman opened a dry goods store. They received their financing from New York City. Isadore Blumenthal, also born in Bavaria, joined Lewison and Bettman in a partnership. On Dec. 1, 1869, they announced the opening of their Tampa Dry Goods and General Merchandise Store. Between the Tampa Cedar Mills and the area stores they promised direct communications with Germany. They paid the highest prices in cash. Gustave Oppenheimer opened an oyster bar, which became the Riverside Restaurant and Oyster Saloon.

In 1870, I. Blumenthal & Co. was opened. In September 1870, S. Sternberger announced that he was opening a store at Manatee. This large store was opened in January 1871, in today's Bradenton. He carried a variety of dry goods including clothing. He paid cash for all farm items. Charles Slager arrived in Tampa in late 1870 and opened a store. Jacob R. Cohen, an experienced retail merchant, joined cattleman Julius C. Rockner, who had $50,000 to invest from his sale of cattle. Cohen who had come from Prussia, and then Savannah, was the beginning of another migration of Jewish families to the Tampa Bay area. The Franco-Prussian War which started in 1870, shut off the export of cedar from Tampa to Germany. This calamity was followed by David Levy Yulee's fight against a railroad being built to Tampa, which would be in competition with his railroad. This resulted in the dissolution of various Jewish partnerships, and then the second major attack of yellow fever in 1871, which caused further damage to the economy. Charles Slager became the first Jewish postmaster, sheriff, and tax collector. Isadore Blumenthal was appointed by the governor to be a county commissioner. An economic downturn later on resulted in the closing of many stores, including Jewish ones.

Herman Glogowski

(top) Abraham and (below) Isaac Maas. Drawings from an 1890 edition of the Tampa Tribune, Tampa, FL

Herman Glogowski

Herman Glogowski served as mayor of Tampa for four one year terms between 1886 and 1893. As mayor, he helped lay the groundwork for Tampa's emergence as Florida's leading manufacturing center. He promoted private investment, development, and work to improve public works and sanitation. He recommended the hiring of a public-health physician. Tampa grew from about 700 people in 1880 to approximately 16,000 in 1900. He was a charter member of Congregation Shaarai Zedek. He was born on April 29, 1854 in Wilhelmsbruck, Germany and came to New York in 1869. Within ten years, he relocated to Gainesville, where he was first a clerk and then opened his own dry goods, clothing, and footwear store. He networked with fellow Masons. He married Bertha Brown, a native of Prussia, and the two of them moved to Tampa in late 1883 or early 1884, when a railroad reached that area. He opened a clothing and gentleman's furnishing goods store. He became part of the Masonic order, was Grand Master of the Hillsborough Masonic Order #25 in 1899-1900 and 1903, and helped pioneer the Tampa Board of Trade On July 26, 1888, he laid the cornerstone for the Tampa Bay Hotel for Henry Plant. On August 16, 1899, he laid the cornerstone for Congregation Schaarai Zedek, (Gate of the Righteous). He also helped bring electric lights to downtown Tampa.

Ybor City Jewish Businesses

In 1886, Ybor City had wooden side-walks and gaslights. The cigar industry, which was started by Vincent Ybor attracted Jewish cigar makers, merchants, manufacturers, and laborers from Cuba and Key West. Jewish families including Annis, Gottsagen, Regensberg, Hammer, and Seckbach played an important role in the growth of the Tampa economy. They opened stores and businesses that served the community in many different ways. Early merchants also came from South Carolina and Georgia and opened stores to serve the growing community. In 1891, because of the peddler's tax in Key West, many of the Jewish merchants were now drawn to Tampa's Ybor City, where they opened small stores in the Spanish neighborhoods and some of them went into the cigar manufacturing business. The Rippa family moved its cigar factory to Tampa from Key West. Isadore Kaunitz opened a dry goods business.

Maas Brothers

In 1886, the Maas Brothers, Abraham and Isaac, opened the first Maas Brothers Department Store, originally called "The Palace". It became Florida's largest department store chain. It operated from 1886 to 1991, and there were nineteen stores in Florida. The Maas Brothers retired in 1929 and their nephew, Jerome Waterman, became the chief executive officer.

Abraham Maas was born in Dolgsheim, Germany in1855. His father was Joseph Maas and his mother was Fannie Bacherach. In 1880, Abe Maas, a penniless immigrant boy of 15, carrying a half-eaten watermelon, got off the train in Cochran, Georgia to join his brothers Sol and Jacob. He had come to America to escape conscription in the Army. His father, Joseph Maas, had saved some money from his little farm and used it to purchase a steerage ticket which meant freedom for Abe. When the older brothers had arrived in America in 1877, they were penniless and knew no English. They worked for a German friend in New York, saved a little money and learned how to get along in the English language. They decided to go to Cochran, Georgia and open a general store they called Maas Brothers. They sold general merchandise, bulk food, groceries and feed, and dealt in cotton. Abe, then Isaac and then Julius came and served as clerks for their brothers. Sol, the head of the whole enterprise, was involved in a shooting episode and died a year later of pneumonia. The brothers then broke up and went into different businesses. Jacob went into the wholesale grocery business in Macon, Georgia. Julius moved to Savanna and became a traveling salesman for a wholesale dry goods firm. He later opened a haberdashery in Tampa. Isaac opened a millinery shop in Ocala. Abe opened a small dry goods store in Dublin, Georgia. He had already married Bena Wolf, a beautiful, redheaded girl from a small village in Germany.

They named their son, Solomon, after Abe's beloved brother. Solomon became a merchant and died September 21, 1944. Later they had a daughter, Jessie. Abe's business was not going well because of the economy. He decided, like Isaac, to go to Florida and chose Tampa, which was little more than a fishing village. The railroad terminus had already gone from Cedar Key to Tampa and the first cigar factory had transferred from Key West. A fine port was going to be built and the beginnings of the Maas Brothers chain was imminent.

In 1887, the Palace Dry Goods Company opened. Isaac joined the company and brought with him a handful of hats and ribbons from his Ocala shop. Abe sent out notices to all customers and ran ads in the newspaper saying, "My brother Isaac has joined me, and the business henceforth will be conducted under the name of Maas Brothers."

In 1893, Abe and Isaac brought their 13-year-old cousin, Ernest, from Germany. Abe put Ernest to work as a porter whose main job was to drive a cart and pony to deliver goods. He couldn't speak a word of English at that time. His daughter, Audrey Maas Shine, in later years said that it was family lore that he promised to teach German to some of his fellow deliveryman if they would teach him how to speak English. Within three months he was speaking English, and before long he was dealing with customers behind the counter at the Maas Brothers store on Franklin Street. Eventually, he became the buyer in the ready-to-wear department. By 1910, Ernest was well-established in business, religious and fraternal circles in Tampa. He married Maude Alice Baer of Washington, D.C.. Besides their daughter, Audrey, they also had a son, Ernest Jr..

Ernest Maas, a tall handsome man, became a director of Maas Brothers. He died in 1947. His wife Maude Baer was born in 1890, in Washington DC. She died in October 1964. Ernest Jr., also an important member of Schaarai Zedek, was born in Florida on November 4, 1910, and died on February 27, 1995. His sister, Audrey, was born in 1919 in Florida. She married Mark Shine, the son of a merchant family.

Ernest Maas expanded his role in civic

affairs by becoming involved in numerous organizations. He was the exalted ruler and then President of the Tampa Elks Lodge. He was President of the Tampa Merchants Association. He helped organize the University of Tampa and served as its treasurer in its early years. He was chairman of the Young Men's Hebrew Association, a forerunner of the Jewish Community Center. In 1929, when Maas Brothers became part of Hahn Department Stores, Ernest left to start his own women's clothing store, Ernest Maas Inc., on Tampa Street. In 1936, he received the Tampa Civitan Club's Citizen of the Year award for organizing a fund-raising drive to save Boy Scout Camp Owen Brorein. He had been President of the Tampa Lions Club, a member of the Board of Directors of the Hebrew Orphans Home at Atlanta, past President of the Boy Scouts of Tampa, and secretary-treasurer of the Maas Realty Co..

In 1937 he joined with his cousins Julius Maas and Julius Weil, who had a company called Maas the Haberdasher. The combined store opened at Franklin and Twiggs Street as Weil-Maas. He was active in the business until 1946. He died September 17, 1947, at age 66.

During the 1920s, Maas Brothers continued to acquire land and buildings. Isaac died in 1935 and Abe died in 1941. Mrs. Sol (Julia) Maas said about Abe, "He never seemed to realize, his importance to the country nor what he had accomplished. He never was a snob. He was Uncle Abe to everyone. Isaac, on the other hand, was aristocratic and restrained. A granddaughter Ashby Emily Moody said, "He brought

The Palace Dry Goods Co., first Maas store in Tampa (later renamed Maas Brothers). Abe is at right; Ernest is the boy to Abe's right.

Ernest Maas

many Jews beside his own family to this country during Hitler's regime. He spent much money to help them get a new start in life. He also contributed generously to the Sacred Heart Catholic Church in Tampa. One of the priests was his close friend."

Jerome Waterman

Jerome A. Waterman, a nephew of the Maas family, became the next leader of the Maas Brothers Department Store. Jerry was born in Hawkinsville, Georgia in November of 1883. He graduated from high school as Valedictorian with First Honors and from Mercer University in 1902 with a B. S. Degree. He was married to Daisy Guggenheimer in 1922 and they had two children. Cecile married Marvin Essrig, and for many years she was the only woman elected to the school board in Hillsborough County. She also had the distinction of being one of the longest serving members of that body and at her retirement was honored by having a school named for her. She has two daughters: Lee, who is a practicing attorney and consultant and Kathy, who is a Circuit Judge in Hillsborough County. His other daughter, Regena (Gena), married Stephen Bragin and has two children, Janet and Marc, who are both lawyers.

Daisy died in 1945, having been very active in the Jewish community and in particular in helping the blind. The Daisy G. Waterman Lighthouse for the Blind in Tampa is still in operation today and is a reflection of that devotion.

Jerome came to Tampa to work for his Uncles, Abe and Isaac Maas, for $85.00 a month, as a bookkeeper in 1907. The brothers had a small dry goods store in town. "Jerry," as he was known to his multitude of friends from around the world, had some different ideas about how to run the store and Abe and Isaac would tell him "If you're so smart, you do it," and he did. Abe and Isaac retired in 1929. Jerry became the President and General Manager and built that store into the Maas Brothers chain of some 30 department stores, that were the most dominant in Florida.

He had legendary energy coupled with an inquisitive and inquiring mind and he had the courage to follow his instincts.

During the time he was building this chain of stores he had time to learn to fly. His pilots license was signed by Orville Wright, who became a correspondent of his. His passion for flying had a positive effect on the growth of Florida. He was the second private plane owner in the state. He did some "barnstorming" and competed in a number of air races. In 1935-36, he was instrumental in securing Pan American Airways to operate a route from Tampa to Havana, Cuba. During that period he organized, and was President of, Gulf Airways, which in 1938 merged with Ted Baker and was then called National Airlines. Ted was the President and Jerry was a director and served continuously till his death. That airline became the fifth largest in the U.S. and had routes from coast to coast. For a long time, National had the best routes from Florida to some of the major cities in the North during some of the fastest population spurts in Florida. In 1936, he convinced the Governor of Florida to set up an Aviation Division of the Road Department and in 1939, as a member of the Tampa Citizens Committee he was successful in securing MacDill Field for the Air Corps. In 1940, Jerry worked out the details with city and county officials to secure Drew Field (now Tampa International Airport) for use by the Air Corps.

In 1937 he was the driving force behind the creation of Peter O. Knight Airport on the North end of Davis Island, which was for many years the City of Tampa's airport. It is still in use today, but mainly for private planes. In 1964, Jerry originated the Tony Janus Award in celebration of the 50th anniversary of the first commercial airplane flight in the United States. Tony was the pilot on this flight, which was between St. Petersburg and Tampa. This award is given annually and has become one of the prestigious awards given in the field of aeronautics. The list of recipients are a who's who of the aviation field including such people as Eddie Rickenbacker, Richard Branscum and many others. Jerry was active in both World Wars and eventually retired as a Lt. Colonel in 1948. He remained active in military affairs and activities till his death on May 2, 1970. He founded the Florida West

Coast Chapter of the Air Force Association, the first in the state. At his death the chapter was named for him. The chapter yearly awards a Waterman scholarship to a high school graduate to attend college, who exhibits excellence and has need.

While helping to build the Maas Brothers Department Store chain, he went to Europe on a vacation/buying trip. The stock market crash happened while he was on board ship. He was broke and owed a lot of money. He came back to Tampa and told his banker that he would not declare bankruptcy, but would pay off all that he owed if the banker would give him time. As a token he gave the banker his diamond ring as security telling him he would be back for the ring when his debts were paid. That ring is on the finger of a family member today.

By 1948, Maas Brothers had become affiliated with Allied Stores, a national department store chain. The President was Earl Puckett. Jerry convinced him that Maas Brothers needed a store in St. Petersburg. Puckett's advisors did not think so, but he went ahead anyway. It was the first store built in the U.S. after WW II and the first Allied Stores branch in the country and for two years was known in the industry as "Puckett's Folly," but it then became one of the most profitable and Puckett became a visionary and others followed that vision.

In the early days of the movie business, Jerry founded Consolidated Amusement, Inc. He was the President of the company that went on to build all the movie houses in downtown Tampa. They included the Victory, the Strand, the still existing Tampa Theater, and others. He also founded the Victory National Insurance Co., of which he was the treasurer. The insurance company later merged with Gulf Life Insurance Company.

Jerry was also a writer, poet and philosopher. Despite his involvement in many projects, he found time to write a Sunday column called, "My Column" for the Tampa Tribune. He did that for twelve years. He later published a book entitled, "An Inspiration a Day", which included the best of his columns. It gave him great satisfaction to pass on his observations of the time period he was living in, as well as the wonder he felt for the miracles of future generations.

Jerry was a man of enormous vision, unbridled enthusiasm, practical reasoning, innovative and passionately patriotic. His multitude of business deals were always said to be fair and his many business partners spoke often of his integrity. He was able to create so many "firsts," airlines, poetry, airfields, while participating in World War I and World War II, and building a chain of movie houses, and the dominant department store chain of Florida. He had the vision and the drive to make it happen. The fast pace was a hallmark of his life, but he never failed to enjoy life to its fullest and he loved to be out for the evening, having a good time with pleasant and interesting company and a good drink. Twenty years after his passing you will still hear "Jerry Stories" being told among friends. When Jerry died he was 86 years young, having lived a 110 year life on this earth.

Jewish Community of Tampa

A substantial discussion of the early years of Schaarai Zedek Congregation of Tampa follows. This Congregation has direct ties to the Jewish community of Pinellas County through its business connections, officers, members and rabbis. This early Jewish history is a good example of what was occurring in the Tampa Bay Jewish community from the late 1890's to the end of World War II, and can serve as an example of Jewish life on the west coast of Florida. A brief history of Rodeph Sholom from 1903 to the end of World War II will follow the Schaarai Zedek discussion, since this congregation split from Schaarai Zedek and also had direct ties to Pinellas County. The types of problems faced by the Jewish people of Pinellas County in the early years were probably similar to those of the people of Schaarai Zedek and Rodeph Sholom.

The Jewish people of Tampa apparently tried to form a formal Jewish congregation prior to 1894. In 1893, Jewish services were held in the Masonic Temple, and Marcus Endel served as Grand Master of Florida's Grand Lodge of Masons that year. During this time the Orthodox, Conservative, and Reform groups worked together to try to form a congregation that would meet the needs of all the Jewish people in Tampa.

Schaarai Zedek

In 1894, Schaarai Zedek Congregation (Gates of Righteousness) was founded on Sunday Oct. 14, as Florida's fifth Jewish Congregation. A meeting was held at the home of M. H. Cohen Sr. at 4:00 p.m. for the purpose of forming an organization for the erection of a synagogue in Tampa. Abe Maas was elected temporary chairman by acclamation. M. Henry Cohen, the son, was elected temporary secretary by acclamation. Judge Cohen was secretary until 1928, when he became President. The proposal was approved and the charter members of the synagogue were enrolled. They were M. H. Cohen, Mrs. M. H. Cohen, Abe Maas, Mrs. Abe Maas, Herman Glogowski, Mrs. Herman Glogowski, T. Brown, Mrs. T. Brown, B. A. Brown, Mrs. B. A. Brown, L. Steinberg, Mrs. L. Steinberg, S. Aaron, Mrs. S. Aaron, S. Abramovitz, Mrs. S. Abramovitz, A. Solomon, Mrs. A. Solomon, M. Weissman, Mrs. M. Weissman, M. Britwitz, Mrs. M. Britwitz, M. Henry Cohen, Mrs. Ike Maas, Joe T. Brown, Mrs. Max Edelstein, Fred Wolf, Mrs. M. Schoenfield, A. Cooperman, Mrs. P. Berkowitz, and M. Gracowaner. A committee was approved to draft a constitution and by-laws. Committees were also approved for membership and for selection of a site for the erection of a synagogue. At a meeting on Oct. 21 at 8 PM, fourteen new members were present and were voted by the charter members to be included also as charter members. They were: Mr. M. Steatz, Mr. J. Simpson, Mr. A. Waterman, Mr. Geo. I. P. Dzialynski, Mr. Isidor Keanuitz, Mr. S. Goldberg, Mr. J. Rudestein, Mr. M. Weinstein, Mr. J. Aamias, Mr. S. Solomon, Mrs. Geo. I. P. Dzialynski, Mrs. Isidor Keanuitz, Mrs. S. Goldberg, and Mrs. J. Reudestein. H. Glogowski was voted to become chairman of the organization. M. Henry Cohen was elected secretary by acclamation. The temporary organization became a permanent organization and the by-laws were proposed by a committee. Article 2 of the bylaws, was Form of Worship. It was proposed that worship was to be Minhag(custom) Orthodox. However, there were objections from people who wanted to use Minhag America(the American Siddur, published by Rabbi Isaac Mayer Weiss). It was decided that the services would be in Hebrew as well as English. In Article 6, a minister was to be elected for a one year period and was to be subject to the direction of the President. The minister was to keep a record of the dates of the birth of children, of marriages he performed, and dates of deaths, names, and places of nativity.

The preamble to the subscription list stated, "We the undersigned Israelites of Tampa appreciating the need of a house of worship and a place where in our children may be taught the tenets of our faith, hereunder subscribe our names and the amount of our donation for the purpose of erecting a synagogue in the City of Tampa, Hillsborough County, Florida."

The first services of the new congregation were conducted by M. Henry Cohen Sr. at the old Masonic Temple, corner of Franklin and Washington Streets. M. Henry Cohen (the son) over the course of the next 36 years conducted services whenever a rabbi was not available. This learned attorney, who later became a judge, even conducted services at Temple Beth-El in St. Petersburg.

A Sunday school was discussed almost immediately. Several ladies and gentlemen offered their services as teachers in this Sunday School and were accepted. Mrs. Baker offered her dancing academy on Florida Avenue for fifty cents for each Sunday to be used as a Sunday School. The proper types of textbooks to be used were discussed on November 14, 1894. A motion was made to contact Dr. Kerauskopf of Philadelphia and Dr. Wise of Cincinnati to get further information. Herman Glogowski, the President, donated the first teachers books. The children's books cost fifty three cents each. The next concern was a cemetery for Jewish burial.

A discussion was held about getting a permanent charter and publishing the articles of incorporation. M. Henry Cohen was appointed as the attorney to oversee the matter. On Dec. 16, 1894, attorney Cohen reported that the Articles of Incorporation had been published the previous day as required by law and had been approved by the Judge of the Circuit Court. Now the

Congregation was a legally incorporated body under the Laws of the State of Florida.

Abe Maas

On Jan. 6, (or 15) 1895, Abe Maas was elected President of the new congregation. which position he held until Jan. 1928, with the exception of two years. Henry Brash was President in 1898 and Herman Glogowski was President in 1899. In 1928, because of his long tenure, his extreme dedication, and his many philanthropic contributions to the Jewish and outer community, the following resolutions were passed by the Board of Trustees and entered on page 88 of the permanent minutes of Schaarai Zedek synagogue.

"The life of Abe Maas is indissolubly bound with the history of Schaarai Zedek Congregation, since its organization on October 14, 1894, at which time he was elected as Temporary Chairman. After the incorporation of the congregation on Nov. 15, 1894, he was elected its first President, at the first Annual Meeting in January, 1895, and since which time, with the exception of two years, he has always held the office of President.

Abe Maas has always been an honored member, a faithful officer, a generous contributor and a zealous worker in every movement, not only in behalf of the congregation, but his influence has ever been felt in every cause tending to the betterment of humanity and of Judaism.

He has not ceased in his activity nor in the vigorousness of his efforts, but Father Time demands that at this good ripe age he lay aside the cares and duties of the office of President, which he has so well and faithfully occupied for these many years, and the announcement of his retirement from further service as the President of the congregation comes with deep pangs of regret to its membership.

His sound advice and excellent counsel was always given freely during the many years of his incumbency in the office of President, and will always be sought in the future. He has voluntarily laid aside the robes of office, and the members of Schaarai Zedek Congregation desire to tender him this memorial of their appreciation of his valued services while he may yet enjoy their commendation.

It can well be said of his efforts on behalf of Schaarai Zedek Congregation that, "It is not the first mile-post, but the last, that tells the story." Therefore, be it RESOLVED, that his good deeds are an invaluable legacy for the betterment of Judaism and of humanity, which shall forever be enshrined in the hearts of the members of Schaarai Zedek Congregation, and by his devotion to the congregation he has builded a monument more enduring than marble. Be it further RESOLVED, That much of the success of the Congregation is due to his unselfish and untiring devotion, and that in just recognition of his long and valued services he is hereby elected as President emeritus of Schaarai Zedek Congregation. Be it further RESOLVED, That this resolution be inscribed on a page of the records of the congregation."

1895 Continued

On Jan. 13, A. Goldberg and Offin Falk were elected to membership. A motion was made to adopt the by-laws at the next regular meeting. Since the meetings were being held in private homes, the congregation voted that smoking be prohibited and that this be part of the bylaws of the Congregation. On Jan. 20, 1895, a motion was made to thank Mr. E. H. Steinberg of Key West for making a donation of $18. It was also decided to solicit financial aid from Jacksonville and Key West co-religionists.

On January 27, the meeting was called to order to approve the by-laws of the congregation. The previous discussion about the mode of worship was not included in the by-laws. Article 2 stated that ten members had to be present for a quorum to hold a meeting. A discussion was held concerning a Jewish cemetery and a motion was made to ask the city to grant the congregation one-half of a certain piece of land to be used as a cemetery, which would be properly fenced and improved by the congregation. Jewish people who were not members of the congregation could purchase a lot in the cemetery if they applied to the Board of Trustees who regulated the price. The President of the Congregation would determine the fee for the use of the minister.

Mr. Weissman reported a sick and needy Israelite stranger in Tampa. After some discussion, a motion was made and seconded that Mr. Weissman offer to have him placed in the city hospital. The congregation organized a charity committee which was named the Hebrew Benevolent Society of Tampa. Each person who wished to join paid ten cents a week to help others. The initial collection was $14.50. Five dollars was given to the sick man in the hospital.

Article 5, of the by-laws, Duties of Members, stated that the members had to pay their assessment and pew rent promptly. They were called upon to observe proper decorum during divine services and to attend regular and called meetings of the congregation. Article 6, Section 1 stated the duties of the President. He was to preside at all meetings of the congregation, preserve order at meetings and during divine services, have supervisory power over the spiritual and religious affairs of the Congregation, appoint a school board, etc. Under the Rules of Order, the subject of proper decorum in the synagogue and meetings was included as extremely important. The Reform movement was far more formal than the Orthodox or Conservative movements.

The collector not only collected dues, but also served as the Administrator of the Congregation. He had to provide a $1000 bond.

For the welfare of the congregation, the Board of Trustees appointed the Committee on Finance, Committee on Supplies and Repairs, Committee on order in Synagogue, Committee on Choir, and Committee on Cemetery.

Pews and seats were sold to the highest bidder for Rosh Hashanah in order to raise money. Article 9, section 3 stated that persons of either sex may occupy the same pew and the family of the pew holder was entitled to seats in the pew.

On February 11, a special meeting was called to verify the purchase of a lot for $1,000 for a synagogue on Florida Avenue from Mary A. Taylor. From the beginning it had been recognized that it was very important to have a synagogue.

On March 17, a person in New York City offered to sell to the Congregation a Sefer Torah and all furnishings for $100. The secretary wrote to Rev. D. Loewenthal of New York to examine the Torah and to determine its condition. At the following meeting the Torah was purchased.

An Israelite died in Tampa and the Congregation paid for the funeral and burial expenses. His name was Joseph Einhorn from Nashville, Tennessee and he died on March 10, 1895.

On September 15, it was decided to hold the High Holy Day Services at the Masonic Hall. Arrangements were made for seating and for an appropriate place to display the Torah. M. Henry Cohen delivered a lecture and conducted the services.

In the early years, meetings were held several times a month or at a minimum once a month. Everyone was deeply involved in making all kinds of decisions about the new synagogue and Sunday school, which was held at Baker's Seminary at 10:00 a.m. on Sundays. The superintendent was M. Henry Cohen. He was also responsible for taking care of the Torah. M. Henry Cohen, the secretary of Schaarai Zedek, served two terms as a municipal judge in Tampa in the early and mid 1900s.

1896

The Hillsborough Lodge of the Masons was used for the High Holy Day services. It was located at the corner of Franklin and Fortune Streets. J. Weiss was given $40 for conducting the services. Seats for the High Holy Day services cost three dollars, if the people were not members of the Congregation. Miss Baker's school on Florida Avenue was used for the Sabbath School and Mr. M. Weissman, a teacher of Hebrew, offered his services to the congregation. Rev. D. Jacobson was named the first rabbi of the congregation for a term of three months from February !st, 1896 to May 1, 1896, with an option to continue for another year, at a salary of $50 per month. At a later meeting he was given a special thank you for the manner in which he had conducted services. He was offered a contract until January 1, 1897, but decided to resign in July of 1896. The schedule of services approved by the Congregation included a Divine Service with a lecture, to be held at 7:30 on Friday evening; biblical instruction to the children from 8:30 to 9:30 a.m. on Saturdays; Divine Services at 9:30 a.m. on Saturdays and instructions to children at 9: a.m. on Sunday.

The Congregation purchased a parcel of land to be used as a cemetery. A cemetery deed from the City of Tampa, Florida, was dated June 3, 1896, and recorded June 20, 1896, in Deed Book T. I. on page 350, records of Hillsborough County, Florida. A fence was erected around the purchased land for $150. Over the ensuing years there were numerous problems with the fence and maintenance of the Cemetery. A committee of Israelites of the community had asked for a special meeting, so they could participate in the establishment of a cemetery. One hundred and thirty dollars was raised for this purpose. This special fund had to be established since each member paid only two dollars per month to the Congregation. A dead body was removed from the Christian cemetery and put into the new Jewish Cemetery. Mrs. Rippa of Key West, the child of N. Falk, and the child of S. Goldberg, were the first three burials in the cemetery.

1897

H. Brash became President of the Congregation for a one-year period. The major issues were the erection of a synagogue, the revival of the Sunday School, working with "Our Circle," the Young People's group to get assistance with the Sunday school, and the securing of a hall for the High Holy Days.

1898

Herman Glogowski became President of Schaarai Zedek. Abe Maas became Vice President, and M. Henry Cohen became Secretary again, a job he kept until 1928. Purim Services were held at the G. A. R. Hall, on the corner of Franklin and Fortune streets. High Holy Days Services were conducted by Mr. Steinhauser and Mr. Fiur. The services were held at 6:00 in the evening and 8:00 in the morning, which was more

in keeping with the way Orthodox services were held. Ernest Maas became a member.

1899

Abe Maas became President again and held the position until 1928. Robert Bucksbaum was elected Vice President, a position he held until his death in 1925. The Temple Guild Sisterhood was formed (no official date appears to be available). The charter members were Mrs. J. L. Mairson, Mrs. O. Falk, Mrs. Abe Maas, Mrs. A. Levin, Mrs. Robert Bucksbaum, Mrs. Sam Borchardt and Mrs. Henry Brash.

The synagogue became a reality. Dues were $1 per month and fourteen members pledged a total of $135 for the new synagogue fund. The law firm of Cohen and Friedman pledged $50 and $100 if necessary. The contract for the building on Florida Avenue was awarded to Hester and Walker, for $2,350. The architect, R. B. Mc Gackin received $100 to supervise the project.

The cornerstone of the building was laid on Wednesday August 16, 1899, at 10:30 a.m. The Hillsborough Lodge and John Darling Lodge as well as the St. Petersburg Lodge of Masons performed the ceremony. The ceremony was very formal. It consisted of a series of individuals walking to the site with drawn swords, white rods, square, level, and plumb. Silver vessels were used for oil and wine. A golden vessel was used for corn. A prayer was said: "Almighty and everlasting God, who didst inspire Thy servant David, King of Israel, to found a temple at Jerusalem, erected to Thee and dedicated to Thy holy name, and did graciously except the House which Solomon, his son built to Thy glory, that the light of Thy countenance shine on us, Thy servants, who following their example, have assembled in Thy name and presence to lay the foundation stone of this building...." Artifacts were placed in the box. The cornerstone was appropriately laid. Corn was poured on the stone as a symbol of plenty and so that the people using the structure be inspired with virtue, wisdom and gratitude. Wine was poured on the stone as a symbol of refreshment and gladness. Oil was poured on the stone as an emblem of peace and joy. The oil of joy was poured upon the hearts of the widowed, the fatherless, and the distressed, until sorrow and stress would be no more. M. Henry Cohen delivered a speech on behalf of the congregation and S. Zellincker performed the Hebrew and English services. A large crowd of interested spectators were present. The Temple Guild served refreshments.

The High Holy Days were held at the new synagogue. Services were conducted by M. Henry Cohen, N. Falk, N. Katz, H. Brash, and S Gelluicker. The Temple Guild contributed substantially to the furnishing of the new synagogue and to the reduction of the mortgage over a period of time. M. Henry Cohen became the Superintendent of the Sabbath School. Mrs. Abe Maas and Mrs. H. Brash volunteered to be teachers.

1900

Much of the year was dedicated to the furnishing of the synagogue, the ordering of pews, and dealing with the various finances involved. On April 8, 1900, the Congregation decided to inquire about the hiring of a rabbi. They wanted one who could conform to the various views of the members of the Congregation, with some being Orthodox and others being Reform. Philip Dzialynski left the Tampa community. It was decided that Passover services would begin at 6:30 p.m. on Friday evening and 9 a.m. on Saturday and Sunday. This was a nod to the more Orthodox members of the Congregation. On May 6, a total of fifteen members pledged to pay $432 toward the hiring of a rabbi. This was over and above the one dollar per month that was being paid in dues. The Sunday School was in operation and the teachers, Mrs. Abe Maas, Mrs. Henry Brash, and Miss Minnie Bucksbaum had been productive and had taught the children excellent spiritual and religious principles. The Temple Guild had paid half of the $1,000 mortgage on the synagogue. A new charitable society was started to help co-religionists who were in need. The President was asked to talk to the President of the Theological Seminary in New York to determine if there was a rabbi available for the Congregation.

1901

A rabbinical fund was started. On January 6, there were twenty members present at the monthly meeting. Six new families were added. A charitable society was once again formed to assist needy Jewish people. The Temple Guild ladies collected $122 in back dues, whereas the collector collected $15 in back dues. Olfim Falk, trustee, was authorized to meet with the President of the Theological Seminary in New York about hiring a rabbi. On March 3, Julius Maas became a member. On March 31, Rev. Friedman came to Tampa to be interviewed and to discuss the arrangement for Passover Services. The Temple Guild paid the balance of the note of $541.67 to the Citizens Bank. Apparently the mode of service whether it be Orthodox or Reform was still a concern. A change in the bylaws put the supervision of the rabbi under the Board of Trustees and gave the board the power to regulate the mode and custom of the congregation. Rev. H. Friedman was hired as the rabbi for one year for $1,000. There were twenty nine members of the congregation at that time. The vote was twenty seven to two. A special meeting was called with the rabbi present to determine the type of ritual to be used by the Congregation.

At the April 7 meeting, six new members were elected. It was determined that members who were up-to-date would have a seat or pew without further cost and then allow wives, parents and families to be part of the seating. However, sons over twenty one years of age had to be members. Resident nonmembers were not to have a seat for the High Holy Days. Visitors to the city would always have a seat. People who did not pay their dues for two months, would be denied seating. The individual members determined what they were able to pay in annual dues. Mr. E. M. Burgmann conducted Purim Services.

At the May 5 meeting, it was announced that a devastating fire had hit Jacksonville and that a number of co-religionists were desperately in need. The fire virtually destroyed Jacksonville. It was the largest fire to occur in any southern city other then the Civil War, up to 1924. The Jewish citizens of Tampa raised $100 to help the Jewish people of Jacksonville. At the June 2 meeting, it was reported that two chandeliers have been installed in the synagogue and the third one had been ordered. Bibles in Hebrew and English had been purchased. The Sabbath School continued through the summer.

On July 7, the Ritual Committee for Services for the High Holy Days presented their report on how to conduct services. The President ruled them out of order. The subject of rituals was brought up again on July 28, Rabbi Friedman was named an ex-officio chairman of the committee and although the committee sought to reconcile the needs of the Orthodox and Reform groups, it did not happen. A concession was made to the Orthodox group by starting the services at 6:00 p.m. and 8:00 a.m.. On November 30, a conference was held by the President and Chairman of the Trustees to try to harmonize the existing differences between the two groups. The rabbi was strictly Reform. When a vote was taken, on December 15, for his reelection there were eighteen in favor and nineteen against.

Abe Maas, Herman Glogowski, and Ernest Kreher along with thirty seven other leading German-born Americans in Tampa formed the German-American Club. It was a major social organization, where the German culture was promoted. In 1908, a three-story building was built on Nebraska Avenue and the membership eventually grew to 1,000 people. Ernest Kreher founded Tampa Shipbuilding and Engineering Company.

Jewish merchants owned numerous retail establishments on North Franklin Street in Tampa. German Jewish merchants were established by 1901. They included the Hamburger family, the Regensburg family, and the Bucksbaum family. They sold dry goods, fabrics, clothing, and housewares. By 1903, there were 16 Jewish-owned stores there, and by 1926 there were 40. Morris Wolf, a clerk for the Maas Brothers, opened his own custom clothing store. This concentration of Jewish businesses, which influenced an entire region in their buying

habits, was similar to those established in other large and small cities. You could find these areas in Philadelphia, New York, Cincinnati, St. Louis, Terre Haute, Indiana, Indianapolis, Boston, Chicago, Milwaukee, St. Petersburg, Florida, etc. Many of these areas disappeared with the advent of shopping malls.

1902

At the Congregational meeting of January 5, a great many outsiders and nonmembers came into the meeting and created such a disturbance that the congregation was unable to proceed with its business. On March 2, the collector reported that members of the Orthodox group had paid their dues to somebody else instead of the congregation. Twenty members refused to pay dues. An attempt was made to obtain the money for the rabbi's salary. Because of the financial problem and the conflicts in the Congregation, the rabbi was given three months notice with termination to be August 1. The Orthodox congregants sued the Reform congregants for control of the synagogue and its facilities.

The treasurer for the congregation was Fred Wolf, who served in that position until 1927. On May 4, it was voted that the rabbi be retained month by month at $66.33 per month until August.

On Aug. 3, Article 2 of the Constitution of Schaarai Zedek Congregation, was amended to read as follows: "The form of worship of this congregation shall be in accordance with Reform services. That all laws and parts of laws in conflict with the foregoing be and the same are hereby repealed. That this amendment to the Constitution go into effect immediately from its passage". It was also decided to hire a Union College student for the holidays. However, Dr. Lewis D. Mendoza of the Hebrew Union College faculty of Cincinnati officiated during the holidays.

On November 1, it was reported that the outhouses had to be placed in a safe and sanitary manner. Herman Glogowski's special committee made sure that this was accomplished. The poor condition of the cemetery continued to be an ongoing problem.

Court Case

Rabbi Frank N. Sundheim, who was the rabbi in the late 1970s and early 1980s, after reviewing the 302 pages of the court case which ensued when the Orthodox group of the Congregation in 1902 sued the Reform group, summarized the unsuccessful effort by stating that the Reform group's dirty tricks consisted of not starting the meetings and services on time, using a voice vote rather than a roll call, and adding three new reform members to make it a reform majority. The attorney's fees were $250, which was a tremendous amount of money that could have been used for other purposes, but instead was used to try to resolve an issue of how services should be conducted. Dr. Oppenheimer, a man who called himself a peacemaker, testified in the case. He said that the Orthodox faction revealed, both by speech and ideas, the ways of an immigrant generation. The result of the trial was a classic example of the ambivalence of a Jew living in the South at the turn-of-the-century. The Orthodox faction felt that when you reformed your religious practices you would continue to do so and thereby leave Judaism. The Reform faction felt that the Orthodox were old-fashioned and not prepared to live in the new country.

In later years in St. Petersburg the first synagogue was Schaarai Zedek, Reform, which lasted six months to one year. A split occurred in 1922, and the Orthodox in 1923, formed Congregation B'nai Israel, which became conservative. The original Reform synagogue went out of business. A new Reform effort began in 1926 and in 1929 became Temple Beth-El. In Clearwater in 1949, Temple B'nai Israel was supposed to be Conservative but became Reform. In 1955, when Temple B'nai Israel joined the Union of America Hebrew Congregations, a group walked out and formed the conservative synagogue, Congregation Beth Shalom. Although over the years there has been a difference in some portions of the religious practices, the Jewish people have always helped each other and helped others.

1903

Our Circle, the young people's social and literary society stopped meeting. The $100 balance in the treasury was requested for the use of the congregation. In March, application was made for membership in the Union of America Hebrew Congregations. On June 7, the congregation was admitted to the union. A fee of 50 cents per person per six months was paid for the twenty members. During this time, as in all prior years, the women's group, Temple Guild, assisted the synagogue in many activities including paying for music and a choir, helping pay for student rabbis for the High Holy Days, helping pay indebtedness, and providing many amenities for the synagogue. Mr. Aaron Shapero, a Hebrew Union College student, was hired for the High Holy Days at a cost of $75 and expenses. The Board paid an additional $10 to the rabbinical student because he was so good.

The congregation protested the action of the Russians at Kishinev. Nicholas II, who succeeded Alexander III, in 1894, tried to enforce the fundamentals of autocracy with the same strictness as his father had done. Peasants, workers, and students rioted to achieve political reforms, freedom of speech, and universal suffrage. The Russian government tried to deflect the revolutionary movement at home by starting a war with Japan and with violent anti-Semitic campaigns. A terrible pogrom occurred in Kishinev in 1903, resulting in forty five people being murdered and 1,300 homes and shops being plundered. The editor of the local newspaper, Bessarabets, had received money from the Minister of the Interior, Viacheslav Plehve, to stir up violence against the Jewish population. When the perpetrators of the horror were tried, they received very light sentences, indicating that pogroms had now become an instrument of government policy. The Jewish people began to form self-defense units. During the war with Japan, the anti-Semitic press blamed the Jewish people for conspiring with the enemy. These campaigns led to a series of pogroms after the Russians were beaten badly by the Japanese. The Black Hundreds, who openly declared the extermination of the Jewish people, were a group of reactionary, anti-revolutionary, and anti-Semitic groups formed in Russia during and after the Russian Revolution of 1905. One of their major aims now was to destroy Judaism.

1904

A fourteen-year-old boy was very sick and a request was made to the Board of Trustees to give assistance to the child. The ladies of the Guild and men provided necessary assistance. At this time the synagogue was always looked to for assistance whenever there were specific needs such as sickness, hunger, poverty, and death. The Sabbath School and Sunday School were reorganized. Horace J. Wolf, a student of Hebrew Union College, was engaged for the High Holy Days. An informal discussion was held about the question of having the Orthodox group be admitted to membership in the synagogue. There were twenty two members of the congregation on December 4.

The secretary was authorized to insert an advertisement in the American Israelite that the congregation was in need of a rabbi, a single man who could lecture in English and conduct Reform services.

Herman Glogowski, except for the year he was President, was Chairman of the Board of Trustees until 1904. Ernest Maas was the collector, and Julius Maas was the Sexton. Mr. Rippa was a member of the congregation. He had relatives in Key West and members of his family were buried in Tampa.

1905

The Board of Trustees offered the sum of $900 a year for a rabbi. There were twenty four members. Rabbi H. S. Stollnitz was engaged for a period of one year for $1,200. On January 3, M. H. Cohen died in Jacksonville FL. He was an extremely honored and beloved member of the Jewish community of Tampa, who had as a founding trustee of the synagogue, worked extremely hard to unite the Jewish people of Tampa. On February 26, Mr. E. H. Steinberg of Congregation Rodeph Sholom approached the President of Schaarai Zedek to see if the two congregations could become affiliated and build together a new synagogue on a lot which they were purchasing. The merger never occurred, but the two congregations did work together in relationship to the cemetery. S.M Abramovitz's son was confirmed. The Union of American Hebrew Congregations requested that special services be held on Thanksgiving day, November 30, to commemorate the 250 year anniversary of the settlement of the Jewish people in the United States. Rodeph Sholom Congregation members were invited to attend this ceremony.

On December 10, the congregation received a letter from the Union of American Hebrew Congregations about the calamity the Jews were facing in Russia. The czar was forced to grant a constitution in October. A series of pogroms were carried out in more than 300 towns and cities with the help of local government officials, leaving almost 1,000 people dead and many thousands of people wounded. In Bialystok and Zhitomir, Russia, the Jewish people fought back when they were attacked on Easter, April 24 and 25. The police prevented the Jewish self-defense organization from protecting their property resulting in the deaths of fifteen Jewish volunteers and one non-Jewish volunteer. The governor did nothing to stop this from occurring until a number of Jewish men broke into his office and threatened him. The pogroms ceased almost immediately.

1906

On January 7, only fifteen members attended the annual meeting. The Temple Singing Circle was formed and became the choir. The rabbi wanted them to perform a sacred concert for the non-Jewish community. There was a discussion about holding a public Seder during Passover, but it was never done. The President spoke about nonattendance at services. Rabbi Stollnitz was elected for another year. There were seventy members in January and fifty two members by September. At the High Holy Days, the Rabbi refused to sing the Kol Nidre. At the meeting of the Board of Trustees on October 7, with Ernest Maas as Chairman (he remained chairman until 1940), it was brought to the attention of the congregation that the rabbi had appeared before the County School Board regarding the teaching of religion in the public schools. Information about this had appeared in the daily newspapers. Members of the congregation who were attempting to maintain a low-profile were not happy with this. The rabbi was told to follow orders or resign.

1907

The Union of American Hebrew Congregations sent a letter to the synagogue requesting that delegates be sent to the 20th Council to be held in Atlanta, Georgia on January 16. By Apri,l there were seventy three members of the synagogue. The National Conference of Jewish Charities in the United States asked the congregation to become a member. They didn't become a member because of financial problems. They also decided to do without a rabbi after the current contract expired. On May 5, there was a confirmation service. Dr. Jacob Singer of Buffalo, New York officiated during the holidays.

1908-1920

On Sunday, March 1, 1908, in Tampa, eighteen city blocks were leveled by a disastrous fire. The losses exceeded one million dollars, 171 homes burned, forty two business buildings and five cigar factories burned. Half the losses were not covered by insurance. This was also a disaster for Congregation Schaarai Zedek. Its membership became depleted as well as its treasury. People lost interest in attending the annual meetings and participating in the synagogue. This crisis continued until 1920.

At the annual meeting of 1908, only eleven members attended. There was a balance of $37 in the treasury. Another meeting could not be held until December 6, because of the lack of a quorum. A question came up about the possibility of selling the synagogue and the land, because it was located at an undesirable site. They thought about building elsewhere where they could attract more Jewish people. On May 2, 1909, the only meeting

of the year was held with Congregation Rodeph Sholom to see if they would help pay for a new fence at the cemetery since the last one was destroyed by fire.

On December 3, Herman Glogowski died in an accident. He had been held in such high esteem by the people of Tampa that the flag on top of City Hall flew at half mast during the funeral procession, which was six blocks long. He was considered to be Tampa's first citizen.

On December 11, 1910, a meeting was held with eleven members present, including four of the Maas family (Abe, Isaac, Julius, Ernest) and M. Henry Cohen, the longtime secretary. The group was concerned about the lack of interest in the congregation. There was $13.03 in the treasury and an accumulated debt of $325.13. Sol Maas and Jerome Waterman joined the congregation.

On January 21, 1911, a discussion was held concerning a discriminatory article written in the Tampa Daily Times. The various Jewish groups worked together to counter this article. Discussions were held concerning the hiring of a new rabbi. An advertisement was placed in the American Israelite. A salary of $1,500 a year was offered. Meanwhile, M. Henry Cohen officiated at the services on the High Holy Days. Apparently, a rabbi was not hired.

No minutes of meetings were available from December 3, 1911 until September of 1913. At that time, M. Henry Cohen was asked to officiate at the coming High Holy Days Services. The ladies of the Temple Guild were requested to arrange for the necessary music. On Oct. 19, 1913, seven people attended the meeting. Finances were in terrible shape. The Union of American Hebrew Congregations informed the congregation that it would be suspended for nonpayment of dues.

In 1914, there was $18.69 in the general fund and $37.50 in the cemetery fund. There was an attempt to sell the synagogue. M. Henry Cohen was asked to officiate at the High Holy Days.

In 1915, the Hebrew Free School had been organized and asked to rent the synagogue for a year at $10 a month. They would pay for all maintenance and insurance costs. The synagogue would be available for the Congregation for the High Holy Days.

On Aug. 20, 1916, the Hebrew Free School offered to buy the synagogue for a price of $5,000 with a cash deposit of $50 and $450 by Nov. 1, 1916. The Congregation would be allowed to use the building for the High Holy Days. M. Henry Cohen conducted the services on the High Holy Days. On October 28, it was reported that the Hebrew Free School owed rent for August, September and October. Its lease was terminated on November 1.

From October 28, 1916, until November 25, 1917, there were no meetings. The Hebrew Free School Congregation owed $50 in back rent. President Abe Maas presented the proposition to Rabbi Hershon to affiliate the members of Congregation Schaarai Zedek with Congregation Rodeph Sholom and that the services would be reform as was done at the present time. It was a consensus of the meeting that the members join individually. There were no minutes available after November 25, 1917 until May 1920.

1920

In May of 1920, a meeting was held at the home of Abe Mass, President of the Congregation. Ernest Maas had just returned from the north and stated that he had met Rabbi George Benedict, who was desirous of coming to Tampa to take charge of the Congregation and who impressed him as being a rabbi who would fill the pulpit satisfactorily. After some discussion, the members present felt that there was a large enough voluntary subscription to ask him to come to Tampa to conduct services prior to his engagement, since twenty seven hundred and fifty dollars had been subscribed to hire the rabbi. He would receive a salary of $2,500 a year and then expenses would be paid for his move to Tampa. He would start on Aug. 1. There were thirty six members at that time. The ladies of the Temple Guild, along with the Chairman of Trustees were to meet with the rabbi to arrange for the High Holy Days Services. Rabbi Benedict spoke to the members about the success of the congregation and its possibilities in the future for including all Jewish people in the City of Tampa, who were unaffiliated

with any congregation, to join Schaarai Zedek. Everyone was invited to participate in the High Holy Days Services. Monthly meetings had resumed. By the meeting of October 5, 1920, most members had paid their back dues. The synagogue loaned benches to Congregation Rodeph Sholom. Rabbi Benedict's salary was considered to be inadequate by the congregation and they therefore raised it from $200 a month to $250 a month. Rabbi Benedict and President Abe Maas were asked to visit the parents of children who were attending the Sabbath School and invite them to become affiliated with the congregation. It was this kind of movement, toward enhancing the synagogue membership and the needs of the St. Petersburg Jewish community, which led to the first Jewish congregation in St. Petersburg in 1921. Schaarai Zedek approved Rabbi Benedict going to St. Petersburg twice a month. On November 21, 1921, there were thirty seven members in the congregation. On December 4, 1921, the treasurer reported that he had received $65 in August and $157 in November from the Jewish community in St. Petersburg, Florida, making a total of $222.

During the January 1, 1922 annual meeting there was a major concern about the conditions of the graves in the Jewish cemetery and the fact that improper burials were being made and no records of interments were being kept. The congregation decided to rejoin the Union of American Hebrew Congregations at $1 per person per year. The Rabbi spoke about beginning a campaign to produce funds for a new temple. President Abe Maas contributed the first thousand dollars. On May 11, 1922, a special meeting of the congregation was called to order by the President concerning the election of a rabbi, and Rabbi Benedict was re-elected for another year. There were thirty one members present. The President was authorized to negotiate for the sale of the synagogue at 1205 Florida Avenue with a view to the erection of a synagogue in Hyde Park. The fence between the two Jewish Cemeteries was to be removed. On June 4, 1922 a bill for $4 was processed for supplies for the Boy Scout Troop. There were forty seven members in the Congregation. Mr.

J. Pasternack expressed his appreciation for the courtesies extended himself and his family upon the confirmation of his son. His son and another boy were confirmed with Goldie Schuster from St. Petersburg. On Nov. 4, 1922 Mrs. Fromer became the first lady to become a member of the temple on her own.

On January 7, 1923, discussions were held concerning the hiring of a new rabbi. On January 21, 1923, the congregation voted unanimously to continue the Sunday School. On February 4, 1923, the trustees requested that the party in St. Petersburg pay $25 for the cemetery lot which was purchased. Rabbi Benedict had taken a new pulpit in Roanoke, Virginia in January or February. The Union of American Hebrew Congregations requested that the congregation rejoin. On March 25, 1923, a lot was purchased at De Leon Street and South Delaware Avenue from Cora L. Hawkins for $3,500. In May of 1923, there were forty five members of the Congregation. At the June 3rd meeting, the Hebrew Orphans Home of Atlanta, Georgia's letter was read requesting contributions. The congregation had worked with them before. A night letter was sent to Rabbi Harvey B. Franklin requesting that he reply to the letter sent by President Maas relative to his engagement as Rabbi for the Congregation. Friday, June 29, was designated as the date of the final and closing services in the old synagogue building. Judge M. Henry Cohen once again conducted the services. At the final meeting on July 1st, in the building, the contract of $29,306 was approved for the erection of the new building.

Judge M. Henry Cohen

Mr. Offin Falk announced that the Temple Brotherhood had adopted a resolution commending Brother M. Henry Cohen for the outstanding service rendered by him to the Congregation. The resolution is as follows:"This organization has as its foundation the highest principles of Brotherly Love, which is so strongly presented in our Faith and our Teachings. We are indeed fortunate to have as a member, one whose untiring efforts in our behalf, have been toward the uplifting and teachings of these principles, and we are presented with an opportunity of not only showing our appreciation but of exercising the right at this time of so doing toward one whose sole ambition was, and is to hold together by task, words, and deeds the strongest zeal of the Brotherly Love... he has shown faithful duty and worked strenuously to enforce by precepts and examples the steady obedience to the tenant of Judaism." M. Henry Cohen served in many capacities in over thirty years of being one of the pillars of the congregation. He was secretary for approximately thirty years, President of the congregation, religious leader on innumerable occasions, including conducting numerous services on the High Holy Days. He was born in New York in 1872. He had been a judge and had practiced general law for many years. His wife Julia was born in Germany in 1875. He died in Florida in 1943. Henry's son, Marcus H. Cohen, was born in Florida in 1909.

Offin Falk

Offin Falk, a longtime member of the congregation and the Board of Trustees, was born in Russia on April 23, 1873. He came to the United States in 1889. His wife, Emma was born in Russia on March 15, 1875. She died on August 26, 1964. He was the founder of O. Falk Department Store in Tampa. He died on March 21, 1941. Ernest Jr. was born on November 4, 1911. Their son David, was listed in the World War I draft. He was born on May 18, 1896, in Tampa. He died on June 5, 1960.

Time of Renewal

On Sept. 2, 1923, it was decided the Pythian Castle Hall had to be secured for the High Holy Days. M. Henry Cohen was asked to officiate at the services. The First Congregational Church approved the use of the church on Florida and Francis Avenues for Yom Kippur Services. Services were also conducted at the Hyde Park Methodist Church. The three facilities were used until June 8, 1924. The reopening of the Sunday School at the High Park Primary Public School was discussed.

In 1924, deeds were issued to the Hebrew Free School Congregation for the cemetery. There were forty members in the Congregation. The cornerstone for the old building as well as the new building were placed in the new structure. The religious school reopened and was making satisfactory progress. An organ was purchased for $3,500. On April 6, 1924, a letter was received from the Probation Officer of Pinellas County, Florida, that a Jewish child, Carrie Jeannette Myers, of Tarpon Springs, nine or ten years old, was in destitute circumstances since the death of her father and the continued illness of her mother, and requested that an effort be made to place the child in the Hebrew Orphans Home in Atlanta, Georgia. The Congregation complied with the request. On May 14, she was taken to the Hebrew Orphans Home. The Jewish community was asked to support her. On June 1, Rabbi Louis Elliot Grafman, a graduate of Hebrew Union College that year, was invited to Tampa on a trial basis. He was hired as Rabbi starting September 1, for $4,250 a year. He continued as the Rabbi until 1929. On August 3, 1924, an invitation was received from the Young Men's Hebrew Association to the dedication exercises. On Sept. 21, 1924 the secretary was requested to write a letter to the Young Men's Hebrew Association of St. Petersburg and to a newspaper in St. Petersburg calling attention to the Holidays, extending an invitation to co-religionists stating that there would be no charge.

The dedication of the new temple was held on December 19, 1924. Professor Carl Geisser, organist, played various selections. Rabbi Grafman performed the service. Rev. C. H. H. Branch gave a presentation on behalf of the Ministerial Alliance. Rabbi Israel L. Kaplan of Temple Ahavath Chesed of Jacksonville gave the dedication address, and Rev. Adolph Burger, rabbi of Rodeph Sholom Synagogue gave the benediction.

In 1925, on February 1, a resolution of sorrow was read on the death of Mr. E. H. Steinberg, a long time resident of Tampa and formerly President of Congregation Rodeph Sholom and President emeritus. Robert Bucksbaum, Vice President of Schaarai Zedek almost continuously since its founding, died in February. He was a man of simple life, big-hearted, genial, generous, a tender and devoted husband, a loving father, and he lived within the loftiest standards as an officer of the congregation, and as a delightful human being working within the Jewish and general communities. He was thoroughly devoted to Judaism and his life was a shining example for all to follow.

On May 17, 1925, the Congregation decided to rehire the rabbi for another year at a higher salary. In addition, he was given a three-month vacation. He was extended a vote of confidence by the congregation. At the same meeting, the congregation was told about a highly defamatory article relating to the Jewish people published in the Sunday Tampa Tribune written by Mr. Lizotte. The members in no uncertain terms responded angrily about this attack on the Jewish people. They voted unanimously that President Abe Maas, Mr. Fred Wolf, and Mr. Dave Falk be appointed as a committee to call upon the Tribune and requested action be taken and published showing that the statements expressed in the article are not those which the Tribune concurred with and that the policy of the paper and its ownership was against this type of discriminatory expression. Further, they appointed a committee who would highlight the accomplishments of the Jewish people in contradiction to the original article. Because of the increasing membership, three dozen additional prayer books, holiday prayer books, and hymn books were ordered. On Sept. 6, 1925, eleven new members were added to the Congregation. On October 11, 1925, twenty nine new members were added to the Congregation. A reception was planned in honor of the rabbi and his new wife. It was held at the Tampa Yacht and Country Club. This is interesting to note since in St. Petersburg and in Clearwater, Jews were not allowed in the yacht clubs.

In 1926, the major concerns included better attendance at services, and of course, the constant need to raise money to meet obligations. The Temple Sisterhood agreed to pay the salary of the organist. On May 17, 1926, the congregation voted to reelect Rabbi Grafman for another year, at a higher salary of $6,000. The rabbi stated that he intended to endeavor to increase the membership and requested that the Trustees appeal to the congregation to cooperate with them. Twenty five men voluntarily increased their dues by a total of $1,381. On June 6, 1926, Mr. Henry Schutz, the first Jewish person in St. Petersburg, contributed $25 to Schaarai Zedek Congregation. Since the rabbi had discontinued services during his vacation, Judge M. Henry Cohen was asked to conduct the services and he accepted. At a meeting on November 7, 1926, thirty one members were stricken from the membership as a result of nonpayment of dues. Eight new people were elected to membership.

In 1927, Mr. Ernest Maas raised $1,500 for the payment of a choir by preparing and selling a Blue Book. On April 3, 1927, eleven members were suspended for nonpayment of dues. It was decided to hold a public Seder. On May 15, 1927, the rabbi was reelected for another year. It was also decided to send the rabbi to the Conference of Rabbis and that his expenses of $150 be paid by borrowing the money from the Building Fund. On October 2, 1927, it was decided to hold Succoth services. Eight new members were enrolled in the congregation, including a widow. The Hebrew Free School Congregation asked to purchase more cemetery lots. On Nov. 6, 1927, it was stated that certain coreligionists in St. Petersburg were desirous of becoming members of the congregation. A committee of officers, including Abe Maas, Offin Falk, and Samuel E. Fink were asked to meet with them. On December 5, 1927, the following people from St. Petersburg, Florida were elected as members: Henry Schutz, A. Cohen, D. H. Blumberg. Mr. Abe Maas stated that he would not seek the presidency in 1928 or later, because of his health. The secretary of the congregation presented a resolution of thanks for his long, faithful, and valued services. He was then elected unanimously as President emeritus.

In 1928, M. Henry Cohen was elected President, Fred Wolf Vice President, M. J. Mackler secretary, Hyman Wertheim treasurer. A discussion was held concerning the viability of having Saturday morning services. Mrs. Fanny Levy, in discussing the Sunday School, stated that the Torah would be exhibited to the children along with all other items related to Judaism. Mr.

Offin Falk discussed the value of the Torah and the knowledge of the existence of same, to the children. The Board of Trustees was enlarged to seven members including two ladies from the Sisterhood. It was decided that the President of the congregation should not exceed two consecutive terms of one year each. Myrtle Hill Cemetery offered to set aside a large plot for a Hebrew Cemetery. On May 20, 1928, there was considerable disagreement between the congregation and the rabbi concerning the operation of the synagogue. Apparently, there were members who wanted to have Saturday morning services and celebrate all the holidays and the rabbi did not appear to be for this. After an understanding had been reached with the rabbi concerning the congregation's wishes, he was rehired for another year. He set a goal of eighty five members for the coming year. In September, there were to be four Saturday morning services as a test of the attendance. The rabbi presented a talk concerning the needs and responsibilities of temple members. A meeting was scheduled of the Brotherhood and Sisterhood for the purpose of creating harmony and outlining temporal and religious subjects to be discussed. Because of limited attendance at Saturday morning services, a recommendation was made to have Sunday morning lectures instead.

In 1929, Fred Wolf became President, Offin Falk Vice President, M. J. Mackler secretary, Hyman Wertheim treasurer. In the meeting of January 14, 1929, letters were received from congregants asking for dues reductions because of severe economic conditions. The rabbi was informed that his salary would not be paid on time. There was a discussion of the possibilities of closing the temple, employment of a cheaper rabbi, or obtaining new members. Everyone agreed that the temple would never be closed. The first social function of the temple to be held after Friday night services occurred on March 1. This social which was in fact an Oneg Shabbat, was extremely well received. On April 7, 1929 it was announced that Rabbi Kaplan of Miami would fill the pulpit in Tampa while Rabbi Grafman would fill the Miami pulpit for the same night.

On April 17, 1929, it was reported that

there were fifty four members that could be counted on for the coming year and the receipts from these individuals would be insufficient to meet the bills of the temple including the salary of the current rabbi. In order to keep this rabbi, people even thought about combining all of the synagogues in Tampa. Everyone agreed that he had proven to be a great asset to the Jewish people of Tampa and the state of Florida and that he had been the cause of a better understanding between Jew and Gentiles in this section of the United States. The building was once again in a state of disrepair. On Sept. 17, 1929, the Jewish families in Lakeland, St. Petersburg, Sarasota, and Bradenton were offered an opportunity to attend holiday services in Tampa . Because of financial problems, the rabbi was offered a salary of $4,000 instead of $6,000. He agreed to accept $500 a month with his contract expiring on May 1, 1930.

In 1930, President Wolf stated that with all of the financial reverses and bank failures he believed that the congregation had touched bottom and was now on its way up. He thanked the Temple Sisterhood for their cooperation. He stated that they were the backbone of the Temple. He said that the building was desperately in need of repairs and that the money that would have been used for a choir should be used to repair the building. Attendance at Friday night services had increased. The rabbi held bible classes where twenty seven people attended with twenty being non-Jewish.

Mr Abe Maas was congratulated on his 75th birthday. Mrs. Sol Maas acted as the organist for the congregation without pay. Rabbi Grafman made sure that confirmation was completed before he left the congregation. A professional organist was hired for the High Holy Days.

Rabbi David L. Zielonka

On April 29,1930, Dr. David L. Zielonka of Texas, a graduate of the 1929 class of Hebrew Union College, was considered for rabbi of the congregation. A salary of $3,600 a year was allotted for him . He was selected the Rabbi on September 1, 1930. In his first year, Rabbi Zelonka was granted time to go to El Paso, Texas to help in the celebration of

Rabbi David L. Zielonka

his father's 30th anniversary as the rabbi of that Congregation. Rabbi Zielonka served with great distinction, as spiritual leader, for forty years. In addition to this, in 1931 he became a member of the founding faculty of the University of Tampa. He taught in the departments of sociology, philosophy, and religion for forty years and headed up the department from 1963-1970. He was a recipient of numerous awards from religious, cultural, civic and educational organizations. He became an Eagle Scout at age forty seven. His retirement dinner program read, "It is the dream of every man to see his labors come to fruition. Few men are fortunate enough to realize this dream. David Zielonka is one of the few. He has endeavored and succeeded in transforming a faltering congregation of 50 into a strong, active congregation of 400 families...(in 1970). He has untiringly and unceasingly given of himself to bridge any factor that causes prejudices and animosities among men." He died on September 24, 1977.

Carol Zielonka

Carol Zielonka, wife of the rabbi, made numerous contributions to the synagogue and to the general community. She described the conditions of the Tampa Bay area in 1930 in a speech entitled, "How Things Were." "It was the era of the great depression, stock market crash and the bank holidays not only for Florida, but also for the whole country....There were rabbis in Jacksonville, Miami and Pensacola. David was the only rabbi in this area and he was called on for occasions of joy and sorrow, as well as interfaith and community gatherings for the entire west coast of Florida. It was a busy life!...Tampa had little anti-Semitism. There were Jewish members in all the service clubs, country clubs, and civic and community organizations. Our business and professional men were highly respected members of the community, just as today.

University of Tampa

The establishment of the University of Tampa in 1931 was an important event. It was the first institution of higher learning in the area, and David was a member of the original faculty. He taught Old Testament and other courses and religion to many students who had never seen a Rabbi.... During his thirty nine years of teaching there, he brought an appreciation and respect for the Jewish people and Judaism to students who have become leaders in our community, including two mayors."

1930's

In the 1930s, Polish Jewish immigrants founded the major strawberry firm of Wishnatzki and Nathel Inc., in Plant City. Other Jewish businesses flourished including Maas Brothers. Julius Maas retired from Maas Brothers but still came to the store and was active. By then Jerome Waterman was in charge of everything. He instituted many of the modern changes in the operation of the store. Jerome's wife, Daisy, was Sisterhood President of Schaarai Zedek in 1928 and 1929. Shirley Collman's mother was also President of Congregation Schaarai Zedek's Sisterhood in 1935-1937. Mel Stein and his wife Connie came to Tampa around 1941 or 1942 to be the manager of the Maas Brothers store while Jerome Waterman was the chief executive officer. Ernest Maas Sr. moved away from Tampa in the 1940s. He returned at a later date and was once again active in Jewish affairs.

1931-1945

In 1931, President Wolf said that conditions had deteriorated even worse than expected. He thanked everyone for their hard work but especially the loyalty and untiring effort of the Temple Sisterhood. They had been the backbone of the congregation for many years and without them the congregation would've failed. The Sisterhood provided for the religious school, provided for the music, and for many other necessities of the congregation. Rabbi Zielonka talked about the poor condition of the Sunday school rooms and urged immediate attention to the needs of the children. Mr. Offin Falk was elected unanimously as President. Mr. Ernest Maas was elected Vice President. M. J. Mackler was the secretary.

The board voted unanimously on the suggestion of the rabbi to cooperate with the Unitarian Congregation of Tampa. The Unitarians were given the right to hold their services at the temple for a six-month period. The temple borrowed $8,000 for operating expenses. The Sisterhood continued its ongoing program of contributing to the expenses of the Temple by donating $500. Bonds were purchased by board members for the National Jewish Hospital in Denver. The president of the temple and the president of the brotherhood made arrangements to conduct summer services.

In 1932, Ernest Maas became President of the congregation. There was a preoccupation with the operation of the Sabbath school and its financing. The serious financial problems of the congregation continued. Rabbis Zielonka recommended that memorial services be held at both Woodlawn Cemetery and Myrtle Hill Cemetery.

In 1933, Rabbi Zielonka conducted a series of open forms on Judaism. The people of Tampa were invited to this series of programs to help them understand the meaning, practices, rituals and philosophy of Judaism. In the difficult times that were occurring in Europe and the adverse teachings of Hitler, this was a way to breakdown religious prejudice and bigotry and to truly show the contributions of the Jewish people to the general community.

Because of the condition of the synagogue, plans were being discussed on how to improve the structure and how to get more Jewish people involved. Many congregants were seeking reduction in their dues because of the severe financial situation in the country. In order to keep this synagogue going it was essential to recruit new members. A fee of $.50 per child per Sunday school session was approved where the children's parents were not members of the synagogue.

In 1934, Fred Wolf was Chairman of the Board of Trustees and Leo Weiss was the President. The Temple had been completely overhauled and redecorated at a cost of $1,263.50. The entire sum had been pledged and paid. The New Year's Eve ball had been a great success and produced $487.58 for the synagogue general fund. The officers, Rabbi Zielonka and the board members were invited to attend the dedication of Temple Beth El's new synagogue building in St. Petersburg on January 19. The Bilgore family, whose business was in Clearwater, were asked to join Schaarai Zedek. The Hebrew Free School asked to purchase space in the cemetery. Rabbi Rosenblatt from St. Petersburg offered his assistance during the absence of Rabbi Zielonka. The Sisterhood helped reduce the indebtedness of the Temple, as they had done in past years.

In 1935, Isaac Maas left in his will the sum of $1000 to Schaarai Zedek. Rabbi Zielonka scheduled short services at 7:30 p.m. on Friday evenings during the summer. The congregation sent to the Hebrew Orphans Home of Atlanta, a five dollar contribution as a memorial for Mrs. Flora H. Jacobs. A Jewish transient, Gus Miller, was buried in the Jewish cemetery for free. Music for the New Year's Eve dance was arranged by Mr. Ernest Maas Jr.. The sale of cemetery lots helped improve the finances of the synagogue.

In 1936, Dr. Daniel Rachelson became President while Mr. Ernest Maas continued as chairman of the board. A resolution of sympathy was included in the minutes of the Board of Trustees to Mrs. Ernest Maas for the loss of her mother and brother.

Ernest Maas reported that he had received a letter from the Anti-Defamation League relative to the picture, "Wandering Jew". The movie was determined to be discriminatory to all Jewish people and Ernest had a conference with the owners of all of the local movie houses and obtained from them a promise that the picture would not be shown in Tampa. The 40th anniversary celebration was held on December 7. Rabbi Rosenblatt of St. Petersburg was the main speaker at the anniversary dinner. In addition Mr. and Mrs. Sol Halaczer of St. Petersburg attended.

Dr. E. C. Nance, pastor of the First Christian Church asked the temple for financial assistance. A check for $10 was sent to the church. Ten new members were added to the congregation in September. This was the first substantial increase in many years.

In 1937, Jules Bragin became a member of the synagogue. A bill for $1.05 was paid to the Davis Island Country Club. This was interesting because Jewish people in other areas were not allowed to join country clubs or have affairs at country clubs.

In 1938, Abe Maas and others developed plans for paying off the mortgage. Judge M. Henry Cohen conducted Friday night services during the absence of Rabbi Zielonka, who went to El Paso, Texas because of the death of his father.

In 1939, Ernest Maas continued as Chairman of the Board of Trustees while Sol Jacobs served as President. Rabbi Zielonka suggested that the word Israelite be erased and changed in all documents and be replaced with "Any person of Jewish Faith".

In 1940, Lewis Wellhouse was President and Jules Bragin was Vice President. Proper resolutions were drawn up on the death of three past Presidents, Abe Maas, Sol Jacobs and Offin Falk.

In 1943, the congregation elected its first woman officer. Mrs. Margaret Hammer, had the dual honor of being Secretary of the Congregation and of the Board of Trustees.

In 1944, the congregation had two Torahs valued at $150 each and an organ valued at $3500.

1945-1956

In 1945, Jules Bragin became President of the synagogue. There was an increase of 20% in Temple membership. Because of the terrible physical condition of the temple he requested that a new temple and Sunday school be built. The cemetery was in terrible condition. Through the years, as new cemetery lots were sold, the money was put into the general fund and maintenance was totally ignored.

In 1948, Jules Bragin reported that there had been a 20% increase in membership and that there was active participation in the Sabbath services, Sunday school, men's club, and many other activities of the congregation. However, a particularly serious problem occurred in the congregation, one that probably was faced by other congregations in other parts of the country. The creation of the State of Israel was welcomed by some, not welcomed by others and ignored by still another group. President Jules Bragin firmly believed that this difference of opinion should not affect the cohesiveness of the congregation. He said, "...None, I'm sure fail to realize the terrible plight of our unfortunate brethren overseas; many of these are homeless, helpless and unfortunately almost bereft of hope. To them Palestine is the land of promise and we, regardless of our political affiliation, are all Jews and must continue to extend a helping hand so that the remnants of our people may be saved." The United Jewish Appeal was an instrument by which funds could be raised for the Jewish people who longed to go to Israel. He urged every person to contribute as much as possible to this cause. President Bragin's other major concerns were the conditions of the cemetery, synagogue and Sunday school. He also urged the community to increase the salary of the rabbi because he was grossly underpaid.

Rabbi Zielonka urged the congregation to come alive and to put aside the lethargy of the depression years and the war years. He courageously evaluated the current condition of the congregation and the facilities and said, "...For a number of years we have seen very little real progress in our Temple." He said that we have added new members but not because of a substantial drive by the congregation. In fact a new member committee didn't even exist, although the Jewish population of Tampa had grown greatly. When money was plentiful, no one tried to create a substantial building fund. When money was easily raised, no one attempted to create new facilities, although the physical structure had deteriorated to the point where the electrical wiring was rotting and where there were constant leaks in the facility. He said, "... unless our temple becomes more alive to its responsibilities and more adequately provides for its Rabbi, I would feel impelled (much against my own wishes, I assure you) to find another pulpit." He could not even provide adequately for his own family although he had seventeen years of seniority over every other Rabbi or Jewish organization director in Tampa. He was forced to carry a full load at the University of Tampa in order to provide for his family.

It was the straightforward statement

of problems of the congregation by both President Bragin and Rabbi Zielonka which led to the revitalization of the first synagogue in Tampa and the creation of the vibrant congregation which it is today.

1957- 2004

On January 26,1957, the present temple structure groundbreaking took place. Schaarai Zedek resolved its numerous structural problems by opening its new facility at 3303 Swann Avenue. This structure contains the cornerstones from the first building built in 1899 and the one built in 1924 located at Delaware Avenue and De Leon Street. Rabbi Zielonka served as spiritual leader until 1970. Rabbi Frank N. Sundheim became associate Rabbi in 1967. He became senior rabbi in 1970 and served until 1986. Rabbi Richard J. Birnholz became senior rabbi in 1986 and has served until the present. Rabbi, Mark Strauss-Cohn, was appointed Assistant Rabbi in July 1998.

Congregation Rodeph Sholom of Tampa

Congregation Rodeph Sholom was formed in 1903, as a result of the split with members of Congregation Schaarai Zedek and the court trial that followed. A meeting was held in the home of J. L. Mairson, at which time twenty families, who wanted to follow conservative practices and rituals, became the founders of Congregation Rodeph Sholom. This new synagogue went through a period of rapid growth at the turn of the century, when an increasing number of Jewish families came to Tampa. Rodeph Sholom was orthodox for many years before joining the Conservative Movement. The first synagogue building was on Palm Avenue in 1903 and in 1909, a larger structure was built on the same premises with the original building being used for Religious School.

In 1912, Rabbi Shaso married Louis Frank of Clearwater to Annie Levy of New York. In 1925, a new synagogue was completed at a cost of $85,000 and seated 250 people. From 1903-1943, six rabbis served the congregation beginning with Rabbi Julius Hess in 1903. Rabbi Adolph Burger served the longest, first in 1923 and from 1930-1942 until his death at age fifty two. Rabbi Benjamin Eisenberg was then appointed. In 1917, the Ladies Auxiliary of Congregation Rodeph Sholom, the forerunner of Sisterhood, was founded. In 1918, the Religious School was reorganized with four girls and one boy, who became the first confirmation class. In 1924, Rabbi Burger organized a choir of seventeen young people. By the 1930s, Hebrew classes were being taught three times a week.

During the depression, Sabbath services were extremely well attended. Of approximately 175 families, 100-125 individuals regularly attended services on Saturday mornings. During World War II, under the guidance of Rabbi Benjamin Eisenberg, congregational life functioned well. There was a sense of family within the congregation. Everyone knew that their friends would be present at the services.

Rabbi Henry Wernick was in the pulpit from 1947-1953. He also acted as a cantor. In the mid-1950s, Rabbi Jerome Kestenbaum helped the Sisterhood and the Men's Club become very successful. There were many Sisterhood sponsored dances, model seders, other kinds of parties, and home-based cultural programs and book reviews following Shabbat services. The Men's Club reached a peak in the fifties. Typically 200-250 men attended monthly meetings. People came for the food and the fellowship.

In 1959, Rabbi Stanley Kazan became the spiritual leader until 1973. In order to provide what he called a "living faith", he organized a junior congregation, an adult bible study group, expanded adult education, and held a training program for prospective teachers in the congregation. He established the Institute of Adult Jewish Studies and was assisted in presenting a series of courses including Beginning Hebrew, Conducting Morning Services, Understanding Your Religion, and the Bible Speaks to Us, by Cantor William Hauben and Raphael Pellach. Rabbi Kazan was also instrumental in establishing the Hillel School of Tampa. During his service, the land for the current synagogue was purchased in 1964 and the congregation had its new home in 1969.

In the sixties, the first Interfaith Tea and the First Annual Jewish Music Festival occurred. Rabbi Sanford Hahn followed in 1973. He initiated the chavurah movement. There is now a preschool, the Irving Cohen Center, where the children start their Jewish education. Rabbi Hahn felt that, "The job of the synagogue was to motivate families to live more Jewishly, and to help people grow personally and in groups."

Some of the greatest changes in the 1970s related to women. Women were granted the right to participate in the minyan and to become B'nai Mitzvah. Women were allowed to carry the Torah around the sanctuary on Simchat Torah. Women were now present on the bimah and recited the Torah and Haftorah blessings.

In 1979, Rabbi Martin Sandberg became the spiritual leader. In 1981, Rabbi Kenneth Berger assumed the pulpit. He and his wife, Eviva, died in a plane crash in 1989. Rabbis Hillel Miligram and Arthur Lavinisky followed. They tried to maintain the balance between tradition and change. Rabbi Marc Sack is currently the congregational spiritual leader since 1995. The congregation has always struggled with key issues of synagogue life. The central issue in the early years, much as it is now, was to make worship attractive and enlightening to the congregants without sacrificing central traditions and rituals. The congregation continues to work on blending tradition and change.

Congregation Beth Israel

Congregation Beth Israel was founded in 1917 as the Hebrew Free School. It later changed its name to Knesseth Yisrael.

In 1924, the Young Men's Hebrew Association was founded. It occupied the structure that had been originally used by the German-American Club founded in 1901. The YMHA lasted from 1924 to 1944 and was a forerunner of the Jewish Community Center now located on Community Campus Drive.

CHAPTER 5

PINELLAS COUNTY HISTORY

Pre-History

The word Pinellas comes from the Spanish words Punta Pinal meaning "point of pines." The peninsula was inhabited by Tocobagan Indians, an agricultural tribe living in this area for hundreds of years, until the Spanish arrived. Around 1000 A.D., was the height of their civilization in the Safety Harbor area. They grew squash, corn, pumpkins and sweet potatoes. They gathered wild grapes and supplemented their diet with wild game and seafood. Indian mounds were found in Safety Harbor, near Bay Pines, and along Pinellas Point from the old ferry site to Eckerd College.

In 1528, Clearwater was discovered by Panfilo de Narvaez. He was looking for gold and silver, but instead left a massive path of destruction among the Indians. He and his men treated them cruelly, ransacking their homes, and pillaging their ceremonial mounds. He was followed in 1539 by Hernando de Soto who established a base camp on what was formerly Indian land. This occurred thirty seven years before St. Augustine was founded. By the 1570s, a Jesuit mission was established among the Tocobagan Indians at Safety Harbor. The mission was later massacred by the Indians. By 1710, the Tocobagan civilization in Florida was destroyed by disease and by attacks from other Indian tribes sponsored by the British. The Pinellas Peninsula became largely unoccupied.

In 1745, Capt. David Cutler led a British exhibition to map and survey the Pinellas Peninsula and the surrounding areas. In 1757, Jose Jimenez, a Spanish naval officer, named this area, "Punta del Pinal" or Point of Pines, which became the word Pinellas. He developed one of the first charted maps of the area. In 1765, an English chart maker, George Gauld, detailed the land further. On the chart he wrote "a pretty good place for a settlement." There were many pirates along the coastline, including the infamous Captain Gomez. The area also was visited by Spanish and Cuban fishermen who came ashore to fill their water containers with fresh water from the springs.

Colonial Times

After the American Revolutionary War (1776-1783), Spain regained control of Florida from Britain as part of the Treaty of Paris. The Spanish government gave land grants to people who would come to Florida. Even the Seminole Indians were encouraged to set up farms. Escaped slaves came to Florida where their U. S. masters had no authority over them. The Spanish hoped that these new people would create a buffer between the United States and Spanish Florida. However, the area became more American than Spanish.

In the 18th century, Creek Indians, who had been displaced by white settlers in the Southeast, moved southward to Florida and became known as Seminole Indians. Cuban fishermen in search of mullet set up temporary camps on shore to process the fish. They were later joined by fugitive African-American slaves who worked in the Cuban fish camps. The U. S. Army was sent to burn the camps between Tampa Bay and Charlotte Harbor and captured about 300 fugitive slaves. Many of the coastal settlers fled to the Florida Keys or the Bahamas.

1800-1820

During the time Britain controlled Florida, the British often incited the Seminoles to attack American settlers who were migrating into their territory. This, along with the fact that the Seminoles accepted escaped black slaves, created a lot of anger. The U.S. Army, in response, attacked the Seminoles and the result was the First Seminole War of 1817-1818, fought in Florida and Southern Georgia. General Andrew Jackson, a hero of the battle of New Orleans, received orders on December 26 to subdue the Seminole (the Spanish word for runaways) Indians around the West Florida border.

1820-1840

The United States did not want to have a foreign country own land next to the Georgia border and pressured Spain to give up its profitless colony through the Adams-Onis Treaty, signed in 1821. It gave East Florida and West Florida to the United States in exchange for assuming $5 million in claims against Spain.

In 1821, David Levy Yulee engineered a scheme for building railroads which made Florida's growth and development possible. This was the first of many railroads that he was responsible for building.

The Indians signed the Treaty of Camp Moultrie with the United States and agreed to move to a reservation which was south of Ocala and north of the Charlotte River. This was not the end of the trouble between the Seminoles and the settlers. The federal government established its first army fort at the mouth of the Hillsborough River to oversee a 256 square-mile Indian Reservation. The Pinellas Peninsula was not part of this reservation.

In 1832, Dr. Odet Philippe, a titled Frenchman and a surgeon in the French Navy, apparently became the first white settler on the Pinellas Peninsula. He set up residence on the bluffs, which is now Safety Harbor. He established his plantation, St. Helena, and planted the first citrus grove in the area.

In 1834, Pinellas County was part of Hillsborough County and known as West Hillsborough. Hillsborough County had just been created by an Act of Congress.

From 1835–1842, the Second Seminole War was fought. Chief Osceola led a group of holdouts who refused to be removed to the west. This was a classic example of guerrilla warfare. A few thousand poorly armed warriors fought against more than 200,000 troops. Over 1,500 soldiers and uncounted American civilians died. The Seminole Indians who did not leave for the West were allowed to live in the Everglades.

1840-1860

In 1841, the first health resort was established at Ft. Harrison on the Pinellas Peninsula, which is modern day Clearwater. It was a convalescent post established for soldiers from Tampa.

In 1842, the Federal Armed Occupation Act gave Americans the opportunity to have 160 acres of land if they would bear arms, live on the land for five years, and cultivate at least five acres. Very few pioneers came to the Pinellas Peninsula during the period from 1840-1880. Only fifty families lived in the area when the Civil War began, and fewer were there after the war.

James Stevens, the father of Clearwater, filed the first of more than 1,300 claims under this act. Samuel Stevenson settled in north Clearwater in the early 1840s. The first of the seven McMullen brothers, Capt. James P. McMullen initially visited Florida from Georgia in 1841, and returned around 1850 to build a log house in east Clearwater.

In 1843, Antonio Maximo secured a land grant from the United States government for services he had performed during the Seminole war. He established a fish ranch at the end of the Pinellas Peninsula. Three years later William Bunce joined him in business and created an opportunity to provide large supplies of fish to the Cuban market.

In 1848, on Sept. 22nd winds from the southwest pushed the waters of the Gulf of Mexico into Tampa Bay. The winds rose to 90 and 100 mph causing all the islands along the coast from Sanibel to thirty miles north of Tarpon Springs to become inundated.

In 1849, the Hillsborough County Commissioners authorized the first road from Tampa to Clearwater Harbor.

During the early 1850s, the seven McMullen brothers, who were of Scottish decent, came from southern Georgia and settled near Safety Harbor and in Largo. The McMullen family had originally come during Colonial days to Virginia. James came to Pinellas County first and bought land in 1853, in the area that later became Coachman.

From 1855 to 1858, the Third Seminole War occurred. The whites aggravated Seminole Chief Billy Bowlegs until he

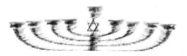

retaliated. The war ended inconclusively with some of the Indians moving to the west and the others staying in the Everglades.

In 1857, Silvan Abbey Cemetery became the first cemetery on the peninsula.

In 1859, the only post office on the peninsula was in Clearwater. It was suspended during the Civil War and reopened after the Civil War.

1860-1880

From 1859-1865, the eastern part of the peninsula was known as Old Tampa. In 1861, Florida seceded from the Union.

In 1865, at the close of the Civil War, only William Coons and his wife lived on the peninsula. In the1860s, Samuel E. Hope became the first landholder in the Tarpon Springs area when he acquired property along the north bank of the river. Soon afterwards, the Thompson and Meyers families arrived.

In 1871, the first black settlers, John Donaldson and Anna Germain, freed former slaves, married and purchased forty acres of land in St. Petersburg. They had come to Gainesville by train and then by covered wagon. They traveled for 250 miles to reach St. Petersburg. They became successful farmers.

In 1876, A. W. Ormand and his daughter, Mary, came from South Carolina and built a cabin near the bank of Spring Bayou. In 1877, Joshua Boyer sailed into the Anclote River. He married Mary, who named the area Tarpon Springs because of all the tarpon in the bayou waters.

In 1878, E. Neeld opened the first general store at Pinellas Village. Customers came by boat, including those from Cuba and Key West.

In 1879, It took Gen. John C. Williams a month to travel with his family in four covered wagons from Gainesville to the Pinellas Peninsula because of the primitive state of transportation. Cotton and cattle were the only things that brought money into the area. Every farm had a small seedling orange growth, but the farmers were unable to market the citrus because of the lack of transportation.

1880-1900

In the 1880s, social organizations were created by family and clan connections. Tourism was in its neophyte years. The Orange View Hotel was built in 1880 and was the start of tourists coming to the community.

In 1881, Hamilton Disston started the first real estate development by purchasing four million acres of land from the state of Florida. He built the first hotel in St. Petersburg and a group of stores.

In 1884, Henry Bradley Plant's South Florida Railroad complex completed construction of a railroad from Kissimmee to Tampa. Plant's South Florida Railroad put Tampa on the map and connected the sparsely populated West Coast with the rest of the world. David Levy Yulee, Henry Plant and Henry Flagler,(East Coast railroads) built the railroad systems in the state of Florida.

Henry Flagler

Henry Flager was the co-founder of Standard Oil as well as a New York railroad magnate. He launched the snowbird phenomenon in the 1880s after his honeymoon in St. Augustine. He was disappointed with the lack of quality accommodations so he commissioned the architects John Carrere and Thomas Hastings to design an opulent hotel off of the main square. The Ponce de Leon Hotel, now Flagler College, was built in the Spanish Renaissance style with colonnades and open courtyards. It opened in 1887. It had Tiffany stained-glass windows, tile mosaics, and terra-cotta relief work on the walls and ceilings. Henry Flagler and Henry Plant not only wanted to move goods and corner the lucrative Cuba trade, but they wanted to develop tourism, which they felt was a tremendous financial resource for the future. They built the first hotels that tourists would ride the trains to see, and where they would spend their money. Initially, the people who came to Florida came because of their health. The pleasant weather would help them recover. They lived in spartan to comfortable accommodations. The two Henrys wanted to attract people with lots of money who travel for pleasure. They built beautiful hotels with all types of activities so that the visitors would never have to leave the grounds. They created the image of Florida as a comfortable, pleasurable, and even utopian destination. Despite hurricanes and erratic business cycles, their vision has succeeded.

1884-1885

The St. Petersburg Times started on Jul. 25, 1884 in Dunedin and was known as the West Hillsborough Times. In 1885, at an American Medical Society Convention Dr. W. C. Bibber of Baltimore, Maryland, a nationally known physician, praised Clearwater and the surrounding areas for its healthy living conditions.

Tarpon Springs

In 1887, Tarpon Springs became the first incorporated city on the Pinellas peninsula. The Orange Belt Railroad arrived on the Peninsula at Tarpon Springs bypassing the older settlement of Anclote. Many wealthy Philadelphians came to Tarpon Springs for sportfishing. The area was promoted as a sport and water resort, even though it was remote from the rest of Florida. The Tropical and Tarpon Hotels were built to accommodate tourists. Tarpon Springs was now cosmopolitan with grand hotels, opera, band concerts, famous artists and plays. Since the Key West sponge industry had suffered because of bad weather and the threat of the Spanish-American war, the Bahamians and Cubans were invited to come to Tarpon Springs to build a sponge exchange on the docks.

Tarpon Springs Avenue Looking West

St. Petersburg

In 1888, the Orange Belt Railroad reached St. Petersburg. It was completed by Peter A. Demens, a Russian immigrant. St. Petersburg became a settlement, with a total of thirty people. All of the small communities along the railroad prospered including Tarpon Springs, Palm Harbor, Ozona, Clearwater, Largo, and St. Petersburg. According to the Federal Census, in 1890, the population of St. Petersburg was 273 people with most living around 9th Street. The fishing industry grew rapidly as a result of the beginning of the operation of the Tampa Bay Ice Company. By 1900, 250 fishermen shipped over three million pounds of fish a year. In St. Petersburg, the ladies of the village raised money to build a wooden sidewalk on Central Avenue from 9th Street to the bay. It was the first recorded public improvement in St. Petersburg history.

In 1892, St. Petersburg was incorporated and became a summer resort. The vote was fifteen for incorporation and eleven against. It was ratified by the state legislature in 1893.

In 1894-95, the freeze and storm were the coldest days in Florida history. The citrus crops were destroyed and many groves were killed. Many growers and gardeners lost their entire income. Farmers diversified into other types of crops. Florida citrus growers moved south to areas like the moderate Pinellas Peninsula.

In 1896, Frank A. Davis, a Philadelphia publisher, publicized St. Petersburg as the future Chicago of the South, in a 132 page book pushing the Pinellas Peninsula for the relief of many diseases and the prevention of others.

In 1897, in St. Petersburg, there were three general stores, a jewelry shop, a novelty store, two drugstores, a barber shop, a bicycle store, a livery stable, an ice company, a cigar factory, a steam laundry, a tailor, two bakeries, two millinery shops, a blacksmith, a wheelwright, a sawmill, several hotels and boardinghouses, an opera house, five doctors, two lawyers, a dentist, and a funeral home.

There were special excursion fares from Wisconsin to Tampa Bay for $38. You could then take a boat across Tampa Bay to St. Petersburg. Upon arrival, you would hear mockingbirds singing and the air was heavy with the fragrance of magnolias and jasmine. The orange groves were irresistible. St. Petersburg also received electric service.

In 1898, because of preparations for a conflict with Spain in Cuba, Mullet Key and Edgemont Key were fortified with coastal artillery units. On August 12, after Spain's surrender, the United States occupied Cuba and returning soldiers spend ten days at a 1,000 tent hospital in a quarantine station on Edgemont Key.

In 1899, a waterworks system was voted on by the citizens of St. Petersburg and the first reservoirs were established at Mirror Lake. The first public telephone system was established (some people believe it was 1898).

Clearwater

In 1891, Clearwater was incorporated. The Bellevue Biltmore was completed by Henry B. Plant. It was the largest occupied wooden structure in the world and did more to promote the area as a first class resort and elevate the class of visitors than any other single structure. It was supposed to be the focal point of a new model city. The Plant railroad system brought more and more people to the Clearwater area. Morton F. Plant, his son, oversaw the project after his father died.

Dunedin

The city of Dunedin was settled by cotton farmers and it was originally called Jonesboro. In 1882, two merchants from Edinburgh, Scotland opened a store and petitioned the government to establish a post office. They called the area Dunedin. Wealthy mid-westerners joined them and developed a fancy winter social life. They built mansions, organized the Dunedin Yacht Club and bought land to keep outsiders away. The city was incorporated in 1899 to keep hogs from forging freely. In February 1924, Dunedin joined the Florida land boom. A large tract of land bounding Edgewater Drive was purchased and other land development was platted. In 1925, a subdivision opened and plans for a golf course were announced. A 1,500 acre tract of land north of Dunedin was sold for

development purposes. The Kellogg cereal company invested in land to be developed as Dunedin Isles. A 200 man crew cleared land, surveyed, platted, and promoted Dunedin. Trains and buses brought people from the north with money to spend. By January 1926, the $3 million value of the land project had risen to $63 million. By 1928, large numbers of properties were delinquent and Dunedin Isles was left with palm-lined streets, an attractive residential waterfront, a number of large homes, the Dunedin Country Club golf course and what was left of the Florida boom. In 1967, the city had its first Scottish Festival and Games.

Clearwater Railroad Station

1900-1920 in Pinellas County

In the 1900 Census, there were 1,573 people in St. Petersburg. The Clearwater population was 343. The Dunedin population was 113. The Tarpon Springs population was 541. Tourists were attracted to the Pinellas County area. The first hotel was established on Pass-a-Grille. In Clearwater an ice plant was built and a water main was installed providing the city with its first water system.

In 1901, St. Petersburg was still a sleepy village with no paved streets or sidewalks.

In 1902, in St. Petersburg, the first tourist society was organized by winter residents from Illinois. In Clearwater, the waterfront was developed and a recreational pavilion and public dock were built.

In 1903, a telephone exchange was established in Clearwater and St. Petersburg was incorporated as a city by the state legislature.

In 1904, electric street car service started in St. Petersburg. It was extended from

Tampa Bay to Boca Ciega Bay in 1913.

In 1905, the former Disston City, later known as Gulfport, was dedicated, but not incorporated, as Veterans City. It was a place for Civil War veterans to retire. A casino was built along the waterfront near a pier. In Clearwater, an electric light franchise was awarded.

Largo

On June 6, Largo became a city. It was established in 1888, when it became a railroad midpoint between Clearwater and St. Petersburg for farmers and grove owners to bring produce to be shipped to market. Women weren't allowed on the streets without an escort after 9 in the evening. Drivers could be fined $5 and given three days in jail for going over the eight mile speed limit. The area was extremely rural and until the 1950s and 1960s, was the largest citrus shipping point in Florida. A killing freeze, rising taxes, and increased land values changed it from rural to urban.

Greeks of Tarpon Springs

In 1905, a Greek sponge diver, John M. Cocoris, from New York, was hired for sponge harvesting. He was encouraged to bring Greek divers from the Aegean Sea, who were experienced spongers. They brought their own equipment and built sponge boats. Using diving suits they harvested rich sponge beds at depths of 30 to 130 feet. They made a substantial profit, which encouraged people from small Greek villages to come to America and Tarpon Springs. It became a Greek Village with a Greek culture. The sponge exchange in Tarpon Springs was created and on Tuesday and Friday mornings auctions were held. Louis Pappas came to Tarpon Springs in 1904 with his father. In World War I, he was the chef for Gen. John Pershing. In 1925, with his wife he opened the Riverside Café opposite the sponge docks. In 1975, the Pappas family consolidated their efforts in a new two-story restaurant on the docks. The city became a site for the Greek Orthodox Church. In 1947, the sponge industry was hit by the red tide, wiping out much of the original economic base. Tarpon Springs became a tourist community.

1906

The Brantley Pier was torn down and was replaced by the 3,000 ft. Electric Pier lighted by the Davis Power Plant and serviced by the trolley. A 400 passenger steamer, the Favorite, arrived at the port on October 17. The old pier was close to the current Municipal Pier. On June 6, Governor N. B. Broward approved a Florida legislative act incorporating the municipality of Largo. On November 25, the St. Petersburg Times published a hotel register identifying 675 rooms in St. Petersburg.

1907

In January a group of motorists traveled from Ocala to St. Petersburg, in a trip that took 3 days, over dirt roads covered with pine needles. On Feb. 23rd, St. Petersburg Times editor, William Straub wrote an appeal, which became known as the "Pinellas Declaration of Independence," to separate Pinellas County from Hillsborough County.

1908-1909

The Board of Trade of St. Petersburg, which later became the Chamber of Commerce, issued a report about the appearance of the land between the two docks on the bay and urged the community to condemn the waterfront property and develop it into a park with a basin for small boats and pleasure craft. In 1909, the improvements were made on the downtown waterfront as St. Petersburg started to grow.

1910

The first hospital, Augusto Hospital, now the Bayfront Medical Center, opened. The St. Petersburg Times sent newspapers to the entire state legislature to try to get them to declare Pinellas County a separate entity. On June 24, much of downtown Clearwater was destroyed by a fire which consumed many of the buildings on the north side of Cleveland Street. The Clearwater Fire Department was established and fire codes similar to those in other cities across the country were put into effect. New buildings were built and bond issues were utilized to construct new roads, water and sewage. Congress appropriated $29,000 for the purpose of dredging Clearwater and Boca Ciega Bays.

On October 12, 1910 the city charter for Gulfport was drawn up at a meeting of registered voters and was filed on November 29. The first permanent settlers in that area were Captain James Barnett and his wife Rebecca. He died in 1886 and she died on January 25, 1907. The earliest stone found in the cemetery in Golfport was that a Spaniard named Emanual Fernandez who died in 1881.

1911–1912

On May 23, 1911, Florida Governor Albert Gilcrist signed the Pinellas Independence Bill into law. On January 1, 1912, Pinellas County became an official county, with Clearwater as the county seat. At the very first meeting of the county commissioners, there was a disagreement about the location of the county seat. St. Petersburg wanted to be the county seat and centrally located Clearwater was just as anxious to have that honor. Clearwater had control of the county commissioners and out voted the down county commissioners 3 to 2. A county courthouse was built, and there was such a protest from St. Petersburg that the Clearwater-Largo Road was barricaded to keep unwanted visitors away. Torches were used around the building so that the workers could work through the night. Armed guards patrolled because of rumors that St. Petersburg residents would come and burn down the new courthouse. The population of the county was 13,000. Pinellas County became divided into up county and down county or north county and south county. The Mason-Dixon line became either Ulmerton Road or Park Boulevard, depending on who was discussing the topic.

On February 16, W.L. Barney brought a brand-new Wright biplane to St. Petersburg and made the first flight in Pinellas County. Clearwater voted for a $40,000 bond for paving, pier construction, and an island park improvement for Clearwater Beach.

Pinellas Park

In 1913, Pinellas Park was incorporated. It was to be an agricultural community that would attract farmers and workers for a proposed cane and sugar mill. Cane fields were planted. A professional agriculturist came to start a perishable flower business. New residents began moving into Pinellas Park after World War II. They came because the land was cheap and there was room to grow.

1913-1914

A company was formed to bring major league spring training to St. Petersburg. On December 15th, the new Municipal Pier opened in St. Petersburg. The population of St. Petersburg had grown so that there were now twenty five schools with approximately 3,300 children enrolled.

On January 1, 1914, the first passenger flight from St. Petersburg to Tampa took 23 minutes. On February 27, the St. Louis Browns became the first major league baseball team to open spring training in St. Petersburg. 4,000 baseball fans attended the game against the Chicago Cubs. Albert F. Lang brought baseball to St. Petersburg.

1915

Morton F. Plant, son of railroad builder Henry Plant, donated $100,000, in 1914, as an endowment for a hospital in Clearwater. The Morton F. Plant Hospital was opened in 1915. A second railroad, the Tampa and Gulf Coast Railroad, was built through Clearwater. Clearwater was beginning to prosper with schools, a newspaper, hospital, churches, and its new independence as a county seat. Its beautiful homes and healthful climate added to its appeal. Clearwater expanded westward to Clearwater Beach.

St. Petersburg had become an enchanting city. The ride up Central Avenue was pretty. The green benches were for relaxing and people spent quite a bit of time at the pier fishing. Unfortunately blacks were not allowed to sit on the green benches. Orange and grapefruit trees bloomed in every yard and every yard had St. Augustine grass. Flowers were everywhere. The combination of the fragrance of the flowers and the salt air, coupled with the sparkling and dazzling light, made the city look like a fairyland, a picture of health. There were approximately 7,200 people in the city during the off-season and 50,000 during the tourist season. No one locked their doors at night.

The Philadelphia Phillies played the Chicago Cubs in the first spring training game in Clearwater. The Coachman Building was the most modern and only five-story brick commercial building in Pinellas County. It was completed in 1917.

In 1916, the St. Petersburg Times has a special section that discussed the importance of tourism in pre-booming St. Petersburg by identifying all of the hotels and boardinghouses, their amenities and their prices. A $10,000 bond issue was voted upon in Clearwater to help in building a wooden bridge to Clearwater Beach, which was completed in 1917.

Oldsmar

In 1917, Oldsmar became a city. In 1915, Ransom E. Olds, the maker of the Oldsmobile, traded his Daytona, Florida apartment for land on old Tampa Bay, where he purchased 34,541 acres. He planned a model community for agriculture and industry, but not for affluent tourists. It was located at the intersection of the road to Tampa and the Seaboard Airline Railway. His target area was Detroit, Michigan. Excursion trains brought prospective buyers to see the area

Later, the name of the town was changed to Tampa Shores and then back to Oldsmar. Ransom E. Olds purchased fifty eight square miles of land in Oldsmar (named for him) to build a 4.5 million dollar project for retirees from his factory. He sold it in 1923 and it went bust in 1927. When the Florida bubble burst, building stopped, unsold lots were overgrown with weeds and palmettos, and a storm at high tide inundated everything. Many of the houses were washed away by the flood. With the final crash of the stock market in 1929, many of the people put their houses on barges and floated them to St. Petersburg. By the 1930s the only residents lived in a downtown trailer park. The population of 300 people remained unchanged until the

postwar boom of 1946 to 1980. The racetrack reopened and later became Tampa Downs. Oldsmar today is a booming modern community. The population increased from 345 in 1950 to 8,361 in 1990.

1917

The Davis Companies, which were built by Frank Davis but controlled by H. Walter Fuller since 1909, went into bankruptcy sending shockwaves throughout St. Petersburg. The properties included trolley lines and vanished real estate holdings. This was the first major financial bust. In Clearwater, the first development of Clearwater Beach was the construction of the Clearwater Beach Hotel, and the building of several frame residents at the mid-beach area around the end of the bridge. Later during the boom, stucco apartment buildings and residences were constructed in this area.

Safety Harbor

The City of Safety Harbor was incorporated in 1917 with a population of 200 people. In 1960, the population was 1,787, and in 2000, the population was 17,200.

It is at the site of the Indian temple town of Tocobaga, first visited in 1567 by Pedro Menendez de Aviles. He negotiated with Carlos, a Calusa chief, to convert the Indians to Christianity. They built a stockade as a mission for Father Rogel and thirty soldiers to colonize the area. It was first recognized as a health center when Hernando de Soto landed in the area on May 18, 1539. He named this beautiful area Espiritu Santo, Feast of the Holy Spirit, after the church festival that occurred on that day. He discovered the five artesian springs that have been the source of much of the income and importance of the town for many generations. Spring 1 has a high magnesium content. Spring 2 has a high sulfur content. Springs 3 and 4 are of drinking water quality. Spring 5 is used as a water source for the spas. In later years a large Indian mound, from the time of the mound builders, was found north of the springs and there was evidence of many centuries of Indian life here. Spanish rifles and remnants of a Spanish fort were also found.

The first permanent settler was Dr. Odet Philippe, who arrived with four daughters in 1842 (This date is questioned by scholars, since he was already in South Carolina between 1819 and 1822 and records show his presence in Tampa at the end of the 1830s). Odet claimed he was born in Lyons, France and was a nephew of King Louis XVI. He was an excellent student who spoke several languages and was a good artist. He went to medical school and allegedly graduated as a surgeon. His boyhood friend, Napoleon, appointed him to be Chief Surgeon in the French Navy. In 1805, he was captured, sent to England, and finally given a parole if he promised never to go back to France or England again. He was released in the Bahamas, where he learned about citrus, and then traveled to Charleston, South Carolina, Havanna and finally to Florida. While in Charleston, Philippe became a wealthy plantation owner growing cotton and tobacco. He also owned trading ships. In the mid 1830s, he sailed into Tampa Bay on his vessel, the Ney. Between 1834-1838, he was listed as a cigar maker in Key West. He also owned a coffee shop, a ten pin bowling alley and a billiard room.

Philippe built, in Safety Harbor, a plantation called St. Helena, named after Napoleon's place of exile. He used materials from Havana to build his home, which is now Philippe Park. He brought from the West Indies flowers and fruits including mangoes, avocados, guavas, tangerines and grapefruits. He planted the first grapefruit trees in Florida. In 1844, his nearest neighbor, Hugh McCarty, was located near the current intersection of Gulf-to-Bay Boulevard and Bayshore Boulevard. Hugh built a wharf which was deep enough for shipping cattle and produce to Cedar Key and Cuba. Safety Harbor was later settled in 1853 by John D. Young and William Mobley.

Safety Harbor Spa

The five springs, Espiritu Santo Springs, have had various names over the years. Colonel William J. Bailey when fighting the Seminole Indians, captured a sick Indian who took him to the springs. He liked the springs so much that he bought the property sometime between 1850-1857. Bailey was the first person to own the springs after the United States acquired Florida from the Spanish. At one time, it was called Bailey Springs and at another time Green Springs. The resort was first developed by James F. Tucker who built a pavilion, bottling house, and shelter over the springs. After the railroad came through in 1888, a building boom occurred. A brick road was built to Tampa and then completed to St. Petersburg. People were attracted to the Green Springs, which were thought to have healing powers. Many written testimonials were gathered by the owners of the springs and were published nationally. Winter tourists came from other resorts to bathe in the springs. The prosperity of the springs brought increased money for civic improvements.

In the early 1900s, Dr. Jesse T. Green, bought the property and used it as a healing resort. He claimed it had healed his paralysis. He publicized this throughout the country. By 1923, the Espiritu Santo Springs Company had been created to develop the resort. In 1928, a second bathing establishment was opened by Dr. Con F. Barth. It used the mineral waters of the Pipkin Mineral Wells across the street from the first spa. Both bathing establishments attracted many visitors to Safety Harbor.

During the 1920s, there were great plans for Safety Harbor and developers believed they were going to build a vast resort around the springs. The Great Depression arrived and the property changed hands several times. In the 1930s, Dr. Alben Jansik purchased the property and the St. James Hotel for taxes. The facilities were used especially to dry out rich alcoholics. Dr. Jansik had come from the Garment District of New York and therefore had a Jewish following along with his other customers. He also, at some point along the way, brought in Dr. Salem Baranoff to assist him during the winter months. Dr. Baranoff had opened, along with his wife, Lisa, and his sister-in-law, Dena, a health resort in Spring Valley, New York. Lisa was nutritionally oriented and Dena was a physical therapist. The Spring

Dr. Salem Baqranoff

l. to r. Lisa Baranoff, Dena Landis, Lucille Moscowitz, Reva Kent.

Valley facility was very successful, but limited by the weather and the size of the facilities. In 1945, he sold the facility in Spring Valley, New York and purchased the Safety Harbor Spa. When the facility actually was named the Safety Harbor Spa is uncertain. Dr. Baranoff brought with him many of his patients from New York and then the Safety Harbor Spa proceeded to grow at a substantial pace. It was used by many very famous Jewish individuals to improve their health through good nutrition, exercise and positive thinking. At one point it was the largest Jewish hotel of its nature in the United States. In 1961, Salu Devnani came to the Safety Harbor Spa as a low level manager and over the years, because of his integrity and his managerial skills, became a managing director of the corporation. Dr. Richard Gubner, one of Dr. Baranoff's staff doctors, purchased the facility.

End of World War I

In 1918, the end of WWI brought thousands of tourists to Florida. The visitors had large amounts of money from the postwar economic boom. They arrived by automobile and train. Henry Ford's inexpensive Model T enabled people of moderate income to make the trip to Florida. The population of St. Petersburg had grown again and there were now thirty four schools with approximately 4,800 children enrolled.

In 1919, on February 4, a bridge was connected from St. Petersburg to one of the keys, Long Key, for the first time. Pass-a-Grille on Long Key was one of the oldest island resorts in Florida. The Spanish explorers landed here. John Gomez of Tampa ran excursion boats in 1857. No one knows when the island was first inhabited.

1920-1930

The time between 1920-1930 was a period of immense growth due to outstanding self-promotion and the booming Florida and American economies. St. Petersburg and Clearwater become thriving tourist destinations. Developers build a large number of hotels and other commercial enterprises to be used for visitors, especially in St. Petersburg. The housing supply became inadequate and resulted in a frenzy of home building. Real estate became the investment of choice. Automobiles increased dramatically. Road systems were constructed in Pinellas County and throughout Florida, allowing visitors to easily reach St. Petersburg, now called the Sunshine City. One hundred and sixty seven miles of new roads, large bridges, and three causeways were built to connect the mainland with the Gulf Beaches. Gulf Boulevard was completed as a highway along the Keys. The Gandy Bridge, connecting St. Petersburg to Tampa, was opened on November 20, 1924. Thousands of tourists came by train and car and discovered the Pinellas Peninsula. Baseball became a favored attraction and the Boston Braves played in St. Petersburg from 1921 through 1937 during spring training.

In 1920, the St. Petersburg population was 14,237. The Clearwater population was 2,427. The Dunedin population was 642 and the Tarpon Springs population was 2,105. The Rotary Club of St. Petersburg was founded with twenty five charter members. Other clubs followed in succeeding years such as the Civitan Club, Kiwanis Club, Optimistic Club, Lions Club, St. Petersburg Exchange Club, Junior League of St. Petersburg, and many other neighborhood, fraternal, civic, charitable, sports, patriotic, and community organizations. The county population was 28,265 people.

In 1921, on Oct. 25, at 3 in the morning, the worst hurricane in St. Petersburg's history hit the city with 100 mile per hour winds, which blew down communications lines and left the city isolated for hours. Municipal Pier and the Pass-a-Grille and Seminole bridges were washed away. In Clearwater, at the height of the storm, 100 mile per hour winds and 10 foot tides caused severe damage. A tornado touchdown occurred around Tarpon Springs. It caused considerable damage to trees and citrus groves. In the winter of 1921-1922 the largest number of tourists in St. Petersburg city history arrived. Hundreds of them bought lots in the city. From 1920-1925, the total value of real estate in St. Petersburg rose 300 percent. In Clearwater, land speculators began developing large portions of the city. The streets, sidewalks, and other improvements were laid out for structures to be built later. On November 9, 1921, the United States Congress passed the Federal Highway Act, which provided $75 million for highway construction of which Florida received $4.6 million.

In 1922, on March 5, the Boston Braves arrived in St. Petersburg to begin spring training. They were greeted by 5,000 fans at the train station. In Clearwater Beach, L. B. Skinner began a huge subdivision called Mandalay, the island of 1,000 palms. The Mandalay Hotel with 250 rooms was finished in 1926.

In 1923, on June 5, county residents voted to approve $2,863,000 in bond issues for the construction of roads and bridges. During the early 1920s, St. Petersburg spent over $12 million on road paving and bridges to make the city more desirable for development. In addition, more money was spent on the trolley system. A power plant was built.

In 1924, on September 19, the Ku Klux Klan held an initiation ceremony for new members in a field on 9th Avenue North in St. Petersburg. Several other initiation ceremonies had been held in St. Petersburg during the previous months and others were planned.

On November 20, Governor Carey Hardee untied a knot holding a rope of flowers to officially open the 2.5 mile Gandy Bridge, which had an additional 2.5 miles of causeways attached to it. Construction had started in 1922. It reduced the trip to Tampa from forty three miles to nineteen miles.

During the winter tourist season signs were placed on Gandy Boulevard and Fourth Street by organizers of a local Ku Klux Klan branch, "Gentiles Only Wanted-No Jews Wanted Here." Jewish people were barred from St. Petersburg's private clubs and organizations, neighborhoods and hotels. The surging popularity of the Ku Klux Klan and racial and religious discrimination during the early and mid-1920s not only was directed at black people, but also at the Jewish people of Pinellas County. The blacks suffered far more than anyone because of neglect of living conditions, medical care, and the constant insults inflicted upon

them. Blacks had been recruited from 1921 to 1926 from Alabama and Georgia to help build the roads, highways, homes, businesses and hotels. The local black community reached 7,400 or 18 percent of St. Petersburg's population. The Jim Crow system of cradle to grave segregation was not only enforced by the Ku Klux Klan, but was also helped along by the indifference of the various community leaders. Blacks could not use city parks or benches, and all new housing had restrictive "Gentlemen's Agreements" to exclude blacks and Jews. The surging popularity of the Ku Klux Klan during the early and mid-1920's made it extremely dangerous for blacks to speak out against racial segregation.

Gandy Bridge

Jim Coad, the outspoken secretary, of the St. Petersburg Chamber of Commerce, was a militant anti-Semite who called for a return to the old stock Americanism. In his ignorance, he not only failed to understand the positive impact of Judaism and Jewish people on American society from colonial days forward, but also symbolized the hatred and power that a single person can wield, when people are afraid to challenge him/her or go along with him/her because of innate discrimination. The Jewish people socialized together and quietly worshiped in their own homes, as well as in a storefront synagogue. Although many of St. Petersburg's non-Jewish citizens rejected Jim Coad's virulent behavior, the local leaders took no responsibility for the controversial signs and no one would remove them. He became Executive Vice President of the Chamber of Commerce in 1926. Some of the leading citizens of the city belonged to the Ku Klux Klan.

In 1925, people swarmed into St. Petersburg. They came by car and on every Atlantic Coast Line and Seaboard train. Single and married men, single and married women and girls and families came to find jobs, to open shops, or go into real estate as salespeople. Every empty store was soon occupied by a real estate office. People stayed out until midnight. Bands played in front of the stores and there were free bus rides and free lunches. There was a huge amount of construction, including the Soreno, Vinoy Park, Don CeSar, Jungle, and Rolyat Hotels. Golf courses were going up in many areas. Every house with an extra bedroom was soon taking in boarders because the rooming houses were filled. The movies were jammed and the streets were crowded with men in knickers and white suits.

On February 23, the New York Yankees started spring training in St. Petersburg. They were welcomed by a large crowd of people. On April 28, all of Pinellas Point and a large area north of the city were annexed into St. Petersburg increasing the incorporated area by about forty square miles. On October 14th, developer Terry Snell announced the development of Snell Island with lot sales exceeding $7 million. In October, the Minnesota Department of Conservation issued an Immigration Bulletin, warning its citizens against investing in Florida and predicting a terrible crash to come. A *Barons Magazine* article estimated that twenty million lots had been laid out for speculation sale in Florida, which was enough to house half of the United States. Ohio passed a law prohibiting the sale of Florida real estate in Ohio. The Massachusetts Savings Bank Association cautioned depositors about Florida investments after 100,000 people withdrew money. On November 5, the Thursday edition of the St. Petersburg Times contained sixty four pages with advertisement for real estate development throughout the city. The Sunday edition of the St. Petersburg Times used ninety of its 134 pages for real estate advertisements. In December, a convention of the Investment Bankers Association of America launched a campaign to promote restrictions on the sale of speculative Florida real estate. There was a significant drop in real estate sales, developers were forced to stop work on subdivisions, home values dropped dramatically, people lost their savings, banks weakened, and workers began to leave the city. The number of city building permits dropped from over 24,000,000 in 1925 to under 3,000,000 in 1927 and 278,000 in 1932. The bank deposits fell from $46 million in 1925 to less than $22 million in 1927 and to under $4.4 million in 1931. Deposits did not return to the 1925 level until 1944.

Palm Harbor

In 1925, the unincorporated area of Palm Harbor, a thirty square mile section of the county, adopted its new name. It started in 1878 as the St. Joseph Post Office, became Sutherland in 1888, and Palm Harbor in 1925. In 1985, the Florida Legislature and the Pinellas County Commissioners created a special taxing district for Palm Harbor, allowing citizens within the district boundaries to tax themselves for services that the county did not provide. It also set up a means of preventing annexation by neighboring cities. In October 1985, the Palm Harbor residents overwhelmingly approved a referendum to levy taxes for a public library and recreational services and facilities. Citrus growing was an important part of the early economy. Many groves were planted and the packing houses shipped thousands of dollars worth of fruit by 1900. The citrus business was destroyed in 1930 by an epidemic of the Mediterranean fruit fly. Arsenic was sprayed on the oranges and all of the crop was destroyed. The Army was stationed in the groves to inspect all the trucks to make sure that none of the citrus left the area. After World War II, citrus again became Palm Harbor's chief crop.

St. Petersburg Hotels

In 1926, the Vinoy Park Hotel was built at a reported cost of three and one half million dollars. On September 10, the air cooled, 2,300 seat, million dollar Florida Theater opened on Central Avenue. A public transportation bus service was inaugurated in St. Petersburg. The Million Dollar Pier was built in St. Petersburg. The Fort Harrison Hotel was completed and provided Clearwater with its first skyscraper. The Florida, St. Petersburg, and Clearwater building booms came to a disastrous end.

In 1927, the radio station known as WSUN (why stay up north) in St. Petersberg was acquired by St. Petersburg. St. Petersburg Junior College held its first classes in the east wing of the former St. Petersburg High School building. In Clearwater, the million dollar causeway was completed from Cleveland Street in the downtown area to Clearwater Beach. It replaced the old wooden Bridge

In 1928, the Don CeSar Hotel opened on St. Pete Beach at a cost of $1.5 million. Despite the Florida land bust, St. Petersburg had a record 30,382 registered tourists.

In 1929, from October 24 to October 29, the stock market lost $16 billion. America entered the Great Depression. Pinellas County's population from 1920 to 1930 had grown 120 percent and was over 40,000 people.

Gulf Beaches

There was still steady growth along the Florida Gulf beaches during the time between 1930 and 1940, although a major depression had struck the rest of the country. Since industry was lacking in this area, the major sources of finance came from the tourism and fishing industries. Cottages, houses, apartments, stores, bathing pavilions, and food establishments were all created for the tourists, who came to live and enjoy, if only on a temporary basis, the beautiful climate of Pinellas County. Sunken Gardens, a major tourist attraction, opened in 1936. The St. Louis Cardinals moved their spring training camp to St. Petersburg in 1938. Pinellas County received a considerable amount of federal financial help, which enabled the development and construction of Albert Whitted Municipal Airport, a new campus for St. Petersburg Junior College, new parks, new and extended sewers, St. Petersburg City Hall, Bay Pines Hospital and Veterans Administration Center, a causeway extending Central Avenue from St. Petersburg to Treasure Island, a U.S. Coast Guard air station, a channel through Boca Ciega Bay, low income housing, etc.. By the end of the 1930s, economic growth had resumed in Pinellas County and the population had grown by about 48 percent, especially in St. Petersburg and Clearwater.

1930

The population of St. Petersburg grew to 40,425. Prices fell and land speculators went bust. Every major bank in St. Petersburg became insolvent and the investors and depositors lost millions of dollars. The city government had borrowed heavily to finance the improvement of the infrastructure during the 1920s boom. The city was now unable to pay its bonds and meet its payroll. It took seven years to restructure its bonds. Racial friction was high. Citrus was the most important agricultural product of the county.

1931-1940

There were two different economies in the area. One provided by the tourists, and the other provided by the local community. In 1931, cruise ships and the railroads kept tourists coming to St. Petersburg. In 1932, the Pinellas County school board laid off its entire maintenance staff and telephones were disconnected at most schools. Teachers only received thirty percent of their first month's salary. In 1933, St. Petersburg merchants accepted travelers' checks in order to keep local business going. In 1934, the New York Yankees came for spring training. On June 28, the 9.5 mile Davis Causeway Toll Road opened from Pinellas County to Hillsborough County connecting Clearwater to Tampa. After World War II, it became the Courtney Campbell Parkway. In 1935, St. Petersburg received its first grant from the Work Projects Administration and hired people who were out of work.

In 1939, the Treasure Island Causeway opened, at a cost of over $1 million to build. This led to the incorporation of beach communities. Treasure Island became a city in 1938. St. Petersburg Beach became a city in 1943. Reddington Beach became a city in 1945. Madeira Beach became a city in 1947. Indian Shores became a city in 1949. Belleair Beach became a city in 1950. North Reddington Beach became a city in 1953. Reddington Shores and Indian Rocks Beach became cities in 1956.

1940-1950

From 1940-1950, the Pinellas County economy began to recover from the Great Depression. The population was 91,852 people in the county, and 60,812 people in St. Petersburg

After Pearl Harbor, St. Petersburg became a military city and its boom-era hotels were converted into military barracks. Military tent cities were set up on local golf courses. They were used by thousands of military and merchant Marine trainees who arrived in the city. In January of 1942, German submarines were operating in the Gulf of Mexico and in the Atlantic near Florida. They sunk twenty four freighters and tankers. Servicemen continued to come into the area and they went to the barrier islands to guard them. St. Petersburg became a basic training location for the Air Corps. This gave the economy an excellent boost of ready cash. St. Petersburg continued to advertise that it had room for thousands of tourists. During the war, 120,000 trainees visited St. Petersburg. In December, the Don CeSar Hotel reopened as a military hospital. In Clearwater, the Bellevue Biltmore Hotel, the Fort Harrison Hotel, and the Gray Moss Inn were occupied by soldiers. Honeymoon Island off Clearwater was offered to honeymooners from the North as a publicity gimmick. It was reported by all the major news organizations. The honeymooners did come, and local people saw a renewal of tourists. Clearwater started a steady growth which continues to the present. In the 1940s the Philadelphia Phillies selected Clearwater as their spring training home.

From 1943-1945, the economy of St. Petersburg and Pinellas County continued to flourish because of the presence of service people. In 1945, the population of St. Petersburg was 85,184.

In 1946, thousands of veterans came back to the area as tourists and residents causing a major postwar housing and population boom. Social Security and private retirement pensions allowed thousands of retirees to migrate to Pinellas County. Many other thousands of people had worked hard during the war and saved their money and now came to this lovely area to live. The new prosperity allowed large numbers of individuals to take vacations, creating a huge Florida vacation industry. During the war, building was at a complete standstill. Air-conditioning was spreading, although still a novelty. By 1960, 18.3 percent of homes were air-conditioned. By 1980, 84 percent of homes were air-conditioned.

In 1947, on March 12, a new spring training major league baseball field was completed in St. Petersburg. On July 2nd, the steelwork began for the construction of the Maas Brothers downtown department store. It was completed in 1948, and employed 500 people. A new bridge was planned to connect St. Petersburg to Manatee County.

In 1948, on May 3, the United States Supreme Court held that state courts could not enforce restrictive covenants and deeds if the enforcement resulted in the violation of a potential purchaser's fourteenth amendment equal rights protections. An example of these deed restrictions existed in the Glenwood neighborhood in Clearwater, which prohibited conveyance of the property to people of African descent or to any Jew or Hebrew. There were similar restrictions at West Seminole Terrace in Seminole, BelleVista in Safety Harbor, Snell Isle and others. On July 29, the beaches obtained their first bank. From 1949 through 1989, beach property values increased from about $3.5 million to over $2.8 billion. They are still increasing sharply today. There are over 14,000 motel units and 5,100 hotel rooms from Belleair Beach to Pass a Grille.

In 1949, the trolley system that had been so important to the early economy of St. Petersburg shut down. Mass transportation as it was known at that time had changed radically.

1950-1960

The most spectacular growth in the history of Pinellas County occurred during this decade. The population rose 135 percent from approximately 159,000 people in 1950 to approximately 375,000 people in 1960. Areas that had been used for citrus groves and other agricultural enterprises were now being developed into urban living facilities. The demand for waterfront property rose so dramatically that developers started dredging sand to turn parts of shallow bays into dryland. By the late 1950s, several large electronic and aerospace companies began locating their manufacturing facilities in Florida.

Shopping centers were being considered. Shifts in residential pattern and means of transportation prompted the change. More people were living in suburbs further away from downtown areas, which were the traditional shopping districts. The shopping centers were built by a single developer on a single parcel of land instead of many parcels of lands used by downtown stores. The shopping centers had large parking lots and were designed to accommodate large numbers of cars. The enclosed shopping mall caused the demise of many downtown areas.

In 1950, the Clearwater population was around 15,000. Two subdivisions were opening and homes and motels were being built. In the early 1950s, two marinas were built on Clearwater Beach. The charter fleet provided recreation and sport for tourists and residents. The beautiful white sand beach drew tourists to the area. The population and the needs for housing continued to grow throughout the 1950s. Another development was the mobile home. It was a low-cost dwelling, which was especially popular with retirees. By the early 1960s, Pinellas County contained more mobile homes than any other county in the state.

In 1953, on March 30 at about 3:30 a.m., a fire destroyed the Littlefield Nursing Home, south of Largo, killing thirty two of the estimated fifty nine people inside. It was the worst tragedy in Pinellas County history.

In 1954, on May 17, the United States Supreme Court handed down a ruling that racial segregation in public schools was a violation of the fourteenth amendment. Pinellas County ignored the Supreme Court decision and built seven new schools for black students between 1954-1962. The local school system was segregated until 1962. It became fully integrated by means of busing to schools in 1971.

On September 6, at 10 in the morning, the $22 million Sunshine Skyway Bridge opened from St. Petersburg to Manatee County. The bridge was 4.25 miles long and reduced the overland trip from St. Petersburg to Bradenton by forty miles. The St. Petersburg Times published a 108-page, seven section special edition, introducing the world to St. Petersburg business, economy, industry, real estate, government and tourist attractions.

In February 1955, the Tampa Tribune's new television station, WFLA–TV, Channel 8, came on the air. Most of the people worked in service industries for tourists or were retired residents.

From 1952-1956, thirty seven new industries came into Pinellas County. The national manufacturers were: Aerosonic Instrument Corp., which made aircraft instruments, moved from Cincinnati to Clearwater with Herbert J. Frank as President; Air Associates Inc., which made aeronautical equipment moved from Teterboro, New Jersey to the Pinellas County International Airport with Frank C. Godsey, Jr. as President; Babcock and Wilcox Company, which had a design and engineering facility for power-boiler manufacture with C.E.Wilson as Manager; Bee Bee Togs, which was a children's apparel maker from Brooklyn that went to Tarpon Springs with Irving C. Baker as President; Circuit Instruments Inc., which was an electronics instrument manufacturer subsidiary of International Resistance Company, went to St. Petersburg with Irwin Braun as President; Crest Leather Manufacturing Company, a division of Jacques Kreisler Manufacturing Company of New Jersey, which made watch bands, went to St. Petersburg with A. J. Pardoll as President; Futuronics Manufacturing Company; General Electric Company X-ray Division, subcontracting for the Atomic Energy Commission, went to the vicinity of Pinellas Park with A. F. Persons as General Manager; Guild Industries Inc. which made children's furniture went from Brooklyn to St. Petersburg with Maurice Goldblatt as President; Hamilton Standard Division of United Aircraft, which was an engineering and design facility for aeronautical equipment went to St. Petersburg with R. P. Lambeck as Manager; Lockheed Aircraft Corp., which had an engineering and design facility for aeronautical equipment in Dunedin with Ed L. Rider as General Manager; Minneapolis-Honeywell Regulator Company, aeronautical division, engineering, design and model-making facility for guidance systems, near Pinellas Park with M. P. Fedders as Vice President; and Pan Laminates Inc., an affiliate of Polyplastex Inc., which made decorative plastics went to St. Petersburg with Albert W. Ehlers as Manager.

The regional and small national manufacturers were: A-B-C Packing Machine Corporation a branch of the Quincy Illinois plant which made custom packaging machines went to Tarpon Springs with Morris P. Neil Sr. as President; Allied Products Corp., which made windows and other construction components went to St. Petersburg with Al Feldman as President; Carousel Fashions Inc., which made women's sports apparel, went to St. Petersburg with Michael K. Jangie as President; Detroit Waste Works went to Tarpon Springs with Norman E. Gallagher as President; Gator Chemicals, which made cleaning supplies, went to St. Petersburg with H. B. Browne as President; Hazelwood Industries Inc., which made metal working machinery went to Tarpon Springs with C. N. Hazelwood as President; Milton Roy Company, a branch of a Philadelphia chemical-pump plant went to St. Petersburg with Robert Sheen as President; Oravisual Company Inc., which made visual training aids went to St. Petersburg with Jean deJean as President; Pinellas Industries Inc., which made concrete tile and other cement products went to St. Petersburg with W. L. Cobb as President; Sealed Units Inc., which made and rebuilt compressor and pump equipment went to Pinellas Park with James H. White as President; Southern Cutting Tool Company, which made cutting tools went to St. Petersburg with Milton O. Denker as President; Tape Production Corp., which made ready punched typesetting tapes moved from New York to St. Petersburg with F. O. Ruff as President; Tweezer Weld Corp., a subsidiary of Federal Tool and engineering Company of New Jersey moved to Pinellas Park with A. J. Pityo as Vice President; and Tele-Vue Tower Inc., which made tubular metal products went to St. Petersburg with Donald A. Smith as President.

Other categories included nuclear design and regional administrative offices. General Nuclear Engineering Corp., which did design and engineering for nuclear applications went to the Dunedin area with Dr. Walter H. Zinn as President; and Allstate Insurance Co., which was involved in automobile insurance and other forms of insurance went to St. Petersburg with Richard A. Parker as Manager.

Industrial services and supply companies included: Aircraft Marine Products, which specialized in tools and dies went to Clearwater with Harry Saunders as General Manager; Bramlett Tool and Die Company, which made tools and dies went to St. Petersburg with Albert Bramlett Jr. as President, Glace Engineering Corp., a branch of Washington Office Public Works Designers went to Treasure Island with I. M. Grace Jr. as President; Gulf Coast Industrial Supply Company who were equipment and supply dealers went to St. Petersburg with J. F. Wilkinson as President; Helicopters International Inc., which provided aeronautical training and charter service moved from Warwick, Rhode Island to Pinellas International Airport with L. W. Plympton as President; Modern Tool and Machine Company, which performed precision machining moved to Pinellas Park with George Ruffel as President; Rader and Associates, a branch of a Florida firm, who were involved in public works design moved to St. Petersburg with E. R. Lampp as manager; and Smith and Gillespie, a regional branch for a national engineering firm, who were public works designers went to St. Petersburg with John A. Anderson as Manager.

The Chamber of Commerce honored these thirty seven companies, who employed more than 4,500 people with a conservative payroll of over $15 million. Many of these individuals became important members of the Pinellas County community and for those who were Jewish of both the Jewish communities and general community.

In addition to these companies, such individuals as Sidney Colen, Charles and Arthur Rutenberg and Marshall Kent helped build contracting firms that created new, well-built housing, which provided for the needs of the public at a reasonable price. They brought to this community a large number of additional people who not only earned their living hear but made exceptional contributions to this society.

A second span of the Gandy Bridge was dedicated. On June 29, President Eisenhower signed the Federal Highway Act, which authorized $33.5 billion to be spent on road construction over the next 13 years. Of the 41,000 mile interstate system, Florida was awarded 1,164 miles. In December, the State Board of Education established the University of South Florida. In Clearwater, the construction industry totaled more than $1 million and the summer tourist season was beginning to catch on. Local officials advertised Pinellas County in movies and any other way possible.

In 1957, Clearwater was the second fastest-growing city in the United States. The population grew from 15,000 to 33,000 by early 1956, and 40,000 by 1957. The local manufacturing employment base rose dramatically with an increase in military and other manufacturers in the area. U.S. 19, the Gulf Coast Highway, was completed. Clearwater expanded, annexing subdivisions, which increased the city size by fifteen square miles. The Cleveland Plaza, Clearwater's first shopping center was built just before 1960.

In 1958, an Indian burial mound was excavated at Tyrone Boulevard and Park Street.

1960-1970

From 1960-1970, there was a large increase in the development of mobile homes and mobile home parks, which added a substantial number of people to the community. The manufacturing sector of Pinellas County continued to grow. However, retail trades and service sectors were dominant sources of employment because of the large number of tourist and retirees. The population surpassed Hillsborough County. Local leaders tried to change the image of St. Petersburg from a retirement center to a young vibrant tourist center. There were large numbers of civil rights efforts, including sit-ins, boycotts and picketing.

In January of 1960, the Howard Frankland Bridge opened. The population of the county was 375,000. The population of St. Petersburg was 181,298. In Clearwater, the largest industry was tourism. However light manufacturing plants were increasing in number and beginning to have an impact on the local economy. In the 1960s, an increasing

number of single-family homes and the service facilities needed to support them were built for the people who became permanent residents. The Pinellas County Courthouse went through a massive expansion.

In 1962, an article in the St. Petersburg Times reported that St. Petersburg Negroes and Jewish people were still barred from all the better places by unwritten and unbroken rules. Jewish people could not belong to the St. Petersburg Yacht Club, play golf or swim at Lakewood Country Club, swim or dance at the Bath Club, or check in at many of the leading hotels.

In 1963, on June 24, a group of 200 local business and civic leaders from the St. Petersburg Council on Human Relations attempted to desegregate the entire community. On June 27, the St. Petersburg Area Chamber of Commerce, Board of Governors passed a resolution urging all people and institutions to face up to the moral responsibility of equal rights for all people. In Clearwater, the Clearwater Pass Bridge was opened forming a link from Clearwater to Clearwater Beach, Sand Key, Belleair Beach, and the rest of the Gulf beaches, thereby adding to the economy of the local areas. Pier 60 off of Clearwater Beach became an instant attraction.

In January of 1964, St. Petersburg had an unprecedented snowstorm. On February 23, St. Petersburg dedicated its new $1 million, 225,000 volume book main library on 9th Avenue North. In October, construction was finished on Interstate 4 in Hillsborough County, which eventually connected St. Petersburg to Daytona Beach.

On February 7, 1965, the St. Petersburg Fine Arts Museum opened. On May 5, the $4.5 million Bayfront Center opened. A convention with 18,000 people attending was held in the new center. On August 6, the President signed into law the Voting Rights Act of 1965, prohibiting states from using poll taxes, literacy tests, or other means of impeding voter registration for minorities. Bruce Marger integrated African-Americans into the St. Petersburg Bar Association. The first two African-Americans were Fred G. Minnis and Isaiah W. Williams. Attorney Eric E. Ludin, past President of the St. Petersburg Bar Association and Congregation B'nai

Israel of St. Petersburg said of Bruce Marger, "I am certain that it required a great deal of courage for a young attorney to take the position Bruce took during that time in our history."

In 1967, the Million-Dollar Pier was torn down so it could be rebuilt. This was a major attempt to revitalize the downtown area. The Religious Community Services was founded. By 1976, thirty six member congregations, including Temple B'nai Israel of Clearwater were active members of this organization, which helps many people in need. The organization provides emergency housing programs, assistance with children, Meals on Wheels, food banks, free clinics, help with the elderly, help with the hungry, help with the homeless, and help with the abused.

1970–1980

From 1970 to 1980, the county experienced rapid growth and development with the population growing by 39.5 percent, an increase of more than 206,000 people. A large number of younger adults became residents. There was a substantial growth in residential construction in Pinellas County. Over 30,000 building permits were issued in 1972 and in 1973. From 1970 to 1974, construction of multifamily housing or condominiums were substantially more than single-family homes. The county's number of housing units increased by 64.8 percent. The Countryside area northeast of Clearwater was developed and started to boom when U.S. Home Construction built residential, commercial, and office projects. Countryside was later annexed by Clearwater.

Other parts of the county with strong growth patterns included, Palm Harbor, East Lake Tarpon, Highpoint, Largo, Indian Shores, Safety Harbor, Tarpon Springs, South Pasadena, Belleair Beach, and Oldsmar. The boom time of the early '70s, especially in 1972 and 1973, resulted in the issuance of 30,000 permits yearly, predominantly for multi-family housing. There was a huge amount of condominium construction. The growth in population, as well as growth in housing, could be attributed to the maturing of the baby boom generation in

combination with expanded employment opportunities in the area and the excellent climatic conditions. All of the growth and development caused severe environmental problems, including shortage of potable water, severe sewage disposal and waste disposal problems, an increase in need for schools, highways, businesses, health facilities, recreational facilities, and other infrastructure. The rapid population growth led to the development of large regional shopping malls including Tyrone Square Mall, opened on October 5, 1972, with 110 stores located on 71 acres, Clearwater Mall in 1973 (later torn down for a new type of outside mall), Countryside Mall in 1975, and Pinellas Square Mall (Parkside Mall) (later torn down for a new type of outside mall) in 1977. This was the beginning of the demise of many of the small family stores, including the stores owned by Jewish people.

In 1970, the population of St. Petersburg was 216,232. The population of Clearwater was 56,602. People generally worked together very well. However, in the evening hours, various religious and ethnic groups were still segregated.

On April 14, 1971, the new $83 million Tampa International Airport was dedicated. On April 20, the United States Supreme Court ruled that if school authorities cannot create a unitary system to eliminate racial discrimination, the Federal District Courts have broad powers to determine the remedy. On June 2, the Pinellas County School Board voted to desegregate all schools with the use of busing. On October 1, Walt Disney World opened outside of Orlando, changing and enhancing the tourism industry in Florida permanently.

On January 20, 1973, five years after the demolition of the Million Dollar Pier casino, the new inverted Municipal Pier opened. On November 24, the Don CeSar Hotel, which had not served hotel guests since 1942, reopened.

On October 27, 1975, Clearwater's Fort Harrison Hotel was purchased and became the Church of Scientology. This altered downtown Clearwater.

During the 1970s there was a battle between residents of St. Petersburg, who wanted to have waterfront development and growth in the downtown area, and those who were afraid that the taxes would rise sharply. By the end of the decade, the downtown district became a center of culture, museums, performing arts centers, galleries, specialty stores, upscale condominium projects, entertainment, office buildings, and retail centers. The population of Clearwater was 92,180. Largo Medical Center was opened in 1979. David Korones was its first President.

1980–1990

From 1980-1990, there was substantially more interest in the arts and higher education. Museums, marine science centers, educational centers, theaters, parks and other leisure areas were built. The Geological Survey Center for Coastal Ecology, Florida Marine Research Institute, Galbraith Marine Science Laboratory opened. St. Petersburg Bayfront Center had a $26 million renovation resulting in an 8,400 seat arena and the 2,000 seat Mahaffey Theater. The St. Petersburg Campus of the University of South Florida began a major expansion increasing from eleven to forty six acres and building a new $15 million library. The United States Coast Guard relocated to St. Petersburg. Tourism continued to be extremely important to the Pinellas County community. The area became a popular summer vacation place for Europeans. The Vinoy Hotel went through a major renovation. The county continued to attract new residents. The population was 851,659, a gain of more than 123,000 people since 1980. The greatest population growth occurred in the unincorporated areas including Palm Harbor, as well as in the cities of Clearwater and Pinellas Park. The largest population increases percentage wise were in the Oldsmar and Safety Harbor areas. Although suburban shopping centers and office parks removed a considerable amount of commerce from traditional downtown areas in the County, a number of the communities during the 1980's and the 1990s undertook downtown revitalization projects. Thousands of acres of land were acquired for public parks and natural preserves and new recreational

facilities were opened.

On February 16, 1980, a 720 foot oil tanker slammed into one of the main piers supporting the steel superstructure of the southbound span of the Sunshine Skyway Bridge. On May 9, at 7:34 in the morning, another ship crashed into the southbound span of the Sunshine Skyway Bridge, causing the bridge to collapse, killing thirty five people.

In 1982, the Salvador Dali Museum opened in St. Petersburg, with the world's largest private collection of works by the famous Spanish surrealist. In 1983, Ruth Eckerd Hall at the Richard B. Baumgardner Center for the Performing Arts, a state of the art performing arts center, opened in Clearwater.

On February 1, 1984, the Amtrak Silver Meteor left St. Petersburg for the last time, ending passenger train service to the city and Pinellas County. This was the end of a magnificent era for Pinellas County, which awakened the peninsula and turned it from a rural enclave into a metropolis.

In late August, 1985, Hurricane Elena stalled fifty five miles off of St. Petersburg, hitting the West coast for days with 100 mile per hour winds, high tides and heavy rains. Three hundred thousand people were evacuated in Pinellas County.

On November 22, 1986, St. Petersburg broke ground for a baseball stadium. This was the end of many small businesses in the area, including the grocery store of Abe and Bunnie Katz.

1990–2000

In 1990-2000, most of the jobs in the County were either in trade or service sections. A new 150,000 square-foot entertainment and retail center called Bay Walk opened in downtown St. Petersburg. The Florida Holocaust Museum opened in downtown St. Petersburg in 1998.

In 1990, the population of the county was 851,659. The population of Clearwater was 105,436. The Florida Suncoast Dome, the St. Petersburg baseball stadium, which cost $110 million, was opened.

On March 13, 1993, the No-Name Storm hit Pinellas County, causing $500 million in damages along the Gulf Coast. Once again Pinellas County survived and the growth of the county increased sharply.

On January 10, 1995, the New York Post wrote an article about St. Petersburg, saying that it was no longer a haven for retirees, and there was now an influx of young families and vacationers of all ages. On January 11, the Florida International Museum opened in the former Maas Brothers Store. On March 9, major league baseball gave a franchise to the Devil Rays.

In 1997, the population of the county was approximately 893,000, with another 41,000 seasonal residents and an estimated 4,250,000 visitors. In 2000, the population had grown to 921,482.

By the year 2000, Pinellas County had reached a point of buildout. There was very little new land in highly desirable areas that could be built on. The challenge for the county, with 280 square miles and 400 lineal miles of coastline and now a population of residents and visitors of well over one million people, is to build the infrastructure and provide the necessary facilities and services to take care of the residents. More and more mom-and-pop hotels on the beaches are being torn down and expensive condos are being built. The challenge for the future will be to appropriately use the natural resources, especially water, in a productive manner to provide for all people within Pinellas County.

INTRODUCTION

The history of Jewish life in the United States, Florida, and the Tampa Bay area, serves as a basis for the Pinellas County Jewish story. This story is about a select group of Jewish people in Pinellas County, who individually and collectively, made this area a better place to live. It talks about the lay leaders of the Jewish community as well as other significant Jewish people and the rabbis of the various congregations. It talks about their lives, their experiences, their contributions to their families, to the Jewish community and to the general community. It discusses the origins of the various Jewish communities, the founding of synagogues and other Jewish organizations, and the events which shaped them. It is an exploration of the roots of the Jewish community in the north and south, and of the unique Jewish American lifestyle they created on the west coast of Florida. The total manuscript includes factual data along with the little stories about people and events that makes the history come alive.

The author has arbitrarily selected all Jewish people present in South County and St. Petersburg up to 1930 and all Jewish people in North County and Clearwater up to 1950 as Jewish Pioneers of Pinellas County. The reason for the discrepancy in dates between the two parts of Pinellas County is that the concentration of Jewish Pioneers, other than the Blum family and the original Jewish people in the early years, were predominantly in St. Petersburg, with but a few in Clearwater, Tarpon Springs, and North County. Where possible, a short genealogical tree of members of an early family will be mentioned. Chronologically, individual members of this family will be discussed if they lived within Pinellas County or possibly in Tampa, or if they were involved with Pinellas County.

CHAPTER 6

CHRONOLOGICAL LISTING OF EVENTS
PINELLAS COUNTY JEWISH HISTORY 1883–1920

The Original Jewish Settlers

Edward A. Blum

The story of the Jewish people of Pinellas County starts before September 25, 1883, when Edward A. Blum, a Russian Jew, formally applied to open a post office in Tarpon Springs to serve the forty five people within the village and approximately one hundred and fifty people total. Prior to that time, he had already opened a grocery store. On November 27, 1883, Edward(Ed) A. Blum was appointed the first Postmaster of Tarpon Springs. He was born in Russia in July 1839. His wife's name had been Gracie. She died prior to 1880. His daughter, Gracie I., was born in Missouri in November, 1872. She married Mr. Knickerbocker. Edward's father, Adolphus, who was a fur dealer, and mother, Julie, also moved to Tarpon Springs. Russian fur traders had arrived in America in 1747 in Alaska. It was well known that the fur trade in the United States was an excellent way to make a livelihood. This probably helped prompt Adolphus and Julie to emigrate with their family to this country.

St. Louis was be a natural place to reside because of the opportunity to engage in the fur trade and because of a thriving Jewish community. Adolphus was seventy two in 1884 and Julie was sixty seven. In the business directories of St. Louis in 1857 and in 1859, none of the Blum family are listed. It would appear that they arrived either in late 1859 or early 1860. It cannot be determined if they came directly from Russia to a port city in the United States and on to St. Louis, or if they stayed in another city for a period of time. The 1860 census shows Adolphus to be ten years older than his wife, rather than five years older. The Blum family had lived in St. Louis from at least 1860-1880. Living with them in 1860 was Catharine Schully, a twenty one year old, who was deaf and unable to speak. She had been born in Russia and had been brought to the United States with the Blum family. No relationship was listed. Also listed with them in 1860, was a son Edward, twenty one years old, and a watchmaker. A second son was Robert, who was eighteen years old, and a carriage maker. In 1873 and 1880, in the St. Louis City Directory, Edward A. Blum and his father, Adolph Blum, are both listed in a fur business at 1522 Pine Street. Adolphus and Julia had both been born in Russia. In the 1880 census, Edward is listed as a bookkeeper.

The post office was on West Tarpon Avenue. R. F. Pent, author of the book, *Story of Tarpon Springs*, said that "Edward came to Tarpon Springs in search of further adventure." He said that "the history of the Jew is such that on the frontiers of commerce and industry you find him. He seldom if ever goes into bankruptcy. He is both wise and has ingenuity and therefore operates a good business, and nine times out of ten he is successful." It was easy for Edward to start a business and become an influential member of the community because a large percent of the newer arrivals in the area since 1882 were of English descent from the West Indies and didn't care about the Civil War. People from the North came here to help build the town. On June 1, 1881, Gov. William D. Bloxham of Florida signed an agreement with Hamilton Disston of Philadelphia to purchase four million acres of land in Florida. This helped lead to the expansion of Florida and the creation of Tarpon Springs. The Blum family made a great contribution to the commercial and social life of the town. Dr. Robert Blum, who built his home across Spring Bayou, was the first dentist. The young ladies and young men contributed their part to the social life of the community. A few yards to the west of the Blum store was a millinery shop operated by Mrs. George, Edward's sister. She had a son, a daughter, Florence O., born in Illinois in 1862, and another daughter. The oldest daughter married Mr. Platt, the town marshal.

The post office was located between Mrs. George's store and the Blum grocery store, which was located at the end of Tarpon Avenue and Spring Bayou. Edward,

the first postmaster, held his position until November 27, 1885. He earned $275.26 as postmaster in the fiscal year ending June 30, 1885. He was a member of the Tarpon Springs Charter Commission. His signature appears in the minutes of a meeting in Tarpon Springs on February 12, 1887, which led to the chartering of the town. He erected a two-story building in the 1880s with a general merchandise store downstairs and living quarters upstairs. He also built a pier. His father, the merchant, built a large warehouse for storing merchandise at Spring Bayou. In the early days, people had to take the train to Cedar Key, and come the rest of the way by boat to Tarpon Springs, thus the need for the Spring Bayou Pier. This area is now the site of the annual Epiphany rites held on January 6th.

There is no 1890 U.S. census available because of a fire years ago, and only fragments were salvaged. The 1900 census lists Edward A. Blum in Jacksonville, Florida. Edward was living with his daughter, Gracie, Grace Brook, age 6, Gracie's second husband, and their son Andrew Knickerbocker, who was born in Florida, November 1899. Edward was last listed in the business directory of Jacksonville, Florida in 1904, as having a watch repair business.

HIGHLIGHTS of 1900-1920

The first settlers who stayed in Pinellas County arrived in St. Petersburg in 1901, started small businesses, and merged into the life of the community. As time passed, especially in the 1910s and in the 1920s, more Jewish people arrived. As a mishpuha, they formed close ties, and as a religious community, they formed uniquely Jewish organizations, including synagogues. These people, and those who followed, became active members of the total community and helped all people who were in need, not just Jewish people. The story is about people and events. The Jewish pioneers and their original experiences will be discussed in the earlier sections and then there will be separate chapters for the synagogues and organizations. It is recommended that each of the stories be expanded in future histories, in order to gain the full significance and beauty of what has occurred, and carry forth this effort into the future.

Henry Schutz

Jewish people were reportedly in St. Petersburg at the turn of the 20th century, however, the first known Jewish person was Henry Schutz, who arrived in 1901. Henry lived in St. Petersburg for twenty eight years and became a very productive citizen. He was born in Hirschaid, Bavaria, Germany in 1860, and came to the United States about 1881, at age twenty one. He arrived in New York City and then went to Savannah, Georgia to learn business methods. He was listed in the 1900 census in the third Militia District of Savannah, Chatham, Georgia. His date of birth was listed as January 1865. He was single and his occupation was a storekeeper. His year of immigration is shown as 1883. There is some conflict between the two data sources. He spent a short time in Orlando. He heard of a business opportunity in St. Petersburg, which was closed when he arrived. He formed a business venture with Mrs. Lena Windreich, a dealer in hats and notions, and three months later, he purchased her interest in the business. He then opened a dry goods store at 341 Central Avenue. The store had a basket on a pulley. The clerks would put money into it and it would be pulled to the balcony where change was made. He was also located at 473 Central Ave and 4th Street and Second Avenue. He went into the women's clothing business at 551 Central Avenue, a beautiful shop with modern apartments upstairs.

When Henry arrived here, there were about 1,600 people in St. Petersburg who were permanent residents and the town was almost two square miles in size. It was little more than an overgrown village. There was a public water supply, electricity, and telephone service. In an illustrated advertising booklet about St. Petersburg published in 1908, there was an article about Henry Schutz as follows: "Henry Schutz–Dry Goods, Notions, Hosiery and Ladies Furnishing Goods, 341 Central Avenue. As a dry goods emporium, where all the latest ideas and styles prevail, there is no better store in St. Petersburg than that

of Mr. Schutz's, which has been a popular place for the last seven years, and one where a dollar goes further in making purchases than any other place, and where quality as well is a potent factor in the business. One of the largest stocks in the city is carried at this establishment, and prices charged are the most reasonable, for the nature of the goods desired. The store opened in a small way seven years ago, and through perseverance and zeal has grown to its present large proportions, and the customage of the house has grown with it to where at the present time no better place in the city can be found."

Henry Schutz

Mrs. Marguerite Blocker Bartlett, a teacher at St. Petersburg High School and St. Petersburg Jr. College from 1916 to 1935, a daughter of a pioneer family, and a member of Pinellas County Historical Society, gave this article to Goldie Schuster. Mrs. Bartlett said that Mr. Schutz was a respected and well-liked merchant and that she was not aware of any discrimination against him.

On September 26,1908, the St. Petersburg Times published an article entitled "Jewish Holiday." The information in the article was so accurate that it would seem that a Jewish person had provided it. The article stated that, " All business houses of Jewish people throughout the country closed in observation of the Jewish New Year, Rosh Hashana, the first of the year, 5669, computed from the beginning of the world. The new year came with the beginning of the seventh month, Tishri, in celebration of the redemption of the Jews from the long Egyptian bondage. Through history that day had been appropriately observed with religious services wherever the Jews were found. The day had been properly observed here by Mr. Henry Schutz, the only representative of the race in this city, who closed his store at sundown yesterday and will remain closed until sundown today." The article went on to talk about Yom Kipur and the fact that synagogues in the whole world would offer prayers for the sick, poor, and dead.

In the census of 1910, Henry was listed as being forty eight years of age, single, and a lodger. He was a proprietor of dry goods. There is an age discrepancy between his obituary and the 1910 census. Emma was born in Germany in 1889, and came to the United States in 1909. They married between 1910 and 1912. They had no children. In the 1930 census, Emma is shown as forty one years of age and a widow. She was a proprietor of a ready to wear store. Her niece, Babette Fleishman, who lived with her, came from Germany in 1922. Babette was a proprietor of a ready to wear store. In 1929, Henry and Emma sold the Schutz store building on Central Avenue to the Woolworth company, which tore down the building and build a new structure. He had sold all of his stock and he was planning to open a new business. In 1930, after Henry's death, Emma opened up Schutz Inc., an elegant lady's apparel shop. She was President and Babette was Vice President. The store was located at 476 First Avenue North. It remained in business until at least 1960, with Babette serving as President.

Olga Tarapani Manket

Olga Tarapani Manket (Esther Tarapani Lovitz's sister) and Leon Manket came to St. Petersburg in 1908 from New York. Subsequently, her sisters, Esther and Cecelia, and her brother, Abe joined her in St. Petersburg. Abe, Olga and Leon came to the United States in 1907. Leon was born on March 7, 1884 and was a naturalized citizen. He was listed in the World War I draft, which showed him two years younger than he was. He was born in Lodz, Poland, and was a real estate agent. Olga was born in the same place, on June 6, 1885. Olga graduated from college in Lodz, Poland, where she was trained as a pharmacist. She practiced in Lodz before immigrating to America. Olga worked in pharmacies in St. Petersburg but never obtained her license in America.

Olga and Leon opened a dry goods store in the 300 block of Central Avenue. Their daughter, Anne Manket Pearlman, was the first Jewish child born in Pinellas County in 1914. She was ten months older than Tobias. Their son, who was younger than Tobias Lovitz, died of an unknown ailment before age five. There is a discrepancy in Olga's age. She died January 3, 1976, in Jacksonville, Florida. Her sister, Esther Lovitz also spent time in the Jewish nursing home in Jacksonville and died there.

Cecilia Tarapani married Philip Levy, who was the brother of Hannah Frank, the wife of Louis Frank, the owner of the New York Department Store in Clearwater. The Levy's moved to Sarasota and became the first Jewish couple there. The 1920 Sarasota census shows a Philip H. Levy, age thirty eight, born in Russia; a retail dry goods merchant, his wife Cecelia T., age thirty three, born in Russia, his daughter Deborah T., age four born in Florida, his son Abraham P., age one year and four months, born in Florida, and his mother-in-law, Helen Baron Tarapani, age sixty eight, born in Russia. They were one of the founders of Temple Beth Shalom of Sarasota in 1926. Cecelia was the treasurer for twenty seven years.

Benjamin Halaczer

In 1908, Benjamin Halaczer and Yetta, natives of Austria, had a store in St. Petersburg. They had the second or third Jewish business to open. Ben was born on October 26, 1882 and died August 1957 in Pinellas County. In the World War I draft he was listed in Polk County, Florida. He was always inventing things. He was also a locksmith. He came from Europe to Tampa and then to St. Petersburg, where he became a naturalized citizen. He had a gas station and tire store on Central Avenue near 10th Street from 1910. He was a locksmith and before settling in St. Petersburg, had the first Singer Sewing Machine agency on the Florida West Coast. He traveled by horse and wagon to the turpentine camps of west central Florida to sell and service sewing machines. In 1915, the store was located at 652 Central Avenue. They had four children. One child was born in Winter Park, and another in Tampa, and two in St. Petersburg. The children were Max, Abe, Miriam, and Marcus.

Samuel and Esther Lovitz

In 1909, Sam and Esther Lovitz came to St. Petersburg. Sam was born in Salant, Lithuania around 1888 or 1889 and immigrated to America in 1903. He was one of four children who arrived with his mother from Russia and lived for a time in New York City, where he worked in a hat factory initially. He went to Harrisburg, Pennsylvania to join some friends to work in a coal mine. After three days, he became indebted to the company store and decided this was not a life for him, so he returned all his goods. He taught Hebrew school in Harrisburg for six months, since he had been trained at a Yeshiva in Lithuania. He then decided to become a photographer and boarded a train headed for Florida where he planned to take pictures. On board a train, around 1911, he struck up a friendship with Abraham Tarapani, who had also immigrated to the United States around 1903. Abe had been living in New York City with his uncles, his mother, and sisters. Abe was headed to St. Petersburg, Florida to join his oldest sister, Olga. Abe invited his mother and sisters to come down to St. Petersburg. Subsequently, his sister, Esther, married Sam Lovitz in 1913.

Sam may have had a real estate business, was in the insurance business, and had a ready to wear store. In 1915, Sam and Esther owned the New York Supply Company. Their home was at 856 Second Avenue North, St. Petersburg. Abe Tarapani arrived in St. Petersburg around 1909 or 1910 and opened a store. Abe and Sam decided they wanted to go into business together and opened the New York Department Store, a dry goods store in St. Petersburg. After a few years, they thought they would have better business in Tarpon Springs, because Tarpon Springs had sidewalks and St. Petersburg did not. In 1911, Abe opened the New York Department Store in Tarpon Springs. In 1916, the Lovitz family moved to Tarpon Springs. Esther opened a dress shop, The Fashion Shop, next-door to her brother's store. They were the only Jewish people there at that time. They attended holiday services in Tampa. Sam was partners with Abe from 1917-1919, while Abe was in the service. After World War I, Sam went into the real estate business. As a sign of respect, he was called Mr. Jew Sam by the black workers in the town. He even received mail from them addressed to Mr. Jew Sam, Tarpon Springs, Florida. He dealt fairly with everyone, black or white. Sam also opened two dress shop's in the Scranton Arcade in Clearwater. Their shop was called, The Fashion Shop. This was

top:
New York Department Store, Tarpon Springs.
bottom:
Tarapani's Department Store. left: A. Loescher, clerk; middle, Abe Tarapani, partner of Sam Lovitz.

next to Darwin Frank's department store. The other one across the walkway was called the Economy Dress Shop. Unfortunately, the wealth he had accumulated in Tarpon Springs, Clearwater and St. Petersburg was mostly lost in the 1929 stock market crash.

Samuel and Esther Lovitz had three children, Tobias, Julius, and Frances. Tobias, who was born in St. Petersburg, grew up in Tarpon Springs. She went to the Florida State College for Women in Tallahassee, now Florida State University, where she was President of Delta Phi Epsilon, the only Jewish women's sorority on campus. She later became President of the Panhellenic Council, the Administrative Board for all sororities on campus. She graduated at the age of nineteen and came back to Tarpon Springs to teach Spanish, social studies, and civics. During World War II she went to Miami and worked as a translator of Spanish at the Censorship Office. She met Jack Brannen , brother of her roommate and a friend, Blanche Brannen from Texas. Tobias married him and they had a son, Jeff.

Julius graduated from high school at the age of sixteen. He graduated with honors in pharmacy from the University of Florida. See separate entry under Phyllis and Julius Lovitz in Clearwater Chapter for additional information.

Frances, the youngest sister, started college at the University of Tampa in the Fall of 1941. Her education was interrupted by Pearl Harbor. She quit school to join the war effort. She then continued her education in Miami and the Florida State College for Women. She then left to join the war effort in Miami at the Censorship Office and later in Tarpon Springs, working on the rationing board, where she handled gas rationing. She married Phillip Zlotnick and moved to El Campo, Texas, where they owned Zlotnick's Department Store. They had two children, Robert and Terry.

Since there were virtually no more Jewish families in Tarpon Springs, except for the Lovitz and Tarapani children, and since to go to Tampa for formal Jewish religious services was along railroad tracks for twenty long miles, Frances and Julius attended, on occasion, the Methodist Church Sunday School at the invitation of their friends and the minister. Being Jewish in Tarpon Springs didn't mean you were different from anyone else.

Joe and Gussie Soloman and Family

Joe and Gussie Soloman had a dry goods store at 864 Central Avenue. Joe was born on May 25, 1879 and died February 8, 1928. Gussie died on February 17, 1966. They emigrated from Romania and went to Key West before 1905, and then went to New York They settled in St. Petersburg around 1910, because of his health. Their daughter Betty was born in Key West. A son, Louis, was born sixteen months later in New York. Louis left home at age sixteen or seventeen and became a traveling salesman. He was a very enterprising individual who was always considered to be the best dressed man around.

For a number of years, Betty and Goldie Schuster were the only Jewish teenage girls in St. Petersburg. Betty married Harry Fyvolent. Harry graduated from Columbia University with a degree in pharmacy. He met Betty in New York and then came to St. Petersburg after their marriage. He opened a drugstore in St. Petersburg and another one in Bradenton. During those days, all drugs were compounded and the pharmacist was expected to be on call twenty four hours a day, seven days a week. This was so hard and nerve-racking and because Betty was upset with this way of life, Harry and his brother-in-law, Louis, opened a haberdashery in Tampa instead. It was called the College Shop and was located on Twigs Street. He then opened another store in St. Petersburg. Harry was born in Brooklyn. When he was a child, in the evening he sat on the front steps of the apartment building. One of the kids told ghost stories to the younger children. The storyteller was Mort Holt, who in later life became a famous director and producer of Broadway shows, one of them being "Lady in the Dark."

Dr. Joel Fyvolent, Betty and Harry's son, was born on November 27, 1928.

When Joe Solomon died, he had already accumulated a large amount of property in Indian Rocks Beach. He had entrusted the property to a bank. During the Depression, the bank sold phony stock and ended up cheating Gussie out of a substantial amount of money. However, she still owned the GTE building in St. Petersburg. Joe Solomon died of nephritis at the Johns Hopkins Hospital, at age forty four on February 8, 1928. His wife, Gussie, who never recovered emotionally from her husband's early death, died at age seventy seven on February 17, 1966.

Louis and Hannah Frank

In 1912, the New York Department Store was opened in Clearwater by Louis Frank, who was born in Wilcomir, Lithuania in 1873. He was the youngest son in a family of seven boys. He helped his widowed mother run the family grocery store after his father's death. He then went to New York and then Canada for a few years. In 1899, he worked his way across the Atlantic

Ocean on a cattle boat, joined his brother in Glasgow, Scotland, and worked in a bicycle shop until he earned enough money to complete his passage to Capetown, South Africa. In 1900, at age twenty seven, he obtained a British passport and traveled to Bulawayo, Rhodesia, where another brother had a bicycle store. On January 1, 1901, he enrolled in the Colonial Defense Force in Rhodesia and fought in the Bohr War. He served as an engineer, gunner, and mounted infantry man under Lord Baden-Powell, the founder of the Boy Scouts movement. At that time, Louis was described as a man who was 5 ft. 6 inches tall, with a fair complexion, gray eyes, and dark brown hair. He was discharged from the army on April 15, 1903. He had won a bronze medal of Queen Victoria suspended by three bars, commemorating the three battles he had served in. This young adventurer then became a diamond prospector in the Union of South Africa, proprietor of a store in a native compound at the famous Cullinan Diamond Mines in the Transvaal; and then a student of electrical engineering and mathematics at the University of Frankfurt in Germany. While he was at the diamond mines, the 3,000 carat Cullinan Diamond, the largest white diamond in the world, was found. However, because of a flaw, it was cut into three smaller stones, which were all put into the British crown jewels, which are in the Tower of London. In 1908, he applied for a land grant in Canada under the provisions of the Volunteer Bounty Act. He sold the land and went to South Africa.

In 1908, Louis returned to the United States and worked in New York and Chicago until he came to Clearwater four years later. He had $500 to invest and a desire to settle down. He opened the New York Department Store, which was a twenty foot by thirty foot building. He settled here because this was where the train stopped. He was the first Jewish person that the people of Clearwater had ever seen. The City of Clearwater had no paved streets and no sidewalks, just sand, muck and a couple of cars. There were two department stores and a men's clothing store for about five hundred people. The county courthouse was a long wooden building. After six months,

at age thirty nine, he decided he needed a wife and because Jewish women were not available at that time in the Clearwater area, he contacted a matchmaker in New York City. Louis closed his store for a week and went to New York to meet Hannah, court her and then propose to her. He later cut and polished, at Tiffany's in New York, one of the diamonds he had found on his trip to Africa. He had the diamond mounted in an engagement ring at Tiffany's and then gave it to his fiancée, Hannah (Annie). As soon as he was able to make a living, he sent for his fiancée.

Someone in New York was related to the Maas family of Tampa. This person wrote a letter to the Maas family saying that they had a twenty seven-year-old woman who would be coming to Tampa and they wanted the Maas family to make sure that she was properly married, by a rabbi, before they would release her. Louis married Hannah in Tampa on December 18, 1912, at Congregation Rodeph Sholom. The marriage certificate showed that they were married by Rabbi J. Shaso, and the witnesses were Falk and L. Levlfog. At the end of Annie Levy's name was the word Panz. This may have been added afterwards, since the ink appeared to be different and the smearing of the ink appeared to be different. They spent their honeymoon night on the shore of Tampa Bay. They went back to Clearwater by horse and wagon over a dirt road. Her first impression of Clearwater was terrible and if she had not already known that she was pregnant, she would have packed up and gone back to New York City. There was one block of stores and a railing in front of them where people could tie up their horses. They lived in a boardinghouse in one room. Because she was bored, she immediately went to work in the store.

Hannah came to the United States in 1902 from Lithuania. Her sister had opposed the Czar. The czarist soldiers came and took her sister and sister's husband away and exiled them. Because of this, Hannah was shipped to the United States. She was either thirteen or fourteen years old. Two men tried to grab her when she arrived in this country. Luckily, her brother, Phil, showed up and prevented them from harming her.

Louis was an active member of the community. In the early years, because Jewish services were either lacking or at a great distance in Tampa, he would attend local church services to satisfy his need for a formal religious experience. Louis and Hannah's oldest son, David A., was born in Florida on August 17, 1913, and died on January 17, 1989, in Pinellas County. Louis was one of the early leaders of the Jewish community and set an example for his son, Darwin, who in later years became President of Temple B'nai Israel, and an active community leader. Darwin S. was born in Pinellas County in 1919. The home of Louis and Hannah Frank was at 301 North Fort Harrison St.. They had previously lived on Oak street in Clearwater in 1930.

The New York Department Store was renamed Frank's Department Store and was located at 426 Cleveland Street, Clearwater, Florida in the 1920's. The one story store carried notions, women's and children's clothes, shoes, accessories, piece goods, patterns, buttons, etc.. Darwin Frank owned and managed the store from 1948-1975. On Monday, October 9, 1961, Frank's Department Store completed its new edition, a bi-level structure of 10,000 ft. of floor space, which was attached to its remodeled storefront on Cleveland Street. The children's clothing department was now on the balcony. Maxine Frank handled the interior decorating, which included the addition of new glass display cases and clothing shelves. A city parking lot with room for two hundred cars was built across the street from the new Park Street entrance. The store was closed in 1975 because of the economy and the suburban shopping centers.

Abe L. Tarapani in National Guard uniform after serving in WW1, Tarpon Spring, FL, ca. 1920

Abe L. Tarapani Sr.

Abe L. Tarapani was born on February 17, 1892 in Velkonur, Kovno, Russia. This area had been previously Lithuania, but Russia had conquered it. Abe first arrived in St. Petersburg and then opened the New York Department Store in Tarpon Springs. Abe was the brother of Esther Lovitz. He opened a new store in 1936 and renamed it Tarapani's Department Store. His first store was located at the southeast corner of Lemon and Stafford. His second store was at the northwest corner of Tarpon and Stafford. In the year 2000, the department store went out of business and became an antique mall run by Abe Jr.. Abe Sr.'s mother, Helen, also lived with him. Abe Sr. was in France with the 28th division. He was a captain in the Florida National Guard and head of the Air Warning Service for the First Fighter Command at Drew Field, Tampa. He served for sixteen years as the Commander of the local American Legion Post. He built the Post building and also brought the statewide meetings to Tarpon Springs. He was a City Commissioner for four terms, President of the Rotary Club, a member of the Elks, a member of the Odd Fellows, and a member of the Tarpon Springs Yacht Club.

Abe was very active in the Bay Pines Veterans Hospital, active in the Boy Scouts at the county or state level, and was a member of the Selective Service Board for fifteen years. Abe Tarapani Sr. was a very generous man. During Thanksgiving and Christmas, he was the Welfare Association for Tarpon Springs. He not only helped, but also asked other merchants to contribute clothing, shoes, and baskets of food for the poor and needy. He was always there for everyone who was in need. It was said about him that people wished that the world would follow his example of goodness. On July 8, 1960, his funeral was held at the Methodist Church, the largest facility in Tarpon Springs, at that time. Rabbi Zielonka, his good friend, from Schaarai Zedek, conducted the services. His wife, Margaret (Maggie) Mizell, was born May 27, 1895 and died December 6, 1985 in Pinellas County. Margaret was a member of the old Florida pioneering families, the Mizelle's, the Townsend's, and the Hancock's. His daughter, Helen, was born August 4 , 1925, and his son, Abe Jr., was born November 6, 1926.

Abe Tarapani Sr. was able to accomplish so much in his community because Jewish people were not discriminated against in Tarpon Springs. Also, while Jewish people were not accepted as members of the St. Petersburg Yacht Club and Clearwater Yacht Club, they were very welcome in the Tarpon Springs Yacht Club and Tampa Yacht Club.

Israelite Colony

In the March 20, 1911, St. Petersburg Independent, there was an article about five members of the Benton Harbor, Michigan Israelite colony coming to St. Petersburg to see if it would be possible to set up a Jewish colony. These individuals thought the climate was fine and that the thriving city would be favorable. What happened with this effort is unknown.

Abraham and Mary Sierkese

In 1912, Abraham and Mary Sierkese came to St. Petersburg. He was born in Russia on June 15, 1883 or July 30, 1883, as shown in the World War I draft, and came to the United States in 1904. He was a naturalized citizen. He died in December 1965. His wife, Mary, was born in Romania in 1880 and came to this country in 1902. She died in 1957. She worked with him, as manager/co-owner in the various stores he owned. He opened a general store on 9th Street and Second Avenue North, which was the west end of town, and later moved it to 800 Central Avenue in 1915. It became Sierkese Department Store. They also had a men's store at one time on the same block.

Abraham said that when they came to St. Petersburg, "9th St. was woodland, the street itself occasionally was ankle deep with mud and St. Petersburg was nothing more than a fishing village..." When he first arrived in St. Petersburg he liked it so much that he wanted to settle here, despite the fact that relatives in Tampa asked him to settle there. At that time, to go to Tampa you had to take a ferry across the Bay. He wired home for the stock in his Brooklyn store and used it to found the Sierkese General Store. Throughout their business careers , Abe and Mary served the community. They taught their daughter, Jennie, that the most important thing in life was to be fair to others, and they practiced what they preached. They also believed that no matter how you earned your living, as long as it was an honest living, that's what made you a good person. Their employees worked for them for extended periods of time, some forty or fifty years. Abe not only served as an officer in Congregation B'nai Israel for many years but was also active in the Masons and Shriners.

Their daughter, Jennie C., was born in Florida on November 21, 1918. When Jennie was seven or eight years old, Amy Williams, a black woman, was hired to help in the household. She not only took care of Jennie, but also in later years took care of Jennie's children, Larry and Marilyn (Gotfried) as well as Marilyn's children. Amy would go to Colorado along with the family. Amy became a second mother to the family and was beloved by all. Although she was not literate because of a lack of schooling in her early life in rural Georgia, she was extremely smart and both spoke and understood Yiddish. Amy was born May 2, 1902, and died March 22, 1992. She arrived in St. Petersburg in the early 1900s.

In 1930, Abe, Mary, and Jennie lived next door to Emma Schutz. During the Depression, the store sold necessities such as school shoes and overalls. In the 1960s, it changed its name to Sierkese Fabrics and started expanding to other locations. The store was sold in 1985 to make way for a new office complex and parking lot. Abe and Mary were outgoing people who loved to play cards and go to the dog track, Derby Lane. Mary Sierkese was Joe Soloman's sister.

Abe Sierkese.
St. Petersburg Times,
March 2, 1952

Louis (Boston) Cohen

In 1913, Louis (Boston) Cohen came to St. Petersburg with his wife Celia. Louis was born in 1867 and died March 22, 1937 in Pinellas County, and Celia was born in 1880 and died June 30, 1942 in Pinellas County In 1920, they had an open-air bakery on the site of the old Soreno Hotel in the Bayfront section. On Sundays, people would drive to the restaurant to gossip and buy hot bread. When the property was sold prior to the construction of the hotel, the bakery was moved to a building on the corner of 7th Avenue and 9th Street North. Because of Louis's generosity, an empty store in his building was used briefly in 1924 for the newly organized Congregation B'nai Israel. Louis and Celia helped start Temple Beth El. Their son is a newspaper person in Australia.

Other News

On September 29, 1914, the St. Petersburg Independent had an article that stated that all stores of Orthodox Jews in St. Petersburg would be closed the next day for the most sacred day in the calendar, the Day of Atonement, Yom Kipper. In 1914, the Bornsteins purchased hundreds of acres of land in Oldsmar and owned them until 1925. The second Jewish girl born in Pinellas County was Tobiah Lovitz Brannen, sister of Julius. She was born at her parents house in St. Petersburg.

On March 21, 1916, the second Jewish boy born in St. Petersburg was Julius Lovitz, who in 1946 was one of the founders of the social club which became Temple B,nai Israel of Clearwater. Julius met his wife, Phyllis, in London in 1945 and they were married on June 5, 1945. They then settled in Clearwater. He opened the Greenwood Pharmacy at 1012 Cleveland Street in 1947 and retired around 1982. Julius grew up in Tarpon Springs. His family were the only Jewish people in the community for many years. He never recalled any anti-Semitism within the large Greek community. Morris Halaczer was a clerk for Joe Soloman.

In Clearwater, there were two other Jewish families, names unknown, beside Louis and Hannah Frank. A couple (name unknown) had a little general merchandise business on N. Gardner Avenue on the east side of the street near Cleveland Street.

Helen Weber

Helen Freund, later Weber, her mother Rosa, and her father Sigmund, who had lived in Chicago, Illinois and Valparaiso, Indiana, moved to Clearwater in October 1916. Sigmund was born in 1858 in Czechoslovakia. He came to the United States in 1883. Rosa was born in 1865 in Germany. They both spoke German. Helen married Mr. Weber in April, 1920. Helen was born on December 18, 1885 in Chicago, Illinois. They had a child, William Edward Weber, who was born on August 6, 1920.

Aron and Pearl Heller

In 1917, Aron and Pearl Heller came from Boston. Aron was born in 1892 in the province of Grodno. In 1815, the family name was spelled Geller because there is no hard G sound or a letter in Russian. When the family went to Argentina the G sound

Aron Heller and his daugher, Lena.

was pronounced like the German Ch, and it became Cheller. In 1905, when they came to the United States and were asked their name, they said Cheller, which in English is pronounced Heller. Aron's parents, Mordecai and Libbe and the small children went first to Salem, Massachusetts where Mordechai had a sister. The older ones, including Aron, stayed in Argentina for two more years. Mordechai (Max) went into business as a Shochet, a ritual slaughterer, first in Boston and then in Chelsea, Massachusetts. Shortly after Mordechai arrived in Chelsea, he was reported to be one of the founders of the Walnut Street Shul. This is hard to verify because two congregations, Congregation Ohabei Shalom, and Beth Ha Midrash Ha Gadol at some point in time merged into one congregation and apparently brought in a third congregation. They renamed themselves Agudas Shalom, Congregation of Peace. This last congregation is the Walnut St. Synagogue. Pearl was Celia Cohen's sister. They opened a grocery store and meat market near Central Avenue. He was a tall slender man. They brought with them two children, Lena and Harry. Lena married Sam Pearlstein, brother of Mrs. Harry (Lil) Signer, who lives in Orlando. Later Evelyn and Sylvia were born. Evelyn graduated from Florida State Teachers College and became a teacher. Sylvia married Ted Wittner. Aron Heller was the grandfather of Pam Wittner and Sharyn Jacobson Wittner. Pearl died in 1953 and Aron died in 1955.

Harry Hankin

In 1917, Harry Hankin came to St. Petersburg. He owned a fruit market and grocery store. Harry was born in Minsk, Russia on December 14, 1887. He came to this country in 1901 and went on to Hartford, Connecticut. When he came to St. Petersburg, he was a widower and had four children who lived at the Hebrew Orphan Home in Atlanta, Georgia. Goldie Schuster worked for him as a cashier. It was her job to write letters to the children: Eugene A. born on January 19, 1912 in Connecticut and died January 27, 1996, Edith E. (Mrs. Charles Wiebel) born in 1914 in Connecticut, Viola B. born in 1911 in Connecticut, and Alma M. born in 1916 in Connecticut (Mrs. Joe

Keller). Alma and Joe had a shoe repair shop at 6th & Central Avenue for many years. Harry Hankin married Ethel, sister of David Rothblatt, and the children were brought home. Harry later had a meat market at 12, 9th Street South. He died on February 23, 1948 in St. Petersburg. His wife Ethel was also born in Minsk, Russia on December 5, 1884. She came to this country in 1891. She was a salesperson in the grocery. She died on May 5, 1946 in St. Petersburg.

Harry Goldman

In 1918, Harry Goldman and his wife Rosette (Zetta) and their children, Pauline who was born in 1909 and Jerome who was born in 1912 in Lima, Ohio came to St. Petersburg. Harry was born in Pennsylvania, January 28, 1882 and Rosette (Zetta) Irene was born in Ohio approximately 1888. They first came from Cleveland, Ohio to Tampa in 1911 and opened a small cigar factory. In St. Petersburg they opened a dry goods store on 9th Street South. In the 1930 census they were still the proprietors of the dry goods store on Second Avenue South. Harry died in Pinellas County in 1953 and Rozetta died in 1955.

Edward and Evelyn (Jess) Goldman

Ed Goldman was born in October, 1894 in Pittsburgh, Pennsylvania and moved as a small child to Cleveland, Ohio. He came to St. Petersburg in 1919, after serving in World War I and traveling through Europe. He opened his first jewelry store, Ed Goldman's Jewelry Company, at Ninth and Central in St. Petersburg in 1920. Max Davis' store was next-door, Frank Rabin's store was nearby and Abe Sierkese was just down the block. He enjoyed going to the minion (prayer session) at the back of the Max Davis store. His larger main store, The Bell Jewelry Company, was at 529 Central Avenue. Ed's wife, Evelyn Jess, of Chicago was born in Illinois, June 21, 1905. In 1924, Evelyn came to St. Petersburg from the University of Illinois, because her father told her of a very nice man who would be just right for her. Father was right, and Ed and Evelyn married November 10, 1927. Many relatives worked for Ed in his stores on Central Avenue including, May Benjamin,

store manager, and apprentices Aaron and Sidney Mershen, Phillip Benjamin and Ted Wittner. Ed, as head of the extended Goldman family helped one sister buy a house, another sister start a business, and put a nephew through college. He was a mentor to all of his nephews and taught them how to merchandise and become successful businessmen. Ed's formula for success, which he taught to his nephews, was "Keep your hands and mind always busy." Ed was respected by everyone in the St. Petersburg business community. He was elected Treasurer of the St. Petersburg Merchants Association, a position he held throughout the 1940s and into the 1950s. Ed died February 1956 and is buried in Pinellas County. Evelyn died May 23, 1990 and is buried in Pinellas County. They had two children; Jane, who was born October 2, 1930, and married Don Silverberg, and Sanford ,who was born December 27, 1934, and became an architect.

Evelyn Goldman became involved in the civic and social life of St. Petersburg. She chaired many large events. In the mid-1930's, Evelyn helped found and became President of the Judaic Council, which the St. Pete Times, in 1936, said was a very fine woman's organization. This organization became the National Council of Jewish Women in the 1940s and Evelyn Goldman was once again elected President. Through the National Council she did important work in speech therapy for needy children. During World War II, Evelyn and her close friend, Evie Fyvolent, were active volunteers with the American Red Cross and the U. S.O.. Evelyn also sold victory bonds and in 1945 was presented a gold prize for representing National Council and selling $65,025 in victory bonds. Evelyn was involved for many years in the St. Petersburg Community Chest Drive. In January, 1941 she received a special award for her work. Evelyn, her sister-in-law, May Benjamin, and other employees continued operating the Bell Jewelry Company for 14 more years after Ed Goldman died in 1956. In the 1970s, she assisted Jane and Don in their jewelry store. She continued her business activities at Silverberg Jewelry Company until the week of her death in

Harry Hankin, Abraham Rothblatt, Louis Rothblatt, ca 1930s. Photograph courtesy of Margaret A. Dyan.

Ethel Rothblatt Hankin. Photograph courtesy of Margaret A. Dyan.

Alma (Hankin) and Joe Keller, 1939. Photograph courtesy of Margaret A. Dyan.

June, 1990. At 82 years of age she wrote, "I lived a wonderful life with wonderful children, grandchildren, and eight great-grandchildren and great friends. I'm ready to go whenever I'm called. Amen...P.S. I'm called "Mrs. G."at Silverberg's and "Dear" by my grandchildren."

Ed's sisters also came to St. Petersburg. They were Helen, who married Jay Wittner, Ida, who married Lou Mershen, Anna, who married Dave Lobel, and Mae ,who married Joseph Benjamin.

Henrietta and Eva Radzinski

Henrietta and Eva Radzinski arrived in St. Petersburg in 1919. They were both born in Pennsylvania with Henrietta born in 1862 and Eva born in 1886. Henrietta was a widow. Neither one of them were employed. They apparently were not involved with Congregation B'nai Israel since it was conservative. However they became deeply involved with Temple Beth El since it was reform. Henrietta had been active in philanthropic work for many years. She was instrumental in the organization of the Chicago Home for Jewish Orphans and the Chicago Home for the Jewish Friendless,

a workroom for dependent women and a safe haven for their children. She had been President of the Chicago Philanthropic Society and she had organized the Deborah Home for Working Boys. All of her children inherited her passion for philanthropic work and all were interested in athletics. Eva continued her work in St. Petersburg. A son, Major William A., was interested in a boy's camp near Duluth, Minnesota, and another daughter, Mrs. Fred Bender, a former resident of St. Petersburg, was interested in camps for children. Another daughter, Mrs. I. M. Portis, was a member of the Advisory Recreation Board of the city of Chicago. Still another daughter, Adler, devoted a great amount of her time to hospital work in Chicago. Henrietta died in Pinellas County in 1940. Eva S. died in Pinellas County in February 1962.

Celebrating Henrietta's 80th birthday, seated l. to r.: Jane Portis, Henrietta Radzinski, Fred Bender; standing, l. to r.: Mrs. I.M. Portis, Maj. Wilmer Radzinski, Mrs. A.M. Adler, Jack Portis, Eva Radzinski, Mrs. Fred Bender, Edwin Radzinski. Photograph from St. Petersburg Times (date not clear-perhaps 1942).

CHAPTER 7

CHRONOLOGICAL LISTING OF EVENTS
ST. PETERSBURG AND SOUTH COUNTY JEWISH HISTORY
1920–2005

Introduction

In order to not cause confusion, because of the existence of both Congregation B'nai Israel of St. Petersburg and Temple B'nai Israel of Clearwater, and because many of the names of the people and businesses of the various parts of Pinellas County may be similar, the history of St. Petersburg's Jewish community and its environs will be told separately from the history of the Clearwater, Palm Harbor, Tarpon Springs, and other Jewish communities in the northern parts of the county, from 1920 to the present. This is not meant to separate north from south, since the Jewish people in Pinellas County participate in a variety of county wide organizations, and work to create a better life for all people of their communities. Further, the histories of the beginnings of each of the synagogues and Jewish organizations will be discussed at the appropriate originating dates, whether north or south. For the synagogues with an extended history, the majority of the story will be told in a separate chapter for each synagogue. Arbitrarily, the author has decided to discuss the Jewish organizations in either the St. Petersburg or Clearwater Chapters, depending, on where they are located. Once again, where there is significant information available, a separate chapter will be written about the organization. The depth of the written history of the synagogues and organizations was based on the information available to the researcher. If the reader wants to understand the history of a given synagogue or Jewish organization, he or she needs to go to that specific chapter. If the reader wants to understand what occurred chronologically by years in either the south part of the county or the north part of the county, he or she needs to read a specific chapter on that area of the county by years and also read that portion of the various synagogues history for that same years. This may seem awkward, but it avoids considerable duplication. This book was meant to be a starting point for other researchers who will continue to study and write about the various aspects of Jewish life in Pinellas County from 1883-2005 and into the future.

The first Jewish person in St. Petersburg was Henry Schutz. The first generation of Jewish people included: the Tarapani family (Olga and Leon Manket, Esther and Sam Lovitz, Cecelia and Philip Levy, and Abe Tarapani Sr.); Benjamin Halaczer (and later Leon and Lillian, Sol and Regina, Morris, and Nettie); Solomon family (Joe and Gussie Solomon, Abraham and Mary Sierkese); Louis (Boston) and Celia Cohen; Aron and Pearl Heller; Harry Hankin (later part of Rothblatt family); Harry and Rosetta Goldman; Edward Goldman; and Henrietta and Eva' Radzinski.

The number of Jewish people in Pinellas County slowly increased from its origins in 1883 in Tarpon Springs, when the Blum family arrived and participated in the life of the community in a very positive manner. After 1920, there was an increasing number of Jewish people coming to the county.

These new people, along with the existing Jewish residents, helped to create a need for synagogues and other Jewish organizations in the community.

HIGHLIGHTS of 1920

Jacobs Family

In 1906, Hyman Motel Jacobs, of Nomenitze, Lithuania, married Bessie (Bashel) in her hometown, the small Lithuanian village of Aleta or Alyta. Subsequently, he and Bessie and Hyman's father, Isaac, moved to South Wales to seek work. Hyman became a coal miner. The family name in Lithuania had been Probolsky and was changed by an immigration clerk when Hyman's father Isaac entered South Wales. Apparently, Isaac had mumbled the last name and the clerk decided it was Jacobs. Hyman worked in the coal mines in Wales,

Hyman M. Jacobs

until he earned enough money to send for his wife, Bessie, and two of his sisters, Bessie and Celia. He left behind his mother Freda, his sister Ethel, and his younger brother, Harry, who was a deaf mute.

In January 1911, Hyman came to the United States from South Wales and went on to Milwaukee to earn a living and try to bring the rest of his relatives to the United States. He joined his mother's parents, the Goldbergs. In January 1912, during a blizzard, he brought his wife, Bessie, who was seven months pregnant with Annabel, and his daughters, Goldie and Jean, and his sisters, Celia and Bessie, to Milwaukee, Wisconsin. He then brought his mother, Freda, and his sister and brother, Ethel and Harry, to Milwaukee. Hyman, looking for work, had to move on to Madison to work on the new capital there. When that job was completed, he went to Chicago, Illinois and his wife, Bessie, and his daughters Goldie (became Schuster), Jean (became Miller) and Annabel (became Carson) joined him there. Renee (became Silverstein) and Arnold were born later. At a later date, Hyman, once again seeking work in a coal mine, moved the family to Indiana Harbor, Indiana and later back again to Chicago. At some point in time, his father, Isaac, arrived from South Wales. Freda and Isaac divorced before 1920 (date not available, it may have been as early as 1905 or 1906) and Freda stayed in Milwaukee and, at a later date, died there. Isaac, who was a peddler and used a horse and wagon, came to St. Petersburg in 1920 with his son, Hyman M., and his daughter-in-law, Bessie. Isaac lived with Hyman and Bessie. Isaac died in July, 1933, at sixty four years of age.

Hyman, a teacher of Hebrew, was the first permanent President of Congregation B'nai Israel. He was the first Jewish person to be a member of the St. Petersburg Chamber of Commerce. He was a merchant who had a wholesale egg business and sold other things as well. He also owned a bicycle store at 916 Central Ave. He was killed in an automobile accident on January 26, 1938, while he was President of Congregation B'nai Israel. His funeral was held in the synagogue. Many stores of the Jewish and non Jewish communities closed for the funeral.

Goldie (Jacobs) and Harry Schuster

Goldie (Gettie) Jacobs Schuster, daughter of Hyman Jacobs and Bessie (Druckman) Jacobs, was born December 25, 1906 in South Wales. She arrived in the United States in January of 1912. She lived in Milwaukee and Indiana Harbor, Indiana, and finally came to St. Petersburg, Florida with her parents, in September 1920. The first house that she lived in was on the unpaved intersection of 13th Street and 13th Avenue South, which was considered to be out-of-town. Most of the Jewish people lived in or near Central Avenue. Her father, ever a teacher, taught her to read the Yiddish newspaper. Her uncle, Sam Gilbert, arrived in 1921 and joined her father in a produce business. In 1922, she was confirmed in Tampa at Schaarai Zedek. Goldie and two boys were taught by Rabbi George Benedict, who came across from Tampa by boat, to teach the few children who were here. On April 7, 1930, she married Harry Schuster from Wisconsin and had two children, Phyllis Schuster of St. Petersburg and Irwin Schuster of Tampa. Harry was born on January 26, 1906 in Stockton, California. His father was Samuel Shuster, born in Russia and his mother was Sarah Shesolt Shuster also born in Russia. Goldie, at age thirty five, became a naturalized citizen of the United States on February 6, 1942. At that time, she was described as being 5 feet tall weighing 114 pounds with hazel eyes and brown hair.

While First Street in St. Petersburg was the major tourist area in the 1920s, by the 1930s, the tourists started moving to the beaches. Jewish merchants, seeing an opportunity to make a decent living, moved there too.

In 1934, Goldie and Harry became pioneer beach merchants when they opened the first small grocery store on Treasure Island to serve the forty cottages there. They worked seven days a week until midnight. They sold drinking water, since the water was too salty to drink. They warmed baby bottles, made sandwiches, baked cakes, had a newspaper route, delivered milk, raked the beaches, filled kerosene cans, pulled cars out of the sand, and did whatever else was necessary to survive during the Depression.

In 1938, Goldie and Harry bought the St.

Petersburg Beach Drug Store which was next door to their grocery store. They had a post office branch in their business. In 1945, they opened Toddlers-to-Teen Shop, which lasted until 1963. In 1948, they opened Schuster's Menswear Shop on Corey Avenue, which lasted until 1974. Many of the New York Yankees were customers of theirs, including Joe DiMaggio, Lefty Gómez, Whitey Ford, Phil Rizzuto, and the announcer Mel Allen as well as other ballplayers. Most of the Yankees stayed at Pat Sergi's cottages on the Gulf on St. Petersburg Beach. Harry served for two years in the Navy prior to World War II. He was active in forming the St. Petersburg Beach Community Club and was active in the establishment of the St. Petersburg Beach City government. Harry and Isadore performed a tremendous public service when they drove up and down the beach warning tourists if storms, especially hurricanes, were expected to hit the island. Typically the women and children were alone, because the men stayed behind to work. Harry died on July 4, 1955. Goldie was an active member of the National Council of Jewish Women, on the board and Sisterhood of Congregation B'nai Israel, ORT, and the Golda Meir Chapter of Hadassah. In 1969, Goldie started writing a history of the St. Petersburg Jewish community. She had gathered notebooks, clippings, old newspapers, and copies of other Jewish community histories. Unfortunately, it has been very difficult to find most of this material. What has been preserved, has been done so by her cousin, Bunnie Katz. Goldie's lifelong quest to preserve Pinellas County Jewish history is a remarkable story. Her persistence in gathering material and in writing down what she had found is an inspiration to all those who cherish the Jewish way of life. She died November 16, 1987. At that time, she was a resident of Menorah Manor.

Harry's brothers came from Madison, Wisconsin to join them. Isadore came after graduating from high school and helped in the store. Then, Nathan came down with his wife, Dorothy, and two children. Nathan bought a truck from a man who was making crushed shell driveways and Harry and Nathan bought a lot, for $900,

on Madeira Beach near 150th Street, which was full of shell mounds. In the meantime, Rae Weisman, her sister, Isabel, brother-in-law, Nathan, and mother, came down from Bridgeport for a vacation. They were the first Jewish tourists that Goldie and Harry encountered and they became very friendly. The next year, Rae and Isadore were married. They rented an abandoned gas station and cottage at John's Pass for $35 a month. They went into business, worked hard and opened a grocery, a filling station, later cottages, a hotel, and finally a department store, all by 1938. In 1939, another brother, Peter, who was single, a graduate of the University of Wisconsin and a federal government social worker met Buena Finger in Baltimore, Maryland. They were married and bought some land at the tip of John's Pass. They also opened the Hotel Madeira, which they operated until 1969, when the new John's Pass Bridge was built and their home and hotel were taken by the right of eminent domain. It must have been one of these hotels that Ben Bush's parents stayed at, when they came down for the winters.

Harry and Goldie Schuster's "one-stop store" at about 100th Avenue on Gulf Boulevard in Treasure Island, FL.

Goldie Jacobs in the 1920s

Samuel Gilbert, President, Congregation B'nai Israel, 1940–1944.

Samuel (Goldberg) Gilbert

Samuel Phillip Goldberg (originally Kirsniansky) came to the United States through Canada from Lithuania at the age of nineteen. He had arrived in Quebec, Canada on June 19, 1906. Samuel, his wife, Stella, who was born in Chicago in 1887, and their daughter, Fern, went from Milwaukee to Chicago and then to St. Petersburg in 1920. He first opened a bicycle shop, and a year later, went into the wholesale produce

business. Their sons, Jerome and Harold, were born in St. Petersburg. Samuel was active in the Jewish community and was one of the founders of Congregation B'nai Israel. He served in many offices and was President of Congregation B'nai Israel in 1938 or 1939. Stella was President of the Ladies Auxiliary which later became the Sisterhood. Samuel was Hyman Jacobs's uncle and Goldie Schuster's great uncle. The Goldbergs later changed their name to Gilbert. Samuel died on July 14, 1955 and Stella died on August 5, 1970.

Morris Katz

Morris Katz owned a store at 452 Central Avenue. Morris was born on November 15, 1882 in Russia and came to this country in 1905. He was a department store salesman. He came to St. Petersburg in 1920 or 1921. He died February 27, 1958. His wife, Mania, was born on Dec. 14 ,1890 in Russia. She came to this country in 1907. She was the manager of a millinery shop. Mania died on January 11, 1973. Morris's father, Wolf, came with them. A son, Ely R., was born in New York in 1914. A second son, Isadore, was born in New York in 1920. They moved to Miami, Florida, at some point in time. The two sons became attorneys. Ely R. died on March 3, 1972.

Rippa Family

The Rippa family were located in Key West, Florida, and New York City. Mendell Rippa was one of three Jewish men who arrived in the early 1880s in Key West. The other two were Joe Wolfson and Abraham Wolowsky. Although, they were not the first Jewish people in Key West, they stayed on to found the Jewish community. All three of these men had a love for Key West, its climate, lifestyle and potential business opportunity. Mendell Rippa had lived in Jassy, Bassarbia, Romania, which was a capital city with the University and had a very active Jewish community and cultural life. Many of the Jewish people of this community had gone on to New York. One day, Mendell sailed for Tampa, but got off the ship in Key West to survey the town. After continuing on to Tampa, he and his two traveling companions returned to New York and described to their communit

Guss Rippa

the new Israel, which was Key West. All three men had marriages arranged in New York and then returned to Key West. This was the beginning of the Key West Jewish community. Whole families, friends, and community members followed them to Key West. Thus began the essence of Jewish life. David Rippa, Mendel's brother and Guss's grandfather, joined Mendel in the retail business. Guss's father owned the Red Star House, a dry goods store in Key West. In 1902, Uncle Harry Rippa wrote to his future wife Rosie about Uncle Mendel and brother Abe being successful in Key West. They had saved $10,000 in three years, which was quite a fortune in those days. Abe subsequently moved his family to Tampa in about 1908 and opened a large dry goods and department store in Ybor City. Abe learned to speak fluent Spanish, spoke Yiddish and English, and learned to read Hebrew. Eventually, Abe opened a used furniture business in Tampa. Abraham was born in 1873 in Jaska, Romania and died in 1952 in Tampa. Molly was born in 1879 in Romania and died in 1959 in Jacksonville, Florida.

By 1893, the city directory listed over 400 males with Jewish sounding names. The population of Key West was 23,000 people. The Jewish businessmen dealt with everyone: whites, Cubans, and blacks, and extended credit to all people. Because of this, the Ku Klux Klan, which was very active, burned down Jacob Markowitz's store. In 1908, the Jewish community hired their first Rabbi, Rev. Julius Shapo.

Guss Rippa

Guss Rippa, a nephew of Mary Sierkese and Joe Solomon, came to St. Petersburg from Tampa and became the city's first Jewish attorney, after graduating from Stetson Law College. Guss's mom was Molly, sister to Mary and Joe Solomon. His dad was Abraham. They married in 1898. Guss, the oldest son, had two brothers, Isadore and Munos, and a sister Lillian. Guss was born on January 4, 1900, in New York. He arrived in Tampa in 1908, and was living in Tampa with his parents in 1920, before he came to St. Petersburg. He married Hinda Landfield in 1922, when she was eighteen years old. Hinda was born in Crystal Falls, Michigan on March 29, 1904 and died in St. Petersburg on January 11, 1961. Guss and Hinda had three sons. Paul was born on January 12, 1924 in St. Petersburg and died on March 31, 1959 in San Diego, California. Leonard, who lives with his wife in Delaware, was born on September 19, 1927 in St. Petersburg. Sol Alexander (known as Al) who lives in Burlington, Vermont with his wife, was born on November 15, 1925 in St. Petersburg.

Without graduating from senior high school, Guss entered a three-year law program at Stetson Law College in 1916 and graduated in 1919. Although at age sixteen he was the youngest student to study law, he really loved it and passed the bar examination. However, he was too young to be admitted to the bar. He was granted special permission by the State of Florida and moved to St. Petersburg, where at age twenty, he began to practice criminal law. "Rippa Frees Murderer" was a headline in the St. Petersburg Times when Guss defended a man accused of murder and was able to get his client acquitted. He certainly did not like that characterization. Guss practiced law for several years, but decided to go into business during the boom and opened a very successful jewelry store in St. Petersburg. He was following in the footsteps of his father-in-law, who owned a jewelry store in Crystal Falls, Michigan, before moving to St. Petersburg. The Depression caused Guss to go broke, and he and his wife moved back to Tampa. Guss opened a printing company in Tampa called "The Palma Ceia Press." He also published a labor newspaper. The Rippa family date back to at least 1894 in Tampa. Part of the Rippa family came from Key West. The Rippa family may have been the reason the Solomon family came to St. Petersburg.

Sol Alexander Rippa

Al distinguished himself throughout his life. He won a Fleet Appointment to the United States Naval Academy, received his Master's Degree in History from Vanderbilt University in 1948, and his Doctorate in the History of Education from Harvard University in 1958. On June 27, 1954, he married Barbara Frogel. They have two children, Dr. Diane C. Rippa and Joel M.

Rippa. He has spent his entire career teaching and writing. He taught at New Mexico Highlands University, Northern Illinois University, the University of Pittsburgh, and in the Public Schools of Tampa, Florida, and Newton, Massachusetts. He concluded his career at the University of Vermont. He has traveled extensively and is a highly successful author. He has won significant awards including Ford Foundation Teacher Fellowships and was chosen as a visiting scholar at Oxford University.

Peter (Paul) Rippa

Peter attended the University of Tampa for two years before being accepted as a naval cadet at age nineteen in 1942. He was a highly decorated, young naval pilot who received the Navy Distinguished Flying Cross for gallantry in combat. After the war, he earned a Bachelor's and Master's Degree from the Naval Postgraduate College and remained in the Navy. For his Master's thesis he applied Einstein's Theory of Relativity to the problem of returning aircraft preparing for landing. This efficient method to land multiple aircraft was used by the Navy for many years. Commander Peter Rippa was killed in 1959 while leading a training flight of the Naval Attack Squadron, of which he was the Commanding Officer.

Leonard (Len) Rippa

Leonard joined the Coast Guard at age 17, several months before the end of World War II. After the war, he graduated from the University of Alabama and joined the United States Air Force. He graduated from Officer Candidate School and went on to become a Radar Intercept Officer and Master Navigator. Leonard's crew returned the Mercury Space Capsule, that carried Colonel John Glenn into space, to Cape Canaveral from the Caribbean, where the space capsule had landed. Leonard was a decorated veteran of the Vietnam War and received the Legion of Merit, the Distinguished Flying Cross, and the Vietnam Cross of Gallantry with Palm. He retired as a lieutenant colonel from the United States Air Force and went into work for the Pentagon. He was appointed as Special Assistant to the Administrator of the GSA in the Ford Administration. He then became the Business Manager of the United States Chamber of Commerce and then served as the President of the Smyrna Main Street Association, Town Council, and as Vice Mayor.

Landfield Family

There was a large Landfield family in St. Petersburg including: Mrs. Landfield, who came from Russia, and Julius, born about 1890 and died 1963. Julius was a proprietor of a billiard room, and he was married to Dora Marcus, who was born in 1889 and who died in 1963. They had a daughter, Pat Glickstein, born in 1933. They moved to Alabama in 1936. Dora married Arthur Jacobson from South Africa, a successful well-dressed businessman of St. Petersburg. They moved to New Hampshire; Samuel, who was in the United States Coast Guard and who married Margret, a beautician; Hinda; Oscar, who was in the United States Coast Guard and who married Helen. Oscar and Samuel served in both World War I and World War II, and retired as Chief Petty Officers. Many of the Landfield family died in Pinellas County.

HIGHLIGHTS of 1921

Ethel (Jacobs) and David Rothblatt, Chicago, IL, December 30, 1917. Photograph courtesy of Margaret A. Dyan.

Schaarai Zedek of St. Petersburg, 1921–1922

On July 13, 1921, a Jewish congregation, Schaarai Zedek, was organized in St. Petersburg. Rabbi George Benedict of Tampa's Shaarai Zedek, Ernest Maas, President, and Offin Falk, President of the Board of Trustees of Schaarai Zedek of Tampa, were present. They helped the founding members with their advice and how to organize. The officers were: Henry Schutz, President: Abraham Sierkese, Vice President; Morris Katz, Treasurer; Saul Dayan, Secretary; Benjamin Halaczer, Chairman, Trustees; Harry Hankin, Trustee; and Joe Solomon, Trustee. The group met the following Thursday at 2:00 P.M., at the residence of Henry Schutz, 551 Central Avenue. They arranged for temporary quarters for the synagogue and discussed the arrangements for building a new synagogue in the future. All members and other interested people were cordially

invited to attend this meeting. Rabbi George Benedict came from Tampa to participate in the meeting. He was particularly interested in having the Jewish children present. Since a rabbi is primarily a teacher, his great interest was in teaching the children. It was a true labor of love for Rabbi Benedict to come from Tampa, since the Gandy Bridge had not been built yet, and it was a long and difficult trip. The Board of Trustees of Schaarai Zedek of Tampa on June 29, 1921 had approved the acquiring of Rabbi Benedict from at least November,1921 through March, 1922 by the St. Petersburg congregation. On December 24, 1921, the treasurer of Schaarai Zedek of Tampa, reported that the Jewish community in St. Petersburg had paid $65 to the Tampa congregation in August and $157 in November for a total of $222 for the services of Rabbi Benedict. This arrangement may have lasted until early 1923. Since the same people that started the synagogue became the founders of Congregation B'nai Israel, with the exception of Henry Schutz, it may be assumed that the roots of Congregation B'nai Israel started in 1921 instead of 1923. Henry appeared to be far more reform then the rest of the members, who were very conservative or orthodox.

HIGHLIGHTS of 1922

David and Ethel Rothblatt

David was born in Milwaukee on April 12, 1895 and died on March 21, 1958 in Gulfport, Florida. Ethel was born on December 18, 1890 in Lithuania and died on July 19, 1987 in St. Petersburg. David and Ethel met as children in Milwaukee and then married on December 30, 1917. They arrived in St. Petersburg in 1922, and David became a partner with his brothers-in-law, Harry Hankin and Hyman Jacobs, in the O.K. Markets. When the partnership dissolved, each one of them went into their own business. David opened the O.K. Market on 9th Street South and later moved the store to 22nd Street South.

About 1927, he had to have his right leg amputated above the knee. During the Mexican conflict, he served in the infantry along the Mexican border and suffered partial freezing of his feet. This was the cause of Buerger's disease, a rare circulatory ailment. He suffered greatly from coldness and pain in his feet and legs. He could not be fitted with wooden legs. After the last of several surgeries, he had a mechanic outfit his car with hand controls so he could drive. He had purchased a new Oldsmobile so he could comfortably get around town. Afterwards, he became an officer in the Disabled American Veterans of World War I, at the local and state level. In 1931, David and Ethel opened the Southern Market, a grocery store at 1801 Central Avenue. Despite his problem and without any compensation from the government, he build a business to support his family, where he sold staples, fancy groceries, fruits and vegetables, and high-quality fresh and cured meats. He retired from the grocery business in 1940 and bought the Gulf View Apartments at 2727, 49th St. S. Gulfport, which he operated until his death.

David, although he had a limited education, was very knowledgeable about many things because of his native intelligence and his interest in everything around him. He was active in many community organizations including serving with distinction as Grand Patriarch of the Odd Fellows in 1954, and on the Board of the Rebekkahs. He traveled wherever he had to, to attend meetings. He was a founder and board member of Congregation B'nai Israel. He received a Certificate of Merit in April 1955, for his work in the Muscular Dystrophy Campaign.

When asked about his religious beliefs, he said, "Probably foremost in my religion, I find that there is something for which I can always reach, having faith in the Creator, Giver of all things. Through him we find happiness and contentment, and the knowledge that He is there to be called upon for strength and guidance...that can give man the assurance that God is always by his side. It also gives him faith in his fellow man...I also find hope in my religion. Mainly that hope is for a brighter tomorrow when there will be a better understanding among all the peoples of the world and even of man for his God...I enjoy the feeling of responsibility for my friends, for my neighbors and for myself. I also enjoy the feeling of responsibility to seek out the truth and to learn it well and to dispense it to the best to my abilities, and by so doing, I will strive each day to make the most of that day, knowing that the past and the future are in His hands." The title of this presentation was "Hope for a Brighter Tomorrow is Reached Through Knowing God."

Ethel and David had three children. They were: Tobias born on September 16, 1920 in Milwaukee, Audrey born on June 17, 1925 in Milwaukee, and Bernice "Bunnie" born on November 1, 1927 in St. Petersburg. Toby married Jules Snyder, Audrey whose second marriage was to Gilbert Chenken, and Bunnie married Abe Katz. All the children were raised in St. Petersburg, but Toby moved to Philadelphia and Atlantic City, and Audrey moved to Zepher Hills in Pasco County. Audrey was a bank manager, member of the Professional Women's Association, and the first librarian of Congregation B'nai Israel.

Ethel was a partner in a grocery store, founding member of Congregation B'nai Israel, Ladies Auxiliary of Congregation B'nai Israel, Ladies Auxiliary of Elks and Rebeccas, and a life member of Hadassah.

Bernice Rothblatt (October 1959)

David Rothblatt driving his delivery truck.

Rothblatt Family

The Rothblatt family in the United States started with Abraham Solotnick Rothblatt and Tobias Lena Rothblatt. When Abraham and Tobias (known as Tobey or Tibby) immigrated to the United States the immigration clerks had difficulty spelling the foreign names of the individuals passing through the gates. They often guessed the correct spelling. Abraham and Tobias were listed as Rothblatt on the immigration papers because Tobias signed them. Thereafter the Rothblatt name, which was the maiden name of Tobias, was used for the family instead of Solotnick. Abraham was born March 22, 1857 in Hungary, and died in St. Petersburg in 1942. Tobias, date of birth unknown, died October 15, 1914 in Milwaukee, Wisconsin. In 1923 Abraham Rothblatt moved to St. Petersburg from Milwaukee to be with his family. He was

Abraham Solotnick and Tobias Lena Rothblatt. Photographs courtesy of Margaret A. Dyan.

David Rothblatt's father and Bunnie Katz's grandfather. Abraham's family including David and his wife Ethel Jacobs, and his daughter Ethel and her husband Harry Hankin also lived here. He lived with the Hankins for several years and then made his home with his granddaughter, Juliet Schmitz Dayan, and her family. He was strictly kosher. He was a cabinetmaker. He refused to work on the Sabbath or on Jewish holidays. His wife Tobias had also been Orthodox. The author's grandfather, Louis Wax, a wrought iron and barrel maker, also refused to work on Saturday and Jewish holidays, but instead worked on Sundays or extended hours to make up for the lost time. Abraham blew the shofar on the high holidays.

They had eight children: Louis, Ethel, Bessie, Benjamin, Morris, David, Lillian and Rose. Ethel married Harry Hankin in St. Petersburg and proceeded to raise his four motherless children as her own. Bessie married Sigfried Schmitz on June 23, 1906 and they moved to St. Petersburg in the 1920s. Their daughter, Juliet, married Saul H. Dayan, (another early family) on February 25, 1924, in St. Petersburg.

Sigfried and Bessie Schmitz

Sigfried Schmitz and his wife, Bessie, sister of Ethel and daughter of Abraham Rothblatt, came to St. Petersburg in the 1920s. He worked at Sears and operated a small restaurant. He was born in Austria-Hungary on March 6, 1872 and came to the United States in 1898 to avoid serving in the Hungarian army. He was naturalized in 1917. Bessie was born in Russia in 1887, and was fifteen years younger than Sigfried when they married on June 23, 1906 in the United States. Their daughter, Juliet, was born in Illinois, in 1908 , their son, John, was born in Illinois in 1909, their son, Joseph, was born in Illinois in 1911, their daughter, Esther, was born in Illinois in 1914, and their son, Max, was born in Illinois in 1919. In 1930, they lived next door to the Harry Hankin family.

Celia and Samuel Sweet

Celia was born around 1902 and Sam was born in Russia in 1893. Celia and Samuel

Bessie Rifka Rothblatt and Siegfried Schmitz, Chicago, IL, ca 1908. Photograph courtesy of Margaret A. Dyan.

had two children, a son, Avram (Bud), who was a doctor and is now deceased, and a daughter, Jackie Beard, who lives in North Carolina. Samuel and Celia Sweet came to St. Petersburg from Milwaukee, Wisconsin, in 1925. On July 19, 1928, Samuel purchased the business including all wares, merchandise, and fixtures at 732 5th St South for $1150. He renamed it, Sweet's Grocery and Meat Market. He served in the Navy during World War I, was a member of the Jewish War Veterans, a Mason for more than fifty years, and was a member of the drill team of Selama Grotto. In 1981, at age eighty seven, he became the oldest bar mitzvah at Congregation B'nai Israel. He affiliated with Congregation B'nai Israel when he first arrived. He participated in many community wide activities. He died on July 12th 1988. Celia died March 28, 1942.

Bessie and Oscar Silverman

Bessie was born in Russia or Lithuania. She was a machine operator. Oscar was born in Russia on September 4, 1894, and came to the United States in 1909. He served in World War I. He married Bessie in December, 1919. They came to St. Petersburg from Milwaukee in 1925. Bessie and Oscar had three children, a son, Jerome, a son, Fred, and a daughter, Corinne, who married Sidney Goodman. All the children grew up in St. Petersburg. Corinne married in 1945 and moved to Greenville, Mississippi. Fred died in the 1990s and Jerome, who is still alive, remained single. Bessie was active in the American Legion and the Ladies Auxiliary of Congregation B'nai Israel. Bessie died September 25, 1986 and Oscar died October 2, 1977.

Harry and Marie Jacobs

Harry and Marie had no children. Harry, who was a deaf mute, was a printer. He met Marie through a deaf mute organization. Unfortunately, she died at a young age. He never remarried. He was an extremely outgoing and friendly person who loved everyone and was beloved by everyone.

Charles A. and Helen Freudenberg

Charles was retired when he and Helen moved to St. Petersburg. He opened a saloon at a later date. Charles was born in Germany in 1855 and died on December 16, 1943. Charles had been a cabin boy aboard ship and had made numerous trips to the United States before he finally came to live here permanently. Although he had no formal education, he was self-taught and a very literate person. He met Helen Heyn, who was thirty years younger than he was, in Chicago, and they married in December, 1921. Helen had been born in Toledo, Ohio in 1886 and died in 1971. They were both founding officers of Temple Beth-El. Helen served as Treasurer of Temple Beth-El in the late 1920s and early 1930s.Helen enjoyed playing cards, which was one of the big recreational pleasures of the day. In the 1920s and 30s, she played bridge with women from Congregation B'nai Israel, and poker in the 1930s with women from Temple Beth-El. They had one child, Chalene, who was born on February 4, 1923 in St. Petersburg. While in high school in the late 1930s, Chalene worked at the Sierkese dry goods store on Saturdays. Her friends at the time were Evelyn Heller, Thelma Diamond, Jill Grossman, Lillian and Shirley Gordon, Caroline Brehm, and Abe Katz. Chalene graduated from St. Pete Junior College and then attended business school. While at school, she worked for the Learners Shop, where Irving Cypen's wife was the manager. She worked for the VA hospital for several years and then went into the retail cosmetic business, where she owned a six store chain. Her husband, Sam C. Field, is an electronic engineer who graduated from the University of Virginia. Chalene and Sam were married in 1947 and have two daughters. Chalene has been President of the Temple B'nai Israel Sisterhood for four years, and President of the PTA.

Jess Family

Samuel Morris Jess, the maternal grandfather of Jane Silverberg, came to St. Petersburg after retiring as a prosperous men's clothing merchant of State Street in Chicago. His first wife, Ethel Vera Goodman, who died in 1916 in Chicago was the mother of Evelyn. Samuel and his second wife, Ella, bought a large home on 15th Avenue North, which became a hub for the Jewish communities of St. Petersburg and Tampa and their card parties. Many of the Jess adult children also came for periods of time. Their daughter, Sadelle, who is married to Gene Spiegel, soon moved to St. Petersburg. Samuel was born in 1856 and died in 1933. Samuel said, "This is the best city in the world."

HIGHLIGHTS of 1923

Congregation B'nai Israel

In July, Congregation B'nai Israel (Conservative) was formed by thirteen Jewish men and their wives. They were: Abe Sierkese, Hyman M. Jacobs, Samuel Goldberg (later changed to Gilbert), Charles Davis, Max Davis, David Rothblatt, Joe Solomon, Louis (Boston) Cohen, Aron Heller, Morris Katz, Harry Hankin, Ben Halaczer, and Leon Halaczer. The synagogue was founded at the apartment of Mr. and Mrs. Charles Davis at 1024 Central Avenue. Another source said the synagogue was founded in the home of Abraham and Mary Sierkese. All were merchants of Eastern European origin who worshiped individually and together in their homes until the first congregation was formed. The congregation was incorporated on December 9, 1925. See the Chapter on Congregation B'nai Israel for the rest of the history.

Halaczer Family

Ben Halaczer's brother, Sol, was born in Austria on April 4, 1885. He became a naturalized citizen. Sol owned an automobile supply store. Sol died in March 1967 in Hillsborough County. Regina was born in Austria in 1887 and died in Tampa in 1944. Their children were: Gabriel born in 1911 in Florida and died in 1953 in Pinellas County; Lilly born in 1913 in Florida; Julius born in 1917 in Florida; Morris born January 8, 1896 in Austria Hungary and lived in Tampa; Leon (Sonya Miller's and Marilyn Benjamin's father) born August 20, 1897 and died June 1987; and Nettie who opened a jewelry store in 1920, in Tampa. Sol and Regina were also living in Tampa in 1920.

Leon Halaczer

Leon (Leisser Lippe) was born in

Leon and Lillie Halaczer

top: *Leon Halaczer in front of his jewelry store (no date given).*
bottom: *Halaczer's Jewelry Store in downtown St. Petersburg, FL during WW II.*
r. to l. *Sonya Halaczer Miller, Lillie Rubin Halaczer, Leon Halaczer, Celia Rubin.*

Kopyczynce, Austria, on August 20, 1897 and died in St. Petersburg, Florida in June 1987. Leon's father, Hersch, was also born in that city and his mother, Miriam Horowitz Halaczer, was born in a neighboring city, Czortkow. His father was a blacksmith who employed two or three workers. They built wagons from scratch and shoed as many as 150 horses in a twelve hour period. He was very respected in the city and lived a comfortable life. His father was very smart and learned how to read and write on his own. He was always involved in giving help within the community. His father and mother had seven children.

At age four, Leon was put into a cheder, where he learned Hebrew. At age six, he started public school. He already spoke Yiddish and Hebrew and learned German, Polish, and Romanian. At age ten, he started in the gymnasium, which was equivalent of high school in the United States, but two years later, decided to drop out of school and take a three year apprenticeship in watch repairing. In 1912, he caught a severe cold with a chronic cough that persisted for two years. At the advice of his doctor, he was sent to a clinical special treatment resort, Szawnica. In August of 1914, World War I started and all of the people in the resort, except Leon, fled in advance of the Russian Army. His brother, Sol, from Tampa, sent him $100, a fortune at that time, to be used for the summer resort and whatever else was needed to help him to get better.

However, Leon didn't have enough money to go to his hometown, which now was occupied by the Russian Army, so he moved into a small hotel. When the local people discovered that he was living alone, they brought him food, provided homes for him to sleep in on a rotating basis, and loaned him money to go to Vienna. Upon reaching Vienna, which was filled with refugees, he had to register at the police station, and was sent by train to Prague. There he worked in a factory, took sick again, was sent to a hospital, and was finally drafted into the Austrian army in 1916, where he fought on the Italian front.

After the war, feeling insecure about the changing government in his city, he decided there was no opportunity to make a living. He had been writing to his brother Sol, who had immigrated to Tampa earlier, and Sol encouraged Leon to come to America. Departing Paris, he arrived in Ellis Island and went on to Philadelphia to visit a cousin. From there, he went to Tampa to be with his brothers. He worked at his trade as a watchmaker and learned English very quickly, as he was adept at languages. His brother encouraged him to open his own watch repair and jewelry store in St. Petersburg, which he did, in May 1921, after only three months in the United States. He remained in the jewelry business until 1963.

Dora Goldberg, a friend of Leon, introduced him to her niece, Lillie Rubin, who was from Richmond, Virginia and formerly Russia. Lillie's two weeks' visit with Dora lasted a lifetime, as Leon and Lillie were married on July 26, 1926 and lived for the remainder of their lives in St. Petersburg. They raised two daughters, Sonya (Mrs. Irwin Miller) and Marilyn, (Mrs. Phillip Benjamin) and were blessed with six grandchildren. Leon and Lilllie became an integral part of the Jewish Community. They were founding members of Congregation B'nai Israel, board members of both the Congregation and Sisterhood. They helped develop B'nai Brith and the Judaic Council of Women, worked for United Way and many other community organizations.

The most important achievement and legacy, was their love of family, Jewish heritage, and the philosophy "do unto others as you would have them do unto you"

Davis Family

Aaron Davis, a dry goods merchant, came to the United States from Romania, in 1887. His wife, Sarah, came first to the United States in 1885 with their daughter, Ida, and then again in 1888, after the birth of their son, Charlie. They stayed in New York until sometime between 1890 and 1893. They then went to Key West, which had a thriving Jewish business community. They owned a ready-to-wear store in Key West, where all six children grew up. The children were: a daughter, Ida, born in Romania in April 1883; a son, Charlie, born in Romania in January 1888; a daughter, Annie, born in New York in June 1890; a son, Marcus, born in June 1893 in Florida; a son, Max, born in Florida on July 4, 1894; a son, Isadore, born in Florida April 1897; and a nephew, Louis Markowitz, born in January 1882 in Romania and was a dry goods clerk. In the 1930 census, Isadore was living in Tampa with his wife, Jennie, age twenty five, his daughter, Lorraine, and his mother-in-law, Rosa Fishermen, who came to the United States in 1900 from Romania. Isadore was a manager of a retail dry goods store.

Charlie Davis

Charlie and Marie Davis left Key West and went to Jacksonville and then arrived in St. Petersburg before 1923, with their three children, Eunice, Armand, and Dotsy. They bought a ready-to-wear business from Joseph Solomon which was located at 862 and 864 Central Ave. Charlie brought his brother-in-law, Frank Rabin, from Jacksonville, who opened a shoe store next to Harry Hankin between eighth and ninth on Central. Charlie was a founder of Congregation B'nai Israel in St. Petersburg. Charles died in Jacksonville in 1934. Eunice married Ted Gross, Dotsy married Sherman (last name unknown), and Armand married Leatrice (last name unknown).

Max and Lillian Davis

In 1923, Charles sold his store to his brother, Max Davis, from whom the present Davis family is descended. Max and his mother, Sarah Davis, came from Key West. Max married Lillian Hecht in 1925. Lillian was born and lived in Tampa. Lillian

became Max's partner in the business as well as a partner in life. They had three children, Marie, Allan, and Arlene. Allan and Arlene still live in the Pinellas County area, while Marie lives in Georgia. Max became immediately involved in the Jewish community including Congregation B'nai Israel, B'nai B'rith, etc.. He served on many committees in both the Jewish and general communities. He was greatly respected by the Christian community for his efforts to make St. Petersburg a better place to live. At the Festival of States Parade he would close the store after lining the sidewalk with chairs from the shoe department so that people would have a comfortable place to sit and enjoy the festivities. Minyans and meetings were held in the dressing room of Max's store. As soon as the tenth man would arrive, the curtain was drawn, business was put on hold, and a prayer session would begin. Max became the President of Congregation B'nai Israel in 1938 and again at a later time. Arlene remembers, as a child of three or four, running up to the bema and sitting on her father's lap during the service. Max was born on July 4, 1894, and died on March 19, 1965. Lillian H. Davis, was born on August 10, 1904, and died on April 18, 1986.

Arlene and Richard Rosenthal

Arlene, Max and Lillian Davis's daughter, was the Regional Secretary to the United Synagogue Youth. Richard and Arlene became active board members of the Youth Commission and later served on the Board of Congregation B'nai Israel. Arlene was both Treasurer and Secretary at Congregation B'nai Israel. Arlene's brother, Aaron, was also a board member. All these descendents of Max and Lillian Davis, including the grandchildren, still make contributions to both the Jewish and general communities.

Early Jewish Social Life

In 1923, because of Louis Cohen's generosity, one of the empty stores in his building was used for religious services. On Sunday nights, the Jewish families took turns visiting each other's homes. The men played cards, while the women and children visited in the kitchen. Everyone was excited

Max Davis

when they heard of a new Jewish family moving to the community. There would be more children for their children to play with. The Jewish families would drive to the wooden pier on hot summer nights to cool off and would visit. The teenagers went to Pass-a-Grille to meet an excursion boat from Tampa containing Jewish children. Sometimes a boat would pickup passengers in Tampa, dock in St. Petersburg where the Jewish children would board, and spend a day at Anna Maria Beach. In the early 1920's, The Jewish community that was kosher had serious problems because none of the stores stocked Jewish food and kosher meat. It had to come from Tampa and was often spoiled. They families would go joy riding through the county to pick oranges at the groves for fifty cents a bushel or would drive to the waterfront for a swim. Frequent trips were made to the "Fountain of Youth," a spring near the Al Lang Stadium to fill a jug of water which was supposed to give you good health. A shopping trip was a long forty five mile drive around Tampa Bay to Maas Brothers in Tampa. Children were taught on the second floor of the Elk's Club by Rabbi Benedict. The first community Seder was held in 1921, in the rear of Joe Solomon's Dry Goods Store, at 862 Central Avenue. The Jewish men went to Tampa for the High Holy Days.

HIGHLIGHTS of 1924

Saul H. Dayan

Juliet (Schmitz) and Saul H. Dayan. Photograph courtesy of Margaret A. Dyan.

Saul Dayan married Julia Lee Schmitz (of the Rothblatt family) on January 18, in St. Petersburg. He was born on March 5, 1903 in Syria, and she was born on October 18, 1907 in Chicago. He died in October 1983 in New York, and she died on August 26, 1953 in Miami. It was not unusual for people to leave services at Congregation B'nai Israel and walk next door to the Dayan family home to continue to socialize. For eleven years, it was one of the principle places for Jewish people to meet and enjoy each other's company.

Royal Palm Cemetery

On February 24, 1,500 burial sites in a section of Royal Palm Cemetery were purchased as a Jewish cemetery. Wolf D. Katz, father of Morris Katz, was the first burial. He died on February 22nd, 1924 at age eighty one. There were other early burials. Baby Moses, was born on December 3, 1924, and died Dec. 6, 1924. His family moved away from this area. Lillian Goldberg died in 1925. Joe Solomon died February 8, 1928 at age forty four. Morris Dickman died Aug. 31, 1928. Clara Landfield was born in 1899 and died April 1929. Sigfried Schmitz died in 1930. James Schwartz was born on May 12, 1915 and died on June 26, 1931. Prior to 1924, the Jewish people were buried in Tampa.

St. Petersburg YMHA

On March 16, the YMHA bought a lot for a synagogue. The synagogue was never built. There are no records apparently available about the founders of the YMHA, when it started and when it folded. There are references to the YMHA in both the St. Petersburg newspaper and the minutes of Schaarai Zedek of Tampa.

HIGHLIGHTS of 1925

Benjamin and Celia Green

In 1925, a delicatessen and restaurant on 9th Street North just off Central Avenue became a gathering place for the city's Jewish people. It was opened by Benjamin and Celia Green, who came from New York City in 1925. It was the first Jewish deli and families from Clearwater, Bradenton, and Sarasota would meet there. Benjamin, who was born in 1885 in Russia, and Celia, who was born in 1887 in Austria, came to the United States where they met and married in 1907. They came from New York to St. Petersburg in 1925 with their three children. Benjamin died on September 24, 1958 and Celia died on January 22, 1981.

Silverman Family

Bessie and Oscar Silverman and Aaron and Ruth Silverman arrived. Ruth and Aaron were cousins of Oscar Silverman. They opened a small grocery store, which required very little capital. Jacob Miller had a dry goods business at 9th Street and second Avenue South. In 1933-34 he moved between 4th and 5th on Central Avenue, where he had a dress store.

Frank and Alice Rabin

Frank and Alice Rabin (originally Rabinowitz) owned Quality Shoe Store on Central Avenue. Later they also owned Sally's Shoes at 537 Central Ave, Lee Shoes in the 600 block of Central Avenue, and Dixie Credit, a women's clothing and army clothing store. About 1946, Frank and Al Esrick opened a motel called the Breakers on Madeira Beach. Frank was born in 1899 and died in 1979. Alice was born in 1902 and died in 1973 or 1974. They were married in 1925 or 1926 and Sally was born in 1928. They originally came from Jacksonville, Florida. He was a fine athlete who played tennis and softball. Their daughter, Sally Goodrich, lives in Tampa.

Jacob and Harriet Miller

Jacob and Harriet Miller and their three month-old son, Irwin, came to St. Petersburg from Brooklyn. Jacob saved money from transportation by walking to different places during the working day. A nickel saved here and a nickel saved there provided the initial money needed for him to establish his own business in Brooklyn. When they moved to St. Petersburg, they opened a fabric and findings (lace, buttons, etc.) store at Ninth Street and 2nd Ave South, despite the fact that Jake had limited education. Later, they opened Miller Dress Shop between 4th and 5th Street on Central Avenue. In 1941, they built the Rellim Hotel. Jacob was born in northern Poland on February 7, 1890, and died on July 13, 1956. He came to the United States through Ellis Island as a teenager. Harriet was born on January 10, 1889, in New York and died on February 22, 1968. Harriet went to high school in New York. Their children were Lillian, born in New York in 1914, Miriam, born in New York in 1916, Dorothy, born in New York in 1921, and Irwin H., born in New York in 1925. Jacob L. Miller and Harriet S. were founding members of Temple Beth-El. Jacob served as President of Temple Beth-El from 1934-1936, 1937-1938, and 1942-1944.

Fyvolent Family
Evelyn Fyvolent Samuels

Evelyn Fyvolent Samuels was born in New York on March 10, 1901 and died on March 21, 2004. She came to St. Petersburg with her husband, Samuel Fyvolent, and son, Lowell. Another son, David Bradley Fyvolent, was born on May 30, 1929. Evelyn's maiden name was Miller. Samuel's father was Duvid Baer Fyvolent, who died on September 1, 1926 and his mother was Yetta, who died in the late 1930s. Evelyn's parents were Jacob Miller and Bella Green Miller. Samuel and Evelyn married in 1922. Evelyn's parents moved from New York to St. Petersburg in 1929.

Evelyn had worked on Wall Street as an honor clerk who sent buy and sell messages to the Chicago Stock Exchange. Lowell was eighteen months old. David Bradley (Buzzy) was born on May 30, 1929. Her husband Samuel opened a general store called Union Dollars Store on Central Avenue between 7th and 8th St.. She arrived at the end of the great building boom of that era. Most of the Jewish community at that time were not part of the boom and therefore stayed on and nurtured the new synagogues, Congregation B'nai Israel and Temple Beth El. She said that the Jewish families welcomed them as if they were part of a mispuha that had arrived and now would become part of the living fiber of the community. She and her husband, Samuel, were one of the founding families of Temple Beth El. She was part of the women's groups who worked hard to raise money for the new synagogue.

Harriet and Jacob Miller

seated, Miriam; standing, Lillian, Dorothy and Irwin Miller

In 1930, Evelyn was able to leave the children for short periods of time with a helper and was able to participate in helping other people who were less fortunate. She was the first Jewish woman appointed to a charitable board, St. Petersburg Children's Welfare Board. She was appointed by Father Enright, of the Catholic Church. Over the next several generations, she continued her outstanding service to the overall community, as well as the Jewish community. After her husband, Samuel Fyvolent, died on December 17, 1952, she married Mark Samuels, a gentleman farmer from England. He started selling fruit by the piece in New York City and quickly moved on to rent land in many parts of the country clear up to the Canadian border and produce his own fruits and vegetables. He became a major vegetable broker who supplied the A&P stores and others. Mark Samuels' parents were Max and Pauline.

At 102 years of age, on July 1, 2003, Evelyn was the oldest living Jewish person in Pinellas County, Florida. Her life had been a journey of raising a family, helping build a Jewish community, and helping those who were in greatest need, without regard to race or religion. She was an outstanding example of an American citizen, and Jewish person, who sees only the best in others. She was a true woman of valor, and her life was a living example of the truest form of Judaism, for all current and future generations, children and adults alike, to emulate.

Evelyn's two brothers, David and Meyer Miller, also came in the mid to late 1920s. David married Goldie Schuster's sister, Jean, and Meyer married Ann Schwartz in the late 1920s or early 1930s.

David Fyvolent,
President Temple Beth-El,
1974–1976

Samuel Fyvolent

Samuel Fyvolent was born in Odessa, Russia on April 2, 1898 and died on December 17, 1952 or 1956. His father was Duvid Baer Fyvolent (The original origin of the Fyvolent name is uncertain. It apparently was first used in New York around 1920.) Duvid died in late 1929 or early 1930 and Samuel's mother, Yetta, remarried. She died in the late 1930s.

Samuel had a sister, Rose, and brothers, Harry, Barney and Jack. Samuel opened a small apparel store on Central Avenue in the middle of the North Side's 700 block. He later moved to 701 Central Avenue and named the store Bradley's. The original ladies apparel store included army uniforms and supplies during World War II. At one time, Samuel had stores in four neighboring cities. Samuel was active in many Jewish and civic organizations in St. Petersburg and in Congregation B'nai Israel of St. Petersburg. He was one of the founders of the Jewish civic organization called the Covenant Club. He arranged for many famous speakers and performers to come to St. Petersburg to put on programs for the club.

Lowell Fyvolent

Lowell was born on May 11, 1925 and died on September 20, 2001. Lowell Fyvolent attended the Wilkinson School of

Music, where he studied violin. He later studied at the prestigious Juilliard College of Music in New York City. During his high school years, he performed in numerous concerts and many of the large churches in St. Petersburg. He served with distinction in the Navy, where he was a Yeoman on the USS Acushnet, which was an oceangoing tug used to take old ammunition out to sea for disposal. During one such trip, a German submarine fired a torpedo at the ship and a barge loaded with old ammunition. Luckily the torpedo went under the cable between the two and all the lives of the sailors were saved. After the war, he married Carolyn Sudakow of New York and Miami Beach. They had two children, Barbara and Stanley. He and his father in law developed property along the East Coast of the country.

David Fyvolent

David Fyvolent also attended the new Wilkinson School of Music, where he studied piano. He attended local schools and then earned a Bachelor of Science Degree in Business Administration in 1951 from the University of Florida. He entered the Navy as an enlisted man in 1953 and was accepted in Officers Candidate School in Newport, Rhode Island. He became an Ensign and served in several duty stations including Signal Officer on the USS Salerno Bay (an aircraft carrier), and security officer of an Underwater Research Laboratory. He was promoted to Lieutenant. During his time in the service, he married Sally Felson of Jacksonville, Florida. They had three children, Susan Gale, an attorney living in Atlanta, Georgia, Arthur Scott, an independent computer consultant and contractor creating web sites and Web advertising for national corporations, and Douglas Stuart, a regional representative for an international freight company. After Sally died, David married Joan Levinson Esrick in 2000. David has made many contributions to the Jewish and general communities. He served as President of Temple Beth-El. Joan Esrick Fyvolent was a Board Member of Pinellas Association for Retarded Children, Menorah Manor Foundation, and St. Petersburg Fine Arts Museum. She is a founding member of Menorah Manor and past Vice-President of Congregation B'nai Israel.

1925–1926 Merchants

A group of Jewish merchants came from Savannah and Atlanta and opened stores on 9th Street South. Another group came from Jacksonville, Florida, Baltimore and other cities and opened dry goods and grocery stores in the black neighborhoods on 22nd Street South. Some Jewish people left the northern resort cities for the winter and opened seasonal gift and jewelry stores downtown. Ed Goldman and Leon Halaczer opened a jewelry store downtown. Kosher meat was brought from Jacksonville to Tampa and from Tampa to St. Petersburg. Other Jewish merchants were: N. Dunoff and his wife, who had a dry goods store on 22nd Street South and then moved to a shoe store at 8th Street and Central Avenue. Barney Bernstein and his wife arrived in the 1920s. They had three children, Leo, Sidney, and Dinah. They had a grocery store which was moved to 3rd Avenue South in the late 1930s. The Rosenbergs had a dry goods store on 22nd Street South and then moved it to Ninth Street and 3rd Avenue South

HIGHLIGHTS of 1926

Jewish Business People

In 1926, Kosher food was shipped from Tampa. Henry Schutz contributed $25 to Schaarai Zedek of Tampa as reported by M. Henry Cohen on June 6, 1926. On Nov. 6, 1927, it was reported in the minutes of Schaarai Zedek that certain co-religionists in St. Petersburg were desirous of becoming members of the congregation and it was moved, seconded and carried that a committee be appointed to visit St. Petersburg to secure applications for membership. The committee appointed by the President included Abe Maas, Offin Falk, and Samuel E. Fink. On December 5, 1927, A. Cohen, Henry Schutz, and H. Blumberg of St. Petersburg became members of Schaarai Zedek of Tampa.

Other Jewish people who arrived in the mid to late 1920s in St. Petersburg were: Isadore Friedman (Sans Souci),1929; Lou Solomon, Lou's Mens Store, 2601, 1st Avenue South; Jacob and Jennie Solomovitch, Sol's Department Store. Jacob was born on November 21, 1880 in Romania and was naturalized in New York on March 25, 1914. He died in March of 1970 in the Bronx, New York. Jennie was born in 1885 in Romania and Pearl was born in 1905 in New York; Samuel and Stella Goldberg wholesale produce; Harry L. Jacobs salesman and wife, Hattie; Esther Cohen, Smart Shop; Jacob and Rose D. Moses dry goods, 828 Central Avenue; Herman and Molly Rosenberg, Rosenberg Department Store; Henry and Jessie Goldberg, Goldberg's Popular Price Clothing; David and Rose Goldberg; Gabriel Goldberg, Southern Specialty Shop; Mrs Minnie Ross (widow of Jacob), Dr. Adolph Rosenthal (Temple Beth El past President), Hannah Pfeiffer (widow of Abraham), Phil Heller (brother of Hannah), Max and Rose Goodkind. Max was born in Germany in 1863, and came to the United States in 1873. Rose W. was born in New York in 1869; Morris and Carrie Newmark (Newmark Saunders Realty), Leo L. and Helen Donsky (Star Ready to Wear Store). Leo was born in Russia in 1895 and came to the United States in 1910. Helen was born in Russia in 1898 and came to the United States in 1908; Louis and Dora Goldberg (Goldbergs Popular Price Clothing), Joseph and Sarah Spero arrived. Sarah lived in Oyster Bay, New York in 1920. She was forty seven years old. She had been born in Russia. She was listed as a retail merchant. She died in Pinellas County, in January 1959. Her three sons were Hiram, age twenty two, born in New York, Morris, age eighteen, born in New York, and Clarence G. H., age fourteen, born in New York. All three boys spoke Yiddish.

Albert Abraham Esrick

Al, his wife Pauline, and two year old son Jerome (Jerry) Esrick arrived in St. Petersburg and purchased a grocery store, Wesley Dixie Grocery Market, (at Ninth and Central Avenue, one block from Webb's Drug Store), from uncle Max Cypen. Max was a brother of Pauline's mother, Bessie Carrol. Al then opened his own store on Tangerine at 18th on the South Side of St.

Petersburg, where the family also lived. Pauline's father's name was Samuel. Al and Pauline's daughter, Sandra, was born in St. Petersburg on November 1, 1931. Somewhat later, Al and Pauline went into the dog food business, which Al operated for thirty five years. Al had his own large pressure cooker in the garage. You had to use a ladder in order to reach the top of the pressure cooker. There was a special room where Ben Cypen worked packaging and freezing, Frosty Dog Food, the first frozen dog food. Both Al and Pauline were very smart and saw a way of filling a need in the dog business. A. A. Esrick Inc. became the oldest and largest distributor of Greyhound food in Florida. All twenty eight kennels of Derby Lane purchased dog food from this company. So did pet shops, breeding farms, veterinarians, sheriff's departments, the SPCA, and Barnum and Bailey Circus. Al was born in Philadelphia in 1903 and died in St. Petersburg on November 23, 1987 at Menorah Manor Nursing Home. (Three different articles concerning his arrival time in St. Petersburg give dates of 1924, 1926 and 1929.) Pauline was born in Philadelphia in, approximately, 1905, and died in St. Petersburg in 1962. Pauline attended high school in Philadelphia and met Al there and they married. In St. Petersburg, Al was active in both the Jewish and general communities. Al believed in helping children. He always gave to those who were needy and especially tried to help clothe and feed children who were without shoes and adequate food. He was described by many, "As a very good person, a very fair person, a very honest person who always tried to help those who were less fortunate." As a child, Sandra accompanied her father on his deliveries of food and saw the conditions in which these children lived. Al and his wife gave very liberally to all Jewish causes, including the building of Congregation B'nai Israel and Menorah Manor. He belonged to the Egypt Temple Shrine of Tampa, the Nitram Lodge 118 F & A M, and the B'nai B'rith of St. Petersburg. Pauline was very active in the Congregation B'nai Israel Sisterhood and the PTA.

Pauline's mother, Bessie Carroll, had a small grocery store on 22nd Street South.

Pauline's father, Samuel, had died before Pauline and Al came to St. Petersburg. Uncle Max Cypen had three children including Judge Irving Cypen.

Sandra Esrick Arthur married Donald Arthur from Tampa in 1951. Donald is in the insurance business. Sandra attended the University of Miami. Sandra and Donald have a son, Jeffrey, who is a singer and composer, a son, Bradley, who is a sculptor, and a daughter, Dawn, who is an artist. All three children married and have their own children. Sandra said, "I remember how my parents instilled in me the love of God and religion." Sandra in turn has instilled the same love in her children and grandchildren. Sandra started a club in fourth or fifth grade called the Sunshine Club with four girls from her school, because being Jewish meant that she was left out of some of the other activities in school. Her father always provided refreshments for them.

Jerry Esrick

Jerry was born on July 2, 1927 in Philadelphia and died on May 27, 1997. Jerry attended the University of Florida. He married Joan Levinson in 1951. Joan was originally from Logan, West Virginia and later from Sarasota. They had five children: Larry, who married Linda Lowe, and lives in Scottsdale, Arizona; Linda Ann who lives in St. Petersburg; Betsy, who married Leonard Englander and lives in St. Petersburg; Stephen, who married Kiki and lives in Aspen, Colorado; and Michelle, who is an actor and filmmaker, and lives in New York City. Sandra Esrick who had attended the University of Miami married Don Arthur in 1950. Don has been in the re-insurance business during his career. He still has an office in St. Petersburg. After Jerry Esrick died, Joan married David Fyvolent.

Jerry was a Board Member of Pinellas County Commissioners, Committee of 100, St. Petersburg General Hospital, Menorah Manor (founding member), Congregation B'nai Israel, and Temple Beth-El.

Jewish Stores on Central Avenue
479 – Philip Levy Novelties. Philip was
    born in England; his wife Julia A. was
    born in Massachusetts. By1930, they

were in the jewelry business. A cousin, Evelyn P., age. 19, born in Rhode Island, was a clerk in the jewelry store.

551 – Henry Schutz Ladies Furnishings

566 – Morris Katz Millinery– Morris was born in 1896 and died in 1976. His wife, Theresa, was born in 1899 and died in 1972.

569 – Gabriel Goldberg Hosiery

666 – Joseph Solomon Clothing (Department store)

703 – Halaczer Brothers Jewelers

800-06 – Abraham Sierkese Dry Goods.

828 – Jacob Moses Dry Goods. Baby Moses died Dec. 6,1924, and was buried in the Jewish cemetery. Was Jacob the father? They moved to Tampa.

852 – Edward Goldman Jewelers

856 – Gabriel Goldberg Clothing.

860 – Hyman. M. Jacobs, wholesale fruit and vegetable store and warehouse.

864 – Charles Davis Clothing

Jewish stores on 22nd Street South in 1929

604 – Nathan Dunoff, dry goods

628 – J. Brady Goodwin, furniture store

630 – David Rothblatt, grocer

634 – Morris Feldman, dry goods

644 – Barnett Bernstein, grocer

648 – Maurice P. Goldstein, dry goods

731 – Gus Goldblatt (had two daughters), meat

863 – Eli Gelman, dry goods

1101 – Jacob Salmon

HIGHLIGHTS of 1926-1929

Reform Jewish Community

The Reform Jewish community started in 1926 and in 1929, formed Temple Beth-El. Jewish women were the original leaders. They included: Gertrude Siegel Shane, Mrs. Sidney B. Wasserman (Byrd Starr), Ella Gerst, Mrs. Minnie Van Straaten, Mrs. Pauline Strauss, Mrs. Dora Jacobson, Mrs. Hannah Rice, Mrs. Minnie Blumberg, Miss Eva Lehwald, and Mrs. Lilly Cohen. Miss Eva Radzinski, although not initially an officer, was one of the guiding lights of the organization from its beginning until the time she died. Mrs. Wasserman was born in 1891 in Tennessee. She died in February 1958

in Florida. Their daughter, Elsa, was born in 1914 in Missouri. Her husband, Sidney, was born in 1888 in Tennessee. He was a real estate salesman. She was a clerk in the Don Leno Shop.

The first meeting of the group was held at the home of Mrs. Wasserman. The women agreed to unite and function as a religious and philanthropic group, guided by the program of the National Federation of Temple Sisterhoods. Later, services were held at the Wasserman family home at 226 21st Ave. Southeast. In the beginning, the officers were Mrs. Minnie Van Straaten, husband Jacob, President; Mrs. Ella Gerst, husband Milton S., (He died on July 19, 1955, in Mobile County, Alabama, certificate number 14110. In 1910 he was living in Jacksonville, Florida with a cousin, in 1930 he was staying in Southern Pines, North Carolina. His date of birth was April 30, 1888.) Vice President; Mrs. Pauline Strauss, husband Maurice G., Treasurer; Mrs. Dora Jacobson, husband Arthur, Secretary; Mrs. Sidney Wasserman, Correspondent Secretary; Mrs. Hannah Rice, husband Sol C., Chairman Board of Trustees; Mrs. Minnie Blumberg, husband David H., trustee; Miss Eva Lehwald, trustee; Mrs. Gertrude Siegel, husband Harold, trustee; Mrs. Lilly M. or L. Cohen born in Indiana in 1885 , husband Herman H. born in Kentucky in 1874 and a department store proprietor, trustee. They had a son, Alvin, born in Kentucky in 1919.

Minnie Van Straaten worked in the Pelie Shop. She was born in Hesse, Germany in 1869. She came to the United States in 1886. Her husband, Jacob, was born in Belgium in 1867. He came to the United States in 1887. He owned a retail meat market. Their daughter, Gertrude, was born in Georgia in 1896. Their son, Herbert S., was born in Georgia on May 23, 1898 and died in January 1977 in Chicago, Illinois. Their son, Harry J., was born in Georgia on August 23, 1902 and died in September 1976 in Durham, North Carolina. Herbert and Harry J. were clothing salesmen. Their son, Eugene, was born in Georgia in 1908. Ella Gerst's husband was a salesman. Pauline Strauss husband was a salesman. Dora Jacobson's husband owned Jay's Boot Shop. Hannah Rice's husband

Minnie Van Straaten

owned Harris and Rice; Minnie Blumberg's husband was a manager of Davis Loan Office; Gertrude Siegel's husband owned Don's Auto Accessory; Lillian Cohen's husband owned Popular Price Department Store. He was born in Kentucky and she was born in Indiana.

M. H. Friendly's wife, Leah, was a spiritualist. Robert Aronson's wife was Rose, who owned Rose Hat Shoppe. Alan Friedman"s wife was Belle R.. The Arcades on Central Avenue were the forerunners of the strip shopping centers of today. Gus Goldblatt had a store on 22nd Street. He was born in Lithuania on July 15, 1896. He was a retail butcher. He appeared in the 1930 census in San Antonio, Texas. He died in December 1963 in Pinellas County. His wife, Eva, was born on July 18, 1898 in Kiev, Russia and died on May 8, 1978 in Pinellas County.

Virgil H. Pace was born in Texas in 1890. His wife Helen R. was born in Poland in 1895 and came to the United States in 1900. They were both retail merchants in an elegant ladies clothing store on 1st Ave North. Their son, Sherman N., was born in Florida in 1924.

Other businessmen were: Samuel Shapiro who came in the early 1930s. He died in 1948 at age fifty eight and is buried in Royal Palm Cemetery; Alan Beller who owned Alan Apparel and Sport Shop; Jacob L. and Harriet Miller who owned a dry goods store; and Sam Hirsch.

Jacob Miller

Jacob Miller was born on June 7, 1873 and died on August 6,1954. He was a retail merchant, who came from Russia in 1899. His wife, Belle Green, was born on June 15, 1881 and died on February 19, 1946. She also came from Russia in 1899. Jacob Miller conducted services at Temple Beth El when a rabbi was not available. Jacob and Belle Green Miller, owned Union Dollar Store. A son, Louis, was born in New York, on August 14, 1902 and died on June 16, 1997. His wife Pauline G., was born on March 27, 1909 and died on December 26, 1986. Louis, who had been a security trader, was a clerk in his parents' store.. A son Dave, born in New Jersey in 1905, was a department store manager. A son Meyer, born in New York in 1908, was

a department store manager. Jacob and Bella were David Fyvolent's grandparents.

HIGHLIGHTS of 1928

Phyllis Weinstein was born to Meyer and Ella on November 27, the same day that Joel Fyvolent was born. Betty and Harry Fyvolent were best friends with Meyer and Ella. Phyllis married Morti Wachtlar of the Wachtlar jewelry family of New York.

HIGHLIGHTS of 1929

Temple Beth El

Temple Beth El was incorporated on May 24, 1929. The officers and trustees were: Herman H. Cohen, President; B. F. Furst, First Vice President; Myer H. Friendly, Second Vice President; M. D. Katz, Secretary; Virgil. H. Pace, Treasurer. Trustees were Charles A. Freudenberg, M. Alan Friedman, Robert Aronson, Henry Schutz, Emma F. Schutz, Jacob Leon Miller (Irwin's Father), and Henry I. Greenberg. Any Israelite not under the age of twenty one years could become a member of the Congregation and would be admitted to membership upon a vote of a majority of the members present at the meeting of the Congregation following the meeting at which the application was presented. Other founders may have been Alan Friedman, Jacob Van Straaten, the Radzinski's, Dr. Lewis B. Mount, and Lewis Cohen. Judge M. Henry Cohen of Schaarai Zedek came from Tampa from 1929-1932, to conduct services. See Chapter on Temple Beth-El for the rest of the history.

Joseph Silverberg

Joseph Silverberg came to St. Petersburg during the tourist season and was active in the jewelry/diamond business with Young's Auction Company. In the 1930s, he and his wife, Helen, founded their own diamond business, Bromley's Jewelers. He was very much involved in the local civic and business activities, as well as the Jewish community. He served at Temple Beth-El in many capacities, including President for eight years. Helen, was very involved as an active partner in the business and a member of Temple Bethel, National Council of Jewish

Joseph Silverberg, President of Temple Beth-El 1946-1949, 1951-1952, 1955-1957.

Women, and the Needlework Guild. She was chosen, "Best Dressed Woman of the Year" of St. Petersburg. They moved here permanently in 1935 with their children, Don and Henry.

HIGHLIGHTS of 1930

In the 1930s, some of the Jewish people in St. Petersburg probably lived in a very insulated world where the upset around them was not noted, while others faced the full brunt of discrimination. Signs on Gandy Boulevard said, " No Jews Wanted." However, during working hours from nine to five, Jewish people participated with their neighbors. The downtown yacht club would not allow Jewish members .

Minnie Ross was a widow born in Austria in 1856. Her daughter was Aggath Woolner, a widow born in Wisconsin in 1880, and her grandson, was Edward B., born in Illinois in 1920. Also in St. Petersburg were Max and Rose Goodkind and. Leo L. Donsky, clothing merchants. Leo was born in 1895 and died in 1976. Helen was born in 1895 and died in 1962. The Goodkinds and Donskys were born in Russia. There was a Jewish meat market in town. Mordechay Dickman, age 65, died on September 15, 1931. His and Morris Dickman's arrival dates in St. Petersburg are unknown. Morris Dickman was born on June 26, 1896 and died in August 1928.

The Jewish community was continuously involved in helping all individuals who needed financial assistance. This was done by working on Community Chest drives. Evelyn Fyvolent and Evelyn Goldman, mother of the Silverberg family, were exceptionally active in the 1930s.

David Miller, Evelyn Samuels' brother, was married to Jean, Goldie Schuster's sister. He was in the vegetable business with Goldie Schuster's father. A brother, Meyer, and his wife, Ann Miller, were in the grocery business. A brother, Lewis, lived in Bradenton.

Typically, Jewish girls completed their high school education and went on to take specialized courses or started a working career. The boys would be sent to the University of Florida and other colleges. Many of the early young men became

attorneys including: Leonard Cooperman, son of J. L. Cooperman, one of the founders of Temple Beth-El, Eli and Ernie Katz, Morris Rosenberg, Judge Irving Cypen, Jay Schwartz, Izzy Abrams, BenSchwartz, Shavy Weiss, Harry Green and Sam Greene.

The Reform congregation of Temple Beth-El, although without a ordained rabbi until 1933, was constantly helped and supported by Rabbi Zielonka and Judge M. Henry Cohen of Schaarai Zedek of Tampa. Rabbi Zielonka performed all necessary life cycle events and acted as a good father to this small congregation on the other side of the Bay. Judge Cohen, who had been the secretary of Schaarai Zedek, since its inception in 1894, past President, and the leader of many services including the High Holy Days Services, when there was no rabbi, led the services for Temple Beth-El, until the arrival of Rabbi William Rosenblatt. Both Rabbi Zielonka and Judge Cohen, although Tampa residents, should be considered honorary residents of Pinellas County for their goodness and generosity in helping the Jewish community here.

1930 Census

Some of the Jewish people listed in the St. Petersburg 1930 census included: Jacob Rosenthal, a single person, who was born in New York in 1868; Henrietta Radzinski, age seventy four, and her daughter Eva, age forty four, both born in Pennsylvania. Eva was President of the Beth-El Auxiliary for many years; Bert B. Goldberg, age fifty from Latvia, came to the United States in 1866, and his wife Esther came from Russia in 1890; M. Alan Friedman, age forty four came from Poland to the United States in 1893 and was a retail merchant; his wife, Bella R., age thirty two, came to United States in 1910 from Poland, and was a retail merchant of a woman's dress shop; his daughter, Gladys L., age twenty, born in New Jersey, was listed as a sales lady in a dress shop; his daughter, Ruth Y., age sixteen, born in New York. Gladys and Ruth were from a former marriage; Arthur A. Jacobson, age forty five, born in Wisconsin; his wife Dora, age thirty seven, born in Wisconsin, his son Henry I., age fifteen, born in South Africa, a banking clerk; his daughter, Revelle S., age thirteen, born in Chicago; D. H. Blumberg, age thirty three, born in Russia, a sales merchant; his wife, Minnie, age twenty seven, born in Minnesota; his daughter Maine or Maria or Mamie, age ten; his daughter, Rosebud, age eight, born in Alabama; and his son, Lionel, age six, born in Alabama; David H. Blumberg, age forty four, born in Lithuania and came to the United States in 1889, a retail merchant in leather goods, his wife Minnie, age thirty seven, born in Minnesota, a saleswoman in leather goods; his son, Eugene, age fourteen, born in Alabama; his daughter Roslyn, age ten, born in Alabama; Isaac B. Kogan and his wife Lucy both came to the United States in 1891. He was born in Russia in 1863, and she was born in Russia in 1864. They had been living in Chicago in 1920, where they had a dry goods store; Louis and Dora Goldberg had a clothing store. He was born in Russia in 1877 and he came to the United States in 1897. She was born in Lithuania and came to the United States in 1893. Robert Aronson, divorced, owned a hat store. He was born in Lithuania in 1887 and came to the United States in 1895. He had a son Joseph who was born in New Jersey in 1911. There was another Louis Cohen who was born in Russia in 1870 and came to the United States in 1888. He was the proprietor of a stove repair store. His wife's name was also Celia and she was born in Russia in 1887 and came to United States in 1897. Herman Rosenberg and his wife, Molly, owned a dry goods store. Herman was born in Romania in 1877 and came to the United States in 1902. Molly was born in Romania in 1883 and came to the United States in 1904. She died in Pinellas County in 1955. Morris was born in Florida in 1910; the Pearlsteins, who had an Army and Navy Store; the Signers and the Slimmer's who owned Slimmer Dress Shop, also came in the 1930s.

Early Rabbis and Lay Cantors of Congregation B'nai Israel

Rabbi S. C. Salzman came in 1930. Rabbi Lehrer came around 1931. Rabbi Morris Baumel came in the mid 1930s. Rabbi Irving Obstbaum came in 1937. Rabbi Osterbye came in 1938. No exact dates are available for the following lay cantors: Rubén Sabin,

Rabbi S.C. Salzman

Rabbi Irving Obstbaum

Jules Green and Mr. Robbin.

Aaron Mershen

Aaron Mershen was born in Brooklyn, on April 26, 1917. He came to St. Petersburg and lived with his mother, Ida Goldman Mershen, at 920 Arlington Ave, for six months in order to prepare for his bar mitzvah. At a later date, his brother, Sydney, came to St. Petersburg and worked for the Veterans Administration. His father, Louis, who had been a very successful businessman, died in 1928. Aaron's grandparents and father had arrived in the United States in 1904. Aaron's father, Louis, was born in 1879. Aaron's mother, Ida, was born in 1885 and died in St. Petersburg.

Aaron came back to St. Petersburg in 1934 for his senior year in high school and graduated in February 1935. When he went to high school, he recalls that kids were coming to school without shoes on. Black people had to walk in the streets and not on the sidewalks. Aaron graduated from New York University in 1939, majoring in history, English, and public speaking. He went on to Harvard Law School and was in the class of 1942. He enlisted in the Navy, went to Notre Dame, and received a commission. He was trained as a safety engineer and became a torpedo officer. In late 1945, he was aboard an escort ship when President Roosevelt attended the Dakai Conference. He was involved in all the major combat in the Pacific Ocean. After the war, he became a retail trainee for Abram and Strauss, which is now part of Federated Department Stores. He then joined Stearns Department Store and became their most successful Buyer. He retired from Stearns after forty two years of service and came back to live in St. Petersburg.

HIGHLIGHTS of 1932

Dr. Louis B. Mount, a dermatologist from Albany, New York, became the city's first Jewish physician. He came to St. Petersburg with his wife, Rose, and daughter, Charlotte, who taught piano. Bay Pines Veterans Hospital was built, and during World War II many Jewish doctors fulfilled their medical residency requirements here. The Florence

Crittendon Home was supported by the Jewish women's group. They contributed clothing, money, etc. Reba Salzer was on the Board of Trustees. During the Depression, Abraham Rothblatt, who was then in his seventies, walked seventy two blocks a week to collect dues from each of the members of Congregation B'nai Israel. This usually amounted to fifty cents or a dollar a week.

The Judaic Council was organized by a group of young married and single women. Its purpose was to help Congregation B'nai Israel financially as well as help needy Jewish families. It also assisted the non–sectarian Florence Crittendon home for unwed mothers. The first President was Reba (Mrs. William) Salzer. The club disbanded after World War II.

Isaac and Viola Katz, Abe's parents, came from Portland, Maine. They opened a cigar stand on Central Avenue at 6th Street and then a grocery store at 11th St and 3rd Ave South. Isaac and Viola had three other children, Philip, Leah and Ruth.

HIGHLIGHTS of 1933

Rabbi William Harrison Rosenblatt

Rabbi Rosenblatt assumed the pulpit of Temple Beth-El from 1933-1935 after graduating from Hebrew Union College. From St. Petersburg he went to Tucson, Arizona, and San Pedro, California. During World War II, he served as a chaplain in Reykjavik, Iceland. In the last thirteen years of his life, he was the chaplain at the Sawtelle Veterans Administration Center in Los Angeles, California. He wrote *Conversations with Life*. One page became his wife, Fay's, favorite because it symbolized what Bill Rosenblatt, as a rabbi and a man, wanted to be as a human being and what he wanted his life to mean. He wrote, "Man as a creature of God reflects the characteristics of the Divine. As he faces the realities of life he has the opportunity to express these qualities in daily living. Even in his own moments of discomfort and dissolution, he will still strive to lend encouragement to those who are in need; bring a sympathetic understanding and have a genuine concern for those who feel weak in body and mind; and graciously try to extend a helping hand

to lift up the fallen. In truthfulness, the desire of life can best be answered by the earnest and good works of his heart and hands. Then he will be in accord with the thought of the Psalmist: Who is the man that desireth life, and loveth days, that he may seek good therein?"

Rabbi Rosenblatt will always be remembered, from the days of his studies at Hebrew Union College to the day he died in 1959, for his intense and incessant dedication. Despite his own moments of discomfort, he gave encouragement to those in need, and sympathetic understanding to help the damaged bodies and souls of all people. He was described as a unique human being who desired life and loved days that we might see good and do good.

Anne Manket Wedding

Anne had gone to Hendersonville, North Carolina, with Belle Friedman, a St. Petersburg store owner to visit. They stayed at a Jewish boarding house. She met Harry Calley there and he took her to a house party at Lake Laurie, North Carolina, where she met her future husband, Fred.

On December 30, Anne Manket, the first Jewish child born in Pinellas County in 1914, daughter of Mr. and Mrs. Leon Manket, met Fred Pearlman of North Carolina, brother of Mrs. Maurice (Thelma) Rothman. Ann and Fred were the first marriage at Temple Beth El at 759 Arlington Avenue North. The wedding was at twilight with Rabbi William M. Rosenblatt officiating. The altar was banked with white chrysanthemums and palms with hidden candelabras bearing lighted candles shedding a soft glow during the ceremony. A musical program was performed by Mrs. Bertha Mitchell, pianist, Mrs. E. R. Barnard, soloist, and Benjamin Swartz, violinist. Mrs. Rubin Tennebaum was matron of honor and two cousins, Miss Deborah Levy of Sarasota and Miss Tobiah Lovitz of Tarpon Springs, were bridesmaids. The bride was given in marriage by her uncle, Abraham Tarapani, of Tarpon Springs. Her flowers were an arm bouquet of orchids, yellow roses, and lilies of the valley. Anne had attended St. Petersburg Junior College and Fred had attended the University of Michigan. Their reception was held at the French Village. Anne and Fred lived in Asheville, North Carolina. For many years, her mother, Olga, lived with them.

HIGHLIGHTS of 1934

Kleinfeld Family

Rabbi Alexander Kleinfeld

Rabbi Alexander Kleinfeld conducted High Holy Day Services at Temple Beth-El and later assumed the pulpit of Congregation B'nai Israel. He served the congregation from 1934 to 1937, went to West Palm Beach and came back to Congregation B'nai Israel from 1938 to 1943. He was related to Sigmund Freud. Rabbi Kleinfeld died December 27, 1943. Rabbi and his wife, Clara, were both born in Eastern Europe and emigrated to the United States. They had four children, Frank Kleinfeld, Edith Neimeth, Joe Kleinfeld, and Rosalyn Nyman. Rabbi graduated from Columbia University in New York in 1905 and also had a degree in music. He served a total of 13-15 pulpits in and around New York, New Jersey and the southern part of the United States. Larry Kleinfeld, when speaking of his grandmother, Clara, said, "Although she had no formal education, she was a thinker. She was the most liberating experience in my life. When I was very young, she challenged me to analyze an array of subjects, including the nature of life and God. She said, " If there is a God, he has to be everywhere. You don't have to go to a specific building to be with God."

In 1938, Jennie Sierkese married Frank G., the son of Rabbi Alexander and Clara Kleinfeld. Frank was born on August 20, 1914 and died on March 1, 1988 in St. Petersburg. Frank was extremely active in Jewish and general community affairs. He came here in 1937 from Patterson, New Jersey. He was a jeweler and former owner and pharmacist at the Medical Arts Pharmacy located at Fifth Avenue North and Fourth Street. He graduated with a Degree in Pharmacy from Brooklyn College. He was a board member of Temple Beth-El, active in the Sertoma Club Speech and Hearing clinics, a 32nd Degree Mason with Nitram Lodge 188 F&AM, a member of Egypt Temple Shrine, President of the Florida Lodge of the B'nai B'rith where he was

Chairman of the Anti-Defamation League in Florida. He led local efforts against signs and policies that affected minorities. He spent a substantial amount of time working closely with the editor of the St. Pete Times to foster good feelings to all minorities. When Richard Nixon was running for Vice President, he booked accommodations with a resort hotel which was totally anti-Jewish. Frank informed the Nixon campaign and the booking was canceled. He was also a member of the Florida Gators Alumni Association and Southwest Florida Society of Hospital Pharmacies. Larry, in summing up his father's life said, "He was the greatest guy ever, a man of peace and goodness."

Jennie attended Florida State University when it was an all girls school. She was President of the Florence Crittenden Home and was extremely active in many community organizations. She served on the Planning Committee of the Gulf Coast Jewish Family Services for many years and on its Board of Directors from 1981-1998. Michael Bernstein, the Executive Director of the Gulf Coast Jewish Family Services said of Jennie, "Jennie Kleinfeld had a very good heart....She was very generous, giving of herself and donating to the agency to help those we are privileged to serve. She had a strong sense of humanity and humility, and we were so glad to have her advice and guidance through the years." Her name is on plaques in various buildings around St. Petersburg. After their children, Larry, Allan, and Marilyn Gotfried grew up she assumed the management of the Sierkese Fabric Store. Jennie died on June 20, 2002. Her son Larry said of her, "She championed the little guy. She said it was OK to be a ditch digger because it was honest work and the person was doing something for the community as well as earning a living for his family. This individual and all individuals were to be respected."

Larry Kleinfeld and his wife, Lauren, have a daughter, Elizabeth. Larry graduated from the University of Florida, Nova University with a Master's Degree in Psychology, and then Cumberland College of Law, Birmingham, Alabama. He also was on the faculty of the Berklee College of Music in Boston for a six-year period.

Lauren graduated from the University of Florida with a degree in Recreational Therapy.

Marilyn Kleinfeld Gotfried and her husband, Murray, have four children. Stephen is a public relations director for the B'nai B'rith in Washington, DC. Andrew is Vice President of Compliance for Raymond James Associates. Twins Mindy McGrath and Carrie Guise live, respectively, in Raleigh, North Carolina, and Tampa. Marilyn graduated from the University of Florida with a Degree in Special Education and Murray graduated from Seton Hall University with a Degree in Business Administration.

Other Jewish People

Rae Ornstein (Mrs. Morris) arrived in St. Petersburg with her daughter Sally Rivkind, and two teenage cousins she was taking care of for the winter, Louise and Samuel Sanddock. Sally later married Jack Weissman. Harold and his wife, Pauline Rivkind, came to St. Petersburg in 1948 to be with Harold's mother.

Anna (Goldman) and David Loebel opened a dress store in St. Petersburg on Central Avenue at 7th St. David had previously worked for Aaron Mershen's father. Bella Goldman married Morris Hermer and Morris became David's partner in the dress store.

HIGHLIGHTS of 1935

Arnold Argintar

Arnold's Men's Wear, 548 Central Avenue, is owned by Arnold Argintar. He is an eighty seven-year-old gentleman who goes to work each day, six days a week. He graduated from Hillsborough High School in 1935 and went into the clothing business with a loan from his father. He was an army supply lieutenant in India and China. After WWII, when shopping centers began to grow, other businesses left the downtown area, but his continued to prosper. He is an old-fashioned gentleman, who still on a hot July day wears a coat and tie when he goes out to lunch. He sells clothing and shoes to men whose fathers and grandfathers were customers in past

decades. He remembers when well-dressed men wore detachable collars and straw hats. Everybody smoked and he therefore employed a re-weaver just to fix cigarette burns in suits. There were at least thirty other stores selling men's wear in and around downtown St. Petersburg. His father, Max, opened a store in Ybor City in 1908. Max came from Romania in 1902. He became very active with the Masons. Arnold was President of the St. Petersburg Merchants Association and has been an active booster downtown for many years. He was Chairman of the Cemetery committee for Temple Beth El. His mother, Ann Davis Argintar, was born in New York and then went to Key West. Her brother was Charlie Davis who traveled on the road selling shoes and gave his store to her brother Max. Arnold wife's name was Eleanor and his childrens' names are Susan, Debbie and Hilary. Arnold reported that minyans were frequently held at Max Davis and the Sierkese stores between 1935 and 1940.

Max Argintar and brother Sender in their store in Ybor City, 1908. Photograph courtesy of Sam Argintar

Other Jewish People

Joseph and Sadie Fein were transferred by the IRS to St. Petersburg from New Jersey. Joseph who was a CPA, opened his own accounting firm a few years later. Meyer and Sadie Possick came to St. Petersburg from Boston. Meyer was a builder. Izzy and Irene Abramowitz of Tampa apparently were the first Jewish people to live on Madeira Beach. Abe Goldman, one of the founders of the Covenant Club, wanted to buy the St. Petersburg Yacht Club, which discriminated against Jewish people. He wasn't allowed to do it. Abe owned co-op apartments and built new apartments. He came from Detroit and opened the Provident Loan Company.

Rabbi Leonard J. Rothstein

Rabbi Leonard J. Rothstein

Rabbi Rothstein assumed the pulpit of Temple Beth-El in 1935 and remained until 1937. He was an active Rabbi from 1904-1958, during which time he served some ten or eleven congregations, mostly in the South. He was a person of strict personal integrity, but not lacking in kindness and good will. He was a forceful speaker and controversial person who was in constant demand by civic groups. When he was Rabbi in Pine Bluff, Arkansas, he took public issue with a policy strongly favored by the Chamber of Commerce and other civic bodies, including some influential members of his own congregation and the local B'nai B'rith Lodge. While a rabbi in Alexandria, Louisiana, he headed a group of clergyman who protested against the wide-open-town conditions tolerated and encouraged by the municipal authorities and business interests. He appealed over the head of the Mayor to the Governor and finally to the President of the United States to declare the city out-of-bounds for the Soldiers and the adjacent encampments. Throughout his career, he remained a staunch adherent of Classic Reform Judaism. He was a persistent spokesman of the truth, a courageous preacher of social justice, a proponent of the ideals and principles of the great historic Jewish faith, a loyal friend to those who knew him. He died in Cincinnati, Ohio in 1968.

Rabbi Pizer W. Jacobs

HIGHLIGHTS of 1936

Hotels Owned by Jewish People

Several small hotels on the beaches were owned by Jewish people in the mid to late 1930s and the 1940s before the Rellim Hotel was built. Jewish people came to the Sekon n' Palm Hotel in Pass-a-Grille and the Anchor Inn in Pass-a-Grille. The Anchor Inn had a wonderful restaurant that attracted lots of Jewish people who were permanent residents as well as visitors. Rae and Isadore Shuster opened a motel in John's Pass in 1938, and his brother and sister-in-law, Peter and Buena, opened the Hotel Madeira in John's Pass in 1939.

Sam and Lily Sandler

Sam and Lily came to St. Petersburg to visit friends, Dinah and Isaac Schulman, who already lived here. After yearly vacations, they became permanent residents in 1948, thereby joining their daughter, Muriel, and son-in-law, Marty. Sam's hobby of stamp and coin collection had acquired for him pen pals all over the world. He therefore decided to open a philatelic and numismatic shop in the Arcade at Janice Landing. Sam and Lily were married in London in 1920 and shortly thereafter came to Brooklyn, where their two children, Muriel and Robert were born. Sam served as a calvaryman in World War I, in the Royal Bucks Hussars, Jewish Brigade, of the British Army. Sam was born in Manchester, England in 1896 and died in St. Petersburg, Florida in 1972. Lily was born in London, England in 1896 and died in St. Petersburg in 1989.

HIGHLIGHTS of 1937

Rabbi Pizer W. Jacobs assumed the pulpit of Temple Beth-El on August 27, 1937. Rabbi and Mrs. Jacobs came from New York stopping to visit in Jacksonville and Tampa. He had previously been the rabbi for the Reform Temple of Jacksonville for seven years. He had also served in Gary, Indiana, Plainfield, New Jersey, and in New York City. He was a graduate of Hebrew Union College in Cincinnati where he received the Jones prize for oratory. He began his ministry in 1900 and was an active Rabbi for over fifty years. He was one of the elders of the Central Conference of American Rabbis and frequently attended its sessions. He died in September, 1966. Mrs. Jacobs was a native of Columbus, Georgia and a former dramatic teacher in New York.

Hyman M. Jacobs was the chairman of the first United Palestine Appeal, which later became the St. Petersburg Jewish Community Council and finally merged with the Clearwater group into the Jewish Federation of Pinellas County.

Jack Adelman and his wife, Jackie, came to St. Petersburg from Los Angeles, California. Jack had served during World War II, in the United States Army. They had two children, Charles H. and Joseph L. Jack died December 5, 1981 in St. Petersburg. He was born in 1906 in Montréal, Canada.

Gus Goldblatt, brother of Bessie Jacobs, owned a mattress store at 19th Street and Central Avenue. Eli Gelman had a grocery store on 22nd St S. and later moved to 1st Ave North and opened a gift shop. Reba Salzer had a gas station and was in the women's wear business at 6th Street and Central Avenue. She was very active in the Florence Crittendon Home.

Katherine and Maurice Diamond, and their daughter, Thelma, came to St. Petersburg from Newark, New Jersey. In 1938, Maurice opened Stewarts Art Gallery, which was an auction house for fine art and fine jewelry. It was located on Central Avenue between 3rd and 4th Streets on the North Side. Maurice was born in Russia in 1894 and he died in 1962. He came to the United States to New York City in 1905 or 1906. Katherine was born in 1897 in Russia and died in St. Petersburg in 1983. She came to the United States with her family when she was a baby and they settled in Chelsea, Massachusetts. They had their business in St. Petersburg from 1937-1942 and then opened up a new business in Lake Worth, which was near Palm Beach, Florida, where they remained from 1942-1962. After Maurice's death, Katherine came to live with her daughter, Thelma, and son-in-law, Jerry Gilbert.

Joel Grossman, was bar mitzvahed by Rabbi Joseph Shenker at Congregation B'nai Israel. He was the son of Mrs. L. Grossman.

HIGHLIGHTS of 1938

The Jewish people of St. Petersburg started a campaign to raise $10,000 for the work of the United Palestine Appeal, a Jewish social service organization under the leadership of Rabbi Stephen S. Wise and Nathan Straus, for the purpose of financing the movement of Jewish peoplefrom Germany and Poland into Palestine. David Rothblatt was the chairman of the committee. From World War I until 1937, American Jewish people had donated over $18 million to the welfare of European Jews. David Rothblatt declared that the unification of the forces of St. Petersburg Jewry was made imperative by the difficult conditions which faced fellow Jews in many countries in Europe. He felt that the one and only constructive method of solving permanently the problem of Jewish homelessness in Europe was to move the people to Palestine. The featured speaker was Joachim Prinz, past Chief Rabbi of Germany. Over 150 people attended the meeting at Congregation B'nai Israel on May 10.

Samuel(Sol) Green

Samuel (Sol) Green, the son of Benjamin and Celia, who owned the restaurant and deli, went to St. Petersburg High School and the University of Florida Law School. He went to New York, where he met and married Margaret Lang. They returned to St. Petersburg in 1938, where Sol opened a law practice on 4th Street. He was active in the St. Petersburg Bar Association and several of the civic clubs. Neither he nor other Jewish people could join or be a guest at the St. Petersburg Yacht Club. He was an avid golfer and was able to join the Pasadena Country Club and later Seminole and Bardmoor. He, his wife Margaret and his son, Robert, enjoyed summers along with many other Jewish families at the Rellim Hotel on St. Pete Beach. Sol was born in 1909 and died in 1979. Margaret was born in 1914 and died in 1990.

B'nai B'rith

A B'nai B'rith meeting was held on May 29, 1938. The officers were: President M. Alan Friedman, Monitor Rabbi Pizer W. Jacobs of Temple Beth-El, and Past President David Rothblatt. They represented B'nai B'rith Lodge Number 1246 at a Conference of the Southern Regional Lodges in Orlando. Other local officers were: Vice President Arnold Argintar, Treasurer Abraham Sierkese, Recording Secretary Frank Kleinfeld, Financial Secretary Harry Cypen, Guardian Harry Herman, Warden

Louis Bishop, Assistant Monitor Rabbi Alexander S. Kleinfeld, and Trustee Max Davis, Trustee David Rothblatt, and Trustee Sam Trager. The following day, Rabbi Jacobs, his wife and Morris Hermer were injured in an automobile accident when David Rothblatt's vehicle went out of control near the Gandy Bridge.

HIGHLIGHTS of 1939

National Council of Jewish Women

The National Council of Jewish Women's local chapter was organized in St. Petersburg and then was chartered in 1940. This chapter was involved in many worthwhile programs, including the State Youth Employment Service, Nina Harris School, which is still in existence, the Cerebral Palsy Program, Disadvantaged Children's Program, and Retarded Children's Program. The first President was Mrs. Louis Cohen.

On May 24, Rabbi Kleinfeld confirmed ten young people at Congregation B'nai Israel. They were: Donna Rabinowitz, Marie Davis, Corinne Silverman, Lillian Gordon, Shirley Gordon, Irving Herscovitz, Joel Grossman, Phillip Benjamin, Marvin Rabinowitz, and Jerome Goldberg.

HIGHLIGHTS of 1940

Judge Irving Cypen

Irving Cypen, the son of Mr. and Mrs. Max Cypen, graduated from the University of Florida. He married Hazel Abrams. Both of them grew up in St. Petersburg. They went to the same high school and junior college. They married in September 1941. Irving finished law school and enlisted in the United States Navy as an officer. Shortly thereafter, Hazel gave birth to their first son, Steven. In 1958, after serving as an assistant municipal prosecutor and judge, Florida Governor Lee Roy Collins appointed Irving to the Miami-Dade Circuit Court. He resigned in 1963 to resume his private practice. They have five children, Steven, Wayne and Myles who are attorneys, Tad who is an artist, and Bonnie Cypen Epstein, who is a social worker. In 2005, they were honored for fifty three years of volunteer work at the Miami Jewish Home

and Hospital for the Aged. In 1951, they had taken a cottage where twenty three widows and widowers lived and turned it into a state-of-the-art research facility that is home to about 700 residents on twenty acres of land. They have contributed more than $1 million and have helped negotiate the contributions of sixty other million-dollar donors. They are there virtually every day making contributions to the people who reside there.

HIGHLIGHTS of 1941

In June, the greatest concern that the young people had in St. Petersburg was to go to the city's fun spots such as the Spa Beach. Natalie Brader, Thelma Diamond, Caroline Brhem, and Corinne Silverman, all high school students, were part of this group. The Gulf beaches were full of people enjoying themselves. By October, there were concerns of a potential war. Members of the Sunshine City Chapter number 351, A.Z.A., Junior Order of the B'nai B'rith Lodge purchased a $100 National Defense Saving Bond. The officers were Willie Abrams, President; Max Keves, Treasurer, and Phillip Benjamin, Secretary.

Rellim Hotel

In 1941, the Rellim Hotel was built on St. Petersburg Beach by Jacob Leon Miller and Harriet S. Miller. The land was purchased from Thomas Rowe who built the Don CeSar Hotel. Jewish people were barred from area resorts and restaurants in the 1940s, except for the Hotel Rellim. Irwin Miller said, "This was a major reason that Dad opened the hotel. The beaches needed to be for everyone." Jacob L. Miller offered food, relaxation and entertainment to Jewish guests for fifteen years, eventually adding villas to the resort. The family ran the resort for another twenty five years after his death. The small resort offered many of the luxuries of the large resorts on the beach. The hotel provided the Jewish people of St. Petersburg, as well as the visitors, a place to socialize. The land for the hotel was at 3200 Gulf Blvd. Initially, the hotel struggled because Jake knew very little about the hotel business.

Within a year, Jacob leased the forty four room hotel to a cruise ship operator, who converted the hotel into an American plan, which offered lodging and three meals a day for one price. In 1948, Jacob purchased land across Gulf Boulevard and built eight, three room villas. In the early 1950s, the Rellim was first to offer golf at the Pasadena Golf Course to their guests. Irwin Miller became the manager of the Rellim Hotel and Sonya Halaczer Miller, who he had married in 1948, directed the entertainment. Rellim Hotel guests enjoyed dances, movies, bingo, dinners, strolling violinists, antique shows, dog races, and a variety of special events. Sonya's theme parties each month were events that the hotel guests always looked forward to. There was a Mexican fiesta, a Presidential ball, cartoon capers, Mardi Gras, a shipwreck dance, and on and on. The hotel operated from December 15 to April 1 each year, and then as a beach club in the summer. The guests became family and returned year after year. Sonia published a newspaper called the Rellim-Tellim to keep the guests aware of the upcoming events. The Rellim Hotel had wonderful clientele and a great reputation. In November 1980, Irwin Miller decided to sell the hotel.

Covenant Club

In 1942, the Jewish Community of St. Petersburg purchased $100,000 in war bonds. On December 7, 1942, Mayor Robert J. McCutcheon, Jr., the Honorable J. D. Pearce, Postmaster, the Honorable W. W. Mc Eachern, President of the Union Trust Company, Rev. J. Wallace Hamilton, Pasadena Community Church and the rabbis from Congregation B'nai Israel and Temple Beth El attended a special dinner, Servicemen's Night, of the Covenant Club to celebrate the magnificent efforts of the Jewish community and their contributions to fighting the war. An honor roll plaque was dedicated to the various members of the Covenant Club and their children who served in the Armed Forces of the United States. The Covenant Club members and their wives and sweethearts were in attendance. Some of the people mentioned in a letter dated December 7, 1942, addressed to Dear Spanky (Irving Spanierman) were;

Sydney (no last name given), Maury Stein, Stanley Minshall, George Fink Hopkins, Dave Yaffin, Al Esrick, Al Rubin, Louis Cohen, Harry Mogil, Harold Slimmer, Danny Berkman, Sam Fyvolent, Maurice Diamond, Phil Wachtler, Sylvia Kaufman (who married Herb Slocum), Mr. Sierkese, Joe Silverberg, Ed Goldman, Jud Young and Sarla, Milton Lew, Sol Green, Joe Davis, Bob Abrams, Anita Stein, the Argintars, the Kleinfields, Frank Rabin, Max Davis, Irving Greenstone, Ike (Lucius Beebe) Bermant, Ruby and Fern Saborsky, Mack Samuels, Clara Williams. The Covenant Club had been founded in the late 1930s, when the Jewish people were denied membership in the Junior Chamber of Commerce. After World War II, the Covenant Club folded and the men became part of the Louis A. Cohen Lodge of the B'nai B'rith. The money that was left in the treasury was donated to the Child Guidance Clinic of St. Petersburg.

In 1943, the Covenant Club provided the first funding for the Child Guidance Clinic of St. Petersburg. The club members belonged to the Child and Family Committee of the Community Welfare Council of St. Petersburg. Because of the Covenant Club's generous support of the Child Guidance Clinic, the clinic was able to ensure that it would be open at least one day a week. The clinic was dedicated to a program of psychological service to children with emotional, educational or social difficulties and also the clinic fostered an educational program in the field of mental health. In 1948, social worker Harold Rivkind came to the Child Guidance Clinic and served in many capacities for an extended period of time.

HIGHLIGHTS of 1942

Evelyn Goldman and Evelyn Samuels both took Red Cross volunteer courses in nutrition and food handling and then worked as volunteers during World War II. During the war years, the Sisterhood of Congregation B'nai Israel took on the work of the U.S.O., to take care of the needs of the many hundreds of Jewish men in the armed services that were stationed in this area. They participated in many community efforts including work for the blind, interfaith, cultural, and social programs.

Ben Bush

Bush Egg Farm

The Bush family purchased the Eureka Egg Farm and Hatchery in the Fall. It was located at 38th Avenue North and 66 Street North in St. Petersburg. Selig and Ida Bush came during the winter months in the middle to late1930s to Madeira Beach and stayed either at Isadore Schuster's small hotel or Peter Schuster's Hotel Madeira. Looking for a business opportunity at the beginning of World War II, they decided to purchase the egg and chicken hatchery. They brought their sons, Ben and Sam, into the business. At that time, there were over 200 poultry farms in Pinellas County. They were organized into the Pepco Cooperative (Pinellas Egg Producers Cooperative). Sam became the first President. He eventually became the Director of the Poultry and Egg Division of the State of Florida. Ben sold the business in 1958 and then went back to complete his engineering degree, that had been interrupted by the war. Ben graduated from the University of Florida in 1966 with a Degree in Plastics Engineering. His son, Sandy, and daughter, Gayle, graduated at the same time. When he graduated from high school he applied to the Massachusetts Institute of Technology in Cambridge. He took an examination and received a grade of 97.3 percent. When he was interviewed by the registrar he was told that he would not be admitted that year because they already had their quota of Hebrew people. He finally ended up going to City College of New York. It was his experience in Cambridge that made him into the determined person he became. He finished his college degree many years after his normal time, became a successful plastics engineer and inventor, and fought discrimination wherever it would appear. He invented machines which could dispense eggs, bread, milk, doughnuts, Pepsi Cola, and Cuban sandwiches. He also invented a coin changer. He went into the plastics fabricating business .After his wife, Ida, died from cancer he met Iris Beverly Heilweil in 1968 and remarried. Iris had been originally married to Dr. Robert E. Carroll. Iris and her parents, David and Rose, arrived in St. Petersburg in 1944. They joined Iris's Uncle Ray and Aunt Clara Farber who arrived in the late 1930

and owned the Ace Beauty Company.

Ben became active in B'nai B'rith as a Lodge President, a Council President, and finally the President of the Florida State Association. He served as a board member of the Jewish Federation and Chairman of the Community Relations Committee for about thirteen years. He was also Chairman of the Anti-Defamation League for the west coast of Florida from Pensacola to Naples. From 1973 to 1983, he was continually harassed by the Ku Klux Klan and their neo-Nazi friends. His panel truck was disfigured, he received harassing messages, was continuously called at two or three o'clock in the morning, and his house and store were broken into. After he retired from his business he continued his lifelong work of helping other people. He became a tutor at a high school in algebra, geometry, and trigonometry. He helped develop math classes which made the subject much more interesting for high school students. He established chess clubs in all the high schools in the county. He is currently coordinating an Industrial Plastics Program at the Pinellas Technical Education Center in Clearwater, as well as working on new inventions. In March 2002, he was given the B'nai B'rith Citation of Appreciation for sixty years of service to humanity.

HIGHLIGHTS of 1943

Jewelry stores and jewelry auctioneers were big businesses during World War II.

Jewish women served as volunteer hostesses and some others worked at the beach USO home at Pass-a-Grill.

Sarah F. Moss

Sarah Moss arrived in St. Petersburg in the early 1940s. She was a graduate of Hunter College in New York City and spent a career teaching and operating children's camps. She became a teacher and then the principal at Congregation B'nai Israel's Hebrew School. Under her leadership, the school grew and included classes from nursery level to adult level. She was described as, "Winsome, gentle and kind, a most excellent example of Jewish womanhood..." "A tireless worker who worked seven days a week." Father

Otis B. Mason, an Episcopalian priest, told of her qualities as a teacher, "So many teachers lack patience, but not Mrs. Moss. She has an understanding that has led me to a deep appreciation of Judaism." During her career she was honored by many people including a special testimonial dinner at the synagogue where 200 members, friends, and relatives rose to applaud her for her many contributions to the Jewish community and the general community. Dr. Phillip Benjamin said of her, "We are honoring a person who is a philanthropist not in money but in time and love."

HIGHLIGHTS of 1944

Rabbi Rothenberg

Rabbi Rothenberg received his rabbinical training at the Rabbi Isaac Elchanan Theological Seminary in New York City, and was installed as the Rabbi of Congregation B'nai Israel in December. He studied under the late Rabbi Dr. Bernard Hovel, Founder and President of the Yeshiva and Yeshiva College, and Rabbi Moses Soloveichik. Rabbi Rothenberg was ordained in March 1944. He previously served at the Jewish Center of Highbridge, Bronx, New York and the Jewish Center in Long Island, New York.

Beatrice F. Mehl

Beatrice and her first husband, Philip Davis arrived in St. Petersburg on October 6. They bought a small juice stand and operated for two years and then owned several other businesses. She divorced Philip and later married Joseph Michael Mehl. Her father, Nathan Fischman, and her mother, Miriam, moved to St. Petersburg in 1951. Additional relatives arrived over the years.

Rothblatt family

Audrey Rothblatt was given a commendation for contributing more than 500 hours to the Bomb-a-Dears, a group of volunteer young women who helped provide recreation for the serviceman being trained in St. Petersburg. Her mother also helped in the war effort by encouraging families with young children to come to her apartment house and reside there. She became the grandmother to all the

babies and young children, and mother to the young, expectant women away from their homes. She worried as much or more about these children and the husbands overseas than most family members would. In all, she helped take care of twenty five families whose fathers were in the armed forces. A second daughter, Bunnie, had 700 hours of service to the Bomb-a-Dears. On Saturday nights at the Pier and on Tuesday nights at the Maritime Service Station, Bunnie and her partner Jerry Bowman would put on jitterbug dancing performances. In 1941, at age fourteen, Bunnie started her own metal salvage drive by putting a large wooden barrel on the corner of her parents' lot and asking people to contribute scrap metal to the war effort. In a short period of time it was half-full of copper and brass.

Max Keller

Max Keller, grandson of Harry Hankin, was born in St. Petersburg. His father, who was a shoemaker, when he was not hammering nails into shoes, was hammering the importance of an education into Max's head. When Max was in third grade, he decided he'd become a lawyer. Max also married a lawyer. By the time he entered Mirror Lake Junior High School, he was becoming a successful shoe salesman. As a senior at Northeast High School, he built the Shoemobile, a twelve-foot-long and five-foot-high fiberglass shoe mounted on a retired post office scooter. He drove this unusual machine all over St. Petersburg picking up and delivering shoes for his father's Owl Shoe Repair business, which was located on the south side of Central Avenue at 6th Street. He became a workaholic and sold houses, massaging mattresses, vacuum cleaners, and dancing lessons. After graduating from Stetson Law School in St. Petersburg he went into law practice and then later on became involved in producing movies. He sold many of these movies to the networks to be used in television.

1944 A.Z.A. dance
back row:
Dorothy Dayan,
Sylvia Heller Wittner,
Sally Rubin Goodrich,
Bunny Katz, Bernice
"Bunnie" Rothblatt Katz.
front:
Sonya Halaczer Miller,
Mrs. Clara Mitchman.

HIGHLIGHTS of 1945

Empire Hotel

top: Glassman's Kosher
Meat, 1020 First Avenue,
North
bottom: Empire Hotel.

The Empire Hotel, which was a kosher hotel with a kosher restaurant, was located on 11th St between 1st Avenue and Arlington (address was 1099 1st Ave S.), across the street from Congregation B'nai Israel. It was owned by the Glassman family, the parents, Jacob and Ida, and the sons, Sol and Leon. Jacob was born in 1891 in Russia and died in 1953 in St. Petersburg. Ida was born in 1885 in Romania/Hungary and died in 1976 in St. Petersburg. Jacob and Ida had gone to Sarasota to look for a possible business opportunity. They decided to come to visit St. Petersburg in 1944 and bought the Empire Hotel in 1945. Jacob and Ida had previously had kosher restaurants in New York and, therefore, had the knowledge and ability to operate this facility. At first, the hotel provided kosher meals three times a day, and then later two times a day. The hotel and restaurant were open from September to May each year, after the completion of the Festival of States and Passover. Although it was a kosher hotel, Jewish and non-Jewish tourists stayed for extended periods of time. Because of the Empire's close location to the spring training field, a bunch of the baseball crowd elected to come. The Glassman family advertised in the Jewish Forward and drew most of its clientele from New York, New Jersey, and occasionally elsewhere. The Empire Hotel quickly became the place to hold large seders. The hotel was sold in 1973.

After leaving the service in 1945, Sol joined the business. He was born January 3, 1917, and died on September 16, 1996. Sol was a sergeant in the Army. He married Helen in 1947 and had a retail store in Tarpon Springs.

After completing his service obligation in 1946, Leon became a partner in the business. Leon had worked for the United States Postal Service in New York prior to World War II. He served in the Army Air Corps for three years. Leon was born on November 25, 1915 in New York. He married Edna Kolodny on June 19, 1948. They had a daughter, Ellen, who went to St. Pete Jr. College and then the University of South Florida to earn a Bachelor of Science Degree in Sociology in 1971. As a teenager, she earned her allowance by working at the hotel and by driving people to the Jewish Community Center on Elbow Lane. She currently works for a local congressman. Edna was born on October 13, 1923 and died on November 8, 1988. Leon was one of the founders of the St. Petersburg Jewish War Veterans Post, Abe Adler, # 246. He became: Commander of Post #246; President, Pinellas County Veterans Liaison Council; President Men's Club Congregation B'nai Israel; Board Member Congregation B'nai Israel. After he closed the hotel he became the Food Service Director for Stetson College of Law. He was the first person to oversee kashrut at Menorah Manor. He instituted the Four Chaplins Sunday and Veterans' Day Service. Edna was a very likable person who was always part of the working force. She was the President of the Jewish War Veteran Auxiliary at the local and state level.

St. Petersburg Jewish Community Council was founded sometime in 1945 or 1946. The object and purpose of the organization was to further the welfare of the Jewish community by: coordinating the functioning of the affiliated Jewish organizations and the Jewish community at large; centralizing all fund-raising for general Jewish causes and local charities and welfare work to avoid duplication, and create efficiency; supervising all relief aid, social and welfare work in the community; assisting in all social and cultural programs of the affiliated organizations; affording the Jewish community as a whole an opportunity to unite, harmonize and facilitate the activities of all affiliated organizations and all Jewish people. The affiliated organizations included: Congregation B'nai Israel, Temple Beth-El, Ladies Auxiliary of Congregation B'nai Israel, Sisterhood of Temple Beth-El, Louis Cohen Lodge of B'nai B'rith, Covenant Club, Hadassah, Jewish War Veterans Post Number 246, National Council of Jewish Women, Massada, and Zionist Organization of America. Any other interested Jewish organization that had been in operation for at least one year could become a member with the approval of the Board of Directors of the Council.

Ben Bush's sister, Minnie, and her husband, Max Leopold, purchased a poultry farm.

Philip Katz, brother of Abe Katz, and Rosalind F. Katz, owned Phil and Murray's Delicatessen at 123 -- 9th St. North from 1945 to 1960. He died April 2, 1970. She died on September 17, 1986. They were both active in Congregation B'nai Israel.

Louis P. Greenberg, a World War I veteran, was admitted to Bay Pines Veterans Hospital, because of his total disability due to gassing, which led to lung cancer. He had previously had his lung removed in Boston City Hospital by Dr. Stroeder, who had apparently been the first person in Boston to perform such an operation. During World War I, while serving in France, he was gassed by the Germans with mustard gas. He spent time in a French hospital and then came back to Boston, where he opened a store selling store fixtures. He was born on April 19, 1888 and died on August 23, 1947 in St. Petersburg. He came to the United States in 1890 with his parents from Kaslav, Ukraine. Rabbi Chapman officiated at his military funeral and Louis became the first Jewish person to be buried at the Bay Pines Veterans Hospital Cemetery. His son, Allan Green, attended his funeral and subsequently made at least eighteen trips to St. Petersburg to say Kaddish at his father's grave. Allan, who is an attorney, graduated from Brown University and Boston University Law school. While in St. Petersburg, on all of the previous occasions, he has always worshiped at Congregation B'nai Israel as a thank you to Rabbi Chapman for his kindness some fifty eight years ago. When Allan was asked about his father, he said, "I love my father very dearly. He was a symbol of strength and courage. He lived for his last six years totally disabled and in a great deal of pain, but still tried to be helpful to all those around him. During his last six months of life, he said to me, "Be my Kaddish." Allen is a prime example of a

child, although an adult, continuing to honor his/her father and/or mother. Allan has never missed saying Kaddish for his father.

HIGHLIGHTS of 1946

In 1946, after World War II, many of the soldiers who trained in this area liked it so much that they came back to make it their permanent homes. Among them were a group of Jewish servicemen who had enjoyed the hospitality of the Jewish people for Sabbath dinners and seders and thought this was a wonderful place to be. Some married girls from the local Jewish community. Jewish doctors from Bay Pines Veteran's Hospital started practices after World War II in the St. Petersburg area. Dr. Julius Fishman, a dentist, also started a practice then.

Lowell S. Fyvolent and his father-in-law, Michael Sudakow, owned Plaza Realty Associates. They developed Central Plaza, which opened in 1952, as a convenient central shopping center. It was the first shopping center in Pinellas County. It covered a fourteen block area and was the hub of the city along 34th Street (U. S. 19) and Central Avenue. It was the progenitor of today's shopping malls, many of which are managed by Jewish people, including the Simon family and Taubman family.

Jacqueline (Jackie) F. and Murray Jacobs

Jackie (maiden name Feinstein) and Murray Jacobs, owners of Goodyear Rubber Products on Central Avenue at 25th St., helped build the Jewish and non-Jewish communities. They arrived in March, after Murray served in the Army Signal Corps. Jackie's grandfather came from Russia in 1880 and her grandmother in 1885 and settled in New York. Her grandfather served in World War I. Jackie and Murray were both born in Brooklyn. They started the Goodyear Rubber Products Company, in 1948, from the back of their station wagon, delivering garden hoses to hardware stores from New Port Richey to Sarasota. They had stores in St. Petersburg, Pinellas Park, Clearwater, Tampa, Bradenton and Fort Myers. They went into business on Sunset Beach and called it, "Jackie and Murray's

Murray Jacobs

Bar and Restaurant." They owned a resort restaurant and a trucking company in the past and then purchased several pieces of real estate in St. Petersburg, including commercial property.

They joined Congregation B'nai Israel in 1948. She subsequently became Sisterhood President and served on the board for over twenty five years. She was Chairman of the Board of Gulf Coast Jewish Family Services and served on the Boards of Menorah Manor Foundation, National Council of Jewish Women, ORT, and Hadassah. She was a board member of the Florida Orchestra and was a recipient of St. Petersburg's Senior Hall of Fame Award. From 1960-1964, Murray was Vice President and Chairman of the Board of Congregation B'nai Israel and then became President in 1965 and 1966. He served in numerous other offices. He received a special Presidential Citation from the Jewish Theological Seminary of America in 1965. In 1967, Murray was given the Man-of-the-Year Award from B'nai Brith Organization. The two of them helped their fellow Jews and their fellow citizens of the community. In 1960, she became a charter member of the B'nai B'rith Women, Chapter 5, St. Petersburg, Florida. In 1976, Jackie helped originate the United Jewish Appeal Pacesetter Division for Women. She helped raise funds for the synagogue for twenty years by chairing the Committee of the Calendar Book. Murray, as an officer of the 58th Street Land Company, helped raise the funds to buy the land for Menorah Center and Menorah Manor. Murray was President of the Jewish Community Center and Jewish Community Council. He was part of a group who organized the Jewish Federation of Pinellas County. Murray was Chairman and Commissioner of the Pinellas County Housing Authority, a member of the St. Petersburg Chamber of Commerce, and a delegate to the Religious United for Action in Community. He was a Mason and Shriner. In 1970, Jackie and Murray founded a conservative synagogue in Ashkelon, Israel, while they were delegates to the World Council of Synagogues. Murray founded the Pinellas County Union of Temples and Rabbis. They both received numerous awards for their dedication and service. He

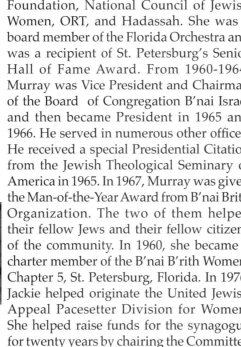

Jerome and Thelma Gilbert

died on January 29, 1986. She died on April 19, 2000.

Jackie was born on July 31, 1921. Her father's name was Saul Feinstein. Her mother's maiden name was Wenocor. Her grandfather came from Russia in 1880 and her grandmother came from Austria in 1885. They first settled in New York and then went on to Massachusetts. Most of their family members then migrated to the United States. Her grandfather died at a young age and, therefore, her grandmother had to raise three small children, five, seven and nine. She worked as a seamstress and dress designer in her home. Jackie's mother told her the story of the great "Chelsea Fire (Massachusetts)" which drove her mother, siblings, and grandmother into the street and to the top of Bunker Hill where they fled to avoid the fire. They watched the entire community being destroyed.

Thelma Gilbert

Thelma spent her winters in St. Petersburg and went to high school here and her summers in Atlantic City. She graduated from St. Petersburg High School in 1941. She returned to St. Petersburg in the Fall of 1946 after her marriage to Jerome Gilbert and worked with him when he first opened his jewelry store, Gilberts Jewel Box. She served in many offices in Congregation B'nai Israel's Sisterhood and became its President in 1963-1965 and again in 1972. She also was the Vice President of Florida Branch Women's League for Conservative Judaism for six years. She was President of the local Jewish War Veterans Auxiliary and became the first Jewish woman to be President of the Veterans Liason's Council Auxiliary, which was comprised of all the veterans auxiliaries in the city. She has been an active volunteer and member of the Pinellas Association for Retarded Children, the League to Aid Retarded Children, and Hadassah.

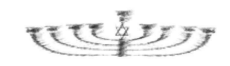

Jerome (Jerry) Gilbert

Jerry Gilbert was born on December 20, 1922 in St. Petersburg. He, Abe Katz, and Phil Benjamin learned Hebrew at the back of a small church which had become the first building for Congregation B'nai Israel. The building was stucco and coquina shells. From 1942-1946, Jerry served in the Coast Guard, mostly in the North Atlantic. In 1947 or 1948, he was the Post Commander of the Jewish War Veterans. In 1947, Dr. Benjamin persuaded him to join the Board of Directors of Congregation B'nai Israel. In 1954, he became President as his father had been many years before. He also served as Chairman of the Board for five years. Jerry recalled that the original board meetings he attended were rather informal. At one meeting, the treasurer, who was one of the most prominent and prosperous members when asked to give a report said "we have enough." This same person at each Yom Kippur appeal would stun the congregation by pledging $100 when most of the pledges were $5 and $10. In the early days, the rabbi's salary was paid by contributions from members, one and two dollars at a time. Jerry has made many other contributions to the Jewish and non-Jewish communities, including President of the Pinellas Association for Retarded Children, in 1974 or 1975. Jerry's sister, Fern Sabin Spoto, was active in the hospital now called Bayfront for many years. She served as President of the Auxiliary, as well as held other offices.

Rabbi Max Kaufman

Rabbi Max Kaufman assumed the pulpit of Congregation B'nai Israel. He had a Master of Arts Degree and Ph.D. from Columbia University. He was the author of several books and had contributed to numerous periodicals over the years. He had previously been the rabbi at Schenectady, New York, and Plainfield, New Jersey.

Wides Family

Vernon and Gladys Wides moved to St. Pete Beach from Boston. In November of 1945, they visited Gladys's parents, Harry and Molly Segal, in the St. Petersburg area during a winter vacation. They went home, settled their affairs, gathered their belongings, and they with their son, Ken moved here. Vernon had been born in Boston on March 13, 1915 to Isaac and Anne Wides, and Gladys had been born in Minneapolis on August 12, 1916. They were married in Boston on July 7, 1940, and had Ken on February 14, 1944, in Boston and Susan on September 13, 1946, in St. Petersburg.

Vernon went into the wholesale produce business selling to beach hotels and stores. Later he had a Mary Carter Paint Store for three years. In 1960, he moved his family to California to go into the junkyard business with his brother-in-law, but returned to St. Pete Beach in 1962 to become a Prudential Life Insurance agent. Kenneth served on the Board of Trustees of Temple Beth-El numerous times. When Vernon was asked what the Temple meant to him he said, "The Temple is for prayer, Simchas, and teaching us to be leaders."

He and his family have always lead by example as well as by word. He retired in the early 1990s and he and Gladys moved into Menorah Manor in May 2002. Gladys worked for the Sierkese family in the 1960s. She became very active in Sisterhood of Temple Beth-El and served as chairperson of many committees for over twenty years. Gladys died on August 30, 2004. Vernon died April 17, 2005.

Rabbi David Susskind's first Bar Mitzvah. l. to r. Harry and Molly Segal, Gladys Wides, Kenneth Wides, Susan Wides, Vernon Wides, Annie Wides.

Kenneth became the first Bar Mitzvah for Rabbi David Susskind and Susan became the first Bat Mitzvah at Temple Beth-El. Kenneth graduated from Florida State University in 1966 with a Bachelor of Science Degree in Economics. He married Elaine Jean Craig on August 19, 1972. They had six children, Sara, Shana, Joshua, Adam, Jesse, and Zachary. Kenneth served on the Temple Board. He was President of St. Petersburg Junior College Alumni Association, Member of the Board of South West Little League and coached Little League for twelve years. He and his wife became major donors to the

Rabbi Max Kaufman

Temple Beth-El Build Now Campaign in 1992, L'Dor V'Dor Campaign in 2000, and donated the Wides Courtyard for the new religious school.

Susan Wides Burnett served on the Temple Board and became Principal of the Religious School. She helped build a solid foundation from which the current religious school has grown with a fine reputation. She was also Secretary of Board of Trustees of Temple Beth El for several years. Susan's daughters, Alison and Jennifer, were also both Bat Mitzvah and confirmed at Temple Beth-El. Susan received an Associate of Arts Degree from St. Petersburg Junior College in 1966, a Bachelor of Arts in Social Science Education from the University of South Florida in 1969, and a Master of Administration/Supervision from the University of South Florida in 1980. From 1969 to 1994, she taught at three high schools, Lakewood, Gibbs, and Dixie Hollins. She was then the Tech Prep Coordinator for the Pinellas County School Board for two years and since then has been the Tech Prep Coordinator for St. Petersburg College. She married Donald C. Burnett on January 3, 1971.

Donald was born on July 25, 1946 and died May 20, 1991. He received his Associate of Arts Degree from St. Petersburg Junior College in 1971, and his Bachelor of Arts Degree from University of South Florida in 1973. He was Manager of Taxes for Florida Power Corp. and was Vice President and Treasurer of Temple Beth-El. He was President of the Florida Power Club.

Elaine Wides

Elaine Wides

Elaine is a person of huge energy. She is everywhere and doing everything to make our society a better place to live. She is the ultimate volunteer. Elaine Jean Craig was born to Robert and Jean Craig in St. Petersburg on April 19, 1950. She graduated from Florida State University in 1972 with a Bachelor of Science Degree in Housing and Interior Design with a minor in Art History. She had spent six months in Italy in the Florence Art Program. In 1973 and 1974, she worked for the Metro Care Development for eighteen months in the advertising department and the Deco Center at Town

Shores Condos in Gulfport. She has chaired and co-chaired numerous committees. She is the co-chair, with Mary Ann Marger, of the Archive Committee of Temple Beth-El, and in this capacity has provided enormous assistance to the author. She has chaired committees of CASA, PTA, St. Petersburg High School, Shorecrest High School, and Southwest Little League. When asked why she was involved in so many activities on a voluntary basis while raising six children, she said, "In contemplating my reasons I finally thought in terms of a tapestry or piece of cloth, that its individual threads taken alone don't necessarily seem important until woven together, where they can tell a story or express a feeling. I'd like to think of myself as a thread that may add to the fabric's story or more importantly, be used to help repair holes or frayed edges that might destroy the fabric and its history. For me discovering and keeping the past alive is just as important as living a productive life in the present and hopefully giving something to the future."

HIGHLIGHTS of 1947

In 1947, Sidney Colen, an interior decorator by profession, was going to San Pao, Brazil. He thought it would be a wonderful place to live. However, he decided to first visit his parents in St. Petersburg. Once here, he never left this area. He met his wife, Ina, in Tampa and they were married on March 28, 1948, in Tampa at Congregation Rodeph Sholom Synagogue.

He evaluated the general pattern of local housing and felt that it did not meet his more exacting standards. He decided that he wanted to build houses that were superior and distinctive and would satisfy the individual tastes of families and, at the same time, would be affordable. Over the years, he typically set the standard for planning and for good affordable housing. Walter Fuller in his book, "St. Petersburg and Its People" said, " Sidney Colen (in his home building) has been, and now is perhaps the greatest of them all....He has done better than swing with the tide–he usually leads the procession."

Rabbi Morris B. Chapman

Dr. Morris B. Chapman was Rabbi of Congregation B'nai Israel from 1947-1972. Rabbi Chapman, was a fair haired, blue-eyed, New Yorker by birth. He and his sister, Rose, graduated from Teachers Institute in 1928. He earned a Master of Arts Degree from Columbia University, was ordained by the Seminary in 1933, and later earned a Doctor of Hebrew Literature degree in 1953. Prior to his time in St. Petersburg, he had pulpits in Lewiston, Maine and Merrick, Long Island, as well as serving as a chaplain in the United States Army. By 1979, he had been the Bay Pines Veterans Hospital's Jewish Chaplain for thirty years. He was one of eight rabbis to be appointed to serve as Civil Defense Chaplain. He received a special commendation for his work during World War II and for his work at Bay Pines Veterans Center. He was a prolific writer whose book, "Over a Barrel" was published in 1979. He also wrote, "For Better or for Worse." He had a feature column in the Jewish Floridian called "10 Points." He spent his retirement years as Adjunct Professor of Hebrew at Eckerd College, teaching continuing education programs at St. Petersburg Junior College, working with the Veterans Hospital, as Vice President of the Jewish Federation of Pinellas County, and in a variety of other programs where he helped all levels of children from the youngest to the most mature.

Rabbi Chapman was deeply involved in the multifaceted Jewish life of the community. He held many important leadership positions, such as first Director of the Southeast Region of the United Synagogue of America, President of the Rabbinical Assembly (Southeast Region), President of the Pinellas County Board of Rabbis, Chairman of local United Jewish Appeal–Federation Combined Campaign, and board member of a large number of non-Jewish organizations including: President of the Visiting Nurses Association, Vice President and a founder of the St. Petersburg's Council on Human Relations, Board Member of the Red Cross, United Givers, and Welfare Council. Rabbi Chapman's motto was typically Jewish, "Judaism is a social gospel–the Jewish

Rabbi Morris Chapman

emphasis is on doing the right: how to help our neighbor, heal the sick, and bring peace and justice into the world."

Florida State Youth Zionist Conclave

On November 6-7, the Second Annual Florida State Youth Zionist Conclave was held at the Detroit Hotel in St. Petersburg. The officers of the St. Petersburg Chapter of Masada were: President Bernice Rothblatt, Vice President Dr. Phillip Benjamin, Recording Secretary Bob Hyman, Corresponding Secretary Esther Wallace, Treasurer Irene Cohen, and Financial Secretary Manuel Kahn. Other working members included: Iris Heilweil, Abe Katz, Dorothy Dayan, Muriel Cohen, Ethel Vera Kahn, Evelyn Oseroff, Ina Cohen, Gregory Gamse, Bill Tuber, Manny Kahn, Rita Rosenthall, Ruth Prince, Selma Resnick, Clair Goldstein, Kay Mendelow, and others. The St. Petersburg chapter had a very successful "Barrels for Israel" drive with Sydney Colen serving as chairman. Seventy large cartons were packed and shipped and $600 was collected and sent to Israel.

Mendelblatt Family
Dr. David Lee and Reba Blacker Mendelblatt

David and Reba came from Pittsburgh, Pennsylvania to St. Petersburg. David became Chief of Ophthalmology for Bay Pines Hospital. He went into private practice in 1953. David graduated from the University of Pittsburgh in 1923, George Washington University Medical School in 1927. He was born on January 9, 1902 and died in 1966. He and Reba were married in 1931. Dr. Mendelblatt was one of the founders of the Jewish Community Center and was very active in helping to found Camp Kadima. He was President of Congregation B'nai Israel from 1961-1962. He had a strong belief in the philosophy of Judaism and in the importance of being involved in community affairs.

Reba was born in 1906 and died in 1977. Reba was President of the Sisterhood of Congregation B'nai Israel in 1954-1956 and 1958-1960. She was a medical secretary. Reba had a strong belief in the importance and value of Jewish family life.

Dr. David Mendelblatt. President of Congregation B'nai Israel 1961-1962.

Dr. Frank I and Katherine Goffman Mendelblatt

Frank was born on July 2, 1935. He graduated from the University of Florida in 1953, the University of Miami School of Medicine in 1960. He is a practicing ophthalmologist who is: Past President of the Tampa Bay Ophthalmological Society; Past Chief of Staff of All Children's Hospital; Associate Professor of Ophthalmology, University of South Florida College of Medicine; Board Member of Board of Directors, University of Illinois, Illinois Eye Research Institute; Chairman of Ophthalmology at All Children's Hospital; Chairman of Ophthalmology at Bayfront Medical Center. Frank was also the Commodore of the Florida Sailing Association and St. Pete Yacht Club.

Katherine married Frank on February 19, 1966. Katherine was born on October 7, 1943. She earned a Bachelor of Arts in Sociology from Upsala College, East Orange, New Jersey in 1996. She arrived in St. Petersburg in 1966 from Bloomfield, New Jersey, after marrying Frank. She was a secretary and transcriptionist in Frank's medical practice. She has been an active member of the Junior League of St. Petersburg, Congregation B'nai Israel Sisterhood, and Salty Sisters of the St. Petersburg Yacht Club. Katherine and Frank have two children, David J. and Mark S.

Dr. David Jeffrey and Amy Sternthal Mendelblatt

Dr. Sidney and Lillian Grau

David J. was born on June 8, 1970. He earned a Bachelor of Science Degree from Tufts University, Medford, Massachusetts in 1992, Doctor of Medicine from University of South Florida College of Medicine–1998. He is an Affiliate Assistant Professor of Ophthalmology, University of South Florida College of Medicine while working in a private practice, and is a member of the Alpha Omega Alpha Medical Honor Society.

Amy was born on December 12, 1974. She married David in June 2004. She has a Bachelor of Arts in Political Science from the University of Pittsburgh, a Master of Social Work from the University of Pennsylvania in 1999, and a Master's in Jewish Communal Service from Gratz College in Philadelphia-1999. Amy worked for the Yale University Hillel Jewish Campus Service Corps. She worked for the Jewish Federation of MetroWest, New Jersey, Jewish Federation of Greater Dallas, and the Sarasota-Manatee Jewish Federation.

Other Mendelblatts

Mark was born February 19, 1973. He earned a Bachelor of Science in Psychology degree from Tufts University in 1995. He was a stockbroker and is now involved in professional sailing. Mark was an Olympian at the Greek Olympic games. He won a gold medal in the Maccabees Games in Israel. Frank's sister, Audrey Berger, came to St. Petersburg in 1947. She graduated from the University of Florida in 1961, with a Bachelor of Arts in Education in 1961. She is now in California, teaching high school English. She also owns a bookstore and arranges lecturers from visiting authors. Frank's brother, Stanley, lived in St. Petersburg. He graduated from the University of Miami with a Bachelor of Arts Degree in 1967. He is in the clothing business in New York.

HIGHLIGHTS of 1948

Dr. Sidney Grau

Sidney and Lillian Grau came to St. Petersburg to get away from the cold. Sidney served in World War II in Europe. He was so cold in combat that he swore he would never be cold again. Afterwards, he applied to the Veterans Administration to work at a hospital in Coral Gables, but ended up at Bay Pines Veterans Hospital in St. Petersburg, were he worked for one year and then acted as a consultant in cardiology for one or two additional years. He then opened his own practice. He needed to establish a year of residency in Florida before he could take his Florida Medical Board Examinations. Sidney graduated from Ohio State University in 1939 with a Bachelor of Arts Degree and then from medical school at Ohio State University in 1942. He rose to the rank of Captain in the Eighth Army in Germany. Sidney was born on November 17, 1917 in Pittsburgh, Pennsylvania.

Sidney Grau has made many contributions to the Jewish and general communities. He has served in the following positions: Board Member of Congregation B'nai Israel; President, Suncoast Art Association; Chief of Staff, Bayfront Medical Center, 1963–1965; President of Board of Menorah Manor; Board Member of the Bayfront Medical Center; Planning Board Bayfront Medical Center; and Member of Board of Florida Orchestra. He received the prestigious Doctor A. J. Gorday Award for Physician of the Year about 1980 and the Dr. Alfred Schick Award-2000. Lillian has served in many positions at Congregation B'nai Israel, including Vice President of the Sisterhood.

When asked why he made his many contributions to humanity he said, "Primarily I have practiced the art and science of medicine in order to protect people and to follow my own personal search for the truth, which ultimately would benefit individuals and the community at large."

Sidney's father, Abraham, was from Poland. Abraham was born about 1879 and died about 1959. Abraham was a traveling salesman. Sidney's mother, Rose, was born about 1880 in Poland and died in 1960. Sidney's wife, Lillian, was born in 1922 in New Jersey. Lillian and Sidney have three children; Stephen, born in 1945 in New Jersey, Barry, born in 1949 in St. Petersburg, and Martha, born in 1953 in St. Petersburg.

Rabbi Albert A. Michaels

Rabbi Albert A. Michaels assumed the pulpit at Temple Beth-El. He was a native of New York City. He was educated at Boston Latin School, University of Michigan, and did graduate work at the University of Wisconsin. He completed his rabbinical preparation at the Jewish Institute, New York, under the guidance of Dr. Stephen S. Wise, where he was ordained and received a Master of Hebrew Literature Degree. He was the holder of several fellowship awards in social services in New York prisons, hospitals and welfare agencies. Rabbi Michaels began his pulpit career in Natchez, Mississippi and later served in Texas where he volunteered as an Army chaplain. After the war, he joined the University of Miami as Director of the Jewish Student Group and lectured in the Department of Religion.

He was given an Award of Merit for his excellent work with the National Conference of Christians and Jews. His wife, Julia Miller Michaels of Pittsburgh, earned her Master's Degree at the University of Pittsburgh.

Rabbi Michaels dreamed of a world free of racial prejudices. He was a man with intense feelings who wanted to right the wrongs of the past and present. While in Miami because of his excellent inter-faith work, he was given the Award of Merit by the National Conference of Christians and Jews. In his sermons, he discussed modern-day problems and ways of resolving them so that people could live a just and equitable life. He always welcomed Brotherhood Week to improve racial conditions throughout the community.

Rabbi Albert A. Michaels

Irwin Miller

Irwin Miller, a hard-working, modest individual, not only owned and managed a hotel for forty years, co-founded the Guardian Bank and First Central Bank of St. Petersburg, invested in and owned several business properties in Pinellas County, but still found time to give of himself to many causes in the Jewish and non-Jewish communities. His work for others represents the true nature of everything that is good in people. He is a past President of Temple Beth-El, as his father before him was, and a board member for over forty years, as well as special projects chairman. He is a Board Member, Founding Member, Past President and Chairman of Menorah Manor, and has been involved in all aspects of campaigns and building plans since the nursing home's inception in 1984. He is a Board Member and Chairman of Menorah Manor Foundation. He has served on the boards of Pinellas Jewish Federation and TOP Foundation. He was a Trustee and Treasurer of All Children's Hospital as well as Trustee of Pinellas County Science Center and NCCJ. He is the recipient of the NCCJ Silver Medallion Humanitarian Award and the Menorah Manor Outstanding Leadership Award.

Irwin was born in New York in 1925 and came to St. Petersburg when he was three months old. He graduated from St. Petersburg High School and went to Cornell University, where he earned a Bachelor's of

Irwin Miller, President Temple Beth-El 1990–1992.

Irwin and Sonya Miller

Science Degree in Engineering in 1944. He immediately enrolled in the Ensign School of the United States Navy and graduated as an ensign. He served in World War II. He married Sonya Halaczer in 1948, who became his lifelong partner in his many ventures, both business and philanthropic.

Sonya Halaczer Miller

Sonya Miller, an equally hard-working, business partner, wife, and mother of three children, was co-owner and Social Director of Hotel Rellim. Sonya has served on the Board of Directors of Temple Beth-El Sisterhood, St. Petersburg Arts Center, Menorah Manor Community, Menorah Manor Travel Club (co-chairperson), Beth-El Art Festival (co-chairperson for twenty years), Menorah Manor Guild, Salvador Dali Museum, Pinellas County Doorways Scholarship, C A S A. She is also a Hadassah Lifetime Member and a Lion of Judah Ruby Sponsor.

Irwin and Sonya Miller jointly have been supportive of many organizations including: Life Founding Member of the Holocaust Museum; Bronze Sponsor of Palladium Theater; Campaign Sponsor of Mahaffey Theater; Event Sponsor of Florida Craftsman; Campaign Sponsor of Eckerd College; Sponsor of American Stage; Leadership Sponsor of United Way; Sponsor of Shorecrest School; Art Sponsor of Gulf Coast Museum; Sponsor of Florida Suncoast Symphony Orchestra; Sponsor of the Academy Foundation; etc.. Jointly they have been the recipients of the Yitzak Rabin Memorial Award for Distinguished Service, Temple Beth-El Outstanding Citizenship Award, and the Israel Bond Peace Medal Award.

Pauline and Harold C. Rivkind

Pauline and Harold Rivkind

Pauline and Harold Rivkind came from Cleveland, Ohio with their three children, Tony, Laurie, and Susan. Harold was born in Cleveland on January 30, 1912 and Pauline was born in Cleveland in 1914. They joined Congregation B'nai Israel in1949, and for the next twenty five years, became enthusiastic boosters of the Jewish community as well as the non-Jewish community.

In 1956, Pauline Rivkind founded the preschool at Congregation B'nai Israel. She was the owner and operator of Pauline Florist in the Central Plaza Sun Mall. She served on many Jewish and community boards including: National Board of Women's League of the United Synagogue of America; National Council of Jewish Women; Haddassah; Women's League; Council of Human Relations; and the first President of the Florida Unit of Teleflora Association. She died on June 1, 1967. Pauline helped build the religious school from its initial eight children to a large sophisticated program. She started a nursery and kindergarten group in rented quarters until the congregation's facilities could be enlarged. She was a founding member of the St. Petersburg Council of Human Relations, Garden Circle, and very active in educational activities. In 1967, Congregation B'nai Israel voted to designate the religious school as the Pauline Rivkind Talmud Torah.

Harold Rivkind came to the Child Guidance Clinic as Acting Director and Administrative Director. The original Child Guidance Clinic had been funded by the Covenant Club, the Jewish men's organization, in 1944. The clinic was dedicated to a program of psychological service to children with emotional, educational, or social difficulties and for developing an educational program in the field of mental health. By 1947, a full-time program was initiated and combined with the Child Guidance Clinic of Clearwater which had been sponsored by the Pilot Club of Clearwater. Paul Penningroth, local psychologist and educator, was hired to lead the organization, and the city provided quarters in the Chamber of Commerce Building. Rivkind said, "...We provided services for referrals and private evaluations, but we worked with parents as well as children. It was always a challenge to help families resolve their difficulties. The clinic was always a very valued organization in the community...." The clinic has always been a positive force in the community for improving mental health for families.

Harold was President of Congregation B'nai Israel from 1954-1962 and 1970-1972. He was the first President of the St. Petersburg Jewish Community Council.

In 1956, while earning his Doctorate of Education from the University of Florida, he was invited to become the first Jewish member of the St. Petersburg Optimists Club. At that time, all the other civic clubs were restricted. In 1958, he was elected President of the Pinellas County Employees Federal Credit Union. In 1961, he was one of the founders of the 58th Street Land Company. In 1967, he married Ruth Phillips, who arrived in St. Petersburg in 1958. Ruth was very active for many years in the Sisterhood of Congregation B'nai Israel. Harold, a psychiatric social worker, retired from the position of Director of the Child Guidance Clinic of Pinellas County in 1976, after thirty years of service to children and families in Pinellas County and forty years in social services. After his retirement, he continued his public service by serving on five different boards including: Gulf Coast Jewish Family Service, Suncoast Mental Health Commission, Menorah Manor, Menorah Center, Etc.. Over his lifetime, he received numerous awards including the Key to the City of St. Petersburg twice.

Thelma and Maurice A. Rothman

Maurice Rothman and Edward L. Kalin founded the first Kane Furniture Store at the corner of 8th Street and Central Avenue in St. Petersburg. Maurice was the husband of Thelma Pearlman of Asheville North Carolina and Edward was Thelma's cousin from Hendersonville, North Carolina. Both men were veterans of World War II. Maurice was operating a pawn shop in New York City that had been started by his grandfather in 1883. Ed and his family had been involved in the retail department store business and then later in lady's ready-to-wear clothing. Thelma's family had operated a retail furniture company throughout North Carolina. Thelma's brother, Fred, had married Anne Manket, the first Jewish child born in Pinellas County. They all decided that they would move to St. Petersburg and start a furniture store. Fred came in 1948 and helped remodel a furniture store that was going out of business. This became the company that grew from one store and six employees in 1948 to seventeen stores and over 900 employees in 2005. The Rothman

family have added substantially to the local economies and the family has made enormous contributions to the Jewish and general communities.

Maurice was born on April 4, 1917 and died April 23, 1997. He attended New York University. He married Thelma Pearlman of Asheville, North Carolina, in 1943 and they had three daughters, Margie, Carol, and Nancy. He was on the Board of Trustees or an officer of: American Red Cross, Bayfront Medical Center, Eckerd College-Executive Committee, Foundation for Florida's Community Colleges Inc., Goodwill Industries, Boca Ciega Kiwanis Club, Museum of Fine Arts, National Conference of Christians and Jews, President, Pinellas County Education Foundation, Ronald McDonald House, St. Petersburg Health Facility Authority, St. Petersburg Jewish Community Center, St. Petersburg Junior College Development Foundation, St. Petersburg Symphony, Sun Bank, Suncoast Chamber of Commerce, Temple Beth-El President, United Way, United Jewish Appeal Chairman. Over the years he received numerous awards: St. Petersburg Chamber of Commerce; Outstanding Contributions to the Betterment of the Community; National Conference of Christians and Jews, Brotherhood Award; Sales and Marketing Executives, Distinguished Businessman; Outstanding Achievement in Furniture Merchandising; Bayfront Hospital Foundation; the William S. "Bill" Belcher Award; Gulf Coast Community Care, Celebrity Award; Personal Enrichment through Mental Health Services, Pace Award; and Governor Lawton Chiles, State of Florida, "Florida's Finest" Award.

Maurice Rothman, President Temple Beth-El 1985–1986

Maury liked to be called M. R. He was a low-profile gentleman who very frequently gave gifts listed only as anonymous. He was a tough, but fair, boss. Other than driving a truck, he would not ask anyone to do anything that he would not do himself. He knew many of the names of his employees, their family status, and their personal details. He was described as an individual, who cared about his friends and was sincerely interested in everything that went on around him. He served the community in the arts, education, religious, civic, and business organizations. In health care, his philosophy was quality not quantity. He believed in giving the children a proper start in life, thereby allowing them to build on a firm foundation. He provided the Neo-Natal Intensive Care Van of All Children's Hospital. He was totally committed and deeply involved in the $20 million expansion program of Bayfront Hospital, where he served on the Board of Trustees for nine years. He persuaded his cousin, Ed Kalin, of Sarasota, and his brother-in-law, David Pearlman, of Orlando, to join with Kanes of St. Petersburg to completely furnish Menorah Manor when it first opened. He was both building chairman and fundraiser who, along with a group of dedicated people, managed to build mortgage free, Temple Beth-El on Pasadena Avenue. In a tremendous act of brotherhood, Maury also helped countless churches, social halls, and schools receive new furnishings, carpets, and accessories. The needs were immediately met by M. R. regardless of race, color, or creed. It was said of Maurice Rothman, "He doesn't work at brotherhood, it's just a way of life with M.R." Maury took great pride in blowing the shofar on the High Holy Days at Temple Beth El, an honor that he received for twenty four years from 1962-1996. His shofar notes were so pure that people came from all over to hear him.

Thelma was born on July 16, 1923 in North Carolina. She attended the University of Illinois and the University of North Carolina at Chapel Hill. Thelma was the co-founder of Kane Furniture and currently is serving as Chairperson of the corporation. She has always been a good mom, grandmother, hard worker, and caring person. She has served on the Boards of Trustees or been an officer of the following organizations: Adult Mental Health Clinic; All Children's Hospital; All Children's Hospital Foundation, Chairman; All Children's Hospital Health Systems Executive Board; Florida Gulf Coast Symphony; Jewish Federation of Pinellas County; Menorah Manor, Secretary and co-founder; Ronald McDonald House; Tampa, Orlando, Pinellas Jewish Philanthropic Fund (T.O.P.); St. Petersburg Symphony; and St. Petersburg Jewish Community Center. She has received

the following awards: St. Petersburg Chamber of Commerce, Outstanding Contributions to the Betterment of the Community; Florida Home Furnishings Representatives Association, the Herman Echenthal Humanitarian Award; Medical Staff, All Children's Hospital, Contributions of Time, Energy and Resources to the Children of Our Community; National Conference of Christians and Jews, Brotherhood Award; All Children's Hospital Foundation, William S. "Bill" Belcher award; and Gulf Coast Community Care, Celebrity Award; Personal Enrichment through Mental Health Services, Pace Award; Governor Lawton Chiles, State of Florida, "Florida's Finest" Award; Phi Delta Kappa-"Laymen of the Year" Alex de Tocqueville; Golden Baton Award-Florida Orchestra; and Hero's Award-Florida Orchestra. Thelma received, in 2006, the highly distinguished International Lion of Judah Kipnis-Wilson/ Friedland Award. President Clinton told this distinguished group of women, on the anniversary of 9/11, "We should move vigorously because private citizens have more power to do public good today than at any time in human history. You have been doing it a long time. On this hallowed day, I urge you to redouble your efforts."

The Rothmans have supported numerous local programs and institutions, through the Maurice A. and Thelma P. Rothman Family Foundation. This includes: The Rothman Chair in Developmental Biology at the University of South Florida Children's Research Institute; The University of South Florida Stavros Institute; Pinellas County Educational Foundation which provides four year college scholarships to deserving children from low-income homes; Eckerd College Jewish Scholarship Program; Eckerd College Kanes Furniture Employees Program; 500 Role Models for Excellence; the National Conference; and many others.

These are the tangible things that Thelma and Maury Rothman have done over the years in the community. Paraphrasing a commentary about Thelma to include Maury, "They have affected many, many people's lives with their willingness to help them in their times of need and in times of great joy. You can ask anyone about them and they will say they are the kindest, most concerned and caring people they know. They strongly feel that they have had the opportunity to give back to St. Petersburg some of what St. Petersburg has given to them. It is one of their greatest pleasures."

HIGHLIGHTS of 1949

Two of the major issues of the St. Petersburg Jewish community were the creation of a Jewish Community Centre (or Center) and the possibility of having both of the synagogues in one large structure with two different services, one being conservative and the other being reform. This would avoid having to build separate new synagogues for each of the congregations. On May 9, 1949, a meeting of the Council was held and a letter was sent by President George Schiller to Mr. George Dikman of the Board of Directors of Congregation B'nai Israel requesting that a meeting be held between the Jewish Community Council and Boards of Congregation B'nai Israel and Temple Beth-El. This meeting was held on May 6th, 1949, with George Schiller acting as chairman and mediator of the meeting, and Iris Heilweil acting as secretary. The individuals in attendance were not only board members of the two synagogues but also leaders of the Jewish community. They included: George Schiller, Rabbi A. Michaels of Temple Beth-El, Mr. A. Freedman, Frank Kleinfeld, Dr. L. Mount, Mr. Samuels, Mr. Sierkese, Mr. Silverberg, Mr. Black, Mr. Kornfield and Mr. Schiller. Rabbi Michaels questioned the authority of the Community Council to call a meeting of Temple Beth-El and Congregation B'nai Israel. Mr. Freedman stated that currently, a Community Center was ill-timed and that all monies collected should go toward the construction of the new Temple. The Jewish community could not afford a third building. The pros and cons of the timing of the Center were discussed. Mr. Frank Kleinfield said that the Community Center had nothing to do with the construction of two new synagogue structures because the Center was a separate corporation. It was suggested that each of the organizations go back to the contributors and find out if a part of the money donated could be allocated for a community center. There were considerable differences of opinion in the group. The functions of the center were spelled out. The community center was to be a business organization for the purpose of supplying a place for physical, cultural and social needs of everyone in the community. It was not to be a religious institution. The community center was to be run by a graduate social worker and to be overseen by a board of directors. A second meeting was held two weeks later, after the board members had an opportunity to meet with the congregations. This meeting was the beginning of the concept of the Elbow Lane Jewish Community Center and the Gulf Coast Jewish Family Services.

On May 26, Morris J. Black, Secretary, sent a letter to Miss Iris Heilweil that the Boards of Congregation Beth-El and Congregation B'nai Israel had initiated a joint meeting under the co-chairmanship of the officers to be held on Monday evening May 30, to discuss their common problems as related to the Jewish community situation. As soon as they would work out the common problems they would respond to the St. Petersburg Jewish Community Council. In November, 1949, a memorandum from President Schiller said that much of the original enthusiasm for the Jewish Community Council was disappearing. He said that unless all of the Jewish organizations gave their active support, the Council could not exist. In December, 1949, Mr. Nathan Rothberg spoke to the St. Petersburg Jewish Community Council. George Schiller said that the Council was an infant organization trying to organize and be successful. George asked Iris to write to Alvin Bronstein, Regional Director, Southeastern Region, Council of Jewish Federations and Welfare Funds in Atlanta, Georgia. George asked that a model constitution be sent to St. Petersburg as soon as possible, preferably before the December 12th meeting. Mr. Bronstein not only sent the constitution, but also offered any help that he could provide to the group. He suggested that he come to St. Petersburg on February 16th and 17th of 1950 to meet with the St. Petersburg Jewish Community Council.

Food for Israel

A Food for Israel drive was conducted by several local organizations including the Zionist Organization of America, Hadassah and Masada, the Zionist youth group. The chairman of the drive was Sidney Colen, assisted by Mrs. Allen Horn, Alfred M. Claven, and Miss Bunnie Rothblatt. Collections were held at the synagogues, Empire Hotel, Phil and Maurice Tropical Food Market, and Luber's.

HIGHLIGHTS of 1950

In 1950, Jewish people belonged to CUCA, an organization of congregations, mostly non-Jewish, who worked together for the betterment of the community.

HIGHLIGHTS of 1951

Bunnie and Abe Katz

Abe and Bunnie Katz

On November 1, 1927, Bunnie (Bernice) Rothblatt Katz was born in St. Petersburg. Her husband, Abraham, was born on October 20, 1921 in Portland, Maine. He came to St. Petersburg in 1932 at the age of ten, due to his father's poor health. His father had been a kosher butcher in Portland. She graduated from St. Petersburg High School in 1945. She was extremely active in both high school and Jewish clubs. She was chairman of the Student Government Improvement Committee, Junior Hadassah, Masada, and was acting President of the Jewish Adult and Youth Club, the Jays. Abe served in the Army Air Corps for three and one half years as an instructor of altitude training technicians. He was the Treasurer of the Jays. They were married on January 7, 1951. Abe's mother gave them their little grocery store, which they ran together with his mother's help. They have two children, Sandra, married to Herbert Brash, and Ilene, married to Marc Horowitz.

Bunnie and Abe have made numerous contributions to the enhancement of the lives of the Jewish community and general community. Abe has been a member of the Board of Congregation B'nai Israel for the last fifty two years. He has also served on the Menorah Manor and Menorah Center Boards. Abe has received numerous awards including: the Mitzvah Men's Club Award– 1993 Man of the Year Award, the Hatan Torah honor, in 1997. Abe is a member of the Jewish War Veterans and B'nai B'rith. Bunnie had been a board member of the synagogue, past President of the Sisterhood, and over the years, has been deeply involved in helping preserve the history of the Jewish people of Pinellas County, as her cousin Goldie Schuster did before her. Bunnie has been the Chairperson of the Archives Committee for an extended period of time and has been a tremendous assistance to the author in the compiling of the research for this book. Abe and Bunnie have won many honors including the Sound of Honor Award, the Citation of Honor of the Jewish Theological Seminary, and the Koach Award from the State of Israel.

In 2004, Bunnie and Abe Katz were the recipients of the Yitzhak Rabin Memorial Award for Distinguished Community Service. It was recalled how "Mr. Abe" extended credit to people who could not afford to pay for their groceries in the 1950s and 1960s. In their store, Katz Discount Foods, located on Eleventh Street at Third Avenue South, Abe and Bunnie employed fourteen full-time people and provided to the community good wholesome food at sensible prices. Abe, when commended for his excellent business practices, said, "My philosophy in business–in life in general–is based on having the right attitude. I love people, and I love what I do. I never look at my job as work, it is really a labor of love. I have always tried to be more than just the neighborhood grocery store. I have always tried to be a friend–like one of the family. I feel I have accomplished that." This was part of the many community services that both of them performed for over fifty years. The presenter, Thelma Rothman said, "Abe and Bunnie's humble and selfless personalities and wry sense of humor continue to inspire volunteers at Congregation B'nai Israel to work hard and achieve results that they can be proud of."

HIGHLIGHTS of 1952

Sidney Colen developed the first-ever condominium complex in Florida in 1952. It was Clearwater Oaks in St. Petersburg. Prior to that time, people who wanted to have ownership in their apartments purchased co-ops. The difference between co-ops and condos was that co-ops were mutually owned and the apartment had to be sold back to the co-op. Condos were individually owned and the person had the right to transfer the title to other family members or to sell it outright. Sidney originally started the condos because he wanted his parents to have a living space that they owned, but one in which all maintenance and other homeowner's problems would be handled by a management team. Unfortunately, because of the age of his parents, it wasn't feasible for them to become occupants.

Sidney and Ina Colen

Sidney Colen was born on March 27, 1919 in Erie, Pennsylvania. He said in his Ethical Will that his early years were difficult and that he was a slow learner. To compensate for this, he trained himself to work harder than anyone else. His main ambition at that time was to be average and to be accepted. He said that he stuttered terribly and, therefore, people would rarely listen to what he had to say. He was constantly being told to slow down. He found schoolwork to be very difficult, which embarrassed him. He was the only Jewish child in his school in the town of Aliquippa, Pennsylvania. The teachers were prejudiced and unsympathetic. The family lived in the back of a produce store with no room divisions, except for used trunks, to mark off the space. His older brother was injured in a truck delivery accident, and his father nearly died from sunstroke while buying and selling in the Pittsburgh Produce Market. They eventually moved to Toledo, Ohio, where it was difficult to understand that teachers could be fairly decent human beings. They were not as anxious to punish with wooden paddles as they did in Aliquippa. He soon learned to enjoy school, but his grades did not improve because of dyslexia. He was a very energetic and hard-working child who had a daily and Sunday paper route, sold eggs from a child's wagon door-to-door, and later sold the Saturday Evening Post door-to-door for $.15 an hour. On Sundays, after delivering papers, he would wash, polish and wax the truck that his father used for freight hauling. Later on, his father bought a bar with his mother and Sidney took over its operation. He graduated from the University of Toledo, majoring in the humanities. When his parents moved to St. Petersburg, Florida he followed, met his wife, Ina, who was from Tampa, and became a resident of St. Petersburg. Being extremely interested in community affairs and always wanting to improve the communities in which he lived or worked, he became an influential member of many Board's of public organizations. They included: the St. Petersburg Planning Board, urging them to study the ever-changing pattern of housing and change rules and concepts before trouble began; Board of Realtors, United Fund, Florida Philharmonic, South Pinellas County Hospital Foundation, Jewish Community Council, etc.. He built whole communities including Kenneth City, Merna Manor, Disston Manor, Leslee Heights, Kendale Park, South Causeway Isles, Sheryl Manor, Merna Park, Clearview Oaks, On Top of the World-Clearwater, On Top of the World-Ocala, etc.. Sidney Colen ended his ethical will with thanks to the people who had helped and guided him throughout his life. In speaking of his wife Ina, he said, "I was grateful to G-D for my wonderful life. Without her in my life, my life would have been entirely different. No greater love can one have and no greater gift, than a devoted, loving wife; for there is nothing as precious, and it is far beyond words that I could utter. Sidney Colen, a humble man, said, "Maybe I should be satisfied, but I'm not. I have left so much undone, or hopefully to be done by others through my legacy, whatever that legacy might be. I had my time, for which I am grateful."

Ina Colen graduated from Florida State College for Women in the summer of 1946. (It became Florida State University in September 1946). She taught geography and history to the seventh, eighth and tenth grades at Brandon Junior High School and

Brandon High School in Tampa for one and one half years before she was married. Her parents, Rose and Perley Gotler, came to Tampa from Springfield, Massachusetts in 1925. They were members of Rodeph Sholom Synagogue, where her mother was active in the Sisterhood. Her father was a glazier on South Franklin St., the home of many Jewish merchants at that time. She gave up teaching and she married Sidney and they had three children. She had been active in Junior Hadassah and the National Council of Jewish Juniors when single. When she married, she became active in the National Council of Jewish Women, Red Cross, Hadassah as a Life Member, Sisterhood of Congregation B'nai Israel. She was a Youth Leader for five years for the United Synagogue Youth, and later was a volunteer Secretary for four years at Congregation B'nai Israel of St. Petersburg. She assisted her husband, Sidney, in his many endeavors which gave them both a sense of accomplishment and a sense of making their values live.

Camp Kadima

Camp Kadima, the Jewish summer day camp, was founded by the Jewish Community Council. The camp opened with sixty five campers and a budget of $6,500. There were two, four week sessions each summer. Initially, it was held at a rented location at 22nd Avenue South about 46th Street. It later moved to the Jewish Community Center on Elbow Lane when the new building was built, and then to a larger location when the Jewish Community Center purchased the old Kapok Tree Restaurant. In 1959, Dr. David Mendelblatt, a founder of the camp, reported that the camp had eighty eight children, with a limit of 100 children, a budget of $12,000, a staff of eighteen counselors, a director and office staff.

HIGHLIGHTS of 1953

Congregation Beth Sholom of Gulfport was formed. It was an independent Conservative synagogue. (See separate chapter on Congregation Beth Sholom of Gulfport.) The Jewish Community Council sponsored the opening of a kosher meat market. A Vad Kasreth Committee was formed to inspect any establishment that sold strictly kosher meat. A committee was appointed to purchase a permanent summer day camp site.

Jane and Don Silverberg

Jane Goldman married Don Silverberg on November 28. Jane was the original Vice President and Comptroller of Silverberg Jewelry Company, which she founded with her husband, Donald A. Silverberg. Jane attended Sophie Newcomb College in New Orleans and then earned Bachelor of Science Degrees in Social Studies and Education from the University of Michigan. In the 1950s, she taught American History at Southside Junior High School in St. Petersburg. Jane and Don have three children, Terri, Edward, and Tom. Jane has had a strong interest in helping children and therefore served as an active Girl Scout Leader and worked with St. Petersburg Community Youth Services, which provided after school academic and cultural support to deprived children.

In the 1960s, she was very active in the civil rights movement. She marched to St. Petersburg City Hall with the city's black sanitation workers to help obtain better working conditions. She and Don helped desegregate many fine restaurants by inviting black friends as their guests for dinner. When Coretta King, wife of Dr. Martin Luther King, gave a concert at Pasadena Community Church in St. Petersburg, Jane and Don entertained her with a beautiful reception in their home.

In the mid-1960s, Jane wrote the newspaper column, "Serving Seniors," that was syndicated by the New York News and Chicago Tribune. This gerontology column, designed to help elderly people with their problems, brought mail from all over the country. Jane served as a Commissioner of the St. Petersburg Housing Authority from 1973-1978. She was active in Pinellas County politics and served as a Democratic Committee Woman. She was a Director of the St. Petersburg Junior College Foundation. In 1982, Jane and Don established the Silverberg Endowment for Academic Excellence which provides funds for academic enrichment of curriculum. Jane is a member of the

American Stage Company, which provides fine theater such as Shakespeare in the Park. From 1979-1985, Jane served on the National Conference of Christians and Jews Board. She was, and still is, committed to improving tolerance between people of all faiths, races, and creeds. She has been a sponsor and participant in the inter-religious and bi-racial Living Room Dialogues. Jane was awarded the Silver Medallion for outstanding service to the community. She and Don were presented the "Prime Minister's Award of Honor" by the State of Israel Bonds for Service to the Jewish Community and received the Second Century Award from the Jewish Theological Seminary.

Don Silverberg was born in Newark, New Jersey on July 23, 1929. He went to Washington University in St. Louis and then graduated from Mexico College in Mexico City with a B.A. in 1950. In 1951, Don joined the United States Army and served as a tank commander with the Second Armored Division and Seventh Army in Europe. When he came home, he went to work in the family business, became a stockbroker, and finally opened his own business, Silverberg Jewelry Company.

Don started his public service at age ten, when his mother took him every Sunday to Bay Pines Veterans Hospital to push disabled veterans in wheelchairs through the gardens. This went on for two years. Don has served the community in many ways as: Member Board of Directors St. Petersburg Junior Chamber of Commerce; Member Board of Directors of Sertona Club; Member Board of Directors of March of Dimes; Member Charitable Solicitation Board of City of St. Petersburg; Chairman of Jewelry Advisory Committee of Tomlinson Adult Vocational Center; Member All Children's Hospital Development Committee; and Bardmoor YMCA. He is a Founding Member of Menorah Manor and was a Board Member of Pinellas County Jewish Day School. He was President of Congregation B'nai Israel. On retiring from the diamond business, Don became a stone sculptor. His marble work has been shown at the annual art show of Temple Beth-El and has been sold to people throughout the United States. At present, Jane is a serious art student at The Arts

Center in St. Petersburg. She also teaches art to seniors at Menorah Manor every week.

Don's brother, Henry (Buddy), was born in Cleveland, Ohio in 1925 and died in St. Petersburg in October, 1983. Henry attended St. Petersburg Junior College and then joined the Air Force and served as a bombardier in World War II. Henry worked in the family jewelry business and then opened Girard Jewelers, a chain of retail stores. Henry married Lu Ellen Neimeth, Rabbi Kleinfelds granddaughter. Henry and Lu Ellen had two children, Lisa and Jeffrey.

Whittner Family–Jacob Whittner and Helen Goldman Whittner

Jacob was born on December 25, 1890, in Folkshani, Romania, twenty miles north of Bucharest. He had a sister, Ghisella, and other siblings. Jacob once played ball with King Carol of Romania! He emigrated to the United States and arrived on the ship "Patricia" in December, 1913, at Hoboken, New Jersey. His cousins, Rosie and Manuel Katz of Tampa, met him there and took him to Tampa to their home. Aboard the ship, he traveled with Morris D. Weissman and Morris's sister, Gisella. Morris was Irving Weissman's father. He worked for the Pearlman's in a dry goods store for several years before World War I. All the other members of his family stayed in Romania. Jacob lost two brothers in the concentration camps in WWII. One of these brothers was named Joseph. Jacob volunteered to go into the army in WWI. He was wounded severely and was unconscious for days. He and Meyer Cutler created Tropical Garment, which manufactured sports clothes and work clothing. Their brand name was Royal Palm.

Jacob and Helen had two sons, Harvey and Ted. Jacob spoke many languages (Spanish, Italian, some French–the romance languages were easy for him). He also spoke Romanian and English, and he spoke Yiddish to his business friends. Jacob died on September 12, 1949.

Helen was the baby of the Goldman family. She was born on March 1, 1895, in Shaker Heights, Cleveland, Ohio. When she was a young woman, Helen worked as a super-secretary for a lawyer in Cleveland. She was a great typist, and she organized this lawyer's life, just like she organized her own family's! Helen came to Tampa in approximately 1920 and married Jacob in 1923.

Helen opened Jay's Five & Ten on Nebraska Avenue in 1939, in an attempt to get Jay Wittner off the road. Jay was a traveling salesman, and Helen was tired of having him gone most of the time. During World War II, items made of metal were next to impossible to find. However, Harvey Firestone was from Cleveland and, somehow, he offered her a train car filled with metal goods to sell in her store.

Helen was extremely active in Rodeph Sholom Synagogue. She served as Sisterhood President for four years.. She was also active in B'nai Brith Women, ORT, Hadassah, etc. She served as PTA President at Robert E. Lee Elementary School in Tampa, when the boys went there, and she was the person who got the hot lunch program started in the public schools in Tampa.

HIGHLIGHTS of 1954

Leonard Lubin

Leonard Lubin, an attorney, arrived in St. Petersburg in 1954. He was born in West Palm Beach, Florida on July 7, 1925 and moved as an infant to Miami where he was reared. He attended the University of Miami before he enlisted in the United States Army during World War II. He was one of the Liberators of the Wels concentration camp in Austria, which was part of the Matthausen Concentration Camp complex. The Holocaust inspired him to be very active in Zionist activities, and he enlisted in the Irgun Underground to help dislodge the British hold on Palestine. He was never called to active duty. He graduated from the University of Miami School of Law in 1949 and practiced law for five years before he came to St. Petersburg. He has pioneered statutory and case law for the rights of mentally incapacitated people, establishing the right to counsel, regular reporting as to conditions, and location and capacity for restoration of full civil liberties. He was married to Lona Lubin, who was born in Miami on April 14, 1927 and died in St. Petersburg in 2001. She attended the University of Miami. They have two children, Lance and Lisa.

In 1960, Leonard assumed the chairmanship of the Congregation B'nai Israel Completion Campaign, which was to raise $100,000. In accepting the chairmanship, Leonard said, "There was a great need to build our Synagogue, and we have a sacred duty to complete it. I'm certain that the congregation and our community will rise to this effort to complete B'nai Israel." As with many other efforts chaired by Leonard Lubin, this was a total success.

Leonard's family came to Key West from Europe. Leonard's paternal grandfather, Abraham (Avrum) Leibovit, was a grain merchant in Batashon (spelled phonetically), Romania. He and his wife, Mollie, had a large family with the oldest child, Jay, being threatened with conscription into the Army. At age fifteen, he would have been cannon fodder for the armies that helped persecute the Jewish people. Jay was sent to America in 1903 and the rest of the family followed around 1905. Terri, Leonard's mother, was born in the United States. The family migrated to Key West, which was disconnected from the mainland, and without water except for cisterns. There were a handful of Jewish families living there including the Rippa family. Leonard's maternal family became merchants and opened a department store. From that time until after World War I, his grandfather represented the Southern American terminal for the Jewish underground. The quota restriction for Jewish immigrants into the United States was limited but there was no enforceable restriction for immigrants in Cuba. A significant number of Jews escaping from Eastern Europe found their way to Cuba. There, the Jewish community readied them for illegal entry into the United States. They were brought in the middle of the night the ninty mile distance that separated Havanna from Key West and were deposited on the Key West beaches. There, Key West Jews collected them, hid them in their homes, and prepared them for shipment out of Key West to the United States' mainland to become lost in the cities. These individuals were furnished money, clothing, information and contacts in the cities in the North. Apparently, a substantial number of Jewish people were processed this way. This information came down to Leonard through verbal tradition and follow-up interviews that he conducted with a number of people throughout the years. When Abraham was challenged about his obvious violation of immigration law, he replied, "I am obeying a higher God's law." He thought of himself as a solid American citizen, who did not feel that it was illegal to help fellow Jewish people. Some members of the family stayed on in Key West, while others went on to Miami and West Palm Beach. They continued as merchants, both wholesale and retail.

Leonard's mother, Terri, and father, Meyer Lubin, came to St. Petersburg from Miami in about 1951 and bought the Jamaican Motel on Treasure Island. They sold out in the mid 1960s.

Other Events

In March, David Rothblatt, Grand Patriarch of the International Order of Odd Fellows, was honored for his service to both the Jewish and general communities. The Jewish Community Council sponsored a Boy Scout troop and a Girl Scout troop.

HIGHLIGHTS of 1955

In February, the St. Petersburg Jewish Community Council officially approved the building of a Jewish Community Center. The Board appointed a special committee entitled Jewish Community Center Committee.

A letter was sent by Lee Weinberg, Chairman of the Jewish Community Center Committee of the St. Petersburg Jewish Community Council to all Jewish people within St. Petersburg and its immediate surrounding areas. It referred to the needs of the growing and expanding St. Petersburg Jewish community. It said, "There is no place in our community, where all Jews, Orthodox, Conservative, Reform or unaffiliated, can congregate, fraternize, and socialize under one roof. There is no place where Jewish children may gather for sports, swimming, and arts and crafts, other than for two months at Camp Kadima. There is no place where Jewish children may get to know each other, grow up together, and

prepare for living together as members of a true community. There is no place for golden agers to gather with other Jews, in a genial atmosphere to have a friendly chat, a game of chess or cards, a friendly place to relieve the monotony of inactivity, forced on them by old age. There is no place for our young people to gather and have parties, dances, and meet others on a community level. There is no place for adults to give an affair in a congenial environment they can call their own. There is no place to adequately give lectures, or to carry on a cultural or recreational program on a Jewish community level. Realizing these facts, the Jewish Community Council, voted last February to create a Jewish Community Center open to all Jews on an equal basis without regard to the religious, fraternal or social affiliations. It will be the crossroads and center of our community where the whole community can meet...."

The Combined Jewish Appeal of St. Petersburg had 642 contributions for over $25,000. Leonard Lubin was the Executive Director of the Combined Jewish Appeal. The Jewish people who contributed were: Mr. and Mrs. Arthur Abrams, Robert Abrams, Mr. and Mrs. George Aghassi, Joseph Anspach, Mrs. I. Applebaum, Mr. and Mrs. A. Argintar, Samuel Aroson, Mrs. B. Ascher, Mrs. G. Ascher, Theodore Ayes, anonymous (7), Mrs. Ella Bailin, Mr. James Ballinger, Mr. and Mrs. Hyman Barak, Dr. and Mrs. R. Bauer, Mr. and Mrs. M. Becker, Mr. and Mrs. Daniel Balsam, Mr. Paul Barnes, Baynard Beach Memorial Chapel, Mrs. Belesky, Mrs. Ella Belofsky, Mr. and Mrs. Lee Benjamin, Mrs. Mae Benjamin, Dr. Phillip Benjamin, Mr. and Mrs. Milton Berger, Mr. and Mrs. Daniel Berkman, Mr. and Mrs. Joseph Berkowitz, Louis Berkowitz, Dr. and Mrs. A. Bernstein, Mr. and Mrs. B. Bernstein, Mr. and Mrs. Dudley Bernstein, Mr. and Mrs. Samuel Bernstein, Beth-El Sisterhood, Hewey Bischoff, Robert Bischoff, Jack Bishow, Morris Black, Mr. and Mrs. S. Blate, Mr. and Mrs. E. Blumberg, Mr. Rudolph Blumberg, Harry Boxman, Mr. and Mrs. Robert Brandt, Edwin P. Braude, Mr. and Mrs. Alex Braun, Mr. and Mrs. Joseph D. Brenner, Mr. and Mrs. A. R. Breyley, Mr. and Mrs. Max Brock, L. Chauncey Brown, Mr. and Mrs. I. Buchalter, Mrs. Rose L. Buchman, Mr. and Mrs. Albert Bunin, Mrs.

David and Ethel Rothblatt

Ben Bush, B'nai Israel Religious School, Beth-El Religious School, Max Caplan, Stanley Caplan, Samuel Carner, Mrs. Annabella Carson, Rabbi Morris B. Chapman, Mr. Joseph and Miss Edythe Cisman, Mr. and Mrs. Josiah Clachko, Mr. Ed Clark, Tillie Chesensky, Mr. and Mrs. L. Claven, Mr. and Mrs. David Coates, Mr. and Mrs. Aron Cohen, Mr. Harry Cohen, Hyman Cohen, Mr. and Mrs. Hyman Cohen, Mr. and Mrs. Sidney Colen, Mr. Al Cooperman, Mr. and Mrs. Martin Cooperman, Mrs. Katherine Cushman, I. R. Cutler, Mr. and Mrs. Bernard Cutson, Dr. and Mrs. Danzinger, Mr. and Mrs. Frank Dee, Mrs. Rose Dessen, Mr. Sidney A. Deutch, Mr. and Mrs. Martin Diamond, Mrs. Theodore Diamond, Mr. and Mrs. George Dickman, Mrs. Gertrude Dinnerman, Mr. and Mrs. William H. Dixon, Mr. and Mrs. Leon Donsky, Mr. William Dropkin, Mr. and Mrs. David Dunetz, Mr. Nathan Dunoff, Mr. Samuel Edelman, Mrs. Lottie Effron, Mrs. Celia Eisenberg, Mr. and Mrs. Sol Eisenberg, Mr. and Mrs. A. Eisenstein, Mr. and Mrs. Joseph Elias, Mr. and Mrs. Max Emsig, Mr. and Mrs. Al Esrick, Mr. and Mrs. Samuel Evans, Mrs. Rose G. Farland, Mr. David Fein, Mr. and Mrs. Joseph Fein, Dr. and Mrs. Harold Feld, Mr. and Mrs. Al Feldman, Mr. Leon Feldman, Dr. C. Fieldman, Mr. Martin Finkel, Dr. and Mrs. J. Fishman, Mr. and Mrs. Nat Fischman, Mr. J. J. Flansburg, Babette Fleishman, Miss Bianchi Fleischman, Mrs. Laura Fleischman, Mr. Fleischmann, Mr. and Mrs. Lou Forscher, Mr. and Mrs. A. Fortunoff, Mr. and Mrs. J. G. Frank, Mr. Lee Franklin, Dr. Leonard Freed, Mr. and Mrs. Isadore Freid, Mrs. Lena Friedberg, Mr. and Mrs. H. Friedman, Mr. and Mrs. M. A. Friedman, Mr. Friedman, Mr. and Mrs. E. Frolich, Mrs. A. J. Frye, Mr. and Mrs. Max Fuente, Lowell S. Fyvolent, Mr. and Mrs. A. B. Gamse, Miss Renee Gamse, Mr. and Mrs. William Garrell, Mrs. Jacob Garry, Mr. and Mrs. Eli Gelman, Miss Anne Gelman, Mr. Louis Gerstkin, Mr. and Mrs. Harold Gilbert, Mr. and Mrs. Samuel Gilbert, Mr. Irving Gilson, Mrs. Mabel Gingold, Mr. and Mrs. A. Ginsburg, Mr. and Mrs. Abraham Katz, Mr. and Mrs. Phillip Katz, Mrs. I. Katz, Mr. and Mrs. Harry Kauffman, L. J. Kauffman, Miss Nancy Kauffman, Mr. and Mrs. Harry Kaye, Mr. and Mrs. Joseph Keller, Mr. and Mrs. Charles Kenegson, Dr. Philip Kitt, Mr. and Mrs. Ben Klein, Mr.

Morris Kline, Mrs. Beatrice Kleinberger, Mrs. Clara Kleinfeld, Mr. and Mrs. Frank Kleinfeld, Mr. and Mrs. H. J. Knight, Mr. and Mrs. Emil Kohn, Mrs. Rose Kosher, Dr. S. D. Kramer, Irving Krigsman, Mr. and Mrs. Abraham Kulberg, Mr. and Mrs. Kutz, Mr. and Mrs. Louis Lackey, Mrs. Mollie Lampl, Mr. Leo Langbein, Mrs. Daniel Lave, Mr. and Mrs. William Lawler, Mr. and Mrs. Dave Lazarus, Mr. and Mrs. A. Leach, Mr. Louis Lefkowitz, Mr. and Mrs. Max Leopold, Mr. and Mrs. Morris Lerner, Mrs. Jean Lesser, Mr. and Mrs. A. Lester, Mrs. Sam Levin, Mr. and Mrs. Al Levin, Mr. and Mrs. H. K. Levine, Mr. Isadore Levine, Mrs. Mildred Levine, Dr. and Mrs. S. Levine, Mr. Samuel Levine, Mr. and Mrs. Irwin Levitt, Mrs. E. Levy, Mr. and Mrs. Samuel Levy, Mr. and Mrs. Milton Lew, Mr. Florence Lewandorf, Mrs. H. F. Licker, Mr. and Mrs. Erwin Lieberman, Mr. and Mrs. Meyer Lieberman, Mr. and Mrs. J. Linn, Mrs. Dora Lipfield, Mr. and Mrs. Jules Lipman, Mr. and Mrs. Morris Lipman, Mr. Aaron Lipwich, Little Dutch Kitchen, Mrs. D. Loebel, Mr. and Mrs. George Loew, Mr. and Mrs. Sandford Lord, Mr. and Mrs. Samuel Lourie, Mr. William Lourie, Mrs. Fred Lowy, Mr. Meyer Lubin, Lugerner and Gleicer, Macy's gift shop, Mr. Morris Mailman, Mr. and Mrs. I. Mardenfeld, Mrs. Selma Maring, Mr. and Mrs. E. Marks, Mr. and Mrs. Stanley Marsh, Colonel and Mrs. William Mashbir, Mr. and Mrs. Samuel Mazear, Dr. P. Mairowitz, Dr. and Mrs. Edward Melich, Dr. and Mrs. D. Mendelblatt, Mrs. Ida Mershen, Mr. and Mrs. Harry Meyer, Mr. and Mrs. Arthur Meyers, Rabbi and Mrs. Al Michels, Mr. and Mrs. J. Milchman, Mr. and Mrs. Irwin Miller, Mr. and Mrs. J. L. Miller, Mr. Louis Miller, Mr. and Mrs. Meyer Miller, Mr. Alex Milman, Milskey, Mr. and Mrs. Julian Moses, Mrs. Sarah Moss, Miss Charlotte Mount, Mr. Arthut Mundorff, Maurice Munraven, Dr. Samuel Myerson, Mrs. G. Nachman, Mr. and Mrs. Myron Navison, National Council of Jewish Women, Mr. H. Neimark, Mr. and Mrs. B. Newman, Mr. and Mrs. James Newman, Mr. and Mrs. Milton Newman, Mr. Moses Newman, Mrs. Carrie Newmark, Mr. Louis Nord, Mr. Israel Nuss, Ethel J. Older, Mrs. Cecilia Oliver, Mr. and Mrs. M. Ornstein, Mr. and Mrs. Meyer Oster, Mrs. George Palikoff, Mr. and Mrs. A. J. Pardoll, Mr. George Paver, Mr. and Mrs. George

Perlman, Mr. and Mrs. E. Perlmutter, Mr. and Mrs. J. F. Pearson, Mr. and Mrs. A. Peskin, Mrs. Teresa Phillips, Mrs. Libby Plain, Mr. and Mrs. A. J. Poll, Mr. and Mrs. J. Posner, Mr. and Mrs. M. Possick, Mr. and Mrs. J. Queen, Mr. and Mrs. Frank Rabin, Mr. and Mrs. S. Rabinovich, Miss Eva Radzinski, Mr. and Mrs. David Rafeld, Mrs. Joseph Reader, Mr. Lawrence Reibman, Mr. Leonard Rauch, Mr. and Mrs. Steven Rey, Mrs. Margarette Rhea, Mr. and Mrs. Sidney Richman, Mrs. Elsie Richman, Miss Belle Richter, Mr. and Mrs. Harold Rivkind, Mr. and Mrs. E. Rivkind, Mr. and Mrs. Samuel Robbins, Mr. and Mrs. Erwin Robiner, Mr. and Mrs. N. Robinson, Mr. Julius Robison, Mrs. Ida Rochelle, Mr. and Mrs. Benjamin Roe, Mr. Louis Roemer, Mrs. Rose Rogalsky, Mr. and Mrs. Harry Rosen, Dr. and Mrs. Louis Rosen, Misses Anne and Rose Rosenberg, Mr. Herman Rosenberg, Mr. and Mrs. M. G. Rosenberg, Mr. and Mrs. Ted Rosengarten, Mrs. Ann Rosenthal, Mr. and Mrs. Bernard Rosenthal, Mr. and Mrs. Jonas Rosenthal, Mr. and Mrs. Meyer Rosenthal, Mr. and Mrs. James Rosenzweig, Mr. and Mrs. Marion Ross, Mr. and Mrs. Max Rosskoff, Mr. and Mrs. D. Rothblatt, Mr. and Mrs. Maurice Rothman, Mrs. J. Rothfarb, Rachel Rothfarb, Mr. and Mrs. H. Routman, Mr. and Mrs. J. Rovell, Dr. and Mrs. H. E. Rubin, Mr. and Mrs. Maurice Rudnick, Dr. and Mrs. Reuben Sabin, Mr. Al Sacks, Mr. and Mrs. Samuel Salk, Mr. and Mrs. William Salzer, Mr. Abe Salzman, Mr. and Mrs. Theodore Samuels, Mr. and Mrs. H. Schimerling, Mr. and Mrs. Saul Schaffer, Mrs. Lee Schindler, Mr. Harry Schine, Mr. and Mrs. Davis Schips, Mrs. D. J. Scheifer, Mrs. Samuel Schloss, Mrs. Jacob Schneer, Mrs. Ida Schneider, Mr. and Mrs. Max Schneider, Mrs. Bessie Schneider, Mr. Richard Schneider, Scholler's, Mr. and Mrs. Nathan Schultz, Mr. and Mrs. George Schunick, Mrs. Goldie Schuster, Mr. and Mrs. I. Schuster, Mr. and Mrs. John Schuster, Mr. and Mrs. J. B. Schwartz, Mr. Williams Seff, Mr. Dave Segal, Mr. and Mrs. Alvin Seligman, Mr. William Seligman, Edith H. Serex, Mr. and Mrs. Abraham Settel, B Shapass, Mr. and Mrs. Benjamin Shapiro, Mr. Philip Shapiro, Mrs. Mary E. Shell, Mr. Benjamin Shenker, Mr. Morris Sherman, Mr. and Mrs. Harry Siegel, Mr. and Mrs. Louis Siegel, Mr. and Mrs. Abraham Sierkese, Mr. and Mrs. Harry Signer, Mr. J. H. Silbar, Mrs. Catherine Silber, Mr. and Mrs. Don Silverberg, Mr. and Mrs. Henry Silverberg, Mr. and Mrs. Joseph Silverberg, Mrs. Ann Silverman, Mr. Aaron J. Silverman, Mrs. Ette Silverman, Mr. Julius Silverman, Mr. and Mrs. O. Silverman, Mr. and Mrs. Harry Simon, Miss Rebecca Simon, Mr. Sigmond Simon, Mr. Morris Sirota, Mrs. Elizabeth Soscovitz, Mr. Harold Slimmer, Mr. and Mrs. M. K. Smith, Mr. and Mrs. Irving Sohon, Mr. and Mrs. C. Solomon, Mr. and Mrs. Henry L. Solomon, Mr. and Mrs. Benjamin Somers, Mrs. Sarah Spero, Mr. and Mrs. Jack Spivak, Dr. Joseph S. Spoto, Dr. Charles Stansky, Mr. Samuel Stavisky, Mr. and Mrs. Jack Stark, Mr. and Mrs. Edward Steiner, Ester Stern, Mrs. F. Stern, Mrs. P. K. Stichler, Mrs. Beatrice Stone, Mr. and Mrs. Morris Stone, Mr. and Mrs. Samuel Sweet, Mr. and Mrs. Jack Tech, Mr. and Mrs. Max Teichberg, Mr. and Mrs. Leonard Temko, Mr. and Mrs. M Thorpe, Saul Tillis, Mrs. Jennie Tinkle, Mrs. E. Torch, Mr. Arthur Trock, Mr. Meyer Tuber, Mr. and Mrs. Irving Turk, Mrs. Tyler, Union Trust Co., Colonel and Mrs. George Wald, Mr. Joseph Walzer, S. B. Wasserman, Mrs. Kenneth Wax, Mrs. Shela Wehunt, Mr. Warren Weil, Mrs. Lillian Weinberg, Mr. and Mrs. Lee Weinberg, Mr. Meyer Weinstein, Mr. and Mrs. Max Weintraub, Mr. and Mrs. S. Weis, Mrs. Miriam Weiss, Mr. and Mrs. Raymond J. Weyl, Mr. and Mrs. Michael Whitman, Mr. and Mrs. Vernon Wides, Mr. William Weichman, Mr. and Mrs. Ted Wittner, Mrs. Rebecca Wolinsky, Mr. and Mrs. David Wolper, Mr. and Mrs. Aaron Wynn, Mr. David Yaffin, Mr. and Mrs. Yanchuck, Mr. and Mrs. R. C. Yedvob, Amanda Yorenker, Mrs. Robert Young, Isadore Zakon, Mr. Charles Zallen, Mr. W. F. Zeigler, Sarah Zimmerman, Irving Zinaman, Mr. A. Zinner, Mr. and Mrs. Herman Zinober, Mr. and Mrs. Al Zwick, Mr. and Mrs. Samuel Adelman, Mr. and Mrs. B. Babbit, Mr. and Mrs. Robert Bramlit, Mr. and Mrs. M. Braunstein, Mrs. G. W. Brodman, Mrs. Karl Brook, Ralph P. Brooks, Adeline Bengehone, Mrs. Amuel Berger, Harris Cohen, Mr. and Mrs. Samuel Cohen, Mr. and Mrs. D. A. Collis, Mr. and Mrs. Phillips Coplon, Mr. and Mrs. D. Dannenberg, Mr. and Mrs. Oscar Davis, Mrs. A. Don, Mr. and Mrs. Benjamin Elders, Mrs. Viola Fanta,, Thomas Fawks, Mrs. Ethel Feinberg, Mr. and

Mrs. H. Forunoff, Mrs. S. Frankel, Mr. and Mrs. M. Freedman, Mr. and Mrs. Jacob Furst, Mr. and Mrs. G. H. Gamse, Mrs. Gussie Ganz, Mr. and Mrs. M. Glimcher, Gluckman, Mr. and Mrs. Alex Goldberg, Mrs. Dora Goldberg, Mr. and Mrs. M. Grubstein, William Hass, David Hersch, Mrs. Clara Hirsch, Charles Hart, Mr. C. A. Harvey, Mrs. Lee Higer, Mrs. Claire Higgins, Mr. Herman Hirschberg, Rebecca Israil, Mr. Itzigson, Mrs. Mary Kapner, Mr. and Mrs. L. Klaskow, Mrs. William Lang, Mr. and Mrs. M. Lasher, Mr. and Mrs. Sidney Leinson, Mr. and Mrs. Lopen, Mr. and Mrs. Harry Miller, Mrs. Cora Mooney, Mr. Theodore Nadel, Mrs. Rose Nanes, Nathan Osterman, Mr. V. P. Parsons, Mr. and Mrs. Jerome Pearl, Mr. and Mrs. Jack Revesz, Mrs. Gussie Rosenberg, Albert Salmonson, Mr. David Schlessinger, Mr. Isaac Schulman, Mr. and Mrs. Samuel Shultz, Mr. Nathan Schuster, Mr. and Mrs. M. Sterenson, Mr. and Mrs. B. Storger, Stanley C. Staniszensky, Mrs. Lou Sugarman, Mrs. Claire Gold Transon, Mr. and Mrs. R. Weinstein, Mr. and Mrs. Harold Welsh, and Mrs. A. Woolner.

The previous list of names, excluding organizations and businesses, represents most of the Jewish people in St. Petersburg at that time. This list, along with the list of members of Temple B'nai Israel of Clearwater from 1959, and Congregation Beth Shalom of Clearwater from 1957, gives the reader and future researchers a good idea of the adults present in the Jewish community of Pinellas County during that time period. Of course, there were many Jewish children in all parts of the county that have not been mentioned.

Maurice (Maury) and Dorothy (Dotty) Goldblatt

Maurice Goldblatt

Maury and Dotty Goldblatt arrived in St. Petersburg on August 1, from Roslyn, New York with their three daughters, Jayne, Fran, and Karen. A fourth daughter, Eileen, was born a few months later. Maury was an unassuming, shy individual who have been described as "a man in a million" by those who knew him best.

Maury's work and commitment to enhancing Congregation B'nai Israel of St. Petersburg was legendary. For many years, he not only taught bar and bat mitzvah lessons,

but he served as a voluntary Cantor and conducted Shabbat services as well as filling the duties of the synagogue's appointed "Gabbai" (Gabbai is a term used for a synagogue position for an individual who is responsible for the distribution of honors, especially during the reading of the Torah. On occasion, the individual also stands by the Torah during the Torah reading to make sure that the reading is done correctly and assists those who receive honors during the Torah service). He personally raised $275,000 in pledges when the synagogue needed to build a new building on 59th St North. His business constructed the large Sukkah for the synagogue, as well as a very large menorah, which is still used today for Hanukkah celebrations. When the congregation sponsored the Globetrotters as a fund-raising effort, he built the basketball floor and installed it in Al Lang Field for the performance. Whatever the synagogue needed throughout the years, if he could, he would build it. He built an Ark, cabinets for the kitchen, office furniture, bookcases for the library, small tables for the pre-school, and larger tables for dinners at both the Jewish Community Center and Congregation B'nai Israel. Maury's greatest pleasure was never saying "no" to his synagogue.

Maury served on the Board of Directors of Congregation B'nai Israel for many years, as well as being President of the synagogue, and President of the Mitzvah Men's Club. He was a founding board member of both the Phillip Benjamin Tower and Menorah Manor, and a major contributor to the Florida Holocaust Museum. He and Dotty were among the original founders of the Pinellas County Jewish Day School. They were both twice honored by Israel Bonds for their support of the State of Israel. Maury received numerous honors throughout the Jewish community over the years, including being the Mitzvah Men's Club Man of the Year, and the B'nai B'rith Man of the Year. As a final, lasting tribute, Congregation B'nai Israel dedicated a Torah found during the Holocaust in his memory, after his death in April, 2000 at the age of eighty.

Maury was born in Brooklyn, New York on February 27, 1920, one of three children born to Annie and Frank Goldblatt. Maury graduated at age sixteen from high school as class valedictorian. He graduated from City College of New York with a degree in statistics and became an Air Force pilot. As a 1st Lieutenant, he flew B-24 bombers in North Africa during World War II. He wrote to Secretary of Labor, Frances Perkins, about a future career. She responded, "Anything that had to do with children would make a good business." This led Maury, who was an inventor, to develop a special feeding table called the "Baby Butler," that had adjustable and extendable legs and could be converted into a swing or play table with small chairs. He moved his business, Guild Industries, from Brooklyn to St. Petersburg in August, because of the opportunity to grow and prosper. His friend, Abe Pardoll, a fellow manufacturer, who already had a successful business in Pinellas County, influenced him. Maury and his brother, Phil Goldblatt, as well as Eddie Jacobson and Kenny Wax, formed Crest Cabinet Manufacturing Corporation in 1962.

Dotty was born in Brooklyn, New York on December 23, 1926 and married Maury on March 9, 1947. Her parents, Sarah and Louis Pincus, and her brother, Harold, and his family all decided to relocate to St. Petersburg in 1955 after Dotty and Maury arrived. Dotty raised four girls while also acting as President of Sisterhood at Congregation B'nai Israel and being very active in the Menorah Manor Guild, Menorah Manor, Hadassah, League to Aid Retarded Children, and ORT.

Maury said that his family taught him, "You live for the betterment of people-to do things to make others happy. It is pretty much the same to be a nice guy as it is to be a bad guy, only the nice guy has an easier time living with himself." Maury never needed anything for himself. He was a simple man who loved everyone and loved living in the St. Petersburg Jewish community, as well as in the general community.

HIGHLIGHTS of 1956

In January, Irving Sohon, in the absence of Chairman Weinberg, reported on the activities of the Center Program Committee. He reported that the response of the Jewish community to the establishment of a Jewish Community Center exceeded all of the expectations of the committee and that there were now fifty four men and women involved in various subcommittee functions. The Building Committee had procured tentative plans and building designs and prospective sites for the structure. The Fund Raising Committee had received pledges of almost $12,000 with $6,250 already collected, although the formal fund-raising drive had not even started yet. It was felt that the Community Center Drive needed to be delayed so that it would not interfere with the Combined Jewish Appeal, because the needs of Israel were paramount to any local needs. The local community was initially going to retain 35% of the Combined Jewish Appeal instead of 15%, but once again the needs of Israel were extraordinary. Another problem occurring was the building of a new synagogue with a budget of $250,000 of which $93,000 had been payable over a period of three years. These conflicts did not stop the concept of a Jewish Community Center but rather delayed the construction.

In 1956, there were no Jewish people on the boards of the banks. Jewish people were also excluded from civic clubs such as the Rotary. Over time, this changed. Many successful businesses such as Ross Chevrolet, Kanes Furniture and the development of Central Plaza helped enormously. Many years later, distinguished Jewish citizens such as Mel Sembler, the Ambassador to Rome, and the developer of Bay Walk, Stephen Raymund, Tech Data Chief Executive Officer, Richard D. Kriseman, City Council Member, and Craig Sher, President and Chief Executive Officer of Sembler Company, made outstanding contributions to the overall community.

The Jewish Community Council urged the Jewish community to increase their contributions to the Combined Jewish Appeal. The disorders occurring in North Africa and the Middle East had a huge impact on Israel and forced an increased rate of immigration of the fearful Jewish people. Forty five thousand Jews had to be transported from Morocco and Tunisia. Egypt was being armed by Russia and was a constant threat to the borders of Israel. The co-chairmen for the drive were Lee Weinberg and Al Feldman. The Executive Chairman was Dr. David Mendelblatt. The Executive Committee consisted of Joe Silverberg, Marion Ross, Jonas Rosenthal, M. G. Rosenberg, Sidney Colen, and Rabbi Chapman. The Treasurer was Frank Dee. The Financial Secretary was Allan Dee. The Executive Secretary was Leonard Lubin.

The officers of the Council were: President, Dr. David Mendelblatt, First Vice President, Marion B. Ross, Second Vice President, Dr. Mark Danziger, Treasurer, Frank Dee, Financial Secretary, Joe Brenner, Recording Secretary, Florence Newman, and Corresponding Secretary, Mildred Levine. The Editor of the Bulletin was Hannah Pearson. Her assistants were Mrs. Ann Sherman, Mrs. H. Wollman, Mrs. M. Cooperman, Ann Goldberg, Lenora Bernstein, and Lorraine Clark. $23,698.50 was collected for the Combined Jewish Appeal, and $5,880.33 was collected for the Community Chest.

The Institute of Jewish Study was being held at Congregation B'nai Israel at a cost of one dollar per family. Class I was "Intermediate Hebrew" with the instructor being Mrs. H. C. Rivkind. Class II was "What Is a Jew" with the instructor being Dr. Morris B. Chapman. Class III was "Ethics for Moderns" with the instructor being Dr. Morris B. Chapman.

The Jewish Girl Scouts had planned several activities. Mrs. Harriet Lieberman sponsored the first annual Chanukah Hop, which was a huge success. The girls then sponsored a class on ballroom dancing, including all the latest dances.

Rabbi David J. Susskind

HIGHLIGHTS of 1957

Rabbi David J. Susskind

Rabbi David J. Susskind became the spiritual leader of Temple Beth El of St. Petersburg in 1957. He became Rabbi Emeritus in 1985. Prior to 1957, he served in Texas, Ohio and Orlando. He was a civilian chaplain at several Air Force bases in Central Florida. He was educated at the Talmudical Academy and Teachers Institute of Rabbi Yitzchak Elchanan Theological

Seminary-1936-1940; Yeshiva College-1944, Bachelor of Arts; ordained from the Jewish Institute of Religion New York's School-1949, Master of Hebrew Letters; Hebrew Union College-Jewish Institute of Religion, 1974, Doctor of Divinity. He had served in leadership positions in numerous Jewish and general community organizations. These include: the Southeast Association of the Central Conference of American Rabbis, as Secretary and then President; Union of American Hebrew Congregations Camp Coleman, served as Dean and board member; represented the Central Conference of American Rabbis Committee on Justice and Peace at the 1964 march in Selma Alabama with Martin Luther King; Religions United for Action in the Community, one of the founders and Chairman for several years; National Conference of Christians and Jews St. Petersburg chapter, board member for nine years; Grievance Committee of the Florida Bar Association, served two-year term; United Way, American Cancer Society, Heart Association, Lung Association, Goodwill, Adult Mental Health Clinic, Hospice, Jewish Family Services, Holocaust Museum, served as a board member in each of these organizations. He has received numerous awards, including the prestigious Liberty Bell Award for Outstanding Citizenship from the St. Petersburg Bar Association, citations and keys to this city from various mayors in Pinellas County. To describe Rabbi Susskind personally is to look at an individual who loves sports, secular entertainment, social amenities, but has a fervent love for Jews and Judaism and is totally committed to helping, not only Jewish people, but all people.

Other Highlights

The Esther Group of Hadassah started in 1957 and lasted until 1965. This group was made up of a large number of younger women who wanted to have their own chapter in St. Petersburg. Estelle Marsh was the first President. The original Hadassah chapter, which started at the end of the 1930s, was founded by May Benjamin who was its first President.

Sidney Colen conceived, planned and

built Kenneth City, which he named for his son. Kenneth City is located between 40th and 54th Avenues North and 54th and 66th Streets. The city was incorporated in 1957, it has over 1200 homes with more than 4000 people. It has a complete government, parks, shopping center, all utilities, a city hall, and police and firemen.

Edward A. Rosenbluth, his wife Dorothy, and his family came from Cleveland to St. Petersburg. He became a land developer and builder of single-family homes as well as offices and shopping centers. He was past President of the Contractors and Builders Association of Pinellas County. He had been Chairman of the Pinellas County Construction Licensing Board, a lifetime Director of the Florida Home Builders Association, and from 1985-1987, he was a member of the St. Petersburg Planning Commission. He served as President of Temple Beth-El from 1973-1974 and 1976-1977. He belonged to the Suncoast Chorus, a life member of B'nai B'rith, and President of the Brotherhood at Temple Beth-El.

HIGHLIGHTS of 1958

Menorah Gardens

In 1958, a group of people from Congregation B'nai Israel sought to buy additional grave sites at the existing Jewish Cemetery at Royal Palms, which was difficult. A meeting was held, chaired by Ted Wittner, to discuss this issue. The group was preparing to make a bid on the grave sites. Phillip Benjamin, who always worked behind the scenes, called Ted and told him not to make that purchase, but rather to get pledges from the participants at the meeting. Phil purchased a thirty three acre tract on Wild Acres Road just south of Ulmerton Road. It took until 1970 for the land to be paid off and necessary improvements made, at a cost of $175,000. The cemetery was divided into a sectarian section, called Menorah Gardens and a non-sectarian section called Chapel Hill Memorial Park. In order to prevent the cemetery from ever being abandoned because of insufficient funds, the non-sectarian section would always provide adequate funding. The cemetery was to be under the direct control

of Congregation B'nai Israel. However, any Jewish people, despite their affiliation or nonaffiliation with this synagogue or other synagogues, could be buried here. The cemetery contains a Genizah, literally defined as a hiding place or store-room for disposition of worn-out books containing the name of God. In the Jewish tradition, such books and manuscripts are buried with the same reverence accorded to deceased persons. The Cemetery Committee, in 1970, consisted of Ted Wittner, Dr. Phillip Benjamin, Rabbi Morris B. Chapman, Joe Klein, Reuben Sabin, William Hirsch and George Dikman. Menorah Gardens was dedicated on September 26, 1971 by Rabbi David Susskind, Temple Beth-El of St. Petersburg, Rabbi Morris Kobrinetz of Congregation Beth Sholom of Gulfport, Rabbi Morris B. Chapman of Congregation B'nai Israel of St. Petersburg, and Rabbi Moshe Frankel of Congregation Beth Shalom of Clearwater.

Edward Rosenbluth, President of Temple Beth-El, 1973-1974 and 1976-1977.

Annette Raymund Family

Annette Leah Raymund was born in 1931. She died on December 30, 2003. Annette was a philanthropist and a volunteer for the Gulf Coast Jewish Family Services for many years. Congressman Davis commended Annette for her philanthropy and volunteerism at the dedication of the Annette Raymund and Family Pavilion at Gulf Coast Jewish Family Services. Congressman Davis described Annette as a "great American who has dedicated so much of herself to one of the best agencies in the United States, serving tens of thousands of people each year." He said, Albert Einstein taught us that "only a life lived for others is worthwhile. Greatness is discovered in goodness, service, humility and character." Michael Bernstein said, "For over twenty years, in times of sickness and health, great joy and tribulations, Tzedakah and Tikkun Olam, the act of charity and repairing the world, one life at a time, has always been a way of life for Annette and her family. Over the years, Annette Raymund and her family have given generously with overwhelming and inspiring humility. She has directly assisted in efforts to feed the poor, visit those who were isolated or sick, provide professional social work support and in being a philanthropist second to none.." At the dedication, a large number of people came to honor her. They were some of the tens of thousands of lives that Annette had touched-from Holocaust survivors, victims of torture, families living with AIDS victims, people with cancer and other illnesses, children and families in crisis, those with mental health needs and many others. Congressman Davis said, "The Annette Raymund family is one that realizes that life is not complete without helping others. Annette is a true philanthropist who has lived the great American dream, but has never lost her humility or forgotten her roots realizing that life is not complete without dedication to helping those in need."

Annette was a retired social worker who worked diligently to also help the Jewish Federation of Pinellas County, Menorah Manor, and Temple Beth-El. She was a hands-on leader in the community and was given the Yitzhak Rabin Distinguished Community Service Award for her excellent efforts. She also participated generously with her time and her money in the Shorecrest Preparatory School, Red Cross, United Way and other community programs. She was awarded the United Way of Pinellas County's Alexis de Torqueville Leadership Award.

Annette moved here from Phoenix, Arizona, with her husband and four children, Steve Raymund, Karen Marder, Eileen Rogachevsky, and Suzanne Sigun. After moving here she went to the University of South Florida and earned a Bachelor of Arts Degree in Social Work.

Steven A. and Sonia Raymund

Steve, born in 1955, is Chairman and Chief Executive Officer of Tech Data Corporation, which was founded by his father, Edward C. Raymund in 1974, in Clearwater. The company provides information-technology products, logistics management, and other value-added services worldwide. It distributes microcomputer hardware and software products, including peripherals, systems, networking and software to approximately 90,000 value-added resellers, corporate resellers, retailers, direct marketeers and Internet resellers.

From December, 1997 through July, 1998, the company donated 200 computers to twenty nonprofit groups under the auspices of the St. Petersburg Family YMCA.

Steve is a graduate of the University of Oregon, with a Degree in Economics. He also attended the Georgetown University School of Foreign Service. Sonia Raymund attended the University of South Florida in St. Petersburg. She studied accounting and graduated in 1985. She and her husband have made numerous contributions to the Jewish, general and educational communities. They endowed a scholarship for minority students at the University of South Florida. Steve is Chairman of the Board of Trustees of All Children's Hospital. Sonia is co-founder of Soulful Arts Dance Academy. Their daughter Monica, who is a dancer, has shown her own good heart as evidenced by her interest in helping the children who were victims of torture, that she had met at the Gulf Coast Jewish Family Services. Monica said that her grandmother, Annette, and parents, Sonia and Steve, had been excellent role models by being champions and leaders in assisting Gulf Coast Jewish Family Services serve hundreds of survivors of torture and tens of thousands of other people in crisis.

Dr. Morris J. and Marilyn LeVine

Morris was born in Chicago. While he was in the United States Army, he received several decorations. After completing his Army service in 1946, he earned a Bachelor of Science Degree from the University of Colorado, a Bachelor of Philosophy and a Doctor of Medicine Degree from the University of Chicago. Morris married Marilyn Fisher of Chicago and then they came to St. Petersburg to open a surgical practice. He proceeded to practice medicine for thirty five years. He has served on the Board of Directors of Congregation B'nai Israel, National Co-Vice President for Programming and Education of Hadassah Associates, has served on the Board of Menorah Manor Foundation, Past President of the Pinellas County Medical Society, and Past President of the 100th Infantry Division Association.

Since retiring, Morris has been teaching Archaeological Studies at the University of South Florida Institute of Learning in Retirement and Adult Education. He has also taught courses at Congregation B'nai Israel and numerous programs in the community at large. His specialty is Biblical Archaeology, Dead Sea Scrolls, Greece, Turkey, Egypt, and the Silk Road. He has been doing this for the last ten years. His interest in ancient times goes back to his honeymoon with Marilyn in 1949 in Israel. Since then, both Marilyn and Morris have participated in thirteen more trips to Israel including an archaeological dig sponsored by the University of South Florida under the direction of Professor James Strange. They have also traveled extensively throughout the United States, Greece, Turkey, Russia, Africa, the Mediterranean, South America, China, Japan, Australia and New Zealand. Morris is able to draw upon his numerous experiences to teach in a very effective manner.

Marilyn received her Bachelor of Philosophy, Bachelor of Science and Master of Arts from the University of Chicago. Marilyn is: Past President of the former Florida Region of Hadassah and the Florida Central Region of Hadassah; President of the Sisterhood of Congregation B'nai Israel; Chairman of the Women's Division of the Combined Jewish Campaign; President of the Auxiliary of the Pinellas County Medical Society; and Member of the Boards of the Jewish Federation of Pinellas County, Menorah Manor Foundation, Jewish Community Center, and Pinellas County Jewish Day School; and Co-Chair of the Israeli delegation of several Folk Fairs. Thanks to her ingenuity, hard work, and determination, there have been many musical productions at Congregation B'nai Israel, which not only provided entertainment, but also served as fund raisers for the synagogue. When Marilyn was asked what motivated her to work so hard in producing so many musical shows and being involved and so many different organizational efforts, she responded, "I always was a creative person. Even as a child I had artistic talent. I created plays and musical productions at a very early age–I directed my creative talents to organizational work benefitting my children, the general and Jewish community–I am very industrious

and feel a sense of responsibility when I have a task to do. And many many people give me task to do–So life has been good to me. When you give, you receive so much more in return."

Marilyn and Morris have received many honors including the Jerusalem Peace Award, David Ben Gurion Award, Shin Award from the Jewish Theological Seminary, American Technion Society Award, and other awards from Congregation B'nai Israel including the Sound of Honor, and the Federation of Jewish Charities.

LeVine Family.
See family picture section
for identification

LeVine Children

Marilyn and Morris have four children: Dr. Mitchell, Dr. Stephen, Sharon, and Dr. David LeVine. They have seventeen grandchildren. Mitchell is a colon and rectal surgeon. He has a Bachelor of Arts Degree in Biology from Emory University, and Doctor of Medicine from the University of Miami School of Medicine. He is an actor in community theater and a winner of several Larry Awards for excellence in community theater. Mitchell's wife, Ellie, is a medical assistant. She holds a Bachelor of Science Degree in Special Education from McGill University in Canada and a Master of Arts Degree from Northwestern University in Chicago. She is founding President of Shoshanim Hadassah. She is also an actor in community theater. Stephen is a vascular surgeon. He has his Bachelor of Science Degree in Biology from Emory University, a Doctor of Medicine from Johns Hopkins in Baltimore. He is Past President of the Pinellas County Medical Society. He is also a member of the Doc Roc band. Stephen's wife, Susan, has a Bachelor of Arts Degree from the University of Florida and has worked in public relations. She is active in Hadassah and Pinellas County Jewish Day School. She is currently Vice President of Congregation B'nai Israel. Sharon Le Vine Rosenthal married David Rosenthal and lives in Richboro, Pennsylvania. Sharon has a Bachelor of Science Degree in Science from Emory University and a Master of Science Degree from the University of Texas. Her husband, David, has a Bachelor of Science Degree from Drexel University and a Master of Science degree from the University of Texas and works in the computer field. David has a Bachelor of Science Degree in Biology from Emory University and a Doctor of Medicine Degree from the University of Miami. Besides his private practice, he is the Medical Director of Menorah Manor Jewish Nursing Home. He is also a volunteer teacher of Israeli dancing. David's wife, Janice, has a Bachelor of Science Degree and Master of Arts Degree from the University of Florida. She is a teacher of music in elementary grades at Pinellas County Jewish Day School. She is a former President of Shoshanim Hadassah. She is a recipient of the Teacher of the Year Excellence Award from the Pinellas Jewish Federation.

Adele and Leonard Morris

HIGHLIGHTS of 1959

Molly Brandt, delegate from the Friendship Club to the Jewish Community Council, reported substantial growth of the senior group to over 200 people in one year. Other reports at that meeting painted a bright and progressive picture of the activities that were going on in the Jewish community of St. Petersburg. The guest speaker for the meeting was Dr. Benjamin B. Rosenberg, Executive Director, Greater Miami Jewish Federation. He spoke on, "The Role of the Jewish Community Council in a Community." He pointed out that the greatest part of the work of the Jewish Community Council was behind the scenes in inspiring community activities and providing necessary information and assistance to others. All Jewish people working together could accomplish far more than a single group working on its own.

The City Council purchased the former building of Congregation B'nai Israel at Eleventh Street and Arlington Avenue North for $60,000 and converted it into the temporary headquarters of the St. Petersburg Science Center.

Dr. Leonard H. and Adele Morris

Dr. Leonard H. Morris and his wife, Adele (Weisman), and two sons, David Allen, age five, and Michael J., age three, came to St. Petersburg in October, so that Leonard could open a dental practice. Adele and Leonard met in Milwaukee and married there in 1953. After Leonard graduated from the Marquette University Dental School in 1954, he opened a practice in Milwaukee. Leonard was born and raised in Sheboygan, Wisconsin, one of seven children, of Russian immigrants. They lived on Treasure Island for seven years and then built a home in St. Petersburg next to Bunnie and Abe Katz. They added two daughters to the family: Wendy Beth, born in 1962 and Julie Kaye in 1964. Their home became the host house for many community/synagogue guests who were Shabbat observants. Leonard passed away in April 1996, at the age of seventy two. He left a legacy of friendship and laughter throughout the community. He is still remembered for his kindness, high professional standards, and his great sense of humor. He led a Yiddish Vinkle, storytelling, at Congregation B'nai Israel for five years in the 1980s. He often said he was inspired by his mother-in-law, Bessie Weisman, who was also a great storyteller and lover of Yiddish. Leonard was President of the Men's Club at Congregation B'nai Israel and active member of the Congregation Board and the primary shofar blower, "Baal T'kiah", for over fifteen years.

Adele Morris has contributed more than her time, energy, and strength to the Jewish and general communities of Pinellas County for the last forty seven years. When Adele has volunteered at Congregation B'nai Israel, Hadassah, Israeli Bonds, Sisterhood, St. Petersburg International Folk Fair, Menorah Manor, Phillip Benjamin Tower, at the home of a family in mourning or at the bedside of a nursing home resident, she has always been a precious example of someone with determination to help all people and the ability to inspire others to do as well. She frequently sparks a glimmer of hope in an individual in need of a friend.

As a teenage girl in Minneapolis, in 1947, Adele set forth her philosophy of life in her synagogue confirmation speech. She said, "If life be a struggle and only the fittest survive, then confirmation is the procedure of sending reinforcements, trained, enthusiastic souls into the battle lines of Jewish life. We, of this year's class, in this congregation, as in thousands of other congregations throughout the land, are new recruits joyously entering the lines, and our Confirmation Service is the rite of initiation and induction during which we pledge our allegiance to God, to Judaism, and to Jewish life." As we can see from her lifetime of effort, this pledge also includes all people of all religions and races.

Adele's organizational skills, leadership skills and dynamic personality have enabled her to hold high offices in many organizations. These include: the first female President of Congregation B'nai Israel in 1981-1983; Chairperson of Torah Procession at the dedication of the new building; co-directed the Israeli Activities Program at the St. Petersburg International Folk Fair for twenty five years; Board of Regional Hadassah; President of local Hadassah chapter; Manager of Hadassah thrift shop in downtown St. Petersburg for a seven-year period; she was the Chairperson of the Israel Bond Drives and dinners long before there was a local professionally staffed office and then continued on as Chairperson of the formal Israel Bond dinners. Throughout her entire life, she has worked diligently to improve educational opportunities for all people of all ages. She has chaired countless committees whose responsibility was to provide excellent programming at all levels of education. She was instrumental in bringing the Pinellas County Jewish Day School to the campus of Congregation B'nai Israel. In 1978, Adele and Leonard received the Israeli Bonds 30th Anniversary Award. She was once again honored by the Jewish community in the year 2000, by being presented the Distinguished Community Service Award

by the Jewish Federation of Pinellas County.

Bruce Marger

Bruce and Mary Ann (Baum) Marger

Bruce Marger, born in New York City, on October 3, 1932, has a Bachelor of Business Administration in Accounting, University of North Carolina, 1954 and Dr. of Jurisprudence, Harvard University, 1959. He is a member of Phi Beta Kappa and Beta Gamma Sigma honor societies. He served in the United States Air Force as a lieutenant from 1955-1957 and then in the United States Air Force Reserve, 1957-1972 as a major in the Judge Advocate Generals Office. He married the former Mary Ann Baum in 1956 and they have three children. They are: William G., born 1959 in St. Petersburg and married to Carol Gray; David S., born 1962 in St. Petersburg and married to Helen Reagor; and Susan Marger Levine, born 1964 in St. Petersburg and married to Dr. Steven M. Levine. When Bruce came to St. Petersburg he became a member and then partner in the law firm that is now Holland and Knight. He has served this law firm for over forty five years. He has been the chairperson of numerous committees in the Florida Bar including the Judicial Poll Committee, Real Property Probate and Trust Law Division, the largest section of the bar. He has served as: Chairperson of the St. Petersburg Board of Florida Gulf Coast Symphony, now the Florida Orchestra; President, Friends of the Library, St. Petersburg; legal advisor, Masonic Home of Florida; and board member, Hospice of the Florida Suncoast Foundation. He is a recipient of the Golden Baton Award and a thirty three degree Mason. He served as President of Temple Beth-El, 1966-1968 and 1987-1989. He has served on the board or as a legal advisor to both Menorah Manor and Phillip Benjamin Tower.

Mary Ann Marger was born in New York City on October 27, 1934, and educated at the University of North Carolina, Greensboro. She was a teacher in the fifth and sixth grade in Florida and Massachusetts between 1956-1959 and 1966-1970. Mary Ann became a freelance writer and wrote for Good Housekeeping, Christian Science Monitor, and numerous other publications from 1959-1975. She was a columnist on issues in education appearing in the Evening Independent, Fort Myers News-Press, and Palm Beach Post early in the 1970s. In the late 1970s and early 1980s, she wrote two books for young adults, "Winner at the Dub-Dub Club" and "Justice at Peachtree" published by Elsevier-Dutton of New York. She was a general assignment correspondent for the St. Petersburg Times from 1976-1987 and then its art critic from 1987-2002. She has been a Member of the Board of both Temple Beth-El and Congregation B'nai Israel of St. Petersburg. She is a member of the Arts Center of St. Petersburg and all St. Petersburg museums. She is also a member of Hadassah, National Council of Jewish Women, and League of Women Voters. She was the founding President of the Evening Branch, St. Petersburg Chapter, National Council of Jewish Women in 1961-1962.

Mary Ann is a Docent of the Florida Holocaust Museum. Of this position she has said, "Leading young people through this museum is the most satisfying thing I've ever done, outside of raising a family! In addition to relating the history of the Holocaust (the motto: Never Again) is the opportunity to instill respect for other human beings of all races, beliefs and abilities, and to encourage them to fight wrongdoing by standing up for what they know is right."

HIGHLIGHTS of 1960

In 1960, the Gulf Coast Jewish Family Services was founded with three staffers who worked in a converted house at the Jewish Community Center. See chapter on Gulf Coast Jewish Family Services for the rest of the story.

The Pinellas Braille Group was organized and sponsored by Temple Beth-El. Mildred Shavlan, certified as a braillist by the Library of Congress, became the teacher of a group of volunteers and continued in this role for many years. She was an active Sisterhood member and community volunteer who continued a family tradition of service. Her mother taught braille to the visually handicapped on a slate and stylus during Mildred's childhood in North Carolina and both parents were active in originating the

Blind Commission in that state. The classes that she taught lasted for approximately nine-ten months. Each student then submitted a thirty five page manuscript to the Library of Congress to receive certification. The classes were so difficult that typically only about 30% of the students completed the work. In 1979, the braillists produced 110 volumes of textbooks and literary works for Pinellas County schools and forty two volumes for the Jewish Braille Institute in New York

HIGHLIGHTS of 1961

The 58th Street Land Company

The 58th Street Land Company Inc. was formed with Dr. Phil Benjamin as President, Mr. Ted Wittner as Vice President, and Murray M. Jacobs as Secretary-Treasurer. Other members included Rabbi Chapman, Charlie Rutenberg, Abe Katz, Jerry Gilbert, Maury Goldblatt, Harold Rivkind. The purpose of the company was to raise money to purchase land and hold the property until the land was needed for the building of a new facility for Congregation B'nai Israel, Menorah Center (Phillip Benjamin Tower), and Menorah Manor. Fifteen men donated $500 apiece toward the land that later became Menorah Center. On April 18, 1961, The 58th Street Land Company bought a piece of property between 58th and 59th Streets North off of 4th Avenue North in St. Petersburg. They later added five more acres to the five acres they had originally purchased. The initial purchase cost $37,000, with $1500 due the 18th day of April each year until 1981, when a payment of $8,500 was to be made. The mortgage was paid as set up. On the 23rd of March, 1970, Congregation B'nai Israel gave a piece of land to Menorah Center Incorporated, 250-58th St. North for $100.

Elbow Lane Jewish Community Center

The land for the first Jewish Community Center in St. Petersburg was purchased on June 15. In February, Sidney Colen, who became the first President, suggested to Al Feldman that a parcel of land that had just come on the market would be an excellent site for a Jewish Community Center. The following Sunday, Al invited a group of men to his home to discuss the details of the land purchase and the proposal for the Jewish Community Center. The land, approximately three acres, was on Elbow Lane running through to Stymie Avenue and just off Park Street. There were half a dozen frame buildings on the property in various states of disrepair. Edward M. Rogall reported that the negotiated price for the property was $36,500, a terrific bargain. Since the Jewish Community Council didn't have any money for this purchase, four men gave individual $2,000 notes to the Citizens National Bank to guarantee the loan. These men included: Edward M. Rogall, Sidney Colen, Al Feldman and Selig Bush.. There was only $3,500 leftover after paying for the land. During the winter of 1962-1963, the main building was burnt down. Arson was suspected. A white supremacy group had a meeting hours before the fire and were condemning the Jewish people for having a Jewish Community Center on the old Eagles Lodge property. Because of the condition of the property, the insurance coverage was very low. George Dikman negotiated a settlement for the fire damage of $16,000. An additional $20,000 was raised and Sanford Goldman was engaged to draw up plans for the new Jewish Community Center. Even after cutting out air conditioning and heating, the bids for the contract way exceeded the amount of money available. Sidney Colen then volunteered to construct the building for whatever money was available and he absorbed the balance. The following winter on a cold Sunday morning, at a council meeting, Dr. Danziger brought up the subject of heating and cooling. Within fifteen minutes all of the members present agreed to lend $200 each to the Jewish Community Center to purchase necessary heating and air-conditioning. Over time, the property was improved and a swimming pool, paved parking area, athletic field, and tennis courts were added without any additional cost to the community or infringing on the funds of the synagogues. Freddy Sohon became the first professional social worker at the Jewish Community Center. Joe Charles and his wife were very active members. Charlie Rutenberg brought furniture from one of his model homes and donated it to the Center.

Marion Samson-Joseph and Bernard Leonard Samson

Marion and Leonard came with their daughter, Dori, to St. Petersburg to live in a better climate than Chicago and to have a better opportunity to succeed. Their children, Barbara and Paul, were born in St. Petersburg. Marion was born to Ida Frankel Lowengard and Julius (Jules) Lowengard on April 10, 1930 in Darmstadt, Germany. Her mother was born on November 6, 1896 and her father was born on April 4, 1891 in Germany. They married on January 20, 1924 in Germany. In 1937, Julius's employer advised him that things were going to get really bad in Germany. Julius obtained a three-month visa for Ida and sent her to the United States to visit her uncle, Louis Frankel. Later, Louis agreed to be the sponsor for Ida, her husband, and two daughters, Marion and Edie. In April 1938, the Lowengard family received their visas and left Germany. Marion's Aunt Jennie came to the United States with her son, Kurt, and then applied for a visa for her husband, Siegbert Seligman. He sailed to America on the St. Louis, which later became known as the Voyage of the Damned. Despite the fact that he had a visa, the ship was denied entry by the United States and several other countries. The ship finally returned to Germany and all on board were arrested and placed in concentration camps.

Marion attended the University of Illinois. She and her sister worked for a period of time in the family restaurant. Later Marion became Assistant Auditor at University National Bank and Hyde Park National Bank in Chicago, Illinois. After the children were born, Marion went from homemaker to businesswoman to philanthropist. Marion was Vice President and then President of Gateway Hospital Corporation, Vice President Atlas Medical Properties Incorporated; Home and Health Professional Services Inc.; Vice-President and Treasurer, Sentinel Service Corp.; She has served on boards and in administrative capacities in many charitable organizations including: Congregation B'nai Israel Board; Congregation B'nai Israel Sisterhood Board; Hadassah; T. O. P.; Menorah Manor; Holocaust Museum; PARC; LARC; Bayfront

Marion Samson-Joseph, President, Menorah Manor Foundation, 1986-1990, 1996-1999; Chair, Menorah Manor Foundation, 1990-1993, Chair, Menorah Manor, 1990-1993, 1999-2001

Center Foundation; All Childrens Hospital. Marion's extremely generous gift to Menorah Manor, made the dream of a Jewish nursing home a reality. The nursing home is honored to be called the Bernard L. Samson building and the synagogue in Menorah Manor is honored to be called the Ida and Jules Lowengard Chapel after Marion's parents.

She is a member of both Congregation B'nai Israel and Temple Beth-El of St. Petersburg. Marion's philosophy of life is, "That life is precious and sometimes much shorter than we anticipate, so material things are only that and not really important in the scheme of things. What is important is living each day to the fullest extent possible and making sure the people in our lives know how much they are appreciated and loved." After Leonard's death, Marion married John J. Joseph, who was born on December 2, 1919. They married on September 6, 1981. During the war, he was a member of the OSS (Office of Strategic Services, the forerunner of the CIA). John served for several years in the United States Army during World War II. He reached the rank of Lieutenant Colonel in the United States Army. Later he became a musician and insurance salesman. He is a Board Member of Menorah Manor and Docent of the Holocaust Museum.

Bernard L. Samson was born on August 18, 1924. Leonard was raised most of his life in an orphanage. He was finally placed in a foster home until he was sixteen years old. He enlisted in the Navy at age eighteen. Leonard married Marion on March 8, 1959. Leonard worked with scrap metal in Chicago before he came to St. Petersburg. He previously had owned a restaurant, a grocery store, a wholesale meat business, and was a Sunday school teacher. He saw the need in Florida for more facilities for good health care. He became the founder and developer of hospitals and medical facilities throughout central and southern Florida. He built and managed: Palms of Pasadena Hospital; Clearwater Community Hospital; Palm Beach Gardens Community Hospital; New Port, Richey Community Hospital and Medical Center; Pembroke Pines Community Hospital; Leesburg Community Hospital; Hubert Rutland Hospital and Medical Center; and Bayonet Point Community Hospital. He was described as, "a man with a dream-developing hospitals. He knew how to put his dream to work and change it into reality." A humble man, he chose to give to numerous worthwhile causes in an anonymous manner. He sponsored many young people in securing their college educations. Leonard and Marion's two daughters have formed a foundation to help fight breast cancer and autism. They're helping to continue their father's legacy by giving back to the community. Leonard was also active in the Rotary Club and Congregation B'nai Israel Brotherhood. Leonard died on July 30, 1976. Leonard's parents, Sam and Lotte, came from Russia.

Barbara Samson wrote poems about her father, Leonard and mother, Marion. Barbara, at age sixteen, wrote "...My father, the greatest man in the world. A man who gave everyone love...A man successful at everything he did. A man who is a friend to everyone he met. I guess one day God just said "I think I will make a great man, who will love like no one else. A great man who will be successful at everything he does. A man who will be so great, he'll be friends with all the world. When God made this man, He gave him to me to be my father. To share his love especially with me, and he did. I must have been the luckiest child in the world, to have been loved by this man...." At age thirty two, she wrote about her mother, "...Today, as a young woman with still so much to learn, I know that I can always look to you, for my respect you have earned. My best friend, my mentor, my conscience, my guide, my confidant, my playmate, my mother, my pride...." Although these poems were written by their child, she speaks for all of us for the great good these two people have returned to the community for the wonderful opportunity they had to grow and prosper in this fine area of the country.

HIGHLIGHTS of 1962

In the April 22nd issue of the St. Petersburg Times, an article was published entitled "A Report on Our Exclusive Clubs" describing the current practices as they related to the inclusion of minorities in the membership. Frank Kleinfeld, President of the Anti-Defamation League of B'nai B'rith, pointed out that the Yacht Club policy can seriously be called in to question since its property was owned by the city, tax-exempt, and leased for one dollar per year. At that time, Herman Goldner, a Jewish person, was the Mayor of St. Petersburg. Leonard Cooperman helped lead the fight to change the rules of the various clubs. Cooperman's brother and others had been rejected by the Junior Chamber of Commerce in the 1930s and early 1940s. Apparently only a few people on the boards of these organizations wanted to continue the practice of discrimination against Jewish people in hotels, civic clubs, and recreational facilities. The majority of the non-Jewish community did not want to restrict the membership of the Jewish community. Once again, as Jim Coad had done in the 1920s and early 30s, a distinct minority of bigots overruled the majority. Fortunately, in later years the situation was corrected by a combination of outstanding Jewish and non-Jewish leaders of the community. Rabbi Susskind said, "Overt acts of discrimination are aberrations and do not reflect the attitudes of the community as a whole."

HIGHLIGHTS of 1965

In 1965, Murray M. Jacobs, President of Congregation B'nai Israel and Elmer Ottenheimer, President of Temple Beth-El, started the Synagogue Council of Pinellas County. They chaired the organization for fourteen years and then became Chairmen Emeritus.

Sanford and Anne Rowe Goldman

Sanford, the brother of Jane Silverberg, married Anne Rowe on January 5. Sanford earned a five-year Bachelor of Architecture Degree from the University of Florida in 1957. He did postgraduate studies with architect Frank Lloyd Wright at both his home and studio in Taliesin, Wisconsin, as well as, Taliesin, Arizona. He received the Architectural Registration from the State of Florida in 1962 and from the National Council of Architectural Registration Boards

in 1974. Charles Benbow said Goldman taught him many things through the years about architecture and the role of the architect. "He took the best of Frank Lloyd Wright. Not the eccentricities, and then he adapted his work to the needs of this area. His houses are very energy efficient and blend in with nature. He built houses for a Floridian to live in Florida." St. Petersburg architect and former mayor, Randy Wedding said, "His work has contributed to the fabric of the city. Time will treat it well." John Stebbins of the Tampa Tribune said, "A Goldman designed house is an exercise in the creative use of space and nature, where the outside freely flows inside." Goldman said, "A house should have a feeling of shelter, rooted in nature. I've tried to keep that feeling in my work."

Sanford currently has a medium sized architectural practice in Brooksville, Florida, designing schools in small rural counties. He and his wife, Anna, have raised three children. Shane Heather was born on November 28, 1969 and married Gerald Davis of St. Petersburg on January 3, 2004. Edward Charles was born on January 30, 1972. Summer Rae was born on June 21, 1977 and married Joe Vecchioli of St. Petersburg on December 24, 2002. All three children had their B'nai Mitzvah on the front lawn of the forty acre ranch, under large oak trees.

Sanford has won several awards for his work, including: First-Place Award Residential, Annual Building Award, Sanford Goldman Residence; Energy Conservation Award, St. Petersburg Municipal Services Building, St. Petersburg, Florida; Energy Conservation Award, Dwight Jones Neighborhood Center, St. Petersburg, Florida; and Energy Conservation Award, Cooperative Extension Facility, Pinellas County, Florida.

Anne L. Goldman was born in Elizabeth, New Jersey, on February 14, 1936 and died in St. Petersburg on February 5, 2003. She came to St. Petersburg at an early age. In 1953, at age seventeen, three days after graduation, she began working in the Times library. Within a dozen years, she became the Women's Editor of the St. Petersburg Times and its sister publication the St. Petersburg Evening Independent. In 1966, she was promoted to News Features Editor, the first woman in the newspaper's history to lead a department that included as many men as women. Three years later, she was in charge of the staff of twenty two editors and writers. Her work drew national attention. She conducted seminars for other journalists at the American Press Institute and served on a Pulitzer Prize Jury. Donald K. Baldwin, a former Times Editor and President said of Anne, "Of all the journalists I've worked with over the years, she was among the very best. She was a gifted writer, but her creative imagination and talent for organizing and bringing to completion any project she undertook really set her apart. The Times is a better newspaper today because of Anne's contributions more than 30 years ago." In 1978, Anne was named Assistant to Eugène Patterson, Editor and President of the Times. She started a hotline column that was extremely successful.

HIGHLIGHTS of 1966

Sound of Honor

Edna Rosenberg created the idea of the Sound of Honor. She and others in the community joined together to pay tribute to outstanding volunteers of Jewish organizations. Their belief was that, "The Spirit of Volunteerism Lives through You." The awards were sponsored by the Jewish Community Center for nine years until 1974. Twenty years later, the Sound of Honor Awards were revived because of the work of Ben Bush. He involved Marcy Levy and Michael Barth, and they became the chairpersons of the committee that re-instituted this beautiful tribute to the women and men of the synagogues and Jewish organizations who have contributed so much to make our lives better. The first honoree was Harriet Lieberman, who was again honored in 1994.

HIGHLIGHTS of 1967

Jay E. and Karen Elias Kauffman

Jay and Karen married at Congregation B'nai Israel in 1973. Jay was born in Scranton, Pennsylvania. After he came to St.Petersburg,

he graduated from high school and then Florida State University in 1973 and received a Juris Doctorate in 1977. He started his community service as President of the Florida State University Religious Council. He was a founding member and Secretary of Congregation Shomrei in Tallahassee, Florida. He served as a member of the Board, Treasurer, and Vice President of Congregation B'nai Israel. He has served as Secretary of the Jewish Federation of Pinellas County, Board Member, President, Vice President and Treasurer of the Pinellas County Jewish Day School

HIGHLIGHTS of 1968

William E. and Sally Ullman Israel

Bill Israel, the son of Oscar Israel of Birmingham, Alabama and Miriam Weinstein Israel of Lumberton, North Carolina was born in Baltimore, Maryland in 1934. He graduated from Riverside Military Academy, Gainesville, Georgia in 1952 and then Georgia Tech in 1956 with a Bachelor of Science Degree in Industrial Management. He served in the United States Army from 1956-1958 and then attended the University of Chicago Graduate School of Business, 1960-1962. He and his wife, Sally, came to St. Petersburg from Atlanta, Georgia.

Bill retired in 1994 from Honeywell after twenty six years at Honeywell's Clearwater facility. He had spent thirty four years in the industrial engineering and engineering management fields primarily in the Aerospace and Defense industry. He was: President of the Florida West Coast Chapter of the Institute of Industrial Engineers for many years; President of the Institute of Industrial Engineers Aerospace and Defense Industries Division; and has served in other positions. He received a special citation from the Institute of Industrial Engineers for outstanding contributions to the field of industrial engineering.

Bill has been extremely active in the Jewish and general communities. He has served as: Brotherhood President of Temple Beth-El; Member of Board of Temple Beth-El; Co-Founder and Vice President of Temple Hillel; Chairman, Jewish Community Relations Committee of the Jewish

Federation; Vice President of the Technion Society of St. Petersburg; Member of Board for the last twenty six years with several terms as Vice President and Treasurer of the Gulf Coast Jewish Family Services; and Charter Member, Treasurer, and President of the Jewish Genealogical Society of Tampa Bay. Bill has served in many offices of community organizations including: Director, St. Petersburg Junior Chamber of Commerce; Vice President of the Council of Neighborhood Associations; Loaned Executive from Honeywell to the United Way Campaign; and Board Member of United Community Associations of Pinellas.

Bill Israel was the first individual in Pinellas County to provide the author with information and contacts in order to start the study of the Jewish community. He subsequently continued to assist the author over a five year period. He was very knowledgeable because of his continued service to the Jewish and general communities and because of his deep interest and commitment to the Jewish Genealogical Society of Tampa Bay.

Sally Ullman Israel was born and raised in Fairfield, Iowa where she was valedictorian in her high school. She graduated with a Bachelor of Arts Degree from the University of Iowa and was Phi Beta Kappa; she has a Master of Business Administration from the University of Chicago, Graduate School of Business, and was the only women in her graduating class. Her early career was in advertising. Later, she was in the Department of Business Administration in Production and Engineering Planning at Honeywell in Clearwater. She met and married Bill Israel in Chicago in 1959. She was very active in the United Way and Chairperson of the Allocations Committee. She served multiple terms as President and held other offices for the last thirty five years in the Pasadena Golf Club Estates Civic Group. She is Vice President of the United Community Associations of Pinellas and is a Member of the Board of the Fire District Task Force.

Their daughter, Sharon A. Israel, was born in Atlanta, Georgia, and at age three came to St. Petersburg. She has received numerous academic honors including Co-Valedictorian, Canterbury School of Florida, St. Petersburg, National Honor Society, Harvard Book Award and was elected a class officer every year at Massachusetts Institute of Technology, where she received a Bachelor of Science Degree in Electrical Engineering. She received her Master's of Business Administration and Doctor of Jurisprudence from Emory University and joined a law practice in Houston, Texas. She served in leadership positions within the American Intellectual Property Law Association, Federal Circuit Bar Association, and Houston, Intellectual Property Law Association.

Sembler Family
Melvin F. and Betty S. Sembler

Mel and Betty came to St. Petersburg and began working in various partnerships to build shopping centers in Central Florida. Mel had previously tested his ability to construct and lease shopping centers in Dyersburg, Tennessee where he developed Green Village. The company always prospered because, according to its President and Chief Executive Officer, Craig Sher, it had three outstanding qualities: "one is integrity; we do what we say and we deliver. Second, the company is financially strong. It has good relationships with the banks. The third strength is the Sembler company's great collection of bright, young people." Craig Sher was one of these bright young people who first was brought to this area by Charlie Rutenberg. The Sembler company has been involved in numerous real estate developments and re-developments, including BayWalk, shopping centers, Publix stores, and Eckerd drugstores.

Mel Sembler became Ambassador to Italy on November 16, 2001. He had been previously the Ambassador to Australia and Nauru. He had been the Chairman of the Board and founder of the Sembler Company, one of the leading shopping center developers in the United States. In 1986-1987, Sembler served as the international leader and spokesman for the shopping center industry as President of the 40,000 member International Council of Shopping Centers, where he had been active worldwide for the previous twenty five years. Mel has served as Finance Chairman for the Republican

National Committee. He was the Chairman of the Drug-Free America Foundation and served on the Board of the Florida Holocaust Museum, Florida Council of 100, and the American Australian Education Leadership Foundation. Mel was born in 1930 in St. Joseph, Missouri and is a 1952 graduate of Northwestern University, where he earned at Bachelor of Science Degree.

Betty Sembler, in 1976, was one of ten founding members of Straight Incorporated, a nonprofit drug treatment program that successfully treated more than 12,000 young people with drug addiction in eight cities, from Dallas to Boston. She, along with Mel, another founder of Straight, have been involved in national drug policy to reinforce the four critical areas to combat drug abuse: education, treatment, interdiction and law enforcement. She has helped form a public policy in the United States against drugs with her participation in the White House Conference for a Drug Free America. She is the founder and President of Save Our Society From Drugs and the Drug Free America Foundation Incorporated. Betty is a Member of the Board of the Florida Holocaust Museum, Florida National Guard Multi-Jurisdictional Counter Drug Training Advisory Board, Jewish Policy Center, and St. Petersburg Menorah Manor.

Greg S. and Elizabeth (Mauer) Sembler

Greg joined the Sembler company after he graduated from the Wharton School of Finance at the University of Pennsylvania in 1983. He earned a Bachelor of Science in Economics Degree with a concentration in Finance. He is Vice Chairman of the company. Greg was born on June 28, 1961. He has been a Member of the Board of Phillip Benjamin Tower, Congregation B'nai Israel, and Pinellas County Jewish Day School. He was deeply involved in the construction of the new synagogue.

Liz was born in New York on April 27, 1962. She earned a Bachelor of Arts in Political Science and Journalism from Syracuse University in 1984, and a Master of Arts in English Literature from the University of South Florida in 1989. She had moved to Pinellas County in 1984 and married Greg on April 13, 1986. She was

teaching at the University of South Florida when she met Rabbi Jonathan Mielke from Congregation Beth Sholom of Gulfport, who was also teaching at the University of South Florida. At that time, he was also Director of Jewish Studies at Pinellas County Jewish Day School. He encouraged her to teach at the Pinellas County Jewish Day School, and when he died in 2001, Liz became the Director of Jewish Studies. Liz has served on numerous boards including: Florida Orchestra, Congregation B'nai Israel, and Chair of Ritual Committee, Pinellas County Jewish Day School, T. O. P., Jewish Federation of Pinellas County, National Young Leadership Cabinet of United Jewish Community, WEDU Educational TV (former Chairman of Board), Board of Overseers of William Davidson Graduate School of Education at Jewish Theological Seminary of New York. She received the Jewish Federation Dr. Edward M. Ludin Young Leadership Award. When asked about her contributions to society she said, "My parents set a fine example for me growing up. It is important to me to do my part to help the community and to teach my children the importance of responsibility to the community."

Brent W. and Debbie Nye Sembler

Brent joined the Sembler Company after he graduated from Florida State University in 1980 with a Bachelor of Science Degree in Speech Communications and a Business Minor. He is Vice Chairman of the company. Brent is involved with the Gulf Coast Jewish Family Services.

Debbie is a graduate of the University of Florida with a Bachelor of Science Degree in Public Relations and Marketing. She has worked in numerous positions including Marketing Director for Old Hyde Park Village Shopping Center in Tampa. She was appointed by Governor Jeb Bush to the University of South Florida Board of Trustees and serves on the Executive Committee of the Tampa Bay Holocaust Museum. She has worked in many charitable and religious organizations over the past eighteen years. She is a recipient of the Gulf Coast Jewish Family Services Honorary Award in 1994 and the "To Life" Award from the Tampa

Bay Holocaust Museum in 2004. She and Brent have three children.

Craig H. and Jan Sher

Craig is President/CEO of the Sembler company. Prior to joining the Sembler Company in 1984, he was Vice President of Finance of the Office Building Division of the Rutenberg Corporation of Clearwater, which he joined in 1981. Craig said about Charlie Rutenberg, "Charlie taught me the world. He was the one who taught me to be a philanthropist, to get involved in a lot of things." Craig began his career with Arthur Andersen & Company. He graduated from Northwestern University with a Bachelor of Science Degree and a Master's Degree in Communication as well as a Master's Degree in Management. He was a Certified Public Accountant and is a Florida Licensed Real Estate Broker. Craig is a native of Minneapolis, Minnesota. He and Jan have three daughters, Alison, Jessica, and Stacey.

Craig is extremely active in the community. He is currently: Vice Chairman Signature Bank; Vice Chairman Sabal Holdings, Incorporated; Co-Chairman Shorecrest Preparatory School Capital Campaign; Director Real Estate Investment Council; Member Board of Trustees All Children's Hospital; St. Petersburg Downtown Partnership Executive Committee; Development Corporation for Israel State of Israel Bonds-National Campaign Cabinet; National Advisory Council, Northwestern University School of Communications; and Chairperson Board of Governors St. Petersburg Area Chamber of Commerce.

Previously, he served in the following offices: Trustee of CASA; President of Temple Beth-El; Director of First Central Bank; Trustee of Jewish Federation of Pinellas County; Trustee of National Conference for Community and Justice; Trustee of Tampa Bay Holocaust Museum; Board Member of Live Arts Peninsula Foundation; Director of American Stage Theater; Director of Bayfront Center Foundation; Director of Bayfront Enterprises Incorporated; Campaign Chairman of Jewish Federation of Pinellas County; and Trustee of Jewish Community Center of Pinellas County.

Craig has won awards for his community service including: Tree of Life Award from the Jewish National Fund; Silver Medallion Humanitarian Award from the National Conference of Community and Justice; and many others.

Other Events

The First Annual Ecumenical Thanksgiving Service was held in St. Petersburg. The shofar was blown to start the colorful procession of the clergy of the Catholic, Protestant, and Jewish faiths. The offering at the service was given to the needy people of St. Petersburg.

Craig Sher, President of Temple Beth-El 1995-1997

HIGHLIGHTS of 1969

Herman and Theresa Baum

Herman and Theresa are the parents of Mary Ann Marger. They retired to St. Petersburg. From 1947-1984, Herman wrote "The House Doctor," a syndicated newspaper column that appeared in more than 100 newspapers including the St. Petersburg Times. He was born in Camden, South Carolina in 1904 and earned a Degree in Electrical Engineering from North Carolina State. He worked his way through college by writing sports for the Raleigh News and Observer. He had worked at the Naval Yards in Boston, Brooklyn, and Charleston, South Carolina and finally at NASA at Cape Kennedy. He died in Menorah Manor in 1997.

Theresa Teiser Baum was born in Wilson, North Carolina in 1906. She earned a two-year degree in Commercial Art at Washington University, in St. Louis, Missouri. She illustrated her husband's column and also worked as a legal secretary. She died at Menorah Manor in 1991. Theresa's sister, Pearl Teiser Kahn, and her husband, Stanley, also retired to St. Petersburg in 1969.

HIGHLIGHTS of 1970

Rabbi Morris Kobrinetz of Congregation Beth Sholom of Gulfport brought kosher meat from Miami. Rabbi Morris Chapman of Congregation B'nai Israel inaugurated a Program with Reverend Preston Leonard of the Christ Gospel Church to have congregants donate money in place of the food they would be purchasing on Yom Kippur. The money was used to help feed the poor of Haiti. Ten dollars helped feed eight people for one month. There was an excellent response from the Jewish community.

Walter P. and Edith Loebenberg

Walter P. and Edith Loebenberg

Walter was born in Germany on May 22, 1924. Edith was born in Germany on March 1, 1926. When Walter was fourteen years old, the Nazis came to take his father, David, the manufacturer and owner of a paint company, to a concentration camp. This was immediately after Kristallnacht, which occurred on November 10, 1938. His father was extremely ill and his mother, Selma, was taking care of his father. Since the Nazis couldn't take Walter's parents, they took Walter to a large facility to process him for the concentration camps. One of the German SS decided that Walter and another young boy should stay behind after the other Jewish people were taken away. Their job was to sweep out the facility so that it would look good for the next group being processed for the concentration camps. This act of pure luck allowed Walter to return to his parents and avoid being murdered. He and his parents obtained visas to enter Cuba. When their ship arrived in Cuba, they were denied entry and sat in the port along with the St. Louis, the Ship of the Damned. Later, an anonymous individual paid for their passage to Ellis Island. Because of the onset of the war and because they did not have a visa to enter the United States, they sat and lived on the hard benches of Ellis Island for four months. Eventually, a distant relative in Chicago assumed responsibility for them, and they were allowed to enter the country provided that they did not seek work. Walter attended school and then spent three years in the United States Army during World War II. Because non-citizens were not permitted to be in the Army, Walter was able to become a United States citizen in a very rapid manner. Afterwards, his parents went to Canada, were readmitted to the United States and were able to become citizens.

Walter's father died in Chicago, Illinois and his mother died in Beverly Hills, California. One sister, Helen, is still alive.

Walter met Edith after the war, and they married on June 20, 1948. Walter went into the restaurant business and then into a vending business. They went to California and then in 1970, they came to St. Petersburg to seek better financial opportunities. They brought their three children, Michael, David, and Sandy, who were born in Chicago with them. Walter said, "Anyone that came to Florida in the 1960s and 1970s could become very successful because of the growth of Florida and Pinellas County. If you worked hard you could achieve almost anything."

Walter went on to become a highly successful businessman and philanthropist. He was President and Chairman of U.S. Health Corporation. He designed, constructed, managed, and owned health facilities including hospitals, medical office buildings, ambulatory care centers, and home health services in Florida and other sections of the southeastern United States. He is currently Chairman of the Board and President of U. S. Enterprises Incorporated., a venture capital and investment firm with offices in St. Petersburg, Florida.

Walter currently is a member of the Board of Directors of Menorah Manor, Gulf Coast Jewish Family Services, and Drug-Free America Foundation. He is a member of the American Hospital Association and Federation of American Hospitals. In his thirty five years in Pinellas County, Walter Loebenberg became a community leader who contributed substantially to the growth of business, education and social developments throughout the Tampa Bay area and the State of Florida, as well as helped advance professional healthcare services throughout the industry and the community. He and Edie have served on numerous boards at the state, national, and international level. Walter is past Chairman of the Board of Governors of the Anne Frank Center USA in New York. He is also a member of the Statue of Liberty-Ellis Island Foundation Committee, and has served on the Florida Commissioner's Task Force on Holocaust Education.

Walter and Edie Loebenberg are

true leaders of the Jewish and general community. Their foresight and vision have continually helped light the flames of hope which fights bigotry, hatred, and prejudice among all people of all races and religions. From their original desire to have a small poster exhibit about the Holocaust and a place where children could learn about this time in history that caused such devastation, they have built one of the finest Holocaust Museums in the world here in St. Petersburg. This fourth largest Holocaust Museum in the United States is a tribute to the millions of people who suffered and perished and a living reminder to the tens of thousands of people who come through the doors each year, that this must never happen again. Multiple times, often anonymously, they have returned to the community what they have received through the opportunity to work diligently and productively in this great country.

HIGHLIGHTS of 1971

Menorah Gardens of Chapel Hill Memorial Park located at 12905 Wild Acres Road, Largo, south of Ulmerton Road between Belcher and Starkey was dedicated as a Jewish cemetery. It was the only Jewish cemetery on the West Coast of Florida owned by a congregation (Congregation B'nai Israel) and was available to all Jewish people affiliated or not affiliated with a synagogue or temple. David L. Robbins was the spokesman for the project.

HIGHLIGHTS of 1972

Temple Hillel
On May 13th, six individuals met with Rabbi Zielonka of Tampa for his guidance and advice on how to start a new reform synagogue. Myron Mench and Leo Wise were part of this group. With the guidance of Rabbi Zelonka and the encouragement of Rabbi Sandy Shapiro of the Union of American Hebrew Congregations, the group elected officers and set out to select a name and find a place to meet. The founding officers were: President, Myron Mensh; Vice President, William Israel; Secretary, Miriam Zwick; Treasurer, Leo Wise. Temple Hillel

was founded by a group of individuals, a dozen or so families, who wanted to have a Chavurah experience. It eventually reached a membership of fifty five or fifty six families with about 100 individual adults. It began with a part-time student rabbi, Michael Charney, who became its full-time Rabbi after his graduation and ordination from Hebrew Union College. He was followed by Rabbi Ronald Goldstein, who served until the Temple was disbanded. Rabbi Goldstein died on December 31, 2003.

Rabbi Ronald Goldstein

The basically young members, with some older family members, formed this new synagogue, where they would have an opportunity to have lots of creative services. The first few meetings were held in individual's homes until a permanent facility was found in St. Petersburg. The congregation had its own portable Hebrew typewriter and, therefore, could write any type of service they wanted, including the appropriate Hebrew. The kids loved the services. Jackie Fleischer was the pianist. The members made their own Ark and obtained a Torah which they placed within. The congregation was an enthusiastic member of the Union of American Hebrew Congregations. Temple Hillel's first home was a converted dental laboratory just off of Park Street at 8175 38th Avenue North, in St. Petersburg. This facility was leased until the end of 1975. The Temple then worked out a sharing arrangement with Calvary United Methodist Church at 11000 110th Avenue North in Largo, to use the church's facility. The move to Largo took place at the beginning of 1976. A religious school was started at the 74th Street Elementary School in St. Petersburg. The structure of the congregation was very informal. President Myron Mensh later served two consecutive terms as President of Temple B'nai Israel of Clearwater.

Myron J. Mensh

A membership list, revised November 20, 1975, indicated the following members: Rabbi Ronald and Sherry Goldstein, Sanford and Joyce Abrams, Mary Baum Allen, Leonard and Madge Auerbach, Robert and Darlene Berkoff, Gene and Bonnie Celeste, Joel and Tina Cohen, Newton and Florence Cohen, Charles and Elaine Collins, Robert and Judy Dew, Sam and Anne Diamond,

Steve and Natalie Fleischaker, Mike and B. J. Altschul Fleischer, Mrs. Marion R. Fleischer, Richard and Jackie Fleischer, Robert and Ellie Geier, Jack and Sheila German, Carl Goldman, Pat Goldman, Mrs. Edith Gordon, Bernard Greenbaum, Gerald and Jo Anne Greenman, Steve and Flo Hersch, Howard and Sheryle Isaacs, Lester and Molly Isaacs, Marilyn Isaacs, Oscar and Miriam Israel, William and Sally Israel, Mrs. Judy Jurin, Skip (Allan) and Pam Kleinfeld, Michael and Francine Kleinman, Wesley and Leona Lay, Julius and Edna Lipman, Peter and Elaine Lipman, Mrs. A. David (Sylvia) Lundy, Myron and Helen Mensh, David and Nancy Meredith, Mrs. Esther Miller, Mrs. Fanny K Moran, Dr. Steve and Pam Newman, Dr. Arnold and Sharon Orlick, Jonathan Orlick, Harold and Carol Plessner, Sidney and Helene Roberts, Larry and Renee Salzer, Dr. Leonard and Caroline Schlessinger, John and Elizabeth Shafer, Richard and Mitze Skrovanek, Allen and Anita Tritt, Ken and Joyce Tucker, Leo and Edith Wise, Albert and Miriam Zwick, Dr. Ray and Helga Zwick, Ms. April Zwick. On September 14, 1976, an additional list of names was added. They were: Patrick and Wendy Adamson, Stan and Annie Behr, Les and Sue Brown, Marshall and Linda Canner, Sidney and Elaine Cutler, Bob and Melanie Dikman, Steven Duke, Ruth and Sadie Isaacs Fishler, Jerome and Ilene Grayson, Cyril and Helen Kleiman, Stanley and Linda Kreps, Joseph and Betty Marlin, Jeff and Judy Person, Martin and Elaine Pilka, Harvey and Sharon Saparow, Stewart and Jane Solomon, and Roger and Victoria Stevens.

The congregation folded in 1978 because of financial difficulties. Temple Hillel, like many small congregations, struggled financially, especially to pay a full-time Rabbi. Dues were not adequate for funding purposes so the congregation started a weekly bingo game at a commercial bingo house in Madeira Beach. Temple volunteers staffed the bingo hall once a week. The source of income, which was vital to produce adequate income to meet budget needs, was uncertain and, therefore, created considerable stress among the members. Also, there was a division of opinion among the Temple members about the need for a

full-time Rabbi. What started out as a caring and loving chavaruh became a divided family and led to the demise of Temple Hillel. The members either joined Temple B'nai Israel of Clearwater or Temple Beth-El of St. Petersburg. The Torah was given to Temple B'nai Israel.

Jewish Bakery

A Jewish bakery, Paradise Bakery, was opened at 167 107th Avenue on Treasure Island. Lorraine and Marty Ismark joined Lorraine's parents in the Tampa Bay area. Marty, a third generation baker, had gone to the Culinary School of Art in Manhattan and graduated in 1957. He had worked in New York City at Jewish bakeries, where everything was made from scratch, no preservatives were used, and everything was fresh. In July 1985, they sold the Treasure Island store and opened La-Mais in the Seminole Mall, which they kept open until 1999.

Lorraine was born in Brooklyn on January 19, 1942, to Sonia and Lou Gollinger. She had attended Brooklyn College prior to their marriage in 1966. Marty and Lorraine have four children. Marty was born in Brooklyn on December 18, 1939. Lorraine has been a member of the Chamber of Commerce of both Treasure Island and Seminole. Marty has been a Member of the Board of the B'nai B'rith.

HIGHLIGHTS of 1973

In 1973, an estimated 1000 members of the St. Petersburg area Jewish community turned out at Congregation B'nai Israel for an Israel Solidarity Rally. Two hundred and fifty thousand dollars was raised to help the Jewish State, which was being menaced on two fronts by the Arab nations. At this urgent appeal, handfuls of cash, boxes of checks, and paper bags containing the contents of children's piggy banks were passed forward to help the Jewish people survive.

HIGHLIGHTS of 1974

Jewish Federation of Pinellas County

The Jewish Federation of Pinellas

County was created out of a merger of the St. Petersburg Jewish Community Council and the Jewish Welfare Fund of Clearwater. See Chapter 22, Jewish Federation of Pinellas County, for the rest of the story to the present.

Slomka Family

Mike Slomka was born on January 3, 1942, in New City, New York. He attended Union College and then graduated from Georgetown University School of Medicine in 1967. He served as a Lt. Commander in the United States Navy at the US Aerospace Medical Center in Pensacola, Florida.

Sandy Slomka was born on October 3, 1942 in Sufferm, New York. She attended Ithaca College for three years and after marrying Mike on June 16, 1963, she finished her education with a Bachelor of Science Degree in Early Childhood Education from the University of Maryland. She taught nursery school in Maryland and then in 1984 went back to school and obtained an additional Degree in Fashion Merchandising. She owned her own business giving seminars, doing personal shopping, and selling a line of clothing.

They have developed a lifelong attachment to Israel through their many trips there and their relatives there. They frequently have chaired State of Israel Bond drives and thus have been honored for their work and their generosity.

In 1974, the Slomka family moved to St. Petersburg, where they rapidly became involved in the general and Jewish communities. Sandy has been a member of the Board of Trustees and Vice President of Congregation B'nai Israel. She has served in many capacities to help build the beautiful new synagogue. She is a past board member of Hadassah and the National Council for Jewish Women. She also has been active in political campaigning. Mike, who practices orthopedic surgery, has served as Chief of Staff of St. Petersburg General Hospital and Chairman of the Governing Board of Palms of Pasadena Hospital. He has been a Member of the Board of the Florida Holocaust Museum, Menorah Manor, and Shorecrest Preparatory School.

Anita and Arlen Helfand

Anita and her husband, Arlen, and two children, Norman and Lorri, came from Rockville, Maryland, and purchased Florida Watch and Jewelers Supply. Anita had taken classes at George Washington University, and then worked for the Central Intelligence Agency for a seven-year period. In St. Petersburg she continued her high level of activity as President of Congregation B'nai Israel's Sisterhood as she had in Maryland. She served in numerous additional positions in the Jewish and general communities including a board member or officer, including President of: Florida Branch of Women's League for Conservative Judaism; Hadassah; Brandeis University National Women's Committee; St. Petersburg International Folk Festival, Israel group; and Menorah Manor Guild. When asked about her numerous contributions, she said, "I am so proud of my heritage, that I became an Adult Bat Mitzvah in April, 1981." This desire to learn and be part of Jewish life continues on in her present position as Secretary of Congregation B'nai Israel.

HIGHLIGHTS of 1975

Congregation Beth Chai

Congregation Beth Chai held High Holy Days Services at 12611 86th Avenue North in Seminole at the Agricultural School for Rosh Hashanah, and at the Jewish Community Center, 8167 Elbow Lane North for Yom Kippur. Rabbi Michael Charney and Cantor Reuben Sabin conducted the services. Rabbi Chapman, Rabbi Emeritus of Congregation B'nai Israel, was a consultant to the new congregation. The leaders of the new congregation met at Rabbi Chapman's dining room table to plan how to operate. Congregation Beth Chai was founded in 1975 and lasted until 1992. The new building, located in the 8400 block of 125th Street North in Seminole, was opened in 1979. Between 100 and 120 families belonged at that time. In 1990, the building was no longer in use and services were held at a church at 108th Avenue off of Alternate US19, in Largo. Initially, lay services were conducted. Later, the rabbis were Michael Charney, Philip Kirshner–1980-85, Stuart L.

Mike and Sandy Slomka

Rabbi Michael Charney

Art Axe with Torah

Sidney Werner

Berman (1988) and Rabbi Jodie Futornick. Rabbi Charney was a reform rabbi, his grandfather an orthodox rabbi, and his father a conservative rabbi. The Presidents were Dr. Edward Lurie, Sid Werner, Art Axe, and Leonard Englander. Charlie Rutenberg gave a contribution of $1,500 to help start the congregation and then made further contributions. Later, Ed and Vivian Lurie donated two acres of land for a new synagogue. An additional two acres of land adjacent to the original tract was purchased by Allen Rosenbaum, Ed Lurie, and others to create enough space for construction to proceed. A construction loan was taken out based on the value of the land. The building was constructed by Allan Rosenbaum, who was a member of the congregation. During and after construction, there were threats against the congregation, swastikas, and a threat that the Rabbi's house would be blown up. A Torah was purchased by the congregation and another one was obtained by a congregant, Dr. Irvin Fineman.

Congregation Beth Chai was established in Seminole because Seminole had a large spurt of growth including a significant Jewish pocket in the west part of Seminole, west of Oakhurst road. Beth Chai had a mix of families, young, middle-aged, and old. Cantor Reuben Sabin was the unpaid Cantor for virtually all of the years of the congregation. He led the choir. Maury Goldblatt helped start Beth Chai. Sam Einstein and his family were important members. Apparently, the Torah or Torahs were lent to the congregation. Unfortunately, it takes a critical mass of people to make a synagogue financially sustainable and this critical mass did not occur. Sid Werner, when asked what was most significant about his membership and his presidency of Beth Chai said, "The effect it had on me was that I had an opportunity as a very young person to assume a leadership role in a synagogue. Because of this, Reva Kent and Charlie Rutenberg recruited me to become chairman of the Federation campaign, which in itself was a wonderful and maturing experience. This in turn led me to become, once again at a very young age, the President of Congregation B'nai Israel." When asked what motivated he

and his family to move on to Congregation B'nai Israel, Sid said, "We were looking for a youth program that would contain lots of good ideas and lots of children. Mark Goodfriend, the Youth Director, was such a person and Congregation B'nai Israel had such programs." Further, he added, "I appreciated almost as an art form the way the service was run and Judaism was practiced. There were a group of members with exceptional backgrounds in Hebrew and prayers, who helped enhance the service with their knowledge and performance."

Dr. Edward J. and Vivian E. Laurie

Dr. Edward J. Laurie, the founding President of Congregation Beth Chai, graduated from John B. Stetson University in 1951, Kirksville College of Osteopathic Medicine in 1955. In addition, he earned his Doctor of Medicine Degree in 1962 from the California College of Medicine at Irvine. Beside having an active practice of medicine, he has served the general community in the following manner: Scoutmaster of Troop 340 in Seminole, 32° Mason, Shriner, Past President Greater Seminole Area Chamber of Commerce, Pinellas County Committee of 100, Citizens Advisory Committee, Board Member YMCA, Board Member SPCA, Vice President and Director Early Childhood Education Foundation, Founder and Organizing Director Seminole Federal Savings Bank, Chairman of Board Seminole Bank, School Advisory Council and Director Seminole Fire Rescue. He has been named a Kentucky Colonel, Rotarian of the Year, and he was awarded the Mr. Seminole Award.

Vivian E. Laurie was a founding member of Congregation Beth Chai along with her husband. She is a life member of ORT and Hadassah and has been active in Congregation B'nai Israel since 1954. She and her husband have been deeply involved with the Early Childhood Education Foundation Inc., where Edward had served as President and Child Care Director from 1976-1995. She has worked with many realtor associations and has been a Member of the Board of Directors of the Greater Seminole Area Chamber of Commerce since 1976. She graduated from Pinellas County School of Practical Nursing, St. Petersburg

Junior College, Pinellas Vocational-Technical Institute, Bob Houge School of Real Estate and St. Petersburg Suncoast Board of Realtors.

HIGHLIGHTS of 1977

Rabbi Jacob Luski

Rabbi Jacob Luski arrived in the United States in 1960 at age eleven with nearly 100 members of his family from Cuba. He had been born in Havanna. The family had originally come from Eastern Europe. They were in the wholesale/retail dry goods business in Cuba. After a year in Miami, Rabbi Luski's immediate family moved to Charlotte, North Carolina, where his father and two uncles established a successful real estate business. Rabbi Luski became President of Temple Israel Youth Group.

In 1971, he received a Bachelor of Science Degree in Industrial Management from Georgia Institute of Technology. During his sophomore year in college, he was asked to assist in the youth program at Ahavat Achim Synagogue in Atlanta. He became the Assistant Youth Director, which was a part-time position. He then took over leadership of the children's services and became a substitute teacher in the Hebrew school. This experience created in him a desire to go forward in the area of Jewish education. He enrolled in a one-year preparatory course at the seminary in New York City. During the year he also married Joanne, a student at Emory University whom he met at the synagogue in Atlanta. He received a Master of Arts, Rabbinic Ordination, and Doctorate of Divinity with honors from the Jewish Theological Seminary in New York. In 1977, Rabbi Jacob Luski became the spiritual leader of Congregation B'nai Israel of St. Petersburg. In 1989, Rabbi Luski became the Jewish Chaplain at the VA Medical Center, Bay Pines. He is a member of numerous organizations and is extremely active in improving the community as well as his congregation and Judaism. He has served on the: Strategic Planning Committee of the Rabbinic Assembly; National Rabbinic Cabinet Executive Committee; State of Israel Bonds; United Jewish Appeal; Hakaschurt of Pinellas County; Board of Jewish Federation of Pinellas County; Founder Tampa Bay

Outreach Lecture Series in Conjunction with Jewish Theological Seminary of America; United Synagogue of Conservative Judaism; and the Rabbinical Assembly. He also is a Board Member, Bayfront Medical Center, Board Member, National Conference of Christians and Jews; President, Clergy Association of Greater St. Petersburg; and Board Member, Religion United in Action for Community. Rabbi Luski has received numerous awards for his work: National Conference for Community and Justice 2004 Silver Medallion Humanitarian Award; Golda Meir/Kent Jewish Center 21st Annual Humanitarian Award; Silver Simha Tribute for twenty five years of service to Congregation B'nai Israel St. Petersburg; Bandera Cubana Grito De Yara, Boston, Massachusetts; Lake Pasadena Neighborhood Association Community, Care and Involvement Award; Twenty Years of Leadership Award, United Synagogue of Conservative Judaism, Southeast Region; Reunification Award, State of Israel Bonds; Leadership Medal, Federation of Jewish Men's Clubs; Service Award, Menorah Center; Presidency Award, United Synagogue of America; Heritage Award, State of Israel Bonds; Outstanding Religious Leader, St. Petersburg Jaycees; and Leadership Award, State of Israel Bonds.

Rabbi Jacob and Joanne Luski

Joanne Luski grew up in Arlington, Virginia. She was president of the Arlington-Fairfax Jewish Congregation United Synagogue Youth. She graduated from Sarah Lawrence College in 1973 with a Bachelor of Arts Degree in Education and in 1976 from Columbia University with a Master of Arts Degree in Education and Curriculum Development. She taught in the SAR Academy in Riverdale, New York and the Solomon Schechter School of White Plains, New York. Joanne was a founding member of the Board of Directors of the Pinellas County Jewish Day School and served on the Executive Board for many years. In 1991 she started volunteering at St. Petersburg High School in the Guidance Department and in 1998 she was awarded the Outstanding Volunteer for St. Petersburg High School. She and Rabbi Luski won the Heritage Award in 1987 and the Star of Peace and Hope Award in 1996. Joanne continues to be very active in a variety of Jewish and community organizations. She and Rabbi Luski have four children: Yael has a Bachelor of Arts Degree in Psychology from Brandeis University and a Master of Science in Dance Therapy from Pratt University; Jeremy has a Bachelor of Science in Hospital Management from the University of Florida; Rachel has a Bachelor of Arts in Sociology-History from Columbia University and a Bachelor of Arts in Modern Jewish Studies from the Jewish Theological Seminary; Naomi is a senior at Emory University.

Estroff Family

Mel and Elsie Estroff became permanent residents of Pinellas County. The Estroff family started coming to St. Petersburg on vacation in 1926 or 1927. Originally, the family came from Russia in 1901 and went to Savannah, Georgia, when his grandfather met a friend who told him about opportunities in the Jewish community in Savannah. Mel was born in Augusta in 1920. In the 20s, when agricultural businesses in Georgia were in difficulty, Jewish people moved to Florida. About one third of the population of the Polk County Jewish community came from Georgia. Mel's father opened the Empire Store in 1925 in Lakeland and later opened stores in other locations, including Tyrone Square. His father helped found the Jewish Alliance of Lakeland, a synagogue.

HIGHLIGHTS of 1980

Jewish Community Growth

The Jewish community grew dramatically from 1975 to 1980. Two new synagogues were formed and membership in the county's five other synagogues increased rapidly. In 1980, there were about 2,000 family units of synagogue membership (approximately 4000-6000 people), versus 1,100 family units in 1975. Membership at Temple Beth-El rose from about 400 to 550 family units. Membership at Congregation Beth Sholom of Gulfport, in the last eighteen months when Rabbi Sidney Lubin arrived, rose from 75 to 150 family units. Membership at Congregation B'nai Israel rose from about 320 families to 425 families. Membership at Congregation

Beth Shalom of Clearwater rose from forty families to 250 families. Membership at Temple B'nai Israel of Clearwater doubled in the five-year period and about a hundred new families were added a year. Between 450 and 500 people attended services on Friday night according to Rabbi Baseman. The increase in membership at Temple B'nai Israel came despite the loss of a large group of families who left to form Temple Ahavat Shalom in Palm Harbor, which grew from forty families to 120 families. In all cases the rabbis reported that they were seeing a new kind of Jewish newcomer. Instead of mostly retirees joining the synagogues, a group of young professionals and businessmen with families were coming to Pinellas County because it was a good place to live. These young people wanted to be involved in the synagogues and demanded the kinds of services that they were used to back north. The Jewish Community Center at 302 South Jupiter Street, despite being a new facility, had already outgrown its physical quarters.

Ed Rogall

In 1980, Ed and Pearl Rogall died in the fire at the MGM Grand Hotel in Las Vegas. Ed served from his appointment in 1964, as a Housing Authority Commissioner and then as Chairman of the Housing Authority from 1968-1979. He was one of the city's leading proponents of public housing and helped provide a better way to offer safe, decent, and sanitary housing to citizens in need in St. Petersburg. More than 5,000 people were the direct beneficiaries of his dedication and labor. He fought a continuing battle for the disadvantaged and elderly.

Pinellas County Day School

The Pinellas County Jewish Day School was founded with twenty seven students. See separate chapter on Jewish Schools.

Wittner family
Ted Wittner

Ted Wittner was born in Tampa and came to St. Petersburg in 1953. Sylvia (Heller) Wittner was born on August 7, 1928, in St. Petersburg and went to St. Petersburg high school. Sylvia graduated from St. Petersburg High School. She was an individual who exhibited love for everyone. She kept a room full of cards and presents and made sure that everyone's birthday or anniversary was recognized. She had a love for flowers and all things beautiful. Sylvia and Ted were married on April 3, 1954. Sylvia died on May 12, 1975 on Mother's Day. It was a very sad day for her family and her many friends.

Ted and Jean Wittner were Chairpersons of the Jewish Federation of Pinellas County and the Combined Jewish Appeal Annual Dinner Dance. Ted was President of the Wittner Company and Jean was President of the St. Petersburg Federal Saving and Loan Association. This was just one of numerous contributions to the community by the Wittner family.

Ted graduated from the University of Florida with a Bachelor of Science in Business Administration in 1950. He married Jean Giles Wittner in 1979. They have three children, Sharyn Wittner Jacobson, Pamela Wittner LeCompte of St. Petersburg, Florida, and James Alan Giles, of Jacksonville, Florida. Ted has been Chairman of Wittner Companies for over thirty years. He is one of the founding directors of the Insurance Exchange of the Americas and a founding member and Director of the R.E. Lee Group, the nation's largest independent wholesaler of life insurance. His real estate development activities include City Center in St. Petersburg. He has been the Chairman of the Board of three different banks, all of which were successful. His civic and religious contributions span over twenty organizations including: Founding Partner of the R. E. Lee Group/US L. P.; President, Commerce Club of Pinellas County; Vice President, St. Petersburg Chamber of Commerce; Chairman Emeritus, Goodwill Industries-Sun Coast; Director, Pinellas Association for Retarded Children (PARC); Trustee, Museum of Fine Arts; Director, Committee of 100/Pinellas County; Trustee, Menorah Gardens Cemetery; President and Director, Congregation B'nai Israel; Member, City of St. Petersburg's Civic Advisory Board; Member, B'nai B'rith International President's Club; Member, Eckerd College Foundation; Chairman, St. Petersburg Progress, Inc.; President, Phillip Benjamin

Ted Wittner

Tower; Founding Chairman, Board of Trustees, Menorah Manor; Trustee, Suncoast Center for Mental Health; Trustee, TOP Foundation; Past President, Golden Triangle Civic Association; Etc.. He has received numerous awards for his many contributions to society including: Sugar Daddy–Florida Diabetes Association, Pinellas Chapter; Great American Tradition's Award–B'nai B'rith International; Top Management Distinguished Service Award–St. Petersburg Sales and Marketing Executives; Menorah Manor Award; Tree of Life Award–Jewish National Fund.

This remarkable and unassuming individual worked closely with Phillip Benjamin, Irwin Miller, Murray Jacob, and others to create the facilities and organizations necessary to help take care of the elderly, the disabled, and those in need in the community.

Sharyn Wittner

Sharyn, a second generation Floridian, said, "Her family instilled in her their strong work ethic and social values. From a very young age, she was expected to begin her responsibilities with helping those less fortunate and to dedicate herself to continuance of her Jewish heritage. One experience was her first trip to Israel where she remembers she made a silent promise "...to our people, to do my best to protect our home, wherever that might be." Sharyn has more than fulfilled her promise by serving on innumerable boards and serving as an officer in many organizations, which contribute to the health and welfare of the community, including: A Founder of Menorah Manor; President, Menorah Manor Foundation; Gulf Coast Jewish Family Services; Florida Center for Survivors of Torture; Founding Member of the Board of Florida Holocaust Museum; Benjamin Tower (formally Menorah Center); President Southwest Region of the Jewish National Fund; Community Action Stops Abuse (CASA); Palladium Theater; Tampa Bay Performing Arts Center; American Stage; Tampa Bay Research; Tampa Bay AIDS Network; American Lung Association; Founding Member of the National Campaign for Tolerance; and Charter Member of the

National Museum of the American Indian. In 1998, she received the illustrious, "Tree of Life" Award from the Jewish National Fund. Dr. David A. Bernstein, Chairman of the Board of Gulf Coast Jewish family services presented Sharyn with an award for her legacy of philanthropy. Dr. Bernstein said, " Sharyn is an inspiration for all of us. She has a true good heart and Gulf Coast is indeed fortunate and honored to have her on our board." Sharyn has been an interior designer for many years and has three children.

Pamela LeCompte

Pam was born on November 3, 1960 in St. Petersburg. She attended the University of South Florida and has been the Human Resources Director of the Wittner Companies for the last twenty years. She has been associated with Next-Generation, Pinellas County Jewish Day School, Juvenile Diabetes, and Susan G. Komen Breast Cancer Foundation.

Jean Giles Wittner

Jean Wittner was born in Atlanta, Georgia and moved to St. Petersburg in 1941. She graduated from St. Petersburg High School and was a member of the National Honor Society. She attended St. Petersburg Junior College and Indiana University. As an astute business person and a philanthropist, she has made innumerable contributions to the growth and development of Pinellas County. Jean is currently, and has been since 1989, President of the Wittner Company, President of Benefit One of America, Inc., President of Wittner and Associates Inc., and Secretary-Treasurer of the Wittner National Group. She also serves on the Board of Directors of Progress Energy Inc., Florida Power Corporation, Carolina Power and Light Company, Raymond James Bank, Eckerd College, Pinellas County Education Foundation. She is a member of the Museum of Fine Arts, Pasadena Yacht and Country Club, Treasure Island Tennis and Yacht Club, the League of Women Voters, and Vinoy Club. She has previously served in innumerable organizations: Centerbanc Savings Association (formerly St. Petersburg Federal Savings and Loan Association)-President, Chief Executive Officer and Director; Colony Bank, Founding Director, Chairman, Executive Committee; St. Petersburg Area Chamber of Commerce, Chairman, 1979-1980 (first woman chairman); United Way of Pinellas County Chairman, 1977-1978 (first woman chairman); St. Petersburg Downtown Improvement Corporation, Founding Member, Board of Directors and Chairman of Board; Florida Savings and Loan League, Director; Tampa Bay Holocaust Memorial Museum and Educational Center, Member of Board and Executive Committee; The Florida Orchestra, Member of Board of Trustees and Secretary of Executive Committee; Goodwill Industries-Suncoast Inc., Member, Board of Directors; St. Petersburg Chapter, American Heart Association, Member, Board of Directors; University of Florida, Member, Advisory Board to the School of Business; Gulf Coast Jewish Family Services, Member, Board of Directors; St. Petersburg Junior College Foundation, Member Board of Directors; Florida Judicial Council; National Conference of Community and Justice, Member, Board of Directors; Pinellas Association for Retarded Children, Member, Board of Directors; Pinellas Suncoast Chamber of Commerce, Chairman, Board of Directors; Presidents Club, Charter Board Member; Public Facilities Financing Committee, Governor's Appointee; The Commerce Club, Member, Board of Trustees; Pinellas County Work- Force Development Board; Menorah Manor Nursing Home, Member, Board of Trustees; Christian Business and Professional Womens' Council, Chairman; and Florida Chamber of Commerce, Member Board of Directors and Executive Committee.

Jean Wittner has received numerous awards for her dedication to her profession and for the betterment of the community. They include: Tampa Bay Business Hall of Fame Award; Business and Professional Woman Management Award; Top Management Distinguished Service Award; Tree of Life Award, Jewish National Fund – jointly with Ted Wittner; National Conference of Community and Justice, Silver Medallion Honoree; Volunteer Activist Award for United Way Leadership; Great American Tradition's Award, B'nai B'rith (jointly with Ted Wittner).

HIGHLIGHTS of 1981

Kosher Foods–Jo-El's

For Jewish people who keep kosher in this part of the West Coast of Florida, it has always been a challenge to provide kosher meat that was properly refrigerated and handled and met the standards of the various environmental health rules and regulations. Originally in the early 1920s, kosher meat was brought from Jacksonville to Tampa and then to St. Petersburg. However, it was spoiled by then. In the 1930s, there were attempts to get local kosher meat, but invariably they failed. In the early 1940s, Harry Hankin had a kosher meat market which he sold to Irving and Rose Halprin. They continued this business for several years. In the late 1940s and early 1950s, the Grubstein Kosher Meat Market took care of the Jewish community. From 1945-1973, the Empire Hotel provided kosher food. They owned a kosher meat market next door to the hotel for a period of time. In 1970, Rabbi Kobrinetz brought kosher meat from Miami. In fact, when a kosher meat market was lacking in the community, typically the meat was purchased in Tampa or Miami.

In 1981, Ellen and Joel Goetz came back to St. Petersburg and purchased a wholesale food distribution business from Rose and Phil Kelmachter. They quickly opened it to the public for retail sales including frozen kosher meat. After three years, they bought the current location in St. Petersburg and turned it into a properly refrigerated air-conditioned large kosher food market. A butcher shop was added and also a small kosher deli. Ellen and Joel started to cater kosher affairs along with the business. Joel became President of the Jewish Community Center of Pinellas County, which moved from Elbow Lane to the old Kapok Tree Restaurant on Madeira Beach. Joel was instrumental in helping raise $3 million to increase the size of the Center. Ellen and Joel have tried to perpetuate "Yiddishkeit" to keep life cycle events kosher for the community. Their store has become a meeting place for people of the Jewish community. Joel was born in the Bronx on September 14, 1941. He originally came with his family to St. Petersburg in 1960. Ellen was born in Brooklyn on November 17, 1941 and came with her family to St. Petersburg in 1955. She earned a Bachelor of Arts Degree in English from the University of Florida and did graduate work at the University of South Florida. She became an English teacher.

HIGHLIGHTS of 1983

Phillip and Marilyn Benjamin

Dr. Phillip Benjamin

Dr. Phillip Benjamin was recognized by the Florida State Cabinet and Governor Bob Graham for his outstanding service to education. He also received the Brotherhood Award from the Bay Area Chapter of the National Conference of Christians and Jews. In his thirty nine years of service in the health and health planning field he had plenty of opportunities to join with others in helping provide health resources to the public. For many years, he helped set policy for healthcare in Pinellas County.

In 1929, when Phil was four years old, he moved with his mother from New York to St. Petersburg. His father was Joseph Benjamin, who sold silk and woolen fabrics. While his mother worked during the Depression, his grandfather, David Goldman, who was a European immigrant, took care of him. David was a very strong person, who could lift a whole keg of wine of 30-50 gallons into his hands. He was a tall, husky man, who lived till age ninety four. David came to this country all by himself, at about sixteen, to get away from the Czarist army. For Jews, the conscription was for forty years! He entered the United States through Galveston, Texas. He obtained a cart and went out West to sell things to the railroads He met Jane Esther Cohen in Pittsburgh, married there, and had their family, with the exception of Helen. David was Orthodox and followed all of the rules carefully.

His mother, May Benjamin, was a kind and gentle person who took care of everyone that needed help. May became the first President of Hadassah in St. Petersburg. Her name is inscribed in the Hadassah Hospital in Jerusalem. Phil learned a great deal about behavior, ethics, and Judaism from his mother, and also observed how his mother kept kosher, despite the fact that it was expensive and difficult to do so in St. Petersburg at that time.

Phil walked to school every day, and also, when he got older to Hebrew school several times a week and to religious school on Sunday. In a book that he wrote to his grandchildren in 1993, Phil recounted that "it was difficult being Jewish in those days" because "there were a lot of hard feelings against almost every minority group." Partly due to this discrimination, the Jewish community, though small, was active, with all the children participating in Purim and Passover plays. His synagogue, Congregation B'nai Israel, was a converted church with a baptismal font, at that time. Throughout high school, Phil's social life revolved around the synagogue, and he also worked after school at his Uncle Ed Goldman's jewelry and luggage store.

When Phil graduated from St. Petersburg High School, he decided to take a summer session at St. Petersburg Junior College in order to get enough credits to attend Northern Illinois College of Optometry. At sixteen and a half, Phil headed to Chicago to go to school, but he also worked as much as he could in order to make enough money to pay for college. When World War II broke out, he was able to work six days a week after school at a hotel, as well as working in a jewelry store on weekends and at a stockyard making dog food. With this money, as well as the money that his family worked to contribute ($42 a month), Phil was able to pay for school.

Phil finished college at age twenty, but never attended his graduation ceremony because he had to take the Florida State Board Examination in Optometry at the same time as graduation exercises, in order to become licensed. Ten days after he took his exam, Phil became a private in the Army where he was sent to an infantry training camp in Texas, before being sent to a training camp for medics. He continued his service by working as an optometrist at various camps.

While Phil was in the Army, he received word that he passed the Florida State Optometry Board exam, becoming the first Jewish applicant in four years to pass the examination. When he returned to St. Petersburg after the war, he worked for several months at Bay Pines Veterans Hospital because he did not have the equipment or office to open his own practice. Soon he was able to rent office space from his Uncle Ed. His mother made sure that the first thing he did was repay the money that his family had lent him to help him go to school.

It was at his office that Phil first met Marilyn Halaczer. He wrote in his book to his grandchildren, "Incidentally, one of the first office girls I hired as soon as I needed help in the office was a sweet beautiful girl named Marilyn...yes, your Nanny!" Marilyn worked for Phil on and off for several years; however they did not begin to date and fall in love until after she stopped working at his office. Phil and Marilyn married in 1955 in St. Petersburg, honeymooned in Havana, Cuba and Jamaica, and then built and owned a four unit apartment building on St. Pete Beach, his first venture into real estate.

During this time, Phil's optometry practice grew, and he expanded his office until, thirty nine years later, when he retired, he had two associates and an office staff of six or seven. According to Phil, his office was prosperous for several reasons: he was active in many groups and he never practiced discrimination. He was proud of the fact that his office was one of the first in St. Petersburg not to discriminate on the basis of race or creed or ability to pay. While most offices at that time only allowed black people to come after office hours, Phil allowed all people at any time and cared for everyone equally.

His non-discriminatory work practices were just one example of Phil's work to eliminate discrimination throughout his life. He broke several barriers himself, becoming the first Jewish person to be accepted in the Junior Chamber of Commerce and the first Jewish member of any downtown civic club (after being blackballed publicly twice at the Lions Club, after giving the club 17 seventeen years of free professional work). He also Chaired the Equal Access/Equal-Opportunity Committee of the State Board of Community Colleges several times.

His dedication to the community extended to many organizations, both Jewish and secular. Phil derived spiritual comfort from his synagogue, and his dedication to Congregation B'nai Israel continued throughout his life. He served on the Board, on nearly every committee, and was one of the most ardent conceivers and supporters of the new building. With his involvement, the synagogue family prospered. In his memoirs, he wrote, "Our Congregation has grown so much and there are so many new members that I was asked by someone at a service if I had just moved to town."

Phil loved to act as a catalyst. He worked with a group of men from the synagogue to conceive of and build a residential apartment building for independent seniors. Until no longer physically able, Phil served as the first President of Menorah Center, now renamed the Phillip Benjamin Tower. He started the Jewish Cemetery, Chapel Hill Memorial Park, and partnered with many to found Menorah Manor, the only Jewish nursing home on the West Coast of Florida. Phil was proud of these projects and believed that they created the foundation for a stronger Jewish community.

In the general community, Phil spent more than twenty five years with the Community College system of Florida. He believed in the mission of this institution and the opportunity it had afforded him personally. St. Petersburg Junior College, founded in 1927 as a private institution, was Florida's oldest two-year College. In June 1975, Phil was part of the Board that approved the Seminole Campus Master Plan. Phil served on the Board of Trustees of St. Petersburg Junior College, from 1971-1996 and was its Chairman for many years. Phil's philosophy was as follows, "Education is more than just book learning, education is not only preparing you for life, but it is an asset that you are adding to your community and your country." In 1984, the Social Arts Building of St. Petersburg Junior College was named in his honor. He was instrumental in establishing the State Board of Community Colleges, was appointed as the first Chairman and then reappointed to the Board, by Governor Bob Graham and five consecutive governors of both political parties. Phil also served on many other boards including the Florida Health Systems Planning Agency, Bayfront Medical Center, the Pinellas Public Utility Advisory

Committee, United Way, TOP Foundation, Chamber of Commerce, Suncoasters and the Jewish Federation of Pinellas County. He was a founding member of the Board of Menorah Manor until his death in 1998. He was also a member of the Menorah Manor Foundation and Maimonides Society, a group of health care professionals affiliated with the Federation of Jewish Charities. He was honored for his work throughout the community with the Liberty Bell Award from the Bar Association.

Though an only child, Phil had a special relationship with his brother-and sister-in-law, Irwin and Sonya Miller. Irwin and Phil were partners in real estate, banking, and many family ventures. Together they started two banks – Guardian Bank and First Central Bank and invested in numerous real estate ventures. Phil cherished his partnership with Irwin and highly valued his intellect and ethics. Together, they made an excellent team.

Despite Phil's accomplishments, he was an unassuming leader. A lot of people liked the limelight, but Phil's style was always to work quietly behind the scenes. The community knew and respected this quality. If someone wanted to get something done, very often they would come to Phil.

Phil's love for people, his service to humanity, and his respect for God had been demonstrated continuously over his lifetime. However, Phil's greatest pleasure was his family. His wife Marilyn, his son, Mark, his two daughters, Judy and Caren, gave him more pride and love and understanding than seemed possible. His grandchildren, Molly, Rebecca, Michael, Peninah and Samuel were the apple of his eye. In his memoirs Phil concludes: "Lord, I'm in no hurry, but if you take me tomorrow, I would praise your name for the bounties that you have bestowed on me."

Phillip Benjamin, health professional, educator, successful businessman, civic leader, philanthropist, fighter for human rights, loving parent, grandparent, and husband was and is a perfect example of how a person should live. In the end he was fulfilling the mitzvah of "...teaching it to the children," when he wrote, "Dear Molly and Rebecca From Grandfather Benjamin," a personal discussion on how to live a good life and how and why to help less fortunate people and those being discriminated against.

Marilyn Halaczer Benjamin

Marilyn Halaczer Benjamin was born and raised in St. Petersburg. She has served on many boards of both Jewish and non-Jewish community efforts including: Congregation B'nai Israel Sisterhood, Art Beautification Committee, Menorah Manor, Phillip Benjamin Tower (Menorah Center), Woman's Campaign of the Jewish Federation of Pinellas County, Red Magen David for Israel, Jewish National Fund, National Council Jewish Women, Mahaffey Theater Foundation, etc.. She also served as President of the Menorah Manor Guild. Marilyn has received many honors over the years. Most recently she received Israel's Declaration of Independence Award. In 2003, she was honored by Menorah Manor for her many years of hard work and support of the nursing home.

Rabbi Ira S. Youdovin

HIGHLIGHTS of 1984 and 1985

Rabbi Ira S. Youdovin was elected Associate Rabbi and then became the Rabbi of Temple Beth-El in 1985 and stayed in that position until 1991. Rabbi Youdovin was the North American Director of the World Union for Progressive Judaism, while serving on the Senior Staff of the Union of American Hebrew Congregations. In 1977, he was appointed Executive Director of the Association of Reform Zionists of America (ARZA). He was selected by the 29th World Zionist Congress in 1978 to membership on the Board of Governors of the Jewish Agency for Israel and the World Zionist Executive. He was the fifth Reform Rabbi to be elected to these positions in the organization. He had served on the Jewish Agency's Budget and Finance Committee, Committee on Rural Settlement, and Board of Directors of the United Israel Appeal. He was on the Board of the Israeli Committee, the Board of the Central Conference of American Rabbis, and also served on its Youth Committee. He was born in the Bronx, New York in 1941, and educated in the New York City Public School System. He graduated from Columbia College in 1962 with a Bachelor of Arts Degree in Psychology. He then

attended the New York branch of the Hebrew Union College-Jewish Institute of Religion and was ordained in June 1968. He served as a chaplain in the United States Air Force. In July 1970, he became Assistant Rabbi of Temple Emanuel in Dorchester, Massachusetts. Rabbi Youdovin traveled extensively in North America and abroad and was guest preacher-lecturer in more than 200 American synagogues as well as many other synagogues in Asia, Europe, Latin America, Australia, and New Zealand. He was the author of numerous publications.

HIGHLIGHTS of 1985

Menorah Manor

Menorah Manor was completed and went into operation. See Chapter 23–Menorah Manor And Other Facilities for the Aging

HIGHLIGHTS of 1988

Jack J. Jenkins of Gulfport, a Board Member of Temple Beth-El, was named to the Executive Board of the National Federation of Temple Brotherhoods. He was a member of the B'nai B'rith International Council and past Vice President of its Board of Governors. He was also a member of the Anti-Defamation League's Regional Advisory Council. He served previously as Brotherhood President at synagogues in Washington, DC, and Alexandria, Virginia.

Rabbi Stuart L. Berman of Congregation Beth Chai of Seminole was appointed to the Community Advisory Board of Straight Incorporated, a drug-abuse treatment program in St. Petersburg. He had received previously, a National Award of Appreciation from the Jewish War Veterans of America, for his outstanding service.

HIGHLIGHTS of 1991

Florida Holocaust Museum

The Florida Holocaust Museum in St. Petersburg was founded by Walter and Edith Loebenberg to satisfy the unmet need of preserving an extremely important part of world history. The Loebenbergs wanted to make sure that all people would be able to learn about the lessons of this horrendous time, in order to prevent it from ever occurring again. See Chapter 18- Florida Holocaust Museum.

HIGHLIGHTS of 1993

Beth Rachamim of St. Petersburg

In October 1993, Beth Rachamim of St. Petersburg was founded. It was established as an alternative to the traditional synagogue to be a positive Jewish setting for gay-Lesbian-bisexual or transgender Jewish men and women, their families and friends. This independent synagogue is Reform although the membership ranges from Orthodox to Reform. There are lay services in both Hebrew and English and the prayer book, Shabbat Va-yinafash is gender neutral and contains gay-specific prayers. The congregation enhances its Jewish identity through study, social action, and participation in the larger Jewish community. Beth Rachamim is a member of the World Congress of Gay, Lesbian, Bisexual, and Transgender Jews.

The Congregation is the caretaker of a Czech Republic Torah, one of more than 1,500 stolen by the Nazis. It is on permanent loan from the Westminster Synagogue in London where the Torahs were eventually taken in 1964.

Beth Rachamim holds Sabbath services on the first and third Fridays of each month at the St. Petersburg Unitarian Universalist Church. The synagogue also offers Havdalah dinners, and annual Hanukkah party, Passover Seder, Hebrew and Torah study, annual spring picnic, and High Holy Day services. It has twenty four members.

HIGHLIGHTS of 2001

Rabbi Michael Torop

In 2001, Rabbi Michael Torop became the religious leader of Temple Beth-El, a diverse community of over 535 families, in St. Petersburg, Florida. He earned a Degree in Political Theory and Anthropology from Brandeis University in Boston Massachusetts where he was Magna Cum Laude, a Master's Degree in Education, with High Honors from Harvard University, and was ordained at Hebrew Union College-Jewish Institute

of Religion in Cincinnati Ohio in 1990. Previously, he served as the Associate Rabbi and Director of Education at the Community Synagogue in Port Washington, New York for a three-year period and as the Rabbi of the Leo Baeck Centre for Progressive Judaism in Melbourne, Australia for eight years. Rabbi Torop's goal is to create communities of learning where Jewish life is explored intellectually and celebrated with joy and a sense of partnership with God. He participates in numerous community and professional organizations including the Central Conference of American Rabbis, the St. Petersburg Ministerial Association and the Coalition for Alternatives in Jewish Education. He is on the Policy Committee of the Florida Holocaust Museum and is a member of the Board of Florida Center for Survivors of Torture.

Rabbi Michael Torop

Rabbi Torop said in a recent sermon, "Learning is a powerful experience. Teaching is a sacred responsibility. Each opportunity to explore Judaism with others brings a sense of renewal and enrichment....When I see faces reflecting a deeper understanding and appreciation of the richness of our heritage, I feel fulfilled."

HIGHLIGHTS of 2002

Rabbi Alter Korf

In 2002, Rabbi Alter Korf came to St. Petersburg to organize Chabad of St. Petersburg, an Orthodox congregation. Rabbi Korf began his training at the Rabbinical College of Canada where he studied from 1991-1992. He then went to Bais Medrash Oholei Torah of Brooklyn, Yeshiva Gedolah of Miami Beach and completed his education at the Rabbinical College of America in Morristown, New Jersey. He has served as the Director of Education of the Yeshiva Summer Program in Morristown, New Jersey, Rabbi at the Chabad Center of the Chabad Lubavitch of Maryland and Rabbi of the Chabad of Rego Park Hebrew School in Rego Park, New York.

HIGHLIGHTS of 2003

In 2003, Menorah Manor celebrated its eighteenth birthday or chai (meaning life) birthday. The honorees at the celebration were not only longtime supporters of Menorah Manor, but leaders of both the Jewish and general communities of Pinellas County. They were: Barry Alpert, Marilyn Benjamin, Ellie and Samuel Fishman, Ruth Glickman, Dr. Sidney Grau, Sydonia Green, Lorette Linsky, Madeleine Liss, Ida Michaels, Irwin Miller, Fagl Oxman, Barbara Rosenblum, Marion Samson-Joseph, Saul and Sue Schechter, Leonard Seligman, James Sobel, Shirley Solomon, Irwin "Wally" Wallace, Marilyn Weissman, Sharyn Whittner, and Ted Wittner. Also honored in remembrance were: Murray Jacobs, Marshall Linsky and Irving Wiseman.

Larry Wasser

Larry Wasser was born in 1946 and died in 2003. He was the Executive Director of the Florida Holocaust Museum. He taught, "you have to do the right thing." He was the son of Holocaust survivors who in 1997 began a campaign that raised $6 million in thirteen months to purchase, renovate, and turn the First Florida Bank Building at 55 5th Street South into the Florida Holocaust Museum.

HIGHLIGHTS of 2004

Rabbi Jacob Luski gave the keynote address at a Catholic convocation entitled "Faith, Traditions – Seeking Understanding." The first four hours of program were dedicated to Catholic-Jewish relations. Three years before, Bishop Robert Lynch spoke before a countywide Jewish audience at Congregation B'nai Israel, discussing Jewish-Catholic relations. The rabbi and bishop are close friends. The conference included the five county Catholic diocese and a dozen rabbis from Hillsborough County and Pinellas County. Bishop Lynch said, "...our priests learned a great deal about the Jewish faith and about our common tradition. These rabbis came to us as friends and they spoke to us as friends. It was enriching. Many of our priests said this convocation was the best ever."

Pinellas County Historical Society at Heritage Village

On December 20th, a Jewish Archive was established for the first time in Pinellas County history. Research material from a study of the Jewish community of Pinellas County, 1883-2005, was donated by Dr. Herman Koren and Temple B'nai Israel of Clearwater. This archive is now identified in the library of Heritage Village as the Special Collections-Multi–Cultural-Jewish. Hundreds of individuals throughout Pinellas County, throughout Florida, and from Boston to San Diego and from south to north in the United States are helping collect the material, which was used by the researcher, Dr. Koren, in preparing this book. This research material will be available for other researchers in Pinellas County and elsewhere. The collection, storage, and proper preservation of these documents from a vast variety of sources here and elsewhere is of great value for any faith-based community getting involved in a project of this nature, and for preserving their original documents.

Jan Luth, Director, said, "Heritage Village, the county's history museum, has a commitment to collect, preserve, and interpret the full breath of the county's history. As a tribute to the museum's dedication to present inclusive history, the Heritage Village Archives and Library was named as the repository for the research materials amassed by Dr. Herman Koren. This special collection will be a legacy for the work that was done, safeguarding it in its entirety for historians and curators in the years to come. Most important, the special collection is preserved for future generations to understand and honor their contribution to the history of Pinellas County."

Heritage Village was opened in 1976 and funded by the Board of County Commissioners and supported in its activities by the Pinellas County Historical Society and other community groups. However, the collection of historical resource materials began in 1964 when there was a small museum housed in the basement of the County Courthouse in Clearwater. Today there are twenty eight structures on twenty one acres, some dating back to the late 19th century, and a historical museum that traces the history from Indian-Spanish times to contemporary times. The Museum also has a special library and archives section.

CHAPTER 8

CHRONOLOGICAL LISTING OF EVENTS OF CLEARWATER AND NORTH COUNTY JEWISH HISTORY 1920–2005

Introduction

The Jewish pioneers of the north county area, their lives, their organizations and their synagogues, are discussed here with the information that was available to the author. As each of the new synagogues and Jewish organizations are introduced, pertinent initial information and people involved will also be discussed. However, because the story of Temple B'nai Israel is intertwined with the story of Congregation Beth Shalom of Clearwater, the beginning information, from 1946 through 1956, is presented in this chapter, and from 1957 on is discussed in separate chapters.

The beginnings of the Jewish community in Clearwater and north county have been discussed in Chapter 6. The Blum family of Tarpon Springs started Jewish life in Pinellas County in the 1880s. The Tarapani family of Tarpon Springs in1911, and the Frank family of Clearwater in1912, started department stores and lived in their respective communities as well as nurtured them for multiple generations.

Highlights of 1916

Helen Weber

In October, Helen Weber and her mother, Rose, and father, Sigmund Freund, arrived in Clearwater. Helen remembered the first wooden bridge built to Clearwater Beach in 1917. On Saturday nights, there were dances and refreshments on the beach, but black people were excluded. The Ku Klux Klan wanted to keep the blacks from participating. They would parade at night down North Garden Avenue. They had electric lights burning on the toes of their shoes. At one time, an order was put out in the newspapers telling the blacks to keep out of the downtown district on Saturday nights when the whites did their shopping.

Sometime in the early years, Helen and her family put on what they believed was the first seder in the Clearwater area. Her sister sent up north for the books for the seder. The sister made the matzo balls. The Frank family were the guests of Helen Weber.

Helen Weber and her father, Sigmund Freund were an active part of the social scene of Clearwater in the 1920s, 1930s, and 1940s. They knew everybody in the

Clearwater area. Helen was included in the society column numerous times. Sigmund was a bridge player and nearly every evening, he played bridge with Professor Tilley, the owner of the jewelry store, Mr. Esterle, who owned a citrus grove, Mr. Batchelar, Editor of the "Sun", and/or Mr Bivers, President of the Bank of Clearwater. Tilley did a lot of business with the ladies who lived at the Bellevue who had lost at gambling and had to pawn their diamonds. Helen and her father were friends with the mayor and most of the prominent people of the area. Around 1926, Helen and Sigmund organized the Clearwater Shuffleboard Club, which had over 300 members. Sigmund became the President of the club and Helen the Treasurer. When Billy Weber went to the North Ward school, Helen was elected President of the PTA. She proposed a cafeteria be started, as some of the children were so poor they foraged in the garbage can for bread crusts. She and her committee turned an open porch into a cafeteria with linoleum on the floor, drapes, newly painted chairs, a donated stove, and icebox. Mrs. O'Hara, the wife of a dentist, was the chairwoman. The poor children were fed free of charge and those who could afford it, paid for lunch.

Highlights of 1920-1929

Highlights of 1920

Mr. Mac (or Mack) built a house in Tarpon Springs and lived there during the winters. Bill and Grace Mack came from Cincinnati for the winter. Bill was an insurance agent. Whether or not Mr.

Mac and Bill and Grace were related is not known. Bill was a member of Rotary. Jewish people owned stores on the dock in Tarpon Springs. The dates are not available. The Jenkins Department Store was owned by a Jewish family. Dates unknown. A group of Jewish people came from the Midwest to Tarpon Springs for the winter. They came as children, and then later as adults. The Merkatz family owned the Hacienda Hotel in New Port Richey in the 1920s and 1930s. They also had a hotel in the Catskills. She was involved with Hadassah.

Highlights of 1921
Bilgore Groves

David Bilgore founded Bilgore Groves. As the years went by, the Bilgore Groves packing house, warehouses, and the first gift store eventually covered the two blocks bounded by Franklin Street, Myrtle Avenue, Park Street, and East Avenue that now house part of Clearwater's municipal building and the parking lot for the St. Pete Times. David later built a cannery on McMullen Booth Road and gift fruit stores in Dunedin and Largo (both on US 19). The company owned orange and grapefruit groves in the Largo area and east and west of US 19 from Clearwater north into Pasco County.

Segregation was very prevalent in Clearwater. The public schools did not really desegregate until 1965 (well after the 1954 Brown v. Board of Education Supreme Court case outlawing segregation). On the first anniversary of Martin Luther King's assassination, there was a confrontation between black and white students at Kennedy Junior High.

Movie theaters had separate "colored" sections into the early 1960s and the so-called Black Beach was actually on Tampa Bay on the Courtney Campbell Causeway. The Bilgore Groves packing house had "White" and "Colored" water fountains and bathrooms in order to do business with certain white companies–something the family despised as a requirement to do business. The Bilgore Groves prided itself on fair treatment for all of its employees. It had very low turnover of both its white and black personnel, and a history of excellent race relations.

Bilgore Groves grew oranges and grapefruit in its orchards, washed, waxed, and packed the fruit in its Clearwater packing house, sold fresh fruit and novelties in its local retail stores, and juiced and canned the fruit in its McMullen Booth Road cannery. It also packed and shipped fruit to national companies like Libby and A&P, and gift fruit packages to customers around the country. It shipped grapefruit for the Harry & David Fruit of the Month Club in the 1960's and 1970's. Howard Lawrence expanded the retail gift stores and a direct mail business that included selling Tampa cigars. During the busy Christmas and winter seasons, many members of the Bilgore/Bragin families (kids too) would be working at the packing house, fruit stores, or cannery. The families' kids would get to ride in old wooden fruit crates on the packing house conveyor belts. After several winter freezes and encroaching development, the Company sold off all of its groves and properties in the early 1980s. The groves had become more valuable for the housing boom than for agriculture.

After working in Bilgore Groves for over twenty five years, in 1976, Howard Lawrence turned the last Bilgore grove on Curlew Road in Palm Harbor into Curlew Hills Memory Gardens Cemetery, Funeral Home and Crematory (one of the first so-called triple combinations in the area). It turned out that the same agricultural zoning for citrus also qualified for cemeteries. He designed Curlew Hills as a beautiful park with several lakes, gardens, and open space, as well as mausoleums, niches, and ground burials. Since the late 1970s, that cemetery has had a dedicated Jewish section, including a Temple B'nai Israel Section for burials. David and Etta Bilgore, Morris and Bert Bilgore, and Howard Lawrence are buried at Curlew. It is still owned by their families today.

David Bilgore

David Bilgore, the founder of Bilgore Groves, was born in Bilgoraj, Poland and immigrated to the United States as a teenager. He married Etta as a young man and lived in Brooklyn, New York. In 1920, he became a wholesale produce broker in

Manhattan. His oldest son, Morris, came into the business with him. David decided that he could do better by owning citrus groves in Florida and shipping the fruit to the East Coast. He started a citrus packing business, David Bilgore & Company, on Cleveland Street in Clearwater. The business was later moved to 702 Franklin St. He then began to buy citrus groves in the Clearwater area. Although David lived permanently in Brooklyn, he spent his winters in Tampa during the citrus season and commuted to Clearwater throughout the 1920s and 1930s, while Morris ran the brokerage business in New York.

Etta Bilgore was born in Poland in 1872, and died in New York in 1945. David was born in Poland in 1870 and died in 1948, at age 72, in Tampa. At the time, his company was building a canning plant on a Bilgore grove near McMullen Booth and Coachman Roads. David's youngest son, Aaron, then joined the business. Aaron lived mostly in New York where he was involved in marketing canned juice. Later in life, Aaron moved to Clearwater.

Morris and Bertha Bilgore

Morris and Bertha (Bert) married on March 25, 1923, and had two children. Morris was born in New York in 1889 and died in 1994. Bertha was born in New York in 1902 and died in 1967. Lila was born on December 19, 1925. Lila received a Bachelor of Science Degree from Drexel University. Lila's husband, Howard Lawrence, joined Bilgore Groves and moved with Lila to Clearwater from Brooklyn in 1951. Paul Bilgore was born April 15, 1930. Paul received a Bachelor of Arts Degree from Yale University and a law degree from Columbia Law School. He married June Michaelove and they had two boys. Paul became a lawyer in New York and did not join Bilgore Groves.

Morris continued the fruit brokerage business in New York for a period of time. As Bilgore Groves expanded in the Clearwater area, it became the principle focus of the family business. Morris and Bert moved to Clearwater Beach in 1953 to work full-time with Jules Bragin and Howard Lawrence. Morris and Jules shared one office with facing partner desks to run the business.

Morris many times bought and sold fruit, at $7,000 or $75,000, on a handshake. He also liked to drive Cadillacs, which he thought were sturdy cars. Morris and Bert were very active in Temple B'nai Israel. Morris became President of Temple B'nai Israel. Morris had a beautiful deep singing voice and loved to sing. He was a regular at Temple B'nai Israel services and could always be heard singing in the congregation. Morris lived to age 95. He was a lifetime member of the Clearwater Kiwanis Club, and served as Chairman, Clearwater Cancer Fund.

On February 3, 1994, Morris's cousin Marge, who was in her 90s at the time, learning of the death of Morris, reflected on the lives of Morris and Bert Bilgore. Marge, in a letter to Lila Lawrence, (talked about the fact that Grandfather Rosenblatt and Grandfather David Bilgore were both very charitable people. Marge said, " I remember that they, (Morris and Bert) went to Europe on their honeymoon. He (Morris) didn't say a word about Europe. He spoke instead about Palestine, long before it was Israel. He said the morning light on the hills of Jerusalem was the most beautiful sight he had seen. He spoke of the color of the city. He was thrilled by it. You know he had a beautiful voice. Molly had a sweet voice. They used to act in all the plays the synagogue put on....He was a truly good person. I never remember him saying anything nasty about anyone. You know that I worked in the office at Bilgore's and there were characters as customers that one really could say something nasty about. But Morris had a sense of humor about them and would laugh off a lot of things. He adored your mother and was so proud of her. I'm sure you and your children have a lot of wonderful memories of him, and what better legacy could anyone ask for."

Morris Bilgore

Jules and Molly Bragin

In the mid 1930s, Jules Bragin, son-in-law of David Bilgore, joined the citrus business. Jules, who had been a dentist in New York, was married to David's daughter, Molly. After joining Bilgore's, Jules and Molly took a freighter (that had carried bananas) from New York to Florida and moved permanently to Tampa (there were more Jews in Tampa than Clearwater at that time). Jules commuted to the Clearwater packing house. During David's winter trips to Florida, he would stay with the Bragins in Tampa and also commute to Clearwater over the then private toll road called the Davis Causeway (now known as State Road 60 or the Courtney Campbell Causeway).

The Bragins have two children, Arla and Stephen, who were born in Brooklyn and moved to Tampa as children. Arla married and moved back to New York. Steve stayed in the Tampa area. Jules became very active in the Tampa (and later the Clearwater) community, and became deeply involved in all forms of charity. He was in charge of collecting money for many non-Jewish people who did not have funds for funerals. The Bragins were members of the Reform Temple, Schaarai Zedek, in Tampa. Jules worked hard to get the management of the Clearwater Country Club and Clearwater Yacht Club to remove their sign that said "No Jews No Dogs". However, it was not until many years later that the signs were eventually removed. Jules and Molly Bragin eventually moved to north Clearwater in 1956 and joined Temple B'nai Israel. They are buried in the Schaarai Zedek Section of Myrtle Hill Cemetery in Tampa.

Steve and Regena (Gena) Bragin

Jules' son, Steve Bragin, was born in New York in 1930, but grew up as a teenager and young adult in Tampa after Jules and Molly Bragin moved there in the 1930's. Steve attended the University of Pennsylvania, Wharton School of Business, before he served in the Korean War. Steve joined Bilgore Groves in the mid 1950's after his service in the Korean War. It was also in the mid 1950s that Howard Lawrence asked Steve and his parents to join the then Clearwater Jewish Community Center in order for them to vote for a Reform Temple. In June 1955, Steve married Gena Waterman, daughter of Jerome (Jerry) Waterman, a nephew of Ike and Abe Maas. Her mother was Daisy Guggenheimer of Virginia. Jerome's mother was Henrietta Maas.

Gena was born on October 15, 1930 in Tampa, Florida. She earned a Bachelor of Science and Marketing Degree from

Steve and Gena Bragin

the Women's College, University of North Carolina. They have two children, Marc Bragin, and Jan, who is married to Anthony Ross. Jan, who is forty four years old, has a Bachelor of Arts Degree from Emory University and a Master's of Business Administration from Rollins College in Orlando. Anthony also has a Master of Business Administration from Rollins College. They have two children. Marc has a Bachelor of Arts Degree from Franklin Pierce University and a Law Degree from Cumberland University. He also has a Master of Science Degree in Jewish Studies from Boston University and is currently a Jewish chaplain at Colgate University.

Steve has been a major officer of David Bilgore & Co. Inc., Trust Officer for Bilgore Trust Company, Officer and Board Member, Curlew Hills Memory Gardens, and Member of the Board of Directors of Nicholas Finance Corporation. He was the Chairman of the Maas Realty Executive Committee. He has served for many years in positions which are essential to the operation of community organizations. From 1992 to 2002, he was Regional Development Director for the University of South Florida. From 2002 to present, he has been the Development Director of the Gulf Coast Museum of Art. He has served in many organizations in the community including: Officer and Founding Member of Springtime Kiwanis Club; Founding Member and Past President, Bay Area Chapter National Conference of Christians and Jews; National Board, National Conference of Christians and Jews; Board Member, Temple B'nai Israel, Clearwater; Past President, Temple B'nai Israel; Past President, Temple B'nai Israel Men's Club; Co-Chairman and first lay appointee, Union of American Hebrew Congregations Commission on Jewish Education; Past Board Member Advisory Board, Anclote Manor Hospital; Past Board Member United Way of Pinellas County; jointly developed concept for 2,500 Seat Performing Arts Center; Founding Director Performing Arts Center of Pinellas County; Past Board Member, Playmakers Theater Group, Tampa, Florida; President, Playmakers Theater Group, Tampa, Florida; Past Officer, Southeast Region Reform

Temples; Member Marketing Committee Morton Plant Hospital; Founding Member Human Relations Council; Founding Member College Fund; Past Member, Committee of 100; Board Member and Treasurer, Florida Gulf Coast Arts Center; and National Board, Union of American Hebrew Congregations.

Howard and Lila Lawrence

Howard Lawrence was born on June 19, 1923 in Brooklyn. He graduated from New York University with a Bachelor of Science Degree in Commerce and Finance. During World War II, he served as an air-sea rescue pilot in the Pacific. He married Lila Bilgore in 1948. Howard was a Levy, and he and Lila changed from Levy to Lawrence before moving to Clearwater. Howard was an accountant in New York before joining David Bilgore & Co. Inc. and serving as its Vice President for thirty five years. He also had a flair for woodworking, magic, and clowning. In 1976, he became the Founder, President, and Chief Executive Officer for a twenty year period of Curlew Hills Memory Gardens.

In 1956-1957, Howard was President of Temple B'nai Israel. In the 1960s, He formed a group of businessmen (called the Madcaps) to dress as clowns and perform for children in local hospitals and the annual Fun 'N Sun festivals. For many of the local businessmen, he was one of the first Jews that they knew. His and the Bilgore's involvement and friendships with the largely Christian business and civic community helped form bridges between the two groups throughout the 1950s and 1960s. Howard was very active with and a leader of the Clearwater Sertoma Club, the Fun N' Sun Festival, Big Brothers, and the Pinellas County Housing Authority. He served on many City of Clearwater and professional boards and commissions. In the late 1960s and mid 70s, he was a driving force in the Pinellas County Democratic Party and its Chairman, 1974-79. Debbie remembers driving Howard and Jimmy Carter to the Tampa airport during Carter's 1976 Presidential campaign. Howard was a founding member of the Board of Governors of Menorah Manor in St. Petersburg and

received awards for service to the City of Clearwater, including Recipient of Medal for Outstanding Service to Community-City of Clearwater. Howard was: Vice President, Clearwater Jaycees; President, Pinellas County Big Brothers; Member, Ruth Eckerd Board of Directors; President, Florida Gift Fruit Shippers Association; Board Member, Florida Cemetery Association; Member, Pinellas County Fair Practices Political Committee; Member Pinellas County Housing Authority; Member, Board of Directors of First Federal Bank, Largo; Member, Board of Directors of Northeast Bank, Clearwater; Instructor for Dale Carnegie Courses; and Founding Member of Operation PAR, a drug treatment and rehabilitation program. Howard had a remarkable career of service to the Jewish community as well as the general community

Howard, Lila, Debbie and David Lawrence, November 1966.

Howard loved to build and create–a perfectionist. Once he had a vision as to how something should be (whether it was in a new Bilgore store, a marketing campaign, the design of Curlew Hills, Temple and community projects, or one of his hobbies), he used all his efforts to try to make that vision come true. He would sweat the details, seek out experts in the field, learn from them, and work with others to make things happen. He made the props used by the Madcaps and made beautiful inlaid wood keepsake boxes, ships in bottles, and stained glass. He would do magic shows in the hospitals and at children's birthday parties. He grew beautiful roses in his yard and for his home. He was a man of many talents and used these talents to make life better and more beautiful for everyone.

Howard and Lila had two children, David and Debbie, who grew up in the 1950's, 1960's, and early 1970's in Clearwater public schools. Since there were very few other Jewish kids in the schools, the Temple B'nai Israel parents made sure that the Jewish kids were involved in activities together. Temple members became extended families to each other. Many were called "aunt" or "uncle" even though there may not have been any blood relationship (e.g., Uncle

Darwin Frank, Aunt Shirley Collman). The Temple acted as the magnet for religious, social, and cultural events. The Bilgore/Bragin/Lawrence women were in charge of the homes and networked with the other women of the community. Bert Bilgore and Lila Lawrence organized dinners, outings, mahjongg and card games, play dates for kids, and school and other group activities that kept Jewish families and kids together, even though the few area Jews lived spread out all over Clearwater.

Relations with Christian neighbors and friends were generally good in the 1960s and 1970s, although David and Debbie didn't advertise their Jewishness to other kids. There were sporadic efforts to convert the Jewish kids. Sometimes Jewish vagrants would travel through Clearwater and be picked up by the Clearwater police. However, the police usually called either Howard or Darwin Frank to come bail out the Jews and buy them a bus ticket to Miami.

For the Lawrence kids, it was a regular weekly family event in the 1950s and 1960s to have Friday evening Shabbat family dinner at Morris & Bert Bilgore's home. There were the usual carryover discussions about the family business. But there were also discussions about issues of the day, the American civil rights movement, politics, importance of family, and the Jewish community. After dinner, everyone (kids as well) usually went to Temple for services. This also meant the kids would miss the Friday high school football games (Rabbi Taxay tried to get the Pinellas School Board to change the days, but to no avail). Sunday morning was Sunday school, where the Jewish kids would gather at the Temple.

David is married and lives with his family in Fairfax, Virginia, where he is a lawyer. Debbie is also married and lives with her family in Marietta, Georgia.

During his 1972 college summer break, David Lawrence worked as a laborer for Vasconi Masonry digging footers and hauling the blocks in the building of B'nai Israel's new Belcher Road Temple.

Morris and Bert Bilgore, Howard and Lila Lawrence, and Steve and Gena Bragin were all very active in the Temple B'nai Israel community. While the Bilgores and Lawrences came from kosher and traditional observant Jewish families in New York and strongly believed in Jewish ideals, they embraced the modernity of Reform Judaism. Lila was President of the Sisterhood. In 1970, David Lawrence (Howard & Lila's son) was on the B'nai Israel Board as youth group President, along with Morris and Howard as past Temple Presidents. Howard was a regular usher at Temple services when the Temple was on Betty Lane. He performed magic for the young kids waiting to go into the Shofar Service at High Holidays, and then would bring them all into the service when the Rabbi was ready for the blowing of the shofars.

The Bilgores and Lawrences also were involved in community activities. Morris and his brother-in-law, Jules Bragin, were members of Kiwanis, where they established the Bilgore Award to be presented each year to a civic minded member of the Clearwater community. Howard & Lila were active in the 1950s in the Jaycees, and later in many Clearwater civic projects and associations. Both Morris Bilgore and Howard Lawrence were on the Temple B'nai Israel committee that interviewed and recommended the hiring of Rabbi Baseman.

Highlights of 1926
Helen Weber met a Jewish man who owned the house on the southeast side of Drew Street. He was a Bohemian Jew (name unknown) who was a winemaker. He had borrowed money to build a warehouse where he was making wine out of oranges. Evidently, the project was not successful, and he lost his property. He ended up in the county home on Largo Road.

Highlights of 1927
Shirley Augustine Collman
Shirley Augustine, who was born on May 1, 1921 started to come to Clearwater Beach with her parents. They came from Tampa by way of Oldsmar and Dunedin. They often stayed at the Kipling Arms Apartments, a boom time project, or one of the small cottages on the street behind them. There was a small store just past the apartments on Mandalay called Mac's, which was a child's delight. It sold candy, and other items

that children loved. The Clearwater Beach Fire Department was right across the street from these apartments. The Palm Pavilion on Clearwater Beach had a food counter with a few stools and later a few tables and chairs were added. The Palm Pavilion floor had slotted wood planks. The structure had dressing rooms, small round dance floor, Ski Ball area, etc. When Shirley was a child, she used to crawl on the sand, underneath the slotted floor of the restaurant to look for change or tokens that had been dropped. Shirley went to Clearwater Joyland with her parents, when they went there to dance. The property of the facility, which was at the foot of the bridge as you came onto the beach, contained trailers, a huge orange dome where people danced near beautiful white sand dunes. Since she was not allowed into the dance hall, she and the other children would climb to the top of the dunes to watch their parents dance, and then had the joy of sliding down the dunes. Clearwater Beach was a quiet, romantic, and delightful place for adults and children. Shirley's parents drove over from Tampa and her mother, Clare Augustine, and Shirley would spend all week. Her father, Lewis Augustine, a dentist, would come on weekends.

Highlights of 1930-1939

There were several Jewish families in Clearwater, but Shirley Augustine never met them. Shirley's family were members of Rodeph Sholom in Tampa and they were Conservative until 1934. They switched to Schaarai Zedek ,where she was confirmed and married. Clearwater was like a small country beach town. Some other Jewish families started to trickle into the Clearwater community during the mid 1930s but with the exception of Fanny Marks, and the Franks, did not remain long. The Nagra (the spelling is uncertain) family came in the late thirties or early forties but did not stay. Shirley knew of Darwin Frank, but he was in college in 1935. There was not much going on for young Jewish children or children in general.

Darwin and Maxine Frank

Maxine was born in West Virginia

on January 10, 1921. Darwin was born in Clearwater at Morton Plant Hospital on May 1, 1918 or 1917. They met in Cincinnati where Darwin was attending college. They were a very important and vibrant part of Clearwater's Jewish history. Darwin was on a work program at college. Maxine had an aunt by marriage, Sylvia Berg, who lived in Clearwater. She was divorced from Maxine's uncle, but Maxine was still very close to her. Maxine and Darwin had a daughter Marilyn, born on February 12, 1952.

Darwin's brother was born in Clearwater on Rogers Street. Darwin, while reminiscing about his childhood, said that his first knowledge of Jewish people was about 1922 or 1923. His mother had a brother in Winter Haven and one in Sarasota. The brother in Winter Haven went to New York to get a bride. As a small child, Darwin and his family traveled by dirt road by car from Clearwater to Tampa to Sarasota. It took about three to three and one half hours each way and then they would get to visit for about one and one and one half hours. They always traveled during the daylight because of the dirt roads. When he was ten or twelve, Darwin and his family would meet all their cousins and other relatives in Tampa at the Hillsborough Hotel. The women would pack food and everyone would socialize, but the kids would run wild. In the late 1920s in Clearwater people did not think about organized Judaism. The only way a boy knew he was Jewish was that he was circumcised. Louis Frank went to a Cheder when he was twelve or thirteen. When Darwin and his brother grew up, there was a lot of anti-Semitism and they were involved in lots of fights. Darwin and his brother learned their Jewishness from their mother who read them Jewish Bible stories. Darwin said that he had no sense of true Jewish identity. He said that he was Jewish because his friends and parents said that he was.

A few Jewish families came during the housing boom years in the 1920s. One of these families was related to Julius Lovitz. These people that came in the 1920s, typically did not stay. More Jewish people came in the 1930s. The Jewish people did not often go into St. Petersburg which was quite a distance, however they did make the sixty

Darwin Frank, President, Temple B'nai Israel, 1949–1951, 1957–1958.

mile round-trip to Tampa from Clearwater by way of Oldsmar. Julius's father was a Mason in the late 1920s or early 1930s. The Solomon family owned a grocery store in the Greenwood area where the black people lived. The Ku Klux Klan paraded once a month through downtown Clearwater in the 1920s and 1930s. However, they never organized any kind of trouble against the department store. During this time, Jewish people were accepted during the day in their businesses but not acceptable at night in social activities. Darwin's parents therefore did not socialize very much. They lived as if they were living in a ghetto. During the late 1940s or early 1950s, Darwin and Maxine wanted to buy a house in Belleair and other areas, but couldn't do it because they were Jewish.

Ike Eisenstein

In the 1930's, Mr. and Mrs. Ike Eisenstein were very active in the local community as well as participated in the very small Jewish community. They continued this participation through the 1940s.

Highlights of 1936

Rabbi Zielonka confirmed Shirley Augustine (later Collman) at Schaarai Zedek in Tampa. Rabbi Zielonka was ultra Reform. He believed in confirmation for both boys and girls, but did not believe in Bar Mitzvahs.

There were about 10,000 people in Clearwater when Fanny Marks opened Lloyd's Dress Shop. Shirley Augustine never met a Jewish person in Clearwater until then. Billy Weber, son of Helen Weber, who owned a real estate office, which was on the North Side of Cleveland Street, was the first and only Jewish teenager that she met. Billy would come into Fanny Marks' store when Shirley and Roberta came over to Clearwater on Saturdays to work.

There were apparently some short-lived Jewish businesses in Clearwater. The owners commuted from Tampa. This was a difficult trip and if the stores were not profitable, the store owners set up businesses elsewhere. Georgia Resnick opened a drug store and lived in Clearwater with his wife, before

1937. Shirley met Mr. and Mrs. Louis Frank in 1937.

Clearwater was a small, quiet, and beautiful town. Although there was no overt prejudice toward Fanny Marks, and her business, there was a sign at the Clearwater Golf Course which read "For Gentiles Only". Several of the prominent hotels and motels would not accept Jewish visitors. The yacht and beach clubs prohibited Jewish use. The Ku Klux Klan was very prominent at the time in Pinellas County. One night they chased a number of blacks out of a baseball park and then had a curfew instituted for the blacks. When Fanny wanted to build a house on Laura Street, after construction had already started she received a letter from a public official that she could not build there because she was Jewish. During this time, the Jewish community participated in civic and social activities, including Red Cross work, and working as gray and pink ladies at the hospital.

Fanny and Simon Marks

Fanny Marks owned Lloyds Dress Shop andalso sold shoes, but lived in Tampa. Simon Marks was a traveling shoe salesman. He was born in Romania on October 14, 1896. He left Romania and his family, at age 14 or 16, and stayed with his aunt and uncle in Saskatchewan, Canada. The aunt and uncle had emigrated earlier to take up an offer of land for Jewish people who emigrate to Canada. The original grant of land was made by Baron de Hirsch, who wanted to set up a model Jewish agricultural center. Sam Bronfman of the liquor fortune bought additional large quantities of land which he offered free to the Jewish people. Simon enlisted in the United States Army in World War I and because of this, he became a United States citizen. The original family name for Simon was Markodice, which was changed to Markowitz, and then changed to Marks.

Fanny was born in Utica, New York on October 13, 1902. Fanny and Simon were married in September 1920. Fanny, was the first President of the Sisterhood. When Simon retired, he loved to fish. He would clean them and gut them and bring them to people as gifts. He loved to make a variety of different foods. Simon died in 1971.

Fanny lived in Clearwater until her death in 1990.

Roberta married Stuart Golding on June 13, 1943. Roberta lived in Clearwater from 1938 to 1943. Stuart was a naval officer. In later years, he built shopping centers and then went into business with Charlie Rutenberg.

Highlights of 1937

There was a private club on Clearwater Beach that would not allow Jewish people. The Clearwater Yacht Club was restricted. There was a sign for Jews to keep out. Despite these shortsighted limitations, there were many non-Jewish people in Clearwater who were very friendly with the Jewish community. Estelle Korones, President of the Sisterhood, went to Tampa to get the theater group from Rodeph Sholom to put on South Persia (Jewish South Pacific) at the Safety Harbor Spa. It netted two thousand dollars.

Sam and Estelle Korones

Sam Korones, his wife, Estelle, and their son, David, came in September, 1939, to visit his brother Sol and wife, Marie, who lived on Indian Rocks Beach. Sol and Marie moved to Indian Rocks Beach in 1934. David, born on April 21, 1937, was a little less than two years old when his parents made the visit. Estelle did not want to bring David up in New York. Sam and Estelle had contacted Louis and Hannah Frank at their department store previously. Louis said there were other Jewish families living in Clearwater in 1939. Sheldon Korones came in 1939. Before that, he was living in St. Petersburg. At the end of World War II, when he came home from the army, Sheldon became a prominent pediatrician and moved to Memphis Tennessee.

Samuel Korones was invited to join and later sponsored the Kiwanis Club in Seminole. The club was to have a meeting at a hotel in Clearwater. There was a sign there, "No Jews, No Dogs Allowed." When the President, Jessie Johnson, found out about this, he canceled the hotel and moved the meeting to the Ft. Harrison Hotel. A group of members called between two hundred and three hundred people in a period of two hours to notify them of the new meeting site.

Sam Korones was the first Jewish person to be inducted into the Clearwater Kiwanis Club which lead to the resignation of seven or eight of the members.

Sam Korones came to Clearwater from Sarasota. His family moved to Sarasota in 1925. He grew up in the school system which he said was not bad at all in comparison to Clearwater where it was very bad. In the early days, there were several instances of discrimination, but most of the Christian neighbors were very nice.

N. David Korones

When David Korones was growing up in the 1940s, the family attended worship services, either in St. Petersburg or Tampa at Rodeph Sholom on Palm Avenue. His Bar Mitzvah was on April 25, 1950 and was performed by Rabbi Henry D. Wernek at Rodeph Sholom. He studied for one year under Sam Good in Clearwater in order to learn how to read Hebrew.

David was virtually the only Jewish student in school from K to 12th grade in Clearwater. There was a period of time when Donald Blum was in school with him, but he and his family denied being Jewish. There was another Jewish boy in high school for a short period of time. He made the high school golf team, but the Clearwater County Club didn't allow Jews as members. The first time he went into the clubhouse for a tournament, there was a sign that said "No Jews or Dogs Allowed." Shortly thereafter, they terminated this policy. He was President of the Student Senate, President of the Spanish Club, Chairman of the Homecoming Event, Business Manager for the Senior Class, and played on various athletic teams. At the same time, David was a member of the Temple youth group.

As an adult, David continued his very active participation in the Clearwater community, and continued to serve it in a variety of capacities. The family stayed in Tampa on the High Holy Days. They stayed at the Floridian Hotel and walked to the synagogue out of deference to his mother's mother who observed Conservative Judaism. The distance was one and a half miles each way. In 1948, David fell and broke his back. Several churches in town, notably

Roberta Marks, 1943. Photographh from [unknown] Morning Tribune, Friday, June 18, 1943.

N. David Korones

Samuel Korones, President, Temple B'nai Israel, 1953–1954.

the Calvary Baptist Church in Clearwater, offered prayers for his recovery. Sam, Estelle, and later, David, became very devoted to the establishment of the Jewish community of Clearwater and North County.

Highlights of 1938

Shirley Augustine came over to Clearwater every Saturday to work with Roberta Marks at Fanny Marks' ready-to-wear shop. Shirley also spent the entire summer with Roberta. During that time, prior to World War II, there was a lot of overt anti-Semitism.

Highlights of 1939

Hilda and George Resnick operated the Greenwood Pharmacy. Saul and Lena Solomon owned a ladies dress shop. Maxwell and Ida Ravel owned the Pepsi Cola Bottling Agency. Helen Weber owned a real estate agency. Missouri Avenue and the new U.S. 19 did not exist at that time. The population of Clearwater in 1939 was about 8,000 people. The Jewish businesses did well, but socially it was another matter for the Jewish people. Sam and Estelle joined Rodeph Sholom Congregation in Tampa. They made friends at the synagogue. Gradually, Jewish people started coming to Clearwater

Leonard Collman moved to Tampa from Sarasota. Leonard worked for National Linen Supply, a nationwide linen supply company, which was founded by his uncle, Isadore Weinstein, in Atlanta. Leonard , who was a salesman, came to St. Petersburg and Clearwater frequently on business. There were quite a few instances of discrimination. People didn't want to deal with National Linen Supply because it was a Jewish firm. Other firms had put out the word.

Arthur and Bessie Collman of Sarasota
Arthur, father of Clarence and Leonard Collman, snuck out of Riga, Russia in 1884. at age twelve. He made up his September 1 birthday date, because he didn't know exactly when it occurred. (At that time, the dates of birth and death were kept on the Yiddish calendar, which did not correspond

each year to the English calendar). He came over illegally, worked as a farmer, and later owned a wholesale liquor business. With the money he earned, he sent for other members of his family. He later owned two different banks. When he was thirty five years old, he decided he needed a wife. He went to Atlanta where he learned that there was a Jewish family that had several daughters. He courted Bessie Goldstein, twenty five years old, and they were married. Arthur changed his name from Kallman to Collman, because he thought that it sounded more American. He always worried that the government would find out that he was in America illegally. He always said that he was born in Atlanta. Leonard's parents, after they married, lived in Alabama, Louisiana, and Arkansas and came to Florida in 1925. Leonard's father owned banks in Louisiana and Arkansas that went broke, however he paid everyone back and no one lost any money.

Bessie was born in Lithuania. The family name had been Brenner, but was changed to Goldstein because it sounded more American.

Arthur started a real estate business in Sarasota and then Collman's Department Store. They had a daughter, Dorothy Collman Colin, who married Barney Colin, a Canadian, and lived in Orlando, and a son Leonard. When Arthur was in Morton Plant Hospital shortly before he died, Shirley told him that Kennedy had been elected President and that there would be a new régime. Apparently, the word régime agitated him terribly and brought flashbacks from the time that he had experienced pogroms. He died the next morning. Gussie Koren, the author's mother, often told the author's wife, Donna, about the horrible memories that she had of pogroms, which she experienced as a child in the Ukraine. Gussie said that she lived in constant terror until she came to the United States in 1914. Arthur and Bessie died within a few weeks of each other in 1960.

Highlights of 1940-1949

Highlights of 1940

In the 1940s and 1950s, Clearwater and St. Petersburg, as well as the surrounding towns, were more seasonal in nature than they are today. When the tourists and snow birds left, life resumed a very simple pattern. Business was at a very low ebb. An example of this phenomenon, in later years, was Flo Failla's department store across from the Safety Harbor Spa. She opened the store in 1959 or 1960 and provided necessary items for the people at the Safety Harbor Spa for the next eight to ten years. She would open in October and have her final sale in May of each year. Today, although Pinellas County has a large tourist and Snowbird population, it also provides many jobs for permanent residents and a vast variety of industries and businesses.

Shirley and Leonard Collman

Shirley Augustine married Leonard Collman, on July 14, 1940. They had originally met on Lido Beach in Sarasota, Florida when she was thirteen years old. Shirley lived in Tampa, but came to Sarasota to visit relatives. Later, Leonard lived in Tampa with his friends, the Segals. This gave him an opportunity to once again see Shirley.

Leonard was born on July 25, 1917, in Louisiana. His brother, Clarence, was born on January 31, 1908 in Louisiana. In 1925, his parents, Arthur and Bessie moved the family to Sarasota. Leonard served in the military in World War II and was discharged in November of 1945. He had spent forty five months at MacDill Air Force Base. His brother, Clarence, moved to Clearwater from Sarasota after World War II, and was one of the originators of Temple B'nai Israel. Leonard and Clarence's father owned a department store in Sarasota that catered to black customers. Leonard and Clarence traveled through the state of Florida looking for a business to buy or a vacant store to rent. They found a newly built store in Clearwater owned by Horner Reality. Leonard and Clarence opened the shoe store near the Korones' jewelry shop in January 1946. The store was fifteen by fifty or sixty feet, and

cost between $100 and $150 a month. Whereas the original store sold shoes for men, women, and children, later in 1949, they opened another store for women only on Cleveland Street.

Leonard and Clarence sold Collman Shoe Store to Eddie Joseph in 1955. Eddie commuted from St. Petersburg every day. They kept Lee's Shoe Store which was opened in 1949, and named for Lee Shirley Collman. Leonard, Louis Brower, and Julius Lovitz developed a five-star mobile home park in 1964. In 1965, it opened in Largo under the name of Colonial Village. The park was sold to the residents in 1975.

Gerald, Shirley, Leonard, Nancy and Steve Collman, May 1961, at Gerald's confirmation.

In the 1950s, Shirley wrote a newsletter that went out every week. She also accumulated much of the information that was found in the 40th anniversary booklet of Temple B'nai Israel in the history section.

Leonard and Shirley have three children, Nancy born in 1943, Jerald born May 10, 1946, and Steve born in 1948. They were the only very young Jewish children in Clearwater at that time. David Korones was older. Max Ravel and his wife, who owned the Pepsi Cola plant, had two teenage boys. The family which had been in Clearwater when Shirley and Leonard arrived, later sold the plant and moved away. Tampa was the only place you could get kosher style food.

The Collman and Korones stores were closed on the High Holy Days. When the Collmans would reopen their store after sundown, people would be waiting in line to buy their children shoes. Leonard was asked to give the benediction at the school PTA once a year. Leonard was asked to join many of the established clubs, Jr. Chamber of Commerce, and service clubs. He did this for a period of time, but could not participate because of business commitments. Children were marked absent on the High Holy Days. Shirley was active in the PTA, Red Cross, March of Dimes, Grey Lady, Pink Lady, etc. In 1949, a builder refused to build Shirley and Leonard a house because they were Jewish. In places, there were restricted areas.

Unfortunately, a few people in the Clearwater and Clearwater Beach areas enforced discrimination against the Jewish people. Tampa, and other areas, had Spanish

Helen Weber

people and Greek people, while Clearwater Beach did not. At one point, there was a proposal to barricade the roads from Tarpon Springs and also from Tampa to Clearwater Beach to keep Clearwater Beach pure.

Leonard Collman's cousins were the Coopermans in St. Petersburg. The Coopermans came to St. Petersburg in the 1920s. Lena Cooperman was a sister of Bessie Goldstein Collman. Lena and Bessie's parents came to Atlanta from Lithuania. The Cooperman's had three children: Leonard, an attorney, deceased, Alfred, deceased, and Nelly.

Highlights of 1942

On a religious note, during WWII, in 1942, Jewish soldiers were quartered at the Belleview Biltmore Hotel. Estelle Korones called the officer in charge and asked to pick up the Jewish soldiers before Yom Kippur and take them to St. Petersburg for services. This occurred two weeks before the High Holy Days. He refused. Estelle called the officer back and said, "If he didn't allow the Jewish soldiers to go to Yom Kippur Services, she would write or call Washington and inform them of his decision." He said, "Let me think about it." The next day, he called back and said that they could go. There were six Jewish soldiers there. The Korones hired a limosine and took the soldiers to dinner, services, and then a hotel to stay overnight before the daytime service. Jewish soldiers had complete run of the Korones house. The thing they wanted most of all was salami and egg omelets. Sandwiches were made and picnics held by the Jewish women during the war for the soldiers. Fanny Marks also entertained Jewish soldiers and provided a home away from home for them. Jewish soldiers were entertained from MacDill and possibly Drew Field in Tampa. Jewish people in Sarasota including Leonard Collman's parents also entertained Jewish soldiers from a training field in Sarasota. Many people in Tampa did the same thing. There was even a community seder at Schaarai Zedek in Tampa.

During the war, the Jewish people of Clearwater already felt the need for a formal Jewish community. The initial discussions concerning the formation of a Jewish organization may well have occurred during this time period. Fanny Marks had a dynamic personality and was one of the early leaders pushing for a formal Jewish community.

Helen Weber

Jewish soldiers, as well as other soldiers were also entertained by Helen Weber. As a real estate agent, she helped many of the service families find living quarters in Clearwater. She received a commendation from the War Housing Authority for her wonderful effort in helping the soldiers. As a notary public, she also married many couples and held receptions for them. About this time a soldier she had assisted noticed a sign posted in the clubhouse of a local country club, Jews were prohibited from the premises. She brought the sign to the attention of the City Council. She berated the Council for allowing this discrimination to go on. Her friend, E. H. Coachman, told her that a Jewish lady had donated $10,000 to build the clubhouse. Judge Ware came over to her and told her that he was indignant about the sign. Her efforts resulted in the desegregation of the Clearwater Golf Club. Helen said there was a lot of prejudice against Jews at that time. She advised one Jewish man not to buy a hotel because of it.

In keeping with the many contributions that Helen Weber made to Clearwater, when Missouri Avenue was being constructed to handle the additional traffic going into Clearwater she contributed a parcel of land to the city. The donated land was a parcel fifty feet by two hundred and thirty feet., which is now the southwest corner of Missouri Avenue and Court Street. In an interview in the Clearwater Sun, Tuesday, December 18, 1979, at age eighty four, she stated the philosophy that she had lived by her entire life: "Many of my friends have passed away. I too, must go. When I do, I'll know that I have helped to develop Clearwater as it is today–a bustling city!" Truly, Helen Weber is a fine example of the contributions that Jewish people make to their communities.

Highlights of 1943

In 1943, Shirley Collman came to Clearwater and met Maxine Frank for the first time. At that time, Frank's Department Store sold a large variety of clothing, shoes, piece goods, and all other things you could find in the typical department store. The store was located across the street from the old post office on Cleveland St., now an official landmark. Shirley had come over to Clearwater to visit for several days with her friend Roberta Marks, who was engaged to Stuart Golding. Jewish family life here was very sparse. There were a few Jewish families in the area, but there was no defined Jewish community. Ethel Schoenfeld, who was Maxine Frank's mother, moved to Clearwater to be near her daughter. Roberta and Stuart Golding's wedding was held at the Clearwater Beach Hotel. It was the first Jewish wedding to be held there. It was previously restricted, but not in 1943. Shirley met Darwin Frank here. Darwin and his brother had graduated from Clearwater High School

Highlights of 1944

Hazel E. Simon, born on March 7, 1904, and Louis Simon, settled in Clearwater on December 8.

Highlights of 1945
Lisa and Dr. Salem Baranoff

Dr. Salem and Lisa Baranoff arrived in 1945 and purchased the Safety Harbor Spa in 1946. He was a naturopath. He lived until age 90. In his later years, he was described as looking like a prophet. He had a slight build, long white hair, about 5'7" tall. He was very knowledgeable in Hebrew and the Torah and led the services at Temple B'nai Israel and then Congregation Beth Shalom of Clearwater, when the congregations were without a rabbi or the rabbi was absent. He was considered to be a very compassionate person.

Salem came to New York with his family in 1904 from Kiev, Russia. His first job was to teach Hebrew school in New York. He attended school to learn English in preparation for college. During this time, he became interested in healing by nature and read and studied the process extensively. Although other members of his family had become rabbis, he wanted to become a physician. He graduated from the American

School of Naturopathy in 1921 and opened his first office in Brownsville. He said, "I use no prescription, no drugs. I concentrate on diet and physical manipulation and correction and I did well." At that time, he was a pioneer, promoting healthful living through physical fitness, proper food, and learning to minimize the aging process so that people could age gracefully. One of his patients offered him an opportunity in Spring Valley to develop a health resort. Even though his facility was not useful for this purpose, Salem was able to rent a small closed hotel, and therefore, started his first health resort, which he operated for nineteen years. He continued to maintain offices in New York City and had a weekly Yiddish radio program to discuss nature, foods, and health. Because his facility in Spring Valley was only available for a limited period of time each year, he decided to come to Florida, especially the West Coast for the winter. Salem knew about the sanitarium in Safety Harbor that had been operated as a place for alcoholics. He came, saw what he liked, and purchased the eighteen acres of land along the bay, including several buildings and the five mineral springs. He purchased the whole complex for $190,000.

Salem wanted to pattern the Safety Harbor Spa after the town of Spa in Belgium. People came there to bathe in the mineral springs and to drink the water. Later, similar mineral waters were found in Austria and Germany, and they also were called spas.

Hernando De Soto discovered the Safety Harbor Springs in 1539 and named them after the Feast of the Holy Spirit, Espiritu Springs. Each spring, which was chemically different from the others, was twenty five feet from another spring. There were stories that the Indians used to come to the springs to cure their ailments Since the mid-1880s, people published testimonials about the cures they achieved at the springs. Later in the century, the area was known as Bailey Springs and Bailey by-the-Sea. The property at that time was owned by Colonel William J. Bailey. In the early 1900s, it became known as Green Springs for its owner, Dr. J. T. Green. In the 1920s, there were thoughts that this area would be another Saratoga Springs,

New York, or Hot Springs, Arkansas. The development did not do well and the Great Depression totally stifled it. Leading up to World War II, the property changed hands several times. Finally, Salem Baranoff purchased the property.

When Salem arrived, Safety Harbor was a hamlet with a budget of $12,000. He immediately became involved in a variety of civic organizations. He provided the spa free of charge for all types of activities. He purchased land for a public library. He also purchased the old police court building as a home for the Safety Harbor American Legion Post, made the down payment, and then paid off the mortgage.

In the first season that the spa was open, 150 people came down from New York. The spa was advertised in the New York Times. Salem's wife, Lisa, and her sister, Dena, worked very hard to make the spa a success. Lisa was the dietitian and Dena was the physical therapist. Salem devised special menus and set up programs of physical therapy and diets. In 1973, there were approximately 200 staff members and 400 guests at the facility.

The spa became world-famous. Salem had a large following from the Catskill Mountain hotels. Many New Yorkers and snow birds came down for the waters and health programs for short or longer periods of time. Sidney Kaplan was head of the NAACP nationally. He and his wife frequently stayed at the Safety Harbor Spa. Dr. Baranoff was like a guru there. He had a very wonderful reputation. The Safety Harbor Spa was open initially during the winter only. Everyone went back north after the season, including the Baranoffs. Many famous Jewish people came from all over the world. The Baranoffs opened the facility to the local Jewish population. They were very generous in allowing the local Jewish community to have a variety of events there. Many weddings were held there including, Marilyn Frank's, Debby Lawrence's, and Mindy Siegel's. The Baranoffs were always in attendance at all Jewish affairs and programs and interested in what was happening.

Dr. Baranoff's philosophy of health and life was ahead of his time in many ways. He preached a program of good health that involved a proper diet, proper thoughts, proper exercise, and adequate rest. He had ten commandments that he wanted everyone to follow in order to have a happier, healthier, and longer life. "These commandments were:

1. Thou shall respect thy body as the highest manifestation of life.
2. Thou shall abstain from all unnatural devitalized food and stimulating beverages.
3. Thou shall nourish thy body with only natural unprocessed live food that thou shall extend thy years in health for loving, charitable service.
4. Thou shall regenerate thy body by the right balance of activity and rest.
5. Thou shall purify thy cells, tissue, and blood with pure fresh air and sunshine.
6. Thou shall abstain from all foods when out of sorts in mind and body. (Take a drink of scotch or a cup of coffee and forget about the food.)
7. Thou shalt keep thy thoughts, words, and emotions, pure, calm, and uplifting. (Instead of thinking negatively, think positively.)
8. Thou shall increase thy knowledge of nature's laws, abide therewith and enjoy the fruits of thy life's labor.
9. Thou shall lift up thyself and thy brother with thine own obedience to all nature's laws.
10. Thou shall stretch thy 600 muscles daily, maintain a positive attitude at all times, and count thy blessings regularly."

Dr. Baranoff said, "I've seen people who follow this program at Safety Harbor Spa and they have benefited by it. I've seen people who came in wheelchairs and, in a couple months, they were on their own and lived another thirty-forty years, living the proper life...Learn how to live. Live and learn how to live...Incidentally, this is also preventive medicine." Finally, Salem's philosophy was "Life can only be understood backwards, but must be lived forwards. Learn from your mistakes and don't repeat them. Your life and your outlook on life will improve immensely."

In 1963, the daily rate of the Safety Harbor Spa was $23. By 1979, it ranged from $65 to $100 a day. There were five doctors on the staff. There was entertainment every night. A recreation director helped make sure that everyone had a joyful time, as well as the very best food. People would receive a physical examination and then would be assigned special diets as well as a variety of exercises, massages, whirlpool baths, and could participate in different arts and crafts. When you left the facility, your physical and mental health had been improved.

Dr. Baranoff was considered to be a very hard-working, sincere, and humble person who gave of himself as well as his financial resources. He was a peacemaker who wanted to unite all people especially the Jewish people. He was active in the original men's club in Clearwater and served as an officer of the original synagogue, Temple B'nai Israel. In 1957, when Isadore Zitlin and Reuben Rutenberg asked him to organize a conservative synagogue in Clearwater, his answer was that if it was important to have a traditional synagogue he would help in every way possible. He became one of the founders of Congregation Beth Shalom and then its President for several years. He became President Emeritus for life. He and his wife, Lisa, not only made a significant contribution to the original synagogue, but contributed freely to its upkeep year by year. He attended services as frequently as possible, took part in cantorial services on holidays and Sabbaths, and blew the shofar extremely well.

Dr. Baranoff contributed and worked for many other Jewish causes including the United Jewish Appeal, Israel Bond drives, and other Jewish organizations. Despite the fact that he had such an active practice, he found time to work diligently for the general community. He was very active in Safety Harbor in the Civic Club, public library, and other civic organizations. He was honored by the community for his many contributions.

Highlights of 1946

After WWII, Jewish businesspeople started to come to Clearwater because, although it was still a small community,

it had tremendous prospects for growth for new businesses. Shirley and Leonard Collman moved to Clearwater. At first, they rented a house on Wilson Street and then bought a small furnished house for $7,500 at 1515 Paloma Lane in Dunedin. The area was so rural that the backyard was full of snakes and there was even one in the attic. At that time, with the exception of the bigger and better houses found on old Druid road and on Clearwater Beach, left over from the Florida boom time, the houses were basically two bedrooms and one bath and very small.

The people of the Jewish community of Clearwater, along with the Jewish families in Safety Harbor, Dunedin, and close by areas, were tired of driving to Tampa for services. Many of them had probably been going to Tampa because they were either from Tampa originally or had family there. There was an increasing need to start a local center to teach the children in all aspects of Jewish life. There were several young families with young children. There was a fervor about developing a Jewish Community Center and synagogue. Fanny Marks was one of the leaders of the time. She gave many speeches concerning the needs of the Jewish community. She was a forceful and active person, who knew how to turn her speeches into action.

Phyllis and Julius Lovitz

Julius went to college in 1932 to become a pharmacist. He graduated in pharmacy in 1937 from the University of Florida. He worked at Dawson's Drug Store in St. Petersburg and then went to work for Walgreens in Miami and made seventeen dollars a week for seventy-one hours a week. Then he worked in St. Petersburg, Pensacola, Austin, Texas in 1939, and then joined the Navy from Austin, Texas in August, 1941. He was a pharmacist mate, second class, and then became a line officer. He went to England where he met his wife, Phyllis Vera Schuman, at a Jewish dance in Bournemouth, England. Phyllis was born in England on March 3, 1924 to Lilly Kaufman Schuman and Emanuel (Manny) Schuman. She and her fraternal twin sister, Elsa Rosenberg, currently of New York City,

Julius and Phyllis Lovitz

were raised in Wesciffe and then moved to London in 1939. For eighteen months during the Blitz, they left London. Phyllis enrolled in Pitman Business College for approximately two years. She worked as a secretary until she met Julius.

Phyllis and Julius were married in London in an Orthodox synagogue on June 5, 1945. Darwin Frank, who was stationed in England, was the best man at their wedding. They held their wedding reception in London. Harold May, a business associate of Abe Tarapani Sr., also attended the wedding.

After the war ended, Phyllis became a member of a women's organization of war brides. She and a few others petitioned the United States Navy, with the help of her Member of Parliament, to speed up the process of reuniting war brides, especially those with children, with their husbands in America. She was the secretary of the organization. She came to this country on the Queen Mary in February 1946. In New York City, she was picked up by the Red Cross and put on a train for the trip to Tarpon Springs, Florida where she was met by Julius, his father, Sam, his Uncle Abe Tarapani, and his sister, Frances.

Julius wanted Phyllis to meet some of the younger Jewish women in the community, so on May 1 he brought Phyllis to meet Shirley Collman and Maxine Frank. They were the only Jewish young women in Clearwater at that time.

Phyllis first did volunteer work at Bay Pines Veterans Hospital in St. Petersburg. She was part of a small group of Jewish women, sponsored by the Red Cross, who came over from Clearwater to help with the wounded veterans. Phyllis was President of the Sisterhood in 1957-1958. She was a charter member of Hadassah. She was the chairwoman of the Temple Halloween UNICEF committee. She was very active in fund-raising for Temple B'nai Israel and for Israel. Phyllis was a volunteer for the local school system for twenty years tutoring children at several elementary schools.

Julius became a partner with George Resnick in a pharmacy on Greenwood Avenue. Julius bought George out a year later and then George built Julius the drug store on Cleveland Street at Five Points. The Resnicks then moved back to Tampa, where they had originally come from. Julius owned three or four pharmacies and real estate. Eventually, Julius owned the largest chain of independent drugstores in the County. Julius worked from 9:00 a.m. to 9:00 p.m. every day of the week for about the first year. Julius was highly respected by the Jewish and general community. There were about 12,000 people in Clearwater.

Julius was an honorary life member of the Jewish Federation Board of Pinellas County. He was on the founding board of Menorah Manor. He was President of Temple B'nai Israel. He served for two terms on the Board of Directors of Morton Plant Hospital, Past President of the Kiwanis Club, Past President of the Clearwater Concert Association, and one of the founding members of the Board of the Exchange National Bank and Trust Company of Clearwater. He was very active in many charitable causes in Pinellas County.

In later years, Julius donated land to the congregation for a religious school next to the old temple at 20 South Betty Lane. Marshall Kent built the religious school below actual cost. Julius was highly respected in the Jewish as well as the non-Jewish Community. In 1972, the Temple cornerstone at Belcher Road was dedicated by the Lovitz family. The word, Shalom (Peace) was prominently displayed on the cornerstone. When Julius died on December 2, 2005, Phyllis said, " Julius had a very wonderful life.The message on the cornerstone was all about Julius and what he meant to the community–a man of goodness, of Shalom-Peace."

Phyllis and Julius have three daughters, Alix, Irene, and Tracey. All of them grew up in Clearwater.

Alix Lovitz Baxter was born on September 30, 1947. She earned a Bachelor of Arts Degree from the University of North Carolina at Chapel Hill in 1969. She then earned a Doctor of Medicine Degree from the University of North Carolina at Chapel Hill in 1981. She served a Residency in Psychiatry at the University of California Los Angeles Neuropsychiatric Institute from 1981-1984. She is in the private practice of psychiatry and psychoanalysis. From 1994-2000, she was Clinical Associate Professor in the Department of Psychiatry at the University of Florida School of Medicine. She married Jeffrey D. Baxter in 1991. Jeffrey earned a Bachelor of Arts in Economics from the University of Missouri at Kansas City in 1969 and a Master of Arts in Economics from the University of Missouri at Kansas City in 1971. He earned a Doctor of Philosophy Degree in Economics from the University of New Mexico in 1976. He served as a special agent in military intelligence for the United States Army. He was self-employed and then was a Forensic Economist for Info Tech Incorporated.

Irene Lovitz earned a Bachelor of Business Administration in Business Administration and Marketing from the University of Miami in 1971. She earned a Master of Science in Family and Child Development from Kansas State University in 1976, and a Doctor of Psychology Degree in Clinical Psychology from the University of Denver in 1979.

Tracey E. Lovitz was born in 1956. She earned a Bachelor of Health Science Degree in Clinical and Community Dietetics from the University of Florida at Gainesville in 1980. She was a Clinical Instructor at the University of Florida at Gainesville. She is currently a Certified Financial Planner for Ameriprise Financial Services Incorporated.

Other Jewish People

Later in 1946, a new group of Jewish people arrived in the Clearwater area. They included: Rosalie and Marvin Byer; Judge Lloyd Marks, son of Fanny and Simon, and Lloyd's first wife, Betsy; Rosita and Phillip Carvel; Hazel and Lou Simon; Mary and Jack Sanders; Marsha and Jack Altschuler; Yetta and Sam Good; the Saul Solomons from Tampa, who owned a retail store; Marsha and Isadore Zitlin; the Paul Weisbergers; the Charlie Gersches; the Sorensas; the Greenwalds, Ike Isenstein of Safety Harbor another Isenstein of Safety Harbor, Anne Gladstone, and Danny Gladstone, who was an optometrist.

Sol Rosensweig, a young single man, moved to Clearwater and established a radio station, WCAM. He sold it in 1947 or 1948 to the Epstein family, and left town.

David and Ada Rosenfeld came from New York in 1948 and opened a ladies shoe store. Their daughter, Bernice Stillman, came with her husband, Stanley, from Birmingham, Alabama and opened a men's clothing store in Clearwater, which was part of a five store chain in Florida.

Clearwater United Jewish Appeal Drive

Louis Frank, and Sam and Estelle Korones conducted the first UJA drive for Clearwater. They also included Largo, Dunedin, Tarpon Springs, and Safety Harbor. They visited each Jewish family. This drive occurred in the middle 1940s. A quota was set by the St. Petersburg group of twenty-five hundred dollars, which the north group exceeded. There were very nice donations from the Christian merchants that Estelle contacted. When Louis Frank put an ad in the paper that they had exceeded their quota, all donations stopped.

Highlights of 1946-1949
Beginning of Formal Jewish Community in Clearwater and North County

From 1946 to 1949, the Jewish people in Clearwater, Safety Harbor, and other north areas frequently met to discuss the start of a formal Jewish community. Oral history reveals that one of the first informal meetings of the Jewish men was held at the old Morrison's Cafeteria on Park Street. Five or six Jewish businessmen from Cleveland Street attended. Also an early meeting was apparently held around a picnic table on the Courtney Campbell Parkway.

The original minutes of the men's club were found under the stage of Temple B'nai Israel. It was because of the insistent urging of Shirley Collman, that the author continued to pursue the existence of these minutes. After there had been a water leak on the stage, Bob Benjamin asked one of the maintenance staff to pull everything out from under the stage. The author went through many boxes of material and found the original minutes of the men's club dated May 1946-June 19, 1947, the original minutes of the Sisterhood dated September 3, 1946, and the original Sisterhood, and Temple bulletins dated November 1, 1954-April 15, 1955.

The first written notice of Jewish people being urged to organize came from the minutes of the Jewish men's club, dated May, 1946, which states, "A group of Jewish residents of the City of Clearwater met at the Palm Cafeteria to discuss the matter of forming a Jewish organization in Clearwater. The necessity for such an organization was pointed out as most urgent and plans were made to proceed with its formation. An invitation was sent to every known Jewish resident of Clearwater and nearby territory to meet at the home of Mr. Saul Solomon on May 20th to discuss this matter further. Mr. Louis Frank was elected temporary chairman and Mr. M. C. Ravel as temporary secretary. Present at this meeting were: Mr. L. Frank, Mr. Saul Solomon, Mr. George Resnick, Mr. Sam Korones, Mr. Louis Simon and Mr. M. C. Ravel."

On May 20, 1946, a meeting was held at the home of Mr. Saul Solomon. It was called to order by temporary Chairman Mr. L. Frank. The minutes of the meeting stated, "Mr. Saul Solomon discussed at length the necessity of a Jewish organization citing incidents and facts that made such an organization necessary. Motion made by Mr. Marks and seconded by Mr. Frank that an organization of Jewish residents of Clearwater and vicinity be formed. Motion carried. Election of permanent officers was held and the following men were elected as follows: Mr. L. Frank, President; Mr. George Resnick, Vice President; Dr. Baranoff, Secretary; and Mr. Saul Solomon, Treasurer. A committee was selected to draft a constitution and By-Laws and to decide the time and place of the next meeting which was to be called within two weeks. The committee included Mr. Sam Korones, Chairman, Mr. A. Rosenbaum, Mr. Ben Krentzman, Mr. Darwin Frank and Mr. Louis Simon.

On June 14, 1946, a special notice was sent out to the Jewish citizens of Clearwater and vicinity by Saul Solomon, acting secretary. He said, "The first formal meeting of the recently organized social society of the Jewish citizens of Clearwater and vicinity will be held at the home of Mr. Louis Frank, 520 Oak Avenue, Clearwater,

Florida on Wednesday, June 19th. This is a very important meeting as we will decide on the organization name, a charter will be drawn up, and by-laws written. Committees have been working on these items and will make their reports at this meeting. Your attendance is earnestly requested. Bring your friends."

On June 19, 1946, the third meeting for the purpose of organizing a men's Jewish community group was held at Mr. Louis Frank's home. Louis was presiding at the meeting as President of the organization. Mr. Ravel was acting as secretary since Dr. Baranoff was unable to attend. The committee was appointed to choose a suitable name for the organization made two recommendations. They were the Jewish Progress Club and the Progress Club. The Progress Club was chosen by the votes of the individuals in attendance. The committee submitted draft By-Laws, which were discussed in detail and amended by the membership. Mr. Altschuler was elected Secretary to take the place of Dr. Baranoff who asked to be relieved of the responsibility.

The Jewish Woman's Club of Clearwater was founded on September 3, 1946. The meeting was called by and held in the home of Mrs. Simon Marks (Fanny), with Mrs. Marks continuing as permanent President until 1953. The minutes of the first meeting identified the temporary officers as follows: Mrs. Simon Marks, President; Mrs. Darwin Frank (Maxine), secretary and treasurer. In attendance were: Mrs. Harry Hurwood, Mrs. Julius Lovitz, Mrs. J. Brannon, Mrs. Sam Korones, Mrs. Ethel Schoenfeld, Mrs. Saul Solomon, Mrs. Jack Altschuler, Mrs. George Resnick, Mrs. Darwin Frank, Mrs. Lou Simon, and Mrs. Simon Marks.

The dues were one dollar per month per person and the first Tuesday of each month was designated as the meeting night, with meetings to be held at the homes of members in alphabetical order. No formal name was selected for the club at that time. The Jewish women discussed various items, including the facts of Jewish life in Clearwater. At that time, there were thirteen Jewish families in Clearwater and Safety Harbor. As a Jewish group, the women recognized that much was lacking. They wanted to be recognized as a formal Jewish community, but had no communal place to gather for meetings or prayers, no place to celebrate a happy event, or to gather in sorrow. There were young children present in the community and neither they nor their parents had a way to feel some sense of Jewish identity. They also felt a need to combat anti-Semitism in Clearwater. At that time, beside the "No Jews or Dogs" signs, the Ku Klux Klan marched periodically through the streets of Clearwater, Tarpon Springs, and St. Petersburg. The desire to have a woman's group was both children and family oriented as well as social in nature. The Jewish women baked cakes and sold them on the corner of Cleveland and Fort Harrison with a big sign on the table" Bake Sale–Jewish Woman's Club of Clearwater." Ethel Schoenfeld would bake and sell her things. It took a lot of nerve for the women to do this because of the fear of potential anti-Semitism. However, the non-Jewish community reacted in a very nice and helpful manner. The Jewish women also gave card parties, ran rummage sales, made special dinners and special luncheons, and ran bingo games as fund raisers. Dr. and Mrs. Salem Baranoff, the owners of the Safety Harbor Spa, allowed the Jewish community to use the facilities for fund raising purposes. Many of the guests donated generously to the cause. Fanny Marks pulled it together. This first small group of Jewish women subsequently became the Jewish Woman's Club of Clearwater, which in 1951, became the Sisterhood of Temple B'nai Israel.

The Jewish Community Club was formally founded on October 16, 1946, with Louis Frank as the first President. An undated newspaper article of apparently that time indicates that the organization was formed the previous May with Louis Frank as President. The article goes on to say, "...that the Jewish Men's Club was looking forward to serve the community and to cooperate in furthering the aims and ideals of its loyal citizens for a greater, more beautiful, and prosperous city. The Jewish Men's Club hopes to bring about a closer relationship between the members of its own faith and the residents of Clearwater and

vicinity to sponsor and encourage social, cultural, religious, and civic activities, good citizenship and good Americanism: to indicate among the members of its own faith the sense of individual obligation to the community, state, and nation."

At the October 16th meeting, the group once again discussed the subject of a suitable name for the organization. The names submitted were: The Jewish Men's Club, the Covenant Club, The Jewish Community Men's Club, and the Jewish Educational League. A secret ballot was held and the name of the organization became "The Jewish Community Men's Club." Under new business, Dr. Baranoff introduced his guests, Mr. Lerman and Mr. Kleiner, and proposed Mr. Lerman become a member of the organization. Saul Solomon moved to have the chairman appoint a committee to investigate the feasibility of purchasing a lot for the purpose of building a community house. It was seconded by Dr. Baranoff and the motion carried. Darwin Frank made a motion to send a check for $4.08 to Rabbi Morris of Ohev Shalom Congregation of Orlando for expenses incurred in coming to the local Jewish community. It was approved. The group agreed to a $10 initiation fee and annual dues of six dollars and a total of $208 was collected. Darwin Frank offered his home for the next meeting.

The fifth regular meeting of the Jewish Men's Club was held on Friday, November 1, 1946 at the home of Darwin Frank, with Louis Frank presiding. The committee assigned to investigate the purchase of a lot gave a report that it was making progress. Sam Korones was chairman of the committee. There was $203.92 in the treasury. Saul Solomon proposed the membership of Harry Browndorff. Harry Hurwitz seconded the motion and it was unanimously approved. Louis Frank appointed George Resnick and Saul Solomon to serve on the membership committee. Saul Solomon moved that the chairman appoint a committee to cooperate with the Jewish Women's Club in meeting new arrivals and visitors to Clearwater and inviting them to take part in community activities. It was seconded by Leonard Collman and approved. Leonard Collman was appointed to this position. Saul Solomon moved to buy a copy of Roberts Parliamentary Rules of Order. It was approved. Louis Simon offered his home for the next meeting.

The sixth regular meeting was held on November 16, 1946 at the home of Louis Simon. A letter was read from the Jewish women's club inviting the Jewish men's club to a joint meeting to be held at the Safety Harbor Sanatorium. The invitation was accepted.

The seventh regular meeting of the Jewish Men's Club was held on December 10, 1946, at the home of the Collmans. The meeting was chaired by Louis Frank. Louis Frank reported for the committee assigned to have racial restrictions removed from the Clearwater Country Club. He reported that he had discussed the matter with Ben Krentzman who promised to take the matter up with the proper authorities. Saul Solomon reported for the committee on purchasing a lot. He reported the availability of several sites, and suggested that the committee be given an idea of how much money the club could spend for that purpose. Simon Marks was appointed to the Lot Committee. Louis Frank discussed with the Masons the possibility of using their facilities. Darwin Frank made a motion to have a Jewish Men's Club meeting once a month and a joint meeting with the Jewish Women's Club during the month. Leonard Collman made a motion to provide the local newspapers with pertinent facts about the club, its ideals, and aims as set forth in its constitution. I. Eisenstein made a motion to appoint a committee to raise funds for the building of a community center. President Louis Frank appointed I Eisenstein, Chairman, George Resnick, Darwin Frank, Saul Solomon, and Dr. Salem Baranoff. The group started a raffle and raised $3.75 for the treasury.

The eighth regular meeting of the Jewish Men's Club was held at the home of Louis Frank on January 7, 1947. The raffle netted $2.50 for the treasury.

The ninth meeting of the Jewish Men's Club was called to order at 8:30 p.m. at the home of Simon Marks. (No date shows on the handwritten minutes.) The Lot Committee was considering the purchase of a lot on the southeast corner of Palm

Bluff and North Garden. The purchase price was $1,300. Saul Solomon made a motion that a Community Seder be held and that a committee be appointed by the chairman to make all necessary arrangements in conjunction with the Jewish Woman's Club and Safety Harbor Sanatorium. The Treasurer reported that there was $294.97 in the treasury. A raffle netted four dollars and Louis Frank donated an additional two dollars. Unfortunately, the records of other meetings of the Jewish Men's Club have not been found.

After Louis Frank gave up the position of President or Chairman of the Jewish Men's Club, the following men served as President of the Jewish Community Club, Reuben Rutenberg, Sam Good, Lloyd Marks, and Isadore Zitlin. The past Presidents of the Jewish Community Club were a who's who of Jewish and community life. Some of the suggested names for the Jewish Community Club were: the Progressive Club, the Jewish Club, the Covenant Club, the Jewish Community Club, and the Jewish Educational Club. The initiation fee was $10 and dues were six dollars a year. Thirteen people joined the club immediately. Several meetings were held between October 16, 1946 and September 1949. One meeting was held at the Solomon's house and one held in Safety Harbor at the Eisenstein's house, one at Collman's house in Duneden, and one at the Korones's home. Julius Lovitz, who didn't have time to participate in many activities outside of work, was invited to one of these meetings at Mr. Louis Frank's house to start to organize a formal Jewish Community Center. He attended the meeting with about fourteen other people including Ben Krentzman, Sam Korones, Darwin Frank, Jack Altschuler, Leonard Collman, Louis Frank, Salem Baranoff, Sam Good, Charlie Gersch, Clarence Collman, the Gladstones, a couple of others from Safety Harbor and Jack Altschuler.

The building committee was having a hard time finding a suitable lot for the Temple building because of the discrimination that existed at that time. People did not want a Jewish Temple in their area. It was standard practice in deeds in 1949 and 1950 to state, "no persons of color or Hebrew can purchase this property."

At one of these meetings, Sam Korones, Darwin Frank, Saul Solomon, and Leonard Collman left in the middle of the discussions to purchase a lot on Betty Lane for $2,500 before the property owners in the area could object to a Jewish organization being built in their neighborhood. The sale of other properties to Jewish people had been denied in the past. This time, Charles Coit, a non-Jewish realtor, who had found the property for the committee, was involved in the sale. The building lot committee already had $208 in seed money collected to help with the down payment. They secured a mortgage for the balance and paid it off quickly. Charlie Gersch, Sam Good, Salem Baranoff, and many others volunteered their time and money to help construct the new Jewish Community Center and synagogue.

The Jewish community of Clearwater in 1947, 1948 and probably 1949 held the High Holy Day services at the Clearwater Garden Club, off of Osceola Avenue. Before Temple B'nai Israel was built, most people went to Tampa for services. Services were not held in any store fronts.

Over the years, many different people claimed that the formal charter meeting was held at their home, but it is hard to tell which one was accurate. Of greatest importance was the fact that the Jewish people were able to work together, although they were young and old, very Orthodox, Conservative, and Reform, and had many different ideas about how the Jewish people should organize to socialize and pray. The younger families had social and religious opportunities for their children and themselves. The older families wanted to provide a home for other Jewish people to get together.

Bruce and Dee Dee Strumpf moved to Clearwater in the late 1940s. They both came from New York. Bruce was in property management. Sissie Angest, later Bierman, moved to the Clearwater area in 1949.

Temple B'nai Israel (Jewish Community Center)

On September 15, 1949, The Articles of Incorporation of the Jewish Community Center were signed by Darwin Frank, Jack Altschuler, Leonard Collman, Clarence Collman, and Samuel Good, in the presence of Ben Krintman and Florence M. Gray. It was filed with the clerk of the Pinellas County Circuit Court on September 19, 1949. The officers were Darwin Frank, President, Samuel Good, 1st Vice-President, Isadore Zitlin, 2nd Vice-President, Simon Marks, 3rd Vice-President, David Shane, Recording Secretary, Clarence Collman, Financial Secretary, Leonard Collman, Treasurer. Other members of the Board of Directors were Harry Hurwood, S. Leventhal, Jack Altschuler, S. H. Baranoff, and S. Brodski. Article II in part states, "The general nature of the object of the corporation is... to promote a closer relationship among the Jewish residents of the Clearwater area, to sponsor and encourage social, religious, and welfare activities, to encourage good citizenship and Americanism, and to incubate among its members a sense of obligation to their community, state, and nation". Temple B'nai Israel was formed with a membership of Reform, Conservative, and Orthodox Jews. To please everybody, they first called themselves B'nai Israel Congregation and Jewish Community Center.

The originating members were: Mr. and Mrs. Jack Altschuler, who was the architect for Betty Lane. He designed the original Temple and supervised its construction. Even though Jack had only one leg, he was physically very active. He and his wife were active in forming the Temple and Jewish Center and participated in or chaired many of the activities; from Safety Harbor; Morris and Lillian D. Brodski from Safety Harbor; Mr. and Mrs. Harry Browndorff; Clarence Collman (Leonard's brother); Leonard and Shirley Collman; Mr. and Mrs. Ike Eisenstein from Safety Harbor; Sam and Yetta Eisenstein; Darwin and Maxine Frank; Darwin's parents, Louis and Hannah Frank; Charles and Rose M. Gersch, who later helped found Congregation Beth Shalom; Mr. and Mrs. Sam Good, a retired couple, who later helped found Congregation Beth Shalom; Mr. and Mrs. Leon Greenwald, a retired couple; Harry and Bessie Hurwood (Bessie was Fanny Marks' Sister); Sam and Estelle Korones; Mr. and Mrs. M. Lerner; S. Leventhal; Julius and Phyllis Lovitz, Mr. Simon Marks

(Fanny's husband); Mrs. Simon Marks (Fanny had a separate membership); Mr. and Mrs. George Resnick; Nat and Naomi Roth, a retired couple (Nat wrote some of the bulletins after Shirley Collman stopped writing them.); Louis and Hazel Simon; Mrs. Ethel Schoenfeld (Maxine Frank's mother); Mr. and Mrs. David Shane from Dunedin; Mr. and Mrs. Saul Solomon; and Mr. and Mrs. Paul Weisberger (Paul always wore rubber sneakers for religious reasons).

Most of the members were retirees and some were businessmen. Many came from Safety Harbor. Lisa Baranoff hosted Hadassah every February. This was the biggest fund raiser held at the Safety Harbor Spa. The younger retirees dabbled in real estate and played the stock market.

Darwin S. Frank

Darwin S. Frank, President of Temple B'nai Israel from 1949-1951, was active in many civic and political causes. He became a Clearwater City Commissioner, because of his sense of humanity and his interest in protecting the small man. Maxine and Darwin Frank were always honored by holding the Torah and dressing it on Yom Kippur. They served on many of the important committees of the synagogue. Darwin believed in being Jewish, but not necessarily in all of the rituals of Judaism. Darwin was a very gregarious individual and a prankster. He was like a little gnome who was full of mischief, but had a good heart. He liked to do and say outrageous things and could get away with it. Once in a Sisterhood musical variety show, he did a takeoff on George Burns. Later on when the curtain was raised again, he was dressed as an angel in a short fluffy dress and wings. He had hairy legs with brown shoes and socks on and was suspended from the ceiling. He never knew a stranger wherever he went. Everyone knew him and thought that he knew their names. When he went to a restaurant he would always get into conversation with the people at neighboring tables and would often ask to taste what they were eating. After his death, every time people would hear an unusual sound or signal, they would say Darwin is trying to get through. Darwin Frank

graduated from Clearwater High School in 1936, and the University of Cincinnati in 1941, with a Bachelor of Science Degree in Business Administration. During World War II, he served in the U.S. Army Corps of Engineers for three years, two of them in London, England. While there, he took a course in public speaking at the University of London, which started him on a lifelong journey of inquiry and further education. In a truly Jewish manner, he understood that if you don't continue to study, you diminished knowledge for all people.

In 1945, when Darwin returned from the service he went to work in the department store established by his father, Louis, and his mother, Hannah, and in 1948 became its owner and manager. During his lifetime, he made enormous contributions to the Jewish and general communities. He served as a Clearwater City Commissioner in 1976 and 1977. He was always concerned about the growth and development of Clearwater. He felt strongly about the need for good public education and was committed to volunteer work and the Jewish community. He was Past President of the Clearwater Merchants Association, a director and Past President of the Downtown Development Board, a director of the Greater Clearwater Chamber of Commerce, a director of Clearwater Federal Savings and Loan Association and a director of the Clearwater Kiwanis Club, and Chairman of the March of Dimes drive to eliminate polio. He was especially interested in helping young boys and girls. He served as chairman of many committees which would help children. He was called Colonel Clearwater for the wonderful things he did for people.

As a private citizen, he rewarded boys and girls from the high school for getting an A grade. If they brought their report cards to Frank's Department Store, they would receive a sizable discount for each A grade. After his retirement in 1985, he did volunteer work for the Religious Community Services, the Pinellas County Education Foundations Doorways Program and the Service Corps of Retired Executives, an organization of volunteers who offered their expertise to help new businesses. He died April 19, 1994. Maxine Frank was born in 1921 in

Huntington, West Virginia. She came from Cincinnati. She worked as an assistant manager at Frank's Department Store, in Clearwater. She had served as a volunteer for thirty two years at Morton Plant Hospital of Clearwater, Past President of Temple B'nai Israel's Sisterhood, and a longtime member of Hadassah.

Highlights of 1950-1959

The times between 1950 and 1960 were very good for the Jewish community. The Jewish people of Clearwater and north county had a synagogue which was growing very rapidly and then a second synagogue forming in the latter part of the 1950s. The children went to Sunday school. There were all kinds of events in the social hall. Everyone worked hard for the common good. There were card games, bingo, rummage sales, Purim carnivals, dances etc.. Many of these affairs were run by the Sisterhood.

In the early 1950s, Bud and Shirley Berolzheimer made parachute ropes during the Korean War and then made shoelaces after the war. Marvin and Marion Bauman owned Bauman's Dress Shop on Fort Harrison Road. They were cousins of Fanny Marks. Fanny had a yarn and knitting store on Clearwater Beach. Danny Gladstone was an optometrist on Fort Harrison Road north of Cleveland Street. He lived in Safety Harbor with his parents. Syd Entel owned a frame and art gallery in Safety Harbor. Richard and June Baumgardner owned the Kapok Tree Restaurant. Arthur Rutenberg arrived in 1954. Charlie Rutenberg arrived in 1955. Cleveland Plaza, an air-conditioned strip mall containing a big Publix, Eckerd Drug Store, and other stores opened. It had been previously a black cemetery. A new Clearwater High School was opened in 1955, and the old Clearwater High School became a black high school. The Courtney Cambell Causeway was the old black beach. Blacks had to leave Clearwater Beach on the 8 p.m. bus at the latest. Reva Kent arrived in February of 1956. She soon became a Sunday school teacher and taught the four, five, and six-year-old children in the kitchen. Dr. Harry Katz came to Largo and opened his medical office. He kept his office open on Saturdays and one half day on Sunday. He built his own hospital in Largo.

The first confirmation class included Jeffrey Lopatin, Anita Bauman, and Mark Rowen. Jeffrey's parents were Harold and Pearl Lopatin. Mark's mother was here. Anita's parents, Marion and Marvin, owned a dress shop on Fort Harrison. They later moved it to Cleveland Street.

Temple functions for the entire community continued for many years As the Jewish population grew, the younger and older members started to socialize in their own groups. Prior to this time, if anyone had a personal party, everyone was invited.

The Jewish people of Clearwater, Safety Harbor, and other North communities, who joined synagogues, basically belonged to Temple B'nai Israel until 1957. In that year, the individuals who were conservative decided to form their own synagogue, Congregation Beth Shalom.

Because the early members of the two synagogues were part of one Jewish community and because most of them had belonged initially to Temple B'nai Israel, it is essential to include in the discussion from 1950-1957, information about all individuals and both synagogues in this chapter. After 1957, information about Temple B'nai Israel will be found in its own separate chapter and information about Congregation Beth Shalom will also be found in its own separate chapter.

Highlights of 1950

In September, the cornerstone was laid for the new congregation, Temple B'nai Israel at 20 South Betty Lane, Clearwater. Mayor Herb Brown of Clearwater and some clergymen spoke at the dedication. Fanny Marks, a highly dedicated member of the Jewish community, also made a speech at that time. She said, "... Today there is a nucleus for what we hope and pray will eventually develop into a Jewish community that will have the prestige and standing amongst all faiths....and it was with these (thoughts) uppermost in our hearts and minds that we formed the Jewish Women's club. The men were in complete agreement with our needs and desires." In her many speeches to a variety of organizations, Fanny always

First building for Temple B'nai Israel. 20 South Betty Lane, Clearwater, FL. Dedicated 1950

remembered "the many people who worked so devotedly for a place of worship." She said that "the congregation stands as a living memorial to all of them and to everyone who gave so much of themselves to make Temple B'nai Israel a unique and wonderful home for the Jewish people. She emphasized that because of our ancestors, we Jews can come to our services in peace with reverence and thankfulness to the one who makes all things possible." Fanny said," I would like to pass on to you, all of you, as it (is) for the future – cherish it and guard it well. May it always be the place in your hearts were you can meet in brotherhood with your fellow man and know God."

The Temple, which was completed, was the culmination of all the planning and hard work of a group of Jewish people who wanted to express their Jewishness within this community. The structure was very simple. There was a small coat rack by the door. Much had to be done to turn it into a house of worship. This was just the beginning. There was a building in need of everything. The women's group planned and carried out more parties, bingo games, dinner parties, luncheons, etc..

The building was 2,400 square feet, forty feet by sixty feet. At one end was a raised stage with a curtain. When the curtain was open, it was a sanctuary and the stage was the Bema. When the curtain was closed, it was a social hall. The draw drape had been donated by the Sisterhood. They also donated drapes for the windows. When entering the front door, the kitchen, rabbi's study, and the bathrooms were to the right. The piano was on the left-hand side in the back of the room and the choir was in front of the piano. On Sunday, the kitchen was sometimes a classroom or a meeting room. Sunday school classes were held in the sanctuary which was divided by folding screens. Because of the wooden floors, all noises were magnified. You could hear every sound including the flushing of the toilet, the moving of the folding chairs, and any other human sounds. The cold, squeaky, hard, folding chairs were finally replaced by Morris Bilgore and Roland Fox who put on a fund drive to obtain padded ones. There were no stained-glass windows in the Temple. The Bema chairs from the Betty Lane Temple are now in the foyer of the current synagogue. In celebration of the dedication of the new synagogue, Mrs. Helen Epstein catered a buffet enjoyed by the Jewish and non-Jewish communities alike.

The Torah used at the dedication of Temple B'nai Israel was lent to the congregation. Julia Berolzheimer and Ethyl Shoenfeld sang at the dedication. Julia may have led the assembly in song. The actual choir came a few years later. The first piano used was an old one and had been donated to the synagogue. Sally Sackheim donated a new piano several years later in the late fifties or early sixties and, then still later Marshall Kent donated an organ. There was a ceremony both inside the structure and outside. It was very hot and there was no air-conditioning inside for a long time.

David Korones, at age thirteen, conducted the first religious service to be held in the Temple on South Betty Lane. He said, "It was awesome and frightening, but I was very proud". The congregation gave him a Star of David and a chain for conducting the service. He lost it several months later in the Gulf and never wore another one afterwards. At first, the members conducted the services. Isadore Zitlin, who was a very learned man, was very active and helped put on numerous religious services. He was highly respected as a lay Jewish leader in the same mode as M. Henry Cohen of Schaarai Zedek of Tampa. Isadore was President of Temple B'nai Israel for a short period of time. He later moved to Congregation Beth Shalom. Sam Good, as well as other men from Safety Harbor, also conducted services. These were typically the older men in the congregation who were conservative or orthodox. They wanted to conduct services and let the younger men be the officers. The younger men, such as Darwin, Julius, and Leonard had not had a bar mitzvah and did not know how to read Hebrew.

Because there was a split between those who were Orthodox or Conservative, and those who were Reform, for a short period of time two types of services were conducted in split shifts . Apparently, this was a very unsatisfactory resolution of the problem concerning how to conduct a religious service. This caused much unrest in the congregation and a lot of grumbling among the leaders. Different rabbis came for the High Holy Days services. Rabbis came for other special services from Tampa and occasionally from St. Petersburg. In 1950 or 1951, Estelle and Sam Korones presented the first Torah to the Temple. A student rabbi, Frank Walding, officiated at the High Holy Days services. He was housed and entertained by the Collmans. Afterwards, other student rabbis presided over the High Holy Day services. They were usually put up in a motel on Cleveland Street and had dinner with various members of the congregation. Rabbi Benjamin Hoffsayer came in September 1953, to preside over the High Holy Day services. When one of the rabbis was eating with the Collmans one night, he said that Jews are supposed to look up instead of down when saying prayers.

Rabbi Zielonka of Schaarai Zedek of Tampa frequently came to Clearwater for various occasions, both religious or community programs. He was highly respected in Clearwater.

Other related Jewish organizations of that time were Temple B'nai Israel Sisterhood, B'nai Brith, Temple B'nai Israel Brotherhood, the Clearwater-Safety Harbor Hadassah, organized by the Safety Harbor ladies. Ann Sanders (husband Jack) helped organize the Hadassah chapter of six women who used a card table by the front door of the Temple for their meetings. Shirley Collman was a charter member. The United Jewish Appeal had been around in the Clearwater area since the 1940s. Some of the chairmen of the 1950s included the Korones, Herb Frank, and Louis Brower.

Temple B'nai Israel Sisterhood was the auxiliary for all women of the congregation. It offered programs in interfaith, outreach, service, educational, Torah study, and social programs, as well as many other fine programs in the community.

Temple B'nai Israel Brotherhood was the men's auxiliary of the Temple. It helped provide ushers for services and held entertaining, informational, and educational programs and was involved with other programs in the community.

Mary and Reuben Rutenberg

Mary and Reuben Rutenberg

Mary and Reuben Rutenberg arrived in Clearwater on September 5, Erev Rosh Hashanah, during the worst hurricane that Clearwater had had since 1913. They had driven from California. They were told to go to Sam Good for an introduction to the Jewish community. He was hammering nails on the building, which was the first synagogue of Temple B'nai Israel. Sam said he needed another hand and Reuben purchased a shovel and some lumber and began to help. Rosh Hashanah services were held that evening in this building on Betty Lane. The Rutenberg family also helped organize Congregation Beth Shalom in 1957, in Clearwater. This was the beginning of the Rutenberg family's enormous contributions to Pinellas County life and prosperity. They have been responsible for contributing large amounts of financial assistance, time, energy, and leadership to numerous nonprofit organizations.

Mary Rutenberg was born October 10, 1898, and died November 18, 1986. She graduated from McKinley High School in Chicago. Mary, as a child, was a tomboy who loved sports. She and the other children were taken to a series of different museums for recreational activities. She would ask numerous questions, which was the first indication of how bright she was. When she was five and one half years old, her brother had to recite a ten stanza poem in school. Her dad, who was home for lunch, while listening to her brother recite the poem, saw interest and recognition on Mary's face. Although Mary could not read yet, he thought she was capable of at least repeating part of the poem. In fact, she repeated the entire thing accurately. Mary took her first piano lesson at age ten and one half. She became so good that she would accompany her brother, Al, who played the violin in a small orchestra which he had founded. Mary's mother decided that she should practice piano instead of doing housework because none of the other children wanted to play the piano. On Sunday afternoons, her father would take her on long trolley rides and share his life with her and his passion for learning and teaching. Mary became an exceptional piano player and a piano teacher for sixty years.

Mary became interested in Sunday School when she completed an excellent course in one year. When she went into the school office to ask about an advanced course, the principal made her a teacher. She had twenty children from the ages of six-eight, no textbook, no preparation, and had to teach. She was fourteen years old. This started a lifelong quest of teaching children as well as adults. She taught children and adults at Temple B'nai Israel in the early 1950s and then taught children from Congregation Beth Shalom on the back porch of her home and then in the sanctuary until 1970. She was a founder of the Clearwater- Safety Harbor Hadassah chapter and became its first President. Her father was a rabbi, who did not want a congregation, but rather to teach. He taught at a synagogue in Chicago. She was a very organized and outgoing person and made friends easily. Although she never sat on any boards, she was always helping people in a variety of different organizations. Mary and Reuben gave a Torah to Temple B'nai Israel and then Mary gave a Torah in memory of Reuben to Congregation Beth Shalom.

Mary's awards fill numerous scrapbooks, including honors from local organizations as well as the State of Israel. An example of the awards was the April 30th, 1972, Clearwater-Israel Dinner of State, where Mary was honored with the highly coveted Shalom Award. Dr. Salem Baranoff said about the significance of this dinner and the award, "a moment expressive of our cherished ties with Israel and the role our community has played in her growth and development. Because we are honoring Mary Rutenberg, this will lend tone and stature to the event."

Mary was involved in many causes, including the human rights of Russian Jews. She said, "With everlasting love hast thou loved the house of Israel, teaching us thy Torah and commandments, thy statutes and judgments. With love for her fellow man,

we hear about the situation of the Jews in Russia, and feel it is incumbent upon us to act, and not only speak up in their behalf. The basic human rights of all people must be upheld, and this includes the right of Jews to live in peace in Russia, or if they choose, to be able to go to the land of their choice to live freely as Jews – as free citizens in a free land. When we utter our ancient prayer proclaiming the unity of God, we feel the unity too of the Jewish people. It is in thanks for these very teachings that we hope to see them shared by Jews in every land. May this beautiful prayer of God's everlasting love bring his blessings to the Jews of Russia and everywhere." Mary summarized her philosophy of life by saying, "Your religion is the way you live."

Reuben was born in a part of Poland occupied by Russia, on September 1, 1892. He came to the United States in 1906. Reuben died on April 21, 1971. When he arrived in this country, he had no money and therefore went to work immediately in a clothing company. At fifteen, he became a corporate President and manufactured trousers for high-class men's clothing stores. Reuben served for a short time in the Army in World War I. He received an honorable discharge on the 10th of August, 1918. Shortly thereafter, he did custom tailoring. He opened a dry goods store and then sought other opportunities as well. He married Mary in 1920, and retired for the first time at age twenty seven. Reuben owned a small chain of furniture and appliance stores in Chicago. Reuben and Mary left the cold of the Midwest and went first to Pasadena, California, but the smog hurt them. They then went to Clearwater and liked it so much that in October 1950, they bought a home on Cleveland Street. Beside his business activities, and his immersion in the religious community, Reuben loved fishing and gardening. In fact, he had his fatal heart attack while tending his beloved garden. Reuben was an avid reader who read everything, including the encyclopedia. He was a man to whom knowledge was life. Mary, like Reuben, was always reading and teaching. She and her husband were constantly involved in all kinds of charitable work. Reuben was truly a righteous man. Written on his tombstone was the phrase, "I never saw a righteous man forsaken."

Mary and Reuben had four children, Morton, Charlie, Arthur, and Dan. Morton was born on October 8, 1921 and died on June 23, 1984. He attended several colleges and became an accountant. He lived in Washington, DC. His wife, Jessica, was an office manager. The biographical information on Charlie, Arthur, and Dan may be found under separate listings.

Mary and Reuben's son, Daniel, best described his parents and their legacy to their children. He said, "Mary and Reuben Rutenberg's defining quality was impatience: with their friends, the community, their family, and even themselves. Why didn't Clearwater have a Hadassah chapter? Why was there not only a Reform temple, but also a Conservative synagogue in Clearwater to afford Jews a choice? Why was there not an adequate Sunday School for Jewish children? Would not an intellectually involved Jewish community benefit from a Jewish cultural society? They never knew the luxury of procrastination; the operative word was "now." They passionately believed in Jewish institutional life, and devoted their energies to fostering it. And that is why all these needs were met within a decade, after their 1950 retirement to Clearwater."

With their children, this commitment to the Jewish community has taken different forms. Charles was philanthropically involved; the Golda Meir Center and UJA were his special interests. Arthur served as President of Temple B'nai Israel and has played a significant role in helping to define and meet its long-range building and financial goals. Daniel, who has served on the Temple board, inaugurated its Gorn Lecture Series. The duty to serve was Mary and Reuben's legacy to them."

Highlights of 1951

The religious school was started by Mary Rutenberg, who was also the official greeter for the congregation. She had eight students: Nancy and Jerald Collman, Alix and Irene Lovitz, Melanie Weiss, and three other students who did not stay in the school. Two of them were brothers. The

families moved away. Mrs. Paul Circus, in 1955, came from St. Petersburg as a paid Sunday school teacher and principal to work with the children. After she left the Sunday school, they went back to volunteer teachers until there were adequate funds and enough children to once again hire paid teachers. There were five children in the Sunday School. The children met in the sanctuary and classes were separated by folding screens. Bible stories, holidays, and later Hebrew were taught to the children. Adult education was conducted by Mary Rutenberg, who taught "Pathways Through the Bible" in members' homes in the early '50s.

Mary Rutenberg started the Temple library. Shirley Collman assisted her. In the beginning, all the books were donated. Much later, new books were purchased.

In 1951–1952, Samuel A. Korones was President of Temple B'nai Israel. The temple dues were $25 for a single person and $50 for a family. Max Sackheim, President of the National Book of the Month Club, was an early and prominent member of Temple B'nai Israel.

The women's group formally became the Sisterhood, a Temple auxiliary for all women of the congregation. It offered many programs including interfaith, outreach, service, education, Torah study, and social programs. The women managed the Judaica shop, handled all the flower arrangements and refreshments for the Oneg Shabbats. Personal gifts were given to all of the children who had been B'nai Mitzvah, confirmed, and completed senior study.

On November 12, the following people were selected to draw up a constitution and bylaws of the Sisterhood: Mrs. Shirley Collman, Mrs. Lisa Baranoff, Mrs. Ann Gladstone, and Mrs. Ann Eisenstein. They affiliated with the national Sisterhood. The brotherhood was formally formed with Mr. Louis Frank as its first President.

Henry, Shirley, and Julia Berolzheimer came to the Clearwater area in January. They lived in Tarpon Springs. The Jenkins' Department Store, which was operated by Jewish people, started business prior to this time.

The first choir members were led by Julia Berolzheimer. The choir consisted

Shirley and Henry Berolzheimer

of Julia, Ethel Schoenfeld, Jessie Jacoby, Larry Friedlander, and then Irving Baker, Harold and Arthur Lopatin joined in 1956. Claire played the piano and sang. Laura Baker was the daughter of Martha and Irving Baker, both deceased now. Martha was very active in Sisterhood until she was too sick to participate. She was the Treasurer for many years.

Julia Berolzheimer

Julia was extremely active in the National Council of Jewish Women. Julia was born on April 10, 1894. She was a charter member of the Chicago Heights section in 1921, Past President, Regional President, national board member for six years, national Vice President for three years, and Chairman of the Committee on International Council of Jewish Women. In 1950, in tribute to Julia, the Chicago Heights Section of the National Council of Jewish women dedicated their bulletin to her. The National Council: unites women interested in the work of religion, philanthropy, and education; improves religious schools and education; works for social reform; and secures the interest and help of influential people to fight religious persecution wherever it exists and whomever is involved.

Highlights of 1952
Lloyd Marks

In 1952–1953, Lloyd Marks was President of Temple B'nai Israel. He was born in Tampa on August 28, 1926. He graduated from Florida Military Academy, St. Petersburg, in 1944 and then served in the United States Navy in World War II, rising to the rank of petty officer. He graduated from the University of Miami School of Law in 1951. He practiced law in Clearwater from 1951-1956 and served as a judge in Safety Harbor, in 1952 and 1953. He then practiced law in Homestead, Florida from 1956-1959. He became a judge again of the Metropolitan Court of Dade County from1959-1965. Lloyd became the city attorney of the City of Florida City in 1982 and in 2005, still holds that post. In 1990, he became a Certified Circuit Court Mediator. He married Ruth B . Marks in 1962. They have a son, Steven Marks, and a daughter,

Lloyd Marks

Jennifer Marks Horsley.

Harold Haftel

The Haftel Family Egg Farm in Tarpon Springs was opened. David and Sadie Haftel moved from Flemington, New Jersey. David had originally come from Poland about 1914. He established the American Grocery Store in Brooklyn. During the Depression, David went broke. He then had a farm and after he lost both legs due to poor circulation, he and his wife decided to move to Florida. Sadie was also in poor health. David was a member of the Knights of Pitheus.

Their son, Harold, joined them. He worked for the United States Department of Agriculture. He was a food inspector. In 1956, they planted an orange grove. They were frozen out in 1962 and then replanted. Harold made the orange grove a huge success. He was environmentally conscious, using a solar panel to help power his home. Long before other farms in the area conserved water, he set up an irrigation system that directly dripped water on the plants roots. He had brought this idea back from a trip to Israel. He also had a real estate firm. Harold helped people in an anonymous manner. He neither wanted praise or thanks. When he sold his orange grove, he decided to make a substantial contribution to the Weizman Institute of Science in Israel. He became a member of their Board of Trustees. He has received numerous honors from the Weizman Institute for his contributions of time, excellent counseling, and funding of programs.

The Weizman Institute of Science was founded in 1934. It is a community of 2,500 scientists, scientists-in-training, and engineers who work on 1,000 or more research projects related to basic medical research, chemistry, biology, agriculture, computer science, and fundamental laws of physics. Their research work is recognized and utilized throughout the world. In the field of cancer, they have been involved in genetic research, bone marrow transplantation, pioneered the use of MRIs, and new therapies. In the field of technology, they have built and introduced powerful computers into the research facilities. They have developed research tools related to lasers. They do brain research with robotics and have built powerful biological computers. In the environment, they have created new strains of food to feed the hungry millions of people in the Third World. They are foremost in solar research, converting salt water to drinking water, and involved in global warming programs. In health, they are involved in the study of blindness, spinal cord injuries, blood tests to screen for schizophrenia, research on stem cells, and the discovery of brain enzymes. In education, they award Ph.D.'s and Master of Science Degrees. They have the first outdoor science Museum. Weizman has the Davidson Institute of Science Education, and are deeply involved in teaching science to young people. The Weizman Institute has eight collaborative agreements with prestigious medical centers and universities throughout the world, including the Pasteur Institute of Paris, Johns Hopkins University, Massachusetts Institute of Technology, NASA, Brookhaven National Laboratory, and Cambridge University of the United Kingdom.

Harold was born on January 31, 1926. He graduated from Delaware Valley College in Doylestown, Pennsylvania in 1950 with a Bachelor of Science Degree in Food Technology. He had previously served in World War II in the Army Air Corps from 1944-1946, and then later in the Korean War from 1950-1951. He was President of the Rotary Club of Tarpon Springs and had served on the Board of Trustees of B'nai B'rith. He went on Medical Missions of Mercy in El Salvador and received numerous awards from Rotary International.

Highlights of 1953

On February 6, Louis Frank was honored by the Jewish community for his 80th birthday. Mr. Frank was a distinguished citizen who enriched everyone by the special strength of his character. His life was an example for Jewish people and non-Jewish people alike of dignity and integrity. He and Hannah built for themselves an enviable reputation as individuals and as Jews. This helped other Jewish people im- measurably in establishing good relations with their fellow citizens. Any Jewish person coming

to Clearwater was immediately referred to Louis. He was always willing to help any Jewish person as well as the community at large. He was a Past Master of the Masons, and affiliated with several different civic organizations. He was the first President of the Jewish Community before the building was even erected. He continued to support the Synagogue-Center with quiet dignity and anonymously. Hannah was affiliated with the Sisterhood and Hadassah chapter. He was still active in his business at age 80.

On June 23, Reuben Rutenberg gave a speech at a Jewish Community Meeting in Clearwater. Reuben tried to balance the needs and desires of various Jewish people while maintaining a cohesive community. The struggle which had appeared at Schaarai Zedek of Tampa in 1902, Congregation B'nai Israel and Temple Beth-El of St. Petersburg in the 1920s, as well as that which was occurring in otherparts of the country, had come to Clearwater. There were older members and younger members, those who wanted to follow strict interpretations of customs and rituals and those who wanted to give them a more modern interpretation, and the usual conflicts which occur when people discuss religion and how best to fulfill your obligation to pray and respect God. Reuben's presentation, which follows, gives real insight into the dynamic conflict occurring in the Jewish community of Clearwater at that time. It also provides information about the period from 1950-1953 in the Clearwater Jewish community. This unique presentation is quoted in its entirety because Reuben tried to hold together a small Jewish community that was fighting over whether to continue to be Conservative or to become Reform. He explains some of the basic similarities and differences between the two movements. He demonstrates his high level of education and reveals part of his philosophy of life.

"Mr. Chairman and members, Clearwater Jewry can be proud tonight with such a large gathering of old and new members. This shows good Jewish spirit and fine American citizenship. We came here tonight to decide a very important issue. Do we want to change the synagogue from conservative to reform? (In the minds of certain individuals including Darwin Frank, the synagogue was always meant to be reform. The congregational charter does not state whether the congregation will follow conservative or reform tradition.) There are quite a few new members here tonight, and we feel they should be informed of the progress of our Jewish community to date, and also get more information as to what conservative and reform stand for. The resolution on which we are to vote tonight calls for a change from "Conservative Traditional Services" to "Reform Traditional Services." There is more than just these words involved in this change. We're crossing dangerous intersections. The stop, look, and listen. Our conservative congregation is organized and chartered under the State of Florida. Our by-laws are not just a copy at random. Our by-law committee met many times to frame the by-laws to suit this community. Every article was carefully considered and discussed. After completion, they were read three times at special meetings, and every word was scrutinized. (Unfortunately, these by-laws have never been found and the record of the meetings held have not been found.) In the by-laws, we did not forget the ladies of our congregation. They are included in all important committees. The religious committee consists of three men and two women. A Sisterhood officer acts as a member of the Board of Directors. We do not believe in taxation without representation, as the ladies have done their share in raising money for the center. Our by-laws stand out as a living instrument. They are very democratic, to suit liberal Jews of 1953.

Solomon Schechter, one of the founders of Conservative Judaism, compared Orthodox Judaism to a road of fire, too hot to walk on comfortably. He compared Reform Judaism to a road of ice, being too cold. He felt the safest road would be a mid-point between fire and ice, without danger, which is Conservative Judaism.

Three years ago, a religious committee was appointed. This committee worked out a service modeled after a very modern conservative synagogue. The committee planned programs, held rehearsals in prayer songs, sent out notices for services, and put notices in the local press for Friday night services. Candles were blessed, prayers were read in English and Hebrew, the Congregation joined the cantor in singing parts of the service, which was followed by an Oneg Shabbat or social hour. Tea and goodies were served by the Sisterhood while Sabbath and Israeli songs were sung. Sometimes, we had outside speakers, and occasionally we had literacy papers read or discussions held. Our membership then was twenty eight, and the first year, we averaged forty people at our Friday night services. Tourists also attended and many of them praised our fine services. The second winter, services were held but the attendance was not as good. The past winter, the attendance at services was very poor most of the time. On a number of occasions, only three or five men appeared and no services were held. We had several exceptions during the winter when the Sisterhood conducted two Friday evenings, which attracted a nice crowd. A couple of Friday evening services were planned by one of our members, and the attendance was up to sixty five people. This goes to prove that when we try hard enough, and a program is planned, we succeed.

When a member has Yahrzeit and wants to say Kaddish, we assembled ten men or more, any day, to accommodate that member. In case of bereavement, when we are called to hold services, we are like a standing army, ready to comfort the bereaved. When a stranger comes to town, should he need financial aid, we are prepared to provide it through our community funds.

Rosh Hashanah and Yom Kippur services were held with an attendance of about seventy six. A young rabbinical student from the Jewish Theological Seminary officiated at our High Holy Day services for the past two years, and most of us were happy with these modern services, especially younger folk. We held Sukkoth, Pesach, and Shavuoth services, when our members can say Yizkor, prayers in remembrance of our departed loved ones. On Simchat Torah we have the usual Hakofet with our Sunday School children taking part in singing Hebrew songs. We celebrate Hanukkah and Purim with dinners and social gatherings where Kosher food is served, to please our own members and a number of tourists from the North, who contribute to our center liberally.

We conducted a modern Sunday School for three years, led by a trained teacher, without cost to the center. Six different Christian religious groups of Clearwater and vicinity, Sunday school pupils and teachers visited our Synagogue, where religious symbols and books were exhibited, and interpretation of Judaism and Jewish religious observance was given. This helps to cement brotherhood in our community.

In the past two years, we have raised $2,587 for the United Jewish Appeal. Our Sisterhood, which is affiliated with the National Woman's League of Conservative Sisterhoods, has helped build and furnish this center. Improvements to the synagogue in the past couple of years amounted to over $5,000 and our treasury is still in fine shape. In the last two years, our community has built up a Hadassah chapter that is a credit to Clearwater Jewry.

Without a permanent rabbi, and at times when the leadership of our community was not dynamic, we still managed to accomplish so much. Some of our members are not satisfied with our services. They are the same people that held offices and chairmanship of the religious committee in the last year or two. During these two years, no formal complaint was registered at any meeting as to the form of services, and in the past year, the officers seldom appeared at Friday night services.

Inspiration without work is worthless. Thomas Edison prescribed 2% inspiration and 98% perspiration. Just changing the name to Reform will not create or modernize a service, making it successful. Planning creative programs, willingness to work, and attendance will create success.

An election of officers was held recently where chiefly young members were elected as officers, with the intention to change to Reform. Immediately after election, a membership drive was held. Some members joined with the intention of retaining their membership only if it became Reform. I think every Jew should be a member of the Community Center, regardless of being Reform, Conservative, or Orthodox.(One

must recognize that the original Jewish organization in Clearwater was not only a synagogue, but also a Jewish community center. This is the reason for Reuben's last comment.) This is not only a place for prayers. It is also a place of learning, of cultural activity, and every Jew must have a place for social activity. In all, about twenty eight new members joined in the last month, some having a preference for Reform and others for Conservative. Clearwater has made a record, raising its membership 75% in a month, whereas in the last two years, we only gained about six members.

At our last regular meeting, where a change was recommended from Conservative to Reform, some members asked a postponement until the Fall when our full membership would be present. This was opposed. It was also suggested that we try to modernize our services by appointing a religious committee composed of modern young people, and give this a few months trial before deciding on a change. This too was opposed. After the meeting, our President was asked for an arbitration committee representing both view points to iron things out before bringing the matter to a vote, but this was not approved. I still plead with you all not to divide our community and make a Korean 38th parallel out of it. Let all our members work for unity under the leadership of a modern rabbi. If we stay united, we can afford to have a rabbi.

Nevertheless, before any vote takes place I should like to call attention to some of the differences between Conservative and Reform. The resolution we are asked to vote on tonight calls for change from "Conservative and in accordance with the principles of traditional Judaism" to "Reform in accordance with the principles of traditional Judaism." How can Reform be called Traditional? Reading in the Torah without wearing hats–is this traditional? Lighting and blowing out the candles by the rabbi at Friday night services–is this traditional Judaism? Smoking in the social hall on Friday night–is this traditional? Eating non-Kosher food in the synagogue – is this traditional? Collecting money during Friday night services – is this traditional? All these things are done in the Reform Temple in Tampa and other cities. How can Reform use a name or label that belongs strictly to Orthodox Jewry. In a large northern city, thirty one Orthodox synagogues have recently organized themselves as the Traditional Union of Orthodox Jews. The news about it is printed in this magazine.

Let us now see: Can we better ourselves by changing to reform? The Reform prayer book has about 25% Hebrew and 75% English. The conservative rabbis of the United Synagogue of America do not tell us how many prayers, or in what language we should pray. This is left to the discretion of each rabbi and his synagogue. There is no sin in changing the style of prayers. They have already been changed many times during the past 2,000 years. One of our great sages said, "Do not make your prayers appointed." "Al Ta-aseh T'filos'cho Kevah". This sage was very modern. He believed in evolution of time.

Reform Jews pray and read the Torah without hats, but do not object to anyone's wearing one at services. Conservative Jews wear hats at service. Reform Jews are allowed to ride in their cars on Sabbaths and holidays. Conservative rabbis are leaning in this direction now. Reform and Conservative alike permit the lighting of lights on the Sabbath. Reform allows non-Kosher food at home and in the temple. Conservative Jews are expected to maintain Kashrut in the synagogue as well as at home. Reform temples have organs, as do a few Conservative synagogues. Although Reform recommends fasting on Yom Kippur, it does not enforce it. Conservative Jews are not allowed to eat on this day. Reform observes the New Year(Rosh Hashanah) only one day; Conservative Jews observe two days for this holiday. Reform observes only the first and last days of Sukkoth and Pesach as full holidays. Conservative Jews observe as full holiday the first two and last two days of these holidays. Reform observes one day of Shavuoth, where as Conservative Jews observe two. Hanukkah and Purim are observed by both alike. Circumcision and name-giving ceremonies are observed by both alike. Confirmation for boys and girls is similar for both. Weddings are very

similar, although Reform is more lenient as regards intermarriage. Funeral rites of Reform and Conservative are very similar. Reform temples today hold Hebrew classes for children two or three times weekly in most temples. Conservative synagogues hold sessions four or five times weekly. Reform Jews count women as part of the Minyan, and call women to be honored in the reading of the Torah. This is done in a few Conservative synagogues also.

Dr. Mordechai M. Kaplan, on his 70th birthday, was honored at a dinner where over 400 rabbis and some prominent Jewish leaders endorsed his philosophy, two thirds of whom were reform rabbis. Dr. Kaplan is Professor of Jewish Religion at the Conservative Rabbinical Seminary in New York, for the past thirty five years. His new and modern philosophy of Conservative Judaism is being accepted by reform and conservative alike. If we look at some of the conservative rabbis in nearby Miami, Rabbi Lehrman of the Miami Beach Jewish Center with a membership of about 1,500 draws such large crowds in his large synagogues that one must come at seven o'clock to get in for the eight o'clock service. Rabbi Shapiro in Southwest Miami, with a membership of 1,000, is in constant demand for interfaith work. What we need is more information and less reformation. Upon comparison of Reform and Conservative Judaism, we can see that the difference is not great. Reform and Conservatism today are trying to meet, Reform going to the right and Conservatism to the left, so that in many instances, they have already met. The Conservative movement is very flexible. It can accommodate modern Judaism and liberal minds. A change in name, or a change in the by-laws, cannot change the philosophy of our loyal and devoted Jews. Spinoza once said, "You can arrest a body, you can not arrest a mind". It would be too much to expect to please everyone.

You must give our organization time to develop in its various capacities. We are expecting too much too quickly. Anything worthwhile must go through a period of trial and error. Everything worthwhile must grow slowly. Let us realize the fact that the interests that we have in common are far greater than the points of difference between us. Let us meet our differences with understanding, not with hatred. We all look toward the synagogue to help us live a fuller and more beautiful Jewish life. Let us consider what is best for the community, rather than for the individual. Let us not tear down the foundations that our elders built. Let us keep the old foundation and build a modern structure on it that will suit both the young and the old. No matter what the outcome of this vote will be tonight, let us work together and build. Let us have Shalom-peace. Without this, there is no religion. I thank you all. Reuben Rutenberg."

The first Seder at Temple B'nai Israel was held on Betty Lane. Clara Zitlin, wife of Isadore, cooked almost the entire meal. The Sisterhood was involved. There was a large crowd. The older men, led by Isadore, conducted the service, but it was a communal reading affair. All of the traditional songs were sung, matzo was hidden, etc.. It was a great success. Other seders were held at the Hotel Fort Harrison Roof Garden, the City Auditorium, and Kapok Tree Inn. The first Temple and Sisterhood bulletins were published in January by Shirley Collman, who was also the editor. She continued in this role through November, 1957.

The Sisterhood of Temple B'nai Israel not only worked hard to build a formal Jewish community, but also provided help to people who were non-Jewish. They worked with the blind and visually impaired. They were involved in various programs, including family education, social justice, equality of women, civil rights, aging and health care, food banks, etc.. The Sisterhood learned Braille from Evon Brower.

The Fort Harrison Hotel became the Jewish country club each Sunday when the Jewish people would gather together there. In the late 1950s, Jewish people made up one quarter of one percent of the population of Clearwater and most non-Jewish people in the community had never met a Jewish person before.

In 1953-1954, Julius Lovitz was President of Temple B'nai Israel. Julius and Leonard Collman flipped a coin and Julius lost. He then had to become the President. Leonard became the President in 1955-1956. Each of

the early founders had to assume the duty in order to keep the synagogue going. This same thing applied to the Sisterhood.

Jane and Arthur Rutenberg

Arthur came to the Clearwater area from Chicago in 1953. Jane came in 1974. Arthur, knowing nothing about construction of homes, needed a builder's license in a hurry. He found a book on carpentry in the public library, glanced through it, and passed the licensing examination. He first started building bungalows for $9,990 in the SkyCrest neighborhood. There was nothing fancy about these 1,000 square-foot, two-bedroom units. Fifty years later, Arthur Rutenberg had provided new homes for 40,000 to 50,000 families. He was one of the founders of US Homes, a national home building giant. He built homes for the upper-end of the market. Gary Catenac, a long-time Rutenberg franchisee in Pinellas County, said, "His (Arthur's) vision and creativity are like nothing I've ever been exposed to in the building industry. It's a great benefit to work with someone in the Builder's Hall of Fame." Much of the open, airy look of Florida homes come from Rutenberg's designs. If he didn't design it, he certainly made it popular. Arthur's brother, Dan, came up with the split bedroom plan in order to give more privacy to the adults. Arthur tried to limit or eliminate hallways to get the most space out of 1,600 square-foot houses. The kitchen, located in the middle of the house, was another Rutenberg staple. Arthur also pushed hard for an open and airy look.

Arthur was born on June 12, 1927 in Chicago. He earned a Bachelor of Science Degree in Chemical Engineering from Northwestern University in 1948. This was quite remarkable, since very few Jewish people earned degrees in the engineering field at that time. He changed his vocation for the future from the oil industry to construction, when his older brother, Charlie, and father, Reuben, bought eight building lots for the family, in a development called Skycrest in Clearwater. He learned the construction business as he went along. Arthur said, "I knew nothing about how to build a house-nothing." After

Arthur Rutenberg

Leonard Colllman, President of Temple B'nai Israel, 1955–1956

Julius Lovitz, President of Temple B'nai Israel, 1953–1954

his first fifty house sales, he placed an ad in the newspaper addressed to "Mr. and Mrs. Clearwater" begging their forgiveness for temporarily freezing orders. Arthur named his business, Rutenberg Homes Incorporated, while Charlie named his construction business, Imperial Homes Incorporated. Each brother had a stake in the other's company. They branched out to St. Petersburg, Sarasota, Naples, West Palm Beach and the rest of the country. In 1969, Charlie and Arthur merged their two companies with a smaller New Jersey company called US Homes. The Rutenbergs owned 64% of the combined company. Arthur became the President and went on a buying spree, acquiring homebuilders around the country. Nineteen months later, Arthur left US Homes, with Charlie staying on as President. In 1980, Arthur founded Arthur Rutenberg Homes. In 1986, Arthur Rutenberg was named National Builder of the Year. He had now developed a full-fledged franchise system, including two in Florida and twenty eight franchises outside of Florida. Arthur Rutenberg's attention to detail and beauty in the homes have made the Rutenberg name synonymous with fine home-building. In 1996, Arthur was elected to the Florida Home Builders Association's Florida Housing Hall of Fame. He was described as, "an innovative homebuilder who designed revolutionary homes for contemporary lifestyles." Arthur was Past Chairman of Outward Bound. He is a Member of the Board of Trustees of Blossom Montessori School for the Deaf.

Jane Bondi Rutenberg was born on January 1, 1948 in Galesburg, Illinois. She attended the University of Arizona and then became a Real Estate Market Analyst. Jane is described by the St. Petersburg Times as "a civic activist who helped organize the Clearwater area's (Family Service Centers) annual Festival of Trees and was an early contributor and fund-raiser for Ruth Eckerd Hall at the Richard B. Baumgardner Center for the Performing Arts." Jane was on the founding Board of Leading Ladies and Co-Chair PACT for All Auction committee.

Jane Bondi Rutenberg is like her great grandfather, August Bondi, who was born on July 21, 1833, in Vienna, Austria.

He believed strongly in what was right and what was wrong. In Austria, in an academic school, at age 14, he was one of 500 students who walked out of school in protest when a teacher slapped one of the students. He encountered and joined people who fought against absolutism, monarchy, and feudalism. In 1848, he and his family fled Austria to escape the Austrian counterrevolution. They went to New Orleans and then on to St. Louis. It was in St. Louis when the Bondi family became part of the Jewish history of Pinellas County. Reverend Isaac Leeser was the house guest of the Bondi family for the winter, when he came to St. Louis in the 1850s to write about the Jewish people of this city. August continued his work toward the freedom of others when he joined John Brown and the abolitionist movement. He later served for thirty seven months in the Union Army. He became a postmaster and then graduated from law school in Kansas. He said about himself, "Even as a child, I decided to dedicate my life to the ideals of progress and freedom. I never deviated from this decision during the course of my long life, a life rich in stormy events. I've remained faithful to the principles I swore to uphold during the stormy days of the 1848 revolution." This was written between 1903 and 1905. Jane said about her ancestor, "I feel lucky to be a descendent of August Bondi. He was a man who was willing to put his life on the line for what he believed in, which always gave our family great pride."

Also, another postmaster came out of St. Louis. He was our first Jewish person in Pinellas County, Edward A. Blum, who was in St. Louis during the time of the Bondi family, and because of the smallness of the Jewish community, must have known them and August.

Rutenberg Children

Arthur and his first wife, Billy, had three children, Barry, Sharon, and Jan. Billy was a nurse. She was very active in Temple B'nai Israel Sisterhood. Arthur and Jane had two children, Julie and Steven.

Barry Rutenberg was born September 6, 1948. He earned a Bachelor of Science Degree from Northwestern University in 1970, and a Master of Business Administration Degree from Harvard University in 1972. He is a homebuilder. He is married to Kirsten Voetmann Rutenberg and they have two children.

Sharon Rutenberg Rosenberg was born on May 23, 1951. She earned a Bachelor of Arts Degree from Northwestern University in 1973, and a Master of Arts Degree in Journalism from Northwestern University in 1975. Before leaving her work to raise her family, she was an award-winning writer for United Press International. She's married to Dr. Michael Rosenberg and has four children.

Jan Rutenberg Morse was born on March 30, 1957. She earned a Bachelor of Science Degree from the University of Denver in 1980. She has two children.

Julie Rutenberg was born on January 28, 1977. She is Director of the Blossom Montessori School for the Deaf. Julie graduated from St. Petersburg Junior College in 1997 with an Associate of Arts Degree in Public Administration. In 2000, she earned an Associate of Science Degree in Sign Language Interpretation from St. Petersburg Junior College and then graduated Cum Laude with a Bachelor of Arts Degree in Educational Interpreting for the Deaf from the University of South Florida. In 2003, Julie founded Blossom Montessori School for the Deaf. After seven years of working with deaf children and their families at the former Friends of Deaf Service Center, she saw a different way to educate deaf children and their families. She brings extensive knowledge of the individual needs and uniqueness of each child and their families to her position. In addition to being the Director of the school, she is a Girl Scout leader and a member of the American Montessori society. Her mother, Jane, is also on the Board of Trustees.

Steven Rutenberg was born on January 21, 1980. He earned a Bachelor of Science Degree in Business from George Mason University in 2002. He is a Florida real estate broker.

Sisterhood News Bulletin

In January, Shirley Collman published the first Sisterhood News Bulletin. Some of the highlights of the bulletin included:

announcement of an ice cream social; the great job being done with the Sunday School children by Mrs. Rutenberg and her assistant, Ms. Francine Glazier; and news of people visiting from out of town. In February, the highlights included: announcement of a card party; announcement of Friday night services; the Sisterhood became the sponsors of the Skycrest Brownie Troop, with Mary Rutenberg acting as liaison officer; discussion of Rabbi David Zielonka, the good friend of the congregation, being heard on a radio program; the Purim play and dance; and various announcements about people visiting from out of town. In bulletin number three, September, the highlights were: Julius Lovitz, President, obtained and had installed a one ton air conditioner. Rabbi Benjamin Hoffsayer of New York was flying in to conduct the High Holy Days services; and there was a lot of chatty information about the comings and goings of the members of the Temple.

People mentioned in the bulletins were: Mrs. E. Joseph, Mrs. J. Janelli, Mrs. Theresa Greenwald, Mrs. Matthews, Mrs. Hartman, Mrs. S. Good, Mrs. Anna and Arthur Gladstone, Mrs. C. Gersch, Mrs. D. Frank, Mrs. Y. Eisenstein, Mrs. Estelle Korones, Mrs. L. Frank, Rosalie and Marvin Byer, Fanny Marks, Roberta and Stuart Golding, Mrs. Ike Eisenstein, Howard Lawrence, Mrs. Dora Eisenstatt, Lou and Hazel Simon, Ethel Schoenfeld, Rebecca Nathanson (a snowbird from Canada), Mrs. Polakoff, Herbie and Renée Avren, Mrs. J. L. Lovitz, Mrs. Howard Lawrence, Mrs. Lou Simon, Mrs. J. Elman, Mrs. Phillip Carvel, Mrs. E. L. Kleinman, Mrs. Teresa Greenwald, Mrs. Charles Gersch, Mrs. Sam Good, Sophie Weiss, Mr. and Mrs. Arthur Collman, Anne and Arthur Gladstone, Rebecca Nathanson.

Highlights of 1954

In 1954 and 1955, Reuben Rutenberg was President of Temple B'nai Israel. Albert and Marion Zucker arrived in the Clearwater area.

Apparently, there was considerable dissension between the various groups in the Temple concerning whether the congregation was Conservative or Reform. The dissension carried over into a discussion of whether or not the kitchen should be kept kosher.

Shirley Collman, in the role of peacemaker, wrote in the bulletin in November the following, "Let's Have a Good Year! Let's forget petty grievances because remember that what we are working for –our Temple or Synagogue–is much more important. I, for one, will put no personal argument (and I mean NONE) before my Temple. If our people throughout the ages had not put first things first, where would we be today? I remember reading somewhere that "The man who never alters his opinion is like standing water, and breeds reptiles of the mind." Remember that when you think that someone else's attitude is wrong, they're probably thinking the same about you. I tell myself these things too. Don't go away–that was the end of the one and only lecture in this bulletin."

People mentioned in the bulletin were: Mrs. Blanche Nemeth, Yetta and Sam Eisenstein, Anne and Ike Eisenstein, Ann and Sam Sanders, Mr. and Mrs. Daniel Goldstein, Mr. and Mrs. Aaron Pepper, Mrs. Sadie Klein, Mrs. Anna Barney, Mr. and Mrs. Jacob Ellman. Rosita and Phillip Carvel moved to New Orleans, where Rosita taught dentistry at Loyola University. Rosalie and Marvin Byer left the area. Newcomers included Jack and Claire Dines, Herb and Cecil Schwartz, Mickey Kleinman (son of Eddie and Shirley), Mr. and Mrs. A. Roth, Leonard and Lee Nerenburg, and quite a few others whose names Shirley did not have.

In order to raise money and have fun, the Sisterhood put on two ice cream socials, a barbecue, and other events. The members of the Sisterhood did all the cooking.

B'nai Israel sponsored the religious school. Mrs. Essie Mae Circus (husband, Paul), who taught religious school at Temple Beth-El in St. Petersburg on Sunday mornings, came to the synagogue to teach the children from 2: 30 p.m. to 4:30 p.m. She was a very dedicated person, who also trained two of the mothers to help her. Essie May and Paul had a store in St. Petersburg, in 1954 called Eagle Crest Food Center. In 1955 they owned the Southern Distributing Company. There were twelve children in three different classes. The religious school committee was made up of Chairman

Paul Weissburger, Julius Lovitz, Leonard Collman, Estelle Korones, and Lila Lawrence.

Sisterhood prepared Thanksgiving baskets for needy families and gave them to the Salvation Army to distribute. This was one of several activities where the Sisterhood helped poor people in the community.

Mary Rutenberg set up the lending library. Salem Baranoff provided the funds to buy the books and the bookcases. Rabbi David Zielonka periodically conducted Friday night services.

Herbert Schwartz

Herbert and his family arrived on September 15, moving from the Chicago area at the request of his employers, Charlie and Arthur Rutenberg. In Chicago, the Rutenbergs owned three stores, a gift shop, appliance store, and furniture store. Herbert was the bookkeeper, credit manager, and helped on the sales floor when needed. In Clearwater, because Arthur was so successful in home sales, he became a building superintendent. When Herbert arrived in Clearwater, there was a population of about 20,000 people, one stoplight at Cleveland Street and Fort Harrison Avenue, and the first two lanes of U.S. Highway 19 were under construction. In the next couple years, the Clearwater area exploded population wise and Rutenberg Construction became the largest builder in the Clearwater area. Charlie then proceeded to shut down the Chicago operations and moved to town. Charlie became the expert land buyer and developer and Herbert became the expert builder.

Herbert and his family joined Temple B'nai Israel. The Temple membership was mainly composed of retired people and a few younger families. The services were conservative in nature. The High Holiday Services were conducted by a student rabbi. As new members joined, there was considerable talk about changing the congregation from conservative to reform. It had been voted down before, but when it came up for approval again, it passed. A significant number of mainly older couples resigned including some of the founders and formed a conservative synagogue,

Congregation Beth Shalom of Clearwater. As the membership grew, the Board of Trustees decided that they could afford a full-time Rabbi. Rabbi Richmond, a retired Rabbi, became the first Rabbi of Temple B'nai Israel. He was a very intelligent scholar with a soft voice and mild nature. He started a full Sunday school program, using every corner of the Temple for classrooms.

In 1957, Herbert decided to form his own building business. Charlie convinced him instead to invest in a land development project he and Arthur were doing called Chesterfield Heights. He became an equal partner and took over lot sales. Sales were so successful that they sold out in ninety days. They formed a new corporation named Chesterfield Homes Inc., a construction company run separately from Rutenberg Construction. The new corporation specialized in building retirement homes on the buyers lots. It took two years and the corporation was so successful that it was merged into the Rutenberg construction companies. Herbert took charge of the construction end of the business. In 1960, Herbert formed his own retirement building business called Schwartz Construction Inc.. Herb operated the business until 1986 and his son until 1995. His son closed the business down to pursue a career in education.

Herb was President of the Clearwater Civitan Club, chairperson of many committees for the Clearwater Lunchtime Kiwanis Club, Board Chairman for Clearwater for Youth, Board of Directors of the Long Center, home to the Upper Pinellas Association for Retarded Citizens, Clearwater Youth and Clearwater Recreation Department, and supervised the construction of the Joe DiMaggio Baseball Complex on Drew Street.

Highlights of 1955

The fifth bulletin and first B'nai Israel Congregation and Sisterhood Bulletin was issued on January 18, by Shirley Collman. Flyers were sent out on a weekly basis to remind people about Friday night services. On January 21, Mr. Jacoby read the Hebrew and Ed Kleinman read the English. There was a guest speaker. Isadore Zitlin was congratulated for doing an excellent job in keeping the Friday night services interesting and dignified. A hundred people attended the Hanukkah dinner which was catered by Mrs. Zitlin, Mrs. Roth, and Mrs. Sher. Newcomers to the community were Sherwin and Estelle Bentauil and Larry and Marion Friedlander. Sherwin owned a driving school. Larry and Marion owned Daniels Men's Store in Clearwater.

In February, the first Sisterhood gift shop was started. Shirley Kleinman became the President of the gift shop. She did a very fine job with very little money and very little space for merchandise. She and her husband, Eddie, were both retired. The first Sisterhood Sabbath was held in March. Isadore Zitlin, the lay religious leader, chanted the Kaddish. He conducted many of the religious services. In 1955-1956, the Sisterhood raised the money for heavy beige drapery fabric to cover the Temple bema and windows.

There were several heated and frustrating meetings at Temple B'nai Israel about becoming a Reform congregation. There was a serious division of opinion between those who wanted more ritual and Hebrew and those who wanted less ritual and more English in the services. This led to the congregation joining the Union of American Hebrew Congregations and a breaking away of a group of members who formed Congregation Beth Shalom. At the meeting where the vote was taken to become part of the Union of American Hebrew Congregations, Reuben Rutenberg walked to the back of the room and called several other members to join him, including Isadore Zitlin, Salem Baranoff, and David Shane. They decided to leave Temple B'nai Israel. (However Congregation Beth Shalom, the conservative synagogue, did not come into being until 1957.) Another problem was the kitchen. At the Sisterhood meetings, there was a heated discussion about keeping the kitchen kosher. However, although it was in the best interest of harmony among the members, the kosher kitchen was voted down. This led to a lot of animosity.

Shirley Collman wrote at the end of the January 18th bulletin, "In closing, let me just say that even though you have other outside interests and friends, don't divorce yourself from your Jewish community or you will only be paying alimony to Mr. Emptiness. And whether or not you like it, that Temple on Betty Lane is YOUR responsibility. (I said it and I am glad.)

> The world is a difficult world indeed,
> And the people are hard to suit,
> And the man who plays on the violin
> Is a bore to the man with a flute.
> And I myself have often thought-
> How very much better it would be
> If every one of the folks that I know
> Would only agree with me.
> But since they will not, the very best way
> To make the world look bright
> Is never to mind what others say,
> But to do what you think is right."

Reuben Rutenberg resigned from the Temple because of the dissension created by the mixed desires of the congregants. One group wanted to join the Reform movement and the group that Reuben belonged to wanted to continue the prayers in a more conservative manner. Reuben was given a vote of thanks for the conscientious job he did while he was in office. Even though there were differences of opinion, which was perfectly normal and healthy, he always performed the duties of his office in an exemplary manner. At a later date, Reuben, a founder of Congregation Beth Shalom of Clearwater, also rejoined Temple B'nai Israel.

Isadore Zitlin, first Vice-President, served out the remainder of Reuben Rutenberg's term as President of Temple B'nai Israel. Isadore had invented the coils that were used in radios. He and his wife lived off of the royalties paid to them by the automobile industry. He was a cantorial soloist, and performed for many years at Congregation Beth Shalom of Clearwater.

Isadore, on becoming President, said, "I am very thankful for the nice remarks that I have received publicly and I wish to express my thoughts in this open letter. As Chairman of the Religious Committee for the task that I have undertaken, and I am willing to continue with enthusiasm. The fine services and speakers we've had so far is shown by the splendid attendance at each

Friday night service. It seems to me that the religious committee has an important job to do, as well as a splendid opportunity to contribute materially to the progress of our Temple. I feel honored that my good friend, the former President of our Temple, appointed me chairman to participate in such worthwhile work and I shall do my best to justify my place as chairman. It is with great regret that you, Reuben, resigned from your post as President. It was your guidance and your practical advice that is responsible for the success of these services. To me, Reuben, you are a teacher and an advisor. I hope your good advice and friendly relationship will continue. I wish you and Mary also, who has been a great help to me, good health and happiness. I also want to thank my committee for their wonderful cooperation."

Shirley Collman wrote at the end of the January 26th bulletin, "And don't forget the reason for the weekly bulletin–please attend Friday night services. We would like to cordially invite all members, friends, and winter visitors to attend our weekly religious services. They begin promptly at 8:15 and are held in the B'nai Israel Temple on Betty Lane and Park Streets. This week, we have an all-star cast. Isadore Zitlin will read the Hebrew, Julius Lovitz will read the English, and Phyllis Lovitz will bless the Sabbath candles. We are very fortunate to have Ben Krentzman, local attorney, as a guest speaker.

Make an effort to attend!...because...a world without a Sabbath (regardless of faith) would be like an ocean without a tide, like a universe without light, or like a life without meaning. It is truly the most satisfying day of the week because without its stubborn observance throughout the years, where would the Jews be today."

Arthur Rutenberg was praised for being a really nice guy. As busy as he was, he gave up every Sunday afternoon to be a music teacher in the Sunday School and help the children learn Hebrew songs. In February, Isadore Zitlin inaugurated the first Saturday morning service. The service was to be conducted in a traditional manner especially for those individuals who were and Orthodox.

Shirley Collman quoted in the February 21st bulletin portions of a sermon by Rabbi Roland B. Gittelsohn. The title of the sermon was, "Who Needs Religion?" "When a Rabbi asks "Who needs religion?" You expect the answer to be as automatically affirmative as when an insurance agent inquires "Who needs life insurance?" However, more and more I am convinced that only a person who has achieved a certain level of insight and maturity needs religion, in the sense that only such a person can understand and accept true religion as distinct from wishful thinking or superstition. The first attribute of the person who needs religion is that he has learned to distinguish between the ends and the means of life.

The second quality of the person who needs religion is that he requires in his life a sense of over-all direction and purpose. He has to have a plan for his life. He must feel that he is a part of something bigger and more final than himself.

Third and finally, you need religion if, in addition to the preceding, you're looking for a sense of commitment in your life. People very often confuse philosophy and ethics on the one hand with religion on the other.

Who needs religion? The person who understands that man is not alone. That inherent in this universe is an ineffable Creative Power from which we derive our own more finite power. That from God alone can we get the right pitch within which to play life's melody in tune."

In April, at the end of Isadore Zitlin's term of office, Leonard Collman was elected President of Temple B'nai Israel. Leonard, upon taking office, tried to bring together the various Jewish groups in Clearwater. He said, "Your new administration and I realize the many responsibilities that face us for the coming year. We are determined to at least equal the fine records of our other past Presidents. To do this, we need to support incorporation of all of our members – which means we must all forget our personal grievances and petty differences so that we may work together to create harmony and understanding. Our group is a small organization. Each member is important! So-let's work together to create unity – always remember that our Temple comes first. There is room in this community for all Jewish organizations. It is actually no reason why individual groups can't work together harmoniously."

Clara Zitlin was congratulated for a wonderful seder dinner. She cooked for about one hundred people who attended this wonderful dinner and service. She was assisted by Ethel Schoenfeld, Gertrude Shane, and Rose Gersch. Rabbi Albert Michaels presented the seder service in a manner that reflected religious dignity, friendliness, and humor

Charles and Isadora Rutenberg

Charlie Rutenberg and his wife, Isadora, a school teacher, came to Clearwater in 1950 to visit his parents. They owned their first brand-new car, which they unfortunately wrecked on the way home. During the Christmas holidays and winter of 1951-1952, they flew back to visit Mary and Reuben again. There was a big land auction being held on a Saturday in Clearwater. Reuben said to Charlie, "We can go to the auction providing you do not buy any land and you do not let me buy any land, since we do not know what we are doing." By the end of the day, Reuben and Charlie had spent $45,000, on the purchase of nine residential lots and several pieces of commercial property on Gulf to Bay. Since the auction was open to everyone, no one questioned that they were Jewish and that they could not purchase the land. They resold some of the lots and went into the building business. Charlie built some 10,000 homes across the Tampa Bay area and some 125,000 homes nationwide. He developed scores of office buildings and shopping centers.

Charlie and Isa Rutenberg

Charlie and Arthur donated the land for the current synagogue structure on Belcher Road. Charlie originally donated four acres on Nursery Road, next to a shopping center for a temple. After thinking it over, he decided this was not a good location and therefore purchased an eight acre piece of land on the east side of Belcher Road, just south of Bellair. This road had just become a four lane highway. The land was in a beautiful setting with many trees and a large open area. He and Arthur donated the land to the congregation and the congregation returned the original lot to Charlie.

Rabbi Baseman said of Charlie Rutenberg, "He was a builder of homes. He was a builder of people. He was a builder of pioneers." Charlie could stare at miles of empty woods and see what the future would be for that area in the Tampa Bay community. He was a developer and a home builder. He had tremendous foresight, and even though others might think that he was not in the right place at the right time, he was correct, time and time again. He helped reshape the Pinellas County community by building large parts of it. One day, in the early days of the company, a man drove up to the Rutenberg's construction trailer, and told Arthur that, he, the visiting older gentleman, had 8,500 permits accounting for 4,500 acres and he wanted to sell them. Arthur talked to his brother, Charlie. Charlie Rutenberg saw the great potential and that's how Countryside Mall and its associated subdivisions came to be. Arthur Rutenberg said of his brother, "Charlie was probably one in a handful of people that could see a piece of land and know what it was right for." He had the same rare ability to see what the needs were for many community organizations and to help shape the community's response to the need. He developed organizations and he developed people that would serve all segments of life. His businesses alone provided a huge economic boost to Pinellas County. His philanthropy provided another huge economic boost to the community. And finally his personal time, that he gave willingly, where his knowledge, experience and drive would make a difference, was the third part of the triangle that helped Pinellas County become what it is today. Although, Charlie faced physical difficulties in later life, he handled adversity with courage and dignity. Charlie never dwelled on his achievements. Charlie never sought recognition. Daniel Rutenberg said of his brother, Charlie, "He never looked through the rearview mirror." Family members said that in his final days, he was still thinking about his next project.

Charlie Rutenberg was one of the early supporters of Ruth Eckerd Hall at the Richard B. Baumgardner Center for the Performing Arts. He became involved in the planning of this future magnificent structure. He agreed to serve as Vice President of Design and Construction, which meant neither to design or to build the building, but to coordinate the entire project to make it one the finest facilities of the performing arts in the world. Charlie and Isa were both cellists. Charlie knew that many performing arts centers around the country look good but did not have the acoustics to match the architecture. He was able to convince the Board to hire the Frank Lloyd Wright Foundation to design Ruth Eckerd Hall at the Richard B. Baumgardner Center for the Performing Arts. This magnificent facility, as well as PACT Incorporated, have been the recipients of the generosity of Charlie and Isa. Even during business down turns, this couple were there to help out. In an obituary in the 2004 Fall Applause, the newsletter of Ruth Eckerd Hall at the Richard B. Baumgardner Center for the Performing Arts, the final paragraph reads, "Ruth Eckerd Hall at the Richard B. Baumgardner Center for the Performing Arts is one of the performing arts jewels in the nation, because of Rutenberg's diligence. His attention to the details and pursuit of acoustic excellence left a legacy that will be enjoyed by thousands of Ruth Eckerd Hall at the Richard B. Baumgardner Center for the Performing Arts visitors for generations to come."

Charlie was one of the founders of the Golda Meir/Kent Jewish Community Center. Because of him and Reva and Marshall Kent, every day for the past twenty five years and into the future for many decades to come, tens of thousands of people of all ages have been and will continue to experience an enhancement of cultural and recreational activities that make a profound difference in their individual life and in their community life.

Charlie was also one of the founders of the Jewish Federation of Pinellas County and the Tampa-Orlando-Pinellas Jewish Foundation. Charlie and Isa were also benefactors of the Clearwater Hospital Development Board, Morton Plant

Hospital, the University of South Florida, the Performing Arts Center and Theater, and Menorah Manor. He also wrote checks for countless other charities in the general community. Charlie and Isa donated a Steinway grand piano to Ruth Eckerd Hall at the Richard B. Baumgardner Center for the Performing Arts in honor of his mother, Mary. He combined his charitable gifts with his vision and ability to inspire others to initiate, nurture, and sustain so many lasting institutions in the community. Reva and Marshall Kent once again were Charlie's partners in all this work.

Charlie Rutenberg was Vice-President for Long-Range Planning of Temple B'nai Israel, as well as the author of a massive planning manual. Charlie Rutenberg has made enormous contributions, both financially and in dedicated hard work, not only to the Jewish community of Pinellas County, but also to the general community. A few of his major accomplishments include: President of the Clearwater Symphony, which became the Florida Symphony Orchestra; Board Member and Financial Vice President of Morton Plant Hospital; President of Large Contributions and Vice President in Charge of Designing Construction for Ruth Eckerd Hall at the Richard B. Baumgardner Center for the Performing Arts Center. He spent countless time, money, and effort in building the facility and the whole concept of a world-class performing arts center. He and his wife, Isa, built the new board room for Morton Plant Hospital, and furnished it.

Charlie served on numerous other boards including: Chairman of the Board and Chief Executive Officer, Republic Bank; Chairman of the Board, Life Savings and Loan; Board of Governors, American Friends of Haifa University; Board of Governors and Treasurer, Hebrew Union College; Charles and Isa Rutenberg Family Foundation; Board of Directors and Chairman of Pooled Income Fund; Vice President, Council of Jewish Federations; Board of Directors, Florida Orchestra; Chairman, Golda Meir Endowment Corporation; Board of Directors and Vice President of PACT; Board of Governors, Menorah Manor; Regional Cabinet, United Jewish Appeal; Board of Directors and President, Jewish Federation of Pinellas County; Board of Directors, Morton Plant Hospital; Chairman, Performing Arts Center; President's Council, University of South Florida.

Charlie received the Mister Clearwater Award from the Clearwater Chamber of Commerce, the Businessman-Citizen of the Year Award from the Harvard Business School Club of Florida West. He was inducted into the Tampa Bay Business Hall of Fame and won the Humanitarian Award from the Golda Meir/Kent Jewish Center.

Charlie continued the teaching of Mary and Reuben Rutenberg when he became the mentor of so many successful people. Charlie taught these people, "Charlie's boys," to be menshes (good people), to give generously. Craig Sher said, "Charlie spent about 50-60% of his time on philanthropy and taught me the importance of giving back." The Strudler family wrote, "Thank you: for your contributions to our community; for your leadership and inspiration; and most of all for our friendship." Pete Monroe of the Paradise Development Group said, "...this tribute to Charlie Rutenberg, as mentor and friend to so many of us in the Pinellas community; as philanthropist, art collector, risk taker, legendary and innovative homebuilder, premier commercial developer, fine family man, and shining example to us all. Charlie, we miss you, but we will endeavor to carry forward the ideas and principles that made you great." And finally, Alan Bomstein said, "I learned so much from Charlie–and none of it was about building! It was about life. Charlie was quite the philosopher, and he never hesitated to share his thoughts with me. He was humorous, gregarious, opinionated, and totally lovable. He understood and taught about giving philanthropy more than anyone I knew. It was Charlie who taught me: "You don't give till it hurts-you give till it feels good." And I still use that line today – it is so true. Charlie also taught me never to begrudge an employee that leaves to move on to other opportunities. Instead, take pride in him, and when he is successful, know that you've played a part in bringing him to a level he achieved. Scores of "Charlie Alumni" inhabit this community, and he took pride in every one of them. He was the consummate mensch (good person)."

At the commemorative dinner honoring the life of Charles Rutenberg on September 28, 2005, there was an incredible amount of love directed at this human being, who had wisdom, humor, integrity, brilliance, and who was as Mary and Reuben's son, a living example of the goodness that they expected from all their children and the type of lives they should live. The Jewish Federation of Pinellas County said, "Charlie set our community on the path to greatness. He was a man whose actions spoke louder than his words, reminding us that Tzedakah is one of the greatest pillars of our faith and that we have a responsibility to support each other in times of need." The people of Old Harbor Bank said, "Old Harbor Bank is proud to honor the life of our friend, Charlie Rutenberg. We admire his accomplishments, his generosity, and most of all, his love for this community. He leaves behind a powerful legacy that will remain an inspiration to our community for many years to come." Liz and Greg Sembler said,, "In memory of Charles Rutenberg, a leader, a teacher, and a friend. May his legacy as a builder of community service be an inspiration to us all." Jane and David Korones said, "Thank you, Charlie, for all the sweet music you made." The Howard Lawrence Family said, "In memory of Charles Rutenberg whose vision could move people as well as mountains-We celebrate his life." Gus and Frances Stavros said, "We will always remember Charlie Rutenberg's outstanding efforts in the construction and support of Ruth Eckerd Hall at the Richard B. Baumgardner Center for the Performing Arts for the benefit of the total Clearwater area." José and Linda Prieto said, "You made a difference to every person you touched, young and old, near and far. May your memory live forever." Ambassador Mel Sembler said, "Charlie set the bar for all of us because he was an outstanding businessman, an outstanding philanthropist, and he always gave back to his community and country." Charlie said, "Difficult matters we take care of right away...The impossible will take longer." Rabbi Arthur Baseman said, "Being a Jew for Charlie was not a role he played, but a life. He put ideas to work...What I learned from

Charlie...was not how to begin, but how to begin again, and again." And finally from the Torah, "He who executes charity and justice is regarded as though he has filled the entire world with kindness."

Charlie Rutenberg was born in Chicago in 1924. Charlie served in the Army in World War II . In 1947, Charlie graduated from the University of Chicago with a Bachelor of Science Degrees in Economics and Political Science. He married his high school sweetheart, Isadora (Isa), about this time.

Charlie died on September 10, 2004. On his tombstone is the phrase, "His eyes undiminished, his vigor unabated." How true a statement this is. Charlie's children and "Charlie's boys" carry on his legacy of good deeds. They too are visionaries.

Isa's parents were Fred and Fanny Kesselman. They came from Russia between 1913 and 1915. Isa was a elementary school teacher in Chicago. Isa was happy to come to the Clearwater area because it was clean, a good place to raise a family, and had a beautiful beach. Isa and Charlie had four children, Alan, Laurie, Marc, and Pamela. Alan was born in 1952. He attended Brown University and earned a law degree from the University of Chicago. He married Anne Marie. Laurie was born in 1954. She was ordained a Rabbi on May 31, 1981, from the Hebrew Union College-Jewish Institute of Religion. She is married to Gary Schoenberg. Marc was born in 1955. He attended college in Berkeley. Pamela was born in 1956. She graduated from Brown University. She purchased the land for the Chabad in Clearwater. She's married to Theodore Tench and they reside in Israel with their seven children.

Highlights of 1956

There was a large influx of Jewish families in 1956-1957. New industries came to the Pinellas County area. Aerosonic made altimeters for airplanes. Hercules, which was north of Drew Street on the west side, came at that time. Three Jewish families came with them. Bee Bee Togs, a children's clothing factory, came to Tarpon Springs and three Jewish families came with them. In 1957-1958, Minneapolis Honeywell opened a factory on U.S. 19 and Ulmerton.

Several Jewish engineers came with them. Some of the Jewish people that came during this time periods were Herb and Miriam Frank,(Miriam lives in Dunedin), Ben Mayer, Irving Schwartz, Harold and Pearl Lopatin, Arthur and Anna Lopatin, Irving and Martha Baker, Flora Harwood Morganstern, Lee Spiegel Harwood, Al and Marion Zucker. Reva and Marshall Kent and the four boys arrived in February 1956. They were family number thirty five at Temple B'nai Israel. They came because of Charlie Rutenberg.

Every Jewish person typically knew all the other Jewish people within the community. When it came to happy occasions, such as weddings, bar mitzvahs, parties, and other special events, all of the Jewish people in the community were invited. This was the major mode of socialization within the community. All of the women belonged to the Sisterhood. The Sisterhood had a fundraiser once a month. There was a party at the temple which netted $1,500.

It was a matter of pride to be selected to put on the Oneg Shabbats on Friday evenings after services. The women would do the dishes after the Onegs. The women wore their fanciest dresses with crinolines under them on Friday evenings. They wore white gloves to the Temple. On Saturday nights, the congregation broke into smaller groups and went to different homes for parties. They went to the: Pelican Restaurant on Clearwater Beach; the Beachcomber Restaurant on Clearwater Beach; the Kapok Tree Restaurant in Clearwater; the Garden Seat owned by the Siple family, in Clearwater across from the Morton Plant Hospital; and, the Fort Harrison Hotel, Crystal Ballroom in Clearwater for special events such as the United Jewish Appeal dinner and fund raiser. There were two movie theaters in Clearwater. The Caribbean Theater, which opened on Cleveland Street in 1956, and the Capital Theater. On Saturday evenings after the movies, everyone would go to Wolfie's Deli in St. Petersburg at US 19 and Central Ave.. This was a great place to socialize with friends from Clearwater as well as the Jewish people of St. Petersburg.

On March 8, Rabbi Joseph Asher of Temple Beth Shalom of Sarasota dedicated a new Torah at Temple B'nai Israel. Rabbi Asher was well-known in international religious affairs. He was educated in London, England, and attended graduate schools of several American colleges, including Hebrew Union College in Cincinnati. During the Second World War, he served in the Australian Army, and later was an advisor on Jewish affairs to the British command in West Germany. Estelle Korones chaired the event and Mrs. Nat Roth and her committee assisted.

Harold and Pearl Lopatin

Harold and Pearl Lopatin, with their sons Jeffrey, age fourteen, and Billy, age ten, drove into Clearwater May 7. They came from Brooklyn, New York, and arrived in this small town where there still was angle parking on Cleveland Street, the main business thoroughfare.He saw Frank's Department Store, parked the car, and went in to meet, hopefully, a fellow Jew. He asked a clerk if he could speak to Mr. Frank. A gentleman with a jovial smile on his face took them by the hand and said to him, "I'm so glad to see you." Mr. Frank invited Harold to come into a room in the back of the store where a board meeting of the synagogue was being held. Attending the meeting were Morris Bilgore, Sam Korones, Julius Lovitz, and maybe Reuben Rutenberg, all local businessmen. They were being addressed by Rabbi Harry Richmond, an elderly gentleman, quite jovial, quite knowledgeable, and very interesting. Harold and his family were welcome to Friday night services and they attended, and, in fact, for the next twenty to twenty five years, Harold and Pearl missed a total of possibly five or six services.

The family found a brand new house and rented it at once.They planned to establish Bee Bee Togs in Tarpon Springs. The original Bee Bee Togs was opened in 1953, in Brooklyn. The owners and operators of the factory were Harold Lopatin, his brother, Arthur, and Irving Baker. Harold arrived first and set up the Florida corporation and then later, Arthur and Irving joined him in Tarpon Springs. Their wives and children also came with them. Arthur, his wife, Anne, and their children, Wendy, age fourteen, and Felice, age seven, arrived in early July. Irving, his wife, Martha, and their children, Laura, age ten, and, Bonnie, age six, arrived a week later. Everyone became immediately involved in the Jewish community and with the synagogue.

The Lopatins always looked forward to Friday night to meet friends, family, and neighbors and share the joy of being together on the Sabbath. Harold had been raised in an Orthodox family and had never attended a Reform service before the one in early May. Jeffrey had been bar mitzvah in New York in an Orthodox synagogue. When Harold first opened the Reform prayer book, he said that he was stunned because all of the prayers that he was accustomed to were within the prayer book, but he was now able to understand the meaning of the prayers because of the English translations. The Hebrew was beautiful as always, but it was now more meaningful to him personally. He said, "I started to realize the depth and real meaning of Judaism. The prayers are in a language I can understand and relate to. My wife and children felt the same way."

Pearl threw a surprise 53rd birthday party for her husband, Harold. This was an unusual number. Apparently, Harold's father, and/or grandfather never lived beyond that age, and that's why she wanted to celebrate the occasion. Harold was dressed in a brown suit and vest and a beautiful lavender and brown tie. He looked like someone out of a smart men's magazine.

Irving died on June 1, 1997 at age 82. He was the retired President of Bee Bee Togs of Tarpon Springs and L. Baker Sales of Largo. He was a veteran of World War II, serving in the Army Air Corps. He was a founding board member of Ellis Bank. He was a member of the Clearwater Lions Club, Touchdown Club, Jewish Veterans of Foreign Wars, and Religious Community Services.

Marion and Marvin Bauman

Marion and Marvin Bauman came to Clearwater in February. They opened a ladies ready to wear shop on Fort Harrison and then later moved to Cleveland St. Their daughter Anita later married Karl Rosenfeld in 1963. Karl was born on November 30, 1936 and Anita was born on February 13, 1942. Marvin's brother also owned a shop.

The members of the Board of Trustees in 1956-1957 were: H. Lawrence, I. Zitlin, C. Collman, N. Roth, J. Coggan, L. Greenwald, S. Korones, Dr. Baranoff, H. Fink, L. Collman, M. Bilgore, D. Frank, J. Lovitz, A Rutenberg, A. Jacoby replaced Dr. Gladstone and L. Lawrence.

Rabbi Harry R. and Helena Richmond

Rabbi Harry R Richmond assumed the pulpit of Temple B'nai Israel, in April. Rabbi Richmond was born in Russia on September 1, 1890 and died in Brooklyn, on August 26, 1976. He came to the United States alone in 1907. He had spent much of his early life in London, England and Canada before arriving in Detroit, where Rabbi Leo Franklin would influence him to enter Hebrew Union College. He first attended The University of Chicago. He received a Bachelor of Arts Degree from the University of Cincinnati and in 1917, he graduated from Hebrew Union College and was ordained. He had earned the Oscar Berman award for scholarship. He had great literary skill. While still a student at Hebrew Union College, he was the assistant editor of the College monthly and was contributing full-length articles to "The American Jewish Israelite" and other publications. In his senior year at the Hebrew Union College, as a committed pacifist, he was the only member of the student body to refuse to sign a telegram to be sent to President Woodrow Wilson in support of the Allied cause against the Axis powers. However, several months later, he resigned his pulpit in Colorado, waved his exemption as a minister, and volunteered as a new recruit with the 34th Division at Camp Cody, New Mexico. This dramatic reversal was motivated by two factors. President Wilson had portrayed the dream and destiny of the United States as a Redeemer Nation, which was fighting the Lord's battle for the preservation of democracy and a war to end all wars. He became an extreme patriot.

Rabbi Richmond said, "(President Wilson) commanded my allegiance, my life and loyalty." He not only served in World War I, but also World War II. Rabbi William

Kloner, a United States Navy Reserve Chaplain, said at the funeral service held at the Army Base in Fort Hamilton in Brooklyn, "Harry R. Richmond exemplified in his lifetime a unique dedication to his faith and to his adopted country. Idealistic and humanitarian, his passion was reserved for the pursuit of peace and justice, his idealism channeled into the service of his country and faith. He was the only Jewish Army chaplain to serve on foreign battlefields in World Wars I and II." In both wars, he was exposed to contagious diseases and battlefield fire, in the hospitals and on the fields of France in World War I, and later at Pearl Harbor on December 7, 1941. After being called back to service, as a reserve chaplain, he was stationed in Hawaii. During this terrible day and despite fire and terror, he reached Fort Shafter to attend to the needs of the wounded and dying arriving during the general confusion. Along with the chaplains of the other religions, he conducted the first mass funeral for the men and women of the Armed Forces who died on that fateful day. Rabbi Richmond was convinced that rabbis must minister to the Jewish personnel away from their homes and community

In 1930, Rabbi Richmond came to a young congregation, Temple Emanuel of Wichita, Kansas. He became their first full-time rabbi and remained as its spiritual leader, except for his service during World War II, until 1955, when he was elected Rabbi Emeritus. In 1947, he was awarded a lifetime contract. After he retired, Temple Emanuel in appreciation and love for their rabbi, built the Rabbi Harry R. Richmond Memorial Library and Lounge. He was not only the spiritual leader of the synagogue, but also served the greater community. Under his direction, a beautiful new structure was built. His work with his fellow Christian ministers and priests resulted in the Roundtable for the National Conference of Christians and Jews. He worked hard to help defeat Gerald K. Winrod, an avowed Nazi sympathizer, who was running for the United States Senate. His interfaith work won him the "Brotherhood Award," given posthumously on March 13, 1977, presented by the Kansas Region, of the National Conference of Christians and Jews.

The citation in part read, "Exemplifying in his life the highest standard of citizenship and brotherhood." It was accepted by his widow, Helena, who had been his friend and helper since she met him in Brooklyn and married him on June 15, 1936.

Rabbi Richmond was retired when Temple B'nai Israel hired him. He had a long and distinguished career, had written extensively, and completed his book, "God on Trial." in 1955. Lloyd S. Cressman, President, Friends University, Wichita, Kansas, wrote about Rabbi Richmond's book, "Any serious-minded reader of these sermons will discover that they are from the pen of a serious-minded author, a man who lives thoughtfully, and who seeks to know the will of God for our generation. He speaks with "concern." His prophetic heart is always sensitive to the tensions and anxieties of distraught people, and it is large enough so that no one of us is excluded. Rabbi Richmond's spirit is ecumenical."

Of the forty two sermons in *God on Trial*, "Applied Religion" is of great significance. Rabbi Richmond said in the sermon, "The period of courtship is the finest prelude to matrimony. It is a period of romance, enchantment, and ecstasy. It is a period when friendship flowers into romance, when romance blossoms into love. Courtship is desirable most, however, in its practical aspect: courtship offers the girl, love and enthralled, a chance to see and observe how the man she is to marry lives and has his being. Life has its strain and stress, situations and circumstances most trying and troubling. Life has periods when love is cruelly tested. Love then is not courtship alone; but love lived, love applied, love practiced.

Even so is religion. There is a period in the life of the individual, when first exposed to religion, it takes on the contour of courtship, and is edged with pageantry, beauty, and enchantment. It is a time when religion is romantic, magical, mysterious. But religion does not end there. All of that and more is but the prelude to religion. Religion is best evaluated not in theory but in practice; not in piety but in action; not in the ceremony but in deed. Religion is what you do with your life; what you do with the

Rabbi Harry Richmond

life of your neighbors; what you do with the living, throbbing, pulsating world about you. So viewed, religion is not the letter of the law; it is the spirit of the law, as applied to life, or if you will, applied to human relationships....

Can we love God and hate man? Can we love God and practice iniquity? Can we love God and live a lie? The man who loves his mother will do nothing to disgrace or dishonor her; he would do everything possible to bring her grace and dignity. Yet the same man may profess love of God and commit every crime on record; a record that dishonors his Father in Heaven.

Responsible for this incongruity in religion is the disparity between profession and practice. Religion is still, to too many, alas! A conventional form, a traditional habit, a routine performance. It is still possible for the same people to assume religious leadership in a group, and to lead in a race riot...

If religion is to have meaning in our day; if society is to be saved by the persuasives, disciplines, and sanctions of religion, there must be no disharmony, no double standard, between religion and life. In the oneness of religion and life is the significance of applied religion. There is but one totalitarianism that I accept: the totalitarianism of religion. It is not a totality that is limiting, crippling, enslaving man. It is rather a totality that ennobles, enriches, enhances human life. It is a totality that sanctifies everything it touches in human experience: the economic, the social, the educational. It is the totality that the Greek envisaged in the triad: the true, the good and beautiful; and the Jew, in the words: "Ye shall be perfect with the Lord your God."

Rabbi Richmond was an avid reader and his favorite hobby was reviewing books. He started this hobby in 1927, because he felt that he could share interesting thoughts hidden within the books and it would be enjoyable for him to do so. He read and reviewed works of nonfiction, especially in the fields of philosophy, psychology, religion, and sociology. He also read and occasionally reviewed fiction works he considered to be outstanding. One of his favorite authors was Bertrand Russell, because his thinking was

so liberal. His favorite fiction writer was Ernest Hemingway. He greatly admired the *Old Man and the Sea*. His book reviews were used to benefit charities such as the Upper Pinellas Girl Scout Camp. During the winter of 1957, he gave seven book reviews for the Clearwater Junior Women's Club. One of the reviews was on *The Three Worlds of Albert Schweitzer* by Robert Payne. Rabbi Richmond chose this book because Dr. Schweitzer was a man of international reputation, a fine Christian and because his doctrine of Holiness had captured the imagination of the most liberal people in the world. Rabbi Richmond had a personal library of many thousands of books which were kept in his home on Keane Road in Largo. In addition, he traveled extensively to Central and South America, most of the European countries and the Orient. When asked what part of the world he liked best he replied, "I love Clearwater, but am at home everywhere. People are the same the world over – they had the same aspirations, defeats and disappointments no matter where they live."

Temple B'nai Israel hired a retired rabbi because the salary required of the younger ones was more than they could afford. Every afternoon, Rabbi Richmond would take a nap on the kitchen table in the synagogue. His study consisted of a card table and a bookcase in the right corner next to the stage. One time, when the Collmans took him to swim at the Fort Harrison hotel swim club, he went to get dressed in the dressing room, but someone had stolen his shirt. On the way back to his temporary hotel, he squatted down in the back seat of the car so no one would see him. His family moved to Clearwater later. The Richmonds had a daughter, Yonah Cheritz, who was a ballerina.

Rabbi Richmond was ultra reform and would not do Bat or Bar Mitzvahs. He believed in confirmations so the child would be kept in the Sunday school to an older age. He would not wear a head covering of any kind. Rabbi Richmond had a tendency to give long sermons. When Herb Frank was the President in 1958-1960, he tried in a diplomatic way to shorten the sermons. Nothing worked! One Friday, Herb installed a large clock on the back wall that would be visible to the Rabbi as they stood on the

Bema. That did not work either. Helena was very active in Sisterhood.

Daniel and Joan Rutenberg

Dan and Joan came to Clearwater. Dan went into the building business with Arthur. Dan invented the four-bedroom version of the split bedroom plan with the master bedroom on the one side of the house and the remaining bedrooms on the other side of the house. This house and the swimming pool were all located on a seventy five foot lot.

Dan was born on September 1, 1929 in Chicago. He earned a Bachelor of Arts Degree in Liberal Arts in 1947, from the University of Chicago. From 1951-1953, he served in the United States Army as an information specialist in Germany. From 1956-1960, he was Vice President of the Rutenberg Construction Company. In 1960, Dan decided to pursue a career in academia. In 1962, Dan earned a Master of Arts Degree in English from the University of Chicago. From 1962-1963, he was Instructor of English at Odessa College in Odessa, Texas and from 1963-1964, he was Instructor of Logic at St. Petersburg Junior College. He joined the faculty of the University of South Florida as an Instructor of Humanities and rose over the years to Chairperson, Humanities, Acting Dean, College Arts and Letters, Professor, Humanities and finally in 1996, Professor Emeritus, Humanities.

In 1962, he took additional education at Texas Technological University in Transcendentalism. Dan earned his Doctorate of English in 1967, from the University of Florida. In 1977, he received a National Endowment of the Humanities Summer Fellowship for Columbia University in the subject area of 19th-century British Painting and Literature. In 1980, he received a National Endowment of the Humanities Fellowship at the University of California, Berkeley in Victorian and Modern Poetics.

Dan has received a series of honors and awards over the years for his academic work and his teaching. Among these has been a Graduate Fellowship at the University of Florida, Phi Kappa Phi, University of Florida, Directory of American Scholars, University of South Florida Annual Award for Outstanding Undergraduate Teaching,

and the University of South Florida Teaching Improvement Award with a $5,000 annual stipend. He has been a Board Member of the Florida Endowment for the Humanities, Chairperson of the Florida Endowment for the Humanities, and has been involved in many relevant professional organizations. He has authored over twenty articles for scholarly journals and has written approximately seventy five capsule reviews.

Dan has not retired, but rather has gone on to perform additional community service as he learned from his parents. Dan was appointed by the governor to the Alafia River Basin Board. He was appointed by the commissioners to the Hillsborough County Citizens Environmental Advisory Committee. He is a member of the faculty of the Community Church College of Sun City, Florida. Dan is on the faculty of the University of South Florida Learning in Retirement Program.

Dan married Joan Stone Rutenberg on March 21, 1954. Joan was born on January 31, 1929. She graduated from the University of Illinois in 1951, with one of the earliest degrees in special education. She raised a family and she taught both cognitively and physically handicapped children in both Illinois and Florida for twenty eight years until her retirement in 1988. Her interest in education continues. She is still an active school volunteer. She's an avid reader and devotee of chamber music and theater.

Dan and Joan have three children, Matthew, Jeremy, and Naomi. Matthew was born on September 9, 1956. He earned a Bachelor of Arts Degree from Harvard University in History and Literature. He is an art consultant in New York City. Jeremy was born on May 5, 1958. He earned a Bachelor of Arts Degree in History from Emory University. Jeremy is a home builder in Atlanta, Georgia. Naomi was born on March 1, 1960. She earned a Bachelor of Arts Degree from Yale University in History, a Master of Arts Degree from the University of Florida in Latin American Studies, and a Doctor of Philosophy Degree from Princeton University in Sociology, Demography. Naomi is married to Robert Burn. Robert earned a Bachelor of Arts Degree in Demography from the University of Newcastle of the

United Kingdom, and a Master of Arts Degree in Demography from the University of Newcastle, United Kingdom. Naomi is a demographer in Washington, DC. Robert is a Logistics Specialist for Management Sciences for Health.

Reva and Marshall Kent

Reva and Marshall Kent

Reva and Marshall Kent, two extraordinary visionaries and leaders of people in the Jewish and general communities, have made an extraordinary impact on the lives of large numbers of very grateful individuals. They have given of themselves, of their time, and their finances to an extraordinary level to help others live a happy, healthy, and dignified life. Reva and Marshall and their two oldest children came to Clearwater from Chicago. They continued their home building business and, along with the Rutenberg family, their close friends, they set out to change the local community for the better.

Reva was born in Chicago in 1926. As a child, during the Depression, she learned the important lessons of helping others from her mother and her grandmother. Her mother would make sandwiches, wrap coins with them, and drop them from the second floor of their house to help the poor and hungry people walking down the street. Reva's mother was constantly and deeply involved in working on charitable projects run by Hadassah and the synagogue Sisterhood. Her grandmother's philosophy was that, "You never get poorer by giving to charity." Reva's maternal grandfather taught her to love Israel. He bought two shares of stock in the Israel B'nai Brak Bank on October 24, 1930, to help support the Jewish people.

Reva's mother, Florence Goldberg, was born on August 15, 1895 in Lithuania and came to the United States at age 19. She was an active member of the PTA, Hadassah, and Sisterhood. Reva's mother and Mary Rutenberg belonged to the same Hadassah chapter in Chicago. Both her mother and father belonged to an extremely conservative synagogue. Florence died on July 22nd, 1986.

Reva's father, Jacob, was born in June, 1891 in Russia and came to the United States at age fourteen. He served in World War I in the United States Army. He had an exceptional religious education. He owned a public garage from the early 1920s until the mid-1940s. The garage was used for the storage and repair of cars. He worked eighteen hour days, seven days a week. He died on February 12, 1960.

Reva's early training by word and deed from her mother, grandmother and grandfather led to a lifetime of unusual and substantial giving of her time and her financial resources to help other people in the Jewish and general communities. Her husband and best friend, Marshall, not only encouraged and supported her efforts in all of her worthwhile programs, but also participated in giving his time and financial resources to make life better for all people.

Reva was introduced to the Rutenberg family when she went to Austin High School with Arthur. This was the beginning of a lifelong connection and partnership between the Kent and Rutenberg families. Reva earned a Bachelor of Arts Degree in Liberal Arts from the University of Illinois in 1947. She and Marshall, who had been sweethearts for years, married in 1948.

By 1956, it was natural for the young Kent family to follow the path of the Rutenberg family and come to Clearwater to create a wonderful life for themselves and for others. Over time, Reva Kent and Charlie Rutenberg became the individuals who brought significant changes to the community. Charlie Rutenberg became the older brother and Reva Kent the younger sister who went out to change the world for the better.

In 1956, Rabbi Richmond immediately involved Reva in the work of the Jewish community. He asked Reva to teach Sunday School. He asked his wife, Helena, to teach Reva what was necessary to work with a class of four, five, and six-year-old's. Since this was the largest class, because of all the young families, it was held in the kitchen at the Temple on Betty Lane. Reva immediately became part of Sisterhood and was involved in every social event that was held on a monthly basis, as a fundraiser. Reva became President of Sisterhood in 1958. She became a Member of the Temple B'nai Israel Board of Trustees in 1960. In 1962, when Stan became a Bar Mitzvah, Reva and Marshall purchased a small Torah for the Temple. Reva and Marshall also elected to support Morton Plant Hospital.

It was Mary Rutenberg who made Reva move into a leadership role outside of the Temple and in the general community, by urging her to become the President of Hadassah in 1962. It was through Hadassah that Reva became involved in the Largo Women's Club in 1959. In 1966, Reva became President of the Pinellas County Federation of Womens Clubs, which served the community from Tarpon Springs to Gulfport. She also became President of the PTA.

In 1968, Marshall and Reva became involved with the Southwest Region Zionist Youth Commission and Camp Judea in Hendersonville, North Carolina. This was the beginning of the concept of the Kent Jewish Community Center. See the separate chapter on Jewish Community Centers.

For several years, Reva chaired the Israel Bond Drive. She became a founding member of the Jewish Federation of Pinellas County and its Campaign Chairman in 1978. That year, Marshall and Reva won"The Israel Humanitarian Award." from the State of Israel Bonds. She became President of the Jewish Federation of Pinellas County for four years, and then also was founding Chairman of "Lion of Judah." She served as a Member of the Board of the National Council of Jewish Federations. She traveled extensively throughout the United States and foreign lands, especially Israel, as part of this office.

In the 1980s, Reva and Marshall became involved with Ruth Eckerd Hall at the Richard B. Baumgardner Center for the Performing Arts-PACT organization, which helped build this unique facility. In 1982, Reva was selected as "The Person of the Year" by the Gulf Coast Jewish Family Services. In 1985, Reva traveled to Israel as part of the "Prime Minister's Mission."She became a Member of the Board of the Florida Region of the United Jewish Appeal. In 1986, Reva became one the founders of TOP and served as its President for two years. At the same time, Marshall and Reva were in the process of founding the Marshall and Reva Kent Jewish Community Center. In 1987,

Marshall, Reva's constant supporter, best friend, and beloved husband became ill and died. This was a great loss not only to Reva and the children, but to the entire community.

Reva was also a founder and a Member of the Board of Trustees of Menorah Manor and the Board of Directors of the Golda Meir Jewish Community Center. In addition, she was selected as the first Jewish woman to be one of the "Ten Best Dressed Ladies in Clearwater."

Reva has never slowed down. Currently, her leadership activities include: President, Jewish Cultural Endowment; Board Member, Jewish Federation of Pinellas County; Board Member, Golda Meir/Reva and Marshall Kent Jewish Community Center; life member Hadassah; life member Florida Holocaust Museum; funded life member Ruth Eckerd Hall at the Richard B. Baumgardner Center for the Performing Arts; supporting member Menorah Manor Guild, B'nai Brith, Brandeis University Women's Group, and the Gulf Coast Jewish Family Services.

Reva Kent's philosophy of life is as follows: "I am in love with the culture from which I came–with the history and traditions of our People–with the customs, the way of life, and everything that enhances my joy of being Jewish. My greatest pleasure and satisfaction comes from my family. I have been blessed with one that has shown an optimum of love, loyalty, and support. Their constant expression of affection and appreciation for our relationship is the strength and impetus to do all the other things that make my life complete...I'm an optimist and I remind them that to be Jewish is to be an optimist...to never let your memories exceed your dreams. I value my family most – and then my Jewish community and institutions. My involvement has enriched the quality of my life and that of Marshall, and my sons and their families. I enjoy starting a project, working for its success, and encouraging and supporting younger leadership so they may excel-and then I move on. I receive pleasure when I can inspire and serve as a mentor, however I do not see myself as a role model. I remain loyal to all ventures and areas of my work and leadership. My involvement with all my activities has

Award given to Marshall and Reva Kent, by T.O.P. Foundation in 1986, reads, "Highest level of Tzedakah is helping man to help himself. Moses Maimonides. Presented to Marshall and Reva Kent in appreciation of your commitment to the ideals of Maimonides."

been a means of meeting and developing lifetime friendships. It has been said that a true friend is the most valuable gift one can secure for...(oneself). I have been blessed with treasured friends whom I hold dear. I consider myself a "people person" and enjoy acknowledging the many talents and abilities of others."

Marshall Kent was born July 5, 1926, in Chicago. At the age of 19, after serving in the United States Army during World War II, he went into the home-building business. Marshall met his dream girl, Reva, and always wanted to be with her. Together, they built a love, a life, and a source of goodness for their family and for many others.

Marshall decided that Temple B'nai Israel needed a religious school, because it was a one-room Temple. In April 1958, Julius Lovitz donated the land and Marshall constructed, below actual cost, the addition; the religious school on the north side of the existing building.

Marshall was a major backer of the Jewish Federation and active in its work for many years. He was an active member and leader in Temple B'nai Israel for more than thirty years. The library at Temple B'nai Israel bears his name, Reva's name, and the names of the children. He was a major philanthropist and gave to Morton Plant Hospital, Roebling Society, PACT, Hadassah, Southern Zionist Youth Commission, and many other charities. He and Reva donated the eleven acre wooded plot in Clearwater for a Jewish Community Center. He was a founder, major contributor, and Treasurer of the Golda Meir Center. Charlie Rutenberg said of Marshall, "I loved him for his sense of fairness and being the first to admit when he was wrong. I loved him for his sense of loyalty to his family and his friends. And I loved him for his sense of Jewishness. Marshall Kent understood what it meant to be a Jew. Marshall Kent gave not only of his money, but of himself. He was a total Jew."

Marshall was outstanding in the building business. He was innovative, he was smart, and he was completely honest. When Marshall decided that something had to be done, it was done properly and was done in the best interest of all people. Arthur Rutenberg said of Marshall at his funeral,

"In later years, Marshall did something few of us ever do. He decided he'd made enough money and from that point on, to not embark on new ventures. He became philanthropic and entered a new phase of his life. He developed a sincere involvement with the community. This is especially evident in the Kent Center, but there are many other examples. I'll miss my friend. I'll miss his clarity and I'll miss his friendship-as I know all of you will."

Marshall died on July 30, 1987, after a long illness. Larry Kent said of his father, "...He was an honest and caring friend, a teacher, a problem solver, a fearless leader, a mentor extraordinaire, and, a philanthropist not only of the pocketbook, but even more so of the heart. One of his greatest attributes was his ability to re-prioritize and change directions in a matter of seconds to help fill someone else's needs. Out of love for others, he would always put his own needs second. Marshall Kent had a heart bigger than this Sanctuary. In it, he had a special place for each and every one of us. We had the fortune of sharing a relationship so unique and individually intimate and we will remember it and cherish it for the rest of our lives."

Finally, Rabbi Baseman said, "Marshall was a man of dedication, distinction, and dynamism. He matched words with works, creed with deed. He had that vitality, that vigor, that spirit to translate thought into action, ideas into reality. He was strong in character and strong in devotion. Despite his pain and his illness, he never surrendered his desire to live. He held his head high, his sense of dignity and purpose never faltered. He exemplified in his life the rabbinic dictum that a successful person is one who has made his little corner of the world a better place—and in that Marshall was a great success. With his Reva, he accomplished so much. Many couples grapple with questions like: Did we make our time together quality time? Did we make our lives meaningful?" Reva and Marshall could answer resoundingly in the affirmative. How protective and committed Reva has always been concerning Marshall. I recall when Reva received a High Holy Day Honor, for example, she would call me to tell me she would rather not do it without Marshall, that the honor should go to Marshall. I surely can hear her Marshall encouraging you, Reva, saying: "You will go on. I know that you can." Our acts live on in people's memories long after we have gone, indeed so that will be with Marshall."

At the end of the memorial service, Kaddish was said. Kaddish, the prayer for the dead, is a sacred duty of all Jewish people. This is a major tradition of love that binds the generations together and special remembrances. It keeps alive the memories of those loved ones who are no longer with us. Kaddish actually never mentions death, but rather honors the living God. Even the small synagogues, Orthodox, Conservative and Reform all maintain the list of the honored dead of the congregants and celebrate the anniversary of their deaths yearly by naming them at services and by individuals saying the Kaddish.

The Kent Family Children

Stan Kent was born in Chicago in 1949. He was the first Jewish child to go through the Largo school system. He graduated from Stetson University with a Bachelor of Science Degree in Business Administration. He founded Contemporary Builders of Deltona and built homes. He later also went into commercial construction. In 1972, Stan married Carolee Jenkins. Carolee earned a Bachelor of Science Degree in Education from Stetson University. They have two children, Stephen and Meredith.

Larry Kent was born in Chicago in 1952. He graduated from the University of Florida with a Bachelor of Science Degree in Business Administration in 1974. He became Vice President of Contemporary Builders and then started Larry Kent Homes. After building 1,200 homes in the Deltona, Florida area, he built a large shopping center and then went into other construction of commercial/rental offices, which he now owns and manages. He was founding Chairman of the Board of Southland Bank in 1987 and Commercial Bank in Ormond Beach in 1989. He now also owns a Burger King franchise. In 1976, Larry married Sandra Seiler of Tampa. Sandra graduated from the University of South Florida with a Bachelor of Science Degree in Fine Arts. She

then received a Bachelor of Science Degree in Education from Tulane University. They are both very active in the Orlando Jewish community, serving at committee and board levels of the Jewish Federation, the Jewish Community Center, and Hadassah. They established a philanthropic fund in the TOP Foundation. They have three children. Justin is an engineer who earned degrees from Massachusetts Institute of Technology in architecture, computer science, and music. Leslie is a professional athlete and filmmaker. Natalie is completing her degrees at the University of Florida in advertising and business. All three of them are following what they have learned from their parents and their grandparents by being innovative and contributing to the good lives of others.

David Kent was born in Clearwater in 1959. He attended Stetson University and then became interested in alternative medicine. He has a clinic in Deltona, Florida and teaches seminars across the United States and internationally. David is very civic oriented and has served on a variety of boards of civic groups and professional organizations. David married Mandy Tweedle of Leesburg, Florida. She earned a Bachelor of Science Degree in Fine Art from the University of Boulder in Colorado.

Joel Kent was born in Clearwater in 1962. He earned a Bachelor of Science Degree in Biology from Stetson University. He then went to the University of South Florida to earn his Doctor of Medicine Degree. He is board certified in Anesthesiology and Family Practice and is Director of the Maryland Pain Center. He married Dr. Trish Amish and they have two children, Emma and Sarah.

Highlights of 1957

Evon and Louis Brower came to the area in February. Louis was born August 29, 1917 and Evon was born on November 16, 1923. They bought a small trailer park in Largo. Evon retired as a speech therapist from Morton Plant Hospital. She was Past President of Temple B'nai Israel Sisterhood, and chaired many committees including teaching, the caring committee, etc. Louis had been the chairman of the United Jewish Appeal

Herbert Frank, President, Temple B'nai Israel, 1958–1959.

and was also on the Cemetery committee.

David and Amelia Davis arrived in the Clearwater area. David was born in 1907 and died in 1970. Roland and Betty Fox arrived in the Clearwater area in September. Hannah and Douglas Wise arrived in the Clearwater area in June. Darwin Frank was once again President of Temple B'nai Israel.

Congregation Beth Shalom

Congregation Beth Shalom was founded by the conservative Jewish community of Clearwater.

Congregation Beth Shalom was a direct outgrowth of the split of the conservative members from Temple B'nai Israel and an increase in Jewish families who wanted to have a conservative synagogue. See Chapter on Congregation Beth Shalom of Clearwater for the rest of the story.

Temple B'nai Israel

See Chapter on Temple B'nai Israel of Clearwater for the rest of the story.

Harold B. and Sally Siegel

Harold and Sally and their daughter, Mindy, moved to Clearwater. Harold opened his first pharmacy in downtown Clearwater on Prospect Street. He was the first person to open a pharmacy inside of a grocery store. Because of its success, he opened additional pharmacies in grocery stores. One Christmas Eve as he was closing the store, he decided to deliver the unsold toys and Christmas decorations to the underprivileged children living in a depressed area of town. He loaded up his car and delivered them himself. The following year, he special ordered extra merchandise, bought a Santa Claus costume, and asked the police to assist him in delivering the gifts to the less fortunate children. Each year, the project grew, and he became known as the "Jewish Santa Claus." This tradition was eventually taken over by the Police Department and is still in operation today. On December 21, 1970, Harold was honored by the City of Clearwater for initiating the program. He was honored over time for his contributions to the Jewish community including having the annual report of the Golda Meir Center of 1993, dedicated to his memory.

Highlights of 1958

In 1958-1959, Herbert Frank was President of Temple B'nai Israel. Herbert founded Aerosonics, which employed many people. He was active in assisting in the athletic events in the school system. He announced the Friday night football games over the loudspeaker.

Burton Hartman came to the area and married Hannah. Her first husband, who had died, was Doug Weiss. Burton built several strip shopping centers and condominiums. Stan and Ida Michels arrived in April. Dorothy and Isadore Goldberg arrived in February. Daniel and Lillian Bandes arrived in the area.

Dr. Robert Keller and his wife, Joan, arrived. He was a gynecologist and obstetrician. She taught archaeology at the University of South Florida. She participated in many digs in Israel. She earned a Master's Degree from the University of South Florida in Archaeology. She had been President of the Sisterhood. During her presidency, as a gag, Phyllis Dorian, Fern Moroff, Hilda, and Ellie Gordon dressed up in hippie clothes from Stan Stillmans Men's Wear Store and went on strike outside the Temple office. They carried signs with very clever Yiddish slogans on them. Stan's wife, Bernice, was related to Bob Rose, who owned the Rose Shoe Bootery.

Florence Pepper was from a very old and distinguished Jewish family from Tallahassee named Mendleson. They had a popular department store in downtown Tallahassee. She moved to Clearwater. Her sister, Marion Friedlander, also moved to Clearwater in the 1950s. Ruth Bush was a realtor. Stanley Michaels was a pharmacist. He owned several drugstores throughout the Clearwater, Largo, and Dunedin areas. He and his wife, Ida, moved to the area in the sixties. Ida established the original speech clinic at Morton Plant Hospital. Dr. Erwin Entel was a radiologist. He and his wife, Syd, moved to Safety Harbor in the 1960s. He practiced at Mease Hospital. She owns a very popular fine arts gallery in Safety Harbor. Morton Gordon was a building contractor. His wife, Dr. Ellie Gordon, is still very active in the community in a variety of Jewish affairs. Albert and his wife, Marian, owned a bakery in Cleveland Plaza, which was the first strip store plaza in the area. The plaza opened in the 1950s and was a huge success. Her parents lived in Safety Harbor. Herb Silverstein, and his wife, Rosalind, moved to Clearwater in the 1960s. They had a business in Tampa. Shirley and Ed Kleinman came to Clearwater in the fifties. Shirley started the first Sisterhood gift shop at Temple B'nai Israel. Ruby and Sam Lempert came in the 1960s. Ruby was President of the Sisterhood. Sam was a traveling shoe salesman. Carl Rosenfeld married Anita Bauman, who was in the first confirmation class at Temple B'nai Israel.

Highlights of 1960

In the early 1960s, programs at General Electric and Minneapolis Honeywell virtually exploded. There was a large influx of professional people including, many Jewish engineers. This helped the Jewish community grow. Charlie Rutenberg brought many new Jewish families to the area.

Rabbi J. Marshall Taxay

J. Marshall Taxay was the Rabbi of Temple B'nai Israel from 1960-1969. On November 26, Rabbi Taxay became the spiritual leader of Temple B'nai Israel. Rabbi Susskind installed Rabbi Taxay. Rabbi Taxay told a series of funny stories, followed by a powerful conclusion that caused the congregation to rise and applaud him.

Rabbi Taxay served the Jewish people of Terre Haute, Indiana from 1924-1944. He went to Temple Israel in Akron Ohio until 1954, Temple Beth El in Daytona Beach, Florida until 1960, and then on to Temple B'nai Israel of Clearwater until 1969. He had a long and colorful career. At the end of the 1920s and during the Depression, the Orthodox congregation of Terre Haute struggled financially and could not afford a rabbi or trained teachers and an administrator for the children in religious school. Rabbi Taxay of Temple Israel, the Reform congregation, and President Ben

Rabbi J. Marshall Taxay

Blumberg developed a consolidation plan for the two synagogues and on March 20, 1935, the first merger of Reform and Orthodox congregations in United States took place. It was decided that the rabbi would be a graduate of Hebrew Union College and that the congregation would belong to the Union of American Hebrew Congregations. The kitchen would be Kosher and the second day of religious holidays would be available to those members who wished to attend. All other Jewish organizations would continue to operate independently for the time being.

While in Terre Haute, Rabbi Taxay was very active in many local, state, and national organizations. He was Grand Chaplain of the Masonic Order of the State of Indiana, President of District 2 of B'nai Brith President of the Terre Haute Clergy Club, Vice President of the Family Welfare Society, Chairman of the Chamber of Commerce Welfare Campaign of 1936 and 1937, and authored a book entitled, *Our Story, the Jewish History in the United States from its Discovery to the Civil War*. He took the summers off and traveled throughout the world. Summer services were always conducted by lay leaders. Rabbi Taxay died on August 12, 1976, at the age of 72.

Bobo/Rophie/Berk Families

Salha and Ralph Bobo were part of a large Syrian Jewish family in Tampa, who owned the Blue-Ribbon Grocery Store in Ybor City. They had seven children. Two of their children, Ezra (Zua) Bobo and Pauline Bobo, came to Clearwater. The Bobo, Rophie, and Berk families have been very active in either Congregation Beth Shalom and/or Temple B'nai Israel.

Gloria and Ezra Bobo

On December 12, 1982, Gloria and Ezra Bobo received the coveted City of Peace Award for their tireless efforts on behalf of temple, community and the State of Israel. Gloria and Ezra had been involved in community and Jewish life since Ezra arrived in Tampa in 1946, and both of them were involved since they married in 1958. He was the youngest person ever to be elected to the Board of Trustees of

Salha Bobo

Congregation Rodeph Sholom of Tampa . At Temple B'nai Israel, he was Coordinating Vice President, Financial Vice President, Treasurer, Secretary, and a member of the Building Committee. He was the Charter President of the Clearwater B'nai Brith. He was also the President of the Merchants Association of Clearwater, a Member of the Board of Governors of the Chamber of Commerce in Clearwater, a Member of the Board of Kiwanis Club, and a Member of the Board of the Jewish Federation of Pinellas County. Gloria was a Member of the Board and life member of Hadassah. She was the first chairman of the Hearing-Screening Program, President of Temple B'nai Israel Sisterhood and a member of the youth commission of Temple B'nai Israel. She was a Member of the Board of the Clearwater High School PTA. She also served as a captain of the March of Dimes and cancer campaigns. Gloria's parents, Mr. and Mrs. Vita I. Grazi, were recipients of the State of Israel Bond award in Brooklyn, New York. Gloria and Ezra had four children: Ralph, Victor, Scot, and Richard.

Pauline (Bobo) and Albert Rophie

Pauline and Albert (Al) Rophie also moved to Clearwater the same year and joined both Temple B'nai Israel and Congregation Beth Shalom. They had four children: Ceci Rophie Betech, who currently lives in Mexico City with her husband and three children; Cheryl Rophie Cohen, who graduated from the University of Florida in 1974 and currently lives in Atlanta, Georgia with her husband and two children; Ralph Rophie who graduated from medical school in 1984 and currently has a family practice in Clearwater. Ralph has a wife and four children; and Alan Rophie.

Alan Rophie earned a Bachelor of Science Degree in Chemistry and Psychology from the University of Florida in 1976. He also earned a Doctor of Optometry Degree from Southern College of Optometry in 1982. He has been in private practice in Dunedin since 1983. Allen's first recollection of synagogue

Alan Rophie's Bar Mitzvah, November 23, 2967 at Congregation Beth Shalom. l. to r. Cheryl, Albert, Alan, Pauline and Cecilia Rophie. Ralph is in front.

life was as a small child, on the High Holy Days, when a dozen Syrian Sephardic families held services in the auditorium of Rodeph Sholom in Tampa. They had neither a rabbi or a cantor, but conducted a very intimate service on their own, and it was rich in tradition. On June 20, 1982, Alan married Sharon Slaughter, moved back to Pinellas County, and joined congregation Beth Shalom. He had been a previous Bar Mitzvah at Congregation Beth Shalom and confirmed at Temple B'nai Israel. Sharon was born in Birmingham, Alabama on November 5, 1957. Sharon earned a Bachelor of Arts Degree in Speech and Hearing Science at Indiana University in 1979. She earned a Master of Arts Degree in Audiology from Memphis State University in 1980, and a Doctor of Audiology from the University of Florida in 2000. She was a Board Member of the Kent Jewish Community Center, a charter member of Lyla Hadassah chapter, member of ORT, and Beth Shalom Sisterhood.

Albert opened Tiny Tots and Teen Town, a business in downtown Clearwater. The store became the Bobo and Rophie Department Store. Eventually, the store became Rophie's Shoes, a business owned solely by Albert. Ezra went back to work at the family Blue-Ribbon Grocery Store in Tampa.

Bernard and Rosalind Berk

Bernie and Roz moved to Clearwater from Indianapolis in 1968 with their children, Tony and Vanessa. They became members of Temple B'nai Israel when it was located on Betty Lane. Bernie was born on June 10, 1938 in New York City. The original family name at that time was Bercovitz. It was legally changed around 1955. Bernie graduated from Purdue University School of Pharmacy in 1958. He entered into a partnership with Michael's Pharmacy in Clearwater, opened his own pharmacy in Druid Hills Nursing Home in Clearwater, and finally opened Berk Drugs in Seminole/Largo. He kept the store until his retirement in 1998. He was President of the Temple B'nai Israel Brotherhood, and also served as Temple Treasurer and Vice President. Roz was born on January 12, 1941 in Indianapolis, Indiana. She and Bernie were married on February 14, 1959 at the Indianapolis Hebrew Congregation. Roz was a Sunday school teacher at Temple B'nai Israel and served in numerous positions in Sisterhood, becoming President from 1972-1974. Both Roz and Bernie became extremely active in the AIDS Coalition Pinellas. They lost their son, Tony, to the AIDS virus in 1988. They were both Members of the Board of the AIDS Coalition Pinellas. Roz became President and Executive Director from 1990-1992. Under her leadership, AIDS Coalition Pinellas provided AIDS education to 30,000 children in Pinellas County schools. Tony had been a National Merit Scholar from Clearwater High School in 1977. He earned his Bachelor's Degree in Theater from Florida State University in 1979. He spent eight years working in New York City as a director and stage manager, including five years at Radio City Music Hall. Bernie and Roz's daughter, Vanessa, married Ralph Rophie.

Vanessa and Ralph Albert Rophie

Ralph, the youngest son of Pauline and Al, married Vanessa Berk, in 1991. They have four children: Victoria Louise, Anthony Daniel, Albert Anthony, and Benjamin Ralph. Ralph earned his Bachelor's of Science in Premed at the University of South Florida in 1980. He earned his Doctor of Medicine Degree at the University of Guadalajara in Mexico in 1984. He returned to Clearwater to open his medical practice. Ralph has served as Chairperson for the Family Practice Department at Morton Plant Hospital. He also has volunteered numerous hours at the local free clinic.

Vanessa had a life-changing experience when her brother, Tony Berk, became ill with AIDS and finally died at a very young age. She became the Educational Outreach Director for the local AIDS coalition. She spoke at various high schools and middle schools as part of the Names Project AIDS Memorial Quilt program. In 1990, she and her mother, Roz Berk, put together a big benefit in a local Clearwater theater for the local AIDS coalition in honor of her late brother. On this special night, Ellie and Mort Gordon introduced Ralph Rophie to Vanessa, and this was the beginning of a wonderful love affair. They were married on

November 30, 1991. The Coalition continues to work at a very high level for AIDS education to help prevent young people from contracting this disease.

Vanessa said, "Being Jewish, to me, is not something I pursue....it just is...and as the traditions continue...so do I continue to live my Jewish life."

Lisl and Dr. Alfred Schick

Lisl and Alfred Schick moved to Clearwater. Lisl, a Holocaust survivor, was born in Vienna, Austria and was then educated in England and the United States. Throughout her life in Pinellas County, she has been deeply involved in both the Jewish and general communities. She is a member of the Executive Board of Directors of the Holocaust Museum, where she also acts as a speaker for students, teachers, and other adult audiences. She was on the first Board of Directors and a founder of Ruth Eckerd Hall at the Richard B. Baumgardner Center for the Performing Arts. She helped establish an educational branch for the Foundation of the Morton Plant/Mease Health Care Center. Lisl and Al received the Generation's Award from Israel Bonds. In 1997, she received the Fourth Annual Celebrity Award from the Gulf Coast Jewish Family Services in recognition of her support and commitment to quality programs and services for the community. In 2003, she was recipient of the Florida Holocaust Museum "To Life" Award.

Lisl and Alfred Schick

If the work she has done in all of these organizations wasn't enough for a single person to do and accomplish, Lisl has spent over thirty two years working in leadership roles in Hadassah, including being the first Floridian to become a National Vice President and still serving on the National Board. In 2005, Lisl was Chairperson of the Hadassah Keepers of the Gate event for the Pinellas County Chapters.

Lisl has constantly shown her strength of conviction and her strength of character. A perfect example of this was her participation in a special Hadassah mission to Russia, in 1988, to visit the Refusnicks. These nine women brought precious material from the outside to Russian Jews, even though they could've been in extreme danger from the Russian authorities. Her leadership in this action, as well as the many others she has been involved in, are an outstanding example of determination and dedication to make this world a better place.

Dr. Alfred Schick was born in Austria on November 17, 1922. He was a Holocaust survivor. Alfred and Lisl took the horror of their childhood and turned it into a positive force for good in the large number of contributions they have made for the health and welfare of all American citizens and citizens worldwide. Al served in World War II in the United States Army from 1943 to 1945.

Al completed his premedical education at Syracuse University and his medical education at the University of Rochester in 1950. He became Chief Resident of the New England Medical Center in Boston. Before coming to Morton Plant Hospital, Al was an Assistant Professor of Radiology at Syracuse University. He then joined the staff of Mercy Hospital in Charlotte, North Carolina and later, Cleveland Memorial Hospital in Shelby, North Carolina.

Al was the first Jewish physician in Clearwater and a Board Certified Radiologist. He was the first Radiologist in Pinellas County to be elected a Fellow of the American College of Radiology, an honor which was granted to few people at that time. He was the Chief Radiologist at Morton Plant Hospital for twenty eight years, Director of Medical Education, and Chairman, Department of Medicine. He was Past President of the West Coast Radiological Society and the Florida Radiological Society. He was Past Director of the Springtime Chapter, Kiwanis Club, Member of Board of Directors, College Fund of Pinellas County, Medical Advisor, St. Petersburg Junior College Program of Radiological Technology, and Member of the Advisory Council of the Junior League of Clearwater-Dunedin. He served in many leadership roles, including President, Temple B'nai Israel. Al, Rabbi Baseman, Charlie Rutenberg, and several other individuals helped start Temple Ahavat Shalom to provide a religious home that was more conveniently located for the Jewish people of the far northern part of the county.

Al received many awards over the years including the President's Achievement Award of the Pinellas County Medical Society, Outstanding Physician Award, Morton Plant Hospital, and Physician Recognition Award, American Medical Association.

Al died on April 25, 1993. There was an outpouring of love and respect for this unique individual known as Al Schick. Lisl published a book of Al's guest columns for the St. Petersburg Times. She also included letters written about him from many people who had been fortunate enough to have their lives touched by him. In the introduction of the book, she described Al. She said, "As will quickly become evident, this is a love story. A love story not only between Al and myself, but between Al and the world. He was a man whose capacity for love was boundless-for people, for his profession, and for all the richness of life that too often, by so many of us, is taken for granted. But not by Al. His curiosity about absolutely everything was unlimited, and his love for learning was endless. This applied not only to his profession, where all who knew him respected and admired him, but included taking courses on just about everything under the sun. Because of his energy and wisdom, as displayed here in his writings, he helped so many to see more, to feel more, and to love more. In a beautifully balanced way, the love in Al's life flowed both ways. Rarely has a man been more universally loved then Dr. Alfred Schick."

To honor the memory of Dr. Alfred Schick, Lisl has endowed the following programs and facilities: Annual Alfred Schick, M.D., Memorial Lecture for Continuing Medical Education at Morton Plant-Mease Health Center; Dr. Alfred Schick Memorial Fund, Gulf Coast Jewish Family Services; an Oncology Treatment Room at Hadassah Hospital in Jerusalem, Israel; Annual Maimomides Society Award, Jewish Federation of Pinellas County; the Office of the Director of Education, Holocaust Museum, St. Petersburg, Florida. A bank of glass windows were dedicated to Dr. Alfred Schick in the new sanctuary of Temple Kol Emeth of Atlanta, Georgia.

Al and Lisl have had a huge capacity

to love everyone and have on a continuous basis tried to improve the richness of life that makes all of our journeys so fulfilling. Their energy, dedication to health and welfare organizations, and wisdom have helped so many to lead productive, healthy, and meaningful lives. Lisl follows Al's motto, "I am not impressed by what people own, but I am impressed with what they achieve. Lisl and Al have four children: Kenneth B. Schick, born April 8, 1953; Nancy Schick Greenberg, born September 7, 1955; Robert O. Schick, born June 15, 1959; and Kathryn Schick Madow, born August 8, 1964.

The Schick Children

Kenneth earned a Bachelor of Science Degree in Journalism and Communications from the University of Florida in 1975. He earned a Master of Business Administration with honors in Marketing and Finance from Georgia State University in 1981. He is General Manager, HBO Closed-Circuit Television Network. He is an active supporter of the Florida Holocaust Museum in St. Petersburg and active in his local community in Atlanta. His wife, Cindy Grusin Shick, was born on June 25, 1956. She earned a Bachelor of Science Degree in Medical Technology from the University of Florida in 1978. She was honored in 2005 as the Volunteer of the Year by the Jewish Family Services of Atlanta.

Nancy Schick Greenberg earned a Bachelor of Arts Degree from the University of Virginia in English in 1977. Nancy has been a Director of Public Relations and Marketing for various hospitals and has served as a consultant to many hospitals and health-care facilities. She has been involved in numerous community projects, and has chaired several them. These include: parent teachers organizations; City of Clearwater Library Foundation; Clearwater-Dunedin Junior League; Pinellas County Jewish Federation's Woman's Division; Board Member of Temple Ahavat Shalom of Palm Harbor; Hadassah. She is a trained docent for the Florida Holocaust Museum and Co-Chairperson of the Anne Frank Humanitarian Award. She graduated from Leadership Pinellas in 2005. Her husband, Will, graduated from Yeshiva University in

1974 and the University of Miami Medical School in 1978. Will, in addition to his practice, is active in the Jewish community. He has served as Chairman of the Pinellas County Jewish Federation Maimonides Division, Abilities Foundation Fundraising Committee, and on the Board of the Pinellas County Jewish Day School.

Robert earned a Bachelor of Science Degree from the University of Florida, with high honors in 1981 and a Doctor of Veterinary Medicine Degree from the University of Florida, with high honors, in 1985. He is a Diplomate of the ACVD. He is a specialist and only one out of approximately 100 Board-Certified Specialists in Veterinary Allergy and Dermatology. He is an active supporter of the Florida Holocaust Museum in St. Petersburg.

Kathryn Schick Madow earned a Bachelor of Science Degree from the University of Florida in Marketing in 1986. She earned a Master's of Business Administration Degree from Georgia State University in Hospital Administration in 1989. She is a medical marketing specialist and physician recruiter for Morton Plant Hospital. She is active in Jewish organizations. Her husband, Dr. Evan Madow, was born on December 18, 1963. He earned a Bachelor of Arts Degree from Stony Brook College in 1985 and a Doctor of Chiropractic Medicine from Life Chiropractic College in 1989. He is the owner of the Florida Health and Wellness Center in Largo. He is active in the Jewish community, and both he and Kathy are supporters of the Florida Holocaust Museum.

Highlights of 1961

Salu De Vinani

Salu De Vinani came to the Safety Harbor Spa in a management position. He went on to become the General Manager of the facility and a trusted advisor to Salem Baranoff. Salu became so involved in supporting Jewish charitable activities that he became known as an honorary Jew. In later years, he was the legal guardian for Salem, Lisa, their children, and Dena. Salu was a sizable contributor and deeply involved in Bonds for Israel. Salu said, "Over the years the Safety Harbor Spa was 99.9% Jewish.

In fact, at one time it was the largest Jewish hotel in the world, and many outstanding personalities came to partake of Dr. Baranoff's healthy way of living. "The Safety Harbor Spa lost its Jewish identity in 1985.

Highlights of 1965

Rabbi Louis Gorod

Rabbi Louis Gorod

Rabbi Louis Gorod assumed the pulpit of Congregation Beth Shalom of Clearwater. Rabbi Gorod previously held pulpits in Sullivan County, New York for seven years, where he was a charter member and officer of the Ministerial Alliance of Sullivan County, and an officer of the Rabbinical Association of Sullivan County. He served a pulpit in Valdosta, Georgia for three years, while also serving as chaplain at Pineview General hospital. He has been President of B'nai B'rith, Auxiliary Chaplain of Moody Air Force Base, and Member Board of Directors Youth Center. He is a graduate of the Rabbi Jacob Joseph Yeshiva and Mesifta in New York and the College of the City of New York. He did graduate work in Biblical Research at the Hebrew University in Jerusalem. His wife, Henrietta, is a graduate of the Columbia University School of Journalism. Many of her stories and poems have been published. They both have been very active in civic and community activities.

Dr. Salem Baranoff

In 1965, Dr. Salem Baranoff, a beloved citizen, was honored. Dr. Baranoff was a sincere and humble man who always worked diligently to improve the welfare of the Jewish community and the general community. In 1957, Isadore Zitlin, the Cantor and First Vice President of Temple B'nai Israel, and Reuben Rutenberg asked Dr. Baranoff to help organize a Conservative synagogue in Clearwater. Dr. Baranoff became one of the founders of Congregation Beth Shalom. He was President of Congregation Beth Shalom for several years, guiding it as a loving parent would. He was the designated shofar blower

Dr. Salem Baranoff, blowing of the Shofar, Isadore Zitlin, cantor, Reuben Rutenberg, President. Sun Photo. date unknown

and assisted in the cantorial services on holidays and Sabbaths. He and his wife contributed freely to the building of the synagogue and its upkeep for many years. He was voted unanimously by the Board of Directors of Beth Shalom to be granted the honor of President Emeritus for life. He believed that teaching Jewish children is an important duty of every Jew. He felt that all Jews are responsible for each other and therefore has worked extremely hard and contributed heavily to the United Jewish Appeal and Israeli Bonds. He has helped thousands of people throughout the United States and abroad to return to normal health through the Safety Harbor Spa. He was constantly involved in the Safety Harbor communal life in the Civic Club, library, and many other organizations.

Highlights of 1967

Sidney Colen

Sidney Colen began the development "On Top of the World" in Clearwater. This was the first all-inclusive active adult community, an innovative concept in retirement including all the amenities expected by the retirees. This 5,000 plus unit condo complex was to be exceeded by a plan for a 30,000 unit housing complex in Ocala. In 1975, the company purchased the Circle Square Ranch in Ocala, Florida. On Top of the World Communities Inc., founded by Sidney Colen, who was Chairman of the Board for over fifty years, has built thousands of homes and provided tens of thousands of jobs to Floridians.

Sidney Colen has always been successful because he made sure that his clients received fair value for what they paid for their homes. In addition, when a family moved in they always had a house or condo that was sparkling clean inside and out and a warranty on all workmanship. Success is measured not by money, but rather by what kind of life people live and whether or not this world is a little bit better when they depart it than when they arrived. Sidney and Ina Colen were fortunate because of their great love for each other, because of their three children and grandchildren and because they extended their love to other people who were less fortunate and also to the community by participating, many times anonymously, in many community endeavors. This has helped improve each community they have lived in.

Sidney helped meet some of the basic needs of life of people because of his philosophy of life. In his Ethical Will he shares his philosophy with his grandchildren. It is well that his philosophy be shared with all children. From, "A Philosophical Summary of My Beliefs" is the following:

1. I believed in strong self-discipline, where one does not heap materialism upon himself.
2. I believed strongly in self-denial, which of course is self-evident. I believe this to be important and realistic.
3. I believed in basic honesty for motives. Never rationalize in order to justify a want or desire.
4. It is very important to be brutally honest with yourself and hopefully honest in your motives.
5. Plan for a well thought-out future. Always provide for outlets in the event there is a miscalculation or a need to retrench.
6. Always bear in mind that there is a redeeming value and purpose for all your decisions. Then proceed, allowing room for miscalculations. Plan in advance for recovery if recovery becomes necessary.
7. Understand that you live in a competitive world and you must be prepared to compete. Avoid cheating. You will progress well by being responsible and having thought out your plans.
8. "With the truth you are able to approach your Deity." However, always have defenses in place. Do not have a jaundiced eye against everything, however.
9. Be compassionate and responsible.
10. Probe under and through problems. Try to understand the basics.
11. Constantly seek the basic truths and thereby you will understand the foundations upon which civilization is founded. Always seek truth for understanding.
12. Self-protection is not dishonesty. A foolish person is naïve.
13. Vested interest is justified; be sure not to misrepresent when dealing in that process.
14. Misrepresentation is wrong. Never let your life be guided in that vein. However, to repeat: honest vested interests, geared in your favor, is not wrong.
15. Family responsibilities are a prime attribute. The Fifth Commandant is a civilized human value, separating humans from lower forms. Keep this Commandant holy.
16. That which you produce and give life to is a never-ending responsibility. Your spouse, children, parents, siblings are all part of your heritage. Keep them sacred.
17. Be grateful for having been given the gift of life. Not all souls have been given that gift; it is holy.
18. Be a responsible human being and contribute to life. This is an awesome responsibility not to be wasted on self. Never hold materialism as your prime purpose.
19. There is nothing wrong with enjoying the fruits of your labor. However, never let it be your only main purpose. Extreme materialism was, in my opinion, sinful waste.
20. Never lose sight of the value of sharing. This too, is holy.
21. Never be fanatically religious to the exclusion of all else. However, value your heritage in which you have your foundation.
22. Learn to be creative. Be creative in your thought process and in your planning. Do not be afraid to do things in a new and innovative way as long as you have thought it out thoroughly and can find a redeeming value. It will always serve you well.

Sidney and his wife, Ina, have practiced over many years the many points which he had expressed as his philosophy of life. In the Torah, God offers life and death and tells us to choose life. In the Torah, God offers us good or evil and he tells us to choose good. This freedom of choice which God has given us and the ability to do good for our families and for other people is truly the capstone of Sydney and Ina's life.

Highlights of 1968

Elinor Z. and Mortimer Gordon

Elinor and Morty Gordon, December 24, 1950.

Ellie and Morty Gordon came to the Clearwater area after Morty responded to an ad in the New York Times, placed by Arthur Rutenberg. He worked for Arthur for one year and obtained a Class "A" license to cover all the jobs under construction at that time. He was a general contractor, engineer, builder and developer who had been involved in construction in the New York and New Jersey areas.

Morty then built condominiums in Pinellas Park and also opened his own real estate agency. He made numerous contributions to the general community including: Member of the Advisory Council for Continuing Education in St. Petersburg Junior College; Member of the Board of Directors of the Pinellas County American Cancer Society; Parent Teachers Association; University of Alabama Alumni Association; consultant to various agencies; Instructor in the Real Estate Brokers Course at St. Petersburg Junior College; and member of Clearwater Largo Realtor's Association.

Morty was born on March 22, 1922 in Brooklyn, New York. He died on September 8, 1993. Morty spoke fluent Yiddish and had a fine voice. He became a soloist at nine years of age in the Machtenberg Jewish Choir. Some of the well-known alumni from the choir were Jan Peerce and Richard Reuven. In his teenage years, Morty acted in the Yiddish Theater on Second Avenue with Molly Picon and Moishe Oysher.

Morty was part of an experimental Speech Pilot Program in the New York high schools and traveled from school to school giving special presentations in public speaking and poetry reading. His work helped Speech become part of the English curriculum in the New York City School System. He was a fine athlete, an excellent student, and a leader in many school activities. He later became a waterfront counselor in summer camps, which was where he met Ellie.

Morty graduated from Brooklyn College in 1942 with a Bachelor of Arts Degree in Science. While working at the Brooklyn Navy Yard, he was advised to go back to college and take up engineering. He scored very well in all of the aptitude tests the Navy had administered, and one of the admirals arranged for him to get into the University of Alabama's School of Engineering.

Morty graduated from the University of Alabama in 1947 with a Bachelor's Degree in Engineering. A very ambitious young man, he worked three part-time jobs while going to college. Morty also continued to express his Jewish background by forming the University of Alabama's first Hillel Chapter and the Hillel Dance Band to play in the local community. Morty was drafted into the Army and became a Second Lieutenant. He came back to the University of Alabama and finished his degree.

Morty was truly a Master Builder and a meticulous craftsman who knew plumbing, electrical work, carpentry, metalwork, and architecture. He built the new Madison Square Garden; Imperial Plaza Shopping Center of Wappingers Falls, New York; Imperial Tower of Wappingers Falls, New York; Cloverleaf Tower, Bronx, New York; 425 Third Ave., New York, New York; etc.. He helped the Yeshiva of the Spring Valley and the Hebrew Institute of Rockland County to expand and renovate at the lowest cost possible. He did this for free.

Prior to his moving to Florida, Morty had been the lead singer in the Senior Adult Choir at Temple Beth-El in Spring Valley, New York. He was also an active member of the Temple Board and served on the Membership and Building Committees.

At Temple B'nai Israel, Morty became President Pro Tem of the resurrected Men's Club, a member of the Building Committee and the Rabbinical Search Committee. He worked diligently to expand the membership of the Temple.

Ellie was born on February 21, 1930, in New York. Her father, David Louis Zahn, graduated from Columbia University School of Dentistry at the age of twenty, one year before he was old enough to obtain his license. He was an excellent athlete and taught his children the love of sports. Her mother, Mildred Ann Bernstein, was a bookkeeper. Mildred loved dancing, and also ice-skating, as her husband did. Her father proposed to her mother while she was a patient in his dental chair, having an impression of her teeth made, with her mouth wide open-she could not respond!

Ellie was very active in high school scholastically, athletically, and musically. She wrote, acted and produced the Senior Talent Show. She graduated at age sixteen and attended Hunter College. She went to summer camp from age eight until age twenty, progressing from camper to Senior Division Head, Athletic Director, and ultimately to Girls Head Counselor. She was always busy being a song leader, writing songs and shows for camp and for the Girl Scouts, where she became a leader. To earn extra money, she organized children's birthday parties with appropriate costumes, games, songs, and poems.

Ellie's scholastic work progressed at the same time as her musical work. She earned a Bachelor of Arts Degree in Speech Correction, Speech, and Theater Arts from Hunter College and worked toward a Master's Degree in Guidance and Counseling, at Montclair State Teachers College. She earned a Master of Science Degree from the University of South Florida in Guidance and Counseling, and a Ph.D. from Nova University in Counseling

In Spring Valley, New York, Ellie taught speech. She was Senior Class Advisor, wrote the Faculty Show, and was a judge in the county-wide oration contest. She worked for Temple Sisterhood, Hadassah, National Council of Jewish Women, and B'nai B'rith, in the educational aspects of these Jewish organizations. She became immersed in the Brandeis University National Women's Committee, a love that would truly change the course of her life when she moved to Pinellas County.

She helped found new chapters of Brandeis University National Women's Committee. She became Expansion Chairman of the Florida Region, and a Member of the National Nominating Committee. She also continued her interest in theater and musical productions. She helped write, produce, and be part of several musicals for Temple B'nai Israel, which became fund raisers. Morty joined her in many of these musical ventures.

Ellie's maternal grandfather, Harry Bernstein, put an extremely high value on education and set very high standards for Ellie to follow; he expected her to know everything the "Quiz Kids" knew. (This was a very popular radio program in the 1940s.) She was tested every Sunday.

As she grew older, her father reminded her that she was fortunate to receive such a fine education. He said, it was incumbent upon her to share this great gift with others to help enrich their lives. Being a nurturing person, having a hard-working, innovative and community oriented husband to help her, she became a committed member of our society who wanted to help others and to improve their quality of life through education, music, and theater.

Ellie and Morty had two sons, Jeff and Philip. Jeff was born on June 2, 1952. He attended Santa Fe Junior College in Gainesville, Florida. He was a paramedic for many years and then decided on a career change into the field of the visual arts. Philip was born on February 27, 1957. He graduated from the University of South Florida with a Bachelor Science Degree. In 1981, He graduated from the South Texas College of Law. He is a practicing attorney.

Highlights of 1969

Rabbi Arthur I. and Renee L. Baseman

On July 7, Rabbi Arthur I. Baseman became the spiritual leader of Temple B'nai Israel of Clearwater. He was born in Boston, Massachusetts and attended Harvard University 1955-1959, where he received a Bachelor of Arts Degree with High Honors in English Literature. While at Harvard, he was a member of the Editorial Board of the Harvard Yearbook, President of the Leverett House Glee Club, a member of Hillel, and was awarded a Harvard Scholarship. He was ordained from the Hebrew Union College-Jewish Institute of Religion, Cincinnati, in 1964, with the Degree of Master of Hebrew Letters. While

Rabbi Arthur and Renee Baseman

at the seminary, he was recipient of the I. Kingdon Fellowship from the American Jewish Archives, the Mother Hirsch Prize for Scholarship, and served as President of his class. Upon ordination, Rabbi Baseman received his commission as Jewish Chaplain with the United States Army and attained the rank of Captain during his tour of duty. He then served as Associate Rabbi at Temple Sinai, Roslyn Heights, New York. He also served as Jewish Chaplain at St. Francis Hospital, Port Washington, New York, the Nassau County Jail and was an officer of the Roslyn Ministerial Association.

By 1969, when Rabbi Baseman had arrived at Temple B'nai Israel from New York, he had already shown the kind of person and Rabbi that he was going to be in the coming years. A letter from the Chaplaincy Commission, The New York Board of Rabbis (Representing Orthodox, Conservative and Reform) stated in part, "...Our loss is Clearwater's gain. This is not just a cliche, it is an earnest statement of fact which the Chaplaincy Commission and our staff here at the New York Board of Rabbis join in most wholeheartedly.... Your great good will and devotion to your profession was always an inspiration and a source of encouragement to me....", Rose Snapperman. In keeping with this statement, Rabbi Baseman said, "One of my major goals, as I begin to serve Temple B'nai Israel, is to make an invisible God visible. I think God (helps) people through people. How else do you sense God with us? I want to be part of that. I want to try to inspire others." Rabbi Baseman has truly been an inspiration to every person he has come in contact with, both Jewish and non-Jewish, and has truly made an invisible and loving God visible to all of us.

In addition to being the rabbi at Temple B'nai Israel for the last thirty five years, Rabbi Baseman has been recognized as a spiritual leader throughout our community and all of Pinellas County. He has served on the Board of the City of Clearwater Community Relations Council and the Clearwater Bicentennial Committee. He has served on the Institutional Review Board of Morton Plant Hospital. He has been President of the Clearwater Ministerial Association and the Pinellas County Board of Rabbis, where he was the first President and served three terms. He has served on the Commission of Synagogue Administration of the Union of American Hebrew Congregations and the Central Conference of American Rabbis. He has also been a Member of the Board of the Jewish Federation of Pinellas County and Golda Meir/Kent Community Center. Rabbi Baseman has spoken to many organizations, churches, schools, and hospitals and has represented the Jewish Chautauqua Society at numerous college campuses.

There are too many stories to tell about Rabbi Baseman during his long and distinguished career in the rabbinate and the many years he has spent at Temple B'nai Israel of Clearwater. The stories go from the very serious to the very funny. He has said, "We have too many critics and not enough models in our society. We would be so much better off if we could just model the kind of behavior we each espouse." "I would like to see people start treating other people more humanely....Hopefully, we can become more sensitive and appreciative of others." "Love is a meeting of the minds and souls, a quiet understanding of the other, and loyalty through good and bad." Rabbi Baseman was asked by a congregant, "Is it a sin for my husband to play golf on a Saturday?" With the usual twinkle in his eyes, the Rabbi answered without hesitation, "The kind of golf he plays is a sin any day of the week."

The following story sums up the person of Rabbi Arthur I. Baseman. On Saturday morning, September 27, 2003, at the Rosh Hashana Services, one of the women in the congregation said to her husband, "Look at the Rabbi." The sun was coming through the window by the Ark and it looked like God was shining a light on him, as he was leading us in prayer. The question was, did we have an angel before us, or did we have a wonderful human being who was our spiritual leader? Over the time that this couple had been coming to Sabbath services, they had seen the many faces of their rabbi. He was funny, he was serious when the occasion warranted it, he was compassionate, as seen by the way he helped the two year old little girl walk down the steps of the Bema and helped the eighty-year-old woman light the candles and recite the blessings. Above all, he has always been friendly and a wonderful teacher. He has always taught by example and with his well-chosen words. His wife, Renee, has helped this extraordinary human being become the person that he is today. The couple and the thousand people in attendance at the services thanked him for his leadership and friendship and for including everyone in the wonderful mishpugha, called Temple B'nai Israel.

Renee Baseman was born in London, England on March 18, 1942. She and her parents, Resi and Stephen Lisser, emigrated to the United States in September 1943. She graduated from Oak Ridge High School in Tennessee, as a National Merit Scholarship Semi-Finalist. She had plans to attend Emory University in Atlanta. After the Temple in Atlanta was bombed, her guidance counselor called her mother and suggested that Renée go to a less dangerous area. Renée attended the University of Cincinnati, her second choice for her college education. On November 20, of her freshman year, she met a rabbinical student, Arthur Baseman. By December, they knew they were meant for each other and in June, 1962, they married. Renée earned a Bachelor of Arts Degree in Psychology in 1963, from the University of Cincinnati and a Master of Arts Degree in Counseling from the University of South Florida in 1995. She has served as a kindergarten teacher at the Temple B'nai Israel Religious School and then Director of the Baseman Early Childhood Center. She has been an early childhood teacher since 1978. Since 1995, she has been a Therapist at the Gulf Coast Jewish Family Service. She has been a very active committee member in many areas including the Clearwater Library Committee and the Public School Student Activity Committee.

Over the years, Renée has taught many different kinds of classes. They included: teaching two-year-olds at the preschool; parenting seminars; caregiver support groups; Holocaust survivors support groups; Jewish bereavement support groups; ninth-grade program in "Sex, Drugs, in Judaism." Renée was the first recipient of the Teacher of Excellence Award presented by the Pinellas County Jewish Federation.

Renée and Rabbi have three children: Adina, born in 1964 and married to M . Eric Sharpstein, in 1987; Jordana, born in 1969 and married to M. Sean McManamon in 1994; and Dalia, born in 1972 and married to M. David Faupel in 1998. All three daughters were consecrated, had a bat mitzvah, were confirmed, and married at Temple B'nai Israel. Adina earned a Bachelor of Arts in Education from the University of Florida. As a teenager, she was national President of the National Federation of Temple Youth. She served as a Temple B'nai Israel Cantorial Soloist and Song Leader. She also served as BIFTY President. She has initiated holocaust study programs in the public schools. Jordana earned a Bachelor's Degree in Special Education from the University of South Florida. She was a special-education teacher in Pinellas County. She's been involved in various Early Childhood Center Committees including editing the monthly newsletter. Dalia earned a Bachelor's Degree in Public-Relations from the University of Florida. She is an editor and communications consultant. As a teenager, she was the Youth Group President and a Cantorial Soloist at Temple B'nai Israel. The Basemans have six grandchildren.

Adina, Jordana, Dalia Baseman

On September 5, Reuben Rutenberg representing Congregation Beth Shalom, came to Temple B'nai Israel to bring Rabbi Baseman greetings and best wishes. Reuben Rutenberg said, "We welcome you, Rabbi Baseman and your family to our community. We hope this marriage between you and Temple B'nai Israel, will be a lasting one, with honor and success. The spiritual values of your pulpit have already risen among your members in the Jewish community of Clearwater, in the short time you have been here. I would like to quote from the Book of Joshua, chapter 1, "God said to Joshua: be strong enough with good courage; as I was with Moses, so I'd be with you. I will not let thee fail, nor forsake thee." As God was with the former Rabbis and Leaders of B'nai Israel, he will be with you, in the coming years. Nineteen years ago, on September 5, Mrs. Rutenberg and I came to Clearwater. The Jewish population of this area then, was about thirty families. Today our Jewish community has grown tenfold. We found the Temple building not quite completed. Mr. Sam Good, may his memory be blessed, Mrs. Rutenberg and I set up the first services for the High Holy Days. The community has progressed, in two congregations, an active Hadassah chapter, a B'nai B'rith group, as well as an effective U. J. A.. The golden age of B'nai Israel, is not in its past, but in its future. Under Rabbi Baseman's spiritual leadership, we can look forward to B'nai Israel, going from strength to strength. May the new year, bring you all, good health, much happiness, and peace in Israel."

Nancy and Alan Bomstein

Ku Klux Klan Rally

A Ku Klux Klan meeting was held at night on the west side of Belcher Road near Ulmerton. Harold and Arthur Lopatin went to the meeting to learn what was happening. They said that when they arrived, there was a cross burning on an empty lot. About 100 people were there in attendance. After about an hour, the crowd dispersed. Nothing further happened.

Highlights of 1970-1979

Highlights of 1970

The Jewish Welfare Fund of Clearwater raised $52,000 from 204 families. The officers were: Darwin Frank, President; Louis Brower, Vice President; Mrs. Sylvia Berman, Treasurer; Mrs. Louise Moskowitz, Secretary. The Director at Large and Publicity Chairman was Morris L. Newman. The Directors were: Mrs. Irving Baker, Mrs. Leonard Collman, Jerry Fish, Dr. Jan Hirschfield, Phillip Merkatz, Mrs. Bea Merkatz, Irving Baker, Philip Katz, Mrs. Isabel Katz, Loren Pollack, Al Rophie, Robert Benjamin, Marvin Peltz, Jeffrey Lopatin, Dale Pollack, Irving Sachs. Ex officio members were Rabbi Arthur I. Baseman, Rabbi Moshe Frankel, Maxwell Sackheim, Mrs. Isadore Goldberg, Ervin Schwartz, Louis Bloom, Norman Bulow, Mrs. Robert Benjamin, Mrs. Semon Amzalak, and Mrs. Cecelia Simon.

Highlights of 1973

After the Yom Kippur War, Charlie Rutenberg helped start the Jewish Welfare Board of Pinellas County. See separate chapter on Jewish Federation of Pinellas County for more information.

Alan and Nancy Bomstein

Alan and Nancy came to Clearwater for a job offer Alan received to start working for Charlie Rutenberg at the US Homes Corporation. Eighteen months later, in 1974, Alan left US Homes Corporation to start Creative Contractors Incorporated, a commercial construction firm. Previously, he had been active in the construction industry in Maryland, since 1967.

Alan was born in Baltimore, Maryland on July 29, 1945. He attended the University of Maryland and majored in accounting. in his words, he grew up "in a world where everyone was Jewish, or so it seemed." In the 1950s and 1960s, there were about 100,000 Jewish people living in approximately a three square mile area in Baltimore. In the Jewish neighborhoods, the public schools were functionally closed on the Jewish holidays. All of his friends were Jewish. Although he met some non-Jewish children in junior and senior high school, basically they were not part of the group he was involved with. All of the social functions he attended were Jewish. Alan and Nancy were married on December 24, 1968, in a kosher banquet hall. Since none of their close friends, at that time, were non-Jewish, it was a totally Jewish affair.

Alan and Nancy came to the West Coast of Florida, a place that most Jewish people from Baltimore simply did not know existed. To them, Florida was Miami and Fort Lauderdale. This meant that Alan and Nancy were now submersed in an entirely new environment, where the social and business local communities were essentially non-Jewish. They regarded this as an opportunity to expand their life and lifestyle, while maintaining their delight in their Jewish heritage and preserving the essence of Jewish life, responsibility for tzedaka, the improvement of life and health for all human beings. Alan set out on his own personal mission to place prominent Jewish people on community boards to help all people broaden their prospective of life. He felt personally that he could make a difference in society, "by genuinely working hard and giving of himself, both in time and money, in charitable and business ways."

Alan learned by example from his parents to always give to others. He said, "My father was a righteous man. At our synagogue, he was known as a "Tzadek." He was an accountant, and made a decent living, but we certainly weren't wealthy. He always gave to charity within his means; but there are no buildings with my parent's name on it. Mom and Dad were active in synagogue and Jewish community life. Dad died when I was twenty four years old. And for years after he died, people who had known him always told me what a wonderful person he was, and what a nice legacy he left. Being a young man when my father died left a remarkable impact on me. For it was then that I came face-to-face with the realization that all you really leave behind is your reputation. Your legacy is not your wealth – it's what you did in your lifetime that outlives you. Could I make my community a better place because of my involvement? Would I be remembered as fondly as my father was? You can't buy reputation; you can only achieve it through your life's actions. And no one can strip you of that. Preserving my reputation has been the guiding force in everything I do. Of all the edifices I've built in my career, the most important thing I have built is my reputation."

Alan's community involvement includes: Chairman, Board of Directors, Baycare Health System; Member and Chairperson, Pinellas County Board of Adjustment; Member of Board, Florida Chamber of Commerce; Member of Board, Pinellas County Economic Development Council; Member of Board Moffitt/Morton Plant Cancer Care; President (twice) Congregation Beth Shalom of Clearwater; Member of Board, First National Bankshares of Florida; Member of Board, First National Bank of Florida; Member of Foundation Board, Executive Board, and Treasurer, University of South Florida; Chairman, Friends of the Phillies; Member of Board of ClearPac (Chamber political action); Member of Board, Morton Plant Mease Health Care; Member of Board, Chairman of Board, Morton Plant Health System; Commissioner,

Judicial Nominations Commission, Florida Sixth Circuit; Chairman, Pinellas County Charter Review Commission; Secretary/ Treasurer, Pinellas County Sports Authority; Member, Pinellas Assembly-Organizing Steering Committee; Member, Foundation Investment Committee, Board Member, Treasurer and Chairperson of the Investment Committee, University of South Florida Foundation; Director, BayCare Health Network; Member of Board, Associated General Contractors of Mid-Florida; Member of Licensing Board, Florida Construction Industry; Member of Board, United Way of Pinellas County; Member, MPO Highway 19 Task Forces; Member of Board, Florida Aquarium; Member of Board, National Conference of Christians and Jews; Member of Corporate Associates Board, Morton Plant Hospital Foundation; Member of Board, Tiger Bay Club; Chairman, Clearwater Downtown Development Board; Member of Community Advisory Board, Junior League of Clearwater/Dunedin; Member of Board, Chairman, Long-Range Planning Committee, Chairman, Facilities Expansion Committee, Ruth Eckerd Hall at the Richard B. Baumgardner Center for the Performing Arts; President, Greater Clearwater Chamber of Commerce; Member of Board, Pinellas Economic Development Council; Vice Chairman, Pinellas Suncoast Chamber of Commerce; Chairman, President's Council, Pinellas Suncoast Chamber of Commerce; Member of Board, the Florida Orchestra; Member of Board, Contractors and Builders Association of Pinellas County; Vice President, Jewish Federation of Pinellas County; President, Tampa Bay Forum; Member of Board, Clearwater Phillies; Vice-Chairman, Dunedin Code Enforcement Board; Member of Board, Clearwater Board of Appeals; Member of Board, Clearwater Marine Science Center; Member of Florida Bar Grievance Committee; Member of Board, Clearwater Progress; Chairman, Tampa Bay Business Journal Advisory Board; Chairman, Advisory Board, Tampa Bay Business Journal; Member, Hall of Fame Jury, Blue-Chip Award Jury, Up and Comers Award Jury; Member, Hall of Fame Bowl Committee; Member of Board, Naisbett Task Force of Pinellas County; Chairman, Bylaws

Committee and Chairman of Planning Committee, Morton Plant Hospital; Member of Board, Pinellas County Arts Council; Member of Board, Pinellas County Task Force for the Medically Needy; Member of Board, Pinellas Higher Education Task Force; Member of Board, Clearwater Club; Chairman, Clearwater Housing Development Corporation; Chairman, Clearwater Housing Opportunities Incorporate; Board Member, WEDU-TV Public Broadcasting Station.

Alan Bomstein was Chairperson of the New Spring Training Stadium Facility for the Philadelphia Phillies; initiated and then spearheaded the merger of Morton Plant Hospital and Mease Hospital; Founder, Director and Vice Chairman of Citizens Bank and Trust and negotiated its sale to F. N. B. Corporation; spearheaded the drive to build the Charles Wharton Johnson Pavilion in Coachman Park in Clearwater; led a successful effort to keep the Florida Department of Transportation from ruining the beauty of the Courtney Campbell Causeway by installing a six-foot chain-link fence; conceived of and chaired the Pinllahassee Day, where 250 Pinellas business leaders traveled to Tallahassee.

Alan has built his business, Creative Contractors, into the second largest locally-owned construction company in Tampa Bay. It holds an outstanding reputation for innovation, performance and value. Alan has built over 1,000 commercial buildings in the Tampa Bay marketplace. He is notable for several of the synagogue and Jewish Community Center buildings. In 1977, Alan did the reconstruction of the former Trinity Presbyterian Church on Belcher Road and and made the structure into the new home for Congregation Beth Shalom. In 1991, he demolished the former church building and constructed a new sanctuary building on the same site. In 1992, he built the new sanctuary building for Temple Ahavat Shalom of Palm Harbor, designed by Tampa architect Sol Fleischman. In 1995, he did a major renovation of Temple Shaarai Tzedek in Tampa, creating a new grand lobby, administrative wing, and enlarging the main sanctuary. In 1999, he built the new structure for Congregation

B'nai Israel in St. Petersburg, a major complex that included a school building, sanctuary, chapel, administrative building, two social halls, and a very large kosher kitchen. Sol Fleischman also designed this complex. Creative Contractors did the initial campus renovation for the Tampa Jewish Community Center, including a new pre-school building and Weinberg Village, an assisted-living facility in Tampa. Alan has made several renovations to the Kent Jewish Community Center in Clearwater.

Alan has built some notable community buildings including: the new Ruth Eckerd Hall at the Richard B. Baumgardner Center for the Performing Arts; a major addition to the Museum of Fine Arts in St. Petersburg; the renovation of the Florida International Museum in St. Petersburg; theLeepa-Ratner Museum on the campus of St. Petersburg College in Tarpon Springs; and the Dunedin Arts Center. He has also built many health care projects including more than thirty at Lakeland Regional Medical Center, with his largest project being a new 320,000 square-foot, nine story hospital building in 2005. In addition, he built the Clearwater City Police building, parking garage and Municipal Service Center, as well as several major projects at Tampa International Airport.

Alan has received numerous awards for his work and his community support. They include: Tampa Bay Business Hall of Fame; Business of the Year Honoree; Alex de Tocquesville Leadership Award from the United Way of Pinellas County; Heavy Hitter Award from the Philadelphia/Clearwater Phillies; Pinnacle Award from the Pinellas County Economic Development Council; Distinguished Alumni Award; Pace Award from PEMHS; Silver Medallion Award from the National Conference of Christians and Jews; Mister Clearwater Award; David Bilgore Memorial Award; Entrepreneur of the Year Award from Arthur Young & Co./Venture Magazine; Liberty Bell Award from the Clearwater Bar Association; Award for Excellence in Architecture from the Florida Chapter American Institute of Architects; Merit Award from the Florida Central Chapter American Institute of Architects; Honor Award from the Young Professional of the Year, Building in Design and Construction Magazine; Florida Design Arts Award from the Florida Arts Council. He is listed in Who's Who in America and Who's Who in South and Southwest.

Nancy Sue (Auerbach) Bomstein was born on August 12, 1946, in Baltimore, Maryland. She attended the University of North Carolina and then graduated from the University of Maryland with a Bachelor of Arts Degree. In 1978, Nancy founded Incredible Edibles, a gift candy business which she ran from her home. In 1979, she opened a retail store on Drew Street next to her husband's office. When Alan bought a building in downtown Clearwater in 1982 for the new home of Creative Contractors, she occupied a corner of the ground-floor for a store and showroom. The business made candy, snacks and gourmet gifts in containers of glass, porcelain, tin, Lucite and woven baskets. She developed a worldwide-national customer base. She sold the business and retired in September, 2002.

Nancy has made many contributions to the community. She has been: Member of Board Junior League of Clearwater/Dunedin; Leadership Pinellas; Member of Board Greater Clearwater Public Library Foundation; Member of Board and chair of other committees, Morton Plant Mease Health Care; Chairman, Patron Gifts, American Cancer Society; Member, Board of Directors, Gulf Coast Jewish Family Services; Participant, Community Policing Institute; Member of Board, Florida Holocaust Museum; Life Member, Keeper of the Gate, National Leadership, Hadassah; Chairman, Community Women's Passover Seder; Chairperson of Committees, Congregation Beth Shalom.

She has received several honors: YWCA Woman of the Year; State of Israel Bonds Honoree; Gulf Coast Jewish Family Services Honoree; Junior League of Clearwater/Dunedin Sustainer of the Year Award.

Nancy and Alan have two children, David and Joshua. David was born on May 12, 1970. He attended Marshall University and earned: an Associate of Arts Degree from St. Petersburg College in 1991; an Associate of Science Degree in 1993 from Hillsborough Community College, where he became a Board-Certified Optician; and

an Associate of Science Degree from St. Petersburg College in 2004, where he became a Board-Certified Radiological Technologist. He is married to Dawn (Jacobson) Bomstein, who was born on February 19, 1977. Joshua was born on December 30, 1975. He earned a Bachelor of Arts Degree in Anthropology from Emory University in 1998. He is married to Lindsay (Batting) Bomstein, who was born on August 24, 1976. She earned a Bachelor of Science Degree from Antioch. Their baby boy, William Asher Bomstein, was born on September 25, 2006.

Alan and Nancy will be remembered not only for the beautiful edifices, Ruth Eckerd Hall at the Richard B. Baumgardner Center for the Performing Arts, Congregation B'nai Israel of St. Petersburg, Congregation Beth Shalom of Clearwater, Leepa Ratner Museum, Temple Ahavat Shalom, etc., but rather for the beautiful life they have created together and for sharing their time, their energy, their finances, and their love with everyone to build a better community of healthier and happier people. They too deserve the title of Tzadek.

top: David and Dawn Bomstein bottom: Joshua and Lindsay Bomstein.

Highlights of 1974

Israel celebrated its 25th anniversary. In Clearwater, Morris L. Newman was honored at this occasion. He had been an outstanding citizen in both the Jewish and non-Jewish communities. He was a charter member of three B'nai B'rith lodges: West Suburban Lodge, of Oak Park, Illinois; Westview Lodge, Elmhurst, Illinois; and Clearwater Lodge, Clearwater, Florida. He served as Blood Bank Chairman of the Florida State Association of B'nai Brith Lodges. He also served as Blood Bank Chairman of District Grand Lodge Number Five, founder and Chairman of the Clearwater Lodge Blood Bank for seven years. Including his many honors and awards in Clearwater, the blood bank was named the Morris L. Neumann B'nai Brith Blood Bank. He served as an officer or Board Member of the B'nai Brith Lodge of Clearwater, Congregation Beth Shalom of Clearwater, Temple B'nai Israel of Clearwater, President of the Friendship Club, etc. He has received many awards from the United Jewish Appeal, B'nai Brith, Jewish Welfare Board of Clearwater, etc.

Highlights of 1975

Rabbi Arthur I. Baseman, and Reva and Marshall Kent were honored at the Masada Award Dinner of the Clearwater Committee for State of Israel Bonds. Reva and Marshall have made outstanding contributions to our society locally, nationally, and internationally. Both of them had been board members of Temple B'nai Israel and the Southern Zionist Youth Commission. Marshall was President of Greenbrier Service Corporation and Kent Corporation. He contributed to Hadassah's Camp Judea in North Carolina.

Reva Kent was a board member of the Pinellas County Jewish Federation, Secretary and Vice President of the Florida Region Hadassah, Past President of Safety Harbor Chapter of Hadassah, and Past President of the Temple B'nai Israel Sisterhood. Just over 1,100 families belonged to five synagogues in Pinellas County.

On December 7, the Long-range Planning Committee, Rabbi Baseman, and the Board of Trustees of Temple B'nai Israel presented a plan to the membership to cap the size of the Congregational family by April 30, 1976. This was deemed necessary because of a surge in growth of the Jewish community of the north area of Pinellas County. There had already been double sessions in the religious school, seating problems at the High Holy Days, and the joyful experience of capacity crowds worshiping on the Sabbath and attending auxiliary meetings. In order to limit the growth of the synagogue, the committee and Rabbi felt that it was imperative to provide an alternative place to worship and carry out Jewish activities for Reform Jewish families. Since the fastest growing sections were in South Pasco County, Dunedin, and the Countryside area, it was determined that a new congregation had to be formed. Under the auspices of Temple B'nai Israel, Rabbi Sanford Shapero, Regional Director of the Union of American Hebrew Congregations, came from Miami to Clearwater to address the organizational meeting and discuss the chartering of a new congregation to serve the needs of Liberal Judaism in the northern portion of Pinellas County and southern Pasco County. The meeting was held at the Countryside Ramada Inn, which then became Temple Ahvath Shalom's first meeting place for their new congregation.

Highlights of 1976

Clearwater decided to establish a public library branch at Countryside Mall. City Commissioner Darwin Frank was unanimously authorized to continue talks with Countryside Mall leasing officer and part owner Loren Pollack on the details of such an arrangement. Bernard Feldman, an Eagle Scout at age fifty, despite terrible pain, continued to work with the Boy Scouts for over thirty nine years. He received a Presidential citation for his unselfish help to other people despite his own unfortunate circumstances.

Temple Ahavat Shalom

Temple Ahavat Shalom was founded in Palm Harbor by eighteen families. Temple B'nai Israel gave the new synagogue a Torah and prayer books and other assistance. The new synagogue was started by a group of young professionals and young married couples. The Ark made by Marion Hirsch was loaned to the congregation by Temple B'nai Israel. Charlie and Isa Rutenberg's daughter was the first rabbi for the High Holy Days. The congregation met in the Ramada on U.S. 19 in Clearwater, moved to a site on State Road 580 in Dunedin, and then to its present location on Curlew in Palm Harbor, during the early 1980s. (See Chapter 14.)

Highlights of 1977
June Baumgardner Gelbart and Richard B. Baumgardner

June came to Clearwater from New York City in 1957, along with her husband, Richard Baumgardner. They founded the world-famous Kapok Tree Restaurant on McMullen-Booth Road in Clearwater. The building, which cost more than $100,000, was designed to take advantage of the 125 foot-high tree, the largest specimen of the Baobob or Monkey Bread tree in the United States. Glass walls allowed diners to see the tree's branches at all times.

After the restaurant closed in 1981, June became the Director and chairman of the

Board of the Kapok Tree Inn corporation. In 1977 she donated thirty eight acres of land to Clearwater for a performing arts center. The memorial gift was given in honor of Richard B. Baumgardner, Sr. The stipulation was that the land be used for a performing arts center and that the development begin by early 1980. On December 15, 1979, the official groundbreaking ceremonies were held for Ruth Eckerd Hall at the Richard B. Baumgardner Center for the Performing Arts. Ruth Eckerd Hall was completed in October, 1983. On November 18, 1986, the Baumgardner Center was recognized for excellence in facility development and received the Governors Design Award.

June was a benefactor and very active in the Jewish community and the general community, and was a patron of the arts. She was a member of Congregation Beth Shalom and Temple B'nai Israel of Clearwater, B'nai B'rith, Hadassah, and a Lion of Judah. She was a founder of Menorah Manor and the Florida Holocaust Museum, and a sponsor of the United States Holocaust Memorial Museum in Washington, DC. She was a board member of: Gulf Coast Jewish Family Services, Golda Meir/Kent Jewish Center, and the Pinellas County Jewish Day School. She supported the Florida Orchestra, Ruth Eckerd Hall, and the Miniature Arts Society, where she presented the first and second place awards on an annual basis. She died at age 71 on March 1, 2002.

Richard grew up in his family restaurant business in Maryland. In his younger days he played jazz saxophone and was a singer for the first Jack Benny radio program in 1932. He continued with NBC for nine years. He served in the U.S. Army Special Services. As he built his restaurant, Richard searched the world and found many beautiful art objects, which made his facility unique. Richard was an art connoisseur who traveled the world collecting art objects, statuary, and paintings to be displayed in the Inn on all of its spacious grounds. The unusual plantings, pools with fountains, and peacocks could be found there. The restaurant had excellent food provided in unique surroundings. He also operated another restaurant called Baumgardners across McMullen-Booth Road. In 1973 he was named Pinellas County Restaurateur of the Year. He died on October 16, 1976, at age 68.

Ruth Eckerd Hall

When June Baumgardner donated the land which became Ruth Eckerd Hall, she did a very Jewish thing: Jewish people throughout the world have been deeply involved in the arts in the Jewish and general communities, whether it be locally during current times, or in Europe during the Nazi times, or in past centuries.

Many Jewish people have been involved in Ruth Eckerd Hall from its inception. Barry Alpert and Aaron Fodiman counseled June to help her with the decision to make the land donation to the city of Clearwater for an arts center. Many people in the Jewish community became Funded Life Members of Ruth Eckerd Hall before the original construction began. The first executive director of Ruth Eckerd Hall was Arnold Breman. Charlie Rutenberg chose the architect, the prestigious Frank Lloyd Wright Foundation in Arizona, headed by Chief Architect William Peters. Charlie was a major fund raiser, and supervised the project to make sure that Ruth Eckerd Hall became one of the foremost centers for the performing arts in the United States. Alan Bomstein carried out the extensive renovation and expansion effort in 2001. The current President and Chief Executive Officer is also Jewish. Robert A. Freedman has thirty three years of arts management experience. He is a graduate of Rutgers University and did postgraduate work at Brooklyn College. He serves on the Clearwater Regional Chamber of Commerce Board, Pinellas County Economic Development Task Force and Board of Congregation Beth Shalom. His wife is Leslie. Their daughter, Lily, graduated Summa Cum Laude from the University of South Florida in St. Petersburg as an English Major.

Highlights of 1978
Rabbi Jan Bresky

Rabbi Jan Bresky assumed the pulpit at Temple Ahavat Shalom. Rabbi Bresky was born in Newark, New Jersey in 1949 or 1950. He graduated from Temple University and Hebrew Union College and was ordained

Rabbi Jan Bresky

Toni and John Rinde

a Rabbi at Hebrew Union College. He was Acting President of the Pinellas County Board of Rabbis in 1983 and Past President of the Palm Harbor Ministerial Association. He had a son, Aaron, and a daughter, Ilana.

Golda Meir Senior Citizens Center

The first executive director was Pam Rutenberg. They had a variety of activities including specialized classes, discussion groups, card games, line dancing, movies and entertainment, hot kosher lunch served five days a week, a studio for ceramics and arts and crafts, and an exercise facility and swimming pool. The center also had a van to pick up and return seniors to their home. The exercise facility was named the Harry and Julia Schwartz Life Extension Center.

Marshall Kent and Charlie Rutenberg were sitting at the dining room table in the Kent home. Charlie said to Marshall, that a Jewish Community Center was needed for the north part of the county. Charlie said he would put up a quarter of a million dollars if Marshall would put up a quarter of a million dollars. They bought four buildings at Jupiter and Rainbow. They also purchased a piece of land, which was needed to make this one entire parcel. This later became the Golda Meir Center. A wide variety of Jewish community center programs were made available to the upper county residents through the new Clearwater facility. These programs included: mother and toddlers programs; junior gymnastics; summer camp for ages two through seventeen; special vacation days programs for children when public school was out. The center was also made available as a meeting place for Jewish organizations and groups.

The Gulf Coast Jewish Family Services established an office in the new Clearwater facility. This helped the G. C. J. F. S. provide help to people who had concerns with social isolation, marital problems, parent-child relationships, single-parent relationships, and assistance to the elderly. The key preventive programs, such as drug and alcohol abuse, were extended to this facility. Congregate dining for the elderly was established at this facility and funded by the Jewish Federation of Pinellas County and the Neighborly Center Corporation.

Toni and Dr. John Rinde

The early life of Toni Rinde may be found in the chapter on Temple B'nai Israel, Highlights of 1985. Toni came to the United States in 1947 with her parents and lived in New Jersey, New York, and Little Rock, Arkansas. She married John in 1959. Toni, earned a degree in Medical Technology from Drexel Institute of Technology in Philadelphia and Glen Cove Hospital on Long Island. She worked as a medical technologist at the University of Arkansas, School of Medicine, while her husband was in medical school.

Toni has been extremely active in the Pinellas County Jewish community. She has been: President of the Women's Division Jewish Federation of Pinellas County, 1986-1988; President Temple B'nai Israel, 1993-1995; General Campaign Chairperson Jewish Federation of Pinellas County, 1988-1990 and 2002-2004; President Jewish Federation of Pinellas and Pasco Counties, 2004-2006. She has been a Member of the Board of Menorah Manor, Executive Board Florida Holocaust Museum, Executive Board Jewish Federation of Pinellas County, Executive Board Temple B'nai Israel, Gulf Coast Holocaust Advisory Committee, and Gulf Coast Advisory Committee on Victims of Torture. She has won many honors including: Pinellas County Jewish Day School-Friends of the Children Award, 1992; Israel Bond Honoree as President of Temple B'nai Israel; Yitzhak Rabin Memorial Award-Distinguished Community Service, 2000; and Israel Bonds Lifetime Achievement Award, 2001.

During her speech for the acceptance of the Yitzhak Rabin Memorial Award, Toni stated, "For the past twenty five years, this community has blossomed into a major Jewish force in Pinellas County. I'm very proud to have been a very small part of that success. We must continue to work together as a unified group with a common goal of strengthening every aspect of Jewish life... With your continued help and involvement, we will grow and prosper and leave a wonderful legacy for children to follow."

The early life of Dr. John Rinde can be found in Chapter 1 under Przemsl, Lwow, and Lublin, Poland and under 1940-1946-

World War II. By 1946, the Rinde family left Poland for France, where they stayed for six years. They came to the United States in 1952 and in 1953. John enrolled at the Massachusetts Institute of Technology and graduated with a Bachelor's Degree in Mechanical Engineering. He also earned several graduate degrees. In 1971, he decided to change his career and enrolled in medical school in Little Rock, Arkansas. He graduated in 1975. In 1978, he established his medical practice in Clearwater and became affiliated with Morton Plant Hospital and Largo Medical Center. He retired in 2003. He has been a: Member of the American College of Physicians; American Medical Association; Florida Medical Association; Pinellas County Medical Society; Board of Governors of the Pinellas County Medical Society; Alternate Delegate to the Medical Executive Committee of Morton Plant Hospital; Chairman of the Utilization Review Committee of Morton Plant Hospital; and Chairman of the EKG Reading Committee of Morton Plant Hospital. He has won several honors including: Tau Beta Pi-National Engineering Honorary Society Member; Pi Tau Sigma-National Mechanical Engineering Honorary Society Member; Sigma Xi-National Research Honorary Society Member; National Science Foundation Fellowship; Fellow of the American College of Physicians.

Toni and John have two children, Debbie Rinde Hoffman, a transplant cardiologist in Tampa, and Barbara Feller, a certified public accountant in Coral Springs, Florida.

Highlights of 1979
Beth Chai Congregation and Rabbi Michael Charney celebrated Sukkot at the Florida Experimental Nurseries in Seminole. The following day, the service was held at the Seminole Fire Station on Vonn Road at 88th Avenue. Rabbi Mehler and Mr. and Mrs. Mordechai Gorn were honored at the Israeli Bond dinner.

Barbara and Mark Birenbaum
Barbara Lapidus Birenbaum and Mark Birenbaum came to Clearwater from Huntington, Long Island, New York, along with many other corporate families during the influx of people going to work for Pall Corporation, Honeywell, General Electric, Sperry Corporation, Superior Manufacturing, etc. Mark was a Corporate Manager who became Vice President of Superior Manufacturing. Mark became a Master Mason and the first Jewish Worshipful Master of Clearwater Lodge Number 127.

Barbara graduated from the University of South Carolina with a Bachelor of Arts Degree in Education and a Master of Education in School Psychology/Special Education. She received a Doctorate in Education in School Psychology/Neuro Psychology from Boston University. Barbara was the Poet-in-Residence at Arts in Education, Pinellas County, Florida from 1980-1982. In 1985, she became a Rehabilitation Psychologist. Also, in 1985, she became an author, illustrator, and composer. In 1996-2000, Barbara was the Literary Representative of the State of Florida, Department of Cultural Affairs. While still in South Carolina, she held many professional positions, including Charter Member of the Council of Exceptional Children, first woman school psychologist, and Charter Member of the National Association of School Psychology.

In Clearwater, as a parent, she was involved in traffic engineering, sidewalks, and water and drainage problems, which ultimately would affect the children of the community. She helped start a newspaper column in the *Clearwater Sun Newspaper* and the *St. Petersburg Times*, that included the creative writing of students. She has been the author/illustrator of several books including, *Lady Liberty's Light*, *The Hidden Shadow*, *Olympic Glow*, *Amazing Bold Eaglet*, *Groundhog Phil's Message*. In 2005, she received the Florida Publishers Association's President's Award for best juvenile book for, *Groundhog Phil's Message*.

Joan and Gerald Benstock
Joan and Gerald came from Huntington, New York to Seminole and established the corporate headquarters for Superior Surgical Manufacturing Company, Incorporated (now Superior Uniform Group, Incorporated).

The Company, which was incorporated in 1922, moved to Pinellas County because the cost of living in New York was very high. Attracting good employees was becoming very difficult. Along with the people coming to staff the headquarters, were twenty Jewish families, who over time, made a significant impact on the Jewish and general communities.

During World War II, the company made hospital specialties for Johnson & Johnson Company as well as for others. Afterwards they went back into the uniform business. In the early 1950s, they made medical supplies for the Armed Forces. It currently employees 240 people and sells a range of apparel and accessories for the medical and health fields, as well as for the industrial, commercial, leisure, and public safety markets. Jeffrey Schwartz, Marketing Manager, is the fifth generation Benstock in the business.

Gerald Benstock, Chairman of the Board of the company, graduated from Admiral Farragut Naval Academy of New Jersey and then earned a Bachelor of Science in Engineering from New York University in 1951. He was born on May 7, 1930. Gerald married Joan in 1951.

Gerald went into the family business that had been established by his step grandfather, Harry Saltz. In the 1930s, during the Depression, his grandmother, Rose, lent money to meet the payroll. In 1934, his father, David, went into the business. David was born in 1906 and died in 1973. His mother, Jane, who married David in 1927 or 1928, was born in 1908 and died in 2001. Jane had gone to business school and was very helpful in the business.

Gerald has been deeply involved in community and charitable work for many years. Some of his activities include: Trustee, Morton Plant Hospital, Clearwater; Vice Chairman, Morton Plant Hospital, Clearwater; Founder and Member of Board of Advisors of Pinellas County Jewish Day School; Member of Dress Circle of PACT; Member, Young President's Organization; Director, Marine Max; Member, Board of Advisors, Manufacturers Hanover Trust Company; officer of Linen Supply Association of America, Institute of Industrial Launderers, American Association of Contamination Control, Suncoast Management Institute; Director, Pinellas County Committee of 100; Cub Scout Pack Master; Member of Council of Economic Advisors of Suffolk County, New York; Member, Economic Development Program Committee; Chairman, United Jewish Appeal for Suffolk County, New York; Member of Metropolitan New York Cabinet; Chairman, Israel Bonds, Huntington, New York; Lecturer at C. W. Post and Hofstra Universities as well as the University of South Florida in the MBA programs; Member, Prime Ministers and Presidents Cabinet-State of Israel; founder, J.C.Penney Charity Golf Classic; Member, Morton Plant Hospital Foundation and Roebling Hospital Society. Gerald ,because of his extensive and highly successful volunteer work, has been the recipient of over thirty awards for outstanding service and dedication.

Joan Benstock was born on March 29, 1932. She attended Syracuse and Hofstra Universities. Joan and Gerald have four children, Susan Schwartz, Wendy Benstock, Michael Benstock and Peter Benstock. Joan's father, Herman Kline, was born in Hungary in 1898. He came to the United States in 1917. Her mother, Ada, was born in New York City in 1905. They married in 1928. They were co-owners of a stationery store.

Joan started her volunteer record of achievement in 1973 in Huntington, New York. She said, "My husband, Gerald, was my mentor. He taught me the significance and importance of making contributions to the community." She was Chairman and President of the Women's Division of the Federation of Suffolk County of New York. Since her arrival in Pinellas County, she has served the Federation in virtually every position including: Major Gifts Chair; Jewish Agency Representative to the Budget Allocations Committee; Women's Division Campaign Chair; Member of the Strategic Planning Committee; Vice President of Budget Allocations; Nominating Committee Chair; Board Member, and Executive Board Member.

Joan served as Southeast Regional Chairman of the Partnership 2000 Consortium of United Jewish Communities. She spearheaded the launching of the partnership and development of the first fiscal cycle projects in the Hadera-Eiron Region in Israel. She has involved teachers and students, both in Pinellas County and in Israel, in an exchange of students, where Israeli teenagers spend two weeks at Camp Or Hashemash at the Kent Jewish Community Center.

Nationally, Joan has served on the Women's Constituency Board and the Southeast Region Lion of Judah Conference Chair. She was named a Member of the Board of Governors of the JAFI, which is a partnership of the world Jewish community through the World Zionist Organization, United Jewish Communities, and the Federations, its governing bodies, the Board of Governors and the Annual Assembly. Joan is the Chairperson of the Oversees Needs Assessment for the Pinellas Federation. Joan is also a member of Hadassah, B'nai B'rith, and Sisterhood.

Joan has been deeply involved in helping Congregation B'nai Israel and the funding of its capital campaign. The Benstock Family Sanctuary at Congregation B'nai Israel is testimony to the Benstock's commitment to the Jewish community. The auditorium at the Pinellas County Jewish Day School is also named for the family.

Joan's philosophy of life can be summed up in the following quotes, "It is proven that people who are educated about an organization or cause will give more to that charity. Tzedekah is an education process. When you teach a man you educate a man; however when you educate a woman, you educate a family and that process will then spill over to all areas of Jewish life and will be perpetuated from generation to generation."

Joan's contribution to the Jewish community is a reflection of her dedication to the leadership roles she has assumed in the past, her passion for Israel, her familiarity and experience with Federation and the United Jewish Communities, and her commitment to her family and synagogue. Joan was the co-winner of the Jewish Federation of Pinellas County's Yitzhak Rabin Award for Distinguished Community Service. In 2005, on a national level, she won the Kippnis Award.

The Benstock Children

Susan was born in 1952. She graduated from George Washington University in Washington, DC in 1974 with a Bachelor of Science Degree in Speech Pathology. She earned a Master of Arts Degree in Speech Pathology in 1976, from Columbia University. She is married to Alan Schwartz, President of Superior Uniform Group. Wendy, born in 1954, earned a Bachelor of Arts Degree at Ithica College in 1976. Michael, born in 1955, attended Lehigh University and then joined the Armed Forces of Israel. He then attended Tel Aviv University. He is now the Chief Executive Officer of Superior Uniform Group. Peter, born in 1961, earned a Bachelor of Science Degree from the University of Miami. He is Executive Vice President of the company. His wife, Tracy, also earned a degree from the University of Miami.

Michael married Margot in 1978. Margot was born and raised in Copenhagen, Denmark. Her father was the sole survivor of the Holocaust in his immediate family. She came to Pinellas County by way of Israel, where she met Michael. She became involved in the Jewish community as the Parent Chairperson of the Preschool at Congregation B'nai Israel. She was President of Pinellas County Jewish Day School Parent Boosters Association. She has served in every major position of the Jewish Federation of Pinellas County. She served as: General Campaign Chairperson; Women's Division President; Covenant Fund Chairperson; Founder and Chairperson of the Teen Council; Member of Young Leadership Cabinet; Chairperson of Southeast Regional Conference Ritual Committee; Member of United Jewish Communities National Woman's Board. She was presented the Ludin "Young Leadership Award."

Michael began his service to the Jewish community in 1974 when he went with the United Jewish Appeal-Federation to Israel on a six-week pilgrimage and remained there for five years. He worked on a kibbutz, attended the University, and served for three years in the Israel Defense forces. He earned a Battlefield commendation and his sergeant stripes for his service in Lebanon. He is: Member of the Board of the Pinellas

County Jewish Day School; Member of the Board and Executive Board of Congregation B'nai Israel; Founding Board Member of Camp Ramah Darom.

The biggest concern of the Benstock family, led by Gerald, was that the children and grandchildren would have a proper Jewish life. The family has therefore made and continues to make highly significant contributions to the Jewish Day School, Congregation B'nai Israel, and the Jewish Federation.

Highlights of 1980-1989
Highlights of 1980

There were about 2,000 Jewish families belonging to seven synagogues within the county. This would indicate a total synagogue membership of 4,000-6,000 people. Two new synagogues had organized. Membership at Temple Beth-El of St. Petersburg had grown from 400 to 550 family units since 1975. Congregation Beth Sholom of Gulfport had grown from seventy five to 150 family units since Rabbi Sidney Lubin had arrived in 1978. Congregation B'nai Israel of St. Petersburg had grown from 320 families to 425 families, had a large youth group, and was the site of the county's first Jewish day school. In Seminole, Beth Chai Synagogue, progressive conservative, which was founded in 1976 by nine families had sixty families and its first building under construction. Congregation Beth Shalom of Clearwater had grown from forty families to 250 families, with 60% of the congregation under forty years of age. Seventy nine new families had joined in the past six months. Temple B'nai Israel of Clearwater grew from 285 families to 570 families with 100 new families being added each year. Rabbi Baseman said attendance at services were incredible averaging between 450 and 500 people. This growth at Temple B'nai Israel had occurred even though there was a large loss of families who left to form Temple Ahavat Shalom of Palm Harbor. Ahavat Shalom had grown from forty families to 120 families. Although they were meeting at a renovated former restaurant on Route 580, they purchased property on Curlew at County Road one, and expected to break ground for their first building in the fall.

Part of this substantial growth of Jewish membership in synagogues was attributed to the increasing number of Jewish people coming to Pinellas County and part of it to the group of young rabbis that came into the community and invigorated the congregations. It was hard to determine the actual number of Jewish people in Pinellas County, because many of them did not join synagogues. A nationwide Gallup Poll put the affiliation rate at twenty percent of the total Jewish population. However, most Pinellas County rabbis estimated that forty-sixty percent of the Jewish families in this area joined synagogues. Other barometers of Jewish population growth included the circulation of the Jewish weekly newspaper, Heritage, published in Orlando. About 3,800 households received this newspaper, which was an increase of 700 households over 1979. The Jewish population appeared to be growing at a much higher rate in Central and West Florida than other areas of Florida. A new Jewish Community Center, founded in 1979 at 302 S. Jupiter Street in Clearwater had already outgrown its facilities. Instead of the typical retirees making up the largest amount of Jewish families coming to Pinellas County, many young Jewish professionals and business people with their children and other members of their family were coming to this area. They wanted to establish a life here and demanded the same kind of Jewish community services they had up north. This influx of Jewish families was a tremendous stimulus to all Jewish synagogues and organizations.

Highlights of 1982
Rabbi Kenneth Bromberg

Rabbi Bromberg was born on August 23, 1928 and died on October 25, 2002. He served as a chaplain in the United States Air Force from 1956-1958; Rabbi of the Jewish Congregation of Oak Ridge Tennessee, 1958-1962; Rabbi of Beth El Congregation of the South Hills, Pittsburgh, Pennsylvania, 1962-1970; Educational Director, Kehillath Israel Congregation in Brookline, Massachusetts, 1970-1972; Director and Founder of Community High School of Jewish Studies, and Jewish Educational Council, Kansas City, Missouri, 1972-1975; and Rabbi of

Beth El Congregation, Omaha, Nebraska, 1975-1982. He earned a Bachelor's Degree in Sociology from Brooklyn College, in 1950. He earned a Master's Degree in Hebrew Literature and was ordained a Rabbi from the Jewish Theological Seminary in 1956. He earned a Master's Degree in Education from the University of Pittsburgh in 1970. He earned an honorary Doctor of Divinity Degree from the Jewish Theological Seminary, in 1982.

Rabbi Bromberg was Past President of the Pinellas County Board of Rabbis and the Upper Pinellas Ministerial Association. He was especially involved in an adult education program called the Community Lay School of Religion. He was on the Curriculum and Religious Affairs Committee of the Pinellas County Jewish Day School. He was an on call Rabbi for Hospice of the Florida Suncoast. He worked as a volunteer tutor in the Pinellas County Adult Literacy Program. He was a docent at the Florida Holocaust Museum and an instructor at Eckerd College in St. Petersburg. He was active in the Civil Rights Movement, supported Jewish women's equal participation in synagogue life and rights, and attempted to influence individuals to live a good life. He loved language and used it well. He read widely, was a news junkie, watched ball games, was a skilled amateur photographer, and fit all this into a busy life of giving exceptional care and love to his family.

Adult Education was always a major interest and concern for Rabbi Bromberg. In several communities, Rabbi and Johanna established WILL, which stood for Women's Institute for Living and Learning, a serious program of contemporary Jewish education for women during the beginning of the movement toward equal treatment of women in the synagogue. WILL evolved into ALL, which stood for Adults for Living and Learning.

The inscription on his tombstone is a reflection of the fullness of this human being. "To understand and ponder, study and teach, preserve and fulfill the teachings of the Torah."

Rabbi Bromberg and his wife, Johanna (Hirsch), were married in 1954 shortly after her graduation in the third graduating class of Brandeis University. She earned a Bachelor's

Degree in near Eastern and Judaic Studies. In 1974, she completed her Master's Degree in Library and Information Science. She taught in afternoon Hebrew Schools, in the Omaha Day School, and in adult education classes in several communities. As a librarian, she served in public libraries in Omaha and in Largo and still is Volunteer Director of the Ray and Nancy Murray Library Tolerance Center of the Florida Holocaust Museum. The Brombergs have three married children and nine grandchildren living in Massachusetts and Rhode Island. Their children and spouses are: Naomi and Yaneer Bar-Yam; Efram and Nancy Bromberg; and Hillel and Chaya Bromberg.

Johanna and Rabbi Kenneth Bromberg

Highlights of 1983

In 1983, Rabbi Jan Bresky, while still the religious leader of Temple Ahavat Shalom, founded the Jewish Media Relations Council. This Council broadcast Rabbi Bresky's message of God's accessibility to people through prayer and God's message of universal love. In 1987, Rabbi Bresky left Temple Ahavat Shalom and devoted himself full-time to the Jewish Media Relations Council. At the same time, Rabbi Bresky held services monthly in various locations.

Highlights of 1985

The Marshall and Reva Kent Jewish Community Center was opened at its present location in North Clearwater. The two centers merged in 1996, to become the Golda Meir/ Kent Jewish Center. The original Golda Meir Center was sold off because the Jewish community had moved further north in the county. The funds from the buildings were used for the combined center. See Chapter on Jewish Community Centers for further information

Highlights of 1986
Dr. Francis N. Dukes-Dobos

Dr. Francis N. Dukes-Dobos was born in Budapest, Hungary in 1920. His father was President of the Budapest Chevra Kadisha, a Member of the Board of the synagogue, and President of the Brotherhood of the Jewish Gymnasium. His mother was President of the greater Budapest Synagogue Sisterhood. During the Holocaust, many members

*Carol and Francis
Dukes-Dobos*

of his family were killed by the Nazis, including two of his sisters. His parents and one of his sisters survived the Budapest ghetto. In 1949, he started his career as Environmental Physiologist at the National Institute for Occupational Health in Budapest, Hungary, while serving on the staff of the Occupational Medicine Clinic at the Institute. He graduated from the University of Budapest Medical School in 1951 with an M.D. degree. He and his first wife, Elizabeth, were married in 1947. They escaped from Hungary during the 1956 uprising against the communist regime and came to America.

In 1956, Francis became a Research Associate at the Johns Hopkins University in Baltimore, Maryland. In 1961, he became a scientist and then later Chief of the Ergonomics and Physiology Branch at the National Institute of Occupational Safety and Health in Cincinnati. He served in this position until 1986, when he retired. Simultaneously, he was Adjunct Professor at the University of Cincinnati, Department of Occupational Medicine. He has published about seventy scientific papers and has contributed to several books. While at NIOSH, he served for two years at the Geneva Headquarters of the World Health Organization. The main topic of his research has been human tolerance to heat and physical work. He developed a method for the assessment of workers' heat stress and established permissible exposure limits which were adopted as a standard world-wide. He has chaired numerous committees for the American Physiological Society, American Conference of Governmental Industrial Hygienics, American Industrial Hygiene Association, International Foundation for Industrial Ergonomics and Safety Research, American Society for Testing and Materials, and the International Commission for Occupational Health. He has received several awards for his research work and was elected a member of the Delta-Omega Public Health Honor Society.

While in Cincinnati, he was President, Cincinnati Lodge Number Four of B'nai B'rith, and Vice-President and Chairman of the Ritual Committee for B'nai Zedek Congregation. In 1972, He received the

"Man of the Year Award."

When Francis arrived in Clearwater, he became an Adjunct Professor at the University of South Florida College of Public Health. He was elected an Honorary Member, Tau Chapter of the Delta Omega Honorary Public Health Society. He published several additional scientific papers and received a patent. When his wife, Elizabeth, died in 1991, he became more actively involved in the B'nai B'rith Unit and served as Chairman of the Anti-Defamation League Committee and then later became President of the unit. In 1994, he received the Sound of Honor Award from the Jewish Federation of Pinellas County. Francis is a Member of the Holocaust Survivors Advisory Board for the Gulf Coast Jewish Family Services

Francis's philosophy of life is based on three factors: his Orthodox upbringing; his education to become a physician and scientist; and his experience with the Holocaust. He believes, "Man has no freedom of choice between evil and goodness because they are affected by their hereditary inclinations, (physical and mental), by the pressure coming from their peers, by the impressions their education left on them, by the influence of the news media, by imagination derived from creative art, by uncontrolled animalistic desires; and last but not least by the inability to resist greed and corruption."

In 1995, he met his current wife, Carol Rubin, who had been the Director of the Jewish Federation of Pinellas County. Carol had also been employed there for several years before she went to work for the Pinellas County Courts. Carol had previously been Director of the Canadian Hadassah-WIZO Organization in Tel Aviv, Israel from 1966-1968, during the Six Day War. She's a life member of Hadassah. She was the Bulletin Editor for the B'nai B'rith Board and received an award for the outstanding Bulletin of the Year in 1996. Carol serves on the Boards of B'nai B'rith and PRIMER.

Rabbi Gary Klein

On July 1, Rabbi Gary Klein became the spiritual leader of Temple Ahavat Shalom of Palm Harbor. Prior to that, he served for nine years as Rabbi of Temple Beth Israel in Altoona, Pennsylvania. While there, he was the Treasurer of the Altoona Hospital, Chairman of the Board of the Altoona Community Mental Health Center, and Vice President of Family and Children's Services of Blair County, Pennsylvania. Prior to that, he served three years as Asistant Rabbi and Director of Youth and Educational Programs for Temple Anshe Sholom in Olympia Fields, Illinois.

In the Tampa Bay Area, he served as Treasurer of Gulf Coast Jewish Family Services and Gulf Coast Community Care. He served on the Mease Hospital Ethics Committee, the Board of Directors of the Long Center and the Board of Directors of the Palm Harbor Chamber of Commerce. He has served as President of the Pinellas County Board of Rabbis. He was a 1988-1989 designee for Leadership Pinellas.

Rabbi Klein is a native of Lakewood, New Jersey. He holds a Bachelor of Arts degree in Political Science from the University of Cincinnati, a Master of Arts in Hebrew letters from Hebrew Union College-Jewish Institute of Religion. He was awarded the honorary degree of Doctor of Divinity from Hebrew Union College-Jewish Institute of Religion in March, 2000. Rabbi Klein, in 1987, stated a belief that he still holds: "I'm very much aware of the significant influence a rabbi can have on people's lives. I appreciate and am careful with the awesome obligation I have. It is my responsibility and priority to strengthen relationships within individual members of families, to foster friendships and caring relationships among member families, to bring the beauty and significance of our Jewish heritage into the lives of our members, to nurture a sense of identity and commitment to our fellow Jews and our fellow men as well."

Highlights of 1988

In February 1988, Young Israel–Chabad of Pinellas County was formed by a few families who wanted to start an Orthodox congregation on the Florida Gulf Coast. A handful of families met originally in downtown Clearwater to organize the congregation. Currently, there are approximately 100 families, with a synagogue in Palm Harbor.(See Chapter on Chabads of Pinellas County)

Highlights of 1989

In 1989, Congregation B'nai Emmunah of Tarpon Springs was formed by Rabbi Jan Bresky, and a small group of Jewish people, who were dedicated to the message he preached. Congregation B'nai Emmunah is a Reform congregation promoting the principles of progressive Judaism. They welcome families and singles of all ages, straight or gay, interfaith families, Jewish or not, who wish to worship, study Torah, and serve God. The congregation is devoted to outreach programs to bring the Jewish hope of a more perfect world closer to all people. The congregation has no dues structure and people give what they think appropriate to support the Synagogue. See separate chapter on Congregation B'nai Emmunah.

Rabbi Gary Klein

Highlights of 1990-1999

Highlights of 1993
Rabbi Robert Schenkerman

Rabbi Schenkerman assumed the pulpit of Congregation B'nai Emmunah of Tarpon Springs. He had previously served as Rabbi of Congregation B'nai Achim of Petersburg, Virginia from 1992-1993, and Temple Beth Jacob of Concord, New Hampshire from 1984-1992.

He earned a Bachelor of Arts Degree Cum Laude in Near Eastern-Judaic Studies from Brandeis University in 1956. In 1958, he earned a Bachelor of Hebrew Literature from Hebrew Union College-Jewish Institute of Religion, New York Campus. In 1961, he earned a Master of Arts, Hebrew Literature, with Honors from Hebrew Union College-Jewish Institute of Religion. In 1961, he was ordained a Rabbi. In 1986, he received his Doctor of Divinity Degree.

Over the years, he taught at a variety of colleges including: Hebrew Union College, Jewish Institute of Religion; Department of Religion and Philosophy, University of Hawaii; Religions/Ethics, Hawaii Loa College and Community College, Honolulu, Hawaii; Religion and Ethics for Huntington Clergy Association, Huntington, New York;

Rabbi Robert Schenkerman

Biblical History of Philosophy, University of South Colorado, Pueblo, Colorado; Department Humanities, Colby Sawyer College, New London, New Hampshire; Religion, St. Leo's College, Fort Lee, Virginia. He also served as Chaplain for: United States Navy, Pearl Harbor, Honolulu, Hawaii; Fort Lee, Virginia; Veterans Administration, Fort Lyons, Colorado; New Hampshire Veterans Administration; St. Paul's Episcopal School, Concord, New Hampshire; Colby-Sawyer College, New London, New Hampshire; New England College Henniker, New Hampshire; House of Representatives, Concorde, New Hampshire; New Hampshire Hospice Programs; Suffolk Development Center, Huntington, New York; Honolulu Police Department, Honolulu, Hawaii. Rabbi Schenkerman, over the years, was involved in many interfaith activities. He was very active in the Board of Rabbis in the communities in which he worked and also in the Ministerial Associations

Highlights of 1997
Congregation Beth Tikvah

In 1997, a group of Jewish people seeking less structure and more fellowship, wanting to form a Chavurah, started Congregation Beth Tikvah of Palm Harbor.(This group came from Congregation B'nai Emmunah, after Rabbi Bresky's death).They originally met in members' homes until they reached seventy families. Today, there are 100 families in the congregation. They now hold bi-monthly services at Coral Oaks Retirement Home in Palm Harbor, where they provide services for the residents. All major holidays are celebrated and a Seder is held.

The congregation conducts Reform services utilizing lay leaders. The congregation stresses an interactive process during the saying of prayers to promote and find answers to satisfy their intellectual curiosity. Each prayer is interjected with a thought or comment, along with an English translation. There are no officers, no committees, no bylaws, no dues, but they are supported through generous contributions of the members. A cantorial soloist enriches the religious experience.

The spiritual leader is Zell Savitz who is assisted by his wife, Jacqueline Perez Savitz.

Rabbi Steven Moch

top: Rabbi Moch with the Springfield Torahs

middle: Rabbi Moch and Rev. Manuel Sykes

bottom: John Stroman, Pastor of Pasadena Community Church (right); Andrew Adams, Professor of New Testament at Eckerd College (middle).

He holds a degree from Gratz College of Philadelphia. He was the principal of a large Religious School in the Philadelphia area, instructional consultant for the Federation of Reform Synagogues in the Mid-Atlantic Region, and taught in the Isaac Mayer Wise Department of Gratz College. He was also the Director. His wife, Jacqueline Perez Savitz, holds a degree from Gratz College. She was also active in both public and Jewish education. She was principal of the largest Reform Religious School in the Philadelphia area. The two of them, along with others, serve on a voluntary basis to enhance the congregation. They adhere to the rabbinic maxim, "He who does not increase his knowledge decreases it."

Today, Beth Tikvah continues as an Independent Congregation, which basically follows Reform tradition. They have designed their own Prayer Book which is a combination of traditional and modern prayers, poems, songs, and inspirational readings. They stress an interactive process among the congregants to produce a sense of spirituality, while also pursuing their intellectual curiosity. They try to bring out what they consider to be the best features of both a Chavurah and a Synagogue.

Highlights of 2000-2005

Highlights of 2000

It was estimated that there were about 25,000 Jewish people in Pinellas County.

Rabbi Steven Fisher Moch

Rabbi Steven Fisher Moch, also known by his Hebrew name Rav Shimon Aryeh ben Ze'ev v'Kayla, has served as Rabbi of Congregation B'nai Emmunah since 2001. Rabbi Moch graduated from George Washington University with a Bachelor of Arts Degree in Religion in 1973, and then studied at Hebrew Union College -Jewish Institute of Religion in Jerusalem and Cincinnati. He received his Master's of Hebrew Letters and was ordained a rabbi. He has taken additional post-graduate courses in biblical studies and pastoral care. On March 9, 2003, he was awarded the Doctor of Divinity degree, for having completed twenty five years of rabbinic service.

Rabbi Moch had served on the pulpit of: Temple Emanuel, Winston-Salem, North Carolina from 1978-1985; Temple B'rith Sholom, Springfield, Illinois from 1985-1991; Temple Beth El, St. Petersburg from 1991-2000. In 2002 he was the resident chaplain at Tampa General Hospital. He has been extremely active in Interfaith activities and civic affairs during his twenty five years. He has been President of Central Illinois and Pinellas County Board of Rabbis, President of clergy associations in Winston-Salem, Springfield, and St. Petersburg. He has served on the boards of homeless shelters and food banks. He has worked on behalf of local issues of social justice. Throughout his rabbinic career he has acted as ambassador for his congregation and for the Jewish community. Rabbi Moch helped found Helping Hands of Springfield, a downtown shelter for the homeless.

Highlights of 2002
Rabbi David Weizman

In August, Rabbi David Weizman became the spiritual leader of Congregation Beth Shalom of Clearwater. He received a Bachelor of Arts degree from Cleveland State University, a Master's of Hebrew Letters, and Rabbinic Ordination from the Jewish Theological Seminary of America. He is working actively with young people and people facing difficulties in their lives. He served as a volunteer Chaplain for the American Red Cross, World Trade Center 911, and flight number 589, including interfaith pastoral duties at the World Trade Center Respite Center and Temporary Morgue at Bellevue Hospital.

Walter P. and Edith Loebenberg

On November 20, Walter P. and Edith Loebenberg received the Humanitarian Award from the Golda Meir/Kent Jewish Center. Walter is Chairman of the Board and President of U. S. Enterprises Inc.. They have been and continue to be true

leaders of the Pinellas County community. They have served on innumerable boards of directors of philanthropic, professional, and civic associations, including Menorah Manor, Gulf Coast Jewish Family Services, and Drug Free America Foundation. Walter is a member of the American Hospital Association, the Federation of American Hospitals, the Statue of Liberty-Ellis Island Foundation Committee, and Past Chairman of the Board of the Ann Frank Center USA in New York. He has served on the Florida Commissioner's Task Force on Holocaust Education. Edith and Walter founded the Holocaust Museum in St. Petersburg. It has been written about them, that, "Their foresight and vision continuously light flames of hope, while fighting bigotry, hatred, and prejudice."

Edith and Walter Loebenberg

Highlights of 2003

On November 12, the Golda Meir/Kent Jewish Center gave its 21st Annual Humanitarian Awards to six Pinellas County rabbis. They were Rabbi Arthur Baseman of Temple B'nai Israel in Clearwater, Rabbi Gary Klein of Temple Ahavat Shalom in Palm Harbor, Rabbi Jacob Luski of Congregation B'nai Israel in St. Petersburg, Rabbi Shimon Moch of Congregation B'nai Emmunah in Tarpon Springs, Rabbi Michael Torop of Temple Beth El in St. Petersburg, and Rabbi David Weizman of Congregation Beth Shalom in Clearwater. Stan Newmark, founding President of the Golda Meir/Kent Jewish Center said, "Since rabbis mean so much to our community, we wanted to honor them as a group. They help us spiritually and bring the people together and give them strength. They were deserving of this honor, deserving of being put in the same category as Graham, Askew, and Levin." The first such ceremony took place in 1983, when former congressmen and United States senator Claude Pepper was honored.

Rabbi Baseman said that the rabbis are recognized for their commitment and devotion to the Jewish people. "We have a passion for Judaism, a love affair with the Torah, a love of the people in the community, a sense of holiness, and we try to repair a

Rabbi David Weizman

world that is fractured by pain and sorrow. People remember what you do longer then what you say. They value what your actions have been. They remember not what you said, but how you made them feel. You have to want to help."

Rabbi Torop said "We, in our congregations, are quite concerned with social justice. At Temple Beth El, one of our projects is to build relationships with the African-American community, to help alleviate the plight of racism within St. Petersburg. What I'm hoping to do next is put together leaders of the community and say, "How do we move forward?"."

Rabbi Moch has worked with Habitat for Humanity and food banks for years. While serving in Springfield, Illinois, one very cold winter day, he organized Helping Hands, an organization of congregations to help move the homeless people indoors and out of the snow.

Rabbi Michael Torop

In accepting their awards, the rabbis said the following: Rabbi Arthur I. Baseman, Doctor of Divinity, "The Purpose of the Laws of the Torah is... to promote compassion, loving kindness, and peace in the world."; Rabbi Gary Klein, Doctor of Divinity, "He who executes charity and justice is regarded as though he has filled the entire world with kindness."; Rabbi Jacob Luski, Doctor of Divinity, "Without a sense of caring, there can be no sense of community."; Rabbi Shimon Moch, "A teacher affects eternity; he can never tell where his influence stops."; Rabbi Michael Torop, "The future belongs to those who believe in the beauty of their dreams."; Rabbi David Weizman, "In every community there is work to be done. In every nation, there are wounds to heal. In every heart there is the power to do it."

Robert Green

Robert Green was born in St. Petersburg in 1942 and graduated from Boca Ciega High School in 1960. He went on to the University of Florida Journalism School and graduated with a Bachelor's Degree in Journalism, in 1964. He then worked as a sportswriter from 1965-1967 at the Fort Lauderdale News. He was in the U.S. Air Force Reserve 1966-1971. He went to Washington D.C. and worked as a reporter and correspondent at the Washington bureau of the Reuters News Agency for thirty years. He covered Congress, the White House, Supreme Court, the Pentagon, the Justice Department, and other major federal agencies. He covered such major stories as Watergate, the Gulf War, the Clarence Thomas hearings, and every Presidential and congressional election from 1968 until he retired in May of 1997. In 1983, he married Aldele Fein. She died in 1995. Robert, because of his many years as an excellent journalist, is one of the proofreaders for this manuscript. He has been very helpful by doing in-depth reviews of the rough drafts of this manuscript.

Highlights of 2004

A new interfaith group called FAST, an acronym for Faith and Action for Strength Together met in St. Petersburg in November to launch a countywide effort to help resolve tenacious social justice issues. Representatives from twenty four congregations, including Temple B'nai Israel, joined together by the hundreds at Bethel Community Church. Their initial concerns were to target and improve education and transportation in Pinellas County. Father Robert Schneider of Espiritu Santo Catholic Church in Safety Harbor referred to those assembled as "God's people working together for peace and justice." Rabbi Baseman said he jumped at the chance to become involved in the interfaith social justice group. "I think that repairing the world is a Jewish imperative that faces every Jew that wants to respond to the covenant with God. We are constantly seeking to do acts of loving kindness in the community daily."

Highlights of 2005
Donna L. and Dr. Herman (Hank) Koren

On June 29, Dr. Herman Koren received the Walter S. Mangold Award, the highest honor in the United States given by the National Environmental Health Association, "for outstanding contributions to the advancement of the environmental health professional." Hank is only the second Jewish person to ever win this award. The first one was Hank's mentor and friend, Dr. Jerrold

M. Michael, who won the award in 1961.

Hank's award citation read, "2005 Mangold Award Recipient – Herman Koren, R.S., M.P.H., H.S.D.

The National Environmental Health Association is proud to present the 2005 Walter S. Mangold Award, its highest honor, to Dr. Herman Koren, Professor Emeritus of Health and Safety, Indiana State University (ISU).

2005 marks Dr. Koren's 50th year in the environmental health profession. A widely recognized and respected leader, who has devoted his life to the advancement of the profession and environmental health education. He has been an inspiration to many environmental health students and peers as a professor, sanitarian, mentor, public speaker, and author.

Koren began his career as a rural field Sanitarian with the Pennsylvania Department of Health in 1955 and in 1959– at the age of twenty six – became the youngest supervisor in the history of the Philadelphia Department of Public Health. Under his leadership at the department, community rodent control programs and immunization programs were developed. Koren then designed sanitation and infection control programs as Chief of Environmental Health and Safety at Philadelphia General Hospital. While working at the hospital, Koren became an Associate at the University of Pennsylvania Medical School, presenting lectures and clinical work in hospital infection control to third-year medical students.

In 1967, Koren started the environmental health program at ISU and was appointed Assistant Professor of Health and Safety and Coordinator of the Environmental Health Internship Program. In his position as Professor, he advised students and graduates, formed a student environmental health association, brought high school students into the classes for ten-week periods, assisted numerous universities in establishing environmental health programs, and traveled to several different states to promote ISU's environmental health program. As a result of Koren's efforts at ISU, the university became one of the first accredited schools of environmental health.

One of Koren's most notable achievements was the creation of a new environmental health internship program at ISU in 1969. Through a U. S. Public Health Service grant, Koren was able to secure paid internships at county health departments and federal agencies for his environmental health students. To his credit, over 1,150 internships in twenty eight states and seventy different programs and over $3 million were provided to students. According to C. Michael Krecek, R.S., M. A., Director/Health Officer of Midland County Department of Public Health, "He's left a true mark upon this nation and world from the more than 500 environmental health professionals he has placed in the field through his work at ISU. His efforts have had a major impact on supplying skilled environmental health professionals to the workplace, who are now leaders in environmental health and public health. I am one of those leaders, and I am convinced it would not have been possible without the mentoring and caring attitude of Hank Koren."

In 1995, Koren retired from ISU, but not from the field of environmental health. His knowledge and expertise continues to reach thousands of students and environmental health professionals through his publications, including *Handbook of Environmental Health* (in two volumes and numerous editions) and *Management and Supervision for Working Professionals* (in two volumes and numerous editions). His latest publication, the second edition of *Illustrated Dictionary and Resource Directory of Environmental and Occupational Health* is a one-of-a-kind environmental health reference book, with over 16,000 entries.

Hank and Donna Koren

Captain John A. Steward, R.E.H.S., M.P.H., with the U.S. Public Health Service, expresses the sentiments of many of Koren's former students: "When I entered the environmental health field, I found myself to have an advantage over other professionals because of the education and experience Doctor Koren had facilitated at ISU. The supervised internships Dr. Koren arranged for me allowed me to develop extensive field experience that others lacked at this stage of their careers...Furthermore, I continued to draw upon Dr. Koren's expert knowledge and insight by using his growing set of environmental health textbooks."

Dr. Koren's Walter S. Mangold Award.

Throughout his career, Koren has been an active member and leader in many local, state, and national organizations. He became a member of NEHA in 1956 and a Fellow of the American Public Health Association in 1967. Because of his vast experience and knowledge, Koren has served as a consultant to the U. S. Public Health Service, the U. S. Environmental Protection Agency, and the World Health Organization. In addition, he has initiated and served as co-chair of several conferences and committees, and has acted as an advisor to many groups–often without gratuity.

Koren has spent a lifetime dedicated to environmental health practice, research, teaching, and public service. He has encouraged many students to consider a degree in environmental health and has written articles and professional publications urging his colleagues around the country to expand their environmental health programs. As expressed by Koren himself, "I still hope to help young people become the best they are capable of being...Teaching to me is essential to my life. I'm trying to return to others what my mentors and professors gave to me. They allowed me to try to help other people to live a better life through the creation of a healthier and safer environment.

It is both a privilege and an honor for NEHA to present this award to Dr. Herman Koren, a man who exemplifies both the spirit and the ideals of the late Walter S. Mangold."

The General Bio of the written presentation by Indiana State University and the Indiana Environmental Health Association entitled, "Dr. Herman Koren–Environmental Health Educator" summarized Hank's early life and the influences on him that led him to become a leader and mentor of young people. ..."Herman Koren was born in Philadelphia on July 1, 1933. He was raised in a very religious and loving family. Although the family suffered from poverty his parents taught him and were examples to him of love and compassion for others. These early experiences were the building blocks for his future career in the public health field.

He demonstrated leadership qualities during the Second World War, when as a child he not only gathered the largest amount of paper and scrap for the war effort, but also organized other children into a group so that they too could be productive. For this, he won an award from his elementary school. He became very active in the Cub Scouts, safety patrol, and then became the captain of the safety patrol for the Vare Elementary School in Philadelphia.

At twelve years of age, Dr. Koren contracted polio. He was paralyzed in all parts of his body with the exception of one hand. The doctors told him that he would never walk again. His tremendous desire to achieve and his persistence to excel despite all odds, not only helped him overcome this almost insurmountable problem, but many of the severe difficulties that he has faced throughout his life. He has instilled the same desire in many of his fine graduates.

At age fourteen, he became the senior den chief of his cub pack of sixty Cub Scouts and six den chiefs. At the same time he was a patrol leader in the scout troop.

At Simon Gratz High School in Philadelphia, he not only became an outstanding scholar, but a student leader, and an athlete...and finally he achieved his goal of winning his athletic letter in tennis.

Dr. Koren earned his Bachelor of Arts Degree from Temple University in Chemistry and Biology. While there, he again demonstrated his leadership qualities and performed services for others. He was the chairman of the blood drive, book exchange, and many other activities. He was President and held many other offices in the Zeta Iota Chapter of Alpha Phi Omega National Service Fraternity. He was the winner of the prestigious Dan Beard Award for outstanding leadership, scholarship, and service....in 1985,...he published a pamphlet entitled "History of Jewish Community, Terre Haute, Indiana," which was highly acclaimed. In 1992, he was nominated for the Research and Creativity Award, Indiana State University and was honored by the Cunningham Memorial Library for excellence in research...in 1993, he became the President of United Hebrew Congregation of

Terre Haute, Indiana. (See About the Author for additional professional information.)

On July 10, Hank Koren received the following e-mail from his friend and mentor, Jerry Michael. Hank has always tried to pattern his life, his professional career, and his need to do something significant for the Jewish and general communities after what Jerry has done. In fact, Jerry wrote a history of the Jewish community of Hawaii, when he was there. Jerry had also made many outstanding contributions to the improvement of the health of millions of people locally, nationally, and worldwide. Jerry's e-mail was entitled, "Your Legacy:"

"Dear Hank:

June 29 was a seminal moment for the field of environmental health as it was a time that your peers recognized you for more than a half-century of contribution to our chosen field.

It was a proud day and your friends, your wife, and your children can be justifiably proud-and yes they can "qvell (be joyful)."It is a special day for colleagues like me as well, for I feel that I have also been rewarded by this act of recognition...

I think now of your legacy and of your record of teaching and research that rivals most of what others have managed to have done.

After the applause from former students and fellow environmental colleagues have faded and the classroom is empty; after the last article has been written, and you are back in the quiet of your own house and the academic gown has been placed in the closet and all the pomp and fanfare has faded, it is rewarding to reflect on those things that endure.

The enduring things that are left are the record of dedication to integrity and excellence and recognition of having done with your life the very best you could to make the world a better and healthier place in which to live through the efforts of those whose lives you've touched by teaching and through example.

That, Hank, lives on into eternity. Your friend, Jerry Michael."

Jerrold M. Michael Sc.D.,Dr.P.H., D.E.E., R.S., Assistant Surgeon General United States Public Health Service (Retired), Emeritus Dean and Professor of Public Health, University of Hawaii, and Adjunct Professor of Global Health, George Washington University."

In the preliminary remarks by Dr. Hank Koren after the presentation of the Walter S. Mangold Award, he said, "For a person to have a single moment of pure happiness in a lifetime is wonderful. For a person to have two distinct moments of pure happiness in a lifetime is remarkable.

My first moment was personal. It was the moment that I met my darling wife, Donna, and fell in love with her, on September 15, 1971 at 7:30 p.m.. Beside being a fantastic wife, friend, and partner, Donna has helped me with everything I have ever written of significance, from my doctoral dissertation to tonight's presentation. She didn't know I was going to talk about her tonight.

My second moment was professional, the Walter S. Mangold Award. This highly coveted award is not only for me, but for all of us here tonight. You are the unsung heroes of the public health field. All of you are being recognized for all that you do to promote good health every single day..."

Donna truly deserves much of the credit for the writing of this, my latest book, It is a unique adaptation of the skills which I learned over the years in conducting numerous research projects in the environmental health science field. Like all of the other research I have done in the environmental health science field, during these 9,000 hours of research and writing, she never complained. In fact, she was extremely encouraging and, she spent over a thousand hours proofreading and acting as a consultant to the work.

Donna was born in Terre Haute, Indiana on August 6, 1940. She was a high honors student when she attended Indiana State University, while raising five children and taking care of an aged father and an aged mother-in-law.

The children are: Sheryl Lynn Koren, born March 17, 1957; Susan Dale Pollard, born May 1, 1958; Debra Lynn Hardas born

June 13, 1961; Scott Lawrence Koren born June 25, 1969; and Laura Michelle Stuckwich born July 12, 1969. Sheryl earned a Bachelor of Science Degree in Nursing from Indiana State University. Susan earned a Bachelor of Science Degree in Special Education from Indiana State University and a Master of Science Degree in Counseling from IUPUI. Debra earned a Bachelor of Science Degree in Environmental Health Science from Indiana State University and an Associate of Arts Degree in Nursing from Indiana State University. She is both a Registered Sanitarian and a Registered Nurse. Laura earned a Bachelor of Science Degree in English from Indiana State University.

Debbie Koren Hardas, when asked why she was going to Poland on January 27, for the 60th anniversary of the liberation of the German death camps said, "I am going because of my father. He is Jewish, was born in the United States, and never had a chance to visit the places I will see." As co-editor of "The New Horizon," she wrote, "...It never ceases to boggle my mind how any particular group of people could hate another so strongly that they could organize and create mass destruction of so many lives before being stopped. But my heart feels sadness at the thought that in so many places the hatred and prejudice continue to thrive, even if on a smaller scale. It is all our jobs to step up to the plate and do what can be done to prevent groups from being targeted for prejudice, ostracism and violence. There are so many lessons to be taught and learned by us all. Let's hope we find the best ones." Yes, the younger generation is engaged and determined that the Holocaust will never be repeated.

In 2001, Hank and Donna joined Temple B'nai Israel of Clearwater. Hank proposed to Rabbi Baseman and the Executive Committee that he write a book about the history of Temple B'nai Israel. Within a period of two weeks, he realized that the history had to be of Jewish life in all of Pinellas County, from its inception to current times. This was the first step toward researching and writing this book.

Dr. Jerrold M. Michael

Jerry Michael's contribution to our society is included in this book because of the highly significant impact he had on the life and career of Hank Koren. Mentors of young people aren't born that way, they learn from others, as Hank learned from Jerry. Jerry was also a Jewish man very much involved with his Judaism and his synagogue, while working and achieving great things in a generally non-Jewish world. This is so reminiscent of the Jewish men and women who first came to Pinellas County and because of their hard work, their goodness, and their desire to make the world better, opened up a new way of life for many Jewish people to come.

Jerry Michael joined the University of Hawaii in 1971, following a twenty-year career in the United States Public Health Service, where he retired as an Assistant Surgeon General holding the rank of Rear Admiral. He served as Dean of the School of Public Health of the University Hawaii for twenty years, and continued as Professor of Public Health until his retirement.

Because of his highly significant contributions to world health, Jerry Michael has received numerous awards. In May of 1985, in ceremonies in Israel, a chair in public health was dedicated at Hebrew University of Jerusalem, in his name. In December of 1987, the Commander of the Most Exalted Order of the Elephant was conferred upon him by the King of Thailand. In 1989, he was awarded the Sang Kancil Gold Medal by the government of Malaysia. He is a prolific writer, who's been recognized for his work in health policy and the politics of health, international health, health management, health leadership, and academic management. Beside being the first Jewish person to win the Walter Mangold Award, he has won the John Shaw Billings Award of the Association of Military Surgeons of the United States. He was awarded several Commissioned Officer Medals from the United States Public Health Service, as well as the Brutsche Award from the United States Public Health Service Commission Officers Association. On June

9, 2005, the Surgeon General of the United States presented him with the Surgeon General's Medallion for a lifetime of service to the Nation in the field of Global Health. The Hebrew University of Jerusalem has awarded him with the Magnes Medal for his work in health services management and international public health. He is an active consultant to the World Health Organization and the China Medical Board.

SYNAGOGUES

Introduction

Although information has already been provided briefly on the origins of the synagogues discussed in this chapter, in the chronological listing of events in Chapter 7, St. Petersburg and south county and Chapter 8, Clearwater and north county, a more in-depth view will be given here. To avoid duplication on a year-to-year basis for each individual synagogue, only major new items or special items will be included. This does not in any way decrease the enormous amount of work and contributions made by various groups over the years. For instance, to list all the activities of the Sisterhoods and Brotherhoods on a yearly basis, would take an enormous number of extra pages for this history. There are many heroes among the Jewish people who have made the synagogues viable Houses of Worship, education and socialization. Unfortunately, it is impossible to determine who all these people were and what they did to create a better Jewish life.

To better understand the significance of the synagogue as a central part of Jewish life it is well to read Rabbi Arthur I Baseman's article entitled "When You Belong to a Synagogue", as follows:

"When you belong to a synagogue you become identified with an institution that has shown a genius for survival, enduring through the ages despite the constant challenge of a brutal historic process of over 4,000 years.

When you belong to a synagogue you become identified with an institution that has consistently represented that there is a moral purpose to the universe and ethical code between people and people and between nation and nation.

When you belong to a synagogue you declare yourself a Jew not merely because you are born a Jew, or choose to be a Jew, or because the non-Jew may exclude you from his company; but because you believe in the mission of the people named Israel, a mission which champions spiritual values, ideals, and beliefs that the world needs to hear.

When you belong to a synagogue you become part of an institution which expresses in majestic terms the yearning of your conscience to better this world by act rather than by word, by "well done" rather than "well said".

When you belong to a synagogue you belong to an institution which expresses in warm and symbolic ways the great stages of your journey from birth to death, from sadness to joy, from despair to hope.

When you belong to a synagogue you become a member of the fellowship wherein you can find friends which cut across boundaries of age, neighborhood, or occupation. Here friendship is founded upon a common commitment to basic truths of life.

When you belong to a synagogue you ensure the continuity of the generations, where your children and grandchildren can learn the history and literature of Judaism, where they can practice the precepts of their faith in the company of other young people. Here they discover that Judaism is joyful and full of vitality, and here they learn of the strengths of family, loyalty, and community.

When you belong to a synagogue you belong to an institution which can help you to become an informed Jew, one who knows what distinguishes the Jewish people from others; an informed Jew who is able to detect, even amidst the blair of discordant sounds, the still, small voice within the individual soul.

....Share your synagogue with others-enable them to find the mood and meaning of this sacred place."

The words of a lay person, Betty G. Smith, also give the reason why we seek out the synagogue as a place of prayer and meditation. "Why am I here in the House of the Lord? I do not know if what I seek can be found here – But I may begin here. I seek my roots and my belonging, For I must be anchored somehow in the flux of time; And in the lonely relativity of space I must stand somewhere. The past, the present and the future converge here, in me, at this moment. I seek in others the fellowship of longing and of hope, of joy in the depths of pain, of courage in the anguish of defeat. Though I am with others at the theater or the ball game, there is no poignancy or depth in that relationship-and the heart is left hungry. I seek the meaning of life in words grown old but not empty – Words that break the heart open to its own transcendence. I seek the meeting with God in the sanctuary of my soul."

CHAPTER 9

CHABADS OF PINELLAS COUNTY

Chabad of St. Petersburg

The Chabad of St. Petersburg was established in November, 2002. It was a synagogue without walls that was using various locations for prayer until a facility was acquired. It is now located at 6151 Central Avenue in St. Petersburg. It is an affiliate of the Chabad-Lubavitch movement and is dedicated to increasing the awareness, knowledge, and observance of Judaism in South Pinellas County. Its goal is to reach out to all Jewish people regardless of their age, affiliation, or level of observance. It conducts Sabbath and High Holy Day services. Its programs include the Jewish Learning Institute lecture series for adults, bar-bat mitzvah lessons, hospital and prison visitation, workshops for the holidays, mezuzah checking and affixing, and home koshering. The synagogue is run by Rabbi Alter Korf and his wife Chaya.

Young Israel-Chabad of Pinellas County-Palm Harbor

The Young Israel-Chabad of Pinellas County was formed in February of 1988. Pamela Rutenberg Tench, daughter of Charlie and Isa Rutenberg, bought the land for the first synagogue which was located on Virginia Avenue in Clearwater. Charlie and Isa established for each of the children a $100,000 grant to be given to a charity of each child's choosing. Pamela, who now resides in Israel, elected to help start an Orthodox congregation on this part of Florida's Gulf Coast. Initially, a handful of families met in downtown Clearwater. The generosity of Pamela Rutenberg and the leadership of Rabbi Shalom Adler and his wife, Chanie, have helped this congregation grow to about 100 member units and it is now housed on a one and one-half acre site in Palm Harbor. The synagogue is located within walking distance of a beautiful neighborhood that offers various levels of housing to the congregants. Young Israel-Chabad is affiliated with two internationally recognized Orthodox outreach organizations, the National Council of Young Israel and the worldwide Chabad-Lubavitch movement. The mission of the congregation is to reach out to every Jewish person to expose him or her to the beauty of Torah, mitzvah, and Yiddishkeit. The synagogue offers a very active women's group and adult education program. It also has a preschool for two-five year olds.

No officers or board members are listed for either Chabad. It is the understanding of the author that the Rabbi serves in all these capacities. The origin of the Chabad-Lubavitch movement may be found in Chapter 1.

CHAPTER 10

CONGREGATION BETH SHALOM OF CLEARWATER

Highlights of 1950-1959

Highlights of 1957

On November 12, Congregation Beth Shalom was chartered by the Circuit Court of the Sixth Judicial Circuit of the State of Florida in and for Pinellas County. The officers were: President-Reuben Rutenberg; First Vice President-Samuel Good; Second Vice President Salem Baranoff; Corresponding Secretary-Mildred D. Goldberg; Recording Secretary-Zelda Bolin; Financial Secretary-Jack Golden; Treasurer-Harold Segal; Board of Directors-David Rosenfeld, Robert Bauman, Jacob H. Goldberg, David Shane, Douglas Weiss, Isadore Zitlin, Al Winston, Ike Eisenstein, and Sid Bolin. The objective of the corporation was: "To promote a closer relationship among the Jewish residents of the Clearwater area, to sponsor and encourage religious activities and conservative religious services among those of the Hebrew faith, to encourage good citizenship and Americanism, and to inculcate among its members a sense of individual obligation to their community, state and nation..."

Jewish families forming Congregation Beth Shalom came from Temple B'nai Israel and new residents in the area. Families leaving Temple B'nai Israel were: Reuben and Mary Rutenberg, Arthur and Billy Rutenberg, Isadore and Clara Zitlin, Salem and Lisa Baranoff, Ike and Annie Eisenstein, Sam and Yetta Eisenstein, Samuel and Yetta Good, Leon and Theresa Greenwald and David and Gertrude Shane. Reuben Rutenberg became the first President. Isadore Zitlin was one of the founders. Further, more people were moving into Clearwater who desired to observe traditional, conservative Judaism. The founding members included: Dr. Salem and Lisa Baranoff of Safety Harbor; Robert and Rita Bauman, owners of Suzanne's Ladies Store and Harvey's Men's Store; Dr. Isadore and Bella Berger; Ezra and Gloria Bobo, Bobo's Gifts located at 530 Cleveland Street; Augusta and Honey Copelan, 304 Pegasus Ave.; Simone and Betty Einstein; Ike and Anna M. Eisenstein, 232 Main St. Safety Harbor; Sam I. and Yetta G. Eisenstein, 146 second Avenue North, Safety Harbor; Ms. Sophie Fink, 400 North Osceola Avenue; Mrs. Beatrice Fisher, 215 Bayshore Dr. Sound, Safety Harbor; Aron and Helen T. Galloway; Jack (Jacob) H. and Mildred D. Goldberg, 1533 Young Avenue; Jack M. and Gertrude Golden, Golden Spot Reality, Safety Harbor; Samuel and Yetta Good, 1962 Harding Plaza; Leon and Teresa Greenwald, 400 North Corona Avenue; David and Sadie Haftel; Louis and Minie Joseph; Dr. Harry and Elizabeth Katz, office 512 First Avenue Southwest, Largo; Marshall and Reva Kent; Mrs. Fanny Kasselman, Isadore Rutenberg's mother; Morris and Eleanor Kohn, 806 A Pine; Ned L. and Lillian Kramer, Lillian B. Kramer's Cancellation Shoes and Tin's Shoe Rack; Nathan and May Leiman, 310 North Jupiter; Philip and Rebecca Merkatz; Simon and Carmen

Pitcheon, Garmane Aerosonic Corporation; Hyman R. and Rose Polakoff, 417 Sixth Avenue, Safety Harbor; Mrs. Mildred Rice; David and Sally Rosenfeld, Rose Bootery; Morris and Judith Rosenstein, Lido Apartments; Arthur and Billy Rutenberg, Eagles West, Bellair; Reuben and Mary Rutenberg; Harry Safchik, 1851 Overbrook Avenue; Jack and Anna Sanders, 1625 Grove; Jacob and Minnie Saunders (Cecilia Schwartz's mother), 1915 McKinley; Harold B. and Sally Segal, Liggett Suburban Drugs and Fussell's Incorporated.; Rebecca Shallat, 15 South Comet; Gertrude and David Shane; Abraham and Celia Simon; Joseph and Vicki Sutton; Mrs. Fanny (Meyer) Tepper, 307 Hillsborough; Lawrence and Lois Volk, Broadway Pharmacy; Douglas and Hannah Weiss, Weiss and Weiss Development Corporation; Alex and Helen Winston, 707 North Highland; Isadore and Clara Zitlin, 1520 Laura.

The first meeting was held at the Sherwood Restaurant on June 12, and about twenty people attended. It was decided to organize the conservative synagogue with a payment of $50 a year per family. About $1000 was raised. The second meeting was held on August 4. Plans were made to have the High Holy Day services at the Clearwater Woman's Club beginning September 25 and extending through October 20.

Arrangements were made for Religious School classes to be held at the Clearwater Women's Club three days each week, including Sundays. A vital part of the congregation was its Sunday and week-day Hebrew school. From the beginning, the goal was to put into each child a love for Judaism and Israel. A children's Sabbath service was started as soon as possible.

The third meeting was held Thursday evening, August 8 at 8 p.m. at the Clearwater Woman's Club, Osceola and Seminole Streets, 700 block north. Reuben Rutenberg was the temporary chairman; Mrs. Sidney Bolin was the temporary secretary; and Harold Siegel was the temporary treasurer. A nominating committee was appointed at the September 5, meeting. On September 22, the Ark was dedicated in a service held at the Woman's Club. On October 3, the nominating committee brought in its slate of officers and board members, and the elections were held. The first official officers of Congregation Beth Shalom were: Reuben Rutenberg, President; Samuel Good, First Vice President; Dr. Salem Baranoff, Second Vice President; Mrs. Sidney Bolin, Recording Secretary; Mrs. Jack H. Goldberg, Corresponding Secretary; Mr. Jack Golden, Financial Secretary; and Mr. Harold Siegel, Treasurer. The Board Members elected for a one-year term were: Mr. David Rosenfeld, Mr. Robert Bauman, Mr. Jack H. Goldberg, Mr. David Shane, and Mr. Douglas Weiss. The Board Members elected for a two-year term were: Mr. Isadore Zitlin, Mr. Al Winston, Mr. Ike Eisenstein, and Mr. Sidney Bolin.

The installation of the officers was held at the Woman's Club on October 19. A strictly kosher dinner was served. Rabbi Harry Richmond from Temple B'nai Israel gave the invocation and installed both the officers and the Board of Directors. Vocal solos were sung by Mrs. Mildred Price and accompanied by Mrs. Charles Rutenberg. The main address of the evening was given by Rabbi Morris B. Chapman of St. Petersburg. Jack H. Goldberg was master of ceremonies and Mrs. Isadore Zitlin was chairman of the installation dinner. The women cleaned and scrubbed after each party, meeting, or service at the Women's Club. These women became the first Congregation Beth Shalom Sisterhood. The money that came from their efforts went into a fund that was used to help build the future synagogue. A month later, the Congregation Beth Shalom Sisterhood had its first installation of officers.

David and Gertrude Shane

David Shane was born in Hungary and came to Ft. Wayne, Indiana in the late 1800s, at the age of 14. Later, he opened a family grocery store in Indianapolis. He married Anna and had five sons: Izzy, Max, Al, Leo, and Syd. Anna died when Syd was eleven years old. He then married his cousin, Bertha Hollander, to raise his boys. The marriage ended in divorce after two years. He married for the third time to Maria, and that marriage also ended in divorce after two years. David's fourth marriage was to Gertrude. She was an artist from St. Petersburg, Florida, who had originally come from Toledo, Ohio. Gertrude had three sons of her own and was widowed. They raised the seven boys in Dunedin, Florida. David and Gertrude were among the original founders of Congregation Beth Shalom, where David was a Member of the original Board of Trustees and Gertrude taught Jewish cooking classes. They returned to Indianapolis because of declining health. Their marriage lasted for twenty five years until David's death in 1961.

Highlights of 1958

Several members of Temple B'nai Israel also had dual memberships in Congregation Beth Shalom. These people wanted to help all Jewish organizations and synagogues prosper. On January 12, 1958, two Torahs were dedicated by: Rabbi Harry R. Richmond, Temple B'nai Israel, Clearwater; Rabbi Morris B. Chapman, Congregation B'nai Israel, St. Petersburg; and Rabbi Jerome Kestenbaum of Tampa. Cantor Nathan Grossman of Tampa helped officiate at the dedication ceremony. At the dedication, President Reuben Rutenberg announced that a new synagogue would be built on Coachmen Road near Belcher Road. The Torahs were presented to the Congregation at the dedication ceremony, which was attended by more than 100 members of the Congregation, city officials, area rabbis, and other guests from the Tampa Bay area. Mr. and Mrs. Al Winston of Clearwater and Indianapolis and Mrs. Winston's mother, Mrs. J. Shallat, led the procession carrying the Torah from Israel, which they had presented to the Congregation. It was given in memory of Mrs. Winston's father, Jacob Shallat and Mr. Winston's father, Samuel Weinstein. The second Torah came from Iraq. It was given in memory of Mrs. Joseph's parents, Lulu and Joseph Isaac. The walls of the Women's Club, where the dedication dinner took place, were lined with the men of the Congregation who passed a Torah from person-to-person. A service of prayers and songs completed the ceremony. Dr. Morris B. Chapman was master of ceremonies and Rabbi Harry Richmond gave both the invocation and benediction. The major

David Shane

speech of the evening was given by Rabbi Kestenbaum. Mayor Lewis Homer and City Attorney Ben Krentzman represented the City of Clearwater. The Clearwater High School String Ensemble, under the direction of Stephen W. Yanetovich, presented several musical selections. Two large silk flags were presented by Mrs. Morris Brodsky, of Safety Harbor in memory of her late husband.

Highlights of 1959

Beth Shalom was located at several different places, including a storefront at 1847 Drew Street and the Clearwater Garden Club. Land was purchased at 2177 Northeast Coachmen Road and a synagogue was built there. A home was also built there for a future Rabbi. At first, all services were conducted by lay leaders. Reuben Rutenberg read from the Torah at the Sabbath services.

Highlights of 1960-1969

Highlights of 1960-1963

In the 1960s, despite all difficulties, synagogue members continued to work for the preservation of Congregation Beth Shalom. The pioneers worked diligently to improve the synagogue structure, the religious rituals and the growing Hebrew school. The leaders at that time were Mr. and Mrs. Reuben Rutenberg, Dr. Salem Baranoff, Samuel Good, Mr. and Mrs. Al Winston, Albert Rophie, Mr. and Mrs. Isadore Zitlin, Ezra Bobo, Harry Landskroner, Mr. and Mrs. Jack Goldberg, and many more people. The congregation had people woes, ego woes, and money woes, but love, dedication, and sacrifice kept the synagogue going. There were worries about how to get new members and teachers and students for the religious school. There was a concern about how much to charge for membership dues and school tuition. Where could the congregation find a proper area for a cemetery? How could they find a proper rabbi and how would they pay for him? The congregation engaged several rabbis, but didn't have the financial resources to keep them. A Sunday school was started by Mary Rutenberg with a handful of young children. As younger families came in, more children arrived and a children's Sabbath service was

added with the older children reading from the Bible or in the Torah service.

Marvin and Ethel Peltz

In 1960, Marvin Peltz came from Tupelo, Mississippi where he had general merchandise stores, including women's ready-to-wear apparel and high-fashion shoes. He became President of Peltz Famous Brand Shoes and opened new stores in Clearwater, Lakeland, and Tampa. He was a member of Congregation Beth Shalom of Clearwater and its Men's Club. He was a member of B'nai B'rith, a Hadassah Associate, and past President of the Lions Club of Tupelo. He died on November 27, 1984 at age 77. His wife, Ethel, was a very productive member of Congregation Beth Shalom and its Sisterhood. She was a member of Hadassah, ORT, B'nai B'rith women and the Order of the Eastern Star of Clearwater. According to Alan Bomstein, "Ethel was a very positive influence on the lives of others. She was very polite and gentle but had a spine of steel. Her mind was agile and she always tried to think of how to help others. She was Miss Daisy, as in the play, "Driving Miss Daisy." She was a person of great humor, while still maintaining her Southern charm." Her contributions to Congregation Beth Shalom were such that the social hall was named for her.

H. Bernard Peltz, son of Marvin and Ethel, opened the first Peltz Shoe Store in 1957 at 542 Central Avenue, St. Petersburg. He later moved to his own building at 526 Central Avenue. Bernard was an advocate of promoting the downtown business area and was instrumental in having Central Avenue reopened to vehicular traffic. Previously, he had served in the United States Air Force in Salzburg, Austria. He had a Bachelor of Science Degree in Advertising and Sales from the University of Alabama. He was a member of the St. Petersburg Chamber of Commerce, Downtown Merchants Association, and Member of the Board of Temple Beth-El of St. Petersburg. He died on January 26, 1982, at the age of forty nine.

An article in the St. Petersburg Times on November 30, 1997 talked about the Center against Spouse Abuse in St. Petersburg and thanked Gary Peltz for donating shoes to the many women arriving at the shelter. CASA's Development Director, Renée McInnis, praised Gary Peltz, co-owner of the shoe store. Renée said, "It takes a whole community to stop domestic violence, and Gary Peltz and his family are true leaders of CASA's community." She presented to the shoe store a "Victory over Violence Award."

Highlights of 1964

Mary Rutenberg wrote several articles which were printed in the local newspapers. The articles discussed the services for Yom Kippur, Succoth, and Simhath Torah. Congregation Beth Shalom held its first Melava Malkah, a Saturday evening program planned as a cultural event. The event opened with the Havdalah service and its cantorial chant, a reading or talk on the Sabbath or related subject, vocal and instrumental solos, and community singing. Refreshments were served and the evening closed with dancing.

The Havdalah service separates the sacred from the profane, the Sabbath from the remainder of the week. Prayers are said over the wine, a lighted twisted candle, and a dish of spices. At this first service ever held at Congregation Beth Shalom, Reuben Rutenberg, the synagogue President, gave the interpretation of the Melava Malkah, which means, the Sabbath Queen is preparing to leave for the remainder of the week. The cultural program included the traditional Havdalah prayers followed by the Hamavdil solo sung by the synagogue cantor, Isadore Zitlin. Mrs. Gertrude Golden read a story by Reuben Rutenberg describing his childhood in a small town in Russia. Mary Rutenberg played a piano solo, "Rondo Brilliant" by Karl Marie Von Weber. Jacob Saunders read an original poem in Yiddish. Mrs. John Greenwood accompanied the communal singing.

In Article II of the Constitution and By-Laws-Object and Scope, the following was written: "The object and scope of this congregation is to help maintain, through the instrumentality of the synagogue and related institutions, the creative continuity of the Jewish people as well help strengthen traditional Judaism as it is interpreted by the conservative movement in Jewish life; to put into practice its way of life; to teach its language, literature and religion; to foster and stimulate the expression of Judaism in everyday living and integrate it into the pattern of American life."

Highlights of 1965

On March 17, Dr. Salem Baranoff was honored by Congregation Beth Shalom at a special dinner. Among many of the honored guests of the general and Jewish community was Rabbi Taxay of Temple B'nai Israel. President Reuben Rutenberg gave the major presentation. He said, "In the name of Beth Shalom, I welcome you all tonight, on this unusual occasion of honoring a beloved citizen among us, Dr. Salem Baranoff....He loves to keep peace, with all people, Jew and Gentile alike. When we chose a name for our Synagogue, it coincided with his name....Dr. Baranoff is a disciple of Aaron. For the past (fifteen) years, I've worked with Dr. Baranoff in different organizations. It has always been a pleasure to work with him, for he is sincere and humble. Eight years ago, Isadore Zitlin, our Cantor and First Vice President, and I asked Dr. Baranoff to help us organize a conservative synagogue in Clearwater. His answer was that if it is important to have a traditional synagogue, I will help you in every way possible. Dr. Baranoff is one of the founders of Beth Shalom. He was President of Beth Shalom for several years, guiding it with his fatherly love. This loyalty and sincerity of his gives warmth and comfort to its members, always hoping for a better and bigger Beth Shalom....he attends services, taking part in the cantorial services on holidays and Shabbat. He blows the shofar extremely well. Dr. and Mrs. Baranoff have contributed freely to the building of our Synagogue and its upkeep from year-to-year, giving from the heart, with gentleness. Recently the Board of Directors of Beth Shalom voted, unanimously, to bestow the honor of President Emeritus for life on Dr. Salem Baranoff...Dr. Baranoff supports Jewish institutions of learning. He believes that teaching Jewish children is an important duty of every Jew. All Jews are responsible for each other....At the (Safety Harbor) Spa, Dr. Baranoff has helped thousands of people from all over the United States and

For Havdalah service. Temple Beth-El collection.

other countries, to return to normal health....
Although he is a busy man, he still finds
time for Safety Harbor communal life, such
as the Civic Club, and library, and other city
institutions. Dr. Baranoff is a humble man....
The accomplishments of Dr. Baranoff speak
louder, and more eloquently, than anything
I can say."

Mary Rutenberg continued in her role
as correspondent for the local newspapers.
In one of her articles, she talked about
Shavuoth, the Feast of Pentacost. The
children presented a religious program
of holiday songs and dances for bringing
the first fruits to the Temple in Jerusalem
in ancient days. The confirmation of boys
and girls took place at the Religious School
ceremony. The religious school for the 1965-
1966 year, started on September 5. Teachers
followed the curriculum recommended
by the Conservative Teachers Division of
the Jewish Theological Seminary, New
York. Additional classes were offered in
Bible and Hebrew, as well as customs and
ceremonies.

On December 19, 1965, Congregation
Beth Shalom dedicated its new Ark and
classrooms on the holiday of Hanukkah,
which means dedication. President Reuben
Rutenberg gave the dedication speech. He
thanked the artist and architect, Charles
Goldsmith, and the building campaign
Chairman, Harry Landskroner. He said
that now that the synagogue had been
materially improved, it was the time to
engage a permanent young conservative
rabbi before the coming high holidays. "The
Talmud advises us, to build a home first and
then get married, Beth Shalom has built its
house of God...and now a (marriage) can be
made between Beth Shalom and a rabbi."
From 1957 to 1965, most of the time, the
congregation utilized its own talents instead
of engaging a rabbi. Whenever they needed
advice on how to conduct services or had
questions about rabbinical laws, they turned
to Rabbi Chapman of Congregation B'nai
Israel of St. Petersburg for help. From 1963
to 1965, the membership increased from
thirty member families to fifty five member
families. It was now felt that a young
Conservative Rabbi would attract younger
couples with small children. It would help

stimulate growth in the religious school,
including the Hebrew school, which is the
foundation of every synagogue.

Rabbi Louis Gorod was chosen to become
the new spiritual leader of Congregation
Beth Shalom.

Highlights of 1966

The synagogue held its 10th annual
Hanukkah dinner. An original play, written
by Henrietta Gorod, was presented by
children of the Religious School. The
children were taught that part of their
Hanukkah money should be shared with
the poor. Mary Rutenberg continued to write
numerous articles for the Clearwater Sun.

Highlights of 1967

Reuben Rutenberg was presented
with a bronze plaque in recognition of
his distinguished service to Congregation
Beth Shalom for over the past ten Years.
Cantor Isadore Zitlin was presented with
a bronze plaque for his ten years of service
to Congregation Beth Shalom. Reuben
Rutenberg's plaque read, " His wisdom has
guided us...through our formative years.
His boundless energy, generosity, and
unwavering loyalty to the synagogue will
always be a glowing (torch)...of dedication
in the richest degree." Isadore Zitlin's
plaque read, "1957-1967 --His love for
traditional liturgical music has enhanced
all the services of our congregation. May
God bless him with many more years of
serving his congregation and community.
April 1967."

President Reuben Rutenberg wrote in his
New Year's message, "... The past year has
been fruitful for Beth Shalom. Its membership
increased, and the services were well
attended. A religious school had an increase
in the number of pupils, and a Sabbath
service was added. This was conducted by
the children who felt the satisfaction in their
service. Our Sanctuary, inside and out, has
a new look. With the spiritual leadership
of our Rabbi we now look forward to
growth in numbers and achievement...."

Highlights of 1969

On January 20, Congregation Beth
Shalom of Clearwater became a member

of The United Synagogue of America-the national organization of Conservative congregations. President Reuben Rutenberg in his New Year's greetings said, "... Congregation Beth Shalom has many plans and it will take many hands to accomplish their fulfillment. We must increase our membership both in our Synagogue and in our school. With additional membership will come increased strength. Beth Shalom must become a true center of Jewish life in the Clearwater community, interesting and attractive to our present and future generations. It is our hope to improve our religious school, where our children will be taught in accordance with the standards and curriculum of the United Synagogue of America, with which we are now affiliated...." Rabbi Baseman of Temple B'nai Israel attended the second day of Rosh Hashanah services and was asked to bless the Torah before and after the reading. There were fifty three member families with thirty eight coming from Clearwater, six from Largo, one from Safety Harbor, one from St. Petersburg, two from Tarpon Springs, and four from New Port Ritchey. On October 1, Reuben Rutenberg, due to personal conditions, resigned as President of Congregation Beth Shalom. Ben Zuckerman wrote to Reuben, "...We wish to express our gratefulness to you for having done so much for Beth Shalom over the years via your leadership and conscientious dedication of time, devotion, and generosity in supporting our projects."

Highlights of 1970-1979

Highlights of 1973

Alan and Nancy Bomstein joined the synagogue in April. When Alan arrived, some of the founding members were still the movers and shakers of the congregation. Dr. Salem Baranoff was always present on the High Holy Days, when he blessed the Torah. Salem, with his shock of white hair, sitting on the bema, made an indelible impression. Harry Landskroner personally ran the Thursday night bingo games. He carried the cash home in a canvas sack at 11 p.m. and went to the bank in the morning with the deposit. If a bingo game was missed one week, the Rabbi's salary was in jeopardy.

Founding member Al Winston, a real estate developer, was instrumental in building the synagogue facility at 2177 NE Coachmen Rd, when the congregation was newly formed. He told Alan Bomstein that in order to get the building permit, the City of Clearwater required a "solid border" of punk trees" (known for their ability to grow quickly), apparently to keep the synagogue from view.

Reuben Rutenberg had already died, but his widow, Mary, remained a stable figure at the synagogue. She was a teacher, supporter, and fundraiser. The Feders, the Feilmans, the Honigmans, the Silvermans, the De Coveneys, the Zimlins, the Orloffs, all were leading families at Congregation Beth Shalom in the 1970s. Pincus Aloof was the rabbi, cantor, and was also a skilled Mohel (a person who performs ritual circumcisions). In September, Cantor Ely Landman conducted the High Holy Days services. (This may have been before the arrival of Pincus Aloof. There is some uncertainty about the dates concerning Pincus.) Joe Stern, Harry Lane, and Lou Danziger were also fixtures of the synagogue. The Horwich sisters were benefactors and active in everything. Another long-standing benefactor was Ethel Peltz. Andrew Sendy and Bernie Panush were also important members.

Highlights of 1975

By 1975, a number of younger families had joined Beth Shalom. The facilities on Northeast Coachmen Road were inadequate for a larger vibrant congregation. David Baker, Mark Michelman, Harvey Kaiser, Arthur Barlis, and Alan Bomstein all took an active interest in the future of the congregation. Rabbi Aloof left to take another position. While attending a United Synagogue event in Orlando, Max Glazer, Arthur Barlis, and Alan Bomstein met a young assistant rabbi, Peter Mehler, from Satellite Beach and shortly thereafter were able to hire him as the Rabbi of the congregation. This started a period of significant growth that doubled the size of the congregation to about 150 families.

David Baker

Arthur Barlis, President, Congregation Beth Shalom, 1977.

Highlights of 1976

Dr.Arthur Barlis became the President of the congregation. As a member of the building committee, Alan Bomstein started to look for options to expand the existing building or to find a site to build a new facility. The congregation purchased the church building of the Trinity Presbyterian Church and proceeded to remodel the sanctuary for the synagogue. Alan insisted that there be a competitive bidding process for the remodeling. His bid was the lowest and he then worked with a young architect, Jane Shapiro, of Columbus, Ohio to remodel the church to meet the specifications of a conservative synagogue. The Trinity Presbyterian Church congregation took the old building at Northeast Coachmen Road as part of the transaction and then sold it off to another church group.

Highlights of 1977

The congregation moved into its new facility in time to celebrate the High Holy Days. The new facility was remodeled through the generosity of the members of Beth Shalom, led by Maurice Hirsty, Manny Goren, Max Glazer, and many others.

The new synagogue was dedicated on the weekend of Friday, October 28, to Sunday, October 30. On Friday night, a proclamation was read by the Honorable Mayor of Clearwater, Gabriel Cazares. He proclaimed the weekend of October 28, 29 and 30, 1977 to be Congregation Beth Shalom Dedication Days in Clearwater. He invited all citizens to join in a spirit of love and brotherhood to welcome the congregation in celebrating the dedication of this beautiful new Sanctuary. He said

that the Jewish people contributed greatly to the spiritual life and moral tone of the community. It was accepted by Dr. Barlis. Rabbi Henry Michelson, assistant chancellor of the Jewish Theological Seminary in New York, related the current construction to the ancient teachings. "Without (the ancient teachings), then in vain do you labor to build; in vain do the policeman labor to protect the city." He said, "The materialism of today, the brick and mortar which too often are the barometers of the quality of life in American communities, are without value unless the old morals, ethics, and teachings are reaffirmed." Michelson praised the spirit of the Clearwater Jewish community and of the community in general. He warned that if the spirit is to survive, the ancient teachings must flourish. Jacob Friedman, the Southeast Regional Director of United Synagogue, the Conservative movement's central organization, presented the key to the synagogue to Beth Shalom's Rabbi Peter J. Mehler. Cantor Abraham Denburg of Beth Tfiloh Congregation in Pikesville, Maryland, led the congregants in traditional Jewish music. Rabbi Michaelson said, "2,000 years ago, universal education became a part of the synagogues. The same Torah studied in Babylonia is studied in Clearwater... Thousands of children will enter halls of learning. How many of them will you inspire to dedicate their lives to Judaism?" The Oneg Shabbat was sponsored by Gert Kurtzman and Belle and Harriet Horwich. Over 200 Jewish people and many others from the Clearwater community attended each of the inspiring services on Friday and Saturday and the special dinner dance held at the Safety Harbor Spa on Saturday evening. Mrs. Alan Bomstein was the dinner chairman.

On Sunday, October 30, at 2 p.m., a Torah processional was held. The Torahs were carried by Rabbis Arthur I. Baseman, Peter J. Mehler, Henry Michelman, Seymour Friedman, Jacob Luski, and lay leaders, under a hoopa into the synagogue. Belcher Road, in front of the synagogue, was blocked in order that the Jewish people and their many non-Jewish friends could march into the synagogue with the Torahs and pay honor to God's word. (This was interesting because the same City of Clearwater that

Torah processional leading to the new Beth Shalom synagogue. St. Petersburg Times, October 31, 1977.

had insisted on punk trees on Northeast Coachmen Road, now closed more than a one mile stretch of Belcher Road on a Sunday afternoon so that the entire congregation could march with the Torahs from Rabbi Mehler's home in Grovewood down Belcher Road to the synagogue.) Congressman Bill Young led the procession. Charles Clark, ritual chairman, presented the mezuzah to Rabbi Henry Michaelman who affixed it to the synagogue. Greetings were given by Dr. Barlis and Mrs. Max Honigman, President of the Sisterhood. A Torah was presented to the synagogue. The officiants at the service were all of the rabbis and Cantor Denburg.

Rabbi Baseman of Temple B'nai Israel of Clearwater gave the dedication prayer. "Eternal God, your people worship you in many different settings: in adorned chapels hallowed by centuries of devotion or in storefront synagogues of quiet simplicity. Old and young come to you full of words or full of thoughts that have no words, responding to your command, 'Make for me a sanctuary that I may dwell among them.' We have a long history of sanctuaries—sanctuaries wherein are heard soft echoes of half-whispered prayers; or faint, tense echos of frustration; or bitter echoes of despair and fatigue; or echoes of aching loneliness; and sanctuaries ringing with joyous song and praise; warmed by true fellowship; reverberating with courage and affirmation of faith. On this day, we add this sanctuary to those of our predecessors, all of which are dedicated to Your name. May it be a sanctuary true to the faith of our heritage, by which we claim kinship with the past and gain strength for the present. May it be a sanctuary ever mindful of the covenant it has with You and Your Torah."

Dr. Arthur Barlis said, "In 1975, there were only forty four families in the synagogue, the facilities were poorly located and they were too small to meet the needs of a growing Jewish community. The congregation didn't even have a Rabbi. This all changed with the arrival of Rabbi Mehler and a decision of the Board of Directors that the Coachman Road facilities were no longer adequate for a conservative synagogue and Hebrew school for the growing Jewish community. Philip

Katz became the chairman of the building committee. While he was looking around the community for a proper location for a new synagogue, he found that the Trinity Presbyterian Church on Belcher Road was for sale. The property was purchased and the Christian House of worship was turned into a conservative synagogue. It is my fervent prayer that the years ahead will be blessed with spiritual, educational, and social growth that we call our successes over these past two years." (Dr. Barlis's date of 1975, appears to be incorrect.)

The religious school enrollment quadrupled over a two and one-half year period. The school went to a full, three-day religious school program to conform with the standards of the conservative movement. The new classrooms provided

Ark and Torahs

Alan Bomstein, President, Congregation Beth Shalom, 1978.

Bernard Panush, President, Congregation Beth Shalom, 1979.

Douglas Zelman, President, Congregation Beth Shalom, 1982.

children sufficient room to learn in a comfortable atmosphere. The most modern teaching tools were made available.

Highlights of 1978

Alan Bomstein became President of Congregation Beth Shalom for the first time. For the next twenty seven years, he would make highly significant and outstanding contributions to Congregation Beth Shalom, the Jewish Community, and the general community.

Highlights of 1979

Bernard Panush became President. He had moved to Clearwater from Troy, Michigan in September. He had served for thirty seven years in the city of Detroit as Deputy Director of the Environmental Protection and Maintenance Department. Rabbi Peter Mehler was the religious leader and Moshe Meirovich was the Cantor and Educational Director. Mayor Corrinne Freeman of St. Petersburg gave an educational presentation. The First Annual Cantorial Concert was held.

Highlights of 1980-1989

Highlights of 1980

Dr. David S. Lifson gave a presentation, "Yiddish Theater and the American Stage." He was considered to be an expert in the field of Yiddish theater and had received numerous awards for his work. A blood drive called "the gift of life" was organized by the synagogue board. The Second Annual Cantorial Concert featured Hazzans Solomon Gisser of Montréal, William Hauben of Tampa, Joseph Schroeder of St. Petersburg, Daniel Gilder of Philadelphia, and Moshe Meirovich of Clearwater. They sang solos, duets, and choral pieces from a rich heritage of Yiddish, Chassidic, Israeli and liturgical music.

Bernard Panush was reelected President for another term. He was cited in Who's Who in American Jewry for his many contributions to the Jewish community and general community. He was the President of the Jewish Community Center of Pinellas County since 1979. He held several offices in the B'nai B'rith, Anti-Defamation League,

Jewish National Fund, the Jewish Historical Society, Chairman of the Clearwater Parks and Recreation Department's Beautification Committee, etc..

Rabbi Shlomo Carlebach, world-renowned interpreter and singer of Chassidic, Yiddish, Israeli, and Cantorial melodies presented an exceptional concert at Congregation Beth Shalom. It has been said of him that he "does more than sing–he reaches the heart, minds, and soul of his audience. He tells details of these people, their hopes, the moments of happiness, and the longing for a better life. He is a visionary with a song in his heart."

The sanctuary was dedicated in the memory of Aaron and Sarah Gurin and Meyer and Fanny Tepper.

Highlights of 1981

Congregation Beth Shalom dedicated a new Judaic library. The $40,000 building, which was located between the sanctuary and social hall, initially housed 1,000 books. The building was a gift from Maurice and Elly Hersty. The feature speaker at the dedication was Rabbi Henry Michelman, Assistant Vice Chancellor of the Jewish Theological Seminary of America.

Highlights of 1982

On September 1, Rabbi Kenneth Bromberg, a graduate of the Jewish Theological Seminary and a member of the Rabbinical Assembly, assumed the pulpit. He arrived during the 25th anniversary of the synagogue. He immediately tried to establish the necessary rapport between a rabbi and congregation. It worked extremely well. He, his wife, Johanna, and their children Naomi, Efrem, and Hillel became outstanding members of the synagogue family.

Jonah Binder, the cantor, led the congregation in melodic prayer. The religious school was organized by co-directors, Anne Gurevitz and Sue Bengele. The religious school met three times a week for a total of five and one-half hours of programs. The children were taught the basic skills and foundation of Judaism, with the ultimate goal of bar and bat mitzvah. The bulletin editors were Shirley Harris and Susan Michelman. The Andrew Sendy

Chapel was dedicated in December.

Rabbi Bromberg presented a three-part series on the" Theory and Practice of Conservative Judaism." This was in response to congregants questions of how Conservative Judaism differed from Reform and Orthodox. The congregants wanted to know about the Shabbat, kashrut, questions of personal status, participation of women in the service, social questions, etc.. They wanted to know what it meant to be conservative Jews, in addition to what it meant to be part of the conservative congregation. They learned that the conservative synagogue and its members are part of a process that seeks to balance tradition and change, old and new, ritual and ethics.

Highlights of 1983

Rabbi Bromberg continued to help the congregation have a better understanding of the Conservative movement. He presented an adult education series which helped the members study the history, development, and content of the relevant rituals. He compared and contrasted contemporary Reform, Conservative, and Orthodox practice. He helped the congregants examine new directions in life-cycle ritual as a demonstration of how tradition could be maintained and yet be flexible enough to meet the needs of the current day. He said that individuals should decide if they wanted to join younger or older generational groups, as their interests dictated.

The congregational members were polled about their desires concerning the role of women in the ritual of the synagogue. One hundred and fifty nine individual responses were received. Seventy percent of the congregants responding approved of women being called to bless the Torah before the Torah reading. Sixty seven percent approved of women chanting the Hebrew blessings before and after the Haftarah. Seventy four percent approved of women opening and closing the Ark and dressing the Torah. Sixty one percent approved of women as Torah readers. Sixty four percent approved of women conducting religious services. Sixty four percent approved of women being counted

in the Minyan. The survey had been developed by the ritual committee and reviewed by the executive committee and the Board of the congregation. Based on these results, Rabbi Bromberg developed a series of presentations to the congregants which discussed religious law and historical precedent related to the participation of women. The ultimate outcome of the wishes of the congregation and the presentations of Rabbi Bromberg led to participation of women in various rituals in the religious services.

Rabbi Kenneth Bromberg

Emanuel Gurin received the coveted Alumni Honor Award of Akron University. He was a world authority in rubber chemistry and was credited with significant discoveries in the chemistry and manufacture of special rubber "blankets" that have considerably advanced the technology of lithographic printing. The main sanctuary was the gift of Emanuel and Rose Gurin in 1977, in memory of their parents, Aaron and Sarah Gurin, and Meyer and Fanny Tepper.

Johanna Bromberg, a very bright and articulate individual in her own right, discussed the essence of Shabbat. She said that it was the sanctification of time. "For six days, she worked and earned a living. On the seventh day, as a free human being she elected to rest, which increased the value of the work on the other days. She said that the rest and refreshment helped restore her spiritual, mental, and human capacities. From the moment she lit the candles for a twenty five hour period, a special love and aura of life embraced her, the children, and her husband. They welcomed the Sabbath bride to their home and enjoyed her visit. The Shabbat was about a peaceful and unrushed time when the family could share the beauty and the uniqueness of this very Jewish day of prayer, song, discussions, and togetherness."

Irwin Kety, President, Congregation Beth Shalom, 1983.

Congregation Beth Shalom Sisterhood established the Woman's Institute for Living and Learning. This was a two-year four semester program to bring Jewish Education to women, especially those without much formal Jewish education. Cantor Elaine Shapiro of Temple Beth El of West Palm Beach presented a concert at the synagogue.

On November 20, Mary Rutenberg was honored for her contributions to the general community, the congregation and the nation of Israel. She received the 35th anniversary Award for Distinguished Service, an event cosponsored by State of Israel Bonds. Singer Judith Steel, a survivor of the Holocaust, who was hidden during World War II by a French Catholic family, was the featured guest artist. Of her contributions to the Jewish and general communities, Mrs. Rutenberg said: "It's important. You can't live in isolation. You live with the world. Giving and living are identical. You have to give. It's a joy to give whether you give of yourself or your wealth."

Highlights of 1984

In 1984, a new Mahzor, or prayer book, was used in the High Holy Day celebration. The editor of the Mahzor, Rabbi Jules Harlow, the Rabbinical Assembly Director of Publications, helped introduce the new prayer book on Rosh Hashanah. Rabbi Harlow was born in Iowa. He was ordained by the Jewish Theological Seminary in 1959. He was an incisive editor, skillful translator, and sensitive liturgist. He also became the editor of the Siddur Sim Shalom, the Conservative prayer book for Shabbat, weekdays, and festivals.

Cantor Simcha Ben Gali of Sarasota provided the music for the High Holy Days. His religious, secular and cantorial evolution began in Warsaw, Poland when he was six years old. At age eleven, he sang as a soloist with the famous Tiomacka synagogue of Warsaw. He graduated from the rabbinical seminary and attended the Warsaw Conservatory of Music. He was awarded the distinguished title of Laureate of Music. He is a certified Cantor by the American Conference of Cantors and United Synagogue of America. The Sisterhood received a national citation for "creative and relevant activity in adult education" for its Woman's Institute for Living and Learning program.

Leo and Vera Plotkin

Leo and Vera Plotkin came to the west coast of Florida from Miami where they had lived since 1957. Leo was raised in South Bend, Indiana. In World War II, he was in the South Pacific. He earned his Bachelor of Legal Letters from Indiana University Law School in 1949. Leo loved the law because of the pursuit of truth and the opportunity to help people. In 1957, he took over a lumber and building supply company in Miami. In 1972, he sold the business, updated his legal knowledge, and passed the Florida Bar Exams. In 1983, Leo and Vera moved to Palm Harbor and Leo started the practice of law. When Amy was born with Down's Syndrome, Leo became an Advocate for the retarded. He fought tirelessly for the rights of people with disabilities and lived to see the enactment of Florida's Chapter 393, which he helped draft. He founded the Association for Jewish Special Education in Dade County, and in Tallahassee, the Leo Plotkin Training Institute to teach advocacy. He worked with the National Association for Retarded Citizens (ARC), was on the Executive Board, served as President of the Florida ARC, President of the Dade County ARC, Board Member of the Upper Pinellas ARC, and Chairperson of the Florida Bar Disability Law Committee. The Governor twice appointed him to the State Human Rights Advocacy Committee, which Leo helped establish. His honors and awards covered a whole wall of the family home. Some of these were: Brotherhood Award, Ray Watson Memorial Award, and the Leo Plotkin Outstanding Legal Service Award. Léo served for two years as President of Temple Beth Shalom. He served as Commander of the Jewish War Veterans Post 243 in Coral Gables. He died on June 12, 2001, at age seventy nine. His wife, Vera, five children, and ten grandchildren were included in the thousands of people, who honored this wonderful man for the enormous good he had done for others.

Vera Plotkin was born in Germany and then moved to Indianapolis, Indiana. She went to Indiana University for two years and met Leo there. She raised their five children and still found time to be involved in many activities at the synagogue, including being very active in the library. She has also been very active in Hadassah through her lifetime.

Thomas Weber, President, Congregation Beth Shalom. (date uncertain–between 1984 and 1989.)

Leo Plotkin

Michael Alan and Marcia Helene Shane

Michael Alan Shane, grandson of David Shane, one of the founders of Congregation Beth Shalom, came to the Clearwater area, after earning a Bachelor of Science in Business Administration and Finance from Indiana University in 1984. He was employed by the Barnett Bank, Rutenberg Corp., then became the owner of On Site Optical, and a real estate broker. Michael was a member of Toastmasters from 1984-1986. He belonged to the B'nai B'rith Youth Organization, Alpha Epsilon Pi Fraternity, and was Vice President of Kent Jewish Community Center and Congregation Beth Shalom. Michael's father, Robert, graduated from Butler University School of Pharmacy. Robert was born on September 26, 1932 and died on January 26, 2003. His mother, Nanette, born on January 27, 1937, now lives in Pinellas County.

Marcia Helene (Meddin) Shane came to the Clearwater area in 1981, with her parents, when they moved here for her father's new job. She graduated from Countryside High School and then earned an Associate of Arts Degree from St. Petersburg Junior College in 1983. In 1985, Marcia earned a Bachelor of Science Degree in Business Administration and Management from the University of Florida. She married Michael in 1987. They have three children: identical twins, Rebecca Ivy and Samantha Laura, born on April 16, 1991, and also Leo Davis, born on June 1, 1994. The three children attended the Kent Jewish Community Center Preschool and summer camp and currently attend the Pinellas County Jewish Day School.

Marcia was a member of the United Synagogue Youth, B'nai B'rith Youth Organization, Hadassah, ORT, and was a little sister for the Alpha Epsilon Pi Fraternity. She was a Member of the Board of Directors of the Pinellas County Jewish Day School. She worked in the bank management field from 1985-1991. Her father, Jeffrey, was born in Savannah, Georgia on December 29, 1946. He graduated from Armstrong State College with a Bachelor of Science Degree in Business Administration and Management in 1972. He has served on the Board of Directors of Congregation Beth Shalom, B'nai B'rith, and the Anti-Defamation League. Her

mother, Jacqueline, was born on June 25, 1944 in Savannah, Georgia. Her mother was a Member of the Board of Directors of Congregation Beth Shalom, and was Past President of the Kent Jewish Community Center. Jeffrey and Jacqueline Meddin now live in Reisterstown, Maryland.

back, l. to r., Samantha and Rebecca Shane; middle, Leo Shane; front, l. to r., Michael and Marcia Shane.

Highlights of 1986

The congregation and the rabbi started to use the new prayer book, Siddur Sim Shalom. It was eleven years in preparation and the first comprehensive (daily, Sabbath, festival and home) prayer book published by the Conservative movement in its 100 years in the United States. It is a judicious blend of the old and the new. It is exceptional because: it incorporates the Holocaust and establishment of Israel into the liturgy; there is a special section on home rituals; there is an attempt to eliminate sexist language; and the text acknowledges the need for less repetition and more variation in the expression of prayer.

The Jewish Theological Seminary of America sponsored a series of four lectures at Congregation Beth Shalom. The mini-course entitled, "The Condition of American Jewry Today" consisted of four lectures by Dr. Jack Wertheimer, Assistant Professor, Department of Jewish History at the Jewish Theological Seminary of America. The four lectures, which were open to the public, were entitled: "The Creation of American Jewry;" "The Religious Life of the American Jew;" "Anti-Semitism-American Style;" and "American Jewry to the End of the Century." Each lecture was held at a different synagogue, which included Congregation Beth Shalom of Clearwater, Congregation Kol Ami of Tampa, Congregation B'nai Israel of St. Petersburg, and Congregation Rodeph Sholom of Tampa. This gave the people of the greater Tampa Bay area an opportunity to participate.

In celebrating the 100th anniversary of the Conservative Movement in the United States, the seminary commissioned a major interdisciplinary study examining carefully where Conservative Judaism was at that moment in time and where it ought to be going. As part of this examination, Rabbi Ismar Schorsch, Chancellor Elect of the Jewish Theological Seminary of America expressed three major tenants of Conservative Judaism. The first tenet was the acceptance of the outside world as a legitimate source of wisdom and experience. The second tenet was that Conservative Judaism embraces critical scholarship, meaning that Jews do not have to parrot the previous generation but can develop their own ideas. The third tenet was that Jews are loyal to their tradition. We live by the laws, but can modify them to meet the needs of the present.

In September, the monthly bulletin was renamed Kol Beth Shalom, The Voice of Congregation Beth Shalom, Clearwater. The bulletin was redesigned to make it more reader friendly. David and Barbara Silvera became the bulletin editors.

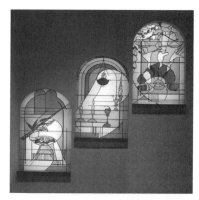

Congregations Beth Shalom and B'nai Israel of St. Petersburg jointly performed a burial of sacred books and ritual objects at Chapel Hill Cemetery. Children attending the religious schools of both congregations, as well as the Jewish Day School of Pinellas County, participated in the ceremony. Any objects or books containing God's name which were no longer serviceable were buried in hallowed land. The children were taught that this was a means of disposing of God's name in a respectful manner.

Dr. Warren Bargad was the Scholar-in-Residence speaker. He was educated at Harvard University, received a Doctor of Hebrew Literature at Brandeis University, and also studied at Hebrew University of Jerusalem. He was Director of the Center for Jewish Studies at the University of Florida, Gainesville. He discussed in two lectures that our perceptions of Israeli-Arab relationships and people were largely shaped by newspaper and television accounts and that these perceptions may

not be true reality

P. Hillel Brummer became the cantor and served until 1989. He received his initial voice training and took general studies at Pressburg Yeshiva. He made his debut as an opera singer in Vienna and later moved to England and enrolled in the Manchester and London Yeshivas. At the age of seventeen he held his first position as a hazzan. He has served as a teacher, choral director, concert artist, and composer. He has held positions in Washington, D. C., Havana, Cuba, Miami Beach, and Pittsburgh.

The Adults for Living and Learning Program started as an outgrowth of the Women's Institute for Living and Learning, which had proved to be so successful. This new program was to help the Jewish people know more about themselves individually and collectively. "We must know who we are, what we are, and why we must endure as a people. We must water the roots of our faith, if we expect to enjoy the blossoms." A new program was also started for high school students.

New stained glass windows were installed in the sanctuary. The windows symbolically represent the sanctification of time exemplified by the sacred days and seasons of the Jewish year. The windows have the following themes: Yamim Noraim, Rosh Hashanah and Yom Kippur; shalosh r' galim, Passover, Shavuot and Sukkot; Shabbat and Rosh Hodesh; minor holidays such as Hanukkah, Purim and Tu B'shevat; the expression of religion in daily life; and Yom Hashoah commemorating the Holocaust and Yom Ha'azma'ut celebrating the establishment of the State of Israel. Lenn Neff was the artist who developed the designs and executed the windows. The windows were the gift of Harriet Horwich and Gertrude Kurtzman in loving memory of their dear ones.

Highlights of 1988

January 22- 24 was the celebration of the 30th anniversary of the congregation and the 10th anniversary of the synagogue at the current location. On Friday night, couples who were married at the synagogue over the past thirty years were blessed by the Rabbi. On Saturday, men and women who were b'nai mitzvah at the synagogue were called to the Torah. On Sunday, a gala dinner dance was held at Ruth Eckerd Hall at the Richard B. Baumgardner Center for the Performing Arts. The anniversary celebration committee was chaired by Phyllis and Erwin Abrams. The committee members were: Paul Applefield, Diane Bernstein, Rabbi Kenneth Bromberg, Rae Feilman, Mr. and Mrs. Paul Freedhoff, Anne Gurevitz, Ethel Honigman, Harriet Horwich, Gertrude Kurtzman, Roslyn Lieberman, Mary Lyon, Mrs. Ethyl Peltz, Marc Silverman, Mr. and Mrs. Mel Silverman, Dorothy Turker, and George Wiener.

Beth Shalom received the Solomon Schechter Award in the Category of Bulletins and Publications for congregations with memberships of up to 250 families in recognition of the excellence attained by Kol Beth Shalom, the monthly bulletin. Individual members recognized for their contribution to the bulletin included Paul Applefield, Diane Bernstein, Johanna Bromberg, Cantor Hillel Brummer, Jane Cowley, Susan Davis, Anne Panush, James Silvera, Dr. Eric Steckler, and Louis Suskin. The bulletin editors were Dave and Bobbie Silvera.

The Scholar-in-Residence was Dr. Jane Gerber whose academic specialty was the history, culture, and relationship of the Islamic and Sephardic Jewish worlds. She was Director of the Institute for Sephardic Studies at the Graduate Center, City University of New York. She had a Doctorate in Jewish and Islamic History from Columbia University.

The demographics of the congregation were starting to change from an older group of individuals to a group that was half older and with half younger families. Although the numbers of the congregant families were not changing, there was now a need for more and more children oriented services and programs.

Highlights of 1989

Rabbi Dov Peretz Elkins was the Scholar-in-Residence speaker. He gave four presentations entitled: "Ten Problems Facing the Jewish Family," "Raising a Jewish Child in This Crazy World,"

"Intermarriage: Preventing It, Facing It, Ignoring It?" and "Jewish Education: Problems and Solutions." Rabbi Elkins has written or edited fifteen books. He was ordained by the Jewish Theological Seminary in 1964 and held a Doctor of Counseling and Humanistic Education from Colgate Rochester Divinity School (1976).

Rabbi Morton Liefman was the guest speaker on the Beth Shalom Torah Weekend. He was the Dean of the Cantors Institute-Seminary College of Jewish Music and Assistant Professor of Liturgy. His special love has always been the deeper understanding of the prayers of the Jewish people and the music to which they are chanted and sung. His presentations were on the music related to drama, history, passion, politics, myth, morals and mortality of the Jewish people. He gave a special presentation on, "The History of Jewish Music."

Paul Applefield, President, Congregation Beth Shalom (date uncertain–between 1984 and 1989).

The Jewish Theological Seminary honored Paul Applefield for his many contributions to Conservative Judaism. He not only served in numerous committees of the synagogue and region, but also was President of Congregation Beth Shalom as well as a member of the Board of Directors of the Southeast Region of the United Synagogue of America.

Cantor Jochanan Bickhardt joined Beth Shalom and served until 1992. He came from Chicago where he was the cantor and ritual director of Congregation Ezras Israel. He studied at yeshivot in New Jersey and under various cantors in New Jersey and Chicago. In discussing prayers and prayer modes which reflects the spirit of the prayers, he said that," Music helps create the necessary mood to make prayer meaningful. Just as studying involves more than reading, listening involves more than hearing...Thou shall sing reverently, for music is a prayer. Cantor and worshiper together must find the proper combination of music and words to produce expressive results leading to the ultimate joy of showing our love for God."

Highlights of 1990-1999

Highlights of 1990

Rabbi Burton Visotzky was the

seminary outreach speaker. He was the Appelman Associate Professor of Midrash and Interreligious Studies of the Jewish Theological Seminary of America. He gave several presentations including: "Word of God or Hand of Moses?" "The Rabbis Were Not Fundamentalists," "Continuing Revelation of Sinai: Two Torahs," "Christians and Jews on Validity of Law," and "Pirke Avot: The Chain of Tradition and Religious Propaganda." He gave presentations at four different synagogues in Tampa, St. Petersburg, and Clearwater.

Rabbi Gordon Tucker was the Scholar-in-Residence speaker. His presentations were: "Jewish Ethics: Do We Know It When We See It?," "Halakah and Ethics: A Tense Partnership," "Jewish Ethics in the Marketplace." In his first presentation, he discussed some of the difficulties we encounter in defining Jewish ethics and in determining what is Jewish about ethical action. In his second presentation, he discussed what happens when Jewish law and Jewish ethics seem to collide. In his third presentation, he discussed the application of conclusions which have been reached about Jewish ethics as they relate to the areas of business transactions, advertising, investment and philanthropy.

Michael, Zachary, Kathy, David Sobel.

Of the 225 families of Congregation Beth Shalom, many of them retirees, there were still found to be a substantial number of young people. There were thirty seven children up to the age of six years. There were thirty one children between the ages of six and twelve years. There were thirty young people between the ages of thirteen and eighteen years. There were eighteen young adults between the ages of nineteen and twenty four years. This indicated that Beth Shalom was not an old people's synagogue. In fact, a fund drive was started to build a new sanctuary. The drive was led by Marc Silverman and Paul Applefield. Alan Bomstein's company, Creative Contractors, Inc., built the new sanctuary, chapel, and social hall which opened in March, 1992. The new facilities made better use of space, replaced old systems, provided the new Peltz Social Hall with the ability by means of a movable acoustical wall to enlarge the sanctuary for special events and the High

Holy Days, while preserving the warmth and intimacy of the sanctuary.

Cantor Bickhardt explained the meaning of mood as it related to music. He said that music can help bring the congregation to the highest spiritual moment. The cantor needs to set the tone, spirit, and proper emotion for the prayer service. In fact, this is the major role of all Jewish liturgical music. He said, " The tone of the voice alone is not able to set the feeling in the congregation. Add spirit to the tone and it assists to create that feeling. Add emotion to the tone and you create spirit."

Michael and Kathy Sobel

Tzedakah has always been a part of the life of Mike and Kathy Sobel, despite their very heavy schedule and their significant involvement in their children's, David and Zachary, scholastic and athletic activities. Mike was President of Congregation Beth Shalom of Clearwater, President of the Golda Meir/Kent Jewish Center, and performed significant activities for Israel Bonds. Kathy served on the Membership Committee of Congregation Beth Shalom, Resource Committee of Gulf Coast Jewish Family Services, and did significant work for Hadassah. As a couple, they chaired three Humanitarian Award Dinners at the Golda Meir/Kent Jewish Center. They received the Volunteers of the Year Award from the Kent Jewish Community Center. Kathy was honored by Hadassah as Woman of the Year. Mike and Kathy were honored by Israel Bonds with the Israel Peace Award.

Their son, Zachary, won two Florida Junior Golf Association tournament titles by age fifteen. He was named Golfer of the Year, while also maintaining a 3.5 average.

Highlights of 1991

Emanuel Goldsmith, Professor of Yiddish Language and Literature, and Jewish Studies at Queens College of the City University of New York presented a series of four lectures. He talked about: "The Romance of the Yiddish Language;" "Momma-Loshen: The Romance of Yiddish Literature;" "Sholom Aleichem: The Humor of Yiddish Literature;" and "H. Leivik: The Conscience of Yiddish Literature." Dr.

Goldsmith, a person who exuded joy and enthusiasm, used solid scholarship in his presentations.

Because of declining interest in a community seder, it was canceled for this year. It was recommended that individuals take people into their home at Passover. It was also recommended that those wanting to attend a community seder contact the Golda Meir Center. Elliot Raskin became the new Executive Director.

Rabbi Bromberg addressed the ever present problem of ritual distinctions between Reform, Conservative, and Orthodox: "My personal practice has always been to refer to the triad of Reform, Conservative, and Orthodox Judaism as the three branches of American Jewry. I prefer branches to denominations because branches suggests common roots and a common trunk. Our common roots are in Torah and its development; our common trunk is Jewish peoplehood. Our commonality extends to our congregations and to the day-to-day problems each faces, especially where the finances of our synagogues are concerned.

When it comes to the stewardship of a synagogue, there are no distinctions to be drawn among a Reform, Conservative, or Orthodox financial squeeze. Recessions do not ask what a synagogue's views are on revelation. Whether congregation observes one or two days of yom tov, reads the Torah on an annual or triennial cycle, has separate or mixed seating, are matters of indifference to those vendors who bill our synagogues for goods and services. We are all in this together." Rabbi Bromberg makes an important point, because throughout the history of the Jewish people we have always been at odds with each other on how best to honor God. However, as Jewish people we must always support, honor, and take care of each other, no matter what the circumstances.

Highlights of 1992

David Levin became the Cantor and served until 1994. Marilyn Hepner became the new Assistant administrator of Congregation Beth Shalom. Marilyn came from Queens, New York. The Maurice and Elly Hirsty Library was dedicated.

A sign was posted at the synagogue with the letters " K K," meaning Kehillah Kedoshah, or sacred community. One of the new stained-glass windows had an inscription which read, "farekha haverekhah" which means "make your books your companions." The full quote was from Judah Ibn Tibbon, who in the 12th century translated medieval Jewish philosophy from Arabic into Hebrew, "Make your books your companions; let your cases and your shelves be your pleasure-grounds and orchards. Bask in their paradise, gather their fruit, pluck their roses, take their spices. If your soul be satiate and weary, change from garden to garden, from furrow to furrow, from prospect to prospect. Then will your desire be renewed and your soul filled with delight." Throughout the history of the Jewish people, literacy and the desire for knowledge has driven the religion to constantly improve itself through the understanding of history, thought processes, and the need to transmit this knowledge to the children.

Congregation Beth Shalom's Holcaust Torah.

A Holocaust Torah was presented to the congregation.

Erwin Abrams was elected Chairman of the Hospice Foundation of the Florida Suncoast Board of Trustees. In this new position, he utilized his twenty seven years of experience in hospital and health care management.

Highlights of 1993

The Scholar-in-Residence speaker was Dr. Peter Pitzele. He spoke on "Psychodrama of the Bible: Mirror and Window of the Soul." Psychodrama is a participatory technique for bringing Bible words alive in order to make sense of the Bible, biblical heroes, scenes, and images. It allows us to better interpret the word of God than by only reading the words. Dr. Pitzele was Director of Psychodrama Services and the Institute for Psychodrama and Group Psychotherapy at Four Winds Hospital in Katonah, New York. His doctorate was from Harvard University and he was a diplomate and certified trainer in psychodrama and group psychotherapy. He was an adjunct faculty member of the Jewish Theological Seminary.

The synagogue presented Cantor David Bagley of Congregation Chevra Chadisha

B'nai Jacob of Montréal, Canada. He gave a concert of Jewish theological music. It should be noted that throughout this manuscript, there have been discussions about Jewish theological music. The reason for this is that music has always been part of Judaism and has always been the way Jewish people approach God in prayer.

Highlights of 1994

Max Goren became the Cantor. The Scholar-in-Residence speaker was Dr. Joel Roth, Professor of Talmud, Jewish Theological Seminary. His major topic was "Critical Issues Confronting American Jewry: Conservative Perspectives." His presentations were: "How Does Jewish Law Evolve and Change," "Human Sexuality and Gender," "Conservatively Speaking, Who Is a Jew" and "Intermarriage and Outreach." In addition, a second Scholar-in-Residence Program speaker was Alan M. Gonsher, who was a rabbi, and child and family therapist. He spoke about "Kids Inc.: Helping Children Develop."

Paul Friedhoff was honored at the 150th anniversary celebration of the B'nai B'rith. Paul who had been a member of B'nai B'rith for fifty eight years was honored for his activities on behalf of Jewish people fleeing Nazi Germany in the mid-1930s. Paul, a recent immigrant from Germany in 1935, served as President of the German-Jewish Club in Philadelphia. He helped members of the club secure proper affidavits to bring relatives out of Nazi Germany. He saved more than 300 Jewish lives.

A special thank you dinner was held for the retirement of Rabbi Bromberg. David Levin was the Cantor and Lonnie Williams was the Administrator. A congregational Seder was held.

Highlights of 1995

Max Goren was the Cantor and Lonnie Williams was the Administrator. Rabbi Gabriel Ben-Or assumed the pulpit. In addressing the congregation, Rabbi Ben-Or said, " I believe that Judaism and the Jewish people throughout the world are vital links in the moral progress of humanity. I believe that Congregation Beth Shalom is a vital link to the good the Jewish people can do.

And I believe that you are a vital link in strengthening this congregation, enabling it to do its good works."

Paul Zim, known as the Jewish music man, presented a concert at the synagogue. He brought his unique blend of music and Jewish heritage to the congregants. Cantor Zim graduated from the Jewish Theological Seminary Cantors Institute of Jewish Music. He also attended the New York Juilliard School and studied Opera at the Metropolitan Opera. He served as the cantor at Temple Beth El in Borough Park, an orthodox synagogue in Brooklyn, and Park synagogue in Chicago. At different times he was a cantor and other times a Jewish entertainer. He said, "When I'm on stage I try to please and communicate with the audience. When I'm a cantor on the bema, I have an audience of one-the Almighty."

Highlights of 1996

Rabbi Bromberg retired and became Rabbi Emeritus. He came out of retirement and served again from 2000 till August 2002.

Rabbi Gabriel Ben-Or served as Rabbi until 2000. The synagogue held a Woman's Leadership Form. Discussions were held in the areas of leadership, the future, how to be a real leader, being alert to opportunity, working for a higher purpose, working together, helping women form visions of their future in the synagogue, and in life in general. The membership committee announced that there were 282 affiliated families.

Highlights of 1997

There were 284 families and eighty five children in the religious school. The Scholar-in-Residence speaker was Rabbi Shaul Maggid. He has lectured widely on the impact of mysticism and the pietistic tradition on contemporary Judaism. His four lectures were entitled, "The Story of Creation: a Kabbalistic Response," "Piety and Law," "Hasidism: Innovation or Tradition," and "The Messianic Roots of Modernity."

Highlights of 1998

On January 24, the congregation celebrated its 40th anniversary. The theme for the celebration was, "Celebrate the Past–Rejoice in Our Future." Rabbi Bromberg talked about the growth and development of Beth Shalom. He said, "With appreciation for process, and with respect for the minority who disagreed, we affected at Beth Shalom the full participation of women in all aspects of Congregational worship. The result has been a release of religious energy and creativity on the part of a significant number of Beth Shalom women resulting in their acquiring synagogue skills they previously would have no reason to develop. In this connection, W.I.L.L. (Women's Institute for Living and Learning) was conceived as a sort of affirmative-action program for women deprived of a proper Jewish education in their youth. The spirit of W.I.L.L. continues today in Rabbi Ben-Or's Bat-Torah program."

The Administrator was Sheila Rolfe. The third annual Congregation Beth Shalom Shabbaton was conducted at the Rotary's Camp Florida in Brandon. The Shabbaton was a retreat for the congregation that included: outdoor Shabbat services, adult study sessions, KADIMA/USY, (youth group) activities, swimming, lakefront activities, campfire, canoeing, arts and crafts, softball, family fun night, etc..

Highlights of 1999

The Charlotte and Werner Gunzburger Chapel was dedicated. The newest fund established was the Burn the Mortgage Fund.

Highlights of 2000-2005

Highlights of 2000

The Jewish Theological Seminary Outreach Program featured Rabbi Gerald Wolpe as the guest speaker. He was Senior Rabbi at Har Zion Temple in Philadelphia for the past thirty years. He was Director of the Finkelstein Institute for the Study of Jewish Ethics at the Jewish Theological Seminary. He served on the Chancellor's Council of the Seminary and the Executive Committee of the Rabbinical Assembly. He was also a member of the American Bar Association's National Coordinating Committee on Bioethics and Law. The theme for his presentation was, "How Does Judaism Define Values In a Rapidly Changing Moral Atmosphere?" The individual topics included: "How Many Clones Make a Minyan: The Jewish Undertone of the Bioethics Revolution," "L'chaim- To Life- As Defined by Congress or by Torah," "Cyberspace and Sacred Space: Judaism As a Guide to the Challenges of the 21st-century," and "The Golem: What Limits Can There Be on the Human Power to Create."

On Sunday, December 17, a Torah was dedicated in honor of Joe Stern. Joe's son, Elliot, gave this very generous and special gift to the synagogue. The dedication was part of the Hanukkah celebration. In November, Rabbi Emeritus Kenneth Bromberg once again assumed the pulpit.

The 50th anniversary of the Torah Fund was celebrated by the conservative movement. The original Torah Fund campaign was initiated in 1942 by the National Women's League. In 1958, a special project was begun to build the Mathilde Schechter Residence Hall. This project provided housing for undergraduate students at the seminary. In recent years, the Torah fund had been expanded and was used for all types of special projects paid for by the Women's League for Conservative Judaism.

Highlights of 2001

On January 13, there was a gala celebration in the Peltz Social Hall to honor the longtime members of Congregation Beth Shalom, Joe Stern and Harry Lane. In a story written in the monthly bulletin, the Ba'al Shem Tov (Hasidic), when asked "Are people still Jewish if they know nothing about the Talmud, Torah, or Psalms said, "Of course they are still Jews! If two such Jews meet on a road and they cannot study Talmud or Bible, nor can they read Psalms or sing a Jewish song, or even remember a Jewish melody, let two such Jews merely love each other. As long as they can still do that, they are still Jews!"

Highlights of 2002

A community wide women's Seder was held at the synagogue. The Passover story was told from a woman's perspective. The Seder was sponsored by the Lylah Pinellas Chapter of Hadassah, North Pinellas

Chapter of Hadassah, Golda Meir/Kent Jewish Center, Congregation Beth Shalom Sisterhood, Jewish Women International, Yachad Group, and Clearwater Chapter of Hadassah and Jewish Federation of Pinellas County. Sheila K. Rolfe was the Administrator of Congregation Beth Shalom and Marlene Siegel, Director of the Religious School.

The Scholar-in-Residence Program speaker was Dr. Naomi Bromberg Bar-Yam, daughter of Johanna and Rabbi Kenneth Bromberg. She graduated from Brandeis University with a Bachelor of Arts degree in Near Eastern and Judaic Studies. She also earned a Master of Social Work degree from the Wurlitzer School of Social Work of Yeshiva University and a Doctor of Social Policy Planning at the Heller School for Social Research of Brandeis University. She presented, "Continuity and Change-New Directions in Jewish Prayer."

Neil Wyman became the Administrator. Rabbi David Weizman began his tenure at Beth Shalom on August 1. His wife, Danielle Upbin, is also a Rabbi. Rabbi Weizman was installed by Rabbi William Leabeau, Dean of the Rabbinical School of the Jewish Theological Seminary. The installation took place on November 17.

In September, Beth Shalom Kol, Rabbi Weizman talked about a River of Hope. He said, "... There is a river that runs through this whole world, a current of energy that connects all things, past and present, and we are all flowing into the future together. So we all have responsibility to keep that river clean. We all must contribute with our own spiritual cleansing, and that is what has led us to this day of Hoshanah Rabbah. If we do that work successfully, then on Simchat Torah, we will be able to sing and dance without inhibition, in the true spirit of freedom...."

At the funeral of Rabbi Kenneth Bromberg, Rabbi Weizman compared Rabbi Bromberg to a tree with few branches but many roots, one that will not cease bearing fruit even in a year of drought. It was his good deeds that even exceeded his wisdom, which was considerable, that spread his roots out through his teachings and his compassion for all people. Twenty years of sermons and lectures, funerals and weddings, b'nai mitzvot and baby namings, gave the congregation and the community a chance to know the man called Rabbi Kenneth Bromberg. There was considerable grief, not only in Congregation Beth Shalom, but also in many other congregations and the community in general, caused by the death of Rabbi Bromberg.

Eileen Jacobs, President, wrote about Rabbi Bromberg, "He was always willing to share his expertise and kindness. That without him, women would not have assumed leadership positions, including ritual chair and congregation President. As a teacher and a crafter of words, he made the greatest contributions to the synagogue. Under his tutelage, a generation of women undertook a two-year course of study to become a Bat Torah and truly became Jewish adults. His unselfish dedication did not stop with his retirement. He continued to contribute not only to the synagogue but too many other community programs, including the Elder Hostel and the Holocaust Museum. When called upon, because of the resignation of the rabbi, he assumed the pulpit again."

Highlights of 2003

Rabbi Reuven Hammer presented " A Prayer and Peace," as part of the Seminary Outreach Program. Rabbi Weizman told a story about a scribe who was brought to a synagogue to examine the ten Torahs in the Ark. The scribe said that this would be very costly and he questioned why it was so important to this congregation to have this done. The rabbi replied, "You know that we Jews have many differences in practice. But the one thing that all Jews have in common is the Torah. It is the one thing that has kept us alive for centuries and will continue to sustain us for generations, as long as we keep all the letters in tact." The story is important to hear. The Jewish people whose lives have been recorded throughout this book have in fact differed in many ways but never in their love and respect for God.

Highlights of 2004

The 19th Annual Seminary Outreach Tampa Bay Lecture Series speaker was Dr. Steven Brown, Dean of the William Davidson

Graduate School of Jewish Education. He gave four presentations entitled: "God Talk-It's All about Metaphors," "Form and Content in the Siddur: Blessings of Enjoyment," "Sources of Authority or How Do We Know What God Wants of Us," and "The Siddur As a Vehicle for Personal and Communal Change: a Self-Help Manual for the Modern Age!"

Congregation Beth Shalom hosted a Jewish learning series entitled, "350 Years of Jewish Life in America." The sessions were entitled: "In the Beginning-First Jewish Settlers," "Local Ancestors, Jewish History of Pinellas County,"-Professor Emeritus Indiana State University, Dr. Hank Koren; "Jews of the Civil War-Brother against Brother," Local Attorney and Historian Gerald Colen; "Jews of the Wild West," "Did you know that Wyatt Earp was married to a Jewish woman," hosted by Gerald Colen.; "Jews of the American Theater"-Robert Friedman, President and CEO of Ruth Eckerd Hall at the Richard B. Baumgardner Center for the Performing Arts discussed the impact of the Yiddish theater and the first Jewish playwrites; "Tides of Change"-Rabbi David Weizman discussed the Jewish renewal movement; "From the Old World to the New," Jewish Food Channel-Dr. Eric Steckler discussed the history of Jewish food in America; "A Place to Worship-the History of the American Synagogue,"-Dr. Eric Steckler; "Take Me out to the Ballgame," Jews in Baseball-Morton Mindell, Associate Curator of the Babe Ruth Museum in Baltimore and Alan Bomstein discussed stars Sandy Koufax, Hank Greenberg, Shawn Green, Ken Holtzman, and others.

Rabbi Weizman discussed the meaning of the morning minyan, or communal prayer. He said that the importance of camaraderie could not be overstated and that Jewish prayer is both personal and communal. "The Talmud says that God hears the prayers of a minyan lower than those of the individual, but for he who does not include private sincere and spontaneous devotion, it is though his prayers are nullified. The Baal Shem Tov emphasized one of the core mystical principles of Judaism: eating food is a form of prayer....We consider every meal an opportunity for unity with all of creation.

Our blessings before and after we eat are meant to bring us to this consciousness.... There really is a religious basis for our focus on food."

The President's Message from Alan Bomstein and Steve Beckerman in September talked about the significance of the time leading up to the High Holy Days. "In a few short weeks, we will celebrate the High Holy Days, the Days of Awe. We're taught that the period preceding the High Holy Days is a time of introspection and making amends for past wrongs we have committed, either intentionally or unintentionally. It is a time... for taking account of where we have been and where we would like to be."

Steve Beckerman

Highlights of 2005

Rabbi Danielle Upbin talked about the great commandment to worship God joyously. "The objective in dancing is, that even when confronted with a great tragedy, the Jews must refuse to yield to the terrible consequences of depression. In striving to live a life of happiness, ...we must seek out the hidden sparks of holiness and light even in the dark places."

Rabbi David Weizman and Rabbi Danielle Upbin.

The Plotkin Museum Display Case was located in the main lobby of the synagogue. The June Gelbart Judaic Collection was given to the synagogue to be housed in this display case. The first annual scholarship brunch was held in honor of Evelyn and Eric Steckler. Over 100 people turned out for this event to honor the Stecklers for their tireless efforts on behalf of Jewish education.

Men's Club

The Men's Club was led by Joe Stern for many years. It sponsors the Holocaust Candles Program. It co-sponsors the Hanukkah party with the Sisterhood. For many years, it has donated money to the Scholarship Fund and has sponsored writing contests for the young people. After several years of inactivity, the Men's Club is once again becoming active under the leadership of Mel Kerman and Lew Levine.

Sisterhood

The mission of Congregation Beth Shalom Sisterhood is to promote the Jewish education of women in the home, synagogue, the local community, and the world community. Monthly programs range from study groups, evenings at the theater, and dancing. Sisterhood lends support to the Jewish Theological Seminary through the Torah Fund. It runs the Judaica Shop, and provides financial support to the synagogue through a series of projects. President Linda Pitchon is currently serving her second term.

Youth Group

The teenagers belong to the United Synagogue Youth. The young people participate in religious, community, social, and fund-raising activities throughout the year. They participate in sub-regional, regional, and international conventions. They run the Shabbat services once a year. President Tovi Snapstailer served in 2004-2005. Co-Presidents, Richard Sadowsky and Brian Roberts are serving in 2005-2006.

Other Groups

Kadima membership is open to sixth, seventh, and eighth grade students. They participated in religious, community, and social programs. Hazak is for individuals fifty five and older. This is a friendship group that meets for fun and educational Jewish experiences such as a museum trips, lunches, theater, and lots more. The Cooking Committee prepares the congregational Kiddush lunches. The Pomegranate Guild design and sew beautiful crafts. The Chesed Committee is a group of volunteers who help members who are having difficulties in their lives. They cook meals for mourners, provide transportation, and call on the home-bound. The congregation holds a Mitzvah Day each year.

CHAPTER 11

CONGREGATION BETH SHOLOM OF GULFPORT

Note: Because of the lack of written records, this chapter includes some narrative, but the majority of the content is a series of names from plaques, which will help to prevent the loss of this information in the future. It is hoped that future researchers will be able to utilize this information to better explain the nature and history of Congregation Beth Sholom of Gulfport.

Around 1953, a group of Jewish men and women met socially, sometimes on Gulfport Beach, sometimes in each other's homes. They referred to themselves as the "Nudnics." This was the beginning of the synagogue. They organized themselves as the Gulfport Jewish Center, which was formed to provide a social and cultural meeting place for the Jewish people of the area. They were led by the renowned writer and poet, Jacob Adler, who served as the President from 1953 to 1958.

The land for a new synagogue was donated by two brothers, Meyer Emsig of Toronto, Canada and Max Emsig of Brooklyn, New York. They raised a large share of the money that was needed to put up a small building around 1953. A lot of Canadian Jews came to Gulfport because Tampa was the terminal for Trans–Canada Airlines. Initially, the services were conducted by the members, then later by Baal Tephillah, and then by a cantor. In 1967, during the presidency of Sam Salk, a new charter was issued by the State of Florida, in which the name was changed to Congregation Beth Sholom.

Jacob Adler

Jacob Adler wrote mainly under the pen name B. Kovner, as well as using fourteen other pen names. His writing appeared in the widely-read Jewish newspaper, *The Forward*. He was born in Dynov, Austria in 1873 and died at the age of 102, on Dec. 31st, 1974. He stopped publishing books and articles at age ninety nine. He contributed more than 30,000 humorous articles, 18,000 poems, numerous plays, and a dozen books. His first poem sold for one dollar, but launched him on a career that earned him the reputation as the Yiddish Mark Twain. He was a frequent guest of Goldie Schuster's

father for dinner and conversation. Jacob Adler was asked how it felt to be a century old. He said, "It's better to be alive for 100 years than to be dead for one week."

Jacob Adler came to the United States in 1873, at the age of seventeen, to be with his aunt and uncle in New Haven, Connecticut. He planned to be a tailor just like his father, who was also a cantor. He worked eighteen hours a day as an apprentice, however, because of lack of adequate food and extreme working conditions he had a nervous breakdown. After trying to write poetry in 1895, he began writing for the labor socialist Daily Forward in New York City for thirty five hours a week. When he was twenty three, he married Celia, who became his inspiration for the next seventy four years. In 1972, Cecilia died and Jacob stopped writing.

Adler's salary grew substantially over the years. He wrote voluminous quantities of material and gave lecturers throughout the United States. In 1924, Jacob Adler left New York and moved to Lakewood, New Jersey, where he befriended Albert Einstein. "They would sit and talk for hours," said one of his five children. Around 1937, after he had stayed in both Miami and in St. Petersburg, he and his wife decided to move to Gulfport. His writing continued and his readership exceeded 275,000 people. Sam Einstein, Past President of Congregation Beth Sholom of Gulfport said, "People used to read his column everyday." Adler wrote in his book, *Cheerful Moments*, "Laughter makes one young. It makes the blood circulate faster, the heart dance and the spirits soar. If I were a doctor, I would advise my patients to resort to laughter. But what doctor would undermine the source of his income?" Meyer Possick, who built the Temple, said: "He wanted to speak only

Jacob Adler. St. Petersburg Times, Saturday, March 9, 1940.

Sam Einstein

in 1978, and became a life member. Harold Ward was President in 1978. Rabbi Sidney I. Lubin was the next rabbi and served from 1978 to approximately 1983. Rabbi Kaplan served from 1989-1990. Rabbi Lawrence Finkelstein served in the 1990s. Rabbi Israel Dvorkin served the congregation (the dates are unknown). There may have been other rabbis prior to Rabbi Milke. Typically, when no rabbi was on the pulpit, Rabbi Morris Kobrinetz would come back and serve. He did this until his death. His son, Rabbi Simeon Kobrinetz, a United States Air Force Chaplain and General, continued this practice on a voluntary basis when he came to this area during the winter months.

The successful growth of the congregation was due to the inspired work of Rabbi Morris Kobrinetz, the lay leadership and the location of the facility. Many Jewish people, such as Jacob Adler, lived nearby and could walk to the synagogue. There were a large number of Jewish families who lived at the Town Shores Apartments. They wanted a synagogue that catered to senior citizens, to the veterans community, and was very close to the Gulf beaches. More Jewish people began to move to Gulfport in the mid 1970s and continued on until the early 1990s.

In addition, Jewish people from the Midwest and Canada wanted a homelike environment in their synagogue. The community did not necessarily need a Hebrew school, but rather wanted to have a large variety of Jewish adult education classes. These classes were extremely well attended. The community also wanted a brief Friday night service with an Oneg Shabbat. On Saturday, they wanted a traditional service with davening. To daven is to pray with fervor and intellect. Davening is described as the way to reach God through prayer. This is the way that these Jewish people were raised as children and they wanted to continue this practice. These individuals were highly intellectual, traditionalist Jews, who felt that a small community atmosphere would make them feel welcome. At the height of growth of the congregation, there were 150 families.

Since the synagogue had increased in size, there was no longer a parking lot. This was a violation of the city ordinance.

Yiddish." Adler also spoke Polish, German, English, and Hebrew.

The Forward

The Forward was and still is a revered institution of American Jewish life. It started out as a Yiddish-language daily newspaper on April 22, 1897. It was a defender of trade unionism and moderate, democratic socialism. Its founding editor was Abraham Cahan. This newspaper became known as the voice of the Jewish immigrant and the conscience of the ghetto. By the early 1930s, its nationwide circulation was over 275,000 customers. Thousands more listened regularly to the Forward's Yiddish-language radio station, WEVD. Nearly every major Jewish writer wrote for the Forward. Mr. Cahan guided the paper for a half-century, until he died in 1950. He also wrote the Bintel Brief, a popular down-to-earth advice column. After World War II, the Yiddish-speaking world of the Eastern European Jews was no more, and now an English weekly publication was launched as a supplement.

In 1969, Rabbi Morris Kobrinetz started part-time at the synagogue and in 1970, he officially became the spiritual leader. The Presidents of the synagogue at that time were Morris Mailman followed by Meyer Possick. In 1971, Saul G. Chason became President and served until his death in 1973. In 1972, a new sanctuary was added and the old sanctuary became a social hall. Rabbi Kobrinetz retired in 1976. He was followed by Rabbi Aaron D. Mauskopf, who retired

Rabbi Aaron Mauskopf

Rabbi Israel Dvorkin

The city fathers of Gulfport made the synagogue possible by waving the existing city ordinance and allowing the congregants to park on the grass across from the synagogue. This was certainly an act of brotherhood on the part of the city fathers.

Meyer Possick

Meyer Possick, Past President, Chairman of the Building Committee, and builder of the enlarged synagogue, was born on December 28, 1912. His wife, Sadie, was born in 1913, and died about 2002. She had a degree in education and was a substitute teacher in Boston before they came to St. Petersburg. They were married around 1933 or 1934 and arrived in St. Petersburg in 1935. Meyer was a baker. They left Boston and were on their way to California, but decided to stop off in Florida to visit a cousin, Isaac Katz, who had a grocery store. After they had a good dinner for $.25, they decided to stay and take up permanent residence here. Meyer served in World War II as a First-Class Seaman. He was on board ships that escorted convoys to England. This took a twenty five day round-trip. It took ten days to cross the ocean, five days to unload the cargo, and ten days to return to Boston. This gave him an opportunity to see his wife. He described the ocean voyage in the following manner, "The ships were from horizon to horizon, possibly as many as 200, and we were on a destroyer escort. We never lost a ship. We spotted a submarine, and we dropped an ash can of dynamite.

After the war, he built businesses, homes, and churches. He built hundreds of homes, mostly in St. Petersburg and had over 140 rental units.

Meyer started the reconstruction of the enlarged synagogue, although from day to day the congregation did not know where the money was going to come from to complete the construction. He built on credit and paid workers out of his own pocket until a small mortgage could be secured. Then he was paid back by the congregation. His motto was, "If you're occupied, you are healthier, your mind works, you feel better, you can make a positive contribution to your society."

Rabbi Jonathan Mielke

Rabbi Mielke came to the United States from South Africa, with his wife, Fey, and five-year-old daughter, Karyn, in 1999. Rabbi Mielke became the spiritual leader of Congregation Beth Sholom of Gulfport and a much loved teacher and Director of Judaic Studies at Pinellas County Jewish Day School. While at the school, he instituted a program that let the students lead the morning prayers. He loved young people and was a fine teacher. At the time of his sudden death, at age fifty five, he was planning a communal program of adult Jewish education. In the two years Rabbi Mielke resided in the community, he made significant contributions to the general society. Rabbi Kenneth Bromberg, Rabbi Emeritus of Congregation Beth Shalom in Clearwater said, "It's interesting, he has been in the community barely two years and has had the impact of someone who has been in the community a lot longer." Rabbi Arthur Baseman of Temple B'nai Israel in Clearwater told the people in the small, crowded Gulfport synagogue that, "A compassionate voice has been silenced and a gentle heart has stopped beating." The funeral service ended with seven-year-old daughter, Karyn, reading the 23rd Psalm. She then sang the priestly benediction. Sam Epstein, President of Congregation Beth Sholom said that Karyn did this on a regular basis.

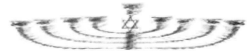

Louis Hersh

Congregation Beth Sholom Wall Plaques and Honors

1. Donated by Sarah Chason and Esther Kleinfeld in honor of the 75th birthday of Saul Chason and Hy Kleinfeld.
2. In loving memory of Louis Hersh, Past President, Congregation Beth Sholom and Past Adjutant and Commander Jewish War Veterans for his unselfish devotion to both organizations.
3. Wall plaque, William "Bill" Nudelman, longtime member, officer and trustee, benefactor and tireless worker for the Congregation–July 20, 1908–September 27, 1999.
4. The Ark and Pulpit were donated by Mr. and Mrs. Israel Rabb.
5. In gratitude to Mr. and Mrs. Meyer Emsig for their gift of a Sefer Torah in memory of their son Mendel, lost in action, and a generous contribution to The Jewish Center of Gulfport.
6. Lectern Microphone and Assembly installed and donated by Nathan A. Rosenzweig in loving memory of his wife, Rose Behrin Rosenzweig.
7. In gratitude to Mrs. Minnie Emsig for the gift of a Sefer Torah.
8. Presented to Louis M. Barnett in recognition of his outstanding effort and sterling leadership in the founding and erection of the Jewish Center of Gulfport, Florida. Dedicated March 8, 1953.

Herman and Helen Robitshek

9. Honoring Jacob Adler, "B. Kovner," poet-writer, one of the founders and first President (1953-1958) in tribute to his untiring devotion for the betterment of Jewish life in our community–Congregation Beth Sholom–December 12, 1970.
10. In honor of the founders, Max and Minnie Emsig, in appreciation of their outstanding effort in making possible the erection of The Jewish Center of Gulfport, Florida – Presented by the Sisterhood-December 14, 1953.
11. Rabbi Morris Kobrinetz–Religious Leader–1970–1978; Rabbi Emeritus, 1978–1997; Spiritual Architect–Expanded Schul; Scholar, Friend, Advisor-November 25, 1903–October 24, 1997.

The Sefer Torahs or Torah Covers

1. Memory of the Gootson Family (Marshall Gootson)
2. Selma Stein (Memory of Polly and Sam Goldenberg)
3. Memory of Joseph and Lillian Ayrons
4. Sisterhood and Congregation Beth Sholom 1994-5754

Building Dedication Plaque

Congregation Beth Sholom dedicated 1972–5733
Morris H. Kobrinetz, Rabbi; Saul G. Chason, President; David H. Kaplan, Vice President; Albert Swartz, Vice President; Joseph Z. Ayrons, Treasurer; Herman Kleinfeld, Secretary; Meyer Possick, Building Chairman; Harry Schwartz, Co-Chairman.

Stained-Glass Windows

1. In memory of Herman and Esther Kleinfeld
2. In memory of David and Anna Applefield
3. Donated by Sylvia Weyl
4. Donated by Julius and Diane Green
5. In memory of Albert Swartz
6. In memory of Morris Green
7. In memory of Morris and Dorothy Mailman
8. In memory of Sherman Lampl

Tree of Life donated by Herman and Helen Robitshek

The added-on building was erected through the generosity of many individuals. The following names reflect most of the members of the synagogue at that time. Some individuals in the Jewish community, although belonging to other synagogues, also made contributions. The individuals were: Mr. and Mrs. Joseph Ayrons, Mr. and Mrs. Julius Green, Mr. and Mrs. Meyer Possick, Mr. and Mrs. Saul G. Chason, Mr. and Mrs. Herman Kleinfeld, Mr. and Mrs. George Pollock, Mr. and Mrs. Al Schwartz, Mr. and Mrs. Sidney Colen, Mr. and Mrs. Morris Mailman, Mr. Robert Collins, Mr. and Mrs. William Nudelman, Mr. and Mrs. Harry Green, Mr. Arthur Sofsky, Mr. and Mrs. Morris Green, Mr. and Mrs. Morris Kavet, Mr. and Mrs. David Kay, Mr. and

Mrs. Mark Ross, Mr. and Mrs. David Applefield, Mr. and Mrs. Harry Goodman, Mr. and Mrs. Albert Kessler, Mr. William Levine, Dr. and Mrs. Leonard Morris (in memoriam), Mr. and Mrs. Edward Rogall, Mr. and Mrs. Ed Tilson, Mr. and Mrs. Ted Diamond, Dr. Mayer Bernstein, Mr. and Mrs. Lou Hersh, Rabbi and Mrs. Morris Kobrinetz, Mr. and Mrs. Eli Machta, Mr. and Mrs. Milton Morris, Mrs. Helen Salkin, Mr. and Mrs. Joseph Weiss, Mr. and Mrs. Morris Grossman, Mr. and Mrs. Herman Cohen, Mr. and Mrs. Arthur Howard, Mr. and Mrs. Frank Kosky, Mr. and Mrs. Sol Mayer, Mr. and Mrs. Sam Morris, Mr. and Mrs. Harry Schwartz, Mr. and Mrs. William Wolf, Louis and Sherry Smith, Mrs. Gertrude Edelman, Mr. and Mrs. Murray Jacobs, Mr. and Mrs. Louis Lackey, Mr. and Mrs. Al Meisner, Mr. and Mrs. Sam Nicoll, Mr. and Mrs. Barney Socol, Mr. and Mrs. Albert Zatlin, Mr. Dave Schahet, Mr.and Mrs. Henry Frank, Mr. and Mrs. David Kaplan, Dr. and Mrs. Morris LeVine, Mr. and Mrs. David Milstein, Mr. and Mrs. Ben Paris, Mr. and Mrs. Harry Stern, Mr. and Mrs. Ben Belon, Mr. and Mrs. Jack Avery, Mrs. Molly Emple, the children of Es and Hy Kleinfeld, honor of Mark Ross, my husband on his 80th birthday, Mr. and Mrs. Al Swartz, in memory of Jack Hecker, in memory of wife, Rose Behrin Rosenzweig, Mr. and Mrs. Isadore Freed, Rabbi and Mrs. Simeon Kobrinetz, Mrs. Esther Salk, Mr. and Mrs. Joseph Weiss, in memory of my son, George Kavet, Mr. and Mrs. Milton Rabbin, in honor of dad, Saul G. Chason, in honor of my husband, David Kaplan, in honor of Morris Mailman, my husband, on his 75th birthday, Sam Salk, the children of Bobby and Al Swartz, in memory of David and Gertrude Mann, in memory of my husband, Irving Edelman, Irwin Kaplan, Mr. and Mrs. Louis Mendelson, Mrs. Helen Salkin, Raymond Schwartz, in memory of Meyer C. Mann, Dr. and Mrs. Harry Eichenbaum, Mr. and Mrs. Morris Kavet, the children of Edith and Ben Paris, Mr. and Mrs. Sam Schneider, in memory of Henry M. Cohen, and in memory of my wife, Tillie Budin.

Currently, there are several significant people who can provide additional information about Congregation Beth Sholom of Gulfport. They are: Elaine Walsh, Past President; Rabbi Simeon Kobrinetz; Dr. Paul Cohen, Past President; Joel Grossman and Lee Liebson of the Grossman family; Claudia Isaacs, who had a slaughterhouse in Tampa; David and Edel Pinsker, who owned U Rental City; Joseph L. Berkowitz; Dottie Feinberg of the Eddie Rosenbloom family; Meyer Possick, builder; Fanny Kaplan, wife of David Kaplan, Past President; Harold Ward, Past President; Bernard Wolk, Past President; Herman Robitshek (wife Helen) Past Executive Director for many years; Myrna Bromwich wife of John Bromwich, Past President; Rabbi Israel Dvorkin, Past Rabbi; Shirley Fishbein, wife of Past President; Helen Hersh, wife of Past President.

Past Rabbi Israel Dvorkin

CHAPTER 12

CONGREGATION B'NAI EMMUNAH/JEWISH MEDIA RELATIONS COUNCIL OF TARPON SPRINGS

Highlights of 1980-1989

Highlights of 1983

On January 2nd, the Articles of Incorporation of the Jewish Media Relations Council, Incorporated, as a nonprofit corporation, were filed with the State of Florida. The officers were: Jan Bresky, President; Jean B. Norkus, Secretary; Bruce H. Bokor, Treasurer. Article II-Purposes and Goals, stated that the nonprofit organization was being organized to disseminate timely, credible information about Jewish people, Judaism and Israel to media and other interest groups. The plan was to coordinate information about various Jewish organizations, produce films about Israel and Jewish life, produce and distribute television shows about Jewish life, train lay religious leaders for media appearances, and to establish a positive Jewish image. Rabbi Bresky established five goals of the Jewish Media Relations Council. They were:

1. To proclaim God's existence to a spiritually searching hungry world; God is Real.
2. To help people pray more effectively; prayer is the vehicle.
3. To teach the ethics of love, toleration and non-harm.
4. To dispel anti-Semitic myths by educating masses of people about Jews and the Jewish religion.
5. To usher in an age of Jewish renewal based upon the renewal of our covenant to be God's people in relationship and action.

Rabbi Bresky also established the parameters of solicitation for the JMRC, which became the parameters of solicitation for Congregation B'nai Emmunah. All contributions were to be voluntary and no plaques, honors, or recognition of any kind was to be given to anyone for making any specific donations. No fund-raising projects of any kind were to be allowed. No dues were to be collected. No boards or committees were to be established to determine budgets and spending. Rabbi Bresky, at his discretion, could choose anyone he desired to help him make certain business decisions and his judgment was to be accepted.

Highlights of 1985-1986

In 1985, Rabbi Bresky started hosting The Spiritual Light, a weekly TV program shown on public access stations throughout Tampa Bay and the northeastern United States. By 1986, he started to distribute literature, which he had written, and he presented television and radio programs as well as speeches. For the next five years, these were sponsored by the Jewish Media

Rabbi Jan Bresky

Relations Council. The Council became an outreach ministry. A periodic bulletin entitled, "The Spiritual Light" was started at the end of 1986. The bulletin was known as, "A newsletter of spiritual growth and inspiration produced by the Jewish Media Relations Council."

Highlights of 1987

Rabbi Bresky continued on as the spiritual leader of Temple Ahavat Shalom of Palm Harbor until July 1. During this four year period, he strove to promote his vision of the Jewish Media Relations Council, while serving as the pulpit rabbi for Temple Ahavat Shalom. This was often a difficult task because of the nature of the differences between the two religious bodies. From 1987–1989, he was a full-time independent radio/television minister.

The JMRC prepared a series of video cassettes of half-hour programs produced by Rabbi Bresky. By April, there were twenty programs available. He also hosted a two hour religious show on talk radio called "It's Your Faith." The program, "Dimensions," was changed into "The Spiritual Light."

Joy Katzen Gutherie added three minute musical segments to the program each week. Rabbi Bresky said, "The core of our religious life is the few minutes we spend every day with God when we pray. Prayer is communication. Sometimes we use words; sometimes we use thoughts; sometimes we just convey feelings. We leave our prayers renewed, refreshed, strengthened and challenged. We leave our prayers with greater wisdom. We leave our prayers with a sense of inner peace." In addition to his programming, Rabbi Bresky conducted Shabbat services starting in July at the Innisbrook Resort in Tarpon Springs.

Highlights of 1988

Rabbi Bresky wrote, "Common Sense Religion for America." He explained his belief that God exists, can be reached through prayer, and is manifested by individuals through ethical behavior. He said, "The goal of the book is to get every person involved in becoming a more spiritual person." Rabbi Bresky said that the first year of his television ministry was important because of the number of people who were reached and the changes that he assumed had occurred in their lives. However, he said that the financial problems were horrible, his health was poor, and that he had made a bad mistake in criticizing existing Jewish institutions and synagogues, because they did not follow his prescribed path to God, prayer and ethics.

Highlights of 1989

Rabbi Bresky's Jewish Media Relations Council became the Jewish Media Relations Council/Congregation B'nai Emmunah. He was backed financially by some members of Temple Ahavat Shalom, who were disappointed that he was leaving, but were willing to help the new ministry. These individuals referred to him as the "Jewish Billy Graham."

Rabbi Bresky developed leukemia and was at Shands Hospital in Gainesville. The new congregation, under lay leadership, met at the Rodeway Inn on US 19 just north of Gulf-to-Bay Boulevard. Rabbi Bresky appeared to recover from leukemia after intensive chemotherapy, radiation

treatments, and a successful bone marrow transplant from his brother. He believed that his recovery was a miracle. Rabbi Bresky said, "I sincerely believe, from a spiritual point of view, that my illness was given to me so I could learn some important lessons: humility, the infinite power of God, and how it feels to be really sick."

In mid-November, Rabbi Bresky spoke at the Sunday service at St. Alfred's Episcopal Church on Curlew Road adjoining Temple Ahavat Shalom. The topic of the rabbi's talk, known as the "miracle rabbi," was "Miracle or Disaster."

Highlights of 1990-1999

Highlights of 1990

The congregation bought a Greek Orthodox Church built in 1922. It was located on the corner of Grand Boulevard and Center Street in Tarpon Springs. Rabbi Bresky encouraged the purchase of the two-story stone building, because the structure was similar to a medieval synagogue, with a warm intimate atmosphere for praying and learning. A Jewish Star of David was inserted into a large stained-glass window near the structure's entrance. A mural of Moses was added at the front of the sanctuary. An Ark was installed on the platform and thereby became the bema. A house next to the church building was renovated as offices for the congregation and for the Jewish Media Relations Council. The congregation had about 135 members and a mailing list of about 400 supporters. Rabbi Bresky obtained a Torah, which had been saved from the Holocaust, for the use of the congregation. It had been given originally by the Westminster Synagogue in London to Rabbi Lori Skopitz, who, in turn, lent it to Rabbi Bresky, who was her classmate. Carrie Weitz was the musician and a cantorial soloist during the formative years of the congregation.

Highlights of 1991

On May 15, Rabbi Bresky died, depriving the congregation of its spiritual leader and leaving the congregation in flux. Before he died, he had built his unconventional B'nai Emmunah into a house of harmony tolerance, and religious ecumenism. Soon afterwards, the congregation split into two factions, with each faction claiming the other one had locked them out of the synagogue. This is reminiscent of schisms that have occurred in other places and other times, such as that which happened at Congregation Schaarai Zedek of Tampa in 1903. A strong leader can typically hold a congregation together. Upon the death of this individual, the differences once again surface. Also, as shown in the breakup of Temple B'nai Israel of Clearwater in 1956 into Temple B'nai Israel and Congregation Beth Shalom.

When the first synagogue starts in a community, typically, Reform, Orthodox, and Conservative groups join together. At some point, a particular group decides that it wants to have its own synagogue and observe certain rituals. However, the synagogues and the Jewish people put aside their differences in times of need and always help each other.

B'nai Emmunah and its parent organization, the Jewish Media Relations Council Incorporated, declared Chapter 11 Bankruptcy. Apparently, part of the reason for this action was due to the congregational mailbox being frozen by the Post Office because of the claims of the rival groups. Much of the dispute seemed to center on the direction the synagogue was taking since Rabbi Bresky's death. Apparently, Rabbi Steven J. Kaplan chose prayers and music which were closer to traditional Judaism than those used by Rabbi Bresky. Rabbi Kaplan had been hired by the three-member Jewish Media Relations Council Board on August 1. Rabbi Kaplan said, "My perception of the basic problem is that I'm trying to make this a bona fide Jewish congregation. They do not want it. They want this generic religious ethical system approach that Jan Bresky had in his media dealings." Sheila Feldman, a newly elected board member, said the dispute, "has to do with the fundamental running of the Jewish Media Relations Council and who is entitled to run it."

Rabbi Kaplan, who was 41 years old, had been the Rabbi at Congregation Beth Sholom of Gulfport, and prior to that, he served on the pulpit of Temple Beth El of Bradenton. He was also a member of the adjunct faculty at the University of South Florida in Tampa, concentrating on Judaic studies. Rabbi Kaplan said that he would continue Rabbi Bresky's practice of welcoming visitors of all faiths to the synagogue, but suggested his approach to eccumenism would be less pronounced and would take a different direction. Rabbi Kaplan said, "Jan was far more comfortable in that realm (eccumenism) than I. My interfaith history has really had an emphasis on Judaic-Islamic issues or even Judaic-Buddhist kinds of issues, as opposed to the Judeo-Christian emphasis that Jan had. Regarding B'nai Emmunah's practice of not charging formal dues, any change would be a decision of the synagogue board. It is a bit alien to me, and certainly from a fiscal perspective, it's a less secure way to function." The B'nai Emmunah congregants insisted on a formal religious school and bar and bat mitzvah programs, as well as a full-scale Adult Education program.

Rabbi Kaplan graduated from Richmond College, part of the City University of New York, with a Bachelor's Degree and a Doctorate Degree in Psychology. He arrived in Florida in 1976 and was active in the 1980s in establishing Hillel chapters on area campuses. He had served as rabbinic advisor and chaplain to Jewish patients at Moffitt Cancer Center at the Research Institute in Tampa and was chaplain at the Florida Mental Health Institute at the University of South Florida.

On August 19, an emergency meeting of the Board of Directors of the JMRC was held at the corporate office, 58 West Center Street in Tarpon Springs, Florida. Two of the three directors were present, Lloyd Tabb and Margret Gerson. The reason for the meeting was to remove the third director, Hilda Schier, from her position. A motion was made by Director Tabb to ratify the previously signed contract of Rabbi Kaplan. It was ratified. A motion was made to appoint Rabbi Kaplan as Managing Director. The motion carried. The next meeting of the Board of Directors was scheduled for August 22.

Meanwhile, on August 29, another group

held a special membership meeting of the JMRC at the Rodeway Inn. Alice Burke was elected President, Sheila Feldman, Secretary, and Bob Lance, Treasurer. The elected Board of Directors were: Alice Burke, Harold Feinberg, Sheila Feldman, Jack Grossman, Bob Lanson, Norman Lurie, Mark Parker, Hilda Schier. Also present were Sue Henry and Steve Rayow who had been nominated from the floor. Shabbat services were to be held at a school on Route 19 in Clearwater.

On August 30, a statement attested to by Hilda Schier, Director and notarized by Martha M. Fiedler formalized the special meeting held on August 29. It listed all of the new directors and the new officers and also stated that ninety five members of the congregation were in attendance at the meeting, and that in addition there were over 200 proxies in support of increasing the Board of Directors from three to nine and electing officers. On the August 30 list, Mae Knotek was included as a director, but not shown to have been elected on August 29. Further, Sue Henry and Steve Rayou apparently were not elected.

On September 3, the nine person JMRC Board met and officially disavowed all actions taken in the name of the JMRC Board by Lloyd Tabb, Peggy Gerson and Rabbi S. Kaplan. They specifically disavowed the contract with the Rabbi. They said, "The only director we legally recognize is Hilda Schier, duly appointed by Rabbi Jan Bresky, and we wish to thank her for all her work to carry out the aims and goals of the JMRC to date."

Several law suits ensued. They were settled or dismissed by March, 1993. Interestingly enough, even though a considerable amount of money was spent on lawyers' fees, as in the lawsuit in Schaarai Zedek, the heat of the moment finally passed and a proper solution was found to the problem. It is unfortunate, that the individuals involved rejected the offer of the use of Rabbi Adler as an arbitrator. One group of the congregation of Rabbi Bresky's followers left the congregation and formed Congregation Aliyah of Clearwater. This group later became defunct.

Highlights of 1992

Since finances were in disarray, over

Rabbi Louis Bogage

the objections of some members the congregation started to sponsor Bingo. This was one of the ways the congregation tried to raise funds to pay for a rabbi as well as other operating expenses. Since there were no formal dues, the synagogue was hard-pressed to meet its financial obligations. A Sisterhood was formed.

Rabbi Louis E. Bogage

Rabbi Louis E. Bogage became the spiritual leader of Congregation B'nai Emmunah and the Jewish Media Relations Council. Rabbi Bogage, age fifty eight, described himself as a progressive liberal of the most contemporary nature. "I feel that life changes daily, our spiritual needs are stimulated in different ways...and that... you must continue to accommodate the changing elements of our spiritual needs." He said, his aims for Congregation B'nai Emmunah coincide with those of the ecumenically minded Bresky. He said, "... Feelings–goes the popular song–we do so much on feelings. We build our lives. We anticipate the future. We make decisions. We move forward. We make the vital choices of life! And so, I have come and I have visited and I've allowed my spirit to soar among those of you who've come out to see me and we have prayed together – that my feelings are good and positive. We will work for one another – teaching each other what we have discovered that we will share the future – as we seek God's blessing together. I will be proud – as a rabbi to serve this struggling group, and I hope all of you will come out to meet me, and let us learn together the ways of our sacred Judaism."

Rabbi Bogage had a Bachelor's Degree in Philosophy from Clark University, Worchester, Massachusetts, a Master's Degree and Doctorate Degree in Hebrew Literature from Hebrew Union College/ Jewish Institute of Religion in Cincinnati, Ohio, and he was ordained by Hebrew Union College. He had been the spiritual leader of Temple Shalom of Port Charlotte and previously served congregations in New York City, Denver, Colorado, and Uniontown, Pennsylvania. He had also served as Regional Director of the Pennsylvania and Southeast Council for the Union of

American Hebrew Congregations.

Highlights of 1993

Rabbi Bogage discussed the importance and significant of time in our lives. He said, "There is just never enough time to love each other, be kind and considerate, experience beauty,...be at ease with those we love, read a book, do something nice for someone, etc.. Judaism teaches us to revere time, and to utilize it with sanctity. There is a time for everything under the sun, says Ecclesiastes and we are challenged to take advantage of every moment – to make it a credit to ourselves and our God. Like the great artists, we can paint a time into our own lives with beautiful color, depth, gentle lines, and strong shades..."

Congregation B'nai Emmunah was relocated to 38577 US Highway 19 North (Cornell Square near Klosterman Road). The High Holy Day services were conducted at Ruth Eckerd Hall at the Richard B. Baumgardner Center for the Performing Arts for more than 800 participants. There were eight children registered for religious school.

The President was Harold Feinberg and the Members of the Board were: Harold Feinberg, Hilda Scheir, Eric Sekeres, Ron Friedman, Norman Lurie, Herman Heilman, Arlene Siegel, and Shelle London. Eric Sekeres said, "...dues were necessary in order for this congregation to survive... Rabbi Bresky's philosophy is not in opposition to this." This brought on considerable discussion and numerous differences of opinion. No action was taken on this matter. A push was made to collect past pledges, without any tangible results. Rabbi Bogage resigned to take a full-time position in Hazelton, Pennsylvania.

Once again, the problem of how to finance the congregation was discussed. The congregation had grossed $18,000 from the High Holy Day Services held at Ruth Eckerd Hall at the Richard B. Baumgardner Center for the Performing Arts. This, plus the eighteen dollars a month requested from each family as a donation, simply was not working. Rabbi Schenkerman had suggested that a formal dues structure be put into place and that eighty percent of

the budget be met in this manner. The other twenty percent would be from gifts and donations. He suggested that each family pay $150-$200 a year and that, in addition, they pay $300 to a building fund. Because of the original philosophy of Rabbi Bresky to requests donations only, this discussion of how to best finance the congregation would continue to be an on going problem of the congregation.

Rabbi Robert Schenkerman

Rabbi Robert Schenkerman assumed the pulpit and remained the Rabbi until 2000. In his first message to the congregation, Rabbi Schenkerman said, "...It is a privilege to serve as the newly-elected Rabbi of our community; it is also a challenge and a unique responsibility. Jan Bresky, founding rabbi, had a dream of which Judaism could be–as proclaimed by the prophets of ancient Israel–and as thought and lived by Rabbi Bresky, with his rare gift, could become a reality. My colleague and friend, Rabbi Buz Bogage, endeavored to establish continuity to Jan's vision...and now, that Tallit of spiritual obligation has been given to me. I pray that I will wear it as befits a rabbi in Israel, and in such a manner that I honor the tradition of values which called it into being. As I come to know, day by day, the leaders and members of our Temple family, I cannot help but conclude that as a rabbi, there is an urgent need for a new focus of energies, and for more of a collective sense of responsibility and involvement on the part of all this Holy Assembly. Rabbi Bresky left us a vision which he was able to perceive from a very high and lofty place. We need to build structure to house that dream; we need to build a foundation of strength, and intra-system of personal involvement and leadership and responsibility. We are an assembly of Emmunah– faith, not reflected only in attitude, but given credence and validity in the work of our hands. A poet once wrote, Faith is the evidence of things unseen. The evidence of all that is hoped for... That poetry does not reflect what is our present need. Our responsibility is to make faith visible and all that is hoped for, something very real and viable. Ten Jews make a minyan; nine rabbis do not! Our Temple

Rabbi Robert Schenkerman

must re-organize and strengthen itself in a systematic, organized and pragmatic manner. Rabbi Bresky taught all of us the thoughts of our sages: Pray as if everything depended upon God. I would hope to teach you the rest of that statement: Act as though everything depended upon you! I ask of all of this congregation and community your prayers and your patience with me as I come to know you and learn and grow with you. We have much to do together–let us begin with individual involvement–each one of us is needed and necessary. Let us relate to each other without conflict and judgment – but only with courtesy, dignity, and respect. May God bless us that, together, we grow from strength to strength–and that the works of our hands endure–that we, who inherit a vision, build a House and community that is strong, self-sufficient, and worthy of a place for prayers and dreams. We may pray for what ought to be–we must work together..."

Rabbi Schenkerman continued the congregation's involvement in the spiritual, religious and communal life of Tarpon Springs. He was involved in adult education programs, open to members of the congregation and the community, religious school for children from grades kindergarten to confirmation, and a preschool program. Rabbi Schenkerman said, "Our Temple is spiritually committed to the prophetic words: "This House Shall Be a House of Prayer for All Peoples." He said, "...God is not in people and places. God is in human relationships. Small congregations are more than places, they are a feeling..." "...Jews in small congregations are the fingertips and toes, the most sensitive receptors and most active organs of outreach of the Reform Jewish body."

Highlights of 1994
William H. Fleece

William H. Fleece was born on October 1, 1935, in Pontiac, Michigan. He earned a Bachelor of Science Degree in Psychology at Ohio State University in 1957, and a Doctorate of Jurisprudence at Indiana University School of Law in 1961. He was admitted to the Florida Bar in 1962. He is a member of the St. Petersburg Bar Association and Florida Academy of Professional

William Fleece, President Temple Beth-El, 1984–1985

Mediators. He was admitted to practice before the United States Supreme Court, United States Court of Appeals, United States District Court, and all Florida state courts. From 1966-1972, he was a Member of the Florida House of Representatives.

William is: Member of the Board, St. Petersburg College Foundation and Member of Finance and Investment Advisory Committee; Member of Community Foundation Board of Menorah Manor; a Co-Trustee of the Herman Forbes Charitable Trust of New York; and Past President, Temple Beth-El of St. Petersburg.

William became the benefactor of Congregation B'nai Emmunah. As one of the three trustees of the Forbes Trust, he provided $20,000 or twenty two percent of the income for Congregation B'nai Emmunah in his first year. High Holy Days contributions were approximately another twenty two percent of the income. In succeeding years, his generosity and the generosity of the Herman Forbes Charitable Trust of New York, has helped sustain the congregation.

Activities

Saturday morning services were started. In February, bingo revenue had reached $2,363 for the month. A valid membership list showed that there were fifty eight families in the congregation. A new Torah was purchased in Los Angeles, by Howard and Lauri. Rabbi Schenkerman started an adult education series entitled, "Amen–An Adventure through the Prayer Book." On the weekend of April 9 and 10, a citywide observance of the Holocaust Remembrance was held in Tarpon Springs, with virtually all denominations gathered in the Sanctuary of Congregation B'nai Emmunah to celebrate this event. The mayor of Tarpon Springs issued a proclamation for the Holocaust Memorial Observance Sabbath. Rabbi Schenkerman led the Tarpon Springs community in helping to make a Ku Klux Klan rally on May 21, a nonentity. Despite considerable pre-publicity and lots of money, the Ku Klux Klan's plan to cause trouble in Tarpon Springs did not work.

On December 8, an Interfaith Community Hanukkah service was held. Clergy from neighboring churches, as well as the local congressman and mayor of Tarpon Springs, were in attendance. The students of the religious school conducted a Friday evening service guided by the Rabbi. Shelle London became President.

Rabbi Schenkerman talked about the origin and significance of Shabbat to the Jewish and non-Jewish community. "... Shabbat represents one of the most unique and significant contributions of the Jewish people to world civilization...The Shabbat is considered the symbol of the perfect life. It is the one day when Jews can forget their troubles and have a foretaste of the world to come. The Shabbat is a time for rest, for the cessation of work, and for leisure. All of God's creatures are commanded to rest on the Shabbat. The Shabbat is the common possession of all, rich and poor, human and beast. All of God's creatures need to be able to rejuvenate themselves. While God is seen as the creator of the universe, people are also blessed with the ability to create and be creative, thereby becoming partners in creation. As partners with God, we share the task of striving to create a perfect world. Shabbat is that very precious and sacred time when the whole world returns to its most natural and authentic state of being. We come to realize ourselves as a loved and a necessary part of the unique design of creation. It is a time of oneness...Shabbat emphasizes the equality of all people, human rights and individual freedom. Shabbat is not the possession of one segment of the society, but is the common possession of everyone...it is with a very special feeling of warmth and friendship, and the bonding of shared experience that we gather in our Synagogue...It is a quiet time to reflect in the circle and the oneness we have made of ourselves, where we have been, what we have done, and where we are going."

Highlights of 1995

Bonnie Whitehurst sang at the High Holy Day services. Cantor Rafael Grossman conducted the musical portion of the service. Bonnie Whitehurst alternated Friday evening services with Joy Katzen-Guthrie. The President was Liesa Gruber. Sheila Weinstock joined the Hebrew teaching staff. The temporary place of worship was

at 38577 US 19 North, Palm Harbor.

Rabbi Schenkerman talked about the temporary place of worship as a step toward a permanent home for the congregation. "Bringing a Torah into a room makes it a place of worship, waiting only for the gathering of Jewish people to learn from the Torah. This temporary facility is now a House of God. Here we shall come to examine what we are in the light of what we can be, aware that it is God before whom we stand. Here we shall offer the service of our hearts in praise of God for all blessings; here we shall renew our faith, seeking comfort and strength....Here we shall share joy and sorrow...Here we shall maintain that covenant together."

Highlights of 1996

The officers selected were: President, Sinclaire Scala; Vice President, Liesa Gruber; Treasurer, Vic Walters; Secretary, Bernice Levin (acting as pro-tem). The Kent Center was used for aarious social gatherings and congregational dinners. A new members drive was started. The proposed dues for new members was $400.

Highlights of 1997

The congregants worked together and converted a house into a synagogue. Vic Walters was the overall Reconstruction Chairman. Sally and Dick McKay took charge of moving day and paid for the rental of the truck to transport the belongings of the congregation from Klosterman Road to 3374 Keystone Road. They also volunteered to pay for the painting of the inside of the building after the construction was completed. The wall was removed between the garage and the living room to create a large room for

Rabbi Moch with Torah

*Holocaust memorial
with shoes of 4 year old
Belgian Girl*

the sanctuary. The level of the floor of the garage was raised to the level of the living room. The Florida room was converted into a classroom. The front bedroom became the Temple office. The rear bedroom became the Rabbi's office. The kitchen was renovated. Tuesday, January 29, was Temple moving day. However, because there were inadequate funds to complete the renovation at that time the congregation moved into temporary quarters at Connell Square.

Six families guaranteed the loan. They were: Sinclair and Enid Scala, Richard and Sally McKay, Robert and Liesa Gruber, Leonard and Kathryn Kornfeld, Katie Newman and Victor and Janice Walters.

The congregation received an additional $75,000 Forbes Charitable Trust grant for the renovation of the facility. William H. Fleece, Co-Trustee of the Herman Forbes Charitable Trust, wrote to the rabbi and congregation concerning the additional $75,000 contribution. He said, "I wish to reiterate the primary reasons that have motivated me, as one of the Trustees, to obtain the past and current contributions for B'nai Emmunah. In the 1980s, I served on the Board and ultimately served as President of Temple Beth-El in St. Petersburg. During that time I was actively involved in the selection process for a new rabbi. I was one of the persons to interview the late Rabbi Jan Bresky for that position. When Jan failed to be selected as that Temple's Rabbi, he went on his way in life to do the reaching out and establishment of the

Jewish Media Relations Council and B'nai Emmunah that is so well-known to many of us. We became friends for the few years that remained in his life and several of us in the Pinellas County area actively supported his dreams and aspirations. Unfortunately, he died at too early an age. He left behind a bold concept, opposed by many, that Jews should reach out and offer formal High Holiday services to those who do not seek to be active members of a synagogue. That concept needs to be continued. It is partially in his honor and memory that a portion of my support is given. Another of the reasons has to do with Rabbi Schenkerman. He is one the most dedicated rabbis I have encountered. He has had to endure difficult working conditions and uncertainty to do those things that rabbis do—teach.... he is most probably undercompensated considering his status and tenure as a Rabbi...Several years ago, I vowed to at least assist in placing you in a position where, as young birds, you could fly on your own. I believe that this contribution should give you the impetus to have a "home" where you can start to attract young families and others that are in the demographic area of your new location. I would request that "The Herman Forbes Charitable Trusts" be noted on your Founders Tablet in Honor of Rabbis Jan Bresky and Robert Schenkerman, D. D."

The congregational seder was held at the Kent Center. The first service at Keystone was Friday, May 2. September 7, was the first day of Sunday school. The religious school staff was made up of Susan Badalament, a Sunday School Teacher at Ahavat Shalom, Elaine Umansky, Jill Umansky, who started at St. Petersburg Junior College, and Sheila Weinstock, who taught Hebrew. Neil Kahn was the Executive Director of the Religious School.

The new Board of Trustees included: Martin Katz, Jan Press, Nick Paull, Liesa Gruber, Leonard Kornfeld, Sinclair Scala, Davida Petrie, Sally McKay, Charles Stone, and Rabbi Shankerman. The officers were, Marty Katz, President; Liesa Gruber, Vice President; Davida Petrie, Secretary; Sinclair Scala, Treasurer. A new dues structure was put into effect. There were sixty two families in the congregation and thirty children in the Religious School. The Herman Forbes Charitable Trust, through Bill Fleece, provided in excess of $100,000 to the congregation.

Highlights of 1998
The new President was Mark Wasserman. There were four children in the confirmation class, Jeff Greenhaus, Robert Hallen, Daniel Brandeis and Justin Klein.

Congregation B'nai Emmunah celebrated the Seder with over 125 congregants from the synagogue and All Saints Episcopal Church, where the Seder was held. A groundbreaking was held for the expansion of the Temple building. By September, the congregation had grown from twenty five families in the latter part of 1996 to almost sixty families and the religious school had increased from four students to over thirty students.

Highlights of 1999
Four children, Lacey Sites, Robin McNicol, Michael Hallen, and Megin Brandeis became B'nai Mitzvot. The entire congregation took part in planting flowers and bushes around the building and enhancing the outer beauty of the synagogue. The adult education courses were well attended. Special committees were appointed to discuss Education, Outreach, and Membership. On May 9, at a special Congregational meeting, it was approved unanimously to proceed with the purchase of the land adjacent to the west of the property. There were fifty one member families.

The Jewish Media Relations Council, Incorporated filed Articles of Amendment to Articles of Incorporation to change its name to Congregation B'nai Emmunah, Incorporated.

Rabbi Schenkerman talked about L'HAYYIM–TO LIFE. "At the very core of who we are as individuals and what we do as a People is the sanctification and affirmation of Life. As human beings and as Jews, we celebrate our journey through the cycle of life, which we share with all creatures, in our unique and venerable way...We are born, we mature, we form families and communities, and we die. Jewish tradition provides through ritual, ceremony, and celebration, a way of appreciating and understanding our journey...We bring in newborns into the Covenant of our People through Brit Milah and naming ceremonies. We welcome the maturing young person into the realm of responsibility of Bar/Bat Mitzvah...We call upon the Eternal's presence when two people commit themselves through Ke'dushin (sanctification through their marriage vows). And we affirm the Living God when our loved ones pass, by saying Kaddish... as we journey through life, L'Hayyim is a statement of belief and benediction...In the prayers for Rosh Hashanah and Yom Kippur, over and over again, the refrain echoes–Remember us O King who desires life, for Your sake, O God of Life...The introspection, prayer, and fasting of Rosh Hashanah and Yom Kippur (fasting is on Yom Kippur only) lead to Sukkot, when we live simply under the stars, sharing food and friendship in a week-long celebration. The inwardness of the High Holy Days thus gives way to and is beautifully balanced by the labors of our hands, a turning outward to gather the harvest with our community around us."

The Temple Dedication Services were held on Friday, December 10. More than 125 people attended. The shofar was sounded and the congregation felt as one, and reverent as the Torahs were carried into the new sanctuary. Many of the local priests and ministers attended the celebration, along with the Congressman and the Mayor of Tarpon Springs. The remarks of the clergy were truly inspirational and reflected an air of brotherhood and love; it was very meaningful and moving.

Highlights of 2000-2005

Highlights of 2000
The congregation had grown from forty five families to sixty four families and the attendance at Shabbat services, which was usually ten-twelve people, had grown to about twenty five. The dues structure had to be raised again. Rabbi Schenkerman and his wife, Arline, were deeply involved in the Tarpon Springs campus of St. Petersburg Junior College and the building of a world-class museum. The congregation lost its cantorial soloist. Sunday School teacher.

Laurie Klein's, twins, Daniel and Melanie, became B'nai Mitzvah.

Cantorial Soloist Colman Reaboi was hired to teach classes, lead services, and serve as lay leader until 2001. He has continued on as a Cantorial Soloist with Rabbi Moch as the religious leader. A new dress code was instituted asking members to refrain from wearing shorts, T-shirts, and other types of athletic equipment. The children were asked to be properly dressed for the Sabbath, out of respect to God and the congregation. The High Holy Day Services were led by Rabbi Lia Bass and chanted by Cantorial Soloist Colman Reaboi.

Highlights of 2001

Since there was the absence of a permanent rabbi and the Temple President was on a temporary hiatus until May, it was very difficult to maintain a religious school, weekly services, and to raise adequate funds for all the expenses that it took to serve the Jewish community on a regular basis. Cantorial Soloist Colman Reaboi had to personally assume a more active role in the religious school, and more responsibility in spiritual leadership. He urged the congregation to step up to the plate in this time of need, both financially and in helping provide leadership. Rachel Kern was Bat Mitzvah and Jeffrey Warford was Bar Mitzvah.

Rabbi Moch, talking about "Consolation and Community," said, "Our tradition wisely directs us in two ways towards consolation and healing. First we are given a ritual for mourning and secondly, we are asked to organize our community to support and console the grieving... Consolation takes effort. Individuals must make the effort to go and visit the bereaved...Communities must organize for the care of entire nations disturbed by a cataclysmic loss. The effort may be taxing at times, but there can be no holier purpose to our living than as a support for the falling and as a staff for the broken and broken hearted. Here we find the true meaning of purposeful and divinely directed living."

Following a tradition established by Rabbi Bresky, Congregation B'nai Emmunah held its High Holy Day services at Ruth Eckerd Hall at the Richard B. Baumgardner Center for the Performing Arts. Rabbi Bresky's philosophy was to provide services for the unaffiliated Jewish people of the Tampa Bay area. Rabbi Moch said, "The High Holy Days are a reminder to us of what we forget most of the year, that we have to make peace with ourselves and others before we can make peace with God."

Sisterhood

Sheila Shear, Sisterhood President, reported on the activities of the Sisterhood of B'nai Emmunah. She said that a group of women informally took care of the chores and the preparation for the Oneg Shabbats for a period of years. From this group of women, grew the concept of forming a Sisterhood. Now in its second year of existence, the Congregation B'nai Emmunah Sisterhood is continuing to grow. Thirty six women joined this year. They are now responsible for the Oneg Shabbats, gift shop, Sunshine Fund, assisting the Hebrew School and Youth Groups, participating in readings/discussion groups, developing a cookbook, and collecting toys for the Gulf Coast Jewish Family Services holiday drive.

First adult confirmation class, May 3, 2003.

CHAPTER 13

CONGREGATION B'NAI ISRAEL OF ST. PETERSBURG

Highlights of 1920-1929

Early Years

The highlights of the early years of people from the Jewish community who were founders of Congregation B'nai Israel, may be found in a previous chapter on the Jewish community of Pinellas County from 1883-1920. Additional information may also be found in the previous chapter on the St. Petersburg and South County Jewish communities.

Highlights of 1923
Max and Lillian Davis

Max Davis, born in 1895, moved to St. Petersburg. He came from Romania, by way of New York and Key West, Florida. Lilly's parents, Alexander and Tillie Hecho, came from Romania and Austria-Hungary to New York and then Tampa in the late 1800s or the beginning of the 1900s. Lillian was born in Florida on August 10, 1904. She died in April 1986 in St. Petersburg. They met in 1923 and were married in 1925. They lived on 14th Avenue, near the Sierkese's and Kleinfeld's. She was a nineteen year old store clerk and he was a twenty eight year old merchant when they met. Max became involved and active in the Jewish community immediately. In 1923, and for a few years after, minyans and small meetings were often held in the dressing room at the back of Max Davis's retail merchant dry goods store. Max was the brother of Charles Davis, and father of Arlene Rosenthal. Arlene remembers, as a small child of three or four, in 1938, running up on the bema to sit on her father's lap during Friday night services. Max was President at that time.

Early Services

The first holiday services were held at the home of Mr. and Mrs. Joe Solomon at 124, 9th Street, North. The first synagogue building was in a storefront at 13th Street and 2nd Avenue North. For a short period of time, the synagogue was located in the Louis Cohen Store building at 7th Avenue and 9th Street North.

Abe Sierkese was the treasurer for many years. Hyman M. Jacobs was the President of the synagogue from 1923 to 1937.

Highlights of 1925
Ladies Auxiliary

The Ladies Auxiliary of Congregation B'nai Israel was founded in 1925. The most-active women at that time included Dora (Mrs. Louis) Goldberg, Bessie (Mrs. Hyman) Jacobs, Stella (Mrs. Sam) Goldberg, Mrs. Abe Sierkese and Yetta Halaczer. They not only raised money for the synagogue, but also gave help to transients and needy families. They provided baskets of food and, where needed, train fares to help people return to their communities. In the 1950s, the name of the auxiliary was changed to the Sisterhood of Congregation B'nai Israel.

Congregation B'nai Israel in 1923. 13th St. and 2nd Avenue, St. Petersburg.

Charter

The charter for Congregation B'nai Israel was notorized on Aug. 14, 1925 when S. G. Shapiro appeared before the public notary, Ina Belle Helms, and verified the signatures of the other officers. On Aug. 29, 1925, the Articles of Incorporation of Congregation B'nai Israel were approved by the members and the synagogue was officially incorporated on Dec. 9, 1925, by M. A. McMullen, Judge of the 6th Judicial Circuit, State of Florida. All members of the Jewish faith, of legal age, were eligible for membership in the organization; anyone, who was so qualified, whose application was approved by a majority vote of the members present at any membership meeting of the corporation, became a member of the congregation, and was entitled to all of the benefits. The corporation was to exist for ninty nine years and could hold real estate valued at $500,000. The officers were Samuel G. Shapiro, President, an insurance agent. (Note: the first operational President was Hyman M. Jacobs.) Samuel's wife's

Max Davis, President, Congregation B'nai Israel, 1938–1940, 1950–1954.

Hyman Jacobs, President, Congregation B'nai Israel, 1923–1937.

Congregation B'nai Israel in 1926. 921 9th St. N, St. Petersburg.

name was Lena; Louis Josselove, First Vice President, the owner of U. and F. Ready-to-Wear Store. His wife's name was Fanny; Henry I. Greenberg, Second Vice President, a real estate broker. His wife's name was Lillian; Joseph Solomon, Treasurer. His wife's name was Gussie. They resided at 2601 1st Avenue South; Hyman M. Jacobs, Secretary, who owned the Central Market.

Highlights of 1926

In 1926, a vacant church was rented at 921, 9th Street North for the first permanent structure for Congregation B'nai Israel. The first Sunday school and Hebrew classes were held there. The first rabbi was hired. The building was used for religious services, fund-raising, meetings, and social events. Services were held there until approximately 1935. Sunday night cafeteria suppers were put on by the Ladies Auxiliary. Evelyn Jess (Mrs. Ed. Goldman) and Goldie Schuster taught Sunday school and directed Purim and Chanukah plays. Rabbi Maurice Lesserox became the first Rabbi of Congregation B'nai Israel.

Highlights of 1928

On September 16, 1928, on Yom Kippur, rain and wind started to batter the synagogue on 9th St North. The congregants quickly left for home. A severe hurricane, category 4, hit Palm Beach County and the Lake Okechobee area and people and homes were devastated. 2,500 people, about five percent of the population of Palm Beach County, died. The Jewish children of St. Petersburg and their parents put on a dance to raise money to help the hurricane survivors.

Highlights of 1930-1939

Highlights of 1930

On October 1, the congregants of Congregation B'nai Israel attended Yom Kippur services at the synagogue at 921 9th Street North. The services were conducted by Rabbi Lapides. On November 13, the St. Petersburg Times honored the Ladies Auxiliary

St. Petersburg Jewish Children at 921 9th St. N, St. Petersburg. Front, l. to r. Melvin Trager, Jackie Sweet Beard, Bunnie Rothblatt Katz, Jerome Silverman, Corinne Silverman Goodman, Jerry Gilbert, Audrey Rothblatt Chenkin, Shelby Trager, Bernie Fuchs, Fern Gilbert Spoto, Max Schmitz?

and Aid Society of Congregation B'nai Israel for the substantial amount of charity work done by the women. The women's organization met every other Tuesday afternoon. Miss Bella Goldman was the President. The men's organization of B'nai Israel met every Thursday night and had a membership of fifty. Louis Boston Cohen was the President.

After Rabbi Lesserox left, Rabbi C. Salzman, then Rabbi Lehrer arrived. Very little information is available about these individuals at this time.

Highlights of 1931

There were between sixty and seventy families in the congregation. There were times during the Depression when there was no rabbi. Lay members, especially Samuel Goldberg, conducted the services. A rabbi would be brought in from Tampa for weddings and funerals. A Chevra Kadisha committee was always available to conduct the necessary rites for the dead.

Highlights of 1933

Members of the Judaic Council of Congregation B'nai Israel held a Cabaret dance at the Elks Club. Mrs. Harry Mogil, Mrs. J. Benson, and Miss Ann Menken were in charge of the entertainment. Mrs. A. Rubin and Mrs. A. Esrick engaged the hall and the orchestra. The group was involved in a sewing project to help others. They held a scheduled meeting on January 8, with Mrs. D. Herman and Mrs. Celia Reuben in charge. Refreshments were served at the close of the meeting by Mrs. S. Fyvolent and Mrs. G. Rippa. They held a radio show and a card party on March 17 at Congregation B'nai Israel for the benefit of the council's building fund. The chairmen were: Mrs. Samuel Fyvolent, Mrs. Leon Halaczer, Mrs. Saul Green, and Mrs. Ed Goldman. During a special meeting held at Mrs. Al Esrick's house, they made arrangements to send a donation to the Hebrew Orphan Home in Atlanta.

Highlights of 1935

A lot was purchased by Congregation B'nai Israel, at 1039 Arlington Avenue North and a synagogue was built for $15,000. The congregation stayed there till 1960 when the congregants built their new synagogue.

Highlights of 1936

Rabbi Morris Baumel was the guest Rabbi. Rabbi Baumel held a Bachelor of Science Degree and Master of Arts Degree from New York University. He conducted services in English on Friday evening and gave a sermon entitled, "Which Comes First?" On Saturday morning, he spoke in Yiddish. He gave a sermon entitled, "The Right Road." On Sunday evening at 8:30 p.m., he lectured on "Maimonides, Principles of Faith." He was invited to become the Rabbi of Congregation B'nai Israel in September, 1936.

Highlights of 1937

On Sunday, December 5, an elaborate Hanukkah celebration program was held. The program included songs, dances, and musical recitals from individuals and groups. There was: a recitation by Phyllis Weinstein; a song by Rabbi Obstbaum; a dance by Sandra Esrick; a piano solo by Grace Wald; a recitation by Marie Davis; a vocal solo by Mrs. Sam Shapiro; a recitation by Bernice Rothblatt; a dance by Corinne Silverman; a cornet solo by Jerry Esrick; vocal solos by Ethel and Doris Spiegal; a recitation by Audrey Rothblatt; a violin solo by Lowell Fyvolent; a piano solo by June Spiegal and songs by the chorus. Rabbi Obstbaum spoke on, "Do We Need Religion Today?" H. M. Jacobs, President and Chairman of the evening's program, gave a speech.

On December 10, Hyman Jacobs was re-elected President, Max Davis, Vice President, Abe Sierkese, Treasurer, Morris Hermer, Secretary. The Board of Trustees elected were: Ed Goldman, Ben Goldberg, David Rothblatt, J. Fuchs, and Sam Fyvolent.

On Sunday, December 19, the new Rabbi, Irving Obstbaum, was installed by Rabbi Burger of Tampa. He was assisted by Rabbi Schlenski of Tampa and Rabbi Pizer W. Jacobs of Temple Beth-El.

Highlights of 1938/1939

In 1938, or 1939, a dinner was held at the synagogue. Thirty six people

attended, including Rabbi Kleinfeld. (photo on page 362)

Congregation B'nai Israel, 1039 Arlington Ave. N, St. Petersburg.

Highlights of 1940-1949

Highlights of 1940

On January 5, Rabbi Kleinfeld spoke on "The Mission of Religion Today." Cadet Lawrence Sherman of the Florida Military Academy, son of Mr. and Mrs. Moe Sherman, was confirmed by Rabbi Kleinfeld. Lawrence spoke on "Service and Duty" and Rabbi Kleinfeld spoke on "The Need of a Living Creed."

Highlights of 1941

In June, six Jewish children were confirmed at Congregation B'nai Israel. They were Victor Dayan, Harvey Adelman, Martin Schindler, Ruth Katz, Sally Lee Rabin, and Lou Ellen Neimeth. Ruth Katz was awarded the coveted Cicia Cieman Memorial and Gold Medal. The valedictory was made by Lou Ellen Neimeth, granddaughter of Rabbi Kleinfeld.

Highlights of 1944
Rabbi Emanuel D. Rothenberg

In December, Rabbi Emanuel D. Rothenberg was officially installed as the Rabbi of Congregation B'nai Israel. He was installed by Rabbi Herbert J. Wilner of St. Petersburg and Benjamin G. Eisenberg of Tampa. Sam Goldberg was installed as President, Frank Rabin was installed as Vice-

Rabbi Irving Ostbaum

Rabbi Emanuel Rothenberg

President, Abraham Sierkese was installed as Treasurer, Reuben Sabin was installed as Secretary, and Max Davis was installed as Chairman of the Board. Rabbi Rothenberg was succeeded in 1946 by Rabbi Max Kaufman.

Highlights of 1947
Rabbi Morris B. Chapman

Rabbi Morris Chapman

Rabbi Morris B. Chapman assumed the pulpit. Prior to his arrival in St. Petersburg, he had pulpits in Lewiston, Maine and Merrick, Long Island. He also was a chaplain for the United States Army. He created a burst of activity and helped pave the way for the growth of the congregation. He was constantly available to not only the Jewish people of St. Petersburg and other communities, but also took an active role in working with the general community, numerous organizations, and many of the local churches. His record of brotherhood activities is long and commendable.

Seder Service 1948, Empire Hotel

Highlights of 1948

In February, the first issue of the B'nai Israel Chronicle was published. It was initially a mimeographed sheet. Somewhat later, the Chronicle was a printed document and Jules J. Green became the managing editor. He worked with an editorial committee. Rabbi Chapman conducted "The Jewish Service of the Air" on WSUN. He also participated in the B'nai Brith Youth Organization and gave numerous presentations to church groups throughout the area. He was frequently called upon to help in dedications of buildings and the installation of officers at synagogues in other parts of the state, such as Orlando, West Palm Beach, Jacksonville, etc.. The adult study groups dealt with books of Jewish interest and with the subject: "Essence of Jewish Religion." The sermon topics included, "Free to be Jews," "The Art of Jewish Giving," "Facing Anti-Semitism Sensibly," "Our Debt to Jewish Womanhood," "The Truth about Truth," etc.. Rabbi Chapman said, "The secret of Jewish survival lives in our ability to strike deep

roots in the past, live fully in the present, and prepare prayerfully for the future... Whatever we have, our life, our speech, our clothes, our religion, our heritage, we owe to the selfless labors of preceding generations. As a token of our appreciation for all the gifts that God, man, and nature have lavished upon us, we must strive to leave the world a better place for those who follow us."

Rabbi Chapman took on the cause of women in Judaism. He talked about the significance of Jewish women and how in good times and bad times they promoted the cultural and spiritual lives of their children and their families. He said that it is part of a great tradition for women to support Judaism through their work, their enthusiasm, and their contributions. Most importantly, they perpetuated Jewish traditions by helping build and maintain the House of God.

On April 23, a seder was held at the Empire Hotel in St. Petersburg. Eighty four people attended, including eight soldiers who were guests of the congregation.

The children in the Sunday school had a joint Purim program at Temple Beth-El. During the summer, the late Friday night services as well as the B'nai Israel Chronicle were discontinued. The congregation had grown to 120 families. In the two hour weekday religious school sessions, the children were acquiring the learning habits and skills central to intelligent participation in Jewish life.

In the Sunday School there was a need for additional classroom space because of the larger number of children participating. The congregation secured the use of Mirror Lake High School for Sunday mornings.

Congregation B'nai Israel sponsored a Junior Congregation which held its first service Saturday morning, December 4th at 11 o'clock. The services were designed to meet the needs of the boys and girls and to train them in the art of Jewish worship. A special prayer book used by conservative congregations was provided and Rabbi Chapman officiated. The congregation used a new prayer book, Siddur, "The Sabbath and Festival Prayer Book," which was used officially by more than 300 Conservative congregations in the United States.

Chevra Kadisha

The Chevra Kadisha, Jewish Burial Society, was reorganized. It is a sacred function of the Hevrah Kadisha to prepare the body, of the deceased, in the traditional fashion that has marked Jewish funerals for thousands of years. Jewish people have always paid reverent tribute to those who have departed. The Hevrah Kadisha discharges its responsibilities at a time when a bereaved family needs people who will help them and do so with dignity and reverence. They follow the following rules: washing and preparing the body; the use of a shroud; avoiding the use of embalming and related procedures unless required by civil law; assisting with shivah(the tradition of morning in the home). The mourners, who sit on low stools in stocking feet, are not expected to be host to those who come to offer condolences. In keeping with Jewish tradition, neighbors and friends prepare the meals to be served at the house of mourning.

Highlights of 1949

Congregation B'nai Israel of St. Petersburg, which had begun as an Orthodox synagogue, had gradually changed to Conservative, and in that year became affiliated with the United Synagogue of America. Rabbi Chapman was instrumental in getting Congregation B'nai Israel to affiliate. The Brandeis Tourist Club gave the gift of $100 to the synagogue, thereby showing the genuine bond of friendship and cooperation between the visitors and the residents of St. Petersburg. The B'nai Israel Community Center building program started with great enthusiasm. A handful of members raised $10,000 without a formal appeal. A new discussion group sponsored by congregation B'nai Israel and chaired by Dr. Sidney Grau received enthusiastic responses and large attendance. The name of the group was changed to the B'nai Israel Forum. There were now 150 member families.

Confirmation exercises were held on Sunday, June 5.

Highlights of 1950-1959

Highlights of 1950

A new addition was built to serve as a social hall, classrooms, library and the Institute for Adult Studies. Groundbreaking was on Sunday, January 15. A special service of consecration was held. The lot was cleared the following day and then construction started. This was a striking advance in the continued growth of Congregation B'nai Israel. This now enabled the congregation to continue to play an indispensable part in Jewish life by providing the threefold function of a synagogue: a Beth Tefillah, a house of Prayer; a Beth Hamidrash, a house of Learning; and a Beth Hak'neseth, an Assembly Hall. President Ben Kornfield gave the greetings, Mrs. Lillian Jacobs led the Star Spangled Banner, Rabbi Morris Chapman gave the invocation, Mayor Stanley C. Minshall gave the principal address. Rabbi Wernick of Rodeph Sholom of Tampa gave a special prayer. The dedication ceremony was directed by Jules J. Green and Stanley Green. The breaking of the ground was directed by Mr. and Mrs. Samuel Fyvolent. The benediction was given by Rabbi Albert Michaels of Temple Beth-El of St. Petersburg. The groundbreaking committee was chaired by Dr. Phillip Benjamin. Rabbi Chapman summing up the beautiful ceremony said, "Let us, in keeping with our sacred traditions, plant wisely today for that beautiful harvest tomorrow."

Mildred Levine, President, Ladies Auxiliary, pledged that the women would, as they always had done in the past, give of themselves untiringly to help build and maintain the shul. A special $100 a couple Donor Dinner was held at the Huntington Hotel on Sunday, February 5, in honor of the B'nai Israel Center. Rabbi Sanders Tofield of the Jacksonville Jewish Center was the principal speaker. Surprise guests were Senator Claude Pepper of Florida and Mayor Harold Turk of Miami Beach. The affair raised over $6,000. The B'nai Israel Center building was used until 1975. The Ladies Auxiliary continued to increase in numbers. Their latest project was to develop a new cook book. On Friday, April 28, the Ladies Auxiliary helped the Rabbi conduct

Ben Kornfield, President, Congregation B'nai Israel, 1947–1950

Sabbath Services. An inspirational message was given by the President-Elect of the Ladies Auxillary, Pauline Rivkind.

Rabbi Chapman addressed the needs for maintaining the dietary laws. He made the following arguments for observing the dietary laws: God ordained them; they have powerful survival value; being kosher was important because Jewish people were a small island initially in a vast sea of idolatry and paganism and being kosher kept the Jewish people from assimilating with their neighbors; being Kosher along with the study of Torah, brotherhood, love, justice, and righteousness helps maintain a unique God-consciousness; the mere act of preparing food links us to God; and being kosher helps you walk in the ways of your fathers. He quoted a philosopher who said, "More than Israel kept the dietary laws, the dietary laws kept Israel."

In February, daily morning services started. The B'nai Israel Library was launched with funds from the Bella Miller Fund in March. Initially, there were sixteen books in the library. The focus of the library was to encourage children to read works of Jewish interest with pleasure and gratification. The Ladies Auxiliary established a library fund to purchase additional books. The response to the library was encouraging because children were becoming avid readers of fine Jewish books. The first librarian was Audrey Rothblatt Vogel.

In discussing the heroes of the Haggadah while celebrating the Seder of the Festival of Passover, the glorious holiday of freedom, Rabbi Chapman said that "the leading character, Moses, is never mentioned. The Jewish people were not ungrateful or disrespectful to their leaders, rather that Jewish thinking dictates that the real heroes are the little people who selflessly support the goals of their leaders. The function of leadership is to give direction and guidance to the followers. However, without the followers, there would be no leaders, and therefore the little people are the unsung heroes."

On May 28, the Children's Services came to a close for the season. It had been very successful and very popular and

consistently had a high attendance. An honor roll was established for those children who came all the time to the services. They were: Raymond Chappan, Cecilia Dayan, Andrew Rivkind, Anthony Rivkind, Laurel Rivkind, Susan Rivkind, Melvin Robiner, Richard Rose, Martin Schwartz, Carol Strauss and William Strauss.

On June 4, the cornerstone of the new B'nai Israel Center was put in place. An evening of entertainment followed. The arrangements committee consisted of Samuel Mazear, Julius Silverman, Meyer Miller, Louis Messenger, Jules Green, Philip Katz, Erwin Robener and Sam Gilbert.

On Sunday, June 5, confirmation exercises were held. The confirmands were: Yale Brevda, Alice Cardon, Sanford Goldman, Mary Graham, Harry Haber, Marcia Kahn, Leslie Levine, Elaine Lippman, Sandra Miller and Ann Newman.

During the summer, the Jewish Adult-Youth Club (JAY's) was activated. Bunnie Rothblatt was the President and Dr. Phillip Benjamin was the Chairman of the Hospitality Committee. They met several times during the summer for beach parties and discussion groups. Many of the college group who were home for the summer joined them. They made plans to hold social and fund-raising affairs as well as have discussion groups and form athletic teams. They volunteered to be responsible for landscaping the front of the new building as well as taking care of the grounds behind the new building. There were thirty young people between the ages of eighteen and thirty five in the group.

The Sunday School, a joint venture between Congregation B'nai Israel and Temple Beth-El, had a total enrollment of 125 children. This had grown from forty five in 1946. The Weekday Religious School had thirty two children enrolled. This was an increase from the previous year when eighteen children were enrolled. The Junior Congregation had been averaging thirty six children and twelve parents for their special Sabbath service.

Mrs. Sarah F. Moss, who had been a teacher at the Congregation's Hebrew school, became the principal. She had arrived in the early 1940s, and was a graduate of Hunter College in New York City. She had retired from the career of teaching and operating children's camps. Dr. Phillip Benjamin said, "We are honoring a person who is a philanthropist not in money but in time and love...." One of Mrs. Moss's Hebrew pupils, Father Otis B. Mason, told of her qualities as a teacher. "So many teachers lack patience, but not Mrs. Moss. She has an understanding that has led me to a deep appreciation of Judaism." Father Mason was a retired Episcopalian priest. Sarah spent many years teaching and guiding children and was honored by Congregation B'nai Israel for her loving work.

Floyd T. Christian, Superintendent of Public Instruction, announced that Jewish children who were absent from public school because they were attending religious services would receive an official excuse. The children would need to bring a note from their parents. This ruling applied to the High Holy Days, Sukkot, Pesach, and Shovouth.

In November, the B'nai Israel Choral Group was formed. It was under the direction of Edith Neimeth. They made their debut in December at a Friday evening service.

Highlights of 1951

The Ladies Auxiliary held its Fourth Annual Purim Dance in the new B'nai Israel Center. A new children's library was started to help provide the youth with adequate Jewish juvenile literature. A new Ceremony of Reaffirmation on the Bar Mitzvah Anniversary was started. Leslie Levine, the first person to participate in the ceremony, did so by chanting the Haftarah from his bar mitzvah. This ceremony applied to both girls and boys alike. The JAY's decided to relax their age restriction by including high school seniors in the group. The congregation sponsored the fourth of the regular monthly teen-age dances. The Pasadena Church sent a contribution of $50 to the B'nai Israel Building Fund. Children continued to chant the Kiddush every Friday evening. The Weekday Religious School enrollment rose to forty two children.

At Chanukah Services on Friday night, December 8, consecration ceremonies for the young children entering the religious school were conducted for the first time.

The children participated in the ceremonies. President Max Davis greeted the children, their parents and the congregation. Dr. Sidney Grau, Chairman of the Education Committee presented miniature Torahs to the children.. They were: Ronnie Balotin, Arthur Carten, Jules Claven, Bonnie Dikman, Phyllis Gilmore, Martha Hankin, David Horn, Larry Kleinfeld, Tora Levine, Arthur Melich, Karen Melich, Martin Meyers, Laurel Rivkind, Arthur Sabin, Dianne Sabin and Doris Topkin.

Highlights of 1952

On February 29, Sheila Green, daughter of Mr. and Mrs. Jules J. Green, became the first Bas Mitzvah of Congregation B'nai Israel of St. Petersburg. Audrey Mendelblatt, daughter of Dr. and Mrs. David Mendelblatt, became the second Bas Mitzvah on March 28. Marilyn Kleinfeld became the third Bas Mitzvah on June 6. The Bas or Bat Mitzvah is the counterpart for girls of the Bar Mitzvah ceremony for boys. It is designed to make Judaism significant for girls and to stress the important part that women play in the preservation and enrichment of our religious heritage.

Under the guidance of Rabbi Chapman, the congregation membership had grown between fourfold and fivefold. A vital spark had been kindled and the congregants became active players in the Jewish and general communities. The Weekday School now had over fifty children and the rabbi had two outstanding teachers helping him. A Youth and Family Hour had been instituted and attendance frequently ran over 100 people. Jewish girls came to the school in droves because they could have a Bas Mitzvah. There was a new flourishing youth program including teenage groups and teenage activities. The JAYS had excellent programs and were making substantial contributions to the congregation as well as having good learning experiences and fun. Adult classes grew significantly and men and women attended and participated in spirited discussions. A new library had been formed for the congregation and for the young and it had grown substantially. The Jr. JAY's, an organization of teenagers, quickly joined the United Synagogue Youth (USY).

They received their charter from the United Synagogue Youth on Friday, December 26, at a Sabbath service. Abe Katz, representing the Youth Activities Committee, presented the Charter to Pete Lipman, the President of the student organization. On August 24-27, a Leaders Training Institute conducted in Miami Beach was attended by Bobby Braun, Carlene Brown, Arlene Davis, Alan Levine, Ross Lew, Peter Lipman, Leroy Milman, Andrew Rivkind, Edwin Shiler, Sharon Silverman and Iris Smith. The attendees' expenses were paid by the congregation. The Institute was designed to help prepare the teenagers for participation in Jewish religious life.

The Augusta Weissman Memorial Youth Fund was started with a check of $500 sent by her children. Augusta was Past President of the Ladies Auxiliary of Congregation B'nai Israel and, throughout her life, was especially dedicated to the cause of Jewish youth. Each year the best all-around student for the year was selected and the child's name was added to a permanent plaque. In addition, the prize-winning student received a $25 government bond. The selection was based on attendance and punctuality at weekly and Sunday religious schools, attendance at Sabbath and holiday services, scholarship, effort, and school and synagogue citizenship.

Thirty four new member families joined the congregation. A men's club was formed with Jules Green heading the provisional committee. Harry Signer was appointed to handle transient welfare cases in the community.

Highlights of 1953

The Board of Directors of Congregation B'nai Israel voted to sponsor the establishment of a Synagogue Council, to be composed of representatives of all St. Petersburg congregations. It was felt that the interests of all the congregations would be best served by creating a forum for determining and resolving problems affecting the welfare of the religious institutions. This may have been the forerunner of the Pinellas County Board of Rabbis.

The Men's Club elected their first officers. They were: Jules J. Green, President; Morris Lerner, Vice-President; Dr. Sherman L. Whalley, Secretary; Harry Signer, Treasurer. The Board of Directors included: Milton Berger, Bernard Cutson, Leon Glassman, David Howard, Abe Katz, Meyer Possick, Jack B. Schwartz, Jack Topkin and David Wolper. Thirty seven men were charter members. Membership then grew rapidly. The Men's Club had its first Annual Picnic on Sunday, April 19.

The Board of Directors voted decisively to uphold the highest educational religious standards. They also decided that it was necessary to have a professional full-time secretary to help in all aspects of the B'nai Israel Synagogue Center. The first person to serve in this role was Mrs. M. Newton. The religious school which had started in 1947, with about a dozen students, all boys, did not provide Jewish training at all for girls. Boys were allowed to have a Bar Mitzvah with only one or two months training. The educational conditions were chaotic. This changed tremendously during the ensuing years and now all children, both girls and boys, were required to meet educational standards.

The United Synagogue Youth (USY) had been helped in the very beginning by Rabbi Chapman's leadership in the synagogue put on much of the service for a large group of congregants on the Sabbath. They had been working to help resolve teen-age problems along with the Youth Activities Committee of the Congregation, the Lady's Auxiliary, and the parent organizations.

During the summer months, Rabbi Chapman took his annual vacation, starting with attendance at the annual convention of the Rabbinical Assembly, and then traveling to enhance his understanding of Conservative Judaism. Each Sabbath eve, a different group of men and women conducted the services. This program started in 1951. On Saturday morning, Sam Gilbert conducted the services. On September 11, Sam Gilbert was honored by his children, Harold and Jane Gilbert, Jerome and Thelma Gilbert, and Reuben and Fern Sabin at a special Oneg Shabbat celebrating his 70th birthday. Rabbi Chapman lauded Sam for his thirty five years of devoted service to the congregation. Hundreds of relatives, friends, and well-wishers attended the service and Oneg Shabbat.

Before the High Holy Days, twenty new members joined the Congregation. The St. Petersburg community was uplifted when the local press told a story in both words and pictures of inter-faith goodwill. Two churches in the community, one Caucasian and one Black, put on their Bulletin Boards, "A Blessed Year to Our Jewish Friends." This gesture of good-will was inspired by the Rev. J. Earl Edwards, a retired Baptist clergyman, who lived in St. Petersburg. He carried on a one-man campaign to foster fellowship toward the Jewish people. The good-will was a tribute to the relationship that had been developed by the Jewish people and their neighbors.

The Augusta Weissman fund for children was expanded further by the generosity of Mr. and Mrs. Jack B. Weissman of Tampa. Mr. and Mrs. Arthur Meyers pledged $1,000 a year to help hire a full-time teacher for the religious school. This was the first concrete step toward professionalizing the teaching staff. The parents and other volunteers had done a wonderful job, but now it was time to have someone who was specifically trained in education. Sarah F. Moss, principal of the Sunday School Department of Beth HaMedrosh Hogadol in Denver, became the head of the Sunday Department and along with the rabbi completely revised the curriculum.

The Congregation honored Rabbi Chapman upon being awarded the degree of Doctor of Hebrew Literature from the Jewish Theological Seminary. Over 300 members and their friends attended the service.

Highlights of 1954

The new kitchen was put into use. New carpeting helped beautify the sanctuary and the lighting was improved.

A new Sefer Torah was dedicated on Sunday, March 14. The highlight of the special service and festivities was the completion of the Torah Scroll by the Scribe in front of the Congregation. He filled in the frames of the letters left unfinished, thereby enabling each of the people present to symbolically write their names as a token of owning a new Torah Scroll. The Torah Scroll was a gift from the Chevra Kadisha.

Rabbi Chapman talked about what he found most important in a synagogue. He said it was not the building, but rather the people, who make up the membership. He said some people were more responsible than others. He said, "The three tests of membership were: do the individuals give of themselves to further the cause of the synagogue; do the individuals promote the spiritual purposes to which the synagogue is dedicated by attending services, cooperating with the religious education of the children, and giving generously to worthwhile causes; do the individuals live as Jews where they contribute financially, spiritually, and ethically to the community."

In September the membership voted for a new site for the synagogue.

Although there had always been an adult education program, Congregation B'nai Israel recognized the need for a formal program of studies. The Congregation sponsored the Institute of Jewish Studies. In the initial programs, fifty four men and women registered for courses given by the Rabbi and Mrs. Moss. The course titles were: "Learning to Read Hebrew," " Know Your Bible," "What Jews Live By," and " Problems of Jewish Parents." Over the ensuing years, this institute grew and provided adult studies for large numbers of people.

Highlights of 1955

The Congregation negotiated for a five acre tract of land for the projected B'nai Israel Center. The land was the entire block between 58th and 59th St., and from Burlington Ave. to Dartmouth Avenue on the North side of the property. Twenty five thousand dollars was paid for the land purchased. At a later date, because of the brilliant foresight of Phillip Benjamin, an additional five acres fronting on 58th St was purchased. The combination of the ten acres of land has been used not only for the new synagogue erected in April of 2000, but also had previously been used as the site for Menorah Manor and Phillip Benjamin Tower.

On April 6, the community seder sponsored by Congregation B'nai Israel was held at the Synagogue Center. On Friday,

Dr. Harold Rivkin, President, Congregation B'nai Israel, 1954–1958, 1970–1972.

June 3, the first Baccalaureate Service in the history of Congregation B'nai Israel was held in conjunction with the Family Sabbath Hour. At that time, the congregation honored the seven high school graduates and the twenty one junior high school and eighth-grade graduates. The Minyan Club, a place for teenagers to have a short discussion on a Jewish topic and then have lunch together, met on Sunday mornings. Forty or more young people met regularly.

During Sabbath services, the congregational family honored President Harold C. Rivkind. Harold was going to spend part of his time in St. Petersburg because he was pursuing an advanced degree in Gainesville. Under his administration, the synagogue flourished in an exceptional manner. As the membership doubled, the scope of activities increased substantially, and the expansion program accelerated. The congregation recognized him for his unremitting efforts, his judicious temperament, his attention to detail, and above all, to his example of Jewish living and Jewish striving.

Fifty six children received awards for perfect attendance at the Youth and Family Hour. Synagogue respect was taking root in the hearts and souls of the children. The Jewish schooling and the support of the parents and teachers helped bring this about.

The B'nai Israel Choral Group was formed. Joel Bressler, former Director of the Hillel Choir at the University of Florida, became the leader.

Maurice Goldblatt

Maurice Goldblatt came to St. Petersburg on August 1. During his lifetime, he donated an extraordinary amount of time, service, and money to Congregation B'nai Israel. He served as volunteer cantor, leading the musical part of the Friday night services. He raised $275,000 in pledges for building and construction. He helped organize and later served as President of the Men's Club. When Congregation B'nai Israel sponsored the Harlem Globe Trotter's basketball team for a fund raising event, he built the basketball court and installed it at Al Lang Field for the performance. When the synagogue needed an Ark in the main sanctuary, he

Bat Mitzvah 1956.
Laurel Rivkind and Rabbi
Chapman.
1039 Arlington Ave.

built it. When a parking lot was needed, he convinced friends to pay for half of it and he paid the rest. He made costumes for plays and tables for synagogue dinners and for the Jewish Community Center. He served on the executive committee and board for many years. He was a rather shy and unassuming man who was embarrassed when the B'nai Israel Sisterhood gave a dinner dance in his honor called, "This is your night, Maury Goldblatt." Maury said, "I don't work for recognition. It is a labor of love, a mitzvah. It is an opportunity to do a good thing. Some have other activities. They go fishing or play golf. I work for the congregation. I get my enjoyment from this work."

Highlights of 1956

On Sunday, October 7, groundbreaking ceremonies were held for the new B'nai Israel Synagogue Center at the five acre site at 59th and 3rd Ave. North in St. Petersburg. This was the second groundbreaking ceremony within a 10-year period, which occurred because of the phenomenal growth in size, influence, and effectiveness of Congregation B'nai Israel.

Congregation B'nai Israel, one of the leaders of the Conservative Movement, was deeply involved in discussions concerning synagogue standards. The United Synagogue, composed of over 600 Conservative congregations, dedicated its entire convention in the summer of 1956 to the consideration of synagogue standards. This organization of Conservative synagogues was extremely concerned about standards of conduct of both the synagogues and the membership in their private lives. Congregation B'nai Israel had already done a credible job in the area of Jewish education. The minimum requirements that had been established for Bar Mitzvah and Bas Mitzvah, as well as confirmation, were being copied by other congregations. Areas of concern in the synagogue were as follows: should deliveries such as flowers and food be permitted at the synagogue on the Sabbath; should fund-raising collections and rummage pickups be permitted on the Sabbath; what is the proper attire at a religious service; should worshipers be permitted to bring presents into the synagogue during a service; should a synagogue ever sponsor a non-kosher affair; should the synagogue get its funds from sources such as bingo games and Monte Carlo nights; should the synagogue ever sponsor entertainment of dubious taste. Discussions concerning personal standards were to be resolved after resolving synagogue standards. By the end of 1957, the United Synagogue issued Standards for Synagogue Practice and Congregation B'nai Israel formally adopted them.

In a deeply moving consecration ceremony held on December 18, fifty five new women were welcomed into the Sisterhood. They were part of a growing family of members joining Congregation B'nai Israel. The congregation provided a Mezuzah and a proper ceremony to all members moving into new homes.

Highlights of 1957

The planning for the new synagogue center continued with the hiring of a professional campaign director. The structure was needed to house the growing membership, about 200 families, and the necessary classrooms for children. A library and a 500 seat sanctuary were to be part of the structure. The site was chosen because the western end of St. Petersburg was growing and because parking was needed. By October, forty seven new member families were added to the congregation. These people helped provide additional funds for the building campaign. The vision of a substantial synagogue center, which was but a dream in 1951, started to become a reality. In a period of seven weeks toward the end of the year, a group of people challenged others to raise $250,000 to make the dream come true. Despite the fact that there were those who felt this was an impossible challenge, the congregation, without holding lavish affairs, over subscribed and pledged $276,580. The leaders of the group said, "Today with a sense of gratitude and deep humility, we only ask that sometime during the next century, those who constitute Congregation B'nai Israel then, would pause for a moment and glance back to the past two months and remember them as the seven weeks

during which the Almighty smiled on St. Petersburg and caused a miracle to occur on the Suncoast of Florida."

Because of the importance of Jewish education at all levels, Menahem S. Aroni was hired to serve as Director of Education. He had previously served in congregational schools in Albany, New York and Charleston, South Carolina. He had degrees in political science and economics and had been principal of several schools in Poland, Israel, and the United States. He served as a political commentator on "The Voice of Israel" and published several syndicated articles.

The 10th anniversary of Rabbi Morris B. Chapman as spiritual leader of Congregation B'nai Israel was celebrated at a testimonial dinner. Since he arrived, the congregation had grown from sixty families to more than three hundred families. The weekday religious school had expanded from thirteen students to sixty students with an anticipated enrollment of seventy five students in the coming year.

Highlights of 1958

On March 26, 1958, Rabbi Abraham Karp, from Rochester, New York, one of the outstanding young leaders of the Conservative movement, delivered a presentation to the congregation. He came under the auspices of the Calalcade Series, an innovation in the field of Adult Jewish Education, where outstanding authorities in their respective fields came to synagogues to share their thinking. His subject was "The History and Philosophy of the Conservative Movement."

On April 13, groundbreaking ceremonies took place at the new five acre site at 59th St. and 4th Ave. North. The invocation was given by Rabbi David Susskind, Temple Beth-El. Greetings were extended by Mayor Samuel Johnson. MA TOVU was sung by Jules J. Green. Thanks from the synagogue family was extended by Jerome C. Gilbert, Chairman of the Board. The groundbreaking message was delivered by Rabbi Jerome Kastenbaum, Rodeph Sholom Congregation, Tampa. A reception followed the ceremony. The founders of the original synagogue were honored as well as those who made the new structure possible. The arrangements committee consisted of Maurice Goldblatt, Chairman, Dr. Phillip Benjamin, Murray Jacobs, Harold C. Rivkind, President of Congregation B'nai Israel, and Rabbi Chapman.

On August 8, the Sun Coast Jewish News reported that the Sisterhood was opening a Nursery School in their new building. The school was to be under the administration of the Education Committees of the Congregation and the Sisterhood. The school was going to be open from nine to noon and would take children between three and five years of age. It was fully accredited and had a qualified teacher leading the program. The cost per child was $15 per month with a registration fee of $5 and insurance of $1.50. A doctor's certificate was required for each child. The children were to receive milk and cookies during the course of the morning. The facilities were made available for the school in early September.

In August, Aaron Stern became Principal and Youth Director. He came from the Tri-City Jewish Center in Rock Island, Illinois. He had attended Warsaw University, Brooklyn College, and Teachers Institute of the Jewish Theological Seminary and Columbia University in New York. Mrs. Walter Smith, a graduate of Brooklyn College who had taught in the lower elementary grades in New York City and Chicago public school systems, became the head of the nursery school program. She was assisted by Mrs. Harold Goldberg who had taught the nursery grades in the Sunday School. Thirty children between the ages of three and five were enrolled in the program. Additional teachers and staff members were hired.

Pauline and Harold Rivkind

As part of the congregation's concentration on young people, B'nai Israel organized both a Boy Scout and Girl Scout Troop. It also created a High School Department for the Jewish children to learn beyond their Bar/Bas Mitzvah.

There was a new spacious sanctuary, auditorium, large meeting rooms, and all the necessary additions to be considered a modern, progressive synagogue center. The architect was Frank Bonsey. Mr. and Mrs. Arthur Meyers endowed the Holy Ark.

Highlights of 1959

In 1959, the Dramatic Club was organized under the direction of Mrs. Morris LeVine. The program consisted of training students for performing on holidays such as Purim and Passover. Milton Jasanoff was the Editor of The Chronicle. The Men's Club, which had slipped in membership and had become inactive, was reactivated. The President of the Men's Club, Alvin Applefield, extended a personal invitation to all members of the congregation to participate in the programs. Forty six new member families joined the synagogue, increasing the membership to 350 families, which was the largest in the history of the synagogue. A new teenage service made up of children who were part of the United Synagogue Youth was started. A luncheon followed each service to help the children socialize.

Jerome M. Gilbert became President of Congregation B'nai Israel. In response to resolving the numerous problems related to new construction, new programs, and necessary financing, he said, "...that without hard work and obligations there is no advancement. In everyone's life there's an empty space that must be filled by helping others, by giving of our energy and if possible, finances. The rewards of service to one's fellow man are many times the effort put forth."

Pauline and Dr. Harold Rivkind

Dr. Harold Rivkind, Past President of Congregation B'nai Israel, was honored on November 11, for his untiring efforts, devotion, and dedicated leadership in guiding Congregation B'nai Israel to its current position in the Jewish Community and in the City of St. Petersburg. Harold received his Bachelor of Arts in Education from Oberlin University. He received his Master's Degree in Education from the University of Pittsburgh. He also earned a Master's Degree in Social Science from Western Reserve University. He earned his Doctorate from the University of Florida in 1958. Since he arrived in St. Petersburg in 1948, he was connected with the Child Guidance Center and was now the Director. He had been a Member of the Board of the United Fund, Aid for Retarded Children,

Menorah Manor, Menorah Center, Gulf Coast Jewish Family Service, and St. Petersburg Optimists. He was Secretary of the Neighborly Senior Citizens and the Mental Health Services of Pinellas County. Harold was Past President of the Southeastern Region of United Synagogue, the Jewish Community Council, and the Florida Conference of Social Welfare. He was elected to the 1986 St. Petersburg Senior Citizen's Hall of Fame. Dr. Rivkind was honored by the White House by being selected as one of three delegates to represent this area at the White House Conference on Youth. The purpose of the Conference was to promote opportunities for children and youth to realize their full potential for a creative life in freedom and dignity. He died on November 30, 2005.

Pauline and Harold Rivkind came to St. Petersburg in 1948, from Cleveland, Ohio. Pauline Rivkind was elected to the Board of the National Woman's League of the United Synagogue of America. She had served four years as President of the South East Branch of the National Woman's League. She helped guide and direct the women of the synagogues to their goals and objectives in the states of Alabama, Florida, Georgia, South Carolina, and Tennessee. Pauline was selected by the women of Congregation B'nai Israel in 1951 to be President of the Sisterhood. She established the synagogue day nursery and kept it running. She was a founder of the Human Relations Group and taught confirmation classes. She served on the Board of the St. Petersburg Garden Club, PTA, Community Chest, Heart Fund, Polio Drive and was involved in other civic affairs. Pauline's work in St. Petersburg helped her gain stature and recognition on the national scene. Pauline was described as a petite person with a perfect spark plug of accomplishment, a human dynamo. Pauline Rivkind's words helped bring out the sweetness of human nature. Pauline died on June 1, 1967.

On May 30, 1968, Harold married Ruth. On his obituary, it shows that he had been married for thirty eight years. He was survived by two sons, Ivan Faggan of Los Angeles and Judah Raviv of Israel. He was survived by three daughters, Carol Berger

of Fort Lauderdale, Laurel Lowy of Florida and Susan Milton of Franklin, Tennessee. He had fourteen grandchildren and nineteen great-grandchildren.

Jerome Gilbert, President, Congregation B'nai Israel, 1959–1961.

Highlights of 1960-1969

Highlights of 1960

The synagogue was dedicated on the weekend of April 29, 30, and May 1. On Friday night, there was a Dedication Sabbath, at which twenty two honorary and memorial plaques were dedicated. Rabbi Chapman's sermon was on, "Let Them Build Me a Sanctuary." Saturday morning, there was a special dedication service in the synagogue. Saturday night, the Synagogue Sisterhood and Men's Club sponsored a buffet dinner dance. The affair was limited to 225 couples. On Sunday afternoon, special guests brought greetings to Congregation B'nai Israel members. The special guests included: Hon. Edward Brantley, Mayor of St. Petersburg; Rev. W. Fred Campbell, President of the St. Petersburg Ministerial Association; and Marion B. Ross, President of Temple Beth-El.

Rabbi Arthur A. Chiel, Genesis Hebrew Center, Tuckahoe, New York, gave the dedication sermon, "The Spirit in Orbit." Rabbi Chiel was ordained in 1946 at the Jewish Institute of Religion in New York City. From 1944 to 1949, he was the Director of Religion of the 92nd Street Y.M. and Y.W.H.A. of New York City. From 1949-1952, he was Director of B'nai B'rith Hillel Foundation of the University of Manitoba in Winnipeg, Canada. He also served on the university faculty as Assistant Professor of Judaic Studies. He helped establish a new conservative congregation, the Rosh Pina, which he served as spiritual leader from 1952-1957. During his time in Canada, he did considerable research on Canadian Jewish

Congregation B'nai Israel, 1960. 301 59th St. N; St. Petersburg, FL

History and wrote about it extensively. He was a member of the Executive Body of the Rabbinical Assembly of America and served as Chairman of the Rabbinical Assembly Convention in 1959. He was Program Editor for Eternal Light Television Program and a lecturer in the Cantor's Institute of the Jewish Theological Seminary of America.

Over the years, Congregation B'nai Israel became a leader in all facets of Conservative Judaism in the Southeast Region. The Sisterhood and educational programs have been widely recognized for their success. Many members of the congregation have held regional offices.

The youth and family hour held on Saturday morning became a tremendous success. Over 100 religious school students gathered together every Saturday morning. After the service, the children always had a light lunch together. This activity helped the children relate to each other and to the synagogue. The religious school provided excellent stimulus for the children. The synagogue met its threefold objective: the acquisition of necessary skills, such as the ability to read Hebrew, participation in the services, chanting the Kiddush etc. in an atmosphere of love and respect for the synagogue; active participation in the religious program of the synagogue, such as the attendance of Sabbath and Festival services; and the application of the teachings of the school and synagogue in their Jewish home.

The Pinellas County License Board granted the synagogue an increase in the number of children who could be taught to a capacity of seventy five.

Maury Goldblatt, President, Congregation B'nai Israel, 1962–1964.

Harry Nadler, President, Senior United Synagogue Youth, was the only young person from the Southeast Region to win a national award at the United Synagogue Youth Convention held in Chicago. Only 150 young people out of 25,000 members received similar awards.

A new Conservative Service was instituted on Saturday morning to replace the old Orthodox Saturday morning service for adults. Many members of the congregation had found the Orthodox Service difficult to follow and felt that they did not receive adequate inspiration from

it. The new service would be no longer than one and one half hours, including English readings, and an abbreviated Torah Service. For those people who still wanted to participate in an Orthodox Service, one would be held in the chapel.

In October, Leonard Lubin, St. Petersburg attorney, was appointed by Dr. David L. Mendelblatt, President of Congregation B'nai Israel to be the chairman of the $100,000 synagogue completion campaign. In accepting the chairmanship, Leonard declared, "There was a great need to build our synagogue, and we have a sacred duty to complete it. I'm certain that the congregation in our community will rise to this effort to complete the B'nai Israel."

Highlights of 1961

Rabbi Chapman wrote about the topic, "How to Enjoy the Services." He said, "... The congregant at services must not be a passive receptacle or funnel through whom words and music pass like a sieve. He must be active even though he may say very little. He must listen, concentrate, be sympathetic, and reverent. He must participate and pay as little attention as possible to the mundane things about him. To a measure, he must shut them out. Above all, to all the elements of the services – prayer, song, Torah, sermon– he invests part of himself." Rabbi Chapman had distinguished himself in the Conservative Movement. He was once again invited by the World Council of Synagogues, on behalf of the International Conservative Movement, to visit a number of European lands and Israel to help promote the Conservative Movement.

Highlights of 1962

J. Marshall Taxay, spiritual leader of Temple B'nai Israel of Clearwater, addressed the Living Ideas Supper Club of Congregation B'nai Israel. He spoke on, "Are Jews Different?" Rabbi Taxay was described as a brilliant speaker who had won many friends through his sincerity and eloquence.

New seats were added to the sanctuary. This was the first in a series of changes designed to enhance the beauty of the synagogue and the solemnity of the services. The Institute of Jewish Studies continued to be very successful. There were special programs on Monday evenings and Wednesday evenings. Attendance was excellent with fifty or more people at each of the sessions.

Highlights of 1963

The daily Conservative services were held in the morning at seven o'clock, except on Sunday when they were held at nine o'clock. The weekday services typically lasted a half-hour and included prayers and discussions. Renovation continued with the addition of carpeting in the sanctuary. The five acre tract adjoining the five acres of the synagogue and its land had its unsightly swamp drained and was turned into a beautiful piece of land.

Rabbi Chapman was honored by the Commission on Jewish Chaplaincy of the National Jewish Welfare Board for completion of twenty years of continuous and faithful performance of duty as a Jewish chaplain in the service of the government of the United States of America. The service started in 1942, during World War II. In 1947, he was appointed Jewish chaplain at the Veterans Administration Center, Bay Pines and continued to serve in that capacity for many years.

On December 1, the charter meeting of the Mr. and Mrs. Club was held. This newly formed group was for young Jewish couples of the St. Petersburg area. They were chartered by Congregation B'nai Israel.

Highlights of 1964

It was recommended that "The New Haggadah" from the Reconstruction Foundation be used in all homes and at the synagogue seder. Rabbi Chapman felt that it was much more relevant for the current time. Rabbi Chapman was part of the Reconstructionist Movement. Reconstructionist Judaism is respectful of traditional Jewish observances, but also open to new interpretations and forms of religious expression.

On April 13, the Ark for the Torahs used in the chapel was dedicated in memory of Julius M. Grossman. The construction of the Ark was done by the B'nai Israel Men's

Club, as a tribute to Jack Grossman, a loyal, active member of both the congregation and the Men's Club. It was made possible by gifts from congregational members, Men's Club members, and other friends of Jack.

The summer layman services were very popular. One hundred or more people came every Friday night. Dr. David L. Mendelblatt was the lay leader.

A synagogue Hevrah Kadisha was once again formed. This announcement was received with great enthusiasm. This Jewish Burial Society is important in Jewish life. In fact, most of the Jewish communities formed in the 1800s including the Jewish community of Terre Haute, Indiana, started with a burial society. In 1849, the Jewish community of Terre Haute officially started with the organization of the Zions Geminda, a burial society.

Highlights of 1965

Dr. and Mrs. David L. Mendelblatt received the Israel Award of Honor in recognition of their distinguished service on behalf of many community and humanitarian causes and for their outstanding role on behalf of the State of Israel. A committee of leading members of the Jewish community had selected them unanimously for this honor. Dave was Past President of Congregation B'nai Israel and Reba was Past President of Sisterhood. Dave had a busy professional schedule including service at the Veterans Administration Center at Bay Pines. The two of them energetically worked with the wider Jewish community as well as the general community. Dave was Chairman of Camp Kadima and the Jewish Community Council.

The congregational family grew to 310 members. Congregation B'nai Israel and Temple Beth-El jointly conducted a membership drive directed at all known non-affiliated Jewish people in the community. Twenty five new families joined the congregation.

Highlights of 1966

The Leo H. Buckman Ramah Fund was established. The fund was designed to provide partial scholarships to help encourage young people to attend Camp

Mrs. Libby Grossman at the dedication of the Torah Ark in the chapel, in memory of her husband, Julius M. Grossman.

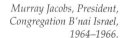

Murray Jacobs, President, Congregation B'nai Israel, 1964–1966.

Ted P. Wittner, President, Congregation B'nai Israel, 1966–1968.

Ramah, a Hebrew speaking, religiously oriented camp under the sponsorship of the United Synagogue of America.

The Sisterhood gave a generous gift to the congregation for the remodeling of the Bimah. The Torah scrolls were repaired according to Jewish Law, since defects or blemishes make them unfit for use. Mr. and Mrs. Leonard Samson and Mr. and Mrs. Maurice A. Goldblatt paid for the repairs.

At the congregational meeting, the congregation voted to endorse a project looking into the possible establishment of a retirement home under the auspices of Congregation B'nai Israel. In fact it was considered as an integral part of the synagogue complex. This was the forerunner of the Phillip Benjamin Tower.

On June 5, at the commencement exercises of the Jewish Theological Seminary, Rabbi Chapman received the degree of Doctor of Divinity, honoris causa. This was the first time that the seminary had bestowed such an honor upon any rabbi in the Southeast. Rabbi Louis Finkelstein, Chancellor of the Jewish Theological Seminary said, "In conferring this degree upon you, the seminary wishes to express its admiration and appreciation for what you have contributed to Judaism, as a rabbi and as a leader of our people. Some of us remember you from your student days, and all of us have followed your career with great delight. It is, therefore, a particular source of happiness for all of us, and most especially to me, to be able to ask you to accept the degree of Dr. of Divinity from the Seminary."

Murray Jacobs received the 80th Anniversary Citation for Distinguished Service from the Jewish Theological Seminary. He was recognized for his leadership in his community and dedicated service on behalf of the cultural and religious traditions of Judaism. He was Past President of Congregation B'nai Israel, chairman of virtually every committee in the synagogue and had given of himself selflessly in the general community as well.

Highlights of 1967

Congregation B'nai Israel and Temple Beth-El had their first joint Thanksgiving Service. Rabbi David J. Susskind of Temple Beth-El gave the sermon while Rabbi Chapman conducted the services. Rabbi Chapman was honored for twenty distinguished years of service. He was also honored by the National Jewish Welfare Board for twenty five continuous years as a chaplain. Congregation B'nai Israel continued to grow. There were thirty eight new member families and twenty two children were consecrated.

Claire and Ron Yogman

Claire and Ron Yogman were married on November 24, 1966 in Savannah, Georgia. They came to St. Petersburg in 1967 and became members of Congregation B'nai Israel.

Ron was born in Brooklyn, New York on May 21, 1943. He graduated with honors from Michigan State University in 1964, with a Bachelor of Arts Degree in Journalism. He was employed by the Times Publishing Company from 1964-1975 as a reporter and then as Business Editor of the Evening Independent and Assistant Financial Editor of the St. Petersburg Times. In 1975, he founded Ron Yogman and Associates, a St. Petersburg-based public relations/advertising agency for professionals, retailers, shopping center developers, home builders, etc..

Ron has made numerous contributions to the Jewish and general communities. He has served on the Board of Trustees of Congregation B'nai Israel in the 1960s and now again in the 1990s. He was instrumental in naming and promoting the five million dollar, "Come Build It", a campaign for the new Congregation B'nai Israel. He also named the Windows of Wonder. Both on a Pro Bono and paid professional basis, Ron was instrumental in both the pre-construction and early promotion of Menorah Manor, "Our Home for Jewish Living." He was a Member of the Board of Phillip Benjamin Tower. He has given his professional expertise to the Florida Holocaust Museum, Gulf Coast Jewish Family Services, Jewish National Fund, etc. He was the key promoter of the Jewish Community Center's "Evening at the Bayfront," coordinating the appearances of David Susskind, David Frost and Ralph Nader. He also did extensive work on

Congregation B'nai Israel's "Jewish Music Festival." Since 1987, Ron has served as Executive Director of the Hillsborough Animal Health Foundation, a nonprofit organization dedicated to strengthening the human-animal bond and promoting responsible pet ownership.

In 2005, Ron was named Chairman of Tikvah. This is a combined campaign of the Jewish communities of Florida's West Coast, from Tampa Bay to Naples, to plan and build a much needed and long-overdue Jewish home for adults with special needs.

Claire Eichholz, a native of Savannah, Georgia, met Ron through mutual synagogue friends in St. Petersburg. Claire and Ron have two grown children, Jann Ian of New York City and Kandice Nicole of St. Petersburg. Claire earned degrees in Early Childhood and Human Development at St. Petersburg College and at Eckerd College. She worked as a preschool teacher at the Pauline Rivkind Preschool at Congregation B'nai Israel from 1967-1992. From 1992-2003, she was a Licensing Specialist for the Pinellas County License Board, supervising the safety and welfare of children in area preschools. From 2003-present, she has worked as Childhood Consultant/Parent Trainer with Directions for Mental Health. She works with parents of children from ages zero to five.

Claire is a lifetime member of Hadassah and has been active in Congregation B'nai Israel Sisterhood, National Council of Jewish Women, where she received the Sound of Honor Award in 1974, and other Jewish organizations. Her community and professional contributions include: Early Childhood Association of Florida, National Association Education of Young Children, and other community organizations.

For more than twenty years, Claire and Ron have maintained the Golden Kipah recognition plaques in the lobby of Congregation B'nai Israel. They deem this effort to be essential to encourage young people after Bar/Bat Mitzvah to continue reading Torah and participating in the synagogue service.

Ron and Claire talking about their arrival in St. Petersburg and their need to become part of the Jewish community said, "As a newly-married couple-also new to the St. Petersburg area-in the late 1960s, we felt the best way to meet friends and establish roots in our new environs was to participate in worthwhile community and charitable endeavors. We never regretted this "outreach"...which paved the way for numerous life-long friendships and "extended family"-especially with our own family dispersed throughout the United States. In effect, learning from our own childhood communities and role models, we have sought to transplant our Judaic roots in our new, chosen, hometown...hopefully this involvement will, in some way, inspire our children's generation."

Highlights of 1968

Twelve of the children entered the National Bible Contest sponsored by the Department of Education and Culture of the Jewish Agency. Temple Beth-El and Congregation B'nai Israel jointly sponsored Rabbi Roland B. Gittelsohn, lecturer and author and President Elect, Central Conference of American Rabbis and Senior Rabbi, Temple Israel of Boston

Reuben E. Halprin, President, Congregation B'nai Israael, 1968–1970.

Highlights of 1969

Cantor Josef Schroeder brought a high level of professionalism to the teenage choir. His influence was such that the choir continued on for generations.

Highlights of 1970-1979

Highlights of 1970

The Jewish Book Council of America awarded the congregation their Library Citation. Congregation B'nai Israel was the only Florida organization to receive this award and only one of eight Jewish religious and cultural organizations throughout the United States to receive the award. The renewed interest in the synagogue library was inspired by Rabbi Chapman and developed by Mrs. Peter Streit, a professional librarian, who served as synagogue librarian for seven years. She was followed as librarian in 1970 by Mrs. Rivy Mencher. The library was part of the educational program at the synagogue. The fifty to sixty adults participating in the Institute of Jewish Studies, taught by Rabbi Chapman, had to read a minimum of four books of Jewish interest each year to qualify for recognition by the National Academy of Adult Jewish Studies. Members of the United Synagogue Youth participated in an honors reading program which included reading and reviewing three recommended books a year. The library also served students from the University of South Florida, St. Petersburg Junior College, University of Tampa, and Florida Presbyterian College, who were doing research in Judaism. The entire community of St. Petersburg was invited to utilize the library resources.

Highlights of 1971

The Bridge Builders Selihot Service was first held in September, to recognize the continuance of generations of congregants within the synagogue. These families had made significant contributions to the congregation for many years.

Highlights of 1973

The monthly bulletin was renamed *Shalom*, with January's issue being volume 1, number, 1. The new editor was Ron Yogman. The Pauline Rivkind Talmud Torah Hanukkah (Chanukah) program attracted more than 150 children from the school, who participated in a program of music and drama, and performed before a capacity audience. Congregation B'nai Israel welcomed fifty new member families. The Men's Club and Sisterhood jointly sponsored a M'Lavah Malkah at the synagogue. People came from as far away as Sarasota and Clearwater, including non-Jewish people. Over 600 people attended. Cantor Josef A. Schroeder's contract was renewed. He first came to St. Petersburg in October 1971 from Atlanta, Georgia. He was a fourth-generation cantor who played the violin, tenor saxophone, and clarinet.

Rabbi Chapman said, "... Jewish women are now seeking equality in synagogue life. Despite the long tradition which insists that the place of the Jewish woman is in the home and not in public worship or ministering in the synagogue, there is no basic reason to disqualify women. It is a powerful survival of prejudice, hardened into practice, that militates against softening the negative

George Feineman, President 1972–1974.

attitudes of the past. We have insisted that girls in our day receive the same basic education in the ideals and practices of Judaism. At age thirteen, a girl becomes a Bat Mitzvah. With girls acquiring the same background as boys in Jewish studies, reading publicly from the pulpit a portion of the Hebrew Scriptures, and even, on occasion reading in the Torah Scrolls, the prescribed section for the Sabbath, playing a novel role as teachers and educational directors in the religious schools (a revolutionary role when one considers that only men were the school teachers originally and that was true in United States as well) – that makes the next step inevitable – namely serving as rabbis. I, for one, unequivocally champion the right of the Jewish women to be ordained as "Rabbi, Teacher, and Preacher in Israel."

Rabbi Morris B. Chapman

After twenty five years service to Congregation B'nai Israel, Rabbi Morris B. Chapman elected to retire from the congregation and became Rabbi Emeritus. Marilyn Benjamin, in writing about Rabbi Chapman, said, "The loves of a man determine the worth of a man, and in our rabbi, we've had a man of many worthy loves. First, has always been his love of education. Starting with absolutely nothing, he built our religious school to a point of national recognition. He has been responsible for the inception of the first Jewish nursery school on the West Coast of Florida. He insisted upon the use of professionals in our Hebrew School. Our Family Sabbath Services, another innovation, had attendance as high as 125 children. His Adult Education Study Programs have received national awards. His D'vat Torahs have always been a part of our meetings and family occasions where he participated, always as a teacher. The second love is for developing youth. Rabbi Chapman has set an example that several generations of our youth will well remember. He helped develop and served as Regional Director of United Synagogue Youth for many years. He was the director of the Southeast Region Leadership Training Institute for eight years. His third love is for humanity. Menorah Center stands as a brick and mortar testimonial to his concern for the pioneers of our Congregation. His use of our High Holiday messages to teach our Congregation concern for diverse groups such as the undernourished in Haiti or the flood victims of Wilkes Barre, (Pennsylvania). His understanding of all needs has led to the founding of Menorah Gardens.

His love of country: Rabbi's service overseas was just the beginning of a long career of service to the military and the veterans. Until this day, he serves as military chaplain at Bay Pines (Veterans Hospital). His love and showing concern for others: Rabbi served as chairman of the Combined Jewish Campaign for two successful years. He is a patron of the Jewish Theological Seminary. He has always been in the forefront of sharing his time and means with our congregation and Jews the world over. The love of citizenship: No community committee or activity was ever refused his time and expertise, in fields as diverse as the Red Cross, Inter-Faith Groups, military chaplains, Visiting Nurse Association, and so many others.

The love of man: Who can forget his joy at a marriage or bris; his countless hours of communicating with those who had a problem whether they sought expert advice or a friendly ear; or his handshake and condolences in a moment of grief. The love of his people, his congregation, his family. Throughout all the short twenty five years, his primary concern has always been for you and I, the members of the congregation and the community of St. Petersburg. He has grown and we have grown, and a measure of our maturity is our appreciation of our Rabbi Morris B. Chapman."

Rabbi Lederman was installed by Rabbi Morris B. Chapman on September 2, Rabbi Chapman urged his successor to attain lofty goals. Rabbi Chapman said "... but rather I would like to talk to you about some personal qualities that are necessary for a successful rabbinate. The first quality is enthusiasm. Each day you have to start your work with enthusiasm, zeal, energy, and a freshness as though it was the very first day of your rabbinate. Unless you bring this sense of excitement to your daily tasks, your work will become stale. Judaism will lose its freshness, its savor. You have to bring

Rabbi Louis Lederman

the sense of excitement at all times if you are to feel the thrill of participating in a great adventure.... Secondly, you have to bring a basic, fundamental conviction – a conviction that what you are doing is important, that you believe in what you are doing. In short, you must serve as a model. There's no room for hypocrisy, no room for compromise. It must be a total commitment. Otherwise your life will become empty and meaningless and you'll lose your effectiveness. There's no substitute for conviction, commitment, and consecration.... In the third place, you have to retain your humility and modesty. This is difficult for a rabbi who stands on the Bimah with people looking up to him garbed in a robe which sets him apart from the people. You, yourself may come to believe that you are set apart. Then your rabbinate, of course, cannot be effective.... And now I address the members of the Congregation saying that they need the same qualities of freshness, conviction, and humility. The rabbi is only another Jew, only more so. The only basic difference is that he is more adept in the tradition.... Rabbi Louis Lederman, I hereby install you as Rabbi of Congregation B'nai Israel and ask God's blessings upon you. When you kindle the lights, may they glow, illuminating the darkness, dispelling all clouds, and set you high bringing freshness and vitality, serving as an inspired model of Jewish life, and retaining your modesty and humility. May your lights glow for many, many years. "

Also participating in the installation ceremony were: Cantor Joseph Schroeder of Congregation B'nai Israel; Rabbi David Susskind of Temple Beth-El; May Benjamin (mother of Dr. Phillip Benjamin); Adele Morris, Jubilee-Installation Chairman of Congregation B'nai Israel; Julius Green, President, Jewish Community Council; Dr. Leonard Morris, President Mitzvah Men's Club; Marilyn LeVine, President Sisterhood of Congregation B'nai Israel; George Feinman, President, Congregation B'nai Israel; Stacey Fogel, President of U. S. Y.; Allyn Goldberg, President of Kadima; and Rabbi Morris Kobrinetz of Congregation Beth Sholom of Gulfport.

Judge Edward Krassner, President, Congregation B'nai Israel, 1974–1976.

Highlights of 1974

On February 15, a special Sabbath service was held, "Marking the fulfillment of fifty years since the founding of Congregation B'nai Israel of St. Petersburg, Florida." The founding members and children who were members included: Mr. and Mrs. Louis Cohen; Mr. and Mrs. Charles Davis; Mr. and Mrs. Samuel Gilbert; Mr. Jerome Gilbert; Mr. and Mrs. Edward Goldman; Mr. and Mrs. Benjamin Halaczer; Mr. and Mrs. Leon Halaczer; Mrs. Phillip Benjamin; Mr. and Mrs. Harry Hankin; Mr. and Mrs. Aron Heller, Mr. Harry Heller; Mrs. Theodore Whittner; Mr. and Mrs. Hyman M. Jacobs, Mrs. Ralph Carson, Mrs. David Miller; Mrs. Harry Schuster; Mr. and Mrs. Morris Katz; Mr. and Mrs. David Rothblatt; Mrs. Abe Katz; Mr. and Mrs. Harry Schutz; Mr. and Mrs. Abraham Sierkese; Mr. and Mrs. Joseph Solomon. The following people and their children had been members of the congregation since 1949 or earlier: Mr. and Mrs. Theodore Ayes; Mrs. Mae Benjamin; Dr. and Mrs. Phillip Benjamin; Mr. and Mrs. Joseph Berkowitz; Mr. and Mrs. Alex Braun; Mr. and Mrs. Irving Buchalter; Rabbi and Mrs. Morris B. Chapman; Mr. and Mrs. Sidney Colen; Mrs. Max Davis; Mr. and Mrs. Richard Rosenthal; Mrs. Oscar Davis; Mr. and Mrs. George Dikman; Mr. and Mrs. Robert Dikman; Mrs. Celia Eisenberg; Mr. and Mrs. Albert Esrick; Mr. and Mrs. Jerome Esrick; Dr. and Mrs. Harold Feld; Mrs. Sadye Frome; Mr. and Mrs. Jerome Gilbert; Mr. and Mrs. Leon Glassman; Mrs. Jacob Glassman; Mr. and Mrs. Sol Glassman; Mr. and Mrs. Harold Goldberg; Dr. and Mrs. Sidney Grau; Mr. and Mrs. Steven Grau; Mrs. Benjamin Green; Mr. and Mrs. Irving Halprin; Mr. and Mrs. Reuben Halprin; Mr. and Mrs. Herbert Sirota; Mr. and Mrs. Joseph Hoffman; Mr. and Mrs. Murray Jacobs; Mr. and Mrs. Robert Jacobs; Mr. and Mrs. Abe Katz; Mr. and Mrs. Benjamin Kornfield; Mr. Alfred Levine; Mr. and Mrs. Hy Levine; Mr. and Mrs. Isadore Levine; Mr. and Mrs. Milton Lew; Mr. and Mrs. Larry Lew; Mr. and Mrs. Ross Lew; Mr. and Mrs. Harold Lyons; Mrs. David Loebel; Mrs. David Mendelblatt; Dr. and Mrs. Frank Mendelblatt; Mr. and Mrs. Meyer Miller; Mrs. Sarah Moss; Dr. and Mrs. Harold Rivkind; Mr. and Mrs.

Samuel Rabinovitch; Mr. and Mrs. Erwin Robiner; Mr. Reuben Sabin; Mr. and Mrs. William Salzer, Mr. and Mrs. E. Stan Salzer and Mr. and Mrs. Lawrence Salzer; Mr. and Mrs. Harry Signer; Mr. and Mrs. Aaron Silverman; Mr. and Mrs. Julius Silverman; Mr. and Mrs. Oscar Silverman; Mrs. Maurice Smith; Mrs. Philip Spiers; Mrs. Beatrice Stone; Mr. and Mrs. Samuel Sweet; Mr. and Mrs. Max Teichberg; Mr. and Mrs. Meyer Weinstein; Mrs. Hilna Wolper; Mr. and Mrs. Isadore Zucker; Mr. and Mrs. Norman Zucker. These sixty six families represented a degree of stability which could only enhance the Congregation B'nai Israel family. New people always add strength and purpose to a congregation. The longtime, existing families are the bedrock of the community.

The Golden Jubilee weekend was held on August 31-September 2. There was an overwhelming sense of warmth and pride of the founders and developers of Congregation B'nai Israel and all of the accomplishments of the synagogue and the people during the last fifty years. Mrs. David Rothblatt and Mr. and Mrs. Leon Halaczer received distinguished citations as founding members and for their half-century of devotion to the congregation. Children of the founders who continued to work hard for Congregation B'nai Israel were also honored. They were: Mr. Jerome Gilbert, Mrs. Phillip Benjamin, Mr. Harry Heller, Mrs. Theodore Whittner, Mrs. Ralph Carson, Mrs. David Miller, Mrs. Harry Schuster, and Mrs. Abe Katz. Sixty six other families received Certificates of Appreciation for twenty five years of service.

Highlights of 1975

In October, the synagogue bulletin was changed from *Shalom* to The *B'nai Israel Review*. Attendance at the High Holy Days services was greater than ever before. Many of the people were part of the thirty six new families who joined the congregation. Longtime members also brought their own families and friends. Leo Chak was Executive Director, Anita R. Lederman was Principal, and Robert Westle was Youth Director. The Men's Club was brought back to life. Twenty five men attended. Chet Levine became the President. Maury

Goldblatt became the director of liturgical music. He took care of the responsibilities for the cantor's side of the bimah. Morris B. Chapman, Rabbi Emeritus, was the guest of honor at the Israel Bonds evening. Rabbi Lederman started a series of ten lectures. Congregation B'nai Israel participated in a community wide Thanksgiving Service with Rabbi Ronald Goldstein of Temple Hillel hosting the other synagogues.

Highlights of 1976

The Marriage Encounter, an approach to strengthening a couple's marriage, where the couple spent forty four hours away from life and its responsibilities, and reacted to each other within a group setting, was started in St. Petersburg. Several couples from Congregation B'nai Israel participated. The second annual Jewish Music Festival was held at the synagogue on March 21.

The new Friday night prayer book, LIKRAT SHABBAT, completely altered the format and mood of the Sabbath services. The Hebrew prayers were essentially intact, but the new and more modern English translations, the readings and transliterations, and the introduction of a formal sermon made a considerable difference in the service. There was a higher level and pitch of participation and enthusiasm during the entire service. Rabbi Lederman said, "One cannot help but feel a deeper and more profound sense of the spiritual and inspirational throughout the services. About the new English readings, there are so many of them. They have been culled from Jewish and non-Jewish sources. They touch upon every facet of life. Nothing human or humane has been omitted. Being in such abundance, it is now possible to have an entirely new Sabbath service each Friday evening. Gone is the repetition and routine of the past. In their place, we now have a new refreshing experience each Friday evening...."

The congregation had been without a cantor for fifty of the fifty three years of its existence. Cantor Joseph Schroeder was the first cantor at the synagogue. During the previous nine months, three fine cantors participated in different services. Fared Dardashti was at the synagogue for Passover.

David Axelrad came on the 7th and 8th of May and Israel Barzak came on the 14th and 15th of May. The greatest beneficiaries of having a professional cantor chant the services each week were the children and teenage youth. It helped develop, within the young people, a familiarity with the liturgical traditions and helped develop a sense of Jewish identity.

Fared Dardashti of Springfield, New Jersey, agreed to serve as a cantor of the Congregation. He was a highly talented, well-trained and fully professional practitioner of vocal music. He studied at Wesley College, 1962-1963, at the Mannes College of Music, 1963-1965, at the Cantors Institute, 1965-1969 and at Union College, 1973-1975. He sang both classical and modern cantorial music. His wife, Sheila, was also a highly accomplished classical guitarist. She was a graduate of the School of Performing Arts at Queens College.

Leo J. Chak resigned as Executive Director of Congregation B'nai Israel and Editor of The B'nai Israel Review. He was leaving for a similar position in a congregation in Toronto, Canada. During his time at Congregation B'nai Israel, he was responsible for many changes and improvements, especially within the framework of the offices and finances.

The Biennial Convention of the Southeast Region of the United Synagogue of America was held at the Don CeSar Beach Resort Hotel, which at one time would not allow Jewish people to even be guests of the hotel. More than 250 men and women representing fifty five Conservative congregations from seven different states were hosted by Congregation B'nai Israel. Richard Mensh, President of Congregation B'nai Israel was the local chairman of the convention. Maury Goldblatt using his truck and crew of men moved a Holy Ark, prayer books, Talleisim, Yarmulkas, and everything else required to set up the convention's Synagogue at the hotel.

In December, the sub-regional United Synagogue Youth Conference was held in St. Petersburg. One hundred and fifty children from various congregations attended. These young people conducted the Friday night services and Saturday morning services.

Richard Mensh, President, Congregation B'nai Israel, 1976–1978.

Dr. and Mrs. Morris J. LeVine were honored by the State of Israel at the culminating event of the St. Petersburg Israel Bond Campaign. Both of them were well known throughout the community for their activities in many organizations and their steadfast devotion to the synagogue, community, and Israel. She is Past President of Congregation B'nai Israel Sisterhood and President of the Florida Region of Hadassah.

Highlights of 1977

In February, the congregation purchased a new piano. Cantor Fared Dardashti was seeking a qualified pianist who could read music and work with the enthusiastic choir.

Irving Bernstein, President, Congregation B'nai Israel, 1978–1980.

Rabbi Lederman completed his 20th year as a rabbi and was completing his fourth year at Congregation B'nai Israel of St. Petersburg. He was now preparing to accept a new, challenging position in North Miami at Temple Beth Moshe. The Rabbi and Anita made this decision because they wanted to have their children have a formal Jewish education, and it was only available in Miami.

Hazzan (Cantor) Fared Dardashti, an internationally renowned concert artist in his own right, presented The Third Annual Jewish Music Festival on Sunday evening, February 27. More than 1,000 men, women, and children were present when he, accompanied by the Symphony Orchestra of the University of Florida under the direction of Professor Bruce LeBaron, and the Chamber Singers of the University of Florida under the direction of Robert Summer, set the tone, created the mood, and provided the professional excellence for a musically perfect evening that was spiritually stirring and emotionally stimulating.

Rabbi Jacob Luski

In August, Rabbi Jacob Luski became the spiritual leader of Congregation B'nai Israel. Rabbi Luski was installed on Sunday, October 30, at 7:30 p.m. One of the major reasons he came to Congregation B'nai Israel of St. Petersburg was because of the dynamic and exciting youth department. The children were highly dedicated and involved in not only youth group activities, but in many of the programs of the synagogue. There was a great deal of enthusiasm.

Rabbi Luski talked about the High Holy Days' themes of life and blessings and emphasized the needs for three action programs: Repentance, Prayer, and Charity. He said, " Teshuvah-The art of repentance. Repentance is a turning; turning in the direction of the good...Tefillah-Prayer is an affirmation that the world represents order rather than chaos. Prayer means that we recognize that life is purposeful and meaningful...Tzedka-(Giving of ourselves) we only receive blessings if we share our blessings."

Highlights of 1978

The congregation presented a cultural gift to Pinellas County, the Annual Music Festival. It was held on February 26, at the Bayfront Center. The music included operatic, Yiddish, Italian, Israeli, French, Hassidic, and Ladino music.

Cantor Josef Schroeder came back after three years to again serve the congregation. He was instrumental in founding the Annual Jewish Music Festival and was going to participate in the Fifth Annual Jewish Musical Festival on March 11, 1979.

There were six special programs identified for the children of various age groups for the summer. They were: Camp Kadima, a day camp of the Jewish Community Center of St. Petersburg; Camp Ramah in Palmer, Massachusetts, for ages nine-sixteen, for either four weeks or eight weeks; Camp Judaea in Hendersonville, North Carolina, for four or eight weeks; U. S. Y. on Wheels, a six-week tour of the United States for ages fourteen-eighteen; U.S.Y. Pilgrimage to Israel, six weeks of touring and study in Israel; and high school and college age programs in a Kibbutz in Israel for ages sixteen-twenty two.

Highlights of 1979

Rabbi Luski quoted the words of Albert Einstein to the Congregation: "Our Jewish Tradition-The pursuit of knowledge for its own sake, an almost fanatical love of justice, and the desire for personal independence –these are the features of the Jewish tradition which make me thank my stars I belong to it. Those who are raging against the ideals of reason and individual liberty and are trying to establish a spiritless state-slavery by brute force, rightly see in us their irreconcilable foes. History has given us a difficult row to hoe; but so long as we remain devoted servants of truth, justice, and liberty, we shall continue not merely to survive as the oldest of living peoples, but by creative work to bring forth fruits which contribute to the ennoblement of the human race, as heretofore."

Cantor Schroeder was seeking a permanent pianist to accompany the Zemer Hen Choir. He called the choir, "A group of faith—faith that our people will survive, and that its thousands of years of history will continue to sustain those who remain, and to welcome those who return. We tell our story in song. Perhaps like no other aspect of its existence, song has, on one hand, been a vehicle for expression and, on the other, a source of sustenance...How beautifully their voices rang out." The choir included: Bette Halprin, Ida Hahn, Rose Halprin, Lauretta and Lee Irwin, Renée and Victor Daniels, Gail and Mike Frye, Ben Rensin, Mel Dinsfriend, Elliot Bader, Eric and Robin Schroeder, Miriam and Kevin Ellicott, Dr. Michael Diamond, Mark Divito, Diane Westle, and Leon Halaczer. Estelle Fox, who attended all of the rehearsals religiously, was the piano accompaniment.

The congregation was quoted the words of Mark Twain from a 1899, Harper's Magazine article. "Evaluation of a Jew-The Jew is not a disturber of the peace of any country. Even his enemies will concede that. He is not a loafer, he is not a sot, he is not noisy, he is not a brawler, nor a rioter, he is not quarrelsome...The Jew is not a burden on the charities of the State, nor of the City; these could cease from their functions without affecting him. When he is well enough, he works; when he is incapacitated, his own people take care of him. And not in a poor and stingy way, but with fine and large benevolence. His race is entitled to be called the most benevolent of all the races of men...Whenever a Jew has real need to beg, his people save him from the necessity of doing it. The charitable institutions of the Jews are supported by Jewish money, and amply. The Jews make no noise about it, it is done quietly, they do not nag and pester

and harass us for contributions, they give us peace, and set us an example which we have not found ourselves able to follow."

Highlights of 1980-1989

Highlights of 1980

Philip Wallace, President, Congregation B'nai Israel, 1980–1981.

Goldie Schuster donated her father's mini Torah and olive wood Book of Esther to the synagogue. He brought them from Lithuania to Wales to Chicago and then to Florida. (Exact date is uncertain).

The library was reorganized according to the Dewey Decimal System. A large number of books were contributed by members of the congregation.

Rose Halprin served as chairman of the Kosher Meat Co-op. The previous year, Reva Pearlstein served as chairman. Rabbi Luski announced that Bernard's Kosher Butchery had opened on Drew Street in Clearwater.

Samuel Sweet, age 87, celebrated his Bar Mitzvah. He fulfilled a lifelong dream, according to his wife, Betty. He attended Hebrew classes at the synagogue and studied under Cantor Schroeder. He spent many hard hours learning his Haftorah portion. Samuel originally came from Madison, Wisconsin and had been a resident of St. Petersburg for over fifty years.

As part of the continuing emphasis on music by the congregation and its leaders, Congregation B'nai Israel sponsored the Sixth Annual Jewish Music Festival at Bayfront Center. Cantor Josef A. Schroeder and Cantor Elaine Shapiro performed international, Israeli, cantorial, Yiddish and English music. The program celebrated traditions in song and dance.

Cantor Elaine Shapiro was the only female Cantor in Conservative Judaism at that time. In 1971, she was accepted at the College of Jewish Music from the Jewish Theological Seminary. She was not permitted to enroll at the Cantor's Institute. She said, "We have to be responsive to the idea that women have a heart and soul, and we want to fulfill our potential as equal participants in the synagogue. The role of American women is changing, and because of this, the role of Jewish women is changing as well. This is the time for us to accept the responsibility of study and prayer, to develop an awareness of our Jewish identity in equality." After five years at the Seminary, during which time she appeared in synagogues throughout the United States and Canada, she was acclaimed for her cantorial work. She became the guest Cantor at a congregation in Manchester, New Hampshire for the High Holy Days. She then became the Cantor for Temple Beth El in West Palm Beach.

Cantor Joseph Schroeder was a sixth-generation Cantor and son of the world famous operatic soprano and concert star, Viola Philo.

Maury Goldblatt supervised the construction of a menorah which was placed outside of the synagogue. It was utilized for a community block party. Rabbi Luski said, "I think it is appropriate that we share the celebration with our non-Jewish neighbors, because of its significance as the first celebration of religious freedom."

President Jimmy Carter in a speech said, "Life is sometimes unfair." Precisely because of this the Jewish sages of over 2000 years ago made the giving of tzedakah mandatory, even for the person receiving tzedakah. The Quotation of the Week in the May, 1980, B'nai Israel Review said, "We Jews do not give "charity." Rather, we perform an act of justice or righteousness, and the word for it in the Jewish vocabulary is tzedakah. In the Jewish tradition, the poor and the unfortunate (like widows, orphans, and the stranger in our midst) had the right-the legal right in Jewish law-to food, clothing, and shelter. It is the obligation of every Jew to give tzedakah, that is, to perform an act of justice by giving help, not out of a momentary whim or sudden philanthropic impulse, but out of our religious duty."

Adele Morris, President, Congregation B'nai Israel, 1981–1983.

Highlights of 1981

Congregation B'nai Israel celebrated with its first adult bat mitzvah class. A group of seven women studied weekly over the previous two years in areas of Jewish History, Hebrew Language, liturgy, customs and ceremonies, and Jewish life cycles. The individuals honored were: Dee Dolgoff, Sylvia Diamond, Anita Helfand, Audrey Kopelman, Marilyn LeVine, Harriett Stein and Sylvia Wiener.

The confirmation class included: Marc Corey Daniels, Matthew Wayne Daniels, Laura Eileen Halprin, Robyn Arlene Koenig, Henry Andrew Maller and Hilary Ann Maller. Confirmation was held on Shavout, the time of the giving of the Torah.

On December 11, the congregation officially welcomed and consecrated sixty five new members. The theme of the evening was, "May the door of the synagogue be wide enough to receive all who hunger for love, all who are lonely for fellowship. May this synagogue be, for all who enter, the doorway to a richer and more meaningful life. Amen."

Harold and Bernice Bressler

Harold and Bernice Bressler came to St. Petersburg from Philadelphia and immediately joined Congregation B'nai Israel. Harold was born October 24, 1916 in Pottstown, Pennsylvania. Harold's father was a junk dealer. Harold said, "(my father) was so sensitive to the plight of others with less means than himself, he would allow the poor children to steal the junk from the yard and pay them to buy it back." This was Harold's first lesson in helping the less fortunate. Harold joined the United States Army during World War II, He designed and operated a highly successful port and military transport system. He served in England, France, and Belgium. When he returned from the war, he was introduced to Bernice Stainsky by their Rabbi and they were married in 1947. He joined his father-in-law and uncles in the family business, Mill's Retail Store, and was its manager for thirteen years. He became very active in many organizations including: founder and President of the Downtown Business Association for Pottstown; Chairperson of the sesquicentennial; founding member of the Jewish War Veterans in Pottstown; State Commander of the Jewish War Veterans; and leadership posts in the Boy Scouts, Toastmasters, and the Lions Club.

In 1956, he completed his college education. He was the Director of the Audit Department of the Governors Justice Commission. At age sixty, he earned his Master's Degree. He came to St. Petersburg to retire, but soon was named Executive

Director of the Chamber of Commerce of Treasure Island. As a Notary Public, he performed many wedding ceremonies on top of the largest sand castle ever built, as certified by the Guinness World Book of Records. He supervised the building of that interesting structure. He then became a guardian through the Florida Guardian Ad Litem program. He went on to become a Member of the Board of Menorah Manor. He became an active member of the speaker's bureau of the Hospice of the Sun Coast. Harold died in May, 1995.

Bernice was born in Philadelphia, Pennsylvania on June 13, 1925. Her father was originally a concert violinist, but was forced to give up his career during the Depression. Bernice learned about giving as she watched her father and uncles provide for the less fortunate. She attended Gratz Hebrew College as well as Temple University, where she received a Bachelor of Arts Degree in Psychology. In 1948, she gave birth to a daughter, Ellen Jane; three years later to a daughter, Amy Ruth; and three years after that to a daughter, Marcia Frances. Bernice, a life member of Hadassah, renewed her commitment to the group in Florida.

In 1982, Bernice went to work for the Gulf Coast Jewish Family Services. She was involved in the Russian resettlement project and in assisting young people to obtain scholarships and loans for college. She helped organize the annual holiday food collection. In 1994, Bernice retired from Gulf Coast Jewish Family Services. Bernice died in 2004.

Harold and Bernice, throughout their lives, helped other people to help themselves. They were caring and giving individuals who learned the true meaning of tzedaka from their parents and passed it on to their children.

Highlights of 1982

A special Shabbat service was held to honor those people who had given to the synagogue fifty years of continuous membership and service. The co-chairs were Bunnie Katz and Toby Snyder. Those honored were: the late May Benjamin, Lillian Davis, Albert and Esther Esrick, Leon Halaczer, Henrietta Kornfield, Ethel Rothblatt, William and Molly Salzer, Bessie Silverman, and Samuel and Betty Sweet.

Rabbi Yaakov Rosenberg, Vice-Chancellor for Development of the Jewish Theological Seminary of America, was the feature speaker at the Great Ideas Weekend. He talked about how Conservative Judaism challenges people in the home, in the synagogue, and in the community. He had been previously involved actively in national and local Jewish affairs.

Six children were confirmed. They were: Matthew Jay Berkman, Michael Thomas DiVito, Andrew Keith Fein, Cynthia Toba Kobin, Sheryl Beth Mizrahi and Ira Marc Slomka. Rabbi Luski said, "...Our time is a pure gift from God–we do not choose it and we cannot give it up! It is a precious jewel entrusted to us so that we walk along the path of life with faith in God and trust in His wisdom. Hopefully, God will endow us with life in the New Year, 5743–so let us not profane it. Rather, let us utilize the precious hours of each day wisely. May God inspire us to realize that it is not the length of life that matters, but how it is lived that counts..."

Cantor Irving Zummer

In August, Irving Zummer became the Cantor of Congregation B'nai Israel. He served in the United States Army. In 1953, he entered the College of Jewish Studies in Chicago and shortly afterwards, began singing for various congregations in Illinois. He then studied with the famous midwest cantor, Todros Greenberg, for a period of three years until Cantor Greenberg decided that he had completed his studies. Cantor Zummer was also ordained by the Cantor's Assembly of America in New York City. Prior to coming to St. Petersburg, he served for seven years at the Temple of Aaron in St. Paul, Minnesota. At Congregation B'nai Israel, he became the Principal of the Hebrew School. Cantor Zummer worked diligently with the teenage choir and the adult choir. The teenage choir had existed since the 1930s. The adult choir was made up of eighteen adult congregants. The cantor put the volunteers through ten, seventy five minute rehearsals before they could accompany him in four-part harmony at the High Holy Day services.

Cantor Irving Zummer

The Cantor said that the practice sessions were not only for reviewing material but creating fresh nuances. He also said, " These volunteers perform a valuable service to the congregation. They certainly enhance what I do." When Cantor Zummer chanted various prayers, he wanted to kindle a flame, a spiritual flame in the congregants. He said, "The rabbi touches them intellectually. I touch them emotionally." "If I'm pleading with God, that's going to come up from inside (of me)." He continued as Cantor until July 1993.

Highlights of 1983

Congregation B'nai Israel presented "60 Years of Show Biz and Shul Biz." This musical spectacular was a continuation of a long history of musical performances given at or supported by Congregation B'nai Israel. It was held in conjunction with the 60th anniversary of the synagogue. The congregation had grown from twelve families to over 400 families over that time period. The congregation also sponsored the Israeli Chassidic Festival. This was the 13th year that this group of singers and dancers came from Israel to present concerts in the United States. Composers from around the world set music to biblical verses, which were then performed by this exceptional group of young people.

The Jewish music festival was revived after a seven year absence. Fared Dardashti, the former Cantor of Congregation B'nai Israel St. Petersburg, along with his wife and children were the performers. The program, celebrating Jewish Music Month included folk music, instrument numbers, and songs in twelve different languages as well as cantorial pieces. General Chairman of the event was Dottie Cohen. Dardashti, was an Iranian born international concert artist whose music encompassed the use of Hebrew, Yiddish, Ladino, English, French, Spanish, Italian, Greek, Persian, Japanese, Arabic and Russian.

Rabbi Luski discussed the nature of failure. He said, "As we approach the High Holy Days, the thought keeps reoccurring in my mind that failures can be converted into successes. When we are left to our own resources, we experiment and try to

Jerald M. Phillips, President, Congregation B'nai Israel, 1983–1984.

copewith our problems and situations. Often, we fail. Babe Ruth struck out more times than he got hits, yet he was the "Home Run King" of the baseball world. We must not think of our experiences or adversities as failures. From every reversal or misfortune, from every encounter or loss, we should profit.. The worst possible consequence of failure is pessimism, bordering on defeatism. Jewish and non-Jewish history is replete with examples of men and women, in all walks of life, who have failed and who have never given up; people who persevered through "thick and thin", and tried again and again until they were triumphant. "Failure is a success" should be our High Holy Day theme this year. For those who would not die or give up, their achievements brought lasting benefits to mankind. From a negative, we should derive a positive. Let us convert every liability into an asset."

Dan Pomerantz was appointed the Director of Youth Activities for the Congregation. Dr. Haim Shaked of the Graduate School of International Studies, University of Miami, an expert on Middle Eastern and Islamic Studies, gave presentations on Israel and the Middle East. Seven children were confirmed. They were: Sheryl Elaine Bader, Kevin Ira Frye, Ian Stewart Kasper, Kimberly Ilene Mallen, Steven Todd Plutchok, Steven Jay Seder, and Howard Peter Slomka.

Highlights of 1984

Jerry and Thelma Gilbert were honored by the Jewish Theological Seminary of America for their longtime leadership of Congregation B'nai Israel and the St. Petersburg Jewish community. Jerry had served as President of Congregation B'nai Israel and Chairman of the Board of Trustees. Thelma had served two separate terms as President of Sisterhood. Rabbi Baruch Frydman-Kohl of Congregation Ohav Shalom of Albany, New York spoke on, "God and Evil." Mark Goodfriend became the Youth Director.

Rabbi Luski discussed the nature of faith. He said, "Gabriel Marcel, of the French school of religious existentialists, once said of faith, that it was a state of not "having," but of "being." He meant that faith was not merely an exercise of the will or intellect, but that it represented a man's total engagement or commitment. In the same way, we may say that Judaism, too, is not concerned only with beliefs; it is not simply the acceptance of a credo or set of dogmas. It has to do with action, and must express itself in everyday life.

The Ten Commandments, which form the central portion of last week's Torah reading, emphasize this very teaching. They were written on two tablets of stone. The first four commandments govern the relationship between man and God; the second set of five regulate the relationship of man to man and his place in society; while the fifth commandment (to honor one's parents) forms a bridge between the two, for, as some of the commentators pointed out, parents are partners with God in creation... Many people think, mistakenly, that the moral laws are sufficient in themselves in a sophisticated modern world. Judaism insists laws are reliable only if they flow from, and are based upon, a Divine sanction.

On the other hand, faith itself, if it does not lead to right doing, is never enough... Faith without action tends to be mere empty lip service; something to be prated and prattled about in Synagogue without imposing any sense of obligation..."

Rabbi Luski discussed the nature of life. He said, "...Life...is a road (Dereh) or a path...First, a road beckons us to move forward. It implies growth, change and an enlargement. Most people resent this aspect of Dereh, resist change, resist the urge to growth. But it is change which makes society and civilization often in the face of resistance possible...Secondly, a Dereh, a way, leads us to other places. It cautions against circumscribing our life and building walls of isolation, which remove us from others. Life would be meaner and pettier were it not enriched by the love and friendship we gain from others...Finally, not every Dereh–not every road is paved with smooth surfaces. Some are in need of repairs; some are imperfect in a variety of ways. Nevertheless, we must travel them. Life's road is never perfectly paved. There's no life without obstacle; without hurt; and without a share of anxiety. We need the road

to challenge us if we are to grow."

Highlights of 1985

The religious holiday, Simchat Torah, was celebrated outdoors. A group of members of the congregation blew shofars together. The Torahs were carried under canopies. The celebration was very unique and meaningful to the community.

The Mitzvah Men's Club received first place recognition for the "Best Fellowship Program" from the Federation of Jewish Men's Clubs at their 53rd International Convention. The program, called the "Brunches," is the main fellowship program for the club. The program encourages brotherhood, education, and service to the synagogue.

Mark Twain's speech of 1899 was again quoted to the congregation. Mark Twain, who in his early years wrote disparagingly about the Jewish people, changed his mind when he met with a group of Jewish war veterans of the Civil War. Mark Twain said, "If the statistics are right, the Jews constitute but 1% of the human race. It suggests a nebulous dim puff of stardust lost in the blaze of the Milky Way. Properly, the Jew ought hardly to be heard of, but he is heard of, has always been heard of. He is as prominent on the planet as any other people, and his commercial importance is extravagantly out of proportion to the smallness of his numbers.

His contributions to the world's list of great names in literature, science, art, music, finance, medicine, and abstruse learning are also way out of proportion to the weakness of his numbers. He has made a marvelous fight in the world in all the ages; and has done it with his hands tied behind him. He could be vain of himself and be excused for it.

The Egyptian, the Babylonian, and the Persian rose, filled the planet with sound and splendor, then faded to dream stuff and passed away; the Greek and the Roman followed and made a vast noise, and they are gone; other peoples have sprung up and held their torch high for a time, but it burned out, and they sit in twilight now, or have vanished.

The Jew saw them all, and is now what he always was, exhibiting no decadence,

Donald A. Silverberg,
President, Congregation
B'nai Israel, 1984–1986.

no infirmities of age, no weakening of his parts, no slowing of his energies, no dulling of his alert and aggressive mind. All things are mortal, but the Jew; all other forces pass, but he remains.

What is the secret of his immortality?"

Highlights of 1986

Cantor Irving Zummer, discussing the Kabbalat Shabbat (welcoming the Sabbath), said, "From ancient times, the Sabbath was personified as a bride and welcomed with rejoicing. Legend tells us that at one time Jews walked to the end of their little towns to greet the Sabbath Bride as twilight approached. Every Friday afternoon six blasts of the shofar were sounded. The first to warn field laborers to stop working, the second to direct business people to close their shops, the third to announce candle lighting time, and the last three to begin Shabbat."

The Adult Studies Commission of Congregation B'nai Israel presented a series of lectures on "The Search for Ideology in Conservative Judaism." Rabbi Neil Gilman, Associate Provost at the Jewish Theological Seminary, presented lectures on "Historical Background: Reform and Neo-Orthodoxy in 19th-Century Germany and the United States," "The Founding Ideology of the Jewish Theological Seminary," "Where Do We Go after the Ordination of Women?" Following these lectures, Dr. Jack Wertheimer, Assistant Professor, Department of Jewish History at the Jewish Theological Seminary of America, presented a series of lectures on "The Condition of American Jews Today." As part of this program, Rabbi Luski discussed the difference between the movements of American Judaism. He said, that they do not lie in the levels of observance, but rather how history is viewed. "I am a Conservative Jew because I recognize that Judaism has evolved over the centuries. I recognize that the Judaism of the time of Moses was radically different from the Judaism that we live today. I am part of the Conservative Movement because, unlike the Orthodox Jew, I believe that there is a history to the development of Jewish tradition...Historical Judaism isn't concerned simply with factual

information, by means that each generation of Jews adds, through its experience, another step in the evolutionary process of Judaism. It is after realizing that centuries of Jews have been through this same process of religious growth and change that we are going through now, that the link between the generations becomes clearly apparent, alive and exciting."

From 1983 to mid 1986, forty children were Bar-Bat Mitzvah. Fourteen children were confirmed.

Highlights of 1987

Estelle Marsh started the project which became the stained-glass windows installed in the sanctuary in 1990. She felt that the frosted windows took away from the beauty of the sanctuary. She involved her husband, Stan, and their good friends, Helen and Aaron Applefield. From the very beginning, it was the idea of one dedicated person, complemented by spouses and friends, who took the initiative to make a change in the congregational home. They immediately approached Rabbi Luski, who thought this was a wonderful idea and he became an integral part of this beautiful and highly successful project.

As part of the celebration of the association of Joanne and Rabbi Luski with the synagogue, they were honored by the State of Israel Bonds at a gala testimonial banquet. Rabbi Luski was installed as President of the Southeast Region of the Rabbinical Assembly. Joanne Luski was a founding Member of the Board of the Pinellas County Jewish Day School and its Treasurer. Joanne and Rabbi Luski took a family sabbatical leave and went to Israel.

Highlights of 1988

Dr. Leonard Morris, assisted by the synagogue's Youth Director, Mark Goodfriend, helped a group of children and adults learn the difficult nuances of holding and blowing the Shofar, a ram's horn. Historically, the shofar was an important element in the lives of the ancient Jewish people. Its sound accompanied the revelation of the Ten Commandments to Moses at Mount Sinai, the coronation of a king, and other significant events in the

Lorraine Maller, President, Congregation B'nai Israel, 1986–1987.

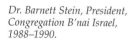

Dr. Barnett Stein, President, Congregation B'nai Israel, 1988–1990.

courtesy of "Windows by V. Berthelsdorf," Kaleidoscope Glass Works, © 1990.

history of the Jewish people. The blowing of the shofar during the High Holy Days contributes to the distinctive character of the Jewish observance and focuses on the spiritual life of the individual.

Highlights of 1989

Rabbi Jules Harlow, editor and translator of Siddur Sim Shalom, presented "What Does the Prayer Book Have To Do with My Life–Breathing New Life into Our Prayers." Leonard Gotler was the Executive Director. The Mitzvah Men's Club sponsored a dinner with the Rabbi. A discussion followed the dinner on what was considered to be a premier book for Conservative Judaism, entitled, "A Guide to Jewish Religious Practice," by Isaac Klein. The annual interfaith Thanksgiving service was held at the Pasadena Community Church. It was sponsored by the Clergy Association of Greater St. Petersburg and the National Conference of Christians and Jews. A Hanukkah Block Party entitled, "A Celebration of Soviet Jewry" was opened to the entire community. The theme of the celebration was, "Give a little light and bring a lot of warmth."

Highlights of 1990-1999

Highlights of 1990
Windows of Wonder

On December 15, the stained-glass windows called the "Windows of Wonder" were officially presented at Congregation B'nai Israel's annual Chanukah party. This was the satisfactory conclusion of three years of extremely hard work. During the presentation ceremony, representatives from each generation of congregants stood under each of the eleven windows and passed the menorah from generation to generation. This was the idea behind the dream of project organizers, Estelle and Stan Marsh, and Helen and Aaron Applefield, to preserve, protect, and beautify the synagogue and pass it on to a new generation. They selected Victor Berthelsdorf, who took two years to complete the 396 square-foot mural.

The eleven panels, each twelve feet high by thirty nine inches wide, reading from right to left, represent the Sabbath and then in chronological order the Jewish holiday cycle, Rosh Hashanah, Yom Kippur, Simchat Torah, Succot, Tu B'Shvat, Purim, Passover, Lag B' Omer, Shavuot, and Tisha B'Av. The center window represents the central theme of Judaism with an open prayer book at the bottom and a giant Mogen David at the top. A large menorah, symbolizing Chanukah, spans eight of the windows. Rabbi Jacob Luski, who was deeply involved in helping the artist accurately depict all of the religious symbols, and in fact in the entire project, said that, "Each of the windows tells its own story, but they are all inter-related. They are not just pretty windows. The symbols representing each holiday are there to be used. It is through doing that our Jewishness comes out."

The description of each window of the "Windows of Wonder" dedication ceremony bulletin is as follows:

"Window number one, Shabbat–The Friday evening table with its Shabbat candles, kiddush cup, and two hallots depicts Friday evening at home. Above the table the conclusion of Shabbat is represented by the Havdala candle, spice box and wine cup. The Tallit represents the prayers of the Jews as they flow upward to God from the Jewish people.

Window number two, Rosh Hashana– One sees the Sefer Hahayim, the Book of Life, into which each Jew prays that he/she be inscribed for the new year. The Shofar-Ram's Horn–which awakens those who slumber and Jacob's Ladder symbolize our striving upwards to improve ourselves during these days of introspection – The Days of Awe.

Window number three, Sukkot–The Harvest Festival is represented in this window, and in the other windows with the symbol of grapes. The Etrog and Luvav–the Arba Minim consisting of the Etrog, Luvav, Myrtle and Willow leaves can also be seen. Simhat Torah, the conclusion of the holiday, is represented through the Torah scroll with the Yad pointing from the heavens.

Window number four, Hanukka– Hanukka is represented by the cruse of an oil-Maccabean style menorah at the bottom of the window. The Dreidel is also found in this window, along with the Shamash which kindles all the lights of the Hanukia-the Hanukka Menorah. The Hanukia is found as a unifying theme throughout the entire set of Windows.

Window number five, Tu B' Shevat–Tu B' Shevat is represented by the blossoming of the almond tree in Israel as well as the fruit of the vine in four different colors corresponding to the four seasons.

Window number six is the central window of the entire series highlighted by the Magen David-the Star of David, the symbol of the Jewish people as well as the Sefarim-the Jewish Books of Study. One can imagine these books to include volumes of the Bible, Mishna, Talmud, Shulhan Aruh, and many more Codes of Jewish Law.

Window number seven, Purim–Purim is represented by the Megillat Esther, the Scroll of Esther and the Gragger.

Window number eight, Passover–one sees the sheaves of wheat in the center in which the matza is to be made. The round matza at the bottom symbolizes the hand-made matza as it was originally prepared in the wilderness of Israel. Elijah's cup is prominently displayed with the hope of future redemption of the Jewish people. The colors also gave one an idea of the sea which the Israelites crossed as they traveled from slavery to freedom.

Window number nine, Lag Baomer– The bonfire and the musical instruments represent the joy of this holiday as we remember when the plague came to an end during Rabbi Akiba's time and all celebrated.

Window number ten, Shavuot–The giving of the Torah is represented by the ten Commandments-The Two Tablets of Stone. The Tefilin boxes, both the head and arm, are included as a symbol of the Jews' daily commitment to the observance of Torah and mitzvot. The fruit once again represents the Harvest Festival.

Window number eleven, Tisha B'Av– One sees the Kotel Maaravi, the Western Wall, which is the only remaining part of the Second Temple, destroyed in the year 70 C. E. in Jerusalem. The stones of the Temple are found in disorder at the bottom of the window, signifying its destruction. At the top of the window we find the sun, symbol of the modern State of Israel. We have hope for a bright and courageous future. This window of Israel illuminates the entire panorama of the Jewish holiday cycle, as Israel is our land."

The artist, Victor Berthelsdorf of Lutz, Florida, had produced throughout the state beautiful stained-glass windows for churches over the past eighteen years. He had never done a synagogue before. Since he was not Jewish, he was unfamiliar with many of the symbols. He went to the library and read everything he could about the Jewish holidays and Judaism. He even explored all the symbols used in the windows, such as the menorah, tallis, shofar, etc. The Marshs and Applefields took numerous trips to the artist's studio to see how the windows were progressing. When the windows were finally installed, the two couples sat in the sanctuary for five hours, to make sure nothing went wrong. Mrs. Marsh said, "We applauded, hugged, and then went out to celebrate." Mrs. Applefield said, "I had been walking out of the synagogue kitchen for forty years, and now I walk out, look at the windows, and feel overwhelmed."

The warm glow of the vivid, bright colors in the modernistic windows permeate the entire sanctuary and social hall. During the day, they are backlit by the natural sunlight. Estelle and Helen said that they never thought that the project could have such an effect on them. Estelle said, "What more can you give to your synagogue than something that will last forever." On March 14, 1992, the Windows of Wonder were officially dedicated. They were subsequently moved to the new structure

Estelle Marsh

Estelle Marsh, during World War II, worked in the Brooklyn Navy Yard as an acetylene torch welder. She was a charter member of that group of welders. She was the first woman in the sheet metal shop and taught about twenty women to weld. She then joined the Air Force. She met her husband Stan, who was also in the Air Force, in 1948. They married in 1950, and moved to Madeira Beach in 1952. They became members of Congregation B'nai Israel and then started volunteering for numerous projects. She produced, with the Center Stage Players, shows at the Jewish Community Center, visited Bay Pines Veterans Hospital with the Jewish War Veterans, became active in Hadassah, of which she was President three times, and initiated the Israel Bond Dinner in St. Petersburg. She and her husband, Stan, were honored twice by the State of Israel Bonds, the last being in 2001.

Highlights of 1991

Rabbi Luski said, "A person's education must continue throughout his or her life... Jewish education is the key to Jewish survival, and any Jew who is concerned with the continuity of Jewish life knows that this is the top priority of the Jewish people..." The Adult Studies Commission presented "The Jewish Family: Problems and Opportunities for the Nineties."

Highlights of 1992

The Adult Studies Commission

presented, "Great Ideas Weekend-the Magic of the Told Tale." Rabbi Eugène and Mrs. Annette Labowitz were the storytellers. In the past, itinerant Jewish storytellers, called Maggidim, crisscrossed Europe telling their tales and stories. They preached the eternal quality of Judaism, the timeless stories of people helping people. The stories are rooted in the past but are still inspiring today.

Anita Helfand of the Sisterhood was the recipient of the Women of Achievement Award. She received it for her outstanding service and dynamic leadership in the synagogue and community. Five young people graduated from the Hebrew High School. Cantor Irving Zummer celebrated his tenth anniversary with the congregation.

Rabbi Luski was honored in New York at the national "Jerusalem 25" dinner, commemorating the 25th anniversary of the reunification of Jerusalem. He was one of twenty five eminent North American rabbis selected for this award. He was honored for his outstanding dedication to the economic future and well-being of the State of Israel.

Estelle Marsh. Above, during WW II. Below, in 1991.

Highlights of 1993

Congregation B'nai Israel Sisterhood and Mitzvah Men's Club presented a breakfast concert featuring Cantor Moshe Friedler and the Mike Eisenstadt Café Muzika Band. There was a very special breakfast and Jewish music including Klezmer, Israeli, Yiddish, Hebrew, and Liturgical music.

The Great Ideas Weekend was held with Dr. Jane Gerber as Scholar in Residence. She was Professor of Jewish History and Director of the Institute for Sephardic Studies at the Graduate Center of City University of New York and Author of "The Jews of Spain: A History of the Sephardic Experience."

The fifth adult B'not Mitzvah class graduated. The members were: Marilyn Halaczer Benjamin, Arline Dresdner, Betty S. Elias, Charlotte Soman Goldberg, Doris Z. Hochman, Susan Goldberg Kagan, Francine Kamerling, Karen Wolchuck Sher, Eileen B. Silverstein. The graduation class of the Hebrew high school included: Benjamin Joseph Friedman, Sharon Eve Grau, Joseph Daniel Kauffman, Yael Hani Luski, Leana Lyons, Jody Beth Phillips, and Samuel Martin Wolfson. The St. Petersburg

Eric Ludin, President, Congregation B'nai Israel, 1990–1992.

Sidney Werner, President, Congregation B'nai Israel, 1992–1994.

Reva Pearlstein, President, Congregation B'nai Israel, 1996–1999.

Judith Gordon, President, Congregation B'nai Israel, 1999–2001.

Dr. Leonard Morris.

College of Judaic Studies was sponsored by Congregation B'nai Israel and Temple Beth-El.

Highlights of 1994

Rabbi Luski said, "If there is one central lesson that we should derive from the High Holy Day season, it is a belief that people can grow, can change, and become better people."

Highlights of 1995

The Adult Studies Commission sponsored the Great Ideas Weekend with Dr. Sheldon R. Eisenberg, Professor of Jewish Studies in Comparative Mysticism, University of Florida as the feature scholar. He spoke about, "Kabbalah: the Secret Story of the Jewish Spirit," "A Personal Guide to Climbing the Mystical Tree of Life," and "Applying Mysticism: Healing and Enriching Your Life." Also, the Mitzvah Men's Club and the Adult Studies Commission sponsored Rabbi Arnold S. Turtetsky, Temple Israel Center, White Plains, New York, who spoke on, "Who Will Save the World?"

The Hevra Kadisha of Congregation B'nai Israel was given special recognition and were honored at a congregational dinner. A special tribute was held for Mark Goodfriend, Youth Director at Congregation B'nai Israel. A quotation from the Sayings of the Fathers summed up the importance of the eleven years he spent at Congregation B'nai Israel, "One who increases Jewish learning adds to life."

Highlights of 1996
Dr. Leonard H. Morris

On Tuesday, April 16, Dr. Leonard H. Morris died. He was a retired dentist and a prominent member of the Jewish community. He served in the Marine Corps in China at the end of World War II. He graduated from the University of Wisconsin and Marquette University School of Dentistry. He started practicing in St. Petersburg in 1959, and shortly thereafter, became one of the area's most accomplished blowers of the shofar. He said, "Hearing the sound of the shofar on Rosh Hashana helps our own spiritual warriors battle firmly against sin and backsliding." "It aims to awaken the conscience, to induce

a searching of the heart and mind and to elicit a moral self-accounting. To be able to blow the shofar, makes me thankful to the Almighty that Israel and the Jewish people live." He frequently trained younger men to carry on the tradition.

Highlights of 1997

Congregation B'nai Israel sponsored the Moscow Synagogue Choir. The Choir made its official debut in 1990. This meant that music that had been suppressed since 1917, the time of the Russian Revolution, could be heard again. They performed musical numbers in Russian, English, Hebrew, Yiddish, French, German, Italian, and Spanish.

Highlights of 1998

On October 25, the groundbreaking ceremony took place for the current synagogue structure of Congregation B'nai Israel. It occurred during the 75th anniversary celebration of the founding of the congregation. Alan Bomstein was the builder. Mayor David J. Fisher of the City of St. Petersburg, President Reva Pearlstein of Congregation B'nai Israel, and President Louis Krosner of Temple Beth-El extended greetings to the audience. The welcome was given by Mike Slomka. He and his wife, Sandy, were the Co-Chairs of the Groundbreaking Committee. Sandy recognized the guests in attendance, the founding families, and the fifty year members. Yona Benstock presented the D,VAR TORAH, which is a sermonette based on the Torah portion for that week. Rabbi Luski presented a stirring message of hope and renewal. Dr. J. Leonard Azneer offered the closing prayer. There was a processional to the groundbreaking site, a musical presentation, the ceremonial groundbreaking, a responsive reading prayer, followed by a reception in the fellowship hall.

Highlights of 2000-2005

Highlights of 2000

On Sunday, April 9, more then 600 men, women, and children followed behind Jerome Gilbert, who was the first one carrying a Torah from the old synagogue to the new synagogue. The procession covered three blocks, but it was a beautiful walk into the future of this congregation. All of the Torahs were carried under canopies, and were accompanied by people singing, dancing and offering prayers. Sheryl Weitman said, "It's just kind of an emotional day. You feel happy and sad. It's a new beginning and ending at the same time." Adele Morris, chairperson of the day's events and Past President of Congregation B'nai Israel, said in a brief presentation bidding farewell to the old building, "My family has experienced every possible life cycle right here." Reva Pearlstein, the immediate Past President, said, "It is the only synagogue that my children remember." But for all these individuals and everyone else in the congregation, new memories will be built rapidly and the new structure will become home. Reva Pearlstein voiced what many others felt, "I truly believe this is one of the most important things that I have accomplished in my life (the building of the new synagogue)." Rabbi Luski reaffirmed everyone's emotions and happiness. He concluded the ceremony with one thought, "Building a synagogue is one of the most significant obligations in Judaism. Building Congregation B'nai Israel's new home is not just construction of a building. It is a noble work of creating a spiritual home for Conservative Judaism in this community."

On December 17, Congregation B'nai Israel dedicated its multimillion dollar synagogue at 300 58th Street North. There were 500 member families in the congregation, and virtually all attended the ceremonies. The program of the dedication was dignified and beautiful. Ron Berzon, Jeff Litt, and Cary Reich blew shofars. Reva Pearlstein gave the welcoming address. Judith Gordon presented a prayer of gratitude. An American flag was presented to the congregation by Congressman C. W. Bill Young. A Jewish flag was presented to the congregation by Sheryl Weitman, Executive Director, State of Israel Bonds. A musical presentation, "Songs of Welcome" was presented by the children, accompanied by Linda and Sam Koppelman and Cary Reich. The recognition of the dignitaries

was done by Reva Pearlstein. A prayer for peace was offered by the Most Reverend Robert N. Lynch, Bishop of St. Petersburg. The adult chorus was conducted by llana Gewitz. Shimon Gewitz was the Cantor. Harry J. Silverman, United Synagogue of Conservative Judaism, Southeast Region, presented, "Synagogue of Excellence." Rabbi Jacob Luski introduced Dr. Ismar Schorsch, Chancellor of the Jewish Theological Seminary of America, who gave the keynote address. "Musical History of Our Miracle," written by Cary Reich and Alan Schwartz was presented by Cary Reich. The candle lighting was entitled, "Come Build It." The dedication prayer was offered by Rabbi Jacob Luski. Klezmer music was presented by Linda and Sam Koppelman and Judy Ludin.

During the course of the total dedication of the new facility, individual plaques, representing the contributions of numerous families, were also dedicated. They included: The Benstock Family Sanctuary, the Benjamin Family Social Hall, the Grossman Family

Rabbi Luski and Congregation B'nai Israel's Torahs.

Tree of Life donated by Fred Buns and Family

Chapel, the Philip M. Schwartz Main Entry Lobby, the Slomka-Reiskind Education Center, the Shirley Burns Early Childhood Center, the Sembler Family Atrium, the Lauri Family Kitchen, the Silverberg Courtyard, the Gordon Family Youth Lounge, the Hall of History (Wittner Family), the Warren Family Bridal Room, Etc..

Highlights of 2001

Three leaders of the congregation were honored. They were Thelma Gilbert, Morris Bornstein and Suzette Adelman. Thelma was honored for her fifty five years on the Board of the Sisterhood. She also had served as President of the Jewish War Veterans Auxiliary, and Board Member of the Veteran's Liaison's Counsel of Pinellas County, Hadassah, Pinellas Association for Retarded Children, Menorah Manor, and Menorah Center. Morris Bornstein was honored for his twelve years of service on the Board of Trustees and as First Vice President of the Synagogue. Suzette Adelman was honored for her many years in education including her role as chairman of a variety of committees." Jewish cyberspace became a new column in the B'nai Israel Review.

Highlights of 2002

Cantor Shimon Gewitz and his wife, Ilana, were honored by the congregation for their years of service and for the many beautiful memories the Cantor created during these years. Cantor Gewitz said, "...I think most of you know how strongly and lovingly Ilana and I feel about our shul and its congregants. You truly have been extensions of our "mishpocha (family)", and having been involved in many of your lives has been an honor for us. The relationship with Rabbi Luski has been a special one and it has been a privilege to have served with him over the seven years."

In July, David B. Sislen became the cantor. When asked about the importance of liturgical music, he responded, "Music plays a vital role in the modern synagogue service. During the average service, the vast majority of the liturgy is sung or chanted in a blend of centuries-old musical traditions and modern innovations that keep the tone of the service simultaneously authentic and

fresh. According to tradition, the roots of the nusach of the service (the traditional melodic patterns that define particular services for particular occasions) go back to the musical modes that were used to chant particular books of the Bible during rituals in the Temple in Jerusalem. This complex system of musical guidelines and motives has remained remarkably intact over the past two millennia, and still makes up the basic stylistic framework of the modern service in all synagogues. But rather than serving as a rigid guideline for liturgical music that constricts the worshiper in the act of prayer, nusach has provided a basis from which many musical innovators have been able to use their passion and talent to enrich the tefilla (prayer) experience, making the experience more meaningful for worshipers.... Adding music to words of liturgy that otherwise would be simply recited, elevates them emotionally and spiritually, creating an atmosphere that helps the worshiper dig deeper and reach higher. "

Highlights of 2003

The Congregation had a substantial audio and visual library. They had thirty four videotapes on a variety of subjects related to the synagogue and synagogue life. In addition, they also had thirteen audiocassette tapes on a variety of subject areas.

Congregation B'nai Israel received honors from the Southeast Region of the United Synagogue of Conservative Judaism in the following categories: Adult Jewish Education, Youth Programming, College Activities, Year-Round Congregational Programming, Family Programming, Community Programming and Support, Publications, Journals, Afternoon Religious Schools, Congregation Library, Holiday Programming, Israel Affairs, Golden Kipah Honor Society, Hevra Kadisha Burial Society, Hebrew High School, and as a Synagogue of Excellence.

Highlights of 2004

Rabbi Luski received the Silver Medallion Award from the National Conference of Community and Justice. He had worked with NCCJ for over two decades and said that he had been enriched

Philip Redisch, President, Congregation B'nai Israel, 2001–2003.

Cantor David Sislen

by the experiences of building a community of fellowship between people. He said, "We gather tonight to seek to break down walls that divide us and to eliminate distrust, misunderstanding and hatred. We cannot live our lives with someone else's heart, spine, lips, or eyes. We must bring to the adventure of living our own heart and soul. Too often we approach life as spectators, rather than as participants. We are content to sit on the sidelines and watch other people live....The truth is that the spectator cannot possibly know the emotions, the feelings, and the satisfactions of the participant." This lesson about life is a key to the ministry of this rabbi in his congregation.

The National Council of Community Justice Interfaith Town Hall Meeting was held at the Woodlawn Presbyterian Church. Both local synagogues participated. The topic for discussion was "Building Friendships and Understanding among Jews, Muslims and Christians in St. Petersburg."

Highlights of 2005

The Jewish Theological Seminary of America presented the Scholar in Residence, Dr. Mayer Rabinowitz, Associate Professor of Talmud. His topics were: "The Conservative Approach to Halakha and The Functioning of the Committee of Jewish Law and Standards," "Homosexuals, Homosexuality, and Halakah," and "Bio-Medical Ethics."

Congregation B'nai Israel Sisterhood

The Congregation B'nai Israel Sisterhood started out about 1929, as the Ladies Auxiliary and Aid Society. As an organization of the synagogue, the ladies raised money through suppers, rummage sales, bake sales, etc.. As new families moved into the St. Petersburg area, the women helped them financially. The women also helped transients with food and lodging. Initially, they cleaned the synagogue and took care of the kitchen.

The Sisterhood became affiliated first with the Southeast Region of Women's League and later in 1960, they became affiliated with the Florida Branch of Women's League for Conservative Judaism. Pauline Rivkind was the first President of the Florida Branch. At a later date, more Presidents of the Florida Branch came from

Congregation B'nai Israel. The Sisterhood is also represented on the International Board of Women's League.

Bunnie Katz described Sisterhood. "Our Sisterhood is an integral part of Congregation B'nai Israel and we provide service in many capacities: youth programs, Judaic Shop, maintain kitchen, Oneg Shabbat, financial support to our Synagogue and youth programs, service Menorah Manor and support the Torah Fund.

Our mission is to strengthen and unite synagogue women's groups; perpetuate Conservative/Masorti (The Masorti Movement is a pluralistic, religious movement in Israel, affiliated with Conservative Judaism. Its philosophy combines commitment to Jewish tradition and halachah (law) with an open and positive approach to the modern world, to democratic culture, and to Zionism.) Judaism in the home, synagogue and community."

Michael Wallace, President, Congregation B'nai Israel, 2004–current.

Mitzvah Men's Club

Phil Redisch described the activities and importance of the Mitzvah Men's Club as follows: a monthly minyan brunch on a Sunday; a continental breakfast each morning following the minyan (prayer session); setup of a 36 x 40 foot Sukkah for the children to decorate and for the congregation to have its meals under the stars during the holiday of Sukkot. Three past Presidents of the Mitzvah Men's Club have become Presidents of the Florida Region of the Federation of the Jewish Men's Clubs in the past ten years, with two of them becoming Presidents of Congregation B'nai Israel; the erection of a 12 x 28 foot replica of the Western Wall each year for a week for the congregation to pray at the Wall in celebration of Israeli Independence Day, Yom Ha'atzmaut; presentation of Friday night services every week at Menorah Manor, on each of the five units in the building, by volunteers; the participation in the Chevra Kadisha, burial honor society; providing the food and service for the Yom Kippur Break-the-Fast; sponsoring a blood drive several times a year at the synagogue; and providing the necessary labor to set up the extra chairs for the High Holy Day Services.

United Synagogue Youth

Congregation B'nai Israel's chapter of the United Synagogue Youth was one of the earliest chapters established in the United States. Since the mid-1950's, it has been consistently active. It meets several times each month to plan and participate in social, athletic, cultural, religious, and educational activities. It also participates in sub regional Shabbatons, regional conventional seminars, and international programs such as Israel Pilgrimage, Wheels, and conventions.

Congregation B'nai Israel Youth Department

Congregation B'nai Israel Youth Department supports all age groups of children under the direction of a professional Youth Director to help support the formal education of the children at the Pauline Rivkind Talmud Torah and the Pinellas County Jewish Day School. Parents are involved as partners with the children in their religious education. A Shabbat morning service is held for children in grades three to seven. This Junior Congregation meets thirty Shabbat mornings during the school year to learn and lead prayers and songs.

Attendance is required of all the students of the Pauline Rivkind Talmud Torah. A K'tongregation is held two Shabbat mornings a month with age-appropriate activities for grades K, 1 and 2. A youth group for third, fourth, and fifth graders meets at least once each month for social, religious, crafts, and sports programs. It is called Halutzim. Kadima, a nationally-affiliated youth group for six, seventh, and eighth graders, meets at least twice a month for social, cultural, and religious programs. The children participate in sub-regional and regional activities such as encampment, convention, and Disney Day.

Philosophy of Conservative Judaism

The philosophy of Conservative Judaism is to attempt to combine a positive attitude toward modern culture, while accepting critical secular scholarship concerning Judaism's sacred texts, and a commitment to Jewish observance. Conservative Judaism believes that the scholarly study of Jewish texts indicate that Judaism has constantly been evolving to meet the needs of the Jewish people in their current circumstances. The central legal authority continues the evolution of Jewish law.

Congregation B'nai Israel, ca. 1938–1939.
Seated, r. to l., Mae Benjamin, Stella (Goldberg) Gilbert, Mrs. Miller, Claire Williams, Rabbi Kleinfeld, Max Davis, Mr. Tannenbaum, Sam (Goldberg) Gilbert, (Jacob) Miller.
Second row, [name unknown], Mrs. Smith (son Harry in front of her), Mrs. Rosenberg, [name unknown], Mr. Schwartz, Mrs. Green (?), Lillian Grossman, Mrs. Abrams, Lillian Davis, Sam Perlstein, Belle Herman, Mrs. Yosem, [name unknown], Mrs. Miller, [name unknown], Mrs. Schwartz, Mr. Loebel.
Third Row, Mr. Smith, Rita Okum, Mr. Rosenberg, Mrs. Moed, [name unknown], Ethel Hanken, [name unknown], Leon Halaczer, [name unknown], [name unknown], Mrs. Loebel.
Fourth Row, Sam Shapiro, [name unknown], Mr. Gilman, Mrs. Gilman, [name unknown], Frank Kleinfeld, [name unknown], Harry Hankin, Murray Yosem, Abe Sierkese.

CHAPTER 14

TEMPLE AHAVAT SHALOM OF PALM HARBOR

Highlights of 1970-1979

With the sharp increase in the growth of membership in Temple B'nai Israel, it was now necessary to provide a new synagogue for the far north portion of Pinellas County. The Board of Trustees of Temple B'nai Israel approved a plan to help the Jewish people of Palm Harbor and north form their own congregation. Rabbi Baseman of Temple B'nai Israel performed Sabbath services for the new congregation on a monthly basis and the children of this congregation went to Temple B'nai Israel for their religious training, until there was a sufficiently large group to form their own religious school.

Highlights of 1976

On May 5, Temple Ahavat Shalom was founded by a group of eighteen families. The name of the corporation was the Reform Congregation of Northern Pinellas County Inc., and its principal place of business and place of worship was the Ramada Inn, 401 U.S. Highway 19 S., Clearwater. Robert L. Shear was designated Resident Agent to accept service of process within the State of Florida. The officers of the corporation were: Cyrus A. Kopit, Chairman/President; David G. Wolstein, Director/Treasurer; Stanley Miller, Director/Vice President; Robert L. Shear, Director/Secretary. Three additional charter families were Charlie and Isa Rutenberg, Reva and Marshall Kent, Eileen Levin and Dr. Harvey Levin. The purpose of the congregation was to promote Judaism in all relations of life by means of public and private worship, by religious education, and through social welfare activities. In the early years, there was constant financial pressure which could have destroyed the congregation if it weren't for the hard work and unfaltering devotion of the pioneering congregants. The new congregation was very concerned with social action. The initial services were led at times by Elaine Wolstein, and occasionally by Charlie Rutenberg's daughter. The first four Presidents of the congregation were Bob Shear, Stanley Miller, Elliott Kahana, who helped raise a substantial amount of money for the social hall, and Myron Graff.

Elaine and Dr. David Wolstein

Elaine Wolstein and her husband, Dr. David Wolstein, arrived in Pinellas County in 1969-1970. They became members of Temple B'nai Israel and then founding members of Temple Ahavat Shalom of Palm Harbor. Elaine's Jewish education began in elementary school in Brooklyn, New York at Beth Jacob Yeshiva for girls. She then attended New York Far Rockaway High School, and also received four years of Hebrew training. At Brooklyn College, she studied Hebrew literature and grammar. Elaine holds a Bachelor of Arts Degree in Education from Roosevelt University in Chicago and a Degree in Jewish Studies from the Union of American Hebrew Congregations. She began tutoring students in Hebrew in both high school and privately. She taught Sunday and Hebrew School throughout her college years, the early years of her marriage, and continuing on to today.

When Elaine came to the Clearwater/Dunedin area, she immediately began teaching at the Religious School of Temple B'nai Israel of Clearwater. She has been deeply involved in the cause of Jewish education and founded the Temple Ahvat Shalom Religious School. She served as the congregation's Director of Education and a member of its faculty for many years. Much of this work was done as a volunteer. Currently, she teaches Hebrew to the B'nai Mitzvah students. She also is the Principal of the weekday afternoon Hebrew School, an adviser to the current Director of Education, and she is a teacher of Hebrew and Judaic studies to adults. She is very active in the Women's Philanthropy of the Jewish Federation. She is a founder and member of the Tampa Bay Jewish Educator's Council, member of the Dunedin Junior Service League, Lifetime Member of Hadassah. She and her husband, David, received the

Tree of Life Award from the Jewish National Fund in 2002 and were honored by Israeli Bonds in 1996. In 2004, she was the winner of the Educator of Excellence Award. When asked what has motivated her to continually work toward the improvement of Jewish education, she said, "It is with great love and devotion in the teachings of Torah that keeps me involved in Jewish education. It is also my life's passion-in both the Jewish and secular world to impart a strong feeling of pride and commitment in our Jewish heritage in Israel."

Highlights of 1978

On June 14, Temple Ahavat Shalom was admitted to the Union of American Hebrew Congregations. On December 6, the name of the congregation was changed to Temple Ahavat Shalom Inc.. The officers of the congregation were: Stanley M. Miller, President; Bob Eisenberg, Vice President; Eric Adler, Vice President; Jules Goldstein, Secretary; Myron Graff, Treasurer; Marilyn Jacobs, Corresponding Secretary; and Directors, Mr. Harry Agoada, Dr. Elliott Familant, Steven Hatton, Dr. Harvey Levin, Dr. Sanford Plevin and Dr. David Wolstein. Rabbi Jan Bresky assumed the pulpit. He immediately asked Eileen Levin to become the cantorial soloist.

Eileen Levin

Eileen Levin, is a Jewish mother, model, and cantorial soloist. Her father, Louis Pollock, and her mother, Marion, were both physical education teachers, who graduated from Temple University. They continued teaching until their retirement. They owned a kosher children's camp, Nock-a Mixon, for thirty five years. Every Friday night and Saturday morning, her father led services and Eileen helped with the singing. Eileen attended Har Zion Temple Hebrew High School in Philadelphia and was confirmed there. She performed in musical theater productions over a number of years. She graduated from Temple University in 1963 with a Bachelor of Science Degree in Education. She went on to obtain a real estate license.

In 1972, Eileen came to the Clearwater/ Dunedin area and joined Temple B'nai Israel.

Eileen Levin. (below) as Yente in "Fiddler on the Roof."

She taught Hebrew classes at Temple B'nai Israel, and was a member of many musical shows. In 1976 Eileen, along with other Temple B'nai Israel families, became charter members of the new synagogue. She sang for the lay services and also helped shape the format of the services at the new Temple. When Rabbi Jan Bresky arrived, he said that Eileen did a fantastic job leading the liturgical songs and made her the cantorial soloist. At that time, it was unusual to have a female musical director at a Pinellas County congregation. Eileen received cantorial training from Cantor Myrovich of Temple Beth Shalom of Clearwater. This musical training, and the day-to-day exposure to her father, Louis, and his knowledge of Hebrew and Yiddish which he transferred to her, helped her to become a cantorial soloist and a better person. Louis felt the necessity to express his love for God by always going to the synagogue, seven days a week, to be part of the prayer session. On the last day of his life, one month after his wife died, he rushed to the synagogue to make sure that there would be ten people there for prayer. He died quietly, while talking to God, and went to meet his beloved wife.

Eileen played many characters in a variety of musical shows, including Fanny Brice in Funny Girl and Yenta the Matchmaker in Fiddler on the Roof. The Kent Center invited Eileen to lead the Passover Seder at their facilities for several years. In the past, she has been a cantorial soloist at Congregation B'nai Emunah, Congregation Alliah, and the University of South Florida Hillel.

She has a son, Richard, a urologist, who married Robbie, who has been involved in the writing process for medical textbooks. A second son, Andrew, is a chiropractor in Pinellas County. His wife, Roxanne, is Professor of Spanish at St. Petersburg College in Tarpon Springs.

Highlights of 1979

The congregation purchased a Pakistani restaurant just west of Belcher on State Road 580 in Dunedin and stayed there until 1982, when they moved into their current home.

Highlights of 1980-1989

Highlights of 1982

On January 31, the groundbreaking for the new facility took place at 1575 Curlew Rd., Palm Harbor. Twenty three families pledged $284,600 for the new synagogue building. Helen and Frank Weaner pledged $150,000. During construction, the structure was defaced. Frank Weaner had a talk with David Duke, the head of the Ku Klux Klan and his fellow Klansmen. This did not occur again. David Duke wanted to make Palm Harbor the state headquarters of the Ku Klux Klan. It did not happen. Frank was not afraid of anyone. He was known for his support in making Palm Harbor a peaceful community and his generosity in supporting good causes. Frank Weaner found bigotry against any human being to be reprehensible.

Frank Weaner

Frank Weaner was born in Detroit, Michigan. He moved to the Tampa Bay area in the early 1960s. He founded the Paradise Fruit Company in Plant City and was Chairman and principal shareholder at the time of his death at age 89, in 1997. He helped found the Palm Harbor Rotary in 1980, was past Chairman of the Palm Harbor Chamber of Commerce, and established the Teacher of the Year Award as well as scholarships for graduating high school seniors. Beside being Temple Ahavat Shalom's largest benefactor, he gave thousands of dollars to a Jesuit High School in Tampa. He not only dropped by frequently to see how the boys were doing, but also made numerous donations of money.

Growth and Expansion

Elaine Wolstein, in addition to being the Educational Director of both the Hebrew and Sunday School, created a Hebrew/Sunday School Curriculum, which included enrichment with art and music. She founded the Youth Group, Confirmation Class, Post-Confirmation Class, Bar/Bat Mitzvah program. Six young people were in the first Confirmation Class. The curriculum included mitzvah projects, community involvement projects, interfaith programs,

Shabbat family services, creative youth services, and a youth choir. Information booklets were developed. The children in the Religious School took field trips to nursing homes, funeral homes, the Holocaust Museum, Art Galleries, etc. Elaine created the adult B'nai Mitzvah program.

Temple B'nai Israel presented to the congregation of Temple Ahavat Shalom a beautifully inscribed Torah pointer. An adult choir was formed to perform on the High Holy Days, as well as once a month during the Shabbat Friday evening services. They were under the direction of Dr. Eugene Szonntagh, organist/choirmaster at the neighboring St. Alfred's Episcopal Church. Ten volunteers rehearsed one evening a week at the Temple.

The love of people brought together two religious leaders of different faiths. Temple Ahavat Shalom's Rabbi Jan Bresky and Rev. David R. Morres of St. Alfred's Episcopal Church became good friends. When the synagogue was constructing its sanctuary on Curlew Road in Palm Harbor, next to the church, swastikas and anti-Semitic slurs were painted on the building under construction. The members of the church helped clean off the nastiness written on the

new synagogue building.

When the new structure was dedicated, St. Alfred's Church gave the Temple a Waterford crystal wine decanter as a gift. The children of both congregations have attended services in each other sanctuaries. The Jewish children have learned about Christmas and Easter and the Christian children have learned about Hanukkah and Passover. Reverend Morres studied Judaism and Rabbi Bresky studied Christianity.

Marcia Satinoff was the bulletin editor.

Highlights of 1984

The Pacesetter's Social Club continued to hold entertaining programs to bring temple members together. Paula Rosoff, one of the early members, taught beginning Hebrew to all students in the religious school. She attended Brooklyn College, where she majored in art. Her husband Jay, a dentist, was deeply involved with her in working for the new temple.

The Bulletin Committee, chaired by Joe Melton, named the bulletin Ner Tamid, Eternal Light. The reason for selecting this name was many fold: to continue the light of information flowing to the membership; to light the way from the darkness of ignorance to the brightness of knowledge of what is happening in our Temple; to tie, symbolically, our glorious heritage of the past to a modern world of life; and to dignify the journal with a respectful identity.

Highlights of 1985

Joe and Miriam Melton were the bulletin editors. The synagogue, under Dr. Norman Gross, continued its role in social action activities. Some of the programs the committee worked on were: Black-Jewish dialogue, Ethiopian Jewery, Soviet Jewery, United Jewish Appeal, drugs, Holocaust education, Israel welfare and understanding, and social action education.

The school was packed. Even the nursery school had a waiting list because of lack of room. Since the children are the highest priority in any synagogue, a new building fund was established to help construct additional school facilities.

The Temple Constitution stated, "The purpose of this congregation shall be to promote Judaism in all relations of life by means of public and private worship, by religious education, and through social and welfare activities."

The Temple Ahavat Shalom Souvenir PhotoJournal of 1985-1986, set forth the meaning of this Synagogue and all synagogues. "Be strong, be strong, and let us strengthen one another, is traditionally proclaimed in unison by the congregation as the reading of each book of the Torah is completed, and as the reading of one book is done, the next is begun... such expression is appropriate, for the very meaning of, and the reason for our congregation. A congregation is a people of many voices with a unison needed to live the past which bore them and carry it to future survival. And the deep wisdom of our Tradition, knowing that no one person can sustain it, enjoins us to congregate. Our Torah cannot be publicly read, our sons (and daughters) cannot be called to Torah, our children cannot be brought to the chupah (wedding canopy), we cannot say Kaddish (a prayer of life said in honor of the dead), without a minyan (a congregation of at least ten men in the Orthodox movement and at least ten men and/or women in the Conservative and Reform movements, who form a prayer group). So we are enjoined to congregate. With all our differences, our variousness as individuals, with our myriad of opinions even as to what a Jew is, we must come together and the many somehow be one, just to be consciously Jewish. So the wisdom of our Tradition is also the source of our ironic humor–it isn't easy to be Jewish."

Rabbi Jan Bresky said, "There is a beautiful Biblical concept called AVODAH, which was the service of the sanctuary in Jerusalem. It meant supporting the ancient Temple in every human way possible. The priests performed the sacrifices. The Levites maintained the structure and cleaned the holy vessels. The Israelites brought their produce and cattle to be offered to God and to support the holy men. Everyone worked together with their individual talents for the good of the sanctuary and of Judaism." He compared the ancient concept of AVODAH to the work done by the congregants to ensure the success of the Souvenir Photo

Journal, which was a major fund raiser for the synagogue.

President Barbara Rosenberg said, "... we must not lose sight of the daily on-going activities which are the backbone of our work. Although in a less dramatic way, the life of the Temple beats continuously, without interruption, seven days a week. Religious Services, Adult Education, Religious School, Nursery School, Youth Groups, Social Action, Bingo, Pacesetters, Sisterhood, and Men's Club meetings combined to make Temple Ahavat Shalom a vibrant force for our Jewish lifestyle in the community. It is now more than ever necessary to preserve the Jewish community in a vital form, so that our children will reap the rewards of our labors."

The Temple officers were as follows: Rabbi, Jan Bresky; Cantor, Robert Marinoff; President, Barbara Rosenberg; Financial Vice President, Martin Satinoff; Vice President, Herman Lichtenberg; Vice President, Robert Weissbein; Treasurer, Harris Blair; Financial Secretary, Morris Krouk; Recording Secretary, Diane Karp; and immediate Past President, Dr. Myron Graff. The trustees were: Maxine Cohen, William Eisenberg, Janet Ettelman, Ellie Geier, Jules Goldberg, Patty Goldstein, Dr. Norman Gross, Miriam Melton, Dr. Paul Reifer, Michael Ribet, Larry Silver, Bernard Slaff, Norman Smith and Hy Turner.

Highlights of 1986

Eight children were confirmed. The Brotherhood had over sixty members. Cantor Weisser formed a chamber ensemble to enhance the service with instrumental music.

Highlights of 1987

Rabbi Klein was welcomed to the congregation. The Temple, as part of its interfaith endeavors, participated in its first annual community-wide interfaith thanksgiving service. Rabbi Klein continued the close relationship with St. Alfred's Episcopal Church.

Cantor Michael Weisser was complemented for his service to the Temple. Shalom and Tobah Rabah wrote a tribute to the cantor, "For your pleasant voice, your knowledge of liturgy, the special services you wrote, your contribution to our High Holiday Services; your work with the children and the choir, you're hospital visits, and your adult education programs...(we honor you)" He and his family left for a new position in Greenville, North Carolina. There were 150 families in the congregation.

Highlights of 1988

In January, Rabbi Klein was installed as spiritual leader of Temple Ahavat Shalom. Rabbi Ira Youdovin installed him in the pulpit. Rabbis Baseman, Bromberg, Luski and Sundheim, Rev. Paul Norcross, Father David Moores, and President Martin Satinoff gave insightful and inspiring presentations. More than 250 people attended the celebration dinner.

Rabbi Gary Klein

The Early Childhood Center was founded. A classroom was dedicated to Elaine Wolstein, in recognition of her outstanding and unselfish service to the Helen and Frank Weaner Religious School of Temple Ahavat Shalom. Another classroom was dedicated to Daniel and Stephanie Melker. Jerry Greenhouse, a temple member, built and donated a new Ark for the Torahs. It was to be used in the sanctuary until a new sanctuary could be built. Nine children were confirmed. A bereavement committee was established. It was designed to provide help to families before, during, and after death in the family.

Highlights of 1989

Marci Linder became the Educational Director upon the retirement of Elaine Wolstein. Twenty children were B'nai Mitzvah. Janet Clement became the Director. Seventy new families joined the congregation. The Young at Heart group was organized under the presidency of Jerry Greenhouse and later, Joe Kreplick. The group became an important social and service arm of the Temple. Their work was supplemented by the daytime adult education program, which included a cultural series. Rabbi Herbert Bronstein of Chicago presented the Scholar-in-Residence program. A men's club was organized under the leadership of Norman Rosenfeld. Selma Bowman became the choir director after Trudy Grushkin retired. The Friday night soloists were Lori Cohen and Lori Seplowe, accompanied on the piano by Martha Glass. An organ was donated by Rita and Stan Fishman. Rabbi Frank Sundheim was the soloist on the High Holy Days. He was accompanied by Arnold Breman and Loweil Adams, a celloist from the Florida Orchestra. The front entrance to the building and the sanctuary were redecorated by the Sisterhood.

Highlights of 1990-1999

Highlights of 1990

Seventy plus new families joined the congregation. The Scholar-in-Residence series provided three visiting scholars: news analyst, Walter Zanger from Jerusalem; Rabbi David Sapperstein, Religious Action Center Director, Union of American Hebrew Congregations; and Dr. Saul Gordon, family educator. The choir was under the direction of Selma Bowman. A new bereavement support group was founded. The Temple was very active in interfaith activities. Twenty seven children were B'nai Mitzvah. A plaque was dedicated in the memory of Max "Bill" Eisenberg from his coworkers and bingo playing friends for his extraordinary labors in promoting bingo to help maintain the finances of the Temple.

Highlights of 1991

Twenty one children were B'nai Mitzvah and thirteen were confirmed. Elaine Wolstein returned to the school as the Interim Director. Sixty new families joined the congregation, bringing the total to 465. This was double the number it had been four years before. The Baby Boomers young couples club was reactivated. Rabbi Klein was appointed to the Board of Directors of the Tampa Region of the National Conference of Christians and Jews.

Highlights of 1992

An effort was made to determine the major contributors to the synagogue in its early years. Although the records and a plaque listing these individuals had been lost, the following names of families were cited: Steve Bowman, Gary Brevoort, Clifford Colin, Andy Gellady, Myron Graff, Elliott Kahana, Jeffrey Karp, Mitch Lowenstein, Richard Maza, Daniel Melker,

Daniel Morris, Sanford Plevin, Arthur Polin, Paul Reifer, Jay Rosoff, Allan Rothschild, Frank Weaner, and David Wolstein. Twenty seven young people were confirmed. A new member dinner was attended by eighty people. A new social group, the Most Happy Kvellers was formed for people in their fifties and sixties. Eleven adults were B'nai Mitzvah. The fund raising goal of $1,300,000 to build a new sanctuary and classrooms was realized. The co-chairpersons were Larry Lieberman and Howard Scala. Groundbreaking was on June 14.

President Ronnie Bernstein, despite an extremely busy schedule, provided large amounts of energy for the Temple. Rabbi Klein said, "Her endeavors on our behalf reflect a sincere commitment to humankind and a sincere believe that Judaism can significantly enhance our lives and through us, the lives of our fellow human beings. In addition to sharing her time and her strength, Ronnie has also given each of us at Temple Ahavat Shalom a little bit of her idealism, her optimism, and her faith in humanity." In completing her final Presidential presentation, Ronnie quoted Solomon Goldman's words concerning the synagogue, as her reason for her dedication. "I come to the synagogue to probe my weakness and my strength, and to fill the gap between my profession and my practice. I come to lift myself by my bootstraps. I come to quiet the turbulence of my heart, restrain its mad impulsiveness and check the itching eagerness of my every muscle to outsmart and outdistance my neighbor. I come for self-renewal and regeneration... I come to be strengthened in my determination to be free... I come to behold the beauty of the Lord, to find Him who put an upward reach in the heart of man."

Betty Salsburg became the new President. Sylvia and Abe Roseoff were two of the early choir members. They went from their 50th wedding anniversary party directly to a Thursday evening practice session. Sylvia said, "There is a special feeling you get making beautiful music."

Highlights of 1993

Eleven children were confirmed. New homes of members were consecrated by Rabbi Klein. A plaque was dedicated in memory of Harriet Wollenberg from her coworkers and bingo playing friends, for her concerns and smiles for everyone who tried to keep the Temple financially solvent.

Highlights of 1994

Harvey Weisenfeld, an accomplished musician and music teacher, became the choir director. There were 475 member families, which led to an expansion in the structure to include a beautiful new sanctuary to help fill spiritual needs. Expanded office space and additional classrooms were also added. The architect for the sanctuary and Ark was Sol Fleischman. The large Torah was donated by Geoff and, of blessed memory, Pat Bild. The small Torah was donated by Barbara and Norman Smith. The new Torah came from a special fund. The stained-glass windows were made by Jim Percy of Orlando.

Sixteen children were confirmed. Twelve adult members of the congregation became B'nai Mitzvah. There were over 300 children in the Hebrew and Sunday School. The sanctuary and the majority of the classrooms, as well as a library and office suite, were completed..

There was a dedication weekend on January 28 and 29, which was magnificent. Rabbi Eric Yoffie, Vice President of the Union of American Hebrew Congregations and Chairman of its Social Action Commission presented several lectures and seminars. On Friday evening, the sanctuary was consecrated. On Saturday morning, there was a brief Shabbat morning worship service, Torah study and luncheon. On Saturday afternoon, there was a family landscaping party and temple beautification party and on Saturday evening there were several adult education courses.

Highlights of 1995

Rabbi Klein talked about his work as a Rabbi. He said his most important job was teaching. He said he taught from the bema through his sermon or Torah study. He taught in the classroom. However the most important teaching took place in the hospital room, at a wedding, preparing a child for bar or bat mitzvah, naming a baby, consecration of a new home, counseling a troubled adult, and helping a couple celebrate the anniversary of their marriage and reaffirm their commitment to each other. To accomplish this, he needs to understand the individuals. Rabbi Klein was granted tenure by the Board of Trustees. Carol Wagmeister became the new administrator.

The duo, KOl B' SEDER (everything is OK) performed at the Temple. These two outstanding composers and performers, Rabbi Dan Freelander and Cantor Jeff Clepper, performed new Reform music. This was in keeping with the wonderful new music for Jewish worship and celebration that had been created in the last twenty years by the Reform Movement. In reaction to their performance, Rabbi Klein said, "Music is one of God's most precious blessings. The music we create and music we hear touch the heart, the mind and the soul in a special way. Listening to music and creating it helps us sense God's presence in our world, in our fellow human beings, and in ourselves. Music has always been an important part of Jewish worship and celebration. Many of our prayers are meant to be sung and even the words of our Torah can be chanted. Our tradition tells us that singing enhances the meaning of the words and helps make the teachings dearer to us."

Highlights of 1996

Rabbi Koenig, a Sofer or Scribe, joined Rabbi Klein in a morning of Torah study. Rabbi Koenig had been commissioned to write a new Torah for Temple Ahavat Shalom. He gave presentations on how to use the quill, ink, and parchment during his twelve months of writing the Torah.

Twenty children were confirmed. Sixty children were B'nai Mitzvah. Twenty five new families joined the congregation.

One morning, Rabbi Klein stayed home to view a rerun of a Donahue show, which had been previously aired several months before. Cantor Michael Weisser, who served a congregation in Lincoln, Nebraska and who had been previously at Temple Ahavat Shalom, had for years received threatening phone calls and vicious hate mail from Larry

Trapp, a well-known Neo-Nazi and Ku Klux Klansman in Lincoln. At first, Cantor Weisser decided not to respond, but then he used an unconventional approach. He called Trapp, who was confined to a wheelchair, and offered to take him shopping for groceries. This led to a wonderful relationship between the two men and Trapp publicly renounced his bigotry and apologized to Jews and Blacks for the pain he caused them. He visited schools and churches throughout the Midwest in an effort to teach people not to hate. He studied Judaism with Cantor Weisser and eventually converted. This is a wonderful example of how to beat discrimination with kindness and education. Hopefully, this book will provide knowledge of the contributions of Jewish people to society and will turn people, who practice bigotry, into reformed Larry Trapps, who vocally help create a world with a better understanding of all people.

Highlights of 1997

Rabbi Klein wrote about the conclusion of David Wolstein's presidency of the congregation. Rabbi Klein said, "David and Elaine were founders of our congregation twenty years ago. They have remained loyal to Temple Ahavat Shalom during every phase of our history. They have set an example of generosity, hard work, integrity, sensitivity, and compassion in all their interaction with their fellow members. They know that each of us, as a child of God, merits his fellow man's respect and understanding. They also know that life is a precious gift from God....." Sixteen children were confirmed.

The three social clubs that the congregation sponsored helped play a major role in the Temple becoming a true community. The three clubs were: the Young Couples Club, for very young couples and singles; the Empty Nesters, for couples and singles whose children have left home; and the Happy Kvellers, for couples and singles who at this stage of their lives could be grandparents. The events they sponsored, combined with those from Sisterhood and Brotherhood, and the congregation as a whole, provided a well-rounded religious, educational, and community program. This was especially helpful for newcomers in the community.

Highlights of 1998

Sixteen children were confirmed. The Temple presented a Scholar in Residence Weekend with guest speakers, Rabbi Fred Schwartz and Mrs. Roberta Schwartz. Rabbi Schwartz was the spiritual leader of Temple Shalom of Chicago. The two of them were recognized scholars and national leaders of the Jewish Reform Movement. Rabbi Jack Stern, Rabbi Emeritus of Westchester Reform Temple of Scarsdale, New York, a leader of the American Jewish Community, gave a guest presentation entitled: "What do we expect of God? What does God expect of us?" He also presented a program entitled: "Is Jewish Humor Funny?" He has been President of the Central Conference of American Rabbis, a trustee of the Union of American Hebrew Congregations, Vice President of the World Union for Progressive Judaism, and Chairman of the Task Force on Jewish Ethics. A new library was opened, with Sylvia Klein and Mildred Schwartz acting as librarians.

Haley and Dr. Lonnie T. Klein

Haley and Lonnie came to the Palm Harbor area for Lonnie to set up a practice of medicine. Lonnie was born on November 24, 1966. He earned a Science Degree in Biology and a Bachelor of Arts Degree in History from the State University of New York at Binghamton, New York. He earned his Doctor of Medicine from New York Medical College in Valhalla, New York in 1992. He was the urology Chief Resident at Columbia University, New York Presbyterian Hospital. He is a Fellow of the American College of Surgeons and Board Certified in Urology. He holds various academic honors and has already written thirteen technical papers. He donates his time at the Good Samaritan Clinic in New Port Richey and also gives community lectures on prostate surgery through Morton Plant Hospital at Countryside Mall. He is a Member of the Board of Temple Ahavat Shalom.

Haley was born on June 3, 1966. She graduated from the University of Michigan in 1988 with a Bachelor's Degree in Pre-law.

She earned the Doctorate of Jurisprudence from Brooklyn Law school in 1991. She currently operates a private business.

Highlights of 1999

Pianist David Syme presented a program, "Jewish Roots and the Classics." An accomplished performer and a Juilliard graduate, who has received critical acclaim around the world, he brought to the congregation a musical discussion of the Jewish strains in the musical masterpieces of the past 200 years. Dan Tichon, Speaker of the Knesset and a member of the Israeli cabinet, gave a presentation at the Synagogue. Mr. Tichon had a degree in economics and international relations from Hebrew University. Twenty children were confirmed.

The Temple presented "An Evening with Alan Dershowitz." Mr. Dershowitz was a noted legal authority, author and professor at Harvard Law school. Among his many books are two books on Jewish life, "Chutzpah" and "The Vanishing American Jew." Mr. Dershowitz frequently spoke to Jewish audiences around the country. In Los Angeles, he discussed the Jewish way of doing things. He related the story which could set some light on why some things are included in the services and some are not and why some traditions are followed and some are not. The story goes: that there was an old inner-city synagogue that had just moved to the suburbs and acquired both a new modern building and modern rabbi. At the first Shabbat service, when the congregation recited the Shema prayer, half the congregation stood up while half remained seated. The standing half yelled to the seated half to stand up, while the seated half yelled sit down to the standing half. The new rabbi was upset by the commotion, and after the service, he asked representatives of both groups to meet with him to ascertain the tradition of the congregation. At the meeting, the sit-down group asked the old rabbi whether it wasn't the tradition to sit down. The old man pondered and then shook his head. " No, my children that is not the tradition." The stand-up group was exultant as it said, then it must be the tradition that we stand

up. Again the old Rabbi pondered and again he shook his head in the negative. " No my children, that is not the tradition. " At this point, the new rabbi's patience snapped and he screamed, "Rabbi I can't take it, half of them stand, half of them sit, they all yell at each other and I can't hear myself think. The old Rabbi pondered and nodded his head in the affirmative. That my children, is the tradition." When Mr. Dershowitz was finished with the story, his mother stood up in the audience and added: "The important thing is that they all say the Shema Yisrael." His mother was right. Traditions change. Although neighborhood, community and synagogue customs determine specific levels and types of religious observance, there is a commonality of shared historical experience and shared beliefs among all Jewish people and that is why Jewish people always come to each other's assistance in times of need and share times of happiness despite their differences concerning the observance of certain customs and rituals.

Ronnie and Evan Weston wrote a guest editorial in the monthly bulletin about the Torah program at the Temple. They quoted Maimonides, "Every Jew is affirmatively commanded to write a Sefer Torah." They said, "Wherever Jews have gone, the Torah has kept us alive. It is our link from generation to generation. We wanted to inform you that our Torah Writing Mitzvah Project has been rejuvenated and we are anxious to get your participation. For most of us, this is a once-in-lifetime experience. Each of us will be able to fulfill the 613th Commandant of having participated in the writing of a Sefer Torah. Every adult and every child, will be united with the Jewish past, present and future and of course with our synagogue, Temple Ahavat Shalom." This noble project not only enriched the congregation in a religious manner but also in a financial manner, since it helped pay off the mortgage.

Two outstanding Jewish scholars, Adrian Sundheim and Joan Keller, presented a six-week course to the congregants. Adrian Sundheim taught for forty seven years. She studied at Beaver College, University of Cincinnati, Hebrew Union College, and Hebrew University of Jerusalem. She taught a course entitled: "The Dirty Dozen," a slightly irreverent look into the lives of twelve women from Jewish literature. She emphasized that typically Jewish people were neither saints nor sinners, but rather fascinating characters.

Joan Keller had a Master of Arts degree in Religious Studies and near Eastern Archaeology. She has published, on the Web, "Dictionary of Judaism in the Biblical Period "on the topic of ancient glass. She has also been an instructor at St. Petersburg Junior College. She taught a course about the pre-history of the Jewish people entitled: "Archaeology and Mythology of the Bible: a Study of Genesis."

The preschool at Temple Ahavat Shalom was renamed the Krieger Early Childhood Center. Hans Krieger was Mr. Bingo. He ran the Temple bingo games, which provided great financial support when there was an extreme need for alternate sources of financing. He was an active member of the Board of Trustees and helped with the religious school and brotherhood. He was grandfather to a generation of children, always there to praise them and to give them their good-morning hug. Landy Gonzalez, when writing about him, said, "There are many children who aren't fortunate enough to have extended family living in our area with whom they can share their daily experiences. Mr. Hans fills that void in many ways."

The Senior Youth Group, which had been active for many years, traveled to West Palm Beach for a youth group conclave. Three hundred and sixteen Jewish teenagers were in attendance. Together under one roof, they sang, danced, and worshiped openly. There were workshops led by Jewish teenagers about issues such as peer pressure, loyalty toward siblings, and how hard it is to observe the traditions of Judaism. Leaders were being born. Although, in this manuscript, because of time and space constraints, little is being written about the junior and senior youth groups in the various synagogues, these young people are the future leaders of the various Jewish organizations. A whole additional volume can be written about these young people. Where available, the Presidents of these organizations are listed in the appendix by synagogue.

Once again, Elaine Wolstein retired from her position as religious school director. She plans to continue helping with the religious school and specifically teaching Hebrew. Penny Barna became the new religious school director. She holds Bachelor and Master Degrees in Education and has worked extensively as an educator. She is a knowledgeable and committed Jewish person who has been a member of the congregation for a number of years.

Highlights of 2000-2005

Highlights of 2000

The Temple received a long-term loan of beautiful tapestries from Roland and Janell Roth entitled, "Homage to Jerusalem." These tapestries, which hang in the sanctuary, are representations of the paintings by the famous Israeli artist, Mordecai Arden. Rabbi Frank Sundheim became Auxiliary Rabbi of Temple Ahavat Shalom on a part-time basis. Rabbi Klein's thirteen years as the spiritual leader was celebrated by the congregation. He married Lou Anne Karlin to Myron Saul Graff, who offered this beautiful saying, "Two hearts, one love, two promises, one covenant, two lives, made one before God."

Lori Cohen, her husband Ed, and her children relocated to Naples, Florida. She had been part of the congregation for the past twenty three years and had, during the past twelve years, served as the cantorial soloist. She enhanced the worship experience by combining her musical talent with her love of Jewish heritage, synagogue, family, and God.

Highlights of 2001

Rabbi Richard Bernholz, Senior Rabbi of Congregation Schaarai Zedek of Tampa, gave a presentation, "Beating the Missionaries at Their Own Game." This program was opened especially to middle and high school students as well as their parents. Eighteen children were confirmed. The Temple presented, "An Evening with the God Squad." The speakers were Rabbi Marc Gellman and Monsignor Thomas Hartman.

Highlights of 2002

Twenty nine children were confirmed. There were 229 students enrolled in the Sunday school and 188 students in the Hebrew school. Thirty four children became B'nai mitzvah. On January 11, a special Shabbat service and oneg was held to celebrate the 25th anniversary of Temple Ahvat Shalom. A formal dinner in honor of the congregation's Presidents was held the following evening.

The Temple library was named the Ariel Goldman Memorial Library. Arial was eleven and one-half years old when she suddenly died. She was to have become a Bat Mitzvah shortly. To honor her and her parents, a special service was held the evening at which she would've been a Bat Mitzvah and the library was named in her honor. Rabbi Klein said, "Our Jewish tradition teaches that we are not alone when we grieve. God is with us through these ordeals. God's presence, at these times, is manifest in many ways. It is notable however, that it is through the companionship of others, that God's gift of compassion is brought to us."

The Temple presented, "An Evening with Charles Krauthammer." He was a syndicated columnist and political analyst for the Washington Post. He was born in 1950, in New York City, grew up in Montréal, and was educated at McGill University. He earned a Bachelors Degree with first class honors in Political Science and Economics. He also studied at Oxford University, where he was a Commonwealth Scholar in Politics at Balliol College. He studied medicine at Harvard University, earned his Doctor of Medicine Degree in 1975, and then practiced medicine as resident and chief resident in psychiatry at Massachusetts General Hospital. He worked for the New Republic magazine as an essayist and editor from 1981-1988. In the mid-eighties, he began writing a syndicated column for the Washington Post and Time Magazine. He had won a Pulitzer Prize and many other awards. His presentation was, "At the Abyss: The Oslo Deception and the Coming Middle East War."

Highlights of 2003-2004

In 2003-2004 Rabbi Klein, writing about the significance of Passover and Shavuot, said, "... Real freedom requires obedience to the divine commandment. People often need to be reminded of the relationship between freedom and responsibility. Even in the United States, many still need to learn that only in a society where everyone is offered the opportunity to enjoy a decent life is freedom safe. Only if we care for those less fortunate than us, are we really free."

The new year started with almost 600 members, 230 children in the Religious School and seventy in the preschool. The top ten early childhood Jewish values being taught at this preschool and all Jewish preschools throughout the county, the state, and the nation were:

1. **Mitzvah or commandment**–since as Jews we are required to do good things and to be good to all people;
2. **Shalom or peace**–since as Jews we know that peace requires action which requires us to mediate our arguments and share with others;
3. **Tza'ar Ba'alay Chayim or compassion to animals**–since as Jews, we are allowed to use animals for our own benefit but we must treat them kindly because they are also God's creatures;
4. **Tikkum Olam or repair of the world**– since as Jews we are required to take care of the Earth and all the things therein;
5. **Bikur Choleem or visiting the sick**-- since as Jews we are required to assist our fellow students, our teachers, family members, and our community;
6. **Hachnasat Orcheem or hospitality to strangers**–since as Jews we are required to help and take care of the stranger within our midst;
7. **Kavod or respect**–since as Jews we are required to show common courtesy and have good manners in our relationships with all people;
8. **Gemilut Chasidim or acts of loving-kindness or good deeds**–since as Jews we are required to help each other willingly and with care;
9. **Tzedakah or justice or righteousness**– since as Jews we are required to feed the poor, help the underdog, improve the lives of all underprivileged people, preferably in an anonymous manner;

10. **K'lal Yisrael or all Jews are part of one people**–since as Jews we are diversified into Orthodox, Reform, Conservative, Reconstructionist, Sephardic, Ashkenazic, American, European, Asian, African, etc., but despite the differences in beliefs, customs, languages, and foods, we all believe in one God and the sanctity of God.

Ehud Barak, former Prime Minister of Israel, provided an excellent lecture entitled, "Evening with Ehud Barak," a fascinating story of Israel. Nine hundred people attended. It was an excellent opportunity for people to learn about the real Israel. Congressmen Michael Bilirakis and his wife, Evelyn, took time from their busy schedules to attend. Bilirakis presence acknowledged the importance of the evening. It was also an excellent fundraiser for the synagogue.

Rabbi Dr. Stanley Yedwab was the Scholar in Residence. He was Rabbi Emeritus of Temple Beth Am of Lakewood, New Jersey. He was also a noted family therapist and teacher of Jewish history. His topic was: "The Great Controversies of Jewish History."

The Rabbi Gary Klein Youth Lounge was completed. It was across the courtyard from the the completely renovated Ariel Goldman Memorial Library. Lynn and Stephen Goldman, Ariel's parents, donated the funds along with many other Temple members to provide this new vibrant media facility in memory of their young daughter. Linda Wexler, volunteer librarian, identified the Temple needs and completed the library with the Judaica resources appropriate for a growing congregation. A new play area was built for the Preschool.

Rabbi Gary Klein Youth Center

Betty Salsburg Klapper

Cantor Deborah Jacobson

Betty Salsburg Klapper, Past President of Temple Ahavat Shalom, came from Wilkes-Barre, Pennsylvania. She was a life- long member of Temple B'nai Brith, a member of its Board of Trustees and Executive Committee, as well as the Executive Committee of the Boards of its Sisterhood and the Pennsylvania Chapter of the National Federation of Temple Sisterhoods. During World War II, she served in the United States Army's Women's Air Corps. In addition to being a wife and mother, she spent twenty five years as

the administrator of a health care facility. She is Past President of the Pennsylvania Chapter of the American College of Health Care Administrators. She has served on the Executive Committee of the: American Healthcare Association, National Conference on Intermediate Care, National Conference on Adult Day Care Centers, National Conference on Consultation Services, Pennsylvania Healthcare Association, and Family Services Association of Wilkes-Barre. She was a delegate to the 1981 White House Conference on Aging.

Rabbi Frank Sundheim

Rabbi Frank Sundheim graduated from the University of Pennsylvania with a Bachelor of Arts Degree, in 1953. He graduated with a Master of Arts in Hebrew Letters from Hebrew Union College-Jewish Institute of Religion, in 1958. He was ordained at Hebrew Union College-Jewish Institute of Religion and has a Doctor of Divinity Degree. He was an Army chaplain, Regional Director of the Southeast Council of the Union of American Hebrew Congregations, and rabbi of three different congregations, including Congregation Schaarai Zedek. He has taught at the University of Tampa and University of South Florida. He has been a cantorial soloist on several occasions. He and his wife, Adrienne, have three children and five grandchildren.

Highlights of 2005

There are currently 600 family members. Temple Ahavat Shalom offers the Krieger Early Childhood Center, Weaner Religious School, youth groups, Sisterhood, Couples Club, Adult Education Institute, and Scholar-in-Residence programs.

Cantor Deborah Jacobson

Deborah Jacobson became the Cantor of Temple Ahavat Shalom in July, 2005. She had served previously for a three-year period at Temple Beth El in Stamford, Connecticut. While completing her studies for her master's degree and ordination, she served as Cantor at the West End Synagogue in New York City.

Deborah Jacobson was born in Cleveland, Ohio on July 19, 1966. She was raised in New Rochelle, New York and graduated from the Westchester Day School in Mamaroneck, New York. She received a Bachelor of Arts Degree in Theater/Voice and Literature from New York University. She became a teacher in public and religious schools, as well as a performer in several off-Broadway plays, including "The Diary of Anne Frank." She appeared in a number of TV shows and in cabaret performances. She wrote, "Survival Jobs: 154 Ways to Make Money While Pursuing Your Dream." It was published in two editions in 1996 and in 1998, and became a Quality Paperback Book Club selection. In 2003, she wrote, "150 Jobs You Can Start Today." In June 2005, her first CD, "Shabbat Unplugged," was released.

Deborah married Jordan Jacobson on July 24, 1994. Jordan is a graduate of New York University and the University of Iowa. He is a professional writer.

In 1997, Deborah decided to pursue cantorial studies and entered the Jewish Theological Seminary in New York City. In 2002, she received her Master's in Sacred Music and a Diploma of Hazzan (Cantor) from the H. L. Miller Cantorial School of the Jewish Theological Seminary in New York City. While studying at the seminary, she spent one year at the Machon Schechter Cantorial School in Jerusalem. Because of her scholarship and potential, she received the H. L. Miller Fellowship. This recognition of excellence is awarded to an individual, "who will make a significant contribution in the musical life of the Jewish communities she/he will serve." Her goals as a cantor include encouraging all congregants to participate more fully in the services and in the community. She looks forward to sharing her great love of Judaism, its texts, music, traditions, and people. "I hope to involve our Temple Ahavat Shalom family in the joy, sacredness, and blessings of our heritage."

Youth Groups

The Junior Youth Group is for grades six through eight and the Senior Youth Group is for grades nine through twelve. The youth groups provide social events, informal Jewish education, Tzedakah/ Caring Community projects, as well as worship services. The youth programs strive to instill Jewish identity, foster commitment to the ideals and values of Reform Judaism, increase synagogue participation among the young members, and maintain a joyful, spirited connection to Judaism. Personal growth and leadership skills are promoted in a wholesome, social, Jewish environment. The youth groups often participate in special events with youth groups of other communities.

Sisterhood

The Sisterhood is a women's organization which strives to help women bond together, learn from one another, and share experiences that enable themselves and their families to grow and lead more fulfilling Jewish lives. The women are of different ages, education, and religious observances. The primary objective of Sisterhood is to provide education and social networking activities that meet the needs of the women of the congregation. Special projects conducted by the women include: Judaica shop; assisting Bar/Bat Mitzvah and confirmation students; rummage sales; youth scholarship fund; women's Purim dinner; and on going fundraising projects that benefit the Temple. The Sisterhood is affiliated with the Women of Reform Judaism.

CHAPTER 15

TEMPLE BETH-EL OF ST. PETERSBURG

Highlights of 1920-1929

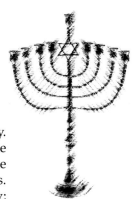

Highlights of 1926-1928

In September 1926, Jewish women who were Reform formed the Temple Beth El Auxiliary. The idea was formulated by Mrs. Gertrude Siegel Shane and Mrs. Sidney Wasserman. The object of the organization was to further Judaism and promote a friendly feeling among the Jewish people. The officers and members were: Mrs. Minnie Van Straaten, President; Mrs. Ella Gerst, Vice President; Mrs. Pauline Straus, Treasurer; Mrs. Arthur Jacobson, Secretary; Mrs. Sidney Wasserman, Corresponding Secretary; Executive Board Chairman, Mrs. Hannah Rice; Board Members, Mrs. Minnie Blumberg, Mrs. Lehwald, Mrs. Gertrude Siegel Shane and Mrs. William Cohen. The woman's auxiliary helped give birth to Temple Beth-El. They met in the home of Mrs. Sidney Wasserman and agreed to function as a religious and philanthropic group guided by the program of the National Federation of Temple Sisterhoods. They also agreed: to carry forth the faith of Judaism; to inspire the ideals of the faith in the young generation; and to become a symbol of the goodness of Jewish life.

Mrs. Jacob Van Straaten was its first President and Miss Eva Radzinski was its guiding spirit during its formative years. Eva was forty years old in 1926 and her mother, Henrietta, was seventy years old. They were both born in Pennsylvania. The second President was Mrs Myer H. Friendly (Leah H.). Myer was born in New York in 1863. Leah was born in Pennsylvania in 1870. Its third President was Eva Radzinski. The constitution was written by two sisters, Misses Holfter of Chicago, who were teachers. The women did everything from scrubbing floors to preparing Passover Seders to raising funds for the religious school and building improvements. They held many parties and presented numerous elaborate affairs which were attended by large numbers of people. They held Purim balls, masquerade balls, bazaars, and sponsored boat trips. All of these affairs were a huge financial success.

Many of the first Reform Jewish people were visitors and tourists who came to St. Petersburg. Later, permanent residents came from a variety of states. As these Jewish people arrived, they found many Jewish people who were Orthodox then later became Conservative. It was a desire of these Reform Jewish people, particularly the women, to establish a Reform Jewish congregation. Initially, since there was no rabbi, Mr. Jacob Van Straaten led the congregation in prayer, although they did not have a Torah or a permanent place to meet.

Highlights of 1928

At the laying of the cornerstone of Temple Beth-El, 400 Pasadena Ave South, on Sunday, March 4, 1962, Mr. M. Alan Friedman gave a first-person oral history of the founding of the beginnings of the Temple in 1928. He was introduced by Maurice A. Rothman, who said that Alan was one of the original founders and charter members of the Temple and also was Past President. M. Alan Friedman related the following: "Like all endeavors the beginning of Temple Beth-El is not an easy one. I believe the greatest handicap was that we were so few in number at the time. However, in 1928, we had our first Reform service. We had no Torah, but we had Union prayer books. How they came about I never did get to know. There were about forty odd persons, men and women, present at that service. It was conducted in a religious hall. I believe it was called the Spiritualist Church, or something. It was caddy corner from St. Anthony's Hospital on 7th Avenue and 11th Street. A couple weeks or so later, a gentleman came in to see me and asked me if I would like to help form a Reform Temple in this community. I said, by all means put us down, we'll be delighted to attend. About two weeks after that, I was asked to come to a place called the Rustic Lodge, which was on 39th Ave North, east of 4th Street. We had a lovely dinner, which was catered by a couple called Mr. and Mrs. Slatehow. After the dinner, we proceeded to organize. I was given the privilege of conducting its first meeting. And it was agreed upon that we have a Reform Temple in the city that was then named Temple Beth-El. Election of officers was held and the gentleman who was instrumental in rounding up quite a few of those attending this meeting was elected its President. We tried to raise some money and we succeeded in raising $1,500 that evening. That sum never escaped me. We met for Friday evening services in different places and we continued services at the Spiritualist Hall for some time. We had some gentleman come over from Tampa to conduct services for us. A few months later, we had another election of officers. We had a better gathering then. The visitors from the North had arrived. A gentleman by the name of Myer Friendly was elected President, a very capable gentleman. We had a man by the name of Furst as Vice President, and David Kapker as Secretary. David Kapker (or Kapkrip) was the business manager for the Pinellas Telephone Company of this city and later transferred to Tampa to hold the same position. After a while, he succeeded in getting a gentleman by the name of Judge M. Henry Sohon (actually it was Cohen) from Tampa, and he conducted services for us for about a year or so. He was brought here every Friday night–he did not drive, but his wife did–and he commuted that way. The following year Mr. Friendly conducted services. After his term of office, Rudy Miller of Plattsburgh, New York, who was a constant visitor here, year in and year out, conducted services. He was Treasurer of our organization. We moved from the Spiritualist Hall to the Knights of Columbus Hall, if you please, where we conducted services for about a year. After that, we rented a store, in an apartment building on 2nd Street, and the corner of Fifth Avenue, where we held the High Holy Days Services, and we engaged the first rabbi, just for the holidays. His name was Rabbi Alexander Kleinfeld, father of Frank Kleinfeld, which most of you undoubtedly know. His services

did not continue with us after the holidays, that was our agreement. Shortly after that he was engaged by Congregation B'nai Israel. The next rabbi was a very young man just out of school, his name was Rabbi William Rosenblatt who was with us about close to two years and later he entered the chaplain service. The next rabbi was Dr. Leonard Rothstein, a very capable man, but he did not remain here too long for reasons of his own. After Rabbi Rothstein, we engaged Rabbi Pizer W.Jacobs, who stayed with us until 1920 (He probably meant to say 1940). Hereafter serving in that capacity was Rabbi E. Wilner who was with us, I believe until 1947. After that came Rabbi Albert Michaels who was with us until 1956 or 1957, I believe. Then we were happy to bring with us our present Rabbi, David Susskind. About 1934, no it was in the early 1940s, we were looking for a location to build. I have omitted the fact that when we built the old Temple in 1932; we just built a shell. Finances were very meager at that time. It was completed however, in 1934. In the early 40s, we looked for another location. Our membership had grown and we bought a lot on 16th Street and 15th Avenue North. It was decided that that was not a favorable place so we sold the lot and instead we remodeled the old building, adding certain facilities, committee rooms, study for the rabbi, social hall, etc., all of which you know. And this about brings us up to date. I must give a great deal of credit to our Sisterhood which has been the right arm of our Temple, but now we have two right arms, I guess one of them you call the "southpaw" and that's our present Brotherhood, who are doing very nice work. And that just about brings us up to date."

About forty men and women attended the first service. Since the group did not have a name, and even though services were being held in various homes because there was no reform synagogue building, Jacob Van Straaten contacted Rabbi Zeppin of the Free Synagogue in Cincinnati and asked if it would be appropriate to use the name Temple Beth-El for the newly formed organization. Rabbi Zeppin said the name was appropriate and could be used and thus Temple Beth-El came into being. A second written document indicates that someone from the congregation discussed this issue with Rabbi Weis (or Weiss) of Cincinnati. A young man, who came during the winter, played the piano. One of the young Jewish girls was the soloist. Services were held on Friday evenings as well as on Saturday mornings.

Temple Beth El was formally organized in 1928. Herman Cohen, a well-known local merchant, was President. Dora Littsfield was an early Sisterhood founder. She gave $25,000 to the Temple. Mary Stichler, who lived to 101 years of age, left $25,000 in her estate to the Temple. J. L. Cooperman was one of the founders of the Temple. His son, Leonard Cooperman, was the second Jewish attorney in St. Petersburg. Myer Friendly moved here from Elmira, New York.

The women were under the leadership of Mrs. Henrietta Radzinski, Mrs. Minnie Ross, Mrs. Adolph Rosenthal, Hannah Pfeiffer (her brother Phil Heller helped), Mrs. Max Goodkind, Mrs. Sidney Wasserman, Mrs. Jacob Van Straaten, and Mrs. Morris Newmark. A piece of land was chosen on Mirror Lake for a synagogue, but was lost to the congregation.

Highlights of 1930-1939

Highlights of 1930

The Beth-El Auxiliary (Sisterhood) continued to sponsor Sabbath services. They sold raffles of homemade crafts, sold candy made by the members, held card parties, and established a fund for the Atlanta Orphans Home. In February, the first Memorial Fund was established in the form of a tree. In November, the women helped with Red Cross drives and were honored for bringing in the largest collection–according to its size–of any other organization. Also in November, the first joint Temple and Sisterhood meeting was held. The congregation had only twelve members–and only nine were active. As a result, Mr. Heller stated his support for having women as members. After much discussion, it was decided that for a nominal fee of five dollars, women could be members of Temple Beth-El. Five of the nine Congregational members voted yes.

The congregation met at the Knights of Columbus Hall at 433 3rd Street South. The Sisterhood also had their meetings there. The Sisterhood was praised by the St. Petersburg Times in an article dated November 13, for giving large sums to charity. Although, the Sisterhood was saving money to help build a new Temple, they took a part of the proceeds from their bazaars, card parties, and membership dues and donated to help needy people in the general community. The Sisterhood membership fluctuated with the tourist season with a high of 100 women during the winter months. Eva Radzinski was President. The Sisterhood met monthly and the Board of the Temple, with President Myer Friendly, met monthly.

Highlights of 1931

Temple Beth El services were held at the Knights of Columbus Building at 339 9th St South (Dr. Martin Luther King Jr. Street South). Myer Friendly was President and helped conduct the services. Frequently, guest speakers gave presentations on Friday nights. Every week, different women cleaned up the facility. To keep warm a small stove had to be replenished with a log of pine every fifteen minutes and a small kerosene heater was dragged by a handle from one end of the hall to another.

Highlights of 1932

Land was purchased for a new temple in April. A building shell was constructed. The Sisterhood voted to participate in fund-raising by sponsoring card parties at the Knights of Columbus at $.50 a ticket, and subsequently at members homes every Wednesday. The women created a hope chest of handmade items that were raffled off.

Highlights of 1933

During the summer, Temple Beth El erected its new house of worship at 757 Arlington Ave.. It was first used in September during the High Holy Days. The Temple was designed by Hadly and Nordstrom, local architects. Conflicting written reports indicate that the building was erected under the guidance of Henry Greenburg, Chairman, and/or Mrs. Henrietta Radzinski, Chairman. Probably both served at one time or another. Members of the building committee were: Mr. and Mrs. Sherman Pace (she became Mrs. Lawrence), Mrs. V. H. Pace, Phil Heller, Hannah Pfeiffer (widow of Abraham), Bert Goldberg (wife Esther), J. Miller, M. Alan Friedman, George Krause, Eva Radzinski (President of Sisterhood), I. B. Kogen and Mrs. H. Pfeiffer. It was built through the efforts of the Sisterhood of Temple Beth El. Over time the Sisterhood continued to substantially provide help to the new synagogue including a brand-new heating system. The officers of the Sisterhood were Mrs. Max Goodkind, President, Miss Eva Radzinski, First Vice President, Mrs. I. Kogen, Second Vice President, Mrs. Agatha Woolner, Secretary and Mrs. Freudenberg, Treasurer. It was a small building without air-conditioning. It had a leaky roof. Seders were held there.

At that time most of the Jewish people of St. Petersburg belonged to both the conservative synagogue and reform temple. They would go to the evening services at Temple beth-El, and the morning services at Congregation B'nai Israel.

Rabbi William H. Rosenblatt

In December, Rabbi William H. Rosenblatt became the spiritual leader of Temple Beth El of St. Petersburg. He graduated from the University of Pennsylvania and Hebrew Union College of Cincinnati. He conducted services in the newly erected temple. He had been highly recommended by the dean of Hebrew Union College, Professor Julian Norgenstern. Prior to the arrival of Rabbi Rosenblatt, Judge Henry Cohen of Tampa, longtime Secretary and Past President of Schaari Zedek of Tampa, conducted the services for several years. Louis Miller of Plattsburg, New York had been the congregational leader.

Rabbi Rosenblatt developed a full program of services and activities to the Jewish, as well as non-Jewish community. Immediately, registration of children started for the religious school. A curriculum was developed for various classes based on the most modern principles of religious education. The Bible study class was started as well as a a series of lectures dealing with the problems of religion and current important events. A men's club, literary circle, and Junior Beth El were organized to meet the interests and needs of the members of the congregation and their friends. Saturday morning services were added to the already existing Friday evening services. One of Rabbi Rosenblatt's first sermon topics was: "The Vision for a New Day." He discussed the transformation of society and the role of religion in the new civilization that was being built. He also presented other interesting topics including: "Time, the Priceless Possession of Man"; "Why We Pray," "At the Altar of Love," "The United States in Transition under the New Deal," and "Living by Your Standard." Rabbi Rosenblatt also presented "Music's Aid to Religious Idealism," "How Shall We Walk Together," "The Hope of the Needy" and "A Forgotten Page in History," which dealt with the Jewish participation in the discovery of America.

Highlights of 1934

On January 19, the Temple Beth El building located at 757 Arlington Avenue was dedicated. About 300 people filled the Temple, many from the non-Jewish community. The Temple was decorated with banks of palms and flowers donated by Mrs. Charles Levinson. Eva Radzinski designed a tablet with the names of all those contributing to the memory of the dedication night.

Rabbi David L. Zielonka of Schaarai Zedek of Tampa delivered the dedication speech. The choir was under the direction of Mrs. Leonora Wilkerson. The choir sang "Lift Up Ye Heads O Ye Gates," "Come Let Us Praise," "Sheheheyonu," "How Lovely Are Thy Dwellings," "To Worship God in Truth," "Our Pious Fathers." There was a solo by Mr. Walter Otto, who had been a cantor in a synagogue in Evansville, Indiana. Rabbi Rosenblatt placed the Torah in the Ark. The officers of the Temple were: J. L. Miller, President, St. Petersburg; I. Kogen, Vice President, Chicago; Louis Miller, Secretary, Plattsburg, New York; and V. H. Pace, Treasurer, St. Petersburg. The key to the synagogue was presented by Mr. H. Greenburg and accepted for the congregation by President J. L. Miller.

The Perpetual Lamp was donated by Mrs. Sophie Mayer. It was lit by a member of the Mayer family. The invocation was given by Judge M. Henry Cohen of Schaarai Zedek. Rabbi Rosenblatt read the Sabbath Service. Greetings were given by Mayor R. G. Blanc, Chaplain E. A. Edwards, who spoke on behalf of the Protestant churches, and Rev. J. F. Enright, who spoke in behalf of the Catholic churches. The dedication sermon was given by Rabbi Zielonka. The Adoration was given by Rabbi Rosenblatt and the final greeting and benediction was given by Rabbi A. Kleinfeld of B'nai Israel Congregation of St. Petersburg.

Rabbi Zielonka in his dedication speech said, "I deem it a singular privilege to be present tonight at the dedication of this splendid little building to the service of God and of man. Since coming to Tampa I have taken a very sincere interest in the gradual unfoldment of your ideals working to the end of taking your rightful place in the realm of liberal religious thinking as a Reform congregation. I have been keenly aware of the many problems that you've had to face and of the splendid courage displayed in striving for better things at a time when organizations were most timid due to the pressure of economic conditions. I congratulate you for your many accomplishments and pray for your continued achievement and success. I'm reminded of the events which transpired for our father, Jacob, at Beth-El, when having perceived a vision as he lay asleep in the great out-of-doors, Jacob awoke thrilled by the experience which had been his and exclaimed: How all-inspiring is this place. Truly this is a house of God and this is a gate of heaven. (Gen.28: 17) The lesson of that utterance should remain with each of us as a constant reminder of the Temple building, whether it be large and ornate or small and simple, is but the outward symbol of the spirit which pervades the membership of that Temple. Your untiring efforts have made this, indeed, a Beth-El, a house of God...(The threefold duty of the synagogue was to be a:)Beth Tefillah, House of Worship; Beth Ha-Midrash-House of Religious Instruction and Education; Beth Ha-Keneseth, House of Communal

Temple Beth-El 1934.

Gathering for Social Betterment...To this threefold duty, I dedicate this Temple – May it prove worthy of the challenge which has been placed before it. May the succeeding years find ever renewed courage. May the blessings of harmonious relationships serve to firmly establish you as a Beth-El, a House of God. Amen"

On the façade, the building declared itself to be "A House of Prayer for All People." People assembled here for the Sabbath, Festival, and High Holy Day services. They had Bar / Bat Mitzvahs, confirmations, weddings, baby naming, and consecration of little children. They spoke tender words of farewell to the departed and repeated the Kaddish for loved ones. "Through war and peace, hope and frustration, joy and sorrow, life and death, Beth-El has been the House of Prayer where the thoughts of all winged their way heavenward to God with the assurance that The Lord is nigh, to all who call upon him in truth. The synagogue has ever been the Jewish House of learning, inspiring our young and old with a hunger for knowledge as the study of their sacred literature and learned the wisdom of the Bible and the lessons of the rabbis. Through the synagogue, the Jew has handed down the ideals of the Torah from generation to generation, obedient to the will of God that "Thou shall teach them diligently unto thy children." (The author of this paragraph is not known.)

A few weeks after the dedication of the new Temple, the Sisterhood helped pay off the mortgage. They contributed $1,120.50 to the Temple building fund, with only $1,000 needed. Eva Radzinski designed a special scroll on which individuals and families were inscribed for a sum of $100 each. The design of the scroll was symbolic, showing the broken columns depicting Jewish faith, the first Temple of King Solomon showing that Judaism lives on, the Star of David and the Sabbath light. The scroll was taken to the home of Miss Radzinski and was supposed to be returned to a permanent place in the Temple on the 10th anniversary of the founding of the congregation. Eva Radzinski said, "A Temple cannot prosper without its women who are always active in the hopes of (creating) a future ."

Rabbi Rosenblatt conducted the first confirmation class. Edward Woolner and Alvin Cohen were the first two confirmants. Edward Woolner spoke on "Our Heritage" and Alvin Cohen spoke on the theme of "The Eternal People." Rabbi Rosenblatt delivered a brief sermon on "A Challenge to Youth." In subsequent weeks, Rabbi Rosenblatt gave presentations on, "Shall Democracy Survive," "The Founding of Liberal Judaism," and "The Future of Religion."

Rabbi Rosenblatt, in his presentation on liberal Judaism, paid homage to Rabbi Isaac Mayer Wise. Rosenblatt said, "All great movements are inspired by men of great vision. Liberal Judaism was founded by Isaac Mayer Wise. This seer of liberal thought through the figure of his personality created not only a liberal Judaism in America, but also inspired a more expansive spirit for religion in general. His life story is a thrilling tale, his life's work is a great monument of human endeavor. The inspiration of his activity led to the founding of several institutions whose work fosters the liberal spirit of religion."

Rabbi Rosenblatt addressed the congregation of the United Liberal (Universalist-Unitarian) Church when he gave his presentation, "The Future of Religion." He said, " Religion is age-old. Its development has been slow, its philosophy of life has been influenced by tradition, and today that philosophy is being challenged.

Is religion as it is constituted today capable of meeting the needs of humanity? Religion may be defined as the expressed desire of man to raise the human personality to a level approximating divine intelligence. In more simple language, religion desires that we live in a God-like fashion. In general, this is the hope of all religions, whether fundamental or liberal, whether Protestant, Catholic, or Jewish. However, the present state of civilization indicates the failure of religion in reaching its ultimate objective. This does not mean that religion has failed, but that the various religions fail to influence the bulk of humanity in its living. There is a great future for religion but that future depends upon an awakening of various religions. Since religion claims to be a dominant world force, and since it has failed to establish a somewhat stable civilization, the time has come when it should examine its way that it may see how to rise above the degenerating forces wrecking the highest form of civilization ever built by man. It must assume a great responsibility for the breakdown of our civilization and precarious condition in which mankind finds itself today. A realization of the true aims of religion will justify its existence and, moreover, demonstrate in a practical way, it's real power and worth. The future of religion depends not upon the solution of economic distress, or other complex problems of our days, but upon the development of a fundamental characteristic lacking in our civilization which will enable us to solve these difficulties and produce a greater happiness for a greater number. The key to the future progress of religion is a development of a religious vision." Reverend Dr. George Gilmore of United Liberal Church and his congregation welcomed Rabbi Rosenblatt and applauded his presentation.

Despite the fact that in 1934 there was substantial anti-Semitism in St. Petersburg, nationally, and throughout the world, Rabbi Rosenblatt was asked to prepare the program for Armistice Day Services on Sunday, November 11. It was under the auspices of the Public Open Air Forum. Rabbi Rosenblatt presented "Religions' Prayer for Peace." President Walter Otto of Pier Chorus, led the audience in musical numbers.

On December 7, Rabbi Rosenblatt gave the anniversary sermon at the 40th Anniversary of Congregation Schaarai Zedek, which had been incorporated December 15, 1894. Rabbi George Solomon of Savannah, Georgia gave the sermon, "The Value of Unity." The President of Congregation Schaarai Zedek was Leo Weiss. Mrs. Annie Laurie Stanley played the organ and Mrs. A. B. Duffer was the sololist. She sang "The Lord Is My Shepherd" and "O Rest in the Lord."

Highlights of 1935
Rabbi Leonard J. Rothstein became the Rabbi for a brief period of time. Rabbi Rothstein conducted the High Holy Day services, as well as Friday night and Saturday's services. He spoke on several topics including, "Why Reform Jews Observe Only A One Day Holiday," "Immortality–Fact or Fiction," "The Sin Re-Interpreted," "Thou Shalt Rejoice–a Significant Command," and "What Is Reform Judaism?" The congregational family was small and the times were very difficult. Therefore, his stay was brief.

Highlights of 1936
Rabbi Leonard J. Rothstein was on the pulpit. He conducted services on Friday evenings.

Highlights of 1937
Rabbi Pizer Jacobs, who was on the pulpit, gave a presentation at Friday night services on "Israel's Philosophy of Life." He also conducted services on Saturday mornings. He invited the entire community to attend services. Hanukkah services were conducted by Rabbi Jacobs. He spoke on "What We Stand For." On Saturday morning, Rabbi Jacobs discussed the Torah portion of the week.

Highlights of 1938
The officers present at a meeting of the congregation on January 19 were, President B. B. Goldberg, Second Vice President V. H. Pace, Secretary and Treasurer Louis Miller, Trustees Mrs. J. Van Straaten, Mrs. H. Radzinski, Mrs. R. Goodkind, M. A. Friedman, J. L. Miller, J. Spearo, and M. Newmark. The President reported that the Temple was in first-class financial condition. The balance on hand as of December 30, 1937, at the Union Trust Company was $1,180.50. As of January 19, the cash on hand was $1,278.25. The savings account at the Florida National Bank was $458.20. The congregation consisted of twenty four members at $25 per year and four members (ladies) at $15 per year. There were $63 in donations and $204.25 in basket collections. Since the office of the Secretary-Treasurer was unconstitutional, two new offices of Secretary and Treasurer were approved and people were nominated for these positions. It should be noted that women were serving as trustees. Rose Goodkind reported on the creation of an organ fund. There was considerable discussion about the erection of a community house. The issue was tabled. Mrs. Pizer Jacobs was hired to help teach in the religious school. The Sisterhood became affiliated with the National Federation of Temple Sisterhoods.

Rabbi Leonard J. Rothstein

Highlights of 1939
Mr. Horace Goldsmith of the membership committee reported that the rabbi had been active in securing memberships for the Temple and at the present time, the congregation was larger than ever before in its history. Considerable work was done to maintain the integrity of the Temple. An organ was installed with Mrs. Rose Goodkind guaranteeing the payments. The Sisterhood started to sell Uniongrams at one dollar per package to establish Hebrew Union College Scholarships, maintain a dormitory, and pay $3.50 for a soloist at Friday evening services. The first payment was made by the organ fund and the second payment was almost ready. The women did community service work by helping with the donations for the American Legion's Iron Lung Fund, the Empty Stocking Fund, and the Denver Orphans Fund. The Women Formed a Red Cross Unit and knitted sweaters for an orphanage in London.

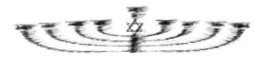

Highlights of 1940-1949

Highlights of 1940

The Memorial Tablet Committee reported progress on the movement to purchase and erect a Memorial Tablet in the Temple auditorium. A $50 fee would be charged for the purchase of a space on the tablet and all Memorial plates would be of uniform size.

Sonia Cohen, daughter of Mr. and Mrs. Louis Cohen, was confirmed by Rabbi Jacobs. There was a special musical program by Louis Hollingsworth, organist, and Walter Otto, soloist. Sonia gave a confirmation presentation. Mrs. Cohen had been honored the same week by being appointed by Major Joseph Bower of New York City, Director of Army and Navy Services of the Jewish Welfare Board, to represent the Board at Bay Pines on behalf of veterans of the Jewish faith. She had for some years independently carried on social service work there.

Rabbi Pizer W. Jacobs was very active in the congregation as well as in the community. He spoke from the pulpit about Abraham Lincoln in Illinois. He addressed the Open Forum at First Congregational Church. He presided at the annual Temple dinner. He gave a presentation to the men's club and arranged for the special speaker, Henry Morganthau, to address the people of St. Petersburg. All this was done in one week. Brotherhood week was shared with the First Avenue Methodist Church. Rabbi Jacobs organized a special luncheon to honor Reverend A. W. Gottshall, the Secretary of the Southern District of the National Conference of Christians and Jews. Temple Beth-El sponsored an open house with games and refreshments for the entire St. Petersburg community. Rabbi Jacobs gave the invocation of the Open Forum of the Mirror Lake Christian Church. At the Sisterhood Sabbath, he spoke on, "World's Greatest Need." Rabbi Jacobs presided over the annual service of the Jewish Youth Council of Temple Beth-El. Rabbi Jacobs was described as an individual who "Displays great skill and untiring skill and devotion."

Rabbi Jacobs was very influential in helping to guide the formation of the St. Petersburg Section of the National Council of Jewish Women. On May 10, Rabbi Jacobs sermon was, "The Power of Women in Human Progress." The first meeting of the chapter was on Wednesday, May 15, at the Central Bridge Studio at 137 2nd Street North. Mrs. Louis A. Cohen was appointed temporary President and Mrs. William Newman was appointed temporary Secretary by the group. The purpose of the organization was, "For betterment of the local community and preservation of democracy through a program of service and civics." The organization was not related to any specific religious organization. Its function was to work with other civic bodies in community affairs and not confine its efforts only to the Jewish community. The members followed a six-point program including, civics, service to the foreign-born, social welfare, social legislation and international peace. The organization conducted a survey of non-citizens in the community to assist them in becoming naturalized citizens. The members started a wardrobe closet to help clothe needy schoolchildren. There were thirty nine paid members who were admitted to charter membership. Mrs. Joseph Wohl and Mrs. Jerry Waterman of the Tampa section outlined a program for the group. Their very first action was to vote to contribute to the American Red Cross War Fund.

The Sisterhood announced its new officers. They were: Mrs. Pizer Jacobs (who had been reelected), President; Mrs. Jacob Van Straaten, Vice President; Mrs. Rose Claven, Recording Secretary; Mrs. Rose Goodkind, Corresponding Secretary; and Mrs. Lee Higer, Treasurer. A full schedule of events including book reviews, rummage sales and luncheons were planned for the following month. The men's organization was newly organized. Mrs. E. Lederer donated flowers to the Temple and Mrs. Sarah Solomon donated an embroidered white satin altar cloth. Mrs. Estelle Klein gave a set of books. Two readings, "Marblehead," and "Especially Jim" were given by Mrs. Rose Baran of New York. She was Past Grand President of the United Order of True Sisters, as well as its founder, and for twelve years, President

Rabbi Pizer Jacobs

of the Philanthropic League for Crippled Children and now Honorary President.

The St. Petersburg Jewish Youth Council participated in the Tampa Fair. They sang in the pageant, "Souls of America."

Don Silverberg's maternal grandmother, Esther Simon, a widow, moved from Cleveland, Ohio to St. Petersburg and lived in an apartment next door to the Silverberg home. She was not a club woman, but was much admired in the community for her concern for helping others. The congregation appreciated her willingness to be in charge of the Oneg Shabbat on many Friday nights. She served her famous Hungarian pastries and hand squeezed orange juice. Don, as a small boy, learned his sense of responsibility for others by helping his grandmother prepare the food and by helping transport the food on a trolley car to the Temple. Many years later, he served in numerous capacities at the Temple, including being President.

Highlights of 1941

Herbert J. Wilner became the rabbi. He served on the pulpit until 1947.

Highlights of 1945

Temple Beth-El was affiliated with the Union of American Hebrew Congregations. They also formally affiliated with the National Federation of Temple Sisterhoods, National Federation of Temple Brotherhoods, and the National Federation of Temple Youth.

Highlights of 1946

The kindling of the Sabbath lights was started at Friday night services in November. Sisterhood members offered the Blessing. When the congregation started to talk about building a new Temple, Sisterhood pledged $30,000 to furnish the kitchen.

Highlights of 1947

In the post-World War II era, the Sisterhood was involved in Meals on Wheels, programs for the blind, and both the men and women made a conscientious effort to join a variety of civic clubs. The Sisterhood started the Pinellas Braille Group that translated printed words into Braille for the visually impaired. Sisterhood has continued to help the Temple and help pay the expense of the Religious School.

Rabbi Herbert H. Wilner helped Temple Beth-El continue to grow. The congregation was rapidly outgrowing the current structure. The Temple drew people from North, South, East, and West and being a tourist city, the Temple swelled and contracted by season of the year. Some outstanding religious and public leaders came during the winter and attended the services, such as Rabbi Emeritus David Philipson, Mrs. Hugo Hartman, and Henry Morganthau Sr..

Jim Alan Friedman, President, Temple Beth-El, 1940–1942, 1944–1946.

Joint sessions of Religious and Hebrew School were held with Congregation B'nai Israel, which at that time was orthodox. Congregation B'nai Israel had been without a religious leader and neither congregation had had enough children to keep a Religious School going. When Rabbi Chapman was hired, he and Rabbi Wilner jointly conducted the Religious School.

Rabbi Wilner worked very effectively to promote goodwill between Christian and Jew in the community. Ministers and teachers outside of the Jewish faith had occupied the pulpit and had been well received. An entire Christian religious school class and their teacher attended the Temple services, which certainly helped to promote understanding and fellowship. Rabbi Wilner spoke regularly on local Jewish religious radio programs.

Rabbi Herbert Wilner

In November, the Temple bulletin for Beth-El was started. There was a great resurgence of building of synagogues in the United States. This interest was carried over into St. Petersburg in the initial planning of an enlarged and remodeled Temple Beth-El to meet the needs of the growing community.

Highlights of 1948

A men's club was organized. It was reorganized in 1954 as the Temple Beth-El Brotherhood with Sol Markman as President.

Highlights of 1949

The congregation purchased a lot for the purpose of building a new synagogue. There were 108 existing families and twenty eight new families were added. A $1,600 deficit

Rabbi Albert A. Michels

Morris Rosenberg, President, Temple Beth-El, 1949–1951, 1953–1954

was reported for the previous year.

Rabbi Michels talked about the significance of the celebration of Passover. He said, "We celebrate not only the deliverance of our war-worn and camp-conscious emigrees from the limbo of European areas and destitution, and the year of the establishment of the free Statehood of Israel, but it brings home to us, the ringing reality of the great tidings, after years of anticipation, of the fulfillment of the dream of our community–the assurance that this year, if possible, and if not, the next year, the building of the new Temple and Temple community house and center. What greater legacy for any community...."

Highlights of 1950-1959

Highlights of 1950

The property which was being considered for the new Temple was at 5th Ave North and 3rd St. However, finances were not in good shape. For the year 1949, there was an actual loss of $931.89. The bank balance on January 19, was $859.31. There was also a building fund balance of $13,966.55 and unpaid pledges of $14,900. There were 128 member families. The Cemetery Committee submitted a contract for $10,000, payable $500 a year with no interest for a period of twenty years. The plot consisted of 208 graves. The congregation decided to buy a $5,000 plot instead of the $10,000 plot.

At a special meeting of the congregation, on May 17, three major items were up for discussion: 1. Merger of Temple Beth El and Congregation B'nai Israel; 2. Rabbi's Contract for 1950-1951; and 3. Budget for 1950-1951. A report of the Merger Committee was made by Mr. M. Alan Friedman, Chairman. After hearing all of the pros and cons, a motion was made to accept the committee's report and carried by a vote of 49 to 3. It was then changed to a unanimous vote for a merger. However, Congregation B'nai Israel rejected the merger proposals.

Beaux Arts, a Temple organization with Irving Sohon as President, invited members and friends to its Purim masquerade and dance. Miss Charlotte Mount, known and admired by all individuals, a patron of the arts, and one of the original founders of

Beaux Arts, presented a concert of various selections.

Julian Morgenstern wrote about how to live Judaism. She said, "Judaism must be lived by our Jewish people confidently, courageously, eagerly, exultantly, with full appreciation of the worth of our heritage, of its indispensability for human salvation and of the lofty role which we, as its bearers and transmitters, are called upon to play in this real momentous and happier act in the drama of human life. It is a proud role indeed, from which we need not shrink, and the burden of which need not terrify us no longer, in which we may assume with faith, with purpose, and with self-consecration."

Highlights of 1951

The synagogue on Arlington Avenue was enlarged and remodeled in order to meet the needs of a larger congregation. A. Parrish was the architect. The cornerstone was laid on Sunday, May 13. In an impressive and inspiring ceremony, after the prayers were said and messages delivered by the many dignitaries, a trowel was raised and the cement set for the cornerstone, which bears witness simply with dignity to the consecration of a new edifice. This edifice, the Temple, is the Sanctuary of Israel. It was born out of Israel's longing for the living God. It has been to Israel, throughout their wanderings, a visible token of God.

On December 28-29, the new Temple and Temple Center were dedicated. The processional into the building was led by the building committee, President, past presidents and officers, and Rabbi Michaels carried the Scroll of the Law. The Torah was deposited in the Ark by Rabbi Albert A. Michels. Building Chairman Jonas Rosenthal presented the key for the new structure to Jack Miller, President of the congregation. Both individuals gave speeches. The perpetual lamp was rekindled by Max L. Abeles, a senior member of the congregation. The invocation was given by Rabbi Morris Chapman of Congregation B'nai Israel. A Hanukkah service was then conducted by Rabbi Michaels. The kiddush was chanted by Leon Donsky and the Hanukkah lights were blessed by Eva Radzinski, President, Temple Beth-El Sisterhood. Greetings were extended by Samuel G. Johnson, Mayor of St. Petersburg; William F. Davenport, Manager of the Chamber of Commerce; Reverend Ben F. Wyland, Executive Secretary, United Churches; Reverend Ernest T. Marble, United Liberal Church; and the Reverend Evan A. Edwards, former Rector, St. Peter's and Paul's Episcopal Church. The organist was Mrs. Bertha Mitchell and the soloist was William Morgan. The dedication sermon was given by Rabbi David L. Zielonka of Temple Schaarai Zedek of Tampa.

Rabbi Zielonka gave the address of dedication some eighteen years before, when the original Temple was built. At the second dedication, he said, "...On January 19, 1934, I urged you to bear in mind the three-fold purpose of the synagogue: a house of worship, a house of religious instruction and education, and a house of communal gathering and social betterment. The years that have intervened have found you constantly striving after these lofty purposes and I take joy in commending you for the high idealism that has guided you through the years and still motivates your growth and activity. Now that we again have assembled during this joyous season of dedication it is well that we reconsecrate Temple Beth-El to a reaffirmation of the past and rededicated to it still further new purposes....Temple Beth-El shall be rededicated to the service of God and to the carrying on of Judaism as we sincerely feel that it should be carried on....It is imperative, therefore, to make clear that for which this house of God shall stand in the future and dedicate it to those ideals. On the tomb of the great German poet and philosopher, Johanna Gottfried van Herder are inscribed three words–Licht, Light, Liebe, Love, Leben, Life. In these three words I would symbolize the objective for which this Temple stands and with these three words I would dedicate this building. In the first place, let this building ever stand for "light" not the light that comes to us through the sense of sight, but the light that comes to us from within, when we take time to reflect. This building stands for the supreme light, "God". ...Now the love for which this Temple shall stand should be first of all love for God. The classic Jewish expression

for this has ever been "Thou shalt love the Lord thy God with all thy heart, with all thy soul and with all thy might." And the Jew has interpreted this verse as referring to every human contact. Every human experience as a benediction. God was felt as the guiding spirit of all human endeavor... And this Temple shall also stand for love of fellow man....If this Temple stands for the light of God and the light of knowledge; if it stands for the love of God and the love of fellowman, it will of necessity stand for "LIFE"....This Temple will ask us to choose life, but at the same time, to choose the right kind of life. In making this choice, we must seek a proper balance between selfishness and unselfishness....Our object in life is not to accumulate riches alone, no matter how pleasant it may be to possess them, but to accumulate friendship and fellowship with their fellow man....And so, I would dedicate this building, this house of God, this monument of your devotion to the Jewish cause, first of all to "LIGHT". May the light of God and the light of knowledge ever find here its finest exponent and expression. I would dedicate this house of God to "LOVE", the love of God and the love of fellow man, and love within the household of Israel. I would dedicate it to "LIFE ", to true conceptions of living here and worthy examples to the world at large. And as this house is thus dedicated, I would ask divine favor upon those who are here assembled. Made these words find lodgment in your hearts and expressions in your lives in the future, "May the words of our mouths and the meditations of our hearts be acceptable before Thee, O Lord, Our Rock and Our Redeemer." Amen.

Eva Radzinski presented a "History of the Formation of Temple Beth-El-Organized 1926." In the written document she said, "My dear mother, Henrietta Radzinski, who was the inspiration of all good deeds in this community from 1919 to the time of her passing, 1940, gave of herself to the unity of our House of Worship, Temple Beth-El. There was also a beautiful poem in this document.

"A weaver sits at the loom of time,
And weaves a cloth of wondrous art,
Neither bought nor sold at earthly mart;

The weaver is God and the cloth he
weaves
Is the green cloth of the human heart."
It was with a feeling of mingled pride and
humility that the people began the process
of enhancing the existing congregation to
meet everyone's needs. However, by 1958,
once again the structure was too small to
accommodate the expanding activities of the
Religious School and Temple membership.

The Sisterhood celebrated its 25th
anniversary. Mrs. Jacob Van Straaten, one of
the founders from 1926 and first President,

told about the founding and
about the first officers. Miss
Eva Radzinski, one of the
founders, past President,
and current President, made
the table decorations, which
were very beautiful. Rabbi
Michels spoke glowingly

*1951. l. to r. Minnie (Mrs
Jacob) Van Straaten, Eva
Radzinski, Mrs. Maurice
Hyman*

of Mrs. Goodkind, who was retiring as
treasurer after many years of excellent
service. He spoke glowingly of her many
years of devotion to the Sisterhood and to
the Temple. Mrs. Shane of Clearwater and
Mrs. Wasserman, also original members
from 1926, spoke a few words. The
Sisterhood and Temple honored Rabbi
Michels by presenting him with a new car.

A dedication and consecration service
was held on Sunday, October 7 for the new
section of Beth-El at Royal Palms Cemetery.
The increasing size of the congregation
made this facility necessary.

Highlights of 1952

The Sisterhood had a special emergency
board meeting on February 7. Eva Radzinski
resigned as President of Sisterhood due to
illness. She had tirelessly worked for the
creation of a Reform congregation in St.
Petersburg, since she arrived in 1919. She
had given of herself in an unselfish manner
and had always led by example.

The additional space available in
the new Temple Center was used to
inaugurate cultural and recreational
activities. Instruction for adults in the
Hebrew language was begun. The series
of discussion lectures were started on
Wednesday evenings because of the requests
of congregants. Rabbi Michels presented a

survey of the problems facing modern men
and solutions every religion must offer
for survival. The Temple Youth became
organized and became part of the National
Federation of Temple Youth. They started
working together with Temple Schaarai
Zedek of Tampa. They presented a special
Sabbath service in honor of Isaac Mayer Wise.

Highlights of 1953

There were 164 member families with
twenty nine new families. The Temple was
in discussion with Congregation B'nai Israel
to form a joint religious day school. The
Brotherhood had reorganized.

The Temple Youth invited the Christian
youth of various churches to join them in a
seder. Rabbi Michels conducted the seder.
The Christian youth asked many questions
about the Jewish symbols and ceremonies.
It was a successful interfaith function.

On October 2, 1953, Rabbi Michels
dedicated the Great Torah. The money used
to purchase the Torah had been contributed
to the William and Rebecca Jacobus Fund
established through the efforts of Rose
Goodkind. The Torah was one of the
precious few rescued from Nazi Germany.
Rabbi Michels said, "As we begin the
readings from the opening portions, may
they become symbolic of the new growth
and augmented interest that is manifest
on all sides in the life of the Temple. It was
reborn for the congregation and gave special
meaning to the Jewish heritage which held
the Torah to be eternal and sacred. The time
spent reading and studying this Torah and
others is essential to a good life, but only if
it leads to ethical action and the benefit of
the world."

Mr. Jack Miller made a gift of $1,000
to the Temple program to help purchase
the Torah. He had previously served as
President of Temple Beth-El, and was one
of the notables who helped in the building
program and made a new structure possible.
Mr. Meyer Samuels procured the building
endowment for the Religious School. Mr.
Jonas Rosenthal erected the new structure.

Rose Goodkind, one of the pioneers of
Temple Beth-El, became the symbol of the
spirit of the congregation. Her devotion to
the finest and the best in religious life of

the Jewish community endeared her to all people. Through her chairmanship of the William and Rebecca Jacobus Memorial Fund, she brought the Temple its organ, menorahs, and eternal light. She celebrated her 85th birthday.

Rose Goodkind decided to leave money to purchase the land for a new synagogue. In 1959, the land was purchased at 400 Pasadena Avenue South, the current location of the Temple. Rose Goodkind's philosophy of life included: a firm belief in God; a pride in the glorious exploits of the Jewish people past and present; an understanding of Judaism which encompassed helping the orphaned and the aged; a joy in living in a free country, where there was a freedom of speech, of press and of worship; a need to do daily tasks as cheerfully and painstakingly as possible, thankful that God had given her the energy and strength to accomplish his work. She said, "The very flowers in my garden, the song of birds, the happy laughter of children, are my constant reminders that God is in everything...To create as much joy and laughter as I can is part of my faith. To try to put some sunshine in the shadows, to hide as much as possible any pain, not to dwell unduly on the sad part of life...I'm comforted with the knowledge that as the sunset of life approaches, that the Lord Is My Shepherd...One clear moonlight night, whenever I look into the sky, my heart responds to the knowledge that, the heavens declare the glory of God and the earth shows his handiwork."

The Temple celebrated its 25th anniversary. A dinner and dance was held in the social hall on Sunday evening, November 15. The speaker was Rabbi Sidney N. Lefkowitz of Congregation Ahavath Chesed of Jacksonville.

Highlights of 1954

As part of Brotherhood Week, the Sisterhood and Brotherhood held interfaith programs including: the Brotherhood Interfaith Religious Service which attracted community wide recognition and many distinguished local clergymen; and Sisterhood Soiree, where the elementary school teachers of St. Petersburg gathered at Temple Beth-El and had an excellent program. Mr. Nate Robinson was Program Chairman of Brotherhood and Mrs. Marion B. Ross was Sisterhood President. When President Eisenhower proclaimed Brotherhood Week, he was following the precept found in the book of Leviticus, "Love thy neighbor as thyself." This precept has been followed by Jewish people for millenniums and has been part of the 300 years of Jewish life in the United States.

Rabbi Michaels wrote an article in the monthly bulletin entitled, "We The Inheritors." He said, "Exactly 300 years ago...a little band of intrepid Jews (came to America)...not as refugees (or) renegades... They had a purpose and a plan. They were within themselves the seeds of what was to blossom out into the enduring principles of a Declaration of Independence and the American Constitution... That hearty handful of divinely determined men and women built their foundation well. Unwanted, they soon became indispensable; independent of soul, unheeded at first, the spark of their genius kindled a mighty and unquestionable flame: the American passion for free, but always fair practices. They insisted on and shared in all the rights and risks of the settlers. They stood guard. They took on the trying task of striving to shape the new society. From a penniless origin by dint of sacrificial living they were able even in a few years to subsidize the first Lutheran Church in America and the historic Trinity Church of what was to be known in later years as New York.(This was called brotherhood in action)...Because of this stalwart stock there has stemmed that unique line of Jewish-American immortals whose genius would have been lost had it not been for their initial shaping of fate by these pioneers: the Jacob Bar Simons, the Aaron Lopez's, the Franks, Hayim Solomons, Levys and Seixas Touros, who became the trailblazers for the spiritual, for the Wises, Brandeis and Einsteins of future generations. This is no idle, vacuous solicitation. It is a SUMMONS TO YOU individually to MEASURE YOURSELF up to the standards set by those who brought you your chance here thirty generations ago!" Rabbi Michaels spoke well for the uniqueness of the Jewish experience in

Joseph Silverberg, President, Temple Beth-El, 1955–1957.

America, its contributions to society at large, and the personal responsibility that each one of us must accept in continuing to build this wonderful society known as the United States of America.

Highlights of 1955

The major blessings to all Jewish people was the Supreme Court decision to abolish racial segregation in the public schools, the condemnation of Senator McCarthy for his violation of human and civil rights, and the friendship expressed by the President of the United States for Judaism and for the people of Israel. The major difficulties facing Jewish people were the development of hate groups and the distribution of arms and weapons of warfare to people in the Middle East to try to destroy the State of Israel.

The sense of brotherhood previously discussed was an ongoing mission of Temple Beth-El, as it was of all the synagogues in the county and in the nation. President Dwight D. Eisenhower said, "The spirit which lies behind our observance of Brotherhood Month is as old as our civilization. It goes back to the answer given to the first man who asked, "Am I. my brother's keeper?"... We live in a period in which the question has a new sharpness and the new age, because there are new forces in the world which divide and threaten men, forces which work to lock each man within the prison of his own mind, which make friend distrust friend, nation distrust nation. In the face of these forces, it is imperative that we heroically, by word and deed, give voice to our faith: that every man is indeed his brother's keeper, that no human being in the world can escape his spiritual involvement in what happens to any other human being, that no man, in the troubled sea of mankind, can be an island."

There were sixty children in the Religious School, with an average attendance of eighty percent weekly. Twelve children attended Tuesday and Thursday classes. Most of the teachers returned their paychecks to the Temple. They taught for free. Seventeen adults enrolled in the Hebrew classes. William Morgan, Cantorial Soloist, also made a significant contribution to the Religious School. He

Rabbi David Susskind

was the Cantorial Soloist from 1954-1957. The Temple participated in the celebration of the Tercentenary observance at Pasadena Community Church. The Sisterhood opened the Rose Goodkind gift shop.

President Joseph Silverberg, in his annual Congregational speech, talked about the period of time when the previous Rabbi had left and the arrival of the new rabbi, David Susskind. The ritual committee used a total of six rabbis and lay leaders during this time. The rabbis were, Sidney Tedesche, Louis I. Newman, Henry Sandman, Israel Gerber, Charles Mantinband, and David J. Susskind. In addition, three local ministers, helped out. They were Reverend Ben F. Wyland, Rev. Dr. J. Wallace Hamilton, and Rev. Dr. Thomas W. Nadel. Judge H. L. Sebring, Dean of Law, Stetson University, also assisted. Dr. Norman L. Goldberg acted as Administrator of the Temple.

Highlights of 1956

Although, he had left the Temple in December 1955, Rabbi Michels still gave the annual addresses to the Needle Workers Ingathering, the Elks Memorial Service, and the Congregational Church Interfaith Luncheon. The Committee on Pulpit Affairs started the process of finding a new rabbi. The Honorable Judge H. L. Sebring, Dean of the Stetson University School of Law, gave a presentation to the congregation. He had been designated by the President of the United States as a member of the Nazi War Crimes Tribunal in Nurenberg, Germany. He had been a member of the prosecution team. The preteen group was very active. House of David Community Church, across from the Temple, emphasized the similarities between the religions and not the differences.

Rabbi David J. Susskind

President Joseph Silverberg announced that Rabbi David J. Susskind would become the spiritual leader of Temple Beth-El. Rabbi Susskind, in his acceptance letter, wrote, "It is my fervent prayer that the covenant we are now entering may be symbolic of an even greater bonded mutual affection and understanding which shall be created between us. I feel confident that in such harmony we shall find many rich and rewarding experiences as we devotedly serve the aims of the Temple and advance the ideals of Judaism." Rabbi Susskind came to the pulpit on July 1.

Rabbi David J. Susskind brought about many innovations. He won the Liberty Bell Award. He started Bat Mitzvah with Susan Wides being the first one. He started a change from an extremely liberal congregation to one that was somewhat more traditional. Rabbi Susskind said, "Our Temple is established upon the precept where faith and friendship meet, will continue to hold aloft the promise of fulfillment to all in our community who desire to join with us in pursuing a rational and a liberal philosophy of Judaism."

Highlights of 1957

Rabbi David J. Susskind was consecrated at a special Sabbath eve service in honor of his ministry at Temple Beth-El, for his community work, and for his consistent effort to expand brotherhood activities throughout the community. Rabbi David Zielonka of Congregation Schaarai Zedek of Tampa delivered the consecration discourse.

The Sisterhood, in keeping with the theme of Brotherhood Month, sponsored an "Institute on Judaism" for public school teachers. The Sisterhood began its Braille program and financially underwrote it. The Braille program originated with the National Federation of Temple Sisterhoods. Seven women started to study braille in order that they could transcribe books for use by the visually handicapped. Six of the seven women were certified by the Library of Congress. The original group was started in St. Petersburg by Mrs. Sybil Kasanof. The group members were Miriam Weiss, Harriet Miller, Esther Belon, Sherrie Richman, Lillian Cordell, June Seligman, and Toby Bresler.

Mr. and Mrs. Louis Gerstkin may have planted the seeds which resulted in the nationally recognized Temple Beth-El Art Festival. They donated to the synagogue an etching, "The Seekers," by the internationally renowned American Artist Joseph Margulies. His work is shown at the Metropolitan Museum of Art, the Brooklyn Museum,

New York Public Library, Yale University, Baltimore Museum of Art, Library of Congress, and the Smithsonian Institute.

Twenty two new member families joined the Temple. At the High Holy Days, Bertha Mitchell was the organist and William Morgan was the cantorial soloist. New projects under development were: a children's choir to accompany Saturday morning worship; formation of a Temple Youth Group of teenagers to affiliate with the Southeastern Federation of Temple Youth; the organization of a Mr. and Mrs. Couples Club for the younger members; a series of adult education courses for study and to acquire the skills of contemporary Jewish life; and cultural programs by guest lecturers and performers of national Jewish prominence. The adult education courses consisted of lectures, discussions, and guest speakers on vital subjects for the American Jew. The course was one of inquiry and search for a mature philosophy of life and the Jewish concepts of God.

In the late 1950s, anti-Semitism in St. Petersburg began to abate and the Jewish people became acknowledged and accepted in the community. Temple members regularly babysat for their Christian neighbors at Pasadena Community Church during Christmas Eve Services. When the church obtained its new carillon, it played Jewish melodies for Temple members as they arrived for Sabbath services

Because of the significant growth of the congregation, a planning commission was appointed to consider expansion needs of the Temple. Lee Weinberg was Chairman. The other members were J. Silverberg, M. Ross, S. Weinman, I. Miller, A. Seligman, Dr. P. Hill, J. Robison, M. Rothman and M. Black. There was a desperate need to expand the religious school because classes were being held in two separate locations and the facilities lacked proper desks or black boards and had acoustical problems.

Rose Goodkind, a Temple pillar, passed away. The land for the new Temple was purchased with the funds which came from Rose's estate. The grounds were dedicated to her memory. She was one of the noblest and best people of the congregation. She was a symbol of love and dedication to all

Marion B. Ross, President, Temple Beth-El, 1957–1962, 1971–1973.

Rose Goodkind

that knew her. Rabbi Susskind said, "Indeed, nothing is truer (the sadness attached to her loss) of our beloved Rose Goodkind, that she was very dear and very precious to all of us. If there be any realization of the misfortune of the solemn hour, it is the recognition that an extraordinary woman has fallen from our midst; one who was so absolutely unique, so great in stature, leadership and inspiration, and so tremendously devoted to our Temple that it is impossible to penetrate the depth of her character or measure the immense vacancy she leaves. There was a mysterious magnetism about her that drew people to her. We all loved her because she loved all of us. She wore an invisible crown of nobility that radiated strength and dignity and which pervaded her presence with majesty and good cheer. But these traits do not in any way exhaust her character. Above and beyond them was her dedicated and stalwart service. Hers was a consecration that sprung from a belief that no one can render greater service than by keeping the lamp of Israel's Eternal Light burning in the sanctuary as a symbol of God's eternal presence in the universe. She exemplified the virtues of Jewish devotion and loyalty with the assets of American womanhood. She was a gracious translation of the...Woman of Valour." A Rose Goodkind Memorial Fund was established as an everlasting tribute to her memory.

Jacob L. Miller, Irwin Miller's father, passed away. The memorial written for him talks about an excellent individual. It reads, "Jacob L. Miller—The congregation, its officers and Board of Trustees of Temple Beth-El mourn the departure unto life eternal of our dearly beloved friend, Jacob L. Miller. His many years of dedicated service and unswerving devotion as a founder, Past-President, and trustee of the congregation ranks him among the stalwarts who pillared our temple. In Jack Miller, we have lost one of our most consecrated spirits, as well as a leading citizen. No monument really needs to be established as a memorial tribute to him, for the continuing existence of our sacred institution stands as an everlasting memorial to his vision and deeds. To the family of our beloved friend, servant and leader, we extend our profound sympathy."

The essence of the previous memorial and what was written is one of the important reasons why documents should be saved and why a history should be written of all synagogues and organizations. How would we know about this great leader some fifty years later when there is no marker at the synagogue, the older congregants are mostly gone, and the newer congregants are unaware of their heritage?

Highlights of 1958

A new Torah was given to the congregation by Mr. and Mrs. Lee Weinberg in honor of their 25th wedding anniversary. They also gave the breastplate, Torah mantle, binder and pointer. The Torah was dedicated on February 2. A second new Torah scroll was a gift from the family and friends of Theodore Carr. The Torah mantle was given by the Carr family. The dedication was held on February 7. Eleven children were confirmed on May 25. Land purchase procedures were started for the current Temple on Pasadena Avenue. There were 200 children in the religious school. Because of the shortage of space the religious school held classes at St. Petersburg Junior College. Twenty five new member families joined the congregation.

Highlights of 1959

The growing needs of the religious school prompted the Religious School Committee to hire a director and an administrator. Six children were confirmed on June 11. Harry Simon was the cantorial soloist.

On November 26, a Consecration of Ground Ceremony was held for the Temple Beth-El sanctuary-religious school. William Morgan sang the national anthem, followed by the invocation by Rabbi Morris B. Chapman of Congregation B'nai Israel. Rabbi David Susskind gave the welcoming address. Greetings were extended by Thomas M. Carney, State Legislator, Edward F. Brantley, Mayor, City of St. Petersburg, and Rev. George R. Savige, Executive Secretary, United Churches of Greater St. Petersburg. Maurice A. Rothman was Chairman, Building Committee. The Benediction was given by Rabbi Harry Richmond of B'nai Israel Congregation of Clearwater.

Highlights of 1960-1969

Highlights of 1960

The existing temple building was purchased by the Order of the Scottish Rite with a closing taking place on November 1. Morris Lapidis, an architect from Miami, was commissioned to design the new Temple. He was one of the outstanding architects in the country and had designed the Fountainebleu, Eden Roc, and Algiers hotels in Miami Beach and synagogues for congregations in Miami, Hewlett, Long Island, and Brooklyn, New York. The architectural committee consisted of Stanley Freifeld, Lowell Fyvolent, Sanford Goldman, David Gorman, Maurice Rothman, Lee Weinberg, Sidney Weinman and Albert Zwick, under the chairmanship of Irwin Miller.

Ten young people were confirmed. The temple office was moved to a temporary location near the new building site.

Highlights of 1961

The cornerstone for the new building was a link between the old and the new. The old cornerstone, which was marble, was removed from the old building downtown and reversed and then was used for the new cornerstone, thereby signifying the continuity of Jewish life from generation to generation.

The Pillar of Light, later known as Jacob's Ladder, was designed to be the backdrop for the new bema. The congregants moved to the current location in time for the High Holy Day services. President M. B. Ross said, "... we have fashioned our Temple in order to worship the Lord in the beauty of holiness and to train our children in the way they should grow." Rabbi Susskind said, "It is evident from our achievement of a magnificent edifice that we have adequately mobilized our resources and energies to successfully respond to our needs for physical expansion. Today, the need for our spiritual growth and deepened knowledge and awareness in the realms of God, Torah, Israel is no less demanding and challenging than our structural needs were before. The same zealous devotion, comparable resources, and total participation is now warranted to

truly complete the purpose,function, and design of our Beth-El."

Temple Beth-El 1960. Middle, original interior in 1962.

Highlights of 1962

There were seven children in the confirmation class. In addition to their academic and religious subjects, they were taught, "there is no dignity without religion," a lesson that was meant to stay with them for the remainder of their lives. The adult Jewish education program presented the topics , "History of Living Bible," " Great Controversies in Judaism," " Basic Jewish Beliefs," "Dynamics of Family Living," "Giants of Jewish History," and "Designs for the Jewish Home." Thirty nine new families joined the congregation.

There had been a considerable demographic change in the congregation over the years. By 1962, sixty percent of

Pillar of Light (Jacob's Ladder) backdrop for the bema. Photo taken at Bar Mitzvah of David Verona.

the congregation earned their livelihood in the community and about forty percent were retired. The congregation family membership was 300, with 175 children in the religious school, and thirty five in the Sabbath weekday Hebrew School. There had been an increase of about 2,000 Jewish families in St. Petersburg and vicinity. A new preschool was opened at the Temple.

Highlights of 1963

The Board of Trustees bought additional property adjacent to the reserve section in Royal Palm Memorial Park. On the weekend of February 22, the house of worship was dedicated and the members re-dedicated themselves to their Jewish faith. The pulpit guest was Rabbi Leon I. Feuer of Toledo, Ohio, the President-Elect of the Central Conference of American Rabbis. Thirteen children were confirmed.

Highlights of 1964
Cecile and Malcolm Berko

Cecile Hoffman Berko was born December 3, 1938, in Chicago, Illinois, and was raised in South Bend, Indiana. She received the Bachelor of Arts Degree in Education from the University of Michigan in 1960, then taught in the South Bend, Phoenix, Arizona, and St. Petersburg, Florida school systems. She was married on August 4, 1963 to Malcolm Jay Berko. He was born in Cleveland, Ohio and raised in Dayton, Ohio. He graduated from the University of Dayton in 1960 and became a stockbroker. He wrote a syndicated column, "Taking Stock." They have two children: Dr. Adam Berko, a family practice physician, married to Patricia. Their three children are Joshua, Zachary, and Hannah. Cecile and Malcolm have a daughter, Hilary Berko, who is a criminal defense attorney in Phoenix, Arizona. She is married to Frank Johnson and has one stepdaughter, Rachel. Malcolm was Brotherhood President from 1966-1968.

Cecile is very significant because of her leadership roles at Temple Beth-El. She and her husband joined the Temple in August, 1964, when they arrived in St. Petersburg. She immediately became active in Sisterhood and became Treasurer. She was the chairperson of many committees for the

Temple. She became the first and only women President of the congregation on two separate occasions in 1986-1987 and 1998-2001.

Cecile said that her parents shaped her Jewish identity of charitable giving and synagogue involvement by example. They had experienced the great Depression and World War II and knew life could be made better if individual people would work to help others. They taught by example and never preached or lectured. "My father was a business humanitarian: making it possible for many to shop in his store, extending credit, and exchanging goods for services. He was also a confidant to many in the community, listening, and supporting with a monetary gift for he had the ability to find the right people to help. I often say that I was raised in the Temple kitchen. My mother cooked and baked for all who asked. She was often the chairperson for gala events that embraced her creative skills in many areas. She was able to enlist the cooperation of so many that her successes were legendary. And, there I was at her side doing whatever she would let me do and I was so proud. I held official positions in Temple Youth Group, B'nai B'rith Girls, the National Council of Christian and Jews, and even was editor of the high school yearbook. It was a natural move to welcome Temple members upon their arrival in St. Petersburg. What a great way to meet people in an environment in which I was so comfortable. After years of living Ida and Milton Hoffman's version of tdzedakah, tikun olam and humility, I set out on my own journey of influence on family and community." And, what a successful journey it has been.

Highlights of 1965

A festival of religious art, original paintings by members of the congregation, and work from their collections was exhibited. Thirty seven new families joined the congregation.

Highlights of 1966

Bruce Marger became President, (1966-1968). He hired the first religious school director and also was responsible for significant repairs at the synagogue. A major musical event was held at the Temple. The sixty-voice choir of St. Petersburg's First Presbyterian Church kicked off five-weeks of music festivals at the synagogue. The Temple Choir, under Dr. Helen Allinger, presented a concert of American Jewish music. This concert was followed by a concert of Jewish religious compositions with the seventy five-voice Florida Presbyterian College Choir under the direction of Dr. R. Waters. The final concerts included a Cavalcade of Jewish Music by the Temple Choir and the St. Petersburg Junior College Choir.

The Sisterhood presented Braille books to seven legally blind children in Pinellas County. Because of the large amount of time and expertise of members of the Sisterhood, these children could continue to effectively participate in classrooms with sighted children. The original Braille transcribing course was started in 1958. Since then, the Sisterhood members have transcribed 300-400 textbooks ranging from elementary school to college. It was estimated that ninety percent of the braille textbooks used in Pinellas County were transcribed by the thirty five active members of the Pinellas Braille Group, an organization of certified braillists. They also transcribed library books and tests with three special education teachers in the county school system.

A testimonial dinner was held in honor of the 10th anniversary of Rabbi David J. Susskind, being the rabbi of Temple Beth-El. An editorial appeared in the St. Petersburg Independent on Thursday, November 10. It read as follows: " DESERVED TRIBUTE– For ten years Rabbi David J. Susskind of Temple Beth-El has been a potent force for good in the social, political and civic, as well as religious life of St. Petersburg. The anniversary of his ministry was observed by a testimonial dinner on November 12 in the Temple's Rothman Social Hall that was attended by religious and civic leaders from many parts of the state. The tribute was well-deserved. Rabbi Susskind is a man of God who believes in personal involvement. He summarized his philosophy sometime ago in these words: "It has become necessary for a religious leader to lead... The laws in the Bible are social laws. They do not operate in a vacuum. Where the will of God is to

create a better world, the least we can do is to advance justice and righteousness." In pursuance of this philosophy, he has given generously of himself in community affairs for advancement of moral and social progress. He has a great capacity for inspiring people. St. Petersburg is a much better place for his being here."

Highlights of 1967

Mrs. Dan Daniels cataloged the Temple Library in accordance with the Dewey Decimal System. A small Torah was presented by the confirmation class of 1966. It was to be displayed in the proposed Temple Museum. Eight children were confirmed. One hundred forty seven students were enrolled in the Sunday Religious School. An average of only thirteen children were missing per session.

Jewish music month was celebrated each Friday in March. On March 3, Mr. Ralph Reed, Director of the Woodwind Trio from St. Petersburg Junior College, with the Temple Choir presented selections from Isadore Freed's Hasidic Service for a Sabbath Eve. On March 10, Music for Worship by Jewish composers who had been influenced by European and traditional modes was presented. On March 17, the topic was "Jewish Liturgical Music of the Synagogue Throughout the Year." On March 24, the children's choir performed in a Purim Service led by Mrs. Leo Berger. On March 31, "The Peaceable Kingdom" was performed by the seventy voice choir under the direction of Dr. Floyd Funk. This half-hour choral rendition was written by Randall Thompson, and based upon the prophecy of Isaiah.

Highlights of 1968

The Temple was re-roofed and there was an extensive renovation of the interior and exterior of the sanctuary. The Founder's Hall finally had a museum which was a repository of Jewish treasure, art, and other objects owned by the congregation. Nine children were confirmed.

Rabbi Solomon B. Freehof, Rabbi Emeritus of Rodeph Sholom Temple, Pittsburgh, Pennsylvania, Past President of the World Union for Progressive Judaism, Past President of the Central Conference

Bruce Marger, President, Temple Beth-El, 1966–1968, 1987–1988.

Leonard Shavlan, President, Temple Beth-El, 1968-1974

of American Rabbis and a prolific writer of numerous books on Bible and Rabbinic Literature, addressed a joint program of Temple Beth-El and Pasadena Community Church. This topic was Jewish Origins of Christian Beliefs.

Highlights of 1969

Temple Beth-El started on its 40th year of Congregational activity. Rabbi Susskind said, "According to the Bible's calculation, forty years is considered to be a generation – the period it normally takes for old patterns to become transformed into new values.... We are the beneficiaries of the founders and builders who forged the Liberal Reform traditions of Judaism we acclaim. Likewise, we are established in a Temple worthy of the name Beth-El, House of God....In our Temple, we need to involve ourselves in all that our Judaism holds sacred and vital religiously, educationally, and socially. The Temple's structure, impetus, and status is in our hands–the new generation...."

A beautifully designed parchment scroll commemorating the 40th Anniversary Year of Temple Beth-El was made available for inscription by members of the congregation. It was put on display so that future generations could know who came before them. The formal religious celebration was held on February 28, with a creative service prepared for this sacred and joyous event. Rabbi Robert P. Frazin, Director of the Southeast Region of the Union of American Hebrew Congregations, gave the major address.

Rabbi Frank Sundheim of Temple Schaarai Zedek of Tampa presented a concert entitled, "A Cavalcade of Jewish Music." The Temple Beth-El Sisterhood and Congregation B'nai Israel Sisterhood jointly sponsored a special production of Rowan and Martin's "Laugh-in." The press reviews were excellent.

Highlights of 1970-1979

Highlights of 1970

Temple Beth-El Museum was opened in February. It was located in the Millers' Founders Hall of the Temple at 400 Pasadena Ave South. The Museum added a new significance to the memorial hall, which is dedicated to those who helped establish the Temple and is the entranceway to the sanctuary. It is a depository of the treasures, culture and heritage of the Jewish people. The museum is dedicated to the memory of Sidney Weiman. The objects on display are symbols of ancient customs and ceremonies. The room itself is contemporary and the accessories are futuristic. This symbolizes the past, present, and future of the religion.

Highlights of 1971

The Temple youth presented a Sabbath service to the residents of a nursing home in South Pasadena. Jewish Music Month was celebrated with music, ritual and drama. The Temple hosted the sixty voice integrated choir of St. Luke's Methodist Church and Beth-El Community Baptist Church for a concert on the theme of "Songs of Faith." At Passover, Rabbi Susskind talked about freedom. He quoted from Rabbi Isaac Mayer Wise who said, "Freedom is the indispensable condition of goodness, virtue, purity, and holiness....Take away freedom from human nature and whatever remains of it is an anomaly, some nameless thing of human form, an animal indifference." Rabbi Susskind, speaking at the annual meeting, said,"the Temple is the inheritance of the entire membership; while it belongs to no one, it is the possession of everyone; while it is administered by the officers and trustees, it is the trusteeship of everyone. It was bequeathed to us by the founders and members of a prior generation in order to preserve and enhance the heritage of Judaism embodied in our building and ennobled by our services and activities, so that we may be the present benefactors and then transmit it to our children and the generations yet to come." He also wrote the slogan for contributions to the synagogue, "The Heart of the Giver Makes Precious the Gift." Fifteen children were confirmed. A new Eternal Light was secured for the Chapel. It was purchased by Mr. and Mrs. Ted Samuels and Mrs. Samuel Logan. There were 250 families in the congregation in April and 389 by December 1. One hundred and fifteen students were enrolled in the Religious School, with twenty nine attending Hebrew school.

Highlights of 1972

Temple Beth-El presented the First Annual Art Show with three internationally acclaimed artists, Syd Solomon, William Pachner, and Norman Laliberte. Members of the congregation were also encouraged to exhibit their Jewish art. Mayor Herman Goldner of St. Petersburg gave a presentation and greeted the guests at a special reception. Mr. Arnold Argintar was Chairman of the Fine Arts Committee. The festivities and entertainment that occurred during this January weekend were designed not only for the pleasure of the individuals, but to enable them all to become part sponsors, donors, and best of all, art collectors. The art creations were in many different media, such as, oils, watercolor, metal, and ceramics. Sonya Miller is a longtime co-chair of the art festival.

Eleven children were confirmed. Donald M. Rolander became the new organist.

Highlights of 1973

The second annual Art Exhibition and Show was held. Thelma Rothman was the chairman. The three artists of the previous years came back and they were joined by sculptors John Johnson, Travis Cundiff, and other artists. David Anderson gave a demonstration of an artist at work. Ralph Patterson, metal worker, gave demonstrations of this art form. The editors of The Scroll were D. Heyman and R. Harris. Rose Shainberg became the library chairman. Don Rolander and the St. Petersburg Choral Society Inc. presented the initial performance of Bach's Sacred Service at the Temple on Friday evening, March 30. It was an outstanding Jewish synagogue musical composition done by the choir and Mr. Rolander, the organist. Twenty six new families joined the synagogue.

Marion B. Ross was selected the first Honorary President of Temple Beth-El, because of his devoted and faithful service for more than two decades on the Temple Board of Trustees and having served as President, three different times. The resolution for this matter was adopted unanimously by the Board of Trustees on October 25.

Mrs. David Fyvolent was the first woman in the history of Temple Beth-El to sit on the Temple's pulpit throughout the Yom Kippur services. A discussion period was added to the Yom Kippur service with Joe Packer presenting a paper on "Concepts of Sin in Judaism" and Dr. Joel Schrager presented "Concepts of Immortality in Judaism." Rabbi Susskind explained the tenet of the Jewish faith, which holds that prayer is not the sole avenue to God's graces. Equally important in God's eyes are deeds of love and compassion.

Highlights of 1974

Edith Chapp and Eleanor Argintar were co-chairmen of the Temple Beth-El's annual Art Festival. It had become one of St. Petersburg's cultural and social highlights of the year. Many artists displayed their work including Sid Solomon, William Pachner, David Anderson, Charlotte Mullendore, Adelia Samaha, John Johnson, Robert Hodgell, and many others. David Anderson gave an excellent demonstration of "The artist at work." John Eckert and Robin Neyman displayed unusual techniques and tricks in making ceramics. Many graphics were on sale in all price ranges.

David Fyvolent, President, Temple Beth-El, 1974–1976.

Sylvia Danto presented the guest editorial in The Scroll. She said, "My religion teaches me to thank God for everyday life.... My faith gives me the incentive to fill my home with truth and to strengthen myself in prayers....My religion means the adoption, as my personal goal, of love, good-will, a positive friendliness toward others. Honesty, integrity, humility, genuine concern for the well-being of all people, belief in the dignity and worth of every man, are personal goals which are re-enforced and renewed by my faith in God. Like social values, these personal values must be translated into daily behavior to have real meaning."

Rabbi and Mrs. Samuel M. Silver gave a musically illustrated lecture, "Is Jewish Music Sad?" The Silvers have presented this program throughout the United States. Mrs. Silver, a noted concert pianist, is a graduate of the Juilliard School of Music, New York City. Rabbi Silver is a former editor of the American Judaism Magazine and the author of "Judaism to Jews and Christians." Rabbi Silver is considered to be the Sam Levinson of the rabbinate because of his sense of humor.

Leonard Lubin was presented the Masada Award by the State of Israel for notable achievement for fortifying the economic foundation of Israel through Israel bonds. The Masada Award symbolizes the heroic struggle on the famed mountain stronghold of the Jewish rebels against Rome where the people chose honorable death to religious and national servitude. Sister Mary of the Sisters of St. Dominic participated in the seder for the congregation. Rabbi Susskind was given the degree of Dr. of Divinity on June 2, for his twenty five years service as a Rabbi. This honorary degree was bestowed upon him for "Your Singular Contribution to the Jewish People and to Reform Judaism." Forty new families joined the congregation bringing the membership to 426 families. There were 110 students enrolled in the religious school. Dual services were held on the High Holy Days to help accommodate the entire congregation. A young adult group was started for those who were ages eighteen to twenty six. Miriam Berger was the soprano sololist.

The total family membership had increased to 426. Regular Saturday morning Torah study and worship was re-instituted. Members of Temple Beth-El supervised the Pasadena Community Church children's choir after they completed their performance. They also babysat for members of the church who wanted to attend Christmas Eve services.

Highlights of 1975

On February 28, the sermon was a "Cavalcade of Music," which traced many events in Jewish history that had significantly influenced the ideals and values that we cherish and teach. This was represented in song and poetry. In March, the neighboring churches were invited to attend the Sabbath worship service to help foster brotherhood and better relations and understanding. The annual art show was once again a great success. Mr. and Mrs. Seymour Chapp were the general chairmen.

A reprint in The Scroll stated, "To accept people as they are and for what they are, to place confidence in them and to encourage them, is to help them become better than they are. To treat people as if they were

what they ought to be is to help them to become what they're capable of becoming. Within every person is the capacity to become something greater than he now is. It is possible for each of us to become better and to help others become what they ought to be." This is truly a wonderful philosophy of life and a road people should travel."

Seven students were confirmed. Beyond the book learning that the young people were exposed to, they were taught that education has a high priority amid Jewish values. Although the book is important, the ideas, understanding, and experiences equipped people for life. Rabbi Stanley Brav, an honored member, helped Rabbi Susskind officiate on the pulpit at the High Holy Day services. Mr. Maurice Rothman blew the shofar. There were 104 children in the religious school. The Temple Young Associates, a group of twenty five couples, formed an organization related to the synagogue. A new volunteer choir was contemplated. Mr. and Mrs. Jake Shainberg completely re-cataloged the library. A confidential counseling service with temple member, Dr. H. Lewis March, as Director was offered to the congregation. Dr. March was a member of Harvard Medical School, Department of Psychiatry, and Chief of the Mental Hygiene Clinic of the Veterans Administration.

Highlights of 1976

In 1976, the Chai Circle was formed from members of the Sisterhood who were unable to participate in daytime activities. The project known as Helping Hand was founded. Money for the fund initially came from the first eight members. Mrs. Gayle from the Jewish Community Center became their advisor. They helped pay dental bills, water bills, etc. for the needy and provided gifts for Jewish patients in nursing homes. The congregants of Temple Beth-El purchased tickets to the annual Starlight Musical '76-"This Land....Your Land" presented by the Pasadena Community Church Choir consisting of 135 adults and 110 children. This relationship between this church and the synagogue was a wonderful example of brotherhood in action.

Rabbi Susskind continued to bring

highly recognized Jewish scholars to give presentations on the pulpit at Friday night services. Frequently, Rabbi Stanley Brav, Rabbi Emeritus of Temple Shalom of Cincinnati participated in services as well as in the special services.

The congregation gave a special tribute to Mr. William Morgan, who served the Temple as soloist for twenty five years. They considered him to be one of their own and showed their deep appreciation for the many years of devoted services he rendered. Nine children were confirmed. Sixteen new families joined the congregation. There were 340 families and 152 single members on the membership rolls.

The Synagogue Council was expanded to incorporate all the congregations in Pinellas County with representation of the rabbi, president, and one delegate. Council objectives were to establish and maintain the spirit of unity between congregations and cooperate with the community for betterment of its spiritual existence, provide programs to enhance the cultural, ethical, and religious life of member congregations; foster administrative rapport between member congregations, and invite the unaffiliated and newly arriving Jewish families to join a synagogue of their choice.

Highlights of 1977

A golden anniversary celebration was held for the Sisterhood celebrating its 51st year in initiating the founding of Temple Beth-El. A past president's plaque was dedicated and put in the Miller Founder's Hall.

A funeral service was held for Rabbi Emeritus David L. Zielonka, who was born October 21, 1904 in El Paso, Texas and died September 24, 1977 in Tampa, Florida. The service was conducted by Rabbi Frank N. Sundheim and Rabbi David Susskind. Rabbi Zielonka served not only Schaarai Zedek of Tampa, but also the Jewish people of Clearwater, Tarpon Springs, Safety Harbor, Dunedin, and St. Petersburg. He was a friend, confidant, teacher, religious leader, and needed helper at all times of emergencies. He helped celebrate all phases of life cycle activities, when there were no rabbis available in Pinellas County. He helped new rabbis

and new congregations grow and prosper. His life was truly a light unto the nations.

Highlights of 1978

In February, the Sisterhood and Brotherhood sponsored the First Annual Opera Highlights in the sanctuary. In July, Temple Beth-El celebrated its 50th anniversary year with a year-long series of religious, social, educational, and cultural events. It started with a new "Tree of Life" sculpture, which was installed in the foyer of the synagogue. The sculpture was designed by Betty Goldstein, New York artist and sculptress. The themes of the sermons of the High Holy Days reflected upon the roots of the congregation and its role and relationship to the membership, as well as the community. The first of the cultural events was a presentation by the St. Petersburg Opera Guild. There was an interfaith institute in conjunction with the National Conference of Christians and Jews. The Hoffman family quartet gave a stirring presentation. The Brotherhood Breakfast series on Sunday mornings, the weekly Thursday Torah sessions, which attracted between sixty and ninety women each week, dinners, and other social events were all held in a manner that reflected the importance of the 50th anniversary celebration. The confirmation exercises reflected the significance of the golden anniversary. David Fyvolent served as chairman of the anniversary activities for the entire year.

Beth Resnick, a graduate of Temple University, Philadelphia, Pennsylvania, became the new religious school principal. She held a Bachelor of Arts Degree in Speech and Hearing Science and a Master of Arts Degree in Elementary Education. She had taught at Gratz College and in schools in Philadelphia and Norfolk, Virginia, before moving to St. Petersburg. Her husband, Dr. Jerrold B. Resnick, was a practicing dentist.

Highlights of 1979

There were 525 family members in the congregation. Reflecting on the first service held in the spacious new sanctuary on Pasadena Avenue on September 10, 1961, Irwin Miller said, "It is most

Edward Rosenbluth, President, Temple Beth-El, 1976–1977.

exciting and overwhelming. The building seemed to be so much more than we really needed, but today we use every inch of it."

The Brotherhood had grown to 171 members. They sponsored health days, blood bank drives, and were active in the Interfaith Coalition on Aging. A former Brotherhood President, the late Dr. Murray Gessner, expanded the Brotherhood Sunday morning breakfast forums.

Highlights of 1980-1989

Highlights of 1980

Rabbi Susskind presented a pulpit prospective on the High Holy Days to the general community. He said, "Rosh Hashanah is here again, renewing within us profound questions about our life, our values, our goals. According to our sacred tradition, it is a time for soul-searching, inner probing, self-examining as we look at ourselves and see ourselves as we really are. In the secrecy of our reflections, we render ourselves a "report card" on which we grade ourselves for our accomplishments and failures. All this is accentuated through the moods and thoughts aroused in us by the prayers...It is a time then for facing reality... The issues for facing reality are crucial even in the understanding and appreciation of Judaism. Rabbis, as you may well have observed, strive mightily to teach Judaism as being practical, applicable, useful and up-to-date. Properly understood, Judaism is eminently realistic; it teaches how to treat ourselves and how to relate to others, how to raise children and how to honor parents, how to be grateful and how to react to evil, how to be charitable and how to be just. It is a treasure house of practical guidance in facing realities. However, the magnificence of Judaism and its rich heritage also has beauty, inspiration, comfort, and culture that can hardly be termed useful in a practical way. Rather, it must be experienced and appreciated in and of itself. The joys and the inspiration which come from the religious expression of prayer and study, hope and faith, are frequently in themselves realistic rewards enough. With the arrival of the New Year, we renew our fervent prayer that a practical and realistic approach to the daily

Sol Markman, President, Temple Beth-El, 1980-1982.

issues of life will result in a Shana Tova (A good year) for you and yours."

The Religious School had over ninety students in its one day a week program. The preschool averaged twenty seven children. There were 524 member families in the congregation and the Brotherhood had its largest membership ever. Rabbi Robert P. Kirzner was hired for a two-year period as an assistant rabbi to specialize in working with the young people of the congregation.

Highlights of 1981

The Temple Beth-El Art Show had forty three professional Bay Area artists participate. They presented paintings, sculptures, ceramics, weavings, prints, photographs, glass, and jewelry. Once again, a gala champagne preview party was held. The chairpeople were Eleanor Argintar and Winfred Klarin.

The fourth annual Opera Highlights featured Roberto Silvano and Rosaline Posno, plus a full chorus of the St. Petersburg Opera Company. They presented an evening of show tunes and light opera.

A new social club was formed geared especially for singles and couples of pre-retirement age.

A Shabbaton for a weekend provided the congregants with an opportunity to devote a full day to Jewish study and enrichment. The feature speaker was Rabbi W. Gunther Plaut, Senior Scholar of Holy Blossom Temple, Toronto, Ontario. He gave a series of lectures on the general topic "Bible Relevance to Contemporary Living." Louise Ressler, who attended, said "it was like a retreat, uplifting and spiritual, as well as educational and instructive. It was pragmatic-holding it on home ground-at Temple Beth-El, making it accessible to the entire congregation, without traveling."

Jewish liturgical compositions were presented to celebrate Jewish Music Month during March. Rabbi Stanley R. Brav provided some of his own versions and adaptations. Rabbi Brav studied under the famous musicologist Abraham Zvi Idelson; sang in the choir at Hebrew Union College; and was one of the editors of "The Union Songster" which includes several of his compositions. He has adapted music by Mozart, Mendelssohn, and Handel to Hebrew prayers. Mrs. Francis Driver and Mrs. Bess Zallen gave a gift of a new piano to the Temple in memory of their husbands, George and Charles. This was meant to help the congregation with future musical presentations.

Rabbi Susskind was honored on his 25th year in the pulpit at Temple Beth-El. As he reflected upon his twenty five years, he talked about times of great suffering and times of redemption. He was referring to the Holocaust and later to the Civil Rights movement in the United States. He said that the Holocaust resulted in the birth of the State of Israel and that the Civil Rights movement resulted in newfound rights for all Americans. He recognized a profound suffering, but also the good that can come later. He said, "See you cannot ask where God is, or where God was at any event or moment in history. You can only see God's power in perspective. It is in the working out of historic forces over a period of time that redemptive power was and is at work." He further reflected that, "Reverence for the past, compassion for all who suffer, hope for the future are these not the things that led me to become a rabbi in the first place? They happened to be my reasons why I never doubted the need for or the validity of the rabbinate. And finally, whatever measure of achievement that has accrued to me, I am exceedingly grateful to my wife and family and who so ever befriended me in the congregation and in the community and thereby gave encouragement to my labors in the vineyard of Judaism."

Eight children were confirmed. President Sol Markman said that the Temple was embarking upon an ambitious project to correct a long-standing shame of neglect, the shut-in segment of the membership. A special committee chaired by Al Lewis was set up to do whatever was necessary to help shut-ins in any way possible, especially to get them to services and other affairs. Four concerts were scheduled.

In the mid-1980s, because of the popularity and fund raising success of the Art Festival, the organizers decided to make this an invitational juried show. It is one of the finest modern art shows in the Southeast. It is

held at the end of January each year and is the host to internationally acclaimed artists who bring their masterpieces to St. Petersburg.

Highlights of 1982

Temple Beth-El presented a musical concert series sponsored by the Sisterhood and Brotherhood. The artists were: Rosaline Posno, St. Petersburg Opera Company; Thomas Palmer, described as, "America's premier baritone;" and Cantor Harold Orbach, described as "a lyric tenor of resonance and enchantment...positively superb." Each individual gave a separate concert. Sylvia Danto was Chairman, Sisterhood and Brotherhood Temple Beth-El Concert Series. The Temple honored the Choir Director, Miriam Berger, and her all volunteer choir members. They also honored Florence Lippman and her late husband, Morris, who served on the Temple choir for twenty five years.

Highlights of 1983

Temple Beth-El participated in the Judaic Exhibit at the Museum of Fine Arts. The St. Petersburg Opera Company held its Opera highlights at Temple Beth-El for the benefit of the Temple. Michael Milkovich became the new Director of the Temple. Rabbi Ira S. Youdovin was chosen as the new Associate Rabbi. The Sheriff of Pinellas County, Gerry Coleman, invited Rabbi Susskind to meet with him concerning recent activity in the area of Pinellas County against members of the Jewish community.

Herbert Goldstein, President, Temple Beth-El, 1982–1984.

Highlights of 1984

The Southeastern Region of the Central Conference of American Rabbis met in Annual Convention in St. Petersburg. Rabbi Ira Youdovin and his wife, Susan, invited small groups of congregants of ten to twenty people to come to their home to share their interests with the Rabbi. They met and exchanged views with more than 350 members of the congregation. This informal kind of long-range fact-finding fulfilled a pledge made by the Rabbi to the Board to get a full understanding of the needs of the congregation. Two general impressions emerged from the meetings. There was strong support for

William H. Fleece, President, Temple Beth-El, 1984–1985.

the Temple, as it existed today. However, the positive feelings were almost entirely among the retired congregants. The younger generation wanted to increase the degree of education for the children and to expand outreach, without taking away from what was currently being done in the Temple. The existing service was considered to be beautiful by the congregants, but the younger members wanted to shorten it and also to add a family oriented service once a month.

A three phase physical expansion of the synagogue was proposed. Additional space was needed for the administrative functions to be all in one area. There was a need for additional classroom/meeting space. A study was suggested for extending the Millers' Founders Hall westward toward Pasadena Avenue.

Because of the Temple's demographics, there was a substantial need for visitations to hospitals, old-age homes, and shut-ins. Since it was physically impossible for the rabbis to do this, a special Human Concerns Committee, under the leadership of Al Lewis, was established. This sacred obligation incumbent upon all Jewish people was now being fulfilled in a far better manner. Further, the Temple took on the responsibility of helping destitute Jewish people living in Pinellas County. These individuals included: elderly Jews who couldn't get or afford their essential medications; Jews who shiver through the winter because they can't pay their electricity bill; and Jews laid off from work who will be evicted because they can't pay the rent.

Maurice A. Rothman, President, Temple Beth-El, 1985–1986.

Highlights of 1985

The project for obtaining new covers for the Torahs to replace the old worn mantles began spontaneously and represented both joyful and sad milestones in the lives of the congregation. It began with the death of Helga Kauffman. Her Saturday morning chapel prayer group (minyan) wanted to honor her. A group of members made a new mantle cover for the Chapel Torah. Her husband then donated the silver ornaments. This led the congregation to have new covers designed for the three Torahs in the sanctuary. Three more donors

made contributions for this purpose. Rose Shainberg honored the memory of her husband, Jake, and his son, Victor. Dr. Stephen and Pam Newman honored their daughter's bat mitzvah. Ralph and Ruth Ann Mizrahi honored their daughter Shelly's wedding. The covers were dedicated on the last night of Hanukkah. This marked the beginning of the 25th anniversary of the use of the current synagogue building.

Rabbi Ira S. Youdovin was Executive Director of ARZA from 1985-1991. Charles Rutenberg was the guest speaker at a Sabbath service to discuss the Federation.

Highlights of 1986

On Hanukkah, four colorful Torah covers replaced the old worn-out ones, which had been used at the Temple for many years. This was the completion of the project started in 1985.

Laurel N. Swerdin

Laurel Swerdin was the Cantorial Soloist from 1986-1989, and again from 1992-1995. She earned a Bachelor of Arts Degree in Music and a Concentration in Accompanying from the University of Miami, Coral Gables, Florida. She took post-graduate studies in voice and music education on scholarship at the University of Miami. She took advanced studies in music education at New York University and Manhattan School of Music. She studied choral conducting at the Juilliard School of Music. She had additional graduate study in piano in France, vocal study in New York City, private study in cantorial music, and Hebrew. She was a member of the Guild of Temple Musicians since 1978, and a member of Sigma Alpha Iota Honorary Music Sorority. She was a music teacher in the New York City public schools and then in Miami. She served as the Cantorial Soloist and Music Director of Temple Judea in Coral Gables, Florida, from 1977-1986.

Highlights of 1987

The Federation Shabbat was held on January 30. The guest speaker was Sid Werner, Chairperson of the current campaign. Sid was a member of The Next Generation, an organization uniting children of Holocaust survivors. He was an attorney, who was perhaps the youngest chairman of any Federation campaign in the United States that year. Rabbi Youdovin agreed to serve as President of the Pinellas County Jewish Federation. He said, "A rabbi's responsibilities are not only to his/her own congregation, although this is a primary, but to the larger community, the Jewish people everywhere, Israel, and, indeed, to all human kind. Federation is an important instrumentality for pursuing these goals... Throughout North America and throughout the world, men and women with incredibly busy schedules serve as Federation officers, while maintaining businesses, legal and medical practices, etc.."

On February 28, a small group of men, who twenty five years earlier led the effort to erect the current Beth-El congregational home, were honored. Two of these individuals were still active in Temple leadership. Maurice A. Rothman, who chaired the committee was President of Temple Beth-El in 1986. Irwin Miller, who had been Past President was now serving as Treasurer. As a result of the foresight and efforts of these individuals, the congregation grew substantially in size and in programming. There now have been thousands of wonderful events held at this edifice including, weddings, Bar/Bat Mitzvahs, religious, educational, cultural and social events.

Highlights of 1989

Rabbi Herman E. Schaalman was the Scholar-in-Residence. He discussed the, "Three Jewish Views of God; The God of Sinai, The God of Auschwitz, and The God of Jerusalem." Ten children were confirmed. They were: Aaron Chausmer, Darlene Green, Jason Green, David Ison, Rod Keskiner, Laura Klein, Beth Newman, Joshua Person, Joshua Pomerantz, and Cassie Zanger.

Michael Brem was the Soloist/Musical Director for 1989-1990. Michael received a Bachelor of Music, Vocal Performance, Incarnate Word College, San Antonio, Texas. He studied vocal performance and cantorial craft with William Sharlin, former Chairman of Music Department, HUC-JIR/Los Angeles and former Cantor of

Leo Beck Temple, Los Angeles, California. In addition, he studied conducting with Lawrence Leighton Smith, Musical Director, Louisville Symphony, Louisville, Kentucky. He previously had been the Assistant Choir Director at St. Andrew's United Methodist Church in San Antonio, Texas, Staff Choral Member, Temple Bethel, San Antonio, Texas, and Cantorial Soloist, Temple Beth-El, San Antonio, Texas.

When commenting on S'lichot service (which means pardon), a traditional time to search your soul in preparation for the High Holy Days, he said, "This music for S'lichot is intimate and subdued, reaching deep inside to the heart, the place that makes us all distinctly human. As we listen to this music, we participate and open ourselves up to a spiritual examination of conscience, and hopefully, to renewal of ourselves." He also discussed the music of Rosh Hashanah and Yom Kippur. He said, "It can be in one moment majestic and dignified, the next moment quiet and supplicatory"

Charles Tatelbaum, President, Temple Beth-El, 1988-1990.

Irwin Miller, President, Temple Beth-El, 1990–1992.

Highlights of 1990-1999

Highlights of 1990

Rabbi Herman Schaalman was the Temple Scholar-in-Residence. He worked with Cardinal Joseph Bernardin in Chicago, as part of the Mayor's Commission to promote interracial and inter religious harmony. He was Rabbi Emeritus of Temple Emanuel of Chicago and taught at Northwestern University and the University of Chicago. He was the President of the Central Conference of American Rabbis and Chairperson of the Committee on Ethics. He gave four presentations: "The Jew in the Modern World;" "The Beginning and the End;" "The Jewish View of Creation;" and "The Jewish view of the Messiah."

Rabbi Youdovin was welcomed to the Pinellas Board of Governors of the National Conference of Christian and Jews. The Jewish Cadet Choir of the United States Air Force Academy performed at a Shabbat service. Max Halle, when discussing the functions of the Tzadaka Committee said, "Tzadaka is more than giving. It is the art of giving." Max Halle presented his Holocaust remembrance program, "Precious Legacy,"

Rabbi Herman Schallman, Rabbi Steven Moch.

at the MacDill Air Force Base in Tampa.

The confirmation class included, Leah Jo Barber, David Berman, Alison Nicole Friedel, Jennifer Denise Gall, Elissa Graham, Denise Marie Green, Marnie Jill Klein, Rachel Anne Krosner, Jonah Person, Elaine M. Rodriguez, Casey Sidney Slott, and Sarah Wides. Rabbi Youdovin said that which the sages taught: "One who saves even a single life is credited with having saved the entire world." Dr. Jacob Neusner, Graduate Research Professor of Religious Studies at the University of South Florida spoke on, "What We Would Not Know About Religion If We Never Learned About Judaism."

President Irwin Miller discussed the imminent departure of Rabbi and Susan Youdovin. Rabbi had been elected to serve the Steven Wise Free Synagogue.

Robert Bruce Marinoff was the Cantorial Soloist from 1990-1992. He had previously held positions at: Temple Beth Judah, Cedar Rapids, Iowa; Congregation Rodeph Sholom, Tampa, Florida; Temple Emanuel, Denver, Colorado; Congregation B'nai Israel, St. Petersburg, Florida; and Temple Ahavat Shalom, Clearwater, Florida. He was educated at the University of Iowa, Goldovsky, Bayerische Staats Conservatory, University of South Florida, Düsseldorf, Germany and Stetson College of Law. He had performed in multiple operas, symphonies, radio and television shows, and stage productions.

Highlights of 1991

Temple Beth-El and Congregation B'nai Israel joined together in support of Operation Exodus. The funds raised in the United States were used to transport Jews out of the USSR to Israel and for direct absorption into the Israeli community. Rabbi Herman E. Schaalman, father of Susan Youdovin, Temple Religious School Director, was once again the Scholar-in-Residence speaker. He spoke on, "Recent Developments in Jewish-Catholic Relations."

Harvey Morganstein wrote about "Jews and Social Action." He said, "The belief in the ability of people to improve themselves and create a better world is one of the basic tenants of Judaism. As result, Jews have always been very active in public affairs. We have fought for social justice. We believe in freedom of choice, without which democracy could not exist. We believe in the ability of people to understand the difference between right and wrong, and determine their own destiny. We have been firmly committed to the liberation of the oppressed and many social movements of our time – for peace, nuclear disarmament, equality for women, anti-apartheid, and human rights. We have helped to shape the miracle of America as an open and pluralistic country with guarantees of religious freedom and the rights of minorities and dissenters; and we are dismayed by evidence of retreat weakening of support for these rights...."

Stephen Fisher Moch became the Rabbi of Temple Beth-El. He had previously served at Temple Emanuel in Winston-Salem, North Carolina and Temple Brith Sholom in Springfield, Illinois. He had a reputation of being an innovative and an action oriented rabbi in the Jewish and general communities. (See Clearwater chapter and Congregation B'nai Emmunah)

Rabbi Moch started with 100 children in the religious school and the numbers grew to 185. New young families continued to come into the community. The congregants and the Temple worked with Habitat For Humanity to provide necessary labor to help build houses for poor families. They also did considerable work with Russian immigrants and worked with mosques and churches to help people in lower economic classes. They were always helping the poor by providing food and clothing.

The Jewish philosophy concerning charity is that, "We are God's partners in the ongoing work of creation." Jewish people believe in interacting with the world, becoming involved, and helping those who are less fortunate. They also believe that education is a lifetime commitment that not only builds your knowledge, but also increases your self-worth. As part of working with other religions, Rabbi Moch established a relationship with the predominantly black Bethel Community Baptist Church.

Once a month, children and families helped lead the services. After confirmation class, young people still continued to study.

Jack Jenkins

Jack Jenkins was named "Person of the Year," because of his active leadership and participation in many facets of Temple life, the Jewish community, and the National Federation of Temple Brotherhoods. He had been: a member, Jewish Chautauqua Society; Member, National Board of National Federation of Temple Brotherhoods; Secretary, Suncoast Council, National Federation Temple Brotherhoods; Treasurer, Florida Region, National Federation Temple Brotherhood; Member, Board of Directors, Temple Beth-El, Alexandria, Virginia; Member, Board of Directors, Washington Hebrew Congregation, Washington, DC; Member, Board of Directors, Temple Beth-El, St. Petersburg; President of the three previous synagogue Brotherhoods; "Man of the Year", Washington Hebrew Congregation; International Vice President, B'nai B'rith International; National Deputy to Veterans Administration Volunteer Services; Board of Directors, Gulf Coast Jewish Family Services; Board of Directors, USO; Distinguished Service Award, USO; Vice Chairman Mayor's Committee on Employment of the Handicapped; Executive Committee Jewish Community Council Greater Washington; Executive Committee United Jewish Appeal; Board of Directors Jewish National Fund; and Hillel Advisory Board, University of Maryland and George Washington University. Jack Jenkins died in November, 1992.

Rabbi Stanley M. Davids

Rabbi Davids served as the Rabbi during the High Holy Days, since Rabbi Moch was not available until November 1. Rabbi Davids had served as Senior Rabbi at the Central Synagogue in New York City. As a graduate of Western Reserve University, magna cum laude, he was ordained and received his Doctor of Divinity at Hebrew Union College, Jewish Institute of Religion, Cincinnati Campus. He served as President of the New York Board of Rabbis.

National Association of Temple Educators

Cara Jablow, Educational Director at Temple Beth-El, along with 750 other men and women from Canada, England, Israel, Australia ,and United States met in conclave with the Biennial Convention of the Union of American Hebrew Congregations. The conference was entitled, "PORTRAITS OF LEARNING." These leaders of religious education in the Reform movement used cutting-edge case problems to help in the development and administration of religious education. This was one more example of the professionalization of Jewish religious education.

Highlights of 1992

Rabbi Moch, in his High Holy Day message, talked about our turning to God. He said, "...our tradition instructs us to examine our past actions-not for the sake of regret or to engender a sense of guilt but to encourage the possibility of improvement....when someone makes a real effort to change his ways he becomes like a new person and he has no connection whatsoever with those undesirable past events. And the rabbis forbade us to ever remind a penitent person of his past. Our job is to help him remain productive today and look ahead to tomorrow. The same must hold true of ourselves....the positive realities of today and the possibility of a better world tomorrow always beckon us ahead."

A quartet of professional singers were added to the choir in 1986 for the High Holy Days. The current professional singers included a Professor of Voice at the University of South Florida, a St. Petersburg Junior College professor, a Largo High School choral director, and a music teacher.

Because of the growth of the Jewish community in St. Petersburg, Temple Beth-El had to expand. The Build Now campaign resulted in a new library, the expansion of the administrative offices, and rabbi 's study and the addition of a new wing on the religious school.

Highlights of 1993

Alicia Appelman-Jurman, the award winning author of "Alicia" shared her astonishing story at a Friday night service on January 22. She survived the Holocaust as a thirteen-year-old girl, not in the camps, but in the fields and forests of Poland and Ukraine, by hiding from murderous Germans, Poles, and Ukrainians. She fought with the Russian partisans and later smuggled Jews across Europe into Palestine. Chaim Potok, the author of the Chosen, described her book as "A powerful, intimate, searingly impressive memoir by a uniquely courageous and unusually intuitive young girl of the Holocaust nightmare and the years following."

Tu Bishevat, the new year for trees, was celebrated on Friday, February 6. Trees were planted in St. Petersburg and in Israel in honor of this festival. A festival meal was prepared from the various fruits of the trees.

Congregations United for Community Action, an organization dedicated to help solve the problems of the community, was formed by 400 people from twenty churches and Temple Beth-El. This became an opportunity to not only help those who are less fortunate, but also to establish a dialogue with churches of all denominations and races to foster understanding and help identify and solve mutual problems in helping others.

Rabbi Moch presented, "Giving of Ourselves to God." He said,"The importance of religion and belief in God comes from the realization that there exists a power that must be greater than ourselves and a presence that exists outside of ourselves, even as it exists within us....Faith must mean looking beyond oneself and religion, must mean serving more than oneself. For that reason, Hillel said, "If I am not for myself, who will be for me? But if I am for myself alone, What am I? And if not now, when?" Those who run our community's social service organizations know that the mainstay of their volunteer force come from churches and synagogues. Their people already give generously of themselves to their home congregations." In fact the giving of oneself is the highest order of giving to God.

Jay Kaminsky became the new Temple Administrator. Over 3,000 pounds of food was collected for distribution to needy people in the area.

Rabbi Stanley Brav, who had retired to St. Petersburg and Temple Beth-El, died. In 1972, he retired from Temple Sholom

in Cincinnati, Ohio. He founded this synagogue many years previously. He also served as Rabbi at Rochdale Temple in Cincinnati and had been on the pulpit in synagogues in Vicksburg, Mississippi and Dallas, Texas. He aided three rabbis with various rabbinic duties from officiating at life cycle events to teaching classes to conducting memorial services. He served with Rabbi Moch and Rabbi Kirzner as a member of the St. Petersburg Reform Beth Din. He taught many individuals on an informal and private basis. He never turned people away who wished to learn something about the Jewish heritage and faith. Rabbi Brav pioneered the causes of social justice and racial equality before they became acceptable positions for religious leaders. Rabbi Moch said, "A great leader of his people has died, but the lessons he taught live on."

The St. Petersburg College of Judaic Studies was co-sponsored by Congregation B'nai Israel and Temple Beth-El. The courses offered were: Beginning Hebrew; Intermediate Hebrew; Jews and Christians in Ancient Sepphoris; The Jews of India; Jews and Muslims Together; Personal Growth with a Jewish Flavor; the Dying World of the Ethiopian Jew; Biblical Lunch Programs with the Rabbi. Also, there were on-going courses including: Bible and Bagels; Shabbat Morning Torah Study; Basic Judaism Class; and Adult Bar and Bat Mitzvah Class. There were special programs including: Family Hanukkah Retreat; Adult Retreat on Spirituality; and Stella Sax Scholar-in-Residence Program, which this year was a continuation of the Adult Retreat on Spirituality. The visiting scholars were Rabbi Lester B. Bronstein and his wife, Cantor Benjie Ellen Schiller, who serve as Rabbi and Cantor of Bet Am Shalom Synagogue in White Plains, New York. They explored "The Texture and Melody of Jewish Life-the Jewish Spiritual Experience."

Rabbi Moch said,"The importance of religion and belief in God come from the realization that there exists a power that must be greater than ourselves and a presence that exists outside of ourselves, even as it exists within us...Faith must mean looking beyond oneself and religion, must mean serving more than oneself..."

Highlights of 1994

The Sisterhood continued its long practice of making contributions to the budget of the Religious School. Over the past fifteen years, the Sisterhood made annual payments to the Religious School of over $50,000 per year. Women made up fifty percent of the total membership of the Temple. They spoke to the important ethical, moral, academic, and charitable issues of the times. The Temple made $60,000 from the art show.

Bishop John C. Favalora, the spiritual leader of 300,000 Catholics in the five-county Diocese of St. Petersburg spoke to the congregation at the March 4, Shabbat service.

Rabbi Moch described the nature of Judaism, synagogues, and people. He said, "This is a lonely world and people seek out a synagogue in order to make friends and celebrate life with other Jews...No other institution, inside or outside of the Jewish community, can fulfill that need as naturally as the synagogue. But the synagogue also provides a place where people who feel confused, people searching for answers, can come to find God and discover the knowledge of what God wants for them. What does Beth-El really stand for? It stands for three things: a communal prayer, holy study and the doing of good deeds...We cannot do any of these things by ourselves in isolation. Therefore, we come together to do them as a group. That is why we have a synagogue. Prayer is emotional. We do it with our hearts. Torah is intellectual. We do it with our heads. The doing of good deeds, is physical. We do it with our hands. Some of us accomplish greater things with our heads. Some of us accomplish greater things with our hearts. And some of us accomplish greater things with our hands. None of us do all three with equal fervor and equal skill. For that reason, we join together in a synagogue – so the strengths of one will make up for the weaknesses of another, and so that together we can do well all three things that Jews are commanded to do."

Highlights of 1995

Dr. John Hope Franklin, author of "Up from Slavery," was the guest speaker at the February 17 Shabbat service. Dr. Franklin was Professor Emeritus of Duke University's History Department and the foremost African-American historian in the country. Rabbi David Sapperstein, Director of the Religious Action Center Reform Judaism, was the Scholar-in-Residence speaker. He addressed the congregation, as well as members of the Congregations United for Community Action.

Sharon M. Brown

Cantor Sharon Brown

Sharon was born on May 4, 1970, in Philadelphia, Pennsylvania. She graduated simultaneously from: Lower Moreland High School of Huntington Valley, Pennsylvania, where she earned a 4.3 grade-point average with honors and awards; and from Gratz College Hebrew High School in Philadelphia, Pennsylvania, where she was class valedictorian. Sharon went on to earn a Bachelor of Music Degree in Voice and a Bachelor of Arts Degree in Spanish from the University of South Florida. She also earned a Master of Arts Degree from the University of South Florida. By 1996, Sharon had earned three degrees, all summa cum laude.

In the early 1990s, a friend of hers recommended that she audition as a song leader at Congregation Schaarai Zedek, where she proceeded to work on Sundays for a period of time. By March of 1992, she became the part-time Cantorial Soloist at Congregation Aliah of Dunedin. Subsequently, she studied with Cantor William Hauben of Tampa. In July of 1995, she became the part-time Cantorial Soloist at Temple Beth-El. During the ensuing years, Sharon was fortunate to have as mentors, Rabbi Shimon Moch of Temple Beth-El, Cantor Shimon Gewitz of Congregation B'nai Israel, Rabbi Michael Torop of Temple Beth-El, and Hazzan David Sislen of Congregation B'nai Israel.

In 2005, Sharon Brown passed her certification examinations at the Conservative movement's Cantor's Assembly in Stamford, Connecticut and the Reform movement's Hebrew Union College in New York.

Sharon Brown always believed that diligence, dedication, and passion for her work would carry her through the most difficult of life's challenges. She found comfort in her studies, family, and community. Quoting Rabbi Michael Torop she said, "We all know that a cantor is more than just a voice, cantors are Klet Kodesh–vessels of holiness–through whom God's blessing can flow. In their work as clergy serving their community, cantors, as opposed to a cantorial soloist, can make a significant impact pastorally, educationally, culturally, and religiously."

Harold Bressler

Harold, a close friend and congregant of Rabbi Moch, died on May 29, 1995. His wife, Bernice, died January 30, 2004. Rabbi Moch said, "Harold may have died, but he has not passed entirely from this world. He left a living legacy through his many deeds of service and devotion to other people, his gentle love of his family and others, and his steadfast faith in God that he did not hesitate to share. Harold did not content himself with living by those exceptional standards; he followed an old Jewish practice and left an "ethical will" or personal testimony of his values and faith that he bequeathed to his family. They cherish those words that they read only after his death."

The ethical will is as follows:" First, I leave to all of you...my children, grandchildren and generations yet unborn, my love. You've had it while I lived and you will have it after my death.... They are not dead who live in the lives they leave behind, so do not mourn for me. Do not grieve; celebrate my life. In days and years to come, when you think of me, perform some act of kindness or charity, do something for another, and do it in my name.

Believe in Yourselves. Recognize your abilities, but with humility. Always do your best...no one can expect more. Remember that there is no such thing as failure, only setback; learn from your mistakes.

Believe in God. Style and form is unimportant, but thank the Almighty for the many blessings that will come to you. Do not, however, blame God for errors or mistakes that you make. Honor the great religious tradition which is part of your inheritance, make it a part of your life and your lives will be more meaningful. Always remember that God does not need your prayers as much as you need them.

Believe in Others. Remember our tradition that teaches, "Do not do to another that which is hateful to you." Respect also the Indian belief, "Do not judge another until you have walked in his moccasins." Do not ridicule, the little, or pass over lightly the opinions of children, as well as adults. A learned Rabbi once taught that every idea is important, each thought counts. You need not agree with everyone, but I respect their right to be heard. Honor your government and its leaders; they may not always be right, but you have the privilege of living under the best system the world has yet devised.

Believe in the Mitzvah of Giving. Give of yourself, as well as of your worldly goods. Help the poor, the homeless, the sick and the friendless; comfort the bereaved. The more of yourself you give away, the more will be left for you; giving can be a very rewarding experience. A poem I once read said that each of us is a "builder for eternity" that in life each of us can build "stumbling blocks or can build stepping stones"...a great philosophy to live by.

Believe in Love. Love family, friends, all of humanity. Love, like hate, flows in greater measure to the giver than it does to the recipient. Love helps one to see the best in others; to understand and overlook their shortcomings and ultimately to know that which is good in ourselves. To love is to honor, to respect, to cherish and so to lift yourselves to a higher plane in the relationship between God and humanity.

Believe in Positive Thinking. Be optimistic and your fondest goals will be realized. Have confidence...what you think can happen, will happen. Predict dark days and you will make this happen...predict success and you can make this happen... your prophecies are often self-fulfilling.

I hope and pray that all of the love, respect, and devotion you have given to your mother and me will be repaid to each of you a thousand times over. Live as you have lived, honoring truth, justice and fair play, so each of you will always be true to yourselves and so true to others, and your lives will have been for a blessing."

Rabbis Moshe and Gedaliah Druin

On December 15, the Renew the Word

campaign was used to restore the Torahs, renovate the bimah and the Ark, and dedicate new sanctuary doors. The Torahs were cleaned and were repaired by a scribe. Rabbi Moshe Druin of Miami performed the work. He studied in Yeshivot of the three main streams of Judaism. He was ordained as a rabbi and scribe in New York, where he met his wife, Ahuva. They moved to Johannesburg, South Africa where he served as Youth Director and Vice-Principal of the Jewish High School, and later as a pulpit rabbi. He and his family moved to North Miami Beach in 1998. Working with Rabbi Moshe Druin was Rabbi Gedaliah Druin, Moshe's father. Gedaliah was ordained in both Miami and New York. Gedaliah was qualified as a Sofer Sta"M, which means Sefer Torah, Tefillin, and Mezuzah. He received his Bachelor of Arts degree from the University of Oklahoma in Psychology, Sociology, and Philosophy and his Master's in Philosophy from the University of Oklahoma. He is currently completing his Ph.D..

Rabbis Druin said, "The Torah is the prized inheritance of the Jewish people. It moves us, motivates us, and unites us as a nation. For 3,000 years, we have learned to live our lives through the teachings, guidance, and messages of the Torah. We are always searching for new ways to bring ourselves closer to it." "The Torah is G-d's gift to the Jewish people. The last and final mitzvah of the Torah is a unique expression of G-d's divinity in this world. There is a commandment upon each and every Jew to write this "Song" – the Torah for themselves. Since the time of its giving, a Sofer(scribe) has completed the sacred task...." Truly, the Rabbis Druin fulfill this sacred duty.

The Torah is made of parchment, which is an animal skin, from a kosher animal. Cow skin is typically used. Goat, sheep, lamb and even deer skin may also be used. The scribes who write the Torahs have an intensive education. Although it is not required that a scribe be a rabbi, he or she typically is one. After ordination, the individual takes intensive training under another scribe and then has to be tested by a board of scribes in the same manner as a rabbi has to be tested prior to ordination.

These individuals are highly motivated to do a perfect job in the copying of one Torah onto a new scroll. Two stories, which are true, tell about the accuracy of the scribes in performing this sacred and most loving duty. Approximately 2,000 years ago, one of the conquerors of the Jewish people wanted to have the Torah translated into Greek. He placed seventy Jewish leaders, who were scribes, into seventy different rooms and ordered them to reproduce a perfect Torah in Greek. Any error or difference between the Torahs would result in death for all seventy. Unbelievably, all seventy Torahs were exactly alike. The other story relates to the Yemini Jews who came to Israel in 1949. They had been separated from the outside society for over 1,000 years. They didn't know who Maimonides was or any of the other Jewish thinkers after that time. They brought their Torahs with them to Israel. When the Torahs were examined, they were found to be perfect, letter for letter and crown for crown. What an amazing act of love the scribes have performed since the Torah was first given to the people Israel. What a person a scribe must be to write and repair Torahs in a totally perfect manner. This is a person who has the greatest respect for God's word.

Torah restoration is both an art and science. Every Torah scroll must be written accurately to be deemed kosher (fit for use) and only a kosher Torah may be read publicly. If an error is found, it is typically because of normal usage or because of deterioration due to environmental conditions. An error is usually due to added or missing letters. Letters may be worn, dirty, or the parchment may be dirty. Worn letters may be filled in with specially made ink. (The ink came down from Sinai originally and the formula and process has been passed from generation to generation through families). Cleaning of the Torah is done with a special soft artist tissue or a special eraser. The use of the computer

Rabbi Gedaliah Druin

now helps identify problems in the specific traditions relating to the formatting of words in a Torah, as well as letters or words that are missing or unnecessary. Human expertise is still a very necessary part of the process. The repair process includes finding and filling in cracked or broken letters, very faded letters, and cleaning. It is recommended by

Rabbis Druin and Moch.

the Rabbis Druin that the Torah restoration take place at the synagogue in order to involve the congregation, especially the children in this loving process. They also recommend that the Rabbi and/or members of the Ritual Committee observe the examination and restoration process. The reason for this involvement by the members and officers of the congregation is for all these individuals to be able to see the problems in the Torahs through the eyes of the scribe. This allows them to become educated consumers and thereby helps prevent further deterioration and damage of the sacred scroll. No special dedication is necessary once the scribe has completed his or her work.

In discussing proper maintenance procedures, he said, "The life of a Torah can be increased with proper care and maintenance.... The number one cause of deterioration in Torahs is moisture." Many times, the Ark is built into an outside wall and therefore moisture unknowingly gets into the Torahs. Rolling the Torah correctly is essential to keep the edges from cracking.

Craig Sher, President,
Temple Beth-El, 1993–1995.

Craig Sher

Craig completed his three-year term as President of Temple Beth-El. During this time period, because of his tremendous energy, innovative approaches, and his dedication to the Jewish community, there was a huge increase in the membership of the Temple, the facility was renovated and

expanded, the congregation became more involved in community affairs, and the budget was balanced each year. As a highly successful manager and leader, he motivated the professional and lay leadership to produce at a consistently higher level and made every effort to see to the needs of each congregant. Craig had built his presidency on the leadership and vision of Mel Estroff and Irwin Miller.

Highlights of 1996

Leonard S. Englander, President of Temple Beth-El, wrote about his experience as a delegate at the UAHC Biennial Convention in Atlanta in December, 1995. He talked about the magical effect of this convention, where over 4,000 Jews of the Reform movement joined together to create goodness and life.

Rabbi Moch talked about the L'Chayim or To Life program, where a home visitor adopted an older, isolated, or home-bound member of the congregation. The home visitor, who visited regularly, offered some human contact and love and made sure that their new friend was safe and well cared for. The individual was asked to bring along a teenager or one of their own children or grandchildren to learn how to help others. Rabbi Moch said, "When our feet run to someone's aid, when our hands reach out to pick someone up, when our mouths speak out against degradation or utter a kind word–God's power becomes manifest in the world. Nothing supersedes the importance of seeing ourselves as God's living power to uplift creation. A new member, Phyllis Birnbaum, and Hugette Levy helped organize the program and Bernice Bressler, along with a local service agency, helped provide some training and orientation for the home visitors."

The Torah Rededication and Celebration entitled "Renewing the Word Fulfilled," occurred on Sunday, May 12. The highlight of the program was a parade where four of the completed Torahs were taken out of the building followed by the visitors, children, and the congregation at large. They joyously danced and celebrated in the street with music, song, and prayer. The Jewish people, according to Jewish law, fulfilled the highest of good deeds, by taking part in the writing of a Torah. It fulfills the obligation of Jewish people to participate and perpetuate the Jewish religion.

The Sisterhood celebrated its 70th anniversary as a highly significant part of the Jewish and general community of St. Petersburg. Its contributions over the years have eased the pain and helplessness of those who would have gone hungry and unclothed. They have been an outstanding example of what Jewish women can do to make the lives of others sweeter.

Highlights of 1997

The Stella Sax lecture series presented Dr. Richard Bredenberg, Academy of Senior Professionals, at Eckerd College. His topic was, "The People behind the Dead Sea Scroll Discoveries."

Highlights of 1998

Terry L. Hirsch talked about the twenty fifth anniversary of the Annual Art Festival. He said, "A twenty fifth anniversary is a time for reflection. It is a time for the celebrants to ponder how they have changed along the road to reaching their milestone and to wonder what the future has in store for them. It is also a time to think of the impact that the years have had on those who hold the celebrants dear." Once again, the extraordinary celebration of the arts proved to be one of the most significant events – in many ways – of Temple life and the Temple year. Twenty five years ago, the Temple membership thought that an art project would be a good way to raise a few needed dollars and provide an opportunity for the Temple members to work together. Temple Beth-El's Art Festival had become one of the most respected art shows in the State of Florida. Its critical success was equal to the financial benefit it brought to the Temple. Under the leadership of festival chairpersons Ellie Argintar, Donna Berman, Sonya Miller, Pam Newman, and Jan Sher, as well as many other fine people over the years, the Art Festival has increased artistically and financially to a level far beyond what was originally predicted.

Beulah Tiepel, Chairperson of the Ritual Committee, talked about the current nature of Reform Judaism. She said, "The evolution of Judaism from rigid orthodoxy to the present progressive reform movement has not changed the sacred covenant and mitzvahs of Judaism. Today, the reverent worship of one God with loving gratitude; the messages of the Torah; and the Ten Commandments are still our holy guides. The sacred ritual of the Sabbath, its services from candle and kiddush to the havdalah are intact. We observe the mitzvahs, which we were taught in childhood....My husband and I attend every Friday service. We enter a holy place where we are enveloped with Shabbat peace. God is always there. Rabbi Moch invites us to join with the ancestors who sacrificed to keep our religion alive. God has not changed. After the final blessing, we take God home with us. Come join us in the spiritual experience."

Louis Krosner, President, Temple Beth-El, 1997–1999.

Rabbi Moch, when describing a significant aspect of Jewish life, said, "Torah learning has always been a critical focus of Jewish life. Our prayer book says that, Talmud Torah, the learning of our sacred text is equal to the doing of all ma'asim tovim, good deeds. But Talmid Torah is never enough. Torah must be transformed into real world doing. Pirkei Avot (The Sayings of Our Fathers) says that a person whose learning exceeds his ma'asim tovim, his goodly acts, is like a tree whose branches are many but whose roots are few, so that any wind that comes can uproot it. But a person whose ma'asim tovim exceeds his learning is like a tree whose branches are few, but whose roots are many so that all the winds in the world cannot uproot it."

Highlights of 1999

The Scholar-in-Residence was Rabbi Michael Chernick. He is Deutsch Professor of Jewish Jurisprudence and Social Justice, Hebrew Union College-Jewish Institute of Religion in New York. His topics were, "Is There a Place for the Lesson of Yesterday in the 21st Century?" He also presented, "Who Pays: Adult Children and Parents." Temple Beth-El offered a workshop on "From Ageing to Sageing." To become spiritually older was to become physically vital, spiritually radiant, and socially responsible elders of the community who converted rich experience into wisdom.

Cub Scout Pack 222, a partnership of Temple Beth-El and Congregation B'nai Israel, was chartered by the Boy Scouts of America. Training was established for volunteer adult leaders.

Rabbi David Susskind

Rabbi Emeritus David Susskind was honored by Temple Beth-El for his fifty years of service as a Rabbi. Rabbi Susskind, in a personal statement, talked about his life. He said, "At my stage in life, we are implored to live one day at a time and thus we do. Having cultivated the garden, it's time to smell the roses and live with an abiding sense of gratitude. I hope it is reflected in my demeanor." He talked about how rich his life has been, although he still lived under a cloud of mourning, reminiscent of the deaths in recent years of his wonderful, beautiful, wife and shortly thereafter, a very talented and gifted son. He said that he was blessed with parents whose devotion to God, Israel, and Torah was synonymous with their love for their six children. He learned from his father faith, reverence, and piety. He learned from his mother the doing of good deeds, compassion for others, a zeal for liberalism, and modernity. All these wonderful traits became part of the fabric of his being.

The havoc and devastation of the Holocaust angered and tormented him. It gave him an overwhelming determination to want to help, to save, and serve Jews. He volunteered to serve with the World Jewish Congress to help in the rescue of Holocaust victims and refugees of the displacement camps. He was too young and they would not accept him. He felt an urgency to learn at the Jewish Institute of Religion and Study under Rabbi Steven S. Wise, who was a voice and advocate of World and American Jewry. He initially wanted to pursue an administrative position with a national Jewish organization. However, after performing the High Holy Day services as a student rabbi and officiating in numerous life cycle ceremonies, he decided to seek a pulpit. He was going to go to Israel and spend his career there, but he was dissuaded because of the unsettled conditions and fortunately was able to become a dedicated rabbi in the United States. The Reform movement was evolving and this young man who was trained initially in the Orthodox schools went on to become part of the Liberal rabbinate. His opportunity to serve a small, but established pulpit in St. Petersburg, Florida, was the realization of a dream. He said, "Even as one seeks to understand God at varying stages of experience in life and re-evaluate beliefs, so did I ever seek to define and refine my life as a rabbi. Sometimes I thought myself successful and other times woefully inadequate, but I believe I gave it my reverential best and respectfully did it my way. My idyllic love for Jews at times faltered, but the love I did receive from the myriads of people in my congregation and community that I was privileged to serve, to teach and to minister to, was sufficiently rewarding so as to be an abiding and cherished blessing. Life as we know it is not without tribulation and I have had my goodly share, even as I have known unmeasured joys. I gratefully pray, "Boruch Hashem yom yom (Praise be God day by day.)."

Highlights of 2000-2005

Highlights of 2000

In the year 2000, the L'DOR V'DOR Endowment Fund was created for a new educational building and an expansion of the Founders Hall. The Temple membership exceeded 500 families.

Rabbi Michael Torop invited local NAACP President Darryl Rouson to attend a Sabbath service and give a talk afterwards.

Highlights of 2001

Temple Beth-El dedicated a new one million, six hundred thousand dollar education wing on Hanukkah. Irving Miller was given much of the credit for this needed addition, since he was instrumental in the L'Dor V'dor (Generation to Generation) three and one-half million dollar capital and endowment campaign, and a driving force behind construction of the new wing. Miller and the late Maurice Rothman headed the construction committee for the congregation's original building on its present site. That building was dedicated in

Terry L. Hirsch, President, Temple Beth-El, 2002-2004.

1962. Miller said, "The thing is, I'm involved because I think it is wonderful for Jewish life and the community, but the idea is building for the future." Rabbi Torop said, "We have already made much of what we were given, by Jewish tradition and by the founders of Temple Beth-El. Now we are showing that what we will make of these gifts is to create a community of learning and joy, filled with a sense of the sacred, dedicated to the pursuit of justice, wholeness and peace." The building will give the congregation of 600 families much-needed room to take care of the needs of approximately 200 children, who were attending the religious school.

Highlights of 2002

The L'Dor V'dor addition to the building was completed. Everyone was able to benefit from the generosity of the congregation. Much of the programming was held in this new addition. It also included Religious or Hebrew School, the Youth Lounge, the Wides Courtyard etc.. The L'Dor V' Dor (generation to generation) fund goal was two million dollars. The fund has a very simple purpose, to ensure the continuation and stability of Temple Beth-El for many years to come.

Craig and Jan Sher

In the same way Temple Beth-El has played a highly significant role in the lives of Craig and Jan Sher and their three daughters, Jessica, Stacy, and Alison, the Sher family has more then returned this love and concern with their activities in support of the Temple. Craig, Past President of Temple Beth-El, led the rabbinical search that resulted in the hiring of Rabbi Stephen Moch. He has also been involved in fund-raising for the Temple and has served on finance and rabbinical liaison committees. Jan was Chairperson of the School Board for many years, and has been Co–Chairperson of the Art Festival, rabbinical search committee, and many other committees. Craig said, "The Temple is our highest philanthropic priority. There is nothing more important than to build and maintain our Temple...We are committed to carry on the Miller Family tradition of being there for the Temple and to carry her family into the fourth generation. We

hope that our children will move back to St. Petersburg and be active in our Temple... We are all equally important at the Temple. It is equally available regardless of means. We believe that everyone should participate in building, rebuilding, and maintaining the Temple. Every gift and everyone is important regardless of the level of their gift. (It is) meaningful for everyone to be a part of building for the future."

Rabbi Michael Torop

Highlights of 2003

Temple Beth-El started the celebration of their 75th anniversary by praising the women of the Sisterhood. The Sisterhood led the way toward the establishment of this reform synagogue. They brought together thirty families who wanted to honor God in a liberal manner. They wanted to celebrate freely their traditions and worship together as a community. Today, there are more than 225 members in the Sisterhood. They continue to make substantial contributions to all facets of the Temple and especially to the educational programs for the children. The Sisterhood puts on a variety of educational events and religious services that focus on women. Since their inception, they have been involved in helping those less fortunate in the St. Petersburg community.

Highlights of 2004

Rabbi Michael Torop wrote the following about Temple Beth-El on its 75th Diamond anniversary: "Our Sages teach: "Blessing is found not only in those things which can be weighed and measured and counted, but in those things which are hidden from the eye". The dimension that matters the most in synagogue life is the one that is hidden from the eye. It is the dimension of depth that accounts for God's presence in our lives. For seventy five years, Temple Beth-El has been a community of great depth. We offer comfort when those in our midst face sorrow. We offer warmth when newcomers cross our threshold. We offer joyous celebration at times of simcha. Temple Beth-El is a glorious synagogue that has earned its place within both the Jewish and general communities because of the dedication and participation of our leadership and our membership throughout our history....Beth-El is also

Michael Shapiro, President, Temple Beth-El, 2004-2006.

a community with one heart....We are unified as we encounter the presence of God, equally valuing the contribution of each and every member, both current and past. On this auspicious occasion, I offer my gratitude to the rabbis who each offered his own vision to help guide our congregation in years past. I share with each of us the debt of gratitude to our founders whose dream has become reality. I acknowledge the many temple leaders and temple members whose legacy we enjoy each and every day."

Rabbi Torop said, "The desire to provide a religious education for their children has always been, and remains today, one of the primary motivations for synagogue affiliation." He believes that the quality of the religious school experience is one of the sustaining pillars of a congregation. Bar Mitzvah and Bat Mitzvah, Pre-School, Hebrew School, Religious School, Confirmation Classes are all part of the educational experience. The enrollment at the Temple Beth-El Religious School was 175 students. One third of the children in the Pre-School were non-Jewish.

Highlights of 2005

Rabbi Torop discussed the need for continuing education for Jewish people. He said that time and again, he encountered people who felt that they were unable to continue their Jewish education because of all of the demands of secular society and their careers. He said to them, "Why study? The rationale behind learning Judaism is so that we can live complete Jewish lives, and to have the knowledge to see the world through Jewish eyes, ultimately, to fill our lives with meaning and our world with purpose." He said this can be accomplished by attending the various educational programs offered through the Temple.

Torahs

The 25 inch parchment plain tip Torah is approximately 125 years old. It is the Temple's first Torah and was acquired when Rabbi Rosenblatt was hired in 1933. There is no information about where it came from. The mantle cover was replaced about 1986. It was designed by an artist in New York by the name of Miriam. The design represents the Hebrew word for "truth." The Torah crown was commissioned in 1976 to celebrate the 25th anniversary of Mr. and Mrs. Jacob Shainberg. It was designed by Kurt J. Mazdorf, silversmith, of New Paltz, New York. The 16 inch ivory tip parchment Torah is inscribed with Jacob L. Miller's name in Hebrew. The mantle cover was designed by the New York artist Miriam. The design represents the Hebrew word for "Peace." The 18 1/2" parchment double roller Torah was purchased in 1959 and donated by Rabbi David Susskind. The mantle cover was designed by the New York artist Miriam. The design represents the Hebrew word for "Light." The 16 3/4" parchment plane tip Torah was inscribed in Hebrew with a tribute to Theodore Carr. The Torah mantle was lovingly handmade by Fanny Morgan in memory of Helga Kaufman.

A review of the Torahs indicated the following dedications: Torah number one had no dedication and therefore it is not known what family contributed it to the Temple; Torah number two was donated in memory of Maurice by Dorothy Goldblatt; Torah number three was donated by Marion Samson Joseph in memory of Bernard L. Samson; Torah number four was donated by Philip, Marilyn, Judy, and Caren Benjamin; Torah number five was donated by Mr. and Mrs. Donald Silverberg and family; and Torah number six was donated by Sharyn and Dick Jacobson, Todd, Mark, and Caron in memory of Sylvia Heller Wittner.

CHAPTER 16

TEMPLE B'NAI ISRAEL OF CLEARWATER

Highlights of 1950-1959

Highlights of 1957

(The early history of Temple B'nai Israel, from 1946-1956, may be found in the chapter on Clearwater and North County) The confirmation class of 1957 was made up of Anita Bauman, Jeffrey Lopatin, and Mark Rowen. The service was conducted on Sunday, June 2. An organ prelude, Arioso by Handel, was played by Grant Jones, the organist. The Temple choir sang, "Create in Me a Clean Heart, Oh God." A floral offering was presented by Anita Bauman. Mark Rowen discussed, "The Ethics of Judaism." Jeffrey Lopatin discussed, "The Fifth Commandment." The Temple Trio performed, "Lift Thine Eyes" by Mendelssohn. During the blessing of the confirmants, a violin solo, "Meditation from Thais," was played by Stephen W. Yanetovich. This was followed by the Temple Choir singing "Bow Down Thy Ear O Lord" by A.S. Arensky. The adoration was spoken, followed by the benediction, and finally an organ postlude, "Sarabaivde" by Bohm. The Temple Choir was under the direction of Julia Berolzheimer, and included Larry Friedlander, Tessie Jacoby, Mary Rowen and Ethyl Schoenfeld. The Temple Trio consisted of Rebecca Hite, Caroline Lesher, and Margret Le Master.

The Board of Trustees changed the by-laws of Temple B'nai Israel to allow people who were members for one year to serve on the board and in various offices. This was a significant moment in the history of Temple B'nai Israel, since it allowed new people to immediately become involved and to bring fresh energy to the congregation. The Sisterhood had a Committee on Emergency Services which provided help for the men and women serving in uniform. They were also involved in the: Serve-a-Camp, Serve-a-Hospital, Serve-a-Chaplain Projects, eighty two military and veterans hospitals, provision of Thanksgiving baskets, seder packages for Jewish servicemen and women overseas, a large variety of local community work, sale of TB seals, collecting can goods for Thanksgiving baskets for the Salvation Army, etc..

Fox Family

Roland Fox, his wife, Betty, and their daughter, Debbie, moved from Dayton, Ohio to Clearwater in September to take the necessary bar examinations and open his own law office. Betty's family also had moved to Clearwater, including her father, Leon Capeluto, her mother, Victoria, her sister, Selma, and her brother, Nace. Leon and Victoria opened the Kiddyland Store.

Roland Fox was born in 1930 in Dayton, Ohio. He served in the United States Air Force. Betty Capeluto Fox was born in 1935 in Montgomery, Alabama, and died in Clearwater in 1992. They had three children. Deborah Lynn Fox was born in 1956 and married Edmund Shapiro of Richmond, Virginia. Debbie graduated from Sophia Newcomb College in New Orleans. She lives in Potomac, Maryland, where she is President of the Har Shalom Congregation. They have three children, Daniel, Jenna, and Michael. Gregory was born in Clearwater in 1958 and married Barbara Rocker of New Delhi, India. They have two children, Allyson and Brett. Leon was born in Clearwater in 1960 and married Jill Fogel of Miami. Leon graduated from the University of Florida. He has served as Treasurer of Congregation Beth Shalom of Clearwater. They have three children, Nolan, Jarrod, and Brody. Roland married Marjorie Diamond in 2000. Marjorie was born in 1939 in Cleveland, Ohio.

Roland became very active in both the general community and Temple B'nai Israel. Howard Lawrence was responsible for introducing him into the significance of serving the greater community. Roland served as a Municipal Judge for eight years. He was President of the Clearwater Seratoma

Roland Fox

Club, Chairman of the first Sertoma Follies, Chairman of the Fun N Sun Committee, founder of the night parade, President of the Belcher Elementary School PTA, Chairman of the Better Business Committee of the Clearwater Chamber of Commerce. He and Betty were very active in a large number of additional charities.

Charlie Rutenberg asked Roland to serve as General Chairman to build the new Temple on Belcher Road. Charlie asked Roland how much Roland was going to pledge for the new Temple. Charlie then taught Roland his first lesson. Charlie said, "You cannot ask for money until you give your utmost." Roland then doubled his pledge. Roland also served Temple B'nai Israel as President, Vice-President, Treasurer, Secretary, Member of the Board for many years, and Chairman of the Rabbi's Selection Committee that brought Rabbi Baseman to Clearwater.

When Rabbi Taxay retired, Roland wanted to reunite Congregation Beth Shalom and Temple B'nai Israel. Beth Shalom was looking for a Rabbi. Roland advertised for a Rabbi to perform a reform service on Friday nights and the first day of Rosh Hashana at Temple B'nai Israel and then conservative services on Saturday morning and the second day of Rosh Hashanah at Congregation Beth Shalom. He received several résumés from rabbis. However, when Rabbi Arthur Baseman heard about this change from the original reform congregation, he asked that his name be removed from the list. Rabbi Baseman explained, "A Rabbi must believe in how he leads and teaches a congregation." Rabbi Baseman's name immediately went to the top of the list.

When the old Temple was sold, a clause was put in the contract allowing the congregation to move the beautiful, but very large, palm tree to the new synagogue. The tree is currently in the courtyard of the Temple complex.

Roland was one of the founders and Past-President of the Jewish Welfare Fund of Clearwater. He participated in the United Jewish Appeal Mission in 1973 and in 1976.

During his years as a municipal judge, the American Bar Association cited the City of Clearwater on four separate occasions for having one of the outstanding court systems in the United States among cities the size of Clearwater. This was accomplished because of the highly successful work of Judge Roland Fox. He started many programs, including helping minors with alcohol problems, and improvement of driver training. Over 2,300 people successfully attended these courses and avoided serious legal actions. The city saved a substantial amount of money in not having to provide jail time for these individuals, and these individuals were rehabilitated.

Gregory A. Fox earned a Bachelor of Science Degree in Management from Tulane University in 1980. He earned a Doctor of Jurisprudence in 1983 from the University of Florida Law School and a Master's of Legal Letters in Taxation from George Washington University in 1984.

Greg said, "My involvement in Temple B'nai Israel began the day I was born. There were very few Jewish families in Clearwater when I was growing up. However, my class at Temple B'nai Israel was one of the largest they had up to this time. There were over twenty kids in my class, starting with consecration and continuing until confirmation. My connection to Temple B'nai Israel commenced my Jewish identity, and continues to this day. I remember fondly the years the Temple spent at Betty Lane and I literally grew up there. My Bar Mitzvah in 1971 was the last Bar Mitzvah held at the Temple on Betty Lane. During those years we did not have Saturday morning services, so my Bar Mitzvah was held on a Friday evening Shabbat service. While the new Temple was being constructed on Belcher Road, I would visit the Rabbi on the site of the current Temple for my Bar Mitzvah training. In high school,... I was a member of Temple B'nai Israel Youth Group (BIFTY)."

After graduating from law school and receiving his Master's in Taxation, he and his father, Roland, formed the firm of Fox and Fox, P.A. Greg immediately became involved in working for Temple B'nai Israel. He was a member of the Temple B'nai Israel Endowment Committee, and served on the Board of Trustees for four years. In 1991, he became a member of the Executive

Committee and served as Assistant Treasurer, Financial Vice President, Coordinating Vice President, and then became President in 1997. He was involved in the expansion of the pre-school, which is considered to be one of the best in the County.

Greg also has been involved in the general community. He was the Treasurer of the Clearwater Bar Association, President of the Pinellas County Estate Planning Council, President of the Sparkling City Commercial Club, and is currently President of the Tampa Orlando Pinellas Jewish Foundation Incorporated.

Barbara Ellen (Rocker) Fox, Greg's wife, was born in New Delhi, India, in 1961. She moved to the United States in 1962 and grew up in Maryland. She moved to Florida in 1979. She earned a Bachelor of Arts Degree in Criminal Justice in 1983 from the University of South Florida. She served as an investigator for the Office of the Auditor General–Division of Public Assistance Fraud–from 1983–1995. She is currently a sales representative.

Barbara has been very active in Jewish and community organizations. She has worked with: Temple B'nai Israel Young Couples Club, Jewish Federation of Pinellas County, Junior League of Clearwater–Dunedin as Co-Chair of various events, Curlew Creek Elementary School, Safety Harbor Middle School, Palm Harbor Middle School, Palm Harbor University High School, and the Magnet Program.

The Fox family has distinguished itself in both the Jewish and general communities. The children of Deborah and Edmund, Gregory and Barbara, Leon and Jill, are examples of what Jewish children are taught in this community and elsewhere, following the trail established by their grandparents and parents: "Become involved in the Jewish and general communities, help all people improve their lives, and you, too, live a good life."

Highlights of 1958

Although there was excellent attendance at Friday night services, there were no Saturday morning services. Rabbi Richmond pleaded for a Saturday morning service, but the individuals in the congregation did not respond. His sermons on Friday nights, although lengthy in nature, reflected the wisdom of the rabbi. They were as if he were presenting arguments to the Supreme Court of the United States. At one sermon, he talked about the idols of the pagan religions, describing them by means of the three L's, licentious, lecherous, and lascivious. Other sermons included topics ranging from "The Quest for Happiness," "The Morality of Ideas," "National Brotherhood," "What Makes Life Worthwhile," etc.. Rabbi Richmond was very accommodating to all members of the congregation. It had been planned years before that Bill Lopatin would be bar mitzvah at an Orthodox synagogue in Brooklyn. Harold was worried about preparing him in an orthodox manner. Rabbi Richmond told Harold not to worry, that Bill would do fine. Rabbi Richmond called the rabbi in Brooklyn and discussed with that Rabbi what Torah portion Bill would have for his bar mitzvah. Under the tutelage of Rabbi Richmond, Bill did a great job in the Orthodox synagogue.

The religious school teachers were parents. The curriculum was set up by Rabbi Richmond and he guided the parents on how to teach the children. They learned Hebrew, Jewish history, Jewish ethics, and other subjects.

On June 6, 1958, a Petition for Change of Name was entered in the court in Pinellas County and the name of the synagogue became officially Temple B'nai Israel. The corporation had been known as Temple B'nai Israel from its beginnings on September 19, 1949.

During all this time, the Brotherhood was very active. Harold Lopatin was President from 1963-1964. He still has his gavel of office. The Brotherhood made numerous contributions to the Temple and Jewish Chatauqua Society.

Marshall Kent had previously decided that Temple B'nai Israel needed a new religious school, because it had outgrown the existing facility. Marshall owned the largest terrazo company on the west coast of Florida. He bought a big flatbed truck and designed an approach to mix the marble chips on the truck with concrete, to be able to pour them together. He was able to use one truck

Howard Lawrence, President, Temple B'nai Israel, 1956–1957.

Laying cornerstone of Betty Lane Religious School, l. to r., Rabbi Harry Richmond, Marshall Kent, Darwin Frank, Howard Lawrence, Clearwater Mayor Lewis Homer.

instead of three trucks to accomplish this.

In April, after Julius Lovitz donated the lot, Marshall Kent poured the floor and constructed the addition to the religious school on the north side of the existing building, below cost. On May 15, the cornerstone was laid for the new school building. Howard Lawrence was the chairman of the building school committee. The cornerstone ceremony was conducted by Howard Lawrence, Mayor Lewis H. Homer, Darwin Frank, President, the children of the religious school, and Rabbi Harry R. Richmond.

Temple B'nai Israel members served as leaders in a variety of community organizations. They sponsored the blood bank at Morton Plant Hospital, with co-chairs, Al Rophie and Phyllis Lovitz. This was also a B'nai Brith project. From the very beginning of the temple, the leadership and membership have been deeply involved in Interfaith activities.

The children formed a youth group for grades nine through twelve, called B'nai Israel Federation of Temple Youth (BIFTY). The youth group was very active. They met at the Temple and celebrated all the holidays, studied Jewish history, and some of the members taught in the religious school. Children from other Jewish communities in Florida were invited to visit. This is how many of the Clearwater Jewish children made friends elsewhere. Bill Lopatin and his wife, Jo Anne, met at just such a conclave. They married in 1967. Bill received a master's degree and Ph.D. from the University of South Florida, moved to Texas, and then South Bend, Indiana. In 1959-1960, Nancy Collman was President. Nancy Collman and Leanne Braun were in the second confirmation class in 1958.

Nancy Collman, who was married by Rabbi Taxay, was the second bride married at the Temple on Betty Lane. She married Robert Gerson. She went back to college after she was married, became a lawyer, and was on the Law Review. She practiced law in

Herbert Frank, President, Temple B'nai Israel, 1958–1960.

Fort Myers for a few years and then retired. She was the first confirmant to be married in the Temple. Her confirmation teacher was Philip Evans. Steve Collman and his bride, Kathy, were the last ones married at the Betty Lane Temple. This occurred at the end of the 1960s.

There were no baby namings in the beginning. The first bris was the son of Marian and Larry Freedlander. It was held in their home and invited guests participated. The older Jewish people were taken care of by their children. For instance, Estelle Korones took care of her mother at her home and Shirley and Leonard Collman took care of Leonard's parents in Shirley and Leonard's home. At that point, the concept of a Jewish nursing home had not reached a crucial point.

Moss Funeral Home usually handled the Jewish funerals. They also provided ambulance service for emergencies and taking patients home from the hospital. Leonard's parents' service was held at Moss Funeral Home and burial was in Sarasota at the Beth Shalom Cemetery that Leonard's father helped found. There is a Jewish section at Sylvan Abbey.

The Temple Board members were: D. Frank, H. Frank, J. Stampleman, L. Friedlander, C. N. Roth, A. R. Samuels, M. Kent, A. Rutenberg, J. Berolzheimer, J. Lovitz, M. Bilgore, I Baker, H. Lawrence, L. Collman, R. Kent, H. Lopatin, David Davis replaced I. Greenwald and M. Baumann.

Highlights of 1959

Attendance at Sabbath services at Temple B'nai Israel averaged about sixty five people. The Temple Board members were: H. Frank, L. Friedlander, D. Davis, E. Schwartz, M. Bilgore, R. Fox, D. Harwood, L. Collman, R. Kent, M. Kent, H. Lawrence, J. Lovitz, I. Baker, and A Rutenberg. On June 2, at a meeting of the Board of Directors of Temple B'nai Israel, Julius Lovitz announced that he would be buying the George Resnick property with 80 ft. fronting on Park Street for his own account and would then donate it to the Temple when the Temple was ready to build a new school facility. Since this piece of property was 40 ft. from the temple, he suggested that the Board negotiate with the owners of the adjoining land and tried to either make a swap or buy it outright.

Julia Berolzheimer continued to teach and lead the Temple Choir for the High Holy Days. Mr. Kassel donated the pulpit chairs. The red drapes from the Temple were offered as a gift to Congregation Beth Shalom. Howard Lawrence continued his excellent job as official greeter, usher, and High Holy Day ticket purveyor. Fifty four children enrolled in the religious school. The Board and the rabbi encouraged the bar mitzvah and confirmation students to attend Friday night services. The first confirmation class included Jeffrey Alan Lopatin, Marc Rowan, and Anita Bauman. They were confirmed by Rabbi Richmond.

Jeffrey and Susan Lopatin

Jeffrey Lopatin graduated from Clearwater High School. In September, he enrolled in the Citadel in Charleston, South Carolina. In 1962, he decided not to make a career in the Army and enrolled in The Fashion Institute of Technology in New York. He studied engineering and graduated in 1963. He returned to Clearwater with his bride, Susan, and became a product engineer with Bee Bee Togs. When Pixie Playmates was formed in 1964, he became Vice President of Production. He became President in 1975 and Chairman when Harold retired in 1990. He and Susan have two children born in Clearwater: Heidi, 1965 and Adam, 1968. Those children attended Hebrew School and were B'nai Mitzvah under Rabbi Baseman. There were seventy two members of the congregation on October 7. The piece of land between that which was purchased by Julius Lovitz and the Temple was purchased by the congregation.

Harold and Sally Siegel

Harold and Sally and their daughter, Mindy, moved to Clearwater. Harold opened his first pharmacy in downtown Clearwater. He was the first person to open a pharmacy inside of a grocery store. He sold everything from aspirins to toys to small television sets to keep up with the competition. One Christmas Eve, as he was closing the store, he decided to deliver the unsold toys and Christmas decorations to underprivileged children. He loaded up his car and delivered them himself. The following year, he special ordered extra merchandise, bought a Santa Claus costume, and asked the police to help him. Each year, the project grew, and he became known as the Jewish Santa Claus. The tradition was eventually taken over by the Police Department and is still in effect. On December 21, 1970, Harold was honored by the City of Clearwater for initiating the program. Despite his business, he found time to be deeply involved in both Temple B'nai Israel and Congregation Beth Shalom. He and Sally donated the necessary funds for an organ for Temple B'nai Israel. Todd was born in 1958. Both Mindy and Todd were married at Temple B'nai Israel. Todd, a pharmacist like his father, is now the Chief Executive Officer of his parents' business. Todd has worked on various planning committees, including Jacob's Ladder, and is a Member of the Board of the Menorah Manor Foundation and Pediatric Cancer Foundation. Todd's wife, Sheila, is a volunteer for the Pinellas County Education Foundation Doorways Program. She has sponsored several children for Florida prepaid college scholarships.

Weiss/Hartman Families

Hanna and Douglas Weiss arrived in Clearwater from Elmhurst, New York with children, Kenneth, age nine and Andrea, age six. They helped form Congregation Beth Shalom and also became members of Temple B'nai Israel. Doug, a builder/developer, built numerous subdivisions, single-family homes, condominiums and a strip mall in Clearwater. He was President of the Temple B'nai Israel Men's Club and a Member of the Board of Directors, as well as on the Temple building committee. Doug died in 1986.

Hanna was born in Germany and emigrated to the United States in 1940, along with her parents and sister. Her father was a physician. She and Doug were married in 1946. She handled the secretarial work in Doug's construction firm. The Clearwater Woman's Club selected her as one of the city's best dressed ladies. She was Financial Secretary of the Sisterhood and participated in the primary schoolchildren's hearing screening program. After the children grew up, she went into real estate sales.

Kenneth became a young Jewish leader under the tutelage of Dr. Taxay. He was a member of Law Review at the University of Florida. He is currently a practicing attorney. Andrea was President of the entire Tampa Bay Federation of Temple Youth. She taught Sunday school at the Temple. She is a reading specialist in the Jacksonville, Florida School system. Her husband, Neal Esserman, is a retail consultant.

In 1992, Hanna remarried. Her husband is Burt Hartman, a retired real estate attorney with a versatile background in New York and Miami.

Temple Family Members in 1959

On April 1, the following families were members of Temple B'nai Israel; Baker, Bauman, Benmayer, H. Berolzheimer, Julia Berolzheimer, Bilgore, Arthur Collman, C. Collman, Dukman, Deutsch, Eisenstadt, D. Frank, L. Frank, H. Frank, Friedlander, Goldstein, Kleinman, Lefkowits, Arthur Lopatin, Harold Lopatin, Julius Lovitz, S. Marks, Miller, Arthur Rutenberg, Charles Rutenberg, M. Sackheim, E. Schwartz, H. Schwartz, Stampleman, Mrs. Baikovitch, Miss Matthews, Mrs. Schoenfeld, Mrs. Gladstone, Salem Baranoff, Brower, Bragin, Burke, Daniel Bandes, Doug Wise, Leonard Collman, R., Davis, Fox, Shirley Harwood Marshall Kent, Samuel Korones, Kaplan, David Lawrence, Michels, Piskin, Podgur, Roth, Ruderman, Rosenheimer, S. Rich, N. Rich, A. Samuels, Salomon, A. Stone, M. Salzman, Zimbal, Zucker, Mrs. Brodsky, Koslow, Mrs. Lebman, Lowen, Morris, Bert Schram, L. Samuels, Mrs. Weiss, Kanner, Mrs. Brodsky, Lowen, Morris, Arnold Jacoby.

On April 1, 1958, there had been sixty six members. Fourteen new members had been added during the course of the year and nine had resigned. Those who had resigned were: Braun, Glazer, Greenwald, Doug Weiss, Zitlin, Talkoff, Faih, Dribben, and Coggan. This made a total of seventy one members. Loren Pollack arrived in September.

Miscellaneous Information

Mrs. Hartman was a widow who lived with her sister in Clearwater Beach from the 1940s until at least 1960. Daniel and Lillian Bandes arrived sometime in the 1950s. Dan and his partner, Doug Wise, were builders. Lillian went for an advanced degree in Miami. This took a lot of courage in those days for a married woman to accomplish this type of success. Leonard Collman and Julius Lovitz opened a five-star mobile home park, Colonial Village Mobile Park, in January 1965. Later, they developed Park Royale Mobile Home Park for Charlie Rutenberg. Bert Schram was already a senior citizen when she arrived in the 1950s. She was a poet and had published several poetry books. She often read one of her poems at various Jewish affairs. Tessie and Arnold Jacoby were honorary members. They were very elderly when they moved to Florida for their health. They taught Sunday school and Arnold taught Hebrew. They made a difference in the lives of the children and the adults.

Lee and Phyllis Dorian

Lee and Phyllis came to the Clearwater area to work for Stanley Freifeld, who was a builder. Lee, a marketing manager, then went to work for Arthur Rutenberg about 1962 or 1963 and then went into his own business around 1965, Dorian Housing Incorporated and Dorian Realty. He started building custom homes. Randolph Farms, Lee's project, was the first cluster homes in Pinellas County. It was very environmentally conscious. As many trees as possible were saved during the construction. Lee helped the economy grow by providing employment for many people. He enhanced the beauty of the community. And in fact, Lee won a beautification award for his work. Lee later donated Randolph Farms Barn to Heritage Village.

Lee Dorian and Herbert Schwartz were the co-chairpersons of the building committee for the present structure on Belcher Road. Both were on-site managers of the sub-contractors while they were both running their own businesses. Herb was also in the construction business and had been brought here by Charlie Rutenberg. Lee took the lead and helped with many of the design features as well as much of the construction supervision. Phyllis said, "That the reason Lee performed this momentous mitzvah was that he knew that the Temple would outlive him and that this would be a wonderful contribution to the Jewish community and society at large."

Lee was extremely generous. Phyllis said, "Many people who needed help received advice and financial assistance from Lee, and this was never publicized." Lee was a community minded person. He was part of the clown group that visited children and also was Chairperson of the Fun and Sun Parade in Clearwater. Lee was Secretary of the Board of Trustees and Secretary of the Executive Committee of Temple B'nai Israel, a Youth Group Advisor, Chairman of the Russian Resettlement Project, a member of the Sertoma Club and the Board of Realtors.

Lee was born on January 14, 1927 and died on February 18, 1983. At the memorial service for Lee Dorian on February 21, 1983, Rabbi Baseman celebrated the short but highly significant life of this remarkable and unassuming leader of people and doer of good deeds.

"What an incredibly beautiful outpouring of love for you, Phyllis, and Robin, and Marc and Solomon, from all of us here, grieving with you on the death of Lee, our youth group advisor. I recall the kind of care and attention Lee gave to every detail. Lee with his ever present tape recorder, whispering things into it– reminding himself of this detail or that detail that had to be implemented. His was a rare gift of leadership. Wherever he functioned, people sought him out. Whether it was sub-contractors or workers, or co-workers – wherever he moved, people turned to him for direction. He helped people do their best. His involvement with the Board of Realtors and as an officer and Board Member of Temple B'nai Israel, as a co-chairman of this building's construction and creation. He also did for so many people–there aren't many of us who don't have something that Lee has given them. Something he created as an artist, as a craftsman, in stained glass. And there's his Randolph Farms from which he drew great pride and satisfaction.

His children described him as the cornerstone of their lives. As a perfect family man. Always there for them–what a

wonderful tribute to a father from children. And you, Phyllis, have been an inspiration to us all. And your devotion to Lee, you and Marc and Robin; and he knew of your love for him and he knew of his love for you.

There is nothing bombastic about Lee's leadership. He never ranted or raved or indulged in histrionics. He spoke softly and people listened. He walked quietly and people followed. A reasoned sentence came from his lips; calm judgment prevailed. It was a quietness within him; and ever certainty. His radiant serenity which compelled respect. And we cannot be in the sanctuary without seeing Lee and sensing his presence. Lee left his signature before our very eyes. The eternal light, the shin. I will never be able to look at the light again without seeing L-E-E etched on its three prongs. And the Ark. There wasn't a detail that Lee did not pursue in terms of our Ark. Once the text was chosen, "And Jacob dreamed a dream, a ladder rooted on earth–the top of it reaching to heaven." From that moment, Lee worked with the artists to create an Ark worthy of our Sanctuary. Stone was placed inside the Ark as well as outside the Ark to demonstrate that the inner person and the outer person must be the same. I am reminded of the story of a sculptor who was once commissioned to fashion a statue to stand high in a Temple with its back against the wall. And the sculptor worked on the entire statue with meticulous care as he strove to make it as perfect as he could. And a friend asked him why he paid so much attention to the back of the statue since it could not be seen by anyone. The sculptor answered, "the statue must be perfect everywhere as God sees everywhere." Well that was Lee. His concern with the hidden part as well as the obvious part, with every detail.

In the Torah, we read that the Ark was to be overlaid with gold and inlaid with gold. So, we have stone on the outside of our Ark and on the inside of our Ark because the outer and inner person were to be represented as one. We must strive to be on the inside –what we appear to be on the

Lee Dorian

Temple B'nai Israel's Ark

outside.

Now, I have left the Bible open since the Saturday morning service. Lee died on the eve of the Sabbath. And I want to read to you the Torah portion of the Sabbath before which Lee died. And this is what we read in the Torah portion,

And the Lord spoke unto Moses, "Speak unto the children of Israel

That they take for me an offering of everyone whose heart makes him willing.

You shall take an offering, and let them make me a Sanctuary

That I may dwell among them and they shall make an Ark.

And thou shalt overlay it with pure gold within and without shall thou overlay it."

Is that mere happenstance? Well, if it is, it is a happenstance that is not peculiar to the God which we often observe. What a fitting portion. What an inspiring portion to reflect upon at this time. What a worthy portion for Lee Dorian.

Lee died on the eve of the Sabbath–the Sabbath that spoke of building a Sanctuary to God. And as the eternal light which he designed, he brightened our life and will continue to do so. His memory is a blessing and we shall vest it with the love and respect, with admiration and honor. "AMEN"

Phyllis and the children had a sculpture made in honor of Lee and placed in the foyer of the Temple. The sculpture is made of Hebrew words which came from the Book of Proverbs Chapter 20: Verse 27, "The Soul of Man is the Light of the Lord."

Phyllis graduated from Hunter College with a Bachelor's of Science in Home Economics and from the University of South Florida with a Master of Arts in Counseling Psychology. She took additional special training at Harvard University to become certified by the Florida Supreme Court to become a mediator in legal actions, especially in family and divorce matters. She has been: Youth Group Advisor; Religious School Teacher; Member of Religious School Committee; Member of Board of Trustees of Temple B'nai Israel; Chairperson of the Adult Education Committee; Vice President of Sisterhood; and Vice President of Hadassah. She is also a member of Brandeis Women.

Phyllis and Lee had two children, a son, Marc, born on January 24, 1955. He graduated from Tulane University with a Bachelor of Science Degree in Political Science. He is a producer for the news show 20/20. Daughter, Robin, studied at Tulane University and Boston University and earned a degree in Broadcast Journalism. She won a CableACE Award for a magazine show produced at Vision Cable. "This is an answer to my true loves...Combining entertainment and journalism this way is great." She is currently a television personality and producer in New York.

Phyllis remarried in 1993 to Irving Schoemberg. Irving was born in Gary, Indiana in 1925 and died in Clearwater in 2001. He earned a Bachelor of Science in Business from Indiana University. He owned a furniture store in East Chicago. After retiring, he performed significant volunteer services through the Service Corps of Retired Business Executives.

Highlights of 1960-1969

Highlights of 1960

On April 21, Rabbi Harry R. Richmond of Temple B'nai Israel announced to the congregation that at the termination of his present contract on June 30, he would be leaving the services of the congregation, because of the deterioration in his health. He said if the congregation could not find a rabbi for the High Holy Days services, he would come back and conduct them. The Board of Trustees sent a letter to the rabbi to thank him for his long and dedicated service to the Temple and for the courtesy of giving such early notice about his intention to retire. Rabbi Richmond was given a two-month severance pay of $1,000. Reverend Smith assumed the pulpit during the illness of the rabbi. A committee was appointed consisting of Arthur Rutenberg as Chairman, Morris Bilgore, Herbert Frank, Larry Friedlander, and Darwin Frank to look into the problem of hiring a new rabbi. Mr. Reuben Rutenberg rejoined Temple B'nai Israel. There was a shortage of space for classrooms for the religious school. The Religious School Committee contacted Rabbi Susskind of St. Petersburg to discuss the programs that Temple Beth-

El had for Bar Mitzvah, Bat Mitzvah and confirmation. A nursery class would be held if there was sufficient enrollment. The Men's Club announced a plan to paint and clean up the sanctuary. Selma Capeluta received permission to have her wedding in the Temple in the early part of August.

On July 5, the congregation pledged $1,000 to be paid to the Union of American Hebrew Congregations. The Board of Trustees felt that the new rabbi should follow the orders of the Board as it relates to services. It was reported that the Men's Club had donated between twelve and fifteen pints of blood to two congregants. Mrs. Shirley Peskin planned an organizational meeting of the Youth Group. The Sisterhood was informed that only kosher style foods can be served in the Temple and that items could not be sold from the gift shop on the Sabbath.

On August 29, it was announced at a Board of Directors meeting that, although a decision was going to be made about selecting a rabbi from the three rabbis who had previously conducted services and had been interviewed by the Board, another rabbi, J. Marshall Taxay, had announced that evening his availability for the pulpit position. Because of the Board's favorable opinion of Rabbi Taxay, the meeting was suspended and the rabbi was given an opportunity to conduct a short service. The meeting was reconvened after the service and the President announced that Rabbi Taxay had been elected to the pulpit position of Temple B'nai Israel at a salary of $10,000. A special meeting of the congregation followed later that day and Rabbi Taxay was hired.

As a classical Reform congregation in the 1960s, sermons and education focused more on social justice, tikkun olam, improving society, and the Jewish prophets, instead of Hebrew and halachah. There was a great pride in the modern State of Israel. Some basic Hebrew was taught and used at the Temple, but congregants were more encouraged to put their Jewish ideals to work in the community at large. In the 1960s, Rabbi Taxay was an amazing orator who gave completely developed sermons without notes or scripts, and spoke on topical subjects of the day and the importance of charity and good deeds, relating them to the Jewish prophets of Micah, Amos and Isaiah. His wife, Mildred, taught most of the children in Sunday School at some point during that decade. Each Friday evening service, he would call on teenagers in the congregation to come up to the bema to read or lead various sections of the service. The Oneg Shabbat was usually served on a table set up at the door to the kitchen in the Betty Lane Temple.

Herb Schwartz said, "Rabbi Taxay was very intelligent and had a strong personality. When he wanted something he usually got it. During his reign, the membership continued to grow and the Betty Lane Auditorium often had overflow crowds."

Rabbi Susskind of St. Petersburg installed Rabbi Taxay. The Rutenberg family torah was given in loving tribute to Reuben Rutenberg. The Kent family torah was given in honor of the four sons becoming Bar Mitzvah, Stan-1962, Larry-1965. David-1972, Joel- 1975. Evelyn Amzalak gave a torah in loving memory of Semon. The Press family gave a torah.

Since Rabbi Taxay was not available until about October 15, it was decided to hire a student or rabbi to conduct the High Holy Day services. The services were conducted by Mr. Frank Waldorf. Anton Music Store loaned the Temple an organ.

At the October Board of Directors meeting, it was announced that there were thirteen new members bringing the congregation total up to eighty seven member families with a goal of one hundred families. Among the new members were Dan Rutenberg, Mr. and Mrs. Loren Pollack, Dr. and Mrs. Harry Katz, Dr. and Mrs. Al Schick, Dr. Norman Stoyer. Seventy one children registered for religious school. The Board of Trustees decided that the President at his discretion could invite the rabbi to the board meetings.

At the November Board of Directors meeting, it was announced that seventy three children were now in the religious school. The children were still being taught by the parents under the direction of Rabbi Taxay. Harold Lopatin taught the history of the Jewish people in the United States and Jewish ethics. The youth group was going to have a fundraiser, the sale of

Arthur Rutenberg, President, Temple B'nai Israel, 1960–1961.

Rabbi J. Marshall Taxay

Morris Bilgore, President, Temple B'nai Israel, 1961–1963.

candy bars. Rabbi Taxay's installation was scheduled for Friday, November 25. There was a discussion about organizing the 10th anniversary celebration of the Temple.

At the December Board of Trustees meeting, it was announced that there were now eighty three members of the congregation. Mr. and Mrs. Arthur Collman had both died. Adult education programs had been scheduled with such topics as: "Why Ceremonies," "Five Great American Jews," " Public Relations," etc., all presented by the rabbi. The Temple Bulletin cost $35 a month to produce and distribute. Mrs. Easton was doing a great job. However, the cost was too high for the synagogue and, as a result of this, Herb Frank agreed to do everything for five dollars a month if Mrs. Easton would provide the copy. At that time, the Temple did not have a mimeograph machine or a typewriter. The 10th Anniversary committee was instructed to have a complete report ready for the special meeting to be held on December 20.

Children of the religious school lighting the first candle. l. to r. David Spiegel, Tracey Lovitz, Debra Lawrence. Times photo by George Trabant. December 2, 1961.

Rabbi Taxay recommended a joint committee be set up with Congregation Beth Shalom to work out mutual problems. Mrs. Matthews donated to the temple an extensive library of Jewish books. Mr. and Mrs. Julius Lovitz donated lot number thirty seven adjoining the Temple to the Temple for a new religious school. They asked that their gift not be publicized.

At the special Board meeting of December 17, held at the Fort Harrison Hotel, Steve Bragin reported on the plans for the 10th Anniversary Dinner to be held at the Palm Garden Restaurant and the charge of three dollars per person.

In the early 1960s, Pearl Lopatin cooked hot lunches for Sisterhood and made a profit for the Temple. The Brotherhood was a member of the National Federation of Temple Brotherhoods. Men who were active at that time were Seymour Morganstern, Saul Fein, Bob Deutsch, and several others. All of the Jewish people knew each other not only from attending the synagogues, but also from visiting each other in their homes

and through contacts with the children at the schools.

Highlights of 1961

At the Board meeting of January 11, Steve Bragin said that the 10th Anniversary Dinner was to be upgraded to a dinner dance at a cost of six or seven dollars per couple. He also reported that the Men's Club would donate a mimeograph machine to the Temple. Darwin Frank reviewed the history of the Temple. Mr. Peskin, chair of the religious school, reported that there were twenty three children enrolled in the Hebrew class.

Nancy Collman graduated from Clearwater High School. There were only three Jewish students out of a class of 550. She was the editor of the Clearwater High School Yearbook, a member of the Honor Society, and earned other honors. Nancy Rich and Leann Braun were the other students. Nancy Collman went on to the University of Florida and after she married, she transferred to the University of Cincinnati where her husband was attending medical school.

The young people confirmed were: Laura Baker, Linda Bauman, Susan Berolzheimer, Jerry Collman, Wendy Lopatin, and Marilyn Miller. The B'nai Israel Choir was accompanied by Robert Wilson. The choir consisted of Irving Baker, Julia S. Berolzheimer, Mrs. Herbert Frank, Mrs. Daniel Goldstein, Mrs. Irving Baker, Mrs. Darwin Frank, Mr. Larry Friedlander, and Mrs. Ethel Schoenfeld.

From 1961-63, Evon Brower was Sisterhood President. Her husband was Lou. They came to the area in 1957. He was Chairman of the United Jewish Appeal one year. He was on the Caring Committee for many years. She was a Speech Therapist at Morton Plant Hospital.

Highlights of 1962

There were many costume parties, including a Cosa Nostra party where everyone was assigned a gangster's name, as he came in with his moll. They had fake bathtub gin, etc. The hostesses wore black fringed shimmy dresses which were made all alike, and also wore feathered headbands.

Maxine Frank took Charleston dance lessons and taught it to the other people. They also had a twist party where the women wore peppermint stripe taffetashort dresses. Maxine Frank took twist lessons and taught it to the group. The Brotherhood had a bowling team which was the Clearwater champion in the bowling league. Harold Lopatin, Steve Bragin, Irwin Schwartz, Irvin Baker, etc. were members.

Syd and Irwin L. Entel

Syd and Irwin Entel came to Dunedin, Florida from New York on December 24. They brought their three children with them. Within a year, Irwin's parents, Bess and Joseph, retired and also moved to Dunedin.

Bess was a New York City schoolteacher and Joseph was the Corporation Counsel for the City of New York.

Syd and Irwin met at Syracuse University and married in July 1954. Irwin, a radiologist, left Montefiore Hospital in the Bronx to join a radiology practice after being admitted to the staff of the Mease Hospital. Syd taught the kindergarten and first-grade on Sundays, under Rabbi Taxay. Irwin became Brotherhood President and Syd, Sisterhood Vice President. Syd was also a Member of the Board of Trustees of Temple B'nai Israel. All three children, Robert, Susan, and Richard graduated from Dunedin High School in the top ten of their class.

Syd was President of the Junior League, President of the Pinellas County Medical Auxiliary, Founder of the Dunedin Fine Arts Center, Member of the Board of the Mease Hospital Foundation, and currently President of the Sterling Society of the Dunedin Fine Arts Center. She serves on the Art and Cultural Advisory Board in Dunedin. She is Past Chairman of the Health Facilities Advisory Board for the City of Dunedin, Member of the Board of the Gulf Coast Jewish Family Services, and a lifetime member of Hadassah.

Irwin was President of the Mease Hospital medical staff and the Board of Pinellas County Medical Society. He is serving as Business Manager of the Dunedin Fine Arts Center. They are founding members of the Performing Arts Center and are members of the Florida Orchestra. Irwin

and Syd received the Friends of the Arts Award of Pinellas County in 2004.

Robert graduated from the University of Miami, and earned a Master's Degree in Public Health and a Medical Degree from the Medical University of South Carolina in Charleston. He is board certified in Diagnostic Radiology, Nuclear Medicine, and Interventional Radiology. He practices with the Morton Plant Mease Radiology Group. He lives in Clearwater. He is Past President of both the Pinellas County Medical Association and the Florida Radiological Society. In April, 2005 he was honored with Physcian of the Year at Mease Hospital. He was President of the Maimonides Society and a Member of the Board of the Holocaust Museum.

Richard graduated from Dartmouth College and has a Doctor of Medicine from Mount Sinai Medical School in New York City. He practices Family Medicine in Maine.

Susan Entel Benjamin graduated from Bowdoin College in Maine. She married Stephen Benjamin, a graduate from Yale University. They had met as children at Temple B'nai Israel Sunday School. Susan operates Susan Benjamin Glass, etc. and Syd Entel Galleries in Safety Harbor with her mother. Susan is Past President of the Junior League of Clearwater-Dunedin, Secretary of the Ruth Eckerd Hall at the Richard B. Baumgardner Center for the Performing Arts P.A.C.T. Foundation, Member of Board of Safety Harbor Chamber of Commerce, and Leadership Pinellas.

Couch, Bess and IrwinEntel; on floor, Rachel Benjamin; by fireplace, Steven, Alyssa and Daniel Benjamin; in back l. to r., Richard, Robert and Syd Entel and Susan Benjamin.

Charles Rosenthal Family

Charles (Chuck) and Altamae (Bunny) Rosenthal moved to Dunedin with their daughter, Lynn K. Chuck was born in 1933 in Bloomington, Illinois and his wife, Altamae, was born in 1935 in Dayton, Ohio. Chuck graduated from Roosevelt University in Chicago with a Bachelor's Degree in Marketing and Advertisement in 1955. Bunnie graduated from Michigan State University with Bachelor of Science Degrees in Radio and TV and Horticulture in 1957. They were married in 1960. Bunny was very active with Hadassah and Sisterhood

Chuck and Bunny Rosenthal.

l. to r. Lynn Rosenthal, Sue Rubin, Nancy Schwartz.

and Chuck with Brotherhood. They were both very active in the Temple B'nai Israel Chai Club. Bunny was a Girl Scout leader and both of them ushered for over ten years at Ruth Eckerd Hall at the Richard B. Baumgardner Center for the Performing Arts. Bunny passed away in 1998 and Chuck in 2001.

Their daughter, Lynn K. Rosenthal, was born in Chicago in 1961. She graduated from the University of South Florida with a Bachelor of Arts Degree in Marketing and General Business Administration, in 1983. She has been a member of Sisterhood and a volunteer with Pinellas County Jewish Federation. She also has volunteered with Americans United for Separation of Church and State. She is a past Member of the Board of NAMI and has followed her parents' interest in this organization. Her father was President in 2000.

Their daughter, Sue A. Rubin, was born in 1964 in Pinellas County. She graduated from Florida State University with a Bachelor of Arts Degree in Public-Relations in 1985. She was a Girl Scout leader. Her husband, Martin D., graduated from Tufts University, Medford, Massachusetts with a Bachelor of Science Degree in Electrical Engineering in 1988. He graduated from the University of South Florida with a Master of Science Degree in Electrical Engineering in 1991. They live in Colorado Springs, Colorado.

Their daughter, Nancy G. Schwartz, was born in Pinellas County in 1970. She graduated from Florida State University with a Bachelor's Degree in Business in 1993. She has been very active in Big Brothers and Big Sisters. She married Raphe Schwartz of Wyckoff, New Jersey. He graduated from Yale University in 1993. Their daughter, Abigail Cara, was born on September 2, 2006.

Highlights of 1963

Temple seders between 1963-1967 were held in the roof garden of the Fort Harrison Hotel. The Religious School enrollment was 105 students. Sisterhood's most important project was to help maintain the school. The national average per student in a Temple School, such as Temple B'nai Israel was $125. Since Temple dues were only $240 per family, Sisterhood provided much of the financial

assistance that kept the school going.

The Maxwell and Sallie Sackheim Award of the twelve-volume Jewish Encyclopedia was given to the student who had shown consistent devotion to Jewish learning and practice and who had served the School with uniform zeal. The award went to Barry Rutenberg.

Highlights of 1964

Martha Baker, President of Sisterhood, in a speech entitled, "From Me to Us-This Is Our Temple's 15th Anniversary Year," said, "...Every Sisterhood member must feel that a sense of personal, individual pride in our share of advancing and simulating the love of our faith, devotion to our Jewish people, loyalty to our beloved America in the hearts of our own sons and daughters – through our School. Having been connected with our School for seven years, observing it advance, both materially and educationally, it is a deep joy to convey this feeling from me, not to you, rather from me to us. Indeed, it is our privilege, our opportunity as a Sisterhood to glorify our faith and render honor unto our Creator. In this trust and dedication we began our 15th year. May He abide with us, you and all our loved ones." Martha, at age 86, died at her home in Clearwater on October 27, 2000.

Roland Fox wrote a congratulatory letter to Irving and Martha Baker. Roland said, "On behalf of the Board and all the members of the Congregation, I want to thank you for your generous donation to the Temple. I believe your contribution was the largest in the history of our Temple. You are one of the families whose sincere and long-standing interest in our Temple has enabled us to progress. Even without this donation, we would always be deeply indebted to you. Through your contribution, many of the items needed by our Temple may now be purchased. A sizable amount will be placed in a special fund for a Youth Activity Center and a new Temple building. The Temple School will immediately have its most pressing problems alleviated. Perhaps the best wish I can have for you is that your generosity be returned many fold in the pleasures of seeing its results." David Winthrop, Treasurer, wrote, "...Tuesday,

November 10, 1964, at a monthly meeting of the Board of Directors of Temple B'nai Israel, when the announcement was made of your wonderful and enormous gift towards several Temple projects, there was a sense of awe, silence, and a remarkable impact among many present, as well as this writer, who felt like he had a lump in his throat, with emotion for your kind deed."

The Maxwell and Sallie Sackheim Award went to Stanton Kent. He had performed in an outstanding manner in the Religious School.

Highlights of 1965

The confirmation class presented the Temple with a Torah in honor of their graduation.

A section of Sylvan Abbey Cemetery was consecrated for Temple B'nai Israel.

Maxwell Sackheim arrived in Clearwater in about 1960. He had retired from a long successful career in advertising in New York City. He opened a business here and then retired twice more. He was a dedicated community leader constantly working to help improve the quality of life for all of the residents of Clearwater. He served as a Director of Morton Plant Hospital, Director of Abilities Inc., which trains and employs handicapped people, Director of the Clearwater Chamber of Commerce, and Director of the Senior Citizen Services.

Highlights of 1966

Mary Rutenberg was asked by Rabbi Taxay to give a talk on "Improving Jewish Education." She said that the current level of learning was not keeping pace with the goals of the new society. She had been interested in improving the standards of Jewish education since 1922. She wanted the children to strengthen their ties with Judaism, to think positively, and to appreciate Jewish values. She felt that adult Jewish education was also extremely important. She recommended that a community wide Jewish school be formed because: there would be less cost per student; there would be one educational director for the entire community, who could be assisted by the rabbis, board of directors, and other Jewish organizations; there would be a training program for Jewish teachers; there would be a feeling of unity among the

Jewish children of the community because they would not only be together but they would also study about one God, one Torah, one nation, one history, one Hebrew language, and one culture; there would be a modern school building fully equipped with large classrooms. She felt that Jewish education was getting inadequate support because of the indifference of the parents and the communities.

Herb Silverstein was family number ninety of Temple B'nai Israel. Leonard Collman and Darwin Frank marched with Martin Luther King.

Joan and Robert Benjamin Jr.

Joan and Bob moved to the Clearwater area in June, after a series of strikes in New York City, culminating with a cold winter transit strike that brought commuting from Queens to Manhattan to a complete stop. They moved here with eight-year-old Peter and six-year-old Nancy, and Joan in her eighth month of pregnancy. They had previously been to the area to visit Joan's sister and brother-in-law, Dee Dee Strumpf, and their daughters, Lori and Jill, who lived in Clearwater. They loved the weather, thought this was a wonderful place to raise children, and they would have a good opportunity to start a new business.

Bob and Joan Benjamin.

There were about 125 Jewish families in upper Pinellas County, and eighty families in Temple B'nai Israel. Today, the area has grown substantially and along with it, there has been a sharp increase in the numbers of Jewish families. Temple B'nai Israel has over 700 families. There are also substantial numbers at Congregation Beth Shalom, Temple Ahvat Shalom, and a smaller number at Congregation B'nai Emmunah. There are some additional congregations in the area.

When Bob and Joan came to the area they immediately became part of the Jewish community. Joan, a former schoolteacher, was selected by Rabbi Marshall Taxay to teach fourth grade, a class of twelve children. Bob was recruited to fill the vacant post of Treasurer by the Board of Trustees. They started on a lifelong involvement in the life of Temple B'nai Israel, the Jewish community, and the national Reform movement. They both served in many chairs

Steve Bragin, President, Temple B'nai Israel, 1965–1967.

at the Temple and Joan became Sisterhood President from 1970-1972. Bob became President of Temple B'nai Israel from 1975-1977. Bob was also the Treasurer of the Jewish Federation of Pinellas County.

Joan and Bob were committed to causes that improved the quality of life for those less fortunate in the community. Joan was involved for many years in a community action agency providing housing for families who were living in sub-standard conditions. She and a colleague opened the first non-profit, Consumer Credit Counseling Service in the area. Joan's last position was with Gulf Coast Jewish Family Services, where she served as Administrator for the Counseling and Family Support Program and Director of Development for the agency. Joan was honored to be the recipient of the National Council of Jewish Women's "For Women Only" award and the Pinellas County National Organization of Women's "An Outstanding Woman of the Year" and the Soroptomist Club's "Woman of the Year Award."

Bob was the Administrator of Temple B'nai Israel. He served on the Board and many committees of the Temple. He was the organizer for Rabbi Baseman's inspired interfaith project, FAST-Faith in Action and Strength Together.

They both became active in the Reform movement nationally. Bob was a Member of the Board of the Union of American Hebrew Congregations, now the Union of Reform Judaism for twenty years. Joan served on the national Social Action Commission of the Union of American Hebrew Congregations, for twenty years. Bob was the President of the Southeast Region of the Union of American Hebrew Congregations and became a troubleshooter with congregations and rabbis for many years.

Marion and Ruth Hirsch

The Benjamin Children

All the Benjamin children distinguished themselves academically. Peter graduated from the University of Florida and then received a Master's Degree in Jewish Communal Services from Hebrew Union College in Los Angeles and another Master's Degree in Social Work from Washington University in St. Louis. Nancy graduated

from the University of Florida as the Four Year Scholar in a field of 2,000 graduates with the highest grade-point average over her four-year career. Julie graduated from the University of South Florida with a Bachelor of Science Degree in Elementary Physical Education. She was recently awarded Elementary Physical Education Teacher of the Year for Pinellas County.

Highlights of 1967

In June, at the start of the Six Day War in Israel, a large meeting was called at the Fort Harrison Hotel for the purpose of raising funds to support Israel. There was a large turnout and money was raised from Jewish and non-Jewish people alike. The money was sent to New York for forwarding to Israel. Arthur Lopatin's daughter, Wendy, was married at the Fort Harrison Hotel in 1967 and his daughter, Felice, was also married there in 1969. The Fort Harrison Hotel was a center for all of the Jewish parties and special functions whenever possible.

Marion and Ruth S. Hirsch

Marion and Ruth Hirsch, after retiring from their printing business in New York, moved to Clearwater. Marion was born in Charleston, South Carolina, and during World War II, married Ruth in New York. They had first met when Ruth was age sixteen. At that time, she wanted to join the youth group but was blackballed by Marion because she was, "too fat, too freckled, too young." She was allowed to join when she was eighteen. Ruth graduated from Columbia University with a Bachelor of Science Degree in Business. They both became actively involved in Temple B'nai Israel. Marion served on the Board of Temple B'nai Israel for four years. He was an integral part of the ground breaking ceremony at the Temple on Belcher. He and Ruth chaired the Temple Seder for several years. Marion was Co-Chairman of the Religious Practices Committee. He established the rules for ushering. Marion and Ruth put out bi-monthly issues of the Temple Bulletin for many years. Marion was President of Brotherhood, Chairman of the Chautauqua Society, and was instrumental in working with Sisterhood on community dinner programs used to strengthen interfaith activities between the various religious denominations. On one afternoon, 750 people attended the dinner and were served traditional Jewish foods and learned about Jewish practices. At most, half of the participants were Jewish. The rest were Catholic, Episcopalian, Presbyterian, Congregationalists, Seven Day Adventists, Baptists, etc. As each group finished dinner, they were escorted to the sanctuary, where three Temple Past Presidents and the Brotherhood President took turns conducting the sessions for fifty or sixty people at a time. The Ark and the Torahs within were discussed. An opened Torah was shown to everyone. Marion constantly read and was involved in study with other people. He was part of the Top of the World's Participation Club which meant attending a bi- monthly series of discussion groups. He began one of the groups on prejudice and cultures of foreign lands. He established a Walk-A-Thon for Channel Markers, a fund-raising effort for the blind.

Judith and Mark S. Klein

Judy and Mark came to the area from New Jersey when Mark accepted a job in management at the Safety Harbor Spa. Judy was born on April 16, 1939. She married Mark on March 11, 1962. Judy attended Rutgers University. She was a member of Hadassah, Temple B'nai Israel Sisterhood, and the Jewish Federation. She was the co-founder of a retail boutique named Applause. Mark was born on October 8, 1935. He graduated from Fairleigh Dickinson University with a Bachelor of Science Degree in Management. He was a Member of the Board of Trustees of Temple B'nai Israel, Jewish Federation of Pinellas County, Morton Plant Mease Hospital. He is a hotel manager, and President of Klein and Heuchan Incorporated, Realtors. He is also President of Florida Gulf Coast Association of Realtors.

Religious Community Services, Inc.

Religious Community Services Inc. was formed in the northern part of Pinellas County with thirty one churches and Temple B'nai Israel as members. Its function was to meet the basic needs and help resolve the problems of distressed persons willingly and with dignity, which were not being met by other means.

Highlights of 1969

A huge change in the direction and growth of the synagogue and its activities occured when Rabbi Arthur I. Baseman arrived on July 1. "Rabbi Baseman is a man of morals and admiration. We have always been proud and honored to have him represent our congregation. He is a man of integrity and sincerity. We love him and Renee', who has worked diligently by his side. The congregation grew mightily under his guidance. He is wonderful with the children. He is very respected in the communities of Clearwater, Largo, Dunedin, and all points north, south, east, and west." Shirley Collman truly spoke for the congregation when she wrote this.

Rabbi Baseman started many programs at Temple B'nai Israel including the Rabbi's Discretionary Fund. This fund can be called by many names, but its function is to provide money for the rabbi that can be used to help people in need and to do it in a confidential manner. It is up to the rabbi to decide how to expand the funds. Over the years, it has been used to provide children with clothing, put food on tables, assist with medical bills, provide graves for indigent families, provide transportation for people, provide funds for Lifeline for the Old, provide medical equipment where needed, provide assistance for the building fund of Congregation Beth Shalom, provide assistance for the United Way, provide assistance for Religious Community Services, provide assistance for Menorah Manor, etc. All of the above are part of the "Acts of Loving Kindness" that all Jewish people are supposed to perform in such a way that the recipient and the donor do not know each other. This is the highest level of charity.

Saturday services started again. It was decided that the children who were becoming Bar or Bat Mitzvah would read from the Torah on Saturday morning. There were eighty families in 1969 when Rabbi Baseman arrived. By 1970, there were 240 families.

Renee and Rabbi Baseman

Alfred Schick, President, Temple B'nai Israel, 1967–1969.

Mark and Judith Klein

Chain of Tradition in the Holy Ark.

Rabbi Baseman, the Board, and Membership Committee energized the congregation and contributed to its tripling in numbers of families in one year. Everyone was welcome to the congregation. These people brought with them a wealth of experience and the ability to work with people. Rabbi Baseman helped plan and motivate everyone involved. He knew the name of every congregant and was available to all when needed. Temple B'nai Israel became the fastest growing Reform congregation in the Southeast region. Prior to the hiring of the first temple administrator, Harry Foreman, who was part time from 1973-1975, the Rabbi and Board administered the Temple. Ruth Hirsch, a congregant, volunteered to be Rabbi Baseman's first secretary.

Synagogue facilities construction was part of the long-range plan developed by Charlie Rutenberg, Rabbi Baseman, the Board, and the Executive Committee of the Temple. Plans for new construction were already being discussed shortly after the arrival of Rabbi Baseman. A new sanctuary was planned for current and future use. The Temple was blessed with outstanding energy and with a group of bold-thinking, far-sighted leaders. Charlie and Arthur Rutenberg donated the land on Belcher Road . Fundraising became a community project. Everyone felt it was a labor of love.

Architects Warren Epstein and Ben Hirsch of Atlanta, were hired to draw plans and oversee construction. Lee Dorian and Herbert Schwartz agreed to supervise the construction. Construction lasted for sixteen months, because there was a nationwide shortage of cement and there were delays in obtaining block and concrete.

Jack German was the Director of the Religious School, 1969-1970. The school philosophy then, as well as now, is that Jewish education is a lifelong process. Programs were offered to children even before consecration and after confirmation. A variety of adult education classes were also offered.

The Brotherhood was started again in the second attempt to bring together the men of the congregation in an organization that would provide fellowship, as well as service to the Temple and the surrounding community. They had been holding entertaining, informational, and educational programs as part of their monthly breakfasts. They also provided ushers for the services and gifts to the bar/bat mitzvah students. They provided a gift to the Temple each year. Bernard Berk was the first President of the newly reorganized Brotherhood, in 1969-1970.

Rabbi Baseman's wife, Renee, suggested that each child receive an ID bracelet for confirmation, to form a chain within the Ark. The first links of the Chain of Tradition came from the first confirmation class that Rabbi Baseman taught in 1969-1970. This Chain of Tradition is carried into the Sanctuary at the beginning of the Confirmation service. During the Sabbath, before the Confirmation service, the young people being confirmed search the current Chain of Tradition and each one helps the other hunt for the bracelet of a brother, a sister, a cousin, a friend to which to link his or her ID bracelet. There are currently over 600 bracelets linked together as a bond of everlasting friendship and love. The Chain of Tradition occupies an honored and permanent place in the Holy Ark.

Jan S. and Gwen M. Hirschfield

Jan and Gwen came in August from Louisville, Kentucky for Jan to start a private medical practice. Jan was born on June 11, 1935. He graduated from Washington University in St. Louis in 1957 with a Bachelor of Arts Degree in the History of Art and Classical Archaeology. He graduated from the University of Missouri School of Medicine in 1961. He specialized in internal medicine and gastroenterology at the University of Colorado Medical Center from 1962-1966. He served at the United States Air Force Hospital, Eglin Air Force Base, 1966-1968, and was Assistant Professor of Medicine, University of Louisville School of Medicine from 1968-1969.

Jan was Chief of Staff at Clearwater Community Hospital, Chairman of Endoscopy Committee at Morton Plant Hospital, Chairman of Crohn's, Colitis Foundation of America, Tampa Region, President of Florida Gastroenterologic Society, and Assistant Professor of Medicine, University of South Florida. He was President of Religious Community Services, a founder of Clearwater Free Clinic and a Member of the Board of Ruth Eckerd Hall at the Richard B. Baumgardner Center for the Performing Arts and Neighborly Senior Services Meals on Wheels. He was a volunteer tutor and mentor at Seminole High School and part of the Academy of Senior Professionals at Eckerd College.

Gwen graduated from the Jewish Hospital School of Nursing in 1961. She attended the University of Wisconsin 1957-1958. She worked at the Endoscopy Department of Morton Plant Hospital in Clearwater from 1990-2006. Gwen has been a member of the Interfaith Committee of Temple B'nai Israel. She and other members of Religious Community Services started a school for pregnant high school students, who were not allowed to attend school. Gwen and the others lobbied the Florida legislature to pass legislation allowing pregnant teenagers to attend school. Gwen has been a member of a multi-denomination woman's book club for over twenty five years, has participated in the annual Mitzvah Day, and is a longtime member of Sisterhood. Everything she does is geared toward helping other people. She has been a member of the Temple B'nai Israel choir for many years. She is a longtime member of the Clearwater chapter of Hadassah. She and Jan were the Co-Chairs of the Temple B'nai Israel, State of Israel Bond Dinners. Professionally, she is a member of the Society of Gastrointestinal Nurses Association.

Their daughter, Elisa P.H.Goldklang, graduated from Duke University in 1984, with a Bachelor of Arts Degree and from City University of New York with a Master of Science Degree in Speech Pathology in 1990. She practices in Scarsdale, New York. She is married and has two children. Her husband, Dr. J. Goldklang, earned a Bachelor of Science Degree from Rochester Institute of Technology in 1980. He earned a Doctor of Chiropractic Medicine from Life University in Marietta, Georgia in 1992.

Son, Eric, earned a B.S. Degree from Indiana University in 1988. He is Managing Director of Packaging and Metals Division, Deutsche Bank, Chicago, Illinois. He is married and has two children. His wife,

Deb Walters Hirschfeld, earned a Bachelor of Arts Degree from the University of Michigan in 1991. She is a partner/owner of Zolo Incorporated, a creative educational equipment firm for children.

Jan and Gwen donated the original Temple pre-school room with the planning of the new Temple in 1972. Throughout their thirty six year association with the Temple, they have been continuous sponsors, supporters, and attendees at most Temple functions. Jan said, "We believe that the most important duty is to establish and maintain a strong Jewish identity at home, in our Temple, and community in addition to the State of Israel and to Jews all over the Earth. We felt a need to bring our Temple into the religious and non-religious aspects of our community."

Ervin Schwartz, President, Temple B'nai Israel, 1969–1971.

Highlights of 1970-1979

Highlights of 1970

The Temple B'nai Israel preschool started as a nursery school in October. On October 25, the membership, represented by 210 voters, unanimously approved the architectural and financial plans for the new Temple. Charles Rutenberg, the Progress and Planning Committee Chairman, and Roland Fox, General Campaign Chairman addressed the congregation prior to this historic decision. The librarian from 1970 to 1972 was Rachel Ward.

Highlights of 1971

Charlie Rutenberg became Chairman of the Building Committee and Arthur did the fund raising. Irving Baker provided the seed money for the new synagogue when he sold his business and gave $10,000 of his funds to the congregation

The Temple B'nai Israel Sisterhood sponsored the first annual Interfaith Institute on February 16, at Temple B'nai Israel. The moderator was Joan Benjamin. The panelists were: Rabbi Arthur I. Baseman of Temple B'nai Israel; Kivie Kaplan, President NAACP; Reverend John Touchberry of Faith United Church of Christ; Howard Harris Jr., Clearwater Neighborhood Action Center. The keynote speaker was Dr. Paul Fitzgerald, Director of People Services, State

Loren Pollack, President, Temple B'nai Israel, 1971–1973.

Department of Education. His presentation was "Humanism–the Emerging New Man." The discussion workshops were led by: Reverend T. A. Johnston of the Church of the Reconciler; Dr. Robert Klein, Pupil Services Division, Pinellas County Board of Public Instruction; Dr. Harry Danielson, Pupil Services Division, Pinellas County Board of Public Instruction; Reverend Walter McMullen, Instructor, St. Petersburg Junior College; Reverend Richard Norsworthy, Unitarian Universalist Church; Reverend A. Phillips Nazro of the Episcopal Church of Ascension; Reverend Donald Airey of the Christ Presbyterian Church; Sister Regina Agnes of the St. Cecilia Catholic Church; Howard Harris Jr., Clearwater Neighborhood Action Center. The discussion topics for the workshops were: "Why are kids turning on with drugs rather than religion;" "Does ecumenism extend to inter-marriage;" "How does the church or synagogue view campus unrest;" " Is your congregation integrated;" "Abortion-yes or no;" "How is the church or synagogue dealing with the new moral code;" "Does the church or synagogue approve of militancy;" "How does the church or synagogue make the youth aware of the needs of the less fortunate members of the community;" "Are the youth in the congregation engaged in community involvement;" "How does the church or synagogue deal with separation of church and state."

The Board of Trustees gave permission for the use of Temple B'nai Israel facilities to the Gables Academy, a school for dyslexic children for ages seven through sixteen. B'nai B'rith sponsored blood banks for the entire community. Temple B'nai Israel Sisterhood on Sunday, November 5, held its first annual public bazaar and served a traditional Jewish meal from noon until 6 p.m.. This was extremely well attended by a large number of non-Jewish people as well as members of the congregation.

Confirmation was held on Sunday May 30, at 7:30 p.m at the Temple at 20 South Betty Lane. The children confirmed were: Jeffrey Brower, David Cohn, Taryn Davis, Marc Dorian, Pam Ginsberg, Mindy Harwood, Amy Jacobson, Robert Meimood, Dede Moroff, Steven Raymund, Alan Rophie,

Nancy Schick, Lori Strumpf, and Helena Zucker. A reception was held at the Fort Harrison Hotel following the Services.

Rabbi Baseman was involved in many community projects. He was President of the Clearwater Ministerial Association. He worked with many local schools. He helped dedicate the Eisenhower Learning Center on April 13, 1971, and the Plumb Elementary School special program, May 18, 1971. By July 1971, the membership of Temple B'nai Israel had grown to 251 families.

Because of the size of the congregation, the High Holy Day services were held at the condominium complex, Top of the World, in the large recreation center. This was due to the courtesy of Sidney Colin. Marion Hirsch made an Ark for the occasion. He found an old bookcase with shelves and doors at the Betty Lane Temple in the storage room. He removed the shelves, cleaned up the bookcase, put blue satin on the outside of the cabinet and doors, and lined the bookcase on the inside with white satin. Shiny gold rope, one inch in diameter, was used to decorate the Ark. A straight students lamp was used as the eternal light. Behind the light, a men's shirt cardboard was covered with blue satin and was used to make a shield around the lamp. A wooden set of the Ten Commandments, which came from the Betty Lane Temple, was put in front of the Ark. This Ark was lent to Ahavat Shalom and used by the congregation there until their sanctuary was completed.

Highlights of 1972

After the Rutenberg family donated the land for the new Temple, everyone pitched in to make the vision of a new sanctuary and home for Temple B'nai Israel a reality. The original Building Fund Recognition Board in the Temple lobby includes family names such as Alpert, Baker, Baseman, Baumgardner, Bellack, Benjamin, Berk, Berolzheimer, Bilgore, Bragin, Brower, Coleman, Collman, Dorian, Entel, Fox, Goldberg, Green, Hirsch, Hirschfield, Jacobs, Kalicka, Karlin, Keller, Kent, Lawrence, Lovitz, Michels, Moroff, Moskowitz, Pollack, Sachs, Schick, Shapiro, Siegel, Silverstein, Strumpf and Weiss.

On January 30, a new cornerstone was set in place with the inscription

"Shalom" etched upon its surface. The cornerstone was dedicated by the Lovitz family. The cornerstone from Betty Lane was laid next to the new stone linking the generations of old with the present and moving toward the future.

The Groundbreaking Ceremony for the new Temple took place on June 6 at 4 p.m. at 1685 South Belcher Road. At the groundbreaking, the past Presidents and other dignitaries sat on an improvised stage which was the flatbed of a semi trailer. The flat bed truck was acquired by Steve Bragin from his uncle Morris Bilgore. Ruth and Marion Hirsch made a skirt which was used as a decoration on the front of the flat bed. The skirt was white and had a blue Star of David on it. It was an awesome occasion, sweet and bittersweet, for those individuals who had helped build the Betty Lane Temple, because of all the memories of the planning and striving that was needed to become a formal Jewish community after World War II. There were many wonderful memories of life cycle events, holidays, social affairs, good fellowship, and the love of a community expressed in the construction and expansion of the Betty Lane Temple. It was now a time for the enlarged Jewish community to move forward. The congregation felt that wherever Rabbi Baseman would lead them would be the right path to follow. The ceremony was followed by a covered dish supper at the Belcher Elementary School just south of the new Temple. Marion Hirsch was the Functions Committee Chairman. Everyone was asked to give as much as they could in order to have the congregation involved in the ownership of the new structure. As an additional fundraiser, a Lucite block 3 in. x 4in. x 1 in. thick was sold as a memento of the occasion. It had the word peace in English and Hebrew on the front and in small letters on top, Temple B'nai Israel, Clearwater, Florida and on the bottom, January 30, 1972 5732.

Marion and Ruth S. Hirsch were part of the dedication service. Charlie Rutenberg donated cooked turkeys for lunch after the dedication.

The dedication of the new synagogue for Temple B'nai Israel on September 29,

September 30 and October 1, 1972, were three days to remember and cherish. They were highly spiritual and gloriously exciting. The celebrations started on Friday evening which was Simchat Torah. The Temple Youth Group prepared an excellent original service complete with apples, flags and happy youngsters leading the way for those who carry the Torahs. During this service, Amy Jacobson's beautiful voice added greatly to the enjoyment. Alan Gallay's drum accompaniment heightened the excitement as the members carrying the Torahs circled the sanctuary.

On Saturday morning, the Dedication Service started outside with all of the dignitaries, congregants and friends of the congregation from the outside community circling the temple behind the Torah bearers in a dignified Torah processional. Within the temple as reported by the bulletin editors, "...The service began with a majestic procession. Rabbi Arthur I. Baseman and Honorable Rabbi J. Marshall Taxay led the way. Dr. Eugene Mihaly, Professor of Rabbinic Literature at Hebrew Union College, Cincinnati, escorted by President Loren Pollack was next, followed by Charles Rutenberg, Lee Dorian, Roland Fox and Herbert Schwartz, each carrying a Torah and escorted by Rabbi Sanford M. Shapero and Rabbi David Susskind. The visiting clergy representing the various churches were next and our Past Presidents completed the procession. Slowly they marched across the rear of the sanctuary and made their way up the center aisle ascending the Bema. The Marshals of the Procession, N. David Korones and Robert T. Benjamin Jr. opened the Ark doors and Rabbi Baseman lovingly set each Torah into its place. It was a climatic and impressive ceremony at a precious moment for us."

"The special service, the choir and reaching out of the congregation all led up to Dr. Mihaly's Dedication Sermon. Rabbi

New cornerstone (1972) with the (1950) cornerstone of the Betty Lane Temple.

Dedication service, September 30, 1972. Rabbis Frank Sundheim, Arthur Baseman, Eugene Mihaly, Sanford Shapero, J. Marshall Taxay, David Zielonka, David Susskind.

Baseman's introduction was warm and personal; it reflected his deep regard and great respect for his teacher. Dr. Mihaly sat through it with a hand over his eyes and it was almost a moment before he rose to acknowledge. His opening remarks were of his pride in his pupil and that he shared Rabbi Baseman's affection and esteem. It was obvious these two men, teacher and disciple, had something between them which few men manage to achieve. As Dr. Mihaly began to speak, this gentle man with a soft rich voice, carried us through the reality of the moment to the true spiritual significance of the occasion. He took us through Europe, after the Holocaust, to a deserted synagogue whose interior was painted white and on whose walls were written thousands of names of Jews who were victims of Hitler's madness. He told us of his tears at the sight and went on to say that whenever he participated in the dedication of a new temple, he felt that he was wiping away a tear. He spoke of God's command to Moses to " build a tabernacle", and Moses trembled. He warned that the building itself was only mortar and brick and that the completion of it was really the beginning for the congregation; that the dedication today was not only of the building, but of the congregation as well. Our task now is to make this Temple a place of worship and study, dedicated to the ideals and advancement of Judaism that is hoping to bring us a little closer to God... Suddenly, becoming aware of the time, he announced that he had prepared too long an address and that he would cut it. We were heartbroken and we would have had him continue. This small, soft-spoken, almost frail man had a power–a power of mind, of heart and, yes of soul. We are deeply grateful that Rabbi Baseman brought us this moment."

The ceremony was greatly enhanced by seven rabbis serving on the Bema. They were, Frank Sundheim, Arthur Baseman, Eugene Mihaly, Sanford Shapero, J. Marshall Taxay, David Zielonka from Sharaai Zedek, and David Susskind. It was further enhanced by the large number of clergymen and their parishioners who came from the various churches to share in the joy of the Jewish community. It was not only a remarkable event for the Jewish community, but also helped enhance the beauty of all religions.

Charles Rutenberg, Past President and General Chairman of the Building Committee, summed up the need for the new temple building. "Throughout our history, Jews have looked to the temple as a symbol. The temple represents the dedication to our faith; a house of worship, not only for ourselves, but for our children and generations to come.

This tie to the future, as well as the past, has always been a fundamental part of Jewish thinking. But beyond these intangibles, the temple also represents a real and physical place: a place for prayer, a place to study, a source of Jewish education, and a place to gather and share our lives.

Now we can add a third meaning to its symbolism, because the temple represents one of the strongest and proudest emotions we can share–our accomplishment...."

Rabbi Baseman's message showed how a structure becomes a holy sanctuary. "This is a proud and triumphant moment for all of us. Much effort, energy, and enthusiasm has been expended, and each of us has had a stake in bringing the dream into a reality.

Now, we must get down to the real business of a temple, that of living out our Judaism. Just as adding love to a house makes it a home; just as adding justice to a city enables it to become a community; so too, adding Mitzvah to mortar can transform a mere building into a temple.

For a temple is not a holy place simply because it honors sacred objects, but because it demands sacred acts; a temple is not to be a place for storing prayerful words, but a site for altering lives.

To the biased and bigoted, may our temple be an adversary; to the noble and decent, may it be an ally; and to the victim and downtrodden, may it be a champion. May its Jacob's Dream-Ladder encourage us to scrape the heavens in our religious quest, and may we snatch from it the lessons by which earth can be made better. May we "dream of things that never were and ask why not."

Charles Rutenberg and Rabbi Baseman, in fact, spoke for all Jewish people, whether Reform, Conservative, or Orthodox, who worked long and hard to build beautiful buildings through the arduous planning, teamwork, and giving of both time and dollars from all segments of the community regardless of which type of synagogue they attend. It always has been and always will be a total effort, because all Jewish people always help each other in trying to create a place where God may be worshiped, children may be educated, and the love of life and family can be demonstrated.

Daniel Glucek, world-famous sculptor, designed and created the metal sculpture for the Ark, which is the focal point of the sanctuary. In 2004, he was still actively involved in receiving commissions for religious architectural installations as well as private and corporate sculptures. His wide-ranging works include various sizes and materials and ranged from a thirty eight foot tall bronze and steel structure entitled "Birds in Flight" which won him the Lincoln Society Award, to an eighteen foot bronze menorah sculpture for Congregation Adat Shalom. His work is applauded from coast-to-coast. The Ark stands twenty five feet tall and was made in four sections, and welded together to form a perfect whole. Each Ark door weighs 500 pounds, but is so delicately balanced that it can be opened with a single finger. The Ark represents Jacob's ladder as described in Genesis 28. Behind the ladder, waves of flames go toward heaven. Above the Ark doors is the Eternal Light shaped in the letter "shin" symbolizing the Hebrew words: Shaddai or Almighty One, Shema or Hear O Israel, Shalom or peace, and Shabbat or Sabbath. The rock formation which flanks the Ark represents the stone upon which Jacob placed his head, and from which emerged the ladder. The Ark is the graphic as well as spiritual representation of the Temple. Rabbi Baseman said, "To me the ladder symbolizes the prayerful relationship between man and God. The base is set on earth and then reaches heavenward. Every prayer and hope for mankind can be seen in this work."

The service was followed by a challah and wine kiddush. On Saturday evening, there was a beautiful dinner and music in the social hall. On Sunday morning, there was a brunch sponsored by the Brotherhood,

with the chefs being Harold Karlin, Ben Kalicka, and Herbert Silverstein. They did as usual a wonderful job in cooking. The speaker was Rabbi Sanford M. Shapero. At noontime, the Sunday School was dedicated and a Mezuzah was placed on each classroom door. From 3 p.m. to 5 p.m., there was a Community Open House and the past Presidents were the hosts and guides. Their wives served punch and cookies in the social hall. Several hundred members of the non-Jewish community participated in this concluding event.

The beauty and holiness of the dedication ceremony of Temple B'nai Israel and the people involved was similar to the dedication ceremony held at Temple Israel in Terre Haute, Indiana on September 25, 1891. The Reform congregation of thirty families had purchased an old church and completely renovated and decorated it in an elegant style with a new organ, Ark, pulpit, chairs, and usual covers for the altar and Ark. The interior decorations were done in excellent taste. The walls were pale blue, which was a nice contrast to the stronger colors of the frieze and ceiling. Both dedications were momentous events in the life of the Jewish and general communities. In Terre Haute as well as Clearwater, there were large audiences far beyond the seating and standing capacity of the sanctuary. In Terre Haute, the non-Jewish community outnumbered the Jewish community substantially. There was also a three-day weekend of prayers, services, and celebration. The dedicating rabbi was Isaac Mayer Wise, the mentor and teacher of Rabbi Alexander Lyons. Rabbi Lyons, who

The new Temple B'nai Israel

Ruth Hirsch tests the hearing of James Jones in the Hearing-Screening Program. (Sun staff photo by Jim Covington–dated Saturday, March 11, 1978.)

led the service, gave a brief presentation on the three-fold lives of people, the physical, the mental, and the spiritual. He called the temple a schoolhouse of the soul. He then lovingly introduced Dr. Wise, who by this time, was seventy two years old and had been described as "walking with faltering steps." When he spoke his age dropped away and he glowed as he vigorously discussed the three parts of Jewish life, "The Past, Present, and Future" (of Judaism). (On April 30, 1999, Rabbi Eric Yoffie, President of the Union of American Hebrew Congregations, at the 150th celebration of the Terre Haute Jewish community presented an updated version of the same topic.) Dr. Wise talked about the old man who was planting a seed beside the road. A young man came by and said "Old man what a foolish thing you are doing. You will never get to see the seed grow into a tree." The old man responded, "Do you see the trees around us, they were planted by other people before us." In this way Rabbi Wise, was telling everyone that the new temple was planted by the congregation for the future growth of the Jewish people. Similarly, Temple B'nai Israel of Clearwater planted a seed for the future growth of the Jewish people of this area.

With the opening of the new Temple, Rabbi Baseman realized his dream of introducing Saturday morning worship services. Now, all Bar and Bat Mitzvahs were scheduled at the service on Saturday mornings. There were 305 families in the congregation at the time of the dedication.

The temple was a beautiful building. The

architects, Epstein and Hirsch of Atlanta, Georgia, created a magnificent edifice to be filled by people honoring God.

The structure was approximately 22,000 square feet. The structure contained the sanctuary, all-purpose room, classrooms for religious school and Hebrew school, social hall, youth lounge, kitchen, library, which was donated by Reva and Marshall Kent, board room, administration office, rabbi's study, principal's office, regular office, Judaica shop and choir loft, and electrical storage room on stage. There were eight classrooms, nursery, kindergarten rooms, and a media center. The structure is twenty five feet tall at its highest point.

The Friendship Club was founded with Morey Newman as its first President. It is an auxiliary of the temple for seniors. One of its major functions was to act as an inter generational exchange with the temple preschool children.

Ernie and Sylvia Schnur, brother-in-law and sister-in-law of Harold Lopatin, moved to Clearwater. They became very active in the Friendship Club for many years. Other people arriving included Harold and Sally Segal. He was a pharmacist who started the Mackey Manufacturing Company, which manufactured single dose pills for hospitals.

The Hearing-Screening Program of three to five-year-olds was started by the Temple B'nai Israel Sisterhood. This was a free service project.

The Sisterhood worked on behalf of the blind, services for youth, efforts to improve social justice and international relations, family education, Head Start Hearing Program, which in 1972, served over 800 children, and interreligious understanding. They were also involved individually as well as a group in a variety of local, state, and national charities.

Benjamin Hirsch

The architects for the new structure were Epstein and Hirsch Architects Incorporated. Benjamin Hirsch was the design partner. He was contacted originally in 1970 by Charlie Rutenberg, Chairman of the temple search committee for an architect to design B'nai Israel's proposed synagogue complex on Belcher Road. Charlie had received his name from the Union of American Hebrew Congregations, since Benjamin was a member of the Architectural Advisory Committee. Benjamin had received a National Design Award in 1968 from the Guild for Religious Architecture for the Memorial to the Six Million, in Atlanta, Georgia. After Benjamin sent his résumé to Charlie, instead of becoming an advisor, he became the architect for the new Temple B'nai Israel building on Belcher Road.

The Sanctuary was designed to expand into the social hall to meet High Holy Days seating requirements. The committee instructed the architect to design the sanctuary and social Hall with plain, stark white stucco walls, without any decorations. This led to the Ark becoming the main focal point of the design of the complex. Benjamin went to the Torah for inspiration. He made the Ark a freestanding pillar with a sculptured metal Ark door assembly depicting Jacob's ladder ascending heavenward. He selected Daniel Gluck, the famous sculptor, to design the doors. To make the Ark freestanding, a skylight assembly with sidelights was designed to make the stone pillar appear to be physically separated from the surrounding structure. The biblical inspiration had come from Genesis XXVIII-22: "And this stone which I have set up for a pillar shall be God's house." Rabbi Baseman had suggested, from the beginning, the incorporation of the theme of Jacob's dream of the ladder and his subsequent feeling of awe in the sanctuary design. Benjamin Hirsch is a practicing architect whose firm designs commercial, institutional, industrial, residential, and religious projects on a national and local level. He has designed many churches, synagogues, and Holocaust memorials. He is responsible for the conceptual development and design of "The Message of Yad Vashem," a multi-media installation that is part of the Atlanta Jewish community's celebration of the State of Israel, and the permanent exhibition of the Zachor Holocaust Center and Educational Resource Center which existed from 1986 until a successor, the William Breman Jewish Heritage Museum, opened in 1996. His "Absence of Humanity: The Holocaust Years," opened on June 30,

1996. Benjamin is listed in *Who's Who in American Jewry*. He served fourteen years as President of Hemshech (Continuation), the organization of Holocaust survivors, second and future generations, living in metro-Atlanta. He is Past President of Congregation Beth Jacob and the Yeshiva High School of Atlanta. He has been a Member of the Board of Trustees of many Jewish organizations in Atlanta.

Benjamin Hirsch was born in Frankfurt, Germany in 1932. In December 1938, less than one month after Krystallnacht, when his father was arrested and sent to Buchenwald, Ben and four older siblings were sent to Paris, France by their mother on a Kinder-Transport. The five Hirsch children, ranging in age from six to thirteen years, survived in a French Jewish network of children's homes that moved them clandestinely throughout France keeping them from the hatred and destructiveness of the advancing Nazi forces. His two older brothers escaped Europe and arrived in New York in June, 1941, and were sent to Atlanta, under the sponsorship of the Hebrew Orphans Home to be near a cousin of their mother. Ben and his two older sisters followed the same escape route and arrived in New York on September 2, 1941. Ben graduated from the Georgia Institute of Technology School of Architecture and earned a Bachelor of Science Degree in Architecture.

Benjamin Hirsch wrote a book entitled *Hearing a Different Drummer-a Holocaust Survivor's Search for Identity.* The book was published by Mercer University Press, Macon, Georgia, 2000. It was a reflection of his childhood, his experience, in the United States Army during the Korean War, and his return to Germany where he truly realized the fate of his parents and younger siblings.

Enid and Stanley Newmark

Stan and Enid came to Clearwater from Buffalo, New York, with their daughters, Lisa and Stefani. Stan graduated with a Bachelor's Degree in Business from New York University in 1954. He worked for Pfizer Laboratories for sixteen years and received the highest awards and honors given to a salesperson. In 1971, he joined Wang Laboratories and was named

Salesman of the Year and Manager of the Year. Subsequently, he worked for theCharles Rutenberg Corporation on various projects. Enid and Stan owned and operated "Put It Together," a relocation service for seniors. He then became a broker salesman.

Stan was Campaign Chairman of the Jewish Federation of Pinellas County, as well as President of the Federation. He was the founding President of the Kent Jewish Community Center and later served as President of the Golda Meir/Kent Jewish Center. He is currently a Member of the Boards of the Federation and the Golda Meir/Kent Jewish Center.

Enid was a 1962 graduate of Queen's College. She taught in the Bedford Stuyvesant section of Brooklyn before moving to Buffalo, New York. After raising her children for a number of years, she became the bookkeeper at the Jewish Federation Office in 1980. She continued in this position until 1985 and also worked as a volunteer. She became a partner in Baby and Me, a maternity and infant store in Clearwater.

Enid was a Member of the Boards of Temple B'nai Israel, Women's American ORT, and the Golda Meir/Kent Jewish Center. She helped form the Women's Division of the Jewish Federation of Pinellas County. She was the Volunteer of the Year for the Golda Meir Center and was recognized as a Woman of Distinction by the Jewish Federation. Enid edits the annual Tribute Journal and selects items for sale at the L' Chaim gift shop at the Center.

Lisa and Stefani both graduated from Florida State University. Lisa is a social worker for the State of Florida and Stefani is a buyer for Dillard's Department Stores. Both daughters and their families live in Clearwater.

The Newmark family were joined in 1976 by Enid's parents, Lola and Curt Mayer. Curt was a Member of the Boards of the Jewish Federation of Pinellas County and the Kent Jewish Center. He has also served as Chairman of the Insurance Committee of both Boards.

Maureen and Dr. Stanley Rosewater

Maureen and Stanley relocated from Ohio to the Clearwater area in order for Stanley to start a practice of medicine. Stanley was born in Cleveland, Ohio on August 23, 1940. Maureen was also born in Cleveland on June 28, 1941. They both went to Shaker Heights High School. They started dating there and were married in June 1961, before Stanley started medical school at Ohio State University. He spent two years in the United States Air Force. They raised their family of three children, Shari, Jim, and Debbie in Clearwater. Debbie was killed in a freak accident in 2003 in Carlsbad, California, where she lived.

Maureen and Stanley have a deep commitment to their fellow Jews. They have said, "It is our responsibility to keep Israel strong so that Jews can live in independence and security in the Jewish state." They both have played an active role in Temple B'nai Israel as Members of the Board of Trustees . Stanley has also been the Secretary of the Board. He was a Member of the Board of the Federation of Pinellas County, and Co-Chairman of the Doctors Division of the Federation. Maureen has been a member of ORT, National Council of Jewish Women, life member of Hadassah, and Chairman of the Women's Division of the Federation. She had the distinction of being in the first adult Bat Mitzvah class at Temple B'nai Israel. She also taught Hebrew for several years at Temple B'nai Israel. They were both honored by the State of Israel Bonds with the City of Peace Award.

Temple B'nai Israel Dedication Plaque

The building of the current Temple at 1685 S. Belcher Rd in Clearwater was the work of a large number of highly dedicated people. These people are recognized on a plaque in the lobby of the Temple. They are as follows: Arthur I. Baseman, Rabbi; Loren Pollack, President; Robert T. Benjamin Jr., Financial Vice President; Lee Dorian, Secretary; J. Marshall Taxay, Honorary Rabbi; N. David Korones, Coordinating Vice President; Charles Rutenberg, Planning Vice President; Bernard Berk, Treasurer; Saul Fein, Financial Secretary; Charles Rutenberg, General Chairman; Roland Fox, Campaign Chairman; Lee Dorian, Herbert Schwartz, Construction Co-Chairmen; Building committee, Rabbi Arthur I. Baseman,

Robert T. Benjamin Jr., Morris Bilgore, Ezra Bobo, Stephen Bragin, Roland Fox, David Jacobs, Robert Klein, N. David Korones and Philip Katz; Challenge Gifts, Morris Bilgore, Arthur Rutenberg, Co-Chairmen; Leadership Gifts, Alfred Schick, Chairman; Congregational Gifts, Robert T. Benjamin Jr., N. David Korones, Co-Chairmen; Women's Gifts, Anne Katz, Shirley Berolzheimer, Co–Chairmen; Youth Gifts, David Lawrence, Chairman; Property Sale, Stephen Bragin, Julius Lovitz, Co-Chairmen; Publicity, Morris Newman, Chairman and Fern Moroff, Loren Pollack, Irving Sachs, Maxwell Sackheim, Alfred Schick, Ervin Schwartz, James Ward, Douglas Weiss; Memorials, Irving Baker, Chairman; and Donations, Fern Moroff, Alfred Schick, Co-Chairmen.

Highlights of 1973

Morris Newman and his wife celebrated their 50th wedding anniversary along with 400 friends and relatives at Temple B'nai Israel on August 31. He was chairman of the Morris Newman blood bank, an interdenominational service for the community. Morris Newman organized the Friendship Club at the Temple in 1972 and was its first President. The library was expanded and new materials were added. The librarian from 1972 to 1977 was Reina Pollack. Regular hours were established for library use. Harold Karlin, President of Brotherhood, started the Sweetheart Breakfast.

An inter-faith forum was sponsored by Temple B'nai Israel and the National Conference of Christians and Jews. The first presentation was given by Dr. Bernard Olson, Director of Religious Affairs of the National Council. Dr. Olson, a Methodist minister, had had a distinguished career in the ministry and had also served as a reporter and music critic. He was the author of "Faith and Prejudice," in which he said, "God has bound Jews and Christians together in a special relationship. Christ's Jewish heritage carried the principles of high ethical monotheism and brotherhood into the new religion which actually began as a Jewish reform movement. Christianity was then grafted onto Judaism..."

The eighth grade of the Religious School under the direction of Zena Sulkes took

as its major theme the concerns of young people as they developed a concept of God. Several children wrote poems to express their feelings. Lauren Benjamin wrote, "God is heaven, God is earth. God is death, and also birth. We are made in His own image, Maybe He even plays football or cribbage. God is up there, away in heaven, the days He created number seven. God created Earth, moon, and sun, God is mine, and only one."

Judy and Sam Winer

Samuel L. and Judith Jacobs Winer

Samuel and Judith came from Philadelphia to Clearwater because of Rabbi Baseman. Samuel earned a Bachelor of Arts and Letters Degree from Pennsylvania State University in 1959. He and Judy were married on June 25, 1961. Samuel became an officer and Member of the Board of Temple B'nai Israel in the late 1970s. He became a founder, a contributor and President of the Golda Meir Center when it was known as the Upper Pinellas Jewish Community Center. Samuel is a businessman and entrepreneur.

Judy earned a Bachelor of Arts Degree from Mary Washington College of the University of Virginia, with a concentration in English. She taught English at middle and high schools in Virginia, Pennsylvania, and New Jersey. She was a member of Hadassah, Vice President of Temple B'nai Israel Sisterhood, a Member of B'nai B'rith Women and ORT. She taught Sunday school at Temple B'nai Israel.

N. David Korones, President, Temple B'nai Israel, 1973–1975.

Highlights of 1974

As of January 1, four of the families who had left to help found Congregation Beth Shalom also rejoined Temple B'nai Israel and therefore had dual memberships. These people were: Dr. Salem Baranoff, Arthur and Billy Rutenberg, Reuben and Mary Rutenberg, and Isadore and Clara Zitlin. They were leaders and movers of the Jewish community and rejoined the original synagogue while supporting both of them. On November 1, there were eight remaining families from the original founders of Temple B'nai Israel. They were: Dr. Salem H. and Lisa Baranoff, Clarence and Lela Collman, Leonard and Shirley Collman, Darwin and Maxine Frank, Sam and Estelle

Korones, Julius and Phyllis Lovitz, Mrs. Fanny Marks, and Mrs. Ethyl Schoenfeld.

Sandra L. Schulman

Sandra graduated in 1957 from a program of interior design training from the Fashion Institute. She was an interior designer for Kent Fabrics of St. Petersburg, Florida. Following that, she was a self-employed interior designer and finally an accountant for Pinellas County Fleet Management. Sandra became a chairperson of many committees for the Temple B'nai Israel Sisterhood. Her parents resided in St. Petersburg since 1972. Her father, Charles, had been a proofreader for the *New York Times* and her mother, Ella, had been a bookkeeper for American Express. Sandra, talking about her reasons for being a synagogue member, said, "I consider the temple not only a house of worship, but a source of solace, kinship, social interaction, and constant learning. I've met many wonderful friends there, including Rabbi Baseman, who I consider a wonderful friend and mentor. My philosophy of life is to make the most of it through constant learning, and leave a vital, meaningful, and lasting contribution to succeeding generations." Sandra led by example and, as a result of this philosophy, earned a Degree in Accounting Technology from St. Petersburg College in 1998.

Octocity

The first annual Octocity was hosted by the youth group with Phil Gordon as chairman. Octocity was a conclave of youth group members from temples from Miami to Sarasota to Orlando to Ormond Beach and all the areas in between. The participants came to Clearwater to celebrate their Jewish heritage and to meet other Jewish young people from around the state. One hundred and thirteen young people attended.

Highlights of 1975

Newcomers to the Clearwater and North area found a dedicated, energetic congregation at Temple B'nai Israel. This was a time of exceptional growth. The Religious School and Preschool expanded rapidly. The congregation gave forth great warmth which led to the sanctuary being full for Shabbat services. In fact, the congregation was getting so large that the Executive Committee and Board of Trustees decided that it was time to encourage members in the Palm Harbor and North areas to form their own congregation, with the assistance of Temple B'nai Israel.

In December, Temple B'nai Israel helped found a sister Reform congregation which became Temple Ahavat Shalom. At the same time, the Board of Trustees set a cap on Temple membership at 550 member units. There were several exceptions to the rules concerning parents and children of members, those being confirmed or Bar and Bat Mitzvah, grandchildren of members etc.. The reason for the cap was that the physical facility could not house an unlimited congregation. However, it was necessary to keep the doors open to families with religious school age children. In 1978, when the cap went into effect, the numbers were raised to 600 family units and again with a variety of exceptions.

A community wide rally was held at Temple B'nai Israel on behalf of Soviet Jewry and Human Rights. The program featured Mayor Gabriel Cazares, Barbara Allison, Lisl Schick, the Temple B'nai Israel Junior Choir, Rabbi Arthur Baseman and Rabbi Peter Mahler. The first annual Chanukah dance was held. First prize in the ticket sale was a trip to a country of the person's choice for two weeks, including Israel, Hawaii, Spain, or a Caribbean cruise.

Father Edward H. Flannery, Executive Secretary of the Secretariat for Catholic-Jewish Relations, a division of the National Conference of Catholic Bishops, spoke at a public forum at Temple B'nai Israel. He discussed the guidelines adopted by Vatican II on promoting inter-religious cooperation and understanding. Father Flannery was the author of the award-winning book, "The Anguish of the Jews: Twenty Three Centuries of Anti-Semitism." He was consultant to the Vatican Secretariat for Catholic-Jewish Relations. In 1965, he received the National Brotherhood Award presented by the National Conference of Christians and Jews.

Harry Foreman was the administrator. Barbie Allison and Marilyn Jacobs were

Robert T. Benjamin, Jr., President, Temple B'nai Israel, 1975–1977.

the bulletin editors. Reina Pollack was the librarian. The fourth annual community dinner was held. This has been an outstanding Interfaith community event.

Highlights of 1976

In January, there were 527 member families with approximately 1,800 people in the Temple family. Three hundred and sixty eight students were enrolled in the religious school and 100 students were attending midweek Hebrew programs. On January 12, Belle Appelbaum became the administrator. By April 4, there were 535 member families. This was the date that the Temple celebrated its 25th anniversary. The chairman of the event was Ezra Bobo. There was a barbecue picnic lunch and then a formal program which was chaired and created by Reina Pollack, featuring presentations by Rabbi Baseman, Fanny Marks, Darwin Frank, Isadore Zitlin, Roland Fox, David Korones, Jim Ward, Ervin Schwartz, Sissy Bierman, and her children, Ann and Ron Angert. Memorabelia and films of the Temple's dedication at Betty Lane were shown. The program was called "This is your life, Temple B'nai Israel." Yolan Ziessman was the temple bulletin editor.

The confirmation class presented to Rabbi Baseman a shofar that was found in the Mea Sharim section of Jerusalem by their parents Joan and Robert Benjamin, Betty and Roland Fox, Dee Dee Strumpf, and Gina Bragin when they traveled to Israel. Rabbi Baseman explained the symbolism of the ram's horn, which was prepared for use as a musical instrument and is curved, indicating humility before God. The shofar is one of the earliest musical instruments known. The confirmation class included Gail Amazon, Nancy Benjamin, Victor Bobo, Janet Bragin, Justin Enfinger, Susan Entel, Leon Fox, Joseph Freeman, Julie Garron, Susan Glorfield, Ricky Green, Mark Michaels, Barbara Nelson, Glenn Opper, Mitchell Schips, Bruce Silverberg, Carin Stemer, Jill Strumpf, and Scott Zeiger.

Rabbi, Renee, Adina, Jordana, and Dalia Baseman sent a New Year's card to friends and relatives with the following inscription which was found in a cellar in Cologne, Germany where Jewish people were hiding from the Nazis. It stated, " I believe in the Sun even when it is not shining. I believe in love even when not feeling it. I believe in God even when he is silent." Rabbi Baseman's message was that the people who make a difference in our lives, whom we remember forever, are not the ones who impress us with their fame, status, wealth, or power, rather those who are the ones who care. The warmth of the touch, a word of encouragement, a sympathetic ear are the ingredients that make a lasting impact on our lives. Do it for those you love.

Changing Role of Women-Getting Back to Basics Program

A new program for women was held at Temple B'nai Israel. It was cosponsored by the Clearwater Chapter of Hadassah, the local chapter of the American Association of University Women, the Clearwater Women's Club, Temple B'nai Israel Adult Education Series, and St. Petersburg Junior College. The program was about the changing role of women in our society and entitled, "Getting Down to Basics." The four main areas of concern discussed were: an introspective look at women; home and family; world of work; and education. The workshop topics were: Your Legal Rights; Families in Transition; Male and Female; Sexuality; Choosing to Assert Yourself; the Good Years Beyond Sixty; Dealing with Guilt: Creatively or Destructively; Divorce: a Time for Change and Growth; the Male Box; Taking Charge of Your Own Life; Responding to Stress; and Loneliness: A Familiar Face.

Arlyn Hutt and Elinor Gordon represented AAUW and Hadassah and became the overall chairpersons. Temple B'nai Israel's Adult Education Program, headed by Arlyn, and the Woman's Living and Learning Center Director, Jane Maddux, helped coordinate the program for three years. This was a great and highly successful community effort that involved a large number of people from all of the organizations. The first program was dedicated to the memory of Audrey and Ray Patouillet, who provided the guidance and inspiration for making the program a reality.

The theme of the conference was well expressed in the following poem.

"You have but one life...
And, daily you choose how it is to be
lived.
You have limited time, energy, emotions,
money...
And how you spend them is decided by
what really matters to you.

We face the end of affluence.
Now is the time to ask: What is really
important in my life?
Now is the time for getting down to
basics!"(author not known)

Sisterhood and Temple Musical Shows

Starting around 1975 or 1976, a series of musical shows were presented at the Temple for the congregation, friends and community. The shows were a fun way of bringing the congregation together while raising funds for the Temple. The Hotel Mountainblue was one of the early shows. The Temple musical shows continued until the early 1980s.

Joseph and Thelma Sefekar

Joseph and Thelma Sefekar.

Joseph was born in New York City on February 20, 1917. He became Chief Clerk, Special Services Staff Section in the Headquarters of the First U.S. Army and served in Europe from 1943-1945. He worked for the United States Civil Service in a variety of positions with the last one being at the Smithsonian Institution as the Administrative Officer. Joseph and Thelma retired to Palm Harbor in 1976. He became deeply involved in B'nai B'rith and also became a substitute teacher. He became the Assistant Budget Officer for the City of Tarpon Springs and then Finance Officer and Budget Manager for Ruth Eckerd Hall at the Richard B. Baumgardner Center for the Performing Arts.

Thelma Lakoff Sefekar was born in Brooklyn, New York on January 16, 1920. She and Joseph married on January 3, 1942. Thelma raised their son, William, and daughter, Bonnie, who is married to an attorney, Lee Landau and lives in Olney, Maryland. Thelma has been a member of many Jewish organizations. She also paints and grows prize winning roses.

Son, William Charles (Bill), came to Palm

Harbor in 1983. He is a transportation planner for Pinellas and Hillsborough Counties. Bill is also the producer of the public access TV show, "B'nai B'rith Presents Jewish Life in Tampa Bay." Bill's wife is Miriam.

Highlights of 1977
Mitchell Levine Family

Mitchell was born on July 31, 1933. He attended classes at Rider College and a business school.

Mitchell and Vicky decided to move to Clearwater with their children, Michael born on June 1, 1962, Marci born on March 19, 1965, and Stephanie, born on June 20, 1973. Mitchell and Vicky successfully operated three Castro Convertibles stores and then later opened the first consignment furniture store, Consignment Furniture Gallery, in Clearwater in April, 1984.

Marci, her husband Matthew, born on December 13, 1959 and their first child, Jacob, born on January 23, 1991, moved to Clearwater from Atlanta to open a sister store, Consignment Furniture Showroom, in St. Petersburg. After Mitchell died on November 1, 1995, Vicky continued to run Consignment Furniture Gallery. Marci and Matthew had a daughter, Rachel, on October 25, 1993. Vicky retired in 1999 and moved to Hendersonville, North Carolina, with her husband, Ed Lieber. Marci and Matthew became the owners of both stores.

Michael had become a Bar Mitzvah in Trenton, New Jersey. Marci and Stephanie became Bat Mitzvah at Temple B'nai Israel. Mitchell was proud of all his children's accomplishments and also the accomplishments of his wife. Because of his involvement in the Hebrew training of his wife, Vicky, and her Bat Mitzvah ceremony, he was asked to say a few words at the end of the ceremony. He said, "As I look around today, I see the glowing faces of the six Bat Mitzvah candidates which reflect the achievements of their studies over the past one and one half years...studies which were taken on because of the keen desire to become a "daughter of the Covenant"...not because of reaching a magical age."

Marci and Matthew were married by Rabbi Baseman in 1988, their children had their baby namings in the Temple, Jacob became a Bar Mitzvah in 2004, and Rachel will become a Bat Mitzvah in 2006.

Mitch's son, Michael, married Tracy in 1985 and they now have three children, Adrienne, Eric, and Alex. Mitch's other daughter, Stephanie, married Dean Saxe in 2003. Michael and Stephanie both live in Atlanta, Georgia, with their families.

Mitchell and Vicky, despite long hours at work and raising a family, became very active at Temple B'nai Israel. Mitchell was on the membership committee and was a Member of the Board of Trustees for several years. He had a desire to provide a suitable office for the Pre-School Director, Sharon Tanner. Marci Levine Sperber said, "He knew how important it was to start our children off on a good foot so they would learn to love their religion as he did, and he felt their director should have a place to meet with parents and children in privacy, formulate lesson plans, and make the pre-school the best it could be." Marci, was very involved in the preschool, as preschool chairperson, Campaign Kinder committee, and a Member of the Board of Trustees.

Vicky and the children wanted to do something to honor the memory of their husband and father, because of his goodness and because he considered Temple B'nai Israel to be his second home. After Vicky talked to Rabbi Baseman, she and her children decided to build offices for the pre–school director. Vicky worked closely with Barry Debowsky, who oversaw the construction of the Mitchell Levine Annex. The Annex was completed in 1997 and dedicated on April 18, 1997. The dedication plaque said, "THE LEVINE ANNEX- Donated in Loving Memory of Husband and Father Mitchell Levine by Vickey Levine and Children-"Teach them faithfully to your children"-Deuteronomy 6:7."

The love between husband and wife and the love between parents and children are truly a hallmark of our Jewish heritage. What Vicky said about Mitchell could easily have been the words of what the author's mother frequently said about the author's father. "Mitchell was a good, kind, loving man who only wanted peace, 'shalom,' in his family, with his friends, and in the world....he was such a loving, peaceful man that we wanted to have a tangible memorial for him."

Highlights of 1978

Al Sulkes, President of Temple B'nai Israel, thanked the Sisterhood for funding the painting of the Temple and the resurfacing of the parking lot. He said, "It seems as if Sisterhood never runs out of ways to support the work of the Congregation and we love all of you for it. May it ever be so!!" The St. Petersburg Jewish Community Center and Temple B'nai Israel developed a cooperative effort for programs, classes and activities to be held at Temple B'nai Israel to serve the northern community.

The social club, CHAI, was formed, with its first President being Felice Zeldin. It was an auxiliary of the temple. It was a club for the middle age group, including couples and singles, who could meet in a social environment.

A demographic study was done of the congregants of Temple B'nai Israel. Four point two percent of the families were under thirty. Thirty nine percent of the families were between thirty and fifty. Fifty six point eight percent of the families were over fifty.

On November 2-5, the Regional Convention of the Union of American Hebrew Congregations was held in Clearwater. The theme was "Clearwater is great in '78." Over 400 people attended.

Prime Timers was an organization formed as an auxiliary of Temple B'nai Israel of Clearwater. The officers were: Ferne Siegal, President; Mort Gordon, Vice President; Renee Polukoff, Secretary; and Howard Kalicka, Treasurer. The objectives of the group were to provide a means for people to meet and to make them feel welcome, to promote cultural and social advancements, to keep alive the spirit of Jewish tradition and heritage. Membership was opened to any person forty years old or older and married couples if one spouse was forty years old or older. The socials included Harvest Moon dances, mystery nights, game nights, mock marriages, hay rides and hotdog roasts, other dances, swim parties, golf outings, and special dinners.

A large number of private nursery

Al Sulkes, President, Temple B'nai Israel 1977–1979.

schools participated in the Sisterhood hearing program.

One of the founders of the Clearwater Jewish community, Estelle G. Korones, died on June 29. She was a charter member and past President of the Ladies of Kiwanis, one of the founders of Temple B'nai Israel, past President of the Sisterhood, a charter member of Hadassah, a member of B'nai Brith Women, founder of the Korones Tournament of the Ladies Division of the Clearwater Country Club, and a member of the Family Counseling Service of Pinellas County.

Dr. Zelda Kaye Snyder

Zelda moved to St. Petersburg from New York. Zelda was born in Jersey City, New Jersey on April 8, 1921. She moved to Brooklyn, New York in 1932 with her family and later earned a Bachelor of Arts Degree from Brooklyn College. She was a scholarship graduate of the School of Religious Education, Federation of Reform Synagogues, New York City. She was awarded a certificate as Teacher of Religion and became a long-term teacher of the Religious School of Union Temple in Brooklyn. She was certified by the New York State Education Department as a Kindergarten Teacher, Elementary School Teacher, Supervisor, and Principal. Zelda graduated from the New York University School of Law, with a Juris Doctor Degree in 1944. She was admitted to law practice in 1945. After thirteen years of practicing law, she decided to enhance her knowledge of the nature and needs of handicapped children. She earned a Master of Science Degree in Education at the College of St. Rose, Albany, New York in 1959. She served as a special-education teacher for eight years and then went on to earn a Doctor of Education Degree from Yeshiva University, New York City in 1962.

Zelda was given the Golden Seal Award, as an Outstanding Teacher, Albany, New York. She was honored when she was named a Fellow, American Association on Mental Deficiency in 1969. She was named Chief, Bureau Special Programs for the Handicapped, Division for Handicapped Children, New York State Education Department in Albany.

After her retirement in 1978, she moved to St. Petersburg, Florida and joined Temple B'nai Israel. She became an active member of the Temple Caring Committee. Since 1988, she has served as a volunteer public speaker on behalf of the Hospice of the Florida Suncoast. In 2005, she was the recipient of the Community Support Award. Also in 2005, she was nominated for inclusion in the City of St. Petersburg Senior Hall of Fame.

Bonnie Tilbe, in her letter of support for the nomination of Dr. Zelda Snyder for the Volunteer of the Year Award said, "I believe that Dr. Snyder exemplifies the traits, actions, and commitment that make a good volunteer a great volunteer...Dr. Snyder is best known in the community through her brilliant public speaking engagements ... (in support of) hospice services and promotes the Hospice Thrift Shops...I find Dr. Zelda Snyder to be a person of extreme commitment, integrity, and giving of herself."

Zelda, reflecting on her long career of helping other people said, "During my early years, and with the example and encouragement of my angel mother, I began to seriously consider the direction I must take in developing a meaningful life for myself. It soon became clear to me that, devoting my personal strengths and talents toward making a positive impact on the lives of those in need, would enable me to discover the depth and scope of my own humanity. The joys of satisfying personal fulfillment soon came to me. Through the years, my life has thereby been enriched beyond measure."

Highlights of 1979

In February, in the Temple B'nai Israel Bulletin, Rabbi Baseman reiterated the teachings of Rabbi Nachman. "A person reaches in three directions, he reaches up to God; he reaches out to other people; and he reaches into his own heart. There is a secret message in this: all three directions are really the same. When we reach out to another person, we find ourselves and God; when we discover God we find others and our authentic selves; when we find ourselves, we reach God and other people."

The board decided that any Jewish person age eighteen or older could become a member of the temple. There were 488 member families.

Prime Timers last President was Howard Kalicka in 1980. Although the organization was short-lived, the people involved had a wonderful time. There were between forty and fifty members.

Other related organizations included: CHAI, a group of middle aged couples and singles. The Presidents were; 1978-79, Felice Zeldin; 1979-80, Janet Baron; Friendship Club an auxiliary of the Temple for seniors, which provided a place for people to meet and have fun. It helped with the Temple preschool children. The Presidents were: 1972-75, Morey Newman; 1975-76, Herbert Bernstein; 1976-80, Edward Corner: and Couples Club which was a club for the younger couples and their families to get acquainted. It helped that age group feel that they were part of the Temple family.

The young people of the Temple worked in interfaith groups to try to get a better understanding of how different religions can exist beside each other and help each other grow. They were involved with Catholic and Protestant children in a series of simulation games about the problems of life. Interfaith activities were an essential part of all organizations of Temple B'nai Israel from adults to children.

The History Committee included Al Sulkes, Chairperson, Martha Baker, Leonard and Shirley Collman, Darwin Frank, Lila Lawrence, Leona Levine, and Sally Siegal.

Between 1975 and 1985, there were many special dinners at the synagogue. One hundred and fifty to 200 people would attend each dinner. Senior citizens helped fund them. The congregation grew very rapidly. There was a tremendous dynamic within the congregation.

Highlights of 1980-1989

Highlights of 1980

The Simcha Tree, a Tree of Life, was donated by the Sisterhood to the temple and put on the wall of the reception hall. It was a permanent place to show all of the happy events of the members of the temple. The Friendship Club, Chai (couples club), Prime Timers for people over forty, were all operating, having fun, and making contributions to the Temple. Janet Baron was the editor of the Temple Bulletin. There were 522 member families. Ethel Schoenfeld, one of the founders of Temple B'nai Israel, mother of Maxine Frank, died on January 19. The confirmands created an original service entitled, "Our Decalogue for a New Decade." The confirmands were: Adina Baseman, Suzanne Bergman, Scott Bobo, Diane Chervitz, Claire Enfinger, Michael Friedman, Bradley Golomb, Michael Haimes, Daniel Harris, Helen Harris, Wayne Ismark, Leslie Klein, Beth Polukoff, Mindy Rothfield, Kathy Schick, Robert Schwersky, Corinne Sherline, Roger Siegal, Greg Solar, Natalie Ward and Elise Zeiger. The Senior Study graduation class consisted of Pamela Hutt, Allisyu Keller, Dawn Nelson, Leslie Tritter and Sheryl Verona.

Barbara Rosenblum, President, Temple B'nai Israel, 1979–1981.

Modern Reform Movement

Temple B'nai Israel, representative of the modern Reform Movement, published a booklet entitled, "This Is Our Temple – It Is Composed of You and Me!" Excerpts from this book help explain the current meaning of Reform Judaism and some of the rituals and symbols of Reform Judaism.

"Reform Judaism is a Liberal interpretation of modern Judaism. Reform not Reformed, in the past tense, underscores the conviction that Judaism is an ongoing, living, dynamic organism, not a static, un–changing, time-completed fact. Reform believes that Judaism is forever contemporary and should be responsive to

the religious needs of successive generations. Reform leaders have deep roots in the past and proudly acknowledge the glory, dignity, and validity of Jewish tradition, which is inherent to all Judaism. Reform identifies with the dynamism found in the evolution of the Jewish faith from its origins to present. Judaism has evolved and Reform is not a different kind of Judaism. It is Judaism, historic, classical, traditional, and eager to do honor to its people and its faith.

Reform Judaism has not abandoned ritual. It seeks rituals which are meaningful for today, which still speak to the Jewish person. A modern prayer book is used, which contains Hebrew and English. Yarmulkas (skull caps) may be worn, if it makes the individual more comfortable. Sabbath services, an integral part of worship, are held every Friday evening and typically every Saturday morning. Yiskor (a special prayer service for the dead) is held on Yom Kippur and Passover. Yahrzeit (the anniversary of the day an individual passed away) is celebrated on Friday night during the week of the individual's death. All religious holidays are celebrated, but only the first day of two day holidays is observed. Consecration takes place on Simchat Torah, when the youngest students are blessed in the presence of the congregation, upon entering religious school. Bar/Bat Mitzvah is a privilege available to all children. They must meet the standards and qualifications established by the Rabbi, the Educational Director, and the Religious School Committee. Confirmation occurs during the holiday of Shavuot, where the 10th grade Religious School students, in a special service, confirm their Jewish faith and at the same time, the congregation confirms their faith in them. Senior seminar is for young people who complete two additional years of study. Baby naming for both boys and girls occurs on Friday evening, when the baby and parents are blessed in front of the Ark by the Rabbi in the presence of the entire congregation. Betrothal blessings in front of the Ark by the Rabbi in the presence of the congregation further strengthens the bond of the engaged couple. The Rabbi officiates at all funerals."

Harold and Gertrude Azarva

Harold and Gertrude Azarva arrived in Clearwater. Harold attended Temple University. He later sold real estate. He and Gertrude have been married for fifty five years. Gertrude attended Temple University. She belonged to Temple B'nai Israel's Sisterhood and the Clearwater Chapter of Hadassah. In 2004, she received the Women of Distinction Award from Hadassah. Before she retired in 1994, she worked as a court reporter for the 11th Circuit in Pinellas County. She is currently Co–President of the League of Women Voters of North Pinellas County.

Highlights of 1981

Five thousand dollars was allocated for a new program of cantorial services. Cantor Norman Belink, Cantor Emeritus of Temple Sinai, Roslyn Heights, New York, was the first cantor hired for the High Holy Day services. Lauri Rutenberg, daughter of Charlie and Isa, was ordained a rabbi. The Sisterhood cook book came out and was a success. Rabbi Baseman celebrated his bar mitzvah year with Temple B'nai Israel.

Extensive remodeling of Temple B'nai Israel was submitted to the Pinellas County Board of Adjustment August 5, and was approved. The internal facilities were remodeled and included six more classrooms, two more meeting rooms, a multipurpose room, additional toilets, additional storage, and fifty eight additional parking spots. Rabbi Baseman was given tenure. The Mental Health Association of Pinellas County thanked the Temple for providing birthday gifts for Project Cheer in December. The Temple Sedar served 247 people, including thirty five children. The rabbi discussed the possibilities of an up-county home for the aged. The first meeting of the Endowment Committee was held. A discussion was made about hiring a full-time Cantor.

The Visiting Scholar Program was devised to bring to the congregants of Temple B'nai Israel and other invited guests a series of experts who could provide new and challenging material to inform as well as stimulate thinking in a variety of areas of Jewish interest. Daria Fane, Xenia's daughter, presented the first educational mini-series on January 1-3. She discussed, "Religion and Politics in the Middle East," "Challenges Confronting Israel in 1982," and a slide program, "Shifting Strategic Balance in the Mid-East." She had also discussed "Iraq's Nuclear Capability, Israel's Nuclear Capability, Nuclear Proliferation in the Mid-East, and Future of the West Bank." She was a researcher for the International Peace Academy of the United Nations and at that time was doing advanced graduate study in international security and strategy at the School of International Affairs of Columbia University. Her photojournalism brought an added dimension to her talks.

Dr. Xenia Fane

Dr. Xenia Fane was born in Brooklyn, New York and moved to Clearwater with her husband, Arthur, in 1978. She was Director of Home Economics Education for New York Board of Education. She taught in the Master's Program at Florida International University. She has taught and supervised every grade level, from nursery school through the graduate level. She was also in a leadership role in her professional organizations at the city, state and national levels. She was the co-author of eleven textbooks on home economics and family living. Some of these were done with her husband, Arthur. She also worked on many filmstrips and films pertaining to family life education, child development, and sex education. Her textbook "Understanding Young Children" had been widely used in the United States and abroad. She was a confirmed antiques collector. Her thimble collection included well over 1,000, items including one that was 2,000 years old, which was from Roman times, and one which was 1,600 years old from the Byzantine times. Both were found on archaeological digs in Israel.

Xenia served Temple B'nai Israel in many capacities. She was a member of the Board of Trustees, the Executive Committee, Chairman of Adult Education, and taught Hebrew to adults and children. In the general community, she was President of Women of Seville, named Clearwater Citizen of the Day, chairman of the state convention

of the Florida Home Economics Association, named Florida Home Economist of the Year, and many many more contributions to a variety of civic associations. When asked how she did all this, she answered from the Talmud, "The day assured, the work is great; it is not up to you to do all the work, but neither can you ignore it." Xenia's secular name means hospitality, her Hebrew name, Tsyona, means Mother of Zion. Arthur was an elementary school principal. She was the founding organizer of the Gorn Scholar-in-Residence program. She started this program with a donation from Mr. and Mrs. Gorn.

Saul Fein, President, Temple B'nai Israel, 1981–1983.

Highlights of 1982

Twenty six children were in the confirmation class. There were 340 children in the religious school, 140 in Hebrew school, and eighty four children who were in the nursery school. There were 644 members in October. In August, the Prime Timers disbanded. Past President Irving Schwartz died. "He gave from his heart. His memory is a blessing we shall endow it with respect."

A community dinner was held with 875 people in attendance. This was a good way to promote fellowship within the general community. Chavurah groups were formed. Sisterhood dues were $12.50 per year. The Temple had a Blood Bank drive.

Rabbi Stanley Dreyfus gave the Scholar in Resident presentations. He was the former rabbi of Terre Haute, Indiana. He and his wife, Mary Ann, assisted Hank Koren in proofreading and providing special information for the 150 Year History of the Terre Haute Jewish Community. Rabbi Dreyfus had written several books and chaired the committee that wrote the current prayer book used by Reform congregations. In 1980, he became the Director of Placement of the Rabbinical Placement Commission.

Gary P. Gormin, President, Temple B'nai Israel, 1983–1985

Highlights of 1983

The Library was renovated and new shelves as well as new carpeting were added. Many new books were made available to the congregants. Lee Jubelirer was the temple administrator. The bulletin editor was Janet Baron. There were 681 families in the Temple. In May or June, Isadore Zitlin, one

of the founders of the congregation and the person who led services during the early years passed away. Jeanette Fein resigned as nursery school director and teacher. Jill Black became the nursery school director.

Cantor Henry Thalheimer and his family were given an extended complementary membership. Cantor Thalheimer had retired from a congregation in Canada. When he was in the area he sang at Temple B'nai Israel on a voluntary basis.

Xenia Fane presented a check in the amount of $25,000 from Mordechai Gorn to be considered the Gorn Endowment Fund. The principal was to be invested and the interest only to be used to fund the Scholar-in-Residence program. Mordechai and Ottilie Gorn continued to be benefactors of this highly acclaimed program. Rabbi Al Vorspan, Vice President of the Union of American Hebrew Congregations, was the Scholar in Residence. He presented, "Moral Tight Ropes We Jews Walk", and a workshop entitled "Our Commitment To Self, Congregation, and Community."

Starting in the fall semester, three and four-year-old children were taught in the nursery school, basic developmental and educational skills through an Apple Computer System. It was very useful for memory development, while helping children learn to select and differentiate between colors, shapes, and sizes.

Highlights of 1984

Temple B'nai Israel was a member of the Religious Commission Services Coalition of Churches and Synagogues. The bulletin editors were Janet Baron, Ann Sobel, and then Sonia Lipschultz. Frank Weiss became the interim administrator. There were thirty two children in the confirmation class. There were 724 families in the temple (on November 20, there were 746 families), with over 100 new families joining. About 300 people attended the children's services for the High Holy Days. There were 307 children in the religious school. Over 1,000 people participated in the Visiting Scholar Program.

On November 4, there was another community dinner which was extremely well attended. After the people from the community ate a good Jewish cooked meal,

they were given a tour of the Temple and were able to ask questions of the Rabbi and the officers concerning the various rituals within the synagogue. Community dinners were very much a part of the Interfaith movement which the Sisterhood, Brotherhood, Youth Group, and temple were involved in within the overall community. The attendance at the High Holy Days services was exceptional. Approximately 600 people attended the early service on Rosh Hashanah Eve, approximately 1,000 people attended the late service, and 1,116 people attended the Rosh Hashanah Day services. Almost 300 people attended the children's services on Rosh Hashanah. There were fifty eight children enrolled in the nursery school and there was a waiting list. One hundred and eighty seven people attended the first meeting of the Sisterhood. There were forty new members.

Rabbi Louis C. Littman

The cantor for the High Holy Days was Rabbi Louis C. Littman, Regional Director of the Union of American Hebrew Congregations Southeast Region. He was a native of Trenton, New Jersey and a graduate of Rutgers University and Hebrew Union College – Jewish Institute of Religion in New York. He was involved with the executive committee of the B'nai Brith Anti Defamation League and was a member of the Interfaith Coalition for Human Rights. He was a host on a weekly public radio program on ethnic music. He was profoundly interested in Jewish community life and was very active in Jewish music. His lecture concert, "Jewish Life in Music" had been performed throughout eastern United States. He, his wife, Phyllis, and their children came to Clearwater for the High Holy Days.

The annual Scholar-in-Residence Program was renamed the Gorn Visiting Scholar Program in honor of Mordechai and Ottilie Gorn. This was a major contribution toward establishing Temple B'nai Israel as an active center of Judaic education. It enabled the members of the congregation to have close contact with some of the great speakers of the time. The Gorn Scholar-in-Residence Program speaker was Gunther Plaut.

Stanley Igel was a member of the Board of Morton Plant Hospital. Ralph Dutcher was a member of the Board of Temple B'nai Israel and also Chairperson of the Cemetery Committee. Mordechai and Ottilie Gorn provided the funding for a mitzvah bus to bring senior citizens to the Temple.

Sheila Weinstock

Sheila received a Bachelor of Science Degree in Marketing from Boston University in 1966. She worked for Arthur Young & Co., a law firm, and United Fruit. Sheila moved to the Clearwater area from Farmington, Massachusetts, a suburb of Boston. She had worked for the Golda Meir Center and for the Hospice of Florida Suncoast. During her time at Temple B'nai Israel she had chaired numerous committees including the Religious School Committee, Caring Committee, Publicity Committee, and had been the editor of the Temple Bulletin as well as a Member of the Executive Committee for many years. She was one of the official hosts of Temple B'nai Israel. She died on March 6, 2006.

Highlights of 1985

Dolores Curphey became the temple administrator. The bulletin editor was Sonya Lipschultz, followed by Phyllis Miller. Twenty five children were confirmed. The Gorn Visiting Scholar was Rhonda Barad of the Simon Wiesenthal Center of New York. She presented, "Global Insights," "The Holocaust: Is It a Dead Issue?," and "Human Rights Update," a multimedia presentation.

The first female cantor at Temple B'nai Israel was Oreen Zeitlan. She was a former Metropolitan Opera regional finalist from Chicago, Illinois. She graduated from the University of Illinois in Urbana and studied at the Eastman School of Music in Rochester, New York and the Hochschule fur Musik Mozarteum in Salsburg, Austria where she received certificates in both Lieder and Opera. On Yom Kippur, she sang special music written for her.

Holocaust Torah

The story of the Reborn Torah was a story of courage, love of the Jewish religion, the

Holocaust, and the Igel family. On Sunday, May 12, at 11 a.m., over 2,000 individuals, including the congregants of Temple B'nai Israel, other Jewish organizations and synagogues, members of various churches, dignitaries, and the general public formed a Torah procession starting on Kersey Road, circled the Temple, and proceeded into the sanctuary for the rededication of this Torah. A special Torah committee had worked for a full year to arrange the acceptance and to honor this Torah, our forebears who died during the Holocaust, and the Christians who suffered trying to help their Jewish countrymen. Despite the horrors and difficulties caused by the Nazis, the Torah had survived the Holocaust. A subscription campaign had gone on for a whole year to have members of the congregation sign the parchment which had been attached to the Torah as part of the Reborn Torah Project. These names were an ongoing and physical link with the Torah and Judaism. The cost per family was minimal to allow everyone to participate. The funds generated were being used to establish an endowment fund and the interest would go to further Jewish education at the Temple.

The history of this Torah was beautifully written in the Temple B'nai Israel Torah Dedication booklet of Sunday, May 12. "The history of Temple B'nai Israel's newest Torah has been tinged with many emotions–love, hope, sorrow, joy, despair, and devotion. Originally commissioned after the High Holidays in 1933, it fulfilled a sacred pledge made by Gustav Igel, Stanley Igel's father. Gustav's wife had been very ill in a sanitarium in Vienna and on Rosh Hashanah, 1933, Gustav, who had remained in Poland, received a telegram informing him that her condition had worsened and was very critical. He got special permission from the rabbi to travel during the Days of Awe and he went to Vienna, but before departing, he promised a special Torah if she recovered. On Yom Kippur, joyous news of her recovery arrived in Poland and Stanley pledged the Torah in his father's name.

The schul to which the Torah was pledged was called Igel's Synagogue. It was on the Igel family property and the family took charge of its maintenance. There was

Jack Geller, President, Temple B'nai Israel, 1985–1987.

Temple B'nai Israel's Holocause Torah.

no official Rabbi, but Gustav and the local men conducted regular services.

The Torah was begun in the fall 1933. During the year it took the scribe to finish it, he lived in the Igel home and the family supported him. The Torah was dedicated in 1934 and was used continuously until late September, 1939. When the Germans approached following the invasion of Poland, the schul was emptied and the Torah scrolls and holy books were taken into hiding.

Although Poland was aware of Germany's impending threat and had mobilized her troops in late summer 1939, nonetheless life had continued somewhat normally until the actual invasion. Stanley and Lusia were married on August 27, even though Stanley had been recalled by his regiment in the Polish army a month earlier. Leo, Stanley's older brother, had graduated from medical school and left for the United States at the beginning of August for a short visit. Thus, the fall of Poland and its division into Russian and German sectors changed the history of the Igel family and this Torah for all-time.

Initially, the Germans controlled the area of the Igel land, but one month after the invasion, the land came under Russian control. From October, 1939 until 1941, Stanley and Lusia lived in Przemysl, and felt that under the Russian occupation they were fairly safe. During this time, they kept the Torah scrolls and holy books hidden in their home, but in 1941, the Russians also began limiting the freedoms of the Jews and they began to fear for their safety. Arrangements were made to give the Torah scrolls to a Gentile friend for safekeeping. The Polish friend risked his life, secreting the scrolls and holy books out of the Ghetto, preserving them from German and Russian hands until the liberation in 1944.

After the Torah Scrolls were safely out of the Ghetto, there still remained Stanley and Lusia's baby daughter, Toni, who needed to be smuggled to safety on the Gentile side. The family entrusted with the Torah Scrolls were able to obtain counterfeit birth certificate and baptismal certificates, and according to a prearranged plan, met the Igels who were wheeling Toni in her baby carriage. The Gentile family then took the carriage and its precious occupant. Because of the bravery of this Polish family, risking the death penalty for harboring and helping Jews, Toni was one of only a handful of children from the area who survived the war.

The Igels were able to find such a family because they had lived in the same part of Poland for several hundred years. All members of the family spoke fluent Polish and they had many dealings with the Polish community. Before the war, Stanley was in the Polish army, so when the war broke out, there were many acquaintances who came to them and offered help. Unfortunately, most of the Jews did not speak Polish, but conducted their lives speaking Yiddish, isolated from the mainstream of Polish community life. These Jews did not have contacts with the Polish underground or with members of the Polish community who could help them.

The elder Mrs. Igel died in 1940 from the stress of the war. Her eldest son, Leo, had remained in America and she knew he was safe, but she would never see him again. Her daughter Sarah's husband was killed by the Russians, and Sarah and her two children, David and Ada, were taken to Siberia.

As the ghetto became more and more perilous, Lusia, Stanley, Gustav, and Martin, Stanley's younger brother, made plans to escape the ghetto to the underground. Stanley, Lusia, and Martin spend the remainder of the war in the forest fighting with the Partisans, while Gustav was hidden in underground Partisan bunkers. (This was extremely dangerous to the Gentiles hiding any Jewish people, because one Gentile Polish family had already been hung for refusing to tell where the Igels were hiding.)

Gustav lived until two months before liberation, enduring in his old age all of the living in bunkers and fleeing from Germans. Stanley, Lusia, and Martin remained in the forest until the liberation in 1944. Only then did they learn that of the 34,000 Jews living in the area, they were among the 170 who survived. Stanley was fortunate –his entire immediate family still lived– but for Lusia there was great anguish. Her entire family had been lost, and she was the lone survivor.

After the liberation and the war's end, Stanley and Lusia reclaimed Toni, their

Torah scrolls, and their religious books. A new life was beginning. Although they could not erase the horror of the war, they did not look back with hatred and despair, but forward with hope and promise for a new tomorrow. With their fluent Polish and Stanley's training as an agronomist, there was much for them to do in the post-war effort. They worked in Poland until 1946 when destiny again summoned them. Stanley became involved in helping 650 children secretly leave Poland. For his efforts, he got into serious trouble with the government, and he was asked to leave the country. He was given safe passage to the border, along with his family and all their belongings, including the Torah.

The family went to Paris for about eight months and then to Czechoslovakia. In Prague, they got a first preference visa to emigrate to the United States and the family arrived in New York City in 1947.

Eventually, they settled in New Jersey where Stanley worked as an agricultural engineer and with the state agricultural program. The Torah scrolls remained in the family's home until 1952 when they were donated to their new synagogue, the Atlantic County Jewish Center. The three Torah scrolls remained in this synagogue until it ceased to exist in 1965. Once again, the Igels took the Scrolls into their home for safekeeping. It is one of these (torahs) that was now being donated to Temple B'nai Israel."

Stanley Igel

Stanley lived on a large farm where his father employed more than 500 workers. A special wing of their home was built to house the synagogue for the area. Stanley graduated from school in Poland with a degree in Agronomics. He served in the Polish Army and Reserve. He was also a member of the Zionist organization, working closely with Menachim Began in 1928. Stanley met Lucia, the daughter of a large department store owner from the city, and they were married on August 27, 1939. He was always very active in Jewish and community affairs. In 1945, he was appointed by the Polish government to serve on a board to deal with over 260,000 survivors. When the Igels were forced to

leave Poland, they arrived in the United States with $18 in their pockets and their treasured possessions, including the Torah. Stanley once again became involved in community life after settling in southern New Jersey. He was the first Jewish person to serve on the county Board of Agriculture. He became President of the Federation of Jewish charities for twelve years and helped build a community center and a synagogue before moving on to New York. In 1975, he started a scholarship at the Hebrew University in Jerusalem in the agricultural field. He has supported Shaarai Zedek Hospital in Jerusalem. In the Clearwater area, he became involved in the Federation of Jewish charities, was appointed to the advisory board of The Jewish Day School, served as a trustee of Temple B'nai Israel, and was a board member of Morton Plant Hospital.

Rabbi Baseman

Rabbi Arthur I. Baseman captured the beauty and significance of the Holocaust Torah when he wrote in the Torah Dedication booklet the following: "The rabbis in the Talmud have declared "Orah Zu Torah"– "Light, that is Torah." By those words they taught that the light of learning, the light of the study of Judaism, will reach into every darkened corner of our globe, the rekindling of every light that has been extinguished by pogrom, persecution, and perfidy.

If the Eternal Light of our faith is dark in Russia, it can be lit and burn more strongly in America; if the Eternal Light is dark in Ethiopia, it can become brighter in Israel. Teachers teaching Judaism, students learning Judaism, Jews living Judaism –"Orah Zu Torah"–"Torah is such a beacon of light."

The Torah we now place in our Holy Ark has been scarred by the ravages of the Holocaust. For too long it has been silent and still a captive of its haunting memories of desolation and despair, its light flickering and faint.

Its spark will now be reignited, and its glow will fill our Sanctuary with its warmth and enwrap us within its spiritual might. Its presence will sanctify us. Indeed, our bringing this Torah into our congregation is our fulfillment of the commandant "Never to forget!."

As we embrace this Torah, we will do so remembering those who embraced it first, peoples' names which we do not know, of a community which is lost forever. Again, Jews will lift it, caress it, kiss it. Children will bless it, adults will adore it. It has come home at last.

This Torah is both a memorial and a precious legacy. It is a memorial to all those martyrs who suffered the inhumanity of the Holocaust. It is a precious legacy of our Jewish brothers and sisters whose handiwork, creativity, and devotion enriched the world for all too brief a time. By this Torah, this Tree of Life, we link ourselves to the roots of our past and to the branches which stretch forward to tomorrow."

Rabbi Baseman completed the ceremony by saying, "One of the highest achievements of any Jew is to participate in the creation of a Sefer Torah (Torah Scroll). The opportunity is being presented to all of us and it is with utmost joy we accept and participate."

The Holocaust Torah joined the other six Torahs in the Ark.

Stained Glass Windows

The stained glass windows originally came from Temple Israel of Gary, Indiana. Temple Israel had sold an older structure to a Christian church after the congregation moved to another area of the community. The Church had promised to treasure the windows as much as the Jewish community had, and they did. However, when the building was destroyed to make way for a convention center, the stained glass windows were removed and the congregation lost

Stained glass windows from Temple Israel of Gary, Indiana.

track of them. The seven windows were probably from the 1920s and the glass was made at the Kokomo Opalescent Glass Company. (Opalescent glass is a term for clear or semi-opaque pressed glass formed with a milky opalescence in the glass like that of an opal.) The glass then went to an artist who completed the work and put all the religious symbols on it.

Temple B'nai Israel was made aware of the stained-glass when two congregants found the windows in the dark dusty corner of a Clearwater man's garage, Mr. Kern Harmon. Mr. Harmon was born on November 1, 1909, in Johnson, Indiana. He and his family later moved to Princeton, Indiana. He moved to Clearwater in 1952 and became a builder of unique homes. He built over 325 custom-built homes, many of which brought him distinction as a builder. He would travel around the country looking for latticework or stained glass or other objects from old buildings that could be put into his new structures. He had purchased the Gary, Indiana, Temple Israel stained-glass windows years before and did not remember exactly where. They were in serious disrepair. It was thought that the windows were made in the United States. This was determined by the design, style, and type of glass of windows which were typically made in the 1920s and 1930s. Windows which came from Europe were typically painted.

Toni Rinde, who was head of Temple B'nai Israel Fine Arts Committee, mentioned finding the stained glass windows to Marcia Sternlieb over lunch. Mrs. Sternlieb was immediately interested because her late husband always felt that the new temple needed stained glass windows in the area left of the Bema. The pieces were restored by Chuck Charmatz of Glass Horizons Inc., of St. Petersburg, who worked with Toni Rinde on the design and layout. The restoration work, the purchase of the stained glass, and the placement of the pieces – which are backlighted– were paid for by Marcia Sternlieb. She donated the windows in memory of her husband. The tribute to Norman Sternlieb and dedication of the windows in his honor took place on September 13. Two of the windows are circles centered with the Star of David. Rabbi Baseman said "The two interlocking triangles represent God and man bonded together. The two triangles reflect the idea that we have the world and the world to come, the afterworld" "that there is God and eternity, heaven and earth."

Nathan Kuperman

Nathan, age 93, is a full-time volunteer who teaches children and Hebrew. He teaches at the Pinellas County Jewish Day School in Clearwater. Nathan started learning Hebrew from his father, and by age six, was enrolled in a Torah School where his education included Judaic studies, culture, laws, grammar and translations. After his bar mitzvah, he spent three and one-half years of intensive study with a rabbi in Massachusetts. He taught a brother his bar mitzvah work and then moved on to tutoring for the rest of his life. He and his late wife, Ruth, moved to On Top of the World in Clearwater. They lived there until her death in October 2002 . In talking about his volunteer work he said, "I always felt like, what good is it going to do me if I have all this knowledge inside me and I don't share it with you? I really think that a volunteer gets more than he gives. I'm a firm believer that we're all here for a reason. When God decides you have fulfilled that reason, that's when you'll go. My reason here is to be with children and help them along." He also said, "It's important that Jewish children learn Hebrew because it provides them a means for speaking to God. If you went to a Christian Church and you couldn't read English, you know what would happen? You would not go to church because you would not understand and would never communicate with your Lord. I think it's important that all know about their religion. I respect every body for who they are. Believe in your God. You don't have to believe in mine, believe in yours, just believe in God."

Highlights of 1986

The Sisterhood was deeply involved in their preschool hearing program at Morton Plant Hospital. This hearing screening program had been a project of Sisterhood since 1971 when Sisterhood provided speech and hearing screening for the Head Start Program throughout Pinellas County. From available records from 1978 through 1985, Temple Sisterhood volunteers screened over 7,000 preschool children.

The bulletin editors were Shari Fuss and Lisa Winner. There were twenty five children in the confirmation class. There were two evening services for both Rosh Hashanah and Yom Kippur. The temple put on a large number of adult education programs. Temple B'nai Israel continued to support Bethel Bethany Home for Retarded Adults.

Temple B'nai Israel was designated as an official site for KEVA, the North American program of recognition for Adult Jewish Education sponsored by the Union of American Hebrew Congregations. It grants students credit units which lead to certification. The program links congregational Adult Jewish Education programs with the Union of American Hebrew Congregations William and Francis Shuster Curriculum. This is a project of the Commission on Jewish Education of the Union of American Hebrew Congregations, the Central Conference of American Rabbis, and the National Association of Temple Educators. The credits can be applied to the Union of American Hebrew Congregations Teacher Certification program.

Ralph G. Dutcher

Ralph G. Dutcher, "Butch", was a man who believed in sharing. He felt that there was no better way to live than to invite friends, Jew or Christian alike, to come together in fellowship and share friendship and respect for each other, which is so valuable to everyone. He believed in giving of himself and his possessions. He wrote, "Those who take but never give–may last for years, but never live." He believed in trying to foster brotherhood and in working to make life better. He believed that even though we may err in what we do, the mistakes could be corrected if we have a true belief in God and the goodness of people. He wrote, "Since nothing we intend is ever faultless, and nothing we ever attempt ever without error, and nothing we achieve without some measure of finitude and fallibility, we are saved by forgiveness."

Mordechai and Ottilie Gorn

Ralph was born in Toledo, Ohio in 1915. His father, Oliver Bert Dutcher, was born in 1880 in Ohio. He was a shipyard worker. His mother, Ella Mae, was born in Michigan in 1884. His grandfather, James, was born in 1866 in New York. His grandmother, Paula, was born in 1868 in Germany. His grandparents lived in Toledo, Ohio, in 1880. Ralph graduated from Michigan State University and Toledo University and had a career in automotive engineering. He worked for the Dana Corporation of Toledo Ohio for thirty five years, where he rose to the position of regional sales manager of the Midwest region.

Ralph married Dorothy Lea in 1944. Ralph and Dorothy moved to Clearwater in 1979 from Dade City, Florida. They became active members of the Pinellas County community. They joined Temple B'nai Israel, where Ralph chaired the Cemetery Committee and then became President of Brotherhood from 1986-1988. Ralph was also an active member of the Golda Meir-Kent Jewish Center, Menorah Manor, PAC of Ruth Eckerd Hall at the Richard B. Baumgardner Center for the Performing Arts, St. Petersburg Florida Orchestra, and other organizations. He was for many years a part of the Kansas City, Missouri, section of the Automotive Engineers and the Society of Automobile Engineers. He was their past secretary.

Zena Sulkes

Zena Sulkes, Director of Education, was awarded the professional title Reform Jewish Educator. It is a professional title awarded to a person who meets high standards of academic preparation and professional experience. The title is awarded and conferred by the Commission on Jewish Education, Central Conference of American Rabbis, Hebrew Union College–Joint Institute of Religion, National Association of Temple Educators. On November 15, 1985, Rabbi Howard Bogot, Director of the Union of American Hebrew Congregations Department of Education presented the title Reform Jewish Educator to Zena W. Sulkes. Zena, at that time, was serving her 14th year as Director of Education of Temple B'nai Israel. She had degrees from the University of Michigan, Wayne State University and the University of South Florida. She had been involved in local, regional, and national efforts to improve the quality of Jewish Education in United States. She was the author of "Proud and Jewish" and a contributor to Compass magazine. She was also a consultant in Reform Jewish Education.

Mordechai Gorn

Mordechai Gorn was born May 25, 1890. His wife, Ottilie, and he donated the innovative and dynamic Gorn Teaching/ Learning Center at Temple B'nai Israel, which contains the latest Judaic resources in audio-visual materials and other materials. Individual study carrels, videotape equipment and a computer helped to make possible the use of programs from the Institute for Computers in Jewish Life. The center is used by children and adults. He has made innumerable contributions to the Jewish and general communities. These include: donating a section of the Weitzman Institute Library, a first aid center for the Mogen David Adom in Israel, a grove of 2,000 trees in the JFK Forest, honorary alumnus of the Hebrew University in Jerusalem; major contributor to St. Joseph Hospital, Stamford Hospital, and a director and major contributor to the Salvation Army. He used the dividends of a living annuity to provide funds for the Gorn Community Service Fund, which is used for a variety of charitable purposes which are nonsectarian. He was an extraordinary person who was a Captain in the Imperial Army of Russia, escaped from an Odessa jail, lived through pogroms, and managed to acquire an engineering education while in Russia. He arrived in Stamford, Connecticut in the 1920's. Although he had no money or even clothing, he managed to start an electrical business. During World War II, he operated the Gorn Aircraft Manufacturing Company and invented the mid-air refueling control system for P84 planes. He wrote *Journey to the Fulfillment*, an autobiography. This man of unlimited talent and fortitude, at age ninety three, had as his motto, "I know not age, weariness, or defeat."

Mordechai Gorn died on Thursday, April 3, 1986. He was a man who loved the country that gave him the chance to enjoy freedom and wealth and shared it with others.

The Gorn Visiting Scholar was Dr. Lawrence E. Mintz, Associate Professor of American Studies at the University of Maryland in College Park, Maryland. His specialty was Jewish humor and how it affected the daily life of the Jewish people. His presentations were: "A Funny Thing Happened to Us on the Way." which is an overview of Jewish humor from biblical times to the present; "The Motives and Functions of Jewish Humor", and "Laughing to Keep from Crying, The Case against Jewish Humor."

Highlights of 1987

Rabbi Baseman celebrated his Chai (18th) year as the rabbi of Temple B'nai Israel. A special service was held on July 19 in honor of Rabbi Baseman and his wife, Renee. The service was part of a multiple-part surprise that the Temple members and officers have been secretly working on for several weeks. The surprise worked. Over 500 members turned out to hear officers, congregation members, a representative of the Christian clergy, and the mayor of Clearwater lovingly describe the work that Arthur and Renee performed for years to help others. The congregation gave Arthur and Renee an all-expense paid, two-week trip to England in August, specifically London and Strafford-on-Avon. The trip was special for the Basemans, since Rene was born in London and Arthur had a degree in English Literature from Harvard.

A story which sums up the person of Rabbi Baseman was published in November in "The Jewish Press." It stated that, " Rabbi Baseman had started his sermon (on Rosh Hashanah)(when) Jack, an elderly congregant sitting in about the 20th row of the sanctuary started to cough violently. "Are you in trouble, Jack?" asked the rabbi from the pulpit. Jack could not answer, he was coughing quite incessantly. The rabbi, instead of delivering his sermon, immediately picked up his glass of water, came off of the pulpit, walked back to Jack and make sure that he drank the water so that it would help him. It did not matter that the sermon, which was being delivered to the largest number of people that would

attend a service during the year, had been interrupted, but rather that he had to come to the aid of a fellow human being."

Myron Mensh served as President from 1987-1991. He said, "The four years of my presidency were some of the best times in my professional career, working with Rabbi Baseman and helping develop leadership among the members of the congregation. It was a thoroughly enjoyable experience."

Myron Mensh, President, Temple B'nai Israel, 1987–1991.

Interreligious dialogue through interfaith programs has always been an important part of every synagogue's experience. In the 1950s and 1960s, Reform Judaism was at the forefront of an interreligious dialogue in North America. The dialogue has always been an attempt to understand each other and to destroy the coalition of hatred and terror that small groups of people try to impose on the majority of good citizens of our country. The Interfaith Event of 1987 at Temple B'nai Israel was entitled "Sharing Our Faith." In attendance at these meetings were representatives of the American Baptist Church, Anona United Methodist Church, Ahavat Shalom Synagogue, Central Christian Church, Christian Science Church, Church of the Reconciliation, Church of God, Church Women United, Catholic Church, Beth Hillel Chai, Espirito Santo, 1st Christian Church Largo, 1st Lutheran Church, 1st Presbyterian Church, First United Methodist Church-Largo, First United Methodist Church-Pinellas Park, F. M. Church, Friendship Methodist Church, Highland Presbyterian Church, Hope Presbyterian Church, Kirk Dunedin, Light of Christ Church, Oakhurst Methodist Church, Our Lady of Lourdes, Prince of Peace Lutheran Church, St. Catherine of Sienna, St. Cecilia Church, St. Jerome Church, St. John Episcopal Church, St. Patrick's Church, St. Paul Lutheran Church, St. Paul United Methodist Church, St. Peter's Cathedral, Skycrest Methodist Church, Temple B'nai Israel, Trinity Presbyterian Church, United Church of Christ, U. U. Fellowship Larger Circle, and Universal Unitarian Church. The various people in attendance shared in the program and presented slides and narrated the similarities and individual differences between the various denominations. The sanctuary, which seats 350 people, overflowed with participants. This reaching out to neighbors by all religious groups in the presence of God built a shared commitment to a moral future, one in which all people could live together in friendship and happiness, but yet approach God in their own special way.

The adult education programs continued to be numerous, interesting, informative, and highly professional. Twenty eight children were confirmed. The Bulletin editor was Dolores Curphey, temple administrator, and Lysa Winner as co-editor. Yolan Ziessman continued as librarian. The Sisterhood, not only continued its support for Religious Community Services (RCS), but established a program to bolster the giving of the congregants. Members were asked to send checks to the Temple to help the needy. A Boy Scout Charter was granted to the Temple. Renee L. Baseman became the first nursery school director. There were double services on Rosh Hashanah eve and Yom Kippur eve. Rabbi Baseman became the rabbi and chaplain of the Jewish War Veterans, Paul Surensky Post # 409. The Chai Club, Young Couples Club continued. A Holocaust Memorial Fund was established.

Religious Community Services is a non-profit agency of sixty four congregations in Pinellas County, established in 1967 to help reduce hunger, poverty, and help with other special-needs. The Food Pantry provides food for families during periods of crisis. Its Food for Tots Program provides baby food and formula. Emergency Housing Program provides temporary shelter for homeless families with children, food, clothing, and counseling. Spouse Abuse Shelter gives temporary housing to adult and children victims of domestic abuse. Stepping Stone offers affordable transitional housing to working low-income families with children. The operating expenses come from the various congregations in the community. A study of the homeless showed that there were between 500 and 600 people who were homeless on any given day, forty six percent of them were families with children, thirty percent of them were single-parent families, thirty eight percent of them had lived in Pinellas County for over one year, and fifty three percent of them were children under

the ages of five years old. The Food Pantry in 1983 fed 11,000 people and in 1986 provided food for 36,000 people in Pinellas County.

The Sisterhood Hearing Program now became the Hearing/Vision Screening Program of three to five-year-old pre-school children. Nine hundred and sixty three children were tested for hearing and 725 children were tested for vision. Twenty four volunteers donated over 300 hours to this project. They received training from the professional audiologists at Morton Plant Hospital of Clearwater. The volunteers traveled from school to school to perform this necessary service. As a result of the screening tests, seventy three children were found to have hearing difficulties and seventy children were found to have possible vision problems.

The Gorn Scholar-in-Residence program featured a series of speakers on a variety of topics. "Our Jewish Cultural Heritage" was presented by Dr. Daniel Rutenberg, Professor of Humanities, University of South Florida. "Modern Jewish Literature" was presented by Zena Sulkes, RJE, Director of Education, Temple B'nai Israel. "Hebrew and Yiddish Folk Music" was presented by Joy Katzen-Guthrie, cantorial soloist. "Purim Shpiel-Biblical Parodies Set to Music" presented by Saul and Tay Caplan, actors. "Jewish Art Today" presented by Syd Entel, owner of Syd Entel Art Galleries. "Jewish Ceremonial Art," presented by Dr. Jan Hirschfield, collector of Jewish ceremonial art.

Highlights of 1988

Temple B'nai Israel conducted the first Living Judaism Scholars Forum on the west coast of Florida. It was sponsored by Hebrew Union College-Joint Institute of Religion, America's oldest institution of higher Jewish scholarship. Rabbi Samuel K. Joseph was the Gorn Visiting Scholar in Residence. He presented, "Asking Ourselves Hard Questions: Moral and Ethical Dilemmas," "Jewish Survival and Identity: The Dilemma of Intermarriage," and "The So-Called Little Dilemmas: a Jewish Response to Everyday Issues." Rabbi Joseph has served many times as a facilitator of a large number of temples in leadership training, including the United Hebrew

Congregation of Terre Haute, Indiana, when the author was President-elect.

Dolores Curphey was both the administrator and the bulletin editor with Associate Editors, Lysa Winner, Robert Winick, and then Shari Fuss. A super auction was held which raised $50,000 for the temple. There were twenty five children in the confirmation class. The new librarian was Mimi Krystel. Zena Sulkes received her Ph D.

Temple B'nai Israel Holocaust Memorial

It was proposed that a Holocaust Memorial become an integral part of Temple B'nai Israel. It was decided that a sculpture depicting the Holocaust tragedy and its eternal lessons for how all people should live and act toward others would be a wonderful addition to the temple grounds. The reason the memorial was put on the temple grounds so that it could be seen by all people was because of a decision of the congregation. At the 1 p.m. Yom Kippur educational session, Rabbi Baseman asked the congregation where the memorial should be placed. The Temple was full of members and also included many of the teenage children. A concern was voiced by the older members that the memorial would be desecrated if not placed in a secure area. Teenager after teenager came to the microphone and said that they wanted it outside because they wanted to be proud of it and of their heritage. They said that if the memorial was defaced, they would personally clean it. At the dedication ceremony, all of the Torahs were carried outside and became part of a wonderful memory.

It was decided that the sixteen foot high art work by Alfred Tibor, the sixty eight year old Hungarian-born artist, a Holocaust survivor, would be one of the most meaningful tributes that the Jewish people of this area could provide as a lasting tribute to those who died and to those looking forward to a better future for all humanity. The sculpture depicts the victims of the Holocaust being swallowed by the flames as the Torah is passed on to the survivors. The main figure is a woman with her arms outstretched pointing to heaven as she is being engulfed by flames. It also shows children being engulfed as they were during

Alfred Tibor

Joy Katzen-Guthrie

the years of the extermination camps. Most importantly, it shows hope and continued life as the Torah is passed from the flames to a survivor standing outside of the fire. Mr. Tibor's works are in synagogues in United States, as well as at the permanent Holocaust Memorial in Israel, Yad Vashem.

Joy Katzen-Guthrie

Joy served as Musical Director for Temple B'nai Israel in 1988-1989. She then became the Cantorial Soloist for the B'nai B'rith Hillel Foundation of Tampa from 1990-1993, and Cantorial Soloist for Temple Shir Shalom in Gainesville in 1994-1999. She was also a Cantorial Soloist for Congregation B'nai Emmunah in Tarpon Springs from 1995-1999. She then became Cantorial Soloist for Congregation Aliyah in Clearwater from 1999-2000, Cantorial Soloist for Temple B'nai Israel of Clearwater 2000-2002, Cantorial Soloist for Temple Beth El of Bradenton 2003-2004, and again at Temple B'nai Israel from 2004-2005. She has also been Music Director for Unity Center for Today in North Tampa since 1998.

Joy, a native of Memphis, Tennessee, came to the Tampa Bay area in 1981. She earned her Bachelor of Arts and Bachelor of Fine Arts Degrees magna cum laude in Broadcast Communications and Music from Stephens College in Columbia, Missouri. Since 1983, she has appeared in concerts regionally and nationally, and is an award-winning writer of musical theater, popular, and spiritual music. Joy's live performances and recordings combine her skills as soloist and bandleader, guest lecturer and teacher, cantorial vocalist, concert artist, Unity Music Director, and contemporary folk, pop, and spiritual songwriter. Her concerts include original songs and compositions, musical stage/film works, and liturgical music of the Jewish Kabbalists (Students of the Jewish Kabbalah) (Kabbalah is a body of mystical teachings of rabbinical origin, often based on an esoteric interpretation of the Hebrew Scriptures.) She also performs Israeli and Yiddish folk tunes and world spiritual music, which she uniquely weaves together with history, storytelling and song.

Highlights of 1989

Rabbi Baseman received a Doctor

of Divinity degree on March 15 for his contributions to Judaism and the Jewish people. Rabbi Baseman, in the Temple Bulletin, later talked about his experiences at the ceremony and the fact that he and the other seven rabbis laughed and carried on, although some people felt that rabbis should always be solemn. He said, "Surely, I am convinced that a rabbi without a sense of humor is at a marked disadvantage. For example, a rabbi teaches, counsels, is sometimes a lawyer, often a social worker, something of an editor, a bit of a philosopher, an entertainer, salesman, and struggling scholar. He visits the sick, marries people, buries the dead, consoles the sorrow laden, works with Bar and Bat Mitzvah kids, plans programs, and amidst it all, prepares a sermon and preaches it on the Sabbath. What then will sustain a rabbi if not a sense of humor when a jovial congregation roars "What a job you got-one hour a week!."

Dedication of the sculpture, "The Light of the Human Soul," by Daniel Gluck, the artist who created the Ark, took place in October, 1989. It was presented to the Temple by the Dorian family in loving memory of Lee. He was the chairperson of the Construction Committee that supervised the creation of the present Temple facility. The inscription reads, "The soul of man is the light of the Lord", Proverbs 27.

The bulletin editor was Dolores Curphey and the assistant editor was Sheila Weinstock. The first adult retreat, "Reform Judaism-Making Knowledgeable Choices", was held. Sixteen children were confirmed and ten graduated from the Senior Study Program. Yolan Ziessman was the Temple librarian from 1977 to 1989. During this time she performed invaluable services and contributed at least fifteen or more hours each week to this task. There were over 700 families in the congregation. The Gorn Scholar was Dr. Moshe Pelli, Director of Jewish Studies, University of Central Florida. He presented, "Jewish Identity: A Modern Phenomenon", "Tensions: Traditional Versus Secular Judaism", and "New Interpretations of the Binding of Isaac."

Preschool Director

From 1970-82, Jeanette Fein was the preschool director. The preschool of Temple

B'nai Israel provides developmentally appropriate activities and enriched experiences in a safe, nurturing, Jewish environment, and encourages all children to explore and discover their expanding world as they move on successfully to grade school. The philosophy of the school is that children learn best by doing. The children participate in individual creativity activities such as creative arts, music, science, dramatic play, fitness, early literacy and computers, outdoor play, and exploration. Children are encouraged to learn at their own pace and in a way that is best suited to them. Children are also taught Hebrew and Spanish. From 1982-1987, Jill Black was the director.

CHAI Presidents were: 1980-82, Mel Fergenbaum; 1982-83, Helene Debowsky; 1983-84, Eric Adler; 1984-86, Nanci Weiss; 1986-87, Robert Klein; 1987-89, Jerri Green; 1989-90, Frank Weiss.

Friendship Club Presidents were: 1980-82, J. Marvin Stern; 1982-83, Lieslott Stern; 1983-88, Hilda Schwartz; 1988-90, Florence Wax.

Yolan Ziessman was the Temple librarian for many years. She wrote a regular column in the Temple Bulletin about things of interest and reviewed new books which were donated to the library. She said that the Temple Library was living proof of the Jewish people's continued respect for books and the study of the writings of Judaism.

Highlights of 1990-1999

Highlights of 1990

There was no Gorn Scholar in Residence Program, since the chairperson, Xenia Fane, was traveling abroad..

40th anniversary celebration

Temple B'nai Israel celebrated its 40th anniversary. The History Committee, chaired by Al Sulkes, prepared a history of the Jewish community of Clearwater and Temple B'nai Israel. The members of the committee were: Martha Baker, Leonard and Shirley Collman, Darwin Frank, Lila Lawrence, Leona Levine, and Sally Siegal. Rabbi Baseman said, "Temple B'nai Israel, the Temple of the "Children of Israel," links its destiny with the Patriarch, Jacob, who later is renamed "Israel," "Champion of

God." We are Jacob's children, the Children of Israel. Our Ark, therefore, symbolizes Jacob's Ladder of Prayer which unites heaven and earth in a common endeavor to better this world. And as Jacob brought a stone on which to rest and dream, so have we brought our stones of effort and dedication upon which to set our dreams and to make our dreams possible – that from within us a divine influence will arise to the heavens and bring down blessings upon generations to come. Upon awakening from his dream, Jacob uttered words which we can echo after forty years of life. We, as Jacob, can look around us, recognize the living spirit of this place, and exclaim, "How full of awe and wonder is this place. This is none other than the house of God and this a gateway to heaven." May it ever be so. The theme of the anniversary was, "Them That Honor Me, I Will Honor."

Holocaust Memorial Consecration Program

The Holocaust Memorial Consecration Program was held on Sunday, April 22. The community proudly stood together that day, Jew and Christian, old and young, black and white, to declare that this kind of atrocity shall never occur again. They remembered the past, connected it to the present, and determined that the future will be one of fellowship and brotherhood. People who love each other do not destroy each other. Rabbi Baseman said, "We pray that our monument will help neighbors stretch their souls toward neighbors, an act of love which could tip the balance. And we pray that our monument will help us rise above our sorrows, for the perished still prevail." He said, "To ensure that those who died did not die in vain; to affirm that those who live, do not live in vain." Rabbi Baseman said, "Under an azure blue sky on that Sunday afternoon, we of Temple B'nai Israel bore witness: Never more will it be said, That we had eyes but did not see; That we had ears but did not hear; That we had mouths but failed to speak.

We remember the victims in order to recall our escape, by luck or providence, or time and place of birth. We remember the victims because we have survived. We remember the victims because we are their living memorials. We remember the victims because they and we are one, and to forget them would be to forget ourselves. We remember the victims so we may live. We remember the Six Million so that we can say to the world...NEVER AGAIN!"

The dedication program started with the lighting of yahrzeit (memorial) candles. This was followed by a procession of rabbis, cantors, and Presidents of congregations in Pinellas County, who carried Torah scrolls from the Temple to the monument. The cantors of Pinellas County led the audience in singing the Star-Spangled Banner and the Hatikvah. The invocation was presented by Rabbi Baseman. Responsive reading was conducted by Rabbi Shalom Adler, Rabbi Kenneth Bromberg, and Rabbi Jodie Futornick. The unveiling of the monument was carried out by the Holocaust committee: Seena and William Baker, Mrs. Barbara Bernstein, Mrs. Sydell Entel, Mr. David Korones, Mrs. Toni Rinde, Lisl and Alfred Schick, Mrs. Claire Stiglitz, Mrs. Judith Winer, Rabbi Arthur I. Baseman, Mr. Ralph G. Dutcher, Mr. Charles Goldsmith, Mr. Howard Lawrence, Mrs. Barbara Rosenblum, Mr. Robert L. Schapiro and Mr. Herbert D. Strauss. The lighting of the Eternal Lamp was done by Toni Rinde. The Message of the Monument was presented by Alfred Tibor, the sculptor. The rabbis, cantors and Presidents of the congregations returned the Torah scrolls to the Ark in the sanctuary.

The Yom Hashoah (Day of Destruction or Day of Whirlwind) Service followed. Cantor Irving Zummer sang Elu Devarim (These Are the Words). Responsive reading was conducted by Rabbi Steven Kaplan and Rabbi Gary Klein. This was followed by Cantor Yochanan Bickhardt singing Ani Maamin (I Fervently Believe). The keynote address, "Humanity, Survival and the Holocaust" was presented by Mark Berkowitz. The kindling of the memorial candles for the Six Million was conducted by Rabbi Jacob Luski and Rabbi Ira Youdovin, survivors and families representing all congregations. Cantor Michael Brem sang El Moleh Rachamim (God Full of Compassion). The words of this beautiful prayer are, "O God, who art full of compassion, who dwellest on high, grant perfect rest beneath the shelter of thy divine presence, in the exalted places among the holy and pure, who shine as the brightest of the firmament to (insert name of person or persons) who has gone to his/her eternal home. We beseech thee, Lord of compassion, shelter him/her evermore under the cover of thy wings, and let his/her soul be bound up in the bond of life, and may he/she rest in peace and let us say, Amen."

Rabbi Baseman recited the thoughts of Elie Wiesel, "Let us say Kaddish (a prayer for the dead that does not mention death but the glorification of God) not only for the dead, but also for the living who have forgotten the dead. And that the prayer be more than a prayer, more than lament; let it be outcry, protest and defiance. And above all let it be an act of remembrance. For that is what the victims wanted: to be remembered, at least to be remembered. For just as the killer was determined to erase Jewish memory, so were the dying heroes and fighting martyrs bent on maintaining it alive. They are now being defamed: or forgotten–which is like killing them a second time. Let us say Kaddish together–and not allow others to betray them posthumously."

Highlights of 1991

The Gorn Scholar-in-Residence was Rabbi David Sapperstein, Co-Director and Counsel of the Religious Action Center of Reform Judaism and Adjunct Professor in Comparative Jewish and American Law at Georgetown University Law School. He presented, "The Supreme Court: What It Means with Regard to Jewish Concerns", and "Ethics Crisis in American Life."

Gail Simon

Temple B'nai Israel is especially concerned about religious education and operates a religious school. The mission of Temple B'nai Israel Religious School is to educate the youth of temple members beginning with pre-school age children through the completion of high school. The curriculum is focused on instilling a positive Jewish identity with a commitment to Judaism. The school uses innovative methods in each of its programs and

Toni Rinde, President, Temple B'nai Israel, 1993–1995.

takes into consideration the individual needs of each student. The Director of Religous Education is Gail Simon. She began teaching Hebrew and religious school in 1975 in Cleveland, Ohio and has taught continuously since then. In 1988, she was awarded a grant to attend the Coalition for Advancement of Jewish Education Conference in Jerusalem which inspired her to change careers and become a full-time Jewish educator. She studied at the College of Jewish Studies in Cleveland Ohio and Hebrew University in Jerusalem. In 1990, she was selected as a recipient of the Ratner Fellowship awarded to outstanding Jewish educators in the Cleveland area. Gail holds a Bachelor's Degree in Library Science from the University of Florida and a Master of Education and Counseling from Kent State University. She has worked as a school and college librarian, as an administrator and teacher, and is certified in several areas including learning disabilities and behavioral disorders.

Highlights of 1992

Renee Baseman was a host of the first Pinellas County meeting of the Tampa Bay Jewish Early Child Educators at Temple B'nai Israel. This group joined the Central Agency for Jewish Education. Renee Baseman retired as preschool director after five years of service. There were two previous directors. Thirteen children were confirmed. Sharon Tanner became the Director of Preschool.

Cheryl Burton was the sololist at temple from 1975-1992. She shared her golden voice with the congregation in many worship services, B'nai Mitzvah, naming of babies and weddings. The congregation, rabbi, and officers held her in the highest level of esteem. She was a true friend and supporter of the congregation Faithfully, and without reservation, she gave of herself to everyone, touching their hearts in so many different ways.

Robert Marinoff became the new cantorial soloist. Harold and Sally Siegel. their son, Todd, and daughter-in-law, Sheila, provided a generous gift to the Temple for the purpose of hiring a cantorial soloist for a three-year period. Mr. Marinoff

had been previously employed by other congregations in the community. He had performed professionally with the Florida Orchestra with various regional opera companies. Temple B'nai Israel presented, "An Afternoon of Opera and Broadway." Robert Marinoff, Dawn Young, a soprano, Michael Berryman, a baritone, Vladimir Khokhlov, a concert pianist, and Rosalie Maresca, an accompanist performed.

The Brotherhood Breakfast of December 13 was held in honor of the rabbi's birthday. Over 250 guests helped share the memories of congregational accomplishments and the role the rabbi had played in its success. He said that, " The breakfast was a superb example that the joy of living is determined not so much by what life brings to us, as by the attitude we bring to life. How true it is that what life does to us depends on what life finds in us."

There was no Gorn Scholar-in-Residence Program. The chairperson was not available to set up the program.

Cantorial Soloist, Robert Marinoff

Bruce Flashenburg

Bruce was born on July 25, 1951. He came to the Clearwater area from Massachusetts in 1992. He graduated from the University of Massachusetts at Amherst with a Bachelor of Science Degree in Public Health and Health Education in 1973. He earned a Certificate from the Cambridge Institute for Computer Programming in Boston, Massachusetts in 1985. Bruce was President of the Brotherhood of Temple Tifereth Israel in Maldem, Massachusetts, Vice President of the New England Conference of the National Federation of Temple Brotherhoods, and President of Temple B'nai Israel from 2001-2003. He has worked in the retail industry, in management positions, and in computer business applications.

Bruce Flashenburg, President of Temple B'nai Israel, 2001–2003.

Mimi Krystel, President of Temple B'nai Israel, 1991–1993.

Highlights of 1993

A new singles group was formed. Twenty one children were confirmed. The Harold Siegel family donated a new organ to the synagogue. The Bereavement Support Group started working with Hospice of Florida Suncoast.

On March 21, Robert Marinoff, cantorial soloist for Temple B'nai Israel presented his

third annual cantorial concert. Joining Robert was Vladimir Khokhlov, concert pianist and Natasha and Eugene Bazhanov, concert violinist. All these artists from Russia were relocated by the Jewish Family Service of Pinellas County. The Gorn Visiting Scholar was Dr. David Ariel, President Cleveland College of Jewish Studies. He presented, "The Mystic Quest, "Changing Jewish Culture" to the teenagers, and "Changing Jewish Culture" to the adults at the Sabbath Service.

A flood occurred in the Temple which damaged the walls and the interior of the Ark.

Aaron and Arlene Chernoff

Arlene and Aaron Chernoff

Aaron, a thirty nine year member of the Army reserve, who retired with the rank of Colonel, was born on July 17, 1928. He graduated from both the University of Pennsylvania and Temple University. He also received an extensive military education including: Command and General Staff College; Industrial College of the Armed Forces; Civil Defense Staff College; and Judge Advocate General School in International Law. He served as a military lay leader on army posts where there were no Jewish chaplains and jointly conducted ecumenical services within his unit. He was awarded the chaplain's tallit, the Army Commendation Medal, twice honored with the Meritorious Service Medal, the George Washington Honor Medal from the Freedom Foundation at Valley Forge, and the Medal of Honor by the Chapel of the Four Chaplains in Philadelphia (Beth also received this honor). In 1955, his design was selected by the Institute of Heraldry to become the insignia of the Civil Affairs Branch. In 1976, he was appointed Bicentennial Projects Officer, and coordinated logistics for the Bicentennial Celebration in Philadelphia. He was a member of the Retired Officers Association, the Reserve Officers Association in Philadelphia, and the Paul Surensky Post 409 of the Jewish War Veterans.

At Temple B'nai Israel, he and Arlene served on the Caring Committee. Aaron was a hospital and nursing-home volunteer chaplain. They both died seven weeks apart in 2004. Daughter, Beth, at her mother's funeral remarked, "they had the same three initials, the same year birth, and the same

year of death. Indeed, my father frequently remarked that they were like "Siamese twins, conjoined at the heart."

Aaron's philosophy of life was, "...As one who has been there, allow me to say that retirement does not have to be an end, but a new beginning. For many retirees here in the Sunshine State, swimming, boating, golf and tennis are the most popular outlets. Arlene and I have gone in a different direction: service to the Jewish community. As part of our congregation's Caring Committee, every Monday we visit the Jewish patients at our local hospital to try to cheer them up, and I offer prayers for their recovery in Hebrew and English. Eight Shabbatim a year, I travel south to St. Petersburg, to conduct services, with a D'var Torah (and interpretation of the Torah text for that week), for the residents of Menorah Manor, the kosher nursing home. As a volunteer lay leader, I have a wonderful congregation – who may be physically frail, but are mentally alert. Their smiles and expressions of gratitude are very rewarding. Retirement will be what you make of it..."

Carol Lawson and Paul W. Kingston II

Caroll moved to Dunedin from East Lansing, Michigan, where she was born on October 21, 1966. She earned a Bachelor of Arts Degree from Michigan State University and a Doctor of Jurisprudence from the Thomas M. Cooley Law School. She married Paul on October 19, 2003. Paul was born in Wesely, Massachusetts on November 19, 1967. Paul owns Kingston Automotive Incorporated. They have a son, Ethan, who was born on June 1, 2005.

Highlights of 1994

There were 720 families in the congregation. There were seven senior study graduates and thirteen children confirmed. Stanley Bush became the temple administrator. He had six years of previous administrative experience in synagogues including his last two at Schaarai Zedek of Tampa. The congregation had over 300 children in religious studies, an excellent preschool, youth groups, auxiliaries, and had built bridges of understanding to the larger Christian community through its many Interfaith efforts contributed to by the

Temple, the Sisterhood, the Brotherhood, and the Youth Groups. The interior of the Ark was beautified by the generosity of Drs. Joan and Bruce Levine. Enhancements were made after the damage done by the flood the previous year. The sanctuary and social hall were also re-wallpapered. The Gulf Coast Jewish Family Service Food Pantry asked all the synagogues to help provide food for the needy in Pinellas County.

The confirmation class consisted of: Diane Yaeger, Adam Greenfield, Karly Schweitzer, Jessie Geller, Lauren Friedman, Jeremy Schwartzberg, Jarred Snyder, Matt Wexler, Willow Duttge, Aimee Salisbury, Alissa Bavil, Marla Rofle and Ben Diamond. The confirmation class traditionally started the confirmation service with a floral offering. Diane Yaeger, speaking for the class said, "In this vase, each type of flower on its own is very different, but put altogether they have great impact, visually and emotionally, forming one beautiful bouquet. Each one of my classmates is as different as each individual flower. But when we come together as a group, we form a bond within Judaism that, like the bouquet, is also beautiful to see. Some of us sitting here today have been friends for over fourteen years. Each of these flowers will eventually wither away. But the experiences, faith, and knowledge all of us have shared as friends, will not die. They will be a part of us forever."

The Gorn Visiting Scholar was Dr. Peter Pitzele. He presented, "The Psychodrama of the Bible." Dr. Pitzele is Director of Psychodrama Services and of the Institute for Psychodrama and Group Psychotherapy at Winds Hospital in Katonah, New York.

The Jubilee Weekend, a celebration of the 25th anniversary of Rabbi Baseman and Renee coming to Temple B'nai Israel was sponsored by the past Presidents group, Sisterhood, Brotherhood, Couples Club, Chai, Temple Youth Groups, and Religious School. Rabbi Robert Frazen from Temple Solel presided over the Shabbat Services on Friday night. At the Saturday Night Gala, Rabbi/stand-up comic, Bob Alpert, who was recognized for his fresh, contemporary, and totally unorthodox comedy delighted the audience as he had done throughout the country on television, radio, and in personal appearances. Rabbi Alpert, a graduate of Lehigh University, was ordained at Hebrew Union College in Cincinnati and was the first Jewish person ever to earn a Doctorate from the Princeton Theological Seminary. He has been a congregational rabbi in New York and Philadelphia.

Many people, during the anniversary service, praised Rabbi Baseman for his skill in family relations, education, teaching, research, administration, problem-solving, and for doing so much to create the wonderful Jewish community that exists in Pinellas County. His warm sense of humor, his friendliness toward everyone, including strangers, his desire to help children, adults, members of the congregation, peers, other people, and other congregations, both Jewish and non-Jewish, indicate the stature of this individual within his adopted community, and respect that he receives from all people.

An article written by Michael Davis, Editor of *The Baltimore Jewish Times*, on September 24, 1993, entitled "The Turning Point," and published in the anniversary prayer booklet, truly expresses the totality of the person of Rabbi Arthur I. Baseman. "Throughout my adolescence, into my college years and beyond, I see the Day of Atonement as twenty five hours of discomfort and denial, an exhausting slow-motion march to nowhere. These are years when separated geographically and metaphysically from my Orthodox roots in Rhode Island, I choose to distance myself from Yom Kippur and many of the rite and obligations of Judaism. I'm adrift thinking I am free.

But then at age twenty seven, something unexpected, exhilarating and clarifying happens in my relationship with God and the day of judgment. It begins on Rosh Hashanah, 1978, along the Gulf of Mexico in the coastal Florida community of Clearwater. Friends invite my wife and me to attend services with them at their Reform temple, B'nai Israel. I resisted first, and imagining my family saying, "Uch! Reform! They're not real Jews. Organs! Choirs!"–but we go.

The congregation is led by Rabbi Arthur Baseman, a Harvard alum and

Red Sox diehard whose zest for life is only exceeded by his passion for social action. He leads an amazing service that night, and the magnificent ushering in of the new year seems to lift me off my seat. There are melodies new to me that enhance my worship experience. There are humorous asides. There are readings in Hebrew and English, with full participation from the congregants, whose attention never seems to waiver. There are no side conversations, and somehow, unbelievably, everyone finds a seat before the service begins.

Madelyn and Richard Liss

It is so fundamentally enjoyable that I actually feel a little guilty in bed that night; after all, one shouldn't have that much pleasure from such a solemn occasion, should one? I show up the next morning for services, and asked to return for Yom Kippur.

Ten days later, it is a Day of Atonement for me and the Boston Red Sox, who blow a one-game playoff to the New York Yankees. When prayers resume after an afternoon interlude, Rabbi Baseman stands at the bimah and announces that since Yom Kippur is a day of forgiveness, he would find it in his heart to forgive Bucky Dent, a light-hitting Yankee infielder who lofted an unlikely home run, driving a stake into the heart of his beloved Red Sox. He has heard of the game's outcome from a lapsed congregant, not unlike myself, and his comment brings the house down.

In Rabbi Baseman, I found my Jewish kindred spirit, and in B'nai Israel my spiritual way station. In the fifteen years since, I have become an unabashed Reform Jew, someone who uses historic tradition to build a more liberal-but no less credible-future."

The congregation, under the leadership and guidance of Nancy and Sheldon Hoffman, made this a memorable weekend. The congregation gave Rabbi and Renee a trip to Israel to show how much the rabbi has always meant to the people of Temple B'nai Israel.

On Wednesday, December 14, 1994, vandals struck Temple B'nai Israel and wrote on the Temple walls "Die Jew," "Go Home Jew," "Yes We Are Back," followed by large swastikas. A large swastika was spray-painted on the Holocaust Memorial. The clergy of the local churches responded immediately in an act of solidarity with the Jewish community. The maintenance staff, within a period of eight hours, removed all the desecration.

Madelyn Liss

Madelyn arrived in Pinellas County from Michigan, following the death of her beloved husband, Richard. She felt a great need to be near her daughter, Sheryl Goff, and her two grandsons who lived in Seminole. Madelyn felt very close to Rabbi Baseman and Temple B'nai Israel. Rabbi Baseman had been deeply involved with her daughter and grandchildren. She said, "Because of Rabbi Baseman's deep concern and caring ways, I found a home at Temple B'nai Israel. Rabbi has filled my life with peace and joy and given me a sense of real belonging. He has helped to fill the emptiness caused by my husband's demise." Madelyn filled this emptiness with a highly significant amount of community service. She was President of the Jewish Community Center of South Pinellas County, President of the Menorah Manor Guild, President of Sisterhood of Temple B'nai Israel, a Member of the Executive Board of Temple B'nai Israel, and an active member of Hadassah.

Madelyn was born in Benton Harbor, Michigan on September 28, 1929. Her husband, Richard, was born on July 16, 1924 in Cleveland, Ohio. After they both lost their spouses, they met and then married on June 14, 1978 in Oak Park, Michigan. Richard passed away on October 16, 1991.

Madelyn received a Bachelor's Degree in Education from Wayne State University in Detroit, Michigan, in 1950. For thirty three years she was a kindergarten teacher in Detroit, and for twenty of those years a Teacher Preparation Counselor for Michigan State University, training future teachers. Her father, Sam Bishop, was a football coach for forty five years at Northwestern High School in Detroit. He was selected as the Educator of the Year by the American Association of School Administrators and then later entered into the Michigan Sports Hall of Fame. Madelyn learned her love of teaching from her father and her graciousness from her mother, Helen.

Highlights of 1995

The Temple and the Sisterhood were recognized for supporting the food pantry of Religious Community Services since 1970. There were 710 families in the congregation and twenty five children were confirmed.

On March 28, a letter was received from the Unity of Spirit, deploring the vandalism at the temple. They said, "In order to express our desire that the healing begin, we want to do three things: 1. We are sending a token of substance as the part of our tithe this week that we trust that in some way be applied toward the restoration of the damaged property, and may also express our desire that the sacred places that you have created be upheld. As the sacredness of the holy places in our culture is revered, all the world is blessed. 2. We offer our willingness to summon volunteers within our own congregation to take turns and keep a watchful eye on your temple property, if that should be desired. As we work together, all can be kept safe. 3. We are with you in prayer, and forming genuine forgiveness for the mistaken beliefs and self-loathing that would cause individuals to commit such vandalism.".

The Gorn Scholar-in-Residence was Trudy Gold of London, England. She spoke about the Jewish people in England during the century.

Western Wall

The Western Wall in the foyer of the temple is a replica of the Western Wall of the Temple in Jerusalem. The Schwersky family, with the able assistance of Toni Rinde, developed the concept for this meaningful artwork as a tribute to the memory of their husband and father, Don, who had brought so much good to his family and his congregation. Toni Rinde knew of two artists, Charles and Kathy Macone, of Clearwater, who took their ideas and turned them into artist's sketches. They then built the sculpture that brings such significance to the western wall of the foyer. The large figure, the Schwersky family feels, represents their beloved husband and father and the three smaller figures represent the universal family. On the side of the sculpture, the Hebrew words "Ani L'dodi l 'dodi Li", are

written. The translation is, "I am my beloved and my beloved is mine." Rabbi Baseman requested that a box be built beside the wall with a slot in it, for people to put prayers in, just as they do in Jerusalem. Gail Simon, Director of Religious Education, has her pre-Bar and Bat Mitzvah class put their prayers in and return at the end of the year to read them and see if they have been answered.

Don and Sandy Schwersky

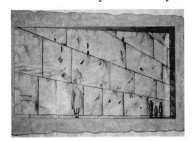 

The Western Wall was dedicated at a beautiful and meaningful Sabbath service in loving memory of Don by Rabbi Baseman and the Schwersky family on May 26. Don was born on September 16, 1933, and passed away at the age of sixty, December 14, 1993. His friends, wife, and children honored and delighted in the life of this fine individual who thought of them, his country, and the Jewish community first and about himself last. Don enlisted in the Navy in 1952 and served until 1956. He, his wife Sandy, and their children moved to Clearwater in 1972 from Sharon, Massachusetts. They joined Temple B'nai Israel right away and Don became a member of the Brotherhood. He served as President of B'nai B'rith three times, two of them in the Clearwater Lodge. During this time, Sandy became President of the B'nai B'rith Women. Together, they planned and put on the B'nai B'rith Follies, first at the Temple social hall on March 4, 1975, and then the following year at the Safety Harbor Spa. Don had a great sense of humor, and was one of the stars of the show. He was a longtime member of the Refrigeration and Air Conditioning Contractors Association, was a longtime board member, and after his death the new Board Room was named the Don Schwersky Room. In 1984, after his son, Steven, and he formed their own company, he took over servicing the temple air conditioners and

Sandy and Don Schwersky

David Greene, President, Temple B'nai Israel, 1995–1997.

did not charge the temple for the service.

Hundreds of people of all faiths filled the sanctuary out of love and respect for Don Schwersky at his funeral. His wife and his children spoke highly of him. His son, Robert, summarized the feelings of all, "The sky was without a moon, yet the night was bright from the light of stars. Looking up, neither my eyes nor my thoughts were focused. But suddenly I saw one of the stars plummeting from where it had been fixed moments ago. It burned out within seconds. Perhaps a farewell message from my father. He knew life was precious and fragile. A kind gentle man who loved his family and friends. Profound in his manner of living. His presence was always heart felt. I think of him when I look up into the night sky. I will always love him to the ends of the universe. May his memory continue to burn as brightly as the stars."

Iris and Stanley Shalit

Iris and Stanley were both born in Boston, Massachusetts. They joined Temple B'nai Israel and became very active members. Iris graduated from Boston University in 1959 with a Bachelor of Arts Degree in Sociology. She and Stanley married in 1960. Iris started working in libraries at age sixteen and finally retired from the Largo Library in 2000. She and Stanley took over the existing Temple B'nai Israel library and re-catalogued the entire system. Iris has been involved in numerous community and Jewish activities. They include: public broadcasting television, Temple B'nai Israel Sisterhood President, Elks Club Ladies Auxiliary President, Community Choir, literacy volunteer, public school aid to Reading Consultant, PTA, Girl Scouts troop leader, consultant, leadership training specialist, Temple B'nai Israel Religious School, Preschool, and Choir, Hadassah, Largo Library Foundation Board, and Friends of Largo Library Board.

Stanley earned a Bachelor's and Master's Degree in Mechanical Engineering in Packaging Technology from Northeastern University. He also was a dedicated individual involved in numerous community and Jewish activities. His activities included: public broadcasting television, Secretary/ Treasurer of the Elks, religious school teacher, Community Choir, Barber Shoppers Singing Society, Knights of Pithias, Temple B'nai Israel Board, Religious School Committee, Brotherhood, Preschool, Choir, and Past-President of the Friends of the Library Board.

Stanley, a distinguished looking gentleman, was committed to his Judaism. He loved to share his excellent Jewish education with others, especially with children. He conducted services at Menorah Manor, once a month and also conducted services at Temple B'nai Israel, especially during the time of the rabbis vacation, during the summer. He was loved and respected by all and was an excellent role model for both children and adults. His burial was on a Monday morning, a time when people are busy with work and their own schedule. And yet, a large number of people came to the Cemetery to pay their respects to this kind human being who lived his Jewish life.

Iris and Stanley's daughter, Janice, graduated from Hicke Business School in St. Louis in 1981. Their daughter, Michelle, graduated from St. Petersburg Junior College in 1984 with an Associate of Arts Degree and then received a Certificate of Completion in Graphic Arts from Mirror Lake Pinellas County Vocational-Technical System in 1986.

Highlights of 1996

The children within the congregation were considerably younger than previous years. Nine children were confirmed and thirty four young children were in the consecration class. The Yitzhak Rabin Teacher of Excellence Award was first given in 1996 and was awarded to Renee Baseman, Jerri Greene, and Raida Goldman.

The Gorn Scholar-in-Residence was Dr. Nathan Katz, Professor and Chair of Religious Studies at Florida International University. He presented "Jews and Gurus," "2,000 Years of Jewish Life in India," and "The Last Jews of Cochin," along with a slide presentation.

From Purim to Pesach, Operation Afikomen, a total Jewish community-wide effort to contribute food for the hungry was coordinated by the Jewish Federation of Pinellas County's Jewish Community

Relations Council and the Women's Division. Although each of the synagogues, agencies, and Jewish individuals within the community always contributed food to the hungry, this was a unique effort where every person was asked to bring a bag of food to the various synagogues and organizations throughout the county to help relieve hunger.

Debbie Friedman, the internationally acclaimed singer and songwriter, made a presentation of her music at Temple B'nai Israel in honor of Jewish Music Month. Debbie pioneered the distinctive development of American Jewish music. Her unique musical style is best exemplified in her recordings of "Sing Unto God," "And You Shall Be a Blessing," and "Mi Shebeirach (The prayer to God for the healing of a loved one.)

The Adult B'not Mitzvah class included: Barbara Baccari, Chalene Field, Donna Feingold, Linda Goldman, Bobby Keiden, Stephanie Rosenbaum and Kathleen Valentine. The service was conducted by Rabbi Baseman and Cantorial Soloist Robert Marinoff. A special thanks was given to the temple educator, Nathan Kuperman. The service was a celebration to the commitment of the study of Torah by these women and all Jewish people. It was dedicated to the memory of Dr. Judith K. Eisenstein, the first young women to become a Bat Mitzvah. This took place in 1922 in New York and the service was led by her father, the famous Rabbi Mordecai Kaplan.

Highlights of 1997

Professor Julius Lester was the Gorn Scholar-in-Residence. He had been awarded all three of the University of Massachusetts's most prestigious faculty awards, including the Chancellor's Medal, the University's highest honor. The Council for Advancement and Support of Education selected him as the Massachusetts State Professor of the Year in 1986. He has published twenty four books including seven non-fiction, fourteen children's books, one book of poetry, and two novels. His books have been translated into eight languages. He presented, "My Journey to Judaism," "Blacks and Jews : Where We Are What We Can Do," and "Jewish Identity and America Today."

Temple B'nai Israel and its Sisterhood were named winners of the prestigious Irving J. Fain Social Action Award for its program "Judaism through the Year." The award presentation was witnessed by over 200 people from eighteen churches, with ten clergy and six nuns in attendance. The congregation was justifiably proud of Sisterhood's President, Wendy Adamson and Nan Reuben, Sisterhood's Religion and Education Vice President, and all the committee members who worked so hard to gain this outstanding recognition. Rabbi Baseman said, "This achievement surely underscores the value of all our Temple Auxiliaries, but this is truly Sisterhood's shining glory. There is no doubt Sisterhood is an idea deeply rooted in the core of the Reform movement. Traditional Orthodox Judaism has treated women as virtual second-class citizens for centuries. It was with Reform Judaism that women were allowed to sit and pray with men and be treated in an egalitarian manner. With the encouragement of early Reform Judaism, women founded their own philanthropic and service organization, the Ladies Hebrew Benevolent Society, in the 1870s in Reform Congregations throughout the country. This group evolved into the Temple Ladies Auxiliary in the 1890s, the National Federation of Temple Sisterhoods in 1913, and the Women of Reform Judaism today. The Temple Sisterhood at B'nai Israel has done so much to make this a wonderful congregation. They have been involved in supporting our Religious School and youth over the years, raised money to help further the goals of education throughout our Congregation, and have participated in every aspect of Congregational life. It is, in so many ways, the backbone of our Congregation."

The Religious School continued to grow both in size and programming. The children were using the library on a regular basis. The library had expanded its collection and even had a Women's Study Section. There were ten senior study candidates and thirteen students were confirmed. The Senior Youth Group hosted a regional conclave of 200 young people. A Temple Survey was conducted to determine the recommendations for future actions by the

Greg Fox, President, Temple B'nai Israel, 1997–1999.

Long-Range Planning Committee.

Rabbi Baseman, in his annual Rosh Hashanah message said, "Rosh Hashanah is not only the beginning of our Jewish New Year, it is also the traditional anniversary of the creation of human life. The Rabbis, in a fanciful Talmudic teaching, portray a fascinating exchange between God and the Ministering Angels at the time of the birth of the human race. The Rabbis suggest that when God proposed to create human beings, the Angels protested: "Why create people? People will lie, steal, cheat and kill. You have made a beautiful world, God. Why spoil it with people who will bring such evil and suffering to it?" God, however, was not dissuaded from His...intention, and created humanity despite the Angels warnings. The question the narrative now raises is "why?" Surely God knew the Angels were correct in their assessment of humans-why did God persist? Our text is uplifting. According to our tradition God created humankind to be "partners in the work of creation." The teaching points out that on the eve of the first Sabbath, God did not say of His...creation, "It's perfect!" God simply said, "It is good. It isn't perfect, but it is good, and I worked long enough. I'm resting now, for it is Shabbat." And so, ever since, we have been created to be God's partners in the work of creation, in the repair and completion of the world (Tzedakah). What does such a message have to do with us? Whether it is how we deal with other people or the physical world, or how we use our natural gift or our resources, Rosh Hashanah calmly and forthrightly presents each individual with the questions, "Was God right or were the angels right? Have I been God's partner or have my actions furthered stymied God's plans and made an unfinished world more incomplete?" It is my personal hope and prayer that each of us be able to claim that he/she has been God's partner in the past year, and may each of us resolve to live the coming year so to make God right and the Angels wrong."

On Yom Kippur, Rabbi Baseman said, "...The Torah is therefore teaching us that the essence of truth and goodness is within our very selves, in our conscience, in the depths of our souls. No external forces are needed to "make us hear it." All that we need to do is to heed that which is already emerging from our innermost being to be heard...The listening is also listening to ourselves."

Rabbi Baseman talked about personal and family health. He said, "Indeed, our entire Jewish tradition is a rich source of spiritual strength to help us confront illness, pain, and suffering in supportive and life-affirming ways. We sense a bond between the individual Jew and the Divine Presence which dwells within us and in the Universe, The Healing Spirit we call God. We, however, must do all that we can to ensure personal well-being and we must establish and confirm our commitment to proper living through self-examination and professional care." Rabbi Baseman announced a new program, in which Temple B'nai Israel joined the Interfaith Health Partnership Program at Morton Plant Mease Health Care. The program was set up at the Temple. The motto of the program was a Yiddish proverb, "There is no wealth like health."

Robert and Carolyn Mintz

Bob and Carolyn moved to Pinellas County from Tampa. Bob was born on November 28, 1940 in Cleveland, Ohio. He graduated from Western Reserve University in 1962 with a Bachelor of Science Degree in Chemistry and Math. He married Carolyn R. Dolin on September 9, 1962. Over the next twenty six years, he worked for the Federated and Allied Stores, with his last position being President of an Allied Store in Pennsylvania. While he was previously working in Syracuse, New York, he was President of the Brotherhood of Temple Society of Concorde and also a Member of the Board of Trustees. Bob and Carolyn joined Temple B'nai Israel because of Rabbi Baseman.

Bob became an active member and leader in the congregation. He was: President of Brotherhood; Board Member of Brotherhood; Member of Youth Committee, Religious School Committee, Membership Committee, Fund-Raising Committee, Security Committee, and Budget Committee; Executive Vice President; Member of Executive Committee; and President of Temple B'nai Israel from 2003-2007.

Robert Mintz, President, Temple B'nai Israel, 2003–2007.

Carolyn Mintz

Bob said, "I accepted the presidency of Temple B'nai Israel because I wanted to be in a leadership capacity at the Temple and to be able to work with Rabbi Baseman. I felt that the Temple needed to continue to grow through its lay leadership and membership and that I could best serve the community by being in the President's chair. I support this history book because all of us and our children need to know the true history of how the Jewish community came to be in Pinellas County. It is important for us to be able to recognize the founding families of our Jewish community, why they came to this area, where they came from and why and how the various synagogues were created. It is also important to know something about the people from the beginning of the Jewish community to the present who have made such wonderful contributions to not only the Jewish community but also the general community. The book is a guide for our children to understand the significance of the Jewish tradition of tzedakah."

Carolyn was born on June 15, 1943 in Cleveland, Ohio. In Syracuse, New York she organized Friday's Sabbath dinners and in Connecticut, she was President of the high school Parent Teacher Student Association. At Temple B'nai Israel, Carolyn has been an active leader. She served on the: Religious School Committee; Chairperson of the Pre-School Committee; Chairperson of the Membership Committee; Member of the Youth Committee; remodeled and operated Sisterhood Judaica Shop; Member of Fund-Raising Committee.

Carolyn and Bob have two children, Scott and Deborah S. Eustace. Scott earned a Bachelor of Arts Degree in Marketing from Southern Connecticut University in 1988. He and his wife, Joy, own a T-shirt retail and wholesale business in Sarasota, Florida.

Bob and Carolyn are outstanding examples of God's helpers on earth.

Highlights of 1998

Dr. Paul Root Wolfe was the Gorn Scholar-in-Residence. He was faculty associate at the Center of Bioethics, where he served as the co-director of the Project on Informed Consent. He is also on the faculty of the University of Pennsylvania. He is a member of many professional societies and lectures widely on issues of bioethics and medical sociology. He presented, "Jewish Bioethics ...," "The Dilemma of Saul: The Jewish View of Suicide," and "If I Am Only My Genes, What Am I."

The First Annual Mitzvah Day was held on March 1. The projects successfully completed included: a Brotherhood sponsored Bloodmobile; preparation and delivery of meals, for eighty people, to Ronald McDonald House; preparing Purim baskets for the homebound Jewish elderly and needy Jewish families and help deliver them on behalf of Gulf Coast Jewish Family Services; etc.. Sandy Levitt was Chairperson of the Mitzvah Day Project.

Rabbi Baseman, talking about Purim said, "Purim reminds us that laughing, having fun, enjoying life in the world that God has given us, is a religious experience as well. Judaism may be serious about life, but it need not be somber...Purim is also a story of human responsibility...It is human intervention and not supernatural intervention that makes things happen... God is the inspirational center of life, and is the One who is at the heart of every step of progress in which the human is the prime doer... God is manifested in the deeds of the people, people who stood together by maintaining Jewish values and a strong Jewish identity."

Sherri Joyer became the new Temple administrator. She had previously been the Membership Director at the YMCA. B'nai Israel Federation of Temple Youth collected food and raised money for the homeless during the annual Super Bowl game. The congregation collected a substantial amount of food for the Religious Community Services Food Basket for the hungry in Pinellas County. A new project, the Mitzvah Crib, which benefits the Haven, a non-profit program which helps women and children get away from abusive environments, was started by the Temple. The Temple also participated in the community wide project sponsored by the Federation called Operation Afikomen which provided food for needy Jewish families. Sisterhood and Brotherhood and other affiliates refurbished the APR room.

Eighteen young people were confirmed and three graduated from Senior Study. Twenty eight children were consecrated.

Rabbi Baseman, talking about the significance of communal worship, said, "... Worship is not a mere performance by a few, but a profound experiencing of the Divine Presence sensed by those who sincerely participate. There is meaning, to be sure, in private devotions, but nothing can compare to the significance obtained by values shared with others in communal worship."

Highlights of 1999

J. J. Goldberg was the Gorn Scholar-in-Residence. He was the author of " Jewish Power: Inside the American Jewish Establishment." He was an award-winning journalist, author and lecturer known for his writing on American politics, Jewish affairs, and the Middle East. His essays on Israeli and American politics, intergroup relations, and the changing religious identity of the American Jew appeared frequently in the New York Times, Newsday, and The New Republic.

Richard Snyder,
President, Congregation
B'nai Israel, 1999–2001.

The religious school programs were enhanced by the active participation of Rabbi Baseman in the school and especially with Bar and Bat Mitzvah and Confirmation students. He was actively involved because he wanted the children to learn more than Hebrew and about Jewish life. He wanted them to learn to love God. Individual attention was paid to children with special needs. The programs were aided by a competent and dedicated Religious School Committee and by numerous Youth Group activities for children.

The goals of the Temple B'nai Israel Preschool were to allow all children to grow and develop in the most positive environment in order to be happy with themselves and the world they are discovering. Their creative potential, their curiosity, and their ability to learn at a very young age helps them discover, experiment, dream, imagine, and express their own ideas in an open free environment.

Rabbi Baseman when talking about the Holocaust observance said, "We all can identify with physical resistance on the part of the Jewish and non–Jewish

Nazi victims, such as the Warsaw ghetto uprising, which went on for forty two days. The Jewish ghetto fighters resisted the Nazi Army, even though they knew they would not win, but still felt impelled to die fighting. But there was another kind of resistance, just as powerful if not more so, a spiritual resistance as exemplified by this remarkable story: As the Nazis were about to execute the Jewish population in a small Ukrainian town, a Jew walked over to the young German officer in charge and told him it was customary in civilized countries to grant a last request of those condemned to death. The young German assured the Jew that he would observe that civilized tradition and asked the Jew for his last wish. A short prayer replied the Jew. Granted snapped the German. The Jew placed his hand on his bare head to cover it and recited the following blessing, first in its original Hebrew, and then in its German translation: "Blessed art Thou, O Lord our God, King of the Universe, who has not made me a heathen." Upon completion of the blessing, he looked directly into the eyes of the German and with his head held high, walked to the edge of the pit and said, " I have finished. You may begin." " Our remembrance of those awful years must honor both kinds of resistance, the physical and spiritual."

Rabbi Baseman discussed the similarities and differences between Reform and Orthodox Judaism. He said, "Both share a commitment to the three basic tenets of Jewish thought: God, Torah, and the people Israel. However, the core of Orthodox Judaism revolves around Halacha, the vast body of Jewish law which tells the Jew what he/she must or must not do in order to live by the Torah. One who lives by the Halacha is called an "observant" or orthodox Jew. Reform Judaism, on the other hand, is not based on the Halacha. Early Reform Judaism divided the traditional commandments into ethical and ritual components. Early Reform defined itself as "Prosthetic Judaism": that strain of Judaism which would keep alive the ethical message of social justice and righteousness. That was and is the focus of this movement of ours. Ritual commandments become a matter of personal choice, and those rituals that bring spiritual meaning and contribute to the survival and vitality of the Jewish people might be observed, while others deemed to be irrelevant could be dropped. As far as Reform Judaism was concerned any theology or ideology which did not have a plan of social action and community involvement is merely a menu without dinner, a creed without a deed. Does this mean Reform Judaism has broken away from its life-source of God, Torah and Israel? Of course not. Reform depends on serious study of the tradition in order to evaluate which ritual or other practice one might meaningfully integrate into one's Judaism. Today, throughout the country, we find a rich diversity in our movement...The point is that the entire Jewish past is our past, and we create from that a core of Jewish meaning that which is right for us. Thus, our religion, our Judaism, will be expressed differently than our Orthodox sisters and brothers, but no less authentically."

An evening of Judaic music was provided by Rabbi Frederick S. Pomerantz and his daughter, Rebecca. The second annual Mitzvah Day was a great success. Thirteen young people were confirmed and six young people graduated from Senior Study.

Highlights of 2000-2005

Highlights of 2000

In March, Michael Medved, a film critic, best-selling author, and national media personality, presented "Mixed Jewish Messages from Hollywood: the Good, the Bad, and the Ugly." He was active in a wide variety of Jewish causes and was co-founder of Pacific Jewish Center. Michael graduated with honors from Yale University and then Yale University Law school. A second Gorn Scholar-in-Residence was Letty Cottin Pogrebin. Her topic was, "Being Female and Jewish in America." She was a founding editor of Ms. Magazine.

Iris and Stan Shalit became the Temple librarians. Cantorial Soloist Colman Reaboi left for a new congregation. Joy Katzen-Guthrie became the new cantorial soloist. Eighteen young people were confirmed. The Religious School had 275 students

and thirty teachers. The annual High Holy Day food drive, sponsored by B'nai Israel Federation of Temple Youth, provided a substantial amount of food for the Religious Community Services food pantry. The new Educational Center was dedicated on December 10.

50th Anniversary Celebration

The weekend of March 10, was the official celebration of the 50th anniversary of Temple B'nai Israel. On Friday evening, a Shabbat dinner, sponsored by the Brotherhood, was held before services and a large number of congregants filled the social hall. The chairpeople for the event were: Bob Mintz, Harold Seltzer and Al Malter. Each table had a Challah (egg twist bread), wine, and white linen tablecloths. A special service followed. The armed services honor guard marched into the sanctuary and presented the American flag. Youth group members then blew shofars to call people to worship. Past Presidents carried the seven Torahs down the aisle and helped place them into the Ark. Past Presidents, Leonard Collman and Julius Lovitz, led the procession. They also represented two of the founding families of the congregation. Steve Bragin and Myron Mensch gave historical presentations using stories of early years. Rabbi Jodi Cohen, Regional Director, Union American Hebrew Congregations presented Temple B'nai Israel with a plaque. She gave a special blessing to Rabbi and Renée Baseman for almost thirty two years of exceptional service to Temple B'nai Israel, the larger Jewish community, and the general community. Mayor Brian Aungst of Clearwater attended Friday night services and presented to Temple B'nai Israel and its congregation a proclamation in honor of the Temple's commitment to the community. The beautiful and meaningful service was followed by an Oneg Shabbat (a special social hour), sponsored by the Sisterhood. The Oneg was equivalent to the reception after a wedding. White tablecloths, centerpieces, and beautifully prepared food were presented in an exceptional manner to the large number of people attending the services.

On Saturday, a special Sabbath service was held. The celebration continued.

Saturday evening, at sundown, the Youth Group conducted a Havdallah Service (a ceremony used to separate the sacredness of the Sabbath from the rest of the week). This was followed by a Gala Ball, with entertainment provided by the Mike Eisenstadt Band. A candle lighting ceremony was held to honor all of the Temple leaders past and present.

On Sunday afternoon, over 300 people participated in a family event and picnic, entitled B'nai Blast. There were arts and crafts and many other outside activities. Adina Baseman Sharpstein provided musical entertainment for the afternoon.

Toni Rinde was the Chairperson of the Anniversary Committee. The other members were: Marci Sperber, Bonnie Szasz, David Greene, Shelley Hoffman, Lusia Igel, Dick Snyder, Rabbi Baseman, Bob Mintz, Carolyn Mintz, Chalene Field, Janet White, Gail Simon, Nancy Hoffman, Sheila Weinstock, Greg Fox, Cal Hyland, Nancy Shapiro, Greg Bachman, Bernice Lipman, and Rhonda Krongold. Toni Rinde said of the anniversary celebration, "Our Temple is the crown and glory of Jewish life, it is our noblest possession. It is that which perhaps more than any other commands the respect of our fellow man. It is a place where the wisdom and experience of many elders can be appreciated and absorbed by the open an inquisitive minds of our youth. It is where our religion and our heritage are passed on from generation to generation.... As putting a fine orchestra together takes the cooperation of many instruments to achieve a beautiful symphony, so putting a 50th anniversary celebration together took the cooperation, commitment and much hard work of many, many fine people....Picture a bouquet in the garden of your thoughts. Put into it seeds of caring and committed hard-working people, lots of love, some disappointments and concerns. Cover it with the earth of fruitfulness and gratitude, water it with love and contentment, and sow on top the seeds of hope, strength and lots of hard work. When the time of harvest comes you will reap the benefits from generation to generation."

Rabbi Baseman said, "...From its very beginning, Temple B'nai Israel was a place not to hide out, but to stand-out. It stands out there on Belcher Road for every passerby to see and be reminded that this sacred place is the headquarters not only of people, but of a value system-a headquarters of decency, compassion, kindness and concern. It is the home address for the virtues by which we try to live, because either Temple B'nai Israel stands for something, or it stands alone –empty, abandoned, forlorn. We don't pull down the shades, nor do we keep the world from intruding on our service and on us. Temple B'nai Israel is a place where eyes do not close, nor do ears stop listening; a place where there is no turning away or giving up; a place where we remember, when others have forgotten. I pray that Temple B'nai Israel will endure for many generations, and that these generations will find here the same inspiration and religious fulfillment that our generations have experienced."

Rabbi Baseman when talking about Shavuot said, "Torah- (is) more than a velvet-covered scroll. "Why are the words of Torah like fire?" The Talmud asks. The answer- "A fire is sustained by many logs, and the words of Torah are sustained through many minds...Let us be serious about our Judaism, and live by its words (Torah) day in and day out."

Highlights of 2001

The Gorn Scholar-in-Residence was Dr. Deborah Lipstadt. She is Professor of Modern Jewish and Holocaust Studies at Emory University. She is the author of, "Denying the Holocaust: The Secret Assault on Truth and Memory," and "Beyond Belief: The American Press and the Coming of the Holocaust." She presented, " Denying the Holocaust: A New Form of Anti-Semitism."

The Cantorial Soloists were Joy Katzen Guthrie and then Barbara Mazer Gross. Sisterhood President, Madelyn Liss and Sisterhood were involved in a variety of Interfaith activities with neighboring churches. Brotherhood President, and Brotherhood were also involved in Interfaith activities and community wide charities. The Young Friends of Temple B'nai Israel Co-Presidents were Alex and Brett Blumencranz. The Temple Boomers Co-Presidents were Susan and

Ellis. The Friendship Club President was Donald Eskin. The Temple B'nai Israel Brotherhood sponsored its first annual Family Sports Night and Spaghetti Dinner.

Rabbi Baseman discussed the significance of the cycle of the Jewish High Holy Days, beginning with Rosh Hashanah, and ending with Simchat Torah, the rejoicing with the Torah as the central connection of the Jewish text to our lives. Rabbi Baseman said, "...Judaism maintains ignorance is unacceptable. Indeed, the Talmud maintains, "An ignorant person cannot be pious." If we are to grow and learn and mature, we need to study more and absorb new insights. It is said that each letter of the Torah has four meanings: it's obvious meaning; its meaning that is only hinted at; the meanings that can be derived from it; and the secrets it contains...The Torah is indeed the heart of the Jewish people...We dance with the Torah Scrolls, we even have a parade with them, not because school is out, but because school is in! For Judaism, school was never out, and learning never stops. We do not read the last verses of the Torah and put it away finished. Oh no. We (immediately) start at the beginning again, and we rejoice. The Torah cycle ends (and starts again at the very same service)." There is so much to be learned by everyone.

Highlights of 2002

An art exhibit was held and ninety eight individuals and companies participated in sponsoring it. The Temple once again sponsored its special preschool summer camp, where children could enjoy developmentally appropriate activities under the supervision of an experienced staff. The staff to child ratio was among the lowest in the country.

The Gorn Scholar-in-Residence was Stephen J. Dubner, the author of "Turbulent Souls: a Catholic Son's Return to His Jewish Family." Stephen earned an undergraduate degree at Appalachian State University in North Carolina. This is where he changed from a music career to a writing career. He earned a Master of Fine Arts in Writing from Columbia University, where he also taught in the English Department. He subsequently was a writer and editor at a New York

Magazine and then in 1994 he became a writer and editor for the Times Magazine, where he stayed until 1999. He spoke on the topic of Catholicism and Judaism.

Rabbi Baseman when describing the significance of Shavout said that, "Sukkot and Passover marks the beginning of the Jewish nation; where as Shavout marks the beginning of the Jewish religion. Thanks to Shavout , the Jewish people and its faith are continually being built." Confirmation services are held at synagogues in conjunction with Shavout. The prime significance of Shavout today lives in its commemoration of the anniversary of the receiving of the Ten Commandments by Moses on Mount Sinai. It is the culmination of the Exodus from Egypt. The revelation of the Torah, both written and oral law, was the beginning of the Jewish religion. Shavout reminds us of the universal principles of the Torah-faith in God, the brotherhood of humanity, and the ideals of justice, compassion, truth, and peace, which is the requirement of the lives of the Jewish people." Further, Rabbi Baseman said, "... Every country has its particular constitution. The Ten Commandments are, in a way, a world constitution, a code of moral laws for all civilized people. Almost every great book that has been written on morality contains ideas that can be traced back to the original Ten Commandments. And yet, the Ten Commandments do not intend to tell us all of our obligations. They contain, rather, the minimum essentials for all people who wish to live a good life."

Temple B'nai Israel started a new permanent fund raising project of newspaper recycling. The motto was help your Temple while saving a tree. Sherri Joyer resigned as Temple Administrator. Robert Benjamin Jr. became the new Temple Administrator. Barbara Mazer Gross became the Cantorial Soloist/Program Director. Ten young people were confirmed. There were twenty seven children in the new consecration class.

The Chavurah Movement was reorganized at Temple B'nai Israel beginning with a Chavurah Shabbat Service on November 1. A Chavurah (plural Chavurot) is a group of singles, couples, or families within the Temple who share common interests and get together regularly to socialize, study, and share Jewish life. Chavurah means to join together in friendship. Each group operates separately to meet the needs of that particular set of members. The Chavurah movement began in Reform temples across the United States during the early 1970s, especially in large congregations. This was a way of bringing a personal touch to each of the members. It represented an opportunity for a more intimate personal involvement and spiritual growth within the context of a strong Jewish environment.

Temple B'nai Israel hosted the Hospice of the Florida Suncoast, while honoring the Temple's own loved ones in a service of Remembrance and Gratitude. Nearly 1,000 people, primarily hospice staff and volunteers, gathered in the sanctuary. Rabbi Baseman gave the invocation. He said, "Death can be overpowering and can darken our world like nothing else. Its antidote is love, love which comforts and heals." He indicated that the Torah says that life continues even after death through those the individual loved and those who love the individual. Rabbi Baseman said, "...life must go on. It is for the living and the loving to complete the lives of our loved ones, carrying forward the ideals by which our loved ones lived in seeking to realize all the dreams of doing....May light and hope triumph over death and darkness."

Barbara Mazer Gross graduated from Washington University in St. Louis with a Bachelor's Degree in Psychology and Music, and a Master's Degree in Psychology. She and her husband, Dr. John Gross, live in St. Petersburg.

Highlights of 2003

The Gorn Scholar-in-Residence was Dr. Howard M. Sachar. He received his undergraduate degree from Swarthmore College and his graduate degree from Harvard University. He was the author of numerous scholarly articles and also the author of fourteen books. He is the Editor-in-Chief of "The Rise of Israel." He is currently, Professor of Modern History at George Washington University, and also Consultant and Lecturer on Middle Eastern Affairs for the United States Foreign Service. The topic

he presented was "The Impact of Jews on Modern Culture."

Twelve young people were confirmed. Brotherhood presented a five-part mini medical school to help congregants prevent disease and injury and promote good health. Dr. Julian Greengold, a congregant, chaired the program. The topics included: preventive medicine; medical emergencies; chronic illness; acute illness; and aging and end-of-life issues. All of the speakers were physicians.

On August 27, Temple B'nai Israel hosted the first Interfaith Symposium in Pinellas County. It was called "Unity Within Diversity" and was sponsored by the National Conference for Community and Justice. Rabbi Baseman and representatives from Muslim, Christian, Baha'i and other faith traditions participated. The panelists were asked what can be done to promote peace. The response from the clergyman was to hold meetings of this sort to show people how the various religions have a common purpose of helping others. In addition, the clergyman talked about setting up long-term service projects to help the needy.

Highlights of 2004

Rabbi Baseman discussed his thoughts on performing mitzvahs. He said, "My personal concept of the afterlife, and one I have shared with you from the pulpit, involves the belief in the immortality of our spirit, that "dust we are and then to dust we return, but the spirit, born of God's Spirit, returns to God who gave it." The extent to which we developed our "soul-muscle," our "personality," our "inner being," is the measure of our immortality-of our bonding with God after death. Nonetheless, in anticipation of our Annual Mitzvah Day effort which will take place on Sunday, February 1, let me share with you this wonderful story of the difference between heaven and hell. I find it delightful and believe that it underscores how we can perform Acts of Loving Kindness for each other. In our narrative, Hell is pictured as a crowded banquet room, with a long table that is filled to overflowing with delicious food and drink. The people sitting around the table cannot bend their arms because their arms are tied to boards. So even though they can touch the food, they cannot feed themselves. They are sick, starving and bickering with each other. Heaven, on the other hand, is a room that is identical to hell in every detail except one, a most important one. In heaven, you see, the people who cannot feed themselves are feeding each other. Each person is healthy and happy and enjoying the companionship of their table mates at the banquet. So it is on Mitzvah Day, February 1. Temple B'nai Israel participants will seek to "feed others", to help bring about better conditions for other people and our community. Let's all reach out to each other and to others, and represent the difference between heaven and hell."

Rabbi Baseman also wrote in the Rabbinically Speaking column of the Jewish Press about the love between a man and women and the sanctification of marriage. "No one can absolutely define love, nor understand it completely. As an example, even though love is elevating and uplifting, in the marketplace of common discourse we talk about "falling in love". What a misrepresentation of the reality of love! And consider the phrase "love is blind"-love is not blind. Love sees everything. What love does do is take note of what is important, and disregards the rest. So what is love? Love is a meeting of the minds and souls, a quiet understanding of the other, a loyalty through good and bad. What is love? Love is sharing and forgiving; it is not dominating but cultivating; it is not gazing at each other, but looking together in the same direction. Love is give and take-you give what is needed and more; you take what is needed and no more. Love is the pledge of respect, devotion, and caring. If you have love in your life, it fills every other emptiness; and makes up for many things you do not have. If you lack love, no matter what you have, it's not enough.

And because of love you marry, not because you belong to each other, but because you belong with each other. And in marriage it is not only two beings who become one, but two worlds become one. How rich we become, not by what we have in our pockets, but what is in our hearts.

In our tradition, the word for marriage is Kiddushin. It means holiness. For the Jew, holiness is to be found in human relationships, and marriage is the most wonderful of all human relationships. When we attempt to create holiness and express it fully through union with another human being, then our life and our love seem to enter the religious dimension of eternity."

The Gorn Scholar-in-Residence was Dr. Carol Ochs. She was Director of the Graduate School and Adjunct Associate Professor of Jewish Religious Thought, Hebrew Union College-Jewish Institute of Religion. She spoke on the topics, "Jewish Spiritual Way," "Finding Our Lives in Torah," and "Women Revitalizing Judaism."

An article appeared in the Temple Tablet in March requesting material and information for the Jewish History Project. Rabbi Baseman said, "Dear friends, The fruit of Hank Koren's efforts will be a resounding affirmation of the Jewish life that has blossomed here, in Pinellas County. I hope that you would do all that you are able to advance this project, and make our history as rich and meaningful as it truly is."

Rabbi Baseman talked about the Jewish History Project of Pinellas County, which he so ardently has supported. He said, "The Mother of All Scrapbooks–For so many family scrapbooks have been the way to record the intimate and treasured details of their daily lives. Pictures, articles, clippings and then lovingly gathered together and carefully pasted, glued and taped onto page after page accumulating an enduring legacy of life. These scrapbooks have functioned as miniature museums, libraries, archives, holding the bits and pieces of personal reflections and memories. How wonderful it is, therefore, that Temple B'nai Israel and its devoted member, Dr. Hank Koren, have been the moving forces in creating the mother of all scrapbooks-a documentary testament of the Jewish community of Pinellas County, and this community's relationship with Hillsborough County and the entire State of Florida."

The Preschool graduating class included eighteen children. Ten young people were confirmed. The concentration class included thirteen children.

Rabbi Baseman discussed the significance of the Festival of Shavuot by telling a story about the Festival sadly complaining to God, that every other Festival had its Mitzvah, its ritual commandment to perform, but Shavuot did not have one. Shavuot began to sadly weep. "God gently drew Shavuot close and replied: You do not require a special Mitzvah, you're the source of all of the Mitzvot because your Festival signifies not only the giving of the Ten Commandments but also the entire Torah with all its Mitzvot. And Jewish youth in the ceremony of Confirmation, will perform your Mitzvah, will be your Mitzvah.... The Festival of Shavuot reminds us, we are its Mitzvah. It is how we act, how we perform the common deed, how we fulfill a friendship,-not the mere performance of a ceremony-that will bring us to the highest peak of spiritual living. Ceremonies are relevant to the human; the Mitzvah is essential to God."

Temple B'nai Israel joined a grouup of churches in a new organization entitled FAST (Faith and Action for Strength Together). The convocation was held at Bethel Community Church in St. Petersburg on November 15. The St. Petersburg Times staff writer wrote, "By chartered bus and car they came by the hundreds, black-and-white, young and old, Christian and Jew and at least one Muslim leader-to launch a countywide effort they hoped would help them tackle tenacious social justice issues....780 people representing twenty four congregations across Pinellas County pinpointed their initial concerns about education and transportation and what to do about them. "These issues really transcend racial, economic, political and religious chasms," the Rev. Clarence Williams of Mount Zion and AME Church in St. Petersburg said afterwards. Father Robert Schneider of Espirito Santo Catholic Church in Safety Harbor, Co-Chair of the conference said of the assembled individuals, "God's people working together for peace and Justice." This involvement by the Temple is the continuation of brotherhood activities, which is at the core of the outreach program of the synagogue.

Rabbi Baseman, reflecting on 350 years of Jewish history in the United States, wrote about some of the early Presidents and their relationship to the Jewish community.

He said, "It was one tiny vessel named St. Catrina that twenty three Jewish passengers sailed into the port of new Amsterdam in 1654. "Twenty-three souls, big and little"-those were the words to describe these exhausted and bewildered refugees from Recife, Brazil, who had been expelled when the Portuguese recaptured the South American colony from the Dutch...George Washington was the first President to write to a synagogue. In 1790, he wrote to the Touro Synagogue in Newport, Rhode Island and described the Government of the United States as one which gives "to bigotry no sanction, to persecution no assistance." He continued, "May the children of the stock of Abraham, who dwell in this land, continue to merit and enjoy the goodwill of the other inhabitants; where everyone shall sit under his own vine and fig tree, and there shall be none to make him afraid." Thomas Jefferson was the first President to appoint a Jew to a Federal Post. In 1801, he named Reuben Etting of Baltimore as US marshal for Maryland. James Madison was the first President to appoint a Jew to a diplomatic post. He sent Mordecai M. Noah to Tunis from 1813-1816. Martin Van Buren was the first President to order an American Consul to intervene on behalf of Jews abroad.. In 1840, he instructed the US Consul in Alexandria, Egypt to use his field offices to protect the Jews of Damascus who were under attack because of a false blood ritual accusation. John Tyler was the first President to nominate a US Consul to Palestine. Warder Cresson, a Quaker convert to Judaism who established a pioneer Zionist colony, received the appointment in 1844. Finally Franklin Pierce was the first President whose name appears on the charter of the synagogue. He signed the Act of Congress in 1857 that amended Bylaws of the District of Columbia to enable the incorporation of the city's first synagogue, the Washington Hebrew Congregation, which is now a prominent Reform Temple."

Donald M. Rolander

Don Rolander celebrated his 25th anniversary as the organist for Temple B'nai Israel. For the past forty four years he ,has been the organist, choir director and director of music at several churches and synagogues. Don's father was a bookkeeper in Princeton, Illinois. His mother was the organist for the Evangelical Covenant Church for thirty seven years. At age eight, his mother started to teach him to play the piano. He earned a music scholarship from Princeton High School in 1960. A child prodigy, at age twelve, he began his professional career as a church organist at First Baptist Church of Princeton. He won numerous awards. During his high school years and at graduation, he was the accompanist to the various choirs and played in the various bands. From 1960-1970, he was the organist and then director of music at several churches including the Evangelical Covenant Church of Austin, Chicago; Berry Memorial United Methodist Church, Chicago; and Arion Male Chorus (Swedish), Chicago.

From 1970–1980, he was the organist-choirmaster at Trinity Lutheran Church, St. Petersburg. He also was the organist-choirmaster at Temple Beth-El of St. Petersburg from 1972-1979. He found time to be director of music at St. Paul's Lutheran Church, Clearwater and the organist at Prince of Peace Lutheran Church, Largo. He has continued this extraordinary career up until the present time at Prince of Peace Lutheran Church of Largo and Temple B'nai Israel of Clearwater. Also, since 1976 when he joined Suncoast Concert Management and Productions Inc. he has been giving concerts and making recordings.

He is a graduate of Sherwood School of Music of Chicago which is affiliated with the University of Chicago. He holds a normal certificate, teacher's certificate and teacher's diploma. In the same manner as cantors and cantorial soloists study under cantors and music teachers of exceptional merit, Don has studied under Benjamin Hadley of the Episcopal Church of the Ascension, Chicago; Max Janowski of the K and M Temple, Chicago; and Diana Bish of Fort Lauderdale. He has attended numerous workshops including one with Sir David Wilcox and was presented a grant by the Prince of Peace Lutheran Church in 1985 to study and attend concerts in Europe. He has been the sub-dean of the St. Petersburg chapter of the American Guild of Organists

Donald M. Rolander

and the Dean of the Clearwater Chapter. He has given numerous recitals and concerts in United States and Europe.

Don believes that religious music is an essential part of life and the love of God. He said, " Whether in the church or the synagogue, God is the chief actor as well as the audience. All other participants are worshipers and/or leaders in worship. Music, being the soul of language, expresses that which can only be communicated best through the art of music. My task has never been to entertain but to represent the people of God. Congregations can sense that those who make music are not giving a recital but worshiping God; and that to pray does not mean to listen to music but to identify oneself with what is being proclaimed in their name. My job is an intimate expression that reveals the inner self as is done in no other way. Working with a variety of cantors over the last thirty five years and especially with Rabbi Baseman has been rewarding and I am most grateful for the honor and privilege."

Donald M. Rolander is the continuation of a long line of non-Jewish musicians going back to 1815, who have helped the rabbi, cantor, cantorial soloist and/or choir create a sense of dignity and beauty in the services of the Reform movement. Within the Orthodox and Conservative movements the rabbi, cantor, cantorial soloist, or a choir unaccompanied by music creates the same sense of dignity and beauty in the services.

Ultimately, to a large degree, Jewish music is the music of the wanderer. Jewish people have taken the ritual music forms from antiquity and creatively adapted these forms into the modern culture. They've added the beauty, the longing for peace, and a love of God, which they have brought from their countries of origin to the United States and have introduced them into this magnificent melting pot of people and ideas. This is why our religious services are so meaningful and so beautiful. For all Jewish people, music is a prayer of the soul.

Highlights of 2005

Rabbi Baseman, in his New Year's message for 2005, said to the congregation, "...Our history, which is being lovingly compiled by Dr. Hank Koren, bids us remember the people who have served us so faithfully in the past and those who do so with willing and dedicated hands now. A new calendar reminds us where we have been this past year. My personal history with Temple B'nai Israel helps me to understand and appreciate the deep connection between the past and the present, and to discern clearly the importance of keeping an eye toward the future. Throughout the nomadic history of the Jewish people, the shul (the synagogue, the temple, call it what you will) has always been the place were the Jewish people have gathered to keep the Jewish soul alive. The shul has always been the original flame from which the numerous, glimmering sparks of Jewish life have emerged. This sacred place, this praying place, the public house of Jewish ideals and commitment, does not sleep-walk through tired routines, but has always been the pilot light by which to ignite Jewish communal existence in many varied forms touching life at every point, foremost at the battle line for the survival of Judaism...Ours is a live shul, and it awaits your presence in its midst."

On January 8, Rabbi Arthur Baseman was honored for forty years in the rabbinate. Some 250 people attended the celebration and dinner. Congregants spontaneously spoke of their love for this distinguished individual who had been with them through good times and bad times and had always represented the finest qualities of Jewish leadership and Jewish life. Had time permitted, the celebration could've gone on through the night. Don Rolander played a piece from Phantom of the Opera on the piano, and led all of us in a song entitled, "What Does a Rabbi Do." The Board of Trustees, to honor the excellent service given by the Rabbi to Temple B'nai Israel, the Jewish community, and the general community of Pinellas County, and by Renée Baseman for her many years of work and devotion to the Preschool, named the Preschool, the Rabbi Arthur I. Baseman DD and Renée L. Baseman Early Childhood Center.

There are hundreds of stories of what Arthur I. Baseman has unselfishly done for others in his forty years as a Rabbi. He is the essence of a human being, because he truly is a religious person and acts in accordance with what should be done to help others live a better life. A representative sampling of the stories are included. The Largo Times, Saturday, January 8, 2005 headline was, " A Calling for Caring-Rabbi Marks Decades of Devotion." "Temple B'nai Israel Today Celebrates Rabbi Arthur I. Baseman's Thirty Five Years with the Congregation." "...Among active reform rabbis in Florida, none has served one congregation longer than Rabbi Arthur I. Baseman. For thirty five years he has internalized their pain, hope and unanswerable questions. Family and friends will call him loving. Testimonies of his respect for different paths to God will reveal his tolerant heart. All will say that, when needed most, he is always there.... On November 23, 1963, Baseman, twenty seven, was asked by fellow rabbis to deliver a eulogy for the slain President Kennedy at a memorial service at Hebrew Union College. The young rabbi spoke confidently, reminding students that hate cannot stain the steel of love.... During his tenure at B'nai Israel, Baseman's small shoulders have helped many in and outside his congregation bear heavy tragedies. Those close to him marvel at his resolve and sincerity. When asked to recall just one memorable moment during his tenure at B'nai Israel, he buried his head in his hands and was silent for nearly ten minutes. Finally, tearfully, he told the story of a handicapped man and his wife involved in an auto accident near the Temple. The wife was killed instantly. The husband survived. Her funeral was held at the Temple and he delivered the eulogy. Near his wife's casket, the man wept and blamed himself for the tragedy. "I tried to relieve him of his guilt, but I couldn't. I couldn't make him feel better." Baseman said, "I just held him in my arms." Such a desire to empathize defines him. "If I'm with Arthur, I am the most important person there is," said the Rev. Joe Diaz of Holy Trinity Episcopal Church in Clearwater, a friend for twenty years. "He climbs up on the principles of caring and respect to reach others."

Rabbi Baseman, reflecting on the 55th year of the congregation said that, "... it continues to be vigorous and successful. Our founding families have every reason to feel a profound sense of pride; their seed has yielded bountiful fruit....A congregation's success is measured by its program and by the spirit that emanates from its program. We are a synagogue, first and foremost, a gathering place for Jewish worship, a community of fellow Jews, and a center for the study of Torah. If we fail to make these purposes central to our very existence, we will be destined to fail....a temple is not a hide-out, rather it stands out. It stands out there on Belcher Road and calls out-loud to every passerby to hear and see. To hear and see, and be reminded that this Temple as a headquarters not only of people but of a value system- a headquarters for decency, compassion, kindness and community concern."

Rabbi David Sapperstein, Director of the Religious Action Center of Reform Judaism, was the Gorn Scholar-in-Residence speaker and also participated in the celebration for Rabbi Baseman. Rabbi Sapperstein has represented the Reform movement to Congress and the administration for the last thirty years. Rabbi Sapperstein is also an attorney. His latest book is: *Jewish Dimensions of Social Justice: Tough Moral Choices of Our Time*. His presentations were: "Jews in America-350 Years-Then and Now;" "Our Shared Core Values-What We Should Know about Each Other (presented to a group of clergy of different religions);" "Is Our First Amendment Alive and Well?;" and "Jewish Dimensions of Social Justice-Tough Moral Choices of Our Times."

In keeping with the many interfaith activities over the years at Temple B'nai Israel, the Sisterhood of Temple B'nai Israel had a special presentation and function in conjunction with the ladies of the Unitarian Universalist Church, Hope Presbyterian Church, St. John's Episcopal Church and Unity Church. Another project which had been going on since the beginning of the synagogue in 1949, has been the feeding of the hungry of all religions and races in Pinellas County and elsewhere. This year's project, which has been sponsored by the Jewish Federation of Pinellas County, was called Grass Roots Tzedakah.

Mitzvah Day was held on April 10. As Jews, the congregation and its members were responsible for tlkkun olam, repairing the world, and this Mitzvah Day was a continuation of the many community service projects which the individuals, of all ages, helped make successful. Hundreds of volunteers worked throughout the community to help others have a better life. This congregation as well as fellow congregations throughout the Tampa Bay area and the rest of the United States have been involved in these communal efforts for many many years. These efforts are truly the physical act of helping others.

By the Fall of 2005, Mitzvah Day 2006 was already in the planning stages. The theme for Mitzvah Day was "How wonderful it is that nobody need wait a single moment before starting to improve the world."–Anne Frank. President Bob Mintz was trying to make this Mitzvah Day better than ever with participation of over 400 congregants. The programs identified included: Veterans Administration Bay Pines-visit nursing home residents; Religious Community Services Thrift Store-organize shelves and clean facilities; Grace House-paint, clean and decorate apartments; Menorah Manor-wash wheelchairs and play balloon volleyball with the residents; beach cleanup-Courtney Campbell Causeway; Moccasin Lake Park-clean park and pull exotic weeds; Everybody's Tabernacle-make peanut butter and jelly sandwiches for homeless shelter; baking for Everybody's Tabernacle Homeless Shelter; arts and crafts-for Gulf Coast Jewish Family Services; Lake Seminole Park-nature preservation; Florida Botanical Gardens-clear brush, prune and plant; storm drains-label them; no bake sweet treats-make them for Gulf Coast Jewish Family Services; UPARC Therapeutic Gardens-mulch, prune and plant; Temple B'nai Israel-outside cleanup and painting; Clearwater Marine Aquarium-landscaping, painting and animal care; BIFTY-car wash off-site to benefit Camp Jenny; visit housebound congregants; Woodside House-interact with hospice patients; and Clothes to Kids-organize, clean and donate new or gently used school clothes. These projects are but a sampling of what all the synagogues do on their individual Mitzvah Days and throughout the year to help improve the world.

Seventeen young people were confirmed. Seventeen children were in the consecration class. As part of the "All Things Jewish" series of programs, Temple B'nai Israel presented a program entitled "Art of the Old Testament." The program featured painting, sculpture, stained glass and other works of art inspired by the Old Testament.

Brotherhood

Temple B'nai Israel Brotherhood is a member of the North American Federation of Temple Brotherhoods. The members are part of a coalition of 30,000 men across North America striving for tikkun olam, repairing the world, through the practice of brotherhood. Brotherhood worked toward making better men and better Jews to increase the participation and involvement of Jewish men in the Reform Movement. Temple B'nai Israel Brotherhood is actively involved in the religious education of the young people, adult education, social action and fellowship activities which contribute to the enrichment of the Temple community. Brotherhood participates in a series of activities including: special brunches and dinners with themes such as sports, Rabbi's birthday, Gorn Scholar-in-Residence presentation; presentation of personalized kiddush cup to each Bar/Bat Mitzvah person; leadership training; providing ushers for Friday's Shabbat services; hosting Yom Kippur Break the Fast; Confirmation Retreat Scholarship Fund; Manny Schwarz Brotherhood Senior Study's Achievement Award; assisting at the Temple's annual Congregational Picnic; sponsoring and participating in blood drives; donating funds to Gulf Coast Jewish Family Services, helping religious school and preschool, Temple library and many charities within the Pinellas County community; etc.. One of the latest programs of brotherhood was the Million Quarter Project. In Ethiopia, children are constantly going hungry. Brotherhood is part of a national effort to collect funds to literally put food in the mouths of the children.

Sisterhood

The Sisterhood of Temple B'nai Israel is affiliated with the Women of Reform Jewry. It is dedicated to working for children, families, Temple and community. Sisterhood provides scholarships for rabbinic and cantorial students attending Hebrew Universities throughout North America and Israel. Sisterhood provides funds to nurseries in Israel, the Jewish Braille Institute, the National Federation of Temple Youth, charities in the community, and numerous other programs. In August, Sisterhood hosted 160 Jewish high school students from all over the State of Florida for leadership training. Sisterhood always presents a copy of the Torah to each Bar/Bat Mitzvah, and a Bible to each confirmand. Sisterhood provides financial assistance to any family that is unable to send their children to religious school. Sisterhood provides funds for the Baseman Early Childhood Center and Temple Religious School. Where there is a need for special teaching materials, Sisterhood is always there. Sisterhood provides monetary support for the Religious Community Services to assist the needy throughout Pinellas County regardless of religious affiliation. Sisterhood sponsors an Interfaith Program every year with the neighboring churches, Universalist Unitarian of Clearwater, St. John's Episcopalian, St. Catherine's Catholic, and Hope Presbyterian Church. Over the years, Sisterhood and various members have received awards for their unselfish dedication to making the world a better place to live. In the past several years, the Jewish Federation of Pinellas County has given this award to Madelyn Liss in 2002, Janet White in 2003, Iris Shalit in 2004, and Donnis Guibord in 2005.

Youth Group

BIFTY is the Senior High School Youth Group of Temple B'nai Israel. It was originally chartered in the late 1960s by the National Federation of Temple Youth. The activities shared by the young people of today are similar to those shared by other young people years ago. They include social activities, Temple activities, as well as general community service. Community activities include working with the Gulf Coast Jewish Family Services, High Holiday Food Drive, Passover Food Drive, gift programs for seniors and families, raising funds for Ethiopia and other foreign countries to help fight world hunger, and assisting victims of violence. The youth program supports Camp Jenny, a week-long program for disadvantaged youth. The program is located at Camp Coleman. The Youth Lounge, which is part of the Levine Annex, has helped bring the youth group out of their homes and into the Temple. The Youth Group helps with services. The Youth Group is student led and responsible for its own programming, under the direction of the Rabbi and the Youth Advisor.

Junior BIFTY is the middle school youth group and open to all Temple youth in grades six-eight. They elect their own officers and board and participate in social and Temple activities. They prepare for advancement to the senior group.

CLUB 3-4-5 is the Temple based program for children in grades three-five. It is usually administered by parent volunteers. Its primary purpose is for young children to be able to interact socially and outside of the classroom setting. They meet six times a year for various programs.

Selichot Service

With the arrival of Cantor Harold Orbach, the first Selichot service was held on October 1. Selichot literally means "prayers of pardon" or "forgiveness." The service was essentially on a spiritual level a preparation for the High Holy Days. It was held late on Saturday evening in keeping with the instructions from the Book of Psalms, "At midnight we rise to give thanks unto You/Because of Your righteous ordinances." Rabbi Baseman said, "Late evening is an unusual time for us to gather in prayer, but it emphasizes the gravity of its message-that of awakening the heart with prayer, meditation, and melody to prepare for repentance." The Youth Group entered the Sanctuary at the sound of the shofar. The young people bore candles of faith and peace. The Torah Mantels were changed to white as a symbolic reminder of how we are about to change ourselves. Cantor Orbach

helped create new and exciting worship experiences with his musical selections.

Cantor Harold Orbach

Harold Orbach, born in 1931, escaped from Hitler's Germany on a Kindertransport to England. (After the Kristallnacht pogrom of November 9 and 10, 1938, where 30,000 Jewish people ended in concentration camps and 100 were killed, the British Jewish refugee committee appealed to members of Parliament to accept Jewish children up to the age of seventeen. A fifty Pound Sterling bond had to be posted for each child to assure his/her ultimate resettlement. The children traveled in sealed trains. The first transport left one month after Kristallnacht and the last one left on September 3, 1939, just before the beginning of World War II. Approximately 10,000 children made the trip. Some of the children were taken into foster homes, others went to orphanages or group homes, and some worked on farms. Most of the children were well treated by their British hosts and developed close ties to these individuals. Approximately twenty to twenty five percent eventually ended up in the United States or Canada.) Harold Orbach came to the United States in 1940.

Cantor Harold Orbach

Harold served as a cantor in his first congregation when he was fifteen years old. This was prior to the establishment of cantorial training schools in the United States. He began his classical career at age eighteen. Harold attended Juilliard School of Music on the prestigious Katherine Long Scholarship. He also attended the Manhattan School of Music. Harold graduated from Hebrew Union College of Sacred Music. He earned a Master of Arts Degree in Education from Tulsa University. He was awarded an honorary Doctorate of Sacred Music Degree from Hebrew Union College. He was honored by his fellow cantors when he was elected President of the American Conference of Cantors.

Harold Orbach was the Cantor of Temple Israel of West Bloomfield, Michigan for forty years before he retired. The Temple had 11,000 people in the congregation. There were three Friday night services and three Saturday morning services every week. There was a dynamic creative Jewish culture at the Temple. He performed large numbers of weddings and Bar/Bat Mitzvahs. While at Temple Israel he presented twelve concerts a year, which were underwritten by members of the congregation.

He is a world-class tenor who has performed innumerable times in all settings within the United States and abroad. He maintains a busy schedule and has appeared in concert from Russia to Germany to Cuba to Japan and from New York's Lincoln Center to Dorothy Chandler Pavilion in Los Angeles. He appeared at a special concert at the Holocaust Memorial Museum in Washington, DC. He participated in the 350th anniversary of the founding of the oldest synagogue in the Western Hemisphere in Curacao. He took part in Jerusalem's 3000 year commemoration and was given the State of Israel Cultural Medal by Golda Meir. Cantor Orbach has been chosen to appear in many world premiere performances, including the first symphony performance of Leonard Bernstein's Dybbuk Variations, David Brubeck's The Gates of Justice, Martin Kalmanoff's A Victory at Masada, Chajes Out of the Desert, and Ellstein's The Thief and the Hangman. He sang at Israel's 25th and 50th birthday celebrations in Tel Aviv, in Caesaria and in Jerusalem. He sang at the 100th anniversary celebration of the Union of American Hebrew Congregations and the Hebrew Union College. He sang at Detroit's 300th birthday, and the United States Bicentennial concert in Philadelphia. He has appeared with Dave Brubeck and Ella Fitzgerald. He was the leading tenor of the American Savoyards and the Piccolo Opera Company. He has made numerous ecumenical appearances including participation in the International Eucharistic Congress and interfaith celebrations in the great Washington Episcopal Cathedral and at the Kennedy Center. This listing does not include many appearances in a variety of operas, concerts, television performances, and recordings.

Harold is one of the cantors who's not afraid to try the "New Sound" of religion. He gave the first published performance of a Jazz Service in a Synagogue when he sang Davidson's "And David Danced Before the Ark." He chanted Raymond Smolover's Rock Service "Edge of Freedom," and Gerschon Kingsley's Service with psychedelic lights and the Moog synthesizer, "Shabbat for Today."

Harold's voice, skill, sincerity, pureness of tone, diction, and beauty of performance has been lauded by many music critics. Robert Sherman of The New York Times said, "sweet-toned singing..." The Detroit News said, "an enchanting tenor voice..." The Cincinnati Post said, "a great tenor voice that shines in every repertoire." The Metropolitan Opera News said "Harold Orbach, as Eleazer, sang with rich, vibrant tones." Harold Orbach has definitely earned the title of the world's "Most Celebrated Cantors", with his vast number and variety of excellent performances in national and international settings.

Harold has brought to Temple B'nai Israel still another dimension to add to the beauty of the services performed by Rabbi Baseman. Harold said, "We are living in a renaissance of Jewish music with the advent of computers and contemporary technology and communications skills." He said, "Reform Judaism means change within the concept of modernity while maintaining traditions. However, many people feel spiritual uneasiness when new melodies enter the worship service, therefore it is always a risk to do something new. Sometimes new is so unique that it is excepted readily and other times it takes time for people to become comfortable. Sometimes the new selections that the Cantor might enjoy, are not completely or even ever excepted by the congregation. This is why the beginning of a new pulpit is like a wedding. It becomes a love relationship between the clergy and the congregation and I eagerly await the future." The future is already the present and the present shows clearly that a beautiful love affair, which will be eternally young, has already started and will grow in depth and significance as the years pass. May Harold Orbach have many happy and healthy years and continue to enhance the beauty of the service, which Rabbi Baseman leads with such love and care.

Harold Orbach's philosophy as Cantor, human being, and Jewish person is, "If there is a God, God is a creator, and for people to be Godlike they must in turn be creators." Toynbe, in the *History of the Jews*, said, "The Jews were a fossilized people." Harold Orbach totally disagreed with Toynbee and set out on a life long quest to challenge this statement through his music, through his relationship to his congregants and all people, and through his belief that Jewish people have always been creative as they have influenced life, in a spectacular manner, over the last 3000 years.

Looking to the present and future he said, "In order for our modern culture to be viable we must continue to be creative, as a result I have dedicated more than fifty years of my cantorate to a blending of the old and the new. I have had the privilege of living through the greatest period of musical creativity in the history of our people. The burgeoning of recordings, CDs and the computer together with easy accessibility to the print media has helped produce a huge amount of Jewish music, both religious and secular. This music is being created on an annual basis. This leads to the question of how individuals can renew their lives each Shabbat. The answer is, add contemporary new approaches and new music, that reflects the spirit of the times, to the older, well accepted music, blend them well together and create a fresh excitement for God and God's word."

What is the significance of the music in the service? Harold Orbach says, "Music is the emotional aspect of the service. It sets an atmosphere, a mood, an opportunity for the participant of the service to be actively involved in the service. Music establishes the spiritual atmosphere to enable the congregants to engage in a dialogue with the Eternal. Music helps the individual get into the spirit of the occasion to be responsive to prayer."

What is the function of the Cantor? Harold Orbach says, "The Cantor helps establish the mood which leads to the service being holy. He/She leads by example. He/She immerses himself/herself in the music and becomes emotionally moved by it and transmits this feeling to the congregants. He/She selects music which emotionally moves him/her. Oftentimes the same music will move the congregants." When the Cantor performs a wedding or Bar/Bat Mitzvah, he/she needs to think of the goodness of the celebrations of life that have actually occurred in his/her experience, in order to get into the proper frame of mind to immerse the recipients in the goodness of the moment. When he/she teaches students, he/she must imagine his/her feeling of the wonder of learning in order to impart the sweetness of knowledge to the young people. Cantor Orbach gave an example of the immersion of the Cantor in the particular part of a service. He said, "I used to sing Kol Nidre (The opening prayer of Yom Kippur) in a loud and dramatic manner. Now, I sing it in soft tones as if I were in a cave as the Moranos were when they asked God to release them from all their vows, many of which were given under duress."

Evelyn Orbach, Harold's wife, is also a musical artist of renown. She is the Artistic Director and Founder of the Jewish Ensemble Theatre (JET) group in West Bloomfield, Michigan. She graduated from the School of Performing Arts of New York, holds a Bachelor of Arts Degree in Drama from Brooklyn College, and has completed significant amount of private study under excellent tutelage.

Think of the nature of hatred, discrimination, repression, and destruction caused by people who want the power to control and destroy others. Think of the loss to society of millions of people who could have made such a difference in the lives of the people of the world. Think of what we would have lost if little Harold Orbach could not have boarded the Kindertransport and gone to England and then onto the United States. Think of all the engineers, doctors, scientists, philosophers, business people, and yes, those with little official recognition, but who still would have made a positive impact on the lives of others. All these names, would have been like honey on the tongues of humanity, for the world would have been a better place because they had lived here. Harold has shown, a single person can make a profound difference. Think what millions of people could have accomplished.

SISTERHOOD AND OTHER TEMPLE ACTIVITIES

An Evening at the Catskills Fashion Show at Betty Lane, date unknown. From left, David Kent, Debbie Lawrence, Laurie Strumpf. (Times Photo, photographer's name unclear).

Informal coffee for board members of Temple B'nai Israel, August 1968. l. to r. Mrs. Gary Steinman, Mrs. Sam Lampert (pouring), Mrs. Irving Baker, Mrs. S.M. Shapiro, Mrs. Jack Berg and Mrs. Darwin Frank. (Clearwater Sun Photo)

Temple B'nai Israel Sisterhood Installation, 1953. From left, Phyllis Lovitz (President 1957–1958), Mrs. Ike Eisenstein, Estelle Korones (President 1953–1954), Mrs. Sam Eisenstein, Fanny Marks (President 1950–1953), Ethel Schoenfeld, Maxine Franks (President 1954–1955).

Children with Rabbi at Temple B'nai Israel's Festival of Sukkas: Lauri Rutenberg, David Lawrence, Joel Peskin, Bonnie Baker, John Schwartz, Frank Schwartz, Rabbi Harry Richmond, Barbara Bandes, Sandy Braun, Felice Lopatin, Larry Kent and Marilyn Frank. (Clearwater Sun Photo) No dates available.

The winning Sukkah at Temple B'nai Israel, date unknown. From left, Joel Kent, David Kent, Reva Kent, Debby Bowman, Rose Bowman and Mrs. Harold Bowman. (Clearwater Sun Photo)

CHAPTER 17

JEWISH ORGANIZATIONS

B'nai B'rith

St. Petersburg B'nai B'rith Lodge 1246

St. Petersburg B'nai B'rith Lodge 1246 came into existence in the mid 1930s. (Unfortunately, very little information has been made available to the author concerning Lodge 1246. Since it was a very active chapter, an important part of Jewish history appears to be lost). Jerry Gilbert remembers being a member of the AZA, B'nai B'rith youth group in 1936 or 1937. A B'nai B'rith meeting was held on December 8, 1937. The officers were: President M. Allen Friedman; Monitor Rabbi Pizer W. Jacobs of Temple Beth-El; and Past President David Rothblatt. Other local officers were: Vice President Arnold Argintar; Treasurer Abraham Sierkese; Recording Secretary Frank Kleinfeld; Financial Secretary Harry Cypen; Guardian Harry Herman; Warden Louis Bishop; Assistant Monitor Rabbi Alexander Kleinfeld; Trustee Max Davis; Trustee David Rothblatt; and Trustee Sam Traeger. Plans were made for the annual dinner-dance on January 18 at the Suwannee Hotel. The committee consisted of Max Davis, Chairman, Sam Hirsch, Morris Hermer, J. Shenker, and Sam Traeger. A B'nai B'rith meeting was held on May 29, 1938. Allen Friedman, Rabbi Jacobs, and David Rothblatt represented the B'nai B'rith Chapter at a conference of the Southern Regional Lodges in Orlando. In 1940, the field representative of the National Council of Jewish Women was the guest speaker. Every man and woman affiliated with any of the Jewish organizations were urged to attend the meeting.

B'nai B'rith sponsored a $5,000 Jewish relief fund for the Jewish people. The local drive was supported by members of different faiths. In a radio broadcast, Rev. J. J. O'Riordan of St. Mary's Catholic Church, Dr. George Gilmore of United Liberal Church, and Rabbi Pizer W. Jacobs of Temple Beth-El asked the St. Petersburg community for its support.

B'nai B'rith Clearwater Unit 2603

The B'nai B'rith Clearwater Unit 2603 was granted a charter on March 17, 1966. The founding members were: Samuel Auerbach, Irving Baker, Arthur Bandes, Samuel Baruch, Robert Bauman, S. H. Baranoff, Simon Bellack, Robert Benjamin Jr., Albert Bexmayor, Saul Berger, Sion Betash, Morris Bilgore, Herbert Blankman, Louis Bloom, Ezra Bobo, Steve Bragin, Louis Brower, Gordon Brown, Nelson Brown, Emil Chayet, Morton Chervitz, Arthur Chorost, Richard Corwin, Leonard Collman, David Davis, Lee Dorian, Irving Dribben, Irving Entel, Saul Fein, Roland Fox, Jacob Ford, Darwin Frank, Herbert Frank, Aaron Galloway, Daniel Gladstone, Charles Goldsmith, Charles Goldstein, Louis Gorod, Leonard Green, Leon Greenwald, Harold Haftel, Saul Hirsher, Phil Katz, Robert Keller, Myron Kimball, David Korones, Sam Korones, Howard Lawrence, Irving Levine, Emanuel Lepkowits, Arthur Lopatin, Harold Lopatin, Jeffrey Lopatin, Julius Lovitz, Phillip Merkatz, Stanley Michels, Harold Moroff, Morris Newman, Marvin Peltz, Loren Pollack, Simon Post, Bernard Rich, Norman Rich, Sidney Rich, Albert Rophie, Charles Rutenberg, Reuben Rutenberg, Maxwell Sackheim, Jacob Saunders, Herbert Schwartz, Alfred Schick, Abraham Simon, Norman Stfuer, Bruce Weiser, Paul Surensky, Marshall Taxay, Douglas Weiss, Alex Winston, and Isadore Zitlin.

The Clearwater B'nai B'rith Chapter held their meetings at Temple B'nai Israel on Betty Lane. The dues were $20 per year. From 1966 through 1974, the lodge grew to 150 male members. The individuals were typically in their thirties and forties, actively working professionals, as engineers, attorneys, pharmacists, doctors, real estate developers, retailers, citrus growers, canners, etc.. At a later date, the age bracket shifted to people in their sixties and over, who were mostly retired. The Clearwater Lodge, as well as the St. Petersburg Lodge, flourished in their early years because of the need to deal with discriminatory practices.

The Clearwater Lodge created a blood bank and had numerous fundraisers for socialization and also to assist others. By the end of the 1970s, the Clearwater Lodge was starting to disintegrate, although it never ceased to function. Howard Feingold stepped in as President and worked very hard with his officers to reinstitute the organization. The Lodge was converted into a Unit, when they joined together with the Women's Chapter. By 1988, formal bulletins were issued. Whereas in 1986, sixteen to twenty people would attend the meeting, by 1988, sixty or more people would attend the meeting. The membership returned to 150 plus people. Some of the speakers over those years were: Dr. Ailon Shiloh, Professor of Anthropology; Dr. Roy Kaplan of the National Conference of Christians and Jews; Dr. Jan Hirschfield of the Anti-Defamation League; James Dawkins of the Jewish Press of Clearwater; Steve Goldman Director of the Holocaust Museum; and Dr. Alice Backal, who spoke about the Jews in Mexico.

In 1993–1994, Janine Porteny took upon herself the immense task of collecting information about the history of the Lodge and the Unit. Harold Haftel was extremely helpful in guiding Janine through the project and helping her find names, telephone numbers, and addresses of old members. She sent out a series of questionnaires in the summer of 1993 and over one half of the individuals responded. This material led to a series of stories about the Clearwater B'nai B'rith Unit, their activities, and some of the people involved in programs.

Mary and Maury Newman moved to Clearwater from Riverside, Illinois in 1961. They rapidly became active in Temple B'nai Israel and became the "Ambassadors of Goodwill" for every Jewish family moving into town. They organized the B'nai Israel Friendship Club. They joined and became lifetime members of B'nai B'rith. Morey became the Blood Bank Chairman. He found that there was an extreme shortage of blood in the community and that the members of B'nai B'rith by themselves could not fulfill this need. He came up with

an idea of donating money for turkeys for Thanksgiving and to give these turkeys to members of the community who would give blood. Also, he did the same thing for Hanukkah and for Christmas. Because of his ideas and his contributions both monetary and physically, the Hunter Blood Bank of Clearwater became self-sufficient. Instead of a shortage of blood, there was a steady supply. Jeff Meddin took over as Chairperson and continued in this role for many years.

At the November, 1987 meeting of the Clearwater B'nai B'rith, Marion and Dick Cole suggested that the B'nai B'rith members become Menorah Manor volunteers. Over the intervening years, the group has continued to perform a large number of services to the Home.

B'nai B'rith became very active in providing food for the Food Pantry of the Jewish Family Services. At each meeting, food has been collected from the members.

B'nai B'rith had its 150th anniversary celebration. Eight synagogues in the community sponsored a special Oneg Shabbat. The chair people of these special events were: David Kalin of Congregation B'nai Israel of St. Petersburg; Judy Stevens of Temple B'nai Israel of Clearwater; Fran Ehrenpreis of Congregation B'nai Emmunah of Tarpon Springs; Rose Shapera and David Kalin of Congregation Beth Sholom of Gulfport; Jack Perlman of Young Israel Chabad of Clearwater; Ed Azar of Temple Ahavat Shalom of Palm Harbor; Harold Haftel of Congregation Aliyah of Clearwater; and Frank Dukes-Dobos of Congregation Beth Shalom of Clearwater.

The Anti-Defamation League is a vital part of the B'nai B'rith. It is dedicated to the fulfillment of America's democratic promise to battle bigotry and strengthen America's pluralistic society. The ADL leads the fight against discrimination. It builds bridges of understanding and friendship among racial, religious, and ethnic groups. It conducts research and provides education and legal remedies to fight prejudice. It confronts threats to the security of the Jewish community and in turn to the security of democracy as we know it. It is an advocate for Israel and the worldwide court of public opinion.

Locally, the members have met with a variety of different groups within the Pinellas County community to establish lines of communication with all individuals, regardless of their race, religion, or ethnic group. Of particular interest was a Jewish-Catholic dialogue held on March 7, 1993. Bishop John C. Favalora of the Catholic Diocese of St. Petersburg and Dr. Jacob Neusner, Distinguished Research Professor of Religious Studies at the University of South Florida were the feature speakers. The program was held in cooperation with the Jewish Federation of Pinellas County, the Tampa Bay Holocaust Memorial Museum and Educational Center , and the Pinellas County Board of Rabbis. Bishop Favalora was well-known to many people in the audience. During his tenure at the Catholic Diocese of St. Petersburg, he has spoken out against anti-semitism and racism, and has continuously reached out to the Jewish community from working on programs at the Holocaust Museum to speaking out against racism, Nazism, and bigotry. Professor Neusner has written, edited, contributed to, or translated more than 300 books. His scholarly analysis of Jewish history, religion, literature and culture have won him numerous honorary degrees from Brown University, University of Chicago, University of Cologne, and the University of Bologna.

The Hillel Foundation is supported by B'nai B'rith. It is a clearinghouse for information that students can use at various universities. It serves as an advocate for Jewish students and Jewish rites. The local Hillel chapter at the University of South Florida received help from the Clearwater B'nai B'rith Unit. In fact, the Clearwater Unit helped keep the Hillel Chapter open at the University of South Florida. In 1993, there were 2000 Jewish students at the University of South Florida compared to 4,000 Jewish students at the University of Florida, 2000 Jewish students at Florida State University, and 2,800 Jewish students at Georgetown University in Washington DC. These other universities with large Jewish student enrollments had significant Hillel programs. It was only natural to keep the University of

South Florida Hillel program alive and viable.

The B'nai B'rith Youth Organization, with over 30,000 Jewish teenagers worldwide, works to help young people reach their potential as individuals and as Jews. The Clearwater Unit provided assistance to the young people and the organizations.

A Young Leadership Action Network of the B'nai B'rith was established. It had become an extremely urgent matter to interest younger people in B'nai B'rith and in various leadership roles. A commitment was made to develop quality programming to prepare the next-generation of leaders. American Jewish communal leaders around the country were speaking out about the need for Jewish continuity. The young Jewish men and women had to be turned on to the significance of their Jewish lives as children and then later continue the wonderful jobs that their elders had done over the years. Democracy and freedom could only be perpetuated and protected by educated individuals who understood the problems of society and how best to contribute to the resolution of these problems. There was a sizable push to increase the number of members, both men and women, in B'nai B'rith. It has been said, "If we lose our own kids, we have lost everything."

Over the last ten years, B'nai B'rith has been involved in a series of programs including: "Jewish Life in Tampa Bay," a cable access TV show; Yearly anti–hate programs featuring Dr. Norman Gross; annual Holocaust remembrance programs and guest speakers who can significantly update the knowledge of the local membership; and provide the members with an opportunity to share their lifelong experiences.

In April, 2003, it was announced that longtime board member, Xenia Fane, had passed away. President Stuart Berger said of Xenia, " Xenia was a woman blessed with intelligence and integrity, kindness, and compassion. Our loss is truly heaven's gain."

Presidential Commentary

Over the past 70 years, a series of Presidents of the United States have written about the significance of the contributions of B'nai B'rith to the society and the welfare of the people of the United States of America.

President Franklin D. Roosevelt said, "B'nai B'rith has effectively served the well-being of American Jewry and the Nation. Its philanthropic achievements are permanently enshrined...its endeavors in the realm of education exhibit a farsighted understanding in the problems of the younger generation...its programs of goodwill strives toward harmony among the compliments comprising our American society."

President Dwight D. Eisenhower said, "I am glad to express my appreciation for B'nai B'rith's achievements in promoting understanding, cooperation, and goodwill among Americans of all races and creeds. I know that the men and women of B'nai B'rith, who so consistently fought for the freedom and equality of all Americans, will continue to work on selflessly for the fulfillment of these great principles."

President John F. Kennedy said, "Voluntary organizations such as B'nai B'rith are an essential part of a free society. The long history and wide range of B'nai B'rith interests have been a positive and constructive force for a good part of the history of our nation."

President Lyndon B. Johnson said, "You have never tired, you have never faltered, you never lost faith in your cause; and your cause has given faith to your nation. You are pro-justice and pro-freedom."

President Richard M. Nixon said, "The perfect standard of B'nai B'rith and of the United States and of humanity, are one and the same today, tomorrow, and all the years to come."

President Gerald R. Ford said, "You, the sons and daughters of the Covenant, have kept your commitment to Judaism and to America. The glow of your compassion illuminates the best of our nation's traditional spirit of voluntary service to others."

President Jimmy Carter said, "The men and women of B'nai B'rith share with me a total commitment to the preservation of human rights, liberty, and freedom of conscience."

President Ronald Reagan said, "For more than 140 years, B'nai B'rith has sponsored religious, cultural, and civic programs; conducted studies of vital issues; combated bigotry; and worked tirelessly

Bill Sefekar

to advance the cause of tolerance and humanity. Because of your efforts today, our country has a purer heart, a deeper sense of the generosity of spirit that must always define America."

President George Bush (the elder) said, "Because it is rooted in a commitment to charity and understanding, your work also has a positive impact far beyond the Jewish community. I applaud your efforts to promote cooperation and tolerance among people of all backgrounds, and it is my sincere hope that, as we move forward with our historic efforts to promote peace in the Middle East, your example will continue to erode barriers of bigotry and mistrust, wherever they exist."

B'nai B'rith Presents Jewish Life in Tampa Bay

B'nai B'rith presents "Jewish Life in Tampa Bay," is a television program aired on public access TV. The Producer and Executive Director, since April 1995, has been Bill Sefekar. The first show aired in September, 1994. The original format for the first two and one half years was for a one-hour program. Subsequently, it became a one half-hour program. Rabbi Jan Bresky began producing the first Jewish television show on cable TV and the Tampa Bay area called the "Enlightenment." This was followed by the current format which talks about Jewish religion, culture, entertainment and organizations, activities and inter-generational concerns.

The program is designed to provide and enhance social integration of the Jewish community; improve education, awareness and the relationship with the non-Jewish community, and combat media anti-semitism. It provides television and media coverage pertinent to Jewish community activities in the Tampa area. It provides information to both Jewish people and non-Jewish people alike to help better understand Jewish life in the community. The program has received awards from the B'nai B'rith's Southeastern District and B'nai B'rith of Florida for Most Outstanding Program. It received honorable mention at the San Francisco Jewish film library. The funding for the show comes from various groups and organizations, including B'nai B'rith and the Jewish Federation of Pinellas County. Over the past twelve years, the program has featured rabbis, cantors, mayors, Nobel Peace Prize Laureates, professors, ambassadors, and other celebrities.

Of the 162 shows produced and shown on public television, the author has selected a few. The entire list can be found at Heritage Village, Largo, Florida, the Pinellas County Historical Society. It is included in a Jewish archives. The shows selected are: July, 1995, Jewish Life in Czarist Russia, and a musical interlude with Cantor Rafael Grossman of Temple B'nai Emmunah in Tarpon Springs; February, 1996, opening of Anne Frank Exhibit at Tampa Bay Holocaust Museum and Shabbat Service by Rabbi Birnholtz of Temple Schaarai Zedek of Tampa; August, 1999, "How to Deal with Hate" Part two, NBC news footage and panel discussion at Kent Jewish Community Center.

Bill Sefekar does all the necessary work on a voluntary basis because he believes, "Jewish life in Tampa Bay or for that matter in America as we know it, is not guaranteed. It will survive with continued efforts from people and organizations that have the vision to learn from the past, live in the present, and leave a legacy for the future. I've spent a good part of my life believing this creed, but it is only in the past twelve years that I am actually living it. I hope to continue my commitment to this effort."

Stuart and Helene Berger

Under the leadership of current President Stuart Berger, B'nai B'rith continues to be a vibrant organization in Pinellas County. "B'nai B'rith has been synonymous with Jewish life and keeps us at the forefront of Jewish advocacy, and I expect to see this expand."

Stuart has been President since 2002, and works for the Jewish Federation of Pinellas County as its Financial Resource Director and Jewish Community Relations Council Coordinator. Stuart received his Bachelor of Arts degree from Eckerd College, and studied briefly at Yeshivot Aish HaTorah in Jerusalen. He has been married for twenty years to his wife, Helene, a Certified Vocational Evaluator for Cascade Disability Management and a University of Florida graduate. They have two children,

Alana, age fifteen, and Daniel, age twelve. His parents, Stan and Arlene Berger, are also active with the Unit.

Helene and Stuart Berger

CHAPTER 18

FLORIDA HOLOCAUST MUSEUM

Introduction

The Holocaust was the state-sponsored systematic persecution and elimination of European Jewry by Nazi Germany and its associated allies. This occurred between 1933 and 1945. In addition to approximately six million Jewish people, Gypsies, people with mental and physical disabilities, Polish people, homosexuals, Jehovah's Witnesses, Soviet prisoners, political dissidents, and anyone else that a person in power had a grievance against, were killed. The word Holocaust comes from the ancient Greek meaning a sacrifice consumed by fire or a great destruction of life.

Holocaust museums have arisen in many countries including Argentina, Australia, Austria, Belgium, Canada, Croatia, Czech Republic, France, Germany, Hungary, Israel, Japan, Netherlands, Poland, South Africa, United Kingdom and the United States of America. In the USA, there are twenty three Holocaust museums and Holocaust memorials including: Albuquerque, New Mexico; Buffalo, New York; Dallas, Texas; El Paso, Texas; Houston, Texas; Farmington Hills, Michigan; Los Angeles, California (four museums); Maitland, Florida; Miami Beach, Florida; Naples, Florida; New Haven, Connecticut; New York (three centers and memorials); Providence, Rhode Island; Boston, Massachusetts; Richmond, Virginia; San Francisco, California; St. Louis, Missouri; St. Petersburg, Florida; Terre Haute, Indiana; and Washington, DC.

In 1973, President Richard M. Nixon signed into law the Ethnic Studies Heritage Act calling for public schools to teach the history and culture of America's minorities. This led to the inclusion of Holocaust studies in schools across America.

On November 1, 1978, President Carter authorized the President's Commission and charged it with establishing a Holocaust Remembrance and Education Center in the United States. In 1980, Congress unanimously passed legislation to establish the United States Holocaust Memorial Council. Elie Wiesel became chairman. The architect for the museum was James Ingo Freed, and the contractor was the Blake Construction Company. The museum cost approximately ninety million dollars to build and an additional seventy eight million dollars was to be spent on the exhibits. The land was donated by the federal government and private donations from 200,000 people funded the museum. The United States Holocaust Memorial Museum was dedicated on April 22, 1993 and opened to the public on April 26, 1993. Dedication speeches were given by President Bill Clinton, Chaim Herzog, Harvey Meyerhoff, and Elie Wiesel. The museum had 36,000 square feet and has been visited, by over twenty two million people, including seven and half million schoolchildren.

In April 1994, the Florida Legislature enacted a mandate requiring Holocaust education in public schools. The Florida Holocaust Museum became one of the resource centers for public education.

Currently, Holocaust museums around the world not only memorialize the victims, but have a universal mission to educate all people and future generations about human rights and tolerance. Whereas the Holocaust represents an example of the horrible evil that can be visited by people who want to decide what is right and what is wrong for everyone else, the total community must learn to reinforce the values, morals, and special identity of all groups of people and teach everyone, especially the children, the importance of coexistence in all aspects of life. Only then, can evil be suppressed and goodness prevail.

Florida Holocaust Museum

The mission of the Florida Holocaust Museum is to honor the memory of the millions of innocent men, women, and children who suffered and died in the Holocaust. The Museum is dedicated to teaching members

of all races and cultures to recognize the inherent worth and dignity of human life in order to prevent future genocides.

Highlights of 1990

On January 30, an authentic railcar used by the Nazis during the Holocaust to transport Jews and other prisoners to their deaths in concentration camps arrived at the Port of Tampa, on its way to the Tampa Bay Holocaust Museum and Educational Center at the Jewish Community Center in Madeira Beach. The railcar, which was fully authenticated, was purchased by Walter P. Loebenberg. The Center had purchased the former Madeira Beach Kapok Tree Restaurant and botanical gardens and converted the restaurant facility to be used for special programming for adults and children. The boxcar was placed on the grounds of this facility. The Tampa Bay Holocaust Memorial Museum and Educational Center rented 4,000 square feet of space for its exhibitions.

The arrival of the railcar, which came from Gdania, Poland, was the culmination of months of planning and hard work guided by Walter Loebenberg, Chairman of the Tampa Bay Holocaust Memorial Museum and Educational Center. He wanted to honor those who were destroyed by the Nazis and to provide an educational experience for all people to learn, not only the horror that people can inflict upon each other, but more importantly, how to prevent this from happening again to any people, anywhere. The railcar was set up on a separate foundation on the same set of tracks used at the killing center of Treblinka. The boxcar became the focal point of the entry to the Museum.

Walter Loebenberg said, "For many involved, such railcars were the first place of death during the Holocaust. Unlike the cattlecars later used, the railcars contained no air slits, so they became suffocation chambers for many of the thousands of victims." Two other such railcars are on display in Dallas, Texas, and Washington, D.C.

Amy and Bruce Epstein

Highlights of 1991

Because of the outstanding visionary efforts of Walter and Edith Loebenberg and Amy and Bruce Epstein, acting as a catalyst to bring in many other people, the Florida Holocaust Museum was founded. It was originally called the Tampa Bay Holocaust Memorial Museum and Educational Center. Walter helped bring together a group of local businessmen and community leaders and guided them as they conceived a living memorial to those who have suffered and died. The group then enlisted the support of others in the community and they involved internationally renowned Holocaust scholars. Thomas Keneally, author of Schindler's List, joined the Board of Advisors and Elie Wiesel was named Honorary Chairman of the Holocaust Center.

This museum was a remarkable dedication to the lives of millions of people who were selected by the Nazis to die simply because of their religion. It was not to be a memorial to death but rather a prayer for life and for the goodness that people can achieve if they allow the God-given spark of life to flourish and excel and produce the wonderful things that people have and continue to contribute in all communities and for all people in the world.

Amy and Dr. Bruce Epstein

Amy Steindler Epstein was born in Cleveland, Ohio on March 23, 1945. She attended Ohio State University and earned a Bachelor of Science Degree in Nursing from Cleveland Community College in 1967. She and Bruce were married in 1965. They have three children: J. H. Epstein, M. D.; Jenny Epstein Alexander, M.S.W.; and Robert A. Epstein, D.C..

Amy is involved in: Woman's American ORT; Hadassah; National Council of Jewish Women; charter member, United States Holocaust Museum; charter member, Ellis Island Foundation; Simon Wiesenthal Center; Lion of Judah, Pinellas County Jewish Federation; Sapphire Society, The Jewish National Fund; Pinellas County Medical Society Auxiliary; and Fine Arts Museum, St. Petersburg, Florida.

Amy's awards and honors in community service are extensive. They include: 2006

Women of Distinction, Jewish Federation of Tampa; Inductee, Cleveland Heights High School Alumni Hall of Fame; Jewish National Fund Tree of Life Award, 1990; Hadassah Woman of the Year Award, 1998; Girl Scouts Leadership Woman of the Year Award; Florida Holocaust Museum "To Life" Award, 2001; Chairman, Woman Awareness Day, Pinellas County Medical Society; Pinellas County Arts Council; President, Jewish Community Center; National Board of the Jewish National Fund; President, Gulf Coast Council of the Jewish National Fund; Member, Menorah Manor Auxiliary Board; founder of Project Sound Off-a crime prevention program; Lazzara Woman's Homeless Shelter; Bayfront Hospital Medical Center; Chairman, Firemen's Balls for the Jewish National Fund; Tampa Bay International Club; Presidential Commission for the Preservation of American Heritage Abroad; Co-Chairperson, and Frank Humanitarian Award (for high school juniors); President, Florida Holocaust Museum-1992-1998; and Chairman of the Board, Florida Holocaust Museum-1998-Present. One of her proudest accomplishments, other than being one of the founders of the Florida Holocaust Museum, is that she has served with distinction since September, 2001, as a member of the United States Commission for the Preservation of America's Heritage Abroad–appointed by the President in 2001 and re-appointed in 2006. Her two projects thus far are the restoration of the Hidden Synagogue in the Terezin Concentration Camp, and the development and construction of a scale model of the concentration camp at Mittlebau-Dora, where the V2 rockets were manufactured

Dr. Bruce A. Epstein was born on April 28, 1943 in Cleveland, Ohio. He graduated from Western Reserve University of Cleveland, Ohio with a Bachelor of Science Degree in Chemistry in 1965. He graduated from the Case Western Reserve University (there was a name change from Western Reserve University) with his Doctor of Medicine Degree in 1968. He received a Honorable Discharge as Major, United States Army Medical Corps, 1971-1973.

Bruce was board-certified from the American Board of Pediatrics. He holds medical licensure in Ohio, California, Texas, Florida, and Arizona. He has hospital appointments at: All Children's Hospital; Bayfront Medical Center; St. Anthony's Hospital; St. Petersburg General Hospital. He is a member of: Phi Beta Kappa; (Fellow) American Academy of Pediatrics; Pinellas County Medical Society; Israel Medical Association; Florida Medical Association; Florida Pediatric Society; American Medical Association; and American Israel physician fellowship.

Bruce has made numerous contributions to the professional literature. In addition he is a contributing editor to the St. Petersburg Times, Parents Magazine, Pediatric Newsletter for Parents. He is the Webmaster for seven different web sites ranging from pediatric health to the Jewish Federation of Pinellas County.

He has received numerous awards and honors including: Media Spokesperson, American Academy of Pediatrics; Legislative Contact, American Israel Public Affairs Committee; Legislative Contact American Medical Association; Legislative Contact American Academy of Pediatrics; Member, Health Advisory Committee for Senator Connie Mack; Trustee, Case Western Reserve University; Recipient, American Medical Association's Physcian Recognition Award; Member, Pediatric Review and Education Program, American Academy of Pediatrics; Lecturer, Bayfront Medical Center; Member, Board of Trustees, University of Arizona Parents Association; Vice President, Jewish National Fund of Tampa Bay; Board Member, Jewish Community Center of Pinellas County; Board Member, Florida Holocaust Museum; Legislative Contact, American Israel Public Affairs Committee, Member, B'nai B'rith, Member, American-Israel Friendship League, Member, Dean's Club, Case Western Reserve School of Medicine; Member, Board of Directors, Straight Drug Rehabilitation Program; Advisory Board, PBS; Recipient, Tree of Life Award, Jewish National Fund; Member, Doctors with Class-a High School AIDS speaker's program; Recipient, Communicator of the Year Award from the Florida Medical Association; Member, Maimonides

Committee; Chairman, Florida Holocaust Museum; Recipient, Alfred Schick M.D. Award; Vice President for Special Events, Florida Holocaust Museum; Member, Board of Trustees All Children's Hospital; Member, Board of Trustees, Menorah Manor; and Co-Chairperson, Jewish Community Relations Council, Jewish Federation.

Amy and Bruce Epstein have made outstanding contributions to the Jewish and general communities. They did this because of their philosophy of life. They said, "Our parents instilled upon us the importance of family, community and heritage. Although they were middle-class Americans with limited financial resources, they always gave of their time to help when needed. Forty years later we still are following our parents tradition and helping our community. By being active in various Jewish related causes, we have received much more than we have given... in the depths of our friendships, the wealth of information about people, and the Holocaust...has greatly enriched our lives."

Highlights of 1992

The museum opened in a small rented space on the grounds of the former Jewish Community Center of Pinellas County in Madeira Beach. It started with one staff member and a small group of dedicated volunteers. In the first month, over 24,000 visitors came to see the exhibit, "Anne Frank in the World." The exhibit poignantly touched all the visitors, and during the next five years, over 125,000 visitors came to see the internationally acclaimed exhibits. Thousands more came for the lectures, seminars, and commemorative events. The center provided, to an eight county area surrounding Tampa Bay, study guides, teacher training programs, and presentations by Center staff and Holocaust survivors. It also provided a growing print and audio-visual library, a photographic archive, a repository for historic artifacts, and a research center for educators and scholars. The museum's major objective was to be a vehicle to actively teach the lessons of the Holocaust which included the accepting of diversity, tolerance and understanding of those who are different

than ourselves.

Highlights of 1993

The museum marked its first anniversary with "Auschwitz-A Crime against Humanity." The exhibit used eighty large-scale photographs, facsimiles of documents, and descriptive texts to graphically portray the history of the Auschwitz/Birkenau Concentration Camp. The Museum played a critical role in helping shape legislation that made Florida the country's first state to mandate Holocaust education in the public schools for kindergarten through 12th grade.

Amy Epstein presided over a ceremony honoring more than 100 American World War II veterans who survived imprisonment in Nazi concentration camps.

Highlights of 1994

The Tampa Bay Holocaust Memorial Museum and Education Center presented its first annual summer institute on the Holocaust for teachers. This was done in conjunction with the formation of the State of Florida Commissioner's Task Force on Holocaust Education. The Museum established a Teacher on Assignment Position with the Pinellas County Public School District. The Museum provides fifty percent of the salary and benefits for a teacher to be actively working with teachers and students on Holocaust Education.

Highlights of 1996

Very large Teaching Trunks were made available to all schools. The materials selected met the standards of local state and federal agencies. The trunks were filled with grade appropriate literature and materials for students. The focus of the material was to create an educational pyramid, with each subsequent year building on the previous year. The first and second graders saw a series of videos with related literature, "Different and the Same." The presentations were about awareness, fairness, understanding, respect, and tolerance. The third and fourth graders studied, "Creating Community." They began to examine the issues at the root of all Holocaust education: immigration, prejudice, families, community, and culture identity. The fifth-graders were involved in the "Beginning Holocaust Studies." Students were introduced to the importance of learning from history, in particular the socio-political and historical context in which the Holocaust took place. There was an emphasis on children, resourcefulness, and creativeness. The middle school students studied, "Investigating Human Behavior." This material focused on the choices individuals and groups made during the Holocaust. The trunk examines the bystander, perpetrator, victim, and rescuer and how their choices affected their lives and the lives of others. The high school students studied, "Historical Perspectives of the Holocaust." The students did a focused study on the historical impact of the Holocaust on the individuals..

The Board of Directors, recognizing the immediate need for a larger facility, approved the purchase of a 27,000 square-foot building in downtown St. Petersburg. The building was to be renovated and occupied by 1998.

Highlights of 1997

Larry Wasser became the Executive Director of the Holocaust Museum. He headed the campaign that raised six million dollars to relocate the museum from its original small facility to the new facility. He provided the guidance that allowed the museum to become internationally known for its educational outreach programs. He was a visionary with a rare ability to encourage people to work beyond their current level of proficiency. He was director of the local Jewish National Fund, a humanitarian, an excellent fundraiser, and a highly successful executive. He died suddenly at age fifty six on Monday, June 2, 2003.

Highlights of 1998

After years of exceptional service to the community and schools, the museum, which had outgrown its 4,000 square-foot facility, moved into the renovated 27,000 square-foot former bank building in downtown St. Petersburg, in February. The grand opening week of festivities was elegant, moving, informative, and educational. It became the fourth-largest Holocaust Museum in the United States, the largest regional Holocaust

Museum in the United States, and recognized as the best educational museum in Tampa Bay. On the first-floor, in a permanent exhibit, is an original boxcar from Poland, once used to transport prisoners. On the second floor, the focus is on the Holocaust in art. The third-floor contains the Ray and Nancy Murray Library and Tolerance Center, classrooms, and Kane's Furniture Hall, a multipurpose gallery available to all museum visitors, community organizations, and companies. The Wall of Witness Project was started when the Education Director joined the Museum instituting educational programming for families, students, docents, and teacher training.

From left, Walter Loebenberg, Elie Wiesel, Edie Loebenberg, and Amy Epstein at the grand opening.

Art set the tone for the museum. Alfred Tibor, the sculptor, the humanist, the survivor was honored by the museum. He presented an outstanding sculpture exhibition. A museum representative said, "His life is his work, his work is his art, and his art is his life." More than 275 of his works were either in public or private collections throughout the world. Alfred Tibor said, "...there is beauty and value to be found in all our lives, for I truly believe that life is a celebration."

The Holocaust Museum was awarded five hundred thousand dollars by the State of Florida, through a cultural facilities grant, to fund vital improvements to the property. In order to be eligible for this grant, the organization had to prove that it could raise two dollars for every one dollar of grant money. Well over one million dollars was raised from the community through the "A Building for the Future-in Remembrance of the Past" Capital Campaign. Paul W. Martin Jr. was President of the museum. The Holocaust Museum Director was Steve Goldman..

"Witness and Legacy," one the most powerful and thought-provoking art exhibits to tour the United States, came to the Holocaust Museum. Steven Goldman said, "Twenty three artists, one third survivors, one third children of survivors, and one third empathizers, had given us an incomparable opportunity to see into their hearts and souls, to join with them in confronting the inconceivable, the Holocaust."

Highlights of 1999

The museum officially changed its name to the Florida Holocaust Museum. The mission statement reflected the use of the museum as a statewide and national resource as well as creating greater awareness and impact beyond the Tampa Bay area. The actual Articles of Amendment to change the name from the Tampa Bay Holocaust Memorial Museum and Educational Center Incorporated to the Florida Holocaust Museum Incorporated were filed on December 17, 1998.

"The Museum's major goal is to make sure that all the suffering and loss imposed upon individuals would never happen again. Prejudice and ignorance creates hate and mistrust. Knowledge creates hope for a better future, where peace and harmony are a reality in all communities, in our country, and in our world."

There were major accomplishments in the past year. Over 60,000 individuals walked through the doors of the museum to visit the permanent and special art exhibits. Educational materials, including curriculum materials and resources, were provided for 100,000 schoolchildren in grades kindergarten through twelve. teacher training and Student Awareness Days were held to help individuals possess the needed tools to promote respect, responsibility, and tolerance. A Summer Institute was held and the First International Scholars' Roundtable was held and was successful.

Description of Florida Holocaust Museum

Nick Benjacob, architect of the Florida Holocaust Museum, wanted the building to convey the sense of a broken shape to sharpen the message of the horrors of the Nazi decision to commit genocide. He used a series of triangles on the outside and in the building, because of their sharp edges, instead of circles or squares which would represent a wholeness instead of a fragmentation. On the second floor, he

useda rust red Bridge of Unity, which joined two balconies, whose railings were six feet and eight feet high, to represent the double fences around the concentration camps. The design of the stairs and bridge is positioned in such a manner to represent "Praying hands," indicating a message of hope for the future.

In the February issue of Southern Living Magazine's article entitled, "From Horror to Hope" there was a description of the Florida Holocaust Museum. "...One area depicts daily life in Jewish neighborhoods before the Nazis. Smiling families celebrate weddings and enjoy picnics. Kids play ball in the streets. Bakers show off the oven paddles of their trade....Life is good–for the moment. But displays of swastika armbands worn by soldiers, of star patches identifying members of the targeted culture, and of ghetto currency exchanged in enclosed communities foreshadow darker times. Photos reflect inhumane conditions forced upon an entire people... A hinge from a gas chamber door heightens a sense of alarm and disgust. Perhaps the biggest shock waits around a corner marked by barbed fencing. Here stands a boxcar, (#1130695-5 resting on original track from the Treblinka Killing Center), actually used to transport innocents to their death. After reaching the sad depth of this museum's story, you begin to glimpse humanity returning." There is a wall filled with poignant images of families, school, and life before the war where you will hear survivors share their own personal triumphs as well as memories. There is a meditation court that allows one to sit and reflect, as well as honor those who died and helped further the cause of freedom.

There are many artifacts in the Florida Holocaust Museum. Among them you will find a gold ring, found in 1998, after the boxcar was pressure cleaned in preparation for its move inside the museum. You also find tiny shoes from a little girl, Doris Mathes, who was born June 14, 1942 and was gassed January 17, 1944 at Auschwitz. When these innocent children died, part of humanity died.

The Holocaust Museum, in its recognition of the past, contributes to the enhancement of the lives of the people of the present and urges us onto a better and more secure future. Walter Loebenberg, you and the many wonderful people, Jewish and non-Jewish, who helped turn a dream about life into reality, are to be thanked by a grateful community. All Holocaust museums throughout the United States and the rest of the world represent the significance of nurturing and preserving life, especially of the innocents.

Highlights of 2000

The St. Petersburg Times published its Newspaper in Education -Anne Frank: Lessons for Today in Human Rights and Dignity, in partnership with the Florida Holocaust Museum. It was a compilation of articles that were published each week in the St. Petersburg Times from September 1999 through May 2000. "The writings of Anne Frank provide an inspiring example of the power of an individual voice and the ability to maintain faith in humanity in the face of prejudice and human destructiveness." This excellent series was reprinted in its entirety as a public service and as a teaching tool for teachers to use with Pinellas County students in grades six to eight. The activities included on the back page of the section were designed to give parents and adults who work with children a guide to discuss topics that increase the children's awareness and appreciation of all people.

Chapter 1, The Human Costs of War, is like the remaining twenty nine chapters in that it takes a topic based on what happened in the Holocaust and expands it to include the related problems of today and how to work to resolve them. Chapter 1 is used as an example of the thought process used in all chapters. Chapter 1 discusses how, despite the advances of modern technology, which should make a better world, the Holocaust was a horrifying example of the opposite, genocide being practiced against many people. However, a still small voice, that of Anne Frank, could still be heard. On July 15, 1944, at age fifteen, she wrote, "It's utterly impossible for me to build my life on a foundation of suffering and death. I see the world being slowly transformed into a wilderness, I hear the approaching thunder that one day, will destroy us too, I feel the

suffering of millions. And yet, when I look up at the sky, I somehow feel that everything will change for the better, that this cruelty too shall end, that peace and tranquility will return once more. In the meantime, I must hold on to my ideals. Perhaps the day will come when I'll be able to realize them!" Remember, when she looked at the sky, it was through a narrow piece of glass. She could never have looked fully through the glass of the attic for fear that she would be seen by someone down below.

Highlights of 2002

The Florida Holocaust Museum made a wonderful contribution to the understanding of Passover by publishing "Freedom Illuminated- The Haggadah-A Mirror of Jewish History-Its Agony and Triumph, edited by Herbert Wollowick. Museum Director, Stephen M. Goldman said, "The Passover is perhaps, the first recorded liberation and redemption for religious persecution...The Haggadah, the book used at the Passover supper, tells the story in excruciating detail. For over 4,000 years, the story remains unchanged and the dictate to retell that story in great detail "as if you yourself were there" remains in place." The story has not changed, but the style of telling has to reflect modern times. Herbert Wollowick said, "Freedom gave birth to Passover; and the Passover gave birth to freedom. The Passover Haggadah is a story of liberty, which has accompanied the Jewish people in all their wandering. Its content has been a source of hope and consolation. Throughout history, no other people have cast aside the sword and taken up the book in its stead! No other nation has devoted itself so completely to the book where the house of study became the house of life and the book a tree of life. It follows that the story of the "People of the Book," the Jewish people, can be told through a book. And of all Hebrew books, the Haggadah most closely reflects the story." Whereas, the Seder (order) is the

1946 Haggadah, printed by the Chief Rabbi's Emergency Council of London. Courtesy of Reva Kent.

festival and ritual meal for the telling of the story of the exodus, the Haggadah is the service book which provides the structure for the Seder.

Highlights of 2003

In July, the Florida Holocaust Museum received full accreditation from the American Association of Museums. Only 800 of the 16,000 museums in the United States have received this distinction. The AAM accreditation signifies excellence in museum administration and exhibition as well as collections management. The accrediting committee required evidence of informed decision making, wise resource allocation, planning, adherence to high standards and strict accountability to the public. At this time, the Florida Holocaust Museum is the only museum in the United States to focus on Holocaust related art and maintains a large permanent collection of Holocaust art. The Florida Holocaust Museum presented Coexistence, an international outdoor exhibition from the Museum on the Seam in Jerusalem, Israel. Several Florida cities, including St. Petersburg, Sarasota, and Boca Raton, participated.

Holocaust, genocide, human rights, and character education were presented to 4,000 more students than the 2002-2003 year.

Highlights of 2004

The Florida Holocaust Museum was visited by a record number of students. Groups came from all over Florida. They came from Suwanee County in the far north, Dade County in the Southeast, Duval County in the Northeast, Collier County in the Southwest, and Palm Beach County on the East Coast. Student groups also came from Georgia, North Carolina, and Alabama. The Teaching Trunks traveled to schools beyond Florida to California, Massachusetts,  New Mexico, New Jersey, Connecticut, Delaware, Idaho, South Carolina, Texas, Mississippi, Kentucky, North Carolina, New York, Pennsylvania, Michigan, and Maryland. In the Larry

Wasser Gallery, "Kaddish for the Children," by Alice Lok Cahana was exhibited. Alice's autobiographical works create a memoir of her experiences, a testament to those lost, and creates a vivid emotional and spiritual experience for the viewer. It is a memorial in prayer for Hungarian Jews who fell victim to the Holocaust.

In another exhibit, "Reservations: Rethinking of the Native American," the museum presented the narrative and art of American Indians because of the many issues raised concerning their demise and Human Rights violations. These issues included: killing members of the group; causing serious bodily or mental harm to members of the group; deliberately inflicting on the group conditions of life calculated to bring about its physical destruction in whole or in part; imposing measures intended to prevent births within the group; and forcibly transferring children of the group to another group. Once again, the museum was in the forefront of helping determine what groups in our society have suffered because of their race, religion or nationality. The museum received the "2004 Top Educational Institution," from the *Tampa Bay Magazine*.

Highlights of 2005

The Florida Holocaust Museum presented a major exhibition of Czechoslovakian native and Tampa artist and winter resident, William Pachner. His many landscapes comment on the people-made changes that take place over time. His work illustrates his artistic thought about the machines that led him to a new life, and his family and millions of others who were killed at the hands of the Nazis.

The Florida Holocaust Museum education staff consists of eight people with an additional seventeen people serving on the Teacher Advisory Board. The museum provides teacher training opportunities, literature based teaching trunks, summer institutes, field trips, and public programs. The Teachers Tribute 2005 was sponsored by the Florida Holocaust Museum, the Salvador Dali Museum, and the Fine Arts Museum. The topic for 2005 was "Integrating Art, History, and Culture."

CHAPTER 19

GULF COAST JEWISH FAMILY SERVICES

Jewish people in the United States have a long and proud history of taking care of the health and welfare of children and adults. In 1801, the first American Jewish orphan care society was established in Charleston, South Carolina.

In 1876, the Hebrew Orphan's Asylum was founded by the B'nai B'rith in Atlanta. In 1901, it changed its name to the Hebrew Orphans Home. From 1886 until 1930, the facility was the home to hundreds of Jewish children throughout the southeastern United States, including several children from Pinellas County. In 1948, the facility was renamed The Jewish Children's Service. In 1988, the name was changed to the Jewish Educational Loan Fund.

From 1928-1948, Jewish social services in Atlanta, as well as elsewhere, underwent a dramatic transformation. The general end of massive immigration, the rise of the Jewish middle class, the Great Depression, the New Deal, the Holocaust, the creation of Israel, and the development of a class of young dedicated Jewish leaders led to an increased role of the Jewish agencies in all facets of the lives of the individuals in need.

Meanwhile, in other big cities, from Philadelphia to New York, throughout the East Coast, and into the Far West, Jewish Family Services came into being to meet the needs of the local communities. For example, in Seattle, Washington the Jewish Family Service was founded in 1892. It started with thirty seven local volunteers and now has become an agency that has over 300 volunteers and ninty professional staff. There were specialized programs developed for seniors, children, adults with mental and developmental disabilities, refugees and immigrants, and families with limited income.

In Tampa, the Jewish Family Services was founded in 1954 and was housed at the Jewish Community Center. In 1973, the all volunteer organization decided it needed to hire professional social workers. Its first professional director came to the organization and the organization grew substantially.

In 1955, when the St. Petersburg Jewish Community Council officially approved the building of a Jewish Community Center, it stipulated that the director of the program would be a social worker. The thought was that the Jewish Community Center would provide various Jewish family support services to the community, including social welfare services.

Highlights of 1960

Apparently, social welfare activities were started informally at the Jewish Community Center by volunteers. It is assumed that these activities were then formalized in the Charter of the Jewish Community Center of St. Petersburg in 1961.

Highlights of 1961

On April 13, the Jewish Community Center of St. Petersburg, Florida (later the Jewish Community Center of Pinellas County) in Article II of the Articles of Incorporation, stated the purpose or purposes of the corporation as follows: " To further the welfare of the Jewish community; through the creation and the erection of the Jewish Community Center to house the philanthropic, social, cultural and educational programs of the Jewish Community, for the benefit of Jewish residents of Greater St. Petersburg and others who may wish to participate in its program...To conduct independently or in cooperation with the Jewish Community or its Council effective programs in social and welfare work...recreational activities and culture and educational programs..." The Gulf Coast Jewish Family Services continued operating under this portion of the charter of the Jewish Community Center of St. Petersburg until it was separately incorporated on July 2, 1974.

Since the Jewish Community Center was an arm of the St. Petersburg Jewish Community Council, it was effectively controlled by the St. Petersburg Jewish

Community Council. In turn, the Gulf Coast Jewish Family Services was also an arm of the St. Petersburg Jewish Community Council. The Gulf Coast Jewish Family Services received financial assistance from both the St. Petersburg Jewish Community Council and the Jewish Welfare Fund of Clearwater.

The predecessor of the current Gulf Coast Jewish Family Services was located in a converted house, at the Elbow Lane Jewish Community Center in St. Petersburg. Freddie Sohon was director of the program. Freddie and Sylvia Gail provided assistance in life management and educational services including: help with basic human needs; emergency financial aid; information, referral, and counseling; student loans; and monitoring isolated seniors who lacked adequate support. The program was supported by the St. Petersburg Jewish Community Council and later by the Jewish Federation of Pinellas County.

Ann Thal of the Tampa Jewish Family Services worked for a period of time with the Gulf Coast Jewish Family Services and helped merge the programs of Pinellas County and Hillsborough County. Sylvia Gail became the Director of the Gulf Coast Jewish Family Services in 1968 and continued in this position until 1978.

Highlights of 1969

On January 1, a larger and more sophisticated program of the Gulf Coast Jewish Family Services was established at the request of the Tampa, St. Petersburg, and Clearwater communities. The new organization was founded to better meet the needs of the communities in the area. Sarasota and Lakeland were invited to participate, but showed no interest.

Highlights of 1972

The Jewish Children's Service (JCS) of Atlanta, Georgia helped provide the seed money for the new program and therefore helped found the current Gulf Coast Jewish Family Services. In appreciation for this most generous gift, the Jewish people of Pinellas County sent a plaque to the Jewish Children's Service, formally the Hebrew Orphans Home of Atlanta.

The plaque read, "In appreciation to the Jewish Children's Service for assistance in establishing the Gulf Coast Jewish Family Service–Your financial and spiritual support in developing a program of child guidance and family counseling demonstrates one of the purist ideals of Judaism – St. Petersburg Jewish Community Council – Clearwater Jewish Welfare Fund – January 25, 1972."

The administrative budget was set at $16,000, with Tampa's contribution to be $4,500, St. Petersburg's contribution to be $2,500, and Clearwater's contribution to be $1,000. The Jewish Children's Service in the first-year contributed one half of the budget up to $8,000. In the second year, the JCS contributed one third of the budget up to $5,335. In the third year, the JCS contributed one fourth of the budget up to $4,000. At the end of a three-year period, the JCS reviewed the division of funds and the services which had been made available. The community agreed to offer the following programs: family counseling; marital counseling; parent-child relationship problems; services for disturbed children; vocational career counseling; evaluation of scholarship loans; services for the aged; and services connected to immigration. The JCS agreed to offer assistance to the agency in program and project establishment whenever necessary.

Highlights of 1974

On July 2, the Gulf Coast Jewish Family Services was incorporated. Its principal office was at 8167 Elbow Lane North, St. Petersburg. The object of the corporation was to provide professional casework counseling and social welfare service under Jewish auspices. It included the total program of a multi-function family service agency handling marital problems, parent-child relationship problems, individual adjustment problems, services to the aging, career counseling, and family life education programs. The officers of the corporation were: President, Alan R. Samuels; Vice-President, Philip Katz; Secretary, Mrs. Herman Zinober; Treasurer, Mrs. Carl Rosenfeld. The members of the Board of Directors were: Allen R. Samuels, Philip Katz, Mrs. Herman Zinober, Mrs. Carl Rosenfeld, Leonard Apter, Mrs. Sidney

Colen, Mr. Stanley Hunter, Mrs. Morris LeVine, Mr. Edward Rogall and Mrs. Edward Rogall.

Highlights of 1978

The Gulf Coast Jewish Family Services was tied to the Jewish Federation. All decisions of the Board of Directors, Gulf Coast Jewish Family Services, was forwarded from President Jack Levy to President Reva Kent of the Board of Directors, Jewish Federation of Pinellas County.

Sylvia Gail, Executive Director for the Gulf Coast Jewish Family Services, wrote to Michael Bernstein regarding the caseload and other agency information he had requested. Sally Siegel, Agency Social Worker, carried on the necessary activities of the social worker, as she had in the past, when Sylvia Gail was on vacation. This was a time of transition between the administration of Sylvia Gail and that of Michael Bernstein, who was hired to replace Sylvia Gail, who was retiring from her position as Executive Director. In the interim, Ron Weisinger, Executive Director of the Jewish Federation of Pinellas County also served as Executive Director of the Gulf Coast Jewish Family Services. Ron reported to the two Boards of Trustees that there was a large amount of cooperation and involvement by local rabbis who had been referring various cases to the Gulf Coast Jewish Family Services.

A new branch office of the Jewish Family Services was opened in November in Clearwater. The office space was made available by Charlie Rutenberg. Murry Goldblatt donated desks and chairs for the office. President Jack Levy informed the Board that under Michael Bernstein's leadership, the Agency was moving ahead in a number of directions. All board members were getting involved in helping to promote and improve the Agency. The Board set out to raise additional funds over and above that which was available to help carry out the many programs offered by a service agency to help the citizens of the community. A plaque was presented to Beverly Zelman and her husband for outstanding service to the community through the Gulf Coast Jewish Family Services.

The Dr. Sidney N. Trockey Educational Loan Fund was approved by Dr. Trockey's estate and accepted by the Board of the Agency.

Michael Bernstein

Michael Bernstein

Michael Bernstein became the agency's Director of Operations on August 15, 1978 and became Executive Director and President in March, 1979. Michael earned a Bachelor of Arts Degree in Psychology from Brooklyn College, Brooklyn New York, in 1973. He was involved in an independent study program in Psychology/Social Work at the University of Helsinki, Finland, 1974-1975. He earned a Master of Science in Social Work Degree in Psychiatric Social Work, University of Louisville, Kentucky in 1974. While completing his fieldwork requirements for the Master of Science in Social Work Degree, He attended the Advanced Institute for Analytical Psychotherapy in New York City. He received ACSW certification in 1976 and Florida Social Work Licensure in 1983.

From October, 1975-August, 1978, Michael was Director of Casework, Jewish Family and Counseling Services, Bayonne, New York. Beside a full caseload, he provided outreach and cooperation with various Jewish and public agencies. From May, 1976-May, 1977, he was Director, St. Timothy's House, Newark, New Jersey. From May, 1977-August, 1978, he was a full-time caseworker for the Jewish Family Services of Central New Jersey, Elizabeth, New Jersey.

Professionally, he has published or co-published eight articles in professional journals. Since 1987, he has given special testimony in front of various committees of the Florida Legislature, United States House of Representatives, and the United States Senate on thirteen separate occasions. Because of his wide-ranging knowledge and his success as a professional, as well as an administrator, he has given special presentations forty four times since 1984. These presentations have been given at local, state, national, and international programs throughout the world.

Michael Bernstein is currently a member of: American Society on Aging; Association of Jewish Family and Children's Services; Florida Advocates for Community Care for Disabled Adults; Florida Association of Jewish Family Agencies; Florida Council for Community Mental Health; Florida Council on Aging; Florida Families First; Jewish Social Service Professionals Association; Jewish Communal Services Association; National Council on Aging; and National Association of Social Workers.

Michael Bernstein's innovative and highly successful approach to caring for others has resulted in numerous special appointments by high-level governmental officials and elections to high offices by his peers, since 1984. Michael Bernstein was: appointed Member-at-Large to the Board of Directors of the Florida Council for Community Mental Health; appointed as Florida Mental Health Institute Advisory Member of the Statewide Mental Health Planning Committee; elected Chairman of the North/Central Florida Association of Jewish Family Services; appointed Chairman of the Florida Blue-Ribbon Task Force on the Mental Health Needs of the Elderly; elected Florida Chapter Representative to the International Board of Directors of IAPSRS; elected President Florida Chapter of International Association of Psychosocial Rehabilitation Services; appointed Legislative Liaison's to the Florida Council for Community Mental Health; elected to the AIDS Coalition Pinellas County Board of Directors; appointed to the Florida Statewide Aging and Adult Services Aging and Mental Health Task Force; appointed by the State Legislature to the Florida Statewide Community Care for Disabled Adults Workgroup; elected Chairman of the Steering Committee for Formation of a Local Center for Independent Living; appointed by Governor Chiles to the Department of Elder Affairs Reorganization Committee; appointed Co-Chairperson for the Florida Council for Community Mental Health Elderly Workgroup; appointed to the International Association of Psychosocial Rehabilitative Services Public Policy Committee; appointed to the Florida Council for Community Mental Health Governmental Relations Committee, and Medicaid Task Force; appointed by Governor Chiles to the State Advisory Council to Study Government Reorganization; elected

Founding Member and President of the North/Central Association of Jewish Family Service Agencies; consultant to University of South Florida/Florida Mental Health Institute; facilitator and evaluator of State Alcohol, Drug and Mental Health delivery system; elected to the Board of Directors of the National Association of Jewish Family and Children's Agencies; member, Task Force on Persons with Disabilities, Florida Developmental Disabilities Council; Appointed to the Executive Board of the National Association of Jewish Family and Children's Agencies; elected Founding President of the Florida Association of Jewish Family Agencies; elected President of Florida Families First; elected founding President of the Florida Advocates for Community Care for Disabled Adults; appointed to the Public Policy Committee of the National Practitioners Network for Fathers and Families; elected to the Executive Board of Jewish Communal Services Association; appointed to the Health Care and Aging Working Group of the United Jewish Communities; awarded Honorary Lifetime Membership on the Board of Directors of the National Association of Jewish Family and Children's Agencies; and appointed by Governor Jeb Bush to the newly-formed seventeen member Governor's Ex-Offender Task Force.

Michael Bernstein has had a tremendous impact on the growth of much-needed social services in Pinellas County, Florida, nationally, and internationally. His highly successful endeavors include: the growth of the Gulf Coast Jewish Family Services from a staff of two people to 565 people; the development of creative and innovative funding streams from all levels of government and foundations; the hosting of highly successful fund raisers for the Agency; the development of a national and international reputation for state-of-the-art programming for seriously and persistently mentally ill elders, as well as long-term residential treatment centers, therapeutic foster homes, psychiatric and mental health care for residents of nursing homes, and suicide prevention; the development of one of Florida's largest case management delivery systems; the development of national and international recognized services for victims of torture and genocide; the development of model mentoring programs for high risk young people; the privatization of children's protective services in Polk County and Pinellas County; the development and implementation of a fully automated client record and billing system.

Michael Bernstein has brought great honor to Pinellas County, the Jewish community, the State of Florida, and the Nation. Everyone shares in his letters of commendation from: President Ronald Reagan; President Bill Clinton; Vice President Al Gore; United States Senator Connie Mack; United States Senator and former Florida Governor Bob Graham; United States Senator Ted Kennedy; United States Senator John Heinz; Governor Lawton Chiles; Governor Bob Martinez; Congressman Bill Young; Neal Brown, Chief of Community Support Services, National Institute of Mental Health; Dr. Mary Harper, United States Department of Health and Human Services; Dr. Jack Habib, JDC-Brookdale Institute Gerontology and Human Development (Jerusalem); Diana Aviv, United Jewish Appeal Federations of North America; and Norman Levine, The Hebrew Immigrant Aid Society.

Highlights of 1979

Pasco and Sarasota Counties started pilot programs for the removal of the senior citizens from state institutions and the placement of them into group homes, or reuniting them with their families.

The Volunteer Committee of the Gulf Coast Jewish Family Services provided extensive free services to clients in the areas of employment, social needs, and professional medication needs. Steven Goodman of Medical Arts Pharmacy and Stan Michaels of Michael's Drug Store were very generous to senior citizens.

Laura Wax set up the Family-Life Education series, in conjunction with the Board of Rabbis at Congregation Beth Shalom of Clearwater. The Family Life Education Series focused on prevention before problems became serious issues. One of the topics of this series focused on the medical, legal, and social needs of the older Jewish adult. Many seniors are struck with severe boredom, isolation, and loneliness, which eventually leads to death. The utilization of support organizations, the Jewish Community Centers, and the synagogues help alleviate these problems.

The Agency received funding from the United Way and Pinellas County government to offer a new program, Emergency Homemaking Services. This program was for frail and isolated seniors. The Homemaking Service which had been given a grant of $12,000 from Pinellas County in October, 1978, was growing at a very rapid rate. The Homemaking Service was providing thirty percent of its assistance to non-Jewish people. To assist in meeting the growing caseload, Doris Meehan, a social work intern from St. Petersburg Junior College, was hired. In addition, interviews were held with Social Work Graduate interns from Florida State University.

The new Gulf Coast Jewish Family Services office in Clearwater became a reality. The Ladies Auxiliary of the Jewish War Veterans and Rabbi Jacob Luski helped provide forty single-parent families and elderly on fixed incomes with Passover Food Baskets. A Congregate Living Facility was proposed to the Department of Housing and Urban Development by the Agency.

Michael Bernstein, in his first annual Executive Directors Report at the first annual meeting said, "In reviewing our last year of basic services I am proud of the birth of many new programs. When I assumed my position with Gulf Coast Jewish Family Services, almost one year ago, I was reviewing a book on Jewish tradition from the Library of B'nai Israel which stated that the mitzvah of helping a fellow Jew suffering and in need, is as great in importance as any of the basic commandments. I am proud that through the help of each of you, GCJFS has fulfilled our basic commitments to provide such help...Not a single child in need of the camp program or class, or a senior or a family was turned away from the Jewish Community Center or synagogues because of an inability to pay. (The synagogues always provide free memberships and services including educational services for anyone unable to pay for them.) Often the question may arise, why the need for a Jewish Family Service. After all, we have County Welfare, a Community Mental Health Center. My response is summed up with keywords of: advocacy, accountability, and commitment, for Jews in desperate need. Most of you know my philosophy of not passing the buck when it comes to meeting a client's need. When a Jew in need, not covered by any insurance and hitting red tape from the bureaucracy, has need for medication, it has been provided by the Jewish community, both medication and medical care."

Annette Raymund, who provided part-time assistance with the needs of aged clients, was cited for her professional services in helping meet the needs previously identified. In addition, she had shown thoroughness, patience, knowledge and concern for her many clients that had been very successful in intervention. Her expertise in having worked with the State of Florida HRS program had proven invaluable in her special efforts to assist with nursing home and foster care placements.

There was an expansion of interest-free loans for college students from broken homes, or for emergency financial problems which had previously caused brilliant and vibrant students to drop out of school. These monies were made available through the Trokey Fund, along with the continuing assistance of the Atlanta Jewish Children's Service.

Charles Saltzman

Charles Saltzman moved to Dunedin from Chicago when he retired from the United States Postal Service. He attended the University of Chicago, where he was a member of Phi Beta Kappa. At age twenty four and preparing to graduate, he was hit by a truck and spent several years, trying to recover from the concussion and other problems that he had. His personal experience led him to be a huge supporter of the Gulf Coast Jewish Family Services. Over the years, he donated not only his time but also over one half million dollars to the organization. Board Chairman David Abelson announced that an annex to the building would be built and named in Charles' honor. Michael Bernstein said, "He

was a kind and generous man who tried to live a good life and never sought recognition for his good deeds." An important part of his life was to share his knowledge with others. He became a guest columnist for the St. Petersburg Times starting in 1980, at age seventy, and continued on for many years. He wrote three books of his essays and columns. Charles died at age ninety five on November 16, 2005. Charles will always be remembered for his generosity, his astute understanding of life, and his ability to help the current generation understand the significance of the past in order to improve the future.

Highlights of 1980

Michael Bernstein, in his annual report, said, "...In our review of the growth of programs and actions of our Jewish Family Services, we, as a Jewish community, have chosen to cling to the heart of humanitarian concern present in the roots of Judaism. We have joined together to meet the emergency needs of those suffering, to each "light our candle of giving and concern rather than to curse the darkness and despair." He said, "...Our agency is not a charitable institution designed to help just the poor or elderly. On the contrary, each client pays for the services according to what he/she can afford." Michael Bernstein also said, "...All of us can relate to the absolute importance of keeping our isolated Jewish elderly at home during a time of physical or emotional crisis, if at all possible. The choice of long-term institutional care is an ugly alternative that should be avoided. We provided approximately 2,000 hours of emergency care with cooking, shopping, cleaning, personal grooming, to keep elderly people functioning in their homes. The cases are usually catastrophic in nature. The stories are not pretty. Oftentimes the aged are suffering with tragic forms of cancer, amputation of limbs, crippling arthritis, broken bones, or emphysema. Such clients are assisted with survival needs until suitable placement or care programs are arranged for a long-term basis."

The City of St. Petersburg contributed funds to the Homemaker Services Program. The first pilot project in Florida, on removing seniors from institutions, was started. The Hacienda Home and Intermediate Group Home were established.

The Adopt-A-Grandchild program was first implemented. It was a way to rectify the problem of the lack of an extended family in a child's life. This provided the opportunity to be with a young child and to help this individual enjoy childhood. For the child, this was an opportunity to have a grandparent who would have the time and patience to be with him/her and to show him/her some of the necessary skills of life.

In December, Gulf Coast Jewish Family Services was awarded a grant to implement the Geriatric Residential Treatment System Program. The program was in response to the local and state needs for seniors who were not getting appropriate care in mental institutions. The GRTS program offered residential care, case management, coordination of financial needs, proper housing, and social services. It served to deinstitutionalize the mental hospital population.

Murray Jacobs, President, spent long hours of planning and consultation at the Jewish Family Services. He was there early in the morning and late at night to help develop quality programming, for fund raising efforts, or to complete any task. His motivation was simply that he cared about people and had the heart and conviction to spend his valuable free time trying to reduce the suffering of Jewish people in the community.

Highlights of 1981

The Agency budget grew from approximately $250,000 in 1980 to approximately $700,000 in 1981. This growth, which represents service dollars for the needy, is mostly credited to the unselfish and courageous individuals associated with the Board of Directors. Albert Einstein stated, "The genius of humanitarian leadership is based on the principal of courage to be involved and allow for the originality to explore new frontiers." Michael quoted Theodore Reich, famous theorist and therapist, "loving and caring, not education, is the material which changes dreams and visions of goodness

into reality." The staff had grown from three people in 1978 to sixty professionals plus numerous volunteers. Michael in his annual report said, "In conclusion, I wish to draw my attention to our President, Murray M. Jacobs. Murray, throughout Jewish history the ideal of helping someone in need is not merely a civic duty, but is a sacred duty. Your leadership, based on sound judgment, sharing of responsibility, and thousands of hours of personal time has served as an inspiration to us all."

The Agency received funding to provide in-home supportive services to low-income adults, eighteen to fifty nine years old, who had severe disabilities and needed assistance to remain independent. The program was considered to be a state model.

Highlights of 1982

Naomi Korn became the new Director of the Adopt-a-Grandchild Program. The program which started with fifty children in the first year, now had 390 children screened and thirty eight volunteers. A new home on 66th Street was set up to service fifteen people. At the Florida Association of Jewish Federations Workshop in Miami, the Gulf Coast Jewish Family Services was singled out as one the most effective and dynamic agencies in programming in the healthy use of public dollars. Quality assurance recommendations for GRTS (Geriatric Residential Treatment System) were developed by Dr. Lewis Belinson.

The requirements for the "Person of the Year Award" were established for general Board approval. They were as follows: every year the Gulf Coast Jewish Family Services would present the Person of the Year Award at their annual meeting; the criteria for the award would be that a person has contributed his/her service to the Gulf Coast Jewish Family Service, the Jewish community, and the community as a whole; nominations would be sought from the entire Jewish community; nominations would be sent in by a specified time with appropriate biographical background of the nominee; and the nominee will be chosen by the Committee based on the quality of the nominee's deeds.

Highlights of 1983

Murray Jacobs was chosen for the first "Person of the Year Award." Michael Bernstein was appointed to the Juvenile Welfare Board Committee to help seek a new Executive Director. Concerning the mission and direction of the Gulf Coast Jewish Family Services the following was reported: approximately seventy five percent of the thousand people helped in 1982 were Jewish; 175 people were helped in the GRTS Program; tuition loans were given to fifteen Jewish children; Federation provided an annual budget of $100,000, which helped forty to fifty Jewish people per week get assistance; many Jewish organizations worked with the Agency, such as Jewish War Veterans, Hadassah, Temple Beth-El, and Temple B'nai Israel; counseling is still the main part of the agency's programs; the link with the Jewish community is as strong as it has been in the Agency's twenty year history; the Homemaker and Adopt-a-Grandchild programs continue to be effective; the Agency, as a Jewish communal organization is commended nationally, as well as, locally for innovative services benefiting both the Jewish and general communities.

Highlights of 1984

Michael Bernstein reported that the elderly population over age seventy is projected to grow from two and one half million to seven million people in the next twenty years. He recommended that the movement toward holistic residential care for the frail elderly in the Jewish and general community continued to be a high priority of the Agency. The Agency was commended by the Florida Department of Health and Rehabilitative Services and the District Mental Health Board for its close, prompt, and attentive work in harmony with them. The Eckerd Foundation awarded the Agency a plaque for giving employment to handicapped people. The GHALP (Group Home Alternative Living Plan) was set up to serve 120 people in one building. Although medication was administered to the individuals, this was not a nursing home custodial program, but rather a rehabilitative facility offering physical medical therapy to those of all ages. Food that was being collected regularly by the Agency was distributed to the following organizations, with the stipulation that none of it could go to overhead expenses: Free Clinic; Catholic Services; Family Service Center; the Center against Spouse Abuse; Alternative Human Services; and the Salvation Army.

Highlights of 1985

Reva Kent, Past President of Federation, was introduced by Harry Green to the Board of the Gulf Coast Jewish Family Services as "Miss Pinellas County of Good Deeds" and "Ms. Federation." The GRTS program status was discussed. The current program consisted of a substantial amount of case management by professional social workers who: screened clients; recommended people movement within the program; helped decide client placement and discharge; assisted the client's guardians; acted as patient advocates; and screened 1,126 potential clients. The GRTS program had been providing service since 1980 to 237 clients. The current caseload of 111 people was a ninety percent utilization of facilities. The clients had been previously confined to psychiatric hospitals for a period of ten to forty five years. Part of the work of the case manager was also to work with people at risk in the community to avoid being placed in a psychiatric hospital.

Michael Bernstein was asked to serve on the Blue-Ribbon Task Force on behalf of the Florida Council for Community Mental Health on the needs of the elderly. Michael Bernstein trained the staff of the Sarasota Jewish Family Service. He donated the money given to him for this purpose, to the Gulf Coast Jewish Family Services. He also continued to give voluntary assistance to other Jewish agencies in the community, such as the Jewish Community Center of St. Petersburg and the Golda Meir Center in Clearwater. He chaired the Governor's Blue Ribbon Task Force on the care of the elderly and helped pass the Children's Mental Health Bill. Typical of what the clients of the Agency feel about the support that they receive is the following comment, "Gulf Coast Jewish Family Service is an Agency with a heart. Makes you feel like a human being. Everyone makes you feel like part of the family." The Agency was the only organization in the Pinellas County area to provide homemaker services to clients under the age of sixty. In the past ten months, service had been given to 359 people.

Highlights of 1986

A program was started to provide supportive psychiatric services to residents of nursing homes. This was the beginning of a formal mental health overlay to the agency. The North/Central Florida Association of Jewish Family Services was formed with Michael Bernstein as Chairman. He was also reelected as President of the Florida Chapter International Association of Psychosocial and Rehabilitative Services. The Executive Director of the Tampa Jewish Family Services came to the Gulf Coast Jewish Family Services for additional training. The Agency continued to apply for grants throughout the United States to improve the care of the residents of this area. The agency applied to the National Institute of Mental Health for special funding for its therapeutic foster home program.

The opening celebration of the Hacienda Home for Special Services was held on Friday, May 30. Governor Bob Graham especially came for this event. Other guest speakers included; Rabbi Stuart Berman, Congregation Beth Chai; Mayor Robert Prior, New Port Richey; Thomas "Chip" Wester, District Administrator of Health and Rehabilitative Services; Dr. Harvey Kaiser, Medical Society of Pasco County; Rev. George Hill, First United Methodist Church; and Mr. James B. Soble, Esq., President, Gulf Coast Jewish Family Services.

Highlights of 1987

The first Jewish refugee family was resettled in this area. Passover baskets were being collected for individuals who were in need. A plaque tribute read "Mental Health Services–Ronald Reagan." The Board approved the initiation of a request for certification by the Family Service Association of America and the Association of Jewish Family and Children's Services. The Homemaker Program has been a model for other programs around the state.

Highlights of 1988

The Surgeon General's Workshop on Health Promotion and Aging was held in March. Michael Bernstein was honored by the federal government to be selected to be one of sixteen people to be a member of the Mental Health Working Group. Their primary concern was the misperceptions and lack of information among public health and healthcare practitioners about mental health problems in later life. Many of the clinically significant changes in individuals had been dismissed as representing the typical mental or behavioral manifestations of normal aging. It was determined that early recognition of these problems could prevent excess patient disability and promote a higher level of health and social functioning, thereby reducing family stress. It was recognized that older persons with mental health, alcohol, and other drug problems typically had physical health problems as well. Although the Gulf Coast Jewish Family Services had always been involved with some form of assistance to the elderly with mental and emotional problems, Michael Bernstein's attendance at this workshop helped bring into focus the tremendous need of the elderly in the local area and served as a stimulant to secure funding for many new programs.

Highlights of 1989

An inter-generational program, Project Growing Together (now known as Adults Mentoring Children) was started. This program, funded by the Florida State Department of Health and Rehabilitative Services, is similar to Big Brothers-Big Sisters, but the children participating must be under HRS supervision because of family problems, such as a history of abuse. This program is also extremely good for senior citizens whose children have now gone on to other life situations. In 1999, Nancy Friedman, Director of Project Growing Together said, "Personally, I think it's important. The children are so disconnected in the foster care program. One of the goals is to provide stability as they move from home to home." Also implemented was Linking Lifetimes, another children's services program, where people thirty five years old and older helped mentor middle school children.

Highlights of 1990

The Florida Health and Rehabilitative Services provided separate funding to the Agency to prevent un-necessary hospital or nursing home placements for individuals with AIDS. A day treatment program was started for adults and seniors with mental illness. The program taught and strengthened the skills needed for independent living. A delegation from Hong Kong visited to observe and learn about the successful programs of the Gulf Coast Jewish Family Services. The volunteer program had grown so large it was now necessary to hire a Volunteer Coordinator. Funding was coming from numerous sources, because of the aggressive actions of the Agency to secure funds for a variety of human service projects.

Michael Bernstein was asked to coordinate the various advocacy groups representing the governor's office, the Health and Rehabilitative Services Program Office, the Area Agency on Aging, Ombudsman Council, Florida Association for Homes of the Aged, and the Florida Council for Community Mental Health. All of these organizations were trying to make a significant positive impact on the Mental Health and Aging Task Force and in trying to find solutions to the problems of the aged and the mentally ill. The Gulf Coast Jewish Family Services, through its Executive Director and with the help of dedicated professionals, resourceful and dedicated volunteers, and an excellent Board of Directors and officers, had moved the Pinellas County area programs into the future to become the standard by which other family service programs would be measured. Governor Chiles selected the Linking Lifetimes Program of the Gulf Coast Jewish Family Services to be one of twenty programs selected statewide to take part in the festivities of his inauguration.

Highlights of 1991

An alternative family program was started. Based upon the therapeutic foster home concept outlined by the National Institute of Mental Health, trained volunteer sponsors opened their homes to adults or seniors with mental illness and welcomed them into their families. The Therapeutic Foster Home project was designed to have a host family specially trained and given a stipend to care for one or two mentally ill clients in their homes. The original Geriatric Residential Treatment Systems Program was used to create the potential for independent living. However, due to the severity of some of the clients' mental health problems, this was not possible. Therefore, the Florida State Department of Health and Rehabilitative Services asked the Gulf Coast Jewish Family Services to institute the foster home model. The Governor's staff also asked the Agency to expand the local Mental Health Overlay Program to Hillsborough County. This program now served ten counties.

The Hacienda, a thirty seven room rehabilitation center for eighty nine mentally ill senior citizens was one of the geriatric residential treatment programs and related services provided by the Gulf Coast Jewish Family Services. Researchers from throughout the world, including Hong Kong and Australia, contacted Executive Director Mike Bernstein to learn how to start their own programs. The program was one the first of its kind in the United States. Bernstein said, " less than ten percent of the 700 residents that the Hacienda had treated had returned to institutions." Prior to 1979, it was thought that little if anything could be done for the mentally ill elderly. The individuals received very little care. The families could not handle the individuals, who were no longer welcome in the community because of their bizarre behavior. Many of the individuals who first came to the Hacienda had been living in state institutions for almost forty years and therefore had no knowledge of current circumstances, such as shopping malls and the growth of society and technology. Individuals living at the Hacienda typically lived there for about two years and then moved on to a group home or back to their family. Social workers and psychiatrists went weekly to the G. Pierce Wood State Mental Hospital in Arcadia, to determine if individuals could respond favorably to the Hacienda program. This program was an outgrowth of several Gulf Coast Jewish Family Services programs begun in 1986 to help seniors and their families cope with mental illness. The other mental health programs include: taking seniors out of state hospitals and putting them in nursing homes, and providing psychiatric services; using a geriatric mental health support team to counsel nursing home residents, evaluate them, and train staff members to better care for them; providing care giver training programs to teach family how to take care of the individual. Michael Bernstein proposed starting foster care programs for the mentally ill elderly and the creation of a mobile crisis team to provide emergency help to seniors when needed.

Michael Bernstein participated in and made presentations at the International Conference on Care for the Elderly in Hong Kong. There were over 400 participants from twenty different countries in attendance. The global issue is that the elderly are living longer and that over fifty percent of older parents live in institutions and not at home. The universal theme was to get people out of the large institutions and back into the local community. It was reported that the largest suicide rate was among the elderly, with depression and isolation being significant factors.

Highlights of 1992

The Family Service Planning Team started deliberations about future planning needs. A plaque tribute read, "Toby R. Bressler-A generous endowment." The State of Florida asked the agency to develop a proposal for a model group home to keep seniors out of hospitals. Dr. Belinson received a certificate from the American Psychiatric Association for over fifty years of dedicated service.

In the Alternative Family Program, sixteen people were taken from the State hospital and only one had to return. This truly shows the value of this program. One hundred and fifty people had been removed from state hospitals and put into nursing homes. The Florida State Department of Health and Rehabilitative Services requested that the Gulf Coast Jewish Family Service expand its Project Growing Together

services in Pasco County to become the Family Service Planning Team for Pasco County. The Agency was invited to present a workshop on building a community-based continuum for the seriously mentally ill at the Florida Council on Aging Statewide Conference. The Agency started an Emergency Alert Services program.

Michael Bernstein was appointed by the Governor to serve as Chairman of the Services Workshop of the Governor's Regional Task Force on Aging. The five priority issues identified by this work group were: mental health; long-term care; transportation; volunteer services; and protective services. All of these issues were currently being addressed in a highly successful manner by the Gulf Coast Jewish Family Services. These issues were also later addressed by the 1993 National White House Conference on Aging.

The Agency was awarded a grant to provide services, along with the University of South Florida, to reach out to mothers and infants with AIDS. The program was held at All Children's Hospital. The State of Florida had the second-highest incidence of pediatric AIDS in the United States. A report published by the National Association of Jewish Family and Children's Services stated that its top priority was to get involved with caring for persons with AIDS. At that time, there were 544 people infected with AIDS in Pinellas/Pasco Counties with fifty percent of these individuals with incomes under $6,000.

Michael Bernstein provided information on mental health programming to the Canadian Mental Health Association in Ontario. The request was sent to Michael because of the international recognition given to the Gulf Coast Jewish Family Services for its mental health programs. Mental health was not only a continuum from early age to old-age, but the programs used to help prevent and correct the problems were internationally considered to be both innovative and cost-effective.

Highlights of 1993

HIV housing was started, with government funding, to house low income individuals in twelve different site apartments located throughout Pinellas

County. A violence prevention school-based program was started in two middle schools in Pinellas County. The agency worked with students, staff, parents, and the community to reduce violence and drug use. The Juvenile Welfare Board provided funding. A plaque tribute read, "Pauline Cunx and David Hanken by Jules Hanken-a loving tribute." A plaque tribute read, "Alfred Schick, M.D.-In loving memory."

The Gulf Coast Jewish Family Services was involved in the Pew Initiative. Monies were made available by the Pew family, majority owners of the Sun Oil Company, to provide services to children and families through grassroots organizations. Florida was one of five states that was selected to receive funds. The goal of the initiative was to improve children's health, child development, and barriers to school development. A site was selected in the St. Petersburg, Gulfport area.

Michael Bernstein gave a presentation to over 500 individuals of twenty one countries in Singapore. After the presentation, he was asked by the Government of Taiwan to send a delegation at the expense of the Government of Taiwan to help train their personnel. He was also asked about the possibility of opening an office in the Government of Taiwan. Oriental cultures see caring for the elderly as an obligation and not a privilege. This made the success of the programs of the Gulf Coast Jewish Family Services, an important part of the modernization of services to the elderly in the Far East.

Florence Fayer received the Sound of Honor commendation. Sy Ripps received the United Way of Pinellas County commendation. The Agency had been invited to participate in a National Institute of Mental Health study. Enid Irving, National Council on Aging, England, representative of the government of Great Britain visited the Agency. She was so thoroughly impressed with the model programs of the Agency, that many were suggested for implementation in England. Special recognition was given to the new Geriatric Mobile Crisis Team. The Alternate Family Program was expanded. The Florida Attorney General's office provided a special grant for the Job-Training

Program. Jane Rutenberg committed herself to raise $50,000, to be matched by the Conn Memorial Foundation, for Project Growing Together. Brent and Debbie Sembler, Annette Raymund, and Jacqueline Jacobs were honored for their outstanding work with the Agency.

Highlights of 1994

A short-term, high-intensity parenting and home care skill-teaching program was started. The program was for parents who were at risk of having their children removed from their home. Services began originally in Pasco County. The Agency assumed ownership and management of the fourteen bed emergency homeless shelter for women and children in Pasco County. The face of the homeless had changed from a middle-aged scraggly looking man to a woman with a child. The shelter was opened to homeless women and their children for a thirty day period. The goals and needs of the women were determined, health-care, food stamps, and other necessities were arranged; help was provided to find a full-time job, and assistance was given to find a permanent residence for the woman and her children. Occasionally, the individuals had to stay longer then the thirty day period. This program was not meant for abusive situations and after the individual and children had been taken care of, they were referred to other agencies.

A Geriatric Crisis Response Team was formed to provide special intervention for elders at-risk of suicide. This innovative program in Pinellas and Pasco Counties furnishes a twenty four-hour in-home outreach and support system for older adults. A team of professional social workers work with the individual to help him/her cope with loss and to gain entrance to a support system of individuals, who will bring meaning back to his/her life. A plaque tribute read, "APA." (American Psychiatric Association)

Many dignitaries, over the years, came to visit the Hacienda Home. Senator Connie Mack came to the Hacienda Home and declared it to be "the epitome of what is right about America." He compared the work being done here to the absorption centers in Israel, where immigrants were given food, clothing, a place to sleep, and a place to learn how to acclimate themselves to a new environment.

The Agency had grown into an internationally respected provider of a diverse spectrum of community assistance with almost 500 professionals and community volunteers working together. This has occurred not only because of the skill of the staff, but also because the Gulf Coast Jewish Family Services continues to work actively with funding organizations, Jewish community organizations, educators, policy makers, professionals, members, and leaders of the community. The Agency has constantly worked at networking with others, providing consulting services, and sharing resources where possible. The Agency continues the 5000 year old tradition, spirit and culture of Jewish life and passes it on through helping families become and remain strong and through tightly woven Jewish communities. In a time that society is changing rapidly, the nuclear family no longer lives with an extended family, and individuals of all ages are subjected to new diseases and new stresses, the Jewish Family Services becomes a beacon of love, guidance, and assistance to all that need it.

Highlights of 1995

A seven-unit complex for low income disabled adults was built with HUD funding in New Port Richey. Case management services was started for adults and children with developmental disabilities in order to assist them in living within the community. A study conducted by HUD in Hillsborough County, indicated that there were 3,000 low-income residents, age seventy five or older, in need of subsidized housing in Tampa. The Gulf Coast Jewish Family Services worked with the Department of Housing and Urban Development (HUD) to help satisfy this need. In 1997, Myrtle Oaks Apartments, 100 small apartments for the elderly, was opened.

A plaque tribute read, "35th anniversary of agency-Bill Clinton." The Gulf Coast Jewish Family Services has provided central assistance to over 11,000 people in crisis-catastrophic physical, medical, psychological, or social situations. The Agency was rated among the top two in the

nation, among 140 Jewish Family Services agencies, as determined by an independent researcher. A plaque tribute read, "Thelma and Maurice Rothman-Generosity and humane efforts."

Dr. David A. Bernstein, Chairman of the Board of Directors said, "In the coming years we must face many critical challenges-shrinking public resources, increased competition for donations, and new reimbursement arrangements. As a practicing physician, I am keenly aware of how fragile human life really is. Catastrophic disabilities-whether due to disease or unfortunate accident-can strike down any one of us at any time, turning our world upside down in an instant. I'm also aware of the very vulnerable, our frail elders, children affected by AIDS, and elders who battled lifelong serious mental illness, all of whom need the compassion and support of our communities. This firsthand knowledge drives us to meet these challenges, and this commitment to those who need us is the bond that strengthens us all." Dr. Bernstein is a practicing physician of internal medicine and is medical director of two nursing homes. He lends an important and unique medical perspective to the Gulf Coast Jewish Family Services. His considerable expertise, his awards, honors, and achievements, including a Grass Foundation Neurobiology Fellowship, a Sigma Xi Biology Honorary, Recipient of the J. Garth Johnson Award, and his many published articles and special studies, make him an indispensable member of the Gulf Coast Jewish Family Services team. All his work for the agency has been done on a voluntary basis.

Highlights of 1996

A Non-Custodial Parent Employment Program was started to help unemployed and underemployed non-custodial parents establish consistent child-support payments by obtaining employment. Instead of putting someone in jail for non-support of children, the individual is ordered into the program by the county courts. The individuals are given assistance in finding jobs and must work and pay child support for at least six months before they are released from the program. Typically, the individuals want to work, but they have been unable to find jobs. The program also helps these individuals in the event of emergencies, which contributes to the individual's and children's welfare. From 1996- 1998, more than 6,200 parents received help finding a job, transportation, clothing, counseling, and whatever else was necessary to go back to work. By 2002, the program had collected in child support, $5,600,000 more than the annual $750,000 cost of the program. The program served an eight county area.

The Agency became the largest provider of in-home sexual abuse treatment services in Pinellas-Pasco Counties. It expanded job training and placement for low income elders to six counties becoming the largest provider in Florida funded by the Department of Elder Affairs. The Agency expanded the People Enrichment Program providing volunteer companions for frail and isolated Jewish elders. It initiated a religious acculturation program for Russian refugees. It expanded geriatric care management services to Hillsborough County. Brent and Debbie Sembler were honored for their support. Thelma and Maurice Rothman were honored at the Gulf Coast Jewish Family Services's annual spring Celebrity Celebration held at St. Petersburg's Museum of Fine Arts.

Highlights of 1997

The Agency provided critical assistance to over 11,000 children, adults and families, in the form of food, shelter, a chance at a new life of freedom, help for the seriously ill, income support for people with physical disabilities, guidance, counseling and compassion for abused children, and community-based support for elderly people with mental illness. It continued to enhance its already excellent service delivery system. Leonard Apter, who had passed away, was honored for his generous donation of time and his enthusiasm for the past thirty six years. He was one of the original board members of the agency.

Highlights of 1998

The Gulf Coast Jewish Family Services was awarded funds from the Hebrew Immigrant Aid Society (HIAS) to establish a regional Jewish Russian

resettlement program. A plaque tribute read, "CARF (Commission on Accreditation of Rehabilitation Facilities) Accreditation- Connie Mack."

Bill Thomas, Employment Specialist for New Directions, a program of the Gulf Coast Jewish Family Services, said, "In the long term, we see this program is helping people change careers if they can no longer do their previous line of work. We think this type of training will give them longevity of work that fits with their disabilities." This AIDS employment training program brought the enrolled clients back into the workplace. The individuals learn computer skills, résumé writing, interviewing techniques, and also received help in the decision concerning whether to disclose their HIV status.

Over 10,000 individuals and families were served by the Agency. The kosher food pantry distributed more than 650 pounds of food each month. The Agency provided consultation to improve services at other Jewish family agencies in Florida. The Agency received numerous commendations from national Jewish advocacy groups including the Council of Jewish Federations, and the National Association of Jewish Family and Children's Agencies. The Gulf Coast Jewish Family Services continued its belief in the Talmudic expression, "The past we inherit, the future we create." It's because of this type of mentality of all people related to the Gulf Coast Jewish Family Services, that the Agency continues to grow and perform exceptional services to both the Jewish and general communities.

Highlights of 1999

The Agency opened the five million seven hundred thousand dollar, US Department of Housing and Urban Development funded, ninety nine-unit Myrtle Oaks affordable housing project for the elderly. A new mentor program was established for Jewish youth. The Non-custodial Parent Employment Program was expanded to the surrounding region. Both the homeless shelter and the Hacienda home received funding for expansion and renovation.

The Agency received the first funding for a Holocaust Survivors Program for Pinellas, Pasco and Hillsborough counties.

The agency started a specialized computer training and job placement program for individuals with disabilities, including HIV/AIDS. The Jewish Family Services received federal government funding to provide mental health services to refugees for a five County area.

Highlights of 2000

A Jail Diversion Program was started to provide assessment and community placement for mentally ill, non-violent offenders in the Pinellas County Jail. The Florida Center for Survivors of Torture was started. This is a treatment center for refugees and others who have survived torture and extreme trauma. As part of a statewide privatization of child protective services, the Child Protection Services Agency of Florida provided funds to the Agency for in-home protective supervision for children referred by state protective service investigators. Services also included out-of-home and foster care supervision and adoption services for children ages six to eighteen. A plaque tribute read, "Ben Gelbart by June Baumgardner Gelbart–In loving memory." A plaque tribute read, "Annette Raymund– Recognition of commitment of serving." A plaque tribute read, "Non-custodial Parent and Employment Program–Al Gore."

The Agency had an eleven million dollar budget with 350 paid professional employees and hundreds of volunteers serving more than 15,000 people in nine counties. Volunteers provided more than 47,000 hours of service. The Gulf Coast Jewish Family Services scored the highest in excellence of care among 140 Jewish family services in the United States. The Agency's Noncustodial Parent Employment Program was highlighted by the White House in a national press conference in Washington DC. The Agency became the largest provider in the State of Florida for case management services to the developmentally disabled. Funding was received to start a community education program focusing on the prevention of medication mismanagement and alcohol abuse among the elderly. Funding was received to initiate a diversion program for mentally ill offenders in the Pinellas County Jail.

Highlights of 2001

The Asian Neighborhood Family Center, located at Bethel Lutheran Church, shares the site with the Southeast Asian Preschool. The Center was operated by the Gulf Coast Jewish Family Services. The center provided after school tutoring in English, GED classes, computer instruction, cultural awareness activities, parenting skills, and a variety of social services. The individuals became acclimated to their new environment and quickly became self-sufficient. (This is reminiscent of the old settlement houses in the Jewish neighborhoods of the big cities). The Juvenile Welfare Board, which had provided the original money for this program, decided that Gulf Coast could manage it effectively and efficiently.

The Florida Center for Survivors of Torture was established in partnership with international and national organizations, including Amnesty International, Harvard University, and treatment centers for victims of torture in San Francisco, New York, Chicago, Washington, DC, and Los Angeles. The center benefits thousands of victims of genocide and torture who now reside in the Hillsborough, Pinellas, and Pasco counties. Congressmen C. W. Bill Young and Senator Bob Graham, supported by Congressman Michael Bilirakis, Jim Davis, and Congresswoman Karen Thurman, helped secure the funding.

The Gulf Coast Jewish Family Services was given this innovative program because of its years of work with Holocaust survivors, and Jewish refugees from the former Soviet Union, who were victims of Nazi atrocities. The agency was serving over 200 people. The program consisted of a center for all individuals who had been tortured. The center provided medical and psychiatric intervention, plus legal support for those who had been horribly traumatized. This included treatment of 100 survivors from seventeen countries during the first year of operation. The center worked in partnership with the University of South Florida Medical School and School of Public Health. Beside treating individuals, the Center is used to teach health professionals how better to serve refugees. The United Nations High Commission on Human Rights also gave the

Gulf Coast Jewish Family Services a special grant for victims of torture and their families.

The Gulf Coast Jewish Family Services provided assistance to over 23,000 needy people in eleven counties. The Agency was given more than one million dollars to initiate the first phase of the privatization of state protective services supervision in Polk County for children at high risk of abuse and neglect. The Agency received funding to double the jail diversion program for the mentally ill in Pinellas County. It received local funding to expand the welfare- to- work program to Orange, Osceola, Manatee and Sarasota counties and received one million dollars to further expand the program in Hillsborough County. It collected and distributed four tons of food, which fed 383 hungry families.

Highlights of 2002

The Tampa AIDS Network merged with the Gulf Coast Jewish Family Services. Harvey Landress, Vice President for Planning for Gulf Coast Jewish Family Services, said "By bringing them together, it will have a better opportunity at the name recognition and the ability to compete for grants because of its regional nature. And it will be able to, in a clearer way, attract clients." Both organizations provide case management, housing vouchers, emergency rent, food and mental health counseling, as well as other services. Service was provided to over 16,000 people in HIV prevention programs. A plaque tribute read, "Herbert J. Frank by Miriam Frank-In loving memory."

The Gulf Coast Jewish Family Services operated with a fifteen million dollar budget, 450 paid employees, and 350 volunteers to provide service to 40,000 needy people in eleven counties. The volunteers contributed 41,000 hours of service. As part of the privatization of state child welfare services, the Agency provided more than two million dollars in services with forty five full-time staff providing supervision to children at risk of abuse and neglect in Polk, Highlands and Hardee Counties. The Agency collected and distributed six tons of food which fed 437 hungry families. It trained over 3,000 professional and para-professional staff in the Tampa Bay area

on working with survivors of torture in medical, psychological, educational, legal and social service agencies.

Highlights of 2003

The Constitution and By-Laws of Gulf Coast Jewish Family Services Incorporated were revised February 18, 2003. The agency's exceptional growth had resulted in a need to make changes.

The emergency homeless shelter of 1994 was enlarged to twenty four beds. The community education program, started in 2001, also began to provide short-term intervention for elders with alcohol and other drug problems in Pinellas County. The Gulf Coast Jewish Family Services was the co-lead agency for case managed services for the elderly, such as home health care, home delivered meals, etc. and monitoring of service. A geriatric residential treatment program was put into effect in Broward County. The intensive sixteen-bed residential program was for seriously mentally ill elders and offered psychiatric services, psycho-social rehabilitation, life skills training, and other supports. The Refugee Family Violence Intervention Program was started by the Agency, through funding by the federal government provided by Congressman Bill Young. Working with local and regional domestic violence shelters, resettlement agency staff, justice system personnel, immigration and family lawyers, health care professionals, educators, social service providers, faith-based community, and other similar groups, the program provided culturally sensitive treatment for refugee and immigrant victims of domestic violence. A plaque tribute read, "Ruth Dikman-Countless volunteer hours." A plaque tribute read, "Yitzhak Rabin Memorial Award-Florida Center for Survivors of Torture."

Highlights of 2004

The Hybrid Clubhouse Program was started to support mentally ill adults and elders through a combination of consumer-directed activities and part-time employment. Other new programs started included Woman-To- Woman, Tampa Bay Real Choice Partnership, Pinellas Pasco

Long-Term Care Partnership, Capable and Caring Parents. The Agency now provided services to twelve counties. Property was purchased to relocate the Hacienda Home residential treatment program for mentally ill older adults and elders. It was awarded four million three hundred thousand dollars by the Sarasota Family YMCA to provide supervision and case management for 1600 children at risk of abuse and neglect in Pinellas County. It provided new services including twelve therapeutic foster home beds, day treatment, psychiatric care, outreach and assessment for welfare recipients with mental health problems and supported employment, in Broward County. The agency collected and distributed over five tons of Kosher and other food which fed 429 hungry families.

A plaque was dedicated for the Annette Raymund Family Treatment Pavilion. It read, "In honor of leadership and support." A plaque was dedicated to Irving and Dorothy Cohen for "Generosity and devotion." A plaque tribute read, "Sharyn Wittner-Generosity and commitment to those in need." A plaque tribute read-, "Dr. and Mrs. Lofty Basta-Generosity and dedication." A plaque tribute read, "Charlotte Gunzburger-Institute for Holocaust Survivors and Other Victims of Genocide."

Highlights of 2005

Yad B'Yad (Hand in Hand) matches caring Jewish adults with Jewish children from single-parent homes to offer support and friendship. The People Enrichment Program utilizes trained volunteers to provide weekly visitations and friendship to isolated Jewish older people and to provide staff assistance performing a variety of needed tasks. Quality-of-life programs help the elderly and disabled persons. Care management services are used for all elderly persons whose families live elsewhere.

The Gulf Coast Jewish Family Services is only one of sixteen programs in the entire country that receives a grant from the United Nations and funding from Washington to establish its historic Center for Victims and Survivors of Torture and Genocide. The Gulf Coast Jewish Family Services and Emergency Food Pantry provide food in over forty programs to over 20,000 people. The Agency provides many people to people, programs including children's programs for high-risk children.

The current Gulf Coast Jewish Family Services programs help more than 20,000 people a year in forty different programs. It is supported by a budget of twenty three million eight hundred thousand dollars and carried out by 550 full and part-time employees providing services in twelve counties.

The Gulf Coast Jewish Family Services has built a tradition of working hand-in-hand with the community to help people make better lives for themselves. They've taken cries for help and recommendations from professionals and lay people and have turned them into action programs which have been cost-effective and innovative, have given immediate help to people in crisis situations, and have also created long-term solutions for these people. Their dedication to quality service is people-oriented and people driven. Their long-term goal is to help people make the most of their potential and to keep people at home and out of costly institutions, while enhancing each individual's innate sense of dignity and independence.

Once again, a single person, Michael Bernstein, was chosen by individuals with a vision for a better tomorrow for all people, despite their financial status or the severity of their problems. Michael Bernstein, in turn presented a vision of a super agency with a heart, that would provide programs to all people from newborn to old-age. He has worked with undue diligence to develop a large number of new programs, publicize them, help secure funds for them, and then help others improve their own communities at a local, state, national, and international level. However, whereas one person has a vision, it takes a community of caring people, professionals, volunteer professionals, and lay people to make the vision a reality. It is to the everlasting honor of thousands of individuals, who have served on Board's and Committees, as well as those who have made monetary contributions and/or contributed large numbers of hours of their personal time,

that the Gulf Coast Jewish Family Services
has been such an outstanding success, and
has truly carried out the ultimate mitzvah
of "Repairing the World."

CHAPTER 20

JEWISH COMMUNITY CENTERS

In 1874- 1875, the Young Men's Hebrew Associations in New York and Philadelphia became the prototypes for 120 more YMHA organizations established throughout the United States from 1875-1890. In the 20th century, many of these organizations evolved into Jewish Community Centers.

In 1884, Samuel A. Barnett, an Anglican clergyman, founded Toynbee Hall, the first settlement house in the slums of East London. The concept was to have university men settle in a working-class neighborhood where they could help relieve poverty and despair and also learn something about the real world and real people.

Several Americans were independently influenced by the English experiment. The American settlement movement diverged from the English one. Women became leaders. There was a greater interest in social research and reform. The American settlements helped a diverse ethnic population, usually immigrants. Most settlement workers started with clubs, classes, lectures, games. They taught English, helped people secure jobs, taught personal health, and pioneered the kindergarten movement.

In 1886, Stanton Coit founded Neighborhood Guild, the first American settlement house, on the lower east side of New York City. In 1889, Jane Addams and her Rockford College classmate, Ellen Starr, founded Hull-House on the west side of Chicago. A week earlier, a group of young college women, many of them graduates of Smith, opened the College Settlement in New York. In 1893, Lillian Wald, after she took care of a sick mother of one of the girls that she was teaching wrote, "Over broken asphalt, over dirty mattresses and heaps of refuse where I went...There were two rooms and the family of seven who not only lived here but shared their quarters with borders (I felt) ashamed of being a part of society that permitted such conditions to exist...What I had seen had shown me where my path lay...I rejoiced that I had a training in the care of the sick that in itself would give me an organic relationship to the neighborhood in which this awakening had come." She dedicated her life to helping others. She,

along with her friend Mary Brewster, established the Visiting Nurses Service. In 1895, Lillian Wald established the Henry Street Settlement.

In 1890, thirteen Jewish centers met in Cincinnati and founded the United YMHA of America, a forerunner of the National Jewish Welfare Board, now the Jewish Community Centers Association of North America. The Association's mission was described as follows: "Jews in North America are to a large extent educated, secure, and integrated into all levels of society. Our task is to nourish their commitment to a creative Jewish community, and to bring them, in everything we do, the fruits of the collective Jewish experience. The individual JCC is uniquely positioned to fulfill this challenging role."

In 1906, in Seattle, Washington, the Seattle Council of Jewish Women's Committee on Philanthropy rented the lower part of a home and started a settlement house. The programs of the settlement house included eight classrooms, social and club rooms, library, clinics, and other equipment. The sewing class of thirty young women in 1906 grew to a class of 142. There was an evening school to learn English. Hundreds of new immigrants received medical and employment assistance, legal services, social orientation, and education there. In 1916, the Settlement House was renamed The Education Center.

The Jewish Community Center's function changed over the years from Americanizing European Jews to its current purpose of helping make American Jews more Jewish. The Center helps bring the unaffiliated back into the mainstream of Jewish life. The Center is the setting for Jews to test, live, and incorporate Jewish values in the innumerable experiences which are its programs. It helps develop a sense of giving and a place for the development of Jewish leadership. The Center is for Jewish youth after school, Jewish adults after work, and for Jewish seniors during the entire day. Jewish singles have a safe and nice place to meet. It turns Jewish strangers into Jewish friends. Its exercise programs help develop the body and mind and helps protect against disease. Further, it reaches out to the handicapped, aged, those with emotional problems, and to all others who need to be able to relate to a family.

Jewish Community Center of Pinellas County–Highlights of 1961

On January 17, Sidney Colen purchased the land and buildings at 8167 Elbow Lane North in St. Petersburg and on May 3rd , assigned all rights, title, and interest in and to the property to the Jewish Community Center of St. Petersburg, Florida, Incorporated. The Jewish Community Center of St. Petersburg was incorporated on April 13.

In Article II of the original Articles of Incorporation, the purposes of the corporation were as follows:

"To further the welfare of the Jewish community; through the creation and the erection of a Jewish Community Center to house the philanthropic, social, cultural, and educational programs of the Jewish Community, for the benefit of Jewish residents of Greater St. Petersburg and others who may wish to participate in its program.

To solicit, collect, and otherwise raise money for philanthropic, social, cultural, and educational purposes in connection with the programs of the corporation, disburse and distribute the same and the income thereof for such purposes...

To conduct independently or in cooperation with the Jewish Community or its Council effective programs in social and welfare work, recreational activities and culture, and educational programs ...

To further the spirit of goodwill and understanding in the St. Petersburg area for Jewish members, residents and others desiring to participate in the activities of the Jewish Community Center."

The first officers of the corporation were: President, A. J. Pardoll; Treasurer, Sydney Colen; Secretary, Irving Sohon. There were

twenty members of the first Board of Directors.

Highlights of 1963

On April 16, the Jewish Community Center facility was destroyed by a suspicious fire. On June 7, "Operation..Up" was underway to raise $30,000 by June 30 to replace the existing burnt out building.

A Letter to the Editor of the St. Petersburg Times, published on Sunday, May 12, 1963, from a non-Jewish person reflected the majority feeling of sadness and anger concerning discriminatory practices and violent actions. It also discussed the need for brotherhood in the community. The letter writer said, "Editor, The Times: I stood in the charred ruins of what was once a modest but proud Community Center for the Jewish at 1703 Park St North (8155 Elbow Lane). The day was April 16, just a few hours after a fire had gutted the building and rendered it useless.

I reflected, too, and thought of the enormity of the miseries to which these courageous people have been subjected throughout the centuries. Lest we forget and to the world's everlasting disgrace, six million Jews (one out of every three in existence) were wantonly slaughtered during World War II while the people of other nations slammed the door on morality, sat idly back and did nothing.

Indignation overwhelmed me when I thought of the existence of the vicious anti-Semitic, witch-hunting meetings headed by depraved fanatics in downtown St. Petersburg. These weekly gatherings methodically and irresponsibly sow seeds of hatred and bigotry without any regard whatsoever for the truth, for human rights or for human dignity. No assembly with such unholy pursuits is more horrendous than this nor more threatening to the peace and security of every home in every community.

Hatred and ignorance are the ugly bed-mates that menace the security of every home and every life. Injustice to anyone, anywhere, is injustice to you, to me, to everyone and necessarily should be of deepest concern to us all.

Every moral and responsible person in St. Petersburg should consider the burning of the Jewish Community Center a personal loss. The damage, estimated between $60,000 and $70,000, is too much for the good members of this community center to withstand since the building was insured for only $20,000.

Here is a sacred opportunity to literally exercise our Christian precepts and prove beyond question that we are truly our "brothers keeper." Perhaps it could be for the atonement of the outrageous injustices we have allowed the Jews to suffer throughout the ages or the decadent restrictions and class barriers we have unwittingly and selfishly imposed. Whatever the motivation, we owe it to ourselves to re-establish our unity with God and the brotherhood of man.

From these ashes must come a new and better building. Let us be internationally acclaimed as the city that refused to allow prejudice to stand in our way. Let us contribute to the best of our ability to the reconstruction of a great new edifice that will stand resplendently as an inspiring monument to the rebirth of tolerance, justice and understanding the world over.

I made my check payable to the Jewish Community Center Building Fund."

As a result of this plea for brotherhood and compassion, by May 20, Ed Rogall said that letters containing cash were being mailed to the Center. He said that it was amazing to realize that many people, including many non-Jewish people had indicated that they wanted to replace the burned out structure.

Highlights of 1965

On August 8, 436 people attended the opening ceremonies of the Jewish Community Center. At 2 P.M., the ceremonies began with the Jewish War Veterans presenting the colors. An invocation was given followed by brief speeches. Mayor Herman W. Goldner of St. Petersburg presented the "Symbolic Key" to Ed Rogall, President of Jewish Community Council, who in turn presented the "Key" to Sidney Colen, newly elected President of the Jewish Community Center. Tween programs (seventh-ninth grade) were established including: knitting, tennis, dancing, photography, judo, and weight lifting. Dances and game nights were

made available. For the adults there were exercise classes, weight control classes, bridge classes, theater production classes, films, dancing, bridge, and Mahjong. They were special classes for children from kindergarten through grade six. A health club was planned for the facility.

The Jewish Community Center published its first newsletter, "Our Heritage" in September. President Sidney Colen announced that there were 160 families as members and each day new families were expressing interest. The membership goal was to have a minimum of 250 families. He said, "I personally am extremely encouraged by the progress and potential of the Center and its organization. We dedicated people partaking in the activities were sincerely interested in the center and its future. With a group such as this, the Center has a bright and glowing prospect, and the Jewish community in St. Petersburg is growing to maturity." The Executive Director was Mrs. Irving Sohon and the editor of the newsletter was Malcolm Berko.

Highlights of 1966

President Sidney Colen talked about the need for personal involvement in all facets of life. He said, "As we sew a seed, so we enjoy the fruits of a bountiful harvest. This is true in every line of human endeavor.

So many of us are reluctant to become personally involved in activities and feel that someone else should, and probably will, take the responsibility for the welfare of our brethren. Personal involvement is necessary and certainly a rewarding experience. Without personal involvement we, as individuals, are apt to stagnate and cease to grow morally and intellectually. For every bit of ourselves that we put out, we receive a like amount in return through personal growth. It is not enough to be just a "belonger." It is our responsibility to accept a challenge and see it through. As we enter an area of responsibility, we emerge at the other end a better and finer person. Not only our bodies need physical exercise, our minds need mental exercise. By denying an organization the benefit of your participation, you deny yourself the opportunity of growth.

In whatever area that your interests may lie, it will be good to become active and give of yourself. Participation and the challenge that it brings is important. Many times I've heard people say, "I am not capable of assuming this responsibility." This I do not believe, as we assume the responsibility and seriously except the challenge, we gain immeasurably as a result.

I am not suggesting that we become so embroiled as to adversely affect our personal life or our business life, but each has a place in a well-balanced personality and each is important to our moral and intellectual growth. Mental laziness seems to be a malady of our time. I assure you that we either go forward or backward but never stand still.

An organization or religious institution of your choice that does not have your participation does suffer as a result but I believe that the individual, in the long run, suffers even more. Benefits do accrue to the mentally alert who are sincere.

Become personally involved. It has many rewards." This personal involvement and thoughtful expression of what people should do to live a good life is something that Sidney Colen practices to this very day. Shalom Park in Ocala, Florida is Sidney's latest and probably greatest expression of his lifelong desire and commitment to help other people realize the best within themselves.

Highlights of 1973-1974

From November, 1973 until September, 1974 the St. Petersburg Jewish Community Demographic and Attitudinal Study was planned, conducted, analyzed, written-up, and submitted. The study raised many important issues for the St. Petersburg Jewish Community Council Board of Directors. It was used to evaluate the need for expanded Jewish Community Center services and facilities. The Council lacked demographic mobility and attitudinal information about the St. Petersburg Jewish community. Louis Solomon, Executive Director of the St. Petersburg Jewish Community Council and Mr. Julius Green, President were involved in the planning process. President Green selected Dr. Joel

Marantz to chair the project.

The study revealed the following results:
1. A total of 1,437 households were contacted by the project interviewers.
2. Data was acquired for 1,562 males and 1,852 females for a total of 3,414 people.
3. Only 3% of the total sample were pre-school children.
4. The 6-18 year-old age group accounted for 17.9% of the population studied.
5. The 19-39 year-old age group accounted for 16.8% of the population studied.
6. The 50 year- old and above age group accounted for almost 50% of the population studied.
7. Most head of households were in a 65 year-old and over category.
8. The retired category was approximately 50% of the occupational category.
9. The permanent residents of the community of St. Petersburg accounted for 97% of the individuals interviewed.
10. Of the individuals interviewed, 61.6% belong to synagogues. The project directors concluded from the use of statistical tests that membership in synagogues would be a good predictor for membership in the Jewish Community Center.
11. In response to the question whether a Jewish home for the aged should be established in St. Petersburg, 79.2% said yes.

Of the 1,736 Jewish households identified in St. Petersburg, 1,437 were successfully interviewed. Only 177 households refused to participate in the study. The authors of the study estimated that the Jewish population of St. Petersburg was 4,535 people and that the community was very stable in nature.

The role of a Jewish Community Center was to satisfy recreational, social, and cultural needs of the total Jewish community. However, in St. Petersburg at the time of the study, the concept of a social group work agency had not yet received universal acceptance. It was recommended to establish a committee to work with the Jewish Community Center Executive

Director and Board of Directors to utilize the data from the study to initiate additional programming that would meet the needs of the community. Because the community was likely to grow, it was recommended that a committee be appointed to discuss the establishment of a Jewish Day School, under the auspices of the St. Petersburg Jewish Community Council. Because of the large proportion of elderly people in the community, it was recommended that a committee explore the building of a Jewish home for the aged. Because of the high level of synagogue membership, it was recommended that a committee explore the possibility of bringing a kosher butcher shop to St. Petersburg.

Highlights of 1976

On May 12, the name was changed to Jewish Community Center of Pinellas County Incorporated. Article III of the Amendments to the Articles of Incorporation states, "This Corporation is organized for the following purposes:

To develop and conduct a comprehensive program of guided leisure time activities utilizing the skills of group work, informal education, and recreation, and aimed at helping individuals to achieve an affirmative identification with Jewish life, and a deep appreciation of their responsibilities as citizens of the United States.

To cooperate with other civic bodies in advancing the welfare of the entire community and furthering the democratic way of life..."

The officers of the Corporation were: President, Ben Bush; Vice President, Mrs. Irving Bernstein; Vice President, Dr. Joel Marantz; Vice President, Dr. Harold Seder; Treasurer, Meni Kanner; Secretary, Mrs. Barry Wax; Past-President, Mrs. Edwin Pearl; Executive Director, Melvin Caplan. There was to be a minimum of twenty five people serving as Directors of the Corporation.

Highlights of 1989

On May 1, Harry R. Rosen of Community Building Consultants submitted his, "Needs Assessment Study-the New Jewish Community Center of Pinellas County" to Joel Goetz, President, Jewish Community

Center, Walter Loebenberg, Chairman, Board of Governors, and Maurice Rothman, Chairman, Capital Campaign. The Executive Director of the Jewish Community Center Pinellas County was Fred Margolis.

From 1974-1989, a significant number of Jewish people had settled in Pinellas County, especially in the past ten years. More recently, younger people with children became the dominant group. Younger professionals and business people have now joined the retirees and have changed some of the needs of the Jewish community. Although the Jewish Community Center on Elbow Lane made a significant contribution to Jewish life in the southern portion of Pinellas County, its physical facilities had now become too limited to meet the emerging needs. The existing program had a strong Pre-School, a popular Day Camp, and a variety of activities for all people.

The study of the needs and desires of the Jewish population consisted of several techniques. A short survey form was mailed out to the entire 4,500 households in the Jewish Federation mailing list. Of this group, 368 households responded. In addition, there were eighteen parlor meetings with 140 people in attendance. A community parlor meeting was held along with a Sunday brunch. Over 300 people attended. Overall, 142 people who did not mail back their survey form filled out a four-page Focus Group Survey. There were a total of 510 responses from the Jewish community. However, the data collection was not uniform and therefore the final data might not be totally accurate. The survey responses came heavily from individuals fifty years old and over. This may also skew the data. Some general findings were:

1. Approximately 50% of the Jewish population had lived in Pinellas County over 10 years.
2. The Jewish people had high levels of college educated individuals, including 75% of the male respndents and 66% of the female respondents to the survey.
3. Synagogue membership included 65% of the respondents.
4. The Duhme Road Jewish Community Center location on Madeira Beach was

considered reasonably accessible to 74% of the respondents.

5. The people participating in the survey felt that the mission of the new Jewish Community Center was to provide a central meeting place for the Jewish community and to bring the Jewish community together.

New Jewish Community Center Campaign

By June 16, The Jewish Community Center of Pinellas County campaign had already raised four million dollars. There were two, one million dollar pledges, and one half million dollars was raised from the sale of the existing property on Elbow Lane. In addition, one million dollars was pledged by the Maimonides Committee, composed of Jewish doctors, dentists, and other health-care professionals from throughout Pinellas County. Dr. Bruce A. Epstein was Chairperson of this group. The money was to be used to build a state-of-the-art gymnasium and physical fitness facility. The Senior Friendship Club committed itself to raise two hundred and fifty thousand dollars. The public portion of the Campaign kicked off on September 18. The Campaign Chairman was Maurice A. Rothman. The Campaign Director was Jay Kaminsky.

Jay Kaminsky talked about the significance of a Jewish Community Center. He said, "...As a Jew, I empathize with the hardships that our forefathers have suffered. As a Jew, I know the road behind us has been difficult. As a Jew, I know that the future must be prepared for and planned thoroughly. All of us, as Jews, need to give that little extra. It is that little extra that will separate our JCC from the others in the country. It is our responsibility to create an environment that will ensure the continuance of Judaism. The vehicle in which we accomplish this task is up to you. The philosophy of a Jewish Community Center is "Community" as well as Jewish. Let us go forward, raise the funds not only to build but also to maintain. We built this Center not only for ourselves but for our children. We must encapsulate our beliefs and involve all who are in dire need of a quality Center and program. Let us look back on this magnificent undertaking" with the words of Judah the Macabe: "A great Miracle happened here." Jay was not only talking about a community center, but more importantly, a center for Jewish living. A place where so many recent arrivals, as well as, our longtime residents could join together in a large amount of healthy social activities.

The Duhme facility, the site of the former Kapok Tree Restaurant, was to be converted into a modern Jewish Community Center. It would have a day-care facility and offer expanded programs, including before-and after-school care for children and day care for toddlers. A health club and banquet hall would be built for 600 people. A swimming pool would be considered at a later date. The facility included 35,000 square feet of enclosed space and another 20,000 square feet open to the outside but covered with a roof.

Highlights of 1998

The Pinellas County Jewish Community Center sold its Dumhe facility and became a Jewish Community Center without walls. The cost of maintenance of the facility had become extraordinarily high.

Highlights of 2000

Camp Kadima was held at Admiral Farragut Academy. President Madeleine Liss said, "Admiral Farragut has beautiful facilities and a great location." In its heyday, Camp Kadima was held at the Jewish Community Center Facility on Elbow Lane.

Highlights of 2004

The Jewish Community Center once again came to life through the efforts of Jay Kaminsky and other interested board members. Jay and his father helped run the center and its programs for many years. The newly revived JCC initially had three main components: general programs for seniors, camp for children, and singles group for retired and semi-retired professionals. They opened an office in Phillip Benjamin Tower and worked with Temple Beth-El of St. Petersburg, Congregation Beth Sholom of Gulfport, and Congregation B'nai Israel of St. Petersburg. Camp Kadima's main facility will be at Temple Beth-El with, the campers using swimming facilities at nearby organizations.

Highlights of 2005

The Board consisting of Madelyn Liss, Ron Frankel, Jay Kaminsky, Susan Turner, Phil London, Emily Rotenberg, Harriet Lieberman, Joyce Seder, and Joel Goetz decided to make a change in the JCC mission statement. The statement follows: "Enriching and embracing their Jewish heritage through enhanced community, family, social, cultural, and recreational program."

A new program director, Jennifer Burnett, was hired to help rebuild the JCC of Pinellas County. She scheduled a community wide family event for October 30. Jennifer is a licensed clinical social worker in Florida. She earned her Master of Social Work Degree from the University of Central Florida in Orlando and holds a Bachelor's Degree in Psychology from the University of South Florida. She is responsible for supervising new and ongoing programs, while coordinating staff, budgeting, marketing, and public relations. Jennifer, a native of St. Petersburg, stressed the importance of creating a welcoming family environment at the JCC.

Golda Meir Center

The Golda Meir Center, a cultural, educational, and social activity Center, designed to enhance the quality of life for senior citizens in a Jewish atmosphere opened in 1980. It was based on the faith and vision of Isa and Charles Rutenberg and Reva and Marshall Kent. They saw the growing need in Clearwater for daily social activities at a Center for the senior population. The concept of the center would be non-residential, creative, educational, and always fun for its participants.

One evening, prior to 1980, the concept of the Golda Meir Center was developed at the home of Marshall and Reva Kent. Charlie Rutenberg and Marshall were sitting at the dining room table in Reva and Marshall's home when Charlie said to Marshall, "If I put up $250,000 will you match it?" Marshall asked, "What for?" Charlie proceeded to describe a day program for seniors which included a cultural lunch program. Marshall liked the concept and asked, "Where will it be located?" Charlie then described the Jupiter and Rainbow property, that had

just come on to the market. Being familiar with these buildings and the concept of a senior citizens center, Marshall agreed to contribute the $250,000 matching funds. The agreement between these outstanding citizens of our community was an answer to the fifth Commandment "Honor your father and your mother, that you may long endure on the land that the Lord your God has assigned to you."

While the building that was purchased was being renovated, Helene Rosenfeld served as Director of the kosher lunch program which was initiated and temporarily being served at Temple B'nai Israel. The Golda Meir Center began with one building and one program–a hot kosher lunch program. With the help of Neighborly Senior Services, the Golda Meir Center served its first kosher lunch to forty five seniors. The lunch was followed by a series of programs where individuals could participate. Senior citizens found a warm and friendly meeting place where they could meet friends, make new friends, and participate in a variety of programs and activities. At the first luncheon at the Golda Meir Center, Reva Kent, President of the Jewish Federation of Pinellas County and Charles Rutenberg were honored as special guests. There was never a charge for the lunch program. However, participants could donate money in an unmarked envelope.

The Board of Directors consisted of President, Charles Rutenberg; Vice President, Gerry Rubin; Treasurer, Herbert Schwartz; Secretary, Marshall Kent: Members Rabbi Arthur Baseman, Bruce Bokor, Salu Devnani, Stanley Igel, Reva Kent, and Pamela Rutenberg Tench. Marcia Pretekin Linder, MSW, was the Executive Director

Over the next several years, the Center housed the offices of the Jewish Federation of Pinellas County and Gulf Coast Jewish Family Services. A qualified professional staff, supported by 150 volunteers, helped the Center flourish. President Charles Rutenberg said, "Activities abound as hundreds of our seniors participate in over fifty different programs. Young seniors, older seniors, very old seniors, people from all walks of life: different religions, different geographic backgrounds; all joining together to learn to enjoy, to exchange memories and ideas; each living his or her own life to the fullest. Our seniors stay young by helping each other and helping the community. The motto of the Center is When You Are Here, You Are Never Old. A Center of interdependence, not of dependence, prevails as people do things together, learn together, help each other, and share the satisfaction of their accomplishments."

Since the Golda Meir Center was not supported by membership or dues, it relied solely on donations from the community. The concept of an Annual Senior Humanitarian Award Dinner was designed to honor an outstanding citizen of the local, state, national, or international community, while also acting as the primary fund raising tool of the organization. The "Humanitarian Dinner," the first of its kind in our community, brought nationally and internationally recognized personalities to speak to our local supporters.

Each year, an elegant dinner chaired by a devoted chairperson and a committee organized a gala function to celebrate and support the Golda Meir Center. The tradition of an annual report which highlighted the honoree's support of the senior population, as well as the highlights of the Golda Meir Center was adopted. The tradition continues to this day.

Highlights of 1983

The first Golda Meir Senior Humanitarian Award was given to Congressman and United States Senator Claude D. Pepper. Senator Pepper made a major impact on the Select Committee on Aging in the United States Senate. CIRFF (Charles and Isa Rutenberg Family Foundation) became a major contributor to the Golda Meir Center.

Highlights of 1984

Charles Rutenberg said, "The purpose of the Golda Meir Center is a simple one–to add joy to the years and years to the joy of life for all of our elders. Here at the Golda Meir Center a year round program of activities enhances the age old traditional Jewish commitment of care, affection, and responsibility for our elders."

The Second Annual Golda Meir Senior Humanitarian Award was presented to the former Governor of the State of Florida, Hon. Reubin Askew. As Governor, he brought Florida into the forefront as a national example for providing humane care for its elderly citizens. He created the Division of Aging, passed the Community Care for the Elderly Act, brought Florida into the Medicaid system, and sought additional tax relief and protection for senior residents. This legislation, served as a foundation for other legislation enabling senior citizens to receive humane care and to live independent existence whenever and wherever possible.

Highlights of 1985

The facilities at the Center were enlarged to allow for more activities. Charlie Rutenberg said," As Board members, we thank all of you for your continued support of the Center. We share with you the privilege of helping our elders in an atmosphere of happiness and comradeship, and the heritage of Jewish togetherness that is the Golda Meir Center." The Golda Meir Center provided medical screening, hot kosher lunches, a series of classes in conjunction with St. Petersburg Junior College, Yiddish and Hebrew classes, folk dancing, exercises designed for senior citizens, holiday parties, transportation, a travel club, films, readings, and entertainment in Yiddish, an outreach program in cooperation with Gulf Coast Jewish Family Services, group counseling for bereavement, financial and legal aid, a Friendship Club and a library with 3,000 volumes. The Adopt a Grandchild Program, through Gulf Coast Jewish Family Services, brought generations together.

Major financial support came from the Golden Founders and Founders of the Golda Meir Center. The Golden Founders were: Mr. and Mrs. Marshall Kent, Mr. and Mrs. Manuel Raimi, The Charles and Isa Rutenberg Family Foundation, Mr. and Mrs. Charles Rutenberg, Mr. Alan Rutenberg, Rabbi Laurie Rutenberg and Rabbi Gary Schoenberg, Mr. and Mrs. Marc Rutenberg, Mr. and Mrs. J. Roger Schaffer, and Mr. and Mrs. Theodore Tench. The Founders were: Mr. and Mrs. William Axelrod, Mr. and Mrs. Salu Devnani, Mr. and Mrs. Ralph Dutcher,

Mr. and Mrs. Frederick E. Fisher, Mr. and Mrs. Stanley Freifeld, Mr. and Mrs. Ben Gelbart, Dr. and Mrs. Lester Greenberg, Mr. and Mrs. Emanuel Gurin, Mr. and Mrs. Reuben Halprin, Mr. and Mrs. Eugene Heller, Mr. and Mrs. Stanley Igel, Mr. and Mrs. Fred Hemmer, Mr. and Mrs. Alfred Hoffman, Jr., Dr. and Mrs. Fred Lieberman, Mr. and Mrs. Elli M.A. Mills, Mr. and Mrs. William Morrison, Republic Bank, Mrs. Mary Rutenberg, Mr. and Mrs. Herbert Schwartz, Mr. and Mrs. Samuel Silberman, and Mr. and Mrs. Sigmund Strochlitz.

The third annual Golda Meir Senior Humanitarian Award honored Bill Gunter, Florida State Treasurer and Insurance Commissioner. He was a key leader and vocal supporter of the Florida Sunshine Law. He was considered one of the most ardent defenders of consumer interests. Through Florida's Outreach Program, he helped curtail the sale of inappropriate insurance policies to the elderly.

Highlights of 1986

The success of the Golda Meir Center brought forth a flurry of requests from people around the country inquiring how to start a Senior Citizens Center in their towns and cities. The Board's goal was to continue to enhance the fullness of life for each and every participant in the programs; to bring them enjoyment, good health, and fulfillment in their lives. More additions were made to the physical plant of the Center. Three buildings on Rainbow Drive were added to the Jupiter Street site. They were used as an Arts and Crafts Center, The Harry and Julia Schwartz Life Extension Center, and facilities for the Jewish Federation of Pinellas County. Renovations to the existing classrooms enabled the Center to have more programs going on at the same time. The head librarian, Bernard Panush, and his large staff of fellow volunteers, helped make the expanded library available to all people.

The recipient of the Fourth Annual Golda Meir Senior Humanitarian Award was Florida Governor Bob Graham. Governor Graham was a pioneer in improving education, environmental protection, and helping elderly Floridians remain self sufficient and productive.

Highlights of 1987

President Charlie Rutenberg reported that this year had been the most important ever. The programs and the staff had expanded. Financial support from the community had increased sufficiently to cover all areas of expense. Over 400 seniors were enjoying the facility and the programs. They shared their lives, loves, and special joys in a place designed especially for them. The kosher lunches were being provided for one hundred people by Neighborly Senior Services. A three week trip to Israel was sponsored by the Center. Curt Mayer, a participant on the trip, said, "It was more than a trip, it was a memory for a lifetime." More than 150 volunteers were involved at the Center.

The Fifth Annual Golda Meir Senior Humanitarian Award was given to Nobel Laureate, Elie Wiesel, winner of the 1986 Nobel Peace Prize. A survivor of Auschwitz and Buchenwald death camps, he wrote over thirty books and numerous plays, essays, and short stories to tell the world the story of the Holocaust.

Highlights of 1988

President Charlie Rutenberg said, "Like an ever growing oak tree, expanding its roots and branches, the Golda Meir Center this year marks yet another milestone in its successful history. I am very proud to announce the opening of the Harry and Julia Schwartz Life Extension Center, the first comprehensive physical fitness center designed specifically for senior citizens. The Life Extension Center is the latest jewel in our crown of dedication to our seniors." More than 500 seniors visited the Golda Meir Center on a regular basis to share a common goal; a goal of independence and personal fulfillment.

The Sixth Annual Golda Meir Senior Humanitarian Award was presented to Theodore Bickel. Mr. Bickel was a world renowned actor, folk singer, and Jewish activist. He was Senior Vice President of the American Jewish Congress and Chairman of the Governing Council of the American Jewish Congress.

Highlights of 1989

The Life Extension Center at the Center served 150 vital members with an average age of seventy two years. The facilities were completely redecorated. The Golda Meir Center was supported totally by the generosity of private individuals and businesses within the community. Charlie Rutenberg agreed with the philosophy that, "People who learned: create and enjoy. Participants at the Center were overheard to say, "The Golda Meir Center has opened a new world for us that would otherwise be quite lonely and dreary. It is a place where one can exercise not only the body, but also the mind." "The Center has enhanced my life not only socially and spiritually, but religiously as well. Our Friday noon Shabbat services are so beautiful and impressive I can't stop the goose bumps that I experience."

The recipient of the Seventh Annual Senior Humanitarian Award was Senator Carl Levin of Michigan. Senator Levin believed that government could and should play a role in helping people lead a better life by promoting social progress in the United States and abroad. Senator Levin was recognized for his commitment to civil and human rights by being named the first recipient to the Alexander Solzhenitsyn Award presented by Christian Solidarity International and the Herbert H. Lehman Ethics Medal presented by the Jewish Theological Seminary of America.

Highlights of 1990

The Golda Meir Center continued to flourish with many programs and activities.

The Eighth Annual Golda Meir Senior Humanitarian Award honored Frederick E. Fisher. In 1986, Mr. Fisher made the single largest gift to the University of Florida of six and one half million dollars for the Fisher School of Accounting at the College of Business Administration. He has been a supporter of the Long Center, St. Paul's Episcopal School, Florida Geriatric Research Foundation, the Community Service Foundation, and a staunch and loyal supporter of the Golda Meir Center.

Highlights of 1991

The Golda Meir Center, true to its original financial philosophy, continued to offer all services at no charge or for a minimal fee. The Center had become a vital part of the lives of its participants. Feelings of loneliness, boredom, uselessness, and stagnation vanished as seniors entered the doors of their home away from home. Stimulating lectures, seminars, and workshops provided information, education, and entertainment to the interested audience.

The Ninth Annual Golda Meir Senior Humanitarian Award was presented to Mr. Fred Buchholtz, the Executive Director of Neighborly Senior Services, one of the largest and most comprehensive social services agencies serving the elderly in the country.

Highlights of 1992

The Golda Meir Center continued to create an atmosphere where every senior citizen was able to enhance his or her worth, while engaging in activities that brought self satisfaction as well as rewards to others. "Our Board of Directors recognizes and understands the needs of seniors for normalcy–for independence rather than a step toward institutions." stated Sue Heyman, Executive Director. A new building was acquired allowing for "Goldie's Attic," a thrift shop. The opening was celebrated by Clearwater Mayor Rita Garvey. "Evening Magic," a fun filled fund-raiser, was supported by Jacobson's, local restaurants and businesses, other non profit agencies, the local media, and the community at large. The Passover Seder drew hundreds of people. The Golda Meir Center had become a major force for promoting the health and welfare of older people in the community. The Life Extension Fitness Center was chosen to be a part of a PBS documentary scheduled for worldwide broadcast in 1993. The senior adults who strengthened their bodies and their minds helped empower their lives and became models of aging for senior populations everywhere.

The Tenth Annual Golda Meir Senior Humanitarian award was received by Art Linkletter and Dr. William Hale. Mr. Linkletter, a television and radio star, was honored for his career in working for the improvement of the lives of people and for his 1989 bestseller entitled "Old Age Is Not For Sissies."

Dr. William Hale was a nationally known physician, community leader, and geriatric researcher. He started the longest running epidemiological study of the aged, the Florida Geriatric Research Program, which has been merged with the Morton Plant Health system. The Florida Geriatric Research Program became one of the largest data bases in the world about the elderly and is now known as the William E. Hale Geriatric Center.

Highlights of 1993

Charlie Rutenberg said that, "The place called the Golda Meir Center succeeded in Clearwater because the people of Clearwater wanted to create it and make it happen. It stayed alive and grew because of the extraordinary Board of Directors, the ten outstanding local, state, national, and world leaders who were honored as the Golda Meir Center's Senior Humanitarians, the Founders and Golden Founders who helped build the financial base, and the community that supported it. All of these people, the staff, volunteers, and the hundreds of local senior citizens who have enjoyed the facilities have made the Center into a living organism that represents the essence of goodness of the Jewish community." The Annual Report in 1993 was dedicated to the memory of Harold B. Siegel in deep appreciation for his generous financial support of the Center and his leadership contributions as a member of the Board of Directors.

The Eleventh Annual Senior Humanitarian Award was given to Major General Uzi Narkis. He was the only man who liberated Jerusalem on two separate occasions. He spent ten years as Director of the World Zionist Organization Information Department. He headed the world wide campaign to rescind the United Nations resolution equating Zionism with racism.

Highlights of 1994/1995

Charles Rutenberg talked about change being as inevitable as the cycle of night and day. Senior social services continued to grow at the Golda Meir Center to meet the ever growing needs of the community. The buildings being used were now at least fifty years old and had outlived their usefulness. The time had come for a new home and the most effective way that this could be achieved was to join with the Marshall and Reva Kent Jewish Center and build a major intergenerational Center known as the Golda Meir/Kent Jewish Center. The major additions to the Kent Center were underway. The new and renovated building would provide new, as well as updated facilities, for all the Golda Meir Center activities, a new preschool wing, new workout rooms, a library, lounges, offices and a kitchen.

Herb Cohen, Executive Director of the new Golda Meir/Kent Jewish Center, talked about the transition which would occur in the near future when the two Centers merged. He said that the Golda Meir Center would be geared toward individuals who have time to develop and expand the second half of their lives. All existing programming would continue and new programming would come about as the needs and interests developed. Merging the two Centers would strengthen each one of them.

The Twelfth Annual Golda Meir Senior Humanitarian Award was presented to Norman H. Lipoff. Mr. Lipoff, a significant leader of the Jewish world, chaired the Jewish Appeal and served as President of the Greater Miami Jewish Federation. He was a member of the Executive Board of the Jewish Agency of the State of Israel and National Chairman of the United Israel Appeal among other positions

The Marshall and Reva Kent Jewish Community Center

In 1963–1964, Marshall and Reva Kent started their quest toward providing a better and more rounded life for all children, when they selected the Hadassah Camp Judeae in Hendersonville, North Carolina, for their children's summer vacation. Reva, at that time, was President of the Clearwater chapter of Hadassah, where she learned about Camp Judeae. Marshall and Reva traveled to Camp Judeae to evaluate its facilities and programs. They saw an opportunity for their sons, Stan and Larry, to have a fun filled summer while developing character through self-knowledge, awareness, and a wonderful Jewish cultural experience. The two boys were immersed in Jewish American life, history, traditions, and family, while exploring the beauty and serenity of the Blue Ridge Mountains and of the total outdoor environment. They came back home more mature, more knowledgeable, and better able to cope with the reality of growing up and becoming successful, productive members of society. Marshall and Reva were so thrilled with the experience their sons had just had, that they wanted all Jewish children to share in this type of experience in the future.

In the 1950s, Camp Judeae started as a two-week program at Camp Blue Star. In 1961, Camp Judeae acquired its own land in Hendersonville, North Carolina. For a short time, Camp Judeae was owned jointly by the Zionist Organization of America and Hadassah. Today, Camp Judeae is completely sponsored by Hadassah and is part of the nationwide Zionist youth movement. Camp Judeae has carried on the vision and mission of Herman Popkin.

Camp Blue Star was conceived in 1948 by Herman Popkin and his brothers, Harry and Ben. Herman had a vision of a child-centered world, where children would be free to grow and to try different skills without being judged for success or failure, while quietly observing Jewish values. Camp was meant to be a place of love, joy, laughter, personal growth, and living Judaism. Miles E. Cutler, former Camp Blue Star Program Director, in his eulogy at the Herman Popkin Memorial said, "Everyone who knew Herman Popkin came away a better person. Psalm 24 states, "Who will go up to the mountain of the Lord, and who will stand in his holy place? He who has clean hands and a pure heart...He who is without vanity and who has not acted deceitfully." Herman Popkin has gone up to the mountain of the Lord. I know in my heart that Herman Popkin is standing in His holy place. Rest in peace Herman – we'll miss you dearly."

From the very beginning of the boys' camp experience, Marshall and Reva became deeply involved with the campand

camp programming. They served for five years on the Camp Committee, an advisory group to the management and staff of the camp. When Camp Judeae was faced with a highly critical problem because of overflowing sewage, Marshall provided $18,000 to the camp to put in a completely new septic system. Marshall and Reva, by word and deed, had already started the process of making this world a better place for children.

In the 1970s, Marshall and Reva had a dream–a dream to one day convert the summer camp experience into an everyday experience for children in North Pinellas County. Their dream was to create a family experience and a family environment where children, and then later people of all ages could partake of high quality, fun filled and educational programs to enhance their lives and their Jewish identity. The children would be challenged in a positive manner to develop and expand their skills and their knowledge while enjoying the social interaction with children of their own age and people of all ages. Marshall and Reva's message on a daily basis, built upon the message of Herman Popkin on a summer basis, "Help young people achieve success and through success achieve happiness." We might add to that statement that Marshall and Reva Kent, over a period of years, gave millions of dollars, but more importantly gave willingly of themselves to help all people achieve happiness. As Herman Popkin has gone up to the mountain of the Lord, so has Marshall Kent. At some date in the distant future, Reva will join Marshall and Herman there. The goodness of people is never measured by their financial situation or the amount of money they give to others. The goodness of these people is found in the sweetness of their heart and their willingness to make life better for others.

Highlights of 1979

As a result of this dream, on April 11, the Articles of Incorporation for the Marshall and Reva Kent Jewish Center, Inc. were filed with the State of Florida. The purpose of the corporation was primarily to acquire and maintain buildings for a community center to serve the Pinellas county community. The Board of Directors of this organization included Elli M.A. Mills, Charles Rutenberg, and Reva Kent. The officers were: President, Elli M.A. Mills; Vice President, Reva Kent; Treasurer, Charles Rutenberg; Secretary, Bruce Bokor.

Subsequently, Marshall and Reva Kent donated a beautiful eleven acre wooded tract of land to the Jewish Federation of Pinellas County to be used for the construction of a Jewish Community Center. This was a continuation of their dream to make facilities available to young people in a Jewish setting; to bring recreation, health, and a spirit of independent development to their lives.

Highlights of 1986

The Federation-Kent Holding Corporation was formed for the purpose of ownership of real property and/or personal property to carry out the purposes of the Jewish Federation of Pinellas County. The Directors of the Corporation were Stanley Newmark, Bruce Bokor and Paul Levine. The officers were; President, Stanley Newmark; Vice President, Paul Levine; Secretary, Bruce Bokor; and Treasurer, Sidney Werner.

The land was now available for the Marshall and Reva Kent Jewish Center to become a reality. Charlie Rutenberg met with Stanley Newmark, then President of the Jewish Federation of Pinellas County and asked him to assume the role of President of the Marshall and Reva Kent Jewish Center, and, to organize the board and help set up the fund-raising effort. A preschool was started on the property with buildings donated from a building site. Karen Zwerling was the first Preschool Director.

From 1987-1990, the Center functioned primarily as a preschool. By 1990, the buildings housing a Junior Olympic swim pool, a kitchen (generously donated by June Baumgardner Gelbart), meeting rooms, and a library were erected on the site.

Highlights of 1990

The Kent Jewish Community Center News reported activities at the Center. They included water aerobics, swimming lessons, a preschool, aerobic exercise, infant care programs, family canoe trips, tennis classes, the Freilich social club, which was a monthly dinner and dance program for seniors, and a summer day camp. Ed Basin, Executive Director of the Center, proudly spoke of all the activities that were going on at the Center. The Center, in its fullest sense, became a place where Jews of all persuasions could come together for a wide variety of purposes. The intention was to provide a multitude of recreational, cultural, and educational programs for people of all ages.

In 1990/91, the President of the Board of Directors was Jackee Meddin. Hans Krieger received the Volunteer of the Year Award; Mike Sobel, Jeff Ulm, and Steve Grant received the President's Award. A Rosh Hashanah dinner, which was homemade, was held for Jewish children and adults. Transportation was made available to senior adults. A community health fair and health screening program were held at the Center, A book fair and Chanukah bazaar were enjoyed by all. There was also an exhibit of the art work of Mordechai Rosenstein.

Highlights of 1991

The Marshall and Reva Kent Jewish Center and the Golda Meir Center agreed to offer reciprocal services to senior adults. The Kent Center offered new programs in tax free investing, fixed income investing, a smoking awareness clinic, a stress management seminar, fitness evaluations, movie marathon, and a coed softball league. A Women's Friendship Club, Retired Men's Club, and Couples Club were started at the Center. A joint Seder was held for the preschool children and the senior adults.

The Kent Jewish Center Day Camp was an eight week summer experience offered in two four week sessions for children aged two through the eighth grade. The camp was located on the eleven acre site and utilized all of the facilities of the Center. A variety of activities was planned for each day, which included swimming, arts and crafts, music, drama, sports, games, trips, and a variety of other camp experiences. Herb Cohen became the new Executive Director.

The Third Annual New Year's Dinner Dance honored Marshall Kent. Reva wrote, "In tribute to the memory of Marshall Kent who dreamed of a Center to meet the cultural, educational, recreational, and

The aquatics center.

Marshall and Reva Kent Jewish Center.

social needs of the Jewish community. Lovingly, Reva."

Highlights of 1992

The Jewish Center and Kiwanis of Dunedin presented the Second Annual Children's Health, Fitness, and Safety Fair. A new dance floor was purchased. Joy Katzen Guthrie gave a concert entitled, "Jewish Music, Past and Present," Cantor Joanna Bickhardt of Congregation Beth Shalom of Clearwater and Cantor Vikki Silverman of Beth Am in Tampa presented "An Evening of Israeli Folk and Modern Hasidic and Much More!" The Center started a series of Sunday children's programs.

The summer camp program was highlighted by overnight camping experiences, coordinated late nights, baseball games, horseback riding and hay rides, in addition to many other activities. The campers also participated in two major tzedakah programs. The first project was to fill the pantry of Gulf Coast Jewish Family Services with canned goods while the second project was to raise $400.00 for Operation Exodus, a humanitarian effort directed primarily toward Soviet Jewry and to help the Soviet Jews become citizens of Israel.

David Abelson.

Highlights of 1993

David Abelson was President of the Board of Directors. The First Annual Tribute Dinner was held in May. Reva Kent was the honoree. Isa and Charlie Rutenberg wrote, "Reva, for more than four decades we have worked together, had fun together, traveled together, shared dreams and sorrows together as we have enjoyed a special relationship of friendship and love. Tonight we join with the entire community to honor you for your extraordinary contributions in every aspect of Jewish life. With love and affection, Isa and Charlie Rutenberg."

Award given Reva Kent, 1993

Logo for the Golda Meier/ Kent Jewish Center. Created 1996.

Highlights of 1994

Jan Orwick, a certified Master Instructor with Infant Swimming Research, provided swimming instruction to infants at the pool at the Kent Center. This increased the usefulness of the center's programs.

Highlights of 1995

To further strengthen the presence of the Jewish people of Pinellas County, the Golda Meir Center and the Marshall and Reva Kent Jewish Center merged to become the Golda Meir/Kent Jewish Center, an intergenerational Jewish Community Center. It offered programs to the very young and the very old, men and women, thinkers and doers, the physically fit and the physically challenged. The next phase of the newly formed Center was to include permanent facilities for the preschool, a new library, a senior lounge, classrooms, and activity areas. For his loyalty and dedication to the Centers, Charlie Rutenberg was named Lifetime Honorary Chairman.

At the Thirteenth Annual Golda Meir/ Kent Jewish Center Humanitarian Award Dinner, there was a special memorial for Yitzhak Rabin The recipient of the 1995 Humanitarian Award was Charles Rutenberg, a major philanthropist and civic activist.

Highlights of 1996

Construction of the Reuben Rutenberg Library and the Lois V. Silberman Senior Lounge, presented by Samuel "Buddy" Silberman in honor of his wife, were underway. The Ahava, meaning Love, was adopted to be used together with the menorah with the dancing children as the logo for the Golda Meir/Kent Jewish Center.

The Fourteenth Annual Golda Meir/ Kent Jewish Center Humanitarian Award was given to Samuel "Buddy" Silberman. He served as President of the New York Federation of Philanthropies and as Vice President of the National Council of Jewish Federations. He was a significant and very generous supporter of the Golda Meir Center, the Marshall and Reva Kent Jewish Center, and the combined Golda Meir/Kent Jewish Center.

Highlights of 1997

Michael Sobel was President of the Board of Directors. The first Tampa Bay film Festival was opened through the cooperation of the Tampa Jewish Community Center/ Federation and the Golda Meir/Kent Jewish Center. This program is dedicated to bringing motion pictures that depict the lives of other Jews throughout the world to the local Jewish community.

The Fifteenth Annual Golda Meir/Kent Jewish Center Humanitarian Award went to Robert J. Strudler. He was the CEO of U.S. Homes. He built homes for senior citizens and was dedicated to making seniors comfortable. Mindy Solomon was recognized as the Volunteer of the Year.

Highlights of 1998

The Center was busy six days a week. The Preschool and summer camp had capacity enrollment. A feeling of warmth and commitment to the Jewish people was felt by everyone who entered the facility.

The Sixteenth Annual Golda Meir/Kent Jewish Center Humanitarian Award was shared by Michael Bernstein of Gulf Coast Jewish Family Services and Marshall Seiden from Menorah Manor. Both of these men have made a huge impact on the health and well being of the Jewish people of Pinellas County.

Highlights of 1999

Mindy Solomon was President of the Board of Directors. She said, "Let us take advantage of the Golda Meir/Kent Jewish Center, and its place in this community as a refuge for all those committed to Jewish continuity. We must prepare for the future. We are a determined and successful people, ever mindful of our responsibility to one another and the beauty of our Jewish heritage. We must share the dream and watch our community grow." The 17th Annual Golda Meir/Kent Jewish Center Humanitarian Award was given to Mel Sembler. He has made many contributions to the Jewish, as well as the general community, both financially and through his service on many Boards of Trustees. Lillian Silberzweig was the Volunteer of the Year.

Highlights of 2000

President Stan Newmark emphasized that "the twenty years of service from the Golda Meir/Kent Jewish Center was not twenty, one year, experiences, repeated over and over again, but rather twenty years of continuous growth from a kosher lunch program for fifty people in a converted office building to a full service multi-million dollar Community Center that has served thousands of people from tots to centurions. The "Burn Our Mortgage" program was the first step in preparation for building the new preschool and enlarging the Center. "We invite our entire community to participate in this campaign to help us to create this center that will be the standard bearer of our struggle for Jewish culture and survival."

The 18th Annual Golda Meir/Kent Jewish Center Annual Humanitarian Award was presented to Dr. James P. Gills. Dr. Gills has donated many millions of dollars to local charities including the Golda Meir/Kent Jewish Center. He is a world class athlete and a deeply spiritual person who is a lay leader of the First United Methodist Church in Tarpon Springs. Enid Newmark was named Volunteer of the Year.

Dan Sultan

Highlights of 2001

Dan Sultan became the new Executive Director. The 19th Annual Golda Meir/Kent Jewish Center Humanitarian Award was received by Bill McBride. He has been a leader in the Tampa Bay community in the areas of health and human services. He has received awards from, among others, the Jewish National Fund.

Highlights of 2002

The introduction of a Rabbi led discussion series and additional special events were the hallmarks of this year. This program presented a series of different viewpoints to the participants.

The recipients of the 20th Annual Golda Meir/Kent Jewish Center Annual Humanitarian Award were Walter P. and Edith Loebenberg. The Loebenbergs are the founders of the Florida Holocaust Museum in St. Petersburg. They are true leaders of the Jewish Community, giving of their time and money for many causes. The volunteer of the Year was Eleanor Abbo.

Highlights of 2003

The Golda Meir/Kent Jewish Center mission statement reads, "The Golda Meir/Kent Jewish Center exits to enhance the quality of life by providing intellectual, social, physical, and cultural programs designed to meet the needs of the Jewish community and the community at large of Pinellas county, in a way that unites, strengthens, nurtures, and enriches all of our lives. The Golda Meir/Kent Jewish Center promotes social interactions that strengthen family unity and binds one generation to another as an interdependent community. The Golda Meir/Kent Jewish Center is an equal opportunity agency."

President Ron Diner stated, "Jewish life in Pinellas County is a tapestry of many voices, needs, interests, cultures, and political viewpoints. More than ever, the Golda Meir/Kent Jewish Center remains steadfast that our role is that of the weaver, bringing together those many facets of our community."

The 21st. Annual Golda Meir/Kent Jewish Center Humanitarian Award was shared by Rabbi Arthur Baseman, Rabbi Gary Klein, Rabbi Jacob Luski, Rabbi Shimon Moch, Rabbi Michael Torop, and Rabbi David Weizman. The Volunteers of the Year were Sylvia and David Stokes.

David and Sylvia Stokes.

Highlights of 2004

The Center made a number of significant improvements to programs and facilities, including the addition of health and fitness equipment, the expansion of programs for senior adults, new cultural enrichment programs for every member of the family, exciting and memorable camp experiences, and advances in the preschool program.

The 22nd Annual Golda Meir/Kent Jewish Center Humanitarian Award was presented to the family of Annette Raymund. Annette, a major philanthropist in Pinellas County, worked tirelessly for the betterment of people. The Volunteer of the Year was Sally Laufer.

Highlights of 2005

A Commemorative Dinner celebrating the life of Charles Rutenberg was held this year. In her opening remarks, President Sally Laufer stated," Our Community Center was made possible through the leadership and vision of Charles and Isa Rutenberg and Marshall and Reva Kent, and the involvement of community leaders, many of whom are with us tonight." Charles Rutenberg left his mark on our

community, as well as, on the Tampa Bay community at large. His involvement in many philanthropic organizations led him to be well known throughout the Tampa Bay community. He was a man of enormous accomplishments, great generosity, and a powerful love for the community." He left a unique legacy that will be an inspiration to all people for all time. The Volunteers of the Year were Kathy and Mike Sobel.

Kent Center Facilities

Today, the facilities at the Golda Meir/ Kent Jewish Center include the Charles and Isadora Rutenberg Aquatic Center, the Harry and Julia Schwartz Life Extension Center, the Ralph and Dorothy Dutcher Social Hall, the Reuben Rutenberg Family Library, the Lois V. Silberman Senior Lounge. In addition to these "named" facilities, there are classrooms and offices which serve the members and guests of the Golda Meir/Kent Jewish Center. The Center is comprised of CENTERS which include:

The Center for Jewish Life which promotes Jewish literacy, learning, exploration, and innovation through classes, workshops, lectures, and public forums. This Center has diverse opportunities for learning and celebration and is open to all people at every level of Jewish education.

The Center for Adult Living and Learning offers programs for all ages of adults allowing them to grow and develop as individuals and to make friends and build a better community. The programs promote intellectual enrichment, creative expression, personal growth, social connections, and development of new skills.

The Center for Youth and Family enriches the lives of young people and their families by providing opportunities for learning, growth, and friendship in a Jewish context. All programs are grounded in Jewish values and traditions. The day camp program and recreational programs enrich the lives of children of all ages.

The Center for Older Adults provides a wide variety of programming, including a balanced combination of recreational, social, intellectual, and physical activities. The Center is dedicated to improving the lives of the aging population of Pinellas County by providing facilities and programs to offset the negative isolation and depression of older adults.

The Center for Health, Fitness and Sport promotes health and wellness for all ages by promoting fitness, aquatics, sports, and educational programs,. Outstanding professionals working at the exceptional facilities help individuals improve their personal fitness, health, and lifestyle.

The Center for Early Childhood Education provides programs that enrich the lives of young children in either a partial or full day setting. Twelve month programs are available for families who require full time child care. Dedicated teachers create stimulating programs inspired by Jewish values in a Jewish setting, with art, music, and field trips that expand the minds of children.

The Center for Summer Camp provides an opportunity for young people to participate in a residential camping environment. Camp Or Hashemesh (Sunshine) provides the opportunity for the children to develop through a variety of activities. Leadership skills are stressed. Lifelong friendships with other campers occur.

CHAPTER 21

JEWISH FEDERATION OF PINELLAS COUNTY

Jewish people have been commanded by Torah to help the widows, orphans, poor, and the stranger in our midst. Leviticus Chapter 19:9 and Chapter 19:10, says, "And when ye reap the harvest of your land, thou shall not wholly reap the corners of thy field, neither shalt thou gather the gleanings of thy harvest. And thou shall not glean thy vineyard, neither shalt thou gather every grape of thy vineyard; thou shall leave them for the poor and stranger..." Judaism has been more than a religion. It has been a way of life in which the community has always helped those who were less fortunate. This has been going on for thousands of years. Everyone in the community made contributions to a central collection box and the elders of the community divided the funds among the individuals who were in greatest need. Every Jewish organization and every synagogue provided assistance. Beside these sources, individuals would travel throughout the country collecting money for orphanages, yeshivas, and for the poor people of Palestine. This multiplicity of Jewish relief and welfare groups fed the hungry, sheltered the homeless, secured jobs, and took care of the sick and elderly.

According to Maimonides, there are eight degrees of tzedakah (acts of loving kindness). The highest degree is a person who helps another person by entering into a partnership with him/her or finds work for him/her, in order that the individual will no longer have to beg from other people. Helping another human being become self-sufficient is the most elevated form of charity. The vast network of Jewish social services and the Federation system of helping provide funds for these services is the true heritage of the Jewish people of this country.

In 1819, in Philadelphia, Rebecca Gratz established the first independent Jewish women's charitable society. This was the forerunner of many of the Jewish charitable societies which would later be joined together and become the Federation of a given community. In 1895, the Jewish people of Boston created a centralized community organization, which later became the Combined Jewish Philanthropies. It brought together all of the different fund-raising groups. It was the first coordinated organized philanthropy formed in this country. Each welfare agency maintained its own independence and its own board but gained from the joint efforts of all organizations. The Boston Federation raised more money and had less expenses than the other communities. From about 1900 to about 1930, the Federations concentrated primarily on local issues of health care, child welfare,

assistance for the handicapped, homes, and housing for the aged. They also opened community centers to help immigrants with their physical health, cultural and recreational activities, and education programs for adults and children. Cultural assimilation became another significant activity, which involved vocational training, day camps, and community development programs. It helped the Jewish immigrant become Americanized.

Meanwhile, external forces in Europe put Jewish lives at risk. In the 1920s and 1930s, the United Palestine Appeal and the American Joint Distribution Committee embarked on a massive campaign to rescue and rehabilitate Jewish people living in extremely dangerous conditions. In the mid-1920s, the Jewish communities of Columbus, Ohio, Detroit, Michigan, Indianapolis, Indiana, and San Francisco, California realized that the local Community Chest would not fund capital investments or national and international Jewish needs. They, therefore, formed Jewish Welfare Funds. In 1936, Atlanta, Georgia, formed its own Jewish Welfare Fund. In 1936, the General Assembly of the National Council of Jewish Federations and Welfare Funds applied pressure on the United Palestine Appeal and the American Joint Distribution Committee to unite their fund-raising campaigns. In response to the Kristallnacht pogrom in Nazi German, the United Jewish Appeal was formed. This organization, in conjunction with the existing UPA and JDC, worked together to provide substantial funds to help rescue Jewish people. Rescue not only meant moving Jewish people to safer locations, but also providing housing, food, medical care and jobs. From World War I until 1937, American Jewish people had donated over eighteen million dollars for the welfare of European Jews.

Before the New Deal legislation of the 1930s and the Great Society legislation of the 1960s, the Federations had established networks of social services. Federal and state funds now became part of the mix in supporting such organizations, such as, Jewish family service agencies and nursing homes. This new development made these Jewish agencies more susceptible to financial problems as financial problems increased at various levels of government.

The changing demographics of the Jewish people of the United States, with half the individuals born in 1955 or later, led to increased needs to strengthen the concept of Jewish giving. A significant number of Jewish people have little direct knowledge of the Holocaust, World War II, and the establishment of the State of Israel. The new issues for the Federation movement, as well as for all Jewish communities, can be identified as follows: the issue of Jewish continuity and identity; the issue of maintaining social policy and human services; the issue of securing necessary financial resources; and the issue of redefining the relationship between Israel and the rest of the Jewish world.

Jewish Federations had become a major influence in Jewish life, internationally, nationally, and locally. In 1985, in the United States over four billion dollars was collected and utilized for local, national, and international relief and programs. More than one million people contributed to these campaigns. More than one million five hundred thousand people annually received services from the agencies supported in part or in whole by the Federations.

Jewish Federation of Pinellas County

Hyman M. Jacobs was recognized as an early leader in the United Palestine Appeal drive in St. Petersburg. On February 5, 1937, plans were made for a banquet at which Rabbi Steven S. Wise and Nathan Straus would be the keynote speakers to help raise funds to resettle Jewish people from Germany and Poland into Palestine. The Jewish people of St. Petersburg and surrounding areas were aghast at the grave plight of the Jewish people of Central and Eastern Europe. There was an extreme urgency to take immediate and united action on behalf of resettlement. On February 17, David Rothblatt was named Chairman of the United Palestine Appeal drive in St. Petersburg and South County. Assisting him were May Benjamin, Hyman M. Jacobs, and Morris Hermer. The main address of the evening was given by Rabbi Max Shapiro of Miami. Father James J. O'Riordan and others also spoke. The Jewish people of St. Petersburg that year raised ten thousand dollars for the work of this Jewish social service organization.

On January 15, 1938, a special meeting, sponsored by B'nai B'rith, was held by all Jewish organizations at Congregation B'nai Israel to hear Simon Levine of the United Palestine Appeal. On January 25, a meeting was held to formally establish a permanent committee to help raise funds for Israel. This committee was made up of Rabbi Joseph Shenker, Sam Goldberg, Hyman M. Jacobs, David Rothblatt, Rabbi Pizer Jacobs, J. L. Miller, Milton Lew, Mrs. Clara Williams, Mrs. May Benjamin, Mrs. Sam Goldberg, Mrs. Myer Weinstein of the Judaic Council, A. Friedman, Rabbi I Obstbaum, Meyer Hermer, B'nai B'rith and others. On May 10, over 150 Jewish people attended the meeting at Congregation B'nai Israel, and raised another ten thousand dollars. The money was used to help resettle Jewish people in Palestine.

Sometime immediately after World War II, Louis Frank and Maxine Korones, of the Clearwater and North County communities, chaired a committee to raise funds for the Jewish people of Europe and Palestine. They were given a quota by the St. Petersburg group. Maxine went to all the businesses, mostly non-Jewish, in Clearwater and asked for and received contributions. When the goal was met, Louis put an article in the newspaper thanking everyone for their generosity.

In 1945 or 1946, the St. Petersburg Jewish Community Council was founded. The object and purpose of the organization was to further the welfare of the Jewish community by coordinating the efforts of all Jewish organizations, centralizing all fund-raising, and working with the affiliated organizations.

Around 1950, the Clearwater and North County Jewish community formed the Jewish Welfare Fund of Clearwater. They conducted independent drives to raise funds for the various Jewish organizations and the Jewish people abroad.

In 1955, the St. Petersburg Jewish Community Council, in their Combined Jewish Appeal of St. Petersburg, collected over twenty five thousand dollars from 642 contributors. Meanwhile, the Jewish Welfare Fund of Clearwater was holding its own drives to help the same organizations that St. Petersburg was funding.

One of the major reasons for the existence of the Federation of Jewish Charities is to avoid duplication of effort. It also provides for much more cost-effective use of funds and for better social services.

Highlights of 1970

The Family Service Committee of the St. Petersburg Jewish Community Council urged the community to develop a corps of volunteers to help Mrs. Gail make friendly visits to clients of the Gulf Coast Jewish Family Services. Mrs. Gail was going to train the volunteers to work with the clients. The St. Petersburg Jewish Community Council cosponsored with Gulf Coast Jewish Family Services, family life education programs for teenagers, adults and senior adults. A recommendation was made to provide funding for the River Garden Nursing Home. The local community raised $174,000.

Highlights of 1971

President Murray Jacobs described the Jewish Community Council of St. Petersburg as the central organization responsible for the fund raising, planning, budgeting, establishment and maintenance of social welfare and community services. In his annual President's Report he not only

discussed the needs and goals of the local organization for community affairs but also the needs of the people of Israel for their welfare and security. The local community raised over $201,000, from 809 families. Both the money raised and the number of participants were the highest in the history of the community.

Murray Jacobs said, "Recognizing the responsibility of the community in providing counseling for individuals and families seeking help to enable them to cope with their emotional problems, we have been a contributing member of the Gulf Coast Jewish Family Services – now on its third year. The steady increase in the caseload reflects the acceptance of the client's relationship with the agency...This year Council is contributing scholarship funds to five young people who expect to spend the summer in Israel. Camp Kadima is about to embark on its 19th year. It continues to attract children from the entire community as well as Clearwater because of its fine reputation." Over 100 children participated at the camp.

On October 17, the Soviet Jewry issue was discussed. Stanley Hunter reported that the main program for Gulf Coast Jewish Family Services currently was to complete a questionnaire throughout Tampa, St. Petersburg, Clearwater, and Sarasota to determine the needs of the aged in those communities. Meyer Possick was waiting for a report from an architect concerning adding on to the Jewish Community Center. The Jewish Community Center had a full set of activities for all ages.

On November 15, the St. Petersburg Jewish Community Council received a report from the local delegates to the 40th General Assembly in Pittsburgh, which is the annual conference of the Council of Jewish Federations and Welfare Funds. The Jewish leaders helped identify current Jewish problems and possible solutions. The leaders learned that there were many young Jewish people who wanted to maintain their Jewish identity and they needed assistance, especially financial, from the established communities to help them. There were over 400,000 Jewish students in the United States and a series of programs needed to be

Murray Jacobs

developed to assist them. A North American Jewish Student Appeal was founded. There was also a discussion about developing young Jewish leadership. It was felt that the middle class had to be brought into the process of helping others. There were sessions on the aging, housing problems, troubled youth, Jewish Social Services, Hillel and Federation.

Highlights of 1972

Frieda Sohon, Executive Director, presented her special report at the annual meeting on May 22. She said, "We are a community that cares. We care about Jewish family life–about our Jewish youth and aged–about Jewish education and culture–about the health of the community–and about Israel and world Jewry. This caring comes from our tradition which requires us to translate our creed to deed." The council raised $217,000. For the first time, a women's division was started under the chairmanship of Adele Morris.

Based on the call to action from national Jewish leaders at the 40th General assembly in Pittsburgh, a Young Leadership Program was started. Young men and women were trained and prepared for total community leadership and involvement. The young Jewish organizations have joined together to help develop young Jewish interest in the community.

Highlights of 1973

Murray Jacobs said that he had been informally discussing with Charlie Rutenberg the possibility of a merger of the St. Petersburg and Clearwater Jewish communities to form a Pinellas County Jewish Community Council. This was the beginning of the Jewish Federation of Pinellas County. It was through the efforts of Charlie and Murray that the two groups merged.

Frieda Sohon, Executive Director, said, "An organized Jewish community is basically concerned with the survival of Jewish people, its culture, institutions and values. Our Jewish Community Council completing its twenty fourth year of service to the Jews locally, nationally and overseas is an example of fulfillment of this fundamental purpose...Before the

Sylvan Orloff

organization of Council, social services were handled by local businessmen who gave a transient a dollar or two, or by the rabbis who gave something from their discretionary funds. Early in the history of Council, social services was handled by a group of volunteers. When the executive director was engaged, professionalism was added to the Council. In 1969, the community, recognizing the need for more social services in the St. Petersburg Jewish community, co-sponsored the Gulf Coast Jewish Family Services with Clearwater and Tampa, partially financed by the Jewish Children's Service, a regional-based agency in Atlanta. After the first year, Tampa withdrew. Mrs. Sylvia Gail, Executive Director, is a professional, trained caseworker with a Master's Degree in Social Welfare and many years of experience and family casework.

Underlying every aspect of community endeavor is the element of leadership. Over the years, we've had to rely on some few dedicated men and women to carry on the needed work of an organized community. Recognizing the need for developing young leaders who will carry on the commitment and service which is a part of community responsibility, St. Petersburg developed its first Young Leadership program under the chairmanship of Dr. Joel Marantz.... Fifteen young couples were invited to participate...

One cannot think of Jewish survival–and I mean survival of individuals as Jews–without recognizing the crucial role of Jewish education...Council has a very definite stake in helping to find ways and means to attract top-notch teachers so as to give more substance and depth to education."

Sylvan Orloff

Sylvan Orloff moved from Des Moines, Iowa to the Clearwater area. He was a founder and first President of the Jewish Federation of Pinellas County. At that time, the principal function of the Federation was to raise funds for the United Jewish Appeal. Some years later, he again was President. He was an active member of Menorah Manor, TOP, Jewish Day School, Gulf Coast Jewish Family Services. Sylvan was born on March

26, 1923. He attended the University of Minnesota. He owned a shoe store supply company and then manufactured shoe laces when he purchased a company in Tarpon Springs from the Berolzheimers. He always supported Jewish charities and also served on the Boards of the Chamber of Commerce and Rotary. His wife, Jean, attended UCLA. They married on June 30, 1946. Jean was one of the founders of the Women's Division of the Federation. She was awarded the Lion of Judah. She was President of ORT, a member of Hadassah, Brandeis University Women, and B'nai B'rith Women. They have five children: Dr. Loni Shelef, Esther Weltman, Louis Orloff, Bruce Orloff, and Ruth Levin. Loni has a Bachelor of Arts Degree in Psychology from Antioch College, and a Master of Arts from Hebrew University in Jerusalem. She earned a Doctor of Philosophy from Union Institute in Cincinnati, Ohio. She is married to Eliezar Jonah Stoppelman-Shelef from Israel.

Highlights of 1974

On August 19, a meeting was held of the Executive Board of the Jewish Community Council of St. Petersburg. It was reported that there had been a series of meetings held between the Clearwater group and the St. Petersburg group to discuss the merger. At that time, there were approximately 1,700 Jewish families in the St. Petersburg group and 720 Jewish families in the Clearwater North group. Whereas the St. Petersburg group was able to use the Jewish Community Center, the Clearwater group worked out of Temple B'nai Israel. Mr. Louis Solomon, the new Executive Director, was asked to try to get adequate facilities for a merged federation. A five-page report was submitted to the board and it was recommended that the full Board of Trustees approve the merger at the September 23rd meeting. It was pointed out that Murray Jacobs had been working with Charlie Rutenberg for the last five years to create such a merger.

The merger committee consisted of Stanley Freifeld, Stanley Hunter, Murray Jacobs, Leonard Lubin, Dr. Joel Marantz, Sylvan Orloff, Charles Rutenberg, Herbert Schwartz, Dr. James Young, Director of

Intermediate Cities Services, Council of Jewish Federations and Welfare Funds, and Louis Solomon, Executive Director, St. Petersburg Jewish Community Council. The issues that were addressed had to do with the implications for local planning of welfare services. They included: a very low birth rate; an aging American Jewish community; the extreme mobility of Jewish people; the need for continuing education for a highly educated Jewish population; the serious problems of intermarriage; the problems of separation and divorce and what to do about the children. The benefits to both communities were discussed. This included increased potential in terms of fund raising and services for a community of 6,000-10,000 people. This is similar in size to the Jewish communities of Akron, Ohio, Atlantic City, New Jersey, Dayton, Ohio, Louisville, Kentucky, Memphis, Tennessee, Omaha, Nebraska, Portland, Oregon, San Antonio, Texas, Toledo, Ohio, and Tucson, Arizona. It also included a single executive director, central administration, board of directors, combined campaign, combined budgeting and planning process, and combined capital fund drives. Ultimately, the community would benefit from this merger.

On September 23, a meeting was held of the Executive Board Members, Delegates-at-Large of all synagogues, and organizations of the St. Petersburg Jewish Community Council. The issue of merging the two welfare funds was discussed and then tabled, because of a variety of issues that had been raised about the merger. On October 14, another special meeting was held of the St. Petersburg Jewish Community Council. At this meeting, President Stanley Freifeld presided. Leonard Auerbach, Secretary, took a roll call and announced that a quorum was present. The individuals in attendance were: Stanley Freifeld, Dr. Joel Marantz, Leonard Auerbach, Irving Bernstein, Dr. Phillip Benjamin, Ben Bush, Dr. Bruce Epstein, Stanley Hunter, Murray Jacobs, Alan Kay, Mrs. Chester Levine, Leonard Lubin, Mrs. Edwin Pearl, Sidney Richman, Roger Schaffer, Louis Smith, Rabbi Morris Kobrinetz, Rabbi Louis Lederman, Bert Green, Meni Kanner, Israel Schulsinger, Albert Swartz, Sherry Smith,

Jean and Sylvan Orloff

Helen Proschan, Larry Haas, Ellen Bernstein, Sadie Possick, Florence Faloba, Helen Weston, Helen Salkin, Mrs. Sidney Richman, Saul Jacobson, Susan Byrd, Ed Rosenbluth, Irving Martin, Mrs. Bernard Greenberg, Leonard Temko, Dr. Murray Gessner, Fred Klitsner, William Israel, Ellen Mensh, Iris Bush, Jerry Kaufman, and Louis Solomon, Executive Director. Mr. Sam Palkin of the National United Jewish Appeal was present.

A motion was made by Lou Smith and seconded by Murray Jacobs. The motion, which was passed on a vote of forty two in favor and two against, where two thirds were necessary for passage, was approved. The motion was as follows: The St. Petersburg Jewish Community Council would merge with the Jewish Welfare Fund of Clearwater. The new organization would be named the Jewish Federation of Pinellas County. The new Board of Directors would consist of thirty delegates-at-large elected by the community. The Presidents of the St. Petersburg and Clearwater organizations would choose nominating committees who would recommend fifteen members each as delegates-at-large. One-third of the new board would serve for a one-year term, one third for a two-year term, and one third for a three-year term. All congregational rabbis in Pinellas County would be ex officio non-voting members of the new board. An Advisory Assembly, consisting of representation from each Jewish organization and synagogue in Clearwater and St. Petersburg would be formed and meet at least twice a year for guidance and informational purposes. "That all land and buildings now owned by the St. Petersburg Jewish Community Council (i.e. Jewish Community Center building and property) be immediately transferred and deeded to the Jewish Community Center Board of Directors with the understanding that if the Jewish Community Center ever ceases to operate, all buildings and properties will be returned to the Jewish Federation of Pinellas County." All business related to the Federation, until the new Board of Directors was elected, was to be conducted by the current Executive Board of the St. Petersburg Jewish Community Council. "The Board of Directors of the Jewish Federation of Pinellas County be charged with the following responsibilities upon election: elect their officers for the first year; approve the initial budget; appoint a Constitutional Committee; prepare and approve a new set of articles of incorporation and by-laws; develop an active committee structure that will involve a broad segment of both communities in the activities of the new federation."

On October 25, President Stanley Freifeld of the Jewish Community Council sent a memorandum to the Executive Board that the merger had been approved by both communities.

On November 26, the first Board of Directors of the Jewish Federation of Pinellas County was elected. From St. Petersburg they included: Stanley Freifeld, Stanley Hunter, Dr. Joel Marantz, Leonard Auerbach, Gerald R. Colen, Alan Kay, Dr. Phillip Benjamin, Irving Bernstein, Mrs. Morris LeVine, J. Roger Schaffer, Mrs. Rosalyn Canner, Louis Smith, Sidney Richman, Dr. Herbert Goldstein, Murray Jacobs, Past President Julius Green. From Clearwater they included: Stanley Michels, Barry Alpert, Harold Haftel, Mrs. Marshall Kent, Dr. Robert Flesch, Sylvan Orloff, Herbert Schwartz, Marvin Feldman, James J. Shapiro, Dr. Alfred Schick, Philip Katz, Mrs. Henry Katz, Roland Fox, Howard Lawrence, Roger Rolfe, and Past President Charles Rutenberg. Ex-Officio members from St. Petersburg were: Rabbi Michael Charney, Rabbi Morris Kobrinetz, Rabbi Louis Lederman, and Rabbi David Susskind. Ex- Officio members from Clearwater were: Rabbi Pincus Aloof and Rabbi Arthur Baseman. Honorary Life Members from St. Petersburg were Mr. and Mrs. Marion B. Ross. Honorary Life Members from Clearwater were Dr. Salem Baranoff, Julius Lovitz and Max Sackheim.

On December 16, elections were held for the first officers of the Jewish Federation of Pinellas County Incorporated. They were unanimously elected as follows: Mr. Sylvan Orloff, President; Mr. Stanley Freifeld, First Vice President; Mr. Stanley Michels, Second Vice President; Mrs. Marilyn LeVine, third Vice President; Mr. Leonard Auerbach, Secretary; Mr. Herbert Schwartz, Treasurer.

Highlights of 1977

A program for feeding the elderly and the disabled was started. Eighty nine meals were served daily, of which thirty nine were home deliveries. The Jewish community provided nine thousand dollars plus the physical work for this effort. This was a coordinated program with Sylvia Gail, Gulf Coast Jewish Family Service, and the Neighborly Center.

Highlights of 1978

The Board was presented proposals for a community Jewish newspaper. Congregation Beth Chai, which published the Seminole Tablet offered to publish the paper for the Federation.

The Abe Adler Post, Jewish War Veterans Auxiliary, provided food for needy families. Seven families received Passover baskets and additional money raised through the congregations.

The First-Year Young Leadership Program advisors reported that a list of over 100 individuals had been established and that forty four active individuals were participating in various sessions on leadership.

Highlights of 1981

On February 19, the initial tri-party organizational meeting of the Tampa/Orlando/Pinellas Jewish Foundation, Incorporated was held in Lakeland, Florida. The Articles of Incorporation and Bylaws of TOP were approved and the following trustees were elected: Tampa Class, Hope Barnett, Leslie Barnett, D. Terry Aidman, Ben Greenbaum and Nathan Gordon; Orlando Class, Elliott Zerivitz, David Ritt, Louis Feinberg, Abe Wise and Sol Schick; and Pinellas Class, Gerald Colen, Reva Kent, Charles Rutenberg, Bruce Bokor, and Charles Ehrlich.

Charles Rutenberg was elected President of TOP. Reva Kent was appointed Chairman of the Investment Committee. Joel M. Breitstein was hired to be Endowment Consultants/Executive Director.

Highlights of 1982

A new transportation program was set up for the Jewish elderly to attend religious and cultural activities. The Pinellas County Jewish community mirrored the national trend of a large and growing number of isolated and frail older Jewish people. Gulf Coast Jewish Family Services also identified a need for transportation for Jewish people in nursing homes and other institutions. Further, there was a need for companionship and visitors. The whole project was geared to help all frail and Jewish elderly, regardless of income.

Beth Chai's newsletter,
The Seminole Tablet.

The Jewish Community Center of Pinellas County held its first Health Fair in conjunction with National Health Fair Week. Over 250 people attended. In cooperation with Palms of Pasadena Hospital they received free hearing tests, eye tests, blood pressure, weight, anemia, pulmonary functions, stress, cancer, mental health information, and other tests. There was a nominal charge for blood tests.

A new Pinellas County senior citizens housing program was started. The Charles and Isa Rutenberg Philanthropic Fund provided $110,000 as seed money.

Camp Kadima had a total of 183 campers in Session I. It had a total of 213 campers in Session II. A special camp within a camp was set up for handicapped children, in order that they could also enjoy a variety of summer activities. Scholarships were made available for children whose families could not afford to send them.

One hundred and fifty members of the Jewish War Veterans had a picnic at the Center. The Senior Friendship Club also had a picnic and had a very large turnout.

Highlights of 1983

Gerald Rubin was the Executive Director of the Jewish Federation of Pinellas County. Fred Margolis was the Executive Director of the Jewish Community Center. Mark Silk was the Executive Director of the Pinellas County Jewish Day School. President Charles Rutenberg spoke of the function of TOP to provide seed money for needed community projects. Twenty five thousand dollars of TOP funds were granted to Mr. Irwin Miller, President of Menorah Manor.

Highlights of 1984

At the April 11 meeting of the Jewish

Federation of Pinellas County, Chairperson Marvin Feldman gave the attendees the background on the donation of the twelve acre Kent Tract to the Federation by Reva and Marshall Kent. He reported on a conceptual plan to utilize the land for the Jewish community. The original "letter of intent" donating the land expressed the hope of the land would be used for the aged and for Federation and community and social purposes. However, with the development of Menorah Manor, Reva and Marshall asked that a facility be built for the needs of all Jewish people. The Rutenberg family offered to donate three movable buildings used for display and models at a development site. They also offered to pay all moving expenses, the expenses of erecting the buildings and a permanent foundation. The Board gratefully accepted the land from Marshall and Reva Kent and the buildings and funds for the erection of the buildings from the Rutenberg family. The Board then voted to name the new facility in perpetuity as "The Marshall and Reva Kent Jewish Center."

Highlights of 1985
American Jewish Mosaic of Florida

The American Jewish Mosaic in Microcosm was a historical and contemporary perspective of the Jewish community in Florida. The report of this traveling exhibit was sent to the Federation. The aims of the exhibit was to explore the rich heritage of the Jewish people of Florida and how they interacted and contributed to the lifestyle and culture of this state. The exhibit had four major themes: immigration, family/synagogue/community, human rights, arts and sciences. Unfortunately, the exhibit gave very little information about Pinellas County because of a series of factors. There was no formal Jewish Historical Society at that time and therefore no formal group that could work with the directors of the exhibit to provide them with local historical information. In addition, with the exception of some local Jewish history collected in St. Petersburg related to Bunnie Katz's family and the beginnings of Congregation B'nai Israel very little material had been collected and analyzed. The emergence of the Jewish

Genealogical Society, the establishment of a Jewish archives at Heritage Village, and this book helps fill in the gaps in the story.

Richard Goldstein made a presentation on behalf of the Hillel Foundation concerning the current financial problems and requesting that the Florida Federations help fund Hillel for the college-age Jewish students. There was a concern that once the young people went off to college, they would forget their Jewish background in the secular world around them. The Hillel movement in Florida started in 1976 at the urging of the Miami Federation because of the concern that Jewish students from many parts of the state were attending colleges in communities too small to support adequate Jewish services for the young people.

A discussion was held concerning the Pinellas Community's Study. The consultant to the study visited the community from May 28-30 and met with fifty community leaders individually or in small groups. These individuals came from the Federation, beneficiary agencies, synagogues and local Jewish organizations. Both laymen and Jewish communal professionals were included in the sample. The preliminary report focused mainly on the perceptions of the interviewees, as expressed openly to the consultant. There were three major concerns: first, and of greatest concern, was a political split in the community between various groups of Jewish people; secondly, the North-South (Clearwater-St. Petersburg) split was terribly divisive; and thirdly, the Federation-agency system in Pinellas County had to be strengthened, since apparently everyone was raising funds for their own specific concerns. Other concerns identified were: the absence of leadership development programs; the inadequate participation of individuals of Pinellas County at regional and national conferences; the development of a closer relationship between the Federation and the synagogues; and lastly, the area of public relations. Many people thought that the Federation was strictly a fund-raising organization and didn't understand all of the unique and excellent contributions that the Federation made to the local community.

Highlights of 1987

Since leadership development was one of the serious concerns of the community, the Pinellas County Jewish Federation Leadership Program was established. The goals of the program were: to recruit the most able people; to develop among these people a sense of motivation and commitment toward common Jewish causes; to educate them about contemporary Jewish issues and community agencies; to encourage their active participation in Jewish community institutions and fundraising; to develop their personal skills for exercising more effective leadership; to have geographic representation; to develop a sense of community and mutual interdependence. There was considerable training concerning the role of the volunteer and the role of the professional in promoting the Jewish community. Over a period of time, the program was very effective.

The Community Relations Committee in conjunction with Federation staff and Board Members, brought a coordinated set of programs and activities to the community. This has resulted in far better communications and has helped decrease the divide within the Jewish community due to a lack of information and poor communications. The strength of the community has definitely been enhanced by everyone pulling together instead of each group trying to resolve the problems of a given program area.

A special Soviet Jewish campaign was started with a goal to raise $120,000 by December 31, 1989. The money was to be used to help resettle Jewish people from the Soviet Union.

Highlights of 1988

The Jewish Community Center site at 8167 Elbow Lane, St. Petersburg was sold. Walter Loebenberg and Stanley Igel met to discuss the development of a Holocaust Memorial Room at the new Jewish Community Center. The Pinellas County Jewish Day School was evaluated by the Soloman Schechter Day School Association and it was given a high rating.

Highlights of 1989

The Board of Directors of the Pinellas County Jewish Day School reaffirmed its decision to move to the Largo site and to start a capital campaign. It was felt that it was important to have a more centralized area in the county for the participation of all families north and south.

The American Jewish community had fought for the right of free emigration for Soviet Jews since at least 1969. Now the Soviet Union had started "Passage to Freedom." In 1988, nearly 19,000 Jews were permitted to leave the Soviet Union. That number was expected to double in 1989. There was a plea for additional funds from the American Jewish community to make this program a reality.

Highlights of 1990

James Sobel informed the Board that the Jewish Community Center had decided on August 7, to cease its Kapok Tree operations. Joel Goetz, President of the Jewish Community Center, explained the options for the continuation of the program.

The Pinellas County Jewish Day School had gone through a considerable number of changes. Its new executive was Dr. Lenora Kopelovich. The Allocations Committee thought that the school had done an excellent job of controlling costs and raising funds.

Sydney Werner reported that the Kent Jewish Community Center had grown greatly in the past year. He said that it had a new facility and a first-rate Executive Director. The Golda Meir Center was able to provide significant financial help to put the Kent Center on an excellent financial footing.

The purpose of the Jewish Federation of Pinellas County was consistent with the draft Mission statement of 1988. That's stated in part, "...the Jewish Federation of Pinellas County is the Jewish community single and central federated Jewish organization. It is the purpose of the Federation to build, strengthen and preserve a thriving Jewish community in Pinellas County and to enhance the quality of Jewish life in the United States, Israel and around the world.

To accomplish this purpose, the federation must serve as the community instrument for building consensus, raising the necessary funds, and developing community priorities (by means of) bringing together all supporters, providers, and consumers of Jewish communal services."

President Jim Sobel gave his annual report. He indicated that Federation was no longer in its infancy but now in its adolescence. The separate St. Petersburg and Clearwater federations were combined. There were no longer two distinct communities. Because of national and local financial problems a new look had a be taken concerning how best to meet the mission statement of the Federation. He said in part, "...Now, in Pinellas County, there are more than twenty municipalities and a continuous urban sprawl from Pass-A-Grille to Tarpon Springs. People live in one community and work in another. Moreover, there are many, like myself, who view this entire Tampa Bay area as one integrated, economic and social region. If that is true, then the distinctions of North and South, which once were very significant in our organizational thinking, must be re-examined. In reality, those distinctions are out of sync with today's circumstances, today's mobility.

Our community has been through some difficult times. Our campaign has been down. We live in very stringent economic times. And our agencies and been fighting for their very existence. Financial resources are more a concern to them and to the Federation.

But, as we take a longer, larger view, we must look at the unique role of Federation in building a community by bringing together scarce resources, by providing a forum for discussion for all elements of our community, and by developing a consensus for making the hard choices to fund the services that appear to have the highest priority to the decision-makers. We must recognize that Federation can only distribute what it receives; we're casting aside the days when Federation distributed funds solely upon the requests of the agencies without taking a significant look at the overall needs of the community and placing these individual agency requests in the context of broader communal needs. The professional leadership of agencies and their supporters must recognize particular interests can best

be served if the total community is strong.

We have also gone beyond the stage when a few relatively large contributors could make commitments for a community. Part of the reason for the financial difficulties of our agencies is due to a failure to build the necessary support systems on a broad-scale basis for the programs in the facilities contemplated. We must have broader participation in the decision-making process over the next several years. Rather than making shabbos for oneself, let's make shabbos for each other. By nursing and strengthening our common interests federation, as an enterprise, will flourish. Leadership of Federation and its agencies is a critical factor...

Having said all this, I believe that our Jewish community has a bright future. We have, in Gulf Coast Jewish Family Services, a first-rate institution...truly a success story; one of the finest institutions of its kind anywhere in the country...Is our glass half-full or half-empty? The only thing I can say with complete certainty is that we have half a glass, perhaps significantly more. It is my hope that our collective efforts will fill that glass and our joined community cup truly will runneth over."

A message from the Holy See was incorporated in a press release of September 11 and put into the minutes of the Board of Directors meeting, since one of the major functions of Federation is to promote and enhance interfaith dialogue. The press release was entitled, "Anti-semitism–a sin against God and humanity." Pope John Paul II had previously said in 1985, "The relationship between Jews and Christians has radically improved in these years. Where there was ignorance and therefore prejudice and stereotype, there is now growing mutual knowledge, appreciation and respect. It is above all, love between us, that kind of love I mean, which is for both of us a fundamental injunction of our religious traditions and which the New Testament has received from the old."

Highlights of 1991

The Albert A. Belson Endowment Fund at the TOP Foundation was established. Half of the income was to go to Menorah

Manor and half of the income was to go to the Federation to be used as needed. The Pinellas County Jewish Day School expected an enrollment of 115 students. The Kent Jewish Community Center had a summer camp enrollment of 191 children. Over 500 children participated in the health fair at the Kent Jewish Community Center. The new Executive Director of the Jewish Community Center of Pinellas County, Teddi Berkowitz, reported that Camp Kadima had 105 children. The Jewish War Veterans reported that the MacDill Air Force Base would have a commemoration of the Holocaust. Paul Hochberg of the Paul Surensky Post No. 409, was the representative of the Department of Florida, Jewish War Veterans of the United States to the Federation Board.

Highlights of 1992

The presentation of awards to Charlie Rutenberg and Reva Kent reads, "As per our Board Resolution of a few months ago, it is our pleasure to acknowledge and thank Charlie Rutenberg and Reva Kent for their work as founding members of the TOP Jewish Foundation and for the subsequent effort they have given it over the past twelve years prior to their stepping down as members of the Board. It is with great pleasure that I present to them this Lifetime Plaque. Both Charlie and Reva also spent many years on the Board of the Federation, and served as officers, including the presidency."

The Federation developed a speakers bureau with individuals who spoke in three major categories "Understanding American Jewry," "Israel and the American Jewish Community," and "Jewish Religious Traditions." Diane Sembler received a special award for her many major roles within the Federation.

The Tampa Bay Jewish Educators Council had a mini-conference with the leader being the Scholar-in-Residence, Danny Siegel. The various workshops were used to examine local curriculum for children, at the various synagogues and other centers of Jewish learning and to make recommendations on how to improve the teaching process.

Highlights of 1993

The Council of Jewish Federations urged Congress to reform health care for all individuals. They called, "... for a plan that offered universal access; comprehensive care, including preventive treatment, risk reduction education, emphasis on primary care provision, reproductive health services for men and women, mental health services, substance abuse treatment, and long-term care; progressive financing; administrative simplification, including standardization of paperwork and reimbursement procedures; efficient use of resources to minimize cost increases, including tort reform regarding medical malpractice; a guarantee of quality, equity, and efficiency; choice of health care providers so as to insure the continuation of existing physician-patient relationship; and continued research and innovation in health care service provision. Reforms must also be sensitive to regional variations in healthcare infrastructure and populations. Appropriate assistance must be made available to poor urban or rural areas, as well as to those areas disproportionately burdened by vulnerable populations."

The Maimonides Society of Pinellas County held its Inaugural Dinner on March 28, at Congregation Beth Shalom of Clearwater. The featured speaker was Professor Norman A. Stillman of the State University of New York at Binghamton. His presentation was entitled, "Moses Maimonides: A Man for All Seasons." The Maimonides Society Steering Committee included: Dr. Mandel Sher, Chairman, Dr. Mark Benjamin, Dr. David Bernstein, Dr. Mitchell Lowenstein, Dr. Arthur Matzkowitz, Dr. James Roberts and Dr. Eric Steckler. Menu arrangements were made by Toni Rinde.

The Jewish community helped the Catholic community celebrate the 25th anniversary of the Diocese of St. Petersburg. The Bishop came to celebrate the Purim Festival with the Jewish community of Tampa Bay. He had previously visited the Holocaust Museum.

Highlights of 1994

The Dr. Edward N. Ludin Young Leadership Award was established by a gift to the TOP Foundation, from Arlene Ludin.

The Maimonides Society had grown to 107 health-care professionals.

Pinellas County Demographic Study

The Jewish Federation of Pinellas County sponsored a demographic study of the Jewish community. The following synagogues and Jewish organizations gave financial support and made the study possible. They were: Congregation B'nai Israel, Gulf Coast Jewish Family Services, Menorah Manor, Pinellas County Jewish Day School, Temple Beth-El and Temple B'nai Israel. The Golda Meir Center provided space for the telephone survey. The results were as follows:

1. Jewish Population Size and Distribution–approximately 30,000 people live in about 13,000 Jewish households. The population in Jewish households increased from 21,000 in 1979, to 29,000 in 1986, to 30,000 in 1990. Of that group approximately 40% live in North Pinellas County, 17% in Central Pinellas County, and 43% in South Pinellas County.

2. Place of Birth–overall 94% of the individuals were born in the United States with 27% born in New York state, and 14% born in Pinellas County.

3. Residency Issues–about half of all the households have been living in the area for less than 10 years. 26% of the households had been living here for 20 or more years. 78% of the households owned their own homes. Very few of the families planned to move elsewhere.

4. Age and Sex–28% of the Jewish population were 65 and over and 13% were 75 and over. 20% of the Jewish population were under age 19. Half the population was under age 46. The distribution of males and females did not differ very much. 47% of the teenagers lived in North Pinellas County and 40% of the teenagers lived in South Pinellas County.

5. Educational Level–97% of the Jewish population had a least a high school degree compared to 78% of the general population of America. 48% of the Jewish population had a least a four year college degree compared to 21% of the general population.

6. Employment Status–36% of the population was retired. The current unemployment rate of those not retired is 2%.

Lisl and Dr. Alfted Schick

7. Religious Profile–3% of the Jewish people considered themselves to be Orthodox. 23% of the Jewish households considered themselves to be Conservative. 39% of the Jewish households considered themselves to be Reform. 36% of the Jewish households considered themselves to be Jewish, without a designation of type of Synagogue to which they might belong.

8. Synagogue Attendance–32% of the respondents never attend services or only do so for special occasions. About 48% of non–members of synagogues attend High Holy Day Services. About 74% of households will join a synagogue at some point in their adult life. About 87% of Jewish children will receive some form of Jewish education.

9. Pinellas County Jewish households are evenly distributed throughout the geographic area and the survey found no identifiable clusters.

Highlights of 1995

The Alfred Schick, M. D. Memorial Award was established by Lisl Schick, in honor of her late husband, Alfred Schick. The Maimonides Society, in cooperation with the Jewish Federation of Pinellas County, presented the award. The criteria for the award includes: significant leadership ability; a high level of involvement in Jewish activities; and the potential for greater leadership responsibility in the future.

The recipients of the award were: 1996, Dr. Mandel Sher; 1997, Dr. David Wolstein; 1998, Dr. Stephen Warren; 1999, Dr. William Greenberg; 2000, Dr. Morris LeVine; 2001, Dr. Sidney Grau; 2002, Dr. David Bernstein; 2003, Dr. Michael Slomka; 2004, Dr. Robert Entel; 2005, Dr. Eric Steckler; and in 2006, Dr. Steven Weiss.

Operation Afikomen was the first-ever total Jewish community wide food drive sponsored by the Federation and the Pinellas County Board of Rabbis. More Than 2,000 items were collected between Purim and Passover. The food was given to the Gulf Coast Jewish Family Service food bank and will provide approximately a three to four months supply of food for 350 clients using the food bank.

Highlights of 1996

The Yitzhak Rabin Memorial Award for Distinguished Community Service was established by the Federation. The criteria for the award is for an individual or a couple to have made a significant difference in the quality of Jewish life in Pinellas County through their personal commitment as a direct service volunteer(s). The Federation's Yitzhak Rabin Memorial Awards Committee selects an individual(s) who is a shining example of distinguished community service by taking an active part in the Jewish community or who has shown extraordinary leadership in the Pinellas County Jewish community.

The recipients of the award were: 1996, Marilyn and Phillip Benjamin; 1997, Sylvan Orloff; 1998, Charles Rutenberg; 1999, Irwin and Sonya Miller; 2000, Toni Rinde and Annette Raymund; 2001, Walter Loebenberg and Adele Morris; 2002, Joan Benstock and John Loftus; 2003, Thelma Rothman and Reva Kent; 2004, Abe and Bunnie Katz; 2005, Ted and Jean Wittner.

The Cardozo Society met on August 28, with twenty five attorneys in attendance. Rabbi Adler spoke about "Jewish Ethics: the Talmud, and American Law." An outreach program, entitled "Unaffiliated Outreach Project" was started to seek out the approximately 10,000 Jewish people in Pinellas County who were unaffiliated with the synagogues.

The Yitzhak Rabin Memorial Recognition Awards committee was established. Gayle Benator was named the chair of the committee.

On April 1, the Jewish Federation of Pinellas County approved a special commission to study Jewish Community Center operations. The committee issued a comprehensive report including recommendations for operation and performance to meet the needs of the Jewish community.

Highlights of 1997

A $100,000 bequest was received from an anonymous donor. The bequest included unrestricted funds to be put into the TOP Foundation and the income to be used at a future date. The Lion of Judah Endowment Program guidelines were approved. An Israeli cultural arts festival was announced.

Bonnie Friedman joined the Jewish Federation of Pinellas County and became Executive Director in 1999. She had previously been the Assistant Director of the Golda Meir/Kent Jewish Center from 1995-1997, and Administrator of the Kent Center Preschool. She graduated from Brooklyn College in 1975 with a Bachelor of Arts Degree in Early Childhood and a minor in Psychology. She was a reading teacher in Freehold, New Jersey in 1984-1992. She is married and has two daughters.

Highlights of 1998

The Jewish Federation of Pinellas County became a member of the newly formed United Jewish Communities, which was the national organization of Jewish federations. The United Jewish Communities was a merger of the United Jewish Appeal, the Council of Jewish Federations, the United Israel Appeal, and the American Jewish Joint Distribution Committee. The United Jewish Communities was established to improve the quality of Jewish life worldwide. Its mission was to nurture Jewish learning, care for those in need, rescue Jews in danger, and enhance the continuity of the Jewish people. The organization established a model of Jewish community and philanthropy and a framework for new opportunities and new Jewish participation that challenges the Jewish people to continue the traditions of education, leadership, advocacy, and responsibility for people and a good life.

The Yitzhak Rabin Memorial Educator of Excellence Award was established by the Federation. This is a special presentation of honor and recognition to an outstanding educator. The criteria established by the Yitzhak Rabin Memorial Awards Committee includes: displays effectiveness as a classroom teacher; demonstrates leadership qualities; displays creativity and innovations; is a role model to students and peers; adapts to new circumstances and shows flexibility; has positive relationships with administration, peers, students and parents; takes advantage of professional growth opportunities; demonstrates involvement in the larger

Jewish community.

The recipients of the award were: 1998, Jerri Greene of Temple B'nai Israel; 1999, Raida Goldman of Temple B'nai Israel; 2000, Lea Thorbecke, of Pinellas County Jewish Day School; 2001, Rabbi Jonathan Mielke of Pinellas County Jewish Day School; 2002, Esther Roth of Temple Beth-El; 2003, Jorie Massarsky of Golda Meir/Kent Jewish Center; 2004, Elaine Wolstein, Temple Ahavat Shalom; and 2005, Janice LeVine.

The Yitzhak Rabin Memorial Program of Distinction Award was established by the Federation. The Yitzhak Rabin Memorial Awards Committee establish the criteria for receiving the award, for developing an original program or project which reflects innovation and creativity, that can serve as a replica role model for other Federations.

The recipients of the award were: 1998, Hanukkah Fest '97, Congregation B'nai Israel; 1999, High School Awareness Day, Florida Holocaust Museum; 2000, 1999 Family Fair, Golda Meir/Kent Jewish Community Center; 2001, Rally for Peace and Solidarity in Israel, Jewish Federation of Pinellas County; 2002, Mitzvah Day 2002, Congregation B'nai Israel; 2003, Florida Center for Survivors of Torture, Gulf Coast Jewish Family Services; 2004, Temple Beth-El Art Show, Temple Beth-El and Advocacy for Israel Committee, Congregation B'nai Israel; and 2005, Women's Community Seder.

Highlights of 2005

The Jewish Federation of Pinellas County serves a variety of functions and conducts an annual campaign to secure maximum funds to meet the financial needs of local, regional, national and international humanitarian organizations and beneficiary agencies. It sponsors: the Jewish Community Relations Council(JCRC), which is involved in resolving issues of human rights, anti-Semitism, human services, social action, and a better understanding of the Middle East; the Tampa – Orlando – Pinellas Jewish Foundation(T.O.P.), which collects and invests funds for current and future needs; Department of Human Resource Development(HRD) focuses on training, placement, and recognition of volunteers; Long Range Planning Committee determines

community needs for the future; a community calendar; the Community Welfare Fund; the Jewish Press, which is available to about 5,100 Jewish households in Pinellas County; the Maimonides Society founded in 1992 by a group of committed health care professionals; the Cardoza Society founded in 1995 by a group of committed practicing attorneys; etc. The Jewish Federation of Pinellas County also provides assistance to the Gulf Coast Jewish Family Services, Menorah Manor, Golda Meir/Kent Jewish Center, Pinellas County Jewish Day School, Tampa Bay Jewish Educators Council, Florida Holocaust Museum, Florida Hillel Council, and the Phillip Benjamin Tower(formerly Menorah Center).

Bonnie Friedman discussed the significance of the Jewish Federation in the life of Pinellas County Jewish people. She said, "As the central address of the Jewish community, our Federation has led the way in convening our agencies, organizations, temples and synagogues through many wonderful and many crisis situations. Whether it was 9-11 or Hurricane Charlie or a community rally for Israel –the Jewish Federation has provided help, information, and spear headed activities, outreach and programming that affect our Jewish lives in a very positive manner.

As the fund-raising arm of the community, we have encouraged seed money for additional Jewish programming as well as provided for the support for those less fortunate in our area. We do this through the Koved Fund which provides emergency assistance to over 1,500 (people) this year, scholarships for education and camp, counseling, food pantry support, subsidies for seniors and youth and much more. We are the link in the chain for our overseas brethren who count on the generosity of the Jewish people to sustain them. Whether it be in Israel, in the former Soviet Union, Argentina or throughout the world, the Jewish Federation answers the call.

Our Federation has a sacred mission of rescuing the imperiled, caring for the vulnerable, and reinvigorating Jewish life throughout the world. Together we have a collective responsibility for Chaverim Kol Yisrael– we are responsible for one another.

We are closely connected with all acts of heart. We believe in the concept of holiness and pursue the ideals of justice, goodness, wisdom and truth.

You may wonder how these values relate to our Federation. Here are a few examples:

Hachnast Orchim–Hospitality: through our Shalom Pinellas and Shalom Baby Program we welcome others to our community. Our outreach activities offer opportunities for people to learn about the Jewish community in Pinellas County.

Talmud Torah–Education: The Pinellas County Jewish Day School, The Kent Jewish Center Preschool and our adult education programs at both the Pinellas County Jewish Center and the Golda Meir/Kent Jewish Center provide many opportunities for learning for our young and our old. (Please note that there is an entire chapter on Jewish educational programs, which includes excellent programming for preschool, for school-age children, and also adult education, in the various synagogues and temples of Pinellas County.)

Hiddur P'nai Zaken–Esteeming the elderly and Kibud Av V'Eym–Honoring our Parents: Our Gulf Coast Jewish Family Services provides services, care and counseling for the community, the elderly, the frail and the indigent.

Tikkun Olan–Repairing the world: Our Jewish Community Relations Council, Women's Philanthropy, and Outreach focus on environmental issues, advocacy, providing food for the hungry and clothes for the needy of all religions and races.

Tzedakah–Charity: The Federation Annual Campaign which raises over $1.3 million allows us to serve at least some of the needs of this community and helps provide life-saving and life-enhancing humanitarian assistance to those in need in Pinellas County, in Israel throughout the world.

Basically, everything that we do in this community and everything we make possible for Jewish people in need wherever they may be, derive direction from our core values. I believe that the Jewish Federation of Pinellas County and its partners-the agencies-do and have done an exemplary job. (Included in this discussion must be the role of each of the synagogues in Pinellas County. See the individual chapters on the synagogues to get a better understanding of their contributions to our society.) Every day, in so many ways, countless Jewish lives are touched by the support of the Jewish Federation of Pinellas County."

Irwin Miller, President of Menorah Manor 1983–1986.

Reuben Halprin

Leonard Seligman, President of Menorah Manor, 1990–1993.

Marion Samson-Joseph, President of Menorah Manor Foundation, 1986–1990.

CHAPTER 22

MENORAH MANOR AND OTHER FACILITIES FOR THE AGING

Menorah Manor

In the 1970s and the early 1980s, there were several attempts to organize community Jewish efforts to enlist the sponsorship of existing Jewish welfare organizations in order to start a Jewish residence for the elderly and a nursing home. The Jewish community's mission was and still is to provide the best possible professional care and a warm, homelike Jewish environment for the elderly.

In 1982, a group that had previously brought government-sponsored elderly housing to the Jewish community, Menorah Center, now organized a regional effort to build a Jewish nursing home. Phillip Benjamin and Murray Jacobs chaired the effort to obtain a Certificate of Need from the State of Florida for a Skilled Nursing Facility and to purchase land for the site of the nursing home. A not-for-profit corporation was formed and Ted Wittner became its first chairman. In March, a site adjacent to Menorah Center and Congregation B'nai Israel was selected. In June, a celebration cocktail reception was held at the new site to share with community leaders the plans for Menorah Manor.

The Miami Jewish Home assisted in the planning. Leonard Seligman, Reuben Halprin, and Irwin Miller were essential participants in this effort. Twenty or twenty five families donated one thousand dollars each as seed money. In October, 1983, formal groundbreaking ceremonies were held and the officers of Menorah Manor, Miller, Marger, Halprin, Wittner, and Seligman began the ceremony. Each community member then present took a turn in breaking ground. This was a symbolic way of showing a total community commitment to the aging and medically needy. Actual construction started in November.

In 1984, Marion Samson-Joseph donated the initial major gift of one million dollars in memory of her deceased husband, Bernard L. Samson. Original founders donated $50,000 or more. Eventually, about 2,400 donors from the Tampa Bay Jewish community gave pledges, cash donations, and gifts-in-kind totaling seven million five hundred thousand dollars. The cornerstone was laid March 31.

The Founding Board of Governors included: Ted P. Wittner, Chairman of the Board; Irwin H. Miller, President; Leonard Seligman, Vice President; Bruce Marger, Secretary; and Reuben Halprin, Treasurer; Executive Board Members, Phillip Benjamin, Murray Jacobs, Richard Jacobson, Walter H. Kessler, A.J. Pardoll, Harold Rivkind, Thelma Rothman and Donald Silverberg; Board of Governors, Barry M. Alpert, Freda Buchman, Rabbi Morris Chapman, Judy Davis, Jerry Esrick, Maurice A. Goldblatt, Harry Green, Julius Green, Victor Greenberg, Mel Gross, Edward Kalin, George Karpay, Reva Kent, Howard S. Lawrence, Beatrice Levine, Eugene Linsky, Marshall Linsky, Walter P. Loebenberg, Julius Lovitz, Ida Michels, Jerry Orns, Marc Perkins, David L. Robbins, Barbara Rosenblum, Charles Rutenberg, Marion Samson-Joseph, Saul Schechter, Col. Philip M. Schwartz, and Betty Sembler.

Ted Wittner, Chair, Menorah Manor, 1983–1987.

Highlights of 1985

Menorah Manor opened on May 20. The first resident was Max Yanchuck followed later that day by Fanny Marks, Goldie Shuster, Joseph Wurzel, and Minnie Dean. During the first month, twenty two residents were admitted, and during the first twelve months, 125 people came to live at Menorah Manor.

From the very beginning, it was meant to be a home away from home where older Jewish people would get quality, loving lifetime care regardless of financial ability. This occurred because of a highly professional staff, large numbers of dedicated volunteers, excellent leadership, and constant advance planning. In the very beginning, an Admission and Resident Services Committee was formed to learn

Barry M. Alpert, President of Menorah Manor, 1986–1988.

Edward W. Vinocur, CEO of Menorah Manor, 1985–1988.

about the care of the elderly and how to utilize the knowledge to provide a sensitive approach to nursing home services and policies which guided the operation of Menorah Manor. The Building Committee ensured that the design, quality, and upkeep of the physical plant would be a constant priority in order to meet the needs of the elderly. The Ethics Committee formulated ethical policy to guide the staff, residents, and families. The Budget and Finance Committee and the Menorah Manor Foundation oversaw the resources of the facility and on a continuous basis, raised funds. The Menorah Manor Guild sponsored and supervised the volunteer programs where people throughout the region helped in every aspect of daily activities, including cultural programs, religious practices, entertainment, resident care, recording oral histories, and all other fund raising, educational, cultural, and social events of importance to Tampa Bay Jewish community life. Because of this the Florida Department of Health and Rehabilitative Services gave Menorah Manor, in its first year of operation, a superior rating.

Ted Wittner was the Chairman of the Board. Irwin H. Miller was the President. Marion Samson-Joseph was the President of the Menorah Manor Foundation. She said, "...We are indeed fortunate for the past support of the many community members, who have made Menorah Manor possible. Our home has merged all of our communities together, in supporting a common goal, the care of our frail elderly..." Ida Michaels was the President of Menorah Manor Guild. She said, "...We have grown in numbers and even more importantly, in the number of volunteer hours of service given....Our goal is to help our Home, in any way possible, to enhance the quality of life for our residents..." The Chief Executive Officer was Edward W. Vinocur, who continued in this position until 1988. (Note: Most of the information concerning the highlights of each year has come from annual reports. The reports are based on a fiscal year from June 30 of one year to June 30 of another year, instead of a calendar year. This may cause a slight error in the reporting of the dates of various events. For example,

something coming from a 1985-1986 year report might show up in the Highlights of 1985 instead of the Highlights of 1986.)

Highlights of 1986

The Menorah Manor Foundation was established to ensure the highest quality of care and continuity for the Home. The officers were: Ted P. Wittner, Chairman; Barry M. Alpert, President; Dr. Sidney Grau, Vice President; Thelma Rothman, Secretary; Walter H. Kessler, Treasurer; and Ida Michaels, President Menorah Manor Guild.

Because of the high level of care given to the residents, Menorah Manor once again received a superior rating from the State of Florida, Department of Health and Rehabilitative Services. The Jewish community of the Tampa Bay area continued to provide considerable funding to help Menorah Manor provide services for those who could not afford it. No one can say that the frail and the elderly, who are financially unable to live in a proper homelike atmosphere, will be deprived because of lack of financial means. The people of the Jewish community have and will continue to take care of their sick and elderly forever. Community support from countless individuals and foundations is considered to be "A Legacy of Love."

Highlights of 1987

Menorah Manor, the regional home for Jewish living, entered its third year. The first two years reinforced the commitment to provide a beautiful home-like setting for parents and grandparents to live as independently as possible with dignity and respect. "Menorah Manor is about caring for the elderly who have so diligently cared for us their entire lives. Now it's their turn, and it's our responsibility to ensure that they are happy, comfortable, and well cared for." A new Alzheimer's Therapy Program, was started. This program was for the residents who needed one-on-one attention. Various therapies were used to aid in sensory stimulation, reality orientation, re-motivation, and re-socialization. The goal was to invoke a response from the individual and encourage participation in life. A Day Resident Program was established as a one-year demonstration project. Three new therapists were added to the Rehabilitation Department.

Florida Governor, Bob Martinez, toured the facility following an unannounced visit by Health and Rehabilitative Services. The officials were highly complimentary of Menorah Manor, its care planning, resident oriented, methods and programs, and family oriented atmosphere. HRS decided to use Menorah Manor as an overall model to measure other nursing homes throughout the state. Governor Martinez said, "This is a place where there is life..."

The officers were: Irwin H. Miller, Chairman; Barry M. Alpert, President; Dr. Sidney Grau, Vice President/President Elect; Walter H. Kessler, Secretary; Saul Schechter, Treasurer; Marion Samson-Joseph, President Foundation Board of Trustees; Shirley Solomon, President Menorah Manor Guild.

Highlights of 1988

Irwin H. Miller said, "Menorah Manor means so much to me and my family. It gives me a warm and good feeling to be part of this fine Home for the Jewish elderly of our Tampa Bay area and to work with our involved Board and community members. We remain committed to our policy of caring and excellence..." Dr. Sidney Grau said, "Our Home for Jewish Living has completed a proud and full fourth year. Our tradition of excellence has continued with the leadership of our new Executive Director and skilled new management in Nursing and Rehabilitation, Finance, and the Dietary Service. We still operate virtually at capacity, a testimony to our reputation, and indeed we always will."

Marshall Seiden was appointed Chief Executive Officer of Menorah Manor and Menorah Manor Foundation and continues in this role until the present. Marshall Seiden said, "Menorah Manor is unique. Our level of care is not surpassed, our love for our residents has no limits and our community friendships are too numerous to be counted. The Menorah spirit is priceless and I am proud to share in it..."

Marshall S. Seiden

In 1970, Marshall Seiden graduated with a Bachelor of Arts Degree from the State University of New York at Stony Brook. He also was a graduate of the University of Hartford, School of Business and Public Administration. In 1983, he received his Certificate in Nursing Home Administration from Long Island University, Department of Health Care and Public Administration. He continues to update his technical and professional skills by attending numerous continuing education seminars in all aspects of health care management. He has authored or co-authored several publications and presentations on various topics related to the health care management and planning fields.

Marshall Seiden, CEO or Menorah Manor, 1988–present.

He served as: Administrative Resident and then Administrative Assistant at University Hospital, State University of New York at Stony Brook, New York; Assistant to the Executive Director and then Assistant Executive Director at Mount Sinai Hospital, Hartford, Connecticut; Assistant Vice President and then Senior Assistant Vice President at Mount Sinai Medical Center, Milwaukee, Wisconsin; Chief Operating Officer and Deputy Executive Director, White Plains Hospital Medical Center, White Plains, New York; Administrator and Associate Executive Director, Daughters of Jacob Geriatric Center, New York, New York; Vice President of Operations, Multi-Care Management, Hackensack, New Jersey; Executive Director, Greater Harlem Nursing Home Division, Jewish Home and Hospital for Aged, New York, New York.

His academic appointments include: Lecturer of the Medical College of Wisconsin; Preceptor, College of New Rochelle; Lecturer, Long Island University; and St. Petersburg Junior College, Health Care Professions Center.

Marshall Seiden is a Licensed Nursing Home Administrator in New York, New Jersey, and Florida. He is also a Certified Health Care Executive by the American College of Health Care Executives. He is a Diplomate of the American College of Health Care Executives and has served on the Board of Directors as well as chaired numerous committees for the Florida Association of Homes for the Aging, Association of Jewish Aging Services, St. Anthony's Hospital, and various other professional and community

Suzanne and Saul Schechter, Co-Presidents of Menorah Manor, 1990–1993

Irving Weissman, President of Menorah Manor, 1993–1995

Marilyn Weissman, Chair of Menorah Manor, 1999–2001.

organizations, and the State of Florida. In 1994, Marshall was honored by the Florida Association of Homes for the Aging as Executive of the Year.

Highlights of 1989

Menorah Manor is the only not for profit Jewish community sponsored skilled nursing home on the West Coast of Florida. The residents come from Pinellas, Hillsborough, Pasco, Polk, Sarasota and Manatee Counties. Irwin Miller said, "... Menorah Manor exemplifies what can be done when an entire community believes, works, and joins together in identifying and fulfilling a need." Dr. Sidney Grau said, "Esprit-I saw it everywhere-I felt it everywhere." Marshall Seiden said, "...This was a year of important new programs, all instituted to ensure that our care remains a standard for the profession." The new programs included: a new medical program; restorative care program; on-site eye care services; increased emphasis on family liaison; improved food service program; etc..

Highlights of 1990

Menorah Manor continued to make significant program improvements. These included: establishment of an in-house dental program; restaurant-style food service and new menu selections; providing services to Menorah Center; participating in statewide elder-care public policy discussions; growing the Membership Program and Building Fund; establishing a greater focus on ethics and environment; commencement of nursing education programs. Marion Samson-Joseph said, "Having had an opportunity this year to observe what and how other homes are doing, I must say that for being the new kid on the block, we are doing a remarkable job." A new program was started to assure that the building, furniture and equipment were maintained properly. An Evolution Committee was formed to investigate the feasibility of expanding the activities within the Home and into the community in conjunction with other agencies. This was geared toward helping the frail Jewish elderly.

The officers were: Marion Samson-Joseph, Chairman, Menorah Manor Board

of Trustees and Menorah Manor Foundation Board of Trustees; Leonard Seligman, President; Irving Weissman, Vice President; Irwin Wallace, Secretary; Karen Sher, Treasurer; Sue and Saul Schechter, Co-Presidents, Menorah Manor Foundation Board of Trustees; Marilyn Weissman, President, Menorah Manor Guild Board of Trustees; Irwin H. Miller, Shalom Geriatric Services Board of Trustees.

Highlights of 1991

An innovative Home Care program was started by Menorah Manor in cooperation with a local agency to offer special services from homemakers, companions, home health aides, physical and occupational therapists, speech pathologists, medical social workers, and registered and licensed nurses. This is now part of the broad mission to provide geriatric care to the Jewish elderly in the area.

Highlights of 1992

In keeping with constantly upgrading the facility to promote excellence in servicing the Jewish elderly, the first-floor and the Alzheimer's unit were renovated and redecorated. An "Activity Wall" was provided to offer self-directed activities to the residents. In order to keep ahead of the financial needs of operating an excellent nursing home, a life insurance program was initiated. Marion and John Joseph once again demonstrated their continuous foresight, commitment, and support for Menorah Manor by purchasing a one million dollar life insurance policy, with the Menorah Manor Foundation named as beneficiaries. To lead by example is a hallmark of the life of Marion Samson-Joseph.

Highlights of 1993

Menorah Manor entered its 9th year of service to the Jewish elderly by being faithful to its mission of providing a caring, safe, Jewish home for the elderly including the finest professional care available. Menorah Manor continued to meet the needs of the community, in terms of residents served, enhanced programming, financial stability, and loving care

The officers were: Leonard Seligman,

Chairman, Menorah Manor Board of Trustees; Irving Weissman, President. Saul Schechter, Chairman, Menorah Manor Foundation Board of Trustees; Loretta and Marshall Linsky, Co-President; Sydonia Green, President Menorah Manor Guild Board.

Highlights of 1994
Menorah Manor History Project

The Menorah Manor History Project started in March and ended in 1995. This was a compilation of oral histories of a variety of significant individuals conducted by a volunteer group. Anita Sher was the Chairperson. Anita Helfand was the transcriptionist. The interviewers were: Helen Applefield, Marilyn Benjamin, Phyllis Braveman, Iris Bush, Marcia Gold, Dottie Goldblatt, Roberta Golding, Syd Green, Audrey Haubenstock, Jacqueline Jacobs, Miriam Kahan, Bunnie Katz, Renée Krosner, Dell Krug, Judy Ludin, Sonya Miller, Adele Morris, Donna Orns, Gladys Osher, Marshall Seiden, Sally Segal, Sheila Weil, Leonard Yager, and Phyllis Zamosky. The people interviewed were: Dr. Phillip Benjamin, Lucy Berkowitz, Lee Colbert, Ina Gotler Colen, Leonard Gotler, Rose Cooper, Maury Goldblatt, Donna Orns, Dorothy Goldblatt, and Lillian Grau, Roberta Golding, Harold L. Goldberg, Marie S. Grant, Joel Grossman, Reuben Halprin, Bunnie Katz, Reva Kent, Horty and Morty Lasher, Howard Lawrence, Julius Lovitz, Ida Michaels, Irwin Miller, Dr. David LeVine, Bruce Marger, Jean Markman, Eleanor and Franklin Rosenblatt, Thelma Rothman, Charles Rutenberg, Saul Schechter, Len Seligman, Betty Siegel, Ted Wittner, Ruth Rivkind, Margaret Smith, Marion Samson-Joseph, Len Yager and Sid Yanchuck. In order to avoid repetition, only portions of some of the interviews are used in this chapter.

The goal of the History Committee was to record Menorah Manor's history as it occurred. Most of the interviews were tape-recorded and then transcribed onto the computer. A special history book was put together and placed on a history pedestal donated by Marion Samson-Joseph. Excerpts of the interviews follow.

Dr. Phillip Benjamin said, "...If I were to say who is the real genesis of Menorah

Manor, I would have to go back to Rabbi Chapman...The Federation at one time tried a proposal to sponsor a Jewish nursing home, but I understand...they were in no position to guarantee any deficit that might occur, so they dropped it. The B'nai B'rith had a committee,... (but it) came to a halt....The first thing we had to do was prepare a Certificate of Need for the Health Systems Agency to approve...Gary Silvers,... helped us tremendously by filling out the form....We received our Certificate of Need on December 2, 1981, but that was the beginning of several battles at that time... The synagogue (Congregation B'nai Israel) agreed to sell Menorah Manor an acre of ground far below its value...Fred Hirt,...Chief Executive of the Miami Jewish Home of the Aged (acted) as a consultant for our project and that saved us from many heartaches. I'm very happy to say that our Jewish community responded very very favorably to the concept of the Jewish Nursing Home. Particularly, I was impressed with the concept of it being kosher even though many of the people were not kosher respecting the religious observances of people who built the community and who needed care...It was built with love and with cash, it all goes together....The main differential between our building once again and so many of the others was in the quality of the building both in design and construction. This Menorah Manor was never intended as a warehouse for elderly people; it's a building designed for living."

Maury Goldblatt said, "...We at the Congregation (Congregation B'nai Israel) had just finished allowing the land for the Day School and the Day School was starting to hum a little bit and I think, at that time, that Rabbi Chapman had suggested that maybe to make a complete complex a nursing home would be an ideal type of situation and I think that is when it started. Older members of our congregation got together and decided that might be something that we ought to work at. I'm talking about Teddy, Phil, and, of course, Irwin, Harold Rivkind, and Rabbi Chapman. The religious services would be as close as possible to a neutral type of situation. It wasn't going to be Orthodox, Conservative, Reform.."

Loretta and Marshall Linsky, Co-Presidents of Menorah Manor Foundation, 1993–1996.

Adele Morris said, "I am sure that this (Menorah Manor) was the most lively supported community event that ever occurred in this community. It touched everybody and everyone anticipated the need for it. I know you are all involved. I know that Mori was involved with the planning and furnishings and you three are very important to this whole project (Donna Orns, Dorothy Goldblatt, and Lillian Grau)…"

Roberta Golding said, "My mother, Fanny Marks, was eighty nine when she died a year ago…She came here (Clearwater) Friday after she married my father…in 1920… She decided to open a store in Clearwater. She commuted every day and then she decided that when I was in the 10th grade (around 1937) that we would move to Clearwater. So we rented our house and rented another house in Clearwater…. Clearwater had two Jewish families when we moved there…She (Fanny) came from Utica, New York and she and my father (Simon) met (when) he was stationed at Utica before he went overseas-before World War I. And the reason they came here was because of Max Argintar (Arnold Argintar's father). He was a good friend of my uncle. My uncle came to Tampa; he got a job. He sent for my aunt and she brought her mother. Her husband had died, so she brought her mother and her sisters and her whole family-the Irving Peckets.

It is interesting that this is the fifth or sixth interview that I have done and each one of the volunteers have said the same thing, that the residents are not looked on as patients; they are residents and they're cared about individually and the staff and the volunteers go to great lengths to help these people retain their identity. Which is, of course, the greatest thing you can do is to let a man and woman remain in their own identity and their independence as much as they can for however much they have, whatever circumstances they are living, so that is a great mitzvah."

Reuben Halprin said, "…Menorah Center and Menorah Manor was always Phil Benjamin's motivation…Everybody that worked to make this thing fly, really worked with Phil under his guidance and direction. He always stepped to the back

and he gave every body the reins and orchestrated it perhaps…Besides Phil and Ted Wittner, there is myself, Murray Jacobs, and Rabbi Chapman was involved. (Initially in planning the nursing home.)…Personally, I had been in other nursing homes and there was a very depressing, disgusting scene. As nice as they try to make it, the overwhelming stench of urine was really such that the cleaning fluids was overwhelming and I thought that this was not necessary and I'm sure that something nicer and cleaner, airy and lighter could and should be provided… The difference between them…and Menorah is just like night and day; you could just see the difference…We had a dream that we hoped that this thing would fly and it did and it is everything we hoped it would be. It is that clean and neat and the management has made it good. The help that works there seems to appreciate it more…"

Bunnie Katz said, "…I remember Abe and me both going there (Menorah Manor) trying to get the building ready for the residents to move and I remember washing basins and toilets,…and doing that housekeeping that needed to be done…(Bunnie and Abe have been involved for twenty years as volunteers in many different roles in Menorah Manor.) People are treated with dignity."

Reva Kent said, "…There was never any doubt that the Jewish (people needed a) Jewish nursing home…I recall early on when Menorah Manor needed seed money and Charlie Rutenberg, who was always a visionary, saw all of these needs coming up…He had placed an amount of money something close to $100,000 in our TOP Foundation and he set up the endowment for senior needs…I do remember their calling it seed money, and at the time, the group only wanted to have ten percent indigents in Menorah Manor in order to keep it afloat and have it more fiscally sound and Charlie insisted that there should be more because we have too many seniors that didn't have funds to get into Menorah Manor…He recommended that $25,000 be used in seed money from his endowment account and the amount of indigents had to be twenty five percent."

Ida Michaels said, "…Probably one of the most exciting parts of being involved with the Guild (Ida was the first Guild President), and Menorah Manor is that everybody wanted to help and everybody did help. They were excited about doing something. This was a new project in there was never any problem getting people to participate....We had to feel our way in deciding what the Guild was going to do, would it be fund raising or would it simply be there to provide volunteer services. The first Guild event was a dinner theater party at Ruth Eckerd Hall at the Richard B. Baumgardner Center for the Performing Arts. That was a sellout and the money was raised from that event to provide a bus for the residents to go to their appointments or to provide outings for the residents....Menorah Manor is a home for the Jewish frail and elderly and has served six counties, so that a lot of the original people on the Board in an effort to get across the knowledge that Menorah Manor existed, formed a Speakers Bureau and went to the various synagogues, temples, clubs, etc. to let the community know that we were there and our information that we were passing along was met with, I would say, a great deal of enthusiasm and support..."

Irwin Miller said, "The need for the home was...studied, discussed through the Federation, through many, many groups for ten years before, but with all the studies there never seemed to be a means of how we can establish a home on the West Coast of Florida, funds, people or expertise that we could structure such a home...Then we enlarged the group and we called a meeting in Ted Wittner's office of about twenty or thirty...Jewish leaders from Pinellas County and some from Tampa. We asked anyone who was interested to put some seed money in and I would say about one hundred percent put in monies which gave us the ability then and the enthusiasm to go forward... Basically we were looking at five million dollars minimum in funds, which was unheard of in 1982 or 1983. I didn't think anyone could have raised that much money. But the need was there and the people felt that the need was there and that was most important that we create this home for Jewish living...then Marion Samson-Joseph came through with a million-dollar endowment

pledge,...we immediately went out to the whole community...to build our home."

Thelma Rothman said, "Long before Menorah Manor received its name, there was a dream in this community to establish a Jewish home for the aged. We had, prior to that, sent all of our people up to Jacksonville to River Garden and it was a terrible separation for the families and we have determined many, many years ago that we needed a Jewish home in our area. Menorah Manor came into being when a few very, very influential people decided that it was going to be in our area... Walking into the home (Menorah Manor) and seeing the residents there and realizing that they have a home away from home, that they are getting quality care, lifetime care, loving care, is really very gratifying. I would say that this is the highlight because it is a realization of a dream for the Jewish community...I think the thing that impresses me most is the continued support of the Jewish community and the continued support of the founders, Board of Directors, and the employees of the home. I think the dedication to the home is beautiful."

Charles Rutenberg said, "Menorah Manor was a dream for a long time before it became a reality. Probably the beginning of Menorah Manor goes back to a company called 58th St. Land Corporation. There was a group of eight investors, including Phil Benjamin, Irwin Miller, Charlie Rutenberg, and others. The discussions about the "58th Street Land Corporation" started in the late 1950s. They purchased five acres of land adjacent to Congregation B'nai Israel. The intention was holding (land) investment and probably to be donating it to the Jewish community. This land was north and east and contingent to the synagogue property....At that time I had a company that I owned with my brother, Art, known as Sunshine Oldsmar Farms and we owned earth-moving equipment. The land that we bought was very low and partially swamp and I recall that I put a drag line into the creek running through the middle of the swamp, cleaned it out, and made all the land around the synagogue useful, including some of the land that belonged to the City of St. Petersburg which I believe was the land that was later sold... Sometime after that, a committee was formed to look into the feasibility of building a nursing home... Into the early 60s, I recall that Len Seligman was on (the committee) and I believe, most of the time, headed the committee. Phil Benjamin, Irwin Miller, and Ted Wittner were prime movers...At the same time the Jewish community was in the difficult process of possible combination of two communities (Clearwater and St. Petersburg Jewish communities). When we began this program, I believe Reva Kent was President of the Federation and that was quite a few years, after years of discussion between St. Petersburg and Clearwater should there be two Federations or one Federation. Federation was really not involved (although totally supportive)."

Marion Samson-Joseph said, "... It has been a very gratifying experience. First of all, I work with a Board who is totally cooperative, we don't get any of the dissension that I see at the other boards that I worked on. The cooperation is wonderful. We basically work for the same thing. And like I said, that it is one of the few organizations ... (where) you have complete cooperation and it is fun to work with all these people... Just talk to some of the residents, they are so appreciative of the things that you do for them. It is really very rewarding."

Irwin "Wally" Wallace, President of Menorah Manor, 1995–1997.

James Soble, President of Menorah Manor, 1997–2001.

Officers

The officers were: Leonard Seligman, Chairman, Menorah Manor Board of Trustees; Irving Wiseman, President; Saul Schechter, Chairman, Menorah Manor Foundation Board of Trustees; Loretta and Marshall Linsky, President; Ruth Glickman, President, Menorah Manor Guild Board of Trustees.

Highlights of 1995

A 189 page 10th anniversary Tribute Journal and History was produced by Sue Schechter and Gene Linsky. *The Journal* brought in $140,000 worth of ads. Almost 300 people attended the Guild-sponsored 10th anniversary gala at the St. Petersburg Coliseum. New programs included: formal dementia program; dental clinic; skin and wound care program; comprehensive social and behavioral services; intensive nursing

services; full-scale rehabilitation services; graduate physician training in geriatrics; quality assurance and improvement program. In ten years, Menorah Manor provided 419,000 days of care to 680 residents.

Highlights of 1996

Menorah Manor was awarded its usual Superior Rating, but this time with zero deficiencies. This placed Menorah Manor in the top ten percent of nursing homes in the United States. Approval was granted to expand the facility for sixty more residents. A formal Rehabilitation Department was started with the hiring of a full-time Rehabilitation Director.

Highlights of 1997

Menorah Manor followed the previous year's State and Federal zero deficiency accreditation with a zero deficiency first accreditation by the Joint Commission on Accreditation of Health Care Organizations with Commendation for both Menorah Manor and the Bresler's Alzheimer's Program. This placed Menorah Manor in the top one percent of all skilled nursing facilities in the country. Marshall Seiden said, "Hats off to an outstanding, totally committed staff, the most supportive volunteers, the Trustees, and an incredibly enthusiastic and generous community."

On July 18, the first stake was driven into the ground for the expansion of Menorah Manor. The official Groundbreaking Ceremony of the sixty bed expansion took place on Sunday, September 21. Rabbi Jacob Luski, of Congregation B'nai Israel of St. Petersburg, led the service. From that day on, the community had the opportunity to watch their Home for Jewish Living grow. There were enhanced recreational activities, rehabilitation, and post-hospital care, and much more.

The officers were: Leonard Seligman, Chairperson, Menorah Manor Board of Trustees and Chairperson, Menorah Manor Foundation Board of Trustees; James Soble, President, Menorah Manor Board of Trustees; and Marion Samson-Joseph, President, Menorah Manor Foundation Board of Trustees; Fagl Oxman, President Menorah Manor Guild Board of Trustees.

Highlights of 1998

Suzanne Schechter, Trustee and Coming-of-Age Campaign Coordinator, said, "According to Jewish tradition, the highest status one can achieve is the "Crown of a good name." This crown can be worn only by a person whose life is characterized by good words, charity, and deeds of loving kindness. The world of philanthropy is not only a tradition at Menorah Manor, it is perpetuated by a belief that once we identify a need, nothing is impossible to achieve. Our beautiful new addition, and the response of the community to the Coming of Age Campaign are perfect examples. We have raised three and one half million dollars so far, toward our goal of six million dollars.

Three major new facilities were established: The Irv Weissman Adult Day Center; the Ida and Jules Lowengard Synagogue; and the Weinman Alzheimer's Care Village. At the Dedication Program for the new and enhanced facility, Rabbi Gary Klein of Temple Ahavat Shalom gave the invocation, Leonard Seligman gave the keynote address, and Rabbi Steven Moch of Temple Beth-El dedicated the new building.

Highlights of 1999

Besides the new facilities mentioned in Highlights of 1998, the following new facilities and/or programs were added: The Toby Weinman Jewish Hospice Program; The Kelly and Stewart Lasher Rehabilitation Center; a chaplaincy program, employing a full-time Rabbi. The Coming of Age Campaign raised five million dollars to fund the expansion and renovation. The young people of the Jewish community have become supporters and trustees of Menorah Manor, thereby ensuring the viability of the leadership of the Jewish community. Marshall Seiden said, "We are the Jewish Community Elder Care Experts, a sobering and important responsibility that mandates continual attention to quality and planning for the future."

The officers were: Leonard Seligman, Chairperson Menorah Manor Board of Trustees and the Menora Manor Foundation Board of Trustees; James Sobel, President, Menorah Manor Board of Trustees; Marion Samson-Joseph, President, Menorah Manor Foundation Board of Trustees; Madelyn Liss, President, Menorah Manor Guild Board of Trustees.

Highlights of 2000

Four residents, with an average age of ninety, became Bat Mitzvah. They were: Edith Berger, Evelyn Shultz, Frieda Sohon, and Sadie Wahnon. It was a remarkable act of love on their part, at their ages of eighty six to ninety two, since it takes children one or more years to prepare for this most meaningful event. A large number of Guild members attended and shared in this wonderful occasion. Sue Schechter turned toward Marshall Seiden on the bimah during the ceremony with tears in her eyes and said, "This is what it's about...this is what we do it all for Menorah Manor." This was a wonderful affirmation of life and Jewish living and reinforced the message of Menorah Manor, that this is your home away from home, and that the remainder of your life should be meaningful. Menorah Manor has gone well beyond the quote on the annual report, "Do not cast me off in old age; when my strength fails, do not forsake me!" Menorah Manor stands for light and life, dignity and happiness. These four people looked forward to their future rather than sitting and bemoaning their age and ailments.

Highlights of 2001

The Menorah Manor Marvels won first place in the annual citywide nursing home Balloon Volleyball Tournament. The therapeutic recreation staff helped organize this tournament, with a Menorah Manor Team made up of residents. Menorah Manor was rated the lowest risk potential (highest-quality) in the United States for insurance purposes. Nursing home insurance had increased almost fourteen times over a period of two years. This performance rating was absolutely essential to help keep Menorah Manor in business.

Highlights of 2002

Menorah Manor was selected as one of only six nursing homes, and out of almost 700 nursing homes in the State of Florida to be awarded the Gold Seal of Excellence for

Barbara Rosenblum, President of Menorah Manor, 2001–2003.

Sharyn R. Wittner, President of Menorah Manor Foundation, 2001–2003.

Elinor and Samuel Fishman Co-Chairpersons, Menorah Manor Foundation, 2001–2003.

being recognized as an outstanding skilled nursing facility. The Jewish community and the general community should be so proud of Menorah Manor because the honors keep coming.

The officers were: James B. Soble, Chairperson Menorah Manor Board of Trustees; Barbara Rosenblum, President; Ellie and Sam Fishman, Co-Chairpersons, Menorah Manor Foundation Board of Trustees; Sharyn Wittner, President; Gail Frye, President Menorah Manor Guild Board of Trustees.

Highlights of 2003

In June, the new Toby Weinman Assisted Living Residence opened and it was almost fifty percent occupied. The Jewish community generously came forward with most of the cost of the construction project and a mortgage was not needed. The Boards of Trustees did an intensive review of their bylaws and revised the articles of incorporation to ensure that Menorah Manor would operate very efficiently. A gala event was held to celebrate the 18th year of service to the Jewish elderly.

The officers were: Barbara Rosenblum, Chairperson, Menorah Manor Board of Trustees; Saul Rachelson, Chairperson Elect; Ellie and Sam Fishman, Co-Chairpersons, Menorah Manor Foundation Board of Trustees; Sharyn Wittner, President/Co-Chairperson; Dell Krug, President, Menorah Manor Guild Board of Trustees.

Highlights of 2004

Menorah Manor is currently operating the following programs for the Tampa Bay region. They are: The Bernard L. Samson Nursing Center; The Toby Weinman Assisted Living Residence at Menorah Manor; The Irv Weissman Adult Day Center; the Kelly and Stewart Lasher Rehabilitation Center; the Toby Rothbardt Bresler Alzheimer Program and the Toby Weinman Alzheimer's Care Village; the Ida and Jules Lowengard Synagogue; the Toby Weinman Jewish Hospice Program; the Geriatric Assessment Program; and the Menorah Manor Guild. The next step is to increase services, through the development of the North County Belcher Road property.

Highlights of 2005

Because of the unique role that Menorah Manor plays in the lives of the Jewish people of Pinellas County and surrounding areas, Marshall Seiden was asked by the author to present the needs and solutions to the needs of the elder Jewish population in this area of the West Coast of Florida. He wrote, "A TWENTY YEAR VISION FOR MENORAH MANOR." He said, "We have provided a successful twenty years of care, over one million days of residential care alone, and multifaceted programs and support for the frail elderly. During the next twenty years, the challenge will be much greater. During that period, the children of the post-World War II baby boom will become the population Menorah Manor must serve and those who have already made their retirement home in this area will be much older. The huge population of elderly will have a very large segment that is frail and needing support. The perception of trust, quality, culture and spiritual comfort that Menorah Manor gives to its community will cause it to consider and establish more services, some new, and some to create more capacity in existing services.

We may see the following: additional and multifaceted assisted-living facilities; additional adult day health center capacity and new models of adult day care combining recreational, cognitive, and physical health care modalities targeted to specific sub-groups in the elderly population; more assistance to families trying to understand their elderly parents needs; new ethical, philosophical, and cultural approaches to the care and lives of the elderly that meet the needs and preferences of an American-born population that came of age in the last half of the twentieth century, is highly educated and enjoyed a much healthier life and different standard of living than did their own grandparents; services brought to the private homes of the frail elderly and community support for the Jewish elderly in naturally occurring retirement communities; increased capacity for outpatient rehabilitation and short-term inpatient rehabilitation; more support for end-of-life care and greater expertise and emphasis on palliative care; ever wider support for Jewish community sponsored elder care services that reflect the wishes of the older population and their children.

It is clear that Menorah Manor will be even more important in the life of this Jewish community during the next twenty years. They will be comforted to know that Menorah Manor is planning to provide the assistance they want and need."

Reflections

In the late 1950s, Rabbi Chapman of Congregation B'nai Israel did what rabbis do, he saw a need for taking care of the frail Jewish elderly and he developed a vision of a Jewish home for the aged (Phillip Benjamin Tower) and also a Jewish nursing home (Menorah Manor) for those who needed greater care. He contacted the highly respected Dr. Phillip Benjamin, who worked behind the scenes as well as acted as a role model for others, and discussed his vision with Phil. Phil assembled a group of men including Murray Jacobs, Ted Wittner, Maury Goldblatt, Irwin Miller, Charlie Rutenberg, and two others. With the purchase of the land, the original group expanded and included Leonard Seligman, Reuben Halprin, Bruce Marger, Harold Rivkind, and others. The total Jewish community of Pinellas County and surrounding areas responded and started to develop the financial support necessary. However, it took one person, once again, to move the process from vision to reality by her extremely generous gift. In 1984, Marion Samson-Joseph gave one million dollars to the building of Menorah Manor and on May 20, 1985, Menorah Manor opened. In 1988, Marshall Seiden arrived, and has done an extremely commendable job since then. Add to the mix the professional and support staff, who are highly trained, very productive, and who act lovingly toward the residents. The last part of the mix needed to have a successful home for the Jewish elderly, who are frail, was to bring the love and effort of many hundreds of volunteers who did everything from giving manicures to being the Chairperson of the Board of Trustees. Each and every volunteer must be honored because he/she gave of himself/herself to make our elderly Jewish population happier

and healthier. One person can make such a huge difference in the lives of others.

Phillip Benjamin Tower

In 1968, a group of men of the Jewish community assembled to found Menorah Center, a non-profit and non–denominational corporation to provide affordable housing for Jewish and non-Jewish senior citizens. Its goal was to continue to provide adult independent living, while improving the quality of life in a secure environment. The first officers were: President Phillip Benjamin, Vice President Murray Jacobs, Secretary/Treasurer Ted Wittner, and Assistant Secretary Harold Rivkind. The Board of Directors were: Reuben Halprin, Sidney Colen, Maury Goldblatt, and Rabbi Morris Chapman. Dr. Benjamin remained President from 1969-1997. Ted Wittner, the Treasurer for twenty seven years, was elected President after Dr. Benjamin's retirement. The Board of Directors in 1998, after Dr. Benjamin died, renamed Menorah Center, Phillip Benjamin Tower in honor of all of the community work that Dr. Phillip Benjamin did over his lifetime.

There are 196 units in the Tower. The average is a ninety nine percent occupancy rate. The Phillip Benjamin Tower has been renovated, and a state-of-the-art air-conditioning system as well as new elevators and a new fire safety system have been installed. From the time of its original opening in 1971, the Tower has been the home for many individuals, who would have been lonely and in a poor housing situation without it. The current amenities include: a health center with a nurse on duty five hours a day; three modestly priced kosher lunches for those people who want them; a barber/beauty shop; a mini grocery store; a coffee shop which serves lunches; a pottery program; a free bus; weekly religious prayers for those who want them; a front desk open twenty four hours a day; a nursing home next door; a synagogue next door; and provision for non-Jewish people to attend church. One hundred of the 201 residents are non-Jewish.

The current Board of Directors includes: Ted Wittner, Marilyn Benjamin, Judy Benjamin, Cecile Berko, Michael Bernstein,

Saual Rachelson, Chair of Menorah Manor, 2003–2005.

Sandy Bozeman, Alan Cohan, Dr. Bruce Epstein, Jerry Gilbert, Joel Grossman, David Halprin, Sharyn Wittner, Abe Katz, Rabbi Jacob Luski, Dick Mensh, Ron Oxman, Dr. Harold Rivkind, Greg Sembler, and Ronald Yogman. The Board of Menorah Center Foundation includes: Ted Wittner, Marilyn Benjamin, Jerry Gilbert, Joel Grossman, David Halprin, Abe Katz and Sharyn Wittner.

Philip Benjamin Tower

CHAPTER 23

JEWISH SCHOOLS

Pinellas County Jewish Day School

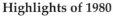

Highlights of 1979

The first community meeting to organize a Pinellas County Jewish Day School was held in February, at the home of Gordon and Helanine Saskin. Interested parents in the community were invited to the meeting. In March, the first planning meeting was held at the home of Michael and Helen Phillips. The first Board of Directors was elected that evening. The Board consisted of Michael Phillips, Jay Kauffman, Reva Pearlstein, Lois Pardoll, Joanne Luski, Ilan Bar Av, Stan Freifeld, Gordon Saskin and Hyman Phillips. In October, the first three community forum meetings for parents were held throughout the county. Parents were able to ask questions of the Board about the proposed school, curriculum, and purpose and goals of the school. Rabbi Jacob Luski offered classrooms at Congregation B'nai Israel, for the new school.

Highlights of 1980

In January, a search committee was formed to hire the first principal. In April, Edwin Frankel was hired to serve in this position. Interviews were then held at the Phillips' house to hire the first secular teacher, Karl Tremmel. Later, a reception was held at the Phillips' home to introduce the new teacher and principal to the community.

It was determined that it was necessary to raise one hundred thousand dollars to open the new school. A community solicitation was made, and the goal was met. The Jewish Federation voted to accept the Pinellas County Jewish Day School as one of its beneficiary agencies. The Federation donated scholarship money to the school. The President of the Pinellas County Jewish Day School served on the Board of the Federation.

The original donors known as Founders were: Mr. and Mrs. Gerald Benstock, Herman Forbes Foundation, Ms. Loretta Freifeld, Mr. Stanley Freifeld, Jewish Federation of Pinellas County, Mr. and Mrs. Maurice Goldblatt, Mr. and Mrs. Stanley Igel, Mr. Ralph Levey, Mr. and Mrs. A. J. Pardoll, Dr. and Mrs. Peter Pardoll, Mr. and Mrs. Hyman Phillips, Mary Rutenberg Foundation, Dr. and Mrs. Gordon Saskin; and Mrs. Helen Silverberg.

The school opened in August at Congregation B'nai Israel with grades K-1 and 2. There were twenty seven students on the first day.

Highlights of 1981

In February, Mrs. Reva Pearlstein, the President of the Pinellas County Jewish Day School, attended the Solomon Schechter national meeting of religious schools, to determine if the local school could become affiliated with the national body. Mark Silk was hired to become the new principal. The school expanded to include third grade.

Highlights of 1982

A trailer was purchased for use as a classroom as the school expanded to include fourth-grade. Mary Ruth Baumgartner was hired to run the office.

Highlights of 1983

The school population grew out of its existing facility. The Phillips family donated a new building to be built on a parking lot of Congregation B'nai Israel.

Highlights of 1984

The school moved into its new facility. The first fifth-grade class graduated.

Highlights of 1986

The school started its first athletic programs with an in-house soccer club. Middle school was now part of the program.

Highlights of 1987

The first Middle School class graduated. The first interschool athletic event was held with the Hillel school in Tampa.

Highlights of 1995

The school was moved to Highland Avenue.

Mission Statement

The Mission Statement of the school is as follows: "The Pinellas County Jewish Day School is grounded in the belief that Jewish education is vital to our children's future and is fundamental to the survival of the Jewish people. Jewish traditions and values infuse and energize the life of the school. We are active members of the Solomon Schechter Day School Association and reflect the philosophy and practices of Conservative Judaism. We strive to provide each student with an outstanding education by encouraging growth and excellence in both Jewish and general studies and by preparing the students to be: ethical and caring human beings; inquisitive learners; knowledgeable and committed Jews; and informed and responsible citizens." The motto of the school is, "Education is an adventure in successful learning."

The family base is diversified. Eleven percent are unaffiliated with synagogues. Eighteen percent are Reform. Eighteen percent are Orthodox. Fifty three percent are Conservative. Two thirds of the parents hold an advanced degree. All families have at least one parent who has attended or graduated from college.

Today, the children can go from kindergarten through eighth grade. It provides typical children's education, along with basic Judaism. All teachers are state certified and participate in continuing professional development. The current director is Pauline Rohrman.

Congregation Beth Shalom

The Congregation Beth Shalom Religious School was founded by Mary Rutenberg in 1958. Today, it is a two-day a week program for children from five to thirteen years old. An eighth grade program meets once a month for dinner and discussion. A Hebrew High School program is available to the older students. The goal of the religious school is to educate the children in Hebrew, in the commandments of mitzvot, tefillah (prayer), Jewish history, holidays, tikun olum (the repair of the world), and, in general, how to be kind and compassionate Jewish people. Each class level has age-appropriate material to cover the various subjects of Hebrew reading, prayer study, history, etc. Attendance at services is integrated into the curriculum to help prepare the student to become a Bar/Bat Mitzvah. Special art projects and musical selections are chosen for each of the Jewish holidays. In addition, on two occasions during the year, the Religious School students lead the services for the congregation. The oldest class is deeply involved in the study of the Holocaust. The students gain a solid understanding of the world political and social environments that allowed Hitler to come to power. The students visit and study at the Holocaust Museum in St. Petersburg. The Religious School is a warm, exciting, and vibrant place. The teachers are committed to excellence and the students possess a strong sense of Jewish identity. Congregation Beth Shalom believes in the partnership between teacher, student, and family and encourages the parents to be part of the children's education.

Congregation B'nai Israel Youth Department

Congregation B'nai Israel Youth Department supports all age groups of children, under the direction of a professional Youth Director to help support the formal education of the children at the Pauline Rivkind Talmud Torah and the Pinellas County Jewish Day School. Parents are involved as partners with the children in their religious education. A. Shabbat morning service is held for children in grades three to seven. This Junior Congregation meets thirty Shabbat mornings during the school year to learn and lead prayers and songs. Attendance is required of all the students of the Pauline Rivkind Talmud Torah. A K'tongregation is held two Shabbat mornings a month with age-appropriate activities for grades kindergarten, one, and two. A youth group for third, fourth, and fifth graders meets at least once each month for a social, religious, crafts and sports programs. It is called Halutzim. Kadima, a nationally-affiliated youth group for six, seventh, and eighth graders, meets at least twice a month for social, cultural, and religious programs. The children participate in sub-regional and regional activities such as encampment, convention, and Disney Day.

Golda Meir/Kent Center Preschool

The Jewish Community Center Preschool curriculum fosters social, artistic, moral, cognitive, and creative development in preschoolers through their own activities, discovery, and exploration. In addition, the child questions thoughtfully and learns to think for himself/herself. The Preschool helps children refine their skills for problem-solving, thinking, reasoning, and creating. Music and music lessons are an important part of the preschool study. Children are taught how to use the classroom libraries, with age-appropriate books, on a daily basis. Also, on a daily basis, children are taught how to use various techniques of art as a means of developing their mind and their own personal resources to deal with new situations. Cooking projects, which are age-appropriate, teach the children about good nutrition and trying new foods. The Preschool children are integrated into the aquatics program.

The Preschool goals are: social development, emotional development, cognitive development, physical development, creative development, and Jewish identity. The child's social development includes cooperating, sharing and interacting with others, making friends, and relating in a positive manner to other children and adults. They are taught how to sit quietly and listen as part of a group. The child's emotional development is specifically related to maintaining a comfortable separation from parents, a feeling of self-esteem and general happiness, and an eagerness to interact with other children and participate in school activities. The child's cognitive development prepares him/her for elementary school. This includes readiness in reading, math, social studies, and science concepts. They are taught listening skills, perceptual skills, and thinking skills. The child's physical development includes gross and fine motor coordination, increased strength and agility,

and the importance of good health habits. This includes nutritious and tasty morning and afternoon snacks and lunch. The child's creative development includes learning how to develop new ideas, new modes of expression, a willingness to reach outside of himself/herself, through art, movement and verbalization. The child's Jewish identity is fostered more through an experiential approach to Judaism. They do this through holiday and Shabbat activities and through Hebrew words, songs, prayers, and an understanding at child appropriate levels of the meaning of the prayers.

Temple Beth-El Pre-School

Temple Beth El Nursery School, now known as Temple Beth-El Preschool, was founded in 1962. The school was donated by Mr. and Mrs. Meyer Samuels. In 1962, Rabbi David J. Susskind helped establish a weekly kindergarten on a nonsectarian basis. It was originally limited to twenty five children. It functioned in the same manner as a kindergarten in the public school system, and was licensed under the laws of the State of Florida and the Pinellas County Board. The main objective of the kindergarten was to provide a foundation for future school endeavors and a healthful and enlightened environment. Mrs. Betty A. Beatty became the first head teacher. She had a Bachelor of Science Degree in Education and six years of experience in Pinellas County kindergartens. By 1967, the Day School had an enrollment of thirty five children. In 1972, the Acting Director was Mrs. Marci Raines, and the new teacher was Mrs. Linda Baron. Linda earned a Bachelor of Science Degree in Early Childhood Education from the University of South Florida and had previously taught on the elementary level in the Atlanta, Georgia school system. She had taught pre-school at the Jewish Community Center in Tampa. Marci Raines received a Bachelor of Science Degree from Central Missouri State University and graduate credits from the University of Kansas City Art Institute. She had previously taught in the Kansas City, Missouri, and Des Moines, Iowa public schools.

In 1973, the Preschool Department had been reorganized and a board of parents was actively involved in administration and programming. By 1974, half of the children enrolled were Christian and a special effort then was made to tie in the annual celebration of Brotherhood in the community with the diverse population of the preschool.

In 1981, the mission and programming of the preschool was based on the recognition of the following statement of childhood. "Early childhood experiences strongly contribute to the development of the child. A program based on the emotional, social, physical, and intellectual growth of the preschooler prepares him or her for the growing years and eventual childhood. Each day, the children are learning new skills. These may range from sharing toys to readiness experience. The scope of education is vast and challenging; the results are gratifying."

In 1987, Cindy Weisburg became the new Pre-School Director and stayed until 2002. Cindy earned a Bachelor's Degree in Elementary Education. She had also passed the Hebrew Regents Examination. There were thirty children enrolled in the 1989-1990 class. By 1991, fifty children were enrolled and by 1992, sixty children were enrolled.

In 2002, Elizabeth Croke became the new Preschool Director. Liz graduated from the University of South Florida with degrees in English and Library Science. She had been a preschool director for six years in Darien, Connecticut.

In 2005, Randi Nash-Ortiz became Director of the Pre-School. She brought with her an expertise in Judaism and a new curriculum with creative ideas. The school currently has an enrollment of fifty six children in various programs for ages two to five. Children may attend half-day sessions, full-day sessions, and also receive before and/or after care.

Religious School

In 1930, private Hebrew lessons were given to children of the congregants. By 1935, a formal school program was established for both congregants and non-congregants. In 1950, a shared Religious School program was operated in conjunction with Congregation B'nai Israel. There were 122 students enrolled. In 1951, the programs split and Dr. Parvey Hill became the first Head of School. The programs continued to grow and members of the congregation helped teach the children. The curriculum included Jewish History, Living Judaism, and Holidays. Since the building was too small for the entire school, the lower classes moved to the YWCA.

The current curriculum includes many facets of Jewish culture, Torah, Hebrew, life cycle celebrations, yearly calendar celebrations and observances. In 2001, a new school wing was dedicated. The state-of-the-art building incorporated a courtyard, a multi-purpose room, and several classrooms. In addition, there is a computer laboratory and a well-equipped Youth Lounge. Laurie Bar-Ness joined the professional team in 2003. Lauri earned a Master's in Jewish Education and the title of Reform Jewish Educator. She also has a Principal's License from the National Board of License, and a Family Educator's License.

Temple B'nai Israel
Baseman Early Childhood Center

When Rabbi and Renée Baseman moved to Clearwater, in June 1969, they had two small children, Adina, age five, and Jordana, who became two in August. They had left a large temple in Roslyn, New York, which included a successful preschool. Adina, Renée, and Rabbi had enjoyed the school. Kindergarten in Clearwater was only for half days. The Baseman's thought that Adina's time could be better utilized if there was a preschool at Temple B'nai Israel. Rabbi Baseman approached Jeanette Fein, a congregant with two children, knowing that she was a teacher, and asked her if she would start a preschool. She did and the first class of the Temple B'nai Israel Nursery School started in September, 1970 with seven girls. The first Teacher/Director was Jeanette Fein and the girls were Jordana Baseman, Julie Benjamin, Deborah Brown, Nancy Fine, Lainie Klein, Wendy Kurland, and Jennifer Thomas. By 1972, the congregation had moved into the new Temple on Belcher Road and the school expanded. Shortly thereafter, the Nursery School was licensed for children under six years of age, by the Pinellas County License Board. The school was then opened to the entire community. Subsequently, the School became one of the five top nursery schools on the recommended list in Pinellas County, and continues in this position until this very day.

In 1978, Jeanette recruited Renée Baseman to teach something unheard of in this area–two year olds! Renée began by teaching Tuesday and Thursday mornings with the ten mothers of the children rotating as assistants in the class. Soon, two classes were created, one on Monday, Wednesday, and Friday mornings, and the original one on Tuesday and Thursday mornings.

Many of the Temple B'nai Israel members, including Karen Zwerling, Pam Morris, Barbara Goodman, Jill Black, Sharon Tanner and Nancy Snyder, were teachers. When Jeanette and Saul Fein (a former Temple President) moved away, Jill Black took over as Director. When Jill decided to teach at Shorecrest, a private school, the Congregational Board hired René Baseman as Director/Teacher from 1985-1992. The school enjoyed exceptional growth. In 1992, Renée Baseman decided to go back to school at the University of South Florida, where she earned a Master's Degree in Counseling in 1995. Sharon Tanner, became the Director of the school and continued until 1999. The Congregational Board asked Renée to serve as interim Director until a replacement, Fran Halpern, was hired in 2000. The Preschool extension was proposed and completed in 2001. Fran Halprin resigned, Renée Baseman was interim Director, until Cheryl Matis was hired in 2001.

Under the leadership of Cheryl Matis, the school has grown and flourished, and is now an Early Childhood Learning Center for more than ninety students. In 2001, there were thirty three students. The programming changed from a one half day morning program to a full day, full-service school, with the half-day retained as a core program for parents who preferred this type of situation. Also, pre-care and after-care programs are available. The extended day enrichment program provides classes in dance, gymnastics, team sports, cooking, science, multi-cultural arts, computers,

and several languages including Spanish, Hebrew, and Americans Sign. The Judaic curriculum also expanded. Shabbat and the holidays are still a central focus. A values curriculum of Mitzvot has been added, as well as Jewish music, Bible stories, and for pre-kindergarten, Hebrew and a weekly parsha (the Torah is divided into fifty four sections or parsha) program.

In the Fall of 2005, Temple B'nai Israel was honored to become accredited by the National Association for the Education of Young Children. The preschool became a Florida Gold Seal School, the only Jewish Preschool in Pinellas County to be recognized in this manner. This was the successful completion of a one and one half year effort. In the Spring of 2005, the Preschool applied to become a state Voluntary Universal Pre-Kindergarten site and was so rewarded. The Center was named the Rabbi Arthur I. Baseman, DD and Renée L. Baseman Early Childhood Center, to honor these two unique people for their dedication to the school and in honor of Rabbi Baseman's 40th anniversary of his wonderful and successful career as a rabbi.

The Preschool also offers an entry-level parent- child program called First Step, for parents and children aged 0-24 months. Toddler Time is a two hour bridge program available to parents and children 24-30 months. Children can start preschool at age two. Both First Step and Toddler Time offer developmentally appropriate toys, activities, parenting tips, and information on growth and development. The preschool has also expanded its license to serve school-age children up to age twelve in its after-school camp programs. During the school vacations in the Fall, Winter, and Spring, fun theme camps are provided. During the summer months, the school provides a camp experience for children age two–seven, in sports, drama, art, camp activities, and Judaics.

The mission of the Preschool of the Rabbi Arthur I. Baseman, DD and Renée L. Baseman Early Childhood Center is, "To provide developmentally appropriate activities and enriched experiences in a safe, nurturing, Judaic environment that encourages all children to explore and discover their expanding world so that they may successfully transition to school." This mission statement is reality. The highly positive comments of the parents and the accreditation by the professional peers of the prestigious National Association for the Education of Young Children attest to the success of the Preschool.

Religious School

The Religious School at Temple B'nai Israel was founded in 1950 by Mary Rutenberg, a volunteer Hebrew and religious school teacher. Later on, Mrs. Paul Circus of St. Petersburg became the first paid principal. She also taught in the school. Jack German was the next Director of the school during the rabbinate of J. Marshall Taxay. He continued briefly during the time of Rabbi Baseman. From the time that Rabbi Baseman arrived when there were only seventy member families in the congregation, until today when there are over 700 member families in the congregation, the Religious School has grown substantially. In Rabbi Baseman's early years, the congregation grew rapidly. The number of children becoming bar or bat mitzvah grew substantially. All of them were prepared to read from the Torah on Saturday mornings. Rosalie Fleischaker became the new school director.

In 1972, Temple B'nai Israel had outgrown its facility and a new sanctuary and school was built on Belcher Road. Zena Sulkes, a highly trained and extremely well educated teacher, became Director of the Religious School and continued for the next seventeen years. Zena was awarded the professional title, Reform Jewish Educator. It was conferred on her on November 15, 1985, by the Commission on Jewish Education, Central Conference of American Rabbis, Hebrew Union College-Joint Institute of Religion, National Association of Temple Educators. She helped bring the enrollment up to nearly 300 students. The school philosophy, then and now, is that Jewish education is a lifelong process. Therefore, programs are offered to children even before consecration in kindergarten and after confirmation in the 10th grade. This was followed by advanced education through the 12th grade, and then a very strong Adult Jewish Education program, which continues until the current time. Temple B'nai Israel was designated as the official site for KEVA, the North American program of recognition for Adult Jewish Education sponsored by the Union of American Hebrew Congregations. The Union granted student credit units, which led to certification. The credits could then be applied to the Union of American Hebrew Congregations Teacher Certification program.

Gail Simon became the Director of Education in May of 1991. The school has a tradition of excellence. Four teachers have been honored as the Yitzhak Rabin Teacher of Excellence, since this award was first given by the Jewish Federation in 1996. Renée Baseman, Jerri Greene, Raida Goldman, and Gail Simon, all award winners, still teach at the school.

Gail Simon received a Bachelor of Arts Degree from the University of Florida in Library Science, in 1967. She completed studies in Jewish and Hebrew education at Cleveland College of Jewish Studies after a fifteen year period in 1990, and also completed studies the same year at Hebrew University in Jerusalem. She earned a Master of Education Degree from Kent State University in Counseling, in 1987. She holds special certifications in Learning Disabilities and Behavior Disorders, K.-12 Media Specialization, Secondary English, Brain-Based Education, and Jewish Meditation. From 1975-1991, she taught Jewish studies and Hebrew at several congregational schools in Ohio. From 1981-1991, she was School Director at New Directions, a treatment center for chemically dependent adolescents, near Cleveland, Ohio. From 1991 until the present, she has been Director of Education at Temple B'nai Israel. In 1990, she received the Ratner Fellowship awarded by the Cleveland Bureau of Jewish Education to an outstanding teacher in a Jewish school. In 2001, she received the Yitzhak Rabin Memorial Award for an Educator of Excellence from the Jewish Federation of Pinellas County. She is a highly significant member of the: Coalition for the Advancement of Jewish Education; National Association of Temple Educators;

Association for Supervision and Curriculum Development; and Tampa Bay Jewish Educators Council.

In 2005, the school decided to offer both Hebrew classes and Judaic students classes on Sunday mornings instead of a split program of Sunday school and weekday Hebrew. Providing the best instruction possible for all students, including those who are learning disabled, remains a high priority and the new schedule allows for extra help to be given to those who seek it during the week. Parent education is also valued and parents participate in several community family education days, as well as a variety of school sponsored programs.

The school offers classes to students from three to eighteen. In addition to the classes, the 250 students participate in excellent youth programs which begin in the third grade, and prepare for a variety of life cycle events, including consecration, Bar and Bat Mitzvah, and Confirmation. Eighth through twelfth graders are encouraged to volunteer as Sunday School aides. There are thirty two student aides and twenty six adult teachers. The youngest teacher is eighteen and the oldest teacher is eighty years old.

The Temple offers scholarships to students, courtesy of the Igel Torah Fund, to attend the March of the Living, where every other year, two or three students have the opportunity to visit the death camps in Poland and then celebrate Israeli Independence Day in Israel. Thousands of young people from all over the world participate in the March of the Living and this becomes an extraordinary experience for those that are able to take part in this program. The author's daughter, Debra, was honored to make such a visit to the death camps in Poland in January, 2005.

The Mission Statement of Temple B'nai Israel Religious School states that the Religious School "...seeks to educate the youth of Temple members, beginning with pre-school age children through the completion of high school. The curriculum is focused on instilling a positive Jewish identity with a commitment to Judaism. The school uses innovative methods in all of its programs and takes into consideration the individual needs of each student." The overall goal of the Temple's educational program is to deepen and broaden the student's Jewish experience and knowledge. Judaism contains helpful answers to the challenges and questions which confront the human spirit and a knowledgeable Jewish person can make full use of the wisdom and the experiences of the centuries. This is accomplished in a challenging, enjoyable, and throughly significant educational experience.

The goal is to help the students become: "Jews who affirm their Jewish identity and bind themselves inseparably to their people by word and deed; Jews who have an appreciation for the heritage of their tradition and the progressive nature of our movement; Jews who express their kinship with the community of Israel by actively seeking the welfare of Jews throughout the world; Jews who affirm our people's historic bonds to the land of Israel and the people of Israel; Jews who understand and participate in Jewish worship; Jews who cherish and study Hebrew, the language of the Jewish people; Jews who esteem the home as the foundation of Jewish life by incorporating Jewish practices and observations into it; Jews who take pride and joy in observing the ceremonies to mark significant occasions, namely consecration, bar/bat mitzvah, confirmation, graduation, marriage, death, and burial; Jews who support and participate in the life of the synagogue; Jews who become people of compassion and character, who "do justly, love mercy, and walk humbly..." The values found in the goal above are shared with the National Commission on Education of the Reform Movement.

Religious School Curriculum
Junior Kindergarten
Four-year-old children learn about being Jewish through their senses. Music, arts and crafts, and playtime are used to introduce the Jewish holidays, basic blessings, Shabbat, the concept of mitzvot, the Synagogue, Torah, and the Jewish way of life.

Kindergarten
Five-year-old children entering

kindergarten in their schools may also participate in the Temple B'nai Israel kindergarten. The students are introduced to Jewish life cycle events, beginning with Consecration in the fall. Shabbat and the Jewish festivals are taught at appropriate times. The life of the child, growing up and changing, are recognized in the context of a Jewish environment.

Grade 1

Students begin to identify themselves as members of the Jewish people, as they explore the relationship to God, Torah and Israel. They celebrate the Jewish festivals. They start learning the meaning of important Jewish concepts. They go to Menorah Manor to learn the Mitzvah of caring for the elderly.

Grade 2

Students study the book of Genesis. They continue to celebrate the holidays and to explore mitzvot in their own lives. The emphasis is on sharing and caring about each other. They use a variety of Hebrew words in games, in connection with holidays, and in Bible study.

Grade 3

Students study a variety of stories in the Torah from Exodus through Deuteronomy. Basic prayers are introduced and the formal study of Hebrew begins.

Grade 4

Students study the major figures and Prophets. They look at the Bible in its entirety and gain a sense of the sequence of events. They participate in activities designed to increase their awareness of what it means to be a Jew. They increase their reading fluency in Hebrew. They become more aware of the prayers used in the synagogue and at home.

Grade 5

Students learn the practical side of giving tzedakah. They explore their covenant with God. In Hebrew class, they continue their study of prayer while emphasizing reading fluency and the mastery and understanding of special prayers.

Grade 6

Students study mitzvot through a variety of special projects. They focus on current events and how these events affect their Jewish lives. In Hebrew class, they concentrate on learning the prayers of the Shabbat evening service. This is the beginning of Bar/Bat Mitzvah preparation.

Grade 7

Students participate in several special projects in order to better understand the concept of mitzvot. Most students have their Bar/Bat Mitzvah during this year. In Hebrew class, the students are involved in intense study for preparation for the Bar/Bat Mitzvah. The students are taught conversational Hebrew.

Grade 8 and 9

Students are part of the High School Department meeting on Monday evenings. They study a variety of subjects with emphasis on relationships with non-Jewish neighbors, with Jewish community, and changing relationships with their peers.

Grade 10 (Confirmation Class)

Students, as part of their culminating year of Jewish education at Temple B'nai Israel, participate in a variety of activities, including a weekend retreat, designed to promote a cohesiveness within the group and dedication to Judaism. They also prepare for a proficiency exam of basic Jewish knowledge which is given just prior to the confirmation ceremony in the late spring.

Grade 11 and 12 (Senior Study)

Students, participating in this optional program, are involved in a stimulating series of classes on a variety of subjects. The controversial nature of many of the subjects discussed promote a high level of interaction among the students and a greater awareness of the relevance of Judaism to daily life. Senior study graduation is the reward for twelve years of growing, and understanding of the individual's Judaism, Jewish life in general, relationships with all people, and how to be a good person.

The Temple B'nai Israel Religious School is a program of progressive Judaism utilized to help develop lifelong skills in the participating students. This program, as well as the programs of all of the religious schools in Pinellas County, aim to promote good citizenship through an understanding of Jewish life and a love of God.

Andrew Rophie blowing Shofar, September 11, 1993, at Pinellas County Jewish Day School.

CHAPTER 24

BROTHERHOODS, SISTERHOODS AND YOUTH GROUPS

Brotherhoods

Conservative Movement

The Federation of Jewish Men's Clubs is an organization of some 270 Conservative/ Masorti Jewish men's groups of about 25,000 individuals across North America and the world. Its objectives are to train and develop leaders to build and strengthen men's clubs; to create and implement programs to involve men in Jewish life; and be an active and influential participant in the Conservative/Masorti Movement. The FJMC helps transform ordinary club events into the extraordinary through innovative programs that enhance spirituality, increase learning, develop leadership skills, and foster fellowship. It empowers its members so that their voices are heard in their communities and in the Conservative movement.

In the mid–1920s, Rabbi Samuel L. Cohen, first developed the idea of bringing together existing Conservative men's clubs into a national federation of Jewish men's clubs. He had a vision that this group would foster an interchange of ideas and focus on common needs. In 1945, the Seminary appointed Rabbi Joel Geffen to help build future leadership through the men's clubs. He guided the organization for forty years. A Layman's Institute was started in 1944, where men's club leaders could go to the Seminary for a Shabbat of prayer and study. This retreat as well as those which followed helped develop a lay leadership that could be useful in all aspects of congregational life including leading prayers. Distinguished Service Awards were initiated and the first one was given in 1948 to Henry Morganthau Jr. Many distinguished Jewish men including Alan Dershowitz, Harvard Law Professor, was so honored. In 1961, the Federation sponsored the first trip to Israel by a Conservative group. The Federation introduced many new programs including: Rosh Hashanah Greeting Cards; the Century Club for the development of a Hebrew Literacy Campaign; Ramah projects to build indoor recreation centers and Jewish camps; Art of Jewish Living series; Holocaust remembrance programs; Shabbat Morning Torah Service Video; Hebrew-Christian series; Hearing the Men's Voices program; promoting the use of Tefillin; and fostering Jewish learning and awareness of the Hebrew Scriptures.

Orthodox Movement

The overall modern Orthodox Movement formed the Union of Orthodox Jewish Congregations of America on June 8, 1898. The Orthodox Union was the outgrowth of the needs of Orthodox Jewish people in America in an ever-changing world.

Reform Movement

Brotherhoods were established at a national level because of the successes of the synagogue sisterhoods. The National Federation of Temple Brotherhoods was founded on January 23, 1923, when sixty five Reform Jewish brotherhoods and men's clubs came together at the Hotel Astor in New York City to form the North American Federation of Temple Brotherhood's, in affiliation with the Union of American Hebrew Congregations. As in the Sisterhoods, the Brotherhoods existed at individual synagogues, as men's clubs for many years prior to the national organization.

The mission of the National Federation of Temple Brotherhoods is the same today as it was when it was founded eighty two years ago. That is: to encourage local Brotherhoods to engage in projects and activities that provide meaningful services to their congregations; to sponsor and promote vitally important nationwide community-building projects; and to give local brotherhood members the opportunity to explore and celebrate their male Jewish spirit.

The purpose of the organization is "to arouse the appreciation for an understanding of our religion among the young men of Jewish faith in this country, and to translate this appreciation and this understanding into action, by being loyal to the best tradition of our faith, and alive to the needs of the modern day. This means humility before God; self respect before man; readiness to eternally serve the weak, the downtrodden, the sick, regardless of race, creed, or color; regard for our fellow man, respect for his feelings and beliefs, and finally willingness to battle against wrong and for right, to battle fearlessly, fairly, and effectively... These are our aims and objectives of our organization. We must study how best we can serve these ends. We must act as a supplementing force ...to strengthen others, as well as ourselves, to be inspired by and to carry on the eternal truths of Judaism." These words were spoken by Roger Strauss, first President of the National Federation of Temple Brotherhoods at the opening national convention.

Beside the numerous jobs performed locally by the brotherhood of a congregation, the national organization as well as the local chapters have been working hard for the, "repair of this world, tikkun olam," through active involvement in youth education, adult education, social action, and fellowship activities. The most important and effective national program has been the sponsorship of the Jewish Chautauqua Society. In 1939, the JCS was adopted as the interfaith education arm of the National Federation of Temple Brotherhoods. The Jewish Chautauqua Society was originally founded in 1893 by Rabbi Henry Berkowitz. It built its image on promoting Judaism and Jewish history. It moved from educating Jewish people about Judaism to interfaith work. Through a variety of lectures, books, grants and films it has become a vital part of explaining Jewish history and the Jewish faith to non-Jewish people in colleges and universities. Its motto is "Understanding through Education."

In the early 1990s, the Jewish Chautauqua Society became a founding partner in the Dillard Center for Black-Jewish Relations. The Center is providing funding to the Thomas More Project, a pilot interfaith project at an inner-city school in Baltimore, Maryland.

The National Federation of Temple Brotherhoods College Youth Program, begun in the 1960s, became the predecessor of the Union of American Hebrew Congregations Youth Commission and in the 1990s the Reform on Campus Program. This program provides funding for lectures, programs, retreats, and all else necessary to help Reform Jewish students maintain their Jewish life in college. Shabbat dinners and weekend retreats are held with rabbis to help keep the students in touch with their Judaism.

The NFTB has conducted a series of projects on: discrimination; Men's Health Initiative; Men's Spirituality Programs; and most recently, the national sponsor of Walking Together, a new nationwide program designed for Jewish, Christian and Muslim fourth to sixth grade school children and their parents, teaching religious diversity through a variety of innovative and educational sessions.

Sisterhoods

Sisterhoods in the various synagogues are like women in the home. They take a structure and turn it into a living entity. The sisterhoods by whatever name they are called are always there in a variety of ways to provide for the needs of all congregants especially the children. Listing all their activities and all their contributions, to each of the synagogues, on a yearly basis, would be a monumental task that would increase the size of this book by hundreds of pages. The conservative synagogues typically belong to the Woman's League of Conservative Judaism. The Orthodox synagogues typically belong to the Woman's Branch of the Orthodox Union of Jewish Congregations of America. The Reform synagogues typically belong to Women of Judaism, the Federation of Temple Sisterhoods.

Although national organizations of sisterhoods did not exist until 1913, individual synagogues from colonial times on, had sisterhoods that were active at the founding of the congregations, kept them alive in times of despair, and helped them grow into the valuable institutions they are today. These sisterhoods, over the years, helped American synagogues expand into new areas of activity. American Jewish leaders felt strongly that women were uniquely suited to save Judaism, the synagogue, and Jewish education. The women who joined the sisterhoods typically were not in the workforce, but they were able to perform an outstanding role in improving society. Sisterhoods have served as: philanthropic organizations to help the poor within the community; fund raisers to help pay for synagogue mortgages, rabbis, interior and exterior decoration, and to provide the amenities needed to make the Sabbath and the holidays more beautiful; religious school organizers, teachers, and promoters of religious education for children and adults; congregational unifiers when disagreements occurred; organizers of interfaith activities; and providers of innumerable other services to their own congregations, as well as the general community. During times of low synagogue attendance, sisterhoods have helped present Judaism as a beautiful, meaningful, and moral way of life that was compatible with American values.

The women's movement of the 1970s and 1980s brought a new challenge to the synagogue and to the synagogue Sisterhood. The feminist movement helped promote an expanded role for women in Jewish religious life. Women wanted to become leaders of the congregations and not just the helpers, problem solvers and financiers. Some of the women wanted to become cantors and rabbis.

Conservative Movement

The Women's League of Conservative Judaism was founded in 1918 by Mathilde Schechter and currently provides service to over 700 Sisterhoods in synagogues in the United States, Canada, Puerto Rico, Mexico, Israel, and other parts of the world. They have a total membership of over 150,000 women. It is dedicated to the perpetuation of traditional Judaism in the home, synagogue, and community. It provides continuing Jewish education to its members. Special projects consist of a Woman's Health Forum, Mitzvah Torah Project of educational and spiritual growth, Distance Learning, and an Israel Connection. The individual synagogue sisterhoods have numerous programs

in: adult education, Jewish education for children and youth, Torah funds, Jewish observance, leadership institutes, Judaica shops, public policy, social action, domestic violence, community services, disaster relief, holiday packages for Jewish military personnel, Jewish Girl Scouts of America, MAZON(Jewish response to hunger), Jewish Braille Institute of America, and an untold number of fund raisers for every project imaginable.

Orthodox Movement

The Woman's Branch of the Orthodox Union of Jewish Congregations of America was founded in 1923. The Women's Branch is the organization of Orthodox synagogue sisterhoods and individual members throughout the United States and Canada. The goals of the organization are: to organize, advise, and serve sisterhoods; to fill Jewish women and youth with the spirit of a Torah Judaism; to reach out to combat intermarriage through information and education. The Woman's Branch provides publications, leadership training, national conventions, regional conferences, speakers bureau, and a sponsor's fund. They help teach the traditions of Orthodox Judaism through: a diversified portfolio of educational material; a newsletter for and about sisterhoods; holiday and special information publications; and through encouraging community responsibility by participating in all areas of Jewish concern. Their national projects include: Stern College for Women of Yeshiva University Scholarship Fund; Touro College for Women Scholarship Fund; Commencement Prizes for Excellence in Judaic Studies at Yeshiva, Stern and Touro Colleges; National Conference of Synagogue Youth; Marriage Committee; Nayros candelabra project using electric candles in hospitals; Political Action Committee; and Jewish Braille.

Reform Movement

The Women of Reform Judaism: National Federation of Temple Sisterhoods was founded in 1913. It is an organization of over 100,000 Jewish women from over 600 sisterhoods throughout the United States, Canada, and several other countries in the world. The organization's preamble to its constitution states, "We, the representatives of the sisterhoods of congregations comprising the Union of American Hebrew Congregations, believing: that the congregation is the foundation of Jewish religious organizations, and that the power of women ought to be exercised in congregational life, and that Jewish values can be furthered by this corporation, Do hereby organize the Federation of Temple Sisterhoods to carry out these aims." This is a powerful statement about the significance of the synagogue within the community and the extreme importance of the role of women in this endeavor.

The Women of Reform Judaism: The Federation of Temple Sisterhoods has numerous significant programs and projects related to providing assistance and materials to the individual synagogues, advancing and strengthening Reform Judaism, the synagogue, and Jewish humanitarian causes. They are involved in all children's programs with a special emphasis on pre- school and parenting, sponsorship of youth activities, teaching of Judaism in educational programs, and service to the interreligious and general community. It initiates and implements programs of social advocacy, especially concerning children, the elderly, and the status of women. In addition to the many program efforts mentioned in the general paragraph on sisterhoods, they are a founder and patron of the Jewish Braille Institute of America, of the Yes Fund(Youth, Education and Special Projects) which provides, among other things, assistance to high school and college age programs, rabbinical students, nursery schools, etc., of the original dormitory for rabbinic students at the Cincinnati campus of Hebrew Union College-Jewish Institute of Religion. They initiated an assumed half of the responsibility for purchase of the land, building, and furnishings of the headquarters of Reform Judaism in New York City; they gave financial support and other assistance for construction of the World Education Center for Progressive Judaism in Jerusalem; they gave support for Kibbutz Yahel Arava, the first reform kibbutz in Israel; they provided assistance to the Leo Beck Education Center in Haifa; and funding for the Religious Action Center in Washington DC.

Youth Groups
Conservative Movement

The United Synagogue Youth (USY) was founded on March 19, 1951 when the National Youth Commission unanimously agreed to concern itself with non-scholastic group work for teenagers. The charter meeting of the new youth group was held in December, 1951. High school aged delegates met at both Columbia University and the Jewish Theological Seminary. Over 500 people, including teenagers and professional youth workers, representing sixty five different communities in fourteen different states, and Canada, attended the first official meeting. At that meeting the aims and objectives of the United Synagogue Youth Constitution were adopted. In late 1951, three more regions were added to the United Synagogue Youth organization. In 1956, the Two-o-Nine tzedakah project began. It was revamped in 1971, becoming Tikun Olam, the social action/charity project of the USY. In 1958, the enrollments increased in the Pilgrimage program. In 1961, the summer programs were expanded and in 1969, the Youth Commission created Camp Kadima, for middle school students. The summer programs continued to expand until this day, including trips throughout the United States and Israel.

It is the philosophy of the United Synagogue Youth that, "People can't go through life being ignorant of their heritage and history, for it may help them understand their present and future. We can't expect the majority of Jewish youth to come voluntarily to Judaism, therefore, USY must bring Judaism to them. Education is necessary in all aspects of life in order to stimulate self-examination and thought. The primary role of USY in education is not to make people believe in G-d, or even in the fundamental concepts of Judaism. The coolest thing about Judaism is that we are allowed to question, and not to accept with blind faith. We...recognize the fact that youth must perpetuate Judaism. Furthermore, we are cognizant of the historical background of our people and shall strive for the betterment of our brethren in foreign lands. In addition, we will promote the realization of the equality of all people in our own land."

Orthodox Movement

The National Conference of Synagogue Youth (NCSY) was formed in the 1950s when local chapters around the country became part of a national organization with well-defined standards set by Jewish law. It is a multi-faceted Jewish Youth Group, which is open to all Jewish youth regardless of background and affiliation. It offers social and educational programming in hundreds of communities across the United States and Canada. It attempts to bring unaffiliated youth an awareness of their Judaism and a relaxed, fun environment to learn about their own heritage. Local Orthodox synagogues typically have NCSY chapters.

Reform Movement

The North American Federation of Temple Youth (NFTY), was founded in 1939 as the youth arm of the Union of Reform Judaism, previously known as the Union of American Hebrew Congregations. It was created at the urging of the National Federation of Temple Sisterhoods to provide an organization for young people to engage in the life of their synagogues. Initially the membership was made up of college-age students, rather than high school students. Its first national officers were in their 20s. The organization continued to grow without significant change until 1948. At that time, it adopted a new constitution that created major structural changes in the organization including: summertime Leadership Institutes; and lowering the membership age to the high school years. In 1951, NFTY entered the camping movement in its newly purchased camp in Oconomowoc, Wisconsin. Currently, there are twelve Union of Reform Judaism camps around the country.

In 1952, the NFTY Bar Mitzvah year, the idea of emphasizing mitzvah programs and projects that serve others rather than ourselves, was introduced. This idea has had a profound influence on the Reform Jewish youth movement ever since. In 1954, the first NFTY Advisors Institute was sponsored, and the first NFTY trip to Israel and Europe occurred.

In 1960, on NFTY's 21st birthday, the theme was, "Coming-Of-Age," and the organization announced its first program to guide local chapters by providing guidelines for excellence in performance. The program was called, "We Will Do and We Will Hearken."

In 1961, NFTY started the Eisendrath International Exchange Program, in which three boys from NFTY went for a semester study to the Leo Beck High School in Haifa, Israel and three Uruguayan girls came to NFTY homes in the United States.

From 1962-1965, NFTY concentrated on innovation in international programming. The Summer Antiquities Tour brought members to Israel and Europe to learn about the culture and history of the countries. The Bible Institute provided experiences in Israel. Mitzvah Corps programs started in Puerto Rico, Israel, Mexico, New York, and Chicago. Today, virtually every region has a Mitzvah Corps Program.

In the late 1960s, NFTY's emphasis on mitzvah led it to leadership in social action programming. In addition, the use of the guitar in NFTY worship services brought a new meaning to the musical worship of Jewish youth, and then the entire Reform Movement.

In 1970, NFTY began outreach programs to its alumni on college campuses. One of the first programs was at the Military Academy at West Point. This was followed by creating musical albums to foster musical religious services.

In 1972, the URJ Kutz Camp began a major innovation. The many programs for fostering leadership skills, Jewish study and creativity which have been offered separately were now combined into the NFTY National Academy. Exceptional professionals and scholars brought their skills to young people and taught them. The NFTY National Torah Corps at the Kutz Camp developed a program of serious Jewish study for people seeking to deepen their Jewish knowledge and identity.

In 2005, NFTY has over 750 groups in nineteen regions throughout the United States and Canada and holds over 150 regional events each year. The organization has influenced both the Jewish community and the general community throughout the world. Graduates of NFTY Programs are prominent in the creative arts, community, politics, and Reform Judaism. Many of these people serve in leadership roles.

The goals of the National Federation of Temple Youth are to: instill Jewish identity; increase synagogue participation among high school youth; foster a long-term commitment to the ideals and values of Reform Judaism: and create today the Reform Jewish congregants of tomorrow. The National Federation of Temple Youth programming includes the promotion and significance of: Jewish education, worship, religious action, leadership development, the Reform Jewish community, personal growth and ethics, the Jewish people, and the land and State of Israel.

Finally, worship and the doing of good deeds are the keys to life. The National Federation of Temple Youth wants its young people to have meaningful experiences for living and praying Jewishly. NFTY helps young people find their connection to God and the role that faith can play in their lives. The worship services and the choice of music to enhance prayer helps the individual become a better person.

CHAPTER 25

OTHER PINELLAS COUNTY JEWISH ORGANIZATIONS

Introduction

The Jewish organizations discussed in this chapter are of no less significance than the Jewish organizations which are discussed in their own chapters. Unfortunately, because of the limitations of the author's ability to obtain significant research material about local chapters of the following organizations, or because of the newness of the organization, the author elected to include the following organizations in a single chapter in alphabetical order. Where possible, information about the national organization may be found either in Chapter 1 or in this chapter. The organizations are: Brandeis University Women; Hadassah; Hillel; Israel Bonds; Jewish Genealogical Society of Tampa Bay; Jewish Press; Jewish War Veterans; Jewish Women International; Jewish Law Students Association at Stetson University; National Council of Jewish Women; ORT; PRIMER; Tampa Orlando Pinellas Jewish Foundation; and a television show entitled B'nai B'rith Presents Jewish Life in Tampa Bay. Future researchers should use this information as a beginning to do additional oral histories and more in-depth study.

Brandeis University Women

In 1948, the Brandeis University National Women's Committee was founded by a group of Boston area Jewish women who had served on various national Jewish organizations. They were, Edith Michaels, Past President Boston Hadassah; Hannah Abrams, President, Women's Scholarship Association of Boston; Augusta Katz, President, Women's District Number One B'nai B'rith; Frances Ritvo, Trustee Jewish Tuberculosis Sanitarium of New England; Flora Silverman, National Chairperson of Women's Auxiliary of the Jewish War Veterans; Dorothy Specter, Past President Boston Hadassah; Tillie Thorner, Secretary Jewish National Fund of New England; and Gertrude Alpert, wife of the first Chairperson, Brandeis Board of Trustees. George Alpert said to these eight women, "We are interested in quality and high caliber, and one of the important considerations in establishing that quality is to have a library which will not only get its accreditation in the University world, but will be a pride to all of us who participate in this undertaking." These ambitious women accepted the challenge to stock the library with large numbers of high quality books and became the permanent organization, the Women's Committee of Brandeis University. From the very beginning, outstanding individuals such as Leonard Bernstein, Eleanor Roosevelt, Martin Buber, Dr. Martin Luther King,

David Ben Gurion, etc. were scholars in residence. See "From the Beginning," editor, Pasternack, Susan, Brandeis University, Waltham, Massachusetts, 1988, and "A Host at Last," Abram L. Sachar, Little Brown and Company, Canada, 1976, for information on programs and speakers.

Suncoast Chapter of Clearwater

The local chapters of the Brandeis University Women's Committee have three major goals. First, to raise funds for the Brandeis University library and for scholarships. Second, to be a well-rounded charitable organization assisting various individuals and other organizations in the community in helping the poor and needy. Third, to be the essence of promoting literacy in the community by being taught by Brandeis University professors, and then sharing the material with other individuals. Also, by promoting individual literacy in children by acting as tutors and mentors.

Highlights of 1982

The Suncoast Chapter of the Clearwater Area was formed. The founder and first President was Ellie Gordon. On December 3, Hannah Abrams, a member of the National Board of the Brandeis University Women's Committee, spoke to fifty women at a tea held at the home of Yolan Ziessman of Clearwater. Hannah talked about the purpose and the history of Brandeis Women.

She discussed activities of local chapters such as university-sponsored academic and cultural programs in literature, theater, music, women's issues and art. Fifty four women had already joined the chapter. The Comparative World Literature Study Group started holding monthly meetings. This program has continued on to the present.

Highlights of 1983

On March 11, Professor Jerrold Bernstein, Chairman of the Fine Arts Department of Brandeis University, presented syllabi for art study groups. A series of art and literature programs were scheduled for the next several weeks. The Sun Coast Chapter was chartered in June, just as the new Farber Library was being dedicated at Brandeis University. The chapter events were both social and intellectual and included study groups prepared by Brandeis faculty, study groups for arts and crafts, and an annual Brandeis professor seminar.

Highlights of 1984

On January 7, the Suncoast Chapter presented Professor John Bush Jones in a special program entitled, "The American Musical Scene since Rodgers and Hammerstein–from Formula to Art Form." A special program included a visit to the studio and home of Clearwater's noted artist, Roger Bansemer. A special program was held on May 5, where Johanna Bromberg, a Brandeis alumna gave the invocation. The program consisted of a humorous and personal reading of contemporary poetry. Other programs of the year were: "Contemporary World Literature," "Jewish Short Stories," " Shakespeare's Comedies," " Survey of World Drama," " Human Dilemma–Focus on Women,"and "Understanding Modern Art." Ellie Gordon was one of 300 delegates attending the 36th annual National Conference of the Brandeis University National Women's Committee on the campus of Brandeis University.

At the first West Coast Conference, over 100 women from the Tampa, Suncoast, and Sarasota Chapters worked together on leadership and leadership development. Even though the program was geared more to improving leadership competencies

for the Brandeis University movement, it also helped train these women for any leadership positions in the community. Barbara Miller, National President of the Brandeis University National Women's Committee, was the keynote speaker.

Highlights of 1985

The visiting professor from Brandeis University was Dr. Robert Greenberg of the Philosophy Department. He presented "Media As the New Philosophy."

Highlights of 1986

The visiting professor from Brandeis University was Dr. Alan Levitan of the Department of Comparative Literature. He presented "Shakespeare in Music from Verdi to Tomorrow."

The Suncoast Chapter was involved in promoting a better understanding of Yiddish movies and the American Jewish immigrant history. They showed excerpts of some 300 Yiddish movies made between 1927 and 1940, with Orson Welles as the narrator. The Jewish Film Festival was sponsored by the Charles and Isadora Rutenberg Foundation, Brandeis University Women, and the Golda Meir Center.

Highlights of 1987

The visiting professor from Brandeis, Department of Romance Languages was Dr. Stephen Gendzier. His presentation was "French Feminism in the Age of Enlightenment."

The Suncoast Chapter worked with the Literacy Program of Upper Pinellas County and the Voluntary Action Center Alternative Human Services. The Chapter received special recognition for its work. The women also helped the visually impaired learn Braille.

Highlights of 1988

The visiting professor from Brandeis was Dr. Jacob Cohen from the American Studies Department. His presentation was "Those Russians–We Americans." The Chapter participated in the Community Outreach Program. The women helped children develop their communication skills and their ability to adapt to the local culture. The women worked as Docents at the Holocaust Museum. They assisted Weinberg Assisted Care Living Facility and the older citizens. They provided a bookcase and books for every floor. The women collected food for the Gulf Coast Jewish Family Services. The project for the Literacy Council of Upper Pinellas continued for many years.

Highlights of 1989

The visiting professor from Brandeis was Dr. Stephen Whitfield of the American Studies Department. He spoke on "How High the Wall?-Church and State in American History." The husbands of the Brandeis University Women became interested in the fascinating programs that their wives were attending. They asked if they could also attend. The top picks ranged from "Leonard Bernstein Retrospective" to jazz, opera, musical theater, classical music, cantorial music, foreign films, lectures, study groups, and trips abroad. The first three husbands accepted were Mortimer Gordon, Max Ben, and Robert Rosenfeld. This practice of naming husbands as associates and allowing them full participation was accepted at the national level in 1992.

Highlights of 1990

The visiting professor from the University of South Florida was Ray Arsenault. He gave a presentation either in 1990 or 1991.

Elinor Gordon attended the Brandeis University National Women's Committees Annual National Conference, "Set Your Sights on Visions of Volume II." Ellie Gordon, who liked to write poetry, summed up the significance of the conference,

"...That our task's far from over
There's much more we must do,
So the youth of tomorrow
Can see their visions come true!"

Highlights of 1992

The visiting professor from Brandeis University was Dr. Jeffrey Abramson of the Legal Studies Department. His presentation was "Justice in America and the New Supreme Court." Brandeis Women were constantly involved in a variety of study groups. Over 100 study groups were

available for this year. Some examples were: "The Jewish Women in America; Thinking about the Environment;" " Issues in United States Foreign Policy;" " What's in a Name? A Study of Genesis;" and "Making Sense of the Gulf War." These topics and the other topics presented by significant scholars then became the basis for material utilized by the women for self-improvement, and more importantly, for helping people understand the issues involved.

Highlights of 1993

The visiting professor from Brandeis University was Dr. John Bush Jones of the Theater Arts Department. His presentation was " The Wendy Chronicles: Wendy Wasserstein from Holyoke to Heidi-and Beyond."

Highlights of 1994

The annual guest speaker was Phil Zitowitz, Elder Hostel Lecturer at Eckerd College. His presentation was "From Hester Street to Hollywood." The Brandeis Women helped collect holiday gift bags for the Alliance for the Mentally Ill.

Highlights of 1995

The visiting professor from Brandeis University was Dr. Sylvia Barack Fishman of the Contemporary Jewry and American Jewish Sociology Department. Her presentation was "Re-Inventing the Cinematic Jew."

Highlights of 1996

The visiting professor from Brandeis University was Dr. Andreas Teuber of the Philosophy Department. His presentation was "Bad Acts and Guilty Minds: the Nature and Meaning of Crime."

Johanna Bromberg, class of 1954 of Brandeis University, led the study group on "Women and the Torah, Women and the Prophetic Writings." Twenty five members studied the Torah, as well as other writings, and interpreted them in relationship to their lives as women. Judy Elkin, a Reform Jewish women, explained why she joined the study group, " I had always wanted to know more about my Judaism, especially from a Conservative Jew, which Johanna is. I think it's a wonderful group. We now shall continue to find a way to challenge us next year." Sheila Feldman, the chapter's study group chairman, said, "For a study group like this, you need a leader who is well-versed in the subject and can read and translate Hebrew. Johanna is a Brandeis graduate and the wife of a rabbi. She has put together a phenomenal course through which women from a wide variety of backgrounds are increasing their knowledge of their Judaic heritage."

Highlights of 1997

The visiting professor from Brandeis University was Dr. Arthur Holmberg of the Drama Department. His presentation was "The Hollywood Dream Machine."

Highlights of 1998

The visiting professor from Brandeis University was Dr. Susan Moeller of the American Studies Department. She was also Director of Journalism. Her presentation was "From Ebola to Princes Diana: How the Media Covers the World."

Highlights of 1999

The visiting professor from Brandeis University was Dr. Margie E. Lachman of the Psychology Department and Life-Span Development Lab. Her presentation was "Everything You Wanted to Know about Memory but Forgot to Ask."

Highlights of 2002

The visiting professor was Dr. Stephen Whitfield. His presentation was "Fiddling with Sholom Aleichman."

Highlights of 2003

The visiting professor from Brandeis University was Dr. David Engerman of the History Department. His presentation was "Nightmare of the Past-How Soviet History Made Today's Russia."

Highlights of 2005

The visiting professor from Brandeis University was Dr. Jonathan Unglaub of the Fine Arts Department. His presentation was "Petrified Passion: The Sculpture of Gian Lorenzo Bernini." All of the visiting

professor programs were shared with the St. Petersburg Chapter.

St. Petersburg Chapter

On December 17, 1984, five women in St. Petersburg came together to form a new chapter of the Brandeis University National Women's Committee. At the next meeting in January, 1985, ten women became paid-up members. The first study group used the syllabus the "Theater of the Absurd." The group worked on publicity, bulletins, book groups, and the organizational structure of the St. Petersburg proposed chapter.

By mid-April, 1985, the required fifty members were enrolled in the organization and the group was advised that they would be chartered in June. They quickly became involved in trying to help with the mission of the Brandeis University National Women's Committee. "To provide financial support for Brandeis University and its libraries. To connect Brandeis, a non-sectarian university founded by the American Jewish community, to its members and their communities through programs that reflect the ideal of social justice and academic excellence."

The concept of learning and experiencing new ideas along with their peers proved to be attractive to women in the community. The study groups continued to grow and diversify. The women also made monthly trips to museums and other libraries. Of particular significance, was the opportunity to study under a Brandeis University professor at least once a year. The chapter has a satellite group in Sun City. The chapter also helps support young people in arts enrichment classes in the high schools. The women work in the community as mentors of young people and reading to students in elementary schools and seniors in nursing homes and other institutions.

The Presidents were: 1984-1987, Francine Kamerling; 1987-1989, Dorene Ben; 1989-1990, Rose Rosenfeld; 1990-1992, Harriet Goff, Babette Husick and Anita Helfand; 1992-1993, Evelyn Weissman; 1993-1995, Jackie Applefield; 1995-1998, Shirley Blau Grossman; 1998-1999, Francine Kamerling and Evelyn Weissman; 1999-2000, Francine Kamerling; 2000-2002, Elaine Kleinmetz;

2002-2003, Natalie Rudin; 2003-2004, Roslyn Geller, Francine Kamerling and Rachel Seldin; 2004-2006, Sarah Slohm.

Hadassah
St. Petersburg Chapters

Because of the paucity of written material available about the St. Petersburg chapters, the author requested that Adele Morris and Marilyn LeVine, longtime members and officers of the St. Petersburg Hadassah, prepare a written statement concerning these chapters. The written statement is from Adele Morris. In addition, there is information about the St. Petersburg Hadassah chapter found in local news reports.

Adele Morris's statement is as follows: "The St. Petersburg Chapter of Hadassah was formed in the late 1930s, with May Benjamin as its primary organizer and first President. The Jewish community was quite small then, but the fund-raising efforts were constant and the Chapter grew slowly. With the influx of new families in the late 1940s and 1950s, there was a marked increase in membership and programming. In 1957, a younger woman's group known as the "Esther Group" was established with Estelle Marsh as its first President, and it became a dominant force for Israel's support. As the community continued to grow, the organization grew in numbers and strength, was modified and altered as needed, and now in 2005, the St. Petersburg Chapter is proud to boast nearly 600 adult members, with more than 500 of them being Life Members.

The Chapter has always been in the forefront of leadership for Hadassah nationally and in the Florida region. It has cultivated women who became leaders and vital volunteers throughout the community. Marilyn LeVine (Mrs. Morris LeVine) is a member of the National Service Committee of Hadassah, and Sophie Friedlander (Mrs. Herbert Friedlander) was National Vice President and continues to serve as a life time member of the national board.

The St. Petersburg Chapter was the first organization to introduce the National Breast Cancer Awareness Project called, "Check It Out." Under the leadership of Sophie Friedlander, the "Check It Out" program was established to present breast-cancer awareness to the high school students (in schools) of Pinellas County. It has provided thousands of students and teachers with valuable, lifesaving information and motivation.

In November 1993, under the leadership of Adele Morris, the Chapter held a unique one day Expo-Bazaar titled "Israel Is Real" at the University of South Florida campus, to showcase Israel's industries, products, entertainment, tourism etc. It involved about 150 volunteer members and attracted close to 3,000 in attendance.

Innovation has always been present in the Chapter as has been cooperation with the Jewish community. Since 2000, the Chapter has held an annual gourmet dinner party to celebrate the success of Hadassah International. Each year, the party theme is of a different country, where there exists an active Hadassah program. For twenty five years, St. Petersburg International Folk Fair Society was a beneficiary of Hadassah volunteers. Annually, Hadassah volunteers deliver Christmas Day Meals-on-Wheels to the homebound.

Currently, there is a monthly book club and a Kabbalah study group, and Hebrew language study. There are both daytime and evening meetings and events to accommodate the schedules and interests of a very diversified membership.

The Chapter has consistently enjoyed a reputation for excellence in every area of its work – and with the enthusiastic leadership of its current President, Chana Olmstead, the future for growth looks good."

Local News Reports

In 1967, Mrs. Saul Katz was President. In 1971, Mrs. Irving H. Halprin was President.

In 1989, the St. Petersburg chapter of Hadassah helped Young Judea, one of the largest and oldest youth movements in the United States, celebrate its 80th birthday. Four individuals were honored for their dedication and work for the youth of the community. They were: Joel Momberg, Vice President of Community Relations for All Children's Hospital; Corinne Freeman, former Mayor of St. Petersburg and Member of the Pinellas County School Board; Gail Robertson,

Department of Licensing, Juvenile Welfare Board; and Jeanne Malchon, State Senator. The feature speaker for the program was Ruth H. Kaslove of Norwalk, Connecticut, Member, National Board of Hadassah.

In 1994, Lil Hoffman, a major fund-raiser for Hadassah, celebrated her 96th birthday. She and her husband, Joseph, purchased Waverley Court, a collection of twenty two units, cottages, and several larger houses, in the middle to late 1940s. She was one of the early members of Hadassah in St. Petersburg. She helped start a small school for Jewish children.

In 1996, 122 women participated in the first ever Hadassah Bat Mitzvah ceremony at the 82nd national convention in Miami Beach. The women ranged from ages thirteen to eighty six, from Reform, Conservative, and Orthodox backgrounds. Sheila Shayne, President of the Aviva Group of the St. Petersburg Chapter of Hadassah, participated. In addition, four other St. Petersburg women participated. They were: Sharon Feen, Sharlene Sakol and Lea Sandler also of the Aviva Group, and Adele Morris, President Golda Meir/Shalom Group of St. Petersburg. Shayne said, "It was a chance to reaffirm my commitment to Judaism. Spirituality is not something that is static. You always continue growing and learning."

In 1998, the Hadassah Thrift Shop closed. The resale store at 671 Central Avenue, had been in the downtown St. Petersburg area for thirty years. Although, the local Chapter had over 700 members, only the older ones were able to do the work and now this was beyond them. Forty volunteers used to work in the store at a time. These volunteers followed the words of Rabbi Harold S. Kushner, "If we are brave enough to love...and to be wise enough to know there's enough love to go around for us, we can achieve fulfillment that no living creature will ever know. We can re-enter Paradise." These women understood the concept well, but they were no longer physically able to do the work.

The St. Petersburg Chapter participated in a nationwide program to help older members of the community celebrate Hanukkah. This was the Hadassah national mitzvah day project.

In 1999, Laurie Reskind, President of the Shoshanim Group of the St. Petersburg Chapter of Hadassah, was among twenty six American women chosen for Hadassah's Young Women's Mission to Israel. She was selected for her outstanding leadership skills. She participated in an intensive program of seminars, study and sightseeing that examined social, cultural, and political issues. She is the daughter of Dr. Michael and Sandra Slomka of St. Petersburg.

In 2001, on Christmas Eve, Dr. Andrea Stolar and a group of helpers made special deliveries of food and other goodies from the Salvation Army to the elderly shut-ins. This is a project of the St. Petersburg Chapter of Hadassah. Renée Lipman, President of the St. Petersburg Hadassah Chapter said, "I think we know that on Christmas Eve and Christmas Day, people who were Christian want to be home with their families, but there is still a need to deliver food to people. So our group decided that this would be a very wonderful thing for us to do." She also said, "We are adding fresh bread and oranges." Jill Engelman started this project in 1998.

Dorene E. Ben died on August 11. She had been the Director of the Volunteer Action Center of Pinellas County, a non-profit agency that trains and coordinates volunteers for other groups. She was a life member of Hadassah.

In 2003, Ruth H. Dikman died at Menorah Manor. She came to St. Petersburg in 1943. She was an Executive Administrator for the Pinellas County School System for more than twenty five years. She was a life member of Hadassah and a member of its chapter board. She also served as a founding board member of the Gulf Coast Jewish Family Service.

Helen Kahan of the St. Petersburg Chapter of Hadassah was named the recipient of the 17th annual Hadassah National Leadership Award.

Clearwater Chapters

The Clearwater-Safety Harbor Chapter was founded by Mary Rutenberg and Lisa Baranoff in 1951. Mary Rutenberg served as the first President. For at least thirty three years, Mary Rutenberg opened the Hadassah meetings with personal reflections or a story. In 1960, the Clearwater-Safety Harbor Chapter formed a new group known as the Deborah Group. In 1962, the Deborah group was reabsorbed into the Clearwater-Safety Harbor Chapter. In 1963-1964, the President was Reva Kent. In 1964, there were 151 members. In 1965, the President was Mrs. Leo Spiegel. In 1966-1967, the President was Mrs. Loren Pollack. In 1969, the President was Mrs. Isadore Goldberg. In 1970, the President was Mrs. Semon Amzalak. In 1980, a new Group was formed called the Shoshana Group. In 1983, the Clearwater-Safety Harbor Chapter was once again remained the Clearwater Chapter as it was in 1951. (See appendix for the rest of the Presidents)

Shoshana Group

The Shoshana Group was disbanded and then became the North Pinellas Chapter in 1983.

North Pinellas Chapter

The North Pinellas Chapter was formed because of the population growth in the 1980s in Pinellas County north of Clearwater. The first President was Ruth Krouk , 1983-1985. The Presidents after Ruth were: 1985-1986, Annette Walter; 1986-1987, Arlene Blitzer; 1987-1989, Ilene Galler; 1989-1990, Janice Caine; 1990-1991, Bernice Gateman, Veronica Harris, Vera Plotkin; 1991-1992, Veronica Harris; 1992-1994, Phyllis Arak; 1994-1996, Evelyn Morrison; 1996-1998, Terry Howard; 1999-2001, Barbara Felder; 2001-2003, Claire Good; 2003-2005, Florence Barnett; 2005, Jackie Albin.

The North Pinellas Chapter meets at Temple Ahavat Shalom on Curlew Road in Palm Harbor. At present, there are 366 members. A study group meets once a month to discuss Jewish history, current events, book reviews, etc. The chapter also has a ten member song and dance group called the Hadassah Honeys.

Yachad Hadassah Chapter

The Yachad Hadassah Chapter President is Selma Kron. (Yachad means together) In 2004, the Moscow Jewish Choir began touring the United States singing about freedom.

They gave a presentation at Temple B'nai Israel for a benefit to raise money for the Yachad Chapter. The choir was a unique group of people because until very recently, they could not sing songs about God or Judaism. The group performed in eight different languages. The program was organized by Selma Kron.

Interfaith Service at Congregation Beth Shalom, 1963. From left, Rev. D.P. McGeachy, Minister of Peace Memorial Presbyterian Church; Rev. M.G. Argeaux, Rector of the Episcopal Church of the Good Samaritan; Reva Kent, President of Hadassah; Rabbi Albert B. Bolton; Rev. Pat W. McBride, President of the Ministerial Association and Pastor of Skycrest Methodist Church; Cantor Sidney Keiser, of Congregation Rodeph Sholom, Tampa. (Clearwater Sun Photo)

Selma and Norman Kron

Selma and Norman purchased a condo in Belleair Beach in 1987 and moved here permanently in 1994. When Norman became ill with cancer, Selma and Norman gifted the Ambler Nursing Home Inc., which they had personally operated for twenty six years, to the Jewish Federation of Philadelphia and established a Charitable Remainder Trust. The Ambler Nursing Home was rated one of the top nursing facilities in the United States. Selma and Norman grew fresh vegetables on their fifteen acre farm and supplied them to the residents within hours of being harvested. They established a pet therapy program long before it became popular.

Norman was born on November 2, 1921 and died in December 1995. He met Selma, who was born on November 11, 1931, on the campus of the University of Pennsylvania, and they were married on August 16, 1953. Norman earned his degrees from the Wharton School of Business and the University of Pennsylvania Law School. He was Editor in Chief of Law Review and upon graduation, became an assistant US attorney. Selma earned a Bachelor of Science Degree in Education from the University of Pennsylvania. Their daughter, Andrea, graduated from Syracuse University with a Bachelor's Degree in Geology. She and her husband, Charles, a physicist, live in Los Alamos, New Mexico, where she is a cartographer, as well as a geologist. Their daughter, Bonnie, graduated from the University of South Florida with a Bachelor's Degree and a major in Dance. She married

Ric Martin and opened an Okinawan martial arts studio in Largo. Their daughter, Debbie, earned a Master's Degree in Social Work at Bryn Mawr College, Pennsylvania. She and her husband, Mark, and children live in Indian Rocks Beach. He is Past President of ASHI Home-Improvement Company. Son, Edward, earned a law degree from Widener College, Pennsylvania and married Garland Pezzuolo, also an attorney.

Selma and Norman were Zionists and became involved in Hadassah. They helped to establish the Gene Therapy Center at Hadassah Hospital in Jerusalem. The department has been on the cutting edge in medicine and the hospital is one of the finest in the world. Selma is a Member of the Board of Project Grace, a nonprofit organization that deals with end-of-life issues. She also was a Member of the Board of Directors of the Jewish Federation of Pinellas County.

Selma said, "Both Norman and I strongly believed that it was not enough just to make money. Tzedahka always has played a large part in our lives. We feel that it is important to share with our family as well as to give to those in need."

Clearwater Chapter

In the State of Florida, there was one large region of Hadassah until 1976. The Clearwater Chapter came in second for the entire state for performance and the recognition of being Chapter of the Year. By 1978, Miami and Miami Beach now had its own region. Lisl Schick became President of the smaller region. In 1986, the Clearwater Chapter won the annual Hannah Goldberg Award at the National Convention for the best study group in the United States. The Clearwater Chapter put on musical shows and fashion shows to raise funds. They also operated bazaars and resale shops from the 1960s until about the 1990s. The first resale shop started in the garage of Lisl Schick on Robinhood Lane in 1976 and then became a formal resale shop. The Lylah Hadassah Chapter President is Terri Tankel.

Hillel

The mission of Hillel, the Foundation for Jewish Campus Life is to maximize the number of Jewish students involved in Jewish activities with other Jewish students. Hillel is open to any Jewish person regardless of the synagogue that they belong to, or if they do not belong to a synagogue.

Hillel at University of South Florida

Hillel offers a substantial amount of programming in social, cultural, educational, and religious areas. This includes the Jewish Adventurers Club, which sponsors camping, hiking, and out-of-state trips. It also has a substantial program for students twenty one and over and young professionals. Hillel teams participate in all intramural sports programs. Hillel sponsors speakers to promote a better understanding on campus of the Jewish community. It offers Shabbat and holiday services. It works in cooperation with the Campus Ministry Association of the University of South Florida.

Hillel at the University of Tampa

Hillel at the University of Tampa sponsors regular Shabbat dinners and holiday programs. They work in conjunction with the University of South Florida Hillel.

Israel Bonds

State of Israel Bonds or securities are issued by the State of Israel to help build and strengthen the nation's economy and infrastructure. The bonds are backed by the full faith and credit of the Government of Israel, which has had a perfect record of payment of interest and principal, since the first bonds were issued over fifty years ago. Well over twenty-five billion dollars have been raised to help build modern highways, ports, schools, water desalination plants, etc..

Early History

At the completion of the War of Independence in 1948, the newly-reborn State of Israel was in complete economic chaos. From Europe and North Africa, Holocaust survivors and displaced persons came into Israel in huge numbers. Israel's treasury was empty, its economy was in danger of collapse, and its meager resources were virtually gone. On September 3, 1950, David Ben-Gurion, Israel's first Prime Minister, met with a group of fifty American and Israeli leaders in Jerusalem. They decided to bring the concept of Israel bonds to the American public and subsequently Golda Meir met with American Jewish leaders in Washington, DC to plan for the launching of the first Israel bond issue in the United States. The Development Corporation for Israel was created in February, 1951 to offer the securities in the United States. In May, 1951, David Ben-Gurion launched the first Israel Bond sales drive in the United States at a rally in Madison Square Garden. This was the third anniversary of Israel independence. The response to Israel bonds was overwhelming, fifty two million six hundred thousand dollars was raised through bond sales. Golda Meir, former Prime Minister, was also a founder of Israel bonds. She said, "You have a stake in every drop of water we pour into our land, in every mile of road built, in every kilowatt of power in every field, in every factory." When she was asked about what collateral she could offer, she said the only collateral she had was the children and future of the State of Israel.

In 1983, Prime Minister Begin at an Israel Bond conference said, "...Ladies and gentlemen, we of course have also a very serious economic problem and I don't have to go into details. Everybody knows about it and you can follow now the Cabinet's deliberations about harsh measures to be taken and therefore we are so grateful to you for the assistance to the Israel Bonds Organization. The Israel Bonds Organization already brought in billions of dollars to develop the economy on the basis of the loan. It is a great phenomenon in the life of the Jewish people and the State of Israel. I've come to you tonight in order to express our deep gratitude and now I would like to say one sentence. Remember, my dear friends, our people suffered much, lost many, on the day, nobody gave us our freedom, we had to fight for it, to give for it sacrifices, to defend it. All of us without exception of party affiliation, and we won. Why? Because our cause is just. Just take note, my dear friends and when you meet your friends, tell them so. Tell them so. There is a rule, unchangeable. The just cause will always win the day."

Local Israel Bonds

About 1953 or 1954, Mary Rutenberg and Lisa Baranoff started selling Israel bonds through Hadassah. In 1968, the regional representative of Israel bonds for this area was located in Sarasota. This person started the special dinners for Israel bonds where members of the community would be honored. St. Petersburg honorees included: 1975, Dr. and Mrs. Morris Levine and Rabbi Morris Chapman; 1976, Mr. and Mrs. Abe Katz; 1977, Mr. and Mrs. Maurice Goldblatt; 1978, Dr. and Mrs. Leonard Morris; 1979, Mr. and Mrs. Jerome Gilbert; 1980, Colonel and Mrs. Phil Schwarz; 1981, Mr. and Mrs. Murray Jacobs; 1982, Mr. and Mrs. Stan Marsh; 1983, Joe Zappala; 1984, Dr. and Mrs. Michael Slomka; 1985, Mr. and Mrs. Maurice Goldblatt and Mr. and Mrs. Irwin Miller; 1987, Rabbi and Mrs. Jacob Luski; 1988, Mr. and Mrs. Richard Mensh, Mr. and Mrs. W. Fleece and Sidney Richman; 1989, Barry Farber; 1991, Mr. and Mrs. Walter Loebenberg; 1992, Mr. and Mrs. Craig Sher and Dr. and Mrs. Mandel Sher; 1993, Jim and Ann Soble and John and Marion Samson-Joseph; 1994, Ron and Fagl Oxman and Eric and Judy Ludin; 1995, Don and Jane Silverberg, Dr. Fred and Emily Gurtman, and Colonel Phil and Lee Schwartz (Lifetime Award); 1996, Rabbi Jacob Luski (Lifetime Award), Rabbi Steven Moch, and Ira and Beverly Mitlin; 1997, Dr. Michael and Sandy Slomka; 1998, Dr. Patricia Cottrille, Dr. Leonard Azneer, and Barbara and Joseph Sterensis; 2000, Bunnie and Abe Katz (Lifetime Award) and Sharlene and Ron Sakol; 2001, Estelle and Stan March and Michelle and Dave Cohen; 2002, Margot and Michael Benstock and Lenny Englander; 2003, Marilyn Benjamin and Sonya and Irwin Miller; 2004, Joan and Philip Redisch and Bonnie and Pat O'Connell; and 2005, Mark and Judy Gordon and David and Patti Gross.

Clearwater honorees included: 1978, Reva and Marshall Kent; 1981, Maureen and Stanley Rosewater; (Records are partially missing for Clearwater)1991, Reva Kent; 1993, Ronnie and David Bernstein, Nancy and Alan Bomstein, and Jill and Jim Shapiro; 1995, Kathy and Dr. Mitchell Lowenstein, Kathy and Jim Sobel, Dorothy and Ralph

Dutcher, and June and Ben Gelbart; 1996, Della and Hans Krieger, Edith and Leonard Seligman, Elaine and Dr. David Wolstein; 1997, Rabbi and Mrs. Gary Klein, Rabbi and Mrs. Arthur Baseman, and Helaine and Zuna Solc; 1998, Rae Feilman, Irene and Dr. Stephen Weiss, and Marilyn and Dr. Allan Katz; 1999, Jean and Louis Kwall, Marlene and Richard Siegel, and Gina and Steve Bragin; 2000, Lynn and Dr. Steven Goldman, Cheryl and Aaron Gold, Helen and Harry Gold, and Jerri and David Greene; 2001, Arlene and Bruce Lowitt, Johanna and Rabbi Bromberg, and Toni and Dr. John Rinde; 2002, Dr. Myron Graff, Dr. Xenia Fane, and William Silver; 2003, Mr. and Mrs. Norman Gross, Mr. and Mrs. Charles Rutenberg, and Roni and Stephen Igel.

Jewish Genealogical Society of Tampa Bay

The Jewish Genealogical Society of Tampa Bay was founded in April, 1999, for the purpose of assisting interested individuals in learning about Jewish genealogy and how to research and document their own family histories. This is accomplished through the exchange of research information, and encouraging and facilitating research activities, arranging genealogical research tours, and presenting monthly programs of interest. The Jewish Genealogical Society of Tampa Bay is one of seventy eight Jewish Genealogical Societies and special-interest groups affiliated with the International Association of Jewish Genealogical Societies throughout the world. Each year, the international group holds a week long international conference in which the local society participates. Some 1,200-1,500 people typically attend these meetings.

Genealogy is one the major hobbies in United States and is either the second or third largest non-commercial use of the Internet. The Internet has made doing family research a much more enjoyable and less tedious task. There are many more databases available today, and they continue to grow in number.

The purpose of the local group is to: facilitate exchange of research information; encourage and coordinate research activities by individuals; educate members to help themselves and others in genealogical research; acquire and organize genealogical research materials and place in a library available to the group; arrange programs at meetings to train and educate individuals in genealogical methods and problem-solving; arrange genealogical tours; contribute findings to international databases; collect, preserve, and disseminate knowledge and information with reference to genealogy; encourage interested persons to pursue and preserve genealogical data; provide opportunities for the sharing of Jewish genealogical information; encourage publication of worthy material in the field of genealogy.

In 2006, the Jewish Genealogical Society of Tampa Bay will start an outreach program to speak to various Jewish organizations in the community to acquaint them with the purposes and actions of the local society. The goal is to help people, who are interested in learning more about their Jewish ancestors, to learn how to research their past in order to better understand their family. A second goal is to develop a database of everyone buried in all the Jewish cemeteries in the Tampa Bay area.

The January 2006 program is "Latest Developments in Lithuanian Research" by Howard Margol. Howard is Past President of the International Association of Jewish Genealogical Societies and Past President of the Jewish Geological Society of Georgia. He travels regularly to Lithuania and Latvia for humanitarian and research purposes. The February 2006 program is "Using the Yad Vashem Holocaust Database" by Alan Koenig. The database, a remarkable tool for tracking family connections and family history, can be accessed on line.

Rita Reuben discussed some of the important databases for genealogical research. They were: World War I draft records and indexes; International Association of Jewish Genealogical Societies Cemetery Project; federal and state census data; New York City Census update for New York State Censuses of 1905, 1915, and 1925; and new Holocaust Databases on JewishGen.

William E. Israel, President, has personally researched his family history for the past nine generations going back to the very late 1700s in Latvia, Lithuania and Belarus. He published a 300 page hardbound book about his father's side of the family.

Jewish Press

The Jewish Press in the United States has appeared in English, Yiddish, Hebrew, German, Ladino, and Russian. The major 19th-century American Jewish newspapers were *The Occident* and *The Israelite*, later known as the *American Israelite*. *The Occident* was founded by Reverend Isaac Leeser in April 1843. *The Israelite* was founded by Reform Rabbi Isaac M. Wise in 1854. Reverend Leeser in Volume I, No. 1, started the new newspaper with introductory remarks. He said that it was customary for an Editor in his first appearance in a publication to discuss the nature and substance of what would be in the newspaper. He said that the idea of a religious periodical did not originate with him, nor did he think it was a good idea when it was first proposed. He thought that newspaper knowledge was at best superficial and would be more pleasing to the general public than instructive. However, over time he realized that people did not have the time to go through the slow process of deep research, which was the true path to knowledge. He began to feel that he could bring well-prepared and well researched information to the general public in order for them to gain knowledge and self-improvement. For those individuals who wanted to learn more, they could do the additional research. He said that he would add to the newspaper works which were translated from Hebrew, French, and German. He endeavored to give one sermon a month. He said that he would not object to controversial articles, if they were written with temperance and were candid. He said that absolute freedom from error was unattainable, but proper care would be given to ensure the greatest accuracy possible. He offered to give accounts of public religious meetings and provide space for congregations and societies to provide information. He said he would be strictly impartial about the reporting of the news, but he would feel free to offer editorials concerning newsworthy items.

Isaac Leeser said, "In conclusion we will state that it is owing to a strict sense of duty that we have embarked on this difficult enterprise; and that it depends altogether upon our religious community to render our task a pleasant one. On one thing we are resolved, to do the best we can, in the full reliance upon that aid from above which is never withheld from those who honestly fulfill their duty. More than that, no man can do, and therefore, this alone can our friends expect from the Editor." This philosophy of Isaac Leeser, written in 1843, is followed this very day by Jim Dawkins, Publisher and Co-Owner and Karen Dawkins, Managing Editor and Co-Owner, of the *Jewish Press* of Pinellas County.

In 1855, the *Deborah*, a German language paper for women was published. This became a supplement to the *Israelite*. This paper reported on synagogues and their auxiliary sisterhoods, religious schools, benevolent societies, and local chapters of national Jewish women's groups.

In 1887, the Philadelphia Jewish Exponent, a Jewish community weekly started. In 1897, the *Jewish Daily Forward*, a Yiddish newspaper, came to be known as the voice of the Jewish immigrant and the conscience of the ghetto. It fought for social justice and helped generations of immigrants enter American life. It was one of the nation's most eloquent defenders of democracy and Jewish rights.

Jewish Press of Pinellas County

The *Jewish Press* of Pinellas County was founded in 1986 jointly by Jim and Karen Dawkins. Jim was the co-owner and publisher and Karen was the co-owner and managing editor. The Dawkins wanted to provide to the Jewish community a credible, professionally done community newspaper similar to the successful ones in large Jewish communities, such as Philadelphia. Desktop publishing gave the *Jewish Press*, as well as other local editors and publishers, more control over their papers. Previously, the small Jewish newspapers were basically used to sell advertisement and news content was of secondary importance. The *Jewish Press* of Pinellas County reversed these priorities. From 1927-1990, the *Jewish*

Floridian, with headquarters in Miami, provided a chain of six newspapers for the Jewish people of Florida. These papers were published in cooperation with the Jewish Federation of the various counties.

Jim and Karen, who held full-time jobs, decided to try to upgrade the quality of the local newspaper. They became part-time editors to collect press releases for the *Jewish Floridian*. Jim, a professional journalist, was an award-winning reporter, designer, and assistant state editor of the Evening Independent, the now defunct evening paper of the *St. Petersburg Times*. He had also been a reporter/writer, bureau chief, and assistant state editor at the Tampa Tribune. Karen was a veteran reporter, bureau chief, and editor for the Tampa Tribune.

The Jewish Federation of Pinellas County liked the improvement of the local *Jewish Floridian* and encouraged Jim and Karen to open their own Jewish newspaper. They became the sole owners and retained editorial control. The Federation then ended its contract with the *Jewish Floridian* and the *Jewish Press* of Pinellas County was born. Two years later, the Tampa Jewish Federation, seeing the success of the Pinellas paper, followed their neighbor's lead and the *Jewish Press* of Tampa was born. The funding of the newspapers came from advertisement sales and the two federations underwrote the home delivery. Approximately 5,000 households in Pinellas County and parts of West Pasco County received the local newspaper. The Tampa paper reaches about 7,000 households. The newspaper has been enlarged from eight pages to forty four pages

The focus of the papers was originally local Jewish news. Today, similar to the Jewish Exponent of Philadelphia, the papers focus on national and international news, along with local Jewish news. Their plans for the future are to add youth and sports news sections, in addition to editorial and op-ed sections.

James Allen Dawkins

Jim Dawkins was born on December 11, 1943 and raised in Kissimmee, Florida. He was a seventh generation Floridian on his mother's side. He is descended from three of Florida's first 100 Pioneer families, Alvarez, Padgett, and Durance. He earned an Associate Degree from Orlando Junior College in 1963. He attended Florida State University and then transferred to Morehead State University in Kentucky where he graduated with a Bachelor of Arts Degree in History, Political Science, and Education. He became a police reporter, and then feature writer of city government for the *Ashland Daily Independent*. From 1969-1971, he was a one-man bureau for the *Lakeland Ledger*. He and Karen were married by Rabbi Baseman on October 4, 1975. Jim took a graduate course in mass communications at the University of South Florida. His level of competency was so high that he exceeded the knowledge being presented in the course. He was approved for a thesis entitled, *The Prototype of a Hebrew-American Newspaper*. He dropped out of the course and three years later, instead of writing a thesis, he and Karen opened a newspaper. Over the years, he has received numerous awards for reporting, writing, and design.

Karen Wolfson Dawkins

Karen Dawkins was born in Omaha, Nebraska in 1951 and moved to St. Pete Beach in 1959. Karen, daughter of Gert and Harold Wolfson, became a Bat Mitzvah at Congregation B'nai Israel in St. Petersburg, with Rabbi Morris B. Chapman officiating. It was believed that she was the first female to read directly from the Torah at her Bat Mitzvah at Congregation B'nai Israel. Karen graduated from the Medill School of Journalism at Northwestern University in Evanston, Illinois, with a Bachelor of Science in Journalism Degree and Master of Science in Journalism Degree. She joined the *Tampa Tribune* in 1974 as a reporter in the West Pasco County Bureau. She became a reporter in the *Tampa Tribune* Clearwater office, where she covered all aspects of the news but concentrated on the court system. Her most memorable story was the collapse of the Skyway Bridge in May, 1980. She became the Bureau Chief of the North West Hillsborough Bureau of the *Tribune*, a copy editor and Night City Editor. Both Karen and Jim are members of the American Jewish Press Association.

Karen and Jim have two children,

Rachel, born February 4, 1979, and Jeremy, born January 9, 1981. Rachel earned her Bachelor of Science Degree and M. D. Degree in the six-year medical school program at the University of Miami. She is currently serving a pediatric residency in New Orleans.

Jeremy received his Bachelor of Science Degree from the Rinker School of Building Construction at the University of Florida. He is a project engineer with a commercial construction company in Orlando.

Philosophy

The Dawkins guiding philosophy has always been, "To provide a professional, credible and unbiased Jewish community newspaper for all Jews focusing greatly on those aspects of Jewish life not readily covered by the general media. Fairness has been an operating principle." Jim and Karen have far exceeded their guiding philosophy, as has been shown through a Jewish demographic study, where 90% of the readership rated the two newspapers as either good or excellent.

Jewish War Veterans

The Jewish War Veterans organization was founded in 1896, and the ladies auxiliary was formed in 1928. The function of the post and auxiliary is to act as a liaison between the American community, the veteran community, and the Jewish community. The Jewish War Veterans organization provides for areas of service including: service to veterans, service to the Jewish community, service to the general community, and service to Israel.

Post and Auxiliary 246 of St. Petersburg

Post and Auxiliary 246 was established in 1957 to help all veterans of South Pinellas County. Members volunteer at the Bay Pines Veterans Hospital in a variety of capacities. The veterans provide special programs on Flag Day and Memorial Day. The Post and Auxiliary make donations to Gulf Coast Jewish Family Services. (Unfortunately, there were no records of Post and Auxiliary 246 of St. Petersburg available to the author. Many of the members of the post were either deceased or extremely old and unable to

provide pertinent information.)

Post and Auxiliary 409 of Clearwater-Paul Surensky Post

The Paul Surensky Post 409 was chartered on May 15, 1971. The charter members were: Bernard Lyon, Art Silverberg, Harold Block, Louis Block, Lawrence Jacobs, Moshe Frankel, Arthur Brosman, Mr. Druz, Milton Ensler, Major Isadore Golden, Harold Haftel, Abraham Simar, Henry Dukalak, E. G. Wiener, Robert R. Baker, H. Benard, Henry Econsus, Jacob Butler, Charles Goldstein, Sidney Kurnitz, George Le Von, Al Peskin and Joseph Zimmerman. Joe Stern was the third Post Commander. In 2005, at age 98, he is the oldest living veteran of Post 409. There has been a Jewish War Veterans presence in the State of Florida, since at least 1952. The Post 409 Auxiliary was established in 1971.

From the inception of Post 409, the veterans group continued to grow to 143 members in the Post and Auxiliary. During that time, there was considerable revenue from the membership and special affairs and the Post and its members were involved in many worthwhile projects. Although the dates of various activities are not available, the activities themselves have been documented by Morris Michaels, current Quartermaster of Post 409.

The Post continues to conduct bingo games at Bay Pines Veterans Hospital. The winners of the games receive canteen books to use at their discretion. This is followed by refreshments served by the Ladies Auxiliary. It provides a needed break for the hospitalized veterans. The Ladies Auxiliary also make lap robes and distribute them at Christmas time.

The Post subsidizes a training program for Candy Stripers at Bay Pines Veterans Hospital. The young people are taught how to work with older Americans and how to perform the mitzvah of bringing their young and enthusiastic presence into the lives of these veterans who have given so much for their country.

The Post hires special buses equipped with wheelchair lifts to take veterans to baseball games. The Post provides the tickets, all food, and people to escort the hospital patients from Bay Pines Veterans Hospital.

Each year, the hospital submits a "Wish List" to the Post. Post 409 has provided computers, televisions, cycles, fishing rods, and golf carts for transportation purposes. The computers were used to help train the veterans for future employment. The golf carts were used to help patients move more easily around the vast facility to meet medical appointments.

The Post goes to bookstores in the community to obtain boxes of books and other reading material for the veterans to make their lives more interesting. The materials can also be used in job training.

The Post supports the National Museum of American Jewish History in Washington, DC. The exhibits deal with the different wars in which the Jewish people fought for the United States. In World War I, 250,000 Jewish men and women served with great distinction. There were 15,000 casualties among the Jewish service people and more than 1,400 awards for bravery were bestowed upon the soldiers of the Jewish faith. In World War II, 550,000 Jewish men and women served with great distinction. Eleven thousand Jewish service people were killed and 40,000 were wounded. There were more than 52,000 decorations awarded to Jewish men and women. In the Korean War, 150,000 Jewish men and women fought with great distinction. In Vietnam, 30,000 Jewish men and women fought in Southeast Asia.

Colonel Jack Jacobs of New Jersey, received the Congressional Medal of Honor. In all subsequent wars, Jewish men and women have fought with valor in numbers far exceeding the percentage of Jewish people in the population of our country. Thus, the financial support of Post 409 to the National Museum is significant, so that the young people of the present can understand the Jewish contributions of the past for the defense of liberty and the United States of America.

Post 409 financially supports: Trees in Israel program, Gulf Coast Jewish Family Services, Golda Meir/Kent Center, and other worthwhile charities and community projects in the Jewish and general communities.

The Post provides programs on "What It Means to Be an American" to the public elementary schools. The members were teachers to help these students write essays on patriotic themes. United States savings bonds are awarded to the first and second place winners and a certificate of merit is given to the third place winner. A special assembly is held in the school for the presentation of the awards. These awards have been given at seven different schools.

Post 409 participates in the annual "Fun in the Sun" parade held by the city of Clearwater in the downtown area. The Post is the lead unit in the parade. The color guard carries the American flag. On national holidays, such as Memorial Day, Veterans' Day, the Post participates in all of the parades and other activities. On Pearl Harbor Day, Post 409 joins the New Port Richey Jewish War Veterans Post in performing a variety of patriotic duties including casting a wreath into the water, providing an honor guard who fire their rifles, followed by taps. Each year, they are involved in the Massing of the Colors, where units from all branches and parts of the Armed Forces in uniform remind the American people of the sacrifice of all veterans in the pursuit of the honor, dignity, and freedom of the United States of America. On Memorial Day, they conduct a special service in the Jewish section of Chapel Hill Cemetery.

The Ladies Auxiliary is an essential part of Jewish War Veterans Post Number 409 of Clearwater. They are involved in many projects that help others. They raise funds and perform work to make the lives of other people happier and more rewarding. Each winter holiday season, the women send a large box of new winter clothing to their adopted hospital, White River Junction Veterans Hospital. They contribute money toward the Wish List at Bay Pines Veterans Hospital. They contribute funds for help in Israel. They are partners with two elementary schools where they give money to teachers in the primary grades to purchase materials helpful for teaching, that are not provided by the school system. The Women's Auxiliary of Jewish War Veterans Post Number 409 provide partial college scholarship awards to a graduating senior from each of two high schools. The students are selected by the school and the funds are sent directly to the bursar of the college selected by the student. The women contribute toys and cooking utensils to the Ronald McDonald House and also clothing and toiletries to abused women shelters. The Ladies Auxiliary has received Certificates of Recognition from the National Department and the State Department of the Jewish War Veterans for their exemplary work in Community Relations, Adopt a Hospital Program, and the Americanism Program.

The author has a deep understanding and special love for the women who make up the Ladies Auxiliary of the Jewish War Veterans. His mother, Gussie Koren, spent many years in the 1930s, 1940s, 1950s working for the Ladies Auxiliary of South Philadelphia Post Number 98, to help the Post grow and prosper. She was the official volunteer cook who provided thousands of meals for hundreds of events that supported Post 98 and the Jewish and general communities. His father, Charles Koren, was one of the early members of Post 98. His father enlisted twice in World War I. He was sent home to die from the influenza pandemic, but he survived and reenlisted. During World War II, Charles continued his service to his country by serving as an auxiliary policemen for five years. His love for his adopted country was instilled in his son. The author's father-in-law, Francis R. Conway, served with distinction on the front lines in France during World War I.

At a special Veterans' Day service, the following Jewish war veterans were honored:

Williams Steckler, Pfc., United States Army, 1944-1945, landed on Omaha Beach five days after D-Day. He and his division fought the Germans east of the Vire River, on July 7, 1944. His company for this action received the Presidential Unit Citation.

Harold Haftel, Sergeant, Army Air Corps, 1944-1946 and 1950-1952, attended the Nuremburg trials as an observer. In 1945, he visited United Nations refugee camps to search for relatives, but found none.

Murray Zolkower, Corporal, United States Army, 1942-1945, as a member of the 120th Medical Battalion, helped liberate Dachau Concentration Camp.

Harry Gold, Staff Sergeant, United States Army, 1942-1945, served in the Judge Advocate section and did investigations of prospective civilian employees at Camp Shanks, New York. Due to poor eyesight he did not go abroad. Prior to service he completed college and law school.

Frances Schlact, Army Nurse, 1945-1947, was stationed at Walter Reed Hospital in Washington, DC. While accompanying wounded soldiers to the White House for tea, she had the opportunity to meet President and Mrs. Truman.

Beth Chernoff, U.S. Army Reserves, 224th Military Intelligence Company, 1979-1985, felt a special bond with Colonel Ilan Ramon, Israel's first astronaut. When he went into space, he took with him a book of Psalms, made kiddush on Friday night, and recited Shema Yisrael as the shuttle flew over Jerusalem. He also took along a Holocaust Torah. Beth, twenty years before when going to ROTC camp at Fort Bragg, North Carolina, took along Shabbat candlesticks she had received for her Bat Mitzvah. On Shabbat, she lit the candles and read the Bible, remembering history, shedding a few tears, communing with her God, and praying for strength.

Mel Kerman, Specialist E-5, United States Army, was a specialist in language who served as an Interpreter/Translator in Russian. He spent a year-long tour of duty on a special secret mission to the Republic of South Africa for Army Security. His mission was to report on Soviet space communications.

Herman Lichtenberg, Staff Sergeant (Surgical Technician), United States Army, 1942-1945, served with the Combat Engineers and the First Calvary Division for twenty two months in the Southwest Pacific. He participated in the Dutch Hollandia and invasion of Leyte in the Philippines. He was awarded the Bronze Star Medal. He participated in administering the plasma infusion to Tojo, Prime Minister of Japan, who tried to commit suicide after the United States troops landed in Japan.

Mark B. Wilson, Lt. Commander, United States Coast Guard, spent twenty years in the Coast Guard. He was involved in Vietnam, Desert Storm, and was the on-scene Acting Senior Safety Inspector of Materials for Greater Northwestern Alaska for the clean up of the Exxon Valdez oil spill in June, 1989.

Mayer Reubenstein, Senior Assistant Surgeon (Major), United States Public Health Service, 1961-1963, was Medical Consultant with the Bureau of Chronic Diseases and assigned to the Wisconsin State Board of Health in Madison. He was in charge of a new pilot program to screen the general public for various chronic diseases. During the Kennedy administration, he was reassigned as a Medical Officer in the United States Coast Guard. He retired as Rear Admiral.

Leo Plotkin, staff Sergeant, United States Army. During World War II, he served for three and one half years and was located in the South Pacific. He took part in the invasion of the island of Biak.

Neil Wyman, Captain, United States Air Force, 1968-1972. He was assigned to Shemya, a small island in the tail of the Aleutian Islands chain, which was only 300 miles from the Soviet Union. His mission was to track launches from the Soviet Union and identify Soviet test missile launches.

Sol Ives, Combat Medic, who was at the Utah Beach Landing in Normandy, France in 1944. He did not carry a weapon, but he wore a helmet with a red cross inscribed on it and a Red Cross armband. Casualties were very heavy and his greatest challenge was to quickly save lives. Sol was in combat for eleven months and was awarded five Silver Campaign Stars, Combat Medic Badge, bronze Star, French Normandy medal. He served with the 79th infantry division, and as a medic attached to 313th Infantry Regiment. He later became a pharmacist for thirty one years in both New Jersey and New York.

Other Members

Morris Michaels was born in Chicago in September, 1919. He entered the Army on July 29, 1942 and served in Guadalcanal, Bougainville, and Luzon in the Philippines where he helped fight the Japanese in Manilla. For his heroic conduct, he received the: Asiatic-Pacific Theater Ribbons with two Battle Stars; Philippine Liberation Ribbon with one bronze Star; and the Good Conduct Ribbon. He was honorably discharged on September 1, 1945.

Joe Stern was born in New Bedford, Massachusetts. He graduated from Boston University. He was a sergeant in the Army Air Corps. He went into the shoe business. He served as Commander of the Paul Surensky Post 409 on five separate occasions. He was a County Commander and held positions in the Jewish War Veterans Department of Florida, as well as being a National Committeeman. His wife, Elaine, was born in Cleveland, Ohio and moved to Florida in 1973. She joined the Auxiliary of Post 246 in St. Petersburg. She married Joe Stern in 1979 and transferred to Auxiliary 409. She was President three times, county President for three years, and volunteered at Bay Pines Hospital for twenty seven years. She graduated from Mather College of Case Western Reserve.

Harold Seymour Ehrenpreis was born in New York City on April 15, 1917. He joined the United States Army on September 12, 1941. He was stationed in Iceland for two and one half years with the Signal Corps and Central Intelligence. He earned the Meritorious Service Unit Insignia, ETO Service Ribbon, Good Conduct Medal, American Defense Service Ribbon. He was discharged on October 21, 1945, with the rank of Sergeant. When he returned home he completed his Bachelor of Science Degree at College of the City of New York in Social Science and then earned a Master of Science Degree in Education, also from CCNY. He worked for the New York City Board of Education as a supervisor in the Bureau of Attendance. After retirement, he earned a Bachelor of Business Administration from Baruch College in New York City. He then worked as an accountant and a tax preparer. He was Past President of Queens Friendship Lodge of B'nai B'rith and belonged to Jewish War Veterans Kew Forest Post 250 of Queens, New York. When he came to Dunedin, Florida, he joined Post 409 and B'nai B'rith Unit 2603 of Clearwater. He died on December 31, 2004.

Harry J. Eiseman was born on January 13, 1920 in the Bronx, New York. He married his first wife and had three sons. He married his current wife, Ruth Silver, in 1977. They won one third of the New York lottery and moved to Clearwater in 1981. After moving to Florida, Harry received his Bachelor's Degree. He worked as a paramedic at the Innsbruck Country Club in the medical department. Harry was the Commander of Post 409 for two terms and also County Commander for Pinellas County. Harry served in the United States Marine Corps during World War II. He earned the Good Conduct Medal, Navy Commendation Medal, National Defense Ribbon, American Defense Ribbon, Marine Corps Achievement Medal, and several other citations. He was discharged as a corporal. He was a man of great honor and was respected by all around him. David Miller wrote about him, "The Title–It cannot be inherited, nor can it be purchased. You or no one alive can buy it for any price. It is impossible to rent and it cannot be lent. You alone and you alone have earned it, with your blood, sweat and lives. You own it forever, the title. "United States Marine." You're a true patriot, God bless you!"

Jess B. Krug

Jess Wasserkrug was born on August 8, 1916 in St. Louis, Missouri. He completed his studies at Washington University in St. Louis.

Jess married Rita Arnowitz on July 2, 1939. Their oldest son, Gerald, was born on February 22, 1940. Their son, Neal, was born on January 26, 1947. A daughter, Nancy, was born on June 21, 1948. Jess currently resides in Clearwater. Rita passed away on July 2, 1989, shortly after they celebrated their 50th wedding anniversary.

At age ten, Jess joined the St. Louis Junior Boy Scouts. He was asked to help direct pedestrian traffic during the 1927 tornado in St. Louis. He became an active member of Troop 30 at the YMHA (Young Men's Hebrew Association).During the summer, he was chosen as a charter member of the "Order of the Arrow," a singular honor. He reached the level of Life Scout, and at a later date, became an Eagle Scout.

Jess was President twice of Lodge 22 B'nai B'rith in St. Louis. He received a plaque from the B'nai B'rith for fifty years of continuous membership. In 2005, Jess is the Treasurer of B'nai B'rith Unit 2603 of Clearwater. In 2006, he will be given the "B'nai B'rith Member of the Year Award."

Jess entered the Navy on May 4, 1944. He became a quartermaster because of his knowledge of Morse Code, which he had learned in the Boy Scouts. He was aboard a ship that was part of the invasion of Iwo Jima. He witnessed the raising of the American flag by the Marines on Iwo Jima. He also served in the action on Saipan and Okinawa. He was honorably discharged from the service on December 28, 1945, with the rank of Quartermaster's Second Class.

In St. Louis, he joined immediately after World War II, Jewish War Veterans Post 346. He served as Adjutant, and then later as Commander. He was elected the Commander of the Missouri State Department. In Clearwater, he was elected Commander of Post 409. Jess, over his lifetime, has demonstrated the qualities of friendship, dedication to his work and organizations, and excellent leadership skills. He has been a source of pride to the Jewish War Veterans, B'nai B'rith, and the entire Jewish community.

Current Leadership

The current leadership of the Paul Surensky Post number 409 is as follows: Commander, Jess B. Krug; Senior Vice Commander, Stanley Berger; Jr. Vice Commander, David Samuels; Adjutant, Ivan Nachman; Quartermaster, Morris Michaels; Chaplain, Murray Zolkower. The current leadership of the Ladies Auxiliary 409 is: President, Charlotte Michaels; Senior Vice President, Paula Sherman; Junior Vice President, Ruth Eiseman; Chaplain, Leona Gallay; Patriotic Instructor, Roz Hochberg; Financial Secretary, Sheila Vidor; Recording Secretary, Ruth Wosk; Fund-Raising, Paula Sherman, Fran Ehrenpreis, and Roz Hochberg.

Jewish Women International

Jewish Women International was founded in 1897 as B'nai B'rith Women. They strive to break the cycle of violence toward women, children, and families through education and social action. They support the Residential Treatment Center in Jerusalem, which has helped thousands of severely emotionally disturbed Israeli children. They also support the Jewish

Women in International Russia Project, which attempts to correct the domestic violence problem in the former Soviet Union. In the United States, they support Esther's Place in Baltimore, Maryland, which provides life skills training, career assessment, job development assistance, and employment retention issues. They also support domestic violence issues resolution through Project Ohr and a variety of resource guides for rabbis and community workers on domestic violence.

Clearwater Chapter
The Clearwater Chapter has sponsored several Project Ohr programs. At Hanukkah, the women in the chapter take gifts to Jewish residents of assisted-living facilities and sponsor Hanukkah parties there. They fill wish lists provided by clients of Gulf Coast Jewish Family Services. They provide food, toiletries, small clothing items. They send Mother's Day flowers to designated abuse shelters. The chapter's annual fund-raiser, a luncheon and fashion show, helps support the Residential Treatment Center in Israel. The Clearwater Chapter has the largest collection of Jewish Women International hand-carved wooden dolls representing famous people who overcame serious obstacles to make a difference in the world. These dolls include one of Helen Keller, Martin Luther King Jr., and Golda Meir. The dolls are taken to elementary schools as part of the teaching program.

Jewish Law Students Association at Stetson University

Jewish Law Students Association at Stetson University in St. Petersburg educates and promotes Jewish ideals and customs to the Stetson College of Law and to the local community. They sponsor or co-sponsor a variety of fund raisers for local Jewish organizations and charities and organize events to promote peace in the Middle East and Israel.

National Council of Jewish Women

In 1893, Hannah G. Solomon of Chicago was asked to organize the Jewish women for hostess duty for the Chicago World's Fair. Hannah, a social activist, along with the other women refused to do this. They felt that their participation should be far more substantive. Hannah then founded the National Council of Jewish Women. She and the Council pioneered the settlement house movement, working with Jane Addams' Hull House in Chicago. The Council went on to: establish Sabbath schools in communities without synagogues; advocate for children in court proceedings; sponsor adult study circles to promote learning and leadership; provide vocational training for girls and women; develop school health programs and free health dispensary; and provide food and other materials for servicemen during the Spanish-American War.

Between 1910 and 1930, the National Council of Jewish Women: established penny lunch programs in public schools; helped settle 65,000 immigrants in port cities nationwide; joined the Red Cross and raised a record-breaking four million dollars for relief of human suffering during World War I; sponsored classes and granted scholarships to unemployed workers; helped bring health care to rural communities through the Farm and Rural Work Program; promoted America's entrance into the League of Nations; send aid to help the Ukrainian Jews in response to a massacre that had occurred; helped organize the international Jewish Women's Organizations Conference in Vienna; helped pass the 19th Amendment on women's suffrage; helped provide job assistance to people suffering from the Depression.

Between 1950 and 1970, the National Council of Jewish Women: started the Freedom Campaign to protect civil liberties during the McCarthy era; started an inter-ethnic coalition to combat censorship; developed a Meals-on-Wheels Program; expanded overseas scholarship programs; and helped build better mental health services and patients rights.

From 1970 to 1990, the National Council of Jewish Women: published "Windows on Day Care", the first nationwide survey of day care facilities and services and the problems found in these programs; received the Achievement Award for dedicated "Services to the Children of America" from the National Council of Juvenile Court Judges; published "Innocent Victims," a comprehensive manual on child abuse detection and prevention; received four major awards for the Council's work with the Court Appointed Special Advocates Project; marched for the Equal Rights Amendment; helped lead the first White House Conference on Families; supported the Roe versus Wade decision on women's reproductive rights.

From 1990 to present, the National Council of Jewish Women: continued to advocate for women, children, and families with considerable success; participated in the National Day of the Working Parent; participated in National Speak out for Children Advocacy Day in Washington, DC; commemorated its 100th anniversary with festivities in the United States and Israel; celebrated the induction of its founder, Hannah G. Solomon, into the National Women's Hall of Fame; participated in White House conferences on race relations, hate crimes, childcare, and early childhood development; launched the National Council of Jewish Women's action alert network to get instant information to members concerning breaking news and legislative actions; published two key studies, "Parents and School Partners" and "Listening to Families;" started STOP, the National Council of Jewish Women's strategies to prevent domestic violence through grassroots efforts; started the Yad B'Yad grant program to nurture knowledge for at risk children and their families in Israel; updated childcare findings in a new study, "Opening a New Window on Childcare;" focused the need for national attention to the childcare crisis; supported the NCJW Women and Gender Studies Program at Tel Aviv University; started Benchmark, a campaign to save Roe versus Wade.

The current statement of purpose is: "National Council of Jewish Women is an organization which, in a spirit of Judaism, is dedicated to furthering human welfare in the Jewish and general communities, locally, nationally, and internationally. Through an integrated program of education, service, and social action, it provides essential services and stimulates and educates the individual and the community toward responsibility in advancing human welfare and the democratic way of life."

Local Chapters

The local chapter of the National Council of Jewish Women was started in St. Petersburg in 1940. Unfortunately, many of the people who probably made so many contributions to the welfare of women and children have now died and the records of their accomplishments are no longer available. This, once again, emphasizes the need for keeping accurate records and then turning them over to Heritage Village, the Pinellas County Historical Society, for proper storage and recovery for future citizens.

Some local news sources provide sketchy information about some people who have been involved with the National Council of Jewish Women. The National Council of Jewish Women's Clearwater Chapter in 1997 was part of a coordinating committee, along with the Church Women United and the National Council of Negro Women, to help in the Women, Infants, and Children's Program. The following information includes brief discussions about the lives of these people.

Florence Lippman

Florence Lippman and nine other residents of Menorah Manor were given the Key to the City of St. Petersburg by Mayor David Fisher in 1997. Florence was recognized for her fifty years of volunteer work. She and her husband, Morris, and small daughter, Elaine (Stupp), arrived in St. Petersburg on December 10, 1941. Later, a second daughter, Lynda (Lockhart), was born. In 1942, Florence joined the St. Petersburg Section of the National Council of Jewish Women and, for the next fifty years, she did virtually all of her community service work through this organization. She loved to help children and youth. In 1960, Florence was appointed to the mayor's Committee for Urban Renewal and also helped with the White House Conference on Children and Youth. Also, in 1960 she helped organize the Youth Employment Service, an outreach program of the National Council of Jewish Women. In 1967, the State of Florida took over the job service and renamed it the Florida State Employment Service Agency Youth Job Corps. Florence worked very hard to convince business owners and corporate executives to make jobs available for underprivileged young people. Florence founded, through the National Council of Jewish Women, the Memorial Scholarship Award. From 1966-1977, she was the bay area representative for Blue Star Camp in North Carolina. She helped St Petersburg children get summer opportunities at the camp, where she personally taught drama, made costumes, and voluntarily cleaned up the dining hall and cooked meals. For a period of time, Florence taught children with learning disabilities in elementary schools and also started an audio taping program for blind students. In February, 1973, Florence was given the prestigious Hannah G. Solomon Award by the National Council of Jewish Women as the outstanding woman in the Jewish community and general community whose achievements fall within the areas of the Council's interest. She received this award for thirty one years of service to the Council and the community. Her activities included: 1942, Secretary and Vice-President of the St. Petersburg Section of the National Council of Jewish Women; 1952-1963, served on a joint venture committee with Needlework Guild to provide clothing to the needy; 1961, President of the St. Petersburg Section; one of the founders of the Evening Branch of the National Council for Jewish Women in Clearwater; helped win "Salute to the Club's Award" for local section because of the unique audio-taping program for blind students; 1962, served on a committee to establish Senior Friendship group at the Jewish Community Center, which operated for twenty seven years; 1966, recipient of Sound of Honor Award for outstanding community service to the Jewish communities; 1984, First Vice President, Florida Suncoast Opera Guild; 1984, Started Tribune Fund Committee to raise money for young people for vocal competition. In 1998, Florence was honored by the Florida Suncoast Opera Guild for her dedicated service and leadership.

Florence married Morris Lippman (Lipwich). Morris was born on July 26, 1907, in Halifax, Nova Scotia. Morris first went into the insurance business in St. Petersburg and then purchased a small dairy store. He sold that business and then entered the salvage business. He owned the Kenwood and New Jersey Apartments in St. Petersburg and the Salvage Center. He and Florence were members of the Temple Beth-El Choir for eighteen years. He was a member of B'nai B'rith and very active in the United Jewish Appeal. He died on January 21, 1974.

Elaine L. Lippman was born in New York City on August 15, 1935. She and her parents left New York and went to St. Petersburg to be with her father's parents, Leah Brina and Aaron Lipwich, because of serious discrimination in New York City. Elaine was musically inclined, as her parents were before her. Elaine played piano in the high school orchestra. She graduated from the University of Florida. She met Mort Stupp and they married in June of 1958. Their son, Gary, was born in November of 1959. She and Mort moved to Gainesville in order for Mort to finish his education. He graduated from the University of Florida and became a CPA. After being in his own business, he became the Chief Financial Officer for Val Pak Direct Mail Advertising. They have two children, Shari and Gary. They both attended the University of Florida and University of South Florida and both graduated. Shari is a nationally certified school math teacher and Gary has made the Army his career.

Lynda Lippman Lockhart was born in St. Petersburg on August 4, 1945. She is a graduate of the University of Florida. She teaches Honors English and Creative Writing at Seminole High School. She is married to Robert W. Lockhart. She has two children, Scott Flesch and Aimee England. She is a writer in her spare time.

Charlotte Mount

Charlotte Mount, the daughter of a professional singer/concert pianist, and Dr. Mount, an early Jewish doctor, who was a dermatologist, arrived in St. Petersburg in the mid-1930s and taught piano lessons from her home. She operated a St. Petersburg music studio for nearly thirty years. Charlotte was a member of Temple Beth-El and its Sisterhood. She was a life member of Hadassah and the National Council of Jewish Women. She was the first President of the St. Petersburg Afternoon Chapter of the Women's American ORT and a founding member and past President of the Judaic Council, an organization of Jewish women from various synagogues. She was a founder of the Fun Club in St. Pete Beach and South Pasadena, a member of the Florida State Music Teachers Association, and the Golden Notes Society of the Florida Gulf Coast Symphony and its guild. She died on July 6, 1997 at the age of eighty four.

Faith H. Sirota

Faith H. Sirota came to St. Petersburg in 1943 from Manchester, Connecticut. She was a collections representative for a mortgage company. She was a member of Congregation B'nai Israel and its Sisterhood, Hadassah, and the National Council of Jewish Women. She died on December 22, 2005 at age sixty-eight.

Suncoast Section

In 1961, a group of young women decided to form their own section of the National Council of Jewish Women. The chapter in St. Petersburg was made up of women who were mainly in their late middle years. These individuals typically met during the day. The young women, who ended up meeting at a Clearwater location, typically Temple B'nai Israel, had young children and were only available to meet in the evenings. Beside the good work that they were doing, they had the opportunity to socialize with other women of their own age group. This group was originally named the Evening Branch of the St. Petersburg Chapter of the National Council of Jewish Women. The first Chairperson of this group was Mary Ann Marger of St. Petersburg. In 1973, on the 80th anniversary of the National Council of Jewish Women, this Section officially became known as the Suncoast Section. This Section provided programs of service, education, and social action to uphold and advance the proudest traditions of democracy and of Judaism and to protect the rights and freedoms which underlie them. An example of one of the community programs was the fingerprinting of children for child safety in conjunction with the Juvenile Welfare Board and Pinellas County Sheriff's Department. The Suncoast Section became defunct around 1990.

The Suncoast Section Presidents were: 1961, Mary Ann Marger; 1962, Susan Gordon; 1963, Audrey Yolken; 1964, Arlene Rosenthal; 1965, Judy Cohen; 1967, Faith Sirota; 1969, Yvette Lew; 1970, Roberta Thorpe; 1972, Judy Jurin; 1974, Beverlee Daniels Blacker; 1976, Marilyn Katz; 1978, Raida Goldman; 1980, Sheila Miller; 1982, Audrey Greenberg; 1984, Marilyn Smith; 1986, Marcy Gall; 1988, Judy Gordon; and 1990, Jean Krause and Judith Elkin.

ORT (Women's American Organization for Educational Resources and Technological Training)

ORT is a national Jewish fund-raising organization that works to strengthen the worldwide Jewish community by empowering people to achieve economic self-sufficiency through technological and vocational education. This is accomplished by providing financial support and leadership to the schools and programs, and by ensuring continued growth of post-secondary technical schools.

Clearwater Chapter

The Clearwater Chapter of ORT is made up of women of all ages including mothers, professionals, and retired people. They work together for the common cause of raising money for the organization to help people learn to be self-sufficient.

St. Petersburg Afternoon Chapter

The St. Petersburg Afternoon Chapter of ORT was established in 1970 with twenty five members. Currently, there are 100 members. They have special luncheons and fundraisers.

PRIMER

PRIMER Incorporated (Promoting Responsibility in Middle East Reporting) is a not-for-profit, non-partisan volunteer media watch group founded by Dr. Norman Gross, in 1992. He continues as the group's President and Editor. The organization is a grassroots media watchdog, whose purpose is to counter anti-Jewish and anti-Israel written, visual, and oral messages through media watch, media response, and the dissemination of accurate information. Its main objective is to continue to help eliminate hate messages on public access TV and work for balanced representation of Jewish and Islamic discussions.

Dr. Norman N. Gross

Dr. Gross received a Bachelor of Arts Degree and a Master of Arts Degree in Education from the University of Rochester. He received a Doctor of Philosophy Degree in Educational Administration from the University of Rochester. He won a Fulbright Fellowship and also served as the John Hey Fellow at Williams College. He served as First Vice President of the Rochester Urban League and a Member of the Board of the NAACP. He has been a board member in various synagogues. He has served as Chairman of the Anti-Hate Committee of the Greater Florida B'nai B'rith and a member of the Holocaust Museum Policy Committee. His personal honors include: B'nai B'rith Community Award; Distinguished Alumnus Award, University of Rochester.

His wife, Shirley is an alumnus of the State University of New York, Brockport. She also completed additional work at the Eastman School of Music. She is a retired elementary school teacher. Their daughter, Deborah Ann Gitmore, is a graduate of Georgetown University, Foreign Service School. She is an archivist for the National Archives. Deborah's husband, Dr. Steven D. Gitomer, has his undergraduate degree from Georgetown University and his medical degree from Georgetown University. Their son, Mark, graduated from the Florida State University, School of Business. He is presently the Decision Support Manager of Moffitt Cancer Center in Tampa. His wife, Sharon, graduated from Florida State University, College of Education, and is currently an English teacher.

Tampa Orlando Pinellas Jewish Foundation

The Tampa Orlando Pinellas Jewish Foundation is a partnership of three Jewish communities. Their goal is to provide permanent resources through endowments to improve the quality of life for Jewish people and non-Jewish people alike locally, in Israel, and abroad. The foundation was established and chartered in 1980. It pools hundreds of private contributions for investment purposes making available better returns on the funds. Through donor-designated grants, the foundation contributes to both Jewish and non-Jewish charities to help in a broad range of social, cultural, and educational initiatives. A Board of Trustees and foundation staff oversee the administration of the funds, management, and investment.

Highlights of 1980

The original Articles of Incorporation were filed on December 12, 1980. The first corporate officers were: Chairman of the Board and President, Charles Rutenberg; Vice-President, Hyman Lake; Vice-President, Leslie J. Barnett; Vice-President, Reva Kent; Secretary, David Ritt; Treasurer, Edward Liebowitz.

The Mission Statement is: the TOP Jewish Foundation, created in 1980, is a supporting foundation of the Jewish Federations of Tampa, Orlando and Pinellas County. Its purpose is to assist these three communities to achieve their immediate and long-term goals through endowment. TOP is dedicated to the continuance and enhancement of the legacy of our forbearers. In partnership with Jewish communal institutions, it seeks to ensure the survival and viability of our local, national, and world Jewish community from generation to generation.

With that guiding principle in mind, TOP's mission is:

To develop a permanent base of support for our communities, and their institutions and programs, through major growth of unrestricted and restricted endowment fund programs.

To support the growth of the Jewish communities of Tampa, Orlando, and Pinellas County and to serve the needs of our people locally, nationally, in Israel, and throughout the world.

To empower and assist families and individuals in achieving their philanthropic goals in the most tax-advantaged manner, working with estate planning, tax, legal and financial planning professionals.

The Lion of Judah Endowment Funds were established in communities in order for women to fulfill all long-term and future commitments to Jewish survival and the quality of Jewish life.

TOP was the first of its kind in the United States to bring together three distinct communities to work together and pool their money to get the best investment results possible for all Jewish people.

Highlights of 1981

The first meeting of the Board of Trustees of Tampa-Orlando-Pinellas Jewish Foundation Incorporated was held at the Hilton Hotel, Lakeland, Florida, at 6 P.M. on Thursday, February 19, 1981. The first elected officers were: Chairman of the Board and President, Charles Rutenberg; Vice-President–Development, Abe Wise; Vice-President–Investment, Reva Kent; Vice-President–Legal and Tax, Leslie J. Barnett; Secretary, David Ritt; Treasurer, B. Terry Aidman.

Highlights of 1982

Charlie Rutenberg reported that after one year and nine months TOP had received $1 million in contributions. He said, "My dream is that each community build its endowment funds through the Foundation, where the principal is sufficient to generate an income equal to the community's annual Federation campaign." Charlie Rutenberg donated $100,000 to start the Pinellas County Senior Citizen Field of Interest Fund.

Highlights of 1984

Joel M. Breitstein, Executive director/Endowment consultant predicted that in the future the TOP Endowment Fund would reach $5 million.

Highlights of 1986

Total assets, as of September 30, for all the funds were $5,000,460,980. Administration of the funds was carried out in a very efficient manner and $24,000 was left over from the administrative budget."

Highlights of 1988

President Reva Kent said that the number of funds over the past two years increased by 72% and the total assets by 49%. The Board's goal was to have $10 million in assets by 1990. From July 1, 1988–June 30, 1989, there were 131 distributions from the TOP Foundation for $371,211 for Pinellas County. Orlando and Tampa had like types of distributions. The monetary gifts were given to: Jewish Federation of Pinellas County; Menorah Manor; Council of Jewish Federations; Kent Jewish Community Center; Gulf Coast Jewish Family Services; Federation of Metropolitan Chicago; Temple Beth-El; American Friends of Haifa University; Jewish Day School; Bayfront Medical Center; P.A.C.T.; Temple B'nai Israel; Congregation B'nai Israel; Young Israel of Clearwater; Hebrew Union College; Straight Foundation; Jewish National Fund; Golda Meir Center; All Children's Hospital; Shorecrest Preparatory School; Jewish Theological Seminary; Temple Ahavat Shalom; American Technion Society; Delta Zeta Foundation; Duke University; Jewish Community Center of Pinellas; Congregation Beth Shalom; Ner Israel Rabbinical College; Hadassah; Upper Pinellas Association for Retarded Citizens; Morton Plant Hospital; National Council of Jewish Women; Tarpon Springs Rotary Club; Goucher College; Great Explorations Incorporated; American Community for the Weizman Institute of Science; Anti-Defamation League; United Way; and Florida Orchestra.

Highlights of 1990

Earned income from all accounts was 8.9%. $1,600,000 was raised to help build phase 1 of the Kent Jewish Community Center.

Highlights of 1992

The Hurricane Andrew Relief Fund was established to help people in South Florida. TOP now had $500,000 in Israel bonds.

From July 1990–July 1992, TOP Foundations distributed $2.4 million in grants. This was truly an astonishing amount of money. Special acknowledgement was given to founding trustees Bruce Bokor, Reva Kent, and Charlie Rutenberg. "His (Charlie's) philanthropy in Pinellas County is virtually legendary."

Highlights of 1994

The Dr. Edward N. Ludin Young Leadership Award was established by Mrs. Arlene Ludin and her family in honor of her late husband. The criteria for selection includes demonstration of significant leadership ability, level of involvement and potential for great leadership in the future. The recipient is also required to have demonstrated a significant involvement in the Federation Annual Campaign, both personally and financially.

The recipients of the award were: 1994, Craig Sher; 1995, Diane Sembler; 1996, Eric Ludin; 1997, David Abelson; 1998, Margot Benstock; 1999, Barbara Sterensis; 2000, Ruth Davidson; 2001, Stephanie Stein; 2002, Mindy Solomon; 2003, Liz Sembler; 2004, Barbara Baccari.

The asset base increased to over $10 million despite the fact that so much money was being returned to the communities. From July 1994–July 8, 1995, there were 715 grants to the three communities with a total of $2,783,871.

Highlights of 1998

As of June 30, TOP Foundation had $16,919,000 in assets. The average return on assets was 17.3%. In 1997 and 1998, $5,515,646 was given to the three communities in grants.

Highlights of 1999

The net income of TOP funds was $11.6%. The use of a diversified portfolio, closely monitored professional investment counselors and highly motivated board members have provided significant returns on funds for the three Jewish communities.

Highlights of 2005

On December 31, the TOP Foundation had assets of $29 million. Eight investment advisory firms were managing the money.

Over the past three years TOP Foundation earned 16.20% per year. Financial help was given to victims of hurricane Katrina.

Of great significance is the involvement of a new generation of children in helping others. This is the ultimate investment in the future of the Jewish people. As Charlie and Isa Rutenberg did in the past, one of "Charlie's boys," Craig Sher, and his wife, Jan, have done for the present and the future. They decided to make a family philanthropy, rewarding, for their daughters, as a means of tightening family bonds, transmitting important family values, and creating a long-lasting family legacy of tzedakah. The Shers worked with the TOP Jewish Foundation to help empower their children in their understanding of philanthropy and leadership. They established the Sher Girls Fund to allow their children to get together once of twice a year, discuss what was significant to them in helping others, and make recommendations for grants. By doing this they have set an example for other Jewish families and their teenage children.

The B'nai Tzedek Program encourages teen Bar/Bat Mitzvah or older young people to contribute $250 or more from their Bar/Bat Mitzvah gift money. The money is combined with a matching $250 from the TOP Jewish Foundation, totaling $500 in a fund named for the individual, and held at the Foundation. Each year 5% of the fund's balance is donated at the teenager's discretion to local or overseas Jewish organizations. This allows young persons to feel empowered in helping others.

TOP Jewish Foundation has set an example for other communities in how to combine the resources from smaller groups to effectively utilize the contributions of individuals to help the many people in need. The founders, the officers, the board members, and the contributors should be recognized for the wonderful commitment of their time and resources to make life better for all people.

CHAPTER 26

JEWISH VALUES

Introduction

Rabbi Arthur I. Baseman weaves together the themes and sets the tone for this chapter on Jewish Values. He said, "Our Jewish tradition speaks to us as follows: "When a person appears before the Throne of Judgment, the first question asked is not "Have you believed in God?" or "Have you attended the House of Prayer regularly?" or "Have you performed the rituals appropriately?" Rather, the first question is "Have you been honorable and faithful in your dealings with other human beings?"

Indeed, the essence of the Jewish value system could be expressed by the simple phrase, "Be holy." It is in Leviticus Chapter 19 verse 2 where this is formally introduced: "You shall be holy; I the Lord your God am holy." How is this to be realized? When we affirm the goodness and sanctity of life. When we recognize the human being as the partner of God in the process of continual creation. When we recognize a covenant relationship between God and the Jewish people. When we acknowledge the institutions of family, synagogue, and community as being essential for developing a sense of purpose in life. When we clearly represent in all our actions that holiness, not happiness, is our goal.

A popular notion, often pictorialized in graphics, illustrates the universe supported on the shoulders of a powerful giant, Atlas.

Not so for the Jews. The answer for the support of the world in the Jewish faith is found in the Ethics of the Fathers: Rabbi Simeon ben Gamaliel said, "The world rests on three things: on truth, on justice, and on peace". By following this timeless teaching, we can indeed "Be holy".

Jewish Values is the author's way of trying to respond to Rabbi Simeon ben Gamaliel's teaching. It extracts from the manuscript key thoughts about Judaism and brings together, in capsule form, the many themes that resonate throughout the history of the Jewish people of Pinellas County, the United States, and the world. It is not a summary, but rather an approach to try to capture the meaning behind some of the essential historical facts that have been discussed. The chapter on Jewish Values is but a beginning. Future researchers should

study the material within the manuscript and add meaningful additions to this chapter. As any history, it is but a snapshot of what has occurred; further interpretation of the history must be left to others to gain the full impact of life as it was observed from the materials which were made available.

Jewish values are crucial to an understanding of Judaism and Jewish people. They are taught to the children by the parents, the grandparents, the community, the religious school, the rabbis, and others. They always include: The importance of ethical conduct; love thy neighbor, whether he is Jewish or non-Jewish; the sanctity of life; the dignity of people; the importance of charity; the importance of social justice; and the importance of giving of oneself to the Jewish and general communities.

Acts of Human Kindness

Jewish people perform acts of human kindness, justice or righteousness, tsedakah. In the Jewish tradition, the poor and unfortunate, the widows, or homeless, and the strangers in our midst, have the legal right in Jewish law to food, clothing, and shelter. It is the obligation of every Jewish person to perform these acts as a religious duty, and not as a sudden philanthropic impulse or momentary whim. Jewish people have always considered the giving of charity to all people to be an integral part of their religious and humanistic lives.

As a small child growing up in an extremely poor but loving and religious home, the author was instructed in the mitzvah of helping others by putting a penny into a pishkah (a small can meant to hold change and collected periodically for those who were less fortunate). During the Depression a penny was a lot of money for a small child.

Jewish people have helped shape the uniquely American nonprofit sector by developing many voluntary organizations. It is reported that the yearly budget of the American nonprofit sector, Jewish and non-Jewish, exceeds the budgets of all but seven countries in the world and that nonprofit organizations employ more civilians than the federal and state governments combined. American Jewish philanthropic tradition not only goes back to the Torah, but also to Maimonides, the establishment of the Charitable Trust in 1601 in England, and the many charities established by Jewish people, managed by Jewish people, and contributed to by Jewish people. There is a strong religious imperative for individualized tzedakah.

Between 1820-1840, Jewish charitable and benevolent associations grew much faster than congregations. In Philadelphia, there were five synagogues and seventeen philanthropic and fraternal societies. In Baltimore there were three congregations and eleven societies.

In large cities and small towns, Jewish men joined lodges to take care of the needs of the individuals and families and to provide a place for socialization. The women were also active in charity. An example of small-town Jewish giving was the Hebrew Ladies Benevolent Aid Society formed in 1872, in Terre Haute, Indiana, to help anyone in the community who was in need of financial assistance.

American Jews have developed a unique model of philanthropy, which greatly influenced the philanthropic structures of all communities. The Jewish culture dictates that you are to take care of your own and also help others who are in need. The Jewish federated philanthropic movement brought together the charitable giving of many people in a pooled manner to help a variety of organizations. This was begun in 1895 with the formation of the Boston Federation. Currently, there are over 7,000 Jewish foundations with assets totaling ten to fifteen billion dollars. The money is apportioned to a variety of health, education and welfare organizations both Jewish and non-Jewish. In addition to this, in every community in the United States, Jewish people are constantly contributing to a broad variety of organizations in order to address the growing complexity of human needs.

An early example of Jewish giving in the United States occurred in 1798 when Emma Lazarus's great grandfather founded the Kalfe Sedaka, a society to help those stricken by Yellow Fever in the epidemic of that year.

Belief in God

Jewish people have not agreed on which rituals and methods should be used in prayer. They formed Orthodox, Conservative, and Reform Movements. However, they always believed in one God, the Torah, and helped each other, despite their differences in how synagogues should be structured and run. There are numerous examples of people breaking away from existing synagogues to form a more ritualistic or less ritualistic form of Judaism. This applies to the Pinellas County Jewish history where there were a group of Reform people who formed Temple Beth El instead of joining the Conservative/Orthodox Congregation B'nai Israel of St. Petersburg and the separation of Congregation Beth Shalom from Temple B'nai Israel of Clearwater.

However, the Olenu, Adoration, is part of every Jewish person's Sabbath prayers. "Let us revere the God of life, and sing the praise of nature's Lord, who spread out the heavens and established the earth, whose glory is proclaimed by the starry skies, and whose wonders are revealed in the human heart. He is our God; there is none else. With love and awe we acclaim the eternal God, the Holy One, Blessed be He."

Discrimination

Jewish people have suffered through anti-Semitism and all forms of discrimination. Much of this has been directed by a few people with the majority of the non-Jewish community not involved. The reason for these actions have been often personal.

More importantly, Jewish people have learned from discrimination and have been at the forefront of the civil rights movement and have always helped less fortunate people achieve the rights that they are entitled to, under the Constitution and Bill of Rights. Jewish people formed the first black organization, the NAACP. It is truly a Jewish value to fight discrimination, wherever and whenever it exists, in an attempt to help all people, regardless of race, creed, nationality, or religious conviction, who may be affected by the hatred of a distinct minority of individuals.

Economic Contributions

Jewish people have been pioneers of our merchant society. From pre-Revolutionary war times through the establishing of the routes for merchandise to flow from the Jewish companies of Philadelphia and the East Coast into the territories in exchange for the fur coming out of these lands, to the outfitting and funding of the George Rogers Clark Expedition, to the opening of stores in the Midwest, the West, the Southeast, the South, and the North throughout the 1800s and 1900s, and now, Jewish people have been essential parts of communities, small and large, and made enormous contributions to these communities. Jewish people have been great financiers and have used their wealth to help others regardless of race and religion

Education

Jewish people believe in education. Rebecca Gratz, a fervent patriot and a profoundly religious woman, believed that Jewish women were uniquely responsible for preserving Jewish life in America and could do this by opening Jewish schools for the children. In 1838, this was accomplished when a school was opened and sixty students enrolled. Rebecca became the school superintendent and served for more than twenty five years. In the same year, Reverend Leeser, who had previously developed the Bible centered approach to American Judaism, published a Hebrew Reader and a year later, the "Catechism for Younger Children." Education has been and continues to be a major focus of not only the Jewish people of Pinellas County but of the

entire country.

Patriotism

Jewish people are patriots, as has been seen from the time prior to the Revolutionary war to the present. In the fall of 1780, on Yom Kippur, General Washington wrote to Robert Morris asking him to please contact Haym Salomon to inform him about the desperate situation faced by the Continental Army. A messenger was sent to the Mikevah Israel Synagogue to request that Haym and the Jewish people of Philadelphia raise $20,000, which was needed immediately. In fifteen minutes, this was accomplished. This occurred despite the fact that there were at most 200 Jewish people in Philadelphia at that time. There are many other stories of Jewish patriots throughout the centuries. Jewish men and women have heroically served in every war with great distinction, in larger numbers than the small percentage of Jewish people in the population, in order to protect the United States.

Political Process

Jewish people have been deeply involved in the political process since colonial times. They served in a large variety of offices at all levels of government and as counselors to Presidents and other high-ranking officials.

Synagogue

The Synagogue is the sanctuary of Israel, born of Israel's longing for God, enduring throughout the wanderings of the Jewish people, as a stronghold of hope and inspiration, teaching us the holiness of life and inspiring in the Jewish people a love of all humanity. The synagogue is built on the foundation of faith, education, fellowship, and a love of God. It is ancient and sacred, and yet contemporary and new. It adapts to the needs of each generation of Jewish people, while preserving the oneness of the Jewish community. Here, the Jewish people offer services from their hearts in praise of God's innumerable blessings. Here, the Jewish people renew their faith while seeking comfort and strength. Here, the Jewish people learn of their heritage and dream of their future. Here the Jewish people share their joys and sorrows as a community rather than living in isolation, for the covenant with God includes each individual standing at Sinai and all the generations to follow. Within the synagogue in the sanctuary, within the Ark, is the Torah. This is the most remarkable book ever written, because it relates the past, sets forth an appropriate and meaningful way to live, and anticipates the future. The Torah is God's gift to people. The Torah tells each person that he or she has freedom of choice and to choose good over evil and life over death. The significance of the Torah to the Jewish people is very clear because the reading of this ancient document never ceases. At the holiday of Simchat Torah, the last of the five books of Moses is read and immediately afterwards, the first book is started again. As Jewish people have moved from country to country and location to location, they have always carried their Torahs with them. Once they became established, they sought to build the synagogue to properly honor the word of God.

Women

Jewish women have traditionally been the founders of the new synagogues, as seen in Tampa and Pinellas County. Their desire to strengthen the family and provide appropriate resources for a good Jewish life in a community led to the founding of the Jewish women's organizations that helped raise the funds and provided much of the work for the building of Jewish congregations and organizations.

Jewish women have been extremely active in nonsectarian women's philanthropic organizations as well as many other organizations. They have also been very active in helping women gain the right to vote and provided a better and more fulfilling life for women and children of all races and religions. Emma Lazarus, as an example, worked to alleviate the suffering of all people and promote the principles of religion, liberty, and law.

AFTERTHOUGHT

This is a final word about the Jewish history of Pinellas County. A group of Jewish people started arriving in Pinellas County in 1883. They came to this wilderness to develop a new way of life in a profoundly American way. They came here for economic and social improvement, but more importantly, to make this world a better place for everyone, because of their sincere belief in God. This book, based on available research material, records the story of the Jewish people of Pinellas County until the end of 2005. From 2006 on, other researchers will need to continue the story.

This book is about events listed chronologically, facts and figures, people, their stories, their hopes, their aspirations, their deeds, and their thoughts. This book talks about the significance of the organizations and synagogues, which were formed to make this a better world. The people, their lives, their synagogues and organizations are woven together in a lovely fabric dedicated to the improvement of life. This book talks about the significance of the various Jewish holidays, God and religion. There are discussions about the various Jewish movements, Conservative, Orthodox, and Reform, their differences, and their similarities.

The research techniques utilized and the preservation of documents, which would have been eventually destroyed, are a gift to all religions and races. All faith communities can follow the outline of this book and can develop their own unique stories and preserve them for their children as an example of how to conduct a good life.

All the hundreds of individuals who participated in this extraordinary effort are to be commended. They have truly followed Deuteronomy 6:4-9. " You shall love the Lord your God, with all your heart, and with all your might. And these words which I command you this day shall be in your heart. Teach them diligently to your children, speaking of them when you sit in your house, when you walk by the way, when you lie down, and when you rise up..." Yes, these people, and all those who came before, have jointly and separately performed a true mitzvah. Their lives have been truly beautiful and worthwhile.

As this book comes to an end, it is truly a new beginning. All people will learn from their own historical research the goodness of yesterday and today so that they can have a structure for all of their tomorrows.

Finally, at the end of the Sabbath service, the prayer, T'FILAT HADERECH, by Debbie Friedman, is sung by the Cantor and the congregation. The music is beautiful and uplifting. It is a prayer of hope, love and compassion for all people. It is a prayer of renewal. It is a prayer that leads us back each week to a new Sabbath service. It truly sums up the yearning of the Jewish people and the beauty of Judaism.

"May we be blessed as we go on our way
May we be guided in peace
May we be blessed with health and joy
May this be our blessing, Amen

May we be sheltered by the wings of
peace
May we be kept in safety and love
May grace and compassion find their way to every soul
May this be our blessing, Amen."

INDEX of JEWISH FAMILY ALBUM

L to R: Adina, Jordana, Dalia

Renee and Rabbi

Renee and Rabbi, Micah, Ari,
Leah, Danielle, Jacob

The Baseman Family

Rabbi, Dave, Renee, Sean, Jordana, Jacob, Adina, Ari,
Micah, Dalia

Top to Bottom: Dave, Dalia, Jordana, Sean, Rick, Adina, Renee,
Rabbi, Resi, Steven, Micca, Ari, Steven, Leah, Danielle, Jacob

L to R: Leah and Danielle

Dr. Vivian Benci, Dr. Saul Lerner, Seth, Maxwell and Francesca

The Benci/Lerner Family

Seth, Francesca and Maxwell

Francesca, Maxwell, Seth

Dr. Vivian Benci and Dr. Saul Lerner

The Bob & Joan Benjamin Family

L to R : back row; Tyler, Peter, Bob, Jerry Woodka, Jed Bandes
front row; Carly Benjamin, Sharri Benjamin, Joan, Julie Woodka, (lap) Jamie Woodka, Nancy Bandes,
Alyssa Bandes, Joshua Woodka

Philip and Marilyn Benjamin

The Philip & Marilyn Benjamin Family

L to R: Judy Benjamin, Mark Benjamin, Caren Appel

L to R: first row; Samuel Benjamin, Michael Appel, Peninah Benjamin second row; Judy Benjamin, Mark Benjamin, Louisa Benjamin, Caren Benjamin Appel, Marilyn Benjamin, Molly Appel, Rebecca Appel.

The Stan and Arlene Berger Family

L to R: back row; Michael, Robert, Debbie (Berger), Jacki and Jason Schwankert
front row; Daniel, Alana, Stan, Arlene, Helene and Stuart Berger

Shirley and Henry Berolzheimer

The Berolzheimer Family

Sister and Brother, Susan Dresnick and
Nathan Berolzheimer

Leah, Trish, Nathan, Benjamin Berolzheimer

Hallie, Matthew, Chad Dresnick

Nancy and Alan Bomstein moved to Clearwater in 1973; married December 24, 1968 in Baltimore, MD.
Children: David, born in Baltimore in 1970; Joshua, born in Dunedin, FL in 1975

The Bomstein Family

Right: Dawn (nee Jacobson) and David Bomstein, married
January 16, 2005 at Congregation B'nai Israel,
St. Petersburg, FL

Below: Joshua and Lindsay (nee Batting) Bomstein,
married November 13, 2004 in Santa Barbara, CA

The Bragin / Ross / Klattel Family

Clockwise from bottom left:
Steve & Gena Bragin, Marl Bragin, Tova Ross, Tom & Janet Bragin Ross, Arla Klattel, Avi Ross.

Johanna and Ken Bromberg

During Monday morning services:
L. to R.: Rabbi, Cecile Bock, Jack Herman

The Bromberg Family

Back, L. to R.; Nancy, Efrem & Max Bromberg, Shlomiiya, Taeer, Naomi & Yaneer Bar-Yam, Chaya & Hillel Bromberg;
Center: Ken & Johanna Bromberg, Tilde Hirsch; Front: Maayan Bar-Yam, Jake Bromberg, Yavni Bar-Yam, Caleb &
Liran Bromberg

Arlene Chernoff
1928–2004

Col. Aaron S. Chernoff
1928–2004

Harvey Alan Chernoff, Esq.
1952–1983

Beth Ellen Chernoff
1956–

Aaron and Arlene Chernoff

The
Chernoff Family

The Leonard and Shirley Collman Family

On the steps of the old Betty Lane Temple B'nai Israel
Jerald Collman–Confirmation (15 years), Shirley Collman, Leonard Collman, Nancy Collman, Steve Collman

Carol J. and Dr. Francis N. Dukes–Dobos

The Edelstein Family

Brian, Al, Mark, Susan, Mikki (in front)

Mark, Lael, Naomi, Daniel, Benjamin (in front)

The Entel Family

Four Generations in 1997

On couch, L to R: Bess Entel, Irwin Entel, Rachel Benjamin (on floor)
Back, L to R: Richard Entel, Robert Entel, Syd Entel, Susan Benjamin
By fireplace: Steven Benjamin, Alyssa Benjamin, Daniel Benjamin

Jerome and Thelma Gilbert

Burt and Linda Goldman

B'not Mitzvah Class of 1996
at Temple B'nai Israel
Rabbi Arthur Baseman & Hebrew Instructor,
Nathan Kuperman
l to r: Donna Finegold, Chalene Feild, Linda
Goldman, Bobbi Keiden, Kathy Valentine,
Stephanie Rosenbaum, Barbara Baccari

Ellie's Grandparents
Harry & Mary Bernstein   Dinah & Philip Zahn

Ellie's Parents
David & Mildred Zahn

Morty's Parents
Ida & Julius Gordon

Elinor and Morty Gordon and Family

Grandson
Michael K. Gordon

Jeffrey's Bar Mitzvah–June 5, 1965
L to R: Jeffrey, Ellie, Morty, Philip

Philip's Bar Mitzvah–March 28, 1970
L to R: Philip, Morty, Rabbi Baseman

The Grau Family

Front: Lillian, Sharon Grau, Linda Grau, Caren Grau, Alex Grau
Back: Dr. Sidney Grau, Steve Grau, David Kimmel, Renée Kimmel, Barry Grau, Teddie Kimmel, Elise Grau,
Marika (Graves) Kimmel, Erica Grau, Aaron Grau

The Greene Family

Standing, L to R: Shirley Hamburger (mother of Jerri), Jerri Greene, David Greene
Kneeling, L to R: Michael Lagassey (husband of Michelle), Michelle Greene, Nat Hamburger (father of Jerri) holding Brandon Newman, Erin Greene Newman, Hadrian Newman (behind Erin)

Leon and Lillie Halaczer

Sonya Miller, Marilyn Benjamin

Sonya and Leon (at right of photo)

Jewish Federation of Pinellas and Pasco Counties
Board Members 2007

David Wolstein
President

Barry Augenbraun
General Campaign Chair

Debbie Sokolov
Women's Philanthropy
President

Joan Benstock
Israel Emergency Campaign
Chair/ONAD Chair

Brian Rolfe
Treasurer

Loren Pollack
Secretary

Mindy Solomon
Budget & Allocations
Committee Chair

Toni Rinde
Marketing Chair

Brian Fox
Young Adult
Division Chair

Les Rubin
Major Gifts

Gordon Goodman
Ben Gurion
Division Chair

Dr. Sheldon Sheinert
Maimonides Society
Chair

Jonathan Bowman
Diplomat Chair

Adam Lopatin
Kick-Off Chair/
Human Resource
Development Chair

**Laurie & Carl
Rutenberg**
Super Sunday
Co-Chairs

Irene Weiss
Women's Philanthropy
Chair

Betty Weintraub & Fran Lasky
Lion of Judah Co-Chairs

Margot Benstock
Missions Chair/
LOJE

Renee Raimi & Claire Stiglitz
Pacesetters Division Co-Chairs

Bonnie Herzberg
Lifeline Division
Chair

Robin Post & Joyce Golden
Main Event Co-Chairs

Sheryl Sutton & Audrey Schechter
Women of Distinction Co-Chairs

Bonnie Friedman
Executive Director

FIVE GENERATIONS OF ROTHBLATT–KATZ FAMILIES

Abraham & Tobias Rothblatt—Isaac & Frieda Jacobs
David & Ethel (Jacobs) Rothblatt   Isaac & Viola Katz
Bernice "Bunnie" Rothblatt   +   Abe Katz

Sandy Katz & Herb Brasch
Elliot Fitzgerald
Benjamin Brasch

Ilene Katz & Marc Horowitz
Jodi Horowitz
Allison Horowitz

Left: Ethel and David Rothblatt
(parents of Bunnie Katz)

Right: Abe Katz with parents,
Isaac & Viola (Possick) Katz–1943

The Katz Family

L to R: Elliot Fitzgerald, Herb Brasch, Sandy Katz Brasch, Benjamin Brasch, Abe Katz, Bunnie Katz, Allison Horowitz,
Ilene Katz Horowitz, Marc Horowitz, Jodi Horowitz–August 1999

The Klein Family

Top L: Mark & Judy Klein–arrived in Clearwater, 1967

Top R: Eugene & Julia Klein, parents of Mark Klein–arrived in Clearwater, 1990

Middle: After college in Washington, Steve brought his bride, Amy Fine, to Clearwater–Mom & Dad, Judy & Mark Klein

Below L: Third generation: Steven & Amy Klein, Jared– born 2000 & Sophie–born 2002

Below R: Three generations of Kleins: Mark, Steven, Jared and Sophie

Marshall and Reva Kent and Family

Justin Kent's Bar Mitzvah
Clockwise from left: David, Trish, Joel, Reva, Larry,
Sandra, Judy, Leo Goldman
Middle: Justin, Natalie and Leslie

Larry, Reva, Stan, Joel and David Kent

Natalie Kent, David Kent, Judy Goldman (Niece), Reva Kent, Larry Kent, Leslie Kent, Justin Kent

Joel and Emma Kent
Dr. Trish and Sarah Kent

Stan Kent

Meredith Kent

Stephen Kent

The Pamela & Gerald Klein Family

The Hank & Donna Koren Family

Koren children, clockwise from top R: Sheryl Koren, Susan Koren Pollard, Scott Koren, Laura Koren Stuckwisch, Debra Koren Hardas

The Kron Family

Standing: Ed & Garland Kron (Son & his wife), Selma Kron, Erica Martin (grandaughter),
Bonnie Martin (Erica's mother)
Seated: Benjamin & Izak Kron, Carrie Cramer, Renee Martin, Nikki Cramer, Debra & Mark Cramer (Mother & Dad)
Front: Tori Martin

Howard, Lila, Debbie and
David Lawrence–November
1966

The Lawrence Family

Rabbi Taxay and Morris Bilgore

Sunday School Sedar–March 1964
L to R: Debbie Lawrence, Howard
Rubin, Rabbi, David Lawrence,
Nancy Schick

Rabbi and Mildred Taxay

Morris & Marilyn LeVine Family

1. Dr. Mitchell LeVine
   (son)
2. Ellie LeVine
   (daughter-in-law)
3. Matthew LeVine
4. Scott LeVine
5. Andrea LeVine
6. Robyn LeVine
7. Stacy LeVine
8. Leslie LeVine

9. Dr. David LeVine
   (son)
10. Janice LeVine
    (daughter-in-law)
11. Naomi LeVine
12. Daniel LeVine
13. Rachel LeVine
14. Shoshana LeVine

15. Marilyn LeVine
16. Dr. Morris LeVine

17. Sharon Rosenthal
    (daughter)
18. David Rosenthal
    (son-in-law)
19. Michael Rosenthal
20. Michele Rosenthal
21. Jeffrey Rosenthal

22. Susan LeVine
    (daughter-in-law)
23. Dr. Steven LeVine
    (son)
24. Jared LeVine
25. Marc LeVine
26. Danielle LeVine
27. Jennifer LeVine

Madelyn & Richard Liss

The Liss Family

Daughters Shelly Gold and Sheryl Goff

Grandson Josh Goff

Grandson Matthew Goff

Julius & Phyllis Lovitz

With Grandson William A. Baxter

The Ludin-Drucker Family

Back Row - L to R Dr. Mark Sokolov, Debbie Sokolov, Eric Ludin, Jacob Ludin, Judy Ludin, Joshua Ludin, Marietta Drucker, Ernest Drucker

Front Row - L to R Ari Sokolov, Jesse Sokolov, Corey Sokolov

Joanne and Rabbi Jacob Luski

1965–We lived in Pinellas Park.
L to R: Al & Evelyn Marks, Barbara, Carolee & Richard Marks

The Marks Family

We moved to St. Petersburg, Florida from Brooklyn, N.Y. in 1956. We packed everything into my dad's homemade boat. Our mother wanted a better life for her family.

Barbara J. age 8, Carolee 11, Richard 9.

Susan & Dennis Martin and Gloria Levin

Edward W. Vinocur
1985–1988

Marshall Seiden
1988–Present

MENORAH MANOR GUILD Presidents

Marilyn Benjamin, Ruth Glickman, Syd Green, Madelyn Liss, Ida Michels, Fagl
Oxman, Shirley Solomon, Marilyn Weissman, Dell Krug, Harriet Kaplan

Barry M. Alpert
President–Menorah Manor
1986–1988

Elinor Fishman
President–Menorah Manor
Foundation 1999–2001
Chair–Menorah Manor
Foundation 2001–2003

Samuel Fishman
President–Menorah Manor
Foundation–1999–2001
Chair–Menorah Manor
Foundation 2001–2003

Sidney Grau, M.D.
President
Menorah Manor
1988–1990

Murray Jacobs
President
Menorah Manor
1981–1983

Loretta Linsky
President–Menorah Manor
Foundation 1993–1996

Marshall Linsky
President–Menorah Manor
Foundation 1999–1996

Irwin Miller
President–Menorah Manor
1983-1986
Chair–Menorah Manor
1987–1990
Chair
Menorah Manor Foundation
1988-1990

Saul Rachelson
Chair–Menorah Manor
2003–2005

Barbara Rosenblum
President–Menorah Manor
2001–2002

Marion Samson-Joseph

President–Menorah Manor
Foundation 1986–1990
Chair–Menorah Manor
1990–1993
Chair–Menorah Manor
Foundation 1990–1993
President–Menorah Manor
Foundation 1996–1999
Chair–Menorah Manor
1999-2001

Suzanne Schechter
President–Menorah Manor
Foundation 1990–1993
Chair–Menorah Manor
Foundation 1999–2001

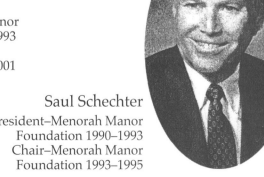

Saul Schechter
President–Menorah Manor
Foundation 1990–1993
Chair–Menorah Manor
Foundation 1993–1995

James Soble, Esq.
President–Menorah Manor
1997–2001
Chair–Menorah Manor
2001–2002

Leonard Seligman
President–Menorah Manor
1990-1993
Chair–Menorah Manor
1993 - 1999

Irwin "Wally" Wallace
President–Menorah Manor
1995–1997

Irving Weissman
President–Menorah
Manor 1995–1997

Marilyn Weissman
Chair–Menorah
Manor   1995–1997

Sharyn R. Wittner
President–Menorah Manor
1995–1997

Ted Wittner
President–Menorah Manor
1995–1997

Irwin & Sonya

2005
Front L to R: Naomi Miller, Irwin Miller, Sonya Miller, Lena Miller, Stacy & Jessica Sher
Back L to R: Paul & Rachel Miller, Howard Miller, Jan & Jay Miller, Jan & Craig Sher, Ali Sher

The Miller Family

Grandchildren 2005
Front L to R: Naomi & Lina Miller
Middle: Stacy Sher, Sonya, Rachel Miller, Jessica Sher
Back: Ali Sher, Paul Miller, Irwin

Irwin's Sisters & Irwin
Seated: Miriam Weiss
Standing: Lillian Berni, Dorothy Halperin

Ron, Heidi, Gabe, Sheila, Marc

The Miller Family

Rabbi Baseman & Gabe
Bar Mitzvah 1985

Back: John Eustace, Bob Mintz, Scott Mintz
Middle: Debbie Eustace, Carolyn, Rachel and Joy Mintz
Front: Karisa Eustace, Connor Eustace, Brittney Mintz

Grandchildren
Top: Karisa Eustace
Middle: Connor Eustace, Brittney Mintz
Front: Rachel Mintz

Back: Debbie Eustace, John Eustace,
Bob Mintz
Front: Karisa Eustace, Connor Eustace,
Carolyn Mintz

Rachel's Bat Mitzvah 1–22–05
L to R: Carolyn, Joy, Scott, Brittney, Rachel, Bob

The Mintz Family

L to R: Dylan, Dan, Sam, Roberta, Jamie

The Mockensturm Family

L to R: Roberta, Sam, Dan, Dylan, Jamie

The Morris Family

Back, L to R: David Morris, Adele Morris, Dr. Leonard Morris, Michael Morris
Front, L to R: Julie Morris and Wendy Morris Haber

Back Row - Eliezar Shelef, Louis Orloff holding Jamie Orloff, Joel Weltman, Esther Orloff Weltman, Jean Orloff, Sylvan Orloff, Stacy Orloff, Bruce Orloff, Nadav Shelef
Front Row - Loni Orloff Shelef, Jessica Weltman, Michelle Weltman, Mark Orloff, Orie Shelef, Brian Orloff, Noam Shelef

The Orloff/Shelef Family

Shelef and Zolc family members on the eve of the Russian Ballet's performance in 1988, at a protest rally organized by Central Florida Council for Soviet Jewry.

Lou & Kay, Jenna, Elliott & Emily Polur   Shari Polur Gold, Alexandra,   Lila, Sarah, Ben, Rob Wrubel
Adrian, Michael Gold

The Polur Family

Lou Polur   Michael Gold   Robert Wrubel   David Polur
Kay Polur   Shari Polur Gold   Lila Wrubel   Ruth Polur

Toni and John Rinde

Debbie Rinde Hoffman & Family: husband, Fred; son, Eric;
daughter, Marissa; Barbara Rinde Feller & Family: husband, Marc;
son, Alec; daughter, Samantha

The Rinde Family

Stella & Maurice Rinde

Lusia & Stanley Igel

Rebecca's Bat Mitzvah, January 19, 2002, at Congregation Beth Shalom
Back, L to R: Aaron Behar, Jeff Cohen, Vicki Rophie, Cecilia Betech, Andrew Rophie, Sharon Rophie, Rebecca Rophie, Alan Rophie, Pauline Rophie, Bill Silver, Tony Rophie
Front, L to R: Adam Cohen, Cheryl Cohen, Pamela Behar, Ali Rophie, Ben Rophie, Vanessa Rophie, Ralph Rophie

Rebecca at Kent Jewish Community Center preschool, 1991

The Rophie Family

Alan's Bar Mitzvah, November 23, 1967, at Congregation Beth Shalom
Back, L to R: Cheryl Rophie, Albert Rophie, Alan Rophie, Pauline Rophie, Cecilia Rophie, Front: Ralph Rophie

Mother's Day 1993: Alan & Rebecca Rophie with Salha "Mama" Bobo

Andrew blowing Shofar, September 11, 1993, at Pinellas County Jewish Day School

Charles "Chuck" Rosenthal and Altamae "Bunny"

The Rosenthal Family

Back: Nancy Rosenthal Schwartz, Sue Rosenthal Rubin,
Middle: Charles " Chuck" Rosenthal, Lynn Rosenthal
Front: Altamae Rosenthal

Lynn Rosenthal, Sue Rubin, Nancy Schwartz

Nancy and Raphe
Schwartz

Marty Rubin holding
Aaron, Jennifer Rubin,
Sue Rubin holding
Mitchell

The Arthur Rutenberg Family

The Sachs Family

Top: Richard Carpel, son-in-law, Hilda and Irving Sachs, Elliott Gordon, grandson
Middle: Arlene, daughter, Marc Sachs, son, Karlyn Sachs, Daughter-in-law, Maggie Gordon, granddaughter
Bottom: Justin Sachs, grandson, Rachel Gordon, granddaughter, Kevin Sachs, grandson

Lisl and Alfred Schick

Alfred Schick, M.D.
November 17, 1922 - April 25, 1993

The Schick Family

November 2004
Back, L to R: Adam Greenberg, Dr. Robert Schick, Kenneth Schick, Dana Nicoletti, Dr. Evan Madow,
Dr. William Greenberg, Bryan Nicoletti
Next Row, L to R: Jeffrey Schick, Justin Schick, Anne Schick, Cindy Schick, Erica Greenberg, Michelle Madow,
Lisl Schick, Dana Nicoletti, Leslie Schick, Nancy Schick Greenberg, Kathryn Schick Madow, Adam Schick
Front, L to R: Jordan Madow, Lance Madow, Alec Madow

Shirley and Harry Felmus, Sherry's parents

Brian and Tracey

The Sherry and Joseph Schwartz Family

Sandy and Don Schwersky

Cameron, Beth, Robert & Jared Schwersky

The SchwerskyFamily

Back: Jared, Robert, Linda, Steve, Jordyn, Monica
Middle: Beth, Sandy, Erica, Diana, Talia
Front: Cameron & Jonah

Diana & Steve Schwersky
Children, clockwise: Jonah & Jordyn
Schwersky, Talia, Erica & Monica Sager

L to R: Jim and Jill Shapiro, Elizabeth and Manny Schwartz, Judith and Barry Schwartz

The Schwartz–Alpert Families

Jason Alpert, Dan and Cassandra Alpert, Jordan and Stephanie Messler, Judith and Barry Alpert

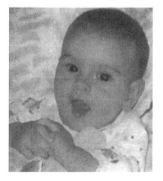

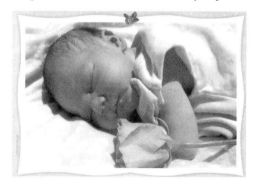

Victoria Alpert   Shayna Beatrice Messler

Jim Shapiro, Heather Shapiro Howell, Greg Howell, Jill Schwartz Shapiro

The Shapiro Family

Jennifer Shapiro Waters & Van Waters with Ethan & Aiden Waters

Emily Shapiro Wenzel & Jay Wenzel

Family Photo June 26, 2005

Lee E. Landau

The Sefekar Family

Thelma and Joe Sefekar 1988

Bill, Bonnie, Thelma and Joe, January 1993

Miriam and Bill Sefekar, Temple B'nai Israel, June 26, 2005

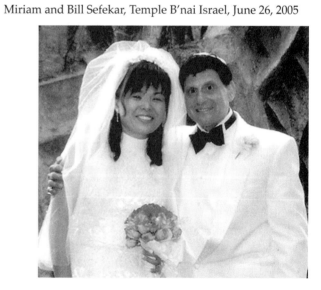

The Shane Family

Back, L to R: Samantha, Rebecca   Middle: Leo   Front, L to R: Michael, Marcia

Michael and Sandy Slomka

The Sobel Family

Michael, Zachary, Kathy & David

The Weizman Family

Assistant Rabbi Danielle Upbin Weizman, Rabbi David Weizman, Zander and Nadav

February 16, 1957 Kenneth N. Wides' Bar Mitzvah, first by Rabbi David Susskind at Temble Beth El (Arlington Building). L to R: Harry & Molly Segal (Maternal Grandparents), Gladys Wides (Mother), Ken Wides, Susan Wides (Sister), Vernon Wides (Father), Annie Wides (Paternal Grandmother)

The Wides Family

November 24, 2001 Wedding of Sara & Edward Nicholson at Tradewinds Resort, officiated by Rabbi Arthur Baseman. L to R: Jesse & Adam Wides (Brothers of Sara), Ken Wides (Father of Sara) Sara & Edward Nicholson, Elaine Wides (Mother of Sara), Shana Wides (Sister of Sara), Joshua & Zachary Wides

Judy, Sam, Scott, Lisa Winer 1983

L to R: Scott Pinheiro, Lisa Pinheiro, Sam Winer, Judy Winer,
Scott Winer, Ona Steele Winer
Wedding of Scott and Ona, June, 1996

The Winer Family

L to R: Max Pinheiro, Lisa Pineheiro, Sam Winer, Scott Pinheiro, Benjamin Pinheiro, Judy Winer, Morley Wyler,
Billie Wyler, Ona Wyler, Scott Wyler at Disney World 2004

The Zimbler Family

Sylvia and Morton
June 9, 1946

Sylvia and Morton Zimbler
Leah DeLorenzo, Rachel Weinthal, Cheryl Zimbler Weinthal,
Stephen Zimbler, Bruce Weinthal, Kathy Hansen Zimbler,
Ethan Trevino, Heather Zimbler-DeLorenzo Trevino,
Dennis DeLorenzo, Debra Zimbler DeLorenzo, November 2004

Heather's Bat Mitzvah, August 29, 1992

Leah's Bat Mitzvah, May 19, 2001

APPENDIX

CHRONOLOGICAL LISTS OF SYNAGOGUE AND ORGANIZATION LEADERS

B'NAI B'RITH

Clearwater Unit 2603, Presidents: 1966-1968, Ezra Bobo; 1969-1971, Saul Fein; 1971-1973, Simon Bellach; 1973-1975, Melvin Silverman; 1975-1978, Donald Schwersky; 1978-1981, Sidney Cutler; 1981-1982, Paul Himelhoch, Sid Fink, and Jerome Granoff; 1982-1984, Paul Hiemlhoch; 1984-1987, Howard Feingold; 1987-1988, Jerome Granoff; 1988-1989, Fran Ehrenpreis; 1989-1990, Lila Lehrer, Judith Stevens, Janine Porteny, Dick and Marion Cole; 1990-1992, Ida Buckstein; 1992-1994, Dr. David Kalin; 1994-1995, Dr. Frank Dukes-Dobos; 1995-1996, Sally Pearl; 1996-2002, Howard Feingold; and 2002-present, Stuart Berger.

CONGREGATION BETH SHALOM OF CLEARWATER

Rabbis: (dates are missing for some of the individuals) Pincus Aloof; Peter Mehler; 1982-1996, Kenneth Bromberg; 1996-2000, Gabriel Ben-Or; 2000-2002, Kenneth Bromberg; 2002-, David Weizman; 2002-, Danielle Upbin, Associate Rabbi.

Presidents: 1957, Reuben Rutenberg; 1958, Dr. Salem Baranoff; 1959, Samuel Good; (dates of service are unknown for Jack Sanders, George Levow, Herman Karp, Harry Landskroner, Herman Zimlin, Sam Brush); 1977, Dr. Arthur Barlis; 1978, Alan Bomstein; 1979, Bernard Panush; (dates unknown for David Baker); 1982, Douglas Zelman; 1983, Irwin Kety;(dates unknown for Paul Applefield, Tom Weber, Marc Silverman); 1990-1992, Michael Sobel;(dates are unknown for Mel Silverman, Leo Plotkin, Eileen Jacobs and Marc Silverman); 1999-2001,Eileen Jacobs and Roni Igel; 2001-2003, Roni Igel; 2003- present, Steve Beckerman and Alan Bomstein.

Sisterhood Presidents: (some of the dates are missing) 1957, Helen Winston; (dates are unknown for Anna Sanders, Clare Zitlin); 1968-69, Ceil Simon; 1969-1970, Bea Merkatz; 1970-1974, Stella Robinson; 1974-1976, Mary Lyon; 1976-1977, Sophie Sulkes; 1977-1979, Ethel Honigman; 1979-1980, Joanna Bakor; 1980-1983, Karin Barnstein; 1983-1985, Francee Weinfeld; 1986-1988, Dianne Bernstein; 1988-1990, Sue Bengele; 1990-1994, Rene Feinman; 1994-1998, Marlene Siegal; 1998-2000, Harriet Starr; 2000-2002, Rosalind Citronowicz and Phyllis Santer; 2002-2006, Linda Pitchon.

Men's Club Presidents: (there is very little information available) 1968-1970, Harry Landskroner; in the 1970s, Arnold Kollenberg and Joseph Stern; 1985, Ed Lanceit; Bob Harvey; 1998, Mike Loebenberg.

Youth Group Presidents: (there is very little information available) 1985, Andi Kaiser; 1986, Juliet Kaiser; 1987, Jeffrey Barlis.

Cantors and Cantorial Soloists: Isadore Zitlin (volunteer); Moshe Meirovich; 1987-1989, Hillel Brummer; 1989-1992, Johanan Bickhardt; 1992-1994, David Levin; (date not available for Max Goren).

Synagogue Administrators: (dates not available for Marie Silverman, Paul Friedhoff, Roberta Frankel, Betsy Mae Troy, Elliot Raskin, Lonnie Williams, Bobby Silvera, and Neil Wyman.

CONGREGATION BETH SHOLOM OF GULFPORT

Rabbis: (the dates of service of the rabbis, names of some of the rabbis, and order of service is not available at this time) Morris Kobrinetz 1970-1978 (his son Simeon is a retired general from the Chaplain Corps); (dates are not available for Aaron Mauskopf, Sydney Lubin, Kaplan, Lawrence Finkelstein, Israel Dvorkin.

Presidents: 1953-1958, Jacob Adler; 1959-1963, Meyer Emsig; 1964-1965, Albert Kessler; 1966-1967, Meyer Possick; 1968, Samuel Salk; 1969, Meyer Possick; 1970, Morris Mailman; 1971-1973, Saul G. Chason; 1974-1975, David Kaplan; 1976, Bernard Dorman; 1977-1978, Harold Ward; 1979-1980, Hyman R. Posner; 1981,

Harold Ward; 1982-1983, Sam Vogel; 1984-1986, John Bromwich; 1987-1989, Bernard M Wolk; 1990, Louis Hersh; 1991-1992, Louis Brodsky; 1993-1994, Sam Einstein; 1994-1995, Mark Jacobs; 1996-1997, Max Roth; 1998-2002, Sam Einstein; 2002-2004, Elaine Walsh.

Sisterhood Presidents: 1964-1966, Fannie Goodman; 1966, Sophia Rudom; 1967-1968, Ann Gordon; 1968-1969, Helen Hersh; 1970-1973, Rose Schwartz; 1973-1974, Rae Cohen; 1974-1975, Lee Itzkovitz; 1975-1976, Helen Vitt; 1976-1978, Zelda Ward; 1978-1980, Libby Applebaum; 1980-1982, Helen Vitt; 1982-1984, Selma Tauber; 1984-1986, Myrna Bromwich; 1986-1987, Felice Abrams; 1987, Bernice M. Rosenberg; 1989-1991, Freda Roth; and 1991-1994, Elizabeth Applebaum.

Mens Club Presidents: 1968-1971, Barnett Socol; 1972-1973, Ben M. Belon; 1974-1977, William Nudelman; 1978, Silas A. Spier; 1979, William Nudelman; 1980-1981, Sam Vogel; 1982-1983, John Bromwich; 1984-1986, Bernard M. Wolk; 1986-1991, Julius Rosenberg; 1992-1993, Max Roth.

CONGREGATION B'NAI ISRAEL

Rabbis (some of the dates of service and the first names of the rabbis are not available at this time): Early 1930s, C. Salzman; 1934-1937, A. S. Kleinfeld; 1937-(completion date not known), I. Obstbaum; 1938, Osterbye; 1939-1945, A. S. Kleinfeld; 1945, Rothenberg; 1946, Max Kaufman; 1947-1973, Morris Chapman; 1973-1977, Louis Lederman; 1977-present, Jacob Luski.

Cantors: lay cantors were Reuben Sabin, Maurice Goldblatt, Robbin and Jules Green (dates not available); professional cantors were 1974, Joseph Schroeder; Fared Dardashti, Irving Zummer, Shimon Gewitz, and David Sislen.

Presidents: 1923-1937, Hyman M. Jacobs; 1938-1940, Max Davis; 1940-1944, Samuel Gilbert; 1944-1947, it is believed that Samuel Gilbert and Benjamin Kornfield each took part of this time; 1947-1950, Benjamin Kornfield; 1950-1954, Max Davis; 1954-1958, Dr. Harold Rivkind; 1959-1961, Jerome Gilbert; 1961-1962, Dr. David Mendelblatt; 1962-1964, Maurice Goldblatt; 1964-1966, Murray Jacobs; 1966-1968, Ted Wittner; 1968-1970, Reuben Halprin; 1970-1972, Dr. Harold Rivkind; 1972-1974, George Feineman; 1974-1976, Judge Edwin Krasner; 1976-1978, Richard Mensh; 1978-1980, Irving Bernstein; 1980-1George Feniman 1981, Philip Wallace; 1981-1983, Adele Morris; 1983-1984, Jerald Phillips; 1984-1986, Donald Silverberg; 1986-1987, Lorraine Maller; 1987-1988, Dr. Paul Cohen; 1988-1990, Dr. Barnett Stein; 1990-1992, Eric Ludin; 1992-1994, Sidney Werner; 1994-1996, Dr. Robert Welsburg; 1996-1999, Reva Pearlstein; 1999-2001, Judith Gordon; 2001-2003, Phillip Redisch; 2003-2005, Michael Wallace.

Sisterhood Presidents: (there are no dates available for the following early Sisterhood Presidents; Dora Goldberg, Belle Herman, Julia Dayan, Celia Kaufman, Stella Gilbert, and May Benjamin); 1947-1949, Henrietta Kornfield; 1949-1950, Mildred Green; 1950-1954, Pauline Rivkind; 1954-1956, Reba Mendelblatt; 1956-1957, Mildred Cohen; 1957-1958, M. Cohen; 1958-1960, Reba Mendelblatt; 1963-1965, Thelma Gilbert; 1965-1967, Dorothy Goldblatt; 1967-1969, Adele Morris; 1969-1971, Jackie Jacobs; 1971-1972, Thelma Gilbert; 1972-1974, Marilyn Levine; 1974-1975, Betty Halprin; 1975-1976, Audrey Kopelman; 1976-1977, Helen Applefield; 1977-1979, Anita Helfand; 1979-1981, Ellen Bernstein; 1981-1983, Dee Dinsfriend; 1983-1984, Pearl Brook; 1984-1986, Bunnie Katz; 1986-1988, Charl Fogel; 1988-1990, Gail Frye; 1990-1992, Gail Frye and Joan Redisch; 1992-1994, Carol Piper; 1994-1998, Naomi Berg; 1998-2002, Diana Litt; and 2002-2004, Gail Weisberg.

Men's Club Presidents: 1959-1960, Alvin Applefield; 1960-1962, Sam Einstein; 1962-1964, Oscar Danes; 1964-1965, George Feineman; 1965-1966, Seymour Maskowitz; 1966-1967, Maurice Goldblatt; 1967-1969, Dr. Harvey Kopelman; 1969-1970, Eugene Merkow; 1970-1971, Herbert Green; 1971-1973, Morton Sherman; 1973-1974, Dr. Leonard Morris and Andrew Cohen; 1974-1976, Chester Levine; 1976-1978, Gerald Lenin; 1978-1980, William Hirsch; 1980-1981, Gerald Lenin; 1981-1982, Dr. Paul Cohen; 1982-1984, Philip Redisch; 1984-1986, Abraham Mellitz; 1986-1988, Leon Glassman; 1988-1989, Dr. Gary Wasserman; 1989-1991, Leon Glassman; 1991-1992, Marc Frye; 1992-1994, Julian Piper; 1994-1995, Scott Hopes; 1995-1997, Neil Smalbach; 1997, Ron Berzon; 1997-1999, Alan Gross; 2000-2002, Jeffrey Litt.

GULF COAST JEWISH FAMILY SERVICES

Presidents: 1977- 1978, Allen Samuels; 1978-1979, Jack Levy; 1979-1982, Murray Jacobs.

Chairman: 1982-1983, Murray Jacobs; 1983-1985, Harry Green; 1985-1989, James Soble; 1989-1993, Jackie Jacobs; 1993-1997, David Bernstein; 1997-2001, Myron Mensh; 2001-2005, David Bernstein.

HADASSAH-CLEARWATER CHAPTER

Presidents: 1951-1953, Mary Rutenberg; 1953-1955, Anna Sanders; 1955-1959, Clara Zitlin; 1959-1962, Bea Merkatz; 1962-1964, Reva Kent; 1964-1966, Irene Spiegel; 1966-1968, Reina Pollack (now Nuernberger); 1968-1970 Dorothy Goldberg Nathanson; 1970-1972, Evelyn Amzalak; 1972-1974, Isabel Katz; 1974-1976, Lisl Schick; 1976-1978, Helaine Rosenfeld; 1978-1980, Hilda Sachs; 1980-1981 Presidents: Ethyl Ferkel, Elsa Eisenberg, Yolan Ziessman; 1981-1983, Betty Slavney; 1983-1985, Elaine Belkin; 1985-1986, Pauline Pollio; 1986-1987, Presidium, Mary Hochhauser, Betty Neuer, Mildred Obolsky; 1987-1989, Mary Hochhauser; 1989-1991, Pauline Rosenberg; 1991-1993, Sylvia Berg; 1993-1994, Presidium, Elaine Belkin, Sylvia Berg, Ruth Brown, Gaye Harfenist, Mary Hochhauser, Pauline Rosenberg, Hilda Sachs, Lisl Schick, Yolan Ziessman; 1994-1997, Rose Shapera; 1997-1998, Presidium, Blanche Gross, Mary Hochhauser, Pauline Pollio, Bea Tokat; 1998-2000, Pauline Pollio; 2001-2003, Elaine Belkin; 2003-2006, Pauline Pollio.

JEWISH COMMUNITY CENTER OF PINELLAS COUNTY

Presidents: Irving Bernstein, Ben Bush, Jerrold R. Colen, Sidney Colen, Arline Dresdner, Amy Epstein, Charles W. Ehrlich, Ron Frankel, Shari Fuss, Joel Goetz, Myra Gross, Murray Jacobs, Meni Kanner, Richard Lane, Harriet Lieberman, Debby Moss, Morty Paul, Lenore Pearl, Edward Rogall, Maurice A. Rothman, Dr. Herbert Goff, and Madelyn Liss. (Dates are not available)

JEWISH FEDERATION OF PINELLAS COUNTY

Presidents: 1974-1975, Sylvan Orloff; 1976-1978, Stanley Freifeld; 1978-1983, Reva Kent; 1983-1984, Charlie Rutenberg; 1984-1985, Saul Schechter; 1985-1987, Stan Newmark; 1987-1989, Rabbi Ira Youdovin; 1989-1991, Jim Soble; 1991-1993, Steve Wein; 1993-1996, Jim Sobel; 1996-1998, Saul Schechter; 1998-2000, David Abelson; 2000-2002, Ron Diner; 2002-2004, Margot Benstock; 2004-2005, Toni Rinde.

MENORAH MANOR

Note: the names and offices of the founding board and officers are found in the Menorah Manor chapter. Also, all other presiding officers for the remainder of the years are found within this chapter.

TEMPLE AHAVAT SHOLOM

Presidents: 1976-1978, Bob Shear; 1978-1980, Stanley Miller; 1980-1982, Elliott Kahana; 1982-1984, Dr. Myron Graff; 1984-1986, Bobbi Rosenberg; 1986-1988, Marty Satinoff; 1988-1989, Lou Kwall; 1989-1990, Raymond Brozovich; 1990-1992, Ronnie Weston; 1992-1993, Betty S. Klapper; 1993-1995, Dr. Kerry Kaplan; 1995-1997, Dr. David Wolstein; 1997-2001, Dr. Myron Graff; 2001-, Nancy Paikoff.

TEMPLE BETH-EL

Rabbis: 1929-1932, Judge M. Henry Cohen (layman); 1933-1935, William H. Rosenblatt; 1935-1937, Leonard J. Rothstein; 1937-1940, Pizer Jacobs; 1941-1947, Herbert J. Wilner; 1948-1956, Albert Michaels; 1956-1985, David Susskind; 1980-1982, Robert Kirzner, Assistant Rabbi; 1984, Ira S. Youdovin, Associate Rabbi;1985-1991, Ira S. Youdovin; 1991-2001, Stephen F. Moch; 2000 – 2001, Jay Kaminsky (layman); 2001-present, Michael Torop.

Cantors and Cantorial Soloists: 1954/1956-1957, William Morgan; May 1956, H. Sisken (Yaffin Bar Mitzvah); 1959, Harry Simon; 1986-1989, Laurel Swerdin; 1989-1990, Michael Brem; 1990-1992, Robert Marinoff; 1992-1995, Laurel Swerdin; 1995-present, Sharon Brown.

Presidents: 1928-1929, Myer Friendly; 1929-1930, Hyman Cohen; 1930-1931, Dr. Adolph Rosenthal; 1931-1933, Bert Goldberg; 1933-1934, Isaac Cogan; 1934-1936, Jacob L. Miller; 1936-1937, Dr. Lewis Mount; 1937-1938, Jacob L. Miller; 1938-1940, Horace Goldsmith; 1940-1942, M. Alan Friedman; 1942-1944, Jacob L. Miller; 1944-

1946, M. Alan Friedman; 1946-1949, Joseph Silverberg; 1949-1951, Morris G. Rosenberg; 1951-1952, Joseph Silverberg; 1952-1953, Nate Robinson; 1953-1954, Morris G. Rosenberg; 1954-1955, Nate Robinson; 1955-1957, Joseph Silverberg; 1957, Jules Robison; 1957-1962, Marion B. Ross; 1962-1964, David Gorman; 1964-1966, Elmer S. Ottenheimer; 1966-1968, Bruce Marger; 1968-1971, Leonard D. Shavlan; 1971-1973, Marion B. Ross; 1973-1974, Edward L. Rosenbluth; 1974-1976, David B. Fyvolent; 1976-1977, Edward L. Rosenbluth; 1977-1980, Stanley Sonneborn; 1980-1982, Saul Markman; 1982-1984, Dr. Herbert Goldstein; 1984-1985, William H. Fleece; 1985-1986, Maurice A. Rothman; 1986-1987, Cecile Berko; 1987-1988, Bruce Marger; 1988-1990, Charles M. Tatelbaum; 1990-1992, Melvin B. Estroff and Erwin H. Miller; 1993-1995, Craig Sher; 1995-1997, Leonard S. Englander; 1997-1999, Louis Krosner; 1999-2002, Cecile Berko; 2002-2004, Terry L. Hirsch.

Sisterhood Presidents: 1926-1930, Mrs. Minnie Van Straaten; 1930, Miss. Eva Radzinski; 1931-1934, Mrs. Benjamin Goodkind; 1934-1938, (the persons are unknown); 1938-1941, Mrs.Pizer Jacobs; 1941-1942, (the person is unknown); 1942-1943, Mrs. Charles Laub; 1944, Mrs. Louis Cohen; 1945, Mrs. Abraham Lippfield; 1946, Mrs. Herbert Wilner; 1947-1948, Mrs. Samuel Rickman; 1949, Mrs. Jack Feist; 1950, Mrs. Maurice Hyman; 1951, Miss Eva Radzinski; 1952-1953, Mrs. M. Bill Newman; 1953-1955, Mrs. Marion B. Ross; 1955-1957, Mrs. Louis Rosen; 1957-1959, Mrs. Jonas Weiss; 1959-1961, Mrs. Sidney Weinman; 1961-1963, Mrs. Henry Russell; 1963-1965, Mrs. David Wellens; 1965-1967, Mrs. David Fyvolent; 1967-1969, Mrs. Marion Ross; 1969-1971, Mrs. Edward Rosenbluth; 1971-1973, Mrs. Mildred Shavlan; 1973-1975, Mrs. David Fyvolent; 1975-1977, Mrs. Stanley L. Sonneborn; 1977-1979, Mrs. Coleman Goldstein; 1979-1982, Mrs. David Ginsburg; 1982-1983, Mrs. Herbert Goldstein; 1983-1984, Mrs. David Ginsburg; 1984-1986, Mrs. Florence L. Fayer; 1986-1987, Mrs. Mae Malin; 1987, Mrs. Joyce Ripps, Mrs. Abe Olitsky and Mrs. Shirley Hay; 1988-1989, Mrs. Joyce Ripps; 1989-1991, Mrs. Jeraldine Freed; 1991-1992, Mrs. Joyce Ripps; 1993-1995, Susan Olsen and Linda Reimer; 1995-1999, Gertrude Debowsky; 1999-2002, Anne Ennis; and 2002-present, Sharon Memmer.

Brotherhood Presidents: 1947-1949, Dr. Parvey Hill; 1949-1950, Marion Ross; 1950-1954,(the persons are unknown); 1954-1955, Sol Markman; 1956-1957, Samuel Mazear; 1957-1958, M. Weiss; 1958-1961, Herbert Vinick; 1961-1962, Al Zwick; 1962-1963, Bruce Marger; 1963-1965, Leonard Shavlan; 1965-1966, William Fleece; 1966-1968, Malcolm Berko; 1968-1970, Stanley Sonneborn; 1970-1971, Karl Goldman; 1970-1972, William Israel; 1972-1973, Barry Wax; 1973-1974, Leonard Auerbach; 1974-1975, Dr. Murray Gessner; 1975-1976, Arthur Eichler; 1976-1977, Dr. Joel Shrager; 1977-1978, Dr. Samuel B. Danto; 1978-1981, Irving Finkelstein; 1981-1983, Irving Kramer; 1983-1984, Phillip Bass; 1985-1987, Max Halle; 1987-1988, Jack Jenkins, Seymour Ripps, and Alfred Lewis; 1988-1989, Dr. Mortimer Elkind; 1989-1990, Alfred Lewis and Seymour Ripps; 1991-1994, Bernard Roth; 1993-1995, Richard Zippin; 1994-1997, Lewis Kroll; 1997-1998, David Joffe; 1998-2000, Donald Ennis; 2000-2003, Ross Preeville; and 2003-2005, David Weiss.

Administrators: 1970, Chuck Metz; 1970, Leo Wise; 1989-1990, Richard Shepherd; 1990-1992, Stanley May; 1992-present, Jay Kaminsky.

Art Festival Chairman: 1971-1973, Thelma Rothman; 1974-1975, Edith Chapp and Eleanor Argintar; 1976, Alene Goldstein and Marilyn Frieman; 1977, Marilyn Frieman; 1978, Marilyn Frieman and Janet Root; 1979-1980, Larry Morse; 1981, Winfred Klarin and Eleanor Argintar; 1982-1985, Eleanor Argintar; 1986-1991, Eleanor Argintar and Sonya Miller; 1992-1997, Eleanor Argintar, Sonya Miller, Pam Newman; 1998-2000, Eleanor Argintar, Donna Berman, Sonya Miller, Jan Sher, and Pam Newman; 2001-2004, Nan Bugatch, Donna Berman, Sonya Miller, Jan Sher, Ann Sobel, Barbara Sterensis.

TEMPLE B'NAI ISRAEL

Rabbis: 1956-1960, Harry R. Richmond; 1960-1969, J. Marshall Taxay; 1969-present, Arthur I. Baseman.

Presidents: 1949-1951, Darwin S. Frank; 1951-1952, Samuel A. Korones; 1952-1953, Lloyd Marks; 1953-1954, Julius Lovitz; 1954-1955, Reuben Rutenberg; 1955, Isadore Zitlin; 1955-1956, Leonard Collman; 1956-1957, Howard Lawrence; 1957-1958, Darwin Frank; 1958-1959, Herbert Frank; 1960-1961, Arthur Rutenberg; 1961-1963, Morris Bilgore; 1963-1965, Roland Fox; 1965-1967, Steven Bragin; 1967-1969, Alfred Schick; 1969-1971, Ervin Schwartz; 1971-1973, Loren Pollack; 1973-1975, David Korones; 1975-1977, Robert Benjamin; 1977-1979,

Al Sulkes; 1979-1981, Barbara Rosenblum; 1981-1983, Saul Fein; 1983-1985, Gary Gormin; 1985-1987, Jack Geller; 1987-1991, Myron Mensh; 1991-1993, Mimi B. Krystel; 1993-1995, Toni Rinde; 1995-1997, David Greene; 1997-1999, Greg Fox; 1999-2001, Richard Snyder; 2001-2003, Bruce Flashenburg; 2003-2007, Robert Mintz.

Administrators: 1973-1975, Harry Foreman; 1975-1983, Belle Applebaum; 1983-1984, Lee Jubelirer; 1984-1985, Frank Weiss; 1985-1993, Dolores Curphey; 1994- (date not known), Stanley Bush (date not known).

Sisterhood Presidents: 1950-1953, Fanny Marks; 1953-1954, Estelle Korones; 1954-1955, Maxine Frank; 1955-1956, Shirley Collman; 1956-1957, Lila Lawrence; 1957-1958, Phyllis Lovitz; 1958-1960, Reva Kent; 1960-1961, Shirley Harwood; 1961-1963, Evon Brower; 1963-1964, Regina Bragin; 1964-1965, Martha Baker; 1965-1967, Ruby Lempert; 1967-1968, Roberta Korones; 1968-1970, Joan Keller; 1970-1972, Joan Benjamin; 1972-1974, Rosalind Berk; 1974-1975, Gloria Bobo; 1975-1976, Judy Steuer; 1976-1977, Annette Ziff; 1977-1979, Billy Rutenberg; 1980-1981, Bette Sharpe; 1981-1984, Jule Kroll; 1984-1986, Ethyl Ferkel; 1986-1988, Charlotte Sherman; 1988-1989, Ann Sobel; 1989-1991, Betty Cohen and Rachel Ward; 1991-1994, Ruth Hirsch;(note-for a number of years the Sisterhood had co- Presidents, which is indicated in the years listed for the individuals) 1994-1998, Wendy Adamson; 1997-1999, Harriet Meier; 1998-2000, Chalene Field; 1999-2001, Janet White; 2001-2003, Phyllis Shapack; and 2003-2005, Madelyn Liss.

Brotherhood Presidents:1969-1970, Bernard Berk; 1970-1972, James Ward; 1973-1975, Harold Karlin; 1975-1977, Harold Gallay; 1977-1978, Arthur Silverberg; 1978-1980, Ernest Schnur; 1980-1982, Robert Ederr; 1982-1984, Marion Hirsch; 1984-1986, Louis Goldstein; 1986-1988, Ralph Dutcher; 1988-1990, Ernest Schnur; 1990-1992, Paul Schwartz; 1992-1994, Paul Hochberg; 1994-1998, Steve Tolkin; 1998, Chet White; 1999-2000, Abe Weintraub; 2000-2002, Robert Mintz; 2002-2004, Richard Kastel; 2004-2006, Gerald Klein.

Senior Youth Group Presidents:1959-1960, Nancy Collman; 1961-1962, Wendy Lopatin; 1962-1963, William Lopatin; 1963-1964, Laura Baker; 1964-1965, Frank Schwartz; 1965-1966, Barry Rutenberg; 1966-1967, Judy Brower; 1967-1969, Sharon Rutenberg; 1969-1970, Cheryl Rophie; 1970-1971, David Lawrence; 1971-1972, Lori Strumpf; 1972-1973, Pam Rutenberg; 1973-1974, Allan Gallay; 1974-1975, Randal Friedlander; 1975-1976, Ruth Ann Orloff; 1976-1977, Sue Rosen; 1977-1978, Gerald Polukoff; 1978-1979, Bruce Levine; 1979-1980, Micah Harris; 1980-1981, Scott Bobo; 1981-1982, Richard Bobo; 1982-1983, Steve Klein; 1983-1984, Tracey Schwartz; 1984-1985, A. Rubin and B. Schwartz; 1985-1986, B. Ismark and S. Sulkes; 1986-1987, Sean McGhie; 1987-1988, Denise Mensh; 1988-1989, Erin Greene; 1989-1990, D. Baseman and S. Koronas; 1990-1992, Michael Namath; 1992-1993, S. Perlman and J. Okun; 1993-1994, Kevin Brahm; 1994-1995, Adam Greenfield and Tanya Abilock; 1996-1997, Jamie Levitt; 1997-1998, Josh Adler; 1998-1999, Rebeka Freilich; 1999-2000, Dana Rosenfeld; 2000-2001, Elisa Dato; 2001-2002, Boreen Dopkin; 2002-2003, Dana Greengold and Melissa Mankin.; 2004- 2006, Jenna Matis.

Junior Youth Group Presidents: 1973-1974, Mark Michaels; 1974-1975, Steven Schwersky; 1975-1976, Larry Bellack; 1976-1977, Jaimi Zwerling; 1977-1978, Adina Baseman; 1978-1979, Elaine Rosenfeld; 1979-1980, Melissa Freeman; 1980-1981, Arthur Rubin; 1981-1982, Scott Winer; 1982-1983, Amy Wilkes; 1983-1984, Elizabeth Katz; 1984-1985, Traci Rubin; 1985-1986, Stuart Debowsky; 1986-1987, Eric Diner; 1987-1988, Robert Black; 1988-1989, Woody Pollack; 1989-1990, Bryan Debowsky; 1990-1991, Howard Brickman; 1991-1992, Alissa Bavil; 1992-1993, Lisa Strikowsky; 1993-1994, Paul Gross; 1995-1996, David Levitt; 1997-1998, Lauren Berger; 1998-1999, Sara Grossman; 1999-2000, Melissa Mankin; 2000-2001, Matt Flashenburg; 2001-2002, Jenna Matis; 2002-2003, Lisa Finegold; 2003-2004, Austin Ruffer; 2004-2005, Stephanie Babcock; 2005-2006, Rachel Daniels.

Chai Presidents:1978-1979, Felice Zeldin; 1979-1980, Janet Baron; 1980-1982, Mel Fergenbaum; 1982-1983, Helene Debowsky; 1983-1984, Eric Adler; 1984-1986, Nanci Weiss; 1986-1987, Robert Kline; 1987-1989, Jerri Greene; 1989-1990, Frank Weiss;

Friendship Club Presidents:1972-1975, Maury Newman; 1975-1976, Herbert Bernstein; 1976-1980, Edward Corner; 1980-1982, J Marvin Stern; 1982-1983, Lieslott Stern; 1983-1988, Hilda Schwartz; 1988-1990, Florence Wax; 1990-1994, Sylvia Schnur; 1994-1997, Ernie Schnur; 1997-1998, Phyllis Shultz; 1998-2004, Don Eskin.

BIBLIOGRAPHY

Anti-Defamation League of B'nai B'rith, *Not the Work of a Day*, New York, New York, 1965.

Apsel, Joyce, "Ann Frank-Lessons in Human Rights and Dignity," Newspaper in Education Series, *St. Petersburg Times*. St. Petersburg, Florida, 2000.

Archives– "A Larger Home for Beth Shalom," Congregation Beth Shalom, Prepared by the Library Committee, Maurice and Ellie Hirsty Library, Clearwater, Florida, 1992

Arsenault, Raymond, "St. Petersburg and the Florida Dream–1888–1950," The Donning Company, Norfolk, Virginia Beach, Virginia, 1998.

Arsenault, Raymond, "St. Petersburg City Centennial, 1888–1988," *St. Petersburg Times*, June 8, 1988.

Ashton, Dianne, Rebecca Gratz, *Women and Judaism in Antebellum America*, Wayne State University Press, 1997.

Baker, Rick, *Mangroves to Major League*, Southern Heritage Press, St. Petersburg, Florida, 2000.

Benjamin, Phillip, Dr., *Dear Mollie and Rebecca-From Grandfather Benjamin*, unpublished manuscript, St. Petersburg, Florida, 1993.

Berger, Miriam, editor, *A Tribute to B'nai B'rith's 150 Years and The 28th Anniversary of B'nai B'rith's Clearwater Unit # 2603*, compiled by Porteny, Janine, self published by B'nai B'rith, Clearwater, Florida, 1994.

B'nai Israel Review, "Congregation B'nai Israel, 1975, 1976, 1977, 1980," St. Petersburg, Florida.

Boswell, Dick, *Sunrise 200-A Lively Look at St. Petersburg's Past*, Times Publishing Company, St. Petersburg, Florida, 1975.

Breibart, Solomon, *The Synagogues of Kahal Kadosh Beth Elohim*, Charleston, South Carolina, 1999.

Brody, Seymour, *Jewish Heroes and Heroines in America*, Florida Atlantic University Libraries, 2003.

Brown, Cantor Jr., *Jewish Pioneers of the Tampa Bay Frontier*, Tampa Bay History Center, 1999.

Central Conference of American Rabbis, Yearbook, Volume LXXXVII, 1977.

Colen, Sidney, *A Philosophical Summary of My Beliefs*, OFF. REC. BK. 11,900 PGS 1139 – 1251, Pinellas County, Florida, March 20, 2000.

Commemorative Dinner Honoring the Life of Charles Rutenberg, Golda Meir/Kent Jewish Center, Clearwater, Florida, September 28, 2005.

Congregation Beth Shalom, "Dedication", Clearwater Florida, October 28-30, 1977

Congregation Beth Shalom, (monthly bulletin), 1982-1986, Clearwater, Florida.

Congregation Beth Shalom, *Beth Shalom Kol, 1986-2004*, Clearwater, Florida.

Congregation B'nai Emmunah/Jewish Media Relations Council Incorporated, Board Minutes, 1991-1997, Tarpon Springs, Florida.

Congregation B'nai Emmunah/Jewish Media Relations Council Incorporated, *The Spiritual Light, 1987-2001*, Tarpon Springs, Florida.

Congregation B'nai Israel Chronicle, 1948, 1949, 1950, 1951, 1952, 1953, 1954, 1955, 1956, 1957, 1958, 1959, 1960, 1961, 1962, 1963, 1964, 1965, 1966, 1967, 1968, St. Petersburg, Florida.

Congregation B'nai Israel Review, 1977-2005, St. Petersburg, Florida.

Congregation B'nai Israel Shalom, 1973, 1974, St. Petersburg, Florida.

Congregation Schaarai Zedek (Centennial Year Book) 1894-1994, Printed by Hillsboro Printing Company, Tampa, Florida, 1994

Connections, "A Guide to Jewish Living in Pinellas County," Jewish Federation of Pinellas County, *Jewish Press* of Pinellas County, Largo Florida, September 2003.

Dayan, Margret Arnaud, "Descendents of Abraham Solotnick and Tobias Lena Rothblatt," West Hills, California, December 1997, a privately published document.

Dedication of Congregation B'nai Israel St. Petersburg, Unpublished Document, St. Petersburg, Florida, December 17, 2000.

Denburg, Moshe, and Learning Resource Center of the Britannia Secondary School, "Jewish Music-An Overview," Vancouver, British Columbia, 1995.

Frank, Darwin, Clearwater Oral History Tapes, November 8, 1989.

Fuller, Walter, *St. Petersburg and its People*, Great Outdoors Publishing Company, St. Petersburg, Florida, 1972.

Golda Meir Jewish Community Center Annual Reports, 1984-1994, Clearwater, Florida.

Golda Meir/Kent Jewish Center Annual Reports, 1995-2005, Clearwater Florida.

Gulf Coast Jewish Family Services Annual Reports, Largo, Florida, 1994-2004.
Gulf Coast Jewish Family Services Board Minutes, Largo, Florida, 1978-1994.

Halevi, Yossi Klein, Jacob Birnbaum and the Struggle for Soviet Jewry, Part I and part II, From the History of the
    Jewish Movement, Angelfire.com, 2004
Halaczer, Leon, "This Is My Life," an unpublished document, St. Petersburg, Florida, 1977.
Hartzell, Scott Taylor, *Voices of America, St. Petersburg, An Oral History,* Arcadia Publishing,
    Charleston, South Carolina, 2002.
Herman, Felicia D.,"Jewish Women Serving a Congregation, the Nomination, American and World
    Jewry," My Jewish Learning.com, 2003.
Hooker, Robert, *St. Petersburg Times-100 Years,* Times Publishing Company, St. Petersburg, Florida, July 25, 1984.

"Jews of City Now Organized," *St. Petersburg Times,* Florida, July 13, 1921.
Jewish Community Council of St. Petersburg, Board Minutes, 1970-1974.
Jewish Educational Loan Fund–Information Kit–Atlanta, Georgia, 2004
Jewish Federation of Pinellas County Incorporated, Board Minutes, 1974-2005

Keller, Joan, "Tampa Bay's Jewish Communities, a Religious History of Tampa Bay," Research Report No.
    5, National Conference of Christians and Jews, Tampa, Florida, 1991.
Kent Jewish Community Center News, Clearwater, Florida, 1990-1995.
Koren, Herman, *Commemorative Book, 150th Anniversary of the Jewish Community in Terre Haute, 1849-1999,*
    United Hebrew Congregation, Terre Haute, Indiana, 1999.
Koren, Herman, Indiana State University-"Environmental Educator-Presentation for Walter S.
    Mangold Award," John Heintz, Indiana State University, editor, unpublished document, National
    Environmental Health Association, Denver, Colorado, 2005.

Levy, B. H. and Belzer, Rabbi Arnold Mark, *History of Mickve Israel,* Arthur B. Levy Memorial Fund,
    Savanna, Georgia, 1994.
Lewis, Theodore, "History of Touro Synagogue", *Bulletin of the Newport Historical Society,* Vol. 48, Part 3,
    Number 159, Newport, Rhode Island, Summer, 1975.
Litvin, Martin, *The Journey–a Biography of August M. Bondi the American-Jewish Freedom Fighter Who Rode
    with John Brown in Kansas,* Galesburg Historical Society, Galesburg, Illinois, 1981.
Lopatin, Harold, Oral History Tape, Boca Raton, Florida, 2004.

Malamed, Sandra Cummings, *The Jews in Early America-a Chronicle of Good Tasting Good Deeds,* Fithian
    Press, McKinleyville, California, 2003.
Manor, Menorah, Oral History Project, Unpublished Document, St. Petersburg, Florida, 1995.
Marcus, Jacob R., *Jews in American Life,* Hebrew Union College–Jewish Institute of Religion, Cincinnati
    Ohio, 1972.
Marcus, Jacob R., *The Jew and the American Bicentennial,* Hebrew Union College–Jewish Institute of
    Religion, Cincinnati, Ohio 1976.
Meir, Golda, Dedication of the Residence Hall of the Jerusalem School, translated from the Hebrew, Israel, 1970.
Michels, Morris, Jewish War Veterans, Paul Surensky Post No. 409, Clearwater, Florida, Personal
    Correspondence, November 8, 2005.
Milgrim, Shirley, *Haym Salomon, Liberty's Son,* The Jewish Publication Society of America, Philadelphia,
    Pennsylvania, 1975.

National Council of Jewish Women History, New York, New York, 2003.
"New Synagogue to Be Erected-Young Mens Hebrew Association Purchases Lot for Building," *St.
    Petersburg Times,* Florida, March 16, 1924.

Pasternak, Velvel, "Song in Hassidic Life," *Jewish Music*: Online, 2004.
Pent, R. F., *Story of Tarpon Springs, Biographical Sketches of Old-timers,* Great Outdoors Publishing Company,
    St. Petersburg, Florida, 1964 (available at the Tarpon Springs Historical Society).
Pinellas County Demographic Study, Sheskin, Ira M., Jewish Federation of Pinellas County, Largo, Florida, 1994.
Pinellas Genealogy Society Inc., *Early Pioneer Families, Pinellas County, Florida, 1845-1945,* Microfilm,
    Largo Library, 1999.

Pinellas County Planning Department, Pinellas County Historical Background, St. Petersburg, Florida, April 1955.

Porteny, Janine and Berger, Miriam, editors, *A Tribute to B'nai B'riths 150 Years and The 28th Anniversary of B'nai B'rith's Clearwater Unit#2603*, unpublished document, Clearwater, Florida, 1994.

Przemysl Poland Memorial Book, Yizkor Book Project, jewishgen.org

Rada, Joe, "From Horror to Hope," *Southern Living Magazine*, February, 1999.

Rajtar, Steve, "Tarpon Springs Historical Trail," by the Internet, Orlando, Florida, 1999.

Rinde,Maurice (alias Wiktor Kroczykowski), "My Experience During the Second World War," unpublished document.

Rosen, Harry R., "The Study for the New Jewish Community Center of Pinellas County, Florida," unpublished Document, St. Petersburg, Florida, May 1989.

Rosengarten, Theodore and Rosengarten, Dale(editors), *A Portion of the People-300 Years of Southern Jewish Life*, University of South Carolina Press, Columbia, 2002.

Rosenzweig, D. M., "History of the Jews in Poland," polishjews.org

"Russian Revolution of 1917," World Book Online Reference Centre

Rutenberg, Mary, Unpublished Personal Papers, 1940s-1970s, Clearwater Florida

Rutenberg, Reuben, Unpublished Personal Papers, 1940s-1970s, Clearwater Florida

Sachar, Howard M., *A History of the Jews in America*, Alfred A. Knopf, New York, 1992.

Saltzman, Charles, *I See It All Again-a memoir*, self published, Clearwater, Florida, 1998.

Sanders, Michael, *Clearwater, A Pictorial History*, The Donning Company, Norfolk, Virginia, 1983.

Schuster, Goldie, "A History of the Jewish People of St. Petersburg," a Partial Unpublished Document, American Jewish Archives, Cincinnati, Ohio, 1988.

Schaarai Zedek , Tampa, Florida, Congregational Minutes, 1894-1950, American Jewish Archives, Cincinnati Ohio.

Schick, Lisl, *Second Opinion-A Doctor's Reflections on Life beyond Medicine*, self-published, Largo, Florida, 1996.

Shiloh, Ailon, Solomon, Louis, Marantz, Joel, The St. Petersburg Jewish Community Demographic and Attitudinal Study, St. Petersburg Jewish community Council, St. Petersburg, Florida, 1974.

Stoughton, Gertrude K., *Tarpon Springs, Florida, the Early Years*, Tarpon Springs Area Historical Society, Inc., 1975.

St. Petersburg Times Archives, 1987-2005, St. Petersburg, Florida.

Tarpon Springs, Hillsboro County, Florida Incorporation, Filed March 10, 1887 (Found in Old Abstracts of Properties).

Tarpon Springs and Meeting Minutes, February 12, 1887, Tarpon Springs Historical Society.

Temple Ahavat Shalom, Ner Tamid, Bulletin, 1984-2004, Palm Harbor, Florida.

Temple Ahavat Sholom, Rabbis Annual Reports, 1984-2004, Palm Harbor, Florida.

Temple Beth-El, (bulletin)1949-1959, St. Petersburg Florida

Temple Beth-El Scrapbook, 1933-1934-1935, St. Petersburg, Florida

Temple Beth-El 5689-5764, 75 Years Rooted in Community, St. Petersburg Florida, 2004

Temple Beth-El Scroll, 1959- 1981, St. Petersburg, Florida

Temple Beth-El Through the Ages, Videotape, Temple Beth El, St. Petersburg Florida.

Temple Beth-El Scroll, St. Petersburg, Florida, 1992-2000.

Temple B'nai Israel – A Celebration of 40 Years, 1949-1990, Clearwater, Florida

Temple B'nai Israel, Audio Tapes of Charter Families, Clearwater, Florida, 1984.

Temple B'nai Israel Bulletins, Clearwater, Florida, 1953-1955 and1975–1995.

Temple B'nai Israel's 50th Anniversary Celebration, March 2000.

Temple B'nai Israel Torah Dedication,(Holocaust Torah), May 12, 1985.

They Came for Good-A History of the Jews in the United States: 1654-1820, Videotape, Novak Amram and Starr Manya, Novak Associates, 2001.

Tobias, Thomas J.(revised by Solomon Breibart), "Tombstones That Tells Stories-the Historic Coming Street Cemetery of Congregation Beth Elohim," Charleston South Carolina, 2000.

TOP Foundation, Incorporated, Board Minutes, 1980–2005

Twain, Mark, *Concerning the Jews, The Man That Corrupted Hadleburg and Other Stories and Essays* (New York: Harper and Brothers, 1900), edited by Jim Zwick, 1995-2005.

Walnut Street Synagogue, *Congregation Aqudath Shalom, 103rd Anniversary Historical Tribute Book*, Chelsea, Massachusetts, 2003.

Temple Beth-El Scrapbook, 1933–1935

Yad Vashem, Dr. Albert Battel, *The Righteous Among the Nations*, the Holocaust Martyrs and Heroes
    Remembrance Authority, 2004.
Young, June Hurley, *Florida's Pinellas Peninsula*, by Byron Kennedy & Company, St. Petersburg, Florida,
    1984.

Wollowick, Herbert E., *Freedom Illuminated-The Haggadah-A Mirror of Jewish History-It's Agony and Triumph*,
    Florida Holocaust Museum, St. Petersburg, Florida, 2002.

Zahav, Jonatan, "The Key West Jewish Community–One Hundred Years," Unpublished Document, Key
    West, Florida, 1987.

OTHER SOURCES

Breman Museum, Ida Pearle and Joseph Cuba Archives, Atlanta Georgia
Congregation Rodeph Sholom of Tampa, History of Rodeph Sholom, rodephsholomhistory.doc, 2003
Florida Death Index on the Internet
Florida Jewish Heritage Trail, Florida Department of State, the Internet
Gateway Family Historian, genealogy newsletter of the St. Louis Public Library.
Gates to Jewish Heritage
Genealogy.com
Internet Modern History Sourcebook
Jewish Women's Archives
Judaic Treasures of the Library of Congress, Jewish Virtual Library, the Internet
My Jewish Learning.com
North American Jewish Data Bank on the Internet
Royal Palm Cemetery Burial List-St. Petersburg Florida on the Internet
Social Security Death Index on the Internet
Today in Florida History, the Internet
United States Census on the Internet-1900
United States Census on the Internet-1910
United States Census on the Internet-1920
United States Census on the Internet-1930
United States Census Household Record
World War I draft registrations 1917-1918 on the Internet

ORAL HISTORIES

Argintar, Arnold, Temple Beth El, May 15, 2003

Baker, Laura, Temple B'nai Israel of Clearwater, October 5, 2004
Benjamin, Marilyn and Miller, Sonya, St. Petersburg Beach, June 15, 2004
Benstock, Gerald and Joan, Belleair Beach, May 24, 2005
Bernstein, Michael, Gulf Coast Jewish Family Service, Largo, August 23, 2004
Bomstein, Alan and Nancy, Congregation Beth Shalom, Clearwater, Florida, March 26, 2004
Bragin, Steve and Gena, Temple B'nai Israel, Clearwater, Florida, December 3, 2002
Bromberg, Johanna, Congregation Beth Shalom, Clearwater, Florida, June 22, 2004

Colen, Sidney, Congregation Beth Shalom, Clearwater, Florida, April 22, 2004

Fane, Xenia Dr., Temple B'nai Israel, Clearwater, Florida, June 10, 2002 and June 19, 2002

Glassman, Leon and Ellen, St. Petersburg, Florida, March 16, 2005
Golding, Roberta, Tampa Florida, August 2, 2003
Gordon, Elinor, Largo, Florida, October 31, 2005.
Grau, Sidney, Dr., Treasure Island, Florida, February 24, 2005

Haftel, Harold, Tarpon Springs, Florida, May 29, 2003
Hirsch, Ruth S., Temple B'nai Israel, Clearwater, Florida, May 28, 2002, June 17, 2002 and June 25, 2002

Igel, Lusia, Temple B'nai Israel, December 10, 2003

Joseph, Samson Marion, Pasadena, Florida, April 5, 2005

Katz, Bunnie, Congregation B'nai Israel, St. Petersburg Florida, December 9, 2002, March 13, 2003, and
    October 28, 2003
Kent, Reva, Temple B'nai Israel, Clearwater, Florida, June 29, 2004, July 13, 2004, May 9, 2005
Kobrinetz, Rabbi, St. Pete Beach, Florida, April 4, 2005

Lawrence, Lila, Temple B'nai Israel, Clearwater, Florida, March 25, 2004
LeVine, Marilyn, Temple Beth El, St. Petersburg, Florida, June 3, 2003 and August 10, 2004
Loebenberg, Walter, St. Petersburg, Florida, April 5, 2005
Lovitz, Phyllis, Clearwater Beach, Florida, September 22, 2005
Lubin, Leonard, Congregation B'nai Israel, St. Petersburg Florida, January 14, 2003

Mensh, Myron, Temple B'nai Israel, Clearwater, Florida, March 13, 2005
Mershen, Aaron, St. Petersburg, Florida, February 22, 2005
Miller, Irwin and Sonya, Temple Beth El, December 10, 2002, May 19, 2004
Moch, Shimon, Rabbi, Congregation B'nai Emmunah, April 13, 2004

Newmark, Enid and Kent, Reva, Clearwater, Florida, January 31, 2006

Orbach, Harold Cantor, Temple B'nai Israel, Clearwater, Florida, December 13, 2005.

Possick, Meyer, Congregation Beth Shalom of Gulfport, Florida, March 29, 2005

Rinde, Toni and John, Temple B'nai Israel, December 10, 2003
Rutenberg, Charles, Temple B'nai Israel, 2003
Rutenberg, Isa, Temple B'nai Israel, May 23, 2005
Rutenberg, Jane, Temple B'nai Israel, May 21, 2004

Samuels, Evelyn, Temple Beth El, St. Petersburg, Florida, December 5, 2002, March 27, 2003
Schick, Lisl, Largo, Florida, August 17, 2004
Siegal, Sally, Largo, Florida, August 11, 2005
Susskind, David Rabbi, Temple Beth El, St. Petersburg, Florida, December 4, 2002

Weinstock, Sheila, Temple B'nai Israel, Clearwater, Florida, May 30, 2002
Whittner, Ted, Congregation B'nai Israel, St. Petersburg, Florida, May 27, 2004
Werner, Sid, Congregation B'nai Israel, St. Petersburg, Florida, March 17, 2005
Wolstein, David, Temple Ahavat Shalom, Palm Harbor, Florida, August 26, 2004

TELEPHONE INTERVIEWS
In order to complete the Jewish history research, telephone interviews, followed by e-mail confirmation and
review of written documents, were used to help gather essential information about people and events. The
author did not keep a record of telephone interviews from 2001–2003.

Arthur, Esrick, Sandra, Miami, Florida, February 28, 2005

Baker, Laura, Temple B'nai Israel, August 4, 2004
Berman, Sandra, Breman Museum, Atlanta, Georgia, August 25, 2004
Bromberg, Johanna, Clearwater March 17, 2004

Cypen, Irving Judge, Miami, Florida, March 18, 2005

Druin, Moshe, Rabbi, Miami, Florida, July 25, 2004

Eppsteiner, Cheryl, Jewish Education Loan Fund, Atlanta Georgia, August 24, 2004

Fyvolent, Joan Esrick, St. Petersburg, Florida, January 4, 2005
Fyvolent, Joel Dr., Tampa, Florida, February 8, 2005

Gilbert, Jerry, Congregation B'nai Israel, St. Petersburg, Florida, January 3, 2005
Glickstein, Pat, West Palm Beach, Florida, February 13, 2005
Goldblatt, Dorothy, Congregation B'nai Israel, St. Petersburg, Florida, January 30, 2005
Goodrich, Rabin, Sally, Tampa, Florida, January 10, 2005
Green, Allan, Cambridge, Massachusetts, April 3, 2005
Green, Robert, St. Petersburg, Florida, March 15, 2004.

Helfand, Anita, Congregation B'nai Israel, St. Petersburg, Florida, July 9, 2004
Heller, George, Boston Massachusetts, June 6, 2004

Ismark, Martin, Temple B'nai Israel, Clearwater, Florida, November 28, 2004
Israel, William, St. Petersburg, Florida, November 12, 2002

Kantor, Anne, Tampa, Florida, February 8, 2005
Klein, Gary,Rabbi, Ahavat Shalom, Palm Harbor, Florida, June 29, 2004
Kleinfeld, Larry, St. Petersburg, Florida, January 18, 2005
Kupersmith, Herb, Chelsea, Massachusetts, June 5, 2004

Lawrence, David, Fairfax, Virginia, August 20, 2004
Levine, Eileen, Belleair, Florida, March 17, 2004
Liss, Madelyn, Temple B'nai Israel, Clearwater, Florida, July 1, 2004
Lopatin, Harold, Boca Raton,Florida, April 8, 2004

Marks, Lloyd, Miami, Florida, March 30, 2004
Marsh, Estelle, St. Petersburg, Florida, June 19, 2004

Rippa, Barbara, Tampa, Florida, February 9, 2005
Rosenbaum, Allen, Congregation Beth Chai, Seminole, Florida, March 24, 2005
Rothman, Thelma, St. Petersburg, Florida, February 27, 2005

Samuels, Lee, San Francisco, California, June 8, 2004
Schier, Saul, Congregation Beth Tikvah of Palm Harbor, Florida, November 3, 2004
Schine, Audrey Maas, Tampa, Florida, November 3, 2004
Schuster, Phyllis, St. Petersburg, Florida, January 11, 2005
Sembler, Liz, Clearwater, Florida, April 20, 2005
Sislen, David B., Cantor, Congregation B'nai Israel, St. Petersburg, Florida, July 28, 2004

Archivists

Katz, Bunnie, Congregation B'nai Israel, St. Petersburg, Florida
Wides, Elaine, Temple Beth-El, St. Petersburg, Florida

Index

Symbols

1946 Haggadah 497
19th Amendment 40
1st Christian Church Largo 455
1st Lutheran Church 455
1st Presbyterian Church 455
58th Street Land Company 152, 178

A

A-B-C Packing Machine Corporation 104
A. A. Esrick Inc. 136
Aamias, J. 70
Aaron, Mrs. S. 70, S. 70
Aaron Diamond Foundation 53
Abeles, Max L. 386
Abelson, David 530, 602, 677
Abilock, Adam Greenfield & Tanya 679
Abram and Strauss 140
Abramovitz, Mrs. S. 70, S. 70, S.M. 77
Abramowitz, Izzy & Irene 143
Abrams, Bob 147, Erwin 305, Felice 676, Hannah 579, Hazel 146, Izzy 139, Mr. & Mrs. Arthur 167, Mrs. 362, Robert 167, Sanford & Joyce 187, Willie 146
Abramson, Dr. Jeffrey 581
Academy of Fine Arts 10
Ace Beauty Company 148
Acts of Human Kindness 603
Adams, Loweil 368
Adams-Onis Treaty 90
Adamson, Patrick & Wendy 188, Wendy 467, 679
Addams, Jane 517
Adelman, Charles H. 145, Harvey 329, Jack & Jackie 145, Joseph L. 145, Mr. & Mrs. Samuel 169, Suzette 360
Adler, Cecilia (Celia) 311, Eric 364, 459, 679, Jacob 311, 314, 675, Josh 679, Mrs. A.M. 120, Rabbi Shalom 320, 460, 547, Rabbi Shalom & Chanie 289
Admiral Farragut Academy 522
Adult Mental Health Clinic 160, 172
Adults for Living and Learning Program 302
Adult Studies Commission of Congregation B'nai Israel 354
Advisory Commission of the Council of National Defense 36
Aerosonic 242
Aerosonic Instrument Corp 103, 252
Afterthought 607
Aghassi, Mr. & Mrs. George 167
Agnes, Sister Regina 432
Agoada, Harry 364
Agudas Shalom 118
Ahavath Chesed Congregation 63
Ahavat Shalom ii, Synagogue 455
Aidman, B. Terry 601, D. Terry 541
Air Associates Inc. 103
Aircraft Marine Products 104
Airey, Reverend Donald 432
Aish HaTorah 35
Akiva, Rabbi v
Al-Andulus 4
Alachua County 62
Alan Apparel & Sport Shop 138
Albert A. Belson Endowment Fund 544

Albert Einstein College of Medicine 35
Albert Whitted Municipal Airport 101
Albin, Jackie 585
Aleph Zedek Aleph (AZA) 23, 146
Alexander, Jenny Epstein 492
Alexander II 3, 28, III 3, the Great 1
Al Lang Field 170, Stadium 132
All Children's Hospital 156, 157, 160
Allen, Mary Baum 187, Mel 123
Allied Products Corp. 104
Allied Stores 69
Allison, Barbara 440
All Saints Episcopal Church 325
Allstate Insurance Co 104
Aloof, Rabbi Pincus 295, 540, 675
Alpert, Barry M. 200, 269, 540, 551, 552, 553, 646, Dan & Cassandra 664, George 579, Gertrude 579, Jason 664, Judith & Barry 664, Rabbi Bob 463, Victoria 664
Al Rahman III 4
Altschuler, Jack 220, 221, Marsha 218, Marsha & Jack 217, 221
Amazon, Gail 441
American: Baptist Church 455, Cancer Society 172, Federation of Labor 31, First Committee 4, Intellectual Property Law Association 183, Israelite, The 589, Jewish Archives 2, 52, Jewish Assembly 48, Jewish Committee 35, Jewish Joint Distribution Committee 547, Jewish Yearbook 37, Joint Distribution Committee 535, Press Institute 182, Red Cross 29, 47, 159, Red Cross War Fund 384, Stage 158, Telephone and Telegraph 36
Amtrak Silver Meteor 107
Amzalak, Evelyn 423, 677, Mrs. Semon 264, 585, Semon 423
Anchor Inn 144
Anderson, David 397, John A. 104, Sister Alma Mary vi
Angert, Ann & Ron 441
An Inspiration a Day 69
Anne Frank Center USA in New York 186
Annette Raymund Family Pavilion 173
Annis family 66
Anona United Methodist Church 455
Anspach, Joseph 167
Anti-Defamation League (ADL) 22, 38, 142, 148, 486
Anti-semitism 544
Appel 63, Caren Benjamin 612, Michael 612, Molly 612Rebecca 612
Appelman-Jurman, Alicia 405
Applebaum, Belle 679, Elizabeth 676, Libby 676, Mrs. I. 167
Applefield, Alvin 338, 676, David & Anna 314, 315, Helen 555, 676, Helen & Aaron 354, 355, Jackie 582, Paul 303, 304, 675
Apte family 62
Apter, Leonard 500
Arafat, Yasser 54
Arak, Phyllis 585
Arcades 138, on Central Avenue 138
Arden, Mordecai 372
Argeaux, Rev. M.G. 585
Argintar, Arnold 145, 397, 485, 684, Arnold & Eleanor 143, 167, Debbie 143, Edith Chapp & Eleanor 678, Eleanor 397, 400, 678, Hilary 143,

Max 143, 556, Max & Ann Davis 143, Sam 143, Sender 14, Susan 143, Winfred Klarin & Eleanor 678, Family 147
Ariel, Dr. David 462
Ariel Goldman Memorial Library 373
Armour 36
Aroni, Menahem S. 337
Aronson, Joseph 140, Robert 138, 140
Aronwitz 63
Aroson, Samuel 167
Arsenault, Ray 581
Art Beautification Committee 198, Exhibition and Show, second annual 397, Festival, annual 397, Show, First Annual 397
Arthur, Bradley 136, Dawn 136, Donald & Sandra Esrick 136, Jeffrey 136, Sandra Esrick 685
Arthur Rutenberg Homes 234
ARZA 52
Ascher, Mrs. B. 167, Mrs. G. 167, Rabbi Joseph 243
Ashkenazic 12
Asia Minor 2
Asian Neighborhood Family Center 513
Askew, Hon. Reubin 524
Associate Justice of the United States Supreme Court 38
Association of Reform Zionists of America 52
Atlanta Hebrew Orphan's Home 27, Jewish Children's Service 504, Jewish Community 21
Atlantic Coast Line 99
Auerbach, Leonard 539, 540, 678, Leonard & Madge 187, Samuel 485
Augenbraun, Barry 629
Augnst, Mayor Brian 471
Augusta Weissman Memorial Youth Fund 334
Augustine, Lewis & Clare 207, Shirley 208, 210
Augusto Hospital 94
Auschwitz 496, / Birkenau Concentration Camp 494
Avery, Mr. & Mrs. Jack 315
AVODAH 366
Avren, Herbie & Renée 235
Axe, Art 190
Axelrad, Cantor David 347
Axelrod, Mr. & Mrs. William 524
Ayes, Mr. & Mrs. Theodore 346, Theodore 167
Ayrons, Joseph & Lillian 314, Joseph Z. 314
Azar, Ed 486
Azneer, Rabbi J. Leonard i, 358, 587

B'nai B'rith 22, 130, 145, 485, Chapter, first in Florida 63, Clearwater Unit 2603 485, Girls (BBG) 23, International Council 198, Lodge 11, Lodge 1246 145, of St. Petersburg 136, presents "Jewish Life in Tampa Bay" 488, Youth Organization 487
B'nai Israel Choral Group 333, Chronicle 330, Men's Club 341, Religious School 168, Review 346, Synagogue Center 336
B'nai Tzedek Program 602
Baal Shem Tov 7, 309
Babbit, Mr. & Mrs. B. 169

Babcock & Wilcox Company 103
Babcock, Stephanie 679
Babylonian exile 1
Baccari, Barbara 467, 602, 624
Bacherach, Fannie 66
Bachman, Greg 472
Backal, Dr. Alice 486
Badalament, Susan 324
Baden-Powell, Lord 115
Bader, Elliot 349, Sheryl Elaine 352
Baer, Lewis 62, Maude Alice 67
Bagley, Cantor David 305
Baikovitch, Mrs. 420
Bailey, Col. William J. 97, 213
Bailey Springs 97, 213
Bailin, Mrs. Ella 167
Baker 420, Bonnie 244, 484, David 295,
    675, I. 418, Irvin 425, Irving &
    Martha 228, 243, 426, Irving C. 103,
    228, 264, 424, 431, 439, 485, Laura
    228, 244, 424, 679, 684, 685, Martha
    264, 424, 426, 445, 459, 484, 679, Mrs.
    70, Robert R. 591, Seena & William
    460, Ted 68
Bakor, Joanna 675
Balfour Declaration 39
Ballinger, James 167
Balotin, Ronnie 333
Balsam, Mr. & Mrs. Daniel 167
Bandes, Alyssa 611, Arthur 485, Barbara
    484, Daniel 420, Daniel & Lillian
    252, 420, Jed 611, Nancy 611
Bar-Ness, Laurie 566
Bar-Yam, Dr. Naomi Bromberg 308,
    Maayan 617, Naomi Bromberg &
    Yaneer 275, 617, Shlomiiya 617,
    Taeer 617, Yavni 617
Barad, Rhonda 449
Barak, Ehud 374, Mr. & Mrs. Hyman
    167
Baran, Rose 384
Baranoff, Dr. Salem H. 97, 220, 221, 226,
    236, 237, 244, 289, 291, 292, 293, 295,
    420, 439, 485, 540, 675, Dr. Salem H.
    & Lisa 213, 219, 290, 439, Lisa 97,
    222, 227, 584, 587
Bar Av, Ilan 563
Barber, Leah Jo 404
Bargad, Dr. Warren 302
Barlis, Dr. Arthur 295, 296, 297, 675,
    Jeffrey 675
Barna, Penny 372
Barnard, Mrs. E. R. 141
Barnes, Mr. Paul 167
Barnett, Capt. James 95, Florence 585,
    Hope 541, Leslie J. 541, 600, 601,
    Louis M. 314, Rebecca 95, Samuel
    A. 517
Barney, W.L. 95
Barnstein, Karin 675
Baron, Janet 445, 447, 448, 679, Linda
    565
Baron de Hirsch Fund 28
Bar Simons, the Jacob 389
Barsimson, Jacob 8
Barth, Dr. Con F. 97, Michael 182
Bartlett, Marguerite Blocker 111
Baruch, Bernard Mannes 39, Samuel 485
Barzak, Cantor Israel 347
Baseman, Adina 441, 445, 609, 679, Dalia
    441, 609, Jordana 441, 566, 609,
    Rabbi Arthur I. i, vi, 240, 242, 250,
    264, 268, 279, 280, 287, 296, 297, 313,
    363, 367, 416, 429, 433, 434, 438, 440,

451, 460, 463, 472, 474, 478, 523, 532,
    540, 603, 624, 625, 671, 678, Rabbi
    Arthur I. & Renée Lisser 261, 262,
    588, 609, Renée 430, 461, 567, 568
Baseman Early Childhood Center 566
Basin, Ed 529
Bass, Phillip 678, Rabbi Lia 326
Basta, Dr. & Mrs. Lofty 515
Batchelar, Mr. 201
Bath Club 105
Battel, Dr. Albert 45
Bauer, Dr. & Mrs. R. 167
Baum, Herman & Theresa Teiser 185
Bauman 420, Anita 223, 415, 419, Linda
    424, Marion & Marvin 223, 244,
    Robert 289, 291, 485, Robert & Rita
    290
Bauman's Dress Shop 223
Baumann, M . 418
Baumel, Rabbi Morris 140, 329
Baumgardner's Restaurant 269
Baumgardner, Richard & June 223,
    Richard B. 268
Baumgartner, Mary Ruth 563
Bavil, Alissa 463, 679
Baxter, Alix Lovitz 216, William A. 640
Bayfront Center 105, Medical Center 94,
    153, 159
Baynard Beach Memorial Chapel 167
Bayonet Point Community Hospital 180
Bay Pines Hospital 101, Veterans
    Hospital 140, 155
Bay Walk 171, 183
Bazhanov, Natasha & Eugene 462
Beach, Anna Maria 132
Beachcomber Restaurant on Clearwater
    Beach 243
Beard, Jackie Sweet 328
Beatty, Betty A. 565
Becker, Mr. & Mrs. M. 167
Beckerman, Steve 309, 675
Bee Bee Togs 103, 242, 243
Begin, Prime Minister 587
Behar, Aaron 657, Pamela 657
Behr, Stan & Annie 188
Belesky, Mrs. 167
Belief in God 604
Belink, Cantor Norman 446
Belinson, Dr. Lewis 505
Belkin, Elaine 677
Bellach, Simon 675
Bellack, Larry 679, Simon 485
Belleair Beach 101, 106
Beller, Alan 138
Bellevue Biltmore Hotel 93, 102
Bell Jewelry Company 119
Belofsky, Ella 167
Belon, Ben M. 676, Esther 391, Mr. &
    Mrs. Ben 315
Belorussia 3
Belzec concentration camp 45
Ben, Dorene E. 582, 584, Max 581
Ben-Gurion, David 579, 586
Ben-Or, Rabbi Gabriel 306, 675
Benard, H. 591
Benbow, Charles 181
Benci, Dr. Vivian 610
Bender, Fred 120, Mrs. Fred 120
Benedict, Rabbi George 79, 122, 126, 132
ben Eliezer, Rabbi Israel 7
Ben Gali, Cantor Simcha 300
ben Gamaliel, Rabbi Simeon 603
Bengehone, Adeline 169
Bengele, Sue 298, 675

Benjacob, Nick 496
Benjamin, Alyssa 425, 622, Bob 217, 611,
    Caren 197, 414, Carly 611, Daniel
    425, 622, Dr. & Mrs. Phillip 346, Dr.
    Mark 545, Dr. Philip 149, 155, 167,
    173, 178, 195, 331, 332, 338, 539, 540,
    555, Joan 264, 431, 611, 679, Joan &
    Robert Jr. 427, Joseph & May 120,
    195, Judah P. 26, Judy 197, 414,
    561, 612, Julie 428, 566, Lauren 439,
    Louisa 612, Mae Goldman 120,
    167, 346, 362, Marilyn Halaczer 129,
    198, 200, 344, 346, 357, 414, 555, 561,
    562, 587, 628, 645, 684, Mark 197,
    612, May 119, 345, 351, 536, 676, Mr.
    & Mrs. Lee 167, Nancy 428, 441,
    Peninah 612, Peter 428, 611, Philip
    119, 130, 146, 173, 414, 551, Philip &
    Marilyn 195, 547, 612, Rachel 425,
    622, Robert 264, 678, Robert T. Jr.
    433, 438, 440, 473, 485, Samuel 612,
    Sharri 611, Stephen & Susan Entel
    425, Steven 425, 622, Susan 425,
    622, Tyler 611, Family 62
Benjamin Family Social Hall 359
Benjamin N. Cardozo School of Law 35
Benmayer 420
Benny, Jack 269
Benson, Mrs. J. 328
Benstock, David & Jane 272, Joan 547,
    629, Joan Kline & Gerald 271, 563,
    684, Margot 602,629, 677, Margot
    & Michael 272, 587, Peter & Tracy
    272, Wendy 272, Yona 358
Benstock Family Sanctuary 359
Bentauil, Sherwin & Estelle 237
ben Yosef, Gershom 62
Berg, Mrs. Jack 484, Naomi 676, Sylvia
    3, 207, 677
Berger, Alana 489, 613, Audrey 156,
    Carol Rivkind 339, Daniel 489, 613,
    Debbie 613, Dr. Isadore & Bella
    290, Edith 559, Lauren 679, Michael
    613, Milton 334, Miriam 401, Mr. &
    Mrs. Milton 167, Mrs. Amuel 169,
    Mrs. Leo 395, Rabbi Kenneth 87,
    Robert 613, Saul 485, Stan & Arlene
    489, 613, Stanley 595, Stuart 675,
    Stuart & Helene 489, 613
Bergman, Suzanne 445
Berk, Bernard 430, 438, 679, Bernard &
    Rosalind 254, Rosalind 679, Roz
    255, Tony 254, 255
Berk Drugs 254
Berkman, Danny 147, Matthew Jay 351,
    Mr. & Mrs. Daniel 167
Berko, Cecile 394, 561, 678, Cecile &
    Malcolm 394, Dr. Adam & Patricia
    394, Hannah 394, Joshua 394,
    Malcolm 519, 678, Zachary 394
Berkoff, Robert & Darlene 187
Berkowitz, Joseph L. 315, Louis 167,
    Lucy 555, Mark 460, Mr. & Mrs.
    Joseph 167, 346, Mrs. P. 70, Rabbi
    Henry 33, Teddi 545
Berlin, Irving 39
Berliner, Emile 32
Berman, David 404, Donna 678, Rabbi
    Stuart L. 189, 198, 507, Sandra 685,
    Sylvia 264
Bermant, Ike (Lucius Beebe) 147
Bernal, Maestro 5
Bernard's Kosher Butchery 349
Bernardin, Cardinal Joseph 403

Bernholz, Rabbi Richard 372
Berni, Lillian (Miller) 649
Bernstein, Barbara 460, Barnett 137,
    Barney 135, David 587, 677, Diane
    303, Dianne 675, Dinah 135, Dr.
    & Mrs. A. 167, Dr. David A. 511,
    545, 546, Dr. Mayer 315, Ellen 540,
    676, Harry 261, Harry & Mary
    625, Herbert 445, 679, Herman
    35, Irving 348, 539, 540, 676, 677,
    Lenora 172, Leo 135, Leonard 579,
    Michael 142, 173, 501, 506, 508,
    509, 531, 561, 684, Mr. & Mrs. B.
    167, Mr. & Mrs. Dudley 167, Mr. &
    Mrs. Samuel 167, Mrs. Irving 521,
    Professor Jerrold 580, Ronnie 368,
    587, Sidney 135
Berolzheimer, Benjamin 614, Bud &
    Shirley 223, Henry 227, 420, J. 418,
    , Julia 224, 227, 228, 415, 419, 420,
    424, Leah 614, Nathan 614, Shirley
    227, 439, Shirley & Henry 614,
    Susan 424, Trish 614
Berryman, Michael 461
Berthelsdorf, Victor 355, 356
Berzon, Ron 676
Betash, Sion 485
Betech, Cecilia Rophie 254, 657
Beth-El Auxiliary (Sisterhood) 379,
    Community Baptist Church 396,
    Religious School 168, Sisterhood
    167
Bethel Community Church 476,
    Lutheran Church 513
Beth Elohim 11, Hak'neseth 331,
    Hamidrash 331, Ha Midrash
    Ha Gadol 118, Hillel Chai 455,
    Rachamim of St. Petersburg 199,
    Shalom ii, Tefillah 331
Bettman, Edward 65
Bevis Marks Synagogue in London,
    England 10
Bexmayor, Albert 485
Bibber, Dr. W. C. 92
Bible iii, 1
Bickel, Theodore 525
Bickhardt, Cantor Jochanan (Yochanan)
    303, 304, 460, 675
Bierman, Sissie Angest 221, 441
BIFTY and BIFTY Junior 481
Bild, Geoff & Pat 369
Bilgore 420, Aaron 203, David 203,
    David & Etta 202, Morris 203, 224,
    243, 244, 418, 422, 424, 433, 439, 485,
    637, 678, Morris & Bertha 202, 203,
    206, Paul & June (Michaelove) 203,
    Family 85
Bilgore Groves 202
Bilgore Trust Company 204
Bill of Rights 14
Binder, Cantor Jonah 298
Birnbaum, Asher 51, Nathan 51, Phyllis
    410
Birnholz, Rabbi Richard J. 86
Bischoff, Hewey 167, Robert 167
Bish, Diana 477
Bishop, Louis 145, 485, Sam & Helen
    464
Bishow, Jack 167
Bivers, Mr. 201
Black, Jill 448, 567, Morris J. 161, 167,
    391, Mr. 161, Robert 679
Blacker, Beverlee Daniels 599
Black Hundreds 35, 76

Blair, Harris 367
Blanc, Mayor R. G. 381
Blankman, Herbert 485
Blate, Mr. & Mrs. S. 167
Blitzer, Arlene 585
Block, Harold 591, Louis 591
Bloom, Louis 264, 485
Bloxham, Gov. William D. 110
Blum, Adolphus & Julie 109, Donald
    209, Dr. Robert 110, Edward A. 24,
    109, 234, 605, George 65, Gracie
    109, Family 109, 110, 121, 201
Blumberg, David H. & Minnie 140,
    Eugene 140, H. 135, Lionel 140,
    Maine or Maria or Mamie 140,
    Minnie 377, Minnie & David H.
    137, Mr. & Mrs. E. 167, Rosebud
    140, Roslyn 140, Rudolph 167
Blumencranz, Alex & Brett 472
Blumenthal, Isidore 65
Board of Governors 551, of Trade of St.
    Petersburg 94
Bobo, Ezra & Gloria Grazi 253, 290,
    Ezra (Zua) 253, 292, 439, 485, 675,
    Gloria 679, Pauline 253, Ralph 254,
    Richard 254, 679, Salha & Ralph
    253, Salha "Mama" 657, Scott 254,
    445, 679, Victor 254, 441, Family 63
Bobo/Rophie/Berk Families 253
Bobo's Gifts 290
Boca Ciega Bay 101
Bock, Cecile 617
Bogage, Rabbi Louis E. 320
Bogot, Rabbi Howard 454
Bohr War 115
Bokor, Bruce 602, Bruce H. 317, 523,
    529, 541
Bolin, Mrs. Sidney 290, 291, Sidney 289,
    291, Zelda 289
Bolton, Rabbi Albert B. 585
Bomstein, Alan 241, 269, 292, 295,
    296, 298, 304, 309, 358, 675, Alan
    & Nancy Sue (Auerbach) 264,
    295, 587, 615, 684, David & Dawn
    (Jacobson) 267, 615, Joshua &
    Lindsay (Batting) 267, 615
Bond, August 234
Bondi (Bondy) family 24, August 24
Bonsey, Frank 338
Book of Commandments, The 4
Book of Daily Prayers for Every Day in the
    Year According to the Custom of the
    German and Polish Jews 20
Borchardt, Mrs. Sam 73
Bornstein, Morris 360, Family 118
Boston Braves 98
Bower, Major Joseph 384
Bowlegs, Chief Billy 90
Bowman, Debby 484, Jonathan 629,
    Mrs. Harold 484, Rose 484, Selma
    367, 368, Steve 368
Boxman, Harry 167
Boyer, Joshua 91
Bozeman, Sandy 562
Bradenton 103
Brader, Natalie 146
Bragin 420, Arla 204, Janet 68, 441, Jules
    85, 203, 206, Jules & Molly (Bilgore)
    203, Marc 68, Marl 616, Regina
    679, Steve 68, 204, 424, 425, 427,
    433, 439, 471, 485, 678, 684, Steve &
    Regina (Gena) Waterman 204, 206,
    588, 616
Brahm, Kevin 679

Bramlett, Albert Jr. 104
Bramlett Tool and Die Company 104
Bramlit, Mr. & Mrs. Robert 169
Brandeis, Daniel 325, Louis D. 38,
    Megin 325, Family 389
Brandeis University 49, National
    Women's Committee 49, 579,
    Women's Committee St. Petersburg
    Chapter 582, Women's Committee
    Suncoast Chapter of Clearwater 579
Brandt, Molly 176, Mr. & Mrs. Robert
    167
Brannen, Tobias Lovitz 113
Brannon, Mrs. J. 218
Branscum, Richard 68
Brantley, Mayor Edward F. 339, 392
Brasch, Benjamin 630, Sandy Katz &
    Herb 630
Brash, Henry 63, 73, 74, Mrs. Henry 73,
    74
Braude, Edwin P. 167
Braun 420, Bobby 334, Irwin 103,
    Leanne 418, 424, Mr. & Mrs. Alex
    167, 346, Sandy 484
Braunstein, Mr. & Mrs. M. 169
Brav, Rabbi Stanley R. 398, 399, 400, 406
Braveman, Phyllis 555
Breakers 133, on Madeira Beach 133
Bredenberg, Dr. Richard 411
Breitstein, Joel M. 541, 601
Brem, Cantor Michael 403, 460, 677
Breman, Arnold 269, 368
Breman Museum 684
Brenner, Joe 172, Mr. & Mrs. Joseph D.
    167
Bresky, Aaron 270, Ilana 270, Rabbi Jan
    269, 275, 277, 317, 320, 364, 365, 488
Bresler, Toby Rothbardt 391, 560
Bressler, Amy Ruth 351, Ellen Jane 351,
    Harold & Bernice (Stainsky) 350,
    Harold & Bernice (Stanley) 408,
    Joel 336, Marcia Frances 351, Toby
    R. 509
Brevda, Yale 332
Brevoort, Gary 368
Brewster, Mary 517
Breyley, Mr. & Mrs. A. R. 167
Brhem, Caroline 146
Brickman, Howard 679
Brith Sholom Synagogue 11
Britwitz, M. 70
Broadway Pharmacy 290
Brodman, Mrs. G. W. 169
Brodski, Morris & Lillian D. 221, S. 221
Brodsky, Louis 676, Mrs. 420, Mrs.
    Morris 292
Bromberg, Caleb & Liran 617, Efram &
    Nancy 275, Efrem 298, 617, Hillel
    299, Hillel & Chaya 275, 617, Jake
    617, Johanna 299, 303, 581, 684,
    685, Max 617, Nancy 617, Naomi
    298, Rabbi Kenneth 303, 305, 306,
    307, 308, 313, 367, 460, 675, Rabbi
    Kenneth & Johanna (Hirsch) ii, 298,
    588, 617
Bromwich, John 676, Myrna 676, Myrna
    & John 315
Bronfman, Sam 208
Bronstein, Alvin 161, Rabbi Herbert 367,
    Rabbi Lester B. & Cantor Benjie
    Ellen Schiller 406
Brook, Mrs. Karl 169, Pearl 676
Brooks, Ralph P. 169
Brosman, Arthur 591

Henry M. 315, Herman H. 138, 379, Hyman 168, 677, Ina 155, Irene 155, Irving & Dorothy 515, Jacob Raphael 62, 65, Jane Esther 195, Jeff 657, Joel & Tina 187, Judge M. Henry 70, 73, 74, 78, 80, 82, 85, 135, 138, 224, 378, 380, 381, 677, Judy 599, Julius 62, Julius & Jacob 62, Lewis 138, Lilly M. & Herman H. 137, Louis (Boston) 117, 129, 131, 147, Louis (Boston) & Celia 121, 140, M. H. Sr. 70, Maxine 367, Michelle & Dave 587, Mildred 676, Min 676, Moses 10, Mr. & Mrs. Aron 168, Mr. & Mrs. Herman 315, Mr. & Mrs. Hyman 168, Mr. & Mrs. Louis 346, Mr. & Mrs. Samuel 169, Mrs. Louis 146, 384, 678, Mrs. Louis A. 384, Mrs. M. H. 70, Mrs. William 377, Muriel 155, Newton & Florence 187, Pearl 118, Rabbi Jodi 471, Rabbi Samuel L. 573, Rae 676, Randi *vi*, Samuel 62, Sonia 384, Family 14
Cohn, Abraham 26, David 432
Coit, Charles 221, Stanton 517
Colbert, Lee 555
Cole, Marion & Dick 486, 675
Coleman, Sheriff Gerry 401
Colen, Gerald R. 309, 540, 541, Ina 500, Ina Gotler 555, Jerrold R. 677, Sidney 104, 163, 172, 178, 179, 518, 519, 677, 684, Sidney & Ina 154, 168, 258, 314, 346
Colin, Barney & Dorothy Collman 210, Clifford 368, Sidney 432
College of Charleston 10
College Settlement in New York 517
College Shop 114
Collins, Charles & Elaine 187, Robert 314
Collis, Mr. & Mrs. D. A. 169
Collman, Arthur 420, Arthur & Bessie (Goldstein) 210, Aunt Shirley 206, C. 244, 420, Clarence 210, 211, 220, 221, Clarence & Lela 439, Jerald 211, 619, Jerry 424, L. 244, 418, Lee Shirley 211, Leonard 210, 219, 220, 221, 233, 236, 239, 420, 427, 471, 485, 678, Leonard & Shirley 3, Mr. & Mrs. Arthur 235, 424, Nancy 211, 418, 424, 619, 679, Nancy & Jerald 227, Shirley 42, 212, 217, 225, 227, 233, 235, 236, 237, 239, 264, 429, 679, Shirley (Augustine) & Leonard 211, 215, 221, 418, 439, 445, 459, 619, Steve 211, 619, Steve & Kathy 418
Collman Shoe Store 211
Colonial Village Mobile Park 420
Committee of 100 136
Community Relations Committee 148
Concentration camp 45
Confederate States of America 58
Congregational Gifts 439
Congregation Aliyah of Clearwater 320
Congregation B'nai Israel *ii*, of St. Petersburg 327
Congregation B'nai Emmunah *iii*, 317, of Tarpon Springs 277
Congregation B'nai Israel 76, 117, 122, 129, 136, Youth Department 362, 564
Congregation Beth Chai 189
Congregation Beth Elohim 11

Congregation Beth Israel 87
Congregation Beth Shalom *ii, iv, v*, 76, 289, 564, Religious School 564, Sisterhood 309
Congregation Beth Sholom of Gulfport 164, 311
Congregation Beth Tikvah 278
Congregation Kol Ami of Tampa 301
Congregation of Peace 118
Congregation Ohabei Shalom 118
Congregation Rodeph Sholom 77, 78, of Tampa 86, 684, 301
Congregation Schaarai Zedek 66, 78, of Tampa 319, 374
Congregations of America 34
Congregations United for Community Action 406
Congressional Medal of Honor 33
Conservative 575, Judaism 16, 17, Movement 573
Consignment Furniture Gallery 442
Consolidated Amusement, Inc. 69
Consumers League of New York 32
Continental Army 14
Conway, Francis R. 593
Coons, William 91
Cooper, Rose 555
Cooperman, Alfred 70, 168, 212, J. L. 139, 379, Lena Goldstein 212, Leonard 139, 181, 212, 379, Mr. & Mrs. Martin 168, Mrs. M. 172, Nelly 212
Copelan, Augusta & Honey 290
Coplon, Mr. & Mrs. Phillips 169
Cordell, Lillian 391
Cordoba 4
Cordray, Sharon *vi*
Corner, Edward 445, 679
Corwin, Richard 485
Cossacks 6
Cottrille, Dr. Patricia 587
Coughlin, Father Charles E. 23, 40
Council of Human Relations 158, of Jewish Federations 547
Countryside area 106, Mall 106
Courtney Cambell Causeway 223, Parkway 101
Covenant Club 134, 147, 150
Cowley, Jane 303
Craig, Elaine Jean 153, 154, Robert & Jean 154
Cramer, Carrie 636, Debra & Mark 636, Nikki 636
Creative Contractors 266, 304
Creek Indians 89
Cressman, Lloyd S. 245
Cresson, Warder 476
Crest Cabinet Manufacturing Corporation 171
Crest Leather Manufacturing Company 103
Croke, Elizabeth 566
Crystal Ballroom in Clearwater 243
Cuba 186
Cub Scout Pack 222 412
Cullinan Diamond Mines 115
Cundiff, Travis 397
Cunx, Pauline 510
Curlew Hills Memory Gardens 204, Memory Gardens Cemetery, Funeral Home and Crematory 202
Curphey, Dolores 456, 457, 458, 679
Cushman, Katherine 168
Cutler, Capt. David 89, I. R. 168, Meyer

165, Miles E. 528, Sidney 675, Sidney & Elaine 188
Cutson, Bernard 334, Mr. & Mrs. Bernard 168
Cypen, Ben 136, Harry 145, 485, Judge Irving 136, 139, 146, 685, Max 135, Myles 146, Steven 146, Tad 146, Wayne 146
Czar Nicholas II 38
Czech Republic Torah 199

da Costa, Isaac 10
Daisy G. Waterman Lighthouse for the Blind 68
Dakai Conference 140
Damascus Blood Libel 21
Danes, Oscar 676
Daniels, Marc Corey 350, Matthew Wayne 350, Mrs. Dan 395, Rachel 679, Renée & Victor 349
Daniels Men's Store in Clearwater 237
Danielson, Dr. Harry 432
Dannenberg, Mr. & Mrs. D. 169
Danto, Dr. Samuel B. 678, Sylvia 397, 401
Danziger, Dr. Mark 172, Lou 295, Dr. & Mrs. 168
da Pearle & Joseph Cuba Archives 684
Dardashti, Cantor Fared 347, 676, Sheila 347
da Silva, Antonio José 12
Dato, Elisa 679
Daughters of Zion 37
Davenport, William F. 387
David Bilgore & Co. Inc. 203, 204
Davids, Rabbi Stanley M. 405
Davidson, Ruth 602
Davis 420, Aaron & Sarah 131, Allan 131, Annie 131, Arlene 131, 334, Armand & Leatrice 131, Charles 129, 137, 327, Charlie 143, Charlie & Marie 131, D. 418, David 418, 485, David & Amelia 252, Dotsy 131, Eunice 131, Frank A. 92, 96, Gerald & Shane Heather Goldman 181, Ida 131, Isadore & Jennie Fishermen 131, Joe 147, Judy 551, Lillian 351, 362, Lorraine 131, Marcus 131, Marie 131, 146, 329, Max 119, 129, 131, 143, 146, 147, 329, 330, 333, 362, 485, 676, Max & Lillian H. 131, Michael 463, Mr. & Mrs. Charles 346, Mr. & Mrs. Oscar 169, Mrs. Max 346, Mrs. Oscar 346, Sarah 131, Susan 303, Taryn 432
Davis Causeway Toll Road 101, Companies 96, Island Country Club 85, Power Plant 94
Dawkins, James Allen 486, 590, Jeremy 591, Jim 589, Karen 589, Rachel 591
Dayan, Cecilia 332, Dorothy 149, 155, Julia 676, Juliet Schmitz 128, Saul 126, Saul H. & Juliet Schmitz 128, Victor 329
Dean, Minnie 551
Dearborn Independent 35
de Aviles, Don Pedro Menendez 57, 96
Deborah, The 589
Deborah Home for Working Boys 120
Debowsky, Bryan 679, Gertrude 678, Helene 459, 679, Stuart 679
Declaration of Independence 14
DeCoveneys, The 295

Freehof, Rabbi Solomon B. 395
Freelander, Rabbi Dan 369
Freeman, Corrine 583, Joseph 441,
    Mayor Corrinne 298, Melissa 679
Freid, Mr. & Mrs. Isadore 168
Freifeld, Loretta 563, Mr. & Mrs. Stanley
    525, Stanley 539, 540, 563, 677
Freilich, Rebeka 679
French and Indian War 13
Freud, Sigmund 22, 142
Freudenberg, Charles A. 138, Charles A.
    & Helen 128, Mrs. 380
Freund, Sigmund & Rosa 118, 201
Friedberg, Lena 168
Friedel, Alison Nicole 404
Friedhoff, Paul 306, 675
Friedlander 420, Larry 228, 415, 418,
    422, 424, Larry & Marion 237,
    Marion 252, Randal 679, Sophie
    583
Friedler, Cantor Moshe 357
Friedman, A. 536, Alan 138, Allen 485,
    Belle 141, Benjamin Joseph 357,
    Bonnie 547, 548, 629, Debbie 467,
    Gladys L. 139, Isadore 135, Jim
    Alan 385, Lauren 463, M. A. 383,
    M. Alan 377, 380, 386, 677, 678, M.
    Alan & Bella R. 138, 139, M. Allen
    145, 485, Michael 445, Mr. 168,
    Mr. & Mrs. H. 168, Mr. & Mrs. M.
    A. 168, Rabbi Seymour 296, Rev.
    H. 74, Robert 309, Ron 321, Ruth
    Y. 139
Frieman, Alene Goldstein & Marilyn
    678, Marilyn 678
Friendly, Myer H. 138, 378, 379, 677,
    Myer H. & Leah H. 138, 377
Friendship Methodist Church 455
Frolich, Mr. & Mrs. E. 168
Frome, Mrs. Sadye 346
Frost, David 342
Frydman-Kohl, Rabbi Baruch 352
Frye, Gail 676, Gail & Mike 349, Kevin
    Ira 352, Marc 676, Mrs. A. J. 168
Fuchs, Bernie 328, J. 329
Fuente, Mr. & Mrs. Max 168
Fuller, H. Walter 96
Funded Life Members of Ruth Eckerd
    Hall 269
Funk, Dr. Floyd 395
Furst 378, B. F. 138, Mr. & Mrs. Jacob
    170
Fuss, Shari 453, 457, 677
Fussell's Incorporated 290
Futornick, Rabbi Jodie 190, 460
Futuronics Manufacturing Company 103
Fyvolent, Arthur Scott 134, Barbara 134,
    Barney 134, Betty & Harry 138,
    Betty Soloman 114, David 397,
    David & Joan Levinson Esrick 134,
    David & Sally Felson 134, David B.
    678, David Bradley 133, Douglas
    Stuart 134, Dr. Joel 114, 686, Duvid
    Baer 133, 134, Evelyn 139, Harry
    114, 134, Jack 134, Joan Esrick 686,
    Lowell 329, Lowell & Carolyn
    Sudakow 133, 134, Lowell S. 151,
    168, Mr. & Mrs. Samuel 331, Mrs.
    David 397, 678, Mrs. S. 328, Mrs.
    Samuel 328, Rose 134, Sam 147,
    329, Samuel 133, 134, Stanley 134,
    Susan Gale 134, Yetta 133, Family
    133
G.I. Bill of Rights 48

Gail, Freddie & Sylvia 500, Sylvia 501,
    538, 541
Gainesville 63
Galbraith Marine Science Laboratory 107
Galicia 5
Gall, Jennifer Denise 404, Marcy 599
Gallagher, Norman E. 104
Gallay, Alan 433, Allan 679, Harold 679,
    Leona 595
Galler, Ilene 585
Galloway, Aaron 485, Aron & Helen T.
    290
Gamse, Gregory 155, Mr. & Mrs. A. B.
    168, Mr. & Mrs. G. H. 170, Renee
    168
Gandy Bridge 98, 99, 104
Gans, Joachim 8
Ganz, Gussie 170
Garden Seat 243
Garmane Aerosonic Corporation 290
Garrell, Mr. & Mrs. William 168
Garron, Julie 441
Garry, Mrs. Jacob 168
Garvey, Mayor Rita 526
Gateman, Bernice 585
Gates to Jewish Heritage 684
Gateway Family Historian 684, Hospital
    Corporation 179
Gator Chemicals 104
Gauld, George 89
Gause, Isaac 26
Gayle, Mrs. 398
Geffen, Rabbi Joel 573
Geier, Ellie 367, Robert & Ellie 188
Gelbart, June & Ben 588, June
    Baumgardner 268, 529, Mr. & Mrs.
    Ben 525
Gellady, Andy 368
Geller, Jack 449, 679, Jessie 463, Roslyn
    583
Gellman, Rabbi Marc 372
Gelluicker, S 74
Gelman, Anne 168, Mr. & Mrs. Eli 168
Gemara *iii*
Gemilut Chasidim 373
Gendzier, Dr. Stephen 580
Genealogy.com 684
General Electric 253, 271, Company X-
    ray Division 103
General Nuclear Engineering Corp 104
Gentlemen's Agreements 99
Geological Survey Center for Coastal
    Ecology 107
George Rogers Clark Expedition 16, 605
Gerber, Dr. Jane 303, 357, Rabbi Israel
    390
Geriatric Crisis Response Team 510
Germain, Anna 91
German, Jack 430, 568, Jack & Sheila 188
German-American Bund 23
German Hebrew Society 21, Jewish
    Community 3, Jewish Immigration
    23
Gersch, Charles & Rose M. 221, Charlie
    217, 220, Rose M. 235, 239
Gershom, David 16
Gerson, Margret 319, Peggy 320, Robert
    & Nancy Collman 418
Gerst, Ella 377, Ella & MIlton S. 137
Gerstkin, Mr. & Mrs. Louis 391, Louis
    168
Gessner, Dr. Murray 400, 540, 678
Gewitz, Cantor Shimon 407, 676, Cantor
    Shimon & Ilana 359, 360, Ilana 359

Giddens, George 65
Gilbert (Goldberg), Jerome & Harold
    124, (Goldberg), Samuel 123, 129,
    Fern (Goldberg) 123, Harold & Jane
    334, Jerome & Thelma 145, 152,
    334, 346, 352, 587, 623, Jerome C.
    152, 178, 337, 339, 346, 485, 562, 676,
    Jerry 328, 686, Mr. & Mrs. Harold
    168, Mr. & Mrs. Samuel 168, 346,
    Sam (Goldberg) 362, Samuel 122,
    332, 334, 676, Stella (Goldberg) 362,
    676, Thelma 152, 360, 676
Gilcrist, Governor Albert 95
Gilder, Daniel 298
Giles, James Alan 193
Gills, Dr. James P. 531
Gilman, Mr. 362, Mrs. 362, Rabbi Neil
    354
Gilmore, Dr. George 382, 485, Phyllis
    333
Gilson, Irving 168
Gingold, Mabel 168
Ginsberg, Pam 432
Ginsburg, Mr. & Mrs. A. 168, Mrs. David
    678
Gisser, Solomon 298
Gitmore, Deborah Ann Gross 600
Gitomer, Dr. Steven D. 600, Mark 600,
    Sharon 600
Gittelsohn, Rabbi Roland B. 239, 343
Glace Engineering Corp. 104
Gladstone, Ann 227, Anne 217, Anne
    & Arthur 235, Daniel 485, Danny
    217, 223, Dr. 244, Mrs. 420, Family
    220
Glass, Martha 368, Susan Benjamin 425
Glassman, Edna 150, Ellen 150, Jacob
    & Ida 150, Leon 334, 676, Leon &
    Edna Kolodny 150, Leon & Ellen
    684, Mr. & Mrs. Leon 346, Mr. &
    Mrs. Sol 346, Mrs. Jacob 346, Sol &
    Helen 150
Glazer 420, Max 295, 296
Glazier, Francine 235
Glickman, Ruth 200, 558, 645
Glickstein, Pat Landfield 126, 686
Glimcher, Mr. & Mrs. M. 170
Globetrotters 170
Glogowski, H. 70, Herman 70, 73, 75, 77,
    78, Mrs. Herman 70
Glorfield, Susan 441
Glucek, Daniel 435
Gluck, Daniel 437, 458
Gluckman 170
Gluek, Dr. Nelson 52
Godsey Frank C. Jr. 103
Goetz, Ellen & Joel 195, Joel 521, 523,
    543, 677
Goff, Dr. Herbert 677, Harriet 582, Josh
    639, Matthew 639, Sheryl Liss 464,
    639
Gold, Adrian 655, Alexandra 655,
    Cheryl & Aaron 588, Harry 593,
    Helen & Harry 588, Marcia 555,
    Michael & Shari Polur 655, Shelly
    639, Trudy 465
Golda Meir/Kent Center Preschool 565,
    Jewish Center 269
Golda Meir Center 523, 580, Chapter of
    Hadassah 123, Jewish Community
    Center 249, Senior Citizens Center
    270
Goldberg, A. 71, Allyn 345, Ann 172, B.
    B. 383, Ben 329, Bert 677, Bert B.

Kogen, I. B. 380, Mrs. I. 380
Kohn, Morris & Eleanor 290, Mr. & Mrs.
    Emil 168
KOl B' SEDER 369
Kol Beth Shalom 302
Kollenberg, Arnold 675
Kopelman, Audrey 350, 676, Dr. Harvey
    676
Kopelovich, Dr. Lenora 543
Kopit, Cyrus A. 363
Koppelman, Linda & Sam 359
Korean War 49
Koren, Charles 15, 47, 593, Debra 635,
    Donna vi, 210, Dr. Herman (Hank)
    200, 309, Gussie Wax 34, 210, 593,
    Hank & Donna 635, Laura 635,
    Sheryl Lynn 283, 635, Susan 635
Korf, Rabbi Alter & Chaya 199, 289
Korn, Dr. Bertram W. i, Naomi 505
Kornfeld, Leonard 324, Leonard &
    Kathryn 324
Kornfield, Ben 331, Benjamin 676,
    Henrietta 351, 676, Mr. 161, Mr. &
    Mrs. Benjamin 346
Koronas, D. Baseman & S. 679
Korones, David 107, 209, 211, 224, 441,
    460, 485, 678, Estelle & Sam 209,
    217, 221, 225, 439, Estelle G. 209,
    212, 218, 235, 236, 243, 418, 444,
    484, 679, Jane & David 242, Maxine
    536, N. David 209, 433, 438, 439,
    Roberta 679, S. 244, Sam 218, 220,
    221, 243, 485, Samuel A. 227, 420,
    678, Sheldon 209, Sol & Marie 209,
    Family 225
Kosher, Rose 168
Kosky, Mr. and Mrs. Frank 315
Koslow 420
Koufax, Sandy 309
Kovner, B. 311
Kramer, Dr. S. D. 168, Irving 678, Ned L.
    & Lillian 290
Krasner, Judge Edward 346, Judge
    Edwin 676
Krause, George 380, Jean 599
Krauthammer, Charles 373
Krecek, C. Michael 281
Kreher, Ernest 75
Krentzman, Ben 218, 220, 238, 292
Kreplick, Joe 367
Kreps, Stanley & Linda 188
Krieger, Della & Hans 588, Hans 372,
    529
Krieger Early Childhood Center 372
Krigsman, Irving 168
Krintman, Ben 221
Kriseman, Richard D. 171
Kristallnacht 42, 186, 437, 481
Kroll, Jule 679, Lewis 678
Kron, Benjamin & Izak 636, Edward &
    Garland Pezzuolo 586, 636, Selma
    636, Selma & Norman 585
Krongold, Rhonda 472
Krosner, Louis 358, 411, 678, Rachel
    Anne 404, Renée 555
Krouk, Morris 367, Ruth 585
Krug, Dell 555, 560, 645, Gerald 595, Jess
    B. 595, Nancy 595, Neal 595, Rita
    Arnowitz 595
Krystel, Mimi B. 457, 461, 679
Kuhn 36
Ku Klux Klan 23, 38, 40, 99, 124, 365
Kulberg, Mr. & Mrs. Abraham 168
Kuperman, Nathan 624, Nathan & Ruth

453
Kupersmith, Herb 686
Kurland, Wendy 566
Kurnitz, Sidney 591
Kurtzman, Gertrude 296, 302, 303
Kushner, Rabbi Harold S. 584
Kutz, Mr. & Mrs. 168
Kwall, Jean & Louis 588, Lou 677

L'dor Va'dor iv
La-Mais 188
Labowitz, Rabbi Eugène & Annette 357
Lachman, Dr. Margie E. 582
Lackey, Mr. & Mrs. Louis 168, 315
Ladies Auxiliary of Congregation B'nai
    Israel 327, of Temple Rhodeph
    Sholom 87, of the Jewish War
    Veterans 593
Ladies Hebrew Benevolent Society 467
Ladino 18
Lagassey, Michael & Michelle (Green)
    627
Lake, Hyman 600
Lakewood Country Club 105
Laliberte, Norman 397
Lambeck, R. P. 103
Lampert, Mrs Sam 484
Lampl, Mollie 168, Sherman 314
Lampp, E. R. 104
Lance, Bob 320
Lanceit, Ed 675
Landau, Lee & Bonnie Sefekar 442, Lee
    E. 666
Landfield, Clara 132, Hinda 126, Julius
    & Dora Marcus 126, Margret 126,
    Oscar & Helen 126
Landis, Dena 97
Landman, Cantor Ely 295
Landress, Harvey 514
Landskroner, Harry 292, 294, 295, 675
Lane, Harry 295, 307, Richard 677
Lang, Albert F. 95, Mrs. William 170
Langbein, Leo 168
Lanson, Bob 320
Largo 94, 106, Medical Center 107
Lasher, Horty & Morty 555, Mr. & Mrs.
    M. 170
Lasky, Fran 629
Laub, Mrs. Charles 678
Laufer, Sally 532
Lauri Family Kitchen 360
Lave, Mrs. Daniel 168
LaVilla Neighborhood 63
Lavinisky, Rabbi Arthur 87
Lawler, Mr. & Mrs. William 168
Lawrence, David 205, 420, 439, 484,
    637, 679, 686, Debbie 205, 484, 637,
    Debra 424, H. 244, 418, Howard
    202, 203, 204, 235, 417, 418, 460, 485,
    540, 555, 637, 678, Howard & Lila
    (Bilgore) 203, 205, 206, Howard
    Family 242, Howard S. 551, L. 244,
    Lila 3, 235, 236, 445, 459, 637, 679,
    685
Lay, Wesley & Leona 188
Lazarus, Emma 15, 29, 604, Mr. & Mrs.
    Dave 168, Samuel 15
Leabeau, Rabbi William 308
Leach, Mr. & Mrs. A. 168
Leadership Gifts 439
League to Aid Retarded Children 152
Lebman, Mrs. 420
LeCompte, Pamela Wittner 193
Lederer, Mrs. E. 384

Lederman, Anita R. 346, Rabbi Louis
    345, 539, 540, 676
Lee's Shoe Store 133, 211
Leesburg Community Hospital 180
Leeser, Reverend Isaac 20, 24, 234, 589,
    605
Lefkowits 420
Lefkowitz, Louis 168, Rabbi Sidney N.
    389
Lehrer, Lila 675, Rabbi 140, 328
Lehwald, Eva 137, Mrs. 377
Leibovit, Abraham (Avrum) & Mollie
    166, Jay 166
Leiman, Nathan & May 290
Leinson, Mr. & Mrs. Sidney 170
Le Master, Margret 415
Lempert, Ruby 679, Ruby & Sam 253
Lenin, Gerald 676, V. I. 38
Leo H. Buckman Ramah Fund 341
Leonard, Reverend Preston 186
Leopold, Max & Minnie Bush 151, 168
Lepkowits, Emanuel 485
Lerman, Mr. 219
Lerner, Dr. Saul & Dr. Vivian Benci
    610, Francesca 610, Maxwell 610,
    Morris 334, Mr. & Mrs. Morris 168,
    221, Seth 610
Lesher, Caroline 415
Lesser, Jean 168
Lesserox, Rabbi Maurice 328
Lester, Mr. & Mrs. A. 168, Professor
    Julius 467
Lev, Benjamin B. 26
Leventhal, S. 221
Levey, Mr. Ralph 563
Levin, Andrew & Roxanne 364, Bernice
    323, Cantor David 305, 675, Cantor
    Eileen 364, Dr. Harvey 364, Eileen
    & Dr. Harvey 363, Gloria 644, Mr.
    & Mrs. Al 168, Mrs. A. 73, Mrs.
    Sam 168, Richard & Robbie 364,
    Ruth Orloff 539, Senator Carl 526
Levine, Adrienne 443, Alan 334, Alex
    443, Alfred 346, Beatrice 551, Bruce
    679, Chester 676, Chet 346, Dr. &
    Mrs. S. 168 , Dr. Steven M. & Susan
    Marger 175, 177, Drs. Joan & Bruce
    463, Eileen 686, Eric 443, Irving
    485, Isadore 168, Leona 445, 459,
    Leslie 332, Marci 442, Marilyn 676,
    Michael 442, Mildred 168, 172, 331,
    Mr. & Mrs. H. K. 168, Mr. & Mrs.
    Hy 346, Mr. & Mrs. Isadore 346,
    Mrs. Chester 539, Paul 529, Samuel
    168, Simon 536, Tora 333, William
    315
LeVine, Andrea 638, Daniel 638,
    Danielle 638, Dr. David 555, 638,
    Dr. David & Janice 175, Dr. Mitchell
    638, Dr. Mitchell & Ellie 175, Dr.
    Morris 546, 638, Dr. Morris J. &
    Marilyn 315, 348, 587, 638, Dr.
    Steven 638, Ellie 638, Janice 548,
    638, Jared 638, Jennifer 638, Leslie
    638, Marc 638, Marilyn 345, 350,
    540, 583, 638, 685, Matthew 638,
    Mrs. Morris 338, 501, 540, Naomi
    638, Rachel 638, Robyn 638, Scott
    638, Shoshana 638, Stacy 638,
    Susan 638
Levinson, Mrs. Charles 380
Levitan, Dr. Alan 580
Levite 1
Levitt, David 679, Jamie 679, Mr. & Mrs.

Irwin 168
Levlfog, Falk & L. 115
LeVon, George 591
Levow, George 675
Levy, Abraham P. 112, Andrew 13,
    Annie 86, Asser 8, Cecelia & Philip
    Levy 121, Cecelia Tarapani 112,
    Cecelia Tarapani & Philip 121,
    Commodore Uriah P. 15, Deborah
    T. 112, 141, Evelyn P. 137, Fanny
    82, Hugette 410, Hyman 13, Jack
    501, 677, Marcy 182, Moses Elias
    61, Mr. & Mrs. Samuel 168, Mrs.
    E. 168, Nathan 9, Philip & Julia A.
    136, Philip H. 112, Family 389
Lew, Milton 147, 536, Mr. & Mrs. Larry
    346, Mr. & Mrs. Milton 168, 346, Mr.
    & Mrs. Ross 346, Ross 334, Yvette
    599
Lewandorf, Florence 168
Lewinsky 63, Rebecca 63
Lewinson, Gustave 65
Lewis, Alfred 401, 402, 678
Liberty Boys 13
Lichtenberg, Herman 367, 593
Licker, Mrs. H. F. 168
Lieber, Ed & Vicky Levine 442
Lieberman, Dr. & Mrs. Fred 525, Harriet
    172, 182, 523, 677, Larry 368, Mr. &
    Mrs. Erwin 168, Mr. & Mrs. Meyer
    168, Professor Saul ii, vii, Roslyn
    303
Liebowitz, Edward 600
Liebson, Lee 315
Liefman, Rabbi Morton 303
Lifson, Dr. David S. 298
Liggett Suburban Drugs 290
Light of Christ Church 455
LIKRAT SHABBAT 347
Lilienthal, B.H 62
Lillian B. Kramer's Cancellation Shoes &
    Tin's Shoe Rack 290
Lincoln, President Abraham 20, 26, 58
Lindberg, Charles 47
Linder, Marci 367, Marcia Pretekin 523
Linehan, Sister Patricia vi
Linkletter, Art 526
Linn, Mr. & Mrs. J. 168
Linsky, Eugene 551, Gene 558, Loretta
    646, Loretta & Marshall 555, 558,
    Lorette 200, Marshall 200, 551, 646
Lion of Judah 249, Endowment Fund,
    601
Lions Club 98, of Tupelo 292
Lipfield, Dora 168
Lipman, Bernice 472, Julius & Edna 188,
    Mr. & Mrs. Jules 168, Peter 334,
    Peter & Elaine 188
Lippfield, Mrs. Abraham 678
Lippman, Elaine L. 332, 598, Florence
    597, Florence & Morris 168, 401,
    Morris 597
Lipschultz, Sonia 448, 449
Lipstadt, Dr. Deborah 472
Lipwich, Arron 168, Leah Brina & Aaron
    598
Liss, Madelyn & Richard 639, Madelyn
    Bishop 200, 464, 472, 480, 522, 523,
    645, 677, 679, 686, Richard 464
Lisser, Resi & Stephen 263
Lithuanians 2
Litt, Diana 676, Jeffrey 676
Littlefield Nursing Home 103
Littman, Rabbi Louis C. 448

Littsfield, Dora 379
Livingston, Sigmund 22, 38
Lobel, Anna Goldman 120, Dave 120
Lockhart, Aimee England 598, Lynda
    Lippman 597, 598, Robert W. 598,
    Scott Flesch 598
Lockheed Aircraft Corp. 103
Loeb & Company 36
Loeb, Marcus 62
Loebel, Anna 362, David & Anna
    Goldman 143, Mr. 362, Mrs. David
    168, 346
Loebenberg, David 186, Michael 186,
    Mike 675, Sandy 186, Walter P.
    492, 521, 543, 547, 551, 685, Walter P.
    & Edith 279, 492, 531, 587
Loew, Mr. & Mrs. George 168
Loewenthal, Rev. D. 72
Loftus, John 547
Logan, Mrs. Samuel 396
Lois V. Silberman Senior Lounge 530
London, Phil 523, Shelle 321, 323
Lopatin, Adam, 629, Arthur 420, 428,
    485, Arthur & Anna 243, Bill 243,
    417, Bill & Jo Anne 243, Felice 244,
    428, 484, Harold 417, 418, 420, 423,
    425, 485, 686, Harold & Arthur 228,
    264, Harold & Pearl 223, 243, Jeffrey
    223, 243, 264, 415, 485, Jeffrey &
    Susan 419, Jeffrey Alan 419, Pearl
    424, Wendy 244, 424, 428, 679,
    William 679
Lopen, Mr. & Mrs. 170
Lopez, Aaron 12, Aaron Family 389,
    Sally 19
Lord, Mr. & Mrs. Sandford 168
Louis A. Cohen Lodge of the B'nai B'rith
    147
Louis Cohen Store 327
Louis XVI, King 97
Lourie, Mr. & Mrs. Samuel 168, William
    168
Lovitz, Alix & Irene 227, Esther & Sam
    121, Esther Tarapani 112, 116,
    Frances 113, Irene 217, J. 244, 418,
    Julian 420, Julius 113, 207, 211, 220,
    233, 235, 236, 238, 243, 418, 420, 439,
    471, 485, 540, 551, 555, 678, Julius &
    Phyllis Vera Schuman 215, 221, 424,
    440, 640, Phyllis 218, 235, 238, 418,
    484, 679, 685, Samuel & Esther 112,
    Tobiah 141, Tobias 113, Tracey E.
    217, 424
Lowen 420
Lowengard, Edie 179, Ida Frankel &
    Julius 179, 560, Marion 179
Lowenstein, Dr. Mitchell 545, Kathy &
    Dr. Mitchell 587, Mitch 368
Lowitt, Arlene & Bruce 588
Lowy, Laurel Rivkind 339, Mrs. Fred
    168
Lubin, Lance 166, Leonard 166, 167,
    172, 340, 398, 539, 685, Lisa 166,
    Lona 166, Meyer 168, Rabbi Sidney
    I. 192, 274, 312, 675, Terri & Meyer
    166
Lublin, Poland 43
Ludin, Arlene 545, 602, Dr. Edward N.
    602, Eric 602, 641, Eric & Judy 587,
    Eric E. 105, 602, 676, Jacob 641,
    Joshua 641, Judy 359, 555, 641
Lugerner and Gleicer 168
Lundy, Mrs. A. David (Sylvia) 188
Lung Association 172

Lurie, Dr. Edward 190, Ed 190, Ed &
    Vivian 190, Norman 320, 321
Luski, Jeremy 192, Joanne 191, 354, 563,
    Naomi 192, Rabbi Jacob ii, 191, 200,
    279, 296, 348, 352, 359, 367, 460, 503,
    532, 562, 676, Rabbi Jacob & Joanne
    587, 642, Rachel 192, Yael Hani 192,
    357
Lutheran Church, first in America 389
Lvov 5, 42
Lwow, Poland 43
Lylah Hadassah Chapter 586
Lynch, Bishop Robert N. 200, 359
Lyon, Bernard 591, Mary 303, 675
Lyons, Leana 357, Mr. & Mrs. Harold
    346, Rabbi Alexander 435

M. D. Memorial Award 546
Maamin, Ani 460
Maas, Abraham "Abe" 66, 70, 73, 75,
    81, 83, 85, 135, Audrey 67, Ernest
    67, 73, 77, 82, 84, 126, Ernest Jr. 67,
    Ernest Sr. 84, Henrietta 204, Ike &
    Abe 204, Isaac 63, Joseph 66, Julius
    67, 74, 77, 84, Mrs. Abe 70, 73, 74,
    Mrs. Ike 70, Mrs. Sol (Julia) 67, 83,
    Solomon 78, Family 78
Maas Brothers 66, 67, , in Tampa 13,
    Department Store 63, 102
Mac (or Mack), Mr. 201
MacDill Field 68
Machta, Mr. & Mrs. Eli 315
Mack, Bill & Grace 201, Senator Connie
    510
Mackler, M. J. 82, 84
Macone, Charles & Kathy 465
Madcaps 205
Maddux, Jane 441
Madeira Beach 101
Madison, President James 12, 476
Madow, Alec 661, Dr. Evan 661, Dr.
    Evan & Kathryn Schick 257, Jordan
    661, Kathryn Schick 661, Lance
    661, Michelle 661
Maggid, Rabbi Shaul 306
Mahaffey Theater 107, 158
Mahler, Rabbi Peter 440
Mahzor 300
Mailman, Morris 168, 312, 315, 675,
    Morris & Dorothy 314
Maimonides iii, 4, 371, 535, 604, College
    20, Society of Pinellas County 545
Mairowitz, Dr. P. 168
Mairson, J. L. 86, Mrs. J. L. 73
Malchon, State Senator Jeanne 584
Malin, Mrs. Mae 678
Mallen, Kimberly Ilene 352
Maller, Henry Andrew 350, Hilary Ann
    350, Lorraine 354, 676
Malter, Al 471
Mandalay Hotel 99
Manket, Anne 141, Leon 112, Olga
    Tarapani 112, 142, Olga Tarapani &
    Leon 121, 141
Mankin, Dana Greengold & Melissa 679,
    Melissa 679
Mann, David & Gertrude 315, Meyer
    C. 315
Mantinband, Rabbi Charles 390
Maracaibo 43
Marantz, Dr. Joel 520, 521, 539, 540
Marble, Reverend Ernest T. 387
Marcel, Gabriel 352
March, Dr. H. Lewis 398, Estelle & Stan

558, 561, 648, Mr. & Mrs. Alvin 169,
 Siegbert & Jennie 179, William 169
Sembler, Ambassador Mel 242, Betty
 551, Brent W. & Debbie Nye 184,
 510, Diane 545, 602, Greg 562, Greg
 S. & Elizabeth (Mauer) 184, 242, Liz
 602, 686, Mel 171, Melvin F. & Betty
 S. 183
Sembler Company 171, 183
Sembler Family Atrium 360
Seminole Bridges 98
Seminole Indians 89
Seminole War, First 57, 89, Second 90,
 Third 58, 90, of 1836 57
Send, Andrew 295
Sephardic Jews 10, 12
Sephardim 6
Seplowe, Lori 367
Serex, Edith H. 169
Sertoma Club 142
Settel, Mr. & Mrs. Abraham 169
Shabbat 302
Shafer, John & Elizabeth 188
Shainberg, Jake 402, Mr. & Mrs. Jacob
 398, 414, Rose 397, 402, Victor 402
Shaked, Dr. Haim 352
Shalit, Iris 480, Iris & Stanley 466, 471,
 Janice 466, Michelle 466
Shallat, Jacob 291, Mrs. J. 291, Rebecca
 290
Shalom 373
Shalom Park, Ocala 520
shalosh r' galim 302
Shame of the Cities, The 34
Shands Hospital 318
Shane, Al 291, Anna 291, Bertha
 Hollander 291, David 221, 237, 289,
 291, 301, Gertrude & David 290,
 291, Gertrude Siegel 137, 239, 377,
 Ivy 301, Izzy 291, Leo 291, 667,
 Leo Davis 301, Maria 291, Max
 291, Michael & Marcia 667, Mr. &
 Mrs.David 222, Mrs. 388, Rebecca
 301, 667, Robert & Nanette 301,
 Samantha 667, Samantha Laura
 301, Syd 291
Shapack, Phyllis 679
Shapass, B 169
Shapera, Rose 486, 677
Shapero, Aaron 76, Rabbi Sanford M.
 268, 433, 434, 435
Shapiro, Cantor Elaine 299, 349, Daniel
 415, Edmund & Deborah Lynn
 Fox 415, Emily 665, Heather 665,
 James J. 540, Jane 296, Jenna 415,
 Jennifer 665, Jim & Jill 587, 664, Jim
 & Jill Schwartz 665, Michael 413,
 415, Mr. & Mrs. Benjamin 169, Mr.
 Philip 169, Mrs. S.M. 484, Mrs. Sam
 329, Nancy 472, Rabbi Max 536,
 Rabbi Morris *v*, Rabbi Sandy 187,
 S. G. 327, Sam 362, Samuel & Lena
 138, 328, Samuel G. 327
Shapo, Rev. Julius 124
Sharlin, William 403
Sharpe, Bette 679
Sharpstein, Adina Baseman 472, M. Eric
 & Adina Baseman 263
Shaso, Rabbi J. 86, 115
Shavlan, Leonard 395, Leonard D. 678,
 Mildred 178, 678
Shavuot, Festival of 475
Shear, Bob 363, 677, Robert L. 363,
 Sheila 326

Shearith Israel of New York 9
Sheen, Robert 104
Sheftal, Mordecai 12, 14
Sheinert, Dr. Sheldon 629
Shekhinah *iv*
Shelef, Dr. Loni Orloff & Eliezar Jonah
 Stoppelman-Shelef 539, Eliezar
 654, Loni Orloff 654, Nadav 654,
 Noam 654, Orie 654
Shell, Mary E. 169
Shenker, Benjamin 169, J. 485, Rabbi
 Joseph 145, 536
Shenkerman, Rabbi Robert 321
Shepherd, Richard 678
Sher, Ali 649, Alison 185, 413, Anita 555,
 Craig 171, 183, 185, 241, 410, 602,
 678, Craig H. & Jan 185, 413, Dr. &
 Mrs. Mandel 587, Dr. Mandel 545,
 546, Jan 678, Jan & Craig 587, 649,
 Jessica 185, 413, Karen 554, Karen
 Wolchuck 357, Stacey 185, Stacy
 413, 649, Stacy & Jessica 649
Sher Girls Fund 602
Sherith Israel 11
Sherline, Corinne 445
Sherman, Ann 172, Charlotte 679,
 Lawrence 329, Morris 169, Morton
 676, Mr. & Mrs. Moe 329, Paula 595
Sherwood Restaurant 290
Shick, Kenneth & Cindy Grusin 257
Shiler, Edwin 334
Shiloh, Dr. Ailon 486
Shine, Mark 67
Ship of the Damned, the Saint Louis 186
Shirley Burns Early Childhood Center
 360
Shoemobile 149
Shoenfeld, Ethyl 224
Shorecrest School 158
Shrager, Dr. Joel 678
Shultz, Evelyn 559, Mr. & Mrs. Samuel
 170, Phyllis 679, Goldie 551, Peter
 & Buena 144, Rae & Isadore 144,
 Samuel 122, Sarah Shesolt 122
Shuster, Goldie 551, Peter & Buena 144,
 Rae & Isadore 144, Samuel 122,
 Sarah Shesolt 122
Shutz, Emma 112
Siegal, Ferne 443, Marlene 675, Roger
 445, Sally 445, 685
Siegel, Arlene 321, Betty 555, Danny
 545, Gertrude & Harold 137,
 Harold 290, 291, Harold B. & Sally
 252, 419, 461, Marlene 308, Marlene
 & Richard 588, Mindy 419, Mr. &
 Mrs. Harry 169, Mr. & Mrs. Louis
 169, Todd & Sheila 419, 461
Sierkese, Abe 362, Abraham 119, 126,
 129, 137, 145, 327, 329, 330, 485,
 Abraham & Mary (Soloman) 117,
 121, 129, Jennie C 117, Mr. 161, Mr.
 & Mrs. Abraham 169, 346, Mrs.
 Abe 327
Sierkese Department Store 117, Fabrics
 117, General Store 117
Signer, Harry 334, Mr. & Mrs. Harry
 169, 346, Mrs. Harry (Lil) 118, The
 140
Sigun, Suzanne Raymund 174
Silbar, Mr. J. H. 169
Silber, Mrs. Catherine 169
Silberman, Lois V. 532, Mr. & Mrs.
 Samuel 525, Samuel "Buddy" 530
Silberzweig, Lillian 531

Silk, Mark 541, 563
Silvan Abbey Cemetery 91
Silvano, Roberto 400
Silver, Bill 657, Larry 367, Rabbi & Mrs.
 Samuel M. 397, William 588
Silvera, Bobby 675, David & Barbara
 302, 303, James 303
Silverberg, Arthur 591, 679, Bruce 441,
 Donald A. 119, 139, 353, 385, 676,
 Edward 164, Helen 563, Henry
 139, Henry (Buddy) & Lu Ellen
 Neimeth 165, J. 391, Jane Goldman
 119, 181, Jane Goldman & Donald
 A. 164, 169, 587, Jane Goldman &
 Donald A. & Family 414, Jeffrey
 165, Joe 147, 172, Joseph 390, 678,
 Joseph & Helen 138, Lisa 165, Mr.
 161, Mr. & Mrs. Henry 169, Mr. &
 Mrs. Joseph 169, Terri 164, Thelma
 Rothman & Donald 551, Tom 164
Silverberg Courtyard 360
Silverman, Aaron & Ruth 132, 346,
 Aaron J. 169, Ann 169, Bessie 351,
 Bessie & Oscar 128, 132, Corinne
 146, 328, 329, Eileen Jacobs & Marc
 675, Ette 169, Flora 579, Harry J.
 359, Jerome 128, 328, Julius 169,
 332, Marc 303, 304, 675, Marie 675,
 Melvin 675, Mr. & Mrs. Julius 346,
 Mr. & Mrs. Mel 303, Mr. & Mrs.
 Oscar 169, 346, Sharon 334, Family
 132, 295
Silverstein, Eileen B. 357, Herb &
 Rosalind 253, Herbert 427, 435,
 Renee Jacobs 122
Simar, Abraham 591
Simcha Tree 445
Simon, Abraham 485, Abraham & Celia
 290, Cantorial Soloist Harry 677,
 Cecelia 264, Ceil 675, Esther 385,
 Gail 460, 465, 472, 568, Hazel 218,
 235, Joseph 13, Louis 218, 220,
 Louis & Hazel E. 213, 217, 222, 235,
 Mr. & Mrs. Harry 169, Rebecca 169,
 Sigmond 169, Family 151
Simon Gratz High School in Philadelphia
 10
Simpson, Mr. J. 70, Sampson 13
Sinclair, Upton 34
Singer, Dr. Jacob 78
Siple family 243
Sirota, Faith H. 599, Mr. & Mrs. Herbert
 346, Morris 169
Sislen, Cantor David B. 360, 407, 676,
 677, 686
Sisterhood of Congregation B'nai Israel
 327, 361
Sisterhoods 18, 34, 574
Sites, Lacey 325
Six Day War 50
Skinner, L. B. 99
Skopitz, Rabbi Lori 318
Skrovanek, Richard & Mitze 188
Skycrest Methodist Church 455
Slaff, Bernard 367
Slager, Charles 65
Slatehow, Mr. & Mrs. 378
Slavney, Betty 677
Slimmer 140, Harold 147, 169
Slocum, Herb 147
Slohm, Sarah 583
Slomka, Dr. Michael 546, Dr. Michael
 & Sandra 189, 358, 584, 587, 668,
 Howard Peter 352, Ira Marc 351,